THE PRENTICE-HALL SERIES IN MARKETING

Philip Kotler, Series Editor

ABELL/HAMMOND	Strategic Market Planning
COREY	Industrial Marketing: Cases and Concepts, 3rd ed.
GREEN/TULL	Research for Marketing Decisions, 4th ed.
KEEGAN	Multinational Marketing Management, 3rd ed.
KLEPPNER/RUSSELL/VERRILL	Otto Kleppner's Advertising Procedure, 8th ed.
KOTLER	Marketing Management, 5th ed.
KOTLER	Marketing for Nonprofit Organizations, 2nd ed.
KOTLER	Principles of Marketing, 2nd ed.
LOVELOCK	Services Marketing: Text, Cases, and Readings
MYERS/MASSY/GREYSER	Marketing Research and Knowledge Development
RAY	Advertising and Communication Management
STERN/EL-ANSARY	Marketing Channels, 2nd ed.
STERN/EOVALDI	Legal Aspects of Marketing Strategy: Antitrust and Consumer Protection Issues
URBAN/HAUSER	Design and Marketing of New Products

MARKETING

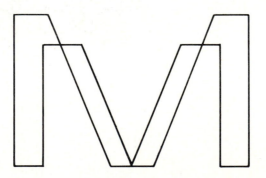

Prentice-Hall, Inc., Englewood Cliffs, New Jersey, 07632

Fifth Edition

MANAGEMENT

analysis, planning, and control

Philip Kotler

Northwestern University

Library of Congress Cataloging in Publication Data

KOTLER, PHILIP.
  Marketing management.

  Includes bibliographical references and indexes.
  1. Marketing management.   I. Title.
HF5415.13.K64 1984   658.8   83–16153
ISBN 0–13–557927–9

MARKETING MANAGEMENT: analysis, planning, and control, Fifth Edition
Philip Kotler

Editorial/production supervision by Esther S. Koehn
Interior and Cover design by Maureen O. Eide
Manufacturing buyer: Ed. O'Dougherty

Printed in the United States of America

10 9 8 7 6 5 4 3 2 1

ISBN 0-13-557927-9

Prentice-Hall International, Inc., *London*
Prentice-Hall of Australia Pty. Limited, *Sydney*
Editora Prentice-Hall do Brasil, Ltda., *Rio de Janeiro*
Prentice-Hall Canada Inc., *Toronto*
Prentice-Hall of India Private Limited, *New Delhi*
Prentice-Hall of Japan, Inc., *Tokyo*
Prentice-Hall of Southeast Asia Pte. Ltd., *Singapore*
Whitehall Books Limited, *Wellington, New Zealand*

This book is dedicated
to my wife, Nancy,
with love

About the Author

PHILIP KOTLER is the Harold T. Martin Professor of Marketing at the J. L. Kellogg Graduate School of Management at Northwestern University. He received a master's degree at the University of Chicago and a Ph.D. degree at M.I.T., both in economics. He did postdoctoral work in mathematics at Harvard and in behavioral science at the University of Chicago.

Dr. Kotler is the author of *Principles of Marketing*, one of the leading undergraduate textbooks, now in its second edition. His *Marketing for Nonprofit Organizations*, now in its second edition, is the most widely used textbook in that specialized area. Dr. Kotler's other books are *Marketing Model-Building: A Decision Making Approach*; *Marketing Management and Strategy: A Reader*; *Creating Social Change*; and *Simulation in the Social and Administrative Sciences*. In addition, he has written over seventy articles for leading journals, including the *Harvard Business Review*, *Journal of Marketing*, *Journal of Marketing Research*, *Management Science*, and *Journal of Business Strategy*. He is the only three-time winner of the coveted Alpha Kappa Psi annual award for the best article published in the *Journal of Marketing*.

Dr. Kotler has served as chairman of the College on Marketing of The Institute of Management Sciences (TIMS), and as director of the American Marketing Association. He is currently on the board of trustees of the Marketing Science Institute and is a director of the Management Analysis Center (MAC) and Deltak, Inc. He received the 1978 Paul D. Converse Award given by the American Marketing Association to honor "outstanding contributions to science in marketing." In 1983, he was honored as Marketer-of-the-Year by the Chicago Chapter of the American Marketing Association.

Contents

PART FOUR   DEVELOPING MARKETING STRATEGIES

The Marketing Planning Process   277

The New Product Development Process   309

Advertising Decisions   635

Sales Promotion and Publicity Decisions   660

Sales Management and Personal-Selling Decisions   675

Preface

Marketing is the business function that identifies current unfulfilled needs and wants, defines and measures their magnitude, determines which target markets the organization can best serve, and decides on appropriate products, services, and programs to serve these markets. Thus marketing serves as the link between a society's needs and its pattern of industrial response.

The Current Marketing Environment

The last decade has been one of trial and tribulation for most companies, here and abroad. Following the Mideast war of 1972, the world economy was plunged into a period of great shortages of oil and of many products that depended on oil. Shortages were shortly followed by double-digit inflation. Efforts to curb inflation led many countries into recession. Consumers' optimism soured into pessimism, and consumers slowed down their spending and proceeded to buy more carefully.

Several major companies tottered under the impact of the hard times, including Chrysler, International Harvester, and Braniff. Some of these companies were not the victims of the times so much as of their own failure to interpret new market forces and consumer requirements. They were victims of weak marketing and weak strategic planning. Other companies showed a high capacity to adapt to changing market needs—Procter & Gamble, IBM, McDonald's, General Mills—and continued to show good profits throughout the period, demonstrating that marketing can make a difference.

On the whole, the United States has been losing industrial leadership during this period. The U.S. foreign trade deficit hit record highs. American firms have been outperformed in many world markets by the Japanese and by some European firms. The U.S. auto industry fell into a weakened position because of its failure to downsize its cars early enough; and the U.S. steel industry is paying dearly for its failure to invest in more modern plants years ago. Many U.S. companies are saddled with high labor costs that prevent their products from being competitive in world markets. U.S. productivity has fallen, and the U.S. reputation for quality products has slipped in the minds of many consumers.

Many critics have placed the blame on U.S. management, saying that it suffers from a too short-run orientation. Top management is judged by annual profitability, and their bonuses are highly related to their current performance. Top management, it is alleged, has stinted on long-run productivity investments, quality improvements, and technological research. The result has been slipping productivity and noncompetitive global costs.

In the meantime another nation, Japan, views market development in much longer-range terms. They plan for global leadership and have succeeded in winning the lion's share of demand in a number of important global markets, including automobiles, cameras, consumer electronics, watches, steel, and shipbuilding. They have accomplished this by going after market share instead of current profitability and also receiving government support in their drive for global industrial leadership.

The marketing challenges thus are greater than at any time in history. Business firms face the following problems:

- [ ] An international market that is moving toward greater protectionism.
- [ ] Many nations that are so debt-ridden that it is hard or risky to do business with them.
- [ ] Foreign companies that receive subsidies from their governments and win business through lower prices.
- [ ] High U.S. wages that make some of our mainstay employment industries uncompetitive in world markets.
- [ ] A cautious consumer population that is price sensitive and increasingly responsive to price discounts and generic products.
- [ ] Old industries like autos and steel that have lost their competitive edge.
- [ ] An insufficient number of new industries in which the United States has a competitive edge and that offer high employment opportunities.

Companies hope that these problems can be solved. Properly viewed, the problems are also opportunities. More companies are recognizing that they need stronger marketing and that they have been mistaking a selling operation for a marketing operation. Selling is what a company does to dispose of the products it makes. Marketing is what a company does to decide on what products to make in the first place. As companies recognize that their marketing can and must be improved, they are taking concrete steps to transform their companies into sophisticated marketing companies. They recognize that the marketplace, not the factory, ultimately determines which firms will succeed. Their challenge is to find ways to reconcile company profitability, customer-need satisfaction, and social responsibility.

Marketing will remain one of the most difficult decision-making areas for companies. Marketing problems do not exhibit the neat quantitative properties of many problems in production, accounting, or finance. Psychological variables play a large role; marketing expenditures affect demand and costs simultaneously; marketing plans shape and interact with other business-function plans. Marketing decisions must be made in the face of insufficient information about processes that are dynamic, nonlinear, lagged, stochastic, interactive, and downright difficult. However, this is not taken as a case for intuitive decision making; rather it suggests the need for improved theory and sharper tools for analysis.

The Nature of This Book

This book on marketing management has the following features:

- ☐ *A managerial orientation*. This book focuses on the major decisions facing marketing executives and top management in their attempt to harmonize the objectives and resources of the organization with the needs and opportunities in the marketplace.
- ☐ *An analytical approach*. This book presents a framework for analyzing recurrent marketing problems. Descriptive material is introduced where it helps illustrate marketing principles.
- ☐ *A basic disciplines perspective*. This book draws heavily on the basic disciplines of economics, behavioral science, and mathematics. *Economics* provides the fundamental tools and concepts for seeking optimal results in the use of scarce resources. *Behavioral science* provides fundamental concepts and findings for the interpretation of consumer and organizational buying behavior. *Mathematics* provides an exact language for expressing the relationships existing between two or more variables.
- ☐ *A universal approach*. This book applies marketing thinking to a wide range of phenomena. Marketing is relevant to industrial as well as consumer markets, service industries as well as goods industries, small companies as well as large ones, nonprofit organizations as well as profit companies, and buyers as well as sellers.
- ☐ *Comprehensive and balanced coverage*. This book avoids a lopsided coverage of strategic, tactical, or administrative marketing. It covers all the topics about which a marketing manager needs some knowledge.

Changes in the Fifth Edition

The fifth edition has been written to reflect the new problems facing companies and the new concepts needed to deal with these problems. The fifth edition has the following objectives:

- ☐ To strengthen the material on strategic marketing because of the increasing necessity for executives to think strategically and not only tactically.
- ☐ To strengthen the material on marketing organization and implementation, because many companies fail to carry out their strategies in an effective manner.
- ☐ To create a stronger chapter flow, which takes the reader through the whole marketing management process—understanding marketing management, analyzing market opportunities, researching and selecting target markets, developing marketing strategies, planning marketing tactics, and implementing and controlling the marketing effort.
- ☐ To introduce the current statistics and new episodes that illustrate effective (or ineffective) marketing.

These objectives have led to the following distinctive features in the fifth edition:

- ☐ Two new chapters, specifically chapter 13 ("Marketing Strategies During Periods of Shortages, Inflation, and Recession") and chapter 18 ("Retailing, Wholesaling, and Physical-Distribution Decisions").
- ☐ Several substantially revised chapters, specifically chapters 1, 2, 6, 9, 11, 12, 19, 22, and 23.

☐ New and expanded material on marketing planning, strategic planning, competitive marketing strategies, marketing warfare, product life cycles, marketing strategies in different economic climates, marketing implementation, negotiation, pricing strategies, retailing and wholesaling, principles of effective marketing communication, and marketing of services.

☐ Substantial revision of the writing style toward shorter and more active prose.

☐ Substantial updating of references and citations of contemporary marketing success stories and empirical findings.

☐ Improved pedagogical aids: new end-of-the-chapter questions, new Instructor's Manual with lecture suggestions and multiple-choice questions, and three new or revised compatible supplementary texts: *Marketing Management and Strategy*: *A Reader*, 3rd ed., Philip Kotler and Keith Cox; *Cases in Marketing Management*: *Issues for the 1980s*, Charles Hinkle and Esther Stineman; *Problems in Marketing Management*: *A Workbook*, Jack Sissors.

The book is organized into six parts. *Part I* develops the societal, managerial, and strategic underpinnings of marketing. *Part II* presents concepts and tools for analyzing any market and marketing environment to discern opportunities. *Part III* presents principles for researching and selecting target markets. *Part IV* deals with strategic marketing and describes how firms can develop their marketing strategies. *Part V* deals with tactical marketing and describes how firms handle each element of the marketing mix—product, price, place, and promotion. Finally, *Part VI* examines the administrative side of marketing, namely, how firms organize, implement, and control marketing efforts.

Acknowledgments

This fifth edition bears the imprint of many persons. I first want to thank my colleagues and associates at the J. L. Kellogg Graduate School of Management at Northwestern University. My colleagues in the marketing department made an important contribution through their zest in blending marketing theory with managerial practice: Bobby J. Calder, Richard M. Clewett, Lakshman Krishnamurthi, Stephen A. LaTour, Sidney J. Levy, Prabha Sinha, Louis W. Stern, Brian Sternthal, Alice Tybout, and Andris A. Zoltners. I also want to acknowledge the valuable assistance of three scholars in our marketing program: Bruce Wrenn, for his work on text material and the instructor's manual; Françoise Simon-Miller, for her valued comments on four chapters; and Lalita Ajay Manrai, for her expert manuscript editing and managing of the workflow process. I also benefited from the excellent secretarial assistance of Marion Davis, Laura Pooler, and Linda Winstead. I also want to thank the Harold T. Martin family for the generous support of my chair at the J. L. Kellogg Graduate School of Management of Northwestern University. Completing the Northwestern team is my dean and longtime friend, Donald P. Jacobs, whom I want to thank for his continuous support of my research and writing efforts.

I am also indebted to the following colleagues at other universities who reviewed this edition and provided insightful suggestions.

C. L. Abercrombie—Memphis State University
William E. Bell—California State University, Fullerton

Peter Bennett—Pennsylvania State University
Marian Burke—Duke University
Julie Edell—Duke University
Jay Klompmaker—University of North Carolina, Chapel Hill
Edward Popper—Northeastern University
Peter Wilton—University of California, Berkeley

My thanks also go to my foreign-edition coauthors for their suggestions on the contents of the fifth edition:

Bernard Dubois—Centre d'Enseignement Superieur des Affaires (France)
Peter Fitzroy and Robin Shaw—Monash University (Australia)
Ronald E. Turner—Queen's University (Canada)

The talented staff at Prentice-Hall deserves praise for their role in shaping the present book. My editor, Elizabeth Classon, offered excellent advice on the form of the fifth edition. I also want to acknowledge the fine editorial work of Esther Koehn, college production editor; the creative graphic design of Maureen Eide, and the marketing research work of Paul Misselwitz.

My overriding debt is to my wife, Nancy, who provided me the time, support, and inspiration needed to regenerate this book. It is truly our book.

PHILIP KOTLER
Northwestern University
Evanston, Illinois

The Role of Marketing in Today's Organizations

1

Marketing is so basic that it cannot be considered a separate function. . . . It is the whole business seen from the point of view of its final result, that is, from the customer's point of view.

PETER DRUCKER

The 1970s and early 1980s have spelled hard times for most of the world's consumers and business firms. The 1973 oil crisis set off a round of further crises: material and energy shortages, rampant inflation, economic stagnation, rising unemployment, dying industries. These developments turned people from a mood of optimism to one of pessimism.

Throughout the 1960s, consumers in industrial nations enjoyed real gains in income and spent their money on a growing number of goods and services: new cars, television sets, dishwashers, foreign travel, higher education, and so on. Consumers in the U.S., Western Europe, Japan, Australia, and a few other nations were feeling relatively well-off. And the citizens of less developed countries, though living on very small incomes, were moving into a mood of "rising expectations," nourished by what they heard and saw in newspapers, magazines, and radio. Sooner or later, they felt, they would participate in the fruits of worldwide industrialization.

The succession of crises starting in the 1970s robbed everyone of these dreams. Prices shot up; incomes stagnated; jobs were lost; competition became keener, even warlike; foreign goods invaded domestic markets and hurt domestic firms; bankruptcies mounted. There was talk of the international financial system collapsing; high protectionism was advocated to close markets to foreign competition; there were proposals to abandon certain industries that were the former employment mainstays of the economy.

Yet one fact stood out: Human needs and wants abounded. Economic stagnation did not come out of satiety or the cessation of wants but out of a failure of the world economic system to work. It had halted and needed to be kicked into action again.

The key to recovery could not rest alone on governments' adopting appropriate fiscal and monetary policies. Business firms had to do a better job of identifying strong needs, innovating better products, and advertising and delivering them more efficiently so that consumers could afford them. In the past, too many companies saw their task as simply selling what they made. When customer interest flagged, these companies prodded their salespeople to sell harder. They would offer premiums or rebates to customers who would buy today. This approach to a reluctant market is called the *sales approach*. And a sales approach often works in the short run, at least in disposing of inventories, if not in increasing profits. But the sales approach provides no long-run answer to the dwindling interest of customers in a company's current products.

The answer in the long run is to monitor the customers' changing needs and wants and to adjust the company's products, services, and methods of distribution to the new needs and wants of the marketplace. This answer is called the *marketing philosophy*. It is the difference between calling on a customer and saying, "I'll sell this to you at a lower price today only," and saying, "Tell me what I can do to help you make or save money and achieve your objectives better." The sales approach is product centered; the marketing approach is customer centered.

If business firms paid more attention to monitoring new needs and wants, they would have no trouble recognizing opportunities. Consumers want more nutritious foods, attractive and affordable clothes, fuel-efficient and repair-free cars, comfortable and trouble-free homes. Industrial customers want more efficient systems and equipment for running their offices; robotized factories to bring down production costs and human drudgery; more efficient ways to deliver their goods to points of purchase. Clearly there are a vast number of opportunities facing business firms. One way to look at marketing is that it is a discipline used by business to convert people's needs into profitable company opportunities.

Technology is the leading force defining the new opportunities. Technology will play the key role in shaping future life styles. We already have portable phones, video recorders and video disc machines, personal computers, large-screen projection TV, cable TV, betablockers for heart-troubled patients, robotized factories, and gene splicing. We will soon have voice-activated typewriters, cancer cures, practical electric cars, and new major energy sources. Yet the invention of a new technology is only half the answer. Its successful marketing is equally challenging. The personal computer industry provides a living illustration of this.[1]

---

[1] See Mitchell Waite and Michael Pardee, *Your Own Computer*, 2nd ed. (Indianapolis: Howard W. Samuel Co., 1981).

Some years passed between the time small desktop computers became available and the emergence of a mass market for personal computers. In 1974, a process control engineer named Johnathan Titus designed the Mark 8 microcomputer and advertised it for sale in *Radio Electronics* magazine. It was in kit form and only appealed to hobbyists. In 1975 a small company called Mits advertised another low cost computer, also in kit form based on a new chip. Other firms entered the market in 1976—Polymorphics, OSI Challenger, Cromemco, etc.—offering their versions, but still appealing to a limited, technically oriented market. The breakthrough came in 1977 when the Tandy Corporation developed the TRS-80 and offered it for sale through its over 6000 Radio Shack Stores at a price of under $600 along with service and teaching as well. Apple came out in 1977 with its integrated desktop computer that was the first to offer true color. Apple and Tandy offered a great range of computer software programs for word processing, game playing, financial record keeping, etc. Their success led more companies to enter the field, and also led to the formation of national retailing chains such as Computerland to facilitate selling, servicing, and training users. Thus building a market and infrastructure for personal computers took several years of patient marketing. And today, the original surviving developers of the market are locked in a life-and-death marketing struggle with IBM, Texas Instruments, Hewlett-Packard, Commodore, and dozens of other firms seeking to figure out the different market segments for small computers (consumers, small business firms, professional markets, etc.), target them carefully, and develop superior products for those markets.

Thus high technology won't be bought until it is shaped to meet the wants of specific customer groups and communicated in a fashion and at a price and with levels of service that are sufficient to motivate the market. All this points to the fact that marketing does not start after the product is made but long before. It is the company's marketing department that must determine whether there is a market out there, its size, segments, perceptions, preferences, and buying habits. Marketing must feed this data to the research and development department so that R&D can design the best possible product for the target market. Marketing must also design the pricing, distribution, and promotion plan for launching the product. Marketing then implements the plan, monitors the results, and introduces corrective actions where the market results are not being met. Thus marketing begins before the product exists and continues long after the product is sold, interpreting all along what is happening in the marketplace and always seeking ways to improve customer satisfaction.

Thus we believe that marketing will play an important role in launching a renewed era of economic activity and rising living standards. One marketing scholar defined marketing as "the creation and delivery of a standard of living."[2] We take this as an inspired and insightful view of the marketing job.

This first chapter will describe the major concepts and philosophies underlying marketing thinking and practice, and we will come back to them again and again throughout the book. This chapter will answer the following specific questions:

☐ What are the core concepts leading to the discipline of marketing?
☐ What are the basic concepts used by marketing management in carrying out its responsibilities?

---

[2] Malcolm P. McNair, "Marketing and the Social Challenge of Our Times," in *A New Measure of Responsibility for Marketing*, Keith Cox and Ben M. Enis, eds. (Chicago: American Marketing Association, 1968).

□ What is the marketing philosophy and how does it contrast to other philosophies of doing business in the marketplace?

□ What role does marketing play in different industries, in nonprofit organizations, and in different countries?

THE CORE CONCEPTS OF MARKETING

Marketing has been defined in various ways by different writers.[3] We would like to propose the following definition of marketing:

Marketing **is a social process by which individuals and groups obtain what they need and want through creating and exchanging products and value with others.**

This definition of marketing rests on the following core concepts: *needs, wants, and demands*; *products*; *value and satisfaction*; *exchange and transactions*; *markets*; and *marketing and marketers*. These concepts are illustrated in Figure 1–1 and discussed below.

Needs, Wants, and Demands

The starting point for the discipline of marketing lies in *human needs and wants*. People need food, air, water, clothing, and shelter to survive. Beyond this, people have a strong desire for recreation, education, and other services. They have strong preferences for particular versions of basic goods and services.

There is no doubt that people's needs and wants today are staggering. In 1978, in the United States alone, 220 million Americans purchased 67 billion eggs, 387 million chickens, 11.4 million hair dryers, 156 billion domestic air travel passenger miles, and over 20 million lectures by college English professors. These consumer goods and services led to a derived demand for more than 150 million tons of steel and 6 billion pounds of cotton. Those are a few of the wants and needs that get expressed in a $1.5 trillion economy.

---

[3] Here are two definitions: "Marketing is the performance of business activities that direct the flow of goods and services from producer to consumer or user." "Marketing is getting the right goods and services to the right people at the right place at the right time at the right price with the right communication and promotion."

FIGURE 1–1
The Core Concepts of Marketing

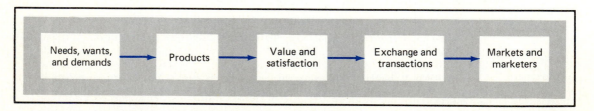

Needs, wants, and demands → Products → Value and satisfaction → Exchange and transactions → Markets and marketers

A useful distinction can be drawn between *needs*, *wants*, and *demands*. A human need is a state of felt deprivation of some basic satisfaction. People require food, clothing, shelter, safety, belonging, esteem, and a few other things for survival. These needs are not created by their society or by marketers; they exist in the very texture of human biology and the human condition.

Human wants are desires for specific satisfiers of these deeper needs. An American needs food and wants a hamburger, needs clothing and wants a Pierre Cardin suit, needs esteem and buys a Cadillac. In another society, these needs are satisfied differently: The Balinese satisfy their hunger with mangoes, their clothing needs with a loin cloth, their esteem with a shell necklace. While people's needs are few, their wants are many. Human wants are continually shaped and reshaped by social forces and institutions such as churches, schools, families, and business corporations.

Demands are wants for specific products that are backed up by an ability and willingness to buy them. Wants become demands when backed up by purchasing power. Many persons want a Cadillac; only a few are really able and willing to buy one. Companies must therefore measure not only how many people want their product but, more important, how many would actually be willing and able to buy it.

These distinctions shed light on the frequent charge by marketing critics that "marketers create needs" or "marketers get people to buy things they don't want." Marketers do not create needs; needs preexist marketers. Marketers, along with other influentials in the society, influence wants. They suggest to consumers that a Cadillac would satisfy a person's need for social status. Marketers do not create the need for social status but try to point out how a particular good would satisfy that need. Marketers try to influence demand by making the product attractive, affordable, and easily available.

Products

People satisfy their needs and wants with products. We shall define products broadly to cover *anything that can be offered to someone to satisfy a need or want*. Normally the word *product* brings to mind a physical object, such as an automobile, a television set, or a soft drink. And we normally use the expression *products and services* to distinguish between physical objects and intangible ones. But in thinking about physical products, their importance lies not so much in owning them as in using them to satisfy our wants. We don't buy a car to look at but because it is a source of a service called transportation. We don't buy a microwave oven to admire but because it makes food preparation easier. Thus physical products are really vehicles that deliver services to us.

In fact, services are also carried by other vehicles, such as *persons*, *places*, *activities*, *organizations*, and *ideas*. If we are bored, we can go to a nightclub and watch an entertainer (person); travel to a warm vacation land like Florida (place); engage in some physical exercise (activity); join a lonely hearts club (organization), or adopt a different philosophy about life (idea). In other words, services can be delivered through physical objects and other vehicles. We will use the term *product* to cover all vehicles that are capable of delivering satisfaction of a want or need. Occasionally we will use other terms for product, such as *offers*, *satisfiers*, or *resources*.

Manufacturers get into a lot of trouble by paying more attention to their products than the services produced by these products. Manufacturers love their products and forget that customers buy them because they meet a need. People do not buy physical objects for their own sake. A tube of lipstick is bought to supply a service: helping the person look better. A drill bit is bought to supply a service: producing a needed hole. A physical object is a means of packaging a service. The marketer's job is to sell the benefits or services built into physical products, rather than just describe their features; otherwise the manufacturer is myopic. Sellers suffer from "marketing myopia:"[4] a tendency to focus nearsightedly on the product rather than farsightedly on the customer's need.

Value and Satisfaction

How do consumers choose among the products that might satisfy a given need? To make the question concrete, suppose Tom Jones needs to travel three miles to work each day. Jones can visualize a number of products that will satisfy this need: walking, roller skates, a bicycle, a motorcycle, an automobile, a taxicab, and a bus. These alternatives constitute his *product choice set.* Let us assume that Jones wants to satisfy different goals in traveling to work, namely speed, safety, ease, and cost. We call these his *goal set.* Now each product has different capacities to satisfy his various goals. Thus a bicycle will be slower, less safe, and more effortful than an automobile, but it will be more economical. Somehow Tom Jones has to decide on the most satisfying product.

The guiding concept is *value.* Tom Jones will form an estimate of the value of each product in satisfying his goals. He might rank the products from the most desirable to the least desirable. The one at the top of the list has the most value to him. Value is the consumer's estimate of the product's capacity to satisfy a set of goals.

We can ask Jones to imagine the characteristics of an *ideal product* for this task. Jones might answer that the ideal product would get him to his place of work in a split second, with absolute safety, no effort, and zero cost. Then the value of each available product would depend on how close it came to this ideal product.

To illustrate, suppose Jones is primarily interested in the speed and ease of getting to work. Figure 1–2 presents a map of the *product space* in terms of these two goals and shows Jones's perception of where each product stands in its ability to satisfy these two goals. His ideal product is also represented by a point. The closer an existing product is to his ideal product, the greater its value (also called *utility*) in his mind. If Jones were offered any of these products free, we would predict that he would choose the automobile. But now comes the rub. Since each product (except walking) involves a purchase price, he will not necessarily buy the automobile. The automobile costs substantially more money than, say, a bicycle. Tom will have to give up more of other things (represented by the cost) to obtain the car. Therefore Tom will consider both the value and the price before making a

---

[4] See Theodore Levitt's classic article, "Marketing Myopia," *Harvard Business Review*, July–August 1960, pp. 45–56.

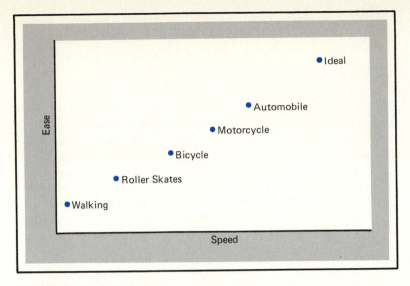

FIGURE 1-2
A Product-Space Map Showing Alternative Product Choices for Satisfying Two Goals Connected with Transportation

choice. He will tend to make the choice that will give him the most value per dollar, assuming that he is a rational, utility-maximizing person.

Thus value is a complicated concept, one that has a long history in economic thought. Karl Marx thought, for example, that the value of an object depended only on how much labor went into its production. So if it took twice as long to produce a motorcycle as a bike, a motorcycle would have twice the value of a bike. If a motorcycle was priced at three times the value of a bike, people would start making motorcycles instead of bicycles, and this would bring the price of motorcycles down to the labor value. This theory of value was discredited by other nineteenth-century economists who felt that value was a subjective, not an objective concept. The consumer decided on the value of different things according to their capacity to satisfy his or her wants. Consumers were thought to possess a cardinal measure of utility, that is, they could assign a measurable number to each product or product bundle. Consumers would then buy the baskets of goods that maximized their total utility. Twentieth-century economists dropped the assumption of cardinal utility; they assume only that consumers have the capability of ranking any two objects in terms of preference. A consumer can state whether he or she prefers A to B, B to A, or is indifferent. On this minimal assumption, it is still possible to build a theory of rational consumer choice.

Modern consumer-behavior theorists have gone beyond narrow economic assumptions of how consumers form value in their mind and make product choices. We will look at modern theories of consumer choice in Chapter 4. These theories are important to marketers because the whole marketing plan rests on assumptions about how customers make choices. Therefore the concepts of value and satisfaction are crucial to the discipline of marketing.

Exchange and Transactions

The fact that people have needs and wants and can place value on products is necessary but not sufficient to define marketing. Marketing exists when people decide to satisfy needs and wants in a certain way that we shall call *exchange*. Exchange is one of four ways in which a person can obtain a product he or she wants.

The first way is *self-production*. A hungry person can relieve hunger through hunting, fishing, or fruit gathering. The person does not have to interact with anyone else. In this case there is no market and no marketing.

The second way is *coercion*. The hungry person can wrest food from another. No benefit is offered to the other party except the chance not to be harmed.

The third way is *begging*. The hungry person can approach someone and beg for food. The supplicant has nothing tangible to offer except gratitude.

The fourth way is *exchange*. The hungry person can approach someone who has food and offer some resource in exchange, such as money, another good, or some service.

Marketing arises from this last approach to acquiring products. *Exchange is the act of obtaining a desired product from someone by offering something in return*. Exchange is the defining concept underlying marketing. For exchange to take place, five conditions must be satisfied:

1. There are at least two parties.
2. Each party has something that might be of value to the other party.
3. Each party is capable of communication and delivery.
4. Each party is free to accept or reject the offer.
5. Each party believes it is appropriate or desirable to deal with the other party.

If these conditions exist, there is a potential for exchange. Whether exchange actually takes place depends upon whether the two parties can find *terms of exchange* that will leave them both better off (or at least not worse off) than before the exchange. This is the sense in which exchange is described as a value-creating process; that is, exchange normally leaves both parties better off than before the exchange.

Exchange must be seen as a process rather than as an event. Two parties are said to be engaged in exchange if they are negotiating and moving toward an agreement. If an agreement is reached, we say that a *transaction* takes place. Transactions are the basic unit of exchange. *A transaction consists of a trade of values between two parties*. We must be able to say: A gave X to B and received Y in return. Jones gave $400 to Smith and obtained a television set. This is a classic *monetary transaction*. Transactions, however, do not require money as one of the traded values. A *barter transaction* would consist of Jones's giving a refrigerator to Smith in return for a television set. A barter transaction can also consist of the trading of services instead of goods, as when lawyer Jones writes a will for physician Smith in return for a medical examination. (See Exhibit 1–1 for examples of modern international barter transactions.)

A transaction involves several measurable entities: at least two things of value, conditions that are agreed to, a time of agreement, and a place of agreement. Usually

Exhibit 1–1

HOW THE NATIONS OF THE WORLD HAVE BEEN MOVING BACK TO BARTER

Most trading in the world takes place in the form of straight cash transactions. The buyer agrees to pay the seller in cash within a certain stated time period. Yet many nations today lack sufficient hard currency to pay cash for their purchases from other nations. They want to offer other items in payment, and this has led to a growing practice called *countertrade*. Approximately 40 percent of trade with Communist-block nations is handled through countertrade. Less developed countries are also pressing for more countertrade agreements when they buy. Although most companies dislike countertrade deals, they may have no choice if they want to win the business.

Countertrade takes several forms:

☐ **Barter.** Barter involves the direct exchange of goods, with no money and no third party involved. For example, the West Germans agreed to build a steel plant in Indonesia in exchange for Indonesian oil.

☐ **Compensation deal.** Here the seller receives some percentage of the payment in cash and the rest in products. A British aircraft manufacturer sold planes to Brazil for 70 percent cash and the rest in coffee.

☐ **Product buyback.** The seller sells a plant, equipment, or technology to another country and agrees to accept as partial payment products manufactured with the equipment supplied. For example, a U.S. chemical company built a plant for a company in India and accepted partial payment in cash and the remainder in chemicals to be manufactured at the plant.

☐ **Counterpurchase.** The seller receives full payment in cash but agrees to spend an equivalent amount of money in that country within a stated time period. For example, Pepsi-Cola sells its concentrate to the U.S.S.R. and agrees to accept rubles and spend it on U.S.S.R. products such as vodka.

More-complex countertrade deals involve more than two parties. For example, Daimler-Benz agreed to sell thirty trucks to Romania and accept in exchange 150 Romanian-made jeeps, which it sold in Ecuador in exchange for bananas, which it brought back to West Germany and sold to a West German supermarket chain in exchange for deutschmarks. Through this circuitous transaction, it finally achieved payment in German currency. Various barter houses and countertrade specialists have emerged to assist the parties to these transactions. Everyone agrees that international trade would be more efficient if carried out in cash, but too many nations lack sufficient hard currency. Sellers have no choice but to learn the intricacies of countertrade, which is a growing phenomenon in world trade. (For further reading, see Robert E. Weigand, "Barters and Buy-Backs: Let Western Firms Beware!" *Business Horizons*, June 1980, pp. 54–61; and John W. Dizard, "The Explosion of International Barter," *Fortune*, February 7, 1983).

a legal system arises to support and enforce compliance on the part of the transactors. Transactions can easily give rise to conflicts based on misinterpretation or malice. Without a "law of contracts," people would approach transactions with some distrust, and everyone would lose.

Businesses keep records of their transactions and sort them by item, price, customer, location, and other specific variables. *Sales analysis* is the act of analyzing where the company's sales are coming from by product, customer, territory, and so on.

A *transaction* differs from a *transfer*. In a transfer, A gives X to B but does not appear to receive anything tangible in return. When A gives B a gift, a subsidy, or a charitable contribution, we call this a transfer, not a transaction. It would seem that marketing should be confined to the study of transactions and not transfers. However, transfer behavior can also be understood through the concept of exchange. Typically the transferer gives a gift and has certain expectations, such as getting back gratitude, or seeing good behavior in the recipient. Professional fundraisers are acutely aware of the "reciprocal" motives underlying donor behavior and try to provide benefits to the donors, such as thank-you notes, donor magazines, and special invitations to events. Marketers have recently broadened the concept of marketing to include the study of transfer behavior as well as transaction behavior.

In the broadest sense, the marketer is seeking to bring about a response to some offer. A business firm wants a response called "buying," a political candidate wants a response called "voting," a church wants a response called "joining," a social-action group wants a response called "adopting the idea." Marketing consists of actions undertaken to elicit a desired response from a target audience toward some object.

To effect successful exchanges, the marketer has to analyze what each party expects to give and receive. Simple exchange situations can be mapped by showing the two actors and the typical resource flows between them. Figure 1–3 shows five familiar exchange situations. The most familiar is the *commercial transaction*—a seller offers a good or service to a buyer in exchange for money. The second is the *employment transaction*—an employer offers wages and fringe benefits to an employee in exchange for the employee's productive services (made up of time, energy, and skill). The third is the *civic transaction*—a police force offers protective services to citizens in exchange for their taxes and cooperation. The fourth is the *religious transaction*—a church offers religious services to members in exchange for their contributions of money and time. The fifth is the *charity transaction*—a charity organization offers gratitude and a feeling of well-being to donors in return for contributions of money and time.

A marketer interested in actualizing a potential transaction will make a careful analysis of what the other party wants and what the marketer might offer. Suppose Caterpillar, the world's largest manufacturer of earth-moving equipment, researches the benefits that a typical construction company may be seeking in buying earth-moving equipment. These benefits are listed at the top of the exchange map in Figure 1–4. A customer prospect wants high-quality equipment, a fair price, on-time delivery, good financing, and good service. This is the *want list* (or *wish list*) of the buyer.

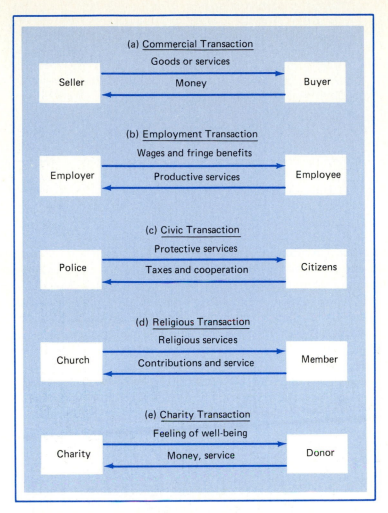

(a) Commercial Transaction

Seller → Goods or services → Buyer

Buyer → Money → Seller

(b) Employment Transaction

Employer → Wages and fringe benefits → Employee

Employee → Productive services → Employer

(c) Civic Transaction

Police → Protective services → Citizens

Citizens → Taxes and cooperation → Police

(d) Religious Transaction

Church → Religious services → Member

Member → Contributions and service → Church

(e) Charity Transaction

Charity → Feeling of well-being → Donor

Donor → Money, service → Charity

FIGURE 1–3
Examples of Exchange Transactions

The wants are not all equally important and may vary from buyer to buyer. One of Caterpillar's tasks is to find out the importance of these different wants of the buyer. At the same time, Caterpillar has a want list that is shown below the Caterpillar arrow in Figure 1-4. Caterpillar wants a good price for the equipment, on-time payment, and good word of mouth. If there is a sufficient match or overlap in the want lists, there is a basis for a transaction. Caterpillar's task is to formulate an *offer* that motivates the construction company to buy Caterpillar equipment. The construction company might in turn make a counteroffer. The process of trying to find mutually agreeable terms is called *negotiation*. Negotiation either leads to mutually acceptable terms or a decision not to transact.

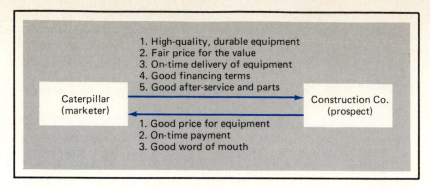

FIGURE 1–4
Two-Party Exchange Map Showing Want Lists of Both Parties

Markets

The concept of exchange leads to the concept of a market. *A market consists of all the potential customers sharing a particular need or want who might be willing and able to engage in exchange to satisfy that need or want.* Thus the size of the market depends upon the number of persons who exhibit the need, have resources that interest others, and are willing to offer these resources in exchange for what they want.

Originally the term *market* stood for the place where buyers and sellers gathered to engage in exchange, such as a village square. Economists use the term *market* to refer to a collection of buyers and sellers. Marketers, on the other hand, see the sellers as constituting the *industry* and the buyers as constituting the *market*. The relationship between the industry and the market is shown in Figure 1–5. The sellers and the buyers are connected by four flows. The sellers send goods and services and communications to the market; in return they receive money and information. The inner loop shows an exchange of money for goods; the outer loop shows an exchange of information.

Business people use the term *markets* colloquially to cover various groupings of customers. They talk about *need* markets (such as the diet-seeking market); *product markets* (such as the shoe market); *demographic markets* (such as the youth market); and *geographic* markets (such as the French market). Or they extend the concept to cover noncustomer groupings as well, such as *voter* markets, *labor* markets, and *donor* markets.

FIGURE 1–5
A Simple Marketing System

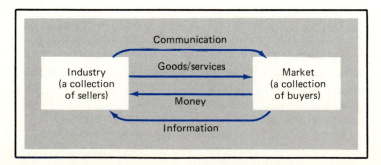

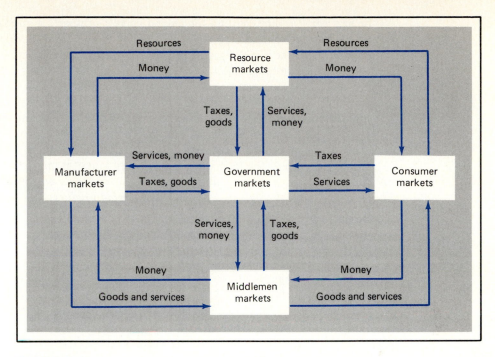

FIGURE 1-6
Structure of Flows in a Modern Exchange Economy

The fact is that modern economies operate on the principle of division of labor where each person specializes in the production of something, receives payment, and buys things needed with this money. Thus modern economies abound in markets. The basic kinds of markets and the flows connecting them are shown in Figure 1–6. Essentially manufacturers go to resource markets (raw-material markets, labor markets, money markets, and so on), buy resources, turn them into goods and services, sell them to middlemen, who sell them to consumers. The consumers sell their labor for which they receive money income to pay for the goods and services they buy. The government is another market that plays two roles. It buys goods from resource, manufacturer, and middlemen markets; it pays them; it taxes these markets (including consumer markets); and it returns needed public services. Thus each nation's economy and the whole world economy consist of a complex set of markets that are linked through exchange processes.

Marketing and Marketers

The concept of markets finally brings us full circle to the concept of marketing. Marketing means human activity that takes place in relation to markets. Marketing means working with markets to actualize potential exchanges for the purpose of satisfying human needs and wants.

If one party is more actively seeking an exchange than the other party, we call the first party a *marketer* and the second party a *prospect*. *A marketer is someone seeking a resource from someone else and willing to offer something-of-value in exchange*. The marketer is seeking a response from the other party, either to sell something or to buy something. The marketer, in other words, can be a seller or a buyer. Suppose several persons want to buy a very attractive house that just came on the market. Each would-be buyer will try to market himself or herself to be the one the seller selects. These buyers are doing the marketing. In the event that both parties are actively seeking an exchange, we say that both of them are marketers and call the situation one of mutual marketing.

Having reviewed these concepts, we are ready to repeat our definition of marketing, that *marketing is a social process by which individuals and groups obtain what they need and want through creating and exchanging products and value with others*.

MARKETING MANAGEMENT

Coping with exchange processes calls for a considerable amount of work and skill. *Persons* become fairly adept at buying to meet their household needs. Occasionally they also undertake selling—selling their car, selling personal services. *Organizations* are more professional in handling exchange processes. They must attract resources from one set of markets, convert them into useful products, and trade them in another set of markets. *Nations* also plan and manage exchange relations with others. They search for beneficial trade relations with other nations. In this book we will focus on *organizational marketing* rather than on personal or national marketing.

Marketing management takes place when at least one party to a potential exchange gives thought to objectives and means of achieving desired responses from other parties. Our definition of marketing management is:

Marketing management is the analysis, planning, implementation, and control of programs designed to create, build, and maintain beneficial exchanges and relationships with target markets for the purpose of achieving organizational objectives.

Marketing management can occur in an organization in connection with any of its markets. Consider an automobile manufacturer. The vice-president of personnel deals in the *labor market*; the vice-president of purchasing, the *raw materials market*; and the vice-president of finance, the *money market*. They have to set objectives and develop strategies for producing satisfactory results in these markets. Traditionally, however, these executives have not been called marketers nor have they been trained in marketing. Instead, marketing management is historically identified with tasks and personnel dealing with the *customer market*. We will follow this convention, although what we say about marketing applies to all markets.

Marketing work in the customer market is carried out by *sales managers, sales representatives, advertising and promotion managers, marketing researchers, customer-service managers, product managers, market managers, and the marketing vice-president*. Each job position carries well-defined tasks and responsibilities. Many of these jobs involve managing particular marketing *resources* such as advertising, sales people, or marketing research. On the other hand, product managers, market managers, and the marketing vice-president manage *programs*. Their job is to analyze, plan, and implement programs that will produce a desired level and mix of transactions with specified target markets.

The popular image of the marketing manager is someone whose task is primarily to stimulate demand for the company's products. However, this is too limited a view of the range of marketing tasks carried out by marketing managers. *Marketing management has the task of influencing the level, timing, and composition of demand in a way that will help the organization achieve its objectives*. Simply put, marketing management is *demand management.*

The organization forms an idea of a *desired level of transactions* with a target market. At times, the *actual demand level* may be below, equal to, or above the *desired demand level*. That is, there may be no demand, weak demand, adequate demand, excessive demand, and marketing management has to cope with these different states. Exhibit 1–2 distinguishes eight different common states of demand and the corresponding tasks facing marketing managers.

Marketing managers cope with these tasks by carrying out marketing research, marketing planning, marketing implementation, and marketing control. Within marketing planning, marketers must make decisions on target markets, market positioning, product development, pricing, channel of distribution, physical distribution, communication, and promotion. These marketing tasks will be analyzed in subsequent chapters of the book. Suffice it to say that marketing managers must acquire several skills to be effective in the marketplace.

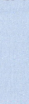

Exhibit 1–2

VARIOUS STATES OF DEMAND AND THE CORRESPONDING MARKETING TASKS

1. **Negative demand.** A market is in a state of negative demand if a major part of the market dislikes the product and may even pay a price to avoid it. People have a negative demand for vaccinations, dental work, vasectomies, and gall bladder operations. Employers feel a negative demand for ex-convicts and alcoholic employees. The marketing task is to analyze why the market dislikes the product and whether a marketing program through product redesign, lower prices, and more positive promotion can change the market's beliefs and attitudes.

2. **No demand.** Target consumers may be uninterested in or indifferent to the product. Thus farmers may not be interested in a new farming method, and college students may not be interested in taking foreign language courses. The marketing task is to find ways to connect the benefits of the product with the person's natural needs and interests.

3. **Latent demand.** A substantial number of consumers may share a strong desire for something that cannot be satisfied by an existing product or service. There is a strong latent demand for unharmful cigarettes, safer neighborhoods, and more-fuel-efficient cars. The marketing task is to measure the size of the potential market and develop effective goods and services that would satisfy the demand.

4. **Falling demand.** Every organization, sooner or later, faces falling demand for one or more of its products. Churches have seen their membership decline, and private colleges have seen their applications fall. The marketer must analyze the causes of market decline and determine whether demand can be restimulated through finding new target markets, changing the product's features, or developing more effective communication. The marketing task is to reverse the declining demand through creative remarketing of the product.

5. **Irregular demand.** Many organizations face demand that varies on a seasonal, daily, or even hourly basis, causing problems of idle capacity or overworked capacity. In mass transit, much of the equipment is idle during the off-peak hours and insufficient during the peak travel hours. Museums are undervisited during weekdays and overcrowded during weekends. Hospital operating rooms are overbooked early in the week and underbooked toward the end of the week. The marketing task is to find ways to alter the time pattern of demand through flexible pricing, promotion, and other incentives.

6. **Full demand.** Organizations face full demand when they are pleased with their amount of business. The marketing task is to maintain the current level of demand in the face of changing consumer preferences and increasing competition. The organization must keep up its quality and continually measure consumer satisfaction to make sure it is doing a good job.

7. **Overfull demand.** Some organizations face a demand level that is higher than they can or want to handle. Thus the Golden Gate Bridge carries a higher amount of traffic than is safe, and Yellowstone National Park is terribly overcrowded in the summertime. The marketing task, called *demarketing*, requires finding ways to reduce the demand temporarily or permanently. General demarketing seeks to discourage overall demand and consists of such steps as raising prices and reducing promotion and service. Selective demarketing consists of trying to reduce the demand coming from those parts of the market that are less profitable or less in need of the service. Demarketing does not aim to destroy demand but only reduce its level.

8. **Unwholesome demand.** Unwholesome products will attract organized efforts to discourage their consumption. Unselling campaigns have been conducted against cigarettes, alcohol, hard drugs, handguns, X-rated movies, and large families. The marketing task is to get people who like something to give it up, using such tools as fear communication, price hikes, and reduced availability.

Source: For a fuller discussion, see Philip Kotler, "The Major Tasks of Marketing Management," Journal of Marketing, October 1973, pp. 42–49; and Philip Kotler and Sidney J. Levy, "Demarketing, Yes, Demarketing," Harvard Business Review, November–December 1971, pp. 74–80.

COMPANY ORIENTATIONS TOWARD THE MARKETPLACE

We have described marketing management as the conscious effort to achieve desired exchange outcomes with target markets. Now the question arises, What philosophy should guide these marketing efforts? What weights should be given to the interests of the *organization*, the *customers*, and *society*? Very often these interests conflict. Clearly marketing activities should be carried out under some well-thought-out philosophy that spells out responsive and responsible marketing.

There are five competing concepts under which business and other organizations can conduct their marketing activity.

The Production Concept

The production concept is one of the oldest concepts guiding sellers.

> The *production concept* holds that consumers will favor those products that are widely available and low in cost. Management in production-oriented organizations concentrates on achieving high production efficiency and wide distribution coverage.

The assumption that consumers are primarily interested in product availability and low price holds in at least two types of situations. The first is where the demand for a product exceeds supply and therefore customers are more interested in obtaining the product than in its fine points. The suppliers will concentrate on finding ways to increase production. The second situation is where the product's cost is high and has to be brought down through increased productivity to expand the market. Texas Instruments provides a contemporary example of the production concept: [5]

> Texas Instruments, the Dallas-based electronics firm, is the leading American exponent of the "get-out-production, cut-the-price" philosophy that Henry Ford pioneered in the early 1900s in connection with developing the market for automobiles. Ford put all of his talent into perfecting the mass production of automobiles to bring down their costs so that Americans could afford them. Texas Instruments puts all of its efforts in building production volume and improving technology in order to bring down costs. It uses its lower costs to cut prices and expand the market size. It goes after and usually achieves the dominant position in its markets. To Texas Instruments, marketing means one thing: bringing down the price to buyers. This orientation is also found in many Japanese companies and makes Texas Instruments well prepared to compete with them in world markets.

Some service organizations also follow the production concept. Many medical and dental practices are organized on assembly-line principles, as are some government agencies, such as unemployment offices and license bureaus. While it results in handling many cases per hour, this type of management is open to the charge of impersonality and consumer insensitivity.

The Product Concept

Other sellers are guided by the product concept.

> The *product concept* holds that consumers will favor those products that offer the most quality, performance, and features. Management in these product-oriented organizations focus their energy on making good products and improving them over time.

These managers assume that buyers admire well-made products, can appraise product quality and performance, and are willing to pay more for product "extras." Many of these managers are caught up in a love affair with their product and fail

---

[5] See "Texas Instruments Shows U.S. Business How to Survive in the 1980s," *Business Week*, September 18, 1978, pp. 66ff. Also see, "The Long-Term Damage from TI's Bombshell," *Business Week*, June 15, 1981, p. 36.

to appreciate that the market may be less "turned on" and may even be moving in a different direction. They say "we make the finest men's tailored suits" or "we make the finest television sets" and wonder why the market doesn't appreciate this. There is a story about an office-files manufacturer complaining that his files should be selling better because they are the best in the world. "They can be dropped from a four-story building and not be damaged." "Yes," agreed his sales manager, "but our customers aren't planning to push them out of four-story buildings."

The Elgin National Watch Company provides a dramatic example of product-centered, rather than market-centered, thinking:

> Since its founding in 1864, the Elgin National Watch Company had enjoyed a reputation as one of America's finest watchmakers. Elgin placed its major emphasis on maintaining a superior product and merchandising it through a large network of leading jewelry and department stores. Its sales rose continuously until 1958, and thereafter its sales and market share began to slip. What happened to undermine Elgin's dominant position?
>
> Essentially, Elgin's management was so enamored with fine, traditionally styled watches that it didn't notice the major changes taking place in the consumer watch market. Many **consumers** were losing interest in the idea that a watch needed superior timekeeping accuracy, had to carry a prestigious name, and must last a lifetime. They expected a watch to tell time, look attractive, and not cost too much. Consumers had growing desires for convenience (self-winding watches), durability (waterproof and shockproof watches), and economy (pin-lever watches). As for **channels,** an increasing number of watches were being sold through mass-distribution outlets and discount stores. Many Americans wanted to avoid the higher markups of the local jeweler, and also often bought on impulse when exposed to inexpensive watch displays. As for **competitors,** many had added lower-priced watches to their line and had begun to sell them through mass-distribution channels. Elgin's problem was that it had riveted its attention to a set of products instead of interpreting and responding to a changing set of wants.

One of the most common manifestations of the product concept occurs with new products that a company invents. Management gets enamored of the product and often loses perspective. They fall into the "better mousetrap fallacy," believing that building a better mousetrap will lead people to beat a path to its door.[6] Consider the following example:

> In 1972, Du Pont researchers invented Kevlar, which it considers its most important new fiber since nylon. Kevlar has the same strength as steel with only one-fifth the weight. Du Pont sent out a call to its divisions to find applications for this new miracle fiber. Du Pont's executives imagined a huge number of applications and a billion-dollar market. Now, a decade later, Du Pont is still waiting for the bonanza. True, Kevlar is a very good fiber for bullet-proof vests, but there isn't a really big market for bullet-proof vests, so far. Kevlar is a promising fiber for sails, cords, and tires, and manufacturers are beginning to nibble. Eventually Kevlar may prove to be a miracle fiber, but it is taking longer than Du Pont expected.[7]

---

[6] Emerson originated this advice: "If a man . . . makes a better mousetrap . . . the world will beat a path to his door." Several companies, however, have built better mousetraps—one was a laser-mousetrap costing $1,500—and most of these companies failed. People do not automatically learn about new products, believe in their superiority, or feel a willingness to pay a higher price.

[7] See Lee Smith, "A Miracle in Search of a Market," *Fortune*, December 1, 1980, pp. 92–98.

The product concept leads to "marketing myopia," an undue concentration on the product rather than the need. Railroad management thought that users wanted trains rather than transportation and overlooked the growing challenge of the airlines, buses, trucks, and automobiles. Slide-rule manufacturers thought that engineers wanted slide-rules rather than calculating capacity and overlooked the challenge of pocket calculators. Colleges assume that high school graduates want a liberal arts education and overlook the shift of preference to vocationally-oriented education. Churches, symphonies, and the post office all assume that they are offering the public the right product and wonder why their sales falter. These organizations too often are looking into a mirror when they should be looking out of the window.

The Selling Concept

The selling concept (or sales concept) is another common approach many firms take to the market.

> The *selling concept* holds that consumers, if left alone, will ordinarily not buy enough of the organization's products. The organization must therefore undertake an aggressive selling and promotion effort.

The concept assumes that consumers typically show buying inertia or resistance and have to be coaxed into buying more; and that the company has available a whole array of effective selling and promotion tools to stimulate more buying.

The selling concept is undertaken most aggressively with "unsought goods," those goods that buyers normally do not think of buying, such as insurance, encyclopedias, and funeral plots. These industries have perfected various sales techniques to locate prospects and hard sell them on the benefits of their product.

Hard selling also occurs with sought goods, such as automobiles:[8]

> From the moment the customer walks into the showroom, the auto salesman "psychs him out." If the customer likes the floor model, he may be told that there is another customer about to buy it and that he should decide on the spot. If the customer balks at the price, the salesman offers to talk to the manager to get a special concession. The customer waits ten minutes and the salesman returns with "the boss doesn't like it but I got him to agree." The aim is to "work up the customer" to buy on the spot.

The selling concept is also practiced in the nonprofit area, by fund raisers, college admissions offices, and political parties. A political party will vigorously sell its candidate to the voters as being a fantastic person for the job.[9] The candidate stomps through voting precincts from early morning to late evening shaking hands, kissing babies, meeting donors, making breezy speeches. Countless dollars are spent on radio and television advertising, posters, and mailings. Any flaws in the candidate are shielded from the public because the aim is to get the sale, not worry about

---

[8] See Irving J. Rein, *Rudy's Red Wagon: Communication Strategies in Contemporary Society* (Glenview, Ill.: Scott, Foresman & Co., 1972).

[9] See Joseph McGinness, *The Selling of the President* (New York: Trident Press, 1969).

post-purchase satisfaction. After the election, the new official continues to take a sales-oriented view toward the citizens. There is little research into what the public wants and a lot of selling to get the public to accept policies that the politician or party wants.

Most firms practice the selling concept when they have overcapacity. Their immediate aim is to sell what they can make rather than make new things that can sell. In modern industrial economies, productive capacity has been built up to a point where most markets are *buyer markets* (i.e., the buyers are dominant), and sellers have to scramble hard for customers. Prospects are bombarded with television commercials, newspaper ads, direct mail, and sales calls. At every turn, someone is trying to sell something. As a result, the public identifies marketing with hard selling and advertising.

Therefore people are surprised when they are told that the most important part of marketing is not selling! Selling is only the tip of the marketing iceberg. Peter Drucker, one of the leading management theorists, puts it this way:

> There will always, one can assume, be need for some selling. *But the aim of marketing is to make selling superfluous*. The aim of marketing is to know and understand the customer so well that the product or service fits him and sells itself. Ideally, marketing should result in a customer who is ready to buy. All that should be needed then is to make the product or service available. . . .[10]

Thus selling, to be effective, must be preceded by several other marketing functions, such as needs assessment, marketing research, product development, pricing, and distribution. If the marketer does a good job of identifying consumer needs, developing appropriate products, and pricing, distributing, and promoting them effectively, these products will sell very easily. When Eastman Kodak designed its instamatic camera, when Atari designed its first video game, and when Mazda introduced its RX-7 sports car, these manufacturers were swamped with orders because they had designed the "right" product based on the marketing homework they had done.

Indeed, marketing based on hard selling carries high risks. It assumes that customers who are coaxed into buying the product will like it; and if they don't, they won't bad-mouth it to friends, or complain to consumer organizations. And they will possibly forget their disappointment and buy it again. These are indefensible assumptions to make about buyers.

The Marketing Concept

The marketing concept is a business philosophy that arose to challenge the previous concepts. Although it has a long history, its central tenets did not fully crystallize until the mid-1950s.[11] (See Exhibit 1–3 for some history.)

---

[10] Peter F. Drucker, *Management: Tasks, Responsibilities, Practices* (New York: Harper & Row, 1973), pp. 64–65.

[11] See John B. McKitterick, "What is the Marketing Management Concept?" *The Frontiers of Marketing Thought and Action* (Chicago: American Marketing Association, 1957), pp. 71–82; Fred J. Borch, "The Marketing Philosophy as a Way of Business Life," *The Marketing Concept: Its Meaning to Management*, Marketing Series, No. 99 (New York: American Management Association, 1957), pp. 3–5; and Robert J. Keith, "The Marketing Revolution," *Journal of Marketing*, January 1960, pp. 35–38.

Exhibit 1-3

HOW OLD IS THE MARKETING CONCEPT AND THE MARKETING DISCIPLINE?

People have offered different speculations as to when some business firms started to apprehend the marketing concept. Peter Drucker thinks the marketing concept was first grasped in the seventeenth century—and in Japan, not in the West.

> Marketing was invented in Japan around 1650 by the first member of the Mitsui family to settle in Tokyo as a merchant and to open what might be called the first department store. He anticipated by a full 250 years basic Sears, Roebuck policies: to be the buyer for his customers; to design the right products for them, and to develop sources for their production; the principle of your money back and no questions asked; and the idea of offering a large assortment of products to his customers rather than focusing on a craft, a product category, or a process.*

Drucker then suggests that marketing appeared in the West in the middle nineteenth century at the International Harvester Company.

> The first man in the West to see marketing clearly as the unique and central function of the business enterprise, and the creation of a customer as the specific job of management, was Cyrus H. McCormick (1809–1884). The history books mention only that he invented a mechanical harvester. But he also invented the basic tools of modern marketing: market research and market analysis, the concept of market standing, pricing policies, the service salesman, parts and service supply to the customer, and installment credit.†

Yet another fifty years passed before the marketing discipline emerged on the academic scene in America. In 1905 W. E. Kreusi taught a course at the University of Pennsylvania entitled "The Marketing of Products."‡ In 1910 Ralph Starr Butler offered a course entitled "Marketing Methods" at the University of Wisconsin. Butler explained how he conceived marketing:

> In considering the whole field of selling I developed the idea that personal salesmanship and advertising had to do simply with the final expression of the selling idea. My experience with the Procter & Gamble Company had convinced me that a manufacturer seeking to market a product had *to consider and solve a large number of problems* before he ever gave expression to the selling idea by sending a salesman on the road or inserting an advertisement in a publication. [italics added]§

Marketing departments within companies first appeared in the early twentieth century in the form of marketing research departments. The Curtis Publishing Company in 1911 installed the first marketing research department (called commercial research at the time) under the direction of Charles C. Parlin. Marketing research departments were subsequently established at U.S. Rubber (1916) and Swift and Company (1917). These departments were viewed as adjuncts to the sales department. Their task was to develop information that would make it easier for sales departments to sell. Over time, marketing research departments accepted additional responsibilities, such as sales analysis and marketing administration. Some time later, companies began to combine marketing research, advertising, customer services, and other miscellaneous marketing functions into marketing departments.

* Peter F. Drucker, *Management: Tasks, Responsibilities, Practices* (New York: Harper & Row, 1973), p. 62.
† Ibid.
‡ Robert Bartels, *The History of Marketing Thought*, 2nd ed. (Columbus, Ohio: Grid, 1976), p. 24.
§ Ibid.

The *marketing concept* holds that the key to achieving organizational goals consists in determining the needs and wants of target markets and delivering the desired satisfactions more effectively and efficiently than competitors.

The marketing concept has been expressed in many colorful ways:

- ☐ "Find wants and fill them"
- ☐ "Make what you can sell instead of trying to sell what you can make"
- ☐ "We have to stop marketing makeable products and learn to make marketable products"
- ☐ "Love the customer and not the product"
- ☐ "Have it your way" (Burger King)
- ☐ "You're the boss" (United Airlines)
- ☐ "To do all in our power to pack the customer's dollar full of value, quality and satisfaction" (J. C. Penney)

One of the best recent statements about making customer satisfaction the central mission of the firm is found in a recent ad by the Advanced Information Systems (AIS) division of American Bell:

> Now . . . today . . . our central focus must be on customers. We will listen to their voices . . . understand their concerns. We will focus on their needs . . . always . . . before our own. We will earn their respect. And we'll build a long-term partnership with them . . . based on mutual respect, trust, and our performance. Customers are our lifeblood . . . our entire reason for being. We must never forget who it is we serve. It's going to be up to us . . . all of us . . . to see that they continue to get what they want . . . when, where, and how they want it. . . . The true measure of how successful this partnership becomes will be directly related to how well we meet customer needs. How well we understand the specifics of their businesses. . . . Now let's get on with it. We've got promises to keep.[12]

Levitt has drawn a sharp contrast between the selling and the marketing concepts.

> Selling focuses on the needs of the seller; marketing on the needs of the buyer. Selling is preoccupied with the seller's need to convert his product into cash; marketing with the idea of satisfying the needs of the customer by means of the product and the whole cluster of things associated with creating, delivering and finally consuming it.[13]

The contrast is further shown in Figure 1–7. The selling concept starts with the company's existing products and calls for heavy selling and promoting to achieve profitable sales. The marketing concept starts with the company's target customers and their needs and wants; the company integrates and coordinates all the activities that will affect customer satisfaction; and the company achieves its profits through creating and maintaining customer satisfaction. In essence, *the marketing concept* is a *customers' needs and wants orientation* backed by *integrated marketing effort* aimed at generating *customer satisfaction* as the key to satisfying *organizational goals*.

The marketing concept expresses the company's commitment to the time-honored concept in economic theory known as *consumer sovereignty*. The determination of what is to be produced should not be in the hands of the companies or in the

---

[12] From a two-page American Bell ad in the *Chicago Tribune*, January 3, 1983.
[13] Levitt, "Marketing Myopia."

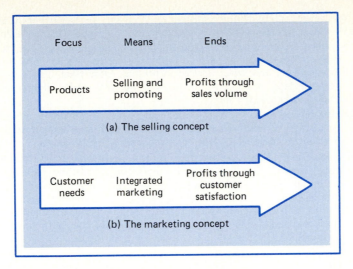

Focus	Means	Ends
Products	Selling and promoting	Profits through sales volume

(a) The selling concept

Focus	Means	Ends
Customer needs	Integrated marketing	Profits through customer satisfaction

(b) The marketing concept

FIGURE 1-7
The Selling and Marketing Concepts Contrasted

hands of government but in the hands of consumers. The companies produce what the consumers want and in this way maximize consumer welfare and earn their profits.

How many companies have adopted the marketing concept? The answer is, not many. Only a small number of companies really stand out as master practitioners of the marketing concept, companies such as Procter and Gamble, IBM, Avon, McDonald's, General Mills, General Foods, Gillette, Kodak, General Electric, Caterpillar, and John Deere.

These companies not only focus on the customer but are organized to respond effectively to changing customer needs. Not only do they have well-staffed marketing departments, but their other departments—manufacturing, finance, research and development, personnel, purchasing—all accept the concept that the customer is king. These organizations have a marketing culture that has deep roots in all of their departments and divisions.

Most companies have not arrived at full marketing maturity. They *think* they have marketing because they have a marketing vice-president, product managers, sales force, advertising budgets, and so on. They have marketing operations, and yet they fail to see the big picture and adapt to changing consumer needs and changing competition. International Harvester is on the verge of bankruptcy; Chrysler almost collapsed; and companies like Harley Davidson, Xerox, and Zenith, one-time leaders in their respective fields, are all rapidly losing market shares to Japanese competitors.

Most companies don't really grasp or embrace the marketing concept until driven to it by circumstances. Any of the following developments might prod them:

☐ **Sales decline.** When companies experience falling sales, they become desperate and start looking for answers. For example, newspapers show falling circulation as more people turn to television news. Some publishers are beginning to realize that they know very little about why people read newspapers and what they want out of newspapers. These

Role of Marketing in Today's Organizations   **23**

publishers are commissioning consumer research and, on the basis of the findings, attempting to redesign newspapers to be contemporary, relevant, and interesting to readers.

□ **Slow growth.** Even slow sales growth gives companies an impetus to cast about for new markets. They recognize a need for marketing know-how if they are to successfully identify, evaluate, and select new opportunities. Dow Chemical, wanting new sources of profits, decided to enter consumer markets and invested heavily in acquiring marketing expertise to carry out the job.

□ **Changing buying patterns.** Many companies are living through increasingly turbulent markets marked by rapidly changing customer wants. These companies need more marketing know-how if they are to continue producing value for buyers.

□ **Increasing competition.** Complacent companies may suddenly be attacked by powerful marketing companies and forced to learn marketing to meet the challenge. Thus American Telephone and Telegraph (AT&T) remained a regulated, marketing-naive company until the 1970s when other companies suddenly were allowed to sell telecommunications equipment to AT&T's customers. At this point, AT&T plunged into the marketing waters and hired the best people it could find to go down the marketing learning curve as fast as possible.[14]

□ **Increasing marketing expenditures.** Companies may find their expenditures for advertising, sales promotion, marketing research, and customer service getting out of hand. Management then decides it is time to rationalize the marketing function.

In the course of converting to a market-oriented company, a company will face three hurdles, those of organized resistance, slow learning, and fast forgetting.

Organized resistance. Some other departments in the company, particularly manufacturing and R&D, do not like to see marketing built up because it threatens their own power in the organization. The nature of the threat is illustrated in Figure 1–8. Initially, the sales/marketing function is seen as one of several *equally* important business functions in a check-and-balance relationship [Fig. 1–8(a)]. A dearth of demand then leads marketers to argue that their function is somewhat more important than the others [Fig. 1–8(b)]. A few marketing enthusiasts go further and say marketing is the major function of the enterprise, for without customers, there would be no company. They put marketing at the center with other business functions serving as support functions [Fig. 1–8(c)]. This view incenses the other managers, who do not want to think of themselves as working for marketing. Enlightened marketers clarify the issue by putting the customer rather than marketing at the center of the company [Fig. 1–8(d)]. They argue for a *customer orientation* in which all functions work together to sense, serve, and satisfy the customer. Finally, some marketers say that marketing still needs to command a central position in the firm if customers' needs are to be correctly interpreted and efficiently satisfied [Fig. 1–8(e)].

The marketer's argument for the concept of the corporation shown in Figure 1–8(e) is as follows:

1. The assets of the firm have little value without the existence of customers.
2. The key task of the firm is therefore to create and hold customers.
3. Customers are attracted through promises and held through satisfaction.
4. Marketing's task is to define an appropriate promise to the customer and to insure the delivery of satisfaction.

---

[14] See Bro Uttal, "Selling is No Longer Mickey Mouse at AT&T," *Fortune*, July 17, 1978, pp. 98–104.

5. The actual satisfaction delivered to the customer is affected by the performance of the other departments.

6. Marketing needs influence or control over these other departments if customers are to be satisfied.

The following situation shows what can go wrong if marketing lacks some control or influence over the other departments:

> The Tender Company (name disguised) is a manufacturer of high-quality packaged sliced meats—bacon, ham, bologna, and salami. The company's products sell in U.S. supermarkets at a premium price to match their premium quality. The vice-president of marketing sees the Tender name as making a promise to the customer that the products are of consistently high quality. Yet from time to time, the manufacturing people fail to exercise adequate quality control: for example, some fatty bacon will be packaged instead of being discarded. Some consumers will find that they have paid a premium price for poor-quality bacon. The company's implicit promise to the customer has been broken. The resulting dissatisfaction can lead to customer loss. Marketing wants the power to insure that this does not happen by having some influence or control over manufacturing.

FIGURE 1-8
Evolving Views of Marketing's Role in the Company

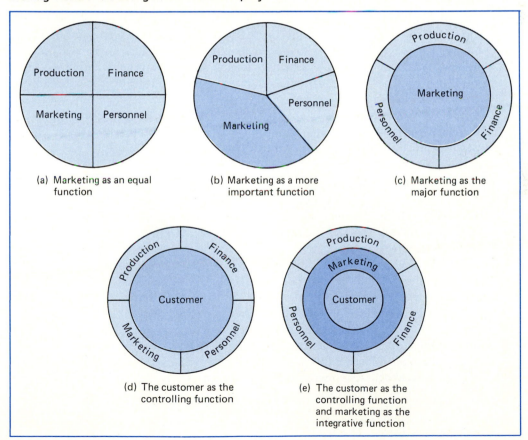

(a) Marketing as an equal function

(b) Marketing as a more important function

(c) Marketing as the major function

(d) The customer as the controlling function

(e) The customer as the controlling function and marketing as the integrative function

Customer satisfaction can be hurt in other ways. Poor production scheduling might result in late deliveries to the trade and out-of-stock conditions facing the customer. Poor R&D may lead to new-product failures. Inadequate funds allocated to marketing may prevent the development of improved packaging. The interests of different departments often come into conflict. Marketing's continuous effort to keep every department's attention riveted on producing customer satisfaction interferes with the felt autonomy of these departments. No wonder other departments react with some resistance to marketing for trying to take center stage in the firm.

The resistance to marketing is especially conspicuous in industries where marketing is being introduced or proposed for the first time, such as in the legal professions, libraries, hospitals, or colleges. Colleges have to face the hostility of professors, and hospitals have to face the hostility of doctors, because each group thinks that marketing their service would be degrading. In the newspaper industry, the hostility of oldtimers is shown by one newspaper editor who wrote a diatribe entitled "Beware the 'Market' Thinkers."[15] This editor warned newspapers not to let marketers in because they do not understand the function of newspapers, which is to print news. Marketing is not the solution, he feels, to the national decline in newspaper readership. Marketers would corrupt all that is good about today's newspapers.

Slow learning.   In spite of resistance in many quarters, companies eventually manage to build up the marketing function in their organization. The company president gives enthusiastic public support to the function; new job positions are created; outside marketing talent is hired; key members of management attend marketing seminars to gain a deeper understanding of marketing; the marketing budget is substantially increased; marketing planning and control systems are introduced. Even with these steps, however, the learning as to what marketing really is comes slowly. In the typical company, marketing enlightenment tends to pass through five stages. These stages are described and illustrated for the banking industry in Exhibit 1–4.

Fast forgetting.   Even after strong marketing is installed in an organization and matures through the various stages, management must fight a strong tendency to forget basic marketing principles. Management tends to forget marketing principles in the wake of marketplace success. For example, a number of major American companies entered European markets in the 1950s and 1960s expecting to achieve outstanding success with their sophisticated products and marketing capabilities. A number of them failed, and a major reason is they forgot the marketing maxim: Know your market and know how to satisfy it. American companies came into these markets with their current products and advertising programs instead of redesigning them on the basis of what the market needed. For example, General Mills went into the British market with its Betty Crocker cake mixes only to have to withdraw a short time later. Their angel cake and devil's food cake sounded too exotic for British homemakers. And many potential customers felt that such perfect-looking

---

[15] William H. Hornby, "Beware the 'Market' Thinkers," *The Quill*, 1976, pp. 14ff. However, see William A. Mindak, "Do Newspaper Publishers Suffer From "Marketing Myopia?" *Journalism Quarterly*, summer 1965, pp. 433–42.

Exhibit 1–4

FIVE STAGES IN THE SLOW LEARNING OF WHAT BANK MARKETING IS ALL ABOUT

Before the mid-1950s, bankers had little understanding or regard for marketing. Banks were supplying needed services. Bankers did not have to make a case for checking accounts, savings, loans, or safe-deposit boxes. The bank building was created in the image of a Greek temple, calculated to impress the public with the bank's importance and solidity. The interior was austere, and the tellers rarely smiled. One lending officer arranged his office so that a prospective borrower would sit across from his massive desk on a lower chair than his own. The office window was located behind the officer's back, and the sun would pour in on the hapless customer, who tried to explain why he or she needed a loan. This was the bank's posture before the age of marketing.

1. Marketing Is Advertising, Sales Promotion, and Publicity

Marketing came into banks in the late 1950s, not in the form of the "marketing concept" but in the form of the "advertising and promotion concept." Banks and other financial institutions were experiencing increased competition for savings. A few financial institutions decided to adopt the marketing weapons of the soap companies. They increased their budgets for advertising and sales promotion and managed to attract many new customers. Their competitors were forced into adopting the same measures and scurried out to hire advertising agencies and promotion experts.

2. Marketing Is Smiling and a Friendly Atmosphere

The banks that first introduced modern advertising and promotion soon found their advantage canceled by the rush of imitators. They also learned another lesson: Attracting people to a bank is easy; converting them into loyal customers is hard. These banks began to formulate a larger concept of marketing, that of trying to please the customer. Bankers had to learn to smile. The tellers had to be retrained. The bars had to be taken off the tellers' windows. The interior of the banks had to be redesigned to produce a warm, friendly atmosphere. Even the outside Greek-temple architecture had to be changed.

The first banks to implement these changes began to outperform their competitors in attracting and holding new customers. Their competitors, however, quickly figured out what was happening and rushed into similar programs of friendliness training and decor improvement. Soon all banks were so friendly that friendliness lost its potency as a determinant factor in bank choice.

3. Marketing Is Innovation

Banks had to search for a new basis for differential advantage. Some banks began to realize that they are in the business of meeting the evolving financial needs of their customers. These banks began to think in terms of continuous innovation of new and valued customer services, such as credit cards, Christmas savings plans, and automatic bank loans. Bank of America, for example, today offers over 350 financial products to customers.

A successful innovation provides the innovative bank with a competitive lead. Financial services, however, are easily copied, and advantages are short-lived. But if the same bank invests in continuous innovation, it can stay ahead of the other banks.

4. Marketing Is Positioning

What happens when all banks advertise, smile, and innovate? Clearly they begin to look alike. They are forced to find a new basis for distinction. They begin to realize that no bank can be the best bank for all customers. No bank can offer all products. A bank must choose. It must examine its opportunities and "take a position" in the market.

Positioning goes beyond image making. The image-making bank seeks to cultivate an image in the customer's mind as a large, friendly, or efficient bank. It often develops a symbol, such as a lion (Harris Bank in Chicago) or kangaroo (Continental Bank in Chicago) to dramatize its personality in a distinctive way. Yet the customer may see the competing banks as basically alike, except for the chosen symbols. Positioning is an attempt to distinguish the bank from its competitors along real dimensions in order to be the preferred bank to certain segments of the market. Positioning aims to help customers know the real differences between competing banks, so that they can match themselves to the bank that can provide them with the most satisfaction of their needs.

5. Marketing is Marketing Analysis, Planning, and Control

There is a higher concept of bank marketing, which represents the ultimate essence of modern marketing. The issue is whether the bank has installed effective systems for marketing analysis, planning, and control. One large bank, which had achieved sophistication in advertising, friendliness, innovation, and positioning, nevertheless lacked good systems of marketing planning and control. Each fiscal year, commercial loan officers submitted their volume goals, usually 10 percent higher than the previous year's goals. They also requested a budget increase of 10 percent. No rationale or plans accompanied these submissions. Top management was satisfied with the officers who achieved their goals. One loan officer, judged to be a good performer, retired and was replaced by a younger man, who proceeded to increase the loan volume 50 percent the following year! The bank painfully learned that it had failed to measure the potentials of its various markets, to require marketing plans, to set quotas, and to develop appropriate reward systems.

---

cakes as those pictured on the Betty Crocker packages must be hard to make. American marketers failed to appreciate the major cultural variations between and even within European countries and the need to start where the consumers are, not where their products are. Sorenson noted:

> In the United States, the marketing concept appears to be well into the mature phase of its own life cycle. It is increasingly being questioned, criticized, and—in some instances—ignored or discarded. By contrast, the marketing concept in Europe is alive and vigorous and just entering the rapid growth stage of its life cycle.[16]

The Societal Marketing Concept

In recent years, some people have raised the question of whether the marketing concept is an appropriate organizational goal in an age of environmental deterioration, resource shortages, explosive population growth, worldwide inflation, and neglected social

---

[16] Ralph Z. Sorensen II, "U.S. Marketers Can Learn From European Innovators," *Harvard Business Review*, September–October 1972, pp. 89–99.

services.[17] The question is whether the firm that does an excellent job of sensing, serving, and satisfying individual consumer wants is necessarily acting in the best long-run interests of consumers and society. The marketing concept sidesteps the potential conflicts between consumer wants, consumer interests, and long-run societal welfare.

Consider the following criticisms:

- ☐ The fast-food hamburger industry offers tasty but not nutritious food. The hamburgers have a high fat content, and the restaurants promote fries and pies, two products high in starch and fat.
- ☐ The American auto industry traditionally catered to the American demand for large automobiles, but meeting this desire resulted in high fuel consumption, heavy pollution, more fatal accidents to those in small cars, and higher auto purchase and repair costs.
- ☐ The soft-drink industry has catered to the American desire for convenience by increasing the share of one-way disposable bottles. However, the one-way bottle represents a great waste of resources in that approximately seventeen bottles are necessary where formerly one two-way bottle made seventeen trips before it was damaged; many one-way bottles are not biodegradable; and these bottles often are a littering element.
- ☐ The detergent industry catered to the American passion for whiter clothes by offering a product that polluted rivers and streams, killed fish, and injured recreational possibilities.

These situations led to a call for a new concept to revise or replace the marketing concept. Among the proposals are "the human concept," "the intelligent consumption concept," and "the ecological imperative concept," all of which get at different aspects of the same problem.[18] We propose calling it "the societal marketing concept."

> The *societal marketing concept* holds that the organization's task is to determine the needs, wants, and interests of target markets and to deliver the desired satisfactions more effectively and efficiently than competitors in a way that preserves or enhances the consumer's and the society's well-being.

The societal marketing concept calls upon marketers to balance three considerations in setting their marketing policies, namely, company profits, consumer want satisfaction, and society interests. Originally, companies based their marketing decisions largely on immediate company profit calculations. Then they began to recognize the long-run importance of satisfying consumer wants, and this introduced the marketing concept. Now they are beginning to factor in society's interests in their decision making. The societal marketing concept calls for balancing all three considerations. A number of companies have achieved notable sales and profit gains through adopting and practicing the societal marketing concept. Here is an example:

---

[17] See Laurence P. Feldman, "Societal Adaptation: A New Challenge for Marketing," *Journal of Marketing*, July 1971, pp. 54–60; and Martin L. Bell and C. William Emery, "The Faltering Marketing Concept," *Journal of Marketing*, October 1971, pp. 37–42.

[18] Leslie M. Dawson, "The Human Concept: New Philosophy for Business," *Business Horizons*, December 1969, pp. 29–38; James T. Rothe and Lissa Benson, "Intelligent Consumption: An Attractive Alternative to the Marketing Concept," *MSU Business Topics*, Winter 1974, pp. 29–34; and George Fisk, "Criteria for a Theory of Responsible Consumption," *Journal of Marketing*, April 1973, pp. 24–31.

Giant Food, Inc., a leading supermarket chain in the Washington, D.C., area, took the initiative and introduced unit pricing, open dating, and nutritional labeling. They assigned home economists to their stores to help consumers buy and prepare food more intelligently. They invited Esther Peterson, formerly the President's advisor on consumer affairs, to join the board of directors and provide guidance on consumer-oriented retailing. According to a spokesman for the company, "These actions have improved Giant's goodwill immeasurably and have earned the admiration of leaders of the consumer movement."

THE RAPID ADOPTION OF MARKETING MANAGEMENT

Marketing management is a subject of growing interest in all sizes and types of organizations within and outside the business sector in all kinds of countries. We will conclude with this brief overview of the rapid adoption of marketing management.

In the Business Sector

In the business sector, marketing entered the consciousness of different companies at different times. General Electric, General Motors, Procter & Gamble, and Coca-Cola were among the leaders. Marketing spread most rapidly in consumer packaged goods companies, consumer durables companies, and industrial equipment companies—in that order. Producers of commodities such as steel, chemicals, and paper came later to marketing consciousness, and many still have a long way to go. Within the last decade consumer-service firms, especially airlines and banks, have moved toward modern marketing. Marketing is also beginning to excite the interest of insurance and stock brokerage companies, although they have a long way to go in applying marketing effectively.

The most recent business groups to take an interest in marketing are professional service providers, such as lawyers, accountants, physicians, and architects. Professional societies, until recently, prohibited their members from engaging in price competition, client solicitation, and advertising. The U.S. antitrust division recently ruled that these restraints are illegal. Accountants, lawyers, and other professional groups are now allowed to advertise and to price aggressively.

The fierce competition engendered by the new limits on corporate growth is forcing accounting firms into aggressive new postures. . . . The accountants insist on referring to their efforts to drum up business as "practice development." But many of the activities that fall under this euphemism are dead ringers for what is called "marketing" in other fields. . . . Accountants speak of "positioning" their firms and of "penetrating" unexploited new industries. They compile "hit lists" of prospective clients and then "surround" them by placing their firms' partners in close social contact with the top executives of the target companies."[19]

In the Nonprofit Sector

Marketing is increasingly attracting the interest of nonprofit organizations such as colleges, hospitals, police departments, museums, and symphonies. Consider the following developments:

---

[19] Deborah Rankin, "How C.P.A.'s Sell Themselves," *New York Times*, September 25, 1977.

Of the nation's 3,000 private colleges, 170 have closed their doors since 1965, unable to attract enough students or funds or both. Annual tuition alone at the top private colleges is now over $10,000. If college costs continue to climb at the current rate, the parents of a child born today will have to spend over $100,000 to pay for a bachelor's degree at one of the top private colleges.

Hospital costs continue to soar, leading to daily room rates in excess of $300 in some large hospitals. Many of the nation's 7,000 hospitals are experiencing underutilization, particularly in the maternity and pediatrics sections. Some experts have predicted the closing of 1,400–1,500 hospitals in the next ten years.

The Catholic Church drew as many as 55 percent of all adult Catholics under thirty years of age to church in a typical week in 1966. By 1975 the figure had fallen to 39 percent, and further declines in weekly attendance are expected.

Many performing arts groups cannot attract enough audiences. Even those that have seasonal sellouts, such as the Lyric Opera Company of Chicago, face huge operating deficits at the end of the year.

Many flourishing nonprofit organizations of yesteryear—the YMCA, Salvation Army, Girl Scouts, and Woman's Christian Temperance Union—are losing members and failing to attract enough financial support.

These organizations have marketplace problems. Their administrators are struggling to keep them alive in the face of changing consumer attitudes and diminishing financial resources. Many institutions have turned to marketing as a possible answer to their problems. Over 10 percent of the nation's hospitals now have a marketing director, in contrast to less than 1 percent a decade ago. U.S. government agencies are showing an increased interest in marketing. The U.S. Postal Service and Amtrak have developed marketing plans for their respective operations. The U.S. Army has a marketing plan to attract recruits and is one of the top advertising spenders in the country. Other government agencies are now marketing energy conservation, antismoking campaigns and other public causes.

In the International Sector

Marketing skills are found in many countries of the world. In fact, several European and Japanese multinationals—companies like Nestle, Beecham, Toyota, and Sony—have in many cases outperformed their U.S. competitors.[20] Multinationals have introduced and spread modern marketing practices throughout the world. This has prodded smaller domestic companies in various countries to start looking into ways to strengthen their marketing muscle so they can compete effectively with the multinationals.

In socialist countries, marketing has traditionally had a bad name. However, various functions of marketing, such as marketing research, branding, advertising, and sales promotion, are now spreading rapidly. In the USSR, there are now over one hundred state-operated advertising agencies and marketing research firms.[21] Sev-

[20] Sorensen, "U.S. Marketers Can Learn."
[21] Thomas V. Greer, *Marketing in the Soviet Union* (New York: Holt, Rinehart & Winston, 1973).

eral companies in Poland and Hungary have marketing departments, and several socialist universities teach marketing.

SUMMARY

Marketing has its origins in the fact that humans are creatures of needs and wants. Needs and wants create a state of discomfort in people, which is resolved through acquiring products to satisfy these needs and wants. Since many products can satisfy a given need, product choice is guided by the concept of value and expected satisfaction. These products are obtainable in several ways: self-production, coercion, begging, and exchange. Most human society works on the principle of exchange, which means that people become specialists in the production of particular products and trade them for the other things they need. A market is a group of people who share a similar need. Marketing encompasses those activities that represent working with markets, that is, trying to actualize potential exchanges.

Marketing management is the conscious effort to achieve desired exchange outcomes with target markets. The marketer's basic skill lies in influencing the level, timing, and composition of demand for a product, service, organization, place, person, or idea.

Five alternative philosophies can guide organizations in carrying out their marketing activity. The production concept holds that consumers will favor products that are affordable and available, and therefore management's major task is to improve production and distribution efficiency and bring down prices. The product concept holds that consumers favor quality products that are reasonably priced, and therefore little promotional effort is required. The selling concept holds that consumers will not buy enough of the company's products unless they are stimulated through a substantial selling and promotion effort. The marketing concept holds that the main task of the company is to determine what a chosen set of customers' needs, wants, and preferences are and to adapt the company to delivering the desired satisfactions. The societal marketing concept holds that the main task of the company is to generate customer satisfaction and long-run consumer and societal well-being as the key to satisfying organizational goals and responsibilities.

Interest in marketing is intensifying as more organizations in the business sector, the nonprofit sector, and the international sector recognize how marketing contributes to improved performance in the marketplace.

QUESTIONS

1. From 1979 to early 1983, over 4,400 auto dealerships in the U.S. went out of business. William Turnbull, president of the National Automobile Dealers Association, stated that if the remaining dealers were to survive, they must change their orientation toward consumers. What might he have meant by that statement?

2. During 1982 and 1983, AT&T ran ads promoting a toll-free number where consumers would talk to a Bell representative on any telephone-related subject (i.e., what effect will the antitrust settlement have on my phone rates, can I buy the phone I'm renting from AT&T, etc.). Is this marketing? Why or why not?

3. Does the marketing concept imply that marketers should confine themselves only to those wants and needs consumers say they want to satisfy?

4. Is there a contradiction between marketing something that has negative demand and practicing the marketing concept?

5. In the face of a long-term energy shortage, many public utilities have sought to reduce their customers' use of electricity. Propose a demarketing plan that will bring down the level of demand and help utilities avoid "brownouts."

6. Do you think that all companies need to practice the marketing concept to some extent? Could you cite companies that do not particularly need this orientation? Which companies need it most?

7. "Marketing is the science of actualizing the buying potentials of a market for a specific product." Does this definition reflect a product, selling, or marketing concept?

8. "Marketing is not simply the job of a group of people in the company who are responsible for selling the company's products. Every member of the firm should function as a marketer." What does it mean for a company recruiter, for example, to function like a marketer?

9. The five stages through which organizations pass as they develop an understanding of marketing were discussed in connection with the banking industry. Discuss them in the context of four-year private liberal arts colleges that are facing declining enrollment.

10. What would a perfume company do differently if its objective was to maximize sales? profits? consumer satisfaction? consumers' lifestyles? quality of life? In other words, how does the company's objective make a difference to its marketing practice?

Strategic Planning and the Marketing Management Process

2

There are three types of companies; those who make things happen; those who watch things happen; those who wonder what happened.

ANONYMOUS

All companies must look beyond their present situation and develop a long-term strategy to meet changing conditions in their industry. They must develop a game plan for achieving their long-run objectives. There is no one strategy that is optimal for all companies. Each company must determine what makes the most sense in the light of its position in the industry and its objectives, opportunities, and resources. Here are vastly different current game plans of four major companies operating in today's rubber tire industry:

> Goodyear Tire & Rubber Co., the world's No. 1 tiremaker, is pouring money into this industry in spite of the industry's slow growth, overcapacity, and price wars. Goodyear is investing heavily in plant modernization to lower costs and improve quality, in R&D to develop more advanced tires, and in marketing and advertising to build up consumer and dealer preference. The result is an increased market share for Goodyear, but it will take a long time for this higher market share to translate into higher profits.[1]

---
[1] See "Goodyear: Will Staying No. 1 in Tires Pump Up Profits?" *Business Week*, July 12, 1982, pp. 85–88.

34

The French company Michelin, the world's No. 2 tiremaker, rose to its high place by leading the industry in innovation. Michelin introduced the steelbelted radial tire, a tire that lasted longer than its competitors'. Michelin's continuous innovation of better tires won it a "Cadillac" reputation for high quality and allowed it to charge premium prices. Although Michelin has lately lowered its prices to gain market share, it still expects to maintain its leadership through technological innovation.[2]

Uniroyal, the fourth-ranked company in the tire industry, has chosen the route of diversification out of the tire business. Its strongest push will be in two nontire businesses, agricultural chemicals and fabricated plastic products, which together account for 33 percent of its sales but over 75 percent of its earnings. Uniroyal has divested its business units making fire hoses, inner tubes, and golf balls, but still has to figure out what to do with the core of the company, namely the domestic tire division, which hangs like an albatross around its neck. Uniroyal is a major supplier of original equipment tires to General Motors, but because of the less than 2 percent growth in the tire industry and the intense price cutting, Uniroyal would be ready to sell its tire business if it could find a buyer.[3]

Armstrong Rubber Co., sixth among U.S. tiremakers, has decided to specialize in making tires almost entirely for the replacement market. It has shown great skill in picking and exploiting specialized niches, such as tires for recreational vehicles and farm equipment. "When you really excel in a market segment, you get paid for it," said Frank R. O'Keefe Jr., Armstrong's president. O'Keefe has sharpened Armstrong's strategic planning process through which Armstrong identifies profitable market segments and its marketing planning process through which it pursues leadership in each chosen market segment.[4]

All of these companies exhibit adaptations to a rapidly changing environment. Each has adopted a different game plan: Goodyear will press for *cost reduction*; Michelin will pursue *innovation*; Uniroyal has chosen the route of *diversification*; and Armstrong will practice *nichemanship* by entering small but highly profitable markets. The difficult task of selecting a corporate strategy for long-run survival and growth is called *strategic planning*.

Marketing plays an important, indeed critical, role in company strategic planning. Corporate strategic planners depend upon the company marketers in at least five ways. First, they depend on marketers for ideas on new products and market opportunities. Second, they depend on marketers to evaluate each new opportunity, specifically, whether the market is large enough and whether the company has sufficient marketing strengths to pursue the opportunity. Third, marketers have the task of developing a detailed marketing plan for each new venture, and spelling out the product, price, distribution, and promotion strategy and tactics. Fourth, the marketing personnel are responsible for carrying out each plan in the marketplace. Fifth, the marketing personnel must evaluate the ongoing results, take corrective actions where necessary, and advise strategic planners when the business is no longer viable. Altogether, the marketing group performs several critical tasks in the company's development and implementation of strategic plans.

---

[2] See "Michelin: Spinning its Wheels in the Competitive U.S. Market," *Business Week*, December 1, 1980, pp. 119–24.

[3] See "Uniroyal: Narrowing Choices As It Clings to the Tire Business," *Business Week*, June 11, 1979, pp. 74–76.

[4] See "The Niche Pickers at Armstrong Rubber," *Fortune*, September 6, 1982, pp. 100–104.

In this chapter, we will look more closely at the relationship between corporate strategic planning and the marketing management process. We will address three questions:

☐ How can companies improve their chances of surviving and prospering in rapidly changing environments?

☐ What are the major *strategic planning tools* used by today's most successful companies?

☐ What are the major steps in the *marketing management process* as practiced by successful companies?

A THEORY OF COMPANY EFFECTIVENESS IN A CHANGING ENVIRONMENT

Before examining the specific ways in which strategic planning and marketing management help companies achieve their objectives, we need to take a broad look at what companies must do to survive and prosper in a rapidly changing environment. Our analysis rests on three concepts: *organization-environment fit*, *environmental change*, and *organizational adaptability*.

Organization-Environment Fit

Every organization interacts with a part of the total environment, which we will call the *relevant environment*. The relevant environment of an automobile manufacturer consists of car buyers, dealers, suppliers, competitors, banks, and various publics. The company's basic task is to design, produce, distribute, and sell attractive goods and services to its target customer market. If its target customers see good value in the company's offer, they will buy its products, and the company will have the money to pay its employees, purchase other factors of production, and pay profits to its stockholders. Thus every company is actively engaged in producing and exchanging values with its environment.

Those companies that are well fitted to their environments will prosper. Porter has identified a set of conditions external to the firm that contribute to its degree of fit with its environment and therefore its profit potential. They are:[5]

☐ **High barriers to entry.** The company operates in an industry that has high barriers to entry. Other firms would find it hard to enter because of such hurdles as patent protection, scarce source of supply, and high capital requirements.

☐ **Weak competitors.** The company faces weak, few, or no competitors making the same product.

☐ **Weak substitutes.** Customers are not able to find satisfactory substitute products or services to replace this product.

☐ **Weak customers.** The company's customers do not possess strong bargaining power to force prices down and reduce the company's profits.

☐ **Weak suppliers.** The suppliers do not possess strong bargaining power to raise costs and reduce the company's profits.

---

[5] See Michael E. Porter, *Competitive Strategy: Techniques for Analyzing Industries and Competitors* (New York: Free Press, 1980), Chapter 1.

Thus General Motors enjoyed very high profits through most of its existence (until recent years) because it was hard for new firms to enter the auto industry, its competitors were relatively weak, customers could find no satisfactory substitutes for the automobile, individual buyers did not have much bargaining power, and the suppliers (steel companies, trade unions, and the like) were not strong enough to bargain away all of General Motors' profits.

These conditions determine the profit potential for any firm currently engaged in that industry. The firm's actual profits depend on the *market size and growth rate*, the *firm's size and positioning strategy* relative to competitors, and *management's ability* to capitalize on its position.

Firms are able to make the most money in large and growing markets. In fact, in these markets, most firms can make a lot of money even if they aren't well managed. There are enough customers wanting the product in relation to the existing supply that all the firms can sell their output. If the market has stopped growing, however, then the leading firms in the industry can still make money; but some of the other firms are likely to make little or no money unless they find a special niche. If the market is actually declining, then most of the companies will experience declining profits or losses.

The company's size and positioning strategy will also determine its profits. Larger companies normally enjoy lower unit costs because of their greater purchasing power. A key factor, however, is the company's positioning strategy in the market. Porter has suggested that a company can pursue one of three generic strategies within a market:[6]

☐ **Overall cost leadership.** Here the company works hard to achieve the lowest costs of production and distribution, so that it can price lower than its competitors and win a large market share. Firms pursuing this strategy must be good at engineering, purchasing, manufacturing, and physical distribution and need less skill in marketing. Texas Instruments is a leading practitioner of this strategy.

☐ **Differentiation.** Here the company concentrates on creating a highly differentiated product line and marketing program so that it comes across as the class leader in the industry. Most customers would prefer to own this brand if its price is not too high. Companies pursuing this strategy have major strengths in R&D, design, quality control, and marketing. IBM and Caterpillar enjoy the differentiation position in computers and heavy construction equipment, respectively.

☐ **Focus.** Here the company focuses its effort on serving a few market segments well rather than going after the whole market. The company gets to know the needs of these segments and pursues either cost leadership, product differentiation, or both, within each segment. Thus Armstrong Rubber has specialized in making superior tires for farm equipment vehicles and recreational vehicles, and keeps looking for other niches to serve.

According to Porter, companies that pursue a clear strategy—one of the above—are likely to perform well. Those firms pursuing the same strategy constitute a *strategic group*. The firm that carries off that strategy best will make the most profits. Thus the lowest-cost firm among those firms pursuing a low-cost strategy will do the best. Porter suggests that firms that do not pursue a clear strategy—*middle-of-the-roaders*—

---

[6] See Porter, *Competitive Strategy,* Chapter 2.

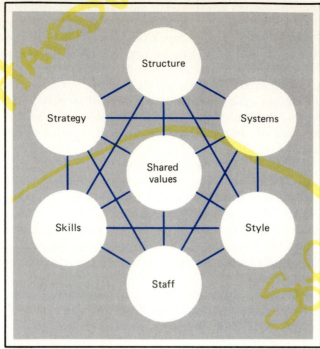

FIGURE 2–1
McKinsey 7-S Framework

SOURCE: Thomas J. Peters and Robert H. Waterman, Jr., *In Search of Excellence: Lessons from America's Best Run Companies.* Copyright © 1982 by Thomas J. Peters and Robert H. Waterman, Jr. Reprinted by permission of Harper & Row, Publishers.

do the worst. Thus Chrysler and International Harvester both came upon difficult times because neither stood out in their respective industries as either lowest in cost, highest in perceived value, or best in serving some market segment. Middle-of-the-roaders try to be good on all strategic dimensions, but since strategic dimensions require different and often inconsistent ways to organize the firm, these companies end up being not particularly excellent at anything.

Even if a firm has a clear strategy and is the leader of its strategic group, it may not be enough. The firm needs to be managed effectively. According to McKinsey & Company, one of the world's leading consulting firms, strategy is not enough. Strategy is only one of seven elements that the best-managed companies exhibit.[7] The McKinsey 7-S framework is shown in Figure 2–1. The first three elements—strategy, structure, and systems—are considered the hardware of success, and the next four—style, staff, skills, and shared values—are the software.

Most management literature has emphasized the hardware elements. Thus a

---

[7] See Thomas J. Peters and Robert H. Waterman, Jr., *In Search of Excellence: Lessons from America's Best-Run Companies* (New York: Harper & Row, 1982), pp. 9–12. The same framework is used in Richard Tanner Pascale and Anthony G. Athos, *The Art of Japanese Management: Applications for American Executives* (New York: Simon and Schuster, 1981).

successful company is one that develops an appropriate *strategy* to reach its goals, builds an appropriate organizational *structure* to carry out this strategy, and equips the organization with effective *systems* of information, planning, control, and reward to get the job done. The key idea has been that strategy, not structure, is the starting point.[8] The company should first decide where it wants to go in the future, and then develop an organizational structure and systems to carry this out. Thus General Motors decides that it must produce small cars in the future, and its task is to reorganize to do this well. This makes more sense than if General Motors avoided this strategy because its current structure was equipped for making only large cars.

Consultants at McKinsey added the four software elements as a result of studying a large sample of excellently managed companies—IBM, P&G, Caterpillar, Delta, McDonald's, Levi Strauss, and so on—and discovering that their strengths went beyond strategy, structure, and systems. These organizations have four more elements. The first is *style*, which means that employees in that company share a common style of behaving and thinking. Thus everyone at McDonald's smiles at the customer, and many employees of IBM are very professional in their bearing and attire. Each successful company exhibits a distinct and widely shared culture that fits its strategy.[9] The second element is *skills*, which means that employees have mastered those skills— such as financial analysis and marketing planning—that are needed to carry out the company's strategy. The third element is *staffing*, in that the company has hired able people and put them into the right jobs to exercise their talents. The fourth "soft" element is *shared values*, in that the employees of the firm share the same guiding values and missions. The well-managed company has a driving purpose and creed that everyone in the company knows and is proud to practice.

Environmental Change

At a given time, an organization's fit with its relevant environment may be excellent. The environment may be rich in opportunity and the organization's seven S's are well aligned with this environment to make a good return. But the company can count on one thing: that the environment will change. And when it does, the company will be pressed to make appropriate adjustments in one or more of the seven S's if it is to continue to prosper.

The extent of the required adjustments depends on the degree, speed, and complexity of the environmental change. Some environments are fairly stable from year to year in their economics, technology, law, and culture, and firms in these environments need not change very much. Other environments are slowly evolving in a fairly predictable way; firms that perceive this evolution can make appropriate adjustments and do well. Still other environments are turbulent and change in major and

---

[8] This theme was first proposed and admirably developed by Alfred D. Chandler, Jr., *Strategy and Structure: Chapters in the History of the American Industrial Enterprise* (Cambridge, Mass.: M.I.T. Press, 1962).

[9] See Terrence E. Deal and Allan A. Kennedy, *Corporate Cultures: The Rites and Rituals of Corporate Life* (Reading, Mass.: Addison-Wesley, 1982). Also see "Corporate Culture," *Business Week*, October 27, 1980, pp. 148–60.

unpredictable ways.[10] During the past decade, companies experienced high inflation, material and energy shortages, new technological breakthroughs, unwanted government regulations, high interest costs, aggressive international competition, and the end of the baby boom. As a result, management has come to believe that the only thing certain will be surprises and more surprises. The question becomes: How should a company carry on its planning in an "age of discontinuity" and "future shock"? A major challenge facing firms is to develop a flexible and adaptable structure so that they can survive in a turbulent environment.

> The American automobile industry is a case in point.[11] The auto industry is central to a vast business ecosystem consisting of rubber, glass, and steel plants, petroleum refineries, gasoline stations, superhighways, the economy of Detroit, and the incomes of millions of people. This business ecosystem had fairly stable characteristics for many years until the early 1970s, when a succession of "blows" left the industry reeling from shock: the oil crises, Nader's attack on automobile safety, government requirement for emission control, the advent of successful small foreign cars and tough competitors, and so on.
>
> American car manufacturers were slow to respond to these environmental changes, in some cases either ignoring them or fighting them. When General Motors, Ford and Chrysler finally started to make small cars to compete with the Japanese, they had already lost their leadership to Toyota, Datsun, and a host of other foreign, especially Japanese, manufacturers. As of today, the Japanese sell 49 percent of the 3.2 million small cars marketed in the United States. Detroit's failure was in not reading the environmental signals early enough and not containing its labor and other costs. U.S. auto workers are paid $8 more an hour in wages and benefits than their Japanese counterparts and it takes them thirty hours, as opposed to fifteen hours in Japan, to assemble a small car. The result is that Japanese car makers have a $2,500 cost edge over U.S. manufacturers.

The sad fact is that U.S. car manufacturers, as a result of overcomplacency and inertia, missed their chance to lead in the rapidly growing small-car market. Small cars became a new opportunity for car manufacturers. A new opportunity, like a window, stays open only for a short time. As the "strategic window" opened on small cars, U.S. manufacturers needed to jump in wholeheartedly and make the necessary investments. By waiting too long, the strategic window started to close, and U.S. car manufacturers came in too late to achieve leadership. Timing is crucial.[12]

A company's *strategic fit* with the environment will inevitably erode. The underlying problem is that the relevant environment will almost always change faster than the company's 7 S's. As a result, we find General Motors operating in a 1984 environment with the leftovers of 1960s strategy, structure, systems, style, staff, skills, and shared values. The company is an *efficient* machine but not an *effective* machine. As Peter Drucker pointed out long ago, it is more important to do the *right thing* than to *do things right*.

---

[10] For a useful classification of types of environment and their implications for organizational planning, see F. E. Emery and E. L. Trist, "The Causal Texture of Organizational Environments," *Human Relations*, February 1965, pp. 21–32.

[11] See "U.S. Car Industry Has Full-Sized Problems in Subcompact Market," *Wall Street Journal*, January 7, 1983, p. 1.

[12] See Derek F. Abell, "Strategic Windows," *Journal of Marketing*, July 1978, pp. 21–26.

Once an organization starts losing its market position through failing to respond to critical environmental changes, it has but a limited number of possible counterstrategies. Thus General Motors can adopt one or more of the following strategies in connection with the small-car market:

1. **Fight harder.** General Motors can lower the prices on its small cars and boost its advertising expenditures, in an attempt to hold on or regain share in the small-car market. General Motors would lose money doing this but buy time to make more fundamental changes.

2. **Develop a better product line.** General Motors can invest heavily in designing better small cars noted for performance, quality, styling, features, or some other combination of desired attributes.

3. **Lower its costs of production.** General Motors can develop better factory-assembly layouts, make greater use of robotic equipment, and design better inventory systems (such as the "just-in-time" system used in Japan). It can move some of its production overseas in search of lower costs. It can form a partnership with a Japanese auto maker for the joint production of certain car models.

4. **Strategic withdrawal.** General Motors can decide to slowly reduce its investment in small-car manufacture and move its resources into more profitable industries.

Thus each company needs to continuously review the level and type of investment needed to stay viable in a given industry and do its best to monitor the changing environment, so that it does not suddenly become an obsolete organization, an economic dinosaur.

Organizational Adaptability

Organizations, especially large ones, have much inertia. They are set up to be efficient machines, and it is difficult to change one part without changing everything. Yet organizations can be changed through leadership, probably in advance of a crisis but certainly in the midst of a crisis. The key to organizational survival is the organization's ability toward self-modification as the environment changes and calls for new behaviors. Adaptable organizations monitor the environment and make changes through anticipatory planning so as to maintain a fairly current strategic fit with the evolving environment.

Environmental scanning is an increasingly important function of the firm. The firm has to identify those components of its environment that can cause the most trouble and/or generate the greatest opportunities. Many companies have set up *issue management programs*, involving information gathering to monitor congressional legislation, foreign competition, raw material availability, and other issues that may affect their future. Ultimately environmental trends and developments can be classified into two groups, those representing environmental threats and those representing environmental opportunities.

We define an *environmental threat* as follows:

An *environmental threat* is a challenge posed by an unfavorable trend or development in the environment that would lead, in the absence of purposeful marketing action, to the erosion of the company's position.

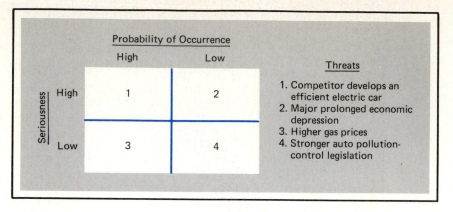

FIGURE 2–2
Threat Matrix

The company's marketing managers should be asked to identify in their marketing plans a list of threats facing the company. The threats should be classified according to their *seriousness* and *probability of occurrence*. Figure 2–2 shows a threat matrix and the location of several threats facing an automobile company. The threats in the upper-left cell are major threats since they can seriously hurt the company and have a high probability of occurrence. The company needs to prepare a contingency plan for each of these threats, which spells out in advance what changes the company can make before or during the threat's occurrence. The threats in the lower-right cell are very minor and can be ignored. The threats in the upper-right and lower-left cells do not require contingency planning but need to be carefully monitored in the event they grow more major.

Similarly marketing executives should identify the major marketing opportunities created by the changing environment. We define a company marketing opportunity as follows:

> A *company marketing opportunity* is an attractive arena for company marketing action in which the particular company would enjoy a competitive advantage.

These opportunities should be classified according to their *attractiveness* and the *success probability* that the company would have with each opportunity (Figure 2–3). The company's success probability with a particular opportunity depends on whether its *business strengths* (i.e., *distinctive competence*) match the *success requirements* of the industry. The best-performing company will be the one enjoying a *sustainable competitive advantage* in meeting the success requirements of the industry. It leads in its ability to generate value for customers.

Looking at Figure 2–3, the best opportunities facing the company are those in the upper-left cell, and management should prepare plans to pursue one or more of these opportunities. The opportunities in the lower-right cell are too minor to consider. The opportunities in the upper-right cell and lower-left cell should be moni-

Suppose General Motors, General Electric, and Sears all become interested in developing and marketing an electric car. Which firm would enjoy the greatest competitive advantage? First consider the success requirements. The success requirements would include (1) having good relations with suppliers of metal, rubber, plastic, glass, and other materials needed to produce an automobile, (2) having skill at mass production and mass assembly of complicated pieces of equipment, (3) having a strong distribution capacity to store, show, and deliver automobiles to the public, and (4) having the confidence of buyers that the company is able to produce and service a good auto product. Now General Motors has distinctive competences in all four of these areas. General Electric has distinctive competences in (1) supply and (2) production but not in (3) distribution or (4) automobile reputation. It does have great know-how in electrical technology. Sears's major distinctive competence is its extensive retailing system, and it has some of the competences through its wholly owned subsidiaries. All said, General Motors would enjoy the major differential advantage in the production and marketing of electric cars.

tored in the event that any of them improve in their attractiveness and success probability.

By assembling a picture of the threats and opportunities facing a specific company, it is possible to characterize its overall situation. Four outcomes are possible. An *ideal business* is one that is high in major opportunities and low or devoid of major threats. A *speculative business* is high in both major opportunities and threats. A *mature business* is low in major opportunities and threats. Finally, a *troubled business* is low in opportunities and high in threats.

Highly adaptable companies won't wait until the environment has changed so drastically that it is too late. They will anticipate their major environmental threats and opportunities and prepare plans to meet them. AT&T, for example, realized in the early 1970s that its environment was undergoing radical change as a result of new competition and technology. It realized that its existing strategy, structure, systems, style, and so on, would be obsolete in the imminent environment. And so it

FIGURE 2-3
Opportunity Matrix

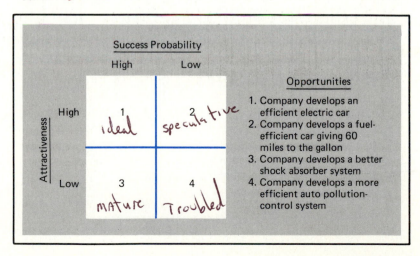

initiated a series of major strategy and structure changes in advance of a crisis, so that it could compete effectively with IBM, Xerox, and other major firms that had a headstart in some of the new markets of the future. Because it took these steps in advance, AT&T has an excellent chance of surviving and prospering.

THE STRATEGIC PLANNING PROCESS

Clearly today's firms have to engage in long-range strategic planning if they are to survive in an increasingly turbulent environment. We define strategic planning as follows:

> *Strategic planning* **is the managerial process of developing and maintaining a viable fit between the organization's objectives and resources and its environmental opportunities. The job of strategic planning is to design the company in such a way that it consists of enough healthy businesses to keep the company going even when some of its businesses are hurting.**

To understand strategic planning, we have to remember how the modern corporation is structured. Most large corporations consist of three organizational levels: the *corporate level*, *business level*, and *product level*. Corporate headquarters is responsible for designing a strategic plan to guide the whole enterprise into a profitable future. Headquarters makes decisions on how much resource support to offer to each business unit (division, subsidiary) as well as which new businesses to start. Each business unit in turn must develop a plan to carry that business unit into a profitable future, given the resources it has to work with from corporate headquarters. Finally, each product level (product line, brand) within a business unit needs to develop a plan

FIGURE 2-4
The Strategic Planning, Implementation, and Control Process

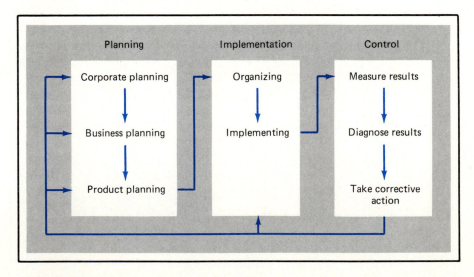

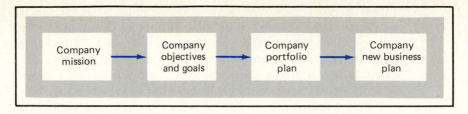

FIGURE 2–5
The Strategic Planning Process

for achieving targeted objectives in its particular product market. These plans are then implemented at the various levels of the organization, results are monitored, and necessary corrective actions are taken. The whole planning, implementation, and control process is shown in Figure 2–4.

Strategic planning itself consists of a set of steps and tools shown in Figure 2–5. We will examine these steps in the following paragraphs.

Company Mission

An organization exists to accomplish something in the larger environment. Its specific mission or purpose is usually clear at the beginning.[13] Over time, its mission may become unclear as the organization grows and adds new products and markets. Or the mission may remain clear, but some managers may lose interest in it. Or the mission may remain clear but lose its relevance to the new conditions in the environment.

When management senses that the organization is drifting, it must renew its search for purpose. According to Peter Drucker, it is time to ask some fundamental questions.[14] *What is our business? Who is the customer? What is value to the customer? What will our business be? What should our business be?* These simple-sounding questions are among the most difficult the company will ever have to answer. Successful companies continuously raise these questions and answer them thoughtfully and thoroughly.

The mission of the organization is shaped out of five key elements. The first is the *history* of the organization. Every organization has a history of aims, policies, and accomplishments. In reaching for a new purpose, the organization must honor the salient characteristics of its past history. It would not make sense for Harvard University, for example, to become a community college, even if such a move were

---

[13] We shall use *mission* and *purpose* interchangeably. However, some authors distinguish the two. Steiner and Miner use *purpose* to describe the economic and ethical motivation of the business, e.g., "to strive for high product quality and corporate integrity." They use mission to describe the product and market domain of the firm, e.g., "to produce educational games for adults." See George A. Steiner and J. B. Miner, *Management Policy and Strategy: Text, Readings, and Cases* (Homewood, Ill.: Richard D. Irwin, 1977), p. 7.

[14] See Peter F. Drucker, *Management: Tasks, Responsibilities, Practices* (New York: Harper & Row, 1973), Chapter 7.

a growth opportunity. The second consideration is the *current preferences* of the management and owners. Those who direct the company have their personal goals and visions. If Sears's current management wants to serve higher-income consumers, this goal is going to influence the statement of corporate purpose. Third, *environmental considerations* influence the purpose of the organization. The environment defines the main opportunities and threats that must be taken into account. The Girl Scouts of America would not get far in today's environment with their former purpose, "to prepare young girls for motherhood and wifely duties." Fourth, the organization's *resources* make certain missions possible and others not. Piedmont Airlines would be deluding itself if it adopted the mission to become the world's largest airline. Finally, the organization should base its choice of purpose on its *distinctive competences*. McDonald's could probably enter the solar energy business, but that would not be making use of its main competence—providing low-cost food and fast service to large groups of customers.

Many organizations are developing formal mission statements that they share with division heads, employees, and in many cases, customers and the public at large. A well-worked-out mission statement provides corporate personnel with a shared sense of opportunity, direction, significance, and achievement. The company mission statement acts as an "invisible hand" that guides widely dispersed employees to work independently and yet collectively toward realizing the organization's goals.

Writing a formal company mission statement is not easy. Some organizations will spend a year or two trying to prepare a satisfactory statement about the purpose of their firm. In the process they will discover a lot about themselves and their potential opportunities.

The mission statement should embody a number of characteristics to make it maximally useful. It should not claim everything. Consider the statement: "We want to be the leading company producing the highest quality products with the widest distribution and service at the lowest possible prices." This sounds good but fails to supply clear guidelines when tough business choices have to be made. The purpose should be stated, if possible, in terms of accomplishing something *outside* the organization. Statements such as "to make money" or "to become the market leader" fail to define a sufficient concept. Profits and leadership are the result of successful accomplishment of purpose rather than the purpose itself.

The mission statement should specify the *business domain* in which the organization will operate. The business domain can be defined, according to Abell, in terms of three dimensions: the *customer groups* that will be served, the *customer needs* that will be met, and the *technology* that will satisfy these needs.[15] Consider, for example, a small company that designs incandescent lighting systems for television studios. Its customer group is television studios; the customer need is lighting; and the technology is incandescent lighting. This company's business domain is defined by the floating cell in Figure 2–6.

This company is at liberty to expand or contract its business domain. For example, it could decide to make lighting for other customer groups, such as homes,

---

[15] Derek Abell, *Defining the Business: The Starting Point of Strategic Planning* (Englewood Cliffs, N.J.: Prentice-Hall, 1980), Chapter 3.

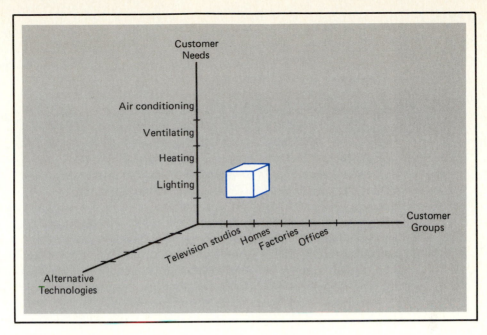

FIGURE 2-6
A Small Lighting Company's Current Definition of Its Business Domain

factories, and offices. Or it could supply other services needed by television studios, such as heating, ventilation, or air conditioning. Or it could design other lighting technologies for television studios, such as fluorescent, infrared, and ultraviolet lighting. Each of the company's businesses is defined by the intersection of the three dimensions. If this company expands into other cells, we say that it has widened its business domain.

In his "Marketing Myopia," Levitt advanced the thesis that market definitions of a business are superior to product definitions of a business.[16] He argued that a business must be viewed as a *customer-satisfying process*, not a *goods-producing process*. Products are transient, while basic needs and customer groups endure forever. A horse-carriage company will go out of business soon after the automobile is invented. But the same company, if it defines its purpose as that of providing transportation, will switch from making horse carriages to making cars. Levitt encouraged companies to shift their business-domain definition from a product to a market focus. Several examples are given in Table 2–1.

In developing a market-based definition of its business, management should avoid a definition that is too narrow or too broad. Consider a lead-pencil manufacturer. If it sees itself as a *small writing-instruments company*, it might expand to the production of pens and other small writing instruments. If it sees itself as a *writing-equipment company*, then it might also consider making typewriters and other equipment that

---

[16] Theodore Levitt, "Marketing Myopia," *Harvard Business Review*, July–August 1960, pp. 45–56.

TABLE 2–1

PRODUCT-ORIENTED VERSUS MARKET-ORIENTED DEFINITIONS OF A BUSINESS

Company	Product-Oriented Definition	Market-Oriented Definition
Revlon	We make cosmetics	We sell hope
Missouri-Pacific Railroad	We run a railroad	We are a people-and-goods mover
Xerox	We make copying equipment	We help improve office productivity
International Minerals and Chemicals	We sell fertilizer	We help improve agricultural productivity
Standard Oil	We sell gasoline	We supply energy
Columbia Pictures	We make movies	We market entertainment
Encyclopedia Britannica	We sell encyclopedias	We are in the information-production and distribution business
Carrier	We make air conditioners and furnaces	We provide a comfortable climate in the home

facilitates writing. The broadest concept of its business is that it is a *communication company*, and this would be stretching things too far for a lead-pencil manufacturer.

Holiday Inns, Inc., the world's largest hotel chain with over 300,000 rooms, fell into this trap. Some years ago it broadened its business definition from the "hotel business" to the "travel industry" of which hotels are only a part. It implemented this by acquiring Trailways, Inc., the nation's second largest bus company, and Delta Steamship Lines Inc. But Holiday Inns failed to manage these companies well and in 1978 divested Trailways and sought a buyer for Delta. Holiday Inns decided to stick to the "hospitality industry" and blanket this industry with alternative room and food systems.[17]

The company's mission statement should be motivating. Employees like to feel that their work is significant and that they are making a contribution to people's lives. When the prosaic task of producing fertilizer is reshaped into the larger idea of improving agricultural productivity to feed the world's hungry, a new sense of purpose comes over the employees. When the task of selling vacuum cleaners is transformed into the larger idea of creating a cleaner and healthier home environment, salespeople feel more challenged.

The corporate mission statement should stress major policies that the company plans to honor. Policies define how employees should deal with customers, suppliers, distributors, competition, and other actors and publics. Policies narrow the range of individual discretion, so that the company acts consistently on important issues.

The company's mission becomes the source and focus of its energy for the next ten or twenty years. Missions are not something to revise every few years in

---

[17] See "Holiday Inns: Refining its Focus to Food, Lodging—and More Casinos," *Business Week*, July 21, 1980, pp. 100–104.

response to environmental changes or new unrelated opportunities. On the other hand, a company has to reconsider its mission when it has lost credence or no longer defines an optimal course for the company.

Company Objectives and Goals

The company's mission must be turned into specific objectives for each level of management, in a system known as *management by objectives*. The most common objectives are *profitability*, *sales growth*, *market-share improvement*, *risk diversification*, and *innovation*. To be useful, the organization's various objectives should be hierarchical, quantitative, realistic, and consistent.

A company always pursues a large number of objectives. These objectives should be stated in a hierarchical fashion from the most important to the least important. An excellent example of hierarchical objectives is provided by Interstate Telephone Company (name disguised).[18] The company has been earning only 7.5 percent in recent years, giving various "stakeholders" a cause for concern.[19] This rate of return is too low to support the company's plans to expand and provide better service and equipment to customers. Management's major objective is to increase its return on investment. Starting from this objective, a whole hierarchy of further objectives are derived and shown in Figure 2–7.

There are two ways to increase return on investment: Increase the total return and/or reduce the investment base. The company is not about to do the latter. To increase its return, the company can increase its billings and/or reduce its costs. To increase its billings, the company can sell more equipment, seek to increase use of present equipment, and increase its rates. Costs could be reduced by increasing the service life of rented telephone equipment. That could be accomplished by doing a better job of matching rented equipment to the actual needs of customers. To the extent that the company sets increased billings as an objective, subsidiary objectives must be set for sales force, advertising, and other marketing functions. For example, each sales district will be assigned a sales quota, and each sales district quota must be broken down and assigned to individual sales representatives. In this way a major objective of the company is ultimately translated into specific objectives for all employees.

To the extent possible, objectives should be stated in *quantitative* terms. The objective "increase the return on investment" is not as satisfactory as "increase the return on investment to 12 percent," or even better, "increase the return on investment to 12 percent by the end of the second year." Analysts use the term *goals* to describe an objective that has been made highly specific with respect to *magnitude* and *time*. Turning the objectives into concrete goals facilitates the process of management planning, implementation, and control.

A company has to choose *realistic* target levels for its objectives. The levels should come out of an analysis of its opportunities and resources, not out of wishful thinking.

---

[18] Leon Winer, "Are You Really Planning Your Marketing?" *Journal of Marketing*, January 1965, pp. 1–8.

[19] "Stakeholders" are the stockholders and all the other parties who have a "stake" in the firm, such as bankers and managers.

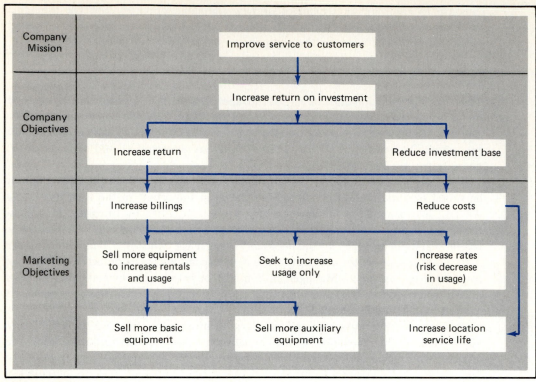

SOURCE: Adapted from Leon Winer, "Are You Really Planning Your Marketing?" *Journal of Marketing*, January 1965, p. 3. Published by the American Marketing Association.

FIGURE 2–7
Hierarchy of Objectives for the Interstate Telephone Company

Finally, the company's objectives need to be *consistent*. It is not possible to "maximize sales and profits," or "achieve the greatest sales at the least cost," or "design the best possible product in the shortest possible time." These objectives are in a trade-off relationship. Weinberg has identified eight basic strategic trade-offs facing any firm.

☐ Short-term profits versus long-term growth
☐ Profit margin versus competitive position
☐ Direct sales effort versus market development effort
☐ Penetration of existing markets versus the development of new markets
☐ Related versus nonrelated new opportunities as a source of long-term growth
☐ Profit versus nonprofit goals
☐ Growth versus stability
☐ "Riskless" environment versus high-risk environment[20]

---

[20] Presented in a seminar, "Developing Management Strategies for Short-Term Profits and Long-Term Growth," sponsored by Advanced Management Research, Inc., Regency Hotel, New York City, September 29, 1969.

A company has to determine the relative emphasis to give to these conflicting objectives, or else the objectives will not serve as useful guidelines.

Company Portfolio Plan

After a company gets clear about its mission, objectives, and goals, it needs to review its current portfolio of businesses and decide what to do with each business. A major task of strategic planning is to decide which businesses to build, maintain, phase down, and phase out.

As a first step, companies have to identify carefully the actual businesses they are in. A company that operates (say) twelve divisions is not necessarily in twelve businesses. A single division of a company may consist of several businesses if the division produces different products for different customer groups. On the other hand, two or more company divisions may be so interrelated that they form a single business. Companies therefore have to freshly identify their distinctive businesses. General Electric went through this grueling exercise some years ago and identified forty-nine different businesses they were in. They called these *strategic business units* (SBUs). A SBU ideally has the following characteristics:

☐ It is a single business or collection of related businesses.
☐ It has a distinct mission.
☐ It has its own competitors.
☐ It has a responsible manager.
☐ It consists of one or more program units and functional units.
☐ It can benefit from strategic planning.
☐ It can be planned independently of the other businesses.

Now each SBU must be evaluated for its strategic profit potential. Top management might have a vague sense that one SBU is a "yesterday has-been," and another is a "tomorrow's breadwinner," and so on. But this impressionistic approach needs to be replaced by a more analytical classification of businesses. In the last decade, several portfolio evaluation frameworks have been proposed, of which the two best known are those of the Boston Consulting Group and General Electric.

Boston Consulting Group growth/share matrix. The Boston Consulting Group (BCG), a leading management consulting firm, developed and popularized an approach known as the *growth-share matrix* shown in Figure 2–8.[21] The eight circles represent the current sizes and positions of eight businesses making up a hypothetical company. The dollar-volume size of each business is proportional to the circle's area: Thus the two largest businesses are 5 and 6. The location of each business indicates its market growth rate and relative market share.

Specifically, the *market growth rate* on the vertical axis indicates the annual growth rate of the market in which the business operates; in the figure it ranges

---

[21] See Derek Abell, *Strategic Market Planning: Problems and Analytical Perspectives* (Englewood Cliffs, N.J.: Prentice-Hall, 1979), Chapter 4.

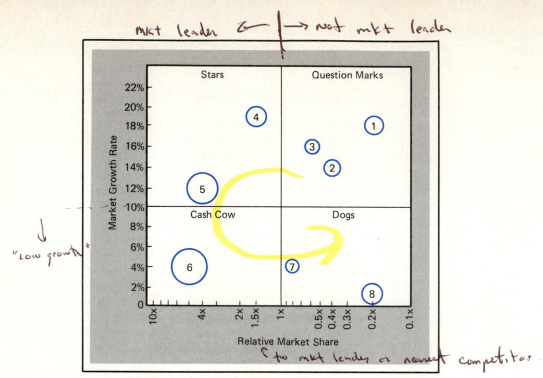

(handwritten annotation above figure:) mkt leader ⟵ ⟶ not mkt leader

(handwritten annotation left of figure:) "Low growth" ↓

(handwritten annotation below figure:) ⟵ to mkt leader or nearest competitor.

SOURCE: B. Heldey, "Strategy and the Business Portfolio," *Long Range Planning,* February 1977, p. 12. Reprinted with permission from *Long Range Planning,* copyright 1977, Pergamon Press, Ltd.

FIGURE 2–8
The Boston Consulting Group's Growth-Share Matrix

from 0 percent to 20 percent, although a larger range could be shown. A market growth rate above 10 percent is considered high.

The *relative market share* on the horizontal axis indicates the SBU's market share relative to the largest competitor. A relative market share of 0.1 means that the company's SBU sales volume is only 10 percent of the leader's sales volume; and 10 means that the company's SBU is the leader and has ten times the sales of the next-strongest company in the market. Relative market share is divided into high and low share, using 1.0 as the dividing line. Relative market share is drawn in log scale, so that equal distances represent the same percentage increase.

The growth-share matrix is divided into four cells, each indicating a different type of business:

☐ **Question marks.** Question marks are company businesses that operate in high-growth markets but have low relative market shares. Most businesses start off as a question mark, in that the company tries to enter a high-growth market in which there is already a market leader. A question mark requires a lot of cash, since the company has to keep adding plant, equipment, and personnel to keep up with the fast-growing market, and additionally, it wants to overtake the leader. The term *question mark* is well chosen because the company has to think hard about whether to keep pouring money into this business or get out. The company in Figure 2–8 operates three question-mark busi-

(handwritten annotation left margin:) CASH drain product.
- Invest Heavily or Divest
- buy out competitor
- Resegment MKT.

nesses, and this may be too many. The company might be better off investing more cash in one or two of these businesses, instead of spreading its cash thinly over all three businesses.

☐ **Stars.** If a company is successful with a question-mark business, it becomes a star. A star is the market leader in a high-growth market. This does not necessarily mean that the star provides a lot of cash throw off for the company. The company has to spend a great deal of money keeping up with the market's rate of growth and fighting off competitors' attacks. Stars are often cash using rather than cash generating; at the same time, they are usually profitable and become the company's future cash cows. In the illustration, the company has two stars, and this augurs well. The company would have to show concern if it had no current stars.

☐ **Cash cows.** When a market's annual growth rate falls to less than 10 percent, the former star becomes a cash cow if it still has the largest relative market share. A cash cow is so called because it produces a lot of cash for the company. The company does not have to finance a lot of expansion since the market's growth rate is low. And since the business is the market leader, it enjoys economies of scale and higher profit margins. The company uses its cash cow businesses to pay its bills and support the stars, question marks, and dogs, which tend to be cash hungry. In the illustration, however, the company has only one cash cow business and is therefore highly vulnerable. In the event this cash cow suddenly loses relative market share, the company has to pump enough money back into its cash cow in order to maintain market leadership. If it uses all the throw-off cash to support the other businesses, its strong cash cow may turn into a weak cash cow.

☐ **Dogs.** Dogs describe company businesses that have weak market shares in low-growth markets. They typically generate low profits or losses, although they may throw off some cash. The company in the illustration manages two dog businesses, and this may be two too many. The company should consider whether it is holding on to these dog businesses for good reasons (such as an expected turnaround in the market growth rate, or a new chance at market leadership) or out of sentimental reasons. Dog businesses often take up more management time than they are worth and need to be phased down further or phased out.

Having located its businesses in the growth-share matrix, the company will determine whether its business portfolio is healthy. An unbalanced portfolio would have too many dogs or question marks and/or too few stars and cash cows.

The company's next task is to determine what objective to assign to each SBU, and what support it will need. Four alternative objectives can be pursued:

☐ **Build.** Here the objective is to increase the SBU's market share, even foregoing short-term earnings to achieve this objective. "Building" is appropriate for question marks whose shares have to grow if they are to become stars.

☐ **Hold.** Here the objective is to preserve the SBU's market share. This objective is appropriate for strong cash cows if they are to continue to yield a large positive cash flow.

☐ **Harvest.** Here the objective is to increase the SBU's short-term cash flow regardless of the long-term effect. This strategy is appropriate for weak cash cows whose future is dim and from whom more cash flow is needed. Harvesting can also be used with question marks and dogs.

☐ **Divest.** Here the objective is to sell or liquidate the business because resources can be better used elsewhere. That is appropriate for dogs and question marks that are acting as a drag on the company's profits.

As time passes, SBUs change their position in the growth-share matrix. Successful SBUs have a life cycle. They start as questions marks, move into stars, then into cash cows, and finally into dogs toward the end of their life cycle. For this reason, companies should look not only at the current positions of their businesses in the growth-share matrix (as in a snapshot) but at their changing positions (as in a motion picture). Each business should be reviewed with respect to where it was last year, the year before, and so on, as well as where it will probably go next year, the year after, and the years after that. If the expected trajectory of a given business is not satisfactory, the company will ask that business's manager to propose a new strategy and the likely resulting trajectory. Thus the share-growth matrix becomes a planning framework for the strategic planners at company headquarters. They use it to try to get each business to perform as well as possible, although some they put out to pasture.

General Electric multifactor portfolio matrix.[22]   The appropriate objective to assign to an SBU cannot be determined solely on the basis of its position in the growth-share matrix. If additional factors are introduced, the growth-share matrix can be seen as a special case of a multifactor portfolio matrix that General Electric (GE) pioneered. This model is shown in Figure 2–9, and seven businesses of a hypothetical company are plotted. This time, the size of the circle represents the size of the market rather than the size of the company's business. And the shaded part of the circle represents that business's absolute market share. Thus business B operates in a moderate size market and enjoys a 25 percent market share.

Each business is rated against two major variables, *industry attractiveness* and the company's *businesses' strength*. These two factors make excellent marketing sense for rating a business. Companies will be successful to the extent that they go into attractive industries and possess the required mix of business strengths to succeed in those industries. If one or the other is missing, the business will not produce outstanding results. Neither a strong company operating in an unattractive industry nor a weak company operating in an attractive industry will do very well.

The real issue, then, is to measure these two variables. To do this, the strategic planners must identify the factors underlying each variable and find a way to measure them and combine them into an index. Table 2–2 illustrates sets of factors making up the two variables. (Each company has to decide on its list of factors.) Thus industry attractiveness varies with the market's size, annual market growth rate, historical profit margins, and so on. And business strength varies with the company's market share, share growth, product quality, and so on. Note that the two BCG factors, market growth rate and market share, are subsumed under the two major variables of the GE model. The GE model leads strategic planners to look at more aspects of an actual or potential business in evaluating it.

Table 2–2 shows that the factors making up each variable are weighted, with the weights summing to 1.00. Management's task is to rate each factor, choosing a whole number between 1 and 5, reflecting how the business stands on that factor. In the illustration, the business is rated 4.00 on overall market size, indicating that the market size is pretty large (a 5 would be very large). Clearly many of these

---

[22] Ibid., Chapter 5.

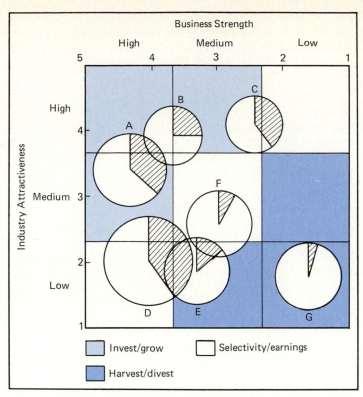

FIGURE 2–9
General Electric's Multifactor Portfolio Matrix

factors require data and assessment from marketing personnel. In any event, the weights are multiplied by the ratings to arrive at the values, which are summed for each variable. The business being evaluated in the illustration scored a 3.45 on industry attractiveness and a 4.30 on business strength, out of a possible maximum score of 5 for each. The analyst places a point in the multifactor matrix in Figure 2–9 representing this business and builds a circle around it whose size is proportional to the size of the market. This business is shown as business A in Figure 2–9. Clearly business A is in a fairly desirable part of the matrix.

In fact, the GE matrix is divided into three zones. The three cells at the upper left show strong SBUs in which the company should *invest/grow*. The diagonal cells stretching from the lower left to the upper right indicate SBUs that are medium in overall attractiveness: The company should pursue *selectivity/earnings*. The three cells at the lower right indicate SBUs that are low in overall attractiveness: The company should give thought to *harvest/divest*. For example, business G represents an SBU with a very small market share in a fair-size industry that is not very attractive

TABLE 2-2

FACTORS UNDERLYING INDUSTRY ATTRACTIVENESS AND BUSINESS STRENGTH IN GE MULTIFACTOR PORTFOLIO MODEL			
	Weight	**Rating (1–5)**	**Value**
Industry Attractiveness			
Overall market size	0.20	4.00	0.80
Annual market growth rate	0.20	5.00	1.00
Historical profit margin	0.15	4.00	0.60
Competitive intensity	0.15	2.00	0.30
Technological requirements	0.15	3.00	0.45
Inflationary vulnerability	0.05	3.00	0.15
Energy requirements	0.05	2.00	0.10
Environmental impact	0.05	1.00	0.05
Social/political/legal	Must be acceptable		
	1.00		3.45
	Weight	**Rating (1–5)**	**Value**
Business Strength			
Market share	0.10	4.00	0.40
Share growth	0.15	4.00	0.60
Product quality	0.10	4.00	0.40
Brand reputation	0.10	5.00	0.50
Distribution network	0.05	4.00	0.20
Promotional effectiveness	0.05	5.00	0.25
Productive capacity	0.05	3.00	0.15
Productive efficiency	0.05	2.00	0.10
Unit costs	0.15	3.00	0.45
Material supplies	0.05	5.00	0.25
R&D performance	0.10	4.00	0.80
Managerial personnel	0.05	4.00	0.20
	1.00		4.30

SOURCE: Slightly modified from La Rue T. Hormer, **Strategic Management** (Englewood Cliffs, N.J.: Prentice-Hall, Inc., 1982), p. 310.

and in which the company has little business strength: It is a fit candidate for harvest/divest.[23]

Management should also plot the projected positions of each SBU under current and alternative strategies. Top management can use the results to decide on the business objective for each SBU and what resources it will be given. Then the task of the SBU's management and marketing personnel will be to figure out the best way to accomplish that objective. Marketing managers in certain SBUs will find

---

[23] The multifactor portfolio matrix has been refined further by the Shell Company, which calls it the directional policy matrix. See S. J. Q. Robinson, R. E. Hichens, and D. P. Wade, "The Directional Policy Matrix-Tool for Strategic Planning," *Long-Range Planning*, June 1978, pp. 8–15; and D. E. Hussey, "Portfolio Analysis: Practical Experience with the Directional Policy Matrix," *Long-Range Planning*, August 1978, pp. 2–8.

that their objective is not necessarily to build sales. Their job may be to maintain the existing demand with fewer marketing dollars or to take cash out of the business and allow demand to fall. *Thus the task of marketing management is to manage demand to the appropriate level decided by the strategic planning done at headquarters.* Marketing contributes to assessing each SBU's potential, but once the SBU's objective and budget are set, marketing's job is to carry out the plan efficiently and profitably.

Company New-Business Plan

The company's portfolio plan for its existing businesses will add up to a certain amount of expected sales and profits. Often, however, projected sales and profit will fall short of what corporate management wants to achieve over the planning horizon. After all, part of the portfolio plan includes dropping some businesses that need replacement. If there is a gap between future desired sales and projected sales, corporate management will have to think of creative ways to fill this strategic planning gap. It will have to develop a plan for obtaining additional business.

Figure 2–10 illustrates this strategic planning gap for a major manufacturer of cassette tape called Musicale (name disguised). The lowest curve projects the expected sales over the next ten years from the company's current portfolio of businesses. The highest curve describes the corporation's desired sales over the next ten years. Clearly the company wants to grow much faster than its current businesses will permit; in fact, it wants to double its size in ten years. How can it fill the strategic planning gap?

A company can fill the gap in three ways. The first is to identify further opportunities to achieve growth within the company's current businesses (*intensive growth oppor-*

FIGURE 2–10
The Strategic Planning Gap

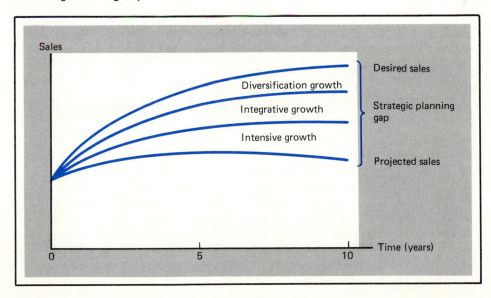

TABLE 2-3

MAJOR CLASSES OF GROWTH OPPORTUNITIES		
Intensive Growth	**Integrative Growth**	**Diversification Growth**
• Market penetration	• Backward integration	• Concentric diversification
• Market development	• Forward integration	• Horizontal diversification
• Product development	• Horizontal integration	• Conglomerate diversification

tunities). The second is to identify opportunities to build or acquire businesses that are related to the company's current businesses (*integrative growth opportunities*). The third is to identify opportunities to add attractive businesses that are unrelated to the company's current businesses (*diversification growth opportunities*). The specific opportunities within each broad class are listed in Table 2–3 and discussed below.

Intensive growth.   Corporate management should first review whether there are any further opportunities for improving the performance of its existing businesses. Ansoff has proposed a useful framework for detecting new intensive growth opportunities. Called a *product/market expansion grid*, it is shown in Figure 2–11.[24] Management first considers whether it could gain more market share with its current products in their current markets (*market penetration strategy*). Then it considers whether it can develop new markets for its current products (*market development strategy*). Finally, it considers whether it can develop new products of potential interest to its current markets (*product development strategy*). Later it will also review opportunities to develop new products for new markets (*diversification strategy*).

Market penetration strategy.   Here management looks for ways to increase the market share of its current products in their current markets. There are three major ways to do this. A company such as Musicale could try to encourage its current customers to buy and use more cassette tapes per period. This would make sense if most of its customers were infrequent buyers of tape and could be shown the benefits of using more tape for music recording or dictation. Or Musicale could try to attract the customers of competitors to switch to its brand. This would make sense if Musicale noticed a lot of weaknesses in the competitors' product or marketing program that it could exploit. Finally, Musicale could try to convince current nonusers of cassette tapes who resemble current users to start using tapes. This would make sense if there were a lot of people who still didn't own tape recorders or tape players.

Market development strategy.   Management should also look for new markets whose needs might be met by its current products. First, it might examine whether there

---

[24] H. Igor Ansoff, "Strategies for Diversification," *Harvard Business Review*, September–October 1957, pp. 113–24. The same matrix can be expanded into nine cells by adding modified products and modified markets. See S. C. Johnson and Conrad Jones, "How to Organize for New Products," *Harvard Business Review*, May–June 1957, pp. 49–62.

	Current Products	New Products
Current Markets	1. Market penetration strategy	3. Product development strategy
New Markets	2. Market development strategy	(Diversification strategy)

FIGURE 2–11
Three Intensive Growth Strategies: Ansoff's Product/Market Expansion Grid

[handwritten margin note:] Appealing because no Development costs. (PC's) School → office + Private LABELING

are any potential user types in the current locations not now buying the product whose interest in cassette tapes might be stimulated. Thus if the company had been selling cassette tapes only to consumer markets, it might consider going after office and factory markets. Second, the company might consider selling through new distribution channels in its present locations to reach other users in these locations. If it has been selling its tape only through stereo equipment dealers, it might add mass merchandising channels. Third, the company might consider expanding to new locations here or abroad. Thus if Musicale sold only in the eastern part of the United States, it could consider adding the western states or opening markets in Europe.

[handwritten margin note:] "easy sale" because its someone you've already sold to Typewriters → word processors

Product development strategy. Next, management should consider some new-product development possibilities. It could develop new cassette tape features, such as a longer playing tape, tape that buzzes at the end of its play, and so on. It could develop other quality levels of tape, such as a higher quality tape for fine music listeners and a lower quality tape for the mass market. Or it could research an alternative technology to cassette tape that allows recording and dictating.

By examining all of these intensive growth strategies—deeper market penetration, market development, and product development—management will hope to discover ways to achieve more sales growth. Still, this may not be enough, in which case management must also examine integrative growth possibilities.

Integrative growth. Management should review each of its businesses to identify integrative growth possibilities. Often a business's sales and profits can be increased through integrating backward, forward, or horizontally within that business's industry. Figure 2–12 shows Musicale's core marketing system. Musicale might consider acquiring one or more of its suppliers (such as plastic-material producers) to gain more profit or control (*backward integration strategy*). Or Musicale might consider acquiring some wholesalers or retailers, especially if they are highly profitable (*forward integration strategy*). Finally, Musicale could consider acquiring one or more competitors, providing that the government doesn't bar this move (*horizontal integration strategy*).

Through looking at possible integration moves, the company will possibly discover additional sources of sales-volume increases over the next ten years. These

Strategic Planning and the Marketing Management Process **59**

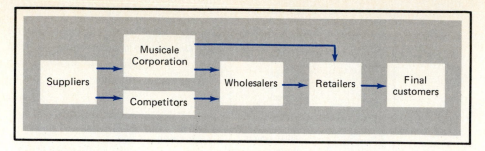

FIGURE 2–12
Core Marketing System Map for a Tape-Cassette Manufacturer

new sources may still not be enough to reach the desired sales-growth level. In that case, the company must consider diversification moves.

Diversification growth.   Diversification growth makes sense when good opportunities can be found outside the present businesses. A good opportunity, of course, is one where the industry is highly attractive and the company has the mix of business strengths needed to be successful. Three types of diversification can be considered. The company could seek new products that have technological and/or marketing synergies with existing product lines, even though the products may appeal to a new class of customers (*concentric diversification strategy*). For example, Musicale might start a computer-tape manufacturing operation based on knowing how to manufacture cassette tape, well aware that it will be entering a new market and selling to a different class of customers. Second, the company might search for new products that could appeal to its current customers though technologically unrelated to its current product line (*horizontal diversification strategy*). For example, Musicale might go into the production of cassette holding trays, even though they require a different manufacturing process. Finally, the company might seek new businesses that have no relationship to the company's current technology, products, or markets (*conglomerate diversification strategy*). Musicale might want to consider such new business areas as personal computers, real estate office franchising, or fast-food services.

Thus we see that a company can systematically identify new business opportunities by using a marketing systems framework, first looking at ways to intensify its work in current product markets, then considering ways to integrate backward, forward, or horizontally in relation to its current businesses, and finally looking at relevant opportunities outside of its current businesses.

THE MARKETING MANAGEMENT PROCESS

We have seen that the strategic planning process consists of setting the company's objectives and developing a business portfolio plan and a new-business plan, all aimed at achieving a desired company future. Each business unit within the company has the task of supplying data and ideas to strategic planners on that business's possible

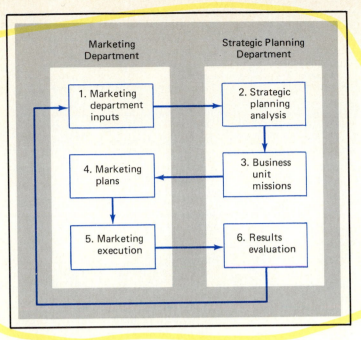

FIGURE 2-13
Relationship Between Marketing and Strategic Planning

future as well as developing a detailed business plan to carry out the agreed-upon objectives of that business with the given level of support.

The relationship between the marketing departments in the various business units and the strategic planning department is shown in Figure 2–13. Each marketing department supplies inputs of information and opinion (Step 1) to the strategic planning department for analysis and evaluation (Step 2). The strategic planning department then sets missions for the business units (Step 3). The marketing departments formulate their marketing plans based on these missions (Step 4) and carry them out (Step 5). The results are evaluated by the strategic planning department, and the process recycles.

Thus each business unit relies upon marketing as the main system for monitoring opportunities and developing marketing objectives and plans for achieving that business's objectives. In fact, the first step in business planning is the marketing step, for this defines the sales targets and therefore the resources needed to achieve these targets. The role of finance, manufacturing, and personnel is to make sure that the proposed marketing plan can be supported with enough money, plant and equipment, and manpower, and also to bring these pools of resources into being.

To carry out their role, marketing managers go through a process called the *marketing management process*. We define it as follows:

> The *marketing management process* consists of analyzing market opportunities, researching and selecting target markets, developing marketing strategies, planning marketing tactics, and implementing and controlling the marketing effort.

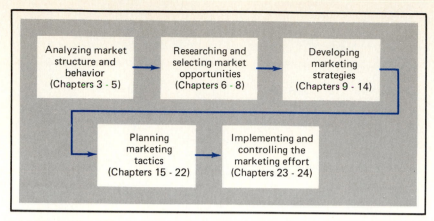

FIGURE 2-14
The Marketing Management Process

These steps are listed in Figure 2–14, along with the chapters in the book that will deal with each step in detail. The remainder of this chapter will present an overview of these steps in the marketing management process. We will illustrate these steps in connection with the following situation:

> Zeus, Inc. (name disguised) is a Fortune 500 company that operates in several industries, including chemicals, energy, typewriters, and some consumer goods. Each area is organized as an SBU. Corporate management is considering what to do with its Atlas typewriter division. At present, Atlas produces standard office electric typewriters that are comparable to the highly popular IBM Selectric typewriters but sell for less. The market for standard electric typewriters is showing slow growth, and this company's brand is dwarfed by the leader. On a growth-share matrix, this business would be called a dog. Zeus's corporate management wants Atlas's marketing group to produce a strong plan for this product line or else face being dropped as a division. Marketing management has to come up with a convincing marketing plan, sell it to corporate management, and then implement and control it.

Analyzing Market Opportunities

The first task facing Atlas's marketing management is to analyze the long-run opportunities in this market for improving its performance as a business division of Zeus, Inc. These managers recognize the abundance of opportunities in the burgeoning business-office-equipment field. The *office of the future* is a major investment frontier in the coming decades, just as the factory was the frontier in the past (the new robotic factory is, of course, another frontier). The U.S. economy is increasingly becoming a service economy, and there are more office workers than factory workers. Yet offices are often poorly organized in terms of such elementary tasks as typing, filing and storing of information and transmitting information, especially in terms of the latest available technologies. Many manufacturers are active in this market and seeking to provide integrated systems of typewriters, microcomputers, copying and duplicating machines, facsimile transmission machines, electronic message systems, and the like. Among them are IBM, Xerox, Olivetti, Exxon, and several Japanese companies. They are all engaged in developing office hardware and software that will increase office productivity, which is the chief buying motive of office-equipment purchasing agents. Xerox, in fact, sees itself not as a copying-machine company but as an office-productivity-improvement company.

Atlas's marketing management's long-run goal is to become a complete office machines manufacturer. At the present time, however, they must come up with a plan to improve their typewriter product line. Even within typewriters, there are many opportunities. Atlas, for example, can scale down its office typewriter to a version for the home market and advertise it as an "office quality" home typewriter. But even larger opportunities lie in incorporating certain technological advances. Just as typing productivity increased greatly in the past when typewriters evolved from manual machines to electric machines and then to electric machines with automatic correction features, they are now evolving further. Atlas could design an electronic or "smart" typewriter, one of the hottest new products in the office-equipment field. Over two hundred thousand have already been sold in the million-unit office typewriter market. An electronic typewriter has only twenty-four moving parts compared to the roughly one thousand levers, springs, gears, and screws inside an electric typewriter; offers more characters; has a memory to carry the last few lines typed; can make automatic corrections; does not jam; and has a number of other useful features. Electronic typewriters are priced from several hundred to several thousand dollars and now include such entries as Smith Corona's Typetronic, Royal's 5010, Olivetti's ET121, Exxon's Qyx, and IBM's electronic Selectrics. Atlas can also consider designing a word processor, which would have more memory and text editing capability than an electronic typewriter and sell for several thousand dollars. Or Atlas can develop a whole computer work station like IBM's Displaywriter system that performs a large number of functions. Ultimately, Atlas can work on voice-activated typewriters, which only require oral dictation.

To enrich its understanding of its opportunities, Atlas has to pay close attention to the *marketing environment* (Chapter 3). The marketing environment consists of a microenvironment and a macroenvironment. The company's *microenvironment* consists of all the actors who help or affect the company's ability to produce and sell typewriters, namely suppliers, marketing intermediaries, customers, competitors, and publics of various sorts. Such questions arise as: What do customers want and look at in buying typewriters? What channels of distribution are growing and shrinking? Which suppliers are most efficient at making components? What are competitors doing? and so on.

Atlas's management also must stay on top of broad trends in the *macroenvironment*, namely demographic, economic, physical, technological, political/legal, and social/cultural developments. It would be myopic to confine attention to the microenvironment and ignore larger changing forces in the society. Such questions arise as: What areas of the country are growing and shrinking? What is the economic outlook, and how will it affect sales of typewriters and the types purchased? What new technologies can be applied to improve typewriter efficiency? and so on. These large-scale forces can have a profound effect on Atlas's market.

To the extent that Atlas considers manufacturing a typewriter for the home, it needs to understand *consumer markets* and how they function (Chapter 4). It needs to know: How many households plan to buy new typewriters? What are they looking for in the way of features and prices? Where do they shop? What are their images of existing competitors? What is the potential influence of price, advertising, sales promotion, personal selling, and so on, on consumer brand decisions?

Atlas's main markets are organizational buyers, including professional firms, large corporations, government agencies, and so on (Chapter 5). Large organizations are staffed with professional purchasing agents, who are skilled at assessing equipment and value. Major equipment decisions are also made by buying committees consisting of different company personnel with different objectives and different degrees of influence on the final vendor decision. Selling to organizations usually involves personal selling through a sales force that is well trained to present the product and show how it can meet the customer's needs. Atlas needs to gain a full understanding of how organizational buyers buy.

Researching and Selecting Target Markets

Atlas's marketing management will have to collect specific data, going beyond its broad scanning of the micro- and macroenvironment and its general understanding of how consumer and organizational markets work. To gain insight into the future typewriter market, Atlas needs to undertake formal marketing research and information gathering (Chapter 6). Marketing research is an indispensable ingredient of the modern marketing concept, in that companies can serve their markets well only by researching their needs and wants, their locations, their buying practices, and so on. There are different degrees of formal research that can be carried on by Atlas. At the very least, Atlas's marketing management needs a good internal accounting system that speedily and accurately reports current sales by typewriter model, customer, industry and size, customer location, salesperson, and channels of distribution. In addition, Atlas's executives should be collecting market intelligence on customers, competitors, dealers, and so on, by keeping their eyes and ears open. The marketing people should go further and conduct some formal research by looking up information in secondary sources, running some focus groups, and conducting telephone, mail, or personal surveys. If the collected data is well analyzed by the latest statistical methods, and some marketing models are applied, the company will probably discover useful information on how sales are affected by various marketing tools and forces.

One of the major information tasks is to measure the size of the overall market and its geographical breakdowns and forecast future sales and profits (Chapter 7). Marketers must be aware of the various techniques available for measuring market potential and forecasting future demand. Each technique has certain advantages and limitations that must be carefully understood by marketers to avoid their misuse.

These market measures and forecasts become key inputs into deciding which markets and new products to focus on. Modern marketing practice calls for dividing the market into major market segments, evaluating them, selecting and targeting certain ones, and deciding on the company's positioning in each market (Chapter 8).

Market segmentation—the task of breaking the total market (which is often too large to serve) into segments that share common properties—can be done in a

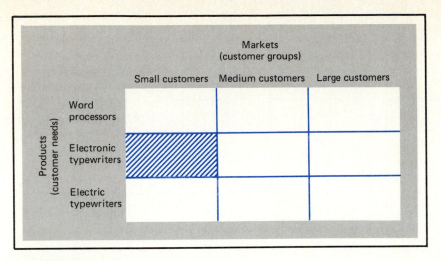

FIGURE 2-15
Product/Market Grid for Typewriters

number of ways. Atlas can segment the typewriter market by customer size (large, medium, small), customer buying criteria (quality, price, service), buyer industry (banks, professional firms, manufacturing companies), and so on.

Market segments can also be formed by crossing two or more variables. Figure 2–15 shows a segmentation of the typewriter market by two broad variables, namely customer groups and customer needs (represented by different products). This particular framework is called a *product/market grid*. Marketing management can estimate, for each of the nine cells, the degree of market segment attractiveness and the company's degree of business strength. Essentially Atlas seeks to determine which product/market cells, if any, best satisfy the company's objectives and resources.

Suppose the best-looking segment for Atlas is the "small customer, electronic typewriter market" that is shaded in Figure 2–15. Even this market segment may be larger than the company can serve effectively, in which case *subsegmentation* can be undertaken. For example, Atlas might decide that its best opportunity lay in designing an inexpensive electronic typewriter whose features will have great appeal to small professional firms. In this way, Atlas will arrive at a clear idea of its *target market*.

Atlas may view this market as its launching pad for later invasions of the larger market. In fact, companies can pursue one of the five *market-coverage strategies* shown in Figure 2–16. In the first, called *single market concentration*, a company niches itself in one part of the market. Usually smaller companies make this choice. In the second, *product specialization*, a company decides to produce only electric typewriters for all customer groups. In the third, *market specialization*, a company decides to make all kinds of typewriters but focuses on small customers. In the fourth, *selective specialization*, a company enters multiple niches that have no relation to each other except that each constitutes an attractive opportunity. This pattern is usually the result of an opportunistic growth strategy. The last pattern, *full coverage*,

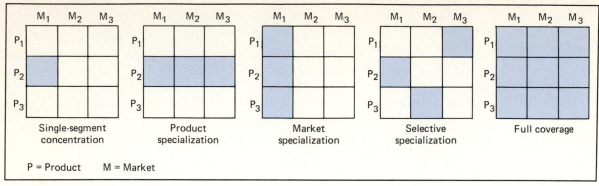

SOURCE: Adapted from Derek F. Abell, *Defining the Business: The Starting Point of Strategic Planning* (Englewood Cliffs, New Jersey: Prentice-Hall, Inc., 1980), Chapter 8 pp. 13–17.

FIGURE 2-16
Five Patterns of Market Coverage

is typically undertaken by larger companies that seek market leadership. They offer a product for "every person, purse, and personality."

Given that Atlas wants to pursue the "electronic typewriter, small customer market," it needs to develop a *positioning strategy* for that target market. Atlas needs to define how it wants to come across to buyers in relation to other competitors selling to that market. Should it be a "Cadillac" firm offering a superior product at a premium price with excellent service that is well advertised and aimed at the more affluent buyers? Or should Atlas build a simple low-price electronic typewriter aimed at the more price-conscious market?

Atlas needs to study carefully the positions taken by its major competitors in the same target market. Suppose companies can be positioned at the very least in terms of their product quality and price. We can develop a *product positioning map* (Figure 2–17) to describe the positions of four competitors currently selling to this market. The four competitors, A,B,C, and D, differ in sales volume as reflected by the sizes of the circles. Competitor A occupies the high-quality/high-price position in this market. Competitor B is perceived by the market to produce an average-quality product at an average price. Competitor C is known to sell a slightly below-average-quality product for a really low price. Competitor D is perceived as a "rip-off artist" because it sells a low-quality product for a high price.

Where should Atlas position itself in entering this market? It normally would not make sense to position itself against Competitor A because then it would have to fight a well-established company for the limited number of customers who want the best typewriter money can buy. However, if Competitor A is rendering poor service or underpromoting, Atlas may decide to attack A. Most marketing-oriented companies generally prefer not to attack an existing competitor (unless it is a weak one) but to find some important needs that competitors are not filling. For example, Atlas might give serious consideration to positioning itself in the high-quality/low-price quadrant (shown by the dotted circle). In this way, it would be "filling a hole" in the market. It must satisfy itself about three things, however. First, Atlas must find out from its engineers if they can build a high-quality typewriter that could

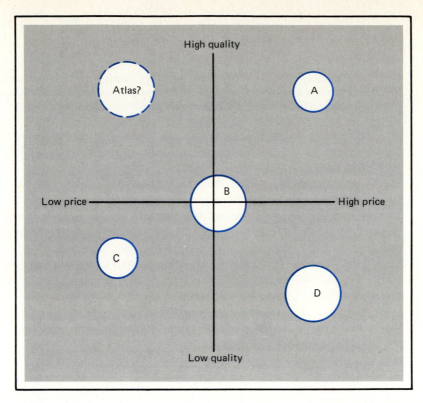

FIGURE 2-17
A Product-Positioning Map Showing Perceived Offers of Four Competitors
and a Possible Position for Atlas

sell at a low price and still make money. Second, Atlas must check whether lots of buyers want a high-quality machine at a lower price. That would be expected, but price might contribute to snob appeal. Finally, Atlas must be able to convince buyers that its typewriter's quality and service are comparable to A's. Many buyers don't believe that lower-price units can be as good as higher-price units, so heavy promotional expenditures may be required.

The main point is that today's companies must choose carefully not only their consumer targets but also their competitor targets. In an era of slow-growth markets, planning for the competitors is as important as planning for the consumers.

Developing Marketing Strategies

The marketing managers must refine the marketing strategy further and be prepared to alter it as time goes on. The marketing strategies are spelled out during the marketing planning process (Chapter 9). The executives sit together and review the current marketing situation, set objectives, and develop marketing strategies and later go on to developing marketing tactics, budgets, and controls.

The marketing strategy spells out the game plan for attaining the business's objectives. We define marketing strategy as follows:

> *Marketing strategy* **is the marketing logic by which the business unit expects to achieve its marketing objectives. Marketing strategy consists of making decisions on the business's marketing expenditures, marketing mix, and marketing allocations in relation to expected environmental and competitive conditions.**

Marketing management must decide what level of marketing expenditures is necessary to achieve its marketing objectives. Companies typically establish their marketing budget at some conventional percentage of the sales goal. Companies entering a market try to learn what the marketing *budget-to-sales ratio* is for competitors. A particular company may spend more than the normal ratio in the hope of achieving a higher market share. Ultimately the company should analyze the marketing work that has to be done to attain a given sales volume or market share and then cost out this work; the result is the required marketing budget.

The company also has to decide how to allocate the total marketing budget to the various tools in the *marketing mix.* Marketing mix is one of the key concepts in modern marketing theory.

> *Marketing mix* **is the mixture of controllable marketing variables that the firm uses to pursue the sought level of sales in the target market.**

There are literally dozens of marketing-mix elements. McCarthy popularized a four-factor classification of these variables called the Four Ps: *product, price, place, and promotion.*[25] The particular marketing variables under each *P* are shown in Figure 2–18.

The company's marketing mix at time *t* for a particular product can be represented by the vector:

$$(P_1, P_2, P_3, P_4)_t$$

where P_1 = product quality, P_2 = price, P_3 = place, and P_4 = promotion.

If Atlas develops product quality at 1.2 (with 1.00 = average), prices it at \$1,000, spends \$30,000 a month on distribution and \$20,000 a month on promotion, its marketing mix at time *t* is:

$$(1.2, \$1,000, \$30,000, \$20,000)_t$$

One can see that a marketing mix is selected from a great number of possibilities. If product quality could take on one of two values, and product price is constrained

[25] E. Jerome McCarthy, *Basic Marketing: A Managerial Approach*, 7th ed. (Homewood, Ill.: Richard D. Irwin, 1981), p. 42 (1st ed., 1960). Two alternative classifications are worth noting. Frey proposed that all marketing-decision variables could be categorized by two factors: the *offering* (product, packaging, brand, price, and service) and *methods and tools* (distribution channels, personal selling, advertising, sales promotion, and publicity). See Albert W. Frey, *Advertising*, 3rd ed., (New York: Ronald Press, 1961), p. 30. Lazer and Kelly proposed a three-factor classification: *goods and service mix, distribution mix,* and *communications mix*. See William Lazer and Eugene J. Kelly, *Managerial Marketing: Perspectives and Viewpoints*, rev. ed. (Homewood, Ill.: Richard D. Irwin, 1962) p. 413.

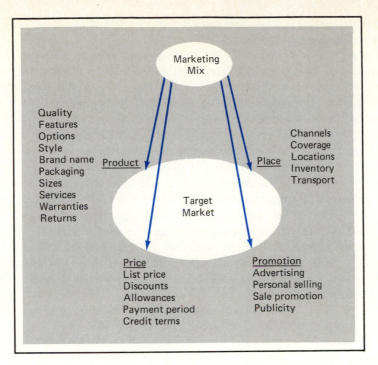

FIGURE 2-18
The Four Ps of the Marketing Mix

to lie between $500 and $1,500 (to the nearest $100), and distribution and advertising expenditures are constrained to lie between $10,000 and $50,000 (to the nearest $10,000), then 550 (2 × 11 × 5 × 5) marketing-mix combinations are possible.

Not all marketing-mix variables can be adjusted in the short run. They vary in their adjustability. Typically, the firm can change its price, increase the size of its sales force, and raise its advertising expenditures in the short run. It can only develop new products and modify its marketing channels in the long run. Thus, the firm typically makes fewer period-to-period marketing-mix changes in the short run than the number of marketing-mix variables suggest.

Finally, management must decide on the *allocation* of the marketing dollars to the various products, channels, promotion media, and sales areas. How many dollars should support Atlas's electric versus electronic typewriters? direct versus distributor sales? direct mail advertising versus trade magazine advertising? East Coast markets versus West Coast markets? We can represent a distinct allocation in the following way: Suppose management sets product quality at 1.2, price at $1,000, a monthly distribution budget of $5,000, and a monthly advertising budget of $10,000 for product i selling to customer-type j in area k at time t. This is represented by the vector:

$$(1.2, \$1,000, \$5,000, \$10,000)_{i,j,k,t}$$

To make these strategic allocations, marketing managers use the notion of *sales-*

response curves that show how sales would be affected by the amount of dollars put in each possible application.

Part of every marketing plan contains a subplan for new-product development (Chapter 10). Atlas, for example, plans to design a new electronic typewriter. But the new-product development process is a road strewn with land mines and booby traps. Too many products never come out of the laboratory, and of those that do, many fail in the marketplace, causing great expense to the company and a loss to society. The art of new-product development calls for organizing this process effectively and using distinct tools and controls at each stage of the process.

After a product is launched under its initial marketing strategy, changes in strategy will be called for. Strategy will have to be modified, first of all, as the product passes through the major stages of the product/market life cycle, namely introduction, growth, maturity, and decline (Chapter 11). Strategy will also vary according to whether the firm's role in the market is that of market leader, challenger, follower, or nicher (Chapter 12). Strategy will have to be adjusted to fit the current economic climate, whether it is one of shortages, inflation, or recession (Chapter 13). Finally, strategy will have to take into account changing global market opportunities and developments (Chapter 14).

Planning Marketing Tactics

Marketing planning calls not only for planning the broad strategies by which the business hopes to achieve its marketing objectives but also for fine tuning the tactics involved in each marketing-mix variable. Many strategies that are well conceived fail in their tactical execution.

The most basic marketing variable is *product*, which stands for the tangible offer to the market, including the product features, packaging, branding, and servicing policies (Chapter 15). Thus Atlas manages a product line consisting of typewriters, which differ in features, quality, and styling. The typewriters are packaged and may carry different brand names and are accompanied by certain levels and types of planned services for customers.

Another important marketing-decision variable is *price*, namely the amount of money that customers have to pay for the product (Chapter 16). Atlas has to decide on wholesale and retail prices, discounts, allowances, and credit terms. Its price should be commensurate with the perceived value of the offer, or else buyers will turn to competitors for their product choices.

Place stands for the various activities the company undertakes to make the product accessible and available to target consumers (Chapters 17 and 18). Thus, Atlas must identify, recruit, and link various middlemen and marketing facilitators so that its products and services are efficiently supplied to the target market. It must understand the various types of retailers, wholesalers, and physical distribution firms and how they make their decisions.

Promotion stands for the various activities the company undertakes to communicate its products' merits and to persuade target customers to buy them (Chapters

19–22). Thus Atlas has to buy advertising, set up sales promotions, arrange publicity, and dispatch sales people to promote its products.

Implementing and Controlling the Marketing Effort

The final step in the marketing management process is implementing and controlling the marketing plan. A plan is nothing "unless it *degenerates into work.*"[26] Therefore the company must design a marketing organization that is capable of *implementing* the marketing plan (Chapter 23). In a small company one person might carry out all of the marketing tasks: marketing research, selling, advertising, customer servicing, and so on. In large companies, several marketing specialists will be found. Thus Atlas has sales people, sales managers, marketing researchers, advertising personnel, product and brand managers, market-segment managers, and customer-service personnel.

Marketing organizations are typically headed by a marketing vice-president, who performs two tasks. The first is to coordinate the work of all of the marketing personnel. Atlas's marketing vice-president must make sure, for example, that the advertising manager works closely with the sales-force manager so that the sales force is ready to handle inquiries generated by ads that are placed by the advertising department.

The marketing vice-president's other task is to work closely with the vice-presidents of finance, manufacturing, research and development, purchasing, and personnel to coordinate company efforts to satisfy customers. Thus if Atlas's marketing people advertise its new electronic typewriter as a quality product, but R&D does not design a quality product, or manufacturing fails to manufacture it carefully, then marketing will not deliver on its promise. The marketing vice-president's job is to make sure that all of the company departments collaborate to fulfill the marketing promise made to the customers.

The marketing department's effectiveness depends not only on how it is structured but also on how well its personnel are selected, trained, directed, motivated, and evaluated. There is a vast difference in the performance of a "turned-on" versus "turned-off" marketing group. The marketing personnel need feedback on their marketing performance. Managers must meet with their subordinates periodically to review their performance, praise their strengths, point out their weaknesses, and suggest ways to correct them.

There are likely to be many surprises as marketing plans are implemented by the marketing organization. The company needs control procedures to make sure that the marketing objectives will be achieved (Chapter 24). Various managers will have to exercise control responsibilities in addition to their analysis, planning, and implementing responsibilities. Three types of marketing control can be distinguished: annual-plan control, profitability control, and strategic control.

Annual-plan control is the task of making sure that the company is achieving the sales, profits, and other goals that it established in its annual plan. The task

---

[26] Drucker, *Management*, p. 128.

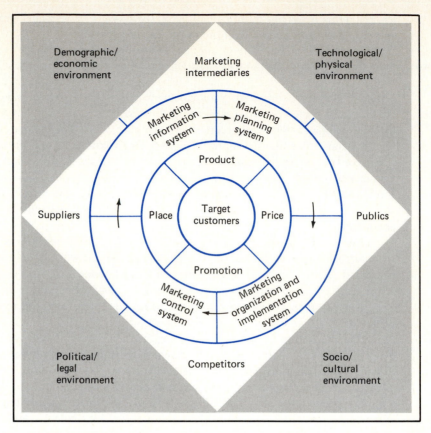

Demographic/economic environment

Technological/physical environment

Marketing intermediaries

Marketing information system

Marketing planning system

Product

Suppliers

Place

Target customers

Price

Publics

Promotion

Marketing control system

Marketing organization and implementation system

Political/legal environment

Competitors

Socio/cultural environment

FIGURE 2-19
Factors Influencing Company Marketing Strategy

breaks into four steps. First, management must state well-defined goals in the annual plan for each month, quarter, or other period during the year. Second, management must have ways to measure its ongoing performance in the marketplace. Third, management must determine the underlying causes of any serious gaps in performance. Fourth, management must decide on the best corrective action to take to close the gaps between goals and performance. It may call for improving the ways in which the plan is being implemented or even changing the goals.

Companies need to analyze periodically the actual *profitability* of their different products, customer groups, trade channels, and order sizes. This is not a simple task. A company's accounting system often is not designed to report the real profitability of different marketing entities and activities. To measure the profit on different typewriter models, for example, Atlas's accountants have to estimate how much time the sales force spends promoting each model, how much advertising goes into each model, and so on. *Marketing profitability analysis* is the tool used to measure the profitability of different marketing activities. *Marketing efficiency studies* might also be undertaken to study how various marketing activities could be carried on more efficiently.

From time to time, Atlas must stand back and critically reexamine its overall marketing game plan and decide whether it continues to make good strategic sense. Marketing is one of the major areas where rapid obsolescence of objectives, policies, strategies, and programs is a constant possibility. Giant companies such as Chrysler, International Harvester, Singer, and A & P, all fell on hard times because they didn't watch the changing marketplace and make the proper adaptations. Because of the rapid changes in the marketing environment, each company needs to reassess periodically its marketing effectiveness through a control instrument known as the *marketing audit*.

Figure 2–19 presents a grand summary of the marketing management process and the forces influencing the setting of company marketing strategy. The target customers stand in the center, and the company focuses its effort on serving and satisfying them. The company develops a marketing mix made up of the factors under its control, the four Ps—product, price, place, and promotion. To arrive at its marketing mix, the company manages four systems: a marketing information system, marketing planning system, marketing organization system, and marketing control system. These systems are interrelated in that marketing information is needed to develop marketing plans, which in turn are implemented by the marketing organization, the results of which are reviewed and controlled.

Through these systems, the company monitors and adapts to the marketing environment. The company adapts to its microenvironment, consisting of marketing intermediaries, suppliers, competitors, and publics. And it adapts to the macroenvironment, consisting of demographic/economic forces, political/legal forces, technological/physical forces, and social/cultural forces. The company takes the actors and forces in the marketing environment into account in developing strategy and positioning an effective offer to the target market.

SUMMARY

Management is the entrepreneurial agent that interprets market needs and translates them into profitable products and services. To do so, management utilizes a strategic planning process and a marketing management process.

The strategic planning process consists of steps taken at the corporate headquarters level to develop long-run strategies for survival and growth. The strategic planning process consists of defining the company's mission, objectives, and goals; portfolio plans; and new-business plans. A clear statement of company mission provides employees with a shared sense of opportunity, direction, significance, and achievement. It should define the company's business domain in terms of customer groups, customer needs, and technologies.

Strategic planning then calls for developing specific objectives, such as sales volume, sales growth, market share, profitability, and innovation, to support the company mission. These objectives should be hierarchical, quantitative, realistic, and consistent.

Strategic planning must then define, for each strategic business unit (SBU) in the company's portfolio, whether that SBU will be built, maintained, harvested, or terminated. Use is made of such tools as BCG's growth/share matrix or GE's multifactor portfolio matrix to evaluate the future of the company's various businesses.

To fill a strategic planning gap between expected sales and desired sales, the company has to develop a new-business plan. The company can generate relevant opportunities by considering intensive growth opportunities within its present product-market scope (such as market penetration, market development, and product development), integrative growth opportunities within its marketing system (such as backward, forward, and horizontal integration), and finally, diversification growth opportunities outside of its marketing system (such as concentric, horizontal, and conglomerate diversification).

Within each business, marketing management must develop marketing data for strategic planners to use, develop marketing plans based on the agreed-upon objectives of the business, and carry them out. In fact, the marketing management process consists of five steps: analyzing market opportunities, researching and selecting target markets, developing marketing strategies, planning marketing tactics, and implementing and controlling the marketing effort.

In the first step, analyzing market opportunities, marketing personnel make careful observations about the changing marketing environment and acquire a deep understanding of how consumer markets and organizational markets arrive at their buying decisions.

The second step, researching and selecting target markets, requires marketing personnel to engage in formal marketing research and data collection, careful measurement of market size and future sales and profits, and careful segmentation of the market so that the most attractive market segments can be selected and proper positions taken by the company in each market segment.

The third step, developing marketing strategies, calls for marketing personnel to master the marketing planning process and the new-product development process and also requires them to prepare to change strategies during the product life cycle, and as the company's market position changes, as the economic climate changes, and as global opportunities open or close.

The fourth step, planning marketing tactics, calls for marketing personnel to fine tune the marketing-mix elements of product, price, place, and promotion so that they are cost effective in reaching the marketing objectives.

The fifth step, implementing and controlling the marketing effort, calls for developing a marketing organization, staffing it, assigning responsibilities for implementing all the activities in the plan, monitoring the plan's performance in the marketplace, and taking corrective action when it is warranted. The overall marketing game plan should be reviewed from time to time through the instrument known as the marketing audit.

QUESTIONS

1. After decades as a marketer of personal-care products to men, Gillette, in the 1980s, began to move into the women's personal-care market with such products as Silkience hair products and Apri skin products. Describe Gillette's strategy, using Table 2–3 (Major Classes of Growth Opportunities) and Figure 2–11 (Intensive Growth Strategies).

2. "With more than 80 percent of the market already in its grasp, Campbell Soup Co. really doesn't need to increase its share of the $1.2 billion of condensed soup sold annually in food stores. What the company does need is to make folks hungrier for soup." What intensive growth strategy is being pursued, and how might they accomplish this objective?

3. Parker Bros., a marketer of traditional board games for adolescents, is concerned about the effect of the video-game market growth on the sale of its product line. How might the company's mission statement affect their response to such an environmental threat, and what counterstrategy might they use to respond to this critical environmental change?

4. Analyze the attractiveness of the beer market by using Porter's indexes.

5. An automotive-parts manufacturer produces three products: mufflers, filters, and silencers. The company is seeking new growth opportunities. Develop a product-market matrix showing some potential expansion opportunities for this manufacturer.

6. What is the major distinctive competence of (a) Sears; (b) Polaroid Company; (c) Procter & Gamble; (d) Ford Foundation?

7. What kind of diversification growth strategy is illustrated by: (a) General Foods' acquisition of Burger Chef, a fast-food service chain; (b) Philip Morris's acquisition of Miller Brewing Company; (c) Mobil Oil's acquisition of Montgomery Ward?

8. A local high school has operated a night school program with only marginal success for several years. Due to a recent tax referendum, the school board has decided it must either significantly increase night school enrollments or cancel the entire program. Suggest a statement of purpose for the night school program and a hierarchy of objectives based upon the intention to increase enrollments.

9. An industrial-equipment company consists of the five strategic business units (SBUs) shown below. Using the Boston Consulting Group portfolio analysts, determine whether the company is in a healthy condition. What future strategies should it consider?

SBU	Dollar Sales (In Millions)	Number of Competitors	Dollar Sales of the Top 3 (In Millions)	Market Growth Rate
A	0.5	8	0.7, 0.7, 0.5	15%
B	1.6	22	1.6, 1.6, 1.0	18%
C	1.8	14	1.8, 1.2, 1.0	7%
D	3.2	5	3.2, 0.8, 0.7	4%
E	0.5	10	2.5, 1.8, 1.7	4%

The Marketing Environment

Everyone lives by selling something.

ROBERT LOUIS STEVENSON

One of the major responsibilities of company marketers is to monitor and search the environment for new opportunities. The marketing environment is constantly spinning out new opportunities, in bad as well as in good years. Table 3-1 shows some of the great marketing success stories in the 1960s, 1970s, and early 1980s. Although the 1970s and 1980s were years of slow growth, there were enough enterprising people around to create marvelous new businesses out of ideas that seem obvious in retrospect. Not listed, of course, are the many new businesses that didn't make it and some that almost did—such as De Lorean automobiles and Freddie Laker's airline.

The marketing environment also spins out new threats—such as an energy crisis, a sharp rise in interest rates, a deep recession—and firms find their markets collapsing. Recent times have been marked by many sudden changes in the marketing environ-

TABLE 3-1

	GREAT MARKETING SUCCESSES	

1960s	**1970s**	**1980s**
McDonald's	Miller Lite Beer	H&R Block	Atari Videogames
Honda Motorcycles	Perrier Water	Hanes L'eggs	Apple Computers
Playboy	Charlie Perfume	Intel's "Chip"	Computerland Stores
Avon Cosmetics	Club Mediterranee	Federal Express	Aquafresh Toothpaste (Beecham)
Levi Jeans (Levi Strauss)	Nautilus	Pac Man	Tandy Computers (Radio Shack)
Crest Toothpaste (P&G)	Häagen-Dazs Ice Cream	Rubik Cube	
Marlboro (Philip Morris)	Prince Tennis Racquets	Kruggerands	
BIC Pens	Adidas and Nike Shoes	Tylenol	
K-Mart	Walkman (Sony)	Pampers (P&G)	
7-11 Convenience Stores	The Limited Stores	Mary Kay	
	Softsoap (Minnetonka)	Penthouse	
	Boeing 747		
	Jovan Toiletries		
	Texas Instrument Pocket Calculators		
	Tagamet (Smith, Klein & French)		

ment, leading Drucker to dub it an *Age of Discontinuity*[1] and Toffler to describe it as a time of *Future Shock.*[2]

Company marketers need to constantly monitor the changing scene. They need to observe the changing environment first-hand and also to rely on marketing intelligence and marketing research systems to track the changing environment more closely. By erecting early warning systems, marketers will be able to alter marketing strategies to meet new challenges and opportunities in the environment.

What do we mean by the marketing environment? The marketing environment comprises the "noncontrollable" actors and forces in response to which organizations design their marketing strategies. Specifically:

> A *company's marketing environment* consists of the actors and forces external to the marketing management function of the firm that impinge on the marketing management's ability to develop and maintain successful transactions with its target customers.

We can distinguish between the company's microenvironment and macroenvironment. The *microenvironment* consists of the actors in the company's immediate environment that affect its ability to serve its markets: the company, suppliers, market intermediaries, customers, competitors, and publics. The *macroenvironment* consists of the larger societal forces that affect all of the actors in the company's microen-

---

[1] Peter Drucker, *Age of Discontinuity* (New York: Harper & Row, 1969).

[2] See Alvin Toffler, *Future Shock* (New York: Bantam Books, 1970), p. 28.

vironment: the demographic, economic, physical, technological, political, legal, and socio/cultural forces. We will first examine the company's microenvironment and then its macroenvironment.

ACTORS IN THE COMPANY'S MICROENVIRONMENT

Every company's primary goal is to serve and satisfy a specified set of needs of a chosen target market at a profit to itself. To carry out this task, the company links itself with a set of suppliers and a set of marketing intermediaries to reach its target customers. The *suppliers-company-marketing/intermediaries-customers* chain comprises the *core marketing system* of the company. The company's success will be affected by two additional groups, namely, a set of competitors and a set of publics. Company management has to watch and plan for all of these actors. These actors are shown in Figure 3–1. We will illustrate the role of these actors in the case of the Hershey Foods Corporation, a major U.S. candy manufacturer. We shall look at the company and its suppliers, marketing intermediaries, competitors, and publics, in that order.

Company

The Hershey Chocolate Company of Hershey, Pennsylvania, racks up over $1 billion of chocolate and confection sales each year. Its product line includes Hershey's Chocolate Bars, Hershey Kisses, Reece's candy, and several other items. Its marketing is handled by a large marketing and sales department consisting of brand managers, marketing researchers, advertising and promotion specialists, sales managers and sales-representatives, and so on. The marketing department is responsible for developing marketing plans for all the existing products and brands as well as developing new products and brands.

FIGURE 3–1
Major Actors in the Company's Microenvironment

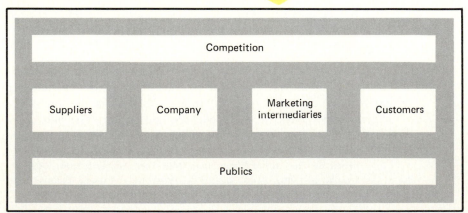

Marketing management at Hershey, in formulating marketing plans, must take into account the other groups in the company, such as top management, finance, R&D, purchasing, manufacturing, and accounting. All of these groups constitute a company microenvironment for the marketing planners.

Top management at Hershey's consists of the president, the executive committee, and the board of directors. These higher levels of management set the company's mission, objectives, broad strategies, and policies. Marketing managers must make decisions within the context set by top management. Furthermore, their marketing proposals must be approved by top management before they can be implemented.

Marketing managers must also work closely with the functional departments. *Financial management* is concerned with the availability of funds to carry out the marketing plan; the efficient allocation of these funds to different products, brands, and marketing activities; the likely rates of return that will be realized; and the level of risk in the sales forecast and marketing plan. *Research and development management* focuses on researching and developing successful new products. *Purchasing* worries about obtaining sufficient supplies of raw materials (cocoa, sugar, and so on) as well as other productive inputs required to run this company. *Manufacturing* is responsible for acquiring sufficient productive capacity and personnel to meet production targets. *Accounting* has to measure revenues and costs to help marketing know how well it is achieving its profit objectives.

All of these departments have an impact on the marketing department's plans and actions. The various brand managers have to sell the manufacturing and finance department on their plans before presenting them to top management. If the manufacturing vice-president won't allocate enough production capacity, or the financial vice-president won't allocate money, the brand managers will have to revise their sales targets or bring the issue before top management. The many potential conflicts between marketing and the other functions are described in Chapter 23. Suffice it to say that marketing management has to work with other groups in the company to design and implement its marketing plans.

Suppliers

Suppliers are business firms and individuals who provide resources needed by the company and its competitors to produce the particular goods and services. For example, Hershey must obtain cocoa, sugar, cellophane, and various other materials to produce its candies. In addition, it must obtain labor, equipment, fuel, electricity, computers, and other factors of production to carry on its business activity. Hershey's purchasing department must decide on which resources to make and which to buy outside. For "buy" decisions, Hershey's purchasing agents must develop specifications, search for suppliers, qualify them, and choose those who offer the best mix of quality, delivery reliability, credit, warranties, and low cost.

Developments in the "supplier" environment can have a substantial effect on the company's marketing operations. Marketing managers need to watch price trends of their key inputs. Rising supply costs of sugar or cocoa may force candy bar price increases that will reduce Hershey's forecasted sales volume. Marketing managers are equally concerned with supply availability. Supply shortages, labor strikes, and other events can interfere with the fulfillment of delivery promises to customers and lose sales in the short run and damage customer goodwill in the long run. Many companies prefer to buy from multiple sources to avoid overdependency on any one supplier who might raise prices arbitrarily or limit supply. Company purchasing agents try to build long-term relationships with key suppliers. Purchasing agents find that they have to "market" their company to suppliers in order to obtain favorable consideration, especially in times of shortages.[3]

The marketing executive is a direct purchaser of certain services to support the marketing effort, such as advertising, marketing research, sales training, and marketing consulting. In going outside, the marketing executive evaluates different advertising agencies, marketing research firms, sales-training consultants, and marketing consultants. The executive has to decide which services to purchase outside and which to produce inside by adding specialists to the staff.

Marketing Intermediaries

Marketing intermediaries are firms that aid the company in promoting, selling, and distributing its goods to the final buyers. They include middlemen, physical distribution firms, marketing service agencies, and financial intermediaries.

Middlemen.   Middlemen are business firms that help the company find customers and/or close sales with them. They fall into two types, agent middlemen and merchant middlemen. *Agent middlemen*—such as agents, brokers, and manufacturers' representatives—find customers and/or negotiate contracts but do not take title to merchandise. Hershey, for example, might hire agents to find retailers in various South American countries and pay commission to these agents based on the amount of orders they produce. The agents do not buy the candy; Hershey ships directly to the retailers. *Merchant middlemen*—such as wholesalers, retailers, and other resellers—buy, take title to, and resell merchandise. Hershey's primary method of marketing candy is to sell candy to wholesalers, large supermarket chains, and vending-machine operators, who in turn resell the candy to consumers at a profit.

Why does Hershey use middlemen at all? The answer is that middlemen are able to produce several utilities for customers more cheaply than Hershey can by itself. As a manufacturer, Hershey is primarily interested in producing and rolling out large quantities of candy from its factory doors. The customer, on the other hand, is interested in finding one bar of candy in a convenient location, at a convenient time, with a related assortment of other goods sought by the consumer, and with an easy payment mechanism. The gap between the large quantities of candy that Hershey rolls out and the consumer's preferred way of buying candy must be overcome. Middlemen come into being to help overcome the discrepancies in quantities, place, time, assortment, and possession that would otherwise exist.

Specifically, middlemen create *place utility* by stocking Hershey candy where customers are located. They create *time utility* by staying open long hours so that

---

[3] This point is elaborated in Philip Kotler and Sidney J. Levy, "Buying Is Marketing, Too," *Journal of Marketing*, January 1973, pp. 54–59.

customers can shop at their convenience. They create *quantity utility* by making candy available in single-bar purchases. They create *assortment utility* by collecting in one point other goods that consumers may seek on the same shopping trip. They create *possession utility* by transferring the candy bar to the consumer in an easy transaction format, namely for a simple payment of cash without the need for any billing. Hershey, to create the same utilities, would have to establish, finance and operate a far-flung network of national stores and vending machines. Hershey, of course, finds it more efficient to work through established channels of middlemen.

Selecting and working with middlemen, however, is not a simple task. At one time, the manufacturer had to contact and sell to numerous small independent middlemen. Today, the manufacturer deals with fewer but larger middlemen organizations. An increasing share of all food distribution is in the hands of large corporate retail chains (such as Safeway and Jewel), large wholesalers and franchised-sponsored voluntary chains (such as Seven-Eleven and White Hen). To cite an extreme case, in Switzerland 70 percent of all food distribution is in the hands of two giant middlemen, Migros and the Coop. These groups have great power to dictate terms or else shut the manufacturer out of some large-volume markets. The manufacturer must work hard to get and maintain "shelf space." The manufacturer has to learn how to manage and satisfy his channels of distribution or face diminishing support or actual exclusion.

Physical distribution firms.   Physical distribution firms assist the company in stocking and moving goods from their original locations to their destinations. *Warehousing firms* store and protect goods before they move to the next destination. Every company has to decide how much storage space to build for itself and how much to rent from warehousing firms. *Transportation firms* consist of railroads, truckers, airlines, barges, and other freight-handling companies that move goods from one location to another. Every company has to decide on the most cost-effective modes of shipment, balancing such considerations as cost, delivery, speed, and safety. (See Chapter 18.)

Marketing service agencies.   Marketing service agencies—marketing research firms, advertising agencies, media firms, and marketing consulting firms—assist the company in targeting and promoting its products to the right markets. The company faces a "make or buy" decision with respect to these services. Some large companies—such as Du Pont and Quaker Oats—operate their own in-house advertising agencies and marketing research departments. But most companies contract for the services of outside agencies. When a firm decides to buy outside services, it must carefully choose whom to hire, since the agencies vary in their creativity, quality, service, and price. The company has to review periodically their performance and must consider replacing those that no longer perform at the expected level.

Financial intermediaries.   Financial intermediaries include banks, credit companies, insurance companies, and other companies that help finance and/or insure risk associated with the buying and selling of goods. Most firms and customers depend on financial intermediaries to finance their transactions. The company's marketing performance can be seriously affected by rising credit costs and/or limited credit.

For this reason, the company has to develop strong relationships with outside financial institutions.

Customers

A company links itself to suppliers and middlemen in order to efficiently supply products and services to its target market. Its target market can be one (or more) of the following five types of customer markets:

- ☐ **Consumer markets.** Individuals and households that buy goods and services for personal consumption.
- ☐ **Industrial markets.** Organizations that buy goods and services needed for producing other products and services for the purpose of making profits and/or achieving other objectives.
- ☐ **Reseller markets.** Organizations that buy goods and services in order to resell them at a profit.
- ☐ **Government markets.** Government agencies that buy goods and services in order to produce public services, or transfer these goods and services to others who need them.
- ☐ **International markets.** Buyers found abroad, including foreign consumers, producers, resellers, and governments.

Hershey sells its products to a number of these customer markets. Its main customer market is resellers who in turn sell Hershey candy to consumers. Another important customer group is institutional buyers, namely, factories, hospitals, schools, government agencies, and other organizations that run cafeterias for their employees. Hershey also sells a substantial volume to foreign consumers, producers, resellers, and governments. Each customer market exhibits specific characteristics that warrant careful study by the seller. The major characteristics of consumer markets and organizational markets (producers, resellers, and government agencies) will be examined in the following two chapters.

Competitors

An organization rarely stands alone in its effort to serve a given customer market. Its efforts to build an efficient marketing system to serve the market are matched by similar efforts on the part of others. The company's marketing system is surrounded and affected by a host of competitors. These competitors have to be identified, monitored, and outmaneuvered to gain and maintain customer loyalty.

The competitive environment consists not only of other companies but also of more basic things. The best way for a company to grasp its competition is to take the viewpoint of a buyer. What does a buyer think about in the process of arriving at the answer to a question that might result in the purchase of something? Suppose a person has been working hard and needs a break. The person asks: "What do I want to do now?" Among the possibilities that pop into his or her mind are socializing, exercising, and eating. (See Figure 3–2.) We will call these *desire competitors*. Suppose the person is mostly motivated to satisfy his or her hunger. Then the question becomes: "What do I want to eat?" Different foods come to mind, such as potato chips, candy, soft drinks, and fruit. These can be called *generic competitors* in that they represent different basic ways to satisfy the same need. At this point, he or she decides on

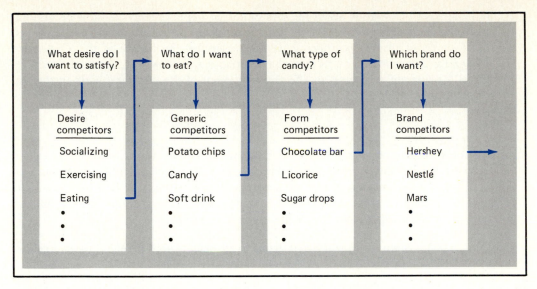

FIGURE 3-2
Four Types of Competition

candy and asks: "What type of candy do I want?" Different candy forms come to mind, such as chocolate bars, licorice, and sugar drops. They all represent *product form competitors*, in that they are different forms for satisfying a desire for candy. Finally, the consumer realizes that he really wants a chocolate bar and faces several brands, such as Hershey, Nestlé, and Mars. These are *brand competitors.*

In this way Hershey's marketing vice-president can determine all of the competitors standing in the way of selling more Hershey chocolate bars. The marketing executive will want to watch all four types of competitors. Company executives have a tendency to focus primarily on the brand competitors and on the task of building brand perference. Hershey wants to be thought of as the leading candy bar producer, and its executives spend their time trying to position its candy as the quality leader and a good value for the money. Hershey relies primarily on product quality, advertising, sales promotion, and universal distribution to build up its brand preference. Its competitive stance against Nestlé, Mars, and so on may range from "live and let live" most of the time to occasional attacks on competitor positions. More often, however, the leading candy bar company is on the defensive against smaller companies that aggressively attack its position.

Candy bar companies are myopic if they focus only on their brand competitors. The real challenge facing candy companies is to expand their primary market, namely the candy market, rather than simply fight for a larger share in a fixed-size market. Candy companies have to be concerned about megatrends in the environment, such as people eating less in general, and eating less candy in particular, or even switching to other forms of candy, such as dietetic candy, and so on. In too many industries, companies focus on the brand competitors and fail to exploit opportunities to expand the whole market or at least prevent it from eroding.

A basic observation about the task of competing effectively can now be summarized. A company must keep four basic dimensions in mind, which can be called the four Cs of market positioning. It must consider the nature of the *Customers, Channels, Competition,* and its own characteristics as a *Company.* Successful marketing is a matter of achieving an effective alignment of the company with customers, channels, and competitors.

Publics

Not only does an organization have to contend with competitors in seeking to satisfy a target market but it must also acknowledge a large set of publics that take an interest, whether welcome or not, in its methods of doing business. Because the actions of the organization affect the interest of other groups, these groups become significant publics to the organization. We define a public as follows:

> A *public* is any group that has an actual or potential interest or impact on an organization's ability to achieve its objectives.

A public can facilitate or impede the ability of an organization to accomplish its goals. Since publics can substantially influence an organization's fortunes, the wise organization takes concrete steps to manage successful relations with its key publics, rather than sitting back and waiting. Most organizations establish public relations departments to plan constructive relations with various publics. These departments monitor the attitudes of the organization's publics and distribute information and communications to build goodwill. When negative publicity breaks out, these departments act as trouble shooters. In the best departments, there is an emphasis on counseling top management to adopt positive programs and to eliminate questionable practices so that negative publicity does not arise in the first place.

It would be a mistake for an organization to leave public relations entirely in the hands of the public relations department. All the employees of the organization are involved in public relations, from the chief officer, who meets the general public, to the financial vice-president, who addresses the financial community, to the field sales representative, who calls on customers.

We believe that public relations should be conceived of as a broad marketing operation rather than a narrow communication operation.[4] A public is a group from which an organization wants some response, such as goodwill, favorable mentions, or donations of time or money. The organization must ask what that public is seeking that it could satisfy. It then plans a benefit package that is designed to build goodwill.

Every company is surrounded by seven types of publics:

☐ **Financial publics.** Financial publics influence the company's ability to obtain funds. Banks, investment houses, stock brokerage firms, and stockholders are the major financial publics. Hershey seeks the goodwill of these groups by issuing annual reports, answering financial questions, and satisfying the financial community that its house is in order.

---

[4] The interrelations between marketing and public relations are examined in Philip Kotler and William Mindak, "Marketing and Public Relations: Partners or Rivals," *Journal of Marketing*, October 1978, pp. 13–20.

- **Media publics.** Media publics are organizations that carry news, features, and editorial opinion; specifically, newspapers, magazines, and radio and television stations. Hershey is interested in getting more and better media coverage.

- **Government publics.** Management must take government developments into account in formulating marketing plans. Hershey's marketers must consult the company's lawyers about possible issues of product safety, truth in advertising, and so on. Hershey must consider joining with other candy manufacturers to lobby against proposed legislation that would harm their interests.

- **Citizen-action publics.** A company's marketing activities may be questioned by consumer organizations, environmental groups, minority groups, and others. For example, some consumerists have attacked candy as having little redeeming value, in that it is high in calories, causes tooth decay, and so on. Hershey must deal with this negative publicity either by counterattacking with positive statements about the benefits of candy or working with the consumerists to achieve a fairer statement of the issues involved. (For a brief account of how consumerism affects company marketing policy, see Exhibit 3–1.)

Exhibit 3–1

THE IMPACT OF CONSUMERISM ON MARKETING DECISION MAKING

Starting in the 1960s, American business firms found themselves the target of a growing consumer movement. Consumers had become better educated; products had become increasingly complex and hazardous; discontent with American institutions was widespread; influential writings by John Kenneth Galbraith, Vance Packard, and Rachel Carson accused big business of wasteful and manipulative practices; John Kennedy's presidential message of 1962 declared that consumers have the right to safety, to be informed, to choose, and to be heard; congressional investigations of certain industries proved embarrassing; and, finally, Ralph Nader appeared on the scene to crystallize many of the issues.

Since these early stirrings, many private consumer organizations have emerged, several pieces of consumer legislation have been passed, and several state and local offices of consumer affairs have been created. Furthermore, the consumer movement has taken on an international character, with much strength in Scandinavia and the Low Countries and a growing presence in France, Germany, and Japan.

But what is consumerism? *Consumerism is an organized movement of citizens and government to enhance the rights and power of buyers in relation to sellers.* Consumerists' groups are seeking, through company persuasion and legislation, to increase the amount of consumer information, education, and protection. Consumerists have advocated—and in many cases won—such proposals as the right to know the true interest cost of a loan (*truth-in-lending*), the true cost per standard unit of competing brands (*unit pricing*), the basic ingredients in a product (*ingredient labeling*), the nutritional quality of foods (*nutritional labeling*), the freshness of products (*open dating*), and the true benefits of a product (*truth-in-advertising*). They want the government to check on the safety of products that are potentially hazardous and to penalize companies that are careless. Some consumerists want companies to elect consumer representatives to their boards to introduce consumer considerations into business decision making.

The most successful consumer group is Ralph Nader's *Public Citizen*. Nader lifted consumerism into a major social force, first with his successful attack on unsafe automobiles (resulting in the passage of the National Traffic and Motor Vehicle Safety Act of 1962), and then through investigations into meat processing (resulting in the passage of the Wholesome Meat Act of 1967), truth-in-lending, auto repairs, insurance, and X-ray equipment.

A number of companies balked at first at the consumer movement. They resented the power of strong consumer leaders to point an accusing finger at their products and cause their sales to plummet, as for instance, when Ralph Nader called the Corvair automobile unsafe, when Robert Choate accused breakfast cereals of providing "empty calories," and when Herbert S. Denenberg published a list showing the wide variation in premiums different insurance companies were charging for the same protection. Businesses also resented consumer proposals that appeared to increase business costs more than they helped the consumer. They felt that most consumers would not pay attention to unit pricing or ingredient labeling and that the doctrines of advertising substantiation, corrective advertising, and counter advertising would stifle advertising creativity. They felt that the consumer was better off than ever, that large companies were very careful in developing safe products and promoting them honestly, and that new consumer laws would lead only to new constraints and higher seller costs that would be passed on to the consumer in the form of higher prices.

Many other companies took no stand and simply went about their business. A few companies undertook a series of bold initiatives to show their endorsement of consumer aims. For example:

> Whirlpool Corporation responded by adopting a number of measures to improve customer information and services. They installed a toll-free corporate phone number for consumers to use if they were dissatisfied with their Whirlpool equipment or service. They expanded the coverage of their product warranties and rewrote them in basic English.

In adopting a "we care" role, several companies increased their market shares and profits substantially. Competitors were forced to emulate them, without, however, achieving the same impact enjoyed by these firms.

At the present time most companies have come around to accepting consumerism in principle. They might oppose certain pieces of legislation on the ground that such measures are not the best way to solve a particular consumer problem. But they recognize the consumers' right to information and protection. Those who take a leadership role recognize that consumerism involves a total commitment by top management, middle-management education and participation, new policy guidelines, marketing research, and company investment. Several companies have established consumer affairs departments to help formulate policies and deal with "consumerist" problems facing the company.

Product managers are finding their role changing as a result of consumerism. They have to spend more time checking product ingredients and product features for safety, preparing safe packaging and informative labeling, substantiating their advertising claims, reviewing their sales promotion, developing clear and adequate product warranties, and so on. They have to check an increasing number of decisions with company lawyers. They have to develop a sixth sense about what the consumers really want and may feel about the product and various marketing practices.

On the other hand, consumerism is, in a profound way, the ultimate expression of the marketing concept. It will compel product managers to consider things from the consumers' point of view. It will suggest needs and wants that may have been overlooked by all the firms in the industry. The resourceful manager will look for the positive opportunities created by consumerism rather than brood over its restraints.

(For an appraisal of the current state of the consumer movement in the United States, see Paul N. Bloom and Stephen A. Greyser, "The Maturity of Consumerism," *Harvard Business Review*, November-December 1981, pp. 130–39.)

- [ ] **Local publics.** Every company comes into contact with local publics such as neighborhood residents and community organizations. Large companies usually appoint a community relations officer to deal with the community, attend meetings, answer questions, and make contributions to worthwhile causes.

- [ ] **General public.** A company needs to be concerned with the general public's attitude toward its products and activities. While the general public does not act in an organized way toward the company, the public's image of the company affects its patronage. To build a strong "corporate citizen" image, Hershey will lend its officers to community fund drives, make substantial contributions to charity, and set up systems of consumer complaint handling.

- [ ] **Internal publics.** A company's internal publics include blue-collar workers, white-collar workers, managers, and the board of directors. Large companies develop newsletters and other forms of communication to inform and motivate its internal publics. When employees feel good about their company, this positive attitude spills over to external publics.

Although companies must put their primary energy toward managing their marketing system effectively, their success will be affected by how various publics in the society view their activity. Companies are wise to spend some time monitoring these publics, anticipating their moves, and dealing with them in constructive ways.

FORCES IN THE COMPANY'S MACRO-ENVIRONMENT

The company, its suppliers, marketing intermediaries, customers, competitors, and publics all operate in a larger macroenvironment of forces and megatrends that shape opportunities and pose threats to the company. These forces represent "uncontrollables," which the company must monitor and respond to. The macroenvironment consists of six major forces, namely, demographic, economic, physical, technological, political/legal, and socio/cultural. We will examine the megatrends in each macroenvironment component and their implications for marketing in the coming years.

Demographic Environment

The first environmental fact of interest to marketers is population because people make up markets. Marketers are keenly interested in the size of the world's population; its geographical distribution; density; mobility trends; age distribution; birth, marriage, and death rates; and racial, ethnic, and religious structure. We shall examine the major demographic trends and their implications for marketing planning.

Worldwide explosive population growth. The world population is showing "explosive" growth. The world population totaled 4.4 billion in 1980 and is growing at 1.8 percent per year. At this rate, the world's population will reach 6.2 billion by 2000 A.D.[5]

---

[5] Much of the statistical data in this chapter is drawn from the *Statistical Abstract of the United States, 1982.* Also see a description of the latest census data in "A Portrait of America," *Newsweek,* January 17, 1983, pp. 20–33.

The population explosion has been a major concern of governments and various groups throughout the world. Two factors underlie this concern. The first is the possible finiteness of the earth's resources to support this much human life, particularly at levels of living that represent the aspiration of most people. The famous eighteenth-century economist, Thomas Malthus, was concerned in his time about the population explosion. He saw the population growing at a geometric rate, while the world's food supply grew at an arithmetic rate. To him, this spelled unavoidable disaster for humankind. If humankind could not regulate its own rate of growth, then natural and other forces such as famine, disease, and war would intervene to keep population down to the available food supply. The Malthusian specter has been resurrected many times since—most recently in *The Limits to Growth*.[6] This book presents an impressive array of evidence that unchecked population growth and consumption must eventually result in insufficient food supply, depletion of key minerals, overcrowding, pollution, and an overall deterioration in the quality of life. One of its strong recommendations is the worldwide *social marketing* of birth control and family planning.[7]

The second cause for concern is that the rate of population growth is highest in the countries and communities that can least afford it. In many developing nations the death rate has been falling as a result of modern medical advances, while the birthrate has remained fairly stable. For these countries to feed, clothe, and educate the children and also provide a rising standard of living for the population is out of the question. Furthermore, the poor families have the most children, and this reinforces the cycle of poverty.

The rate of growth of the world's population has great importance for business. A growing population means growing human needs. It means growing markets, provided there is sufficient purchasing power. On the other hand, if the growing population presses too hard against the available food supply and resources, costs will shoot up and profit margins will be depressed.

Slowdown in U.S. birthrate.   A "birth dearth" has replaced the former "baby boom" in the U.S. The U.S. population stands now at 233 million. It is projected to grow to 264 million by the year 2000. Yet despite the increase in the number of people, the rate of population growth has slowed considerably since the 1950s. The annual number of births peaked at 4.3 million in 1960 and, by the mid-1970s, fell to under 3.2 million births. Recently there has been a slight gain, to 3.6 million births. The population is expected to grow this decade by less than 1 percent a year. Factors contributing to smaller families are the desire to improve personal living standards, the increasing desire of women to work outside the home, and the improved technology and knowledge of birth control.

The declining birthrate is a threat to some industries, a boon to others. It has created sleepless nights for executives in such businesses as children's toys, clothes,

---

[6] Donella H. Meadows, Dennis L. Meadows, Jorgen Randers, and William W. Behrens III, *The Limits to Growth* (New York: New American Library, 1972), p. 41.

[7] See Eduardo Roberto, *Strategic Decision-Making in a Social Program: The Case of Family-Planning Diffusion* (Lexington, Mass.: Lexington Books, 1975).

furniture, and food. For many years the Gerber Company advertised "Babies are our business—our only business" but quietly dropped this slogan some time ago. Gerber now sells life insurance to older folks, using the theme "Gerber now babies the over-50's." Johnson & Johnson responded to the declining birthrate by wooing adults to switch to its baby powder, baby oil, and baby shampoo. Meanwhile industries such as hotels, airlines, and restaurants have benefited from the fact that young childless couples have more time and income for travel and dining out.

Aging of U.S. population.

Recent generations have been blessed with a declining death rate. Average life expectancy is 74 years, a 20-year increase since 1920. The life expectancy of males is 70 and females, 78. The rise in life expectancy and the declining birthrate is producing an aging U.S. population. The U.S. median age is now 30 and is forecast to reach 35 by the year 2000.[8]

Age-group populations show different rates of growth. The 15–24 age group will decrease by 17 percent, or 7.1 million, in the 1980–90 decade. This forebodes a slowdown in the sales growth of motorcycles, baseball and football equipment, denim clothing, records, and college enrollment.

The 25–34 age group will undergo a healthy 14 percent increase in this decade. This bodes well for furniture manufacturers, vacation planners, life insurance companies, and tennis and ski equipment manufacturers, who market products to this group.[9]

The 35–54 age group will undergo the greatest increase of all age groups in the coming decade, namely 25 percent. Members of this group are well established in their work life and are a major market for large homes, new automobiles and clothing.

The 55–64 age group will shrink by 2 percent in this decade. These "empty-nesters," whose children have left home, will have more time and income on their hands. This group is a major market for eating out, travel, expensive clothes, golf, and other forms of recreation.

The over-65 age group will show the second largest increase in the coming decade, up by 20 percent. This group foretells a burgeoning demand for retirement homes and communities, campers, quieter forms of recreation (fishing, golf), single-portion food packaging, and medical goods and services (medicine, eye glasses, canes, hearing aids, and convalescent homes). This group is becoming more self-centered, active, and more leisure oriented than the comparable group in past generations. They are willing to spend more money on themselves and not worry about leaving money to their children.

Companies that used to sell primarily to the youth market have responded to the greying of America by repositioning their products or introducing new ones. We saw that Johnson & Johnson has persuaded adults to use its baby oil and baby shampoo, and that Gerber now sells life insurance to older people. Wrigley introduced a stick-proof gum called Freedent for people who have dentures. And Helena Rubinstein produces a line of skin-care products for women over 50.

---

[8] See "The Graying of America," *Newsweek*, February 28, 1977, pp. 50–65.

[9] For an excellent account of the opportunities provided by this age group, see Landon Y. Jones, "The Baby-Boom Consumer," *American Demographics*, February 1981, pp. 37–42.

The changing American family. The character of the American family is changing as a result of later marriage, fewer children, more divorce, and more working wives. Specifically:

1. **Later marriage.** Although 96 percent of all Americans will marry, the average age of couples marrying for the first time has been rising over the years and now stands at 23.4 years for males and 21.6 years for females. By 1990, over half of the 20–24-year-old women and one third of the 25–29-year-old women will never have married. This will slow down the sales of engagement and wedding rings, bridal outfits, and life insurance.

2. **Fewer children.** The average family size is shrinking. Couples with no children under 18 now make up 48 percent of all families. The newly married are also delaying childbearing longer. Of those families that have children, the mean number of children is 1.07, down from 3.5 in 1955. This means a slowed-down demand for baby food, toys, children's clothes, and other children's goods and services.

3. **Higher divorce rate.** The United States has the world's highest divorce rate, with about 50 percent of all marriages ending in divorce. This has created over a million single-parent families and the need for additional housing units, furniture, appliances, and other household products. About 79 percent of those divorced remarry, leading to the phenomenon of the "blended" family. Currently about 69 percent of all males and 63 percent of all females are married.

4. **More working wives.** Over 50 percent of all married women hold some kind of job. There is less stigma attached to working, a greater number of job opportunities, and new freedom resulting from birth-control acceptance. Working women are a market for better clothing, day-nursery services, home-cleaning services, and more frozen dinners. The growing number of working women means less viewing of television soap operas and less reading of such women's magazines as *Good Housekeeping* and *Ladies' Home Journal*. Their incomes comprise 40 percent of their households' incomes and engender the purchase of higher-quality goods and services. Marketers of tires, automobiles, insurance, and travel service are increasingly directing their advertising to working women. All of this is accompanied by a shift in traditional roles and values of husbands and wives, with the husband assuming more domestic functions, such as shopping (over 40% of all grocery shopping trips) and child care. As a result, husbands are becoming more of a target market for food companies and household-appliance manufacturers and retailers.[10]

The rise of nonfamily households. The number of nonfamily households is increasing, from 19 percent of all households in 1970 to 26 percent in 1980, and possibly 30 percent in 1990. These households take several forms, each constituting a different market segment with special needs:

1. **Single-adult households.** Many young adults leave home early and move into apartments. In addition, many divorced and widowed people live alone. Altogether, nearly 18 million people live alone (23 percent of all households). By 1990, 45 percent of households will be single-person or single-parent households. They are the fastest-growing category of urban home seekers. The SSWD group (single, separated, widowed, divorced) need smaller apartments; inexpensive and smaller appliances, furniture, and furnishings; and food that is packaged in smaller sizes. Their car preferences are different in that they buy half of all Mustangs and other small specialty cars, and only 8 percent of the

---

[10] See Ellen Graham, "Advertisers Take Aim at a Neglected Market: The Working Woman," *Wall Street Journal*, July 5, 1977, p. 1.

large cars.[11] Singles are a market for various services that enable singles to meet each other, such as singles bars, tours, and cruises.

2. **Two-person cohabitor households.** There are 1.9 million households made up of unmarried persons of the opposite sex sharing living quarters. (One sociologist observed that cohabitation is becoming more like the first stage of marriage.) And there are many more households made up of two or more persons of the same sex sharing living quarters. Since their arrangements are more temporary, these households are a market for inexpensive or rental furniture and furnishings.

3. **Group households.** Group households consist of three or more persons of the same or opposite sex sharing expenses by living together. Included are college students and certain secular and religious groups who live in communes.

Marketers should consider the special needs of nonfamily households, since they are growing more rapidly than family households.

Geographical shifts in population. Americans are a mobile people, with approximately one out of five, or 46 million Americans, moving each year. Among the major mobility trends are the following:

1. **Movement of people to the Sunbelt states.** Over the next decade the West will experience a population growth of 17 percent, and the South will experience a growth of 14 percent. The South and West now have 51 percent of the U.S. population, up from 45 percent in 1970. Major cities in the North, on the other hand, lost population between 1970 and 1978 (New York, 7.5 percent; Pittsburgh, 5.2 percent; Jersey City, 8.9 percent; and Newark, 5.2 percent). These regional population shifts interest marketers because of marked differences in regional expenditure patterns. Consumers in the West, for example, spend relatively less on food and relatively more on automobiles than those in the Northeast. The exodus to Sunbelt states will lessen the demand for warm clothing and home heating equipment and increase the demand for air conditioning.

2. **Movement from rural to urban areas.** People have been moving from rural to urban areas for over a century. In 1880, 70 percent of the nation's population lived in rural areas; at the present time, 75 percent live in urban areas. Cities show a faster pace of living, more commuting, higher incomes, and greater variety of goods and services than can be found in the small towns and rural areas that dot America. The largest cities— New York, Chicago, Los Angeles—account for most of the sales of expensive furs, perfumes, luggage, and works of art; and these cities support the opera, ballet, and other forms of "high culture." Recently, however, there has been a slight shift of population back to small towns and rural areas.

3. **Movement from the city to the suburbs.** Many persons live far away from their places of work, owing largely to the development of automobiles, major highways, and rapid rail and bus transit. Cities have become surrounded by suburbs, and these suburbs in turn by "exurbs." The U.S. Census Bureau has created a separate population classification for sprawling urban concentrations: Standard Metropolitan Statistical Areas (SMSAs).[12] Over 75 percent of the nation's population lives in the 323 Standard Metropolitan Statistical Areas, and these SMSAs constitute the primary market focus of firms. Companies use the SMSAs in researching the best geographical segments for their products, in

---

[11] See June Kronholz, "A Living-Alone Trend Affects Housing, Cars, and Other Industries," *Wall Street Journal*, November 16, 1977, p. 1.

[12] An SMSA consists of a county or group of contiguous counties with a total population of at least 100,000 and a central city with a minimum population of 50,000 (or two close-together cities with a combined population of 50,000).

planning on their geographical rollout strategy for new products, in deciding where to purchase advertising time or space, and so on. SMSA research shows, for example, that New Englanders smoke 29 percent more cigarettes than the national average; Chicagoans consume 22 percent more soft drinks; and New Yorkers use 19 percent more paper goods.

About 60 percent of the total population, or 39 percent of the metropolitan population, lives in suburbs. Suburbs show more casual, outdoor living, greater neighbor interaction, higher incomes, and younger families. Suburbanites buy station wagons, home-workshop equipment, garden furniture, lawn and gardening tools and supplies, and outdoor-cooking equipment. Retailers have acknowledged the suburbs by building branch department stores and suburban shopping centers.

At the same time, marketers should recognize a recent countermove back to the central city, especially in cities where urban renewal has been successful. Young adults and older adults whose children have grown up are attracted by the superior cultural and recreational opportunities and are less interested in suburban commuting and gardening. This has led to new high-rise apartment construction and new retail outlets within the city.

Marketers must proceed cautiously when they develop their geographical marketing plans. Marketing researchers use several schemes to segment geographical markets—census tracts, standard metropolitan areas, Nielsen regions, media markets, and so forth. Garreau recently proposed a suggestive new segmentation scheme, which he calls "The Nine Nations of North America." (See Exhibit 3–2.)

A better-educated and white-collar population.
Sixty-six percent of Americans over twenty-five years of age have high school degrees. Sixteen percent of Americans have college degrees, and the percentage continues to rise. The rising number of educated people will increase the demand for quality products, books, magazines, and travel.

In 1980, the total labor force was 97.3 million people. Between 1960 and 1980, the number of white-collar workers rose from 43 to 52 percent, blue-collar workers declined from 37 to 32 percent, service workers increased from 12 to 13 percent, and farm workers declined from 8 to 3 percent. For the 1980s, the U.S. Bureau of Labor Statistics predicts the most growth in the following occupational categories: engineering, science, medicine, computers, social science, buying, selling, secretarial, construction, refrigeration, health service, personal service, and protection.

Changing ethnic and racial population.
The U.S. population is 79 percent white, and blacks constitute another 10 percent. The Hispanic population has been growing fast and now stands at 14.6 million, with the largest subgroups being Mexicans, Puerto Ricans, and Cubans, in that order. The Asian population has also burgeoned, with the Chinese constituting the largest group, followed by the Japanese, Filipinos, Koreans, Vietnamese, in that order. Hispanic and Asian consumers are concentrated in the far western and southern parts of the country, although some dispersal is taking place. Each population group has certain specific wants and buying habits. Several food, clothing, and furniture companies have directed their products and promotion to one or more of these groups.

Exhibit 3-2

THE NINE NATIONS OF NORTH AMERICA

Joel Garreau recently called upon marketers to stop viewing the United States as a "homogenous glob of humanity tied together by TV, WATS lines, and McDonald's outlets, but rather [to view it as] nine distinct regions or 'nations.'" His nine nations are shown on the map and described below:

- ☐ **The Breadbasket.** The integrating factor is the elemental simplicity of farming as a way of life.
- ☐ **Ecotopia.** People here have an ethic of libertarian self-reliance and mystical relationship to the land.
- ☐ **The Foundry.** Declining and gritty industrial cities with an ethic of heavy work with heavy machines. Hard work and yet hard times without work.
- ☐ **The Empty Quarter.** An area of mining and power, with a land grab going on today.
- ☐ **The Islands.** Latin American culture with Miami as its capital.
- ☐ **MexAmerica.** Hispanic values of Catholicism, pride in family, and close community ties.
- ☐ **New England.** Original boundaries of U.S. with traditional values.
- ☐ **Dixie.** The southern culture provides a unifying history, language, food, dress, and charm.
- ☐ **Quebec.** French speaking, it has a culture of its own.

He argues that each region has its own ways of thinking, planning, and living, and marketers who ignore these differences can make big mistakes. Here are a few of his observations:

> One of the reasons the U.S. auto industry was slow to react to imported cars was the industry's management base in Detroit. If auto executives lived in California, they would have seen the trend toward Japanese cars. But when they looked out of their windows in Detroit, all they saw were gas-guzzlers. They just didn't see Japanese cars as a problem.

> Many of the regional labels businessmen use are obsolete or misleading. There are no such places as the "Sunbelt," or the "Midwest," or the "West Coast." Even state boundaries are meaningless in many regards. California is three states (MexAmerica, Ecotopia, and Empty Quarter), which is why it doesn't make any sense.

> The notion of "suburb" and everything that term implies is strictly a Foundry phenomenon. Suburbs were formed in the Foundry because people wanted to get out of the decaying cities, and the people who stayed behind in the cities resented that. But in places like the southwest, suburbs are an accepted fact of existence. Everything is a "suburb."

SOURCE: Joel Garreau, *The Nine Nations of North America* *(New York: Avon, 1981). Some of the quotations are from a speech delivered by Joel Garreau in Denver in late 1982.*

Shift from a mass market to micromarkets. The effect of all these changes—smaller families, more nonfamily households, an aging population, the high growth rates of Hispanic, Oriental, and black consumers—is to transform the American marketplace from a *mass market* into more fragmented *micromarkets*, differentiated by age, sex, geography, lifestyle, ethnic background, education, and so on. Each group has strong preferences and consumer characteristics and is reached through increasingly differentiated media. Companies are abandoning the "shotgun" approach that aimed at a mythical "average" consumer and are increasingly designing their products and marketing programs for specific micromarkets.

These demographic trends are highly reliable for the short and intermediate run. There is little excuse for a company's being suddenly surprised by demographic developments. The Singer Company should have known for years that its sewing machine business would be negatively affected by smaller families and more working wives; yet they were very slow in responding. Alert firms can identify the major demographic trends and spell out their implications for the particular industry.

Economic Environment

Markets require purchasing power as well as people. Total purchasing power is a function of current income, prices, savings, and credit availability. Marketers should be aware of four main trends in the economic environment.

Slowdown in real-income growth. In 1979 American income per capita stood at $8,728, and median household income stood at $19,684. Although money income per capita keeps rising, real income per capita has stagnated for the last decade. Real per capita income has been hurt by an inflation rate exceeding the money-income growth rate, an unemployment rate between 6 and 10 percent, and in increase in the tax burden. These developments have reduced *disposable personal income,* which is the amount people have left after taxes. Furthermore, many people have found their *discretionary income* reduced. That is the amount they have left after paying for their food, clothing, shelter, insurance, and other necessaries. Reductions in discretionary income hurt sellers of discretionary goods and services, such as automobiles, large appliances, and vacations. On the positive side, however, there has been a rise in two-income families, which has increased average family income.

In response to the real-income decline, many Americans have turned to more cautious buying. They are buying more store brands and generics and fewer national brands to save money. Many companies have introduced economy versions of their products and have turned to price appeals in their advertising messages. As for durable goods, some consumers have postponed their purchase of these items, and other consumers have made a purchase out of fear that prices will be 10 percent higher next year. Many families have begun to feel that the American dream of a large home, two cars, foreign travel, and private higher education is now an impossible dream.

Marketers should pay attention to income distribution as well as to average income. Income distribution in the United States is still pronouncedly skewed. At the top are *upper-class consumers*, whose expenditure patterns have not been affected by current economic events and who are a major market for goods (Rolls Royces starting at $100,000) and services (round-the-world cruises starting at $10,000). There is a comfortable *middle class* that exercises some expenditure restraint but is able to afford expensive clothes, minor antiques, and a small boat or second home. The *lower class* must stick close to the basics of food, clothing, and shelter and must husband resources and try hard to save.

Marketers also have to take geographical income variations into account. A city like Houston is growing at a fast rate, while Detroit is languishing. Marketers must focus their efforts on the areas of greatest opportunity.

Continued inflationary pressure. The double-digit inflation of the early seventies brought about a substantial increase in the prices of homes, furniture, medical care, and food. Although the inflation rate is now more modest, there are still several sources of continued inflationary pressure: cartel price fixing of several commodities, including oil; the lack of competition in certain sectors of the economy; the demands of several labor unions for wage increases that exceed productivity gains; the unfavorable balance of foreign trade, which shrinks the value of the dollar and pushes up the prices of foreign goods; the high interest rates; the high expenditures on public services and on nonproductive capital investment; and a psychology of inflationary expectation, which in turn feeds the inflation. Inflation leads consumers to search for opportunities to save money, including buying cheaper brands in larger, economy sizes, buying from less-expensive retail outlets, performing more of their own services, and bartering services with others.

Low savings and high debt. Consumer expenditures are also affected by consumer savings and debt patterns. Eighty-four percent of American spending units hold some liquid assets, the median amount being $800. Savings equaled 4.6 percent of disposable personal income in 1979. Americans hold their savings in the form of bank savings accounts, bonds and stocks, real estate, insurance, money market funds, and other assets. These savings are an important source of funds for financing major purchases.

Consumers can increase their purchasing power through borrowing. Consumer credit has been a major contributor to the rapid growth of the American economy, enabling people to buy more than their current income and savings allowed, thus creating more jobs and still more income and more demand. In 1980, outstanding consumer credit (including home mortgages) stood at $1.4 trillion, or $6,298 for every man, woman, and child in America. The ratio of consumer credit (not including mortgages) to disposable personal income stood at 22 percent in 1980. The cost of credit, however, is also high (with interest rates between 12 and 20 percent), and consumers are spending around twenty-one cents of every dollar they earn to pay off existing debts. This retards the further growth of housing and other durable-goods markets that are heavily dependent on credit.

Changing consumer expenditure patterns. Consumption expenditures in major goods and services categories have been changing over the years. Food, housing, household operations, and transportation use up two-thirds of household income. However, over time, the food, clothing, and personal-care bills of households have been declining percentagewise while the housing, transportation, medical-care, and recreational bills have been increasing. Some of these changes were observed over a century ago by Ernest Engel, a German statistician who studied how people shifted their expenditures as their income rose. He observed that *as family income rises, the percentage spent on food declines, the percentage spent on housing and household operations remains constant, and the percentage spent on other categories (clothing, transportation, recreation, health, and education) and the percentage put into savings increase.* Engel's "laws" have generally been validated in subsequent budget studies.

Changes in such major economic variables as money income, cost of living, interest rates, and savings and borrowing patterns have an immediate impact on the marketplace. Companies that are particularly income sensitive are wise to invest in sophisticated economic forecasting. Businesses do not have to be wiped out by a downturn in economic activity. With adequate forewarning, they can take the necessary steps to reduce their costs and ride out the economic storm.

Physical Environment

The 1960s witnessed a growing public concern over whether the physical environment was being irreparably damaged by the industrial activities of modern nations. Kenneth Boulding pointed out that the planet earth was like a spaceship in danger of running out of fuel if it failed to conserve and recycle its materials. The Erlichs in 1970 coined the term *eco-catastrophe* to symbolize the harmful impact of certain American business practices on the environment. The Meadowses in their 1972 book, *The Limits to Growth*,[13] raised concerns about whether the world would run out of sufficient natural resources to maintain, let alone improve, current living standards. Rachel Carson, in *Silent Spring*[14] pointed out the environmental damage to water, earth, and air caused by industrial activity of certain kinds. Watchdog groups, such as the Sierra Club and Friends of the Earth, sprang up, and concerned legislators proposed various measures to protect the environment. (See Exhibit 3–3 for a discussion of the impact of the environmentalist movement on marketing.)

Marketers should be aware of the threats and opportunities associated with four trends in the physical environment.

Impending shortages of certain raw materials. The earth's materials consist of the infinite, the finite renewable, and the finite nonrenewable. An *infinite resource*, such as air, poses no immediate problem, although some groups see a long-run danger. Environmental groups have lobbied for a ban of certain propellants used in aerosol cans because of their potential damage to the ozone layer of air. Water is already a problem in some parts of the world.

Finite renewable resources, such as forests and food, have to be used wisely. Companies in the forestry business are required to reforest timberlands in order to protect the soil and to ensure a sufficient level of wood supply to meet future demand. Food supply can be a major problem in that the amount of arable land is relatively fixed, and urban areas are constantly encroaching on farmland.

Finite nonrenewable resources, such as oil, coal, and various minerals, pose a serious problem:

> . . . it would appear at present that the quantities of platinum, gold, zinc, and lead are not sufficient to meet demands . . . silver, tin, and uranium may be in short supply even at higher prices by the turn of the century. By the year 2050, several more minerals may be exhausted if the current rate of consumption continues.[15]

---

[13] Meadows et al., *Limits to Growth*.

[14] Rachel Carson, *Silent Spring* (Boston: Houghton-Mifflin Co., 1962).

[15] *First Annual Report of the Council on Environmental Quality* (Washington, D.C.: Government Printing Office, 1970), p. 158.

Exhibit 3-3

THE IMPACT OF ENVIRONMENTALISM ON MARKETING DECISION MAKING

Where consumerists focus on whether the marketing system is efficiently serving consumer material wants, environmentalists focus on marketing's impact on the environment and the costs of serving these needs and wants. *Environmentalism is an organized movement of concerned citizens and government to protect and enhance people's living environment.* Environmentalists are concerned with strip mining, forest depletion, factory smoke, billboards, and litter; with the loss of recreational opportunity; and with the increase in health problems caused by bad air, water, and chemically sprayed food.

Environmentalists are not against marketing and consumption; they simply want them to operate on more ecological principles. They think the goal of the marketing system should be to maximize *life quality*. And life quality means not only the quantity and quality of consumer goods and services but also the quality of the environment.

Environmentalists want environmental costs included in producer and consumer decision making. They favor using taxes and regulations to impose the true social costs of antienvironmental behavior. Requiring business to invest in antipollution devices, taxing nonreturnable bottles, and banning high-phosphate detergents are viewed as necessary to lead businesses and consumers to move in environmentally sound directions.

Environmentalists are more critical of marketing than are consumerists. They complain of too much wasteful packaging, whereas consumerists like the convenience of modern packaging. Environmentalists feel that advertising leads people to buy more then they need, whereas consumerists worry more about deception in advertising. Environmentalists dislike shopping centers, whereas consumerists welcome more stores.

Environmentalism has hit certain industries hard. Steel companies and public utilities have had to invest billions of dollars in pollution-control equipment and costlier fuels. The auto industry has had to introduce expensive emission-controls in cars. The soap industry has had to develop low-phosphate detergents. The packaging industry has had to develop ways to reduce litter and increase biodegradability in its products. The gasoline industry has had to formulate new low-lead and no-lead gasolines. These industries resent environmental regulations, especially when imposed too rapidly to allow the companies to make the proper adjustments. These companies have absorbed large costs and have passed them on to buyers.

Marketers' lives have become more complicated. Marketers have to check into the environmental consequences of the product, its packaging, and its production processes. They have to raise prices to cover environmental costs, knowing the product will be harder to sell. At the same time, many managers recognize the validity of respecting the environment and have introduced environmental criteria in their decision making on product ingredients, design, and packaging. Some companies direct their R&D toward finding ecologically superior products, as the major selling point of the product. Sears developed and promoted a phosphate-free laundry detergent; Pepsi-Cola developed a one-way, plastic soft-drink bottle that is biodegradable in solid-waste treatment; and American Oil pioneered no-lead and low-lead gasolines.

The marketing implications are many. Firms using scarce minerals face substantial cost increases, even if the materials remain available. They may not find it easy to pass these cost increases on to the consumer. Firms engaged in research and development and exploration have an incredible opportunity to develop valuable new sources and materials.

Increased cost of energy.   One finite nonrenewable resource, oil, has created the most serious problem for future economic growth. The major industrial economies of the world are heavily dependent on oil, and until cost-effective substitute forms of energy can be developed, oil will continue to dominate the world political and economic picture. The high price of oil (from $2.23 a barrel in 1970 to $34 a barrel in 1982) has created a frantic search for alternative forms of energy. Coal is again popular, and companies are searching for practical means to harness solar, nuclear, wind, and other forms of energy. In the solar energy field alone, hundreds of firms are putting out first-generation products to harness solar energy for heating homes and other uses.[16] Other firms are searching for ways to make a practical electric automobile, with a potential prize of billions going to the winner.

Increased levels of pollution.   Some industrial activity will inevitably damage the quality of the natural environment. Consider the disposal of chemical and nuclear wastes, the dangerous mercury levels in the ocean, the quantity of DDT and other chemical pollutants in the soil and food supply, and the littering of the environment with nonbiodegradable bottles, plastics, and other packaging materials.

The public's concern creates a marketing opportunity for alert companies. It creates a large market for pollution-control solutions such as scrubbers and recycling centers. It leads to a search for alternative ways to produce and package goods that do not cause environmental damage.[17]

Strong government intervention in natural-resource management.   Various government agencies play an active role in environmental protection. Ironically, their effort often runs counter to the attempt to increase employment, such as when business is forced to buy expensive pollution-control equipment instead of more-advanced production equipment. At times, conservation has to take a back seat to economic growth.

Marketing management needs to pay attention to the physical environment, in terms of obtaining needed resources and also of avoiding damage to the physical environment. Business can expect strong controls from both government and pressure groups. Instead of opposing all forms of regulation, business should help develop acceptable solutions to the material and energy problems facing the nation.

Technological Environment

The most dramatic force shaping people's destiny is technology. Technology has released such wonders as penicillin, open-heart surgery, and the birth-control pill.

---

[16] See "The Coming Boom in Solar Energy," *Business Week*, October 9, 1978, pp. 88–104.

[17] See Karl E. Henion II, *Ecological Marketing* (Columbus, Ohio: Grid, 1976).

It has released such horrors as the hydrogen bomb, nerve gas, and the submachine gun. It has released such mixed blessings as the automobile, video games, and white bread. One's attitudes toward technology depend on whether one is more enthralled with its wonders or its horrors.

Every new technology is a force for "creative destruction." Transistors hurt the vacuum-tube industry, xerography hurts the carbon-paper business, autos hurt the railroads, and television hurts the movies. Instead of old industries moving into the new, they fought or ignored them, and their businesses declined.

The economy's growth rate is affected by how many major new technologies are discovered. Unfortunately, technological discoveries do not arise evenly through time—the railroad industry created a lot of investment, and then there was a dearth until the auto industry emerged; later radio created a lot of investment, and then there was a dearth until television appeared. In the time between major innovations, the economy can stagnate. Some economists believe that the current economic stagnation of the economy will continue until a sufficient number of new major innovations emerges.

In the meantime, minor innovations fill the gap. Freeze-dried coffee probably made no one happier, and antiperspirant deodorants probably made no one wiser, but they do create new markets and investment opportunities.

Each technology creates major long-run consequences that are not always foreseeable. The contraceptive pill, for example, led to smaller families, more working wives, and larger discretionary incomes—resulting in higher expenditures on vacation travel, durable goods, and other things.

The marketer should watch the following trends in technology.

Accelerating pace of technological change.

Many of today's common products were not available even one hundred years ago. Abraham Lincoln did not know automobiles, airplanes, phonographs, radio, or the electric light. Woodrow Wilson did not know television, aerosol cans, home freezers, automatic dishwashers, room air conditioners, antibiotics, or electronic computers. Franklin Delano Roosevelt did not know xerography, synthetic detergents, tape recorders, birth-control pills, or earth satellites. And John Kennedy did not know personal computers, digital wristwatches, videorecorders, or word processors.

Alvin Toffler, in his *Future Shock*, sees an accelerative thrust in the invention, exploitation, and diffusion of new technologies.[18] More ideas are being worked on; the time lag between new ideas and successful implementation is decreasing rapidly; and the time between introduction and peak production is shortening considerably. Ninety percent of all the scientists who ever lived are alive today, and technology feeds upon itself.

In Toffler's later book, *The Third Wave*, he forecasts the emergence of the *electronic cottage* as a new way that work and play will be organized in society.[19] The advent of word-processing typewriters, telecopiers, personal computers, and audio and video links make it possible for many people to do their work at home instead

---

[18] Toffler, *Future Shock*, pp. 25–30.

[19] Alvin Toffler, *The Third Wave* (New York: Bantam Books, 1980).

of traveling to and from offices, which may be located thirty or more minutes away. Eventually people will find that the cost of installing and operating telecommunications equipment in the home will fall below the cost of commuting. As seen by Toffler, the electronic-cottage revolution will reduce the amount of auto pollution, bring the family closer together as a work unit, and create more home-centered entertainment and activity. It will have substantial impact on consumption patterns and marketing systems.

Unlimited innovational opportunities. Scientists today are working on a startling range of new technologies that will revolutionize our products and production processes. The most exciting work is being done in biotechnology, solid state electronics, robotics, and material sciences.[20] Scientists today are working on the following promising new products and services: cancer cures, lung and liver cures, chemical control of mental illness, happiness pills, practical solar energy, practical electric cars, household robots, totally safe contraceptives, and nutritious foods that are nonfattening and tasty. In addition, scientists also speculate on fantasy products, such as small flying cars, single-person rocket belts, three-dimensional television, space colonies, and human clones. The challenge in each case is not only technical but commercial, namely, to develop practical affordable versions of these products.

High R&D budgets. The U.S. leads the world in research and development spending. In 1981, R&D expenditures exceeded $69 billion and are expected to rise at an average of 3 percent annually throughout the 1980s.

The federal government supplied 47 percent of the 1981 total R&D funds. Almost 87 percent of the funds go to applied R&D. The remainder is spent on basic research, more than two-thirds of which takes place in colleges and universities.

The five industries spending the most R&D money are aircraft and missiles, electrical equipment and communication, chemicals and allied products, machinery, and motor vehicles and other transportation. Industries that spend the least on R&D are lumber, wood products, furniture, textiles, apparel, and paper and allied products. Industries at the top range spend between 5 and 7 percent of their sales dollar on R&D, and those in the lowest range spend less than 1 percent of their sales dollar. The average company spends about 2 percent of its sales on R&D. A recent study showed a high correlation between R&D expenditures and company profitability. Six companies—Merck, AT&T, Dow, Eastman Kodak, IBM, and Lilly—averaged 5.7 percent in their R&D expenditures-to-sales ratio, and their profitability averaged 15.3 percent of sales. Another six companies—Boeing, Chrysler, Goodyear, McDonnell-Douglas, Signal Companies, and United Technologies—averaged 3.5 percent in their R&D-to-sales ratio and were much less profitable.[21]

Today's research is carried out mostly by research laboratory teams rather than by lone inventors like Thomas Edison, Samuel Morse, or Alexander Graham Bell.

---

[20] For an excellent and comprehensive list of possible future products, see Charles Panat, *Breakthroughs* (Boston: Houghton-Mifflin Co., 1980); and "Technologies for the '80s," *Business Week*, July 6, 1981, pp. 48ff.

[21] "Corporate Growth, R&D, and the Gap Between," *Technology Review*, March-April 1978, p. 39.

Managing company scientists is a major challenge. They resent too much cost control. They are often more interested in solving scientific problems than in coming up with marketable products. Companies are adding marketing people to R&D research teams, hoping to achieve a stronger marketing orientation.

Concentration on minor improvements rather than on major discoveries. As a result of the high cost of money, many companies are pursuing minor product improvements rather than gambling on major innovations. Even basic-research companies like Du Pont, Bell Laboratories, and Pfizer are proceeding cautiously. Many companies are content to put their money into copying competitors' products and making minor feature and style improvements. Much of the research is defensive rather than offensive.

Increased regulation of technological change. As products become more complex, the public needs to be assured of their safety. Consequently, government agencies have expanded their powers to investigate and ban potentially unsafe products. Thus the federal Food and Drug Administration has issued elaborate regulations on testing new drugs, with the result that industry-research costs are higher, the time between idea and introduction has been lengthened from five to about nine years, and much drug research has been driven to countries with fewer regulations. Safety and health regulations have also increased in the areas of food, automobiles, clothing, electrical appliances, and construction. Marketers must be aware of these regulations when proposing, developing, and launching new products.

Technological change faces opposition from those who see it as threatening nature, privacy, simplicity, and even the human race. Various groups have opposed the construction of nuclear plants, high-rise buildings, and recreational facilities in national parks. They have called for *technological assessment* of new technologies before allowing their commercialization.

Marketers need to understand the changing technological environment and how new technologies can serve human needs. They need to work closely with R&D people to encourage more market-oriented research. They must be alert to the negative aspects of any innovation that might harm the users and thus bring about distrust and opposition.

Political/Legal Environment

Marketing decisions are highly affected by developments in the political/legal environment. This environment is made up of *laws, government agencies, and pressure groups* that influence and constrain various organizations and individuals in society. We will examine the main political trends and their implications for marketing management.

Substantial amount of legislation regulating business. Legislation affecting business has steadily increased over the years. The legislation has a number of purposes. *The first is to protect companies from each other*. Business executives all praise competition but try to neutralize it when it touches them. If threatened, they show their teeth:

ReaLemon Foods, a subsidiary of Borden, held approximately 90 percent of the reconstituted lemon juice market until 1978. In that year, the Federal Trade Commission ruled that Borden had used a selective predatory pricing policy to run its major rivals out of business. They barred Borden from pricing its ReaLemon at "unreasonably" low levels. In 1983, this was modified to allow Borden to price anywhere above its variable costs without having to include its development and marketing costs.[22]

So laws are passed to define and prevent unfair competition. These laws are enforced by the Federal Trade Commission and the antitrust division of the Attorney General's office.

The second purpose of government regulation is to protect consumers from unfair business practices. Some firms, if left alone, would adulterate their products, tell lies in their advertising, deceive through their packages, and bait through their prices. Unfair consumer practices have been defined and are enforced by various agencies. Many managers see purple with each new consumer law, and yet a few have said that "consumerism may be the best thing that has happened . . . in the past twenty years."[23]

The third purpose of government regulation is to protect the larger interest of society against unbridled business behavior. It is possible for the gross national product to rise and the quality of life to fall. A major purpose of new legislation and/or enforcement is to charge business with the social costs created by their production processes or products.

The marketing executive needs a good working knowledge of the major laws protecting competition, consumers, and the larger interests of society. The main federal laws are listed in Table 3–2. The earlier laws dealt mainly with protecting competition, the later laws, with protecting consumers. Marketing executives should know these federal laws and particularly the evolving court interpretations.[24] And they should know the state and local laws that affect their local marketing activity.

Several countries have gone further than the United States in the passage of strong consumerist legislation. Norway banned several forms of sales promotion, such as trading stamps, contests, and premiums, as being inappropriate or "unfair" instruments for the sellers to use in promoting their products. The Philippines requires food processors selling national brands to market low-price brands also, so that low-income consumers will find economy brands on the market. In India, food companies need special approval to launch brands that duplicate what already exists on the market, such as another cola drink or brand of rice. These and other legislative developments have not surfaced prominently in the United States, but they suggest how far regulations might be pushed to constrain marketing practice.

The real issue raised by business legislation is, Where is the point reached when the costs of regulation exceed the benefits of regulation? The laws are not always administered fairly by those responsible for enforcing them. They may hurt

---

[22] "FTC to Relax Pricing Order Against Borden," *Wall Street Journal*, March 2, 1983, p. 46.

[23] Leo Greenland, "Advertisers Must Stop Conning Consumers," *Harvard Business Review,* July-August 1974, p. 18.

[24] See Louis W. Stern and Thomas L. Eovaldi, *Legal Aspects of Marketing Strategy: Antitrust and Consumer Protection Issues* (Englewood Cliffs, N.J.: Prentice Hall, 1984).

TABLE 3–2

MILESTONE U.S. LEGISLATION AFFECTING MARKETING

Sherman Antitrust Act (1890)

Prohibits (a) "monopolies or attempts to monopolize" and (b) "contracts, combinations, or conspiracies in restraint of trade" in interstate and foreign commerce.

Federal Food and Drug Act (1906)

Forbids the manufacture, sale, or transport of adulterated or fraudulently labeled foods and drugs in interstate commerce. Supplanted by the Food, Drug, and Cosmetic Act, 1938; amended by Food Additives Amendment, 1958, and the Kefauver-Harris Amendment, 1962. The 1962 amendments deal with pretesting of drugs for safety and effectiveness and labeling of drugs by generic name.

Meat Inspection Act (1906)

Provides for the enforcement of sanitary regulations in meat-packing establishments and for federal inspection of all companies selling meats in interstate commerce.

Federal Trade Commission Act (1914)

Establishes the commission, a body of specialists with broad powers to investigate and to issue cease and desist orders to enforce Section 5, which declares that "unfair methods of competition in commerce are unlawful."

Clayton Act (1914)

Supplements the Sherman Act by prohibiting certain specific practices (certain types of price discrimination, tying clauses and exclusive dealing, intercorporate stockholdings, and interlocking directorates) "where the effect . . . may be to substantially lessen competition or tend to create a monopoly in any line of commerce." Provides that violating corporate officials could be held individually responsible; exempts labor and agricultural organizations from its provisions.

Robinson-Patman Act (1936)

Amends the Clayton Act. Adds the phrase "to injure, destroy, or prevent competition." Defines price discrimination as unlawful (subject to certain defenses) and provides the FTC with the right to establish limits on quantity discounts, to forbid brokerage allowances except to independent brokers, and to prohibit promotional allowances or the furnishing of services or facilities except where made available to all "on proportionately equal terms."

Miller-Tydings Act (1937)

Amends the Sherman Act to exempt interstate fair-trade (price fixing) agreements from antitrust prosecution. (The McGuire Act, 1952, reinstates the legality of the nonsigner clause.)

Wheeler-Lea Act (1938)

Prohibits unfair and deceptive acts and practices regardless of whether competition is injured; places advertising of foods and drugs under FTC jurisdiction.

Antimerger Act (1950)

Amends Section 7 of the Clayton Act by broadening the power to prevent intercorporate acquisitions where the acquisition may have a substantially adverse effect on competition.

Automobile Information Disclosure Act (1958)

Prohibits car dealers from inflating the factory price of new cars.

National Traffic and Safety Act (1958)

Provides for the creation of compulsory safety standards for automobiles and tires.

Fair Packaging and Labeling Act (1966)

Provides for the regulation of the packaging and labeling of consumer goods. Requires manufacturers to state what the package contains, who made it, and how much it contains. Permits industries' voluntary adoption of uniform packaging standards.

TABLE 3–2
(cont.)

Child Protection Act (1966)
Bans sale of hazardous toys and articles. Amended in 1969 to include articles that pose electrical, mechanical, or thermal hazards.

Federal Cigarette Labeling and Advertising Act (1967)
Requires that cigarette packages contain the statement "Warning: The Surgeon General Has Determined that Cigarette Smoking is Dangerous to Your Health."

Truth-in-Lending Act (1968)
Requires lenders to state the true costs of a credit transaction, outlaws the use of actual or threatened violence in collecting loans, and restricts the amount of garnishments. Established a National Commission on Consumer Finance.

National Environmental Policy Act (1969)
Establishes a national policy on the environment and provides for the establishment of the Council on Environmental Quality. The Environmental Protection Agency was established by "Reorganization Plan No. 3 of 1970."

Fair Credit Reporting Act (1970)
Ensures that a consumer's credit report would contain only accurate, relevant, and recent information and would be confidential unless requested for an appropriate reason by a proper party.

Consumer Product Safety Act (1972)
Establishes the Consumer Product Safety Commission and authorizes it to set safety standards for consumer products as well as exact penalties for failure to uphold the standards.

Consumer Goods Pricing Act (1975)
Prohibits the use of price maintenance agreements among manufacturers and resellers in interstate commerce.

Magnuson-Moss Warranty/FTC Improvement Act (1975)
Authorizes the FTC to determine rules concerning consumer warranties and provides for consumer access to means of redress, such as the "class-action" suit. Also expands FTC regulatory powers over unfair or deceptive acts or practices.

Equal Credit Opportunity Act (1975)
Prohibits discrimination in a credit transaction because of sex, marital status, race, national origin, religion, age, or receipt of public assistance.

Fair Debt Collection Practice Act (1978)
Makes it illegal to harass or abuse any person and make false statements or use unfair methods when collecting a debt.

many legitimate business firms and discourage new investment and market entry. They also may increase consumer costs. Although each new law may have a legitimate rationale, their totality may have the effect of sapping initiative and slowing down economic growth.

Changing government agency enforcement. To enforce the laws, Congress established several federal regulatory agencies—the Federal Trade Commission, the Food and Drug Administration, the Interstate Commerce Commission, the Federal Communications Commission, the Federal Power Commission, the Civil Aeronautics Board, the Consumer Products Safety Commission, the Environmental Protection Agency, and the Office of Consumer Affairs. These agencies can have a major impact on a company's marketing performance. Consider the following example:

In 1973 the rotary-engine Mazda automobile had climbing sales. People were impressed by its smooth ride, low repair costs, and reduced air pollution. Then the Environmental Protection Agency issued a report stating that Mazda's fuel consumption was only eleven miles per gallon in city driving. Mazda executives objected, claiming seventeen to twenty-one miles per gallon. The charge stuck in the public's mind, however, and Mazda sales declined 39 percent in the first five months of 1974, as people became more concerned with fuel efficiency than with reduced air pollution.

These agencies are allowed some discretion in enforcing the laws. From time to time, they appear to be overzealous and capricious. The agencies are dominated by lawyers and economists, who often lack a practical sense of how business and marketing work. In recent years, the Federal Trade Commission has added staff marketing experts, to achieve a better understanding of the complex issues. The degree of enforcement appears to be moderating under President Reagan, with a strong trend toward deregulation.[25]

Growth of public-interest groups.   Public-interest groups have increased in number and power in the last two decades. These groups lobby government officials and put pressure on business executives to pay more attention to consumer rights, women's rights, senior citizen rights, minority rights, and so on. Many companies have established public-affairs departments to study and deal with these groups.

New laws, more enforcement, and growing numbers of pressure groups have combined to put more restraints on marketers. Marketers have to clear their plans with the company's legal and public relations departments. Private marketing transactions have moved into the public domain. Salancik and Upah put it this way:

> There is some evidence that the consumer may not be king, nor even queen. The consumer is but a voice, one among many. Consider how General Motors makes its cars today. Vital features of the motor are designed by the United States government; the exhaust system is redesigned by certain state governments; the production materials used are dictated by suppliers who control scarce material resources. For other products, other groups and organizations may get involved. Thus, insurance companies directly or indirectly affect the design of smoke detectors; scientific groups affect the design of spray products by condemning aerosols; minority activist groups affect the design of dolls by requesting representative figures. Legal departments also can be expected to increase their importance in firms, affecting not only product design and promotion but also marketing strategies. At a minimum, marketing managers will spend less time with their research departments asking "What does the consumer want?" and more and more time with their production and legal people asking "What can the consumer have?"[26]

Socio/Cultural Environment

The society that people grow up in shapes their basic beliefs, values, and norms. They absorb, almost unconsciously, a world view that defines their relationship to themselves, to others, to nature, and to the universe. Here are some of the main cultural characteristics and trends of interest to marketers.

---

[25] See Edward Meadows, "Bold Departures in Antitrust," *Fortune*, October 5, 1981, pp. 180–88.

[26] Extracts from Gerald R. Salancik and Gregory D. Upah, "Directions for Interorganizational Marketing" (unpublished paper, School of Commerce, University of Illinois, Champaign, August 1978).

Core cultural values have high persistence.   People in a given society hold many core beliefs and values that will tend to persist. Thus, most Americans still believe in work, in getting married, in giving to charity, and in being honest. Core beliefs and values are passed on from parents to children and are reinforced by the major institutions of society—schools, churches, business, and government.

People's secondary beliefs and values are more open to change. Believing in the institution of marriage is a core belief; believing that people ought to get married early is a secondary belief. Family-planning marketers could be more effective in arguing that people should get married later than that they should not get married at all. Marketers have some chance of changing secondary values but little chance of changing core values.

Each culture consists of subcultures.   Each society contains *subcultures*, that is, groups of people with shared value systems emerging out of their common life experiences or circumstances. Episcopalians, teenagers, and Hell's Angels all represent separate subcultures whose members share common beliefs, preferences, and behaviors. To the extent that subcultural groups exhibit different wants and consumption behavior, marketers can choose subcultures as their target markets.

Secondary cultural values undergo shifts through time.   Although core values are fairly persistent, cultural swings do take place. The advent in the 1960s of the "hippies," the Beatles, Elvis Presley, *Playboy* magazine, and other cultural phenomena had a major impact on young people's hair styles, clothing, sexual norms, and life goals.

Marketers have a keen interest in anticipating cultural shifts in order to spot new marketing opportunities or threats. Several firms offer "cultural futures" forecasts in this connection. One of the best known is the Yankelovich Monitor, put out by the marketing research firm of Yankelovich, Skelly, & White. The Monitor interviews 2,500 people each year and tracks thirty-five social trends, such as "antibigness," "mysticism," "living for today," "away from possessions," and "sensuousness." It describes the percentage of the population who share the attitude as well as the percentage who are antitrend. For example, the percentage of people who value physical fitness and well-being has been going up steadily over the years, especially in the under-thirty group, the young women and upscale group, and people living in the West. Marketers of foods, exercise equipment, and so on, will want to cater to this trend with appropriate products and communication appeals.

The major cultural values of a society are expressed in people's relationship to themselves, others, institutions, society, nature, and the cosmos.

People's relation to themselves.   People vary in the relative emphasis they place on self-gratification versus serving others. The move toward self-gratification was especially strong during the 1960s and 1970s. *Pleasure seekers* sought fun, change, and escape. Others sought *self-realization* and joined therapeutic or religious groups.

The marketing implications of a "me-society" are many. People use products, brands, and services as a means of self-expression. They buy their "dream cars" and "dream vacations." They spend more time in the outdoors in health activities (jogging, tennis), in introspection, and in arts and crafts. The leisure industry (camping, boating, arts and crafts, sports) faces good growth prospects in a society where people seek self-fulfillment.

People's relation to others. Recently, some observers have pointed to a countermovement from a "me-society" to a "we-society." They think the pendulum has swung and that more people want serious and long-lasting relationships with others, and not just to pursue their self-interest. Some recent advertising is shifting toward featuring people in groups enjoying sharing things with others. A Doyle Dane Bernbach survey showed a widespread concern among adults about social isolation and a strong desire for human contact.[27] This portends a bright future for "social support" products and services that enhance direct communication between human beings, such as health clubs, vacations, and games. It also suggests a growing market for "social surrogates," things that allow a person who is alone to feel that he or she isn't, such as home video games and computers.

In relating to others, people desire open and easy relationships, rather than formal ones. This desire has several marketing implications. People want their homes to be more casual. They want packaging to provide more complete and honest information. They want advertising messages to be more realistic. They want salespersons to be more friendly and helpful.

People's relation to institutions. People vary in their attitudes toward corporations, government agencies, trade unions, universities, and other institutions. Most people accept these institutions, although some are highly critical of particular ones. By and large, people are willing to work for the major institutions and expect them to carry out society's work. There is, however, *a decline in institutional loyalty*. People are giving a little less to these institutions and trusting them less. The work ethic is eroding.

Several marketing implications follow. Companies need to find new ways to win consumer confidence. They need to review their advertising communications to make sure that their messages are honest. They need to review their various activities to make sure that they are coming across as "good corporate citizens." More companies are turning to *social audits*[28] and to *public relations*[29] to build a positive image with their publics.

People's relation to society. People vary in their attitudes toward their society, from patriots who defend it to reformers who want to change it, to discontents who want to leave it. There is declining patriotism and stronger criticism and cynicism as to where the country is going. Recently, the concept of *life ways* has been used for classifying people's relationships to the society in which they live. People fall into one of six *life-way* groups:

---

[27] See Bill Abrams, " 'Middle Generation' Growing More Concerned with Selves," *Wall Street Journal*, January 21, 1982, p. 25.

[28] See Raymond A. Bauer and Dan H. Fenn, Jr., "What Is a Corporate Social Audit?" *Harvard Business Review*, January-February 1973, pp. 37–48.

[29] Leonard L. Berry and James S. Hensel, "Public Relations: Opportunities in the New Society," *Arizona Business*, August-September 1973, pp. 14–21.

□ **Makers.** Makers are those who make the system work. They are the leaders and the up-and-comers. They are involved in worldly affairs, generally prosperous and ambitious. They are found in the professions and include the managers and proprietors of business.

□ **Preservers.** Preservers are people who are at ease with the familiar and are proud of tradition. They are a powerful force in promoting stability in a changing world.

□ **Takers.** Takers take what they can from the system. They live only marginally in the work world, finding their pleasures outside. They are attracted to bureaucracies and tenured posts.

□ **Changers.** Changers tend to be answer-havers; they commonly wish to change things to conform with their views. They are the critics, protestors, radicals, libbers, advocates, and complainers—and a significant segment of the doers. Their focus is chiefly outward.

□ **Seekers.** Seekers are the ones who search for a better grasp, a deeper understanding, a richer experience, a universal view. The pathways of their seeking and the rewards sought tend to be internal. They often originate and promulgate new ideas.

□ **Escapers.** Escapers have a drive to escape, to get away from it all. Escape takes many forms, from dropping out to addiction to mental illness to mysticism.[30]

These types are found in all societies, and over time the relative sizes of the groups change. Mitchell sees American society drifting toward a greater ratio of takers to makers, which does not augur well for future economic growth. He also sees an increasing ratio of escapers to changers, which means that society will grow more conservative and self-indulgent.

Marketers can view life-way groups as market segments with specific symbolic and material needs. Makers are high achievers who collect success symbols, such as elegant homes, expensive automobiles, and fine clothes, whereas changers live more austerely, drive smaller cars, and wear simpler clothes. Escapers go in for motorcycles, chic clothes, surfing, and disco. In general, the consumption patterns of individuals will reflect their orientation toward society.

People's relation to nature. People vary in their attitude toward the physical world. Some feel subjugated by it, others are in harmony with it, and others seek mastery over it. A long-term trend has been people's growing mastery over nature through technology and the attendant belief that nature is bountiful. More recently, however, people have awakened to nature's fragility and finite supplies. People recognize that nature can be spoiled or destroyed by human activities.

People's love of nature is leading to more camping, hiking, boating, and fishing. Business has responded with hiking boots, tenting equipment, and other gear for nature enthusiasts. Tour operators are packaging more tours to wilderness areas. Food producers have found growing markets for "natural" products, such as natural cereal, natural ice cream, and health foods. Marketing communicators are using suggestive natural backgrounds in advertising their products.

People's relation to the universe. People vary in their beliefs about the origin of the universe and their place in it. Most Americans are monotheistic, although their religious conviction and practice have been waning through the years. Church attendance has been falling steadily, with the exception of certain evangelical movements reaching out to bring people back into organized religion. Some of the religious impulse

---

[30] Arnold Mitchell of the Stanford Research Institute, private publication.

has not been lost but has been redirected into a growing interest in Eastern religions, mysticism, and the occult. More Americans than ever are studying yoga, zen, and transcendental meditation.

As people lose their religious orientation, they seek to enjoy their life on earth as fully as possible. They seek goods and experiences that offer fun and pleasure. In the meantime, religious institutions start turning to marketers for help in reworking their appeals to compete against the secular attractions of modern society.

In summary, cultural values are showing the following long-run trends:

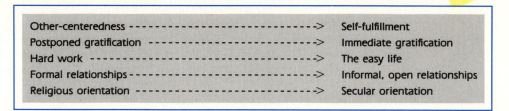

Other-centeredness ---------------------->	Self-fulfillment
Postponed gratification ---------------->	Immediate gratification
Hard work ------------------------------>	The easy life
Formal relationships ------------------>	Informal, open relationships
Religious orientation ------------------>	Secular orientation

Marketers should recognize that each trend is subject to exceptions. A long perspective on cultural change shows that much cultural change follows a model of long-term pendulum swings rather than one-way movements. Every force seems to breed a counterforce, and in many cases, the counterforce eventually becomes dominant.

From time to time, a "futurist" will come out with a major list of trends that cuts across all components of society. Exhibit 3–4 describes the ten "megatrends" recently reported by John Naisbitt, a prominent futurist.

MAPPING A COMPANY'S MARKETING ENVIRONMENT, MARKETING SYSTEM, AND MARKETING STRATEGY

We have seen in this chapter how a company links itself to a set of actors to carry out its marketing task, and how these actors are all affected by major forces in the environment. We shall now use the Hershey Food Company to pull these ideas together and show the relationship between the company's marketing environment, marketing system, and marketing strategy.

Figure 3–3 shows the major components and flows in a candy company's marketing system. The diagram is divided into six elements.

1. The **environment** or, more precisely, those forces in the environment that affect candy demand and supply, such as population growth, per capita income, attitudes toward candy, and raw material availability and cost.
2. The **company's and competitors' marketing strategies.**
3. The **major marketing decision variables** in this market—product characteristics, price, sales force, physical distribution and service, and advertising and sales promotion.
4. The **major marketing channels** that the company uses for this product.
5. The **buyer-behavior model,** which shows customer response to the activities of the manufacturers and the distribution channels as well as to the environment.
6. The total **industry sales, company sales, and company costs.**

Exhibit 3-4

NAISBITT'S MEGATRENDS: A PROMINENT FUTURIST REPORTS ON TEN "MEGATRENDS" OF GREAT IMPORT TO MARKETERS

For the past twelve years, John Naisbitt has been publishing *The Trend Report*, and several major corporations each pay over $15,000 a year to receive three reports. Naisbitt and his staff spot the trends through *content analysis*, namely, by counting the number of times hard-news items appear in major newspapers. The items fall into thirteen broad categories and over two hundred subcategories. Recently Naisbitt published a book based on his findings called *Megatrends*: *Ten New Directions Transforming Our Lives* (Warner Books, New York). Here are the ten megatrends Naisbitt found:

1. The American economy is undergoing a "megashift" from an industrial to an information-based society.
   - Today 13 percent of the total U.S. work force is employed in manufacturing, while 60 percent produce or process information. Those that use or convey information include: teachers, clerks, secretaries, accountants, stockbrokers, lawyers, and insurance people.
   - Between 1970 and 1980 the total labor force increased 18 percent, while managers and administrators increased 58 percent. Health administrators increased 118 percent, systems analysts increased 84 percent, and bankers increased 83 percent.

2. As the society increases in *high-tech*, there will be *high-touch* reactions.
   - Teleconferencing, a high-technology innovation, has not yet caught on because people enjoy the high-touch of face-to-face meetings.
   - The hospice movement to allow people to die in peace if they wish is a high-touch reaction to the high-tech life-support systems recently developed.
   - Many companies try to add high-touch to their high-tech to increase the latter's acceptance. Thus Apple Computer Co. chose the apple and a rainbow to symbolize its "user-friendly" nature. These companies search for "earth values" or "feather values" to soften their products.

3. The U.S. is moving away from isolation and self-sufficiency and recognizing its global interdependence. It is losing its dominance as an economic power.
   - Productivity growth in the U.S. fell to 1 percent per year between 1973 and 1977 and actually declined 2 percent in 1979. Japan is number one in productivity. However, Japan is being challenged by Singapore, South Korea, and Brazil.
   - We need to begin thinking globally and acting locally. Illinois and Florida, for instance, are trading with countries around the globe.

4. U.S. corporate managers are beginning to think about the long term rather than the next quarter.
   - The short-term emphasis was due largely to pressure from shareholders and the fact that managers are rewarded for short-term rather than long-term planning.
   - American auto makers are suffering because of short-term behavior, which led to cutting costs at the expense of quality and durability.

5. We are beginning to build from the bottom up in our companies and are moving away from a centralized structure toward a decentralized structure.
   - In an industrial society, workers have to go to a central plant and work with others.
   - In an information society, all one needs is a telephone and a typewriter.

6. We are returning to an emphasis on self-reliance and deemphasizing help from institutions.
   - No longer do parents automatically send their kids to school. Today an estimated one million families are educating their children at home.
   - No longer are people content to devote their lives to corporations. There has been an entreprenurial explosion. In 1950, 93,000 new businesses were started; today 600,000 new businesses are forming per year.
7. Workers and consumers are demanding and getting a greater voice in government, in business, and in the marketplace.
   - People today want to have a say in decisions that affect their lives.
   - Owing to the availability of information today, it is possible for the average voter to know as much as or more than his or her representatives.
8. The computer is smashing the corporate organizational chart. We are moving from hierarchies to networks.
   - People are forming networks to share ideas, information, and resources, and the networks often cut across hierarchies.
   - Information is power, and the people who have good access to information are increasing their influence in organizations.
9. Workers are moving from the North and Northeast to the South and Southwest.
   - People are leaving the North very rapidly. During the 1970s, Buffalo, Cleveland, and St. Louis lost almost one-fourth of their populations.
   - The cities showing the greatest opportunity are Albuquerque, Austin, Dallas, Denver, Phoenix, Salt Lake City, San Antonio, San Diego, San José, Tampa, and Tucson.
10. People are demanding variety instead of "one size for all."
   - Only 7 percent of the population fits the old traditional family profile; i.e., working father, mother at home, two children.
   - Today there are 752 different models of cars and trucks, 2,500 types of light bulbs, and 200 different TV channels on cable networks.

Naisbitt summed it up in the last statement of his book, "My God what a fantastic time to be alive."

SOURCE: *John Naisbitt,* Megatrends: Ten New Directions Transforming Our Lives *(New York: Warner Books, 1982).*

The various arrows show key flows in the marketing system. Flow 5, for example, would refer to a detailed diagram and description showing types of product-characteristics decisions, the inputs that influence each of these decisions, and the sources of data for each of the inputs.

Let us select one element in Figure 3–3, the *company marketing strategy* box, and list on the right side of this box all the major marketing decisions made by the company (see Figure 3–4). There are two major types of decisions, trade decisions and consumer decisions. To influence the trade, the company uses the wholesale price, trade allowances, credit policy, and delivery policy. To influence consumers, the company uses product characteristics, packaging characteristics, retail price, consumer deals, and consumer advertising.

The next step is to list the various inputs and influences on these decisions, which fall into one of three groups:

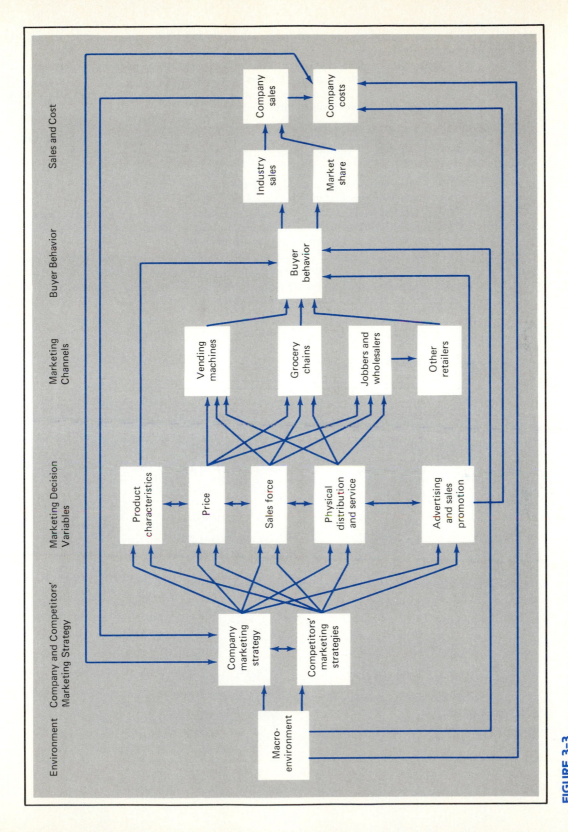

Environment · Company and Competitors' Marketing Strategy · Marketing Decision Variables · Marketing Channels · Buyer Behavior · Sales and Cost

Macro-environment

Company marketing strategy · Competitors' marketing strategies

Product characteristics · Price · Sales force · Physical distribution and service · Advertising and sales promotion

Vending machines · Grocery chains · Jobbers and wholesalers · Other retailers

Buyer behavior

Industry sales · Market share

Company sales · Company costs

FIGURE 3-3
Comprehensive Marketing System Map: Candy Company

1. The company's long- and short-range goals for sales growth, return on sales, and return on investment.
2. Forecastable factors in the environment, such as population growth, disposable personal income, cultural factors, and the cost and supply outlook.
3. Assumptions about the sales effectiveness of different marketing instruments as well as expectations concerning competition.

Any input can be elaborated further. For example, it is possible to isolate four cultural factors that will have a significant effect on future candy consumption:

☐ **Weight consciousness.** If Americans start abandoning the idea that "thin is beautiful," candy sales will rise substantially.
☐ **Cavity consciousness.** As better toothpastes are developed, people will worry less about how sugar affects their teeth; on the other hand, some companies see cavity-consciousness as an opportunity to develop a tasty, sugarless candy.
☐ **Nutrition consciousness.** If publicity on the negative effects of refined sugar on human metabolism continues to grow, more people will steer away from candy.
☐ **Cigarette consumption.** If people reduce their cigarette smoking, we can expect candy, gum, and other oral gratifiers, to replace cigarettes.

FIGURE 3–4
Input-Output Map of Company Marketing Decisions: Candy Company

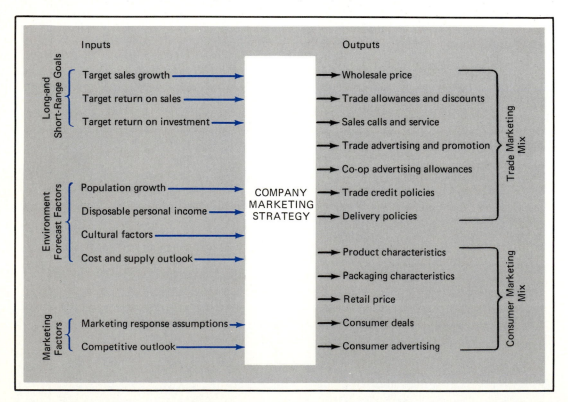

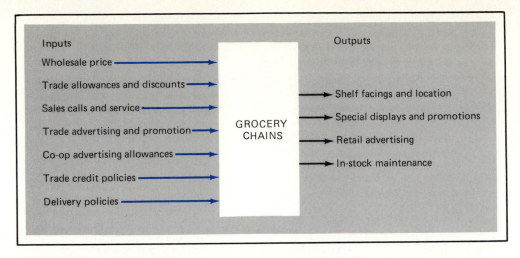

FIGURE 3-5
Input-Output Map of Grocery-Chain Decisions: Candy Company

We can now trace how the various outputs feed into other parts of the system. Consider the output described as the trade marketing mix. This output becomes input into each of the distribution channels—for example, the grocery-chain model (see Figure 3–5). The trade marketing mix becomes the "handle" that the manufacturer uses to influence the retailer to provide favorable shelf facings and location, special displays and promotions, advertising, and in-stock maintenance.

The influence of the dealers' decisions on the final consumers is shown in Figure 3–6 along with influences coming from other parts of the marketing system. The various influences are classified into product and promotion factors (outputs coming from the company marketing decision model), distribution factors (outputs coming from the channels of distribution models), and environmental factors (outputs coming from the environmental model). These factors influence consumers' buying behavior and bring about a certain level of industry sales and brand-share sales of candy bars.

Ultimately, the marketing planner must estimate the quantitative relationships between various key elements. Figure 3–7 shows the estimated effect of a product characteristic—chocolate weight percentage on the sales of one of its soft-center candy bars. The company would like to keep this percentage down because chocolate is an expensive ingredient compared with the ingredients that make up the soft center. Consumer tests, however, reveal that as the chocolate content of the bar is reduced, the bar loses its appeal, and sales decline. The soft center begins to appear through the chocolate and leads consumers to feel that the bar is poorly made. Furthermore, consumers desire more chocolate to offset the soft center. When the layer of chocolate gets too thick (above 35 percent of the weight of the bar), consumer preference for the bar also falls. The consumers begin to think of it not as a soft-centered chocolate candy bar but as a chocolate bar with "some stuff in it." They compare this bar with pure chocolate bars, and it suffers by comparison. Thus Figure 3–7 shows management's best estimate of how sales are affected by a specific product characteristic,

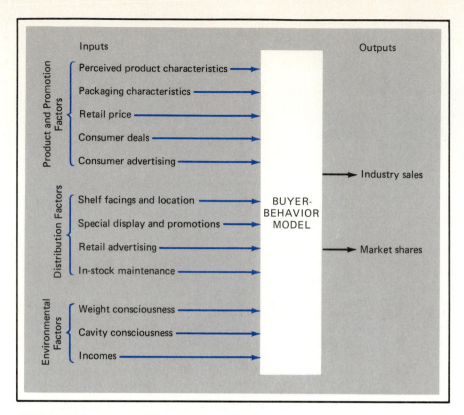

FIGURE 3-6
Input-Output Map of Buyer Behavior: Candy Company

here "percentage chocolate." Any function that shows how sales are affected by a marketing variable under management's control is known as a *sales-response function*.

Given this sales-response function, what is the optimum percentage of chocolate? If the company wants to maximize sales, chocolate should constitute 35 percent of the candy bar's weight. Since the company is primarily interested in maximizing profit, however, management needs the ingredient-cost functions, as well as the sales-response function, to determine the profit-maximizing amount of chocolate.

Other functional relationships should be studied—the relationship between the amount spent on advertising and the resulting sales, the number of sales representatives and the resulting sales, and so on. At some point, the various functional relationships must be put together into a model for analyzing the sales and profit consequences of a proposed marketing plan. A useful device is shown in Figure 3-8.

Quadrant 1 shows a relationship between population and the total sales of chocolate-covered, soft-centered candy bars. The functional relationship shows that sales increase with population but at a decreasing rate. The part of the curve describing candy consumption when the American population was under 220 million is derived through least-squares regression analysis. The part of the curve showing sales for

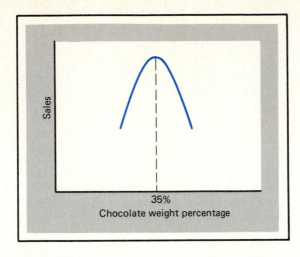

FIGURE 3–7
Functional Relationship Map:
Candy Company

future sizes of the U.S. population is extrapolated and is influenced by anticipated cultural and economic trends. The curve indicates that a population of 220 million consumes approximately $105 million of soft-centered candy bars.

The second quadrant shows the relationship between total sales of soft-centered candy bars and company sales. When industry sales are $105 million, Hershey enjoys sales of $70 million—that is, a market share of approximately 67 percent. The part of the curve toward the lower level of industry sales is derived from historical information; the part toward the higher levels of sales is extrapolated on the assumption of no dramatic changes in company and competitors' marketing efforts. The line indicates that the company expects its share of market to fall slightly as total sales increase. For example, when industry sales are $140 million, the expectation of company sales is $90 million, or an estimated market share of 61 percent, as compared with 67 percent now.

The third quadrant shows a linear relationship between company sales and company profits. Current profits are $7 million on company sales of approximately $70 million, or 10 percent. If company sales rise to $105 million, the company expects profits of approximately $10.2 million—that is, 9.7 percent.

This graphical device allows us to visualize the effect of a particular environment factor and marketing program on company sales and profits. Suppose that the company expects a new antismoking campaign to favor candy bar sales and shift the curve in the first quadrant higher (see Fig. 3–8). Furthermore, suppose the company plans to intensify its marketing effort to capture more market share. The anticipated effect of this on company market share can be seen by shifting the function in the second quadrant to the right, as shown in Figure 3–8. At the same time, the company's marketing costs increase and shift the sales-profit curve to the right, as shown in the third quadrant of Figure 3–8. What is the net effect of this complicated set of shifts? The result is that, although sales have increased, profits have fallen. Apparently, the cost to the company of attaining a higher market share exceeds the profits on

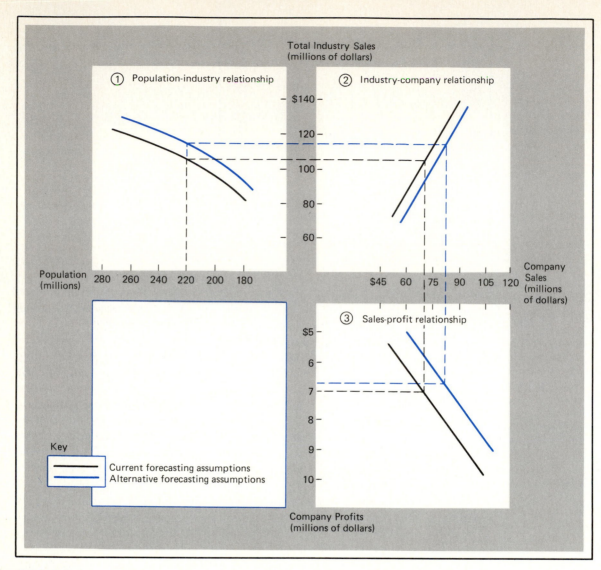

Total Industry Sales
(millions of dollars)

① Population-industry relationship   ② Industry-company relationship

③ Sales-profit relationship

Population (millions)   280 260 240 220 200 180 $45 60 75 90 105 120   Company Sales (millions of dollars)

Key

—— Current forecasting assumptions
—— Alternative forecasting assumptions

Company Profits
(millions of dollars)

FIGURE 3–8
Profit-Forecasting and Planning Map: Candy Company

the extra sales. The company would be wise not to intensify its marketing effort, unless it would have a stronger effect on sales and profits.

The four-quadrant model assists management in visualizing the impact of specific environmental assumptions and marketing plans on final sales and profits. It can be improved further by introducing more variables and representing their relationships in an overall mathematical model of the candy company's marketing system.

SUMMARY

The marketing environment is the place the company must start in searching for opportunities and monitoring threats. It consists of all the actors and forces that affect the company's ability to transact effectively with a target market. We can distinguish between the company's microenvironment and macroenvironment.

The company's microenvironment consists of the actors in the company's immediate environment that affect its ability to serve its markets; specifically, the company itself, suppliers, market intermediaries, customers, competitors, and publics. The company itself consists of several influential departments, all of which have an influence on marketing management's decision making. Suppliers, through their influence on the cost and availability of needed inputs, also have an influence on marketing decisions. The company converts these supplies into useful products and services and uses marketing intermediaries (middlemen, physical distribution facilitators, marketing service agencies, financial intermediaries) to help it find customers and deliver the goods. The target market itself may consist of consumers, producers, resellers, or government agencies, here or abroad. In carrying out its marketing task, the company faces several types of competitors: desire competitors, generic competitors, product-form competitors, and brand competitors. The company also has to deal with various publics that have an actual or potential interest in or impact on the company's ability to achieve its objectives: financial; media; government; citizen action; and local, general, and internal publics. All of these actors make up the company's microenvironment.

The company's macroenvironment consists of six major forces impinging on the company: demographic, economic, physical, technological, political/legal, and socio/cultural. The demographic environment shows a worldwide explosive population growth, a U.S. birthrate slowdown, an aging U.S. population, a changing American family, a rise of nonfamily households, geographical population shifts, and a more-educated and white-collar population. The economic environment shows a slowdown in real-income growth, continued inflationary pressure, changing savings and debt patterns, and changing consumer-expenditure patterns. The physical environment shows impending shortages of certain raw materials, increased energy costs, increased pollution levels, and increasing government intervention in natural resource management. The technological environment exhibits accelerating technological change, unlimited innovational opportunities, high R&D budgets, concentration on minor improvements rather than on major discoveries, and increased regulation of technological change. The political/legal environment shows substantial business regulation, strong government agency enforcement, and the growth of public-interest groups. The socio/cultural environment shows long-run trends toward self-fulfillment, immediate gratification, the easy life, informal and open relationships, and a more secular orientation.

The interaction between the marketing environment and company marketing system and strategy is illustrated for a major candy company that produces a candy bar for the mass market.

QUESTIONS

1. Videotex, also called viewdata, is a two-way interactive system that allows a user to view a presentation over cable TV and then communicate a response via a home terminal to a computer over telephone lines. What implications does this new technology have for marketers?

2. During September and October of 1982 seven people in Chicago died after taking cyanide-laced Tylenol capsules. Tylenol was Johnson & Johnson's best-selling product, with over $400 million in annual sales. In addition to sales losses from permanent or temporary brand switching, J&J spent $100 million on a recall and another $30 million in replacing the product in tamper-resistant packaging and promoting the "new" Tylenol. What actions can be taken by marketers to minimize the threat of such catastrophic environmental events?

3. A major alcoholic-beverage marketer is considering introducing an "adult" soft drink that would be a socially acceptable substitute for alcohol. What cultural factors could influence the introduction decision and subsequent marketing mix?

4. Lifestyle studies have showed a positive trend in the attitude that "meal preparation should take as little time as possible." How might this attitude affect the sales of frozen vegetables?

5. Discuss in some depth how the six macroenvironmental forces discussed in this chapter may affect the marketing of Coca-Cola in 1995.

6. Tell whether you would support or not support each of the following new legislative proposals (give your reasoning): (a) a bill to require companies in concentrated industries to go through federal hearings before each price boost; (b) a bill to allow auto makers to prevent dealers from selling outside their territories; (c) a bill to require manufacturers to grant wholesalers a bigger discount than they give to large retail chains; (d) a bill to protect independent retailers from price competition from a manufacturer who does retailing of his own.

7. Develop a comprehensive marketing system map of some company of your choice. Be sure to show the marketing-mix elements and the channels of distribution.

8. Develop a diagram showing the major publics of a privately owned hospital.

Consumer Markets and Buying Behavior 4

There is an old saying in Spain: To be a bullfighter, you must first learn to be a bull.

ANONYMOUS

Understanding the buying behavior of the target market is the essential task of marketing management under the marketing concept. This chapter will explore the buying dynamics of consumers, and the next chapter will explore the buying dynamics of organizational buyers.

The consumer market consists of all the individuals and households who buy or acquire goods and services for personal consumption. In 1982 the American consumer market consisted of 233 million persons whose aggregate personal income was $2.6 trillion—the equivalent of $11,159 for every man, woman, and child. Each year, this market grows by several million persons and over $100 billion, representing one of the most lucrative consumer markets in the world.[1]

Consumers vary tremendously in age, income, educational level, mobility pat-

_____
[1] *Statistical Abstract of the United States*, 1982.

terns, and taste. Marketers find it useful to distinguish different consumer groups and to develop products and services tailored to their needs. If a market segment is large enough, some companies may set up special marketing programs to serve this market. Here are two examples of special consumer groups:

☐ **Hispanic consumers.** A rapidly growing ethnic group in the U.S. is people of Hispanic origin, particularly Mexican-Americans, Puerto Ricans, and Cubans. Over 75 percent of their members live in the top thirty U.S. metropolitan areas, with particular concentration in New York City, Los Angeles, and Miami. They constitute the second largest ethnic market in the U.S.; the largest is the black consumers. They are consumption oriented and have a strong preference for major name-brand products. Certain companies—such as P&G, Colgate, Bristol-Meyers, Pepsi-Cola—have focused on this target market by advertising in Spanish-language mass media and used Hispanic models in their ads. The result is that Hispanic consumers favor certain brands over others; for example, they are much greater users of Cheer, Pepsi-Cola, and Marlboro. Marketers must also pay careful attention to differences among Hispanic groups. Each major Hispanic subculture has its own beliefs, values, and customs, and therefore an appeal that might work with New York's Puerto Rican community may utterly fail with Miami's Cuban population.[2]

☐ **Elderly consumers.** "Old age" in the U.S. officially begins on a person's sixty-fifth birthday, when retirement usually occurs and certain benefits start flowing in. Accordingly, elderly people make up 12 percent of the population and are the second fastest-growing age group. Marketers tend to make two mistakes with respect to the elderly. They either ignore them on the assumption that they have little purchasing power or assume they are a homogeneous group. The fact is that many elderly people have sufficient economic resources, and furthermore they show a large variety of lifestyles. Many people reaching sixty-five still consider themselves middle-aged; feeling elderly comes around age seventy-five. Some older people are very busy reorganizing their lives and becoming involved in new activities and organizations; others are disengaging and becoming withdrawn. Elderly consumers purchase more medical attention and many leisure-related products, such as travel, entertainment, and other recreation. Marketers should avoid promoting products specifically for the elderly. Heinz launched a line of "senior foods," which failed because the elderly did not want to publicly buy senior foods; they preferred buying baby food and pretending that it was for their grandchildren. Clothing manufacturers and retailers might design their clothing for middle-aged tastes, and the elderly will respond. Marketers should be aware that the elderly are typically price sensitive and have time to shop and make comparisons. Marketers should favor television advertising because the elderly spend a lot of time watching television.[3]

---

[2] See "Spanish Speaking Are $20 Billion U.S. Market," *Advertising Age*, November 21, 1973, p. 56; and "Spanish TV Net Grows, Looks to East," *Advertising Age*, August 18, 1975, p. 214.

[3] See Zarrel V. Lambert, "An Investigation of Older Consumers' Unmet Needs and Wants at the Retail Level," *Journal of Retailing*, Winter 1979, pp. 35–57; Carole B. Allan, "Measuring Mature Markets," *American Demographics*, March 1981, pp. 13–17; Rena Bartos, "Over 49: The Invisible Consumer Market," *Harvard Business Review*, January–February 1980, pp. 140–48; Betsy D. Gelb, "Exploring the Gray Market Segment," *MSU Business Topics*, Spring 1978, pp. 41–46; and Lynn W. Philips and Brian Sternthal, "Age Differences in Information Processing: A Perspective on the Aged Consumer," *Journal of Marketing Research*, November 1977, pp. 444–57.

Other consumer submarkets—the blacks,[4] youths,[5] women,[6]—could be similarly researched to see if focused marketing programs would make competitive sense.

The 233 million American consumers buy an incredible variety of goods and services. (For a classification of these goods, see Chapter 15). Here we will concentrate on trying to understand how consumers make their purchase choices among these goods and services.

A MODEL OF CONSUMER BEHAVIOR

In earlier times, marketers could arrive at a fair understanding of consumers through the daily experience of selling to them. But the growth in the size of firms and markets has removed many marketing decision makers from direct contact with their customers. Increasingly, managers have had to turn to consumer research. They are spending more money than ever to study consumers, trying to learn: *Who buys? How do they buy? When do they buy? Where do they buy? Why do they buy?*

Of central interest is the question, How do consumers respond to various marketing stimuli that the company might arrange? The company that really understands how consumers will respond to different product features, prices, advertising appeals, and so on, will have an enormous advantage over its competitors. Therefore, business and academic researchers have invested much energy in researching the relationship between marketing stimuli and consumer response.

Their starting point is the stimulus-response model shown in Figure 4–1. This figure shows marketing and other stimuli entering the buyer's "black box" and producing certain responses. The stimuli on the left are of two types. Marketing stimuli consist of the four Ps: product, price, place, and promotion. Other stimuli consist of major forces and events in the buyer's environment: economic, technological, political, and cultural. All these stimuli pass through the buyer's black box and produce the set of observable buyer responses shown on the right: product choice, brand choice, dealer choice, purchase timing, and purchase amount.

The marketer's task is to understand what happens in the buyer's black box between the stimuli and responses. The buyer's black box has two components. First, the buyer's characteristics have a major influence on how he or she reacts to the stimuli. Second, the buyer's decision process influences the outcome. The first part of this chapter will examine the influence of consumer characteristics on buying behavior; and the second part will examine how the buyer's decision process leads to buyer choices.

---

[4] See Kevin A. Wall, "New Market: Among Blacks, the Haves Are Now Overtaking the Have-nots," *Advertising Age*, February 11, 1974, pp. 35–36; Mary Jane Schlinger and Joseph T. Plummer, "Advertising in Black and White," *Journal of Marketing Research*, May 1972, pp. 149–53; and Raymond A. Bauer and Scott M. Cunningham, "The Negro Market," *Journal of Advertising Research*, April 1970, pp. 3–12.

[5] See Melvin Helitzer and Carl Heyel, *The Youth Market* (New York: Media Books, 1970), p. 58; and George W. Schiele, "How to Reach the Young Consumer," *Harvard Business Review*, March–April 1974, pp. 77–86.

[6] See Rena Bartos, "What Every Marketer Should Know about Women," *Harvard Business Review*, May–June 1978, pp. 73–85.

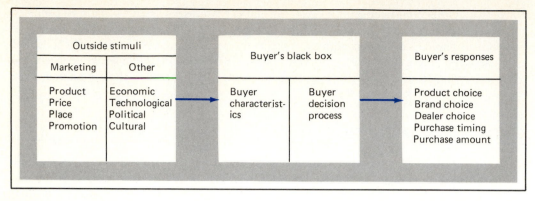

Outside stimuli		Buyer's black box		Buyer's responses
Marketing	Other			
Product Price Place Promotion	Economic Technological Political Cultural	Buyer characterist- ics	Buyer decision process	Product choice Brand choice Dealer choice Purchase timing Purchase amount

FIGURE 4-1
Model of Buyer Behavior

MAJOR FACTORS INFLUENCING CONSUMER BEHAVIOR

Consumers do not make their decisions in a vacuum. Their purchases are highly influenced by cultural, social, personal, and psychological factors. These factors are listed in Figure 4–2. For the most part, they are "noncontrollable" by the marketer but must be taken into account. We want to examine the influence of each factor on a buyer's behavior. We will illustrate these characteristics for a hypothetical consumer named Larry Brown:

> Larry Brown is thirty-five, married, and a brand manager in a leading consumer-packaged-goods company. He received an M.B.A. some years before computers became a regular course in business school curriculums. Larry feels that he may become obsolete if he doesn't learn how to use a computer in his work and home. He is considering buying a personal computer but faces a great number of brand choices: IBM, Radio Shack, Apple, Texas Instruments, Atari, and so on. His choice will be influenced by many factors.

Cultural Factors

Cultural factors exert the broadest and deepest influence on consumer behavior. We will look at the role played by the buyer's culture, subculture, and social class.

Culture. Culture is the most fundamental determinant of a person's wants and behavior. Whereas lower creatures are largely governed by instinct, human behavior is largely learned. The child growing up in a society learns a basic set of values, perceptions, preferences, and behaviors through a process of socialization involving the family and other key institutions. Thus a child growing up in America is exposed to the following values: achievement and success, activity, efficiency and practicality, progress, material comfort, individualism, freedom, external comfort, humanitarianism, and youthfulness.[7]

---

[7] See Leon G. Schiffman and Leslie Lazar Kanuk, *Consumer Behavior*, 2nd ed., (Englewood Cliffs, N.J.: Prentice-Hall, 1983), pp. 404–20.

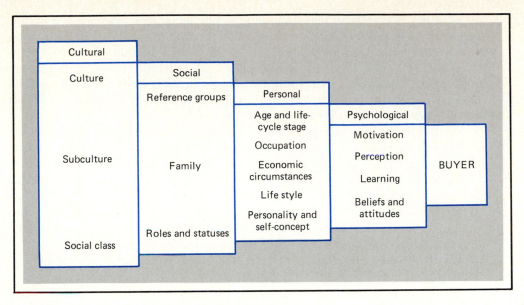

FIGURE 4-2
Detailed Model of Factors Influencing Behavior

Larry Brown's interest in computers is a result of his being raised in an advanced technological society. Computers presuppose a whole set of consumer learnings and values. Larry knows what computers are. He knows how to read instructions on how to operate a computer; he knows that the society values computer expertise. In another culture, say a remote tribe in central Australia, a computer would mean nothing. It would simply be a curious piece of hardware, and there would be no buyers.

Subculture. Each culture contains smaller groups of subcultures that provide more specific identification and socialization for its members. Four types of subcultures can be distinguished. *Nationality groups* such as the Irish, Polish, Italians, and Puerto Ricans are found within large communities and exhibit distinct ethnic tastes and proclivities. *Religious groups* such as the Catholics, Mormons, Presbyterians, and Jews represent subcultures with specific cultural preferences and taboos. *Racial groups* such as the blacks and Orientals have distinct cultural styles and attitudes. *Geographical areas* such as the Deep South, California, and New England are distinct subcultures with characteristic lifestyles.

Larry Brown's interest in various goods will be influenced by his nationality, religion, race, and geographical background. These factors will influence his food preferences, clothing choices, recreation, and career aspirations. His subculture identifications may influence his interest in a personal computer. He may come from a subculture that places a high value on being an "educated man" and this helps explain his interest in computers.

Consumer Markets and Buying Behavior **125**

Social class.   Virtually all human societies exhibit social stratification. Stratification sometimes takes the form of a caste system where the members of different castes are reared for certain roles and cannot change their caste membership. More frequently, stratification takes the form of social classes. *Social classes are relatively homogeneous and enduring divisions in a society, which are hierarchically ordered and whose members share similar values, interests, and behavior.* Social scientists have identified the six social classes shown in Table 4-1 on page 126.

Social classes have several characteristics. First, persons within each social class tend to behave more alike than persons from two different social classes. Second, persons are perceived as occupying inferior or superior positions according to their social class. Third, a person's social class is indicated by a number of variables, such as occupation, income, wealth, education, and value orientation, rather than by any single variable. Fourth, individuals are able to move from one social class to another—up or down—during their lifetime. The extent of this mobility varies according to the rigidity of social stratification in a given society.

Social classes show distinct product and brand preferences in such areas as clothing, home furnishings, leisure activities, and automobiles. Some marketers focus their efforts on one social class. Thus the Four Seasons restaurant in upper Manhattan focuses on upper-class customers whereas Joe's Diner in lower Manhattan focuses on lower-class customers. The social classes differ in their media preferences, with upper-class consumers having greater exposure to magazines and newspapers than lower-class consumers. Even within a media category, the social classes differ in their preferences. Upper-class consumers prefer current events and drama, and lower-class consumers prefer soap operas and quiz shows. There are also language differences among the social classes. The advertiser has to compose copy and—for TV commercials—dialogue that ring true to each social-class target.

Larry Brown probably came from an upper-class background. His family placed a lot of value on education and on becoming a professional person, whether a manager, lawyer, accountant, or physician. As a result, Larry has good verbal and mathematical skills and is not daunted by a computer as someone from a lower-class background might be.

Social Factors

A consumer's behavior is also influenced by social factors, such as the consumer's reference groups, family, and social roles and statuses.

Reference groups.   A person's behavior is strongly influenced by many groups. A person's reference groups are those groups that have a direct (*face-to-face*) or indirect influence on the person's attitudes or behavior. Groups having a direct influence on a person are called *membership groups*. These are groups to which the person belongs and interacts. Some are *primary groups* with which there is fairly continuous interaction, such as family, friends, neighbors, and co-workers. Primary groups tend to be informal. The person also belongs to *secondary groups*, which tend to be more formal and where there is less continuous interaction: They include religious organizations, professional associations, and trade unions.

TABLE 4-1

1. UPPER UPPERS (LESS THAN 1 PERCENT). Upper uppers are the social elite who live on inherited wealth and have a well-known family background. They give large sums to charity, run the debutante balls, maintain more than one home, and send their children to the finest schools. They are a market for jewelry, antiques, homes, and vacations. They often buy and dress conservatively, not being interested in ostentation. While small as a group, they serve as a reference group for others to the extent that their consumption decisions trickle down and are imitated by the other social classes.

2. LOWER UPPERS (ABOUT 2 PERCENT). Lower uppers are persons who have earned high income or wealth through exceptional ability in the professions or business. They usually come from the middle class. They tend to be active in social and civic affairs and seek to buy the symbols of status for themselves and their children, such as expensive homes, schools, yachts, swimming pools, and automobiles. They include the **nouveaux riches,** whose pattern of conspicuous consumption is designed to impress those below them. The ambition of lower uppers is to be accepted in the upper-upper stratum, a status that is more likely to be achieved by their children than themselves.

3. UPPER MIDDLES (12 PERCENT). Upper middles possess neither family status nor unusual wealth. They are primarily concerned with ''career.'' They have attained positions as professionals, independent businesspersons, and corporate managers. They believe in education and want their children to develop professional or administrative skills so that they will not drop into a lower stratum. Members of this class like to deal in ideas and ''high culture.'' They are joiners and highly civic minded. They are the quality market for good homes, clothes, furniture, and appliances. They seek to run a gracious home, entertaining friends and clients.

4. LOWER MIDDLES (30 PERCENT). Lower middles consist of primarily white-collar workers (office workers, small-business owners), ''gray collars'' (mailmen, firemen), and ''aristocrat blue collars'' (plumbers, factory foremen). They are concerned with ''respectability.'' They exhibit conscientious work habits and adhere to culturally defined norms and standards, including going to church and obeying the law. The home is important, and lower middles like to keep it neat and ''pretty.'' They buy conventional home furnishings and do a lot of their own work around the home. They prefer clothes that are neat and clean rather than high style.

5. UPPER LOWERS (35 PERCENT). Upper lowers are the largest social-class segment, the blue-collar working class of skilled and semiskilled factory workers. While they seek respectability, their main drive is security, ''protecting what they have.'' The working-class husband has a strong ''all-male'' self-image, being a sports enthusiast, outdoorsman, and heavy smoker and beer drinker. The working-class wife spends most of her time in the house cooking, cleaning, and caring for her children. She sees being the mother of her children as her main vocation, and she has little time for organizations and social activity.

6. LOWER LOWERS (20 PERCENT). Lower lowers are at the bottom of society and consist of poorly educated, unskilled laborers. They are often out of work and on some form of public assistance. Their housing is typically substandard and located in slum areas. They often reject middle-class standards of morality and behavior. They buy more impulsively. They often do not evaluate quality, and they pay too much for products and buy on credit. They are a large market for food, television sets, and used automobiles.

SOURCE: Adapted from **Consumer Behavior**, 3rd ed. by James F. Engel, et al. Copyright © 1978 by The Dryden Press. Reprinted and adapted by permission of Holt, Rinehart and Winston, CBS College Publishing.

People are also influenced by groups in which they are not members. Groups to which a person would like to belong are called *aspirational groups*. For example, a teenager may hope one day to play for the Dallas Cowboys. A *dissociative group* is one whose values or behavior an individual rejects. The same teenager may want to avoid any relationship with the Hare Krishna cult group.

Marketers try to identify the reference groups of their target customers. People are significantly influenced by their reference groups in at least three ways. Reference groups expose an individual to new behaviors and lifestyles. They also influence the person's attitudes and self-concept because he or she normally desires to "fit in." And they create pressures for conformity that may affect the person's actual product and brand choices.

The importance of reference-group influence varies among products and brands. Hendon asked 200 consumers to specify which of their product and brand choices were strongly influenced by others.[8] He found that reference groups had a strong influence on both product and brand choice in the case of automobiles and color television. Reference groups had a strong influence in brand choice only in such items as furniture and clothing. And reference groups had a strong influence in product choice only in such items as beer and cigarettes.

Hendon also observed that reference group influence changes as products go through the product life cycle. When a product is first introduced, the decision to buy it is heavily influenced by others, but the brand chosen is less influenced by others. In the market growth stage, group influence is strong on both product and brand choice. In the product maturity stage, brand choice but not product choice is heavily influenced by others. In the decline stage, group influence is weak in both product and brand choice.

Manufacturers of products and brands where group influence is strong must figure out how to reach the *opinion leaders* in the relevant reference groups. At one time, sellers thought that opinion leaders were primarily community social leaders whom the mass market imitated because of "snob appeal." But opinion leaders are found in all strata of society, and a specific person can be an opinion leader in certain product areas and an opinion follower in other areas. The marketer tries to reach the opinion leaders by identifying certain personal characteristics associated with opinion leadership, determining the media read by opinion leaders, and directing messages at the opinion leaders.

Group influence will be stronger for products that will be visible to others whom the buyer respects. Larry Brown's interest in a computer and his predilections for various brands will be strongly influenced by some of his membership groups. His cohorts at work and their buying of computers and their brand choices will influence him. The more cohesive the group, the more effective its communication process, and the higher the person esteems it, the more influential it will be in shaping the person's product and brand choices.

---

[8] See Donald W. Hendon, "A New Empirical Look at the Influence of Reference Groups on Generic Product Category and Brand Choice: Evidence from Two Nations," in *Proceedings of the Academy of International Business: Asia-Pacific Dimension of International Business* (Honolulu: College of Business Administration, University of Hawaii, December 18–20, 1979), pp. 752–61.

Family.   Members of the buyer's family can exercise a strong influence on the buyer's behavior. We can distinguish between two families in the buyer's life. The *family of orientation* consists of one's parents. From parents a person acquires an orientation toward religion, politics, and economics and a sense of personal ambition, self-worth, and love. Even if the buyer no longer interacts very much with his or her parents, the parents' influence on the unconscious behavior of the buyer can be significant. In countries where parents continue to live with their children, their influence can be substantial.

A more direct influence on everyday buying behavior is one's *family of procreation*, namely, one's spouse and children. The family is the most important consumer-buying organization in society, and it has been researched extensively.[9] Marketers are interested in the roles and relative influence of the husband, wife, and children in the purchase of a large variety of products and services.

Husband-wife involvement varies widely by product category. The wife has traditionally been the main purchasing agent for the family, especially in the areas of food, sundries, and staple-clothing items. This is changing with the increased number of working wives and the willingness of husbands to do more of the family purchasing. Marketers of staple products would therefore be making a mistake to continue to think of women as the main or only purchasers of their products.

In the case of expensive products and services, husbands and wives engage in more joint decision making. The marketer needs to determine which member normally has the greater influence in the purchase of a particular product or service. Either the husband is more dominant, or the wife, or they have equal influence. The following products and services fall under such:

- ☐ **Husband-dominant:** life insurance, automobiles, television
- ☐ **Wife-dominant:** washing machines, carpeting, non-living-room furniture, kitchenware
- ☐ **Equal:** living-room furniture, vacation, housing, outside entertainment

At the same time, the dominance of a family member varies for different subdecisions within a product category. Davis found that the decision of "when to buy an automobile" was influenced primarily by the husband in 68 percent of the cases, primarily by the wife in 3 percent of the cases, and equally in 29 percent of the cases.[10] On the other hand, the decision of "what color of automobile to buy" was influenced primarily by the husband in 25 percent of the cases, by the wife in 25 percent of the cases, and equally in 50 percent of the cases. An automobile company would take these varying decision roles into account in designing and promoting its cars. (See Exhibit 4–1 for some recent data on women car buyers.)

In the case of Larry Brown's buying a microcomputer, his wife will play an influencer role. She may want him to take up a new hobby, and she may also want to use the computer for certain applications related to her career. She may have

---

[9] See Harry L. Davis, "Decision Making within the Household," *Journal of Consumer Research*, March 1976, pp. 241–60; Harry L. Davis and Benny P. Rigaux, "Perception of Marital Roles in Decision Processes," *Journal of Consumer Research*, June 1974, pp. 51–60; and Harry L. Davis, "Dimensions of Marital Roles in Consumer Decision-Making," *Journal of Marketing Research*, May 1970, pp. 168–77.

[10] See Davis, "Dimensions of Marital Roles."

Exhibit 4-1

WOMEN BECOME A MORE IMPORTANT MARKET FOR CAR BUYING

Laurie Ashcraft, marketing research manager of Minnetonka, Inc., recently made the following observations at a Midwest marketing and research conference:

"Women in car ads have typically been shown sitting on the hood rather than behind the wheel. . . . It seems Detroit is always trying to catch up to changes in consumer demands. . . . And now, they're trying to catch up in their marketing to women. In 1980, women influenced 80 percent of new-car purchases and actually made 40 percent of these purchases. And the increase in car ownership by women has been a steady trend, jumping to 40 percent from 21 percent in 1972. . . . Some auto manufacturers are frantically trying to change their advertising to reflect the reality that women do more than pick out the color of the upholstery. . . . A study . . . revealed that 47 percent of women feel they are not being communicated with effectively in car ads. The women said car ads assume women to be primarily interested in appearance, underestimate women's car sense, and overestimate male influence on women drivers. . . . For example, 60 percent of service contracts are bought by women, and surveys have found that they should be approached differently than men since women are interested in aspects such as safety to a greater degree.

"Detroit and other top management suffer from inertia and cannot be easily persuaded that change is occurring. . . . Marketing decision makers are bringing too much of their own mind-set to the party."

SOURCE: Laurie Ashcraft, "Marketers Miss Their Target When They Eschew Research," Marketing News, January 7, 1983, p. 10.

even initiated the suggestion. Her influence will depend on how much Larry values her views and how strongly she makes the case for buying a computer.

Roles and statuses. A person participates in many groups throughout life—family, clubs, organizations. The person's position in each group can be defined in terms of *role* and *status*. With his parents, Larry Brown plays the role of son; in his family, he plays husband; in his corporation, he plays brand manager. A role consists of the activities that a person is expected to perform according to the persons around him or her. Each of Larry's roles will influence some of his buying behavior.

Each role carries a *status* reflecting the general esteem accorded to it by society. The role of Supreme Court justice carries more status than the role of brand manager; and the role of brand manager carries more status than the role of office clerk. People often choose products to communicate their role and status in society. Thus company presidents drive Mercedes and Cadillacs, wear expensive, finely tailored suits, and drink Chivas Regal Scotch, if their corporate cultures allow such displays of wealth. (Some companies, particularly abroad, tend to associate power with discretion and to disapprove of "exterior signs of success.") Marketers are aware of the potential of products to become *status symbols*. However, status symbols vary for different social classes and also geographically. Status symbols that are "in" in New York are jogging to work, fish and fowl, and cosmetic surgery for men; in Chicago buying through catalogs, croissants and tacos, and telephones in cars; in Houston elegant parties, caviar, and the "preppy" look; in San Francisco sky diving, freshly made pasta, and Izod shirts.[11]

Personal Factors

A buyer's decisions are also influenced by his or her personal characteristics, notably the buyer's age and life-cycle stage, occupation, economic circumstances, lifestyle, and personality and self-concept.

Age and life-cycle stage.   People change the goods and services they buy over their lifetime. They eat baby food in the early years, most foods in the growing and mature years, and special diets in the later years. People's taste in clothes, furniture, and recreation is also age related.

Consumption is also shaped by the stage of the *family life cycle*. Nine stages of the family life cycle are listed in Table 4–2, along with the financial situation and typical product interests of each group. Marketers often define their target markets as certain life-cycle groups and develop appropriate products and marketing plans.

Some recent work has identified *psychological life-cycle stages*. Adults experience certain *passages* or *transformations* as they go through life.[12] Thus Larry Brown may move from being a satisfied brand manager and husband to being an unsatisfied person searching for a new way to fulfill himself. This may have stimulated his interest in computers. Marketers should pay attention to the changing consumption interests that might be associated with these adult passages.

Occupation.   A person's consumption pattern is also influenced by his or her occupation. A blue-collar worker will buy work clothes, work shoes, lunch boxes, and bowling recreation. A company president will buy expensive blue serge suits, air travel, country club membership, and a large sailboat. Marketers try to identify the occupational groups that have an above-average interest in their products and services. A company can even specialize in producing products needed by a particular occupational group. Thus some computer software companies might specialize in designing computer programs useful to brand managers.

Economic circumstances.   A person's economic circumstances will greatly affect product choice. People's economic circumstances consist of their *spendable income* (its level, stability, and time pattern), *savings and assets* (including the percentage that is liquid), *borrowing power,* and *attitude toward spending versus saving*. Thus

---

[11] See "Flaunting Wealth: It's Back in Style," *U.S. News & World Report,* September 21, 1981, pp. 61–64.

[12] Gail Sheehy, *Passages: Predictable Crises in Adult Life,* (New York: Dutton, 1974); and Roger Gould, *Transformations* (New York: Simon & Schuster, 1978).

TABLE 4-2

AN OVERVIEW OF THE FAMILY LIFE CYCLE AND BUYING BEHAVIOR

Stage in Family Life Cycle	Buying or Behavioral Pattern
1. Bachelor stage: young, single people not living at home.	Few financial burdens. Fashion opinion leaders. Recreation oriented. Buy: basic kitchen equipment, basic furniture, cars, equipment for the mating game, vacations.
2. Newly married couples: young, no children.	Better off financially than they will be in near future. Highest purchase rate and highest average purchase of durables. Buy: cars, refrigerators, stoves, sensible and durable furniture, vacations.
3. Full nest I: Youngest child under six.	Home purchasing at peak. Liquid assets low. Dissatisfied with financial position and amount of money saved. Interested in new products. Like advertised products. Buy: washers, dryers, TV, baby food, chest rubs and cough medicines, vitamins, dolls, wagons, sleds, skates.
4. Full nest II: Youngest child six or over.	Financial position better. Some wives work. Less influenced by advertising. Buy larger-sized packages, multiple-unit deals. Buy: many foods, cleaning materials, bicycles, music lessons, pianos.
5. Full nest III. Older married couples with dependent children.	Financial position still better. More wives work. Some children get jobs. Hard to influence with advertising. High average purchase of durables. Buy: new, more tasteful furniture, auto travel, unnecessary appliances, boats, dental services, magazines.
6. Empty nest I: Older married couples, no children living with them, head in labor force.	Home ownership at peak. Most satisfied with financial position and money saved. Interested in travel, recreation, self-education. Make gifts and contributions. Not interested in new products. Buy: vacations, luxuries, home improvements.
7. Empty nest II: Older married. No children living at home, head retired.	Drastic cut in income. Keep home. Buy: medical appliances, medical-care products that aid health, sleep, and digestion.
8. Solitary survivor, in labor force.	Income still good but likely to sell home.
9. Solitary survivor, retired.	Same medical and product needs as other retired group; drastic cut in income. Special need for attention, affection, and security.

SOURCE: William D. Wells and George Gubar, "Life Cycle Concepts in Marketing Research," *Journal of Marketing Research*, November 1966, pp. 355–63, here p. 362. Also see Patrick E. Murphy and William A. Staples, "A Modernized Family Life Cycle," *Journal of Consumer Research*, June 1979, pp. 12–22.

Larry Brown can consider buying a personal computer if he has enough spendable income, savings, or borrowing power and prefers spending to saving. Marketers of income-sensitive goods pay continuous attention to trends in personal income, savings, and interest rates. If economic indicators point to a recession, marketers can take steps to redesign, reposition, and reprice their products so they continue to appeal to target customers.

Lifestyle. People coming from the same subculture, social class, and even occupation may lead quite different lifestyles. Larry Brown, for example, can choose to live a "belonging" lifestyle, which is reflected in wearing conservative clothes, spending a lot of time with his family, helping his church. Or he can choose an "achiever" lifestyle, marked by working long hours on major projects and playing hard when it comes to travel and sports.

A person's *lifestyle*, then, is the *person's pattern of living in the world as expressed in the person's activities, interests, and opinions.* Lifestyle portrays the "whole person" interacting with his or her environment. Lifestyle reflects something beyond the person's social class, on the one hand, or personality, on the other. If we know someone's social class, we can infer several things about the person's likely behavior but fail to see the person as an individual. If we know someone's personality, we can infer distinguishing psychological characteristics but not much about actual activities, interests, and opinions. Lifestyle attempts to profile a whole person's pattern of acting in the world. (See Exhibit 4–2).

In preparing a marketing strategy for a product, marketers will search for relationships between their products or brands and lifestyle groups. A personal-computer manufacturer might find that many target buyers resemble Scott, the successful professional in Exhibit 4–2, whose value and lifestyles are those of an achiever. The marketer may then aim the brand more clearly at Scott's lifestyle. Advertising copywriters can create advertising that is congruent with the symbols in this person's lifestyle:

> He lives in one of those modern high-rise apartments and the rooms are brightly colored. He has modern, expensive furniture, but not Danish modern. He buys his clothes at Brooks Brothers. He owns a good hi-fi. He skis. He has a sailboat. He eats Limburger and any other prestige cheese with his beer. He likes and cooks a lot of steak and would have a filet mignon for company. His liquor cabinet has Jack Daniels bourbon, Beefeater gin, and a good Scotch.[13]

The implications of the lifestyle concept are well stated by Boyd and Levy:

> Marketing is a process of providing customers with parts of a potential mosaic from which they, as artists of their own lifestyles, can pick and choose to develop the composition that for the time seems the best. The marketer who thinks about his products in this way will seek to understand their potential settings and relationships to other parts of consumer lifestyles, and thereby to increase the number of ways they fit meaningfully into the pattern.[14]

---

[13] Sidney J. Levy, "Symbolism and Life Style," in *Toward Scientific Marketing*, ed. Stephen A. Greyser (Chicago: American Marketing Association, 1964), pp. 140–50.

[14] Harper W. Boyd, Jr., and Sidney J. Levy, *Promotion: A Behavioral View* (Englewood Cliffs, N.J.: Prentice-Hall, 1967), p. 38.

Exhibit 4-2

HOW LIFESTYLES ARE IDENTIFIED

Researchers have worked hard to develop a lifestyle classification, based on *psychographic* measurements. A number of classifications have been proposed, two of which will be described here, namely the AIO framework and the VALS framework.

The AIO Framework (Attitudes, Interests, and Opinions)

In this approach, respondents are presented with long questionnaires—sometimes as long as twenty-five pages—seeking to measure their activities, interests, and opinions. The table below shows the major dimensions used to measure the AIO elements, as well as respondents' demographics.

Activities	Interests	Opinions	Demographics
Work	Family	Themselves	Age
Hobbies	Home	Social issues	Education
Social events	Job	Politics	Income
Vacation	Community	Business	Occupation
Entertainment	Recreation	Economics	Family size
Club membership	Fashion	Education	Dwelling
Community	Food	Products	Geography
Shopping	Media	Future	City size
Sports	Achievements	Culture	Stage in life cycle

SOURCE: Joseph T. Plummer, "The Concept and Application of Life-Style Segmentation," **Journal of Marketing**, January 1974, p. 34.

Many of the questions are in the form of agreeing or disagreeing with such statements as:

☐ I would like to become an actor.
☐ I enjoy going to concerts.
☐ I usually dress for fashion, not for comfort.
☐ I often have a cocktail before dinner.

The data are analyzed on a computer to find distinctive lifestyle groups. Using this approach, the Chicago-based advertising agency of Needham, Harper and Steers has identified several lifestyle types, which they have given names to—such as Ben, the self-made businessman, and Candice, the chic suburbanite.

When developing an advertising campaign, the marketers explicate which lifestyle group(s) their product is aimed at and develop an ad appealing to the AIO characteristics of that lifestyle group(s).

The Vals Framework (Values and Lifestyles)

Arnold Mitchell of SRI International recently developed a new classification of the American public into nine lifestyle groups based on analyzing the answers of 2713 respondents to over 800 questions. The nine groups are shown below, with the current estimated percentage of the U.S. adult population in each:

The nine value and lifestyle groups are described below:

- ☐ Survivors (4%) are disadvantaged people who tend to be "despairing, depressed, withdrawn."
- ☐ Sustainers (7%) are disadvantaged people who are valiantly struggling to get out of poverty.
- ☐ Belongers (33%) are people who are conventional, conservative, nostalgic, and unexperimental, who would rather fit in than stand out.
- ☐ Emulators (10%) are ambitious, upwardly mobile, and status conscious; they want to "make it big."
- ☐ Achievers (23%) are the nation's leaders who make things happen, work within the system, and enjoy the good life.
- ☐ "I-am-me" (5%) people who are typically young, self-engrossed, and given to whim.
- ☐ Experientials (7%) are people who pursue a rich inner life and want to directly experience what life has to offer.
- ☐ Societally conscious (9%) people have a high sense of social responsibility and want to improve conditions in society.
- ☐ Integrateds (2%) are people who have fully matured psychologically and combine the best elements of inner directedness and outer directedness.

The classification is based on the idea that individuals pass through a number of development stages, with each stage affecting the person's attitudes, behavior, and psychological needs. People pass from a need-driven stage (survivors and sustainers), into either an outer-directed hierarchy of stages (belongers, emulators, and achievers) or an inner-directed hierarchy of stages (I-am-me, experientials, societally conscious), with a few reaching an integrated stage.

Marketers pay little attention to the need-driven segments because those groups lack economic resources. The other groups are of greater interest and have some distinct demographic, occupational, and media characteristics. Thus a manufacturer of expensive luggage will want to know more about the characteristics of achievers and how to advertise effectively to them; a manufacturer of hot tubs will want to zero in on the experientials. A manufacturer of garbage disposals will direct different appeals to belongers versus societally conscious people. Over forty major corporations now subscribe to VALS and use the data to reach target lifestyle groups effectively.

SOURCE: For further discussion of AIO, see William D. Wells, "Psychographics: A Critical Review," Journal of Marketing Research, May 1975, pp. 196–213; and Peter W. Bernstein, "Psychographics Is Still an Issue on Madison Avenue," Fortune, January 16, 1978, pp. 78–84. For further discussion of VALS, see Arnold Mitchell, The Nine American Life Styles (New York: Macmillan, 1983).

Personality and self-concept.   Each person has a distinct personality that will influence his or her buying behavior. By *personality*, we mean the *person's distinguishing psychological characteristics that lead to relatively consistent and enduring responses to his or her own environment*. A person's personality is usually described in terms of such traits as self-confidence, dominance, autonomy, deference, sociability, defensiveness, and adaptability.[15] Personality can be a useful variable in analyzing consumer behavior provided that personality types can be classified, and strong correlations exist between certain personality types and product or brand choices. For example, a personal-computer company might discover that many prospects have personalities that are high on self-confidence, dominance, and autonomy. This suggests using an advertising approach that projects these qualities to the persons who buy or own computers.

Many marketers use a concept related to personality—a person's *self-concept* (or self-image). All of us carry around a complex mental picture of ourselves. For example, Larry Brown may see himself as highly accomplished and deserving the best. To that extent, he would favor a computer that projects the same qualities. If the IBM personal computer is promoted as a computer for those who want the best, then its brand image would match his self-image. Marketers should try to develop brand images that match the self-image of the target market.

The theory, admittedly, is not that simple. Larry's *actual self-concept* (how he views himself) differs from his *ideal self-concept* (how he would like to view himself) and from his *others-self-concept* (how he thinks others see him). Which self will he try to satisfy with the choice of a computer? Some marketers feel that buyers' choices will correspond more to their actual self-concepts, others to the ideal self-concept, and still others to the others-self-concept. As a result, self-concept theory has had a mixed record of success in predicting consumer responses to brand images.[16]

Psychological Factors

A person's buying choices are also influenced by four major psychological factors—motivation, perception, learning, and beliefs and attitudes. We will explore each factor's role in the buying process.

Motivation.   We saw that Larry Brown became interested in buying a computer. Why? What is he really seeking? What needs is he trying to satisfy?

A person has many needs at any given time. Some needs are *biogenic*. They arise from physiological states of tension such as hunger, thirst, discomfort. Other needs are *psychogenic*. They arise from psychological states of tension such as the

---

[15] See Raymond L. Horton, "Some Relationships Between Personality and Consumer Decision-Making," *Journal of Marketing Research*, May 1979, pp. 244–45.

[16] For more reading, see Edward L. Grubb and Harrison L. Grathwohl, "Consumer Self-Concept, Symbolism, and Market Behavior: A Theoretical Approach," *Journal of Marketing*, October 1967, pp. 22–27; Ira J. Dolich, "Congruence Relationships between Self-Images and Product Brands, *Journal of Marketing Research*, February 1969, pp. 40–47; and E. Laird Landon, Jr. "The Differential Role of Self-Concept and Ideal Self-Concept in Consumer Purchase Behavior," *Journal of Consumer Research*, September 1974, pp. 44–51.

need for recognition, esteem, or belonging. Most of these needs will not be intense enough to motivate the person to act at a given time. A need becomes a motive when it is aroused to a sufficient level of intensity. A *motive* (or drive) is a need that is sufficiently pressing to direct the person to seek satisfaction of the need. Satisfying the need reduces the felt tension.

Psychologists have developed theories of human motivation. Three of the most popular—the theories of Sigmund Freud, Abraham Maslow, and Frederick Herzberg—carry quite different implications for consumer analysis and marketing.

Freud's theory of motivation.   Freud assumes that the real psychological forces shaping people's behavior are largely unconscious. Freud sees the person as repressing many urges in the process of growing up and accepting social rules. These urges are never eliminated or perfectly controlled; they emerge in dreams, in slips of the tongue, or in neurotic behavior.

Thus, according to Freud, a person does not fully understand his or her motivational mainsprings. If Larry Brown wants to purchase a personal computer, he may describe his motive as wanting a hobby or furthering his career. At a deeper level, he may be purchasing a computer to impress others. At a still deeper level, he may be buying the computer because it helps him feel modern and young and potent.

When Larry looks at a particular computer brand, he will react not only to its alleged capabilities but also to other cues. The computer's shape, size, weight, material, color, and case can all trigger certain emotions. A rugged-looking computer can feed into Larry's feelings about being a macho male. The manufacturer, in designing the computer, should be aware of the impact of visual, auditory, and tactile elements in triggering consumer emotions that can stimulate or inhibit purchase.

The leading modern exponent of Freudian motivation theory in marketing is Ernest Dichter, who for over three decades has been interpreting buying situations and product choices in terms of underlying unconscious motives. Dichter calls his approach *motivational research*, and it consists of collecting "in-depth interviews" with a few dozen consumers to uncover their deeper motives triggered by the product. He uses various "projective techniques" to throw the ego off guard—techniques such as word association, sentence completion, picture interpretation, and role playing.[17]

Motivation researchers have produced some interesting and occasionally bizarre hypotheses as to what may be in the buyer's mind regarding certain purchases. They have suggested that

☐ Consumers resist prunes because they are wrinkled looking and remind people of old age.
☐ Men smoke cigars as an adult version of thumb sucking. They like their cigars to have a strong odor in order to prove their masculinity.
☐ Women prefer vegetable shortening to animal fats because the latter arouse a sense of guilt over killing animals.
☐ A woman is very serious when baking a cake because unconsciously she is going through the symbolic act of giving birth. She dislikes easy-to-use cake mixes because the easy life evokes a sense of guilt.

---

[17] See Ernest Dichter, *Handbook of Consumer Motivations* (New York: McGraw-Hill, 1964).

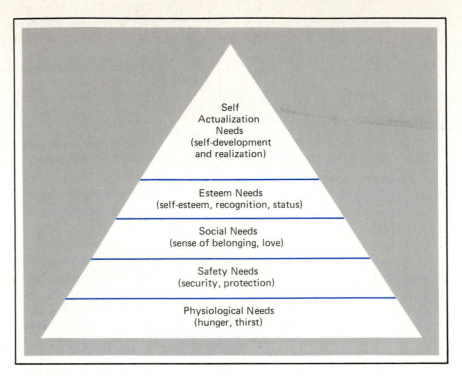

FIGURE 4–3
Maslow's Hierarchy of Needs

Maslow's theory of motivation.   Abraham Maslow sought to explain why people are driven by particular needs at particular times.[18] Why does one person spend considerable time and energy on personal safety and another on pursuing the esteem of others? His answer is that human needs are arranged in a hierarchy, from the most pressing to the least pressing. Maslow's hierarchy of needs is shown in Figure 4–3. In their order of importance, they are *physiological* needs, *safety* needs, *social* needs, *esteem* needs, and *self-actualization* needs. A person will try to satisfy the most important needs first. When a person succeeds in satisfying an important need, it will cease being a motivator for the present time, and the person will be motivated to satisfy the next-most-important need.

For example, a starving man (need 1) will not take an interest in the latest happenings in the art world (need 5), nor in how he is seen or esteemed by others (need 3 or 4), nor even in whether he is breathing clean air (need 2). But as each important need is satisfied, the next-most-important need will come into play.

What light does Maslow's theory throw on Larry Brown's interest in buying a computer? We can guess that Larry has satisfied his physiological, safety, and social needs; they do not motivate his interest in computers. His computer interest

---

[18] Abraham H. Maslow, *Motivation and Personality* (New York: Harper & Row, 1954, pp. 80–106.

might come from a strong need for more esteem from others or from a higher need for self-actualization. He wants to actualize his potential as a creative person through learning to master the computer.

Herzberg's theory of motivation.   Frederick Herzberg developed a "two-factor theory" of motivation, which distinguishes between dissatisfiers (factors that cause dissatisfaction) and satisfiers (factors that cause satisfaction).[19] For example, if the Apple computer did not come with a warranty, that would be a dissatisfier. Larry would like a product warranty. At the same time, the presence of a product warranty would not act as a satisfier or motivator of his purchase, since it is not a source of intrinsic satisfaction with the Apple computer. The Apple computer's fine-color graphics would be a satisfier and enhance Larry's enjoyment of the computer.

This theory of motivation has two implications. First, sellers should do their best to prevent dissatisfiers from affecting the buyer. These dissatisfiers might be a poor training manual or a poor service policy. While these things will not sell the computer, they might easily unsell the computer. Second, the manufacturer should carefully identify the major satisfiers or motivators of purchase in the computer market and be sure to include them. These factors will make the major difference as to which computer brand the customer buys.

Perception.   A motivated person is ready to act. How the motivated person acts is influenced by his or her perception of the situation. Two people in the same motivated state and objective situation may act quite differently because they perceive the situation differently. Larry Brown might see a fast-talking computer salesperson as aggressive and insincere. Another shopper might see the same salesperson as intelligent and helpful.

Why do people have different perceptions of the same situation? We start with the notion that all of us apprehend a stimulus object through *sensations*, that is, flows of information through our five senses: sight, hearing, smell, touch, and taste. However, each of us attends, organizes, and interprets this sensory information in an individual way. *Perception* can be defined as "the process by which an individual selects, organizes, and interprets information inputs to create a meaningful picture of the world."[20] Perception depends not only on the character of the physical stimuli but also on the relation of the stimuli to the surrounding field (the Gestalt idea) and on conditions within the individual.

People can emerge with different perceptions of the same stimulus object because of three perceptual processes: selective exposure, selective distortion, and selective retention.

---

[19] See Frederick Herzberg, *Work and the Nature of Man* (Cleveland: William Collins Publishers, 1966); and Robert J. House and L. Widgor, "Herzberg's Dual-Factor Theory of Job Satisfaction and Motivation: A Review of the Empirical Evidence and a Criticism," *Personnel Psychology* 20 (1967): pp. 369–80.

[20] Bernard Berelson and Gary A. Steiner, *Human Behavior: An Inventory of Scientific Findings* (New York: Harcourt Brace Jovanovich, 1964), p. 88.

Selective exposure. People are exposed to a tremendous amount of stimuli every day of their lives. Looking at commercial stimuli alone, the average person may be exposed to over fifteen hundred ads a day. It is impossible for a person to attend to all of these stimuli. Most of the stimuli will be screened out. The real challenge is to explain which stimuli people will notice. Here are some findings:

☐ *People are more likely to notice stimuli that relate to a current need.* Larry Brown will notice all kinds of ads for computers because he is motivated to buy one; he will probably not notice ads for stereophonic equipment.
☐ *People are more likely to notice stimuli that they anticipate.* Larry Brown is more likely to notice computers in a computer store than a line of radios also carried by the store because he did not expect the store to carry radios.
☐ *People are more likely to notice stimuli whose deviations are large in relation to the normal size of the stimuli.* Larry Brown is more likely to notice an ad offering $100 off the list price of an Apple computer than one offering $5 off the list price.

Selective exposure means that marketers have to work especially hard to attract the consumer's attention. Their messages will be lost on most people who are not in the market for the product. Even people who are in the market may not notice the message unless it stands out from the surrounding sea of stimuli. Ads that are larger in size, or that use four colors where most ads are black and white, or are novel and provide contrast are more likely to be noticed.

Selective distortion. Even stimuli that consumers notice do not necessarily come across in the intended way. Each person attempts to fit incoming information into his or her existing mind-set. Selective distortion describes the tendency of people to twist information into personal meanings. Thus Larry Brown may hear the salesperson mention some good and bad points about a competing computer brand. If Larry has a strong leaning toward IBM, he is likely to distort the points in order to conclude that IBM is the better computer. People tend to interpret information in a way that will support rather than challenge their preconceptions.

Selective retention. People will forget much that they learn. They will tend to retain information that supports their attitudes and beliefs. Because of selective retention, Larry is likely to remember good points mentioned about the IBM and forget good points mentioned about competing computers. He remembers IBM's good points because he "rehearses" them more whenever he thinks about choosing a computer.

These three perceptual factors—selective exposure, distortion, and retention—mean that marketers have to work hard to get their messages through. That explains why marketers use so much drama and so much repetition in sending messages to their market.

Learning. When people act, they learn. *Learning* describes changes in an individual's behavior arising from experience. Most human behavior is learned.

Learning theorists say that a person's learning is produced through the interplay of *drives*, *stimuli*, *cues*, *responses*, and *reinforcement*.

We saw that Larry Brown has a drive toward self-actualization. A *drive* is defined as a strong internal stimulus impelling action. His drive becomes a *motive* when it is directed toward a particular drive-reducing *stimulus object*, in this case a computer. Larry's response to the idea of buying a computer is conditioned by the surrounding cues. Cues are minor stimuli that determine when, where, and how the person responds. His wife's encouragement of his interest, seeing a computer in a friend's home, seeing computer ads and articles, hearing about a special sales price are all cues that can influence Larry's *response* to the impulse to buy a computer.

Suppose Larry buys a computer and chooses an IBM. If his experience is *rewarding*, he will use the computer more and more. His response to computers will be reinforced.

Later on, Larry may want to buy a typewriter. He notices several brands, including one by IBM. Since he knows that IBM makes good computers, he infers that IBM also makes good typewriters. We say that he *generalizes* his response to similar stimuli.

A countertendency to generalization is *discrimination*. When Larry examines a typewriter made by Olivetti, he sees that it is lighter and more compact than IBM's typewriter. Discrimination means he has learned to recognize differences in sets of similar stimuli and can adjust his responses accordingly.

The practical importance of learning theory for marketers is that they can build up demand for a product by associating it with strong drives, using motivating cues, and providing positive reinforcement. A new company can enter the market by appealing to the same drives that competitors appeal to and providing similar cue configurations because buyers are more likely to transfer loyalty to similar brands than to dissimilar brands (generalization). Or it may design its brand to appeal to a different set of drives and offer strong cue inducements to switch (discrimination).

Beliefs and attitudes.   Through acting and learning, people acquire their beliefs and attitudes. These in turn influence their buying behavior.

A *belief* is a *descriptive thought that a person holds about something*. Larry Brown may believe that an IBM personal computer has a larger memory, stands up well under rugged usage, and costs $4,000. These beliefs may be based on knowledge, opinion, or faith. They may or may not carry an emotional charge. For example, Larry Brown's belief that an IBM personal computer is heavier than an Osborne may not matter to his decision.

Manufacturers, of course, are very interested in the beliefs that people carry in their heads about their products and services. These beliefs make up product and brand images, and people act on their beliefs. If some of the beliefs are wrong and inhibit purchase, the manufacturer will want to launch a campaign to correct these beliefs.

An *attitude* describes a person's *enduring favorable or unfavorable cognitive evaluations, emotional feelings, and action tendencies toward some object or idea*.[21] People have attitudes toward almost everything: religion, politics, clothes, music,

---

[21] See David Krech, Richard S. Crutchfield, and Egerton L. Ballachey, *Individual in Society* (New York: McGraw-Hill Book Co., 1962), chap. 2.

food, and so on. Attitudes put them into a frame of mind of liking or disliking an object, moving toward or away from it. Thus Larry Brown may hold such attitudes as "Buy the best," "IBM makes the best computers in the world," and "Creativity and self-expression are among the most important things in life." The IBM computer is therefore salient to Larry because it fits well into his preexisting attitudes. A computer company can benefit greatly from researching the various attitudes people have toward the product and their brand.

Attitudes lead people to behave in a fairly consistent way toward similar objects. People do not have to interpret and react to every object in a fresh way. Attitudes economize on energy and thought. For this reason, attitudes are very difficult to change. A person's attitudes settle into a consistent pattern, and to change one attitude may require major adjustments in other attitudes.

Thus a company would be well advised to fit its product into existing attitudes, rather than to try to change people's attitudes. There are exceptions, of course, where the great cost of trying to change attitudes might pay off.

> Honda entered the U.S. motorcycle market facing a major decision. It could either sell its motorcycles to a small number of people already interested in motorcycles or try to increase the number interested in motorcycles. The latter would be more expensive because many people had negative attitudes toward motorcycles. They associated motorcycles with black leather jackets, switchblades, and crime. Honda took the second course and launched a major campaign based on the theme "You meet the nicest people on a Honda." Its campaign worked and many people adopted a new attitude toward motorcycles.

We can now appreciate the many forces acting on consumer behavior. A person's choice is the result of the complex interplay of cultural, social, personal, and psychological factors. Many of these factors cannot be influenced by the marketer. They are useful, however, in identifying the buyers who might have the most interest in the product. Other factors are subject to marketer influence and clue the marketer on how to develop product, price, place, and promotion to attract strong consumer response.

THE BUYING DECISION PROCESS

Marketers have to go beyond the various influences on buyers and develop an understanding of how consumers actually make their buying decisions. Marketers must identify who makes the buying decision, the type of buying decision that is involved, and the steps in the buying process.

Buying Roles

For many products, it is fairly easy to identify the buyer. Men normally choose their tobacco, and women choose their pantyhose. On the other hand, other products involve a *decision-making unit* consisting of more than one person. Consider the selection of a family automobile. The suggestion to buy a new car might come from the oldest child. A friend might advise the family on the kind of car to buy. The husband might choose the make. The wife might have definite desires regarding the car's looks. The husband might make the final decision with the wife approving. The wife might end up using the car more than the husband does.

Thus we can distinguish several roles people might play in a buying decision:

☐ **Initiator.** The initiator is the person who first suggests or thinks of the idea of buying the particular product or service.

☐ **Influencer.** An influencer is a person whose views or advice carries some weight in making the final decision.

☐ **Decider.** The decider is a person who ultimately determines any part of, or the entire, buying decision: whether to buy, what to buy, how to buy, or where to buy.

☐ **Buyer.** The buyer is the person who makes the actual purchase.

☐ **User.** The user is the person(s) who consumes or uses the product or service.

A company needs to identify these roles because they have implications for designing the product, determining messages, and allocating the promotional budget. If the husband decides on the car make, then the auto company will direct most of the advertising to reach husbands. The auto company might design certain car features to please the wife and place some ads in media reaching wives. Knowing the main participants and the roles they play helps the marketer fine tune the marketing program.

Types of Buying Behavior

Consumer decision making varies with the type of buying decision. There are great differences between buying a toothpaste, a tennis racket, a personal computer, and a new car. The more complex and expensive decisions are likely to involve more buyer deliberation and more buying participants. Assael distinguished four types of consumer buying behavior based on the degree of buyer involvement in the purchase and the degree of differences among brands.[22] The four types are named in Table 4–3 and described below.

Complex buying behavior. Consumers go through complex buying behavior when they are highly involved in a purchase and aware of significant differences existing among brands. Consumers are highly involved in a purchase when it is expensive, bought infrequently, risky, and highly expressive. Typically the consumer does not know much about the product category and has much to learn. For example, a person buying a personal computer may not even know what attributes to look for. Many of the product features carry no meaning: "16K memory," "disc storage," "screen resolution," "BASIC language," and so on.

---

[22] See Henry Assael, *Consumer Behavior and Marketing Action* (Boston, Mass.: Kent Publishing Co., 1981), chap. 4 for a full discussion and documentation of these four types of consumer buying behavior. An earlier classification of three types of consumer buying behavior—extensive problem solving, limited problem solving, and routinized response behavior—is found in John A. Howard and Jagdish N. Sheth, *The Theory of Buyer Behavior* (New York: John Wiley & Sons, 1969), pp. 27–28.

TABLE 4-3

FOUR TYPES OF BUYING BEHAVIOR		
	High Involvement	**Low Involvement**
Significant Differences between Brands	Complex buying behavior	Variety-seeking buying behavior
Few Differences between Brands	Dissonance-reducing buying behavior	Habitual buying behavior

SOURCE: Modified from Henry Assael, *Consumer Behavior and Marketing Action* (Boston: Kent-Publishing Co., 1981, p. 80). Copyright © 1981 by Wadsworth, Inc. Printed by permission of Kent Publishing Co, a division of Wadsworth, Inc.

This buyer will pass through a cognitive learning process characterized by first developing beliefs about the product, then moving toward attitudes, toward the product, and finally making a deliberate purchase choice. The marketer of a high-involvement product must understand the information-gathering and evaluation behavior of high-involvement consumers. The marketer needs to develop strategies to assist the buyer in learning about the attributes of the product class, their relative importance, and the high standing of his brand on the more important attributes. The marketer needs to differentiate the features of his brand, use mainly print media and long copy to describe the brand's benefits, and enlist store sales personnel and the buyer's friends to influence the final brand choice.

Dissonance-reducing buying behavior. Sometimes the consumer is highly involved in a purchase but sees little differences in the brands. The high involvement again is based on the fact that the purchase is expensive, infrequent, and risky. In this case, the buyer will shop around to learn what is available but will buy fairly quickly because brand differences are not pronounced. The buyer may respond primarily to a good price or the convenience of purchasing at that time or place. An example might be in shopping for carpeting. Carpet buying is an involving decision because it is expensive and relates to self-identification; yet the buyer is likely to consider most carpeting in a given price range to be the same.

After the purchase, the consumer might experience postpurchase dissonance because of noticing certain disquieting features of the carpet or hearing favorable things about other carpets. The consumer starts learning more things and seeks to justify his or her decision to reduce the dissonance. Thus the consumer first passed through a state of behavior, then acquired some new beliefs, and ended up by evaluating his choice favorably. The implications for the marketer in this situation are that pricing, good location, and effective sales personnel are important influences of brand choice, and the major role of marketing communications is to supply beliefs and evaluations that help the consumer feel good about his or her choice after the purchase.

Habitual buying behavior. Many products are bought under conditions of low consumer involvement and the absence of significant brand differences. A good example is the purchase of salt. Consumers have little involvement in this product category. They go to the store and reach for the brand. If they keep reaching for the same brand, say, Morton salt, it is out of habit, not strong brand loyalty. There is good evidence that consumers have low involvement with most low cost, frequently purchased products.

Consumer behavior in these cases does not pass through the normal belief/attitude/behavior sequence. Consumers do not search extensively for information about the brands, evaluate their characteristics, and make a weighty decision on which one to buy. Instead, they are passive recipients of information as they watch television or see a print ad. Ad repetition creates brand familiarity rather than brand conviction. Consumers don't really form an attitude toward a brand but select it simply because it is familiar. After purchase, they may not even evaluate it because they are not involved with the product. So the buying process is, brand beliefs formed by passive learning, followed by purchase behavior, which may or may not be followed by evaluation.

Marketers of low-involvement products with few brand differences find it effective to use price and sales promotions as an incentive to product trial, since buyers are not highly committed to any brand. In advertising a low-involvement product, a number of things should be observed. The ad copy should stress only a few key points. Visual symbols and imagery are important because they can be easily remembered and associated with the brand. The ad campaigns should go for high repetition with short-duration messages. Television is more effective than print media because it is a low-involvement medium that is suitable for passive learning.[23] The advertising planning should be based on classical conditioning theory where the buyer comes to identify a certain product by a symbol that is repeatedly attached to it.

Marketers can also try to convert the low-involvement product into one of higher involvement. This can be accomplished by linking the product to some involving issue, as when Crest toothpaste is linked to keeping one's teeth healthy. Or the product can be linked to some involving personal situation, for instance, by advertising a coffee brand in the early morning when the consumer is looking for something to shake off sleepiness. Or the consumer can be drawn in by advertising that triggers strong emotions related to personal values or ego defense. Or an important feature might be added to an unimportant product, for instance, fortifying a plain, tasty drink with vitamins. It should be appreciated that these strategies at best raise consumer involvement from a low to a moderate level; in no way do they propel the consumer into complex buying behavior.

Variety-seeking buying behavior. Some buying situations are characterized by low consumer involvement but significant brand differences. Here consumers are often observed to do a lot of brand switching. An example occurs in purchasing cookies. The consumer has some beliefs, chooses a brand of cookies without much evaluation,

---

[23] Herbert E. Krugman, "The Impact of Television Advertising: Learning without Involvement," *Public Opinion Quarterly*, Fall 1965, pp. 349–56.

and evaluates it during consumption. But next time, the consumer may reach for another brand out of boredom or a wish to experiment. Brand switching occurs for the sake of variety rather than dissatisfaction.

The marketing strategy is different for the market leader in this product category and the minor brands. The market leader will try to encourage habit buying behavior by dominating the shelf space, avoiding out-of-stock conditions, and sponsoring frequent reminder advertising. Challenger firms, on the other hand, will encourage variety seeking by offering lower prices, deals, coupons, free samples, and advertising that features reasons for trying something new.

Researching the Buying Decision Process

Companies will want to research the buying decision process involved in their product category. Consumers can be asked when they first became acquainted with the product category, what their brand beliefs are, how involved they are with the product, how they make their brand choices, and how they rate their satisfaction after purchase.

Different consumers, of course, will vary in the way they buy a given product. In buying a personal computer, for example, some consumers will spend a great deal of time seeking information and making comparisons; others will go straight to a computer store, look at the brands, point to one, negotiate a price, and sign a contract. Thus consumers can be segmented in terms of *buying styles*—for instance, deliberate buyers versus impulsive buyers—and different marketing strategies directed at each segment.

How can marketers identify the typical stages in the buying process for any given product? They can introspect about their own probable behavior, although this is of limited usefulness (*introspective method*). They can interview a small number of recent purchasers, asking them to recall the events leading to the purchase of the product (*retrospective method*). They can find some consumers who are contemplating buying the product and ask them to think out loud about how they would go through the buying process (*prospective method*). Or they can ask a group of consumers to describe the ideal way for people to go about buying the product (*prescriptive method*). Each method results in a consumer-generated report of the steps in the buying process.

A report by a consumer who bought a computer is shown in Table 4–4. The buyer is a married male, who first got interested when his neighbor purchased a computer. He then developed a reason for possibly purchasing one. A few days later, he saw an ad for an Apple computer. Two weeks later he dropped into a computer store just to browse. He liked the salesman, found that he could afford a computer, and purchased one. The computer did not satisfy him completely, and an ad for a competitive brand made him feel a little ambivalent. He was annoyed a few days later when his salesman did not seem very cooperative in answering some questions. The marketing analyst should collect reports from other consumers and attempt to identify one or more typical buying processes for that product.[24]

---

[24] See James R. Bettman, "The Structure of Consumer Choice Processes," *Journal of Marketing Research*, November 1971, pp. 465–71.

TABLE 4–4

REPORT OF A PARTICULAR CONSUMER'S INVOLVEMENT IN BUYING A COMPUTER

3/17 My neighbor just bought a computer. He says he finds it challenging. It would be nice to have a computer; I could keep my financial records on it.

3/19 Here's an ad for an Apple computer showing several applications that I would find interesting.

4/2 I don't have any plans this evening. I'll go over to Computerland and learn something about these computers.
Here comes a salesman.
He's very helpful. I'm pleased that he is not pressuring me to buy one.
I don't think I can afford a computer.
How much would it cost a month to finance?
I can afford it.
My wife also wants me to buy one. I'm impressed with the Apple. I'll buy it and take it home.

4/5 I didn't realize how much time it takes to master.
I wish the screen had eighty columns instead of forty.

4/6 Here's the new IBM advertised. It looks like it has some neat features.

4/8 My other neighbor wants to buy a computer. I told him the good and bad points about the Apple.

4/11 I phoned the computer salesman for some information about a sticky key. He wasn't helpful. He told me to call the service department.

Stages in the Buying Decision Process

Based on the examination of many consumer reports on the buying process, "stage models" of the buying process have been conceptualized by consumer-behavior researchers. Stage models are mostly relevant to complex decision making, i.e., buying expensive, high-involvement products. We will use the model shown in Figure 4–4, which shows the consumer as passing through five stages: *problem recognition*, *information search*, *evaluation of alternatives*, *purchase decision*, and *postpurchase behavior*. This model emphasizes that the buying process starts long before the actual purchase and has consequences long after the purchase. It encourages the marketer to focus on the buying process rather than on the purchase decision.[25]

This model implies that consumers pass through all five stages in buying something. We saw this is not the case, especially in low-involvement purchases. Consumers may skip or reverse some of these stages. Thus a woman buying her regular brand of toothpaste would go right from the need for toothpaste to the purchase decision, skipping information search and evaluation. However, we will use the model in Figure 4–4 because it shows the full range of considerations that come up when a consumer faces a highly involving new purchase.

To illustrate this model, we will allude once again to Larry Brown and try to

---

[25] Several models of the consumer buying process have been developed by marketing scholars. The most prominent models are those of John A. Howard and Jagdish N. Sheth, *The Theory of Buyer Behavior* (New York: John Wiley, 1969); Francesco M. Nicosia, *Consumer Decision Processes* (Englewood Cliffs, N.J.: Prentice-Hall, 1966); and James F. Engel, Roger D. Blackwell, and David T. Kollat, *Consumer Behavior*, 3rd ed. (New York: Holt, Rinehart & Winston, 1978).

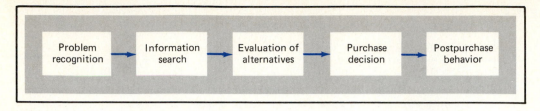

FIGURE 4-4
Five-Stage Model of the Buying Process

understand how he became interested in buying a personal computer and the stages he went through to make the final choice.

Problem recognition.   The buying process starts with the buyer's recognizing a problem or need. The buyer senses a difference between his or her actual state and a desired state. The need can be triggered by internal or external stimuli. In the former case, one of the person's normal needs—hunger, thirst, sex—rises to a threshold level and becomes a drive. From previous experience, the person has learned how to cope with this drive and is motivated toward a class of objects that he or she knows will satisfy the drive.

Or a need can be aroused by an external stimulus. Larry Brown passes a bakery, and the sight of freshly baked bread stimulates his hunger; he admires a neighbor's new car; or he watches a television commercial for a Jamaican vacation. All of these stimuli can lead him to recognize a problem or need.

The marketer needs to identify the circumstances that trigger the particular need or interest in consumers. The marketer should research consumers to find out *what kinds of felt needs or problems arose, what brought them about*, and *how they led to this particular product*.

Larry Brown might answer that he felt a need for a new hobby; this happened when his "busy season" at work tapered off; and he was led to think of computers as a result of a co-worker's buying one. By gathering information from a number of consumers, the marketer can identify the more frequent stimuli that give rise to interest in the product category. The marketer can then develop marketing strategies that trigger consumer interest.

Information search.   An aroused consumer may or may not search for more information. If the consumer's drive is strong, and an affordable gratification object is at hand, the consumer is likely to buy the object then. If not, the consumer's need may simply be stored in memory. The consumer may undertake no further search, some further search, or a very active search for information bearing on the need.

Assuming that the consumer undertakes some search, we distinguish between two levels. The milder search state is called *heightened attention*. Here Larry Brown simply becomes more receptive to information about computers. He pays attention to computer ads, computers purchased by friends, and conversation about computers.

Or Larry may go into *active information search*, where he looks for reading material, phones friends, and engages in other search activities to gather product information. How much search he undertakes depends upon the strength of his drive, the amount of information he initially has, the ease of obtaining additional information, the value he places on additional information, and the satisfaction he gets from search. Normally the amount of consumer search activity increases as the consumer moves from decision situations of limited problem solving to extensive problem solving.

Of key interest to the marketer are the major information sources that the consumer will turn to and the relative influence each will have on the subsequent purchase decision. *Consumer information sources* fall into four groups:

☐ **Personal sources** (family, friends, neighbors, acquaintances)
☐ **Commercial sources** (advertising, salespersons, dealers, packaging, displays)
☐ **Public sources** (mass media, consumer rating organizations)
☐ **Experiential sources** (handling, examining, using the product)

The relative influence of these information sources varies with the product category and the buyer's characteristics. Generally speaking, the consumer receives the most information exposure about a product from commercial sources, that is, marketer-dominated sources. On the other hand, the most effective exposures tend to come from personal sources. Each type of source may perform a somewhat different function in influencing the buying decision. Commercial information normally performs an *informing* function, and personal sources perform a *legitimizing* and/or *evaluation* function. For example, physicians often learn of new drugs from commercial sources but turn to other doctors for evaluation information.

As a result of gathering information, the consumer becomes acquainted with some of the brands in the market and their features. The box at the far left of Figure 4–5 shows the *total set* of brands available to the consumer. Larry Brown will become acquainted with only a subset of these brands, which we will call the *awareness set.* Only some of these brands will meet Larry's initial buying criteria and make up the *consideration set.* As Larry gathers more information about these brands, only a few will remain as strong choices and make up the *choice set.* He makes his final decision from the choice set, based on the decision evaluation process he uses.[26]

The practical implication is that a company must design its marketing mix to get its brand into the prospect's awareness set, consideration set, and choice set. If its brand fails to get into these sets, the company has lost its opportunity to sell to the customer. The company must go further and learn which other brands remain in the consumer's choice set, so that it knows its competition and can plan its appeals.

As for the sources of the information used by the consumer, the marketer should identify them carefully and evaluate their respective importance as sources of information. Consumers should be asked how they first heard about the brand, what information came in subsequently, and the relative importance of the different

---

[26] Originally, Howard and Sheth suggested the term *evoked set* to describe the set of alternatives that the buyer considers. (See Howard and Sheth, *Theory of Buyer Behavior*, p. 26). We believe that the set of brands of interest to the consumer keeps changing as information comes in, and it is more useful to distinguish different sets as he or she goes through the buying decision process. See Chem L. Narayana and Rom J. Markin, "Consumer Behavior and Product Performance: An Alternative Conceptualization," *Journal of Marketing*, October 1975, pp. 1–6.

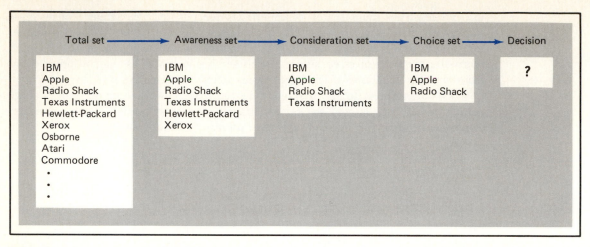

FIGURE 4–5
Successive Sets Involved in Consumer Decision Making

information sources. The marketer will find this information critical in preparing effective communication for the target market.

Evaluation of alternatives.   We have seen how the consumer uses information to arrive at a set of final brand choices. The question is, How does the consumer choose among the alternative brands in the choice set? The marketer needs to know how the consumer processes information to arrive at brand choices. Unfortunately, there is no simple and single evaluation process used by all consumers or even by one consumer in all buying situations. There are several decision evaluation processes. Most current models of the consumer evaluation process are *cognitively oriented*— that is, they see the consumer as forming product judgments largely on a conscious and rational basis.

   Certain basic concepts help throw light on consumer evaluation processes. The first concept is that of *product attributes*. We assume that each consumer sees a given product as a bundle of attributes. The attributes of interest to buyers in some familiar product classes are:

- ☐ **Computers:** memory capacity, graphics capability, software availability
- ☐ **Cameras:** picture sharpness, camera speeds, camera size, price
- ☐ **Hotels:** location, cleanliness, atmosphere, cost
- ☐ **Mouthwash:** color, effectiveness, germ-killing capacity, price, taste/flavor
- ☐ **Brassieres:** comfort, fit, life, price, style
- ☐ **Lipstick:** color, container, creaminess, prestige factor, taste/flavor
- ☐ **Tires:** safety, tread life, ride quality, price

While the above attributes are of normal interest, consumers will vary as to which they consider relevant. Consumers will pay the most attention to those attributes that are connected with their needs. The market for a product can often be segmented according to the attributes that have primary interest to different customer groups.

Second, the consumer is likely to attach different *importance weights* to the relevant attributes. A distinction can be drawn between the importance of an attribute and its salience.[27] Salient attributes are those that come to the consumer's mind when he or she is asked to think of a product's attributes. The marketer must not conclude that these are necessarily the most important attributes. Some of them may be salient because the consumer has just been exposed to a commercial message mentioning them or has had a problem involving them, hence making these attributes "top-of-the-mind." Furthermore, in the class of nonsalient attributes may be some that the consumer forgot but whose importance would be recognized when they were mentioned. Marketers should be more concerned with attribute importance than attribute salience.

Third, the consumer is likely to develop a set of *brand beliefs* about where each brand stands on each attribute. The set of beliefs held about a particular brand is known as the *brand image*. The consumer's beliefs may be at variance with the true attributes owing to his or her particular experience and the effect of selective perception, selective distortion, and selective retention.

Fourth, the consumer is assumed to have a *utility function* for each attribute.[28] The utility function describes how the consumer expects product satisfaction to vary with alternative levels of each attribute. For example, Larry Brown may expect his satisfaction from a computer to increase with its memory capacity, graphics capability, and software availability; and to decrease with its price. If we combine the attribute levels where the utilities are highest, they make up Larry's ideal computer. The expected utility from actual computers in the marketplace will vary below the maximum utility that would be derived from an ideal computer.

Fifth, the consumer arrives at attitudes (judgments, preferences) toward the brand alternatives through some *evaluation procedure*. Consumers have been found to apply different evaluation procedures to make a choice among multiattribute objects.[29]

We will illustrate these concepts in connection with Larry Brown's buying a computer. Suppose Larry Brown has narrowed his choice set to four computers (A, B, C, D). Assume that he is primarily interested in four attributes: memory capacity, graphics capability, software availability, and price. Table 4–5 shows his beliefs about how each brand rates on the four attributes. Larry rates brand A as follows: memory capacity, 10 on a 10-point scale; graphics capability, 8; software availability, 6; and price, 4 (somewhat expensive). Similarly, he has beliefs about how the other three computers rate on these attributes. The marketer would like to be able to predict which computer Larry will buy.

Clearly, if one computer dominated the others on all the criteria, we could predict that Larry would choose it. But his choice set consists of brands that vary

---

[27] James H. Myers and Mark L. Alpert, "Semantic Confusion in Attitude Research: Salience vs. Importance vs. Determinance," in *Advances in Consumer Research* (*Proceedings of the Seventh Annual Conference of the Association of Consumer Research*, October 1976, IV, pp. 106–10.

[28] Some progress has been made in attempting to measure individual and market utility functions. See Exhibit 10–2, pp. 326–30.

[29] See Paul E. Green and Yoram Wind, *Multiattribute Decisions in Marketing: A Measurement Approach* (Hinsdale, Ill.: Dryden Press, 1973), chap. 2.

TABLE 4–5

A CONSUMER'S BRAND BELIEFS ABOUT COMPUTERS				
Computer		**Attribute**		
	Memory Capacity	**Graphics Capability**	**Software Availability**	**Price**
A	10	8	6	4
B	8	9	8	3
C	6	8	10	5
D	4	3	7	8

Note: Each attribute is rated from 0 to 10, where 10 represents the highest level on that attribute. Thus computer A has the highest memory capacity. The consumer is assumed to normally want more of each attribute. Price is indexed, however, in a reverse manner, with a 10 representing the lowest price since a consumer prefers a low price to a high price.

in their appeal. If Larry wants memory capacity above everything, he should buy A; if he wants the best graphics capability, he should buy B; if he wants the best software availability, he should buy C; if he wants the lowest-price computer, he should buy D. Some buyers will buy on only one attribute, and we can easily predict their choice.

Most buyers will consider several attributes but place different weights on them. If we knew the importance weights that Larry Brown assigned to the four attributes, we could predict more reliably his computer choice.

Suppose Larry assigned 40 percent of the importance to the computer's memory capacity, 30 percent to its graphics capability, 20 percent to its software availability, and 10 percent to its price. To find Larry's perceived value for each computer, his weights are multiplied by his beliefs about each computer. This leads to the following perceived values:

$$\text{Computer A} = 0.4(10) + 0.3(8) + 0.2(6) + 0.1(4) = 8.0$$
$$\text{Computer B} = 0.4(8) + 0.3(9) + 0.2(8) + 0.1(3) = 7.8$$
$$\text{Computer C} = 0.4(6) + 0.3(8) + 0.2(10) + 0.1(5) = 7.3$$
$$\text{Computer D} = 0.4(4) + 0.3(3) + 0.2(7) + 0.1(8) = 4.7$$

We would predict that Larry, given his weights, will favor computer A.

This model is called the *expectancy value model* of consumer choice.[30] It is one of several possible models describing how consumers go about evaluating alternatives. (See Exhibit 4–3) As noted earlier, marketers should interview computer buyers to find out how they actually evaluate brand alternatives.

---

[30] This model was developed by Martin Fishbein in "Attitudes and Prediction of Behavior," in *Readings in Attitude Theory and Measurement*, ed. Martin Fishbein (New York: John Wiley, 1967), pp. 477–92. For a critical review of this model, see William L. Wilkie and Edgar A. Pessemier, "Issues in Marketing's Use of Multi-Attribute Attitude Models," *Journal of Marketing Research*, November 1973, pp. 428–41.

Exhibit 4–3

The text described the *expectancy-value model* of how consumers might evaluate alternatives. It can be stated more formally as follows:

$$A_{jk} = \sum_{i=1}^{n} W_{ik} B_{ijk} \qquad (4\text{--}1)$$

where: A_{jk} = consumer k's attitude score for brand j
W_{ik} = the importance weight assigned by consumer k to attribute i
B_{ijk} = consumer k's belief as to the amount of attribute i offered by brand j
n = the number of important attributes in the selection of a given brand

Essentially, a consumer's beliefs about a brand's attributes are multiplied by the respective-importance weights and summed to derive an attitude score. Here are some other models.

Ideal-brand model. This model says that the consumer holds an image of the ideal brand and compares actual brands to this ideal. The closer an actual brand comes to this ideal, the more it will be preferred.

Suppose Larry Brown does not value memory capacity beyond a certain point because he has no use for it, and it adds to cost. And suppose he has a certain price in mind as ideal. Suppose his ideal levels of the four attributes are not (10, 10, 10, 10) as in the expectancy value model but (6, 10, 10, 5). We would calculate how dissatisfied he would be with each brand according to the formula:

$$D_{jk} = \sum_{i=1}^{n} W_{ik} |B_{ijk} - I_{ik}| \qquad (4\text{--}2)$$

where D_{jk} is consumer k's *dissatisfaction* with brand j, and I_{ik} is consumer k's *ideal level* of attribute i. Other terms remain the same. The lower the D, the more favorable consumer k's attitude toward brand j. For example, if there were a brand whose attributes were all at the ideal levels, the term $|B_{ijk} - I_{jk}|$ would disappear, and the dissatisfaction would be zero. Here is Larry Brown's dissatisfaction score with each brand:

Computer A = 0.4 | 10 − 6 | + 0.3 | 8 − 10 | + 0.2 | 6 − 10 | + 0.1 | 4 − 5 | = 3.1
Computer B = 0.4 | 8 − 6 | + 0.3 | 9 − 10 | + 0.2 | 8 − 10 | + 0.1 | 3 − 5 | = 1.7
Computer C = 0.4 | 6 − 6 | + 0.3 | 8 − 10 | + 0.2 | 10 − 10 | + 0.1 | 5 − 5 | = 0.6
Computer D = 0.4 | 4 − 6 | + 0.3 | 3 − 10 | + 0.2 | 7 − 10 | + 0.1 | 8 − 5 | = 3.8

In this case, Larry Brown would have the strongest preference (i.e., least dissatisfaction) with computer C.

To use the ideal-brand model, the marketer would interview a sample of buyers and ask them to describe their ideal brands. The marketer will obtain three classes of response. Some consumers will have clear pictures of their ideal brand. Other consumers will mention two or more ideals that would satisfy them. The remaining consumers will have trouble defining an ideal brand and would find a wide range of brands equally acceptable.

Conjunctive model. Some consumers will evaluate alternatives by establishing minimum attribute levels that acceptable brands must possess. They will only consider the brands that exhibit a *conjunction* of all the minimum requirements. Thus Larry Brown might consider only computers that score better than (7, 6, 7, 2) on memory, graphics, software, and price respectively. These cutoffs eliminate brands A, C, D from further consideration. Conjunctive evaluation in the extreme could eliminate all brands. A consumer might not purchase any computer because no brand meets his or her minimal requirements. Note that conjunctive evaluation does not pay attention to how high an attribute level is as long as it exceeds the minimum. A high level of one attribute does not compensate for a below-minimum level of another attribute.

Disjunctive model. Larry Brown might want to consider only computers that exceed specified levels on one or a few attributes, regardless of their standing on the other attributes. He might decide that he will consider only computers that have strong memory (> 9) *or* graphics (> 9). According to Table 4–5, Larry is left with computers A and B as choices. The model is noncompensatory in that high scores on other variables have no bearing on keeping them in the acceptable set.

Lexicographic model. Another noncompensatory process occurs if Larry Brown arranges the attributes in order of importance and compares the brands on the first important attribute. If one brand is superior on the most important attribute, it becomes his choice. If two or more brands are tied on this attribute, Larry considers the second most important attribute; he continues this process until one brand remains. Suppose Larry "prioritizes" the attributes in the following order; price, software, memory, graphics. He looks at price and finds brand D dominates. At this point he has determined that brand D is his preferred computer.

Marketing implications. The preceding models indicate that buyers can form their product preferences in several ways. A particular buyer, on a particular buying occasion, facing a particular product class, might be a conjunctive buyer, disjunctive buyer, or some other type of buyer. The same buyer may behave as a conjunctive buyer for large-ticket purchases and a disjunctive buyer for small-ticket items. Or the same buyer, in buying a large-ticket item, may behave first like a conjunctive buyer to eliminate many alternatives and then make a final choice as an ideal brand buyer. When we realize that a market is made up of many buyers, it seems almost hopeless to assess the nature of buying behavior in that market.

Yet marketers can gain useful insights by interviewing a sample of buyers to find out how they form their evaluations in that product class. The marketer might find that the majority of consumers in that market use one particular evaluation procedure. In such a case, the marketer can consider the most effective ways to make the brand salient to consumers who are using that evaluation procedure.

SOURCE: For additional discussion of these models, see Paul E. Green and Yoram Wind, Multiattribute Decisions in Marketing: A Measurement Approach (Hinsdale, Ill.: Dryden Press, 1972), Chapter 2.

Suppose most computer buyers say they form their preferences using the expectancy-value process described above. Knowing this, a computer manufacturer can do a number of things to influence buyer decisions. The marketer of computer C, for example, could apply the following strategies to influence people like Larry Brown to show a greater interest in his brand:[31]

- **Modifying the computer.** The marketer could redesign his brand so that it offers more memory or other characteristics that this type of buyer desires. This is called *real repositioning*.
- **Altering beliefs about the brand.** The marketer could try to alter buyers' beliefs of where his brand stands on key attributes. This is especially recommended if buyers underestimate brand C's qualities. It is not recommended if buyers are accurately evaluating brand C; exaggerated claims would lead to buyer dissatisfaction and bad word of mouth. Attempting to alter beliefs about the brand is called *psychological repositioning*.
- **Altering beliefs about the competitors' brands.** The marketer could try to change buyers' beliefs about where competitive brands stand on different attributes. This may make sense where buyers mistakenly believe a competitor's brand has more quality than it actually has. This is called *competitive depositioning*, and is often expressed through running a comparison ad.
- **Altering the importance weights.** The marketer could try to persuade buyers to attach more importance to attributes the brand excels in. The marketer of brand C can tout the benefits of choosing a computer with great software availability, since C is superior in this attribute.
- **Calling attention to neglected attributes.** The marketer could try to draw the buyer's attention to neglected attributes. If brand C is a highly portable computer, the marketer might tout the benefit of portability.
- **Shifting the buyer's ideals.** The marketer could try to persuade buyers to change their ideal levels for one or more attributes. The marketer of brand C might try to convince buyers that computers with a large memory are more likely to jam and that a moderate-size memory is more desirable.

Purchase decision. The decision evaluation stage leads the consumer to form preferences among the brands in the choice set. The consumer may also form a *purchase intention* and lean toward buying the preferred brand. However, two factors can intervene between the purchase intention and the purchase decision. These factors are shown in Figure 4–6.[32]

The first factor is the *attitudes of others*. Suppose Larry Brown's wife feels strongly that Larry should buy the lowest-priced computer (D) to keep down expenses. As a result, Larry's "purchase probability" for computer A will be somewhat reduced. The extent to which another person's attitude will reduce one's preferred alternative depends upon two things: (1) the intensity of the other person's negative attitude toward the consumer's preferred alternative and (2) the consumer's motivation to comply with the other person's wishes.[33] The more intense the other person's negativ-

[31] See Harper W. Boyd, Jr., Michael L. Ray, and Edward C. Strong, "An Attitudinal Framework for Advertising Strategy," *Journal of Marketing*, April 1972, pp. 27–33.

[32] See Jagdish N. Sheth, "An Investigation of Relationships among Evaluative Beliefs, Affect, Behavioral Intention, and Behavior," in *Consumer Behavior: Theory and Application*, ed. John U. Farley, John A. Howard, and L. Winston Ring (Boston: Allyn & Bacon, 1974), pp. 89–114.

[33] See Fishbein, "Attitudes and Prediction."

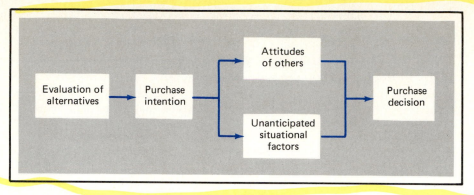

FIGURE 4-6
Steps Between Evaluation of Alternatives and a Purchase Decision

ism, and the closer the other person is to the consumer, the more the consumer will revise downward his or her purchase intention.

Purchase intention is also influenced by *unanticipated situational factors.* The consumer forms a purchase intention on the basis of such factors as expected family income, expected price, and expected benefits from the product. When the consumer is about to act, *unanticipated situational factors* may erupt to change the purchase intention. Larry Brown might lose his job, some other purchase might become more urgent, or a friend might report disappointment in that computer brand. Thus preferences and even purchase intentions are not completely reliable predictors of purchase behavior.

A consumer's decision to modify, postpone, or avoid a purchase decision is heavily influenced by *perceived risk*. Many purchases involve some *risk taking*.[34] Consumers cannot be certain about the purchase outcome. This produces anxiety. The amount of perceived risk varies with the amount of money at stake, the amount of attribute uncertainty, and the amount of consumer self-confidence. A consumer develops certain routines for reducing risk, such as decision avoidance, information gathering from friends, and preference for national brand names and warranties. The marketer must understand the factors that provoke a feeling of risk in consumers and provide information and support that will reduce the perceived risk.

A consumer who decides to execute a purchase intention will be making up to five *purchase subdecisions*. Thus Larry Brown will make a *brand decision* (brand A), *vendor decision* (dealer 2), *quantity decision* (one computer), *timing decision* (weekend), and *payment-method decision* (credit card). The decisions are not necessarily made in this order. Furthermore, purchases of everyday products, in contrast, involve fewer of these decisions and much less buyer deliberation. Thus in buying cigarettes, Larry gives little thought to the vendor or payment method. We deliberately chose

---

[34] See Raymond A. Bauer, "Consumer Behavior as Risk Taking," in *Risk Taking and Information Handling in Consumer Behavior*, ed. Donald F. Cox (Boston: Division of Research, Harvard Business School, 1967); and James W. Taylor, "The Role of Risk in Consumer Behavior," *Journal of Marketing*, April 1974, pp. 54–60.

a product that involves extensive problem solving—here personal computers—to illustrate the full range of behavior that might arise in buying something.

Postpurchase behavior. After purchasing the product, the consumer will experience some level of satisfaction or dissatisfaction. The consumer will also engage in postpurchase actions of interest to the marketer. The marketer's job does not end when the product is bought but continues into the postpurchase period.

Postpurchase satisfaction. What determines whether the buyer is highly satisfied, somewhat satisfied, somewhat dissatisfied, or highly dissatisfied with a purchase? The buyer's satisfaction(s) is a function of the closeness between the consumer's product *expectations* (E) and the product's *perceived performance* (P), that is $S = f(E,P)$.[35] If the product matches expectations, the consumer is satisfied; if it exceeds them, the consumer is highly satisfied; if it falls short, the consumer is dissatisfied.

Consumers form their expectations on the basis of messages they receive from sellers, friends, and other information sources. If the seller exaggerates the benefits, consumers will experience *disconfirmed expectations*, which lead to dissatisfaction. The larger the gap between expectations and performance, the greater the consumer's dissatisfaction. Here the consumer's coping style comes into play. Some consumers magnify the gap when the product is not perfect, and they are highly dissatisfied. Other consumers minimize the gap and are less dissatisfied.[36]

This theory suggests that the seller should make product claims that faithfully represent the product's likely performance so that buyers experience satisfaction. Some sellers might even understate performance levels so that consumers experience higher-than-expected satisfaction with the product.

Festinger and Bramel believe that the most nonroutine purchase will unavoidably involve some postpurchase discomfort.

> When a person chooses between two or more alternatives, discomfort or dissonance will almost inevitably arise because of the person's knowledge that while the decision he has made has certain advantages, it also has some disadvantages. That dissonance arises after almost every decision, and further, that the individual will invariably take steps to reduce this dissonance.[37]

Postpurchase actions. The consumer's satisfaction or dissatisfaction with the product will influence subsequent behavior. If the consumer is satisfied, then he or she will exhibit a higher probability of purchasing the product on the next occasion. The satisfied consumer will also tend to say good things about the product to others. According to marketers: "Our best advertisement is a satisfied customer."

A dissatisfied consumer responds differently. The dissatisfied consumer will try to reduce the dissonance because of a drive in the human organism "to establish

---

[35] See John E. Swan and Linda Jones Combs, "Product Performance and Consumer Satisfaction: A New Concept," *Journal of Marketing Research*, April 1976, pp. 25–33.

[36] See Rolph E. Anderson, "Consumer Dissatisfaction: The Effect of Disconfirmed Expectancy on Perceived Product Performance," *Journal of Marketing Research*, February 1973, pp. 38–44.

[37] Leon Festinger and Dana Bramel, "The Reactions of Humans to Cognitive Dissonance," in *Experimental Foundations of Clinical Psychology*, ed. Arthur J. Bachrach (New York: Basic Books, 1962), pp. 251–62.

internal harmony, consistency, or congruity among his opinions, knowledge, and values."[38] Dissonant consumers will resort to one or two courses of action. They may try to reduce the dissonance by *abandoning or returning* the product, or they may try to reduce the dissonance by seeking information that might *confirm* its high value (or avoiding information that might confirm its low value). In the case of Larry Brown, he might return the computer, or he might seek information that would make him feel better about the computer.

Marketers should be aware of the full range of ways in which consumers handle dissatisfaction. Consumers have a choice between taking and not taking any action. If the former, they can take public action or private action. Public actions include complaining to the company, going to a lawyer, or complaining to other groups that might help the buyer get satisfaction. Or the buyer might simply stop buying the product and/or bad-mouth it to friends and others. In all these cases, the seller loses something in having done a poor job of satisfying the customer.[39]

Marketers can take steps to minimize the amount of consumer postpurchase dissatisfaction. They can do a number of things to help customers feel good about their purchase. Computer companies can send a letter to new computer owners congratulating them on having selected a fine computer. They can place ads showing satisfied brand owners. They can solicit customer suggestions for improvements and list the location of available services. They can write instruction booklets that are dissonance reducing. They can send owners a magazine containing articles describing new computer applications. Postpurchase communications to buyers have been shown to result in fewer product returns and order cancellations.[40] In addition, they can provide good channels for customer complaining and arrange for speedy redress of customer grievances.

There is one more step in the postpurchase behavior of buyers that sellers should watch, namely what the buyers ultimately do with the product. If consumers find a new use for the product, that should interest the seller because the company can advertise the new use. If consumers store the product and make little use of it or actually get rid of it, the product is not permanently satisfying, and consumer word-of-mouth would not be strong. Of some interest is how consumers ultimately dispose of the product. If they sell or trade the product, that will dampen new product sales. All said, the seller needs to study product use and disposal for clues to possible problems and opportunities.[41]

Understanding consumer needs and buying processes is the foundation of successful marketing. By understanding how buyers go through problem recognition, information search, evaluation of alternatives, the purchase decision, and postpurchase behav-

---

[38] Leon Festinger, *A Theory of Cognitive Dissonance* (Stanford, Calif.: Stanford University Press, 1957), p. 260.

[39] See Ralph L. Day and E. Laird Landon, Jr., "Toward a Theory of Consumer Complaining Behavior," in *Consumer and Industrial Buying Behavior*, ed. Arch G. Woodside, Jagdish N. Sheth, and Peter D. Bennett (New York: Elsevier North-Holland, 1977), p. 432.

[40] See James H. Donnelly, Jr., and John M. Ivancevich, "Post-Purchase Reinforcement and Back-Out Behavior," *Journal of Marketing Research*, August 1970, pp. 399–400.

[41] See Jacob Jacoby, Carol K. Berning, and Thomas F. Dietvorst, "What about Disposition?" *Journal of Marketing*, July 1977, p. 23.

ior, marketers can pick up many clues as to how to meet buyer needs. By understanding the various participants in the buying process and the major influences on their buying behavior, marketers can design effective marketing programs for their target markets.

SUMMARY

Markets have to be understood before marketing plans can be developed.

The consumer market buys goods and services for personal consumption. It is the ultimate market for which economic activities are organized. The market consists of many submarkets, such as black consumers, young adult consumers, and elderly consumers.

The buyer's behavior is influenced by four major factors: cultural (culture, subculture, and social class), social (reference groups, family, and roles and statuses), personal (age and life-cycle stage, occupation, economic circumstances, lifestyle, and personality and self-concept), and psychological (motivation, perception, learning, and beliefs and attitudes). All of these provide clues as to how to reach and serve the buyer more effectively.

Before planning its marketing, a company needs to identify its target consumers and the type of decision process they go through. While many buying decisions involve only one decision maker, other decisions may involve several participants, who play such roles as initiator, influencer, decider, buyer, and user. The marketers's job is to identify the other buying participants, their buying criteria, and the amount of influence they have on the buyer. The marketing program should be designed to appeal to and reach the other key participants as well as the buyer.

The amount of buying deliberateness and the number of buying participants increase with the complexity of the buying situation. Marketers must plan differently for four types of consumer buying behavior: complex buying behavior, dissonance-reducing buying behavior, habitual buying behavior, and variety-seeking buying behavior. These four types are based on whether the consumer has high or low involvement in the purchase and whether there are many or few significant differences among the brands.

In complex buying behavior, the buyer goes through a decision process consisting of problem recognition, information search, evaluation of alternatives, purchase decision, and postpurchase behavior. The marketer's job is to understand the buyer's behavior at each stage and what influences are operating. This understanding allows the marketer to develop a significant and effective marketing program for the target market.

QUESTIONS

1. Suppose Larry Brown, the consumer discussed in this chapter, purchased a personal computer. Discuss the information-search stage of the buying decision process for his subsequent purchase of computer software.

2. Jovan has introduced Andron, a cologne containing pheromones—a chemical believed to evoke an aphrodisiac response in members of the opposite sex who are near the wearer of the cologne. What factors are operating to influence a potential purchaser of this product?

3. In 1982 and 1983 Seven-up ran ads with the theme "crisp and clean with no caffeine." What consumer-behavior factors were considered in the decision to run this ad?

4. Apply the five different roles in the decision process to your decision regarding college.

5. A friend of yours plans to buy a new car. He prefers foreign makes and his choice has narrowed down to Volkswagen, Toyota, and Volvo. He looks for three things in a car: economy, quality, and roominess, and he values them at 0.5, 0.3, and 0.2, respectively. He rates Volkswagen at 0.8, 0.8, and 0.2 on the three attributes; Toyota, 0.3, 0.5, and 0.9; and Volvo, 0.5, 0.8, and 0.7. Predict the cars he is most likely to buy and least likely to buy if he evaluates cars according to the expectancy value model.

6. "A person will tend to buy the brand in the product class whose image is most congruent with his or her self-image." Is a person's self-image a highly reliable prediction of his or her brand choice?

7. Develop a map showing the structure of purchase decisions made by potential buyers of paint. Indicate how a paint company such as Du Pont can determine points at which advertising might favorably affect Du Pont's share of the market.

8. A homebuilder plans to design homes for "empty nesters." Can this life-cycle group be further segmented? What kind of home design features fit the needs of empty nesters?

9. Describe the consumer market for briefcases, using the framework developed in this chapter.

Organizational Markets and Buying Behavior

5

Companies don't make purchases; they establish relationships.

CHARLES S. GOODMAN

Organizations constitute a vast market for raw materials, manufactured parts, installations, accessory equipment, supplies, and business services. There are over 14 million organizations buying goods and services. Companies that sell steel, computers, nuclear-power plants, and other goods to organizations must do their best to understand the buyers' needs, resources, policies, and buying procedures. They must take into account several considerations not normally found in consumer marketing.

☐ Organizations buy goods and services to satisfy a variety of goals: making profits, reducing costs, meeting the needs of their employees, and/or meeting social and legal obligations.

☐ More persons typically participate in organizational buying decisions than in consumer buying decisions, especially in the case of buying major items. The decision participants usually have different organizational responsibilities and apply different criteria to the purchase decision.

☐ The buyers must heed formal policies, constraints, and requirements established by their organizations.

☐ The buying instruments, such as request for quotations, proposals, and purchase contracts, add another dimension not typically found in consumer buying.

Webster and Wind define *organizational buying* as "the decision-making process by which formal organizations establish the need for purchased products and services, and identify, evaluate, and choose among alternative brands and suppliers."[1] No two companies buy in the same way, yet the seller hopes to identify enough uniformities in organizational buying behavior to improve the task of marketing strategy planning.

In this chapter, we will look at three organizational markets: industrial markets, reseller markets, and government markets. Industrial buyers buy goods and services to aid them in producing other goods and services. Resellers buy goods and services to resell them at a profit. Government agencies buy goods and services to carry out mandated governmental functions. We will examine five questions about each market: *Who is in the market? What buying decisions do buyers make? Who participates in the buying process? What are the major influences on the buyers? How do the buyers make their buying decisions?*

THE INDUSTRIAL MARKET

Who Is in the Industrial Market?

The *industrial market* (also called the producer or business market) consists of all the individuals and organizations that acquire goods and services that enter into the production of other products or services that are sold, rented, or supplied to others. The major types of industries making up the industrial market are agriculture, forestry, and fisheries; mining; manufacturing; construction; transportation; communication; public utilities; banking, finance, and insurance; and services.

More dollars and items are involved in sales to industrial buyers than to consumers. For a simple pair of shoes to be produced and sold, hide dealers must sell hides to tanners, who sell leather to shoe manufacturers, who sell shoes to wholesalers, who in turn sell shoes to retailers, who finally sell them to consumers. Each party in the chain of production and distribution has to buy many other goods and services as well, and this explains why more industrial buying goes on than consumer buying.

Industrial markets have certain characteristics that contrast sharply with consumer markets. These characteristics are described below.

Fewer buyers. The industrial marketer normally deals with far fewer buyers than does the consumer marketer. Goodyear Tire Company's fate in the industrial market critically depends on getting an order from one of the big three auto makers. But when Goodyear sells replacement tires to consumers, it has a potential market of owners of 105 million American automobiles currently in use.

Larger buyers. Even in populous markets, a few large buyers normally account for most of the purchasing. In such industries as motor vehicles, telephone and tele-

---

[1] Frederick E. Webster, Jr., and Yoram Wind, *Organizational Buying Behavior* (Englewood Cliffs, N.J.: Prentice-Hall, 1972), p. 2.

graph, cigarettes, aircraft engines and engine parts, and organic fibers, the top four manufacturers account for over 70 percent of total production.

Geographically concentrated buyers. More than half of the nation's industrial buyers are concentrated in seven states: New York, California, Pennsylvania, Illinois, Ohio, New Jersey, and Michigan. Industries, such as petroleum, rubber, and steel, show even greater geographic concentration. Most agricultural output comes from a relatively small number of states. This geographical concentration of producers helps to reduce the costs of selling to them. Industrial marketers will want to watch any tendencies toward or away from further geographic concentration.

Derived demand. The demand for industrial goods is ultimately derived from the demand for consumer goods. Thus animal hides are purchased because consumers buy shoes, purses, and other leather goods. If the demand for these consumer goods slackens, so will the demand for all the industrial goods entering into their production.

Inelastic demand. The total demand for many industrial goods and services is not much affected by price changes. Shoe manufacturers are not going to buy much more leather if the price of leather falls. Nor are they going to buy much less leather if the price of leather rises unless they can find satisfactory leather substitutes. Demand is especially inelastic in the short run because producers cannot make many changes in their production methods. Demand is also inelastic for industrial goods that represent a small percentage of the item's total cost. For example, an increase in the price of metal eyelets for shoes will barely affect the demand level. At the same time, producers will use price to decide which supplier to buy from, although it will have less effect on the amount bought.

Fluctuating demand. The demand for industrial goods and services tends to be more volatile than the demand for consumer goods and services. This is especially true of the demand for new plants and equipment. A given percentage increase in consumer demand can lead to a much larger percentage increase in the demand for plant and equipment necessary to produce the additional output. Economists refer to this as the *acceleration principle.* Sometimes a rise of only 10 percent in consumer demand can cause as much as a 200 percent rise in industrial demand in the next period. This phenomenon has led many industrial marketers to diversify their product lines to achieve some balance over the business cycle.

Professional purchasing. Industrial goods are purchased by professionally trained purchasing agents, who spend their work lives learning how to buy better. Many belong to the National Association of Purchasing Agents, which seeks to improve the effectiveness and status of professional buyers. Consumers, on the other hand, are much less trained in the art of careful buying. The more complex the industrial purchase, the more likely that several persons will participate in the decision-making process. Buying committees made up of technical experts and top management are common in the purchase of major goods. Consequently, industrial marketers have to hire well-trained sales representatives and often use sales teams to deal with the well-trained buyers. Although advertising, sales promotion, and publicity play an important role in the industrial promotional mix, personal selling serves as the main selling tool.

Miscellaneous characteristics.   Here are some additional characteristics of industrial buying:

- ☐ **Direct purchasing.** Industrial buyers often buy directly from producers rather than through middlemen, especially those items that are technically complex and/or expensive.
- ☐ **Reciprocity.** Industrial buyers often select suppliers who also buy from them. An example of this reciprocity would be a paper manufacturer who buys needed chemicals from a chemical company that is buying a considerable amount of its paper. Reciprocity is forbidden by the Federal Trade Commission and the Justice Department's antitrust division if it shuts out competition in an unfair manner. A buyer can still choose a supplier that it also sells something to, but the buyer should be able to show that it is getting competitive prices, quality, and service from that supplier.[2]
- ☐ **Leasing.** Industrial buyers are increasingly turning to equipment leasing instead of outright purchase. This happens with computers, shoe machinery, packaging equipment, heavy-construction equipment, delivery trucks, machine tools, and sales-force automobiles. The lessee gains a number of advantages, such as having more available capital, getting the seller's latest products, receiving better servicing, and gaining some tax advantages. The lessor often ends up with a larger net income and the chance to sell to customers who might not have been able to afford outright purchase.[3]

What Buying Decisions Do Industrial Buyers Make?

The industrial buyer faces a whole set of decisions in making a purchase. The number of decisions depends on the type of buying situation.

Major types of buying situations.   Robinson and others distinguish three types of buying situations, which they call *buyclasses*.[4] At one extreme is the straight rebuy, which is a fairly routine decision, and at the other extreme is the new task, which may call for complete negotiation.

Straight rebuy.   The straight rebuy describes the buying situation where the purchasing department reorders on a routine basis (e.g., office supplies, bulk chemicals). The buyer chooses from suppliers on its "list," giving weight to its past buying satisfaction with the various suppliers. The "in" suppliers make an effort to maintain product and service quality. They often propose automatic reordering systems so that the purchasing agent will save reordering time. The "out" suppliers attempt to offer something new or to exploit dissatisfaction so that the buyer will consider buying from them. Out-suppliers try to get their foot in the door with a small order and then to enlarge their "purchase share" over time.

---

[2] See Reed Moyer, "Reciprocity: Retrospect and Prospect," *Journal of Marketing*, October 1970, pp. 47–54.

[3] See Leonard J. Berry and Kenneth E. Maricle, "Consumption without Ownership: Marketing Opportunity for Today and Tomorrow," MSU *Business Topics*, spring 1973, pp. 33–41.

[4] Patrick J. Robinson, Charles W. Faris, and Yoram Wind, *Industrial Buying and Creative Marketing* (Boston: Allyn and Bacon, 1967).

Modified rebuy. The modified rebuy describes a situation where the buyer wants to modify product specifications, prices, other terms, or suppliers (e.g., new trucks, specialized electrical components). The modified rebuy usually expands the number of decision participants. The in-suppliers get nervous and have to put their best foot forward to protect the account. The out-suppliers see it as an opportunity to make a "better offer" to gain some new business.

New task. The new task faces a purchaser buying a product or service for the first time (e.g., custom-built office building, new weapon system). The greater the cost and/or risk, the larger the number of decision participants and the greater their information seeking. The new-task situation is the marketer's greatest opportunity and challenge. The marketer tries to reach as many key buying influences as possible and provide helpful information and assistance. Because of the complicated selling involved in the new task, many companies use a special sales force, called a *missionary sales force,* made up of their best sales people.

New-task buying passes through several stages, each with its own requirements and challenges to the marketer. Ozanne and Churchill have applied an innovation diffusion perspective to the new task, identifying the stages as *awareness, interest, evaluation, trial,* and *adoption*.[5] They found that information sources varied in effectiveness at each stage. Mass media were most important during the initial awareness stage, whereas salespersons had their greatest impact at the interest stage. Technical sources were the most important during the evaluation stage. These findings provide clues to the new-task marketer as to efficient communications to use at different stages of the buying process.

Major subdecisions involved in the buying decision. The number of decisions that the buyer has to make are fewest in the straight rebuy and the most in the new-task situation. In the new-task situation, the buyer has to determine *product specifications, price limits, delivery terms and times, service terms, payment terms, order quantities, acceptable suppliers,* and *the selected supplier.* Different decision participants influence each decision, and the order in which these decisions are made varies.

The role of systems buying and selling. Many buyers prefer to buy a whole solution to their problem and not make all the separate decisions involved. This is called *systems buying*; it originated in government practices in buying major weapons and communication systems. Instead of purchasing and putting all the components together, the government would solicit bids from prime contractors, who would assemble the package or system. The winning prime contractor would be responsible for bidding and assembling the subcomponents. The prime contractor would thus provide a *turn-key operation,* so called because the buyer simply had to turn one key to get everything that was wanted.

Sellers have increasingly recognized that buyers like to purchase in this way

[5] Urban B. Ozanne and Gilbert A. Churchill, Jr., "Adoption Research: Information Sources in the Industrial Purchase Decision," *Proceedings, Fall Conference* (Chicago: American Marketing Association, 1968).

and have adopted the practice of *systems selling* as a marketing tool. Systems selling has two components. First, the supplier sells a group of interlocking products. For example, the supplier sells not only glue but glue applicators and dryers as well. Second, the supplier sells a system of production, inventory control, distribution, and other services to meet the buyer's need for a smooth-running operation. Systems selling is a key industrial marketing strategy for winning and holding accounts.

Who Participates in the Industrial Buying Process?

Who does the buying of the hundreds of billions of dollars' worth of goods and services needed by the industrial market? Buying organizations vary tremendously, from one or a few purchasing agents to large purchasing departments headed by a vice-president of purchasing. In some cases purchasing executives make the entire decision as to product specifications and supplier, in other cases they are responsible for supplier selection only, and in still other cases they only place the order. Typically, they make full decisions on smaller items and carry out the wishes of others on major capital items.

Webster and Wind call the decision-making unit of a buying organization the *buying center*, defined as "all those individuals and groups who participate in the purchasing decision-making process, who share some common goals and the risks arising from the decisions."[6]

The buying center includes all members of the organization who play any of five roles in the purchase decision process.[7]

☐ **Users.** Users are the members of the organization who will use the product or service. In many cases the users initiate the buying proposal and help define the product specifications.

☐ **Influencers.** Influencers are persons who influence the buying decision. They often help define specifications and also provide information for evaluating alternatives. Technical personnel are particularly important as influencers.

☐ **Buyers.** Buyers are persons with formal authority for selecting the supplier and arranging the terms of purchase. Buyers may help shape product specifications, but they play their major role in selecting vendors and negotiating. In more complex purchases, the buyers might include high-level officers participating in the negotiations.

☐ **Deciders.** Deciders are persons who have formal or informal power to select or approve the final suppliers. In routine buying, the buyers are often the deciders, or at least the approvers.

☐ **Gatekeepers.** Gatekeepers are persons who control the flow of information to others. For example, purchasing agents often have authority to prevent salespersons from seeing users or deciders. Other gatekeepers include technical personnel and even switchboard operators.

Within any organization, the buying center will vary in size and composition for different classes of products. More decision participants will be involved in buying a computer than in buying paper clips. The industrial marketer has to figure out:

---

[6] Webster and Wind, *Organizational Buying Behavior*, p. 6.

[7] Ibid., pp. 78–80.

Who are the major decision participants? In what decision do they excercise influence? What is their relative degree of influence? And what evaluation criteria does each decision participant use? Consider the following example:

> The American Hospital Supply Corporation sells nonwoven disposable surgical gowns to hospitals. It tries to identify the hospital personnel who participate in this buying decision. The decision participants turn out to be the vice-president of purchasing, the operating-room administrator, and the surgeons. Each party plays a different role. The vice-president of purchasing analyzes whether the hospital should buy disposable gowns or reusable gowns. If the findings favor disposable gowns, then the operating-room administrator compares various competitors' products and prices and makes a choice. This administrator considers the gown's absorbency, antiseptic quality, design, and cost and normally buys the brand that meets the functional requirements at the lowest cost. Finally, surgeons influence the decision retroactively by reporting their satisfaction with the particular brand.

When a buying center includes many participants, the industrial marketer will not have the time or resources to reach all of them. Smaller companies concentrate on reaching the *key buying influences*. Larger companies go for *multilevel in-depth selling* to reach as many decision participants as possible. Their sales people virtually "live" with the customer when it is a *major account* with recurrent sales.

Industrial marketers must periodically review their assumptions on the roles and influence of different decision participants. For example, for years Kodak's strategy for selling X-ray film to hospitals was to sell through lab technicians. The company did not notice that the decision was being made increasingly by professional administrators. As its sales declined, Kodak finally grasped the change in buying practices and hurriedly changed its marketing strategy.

What Are the Major Influences on Industrial Buyers?

Industrial buyers are subject to many influences when they make their buying decisions. Some marketers assume that the most important influences are economic. They see the buyers as favoring the supplier who offers the lowest price, or best product, or most service. This view suggests that industrial marketers should concentrate on offering strong economic benefits to buyers.

Other marketers see buyers responding to personal factors such as favors, attention, or risk avoidance. A study of buyers in ten large companies concluded that

> . . . corporate decision-makers remain human after they enter the office. They respond to "image"; they buy from companies to which they feel "close"; they favor suppliers who show them respect and personal consideration, and who do extra things "for them"; they "over-react" to real or imagined slights, tending to reject companies which fail to respond or delay in submitting requested bids.[8]

---

[8] See Murray Harding, "Who Really Makes the Purchasing Decision?" *Industrial Marketing*, September 1966, p. 76. This point of view is further developed in Ernest Dichter, "Industrial Buying Is Based on Same 'Only Human' Emotional Factors that Motivate Consumer Market's Housewife," *Industrial Marketing*, February 1973, pp. 14–16.

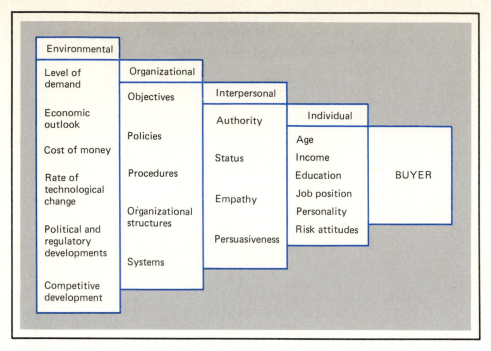

FIGURE 5–1
Major Influences on Industrial Buying Behavior

This view suggests that industrial marketers should pay primary attention to the human and social factors in the buying situation.

Industrial buyers actually respond to both economic and personal factors. Where there is substantial similarity in supplier offers, industrial buyers have little basis for rational choice. Since they can meet organizational goals with any supplier, buyers can bring in personal factors. On the other hand, where competing products differ substantially, industrial buyers are more accountable for their choice and pay more attention to economic factors.

Webster and Wind have classified the various influences on industrial buyers into four main groups: environmental, organizational, interpersonal, and individual.[9] These groups are shown in Figure 5–1 and described below.

Environmental factors.   Industrial buyers are heavily influenced by factors in the current and expected economic environment, such as the level of primary demand, the economic outlook, and the cost of money. In a recession economy, industrial buyers reduce their investment in plant and equipment and attempt to reduce their inventories. Industrial marketers can do little to stimulate purchases in this environment. However, government programs such as investment tax credits can help.

---

[9] Webster and Wind, *Organizational Buying Behavior*, pp. 33–37.

Companies that fear a shortage of key materials are willing to buy and hold larger inventories. They will sign long-term contracts with suppliers to insure a steady flow of these materials. Du Pont, Ford, Chrysler, and several other major companies regard *supply planning* as a major responsibility of their purchasing executives.[10]

Industrial buyers are also affected by technological, political, and competitive developments in the environment. The industrial marketer has to monitor all of these environmental forces, determine how they will affect buyers, and try to turn problems into opportunities.

Organizational factors. Each buying organization has specific objectives, policies, procedures, organizational structure, and systems. The industrial marketer has to know these as well as possible. Such questions arise as: How many people are involved in the buying decision? Who are they? What are their evaluation criteria? What are the company's policies and constraints on the buyers?

The industrial marketer should be aware of the following organizational trends in the purchasing area:

☐ **Purchasing-department upgrading.** Purchasing departments often occupy a low position in the management hierarchy, in spite of managing often more than half of the company's costs. However, inflation and shortages have led many companies to upgrade their purchasing departments. Several large corporations have elevated the heads of purchasing to vice-presidential levels. Caterpillar and some other companies have combined several functions—such as purchasing, inventory control, production scheduling, and traffic—into a high-level function called *material management*. "New-wave" materials managers are actively building new supply sources. Many companies are looking for top talent, hiring M.B.A.'s, and offering higher compensation. This means that industrial marketers must correspondingly upgrade their sales personnel to match the caliber of the new buyers.

☐ **Centralized purchasing.** In multidivisional companies, much purchasing is carried out by the separate divisions because of their differing needs. But recently companies have tried to recentralize some of the purchasing. Headquarters identifies materials purchases by several divisions and considers buying them centrally. This gives the company more purchasing clout. The individual divisions can buy from another source if they can get a better deal, but in general, centralized purchasing produces substantial savings for the company. For the industrial marketer, this development means dealing with fewer and higher-level buyers. Instead of the seller's regional sales forces selling at separate plant locations, the seller may use a *national account sales force* to deal with the buyer. National account selling is challenging and demands a sophisticated sales force and marketing planning effort.[11]

☐ **Long-term contracts.** Industrial buyers are increasingly responding to long-term contracts with suppliers. These contracts call for skillful negotiation, and buyers are adding negotiating specialists to their staffs. Industrial marketers, in turn, will have to add skilled negotiators to their staffs.

---

[10] See "The Purchasing Agent Gains More Clout," *Business Week*, January 13, 1975, pp. 62–63.

[11] See Thomas H. Stevenson and Albert L. Page, "The Adoption of National Account Marketing by Industrial Firms," *Industrial Marketing Management* Vol. 8, 1979, pp. 94–100; and Benson P. Shapiro and Rowland T. Moriarty, *National Account Management: Emerging Insights* (Cambridge, Mass.: Marketing Science Institute, March 1982).

□ **Purchasing-performance evaluation.** Some companies are setting up incentive systems to reward purchasing managers for especially good performance, in much the same way that sales personnel receive bonuses for especially good selling performance. These systems will lead purchasing managers to increase their pressure on sellers for the best terms.

Interpersonal factors. The buying center usually includes several participants with different statuses, authority, empathy, and persuasiveness. The industrial marketer is not likely to know what kind of group dynamics will take place during the buying process, although whatever information he or she can find out about the personalities and interpersonal factors would be useful.

Individual factors. Each participant in the buying decision process brings in personal motivations, perceptions, and preferences. Those are influenced by the participant's age, income, education, professional identification, personality, and attitudes toward risk. Buyers definitely exhibit different buying styles. Some of the younger, better-educated buyers are "computer freaks" and make rigorous analyses of competitive proposals before choosing a supplier. Other buyers are "tough guys" from the "old school" and play off the sellers:

> A good example of a cagey buyer is [the] vice-president in charge of purchasing for Rheingold's big New York brewery. . . . Using the leverage of hundreds of millions of cans a year, like many other buyers, he takes punitive action when one company slips in quality or fails to deliver. "At one point American started talking about a price rise," he recalls, "Continental kept its mouth shut. . . . American never did put the price rise into effect, but anyway, I punished them for talking about it." For a three-month period he cut the percentage of cans he bought from American.[12]

Industrial marketers must know their customers and adapt their tactics to known environmental, organizational, interpersonal, and individual influences on the buying situation.

How Do Industrial Buyers Make Their Buying Decisions?

Industrial buyers do not buy goods and services for personal consumption or utility. They buy things to make money, or to reduce operating costs, or to satisfy a social or legal obligation. A steel company will add another furnace if it sees a chance to make more money. It will computerize its accounting system to reduce the costs of doing business. It will add pollution-control equipment to satisfy legal requirements.

To buy the needed goods, industrial buyers move through a purchasing or procurement process. Robinson et al., have identified eight stages of the industrial buying process and called them *buyphases*.[13] These stages are shown in Table 5–1. All eight stages apply to a new-task buying situation, and some of them to the other

---

[12] Walter Guzzardi, Jr., "The Fight for 9/10 of a Cent," *Fortune*, April 1961, p. 152.

[13] Robinson, Faris, and Wind, *Industrial Buying*.

TABLE 5-1

MAJOR STAGES (BUYPHASES) OF THE INDUSTRIAL BUYING PROCESS IN RELATION TO MAJOR BUYING SITUATIONS (BUYCLASSES)

	Buy Classes		
Buy Phases	New Task	Modified Rebuy	Straight Rebuy
1. Problem recognition	Yes	Maybe	No
2. General need description	Yes	Maybe	No
3. Product specification	Yes	Yes	Yes
4. Suppliers' search	Yes	Maybe	No
5. Proposal solicitation	Yes	Maybe	No
6. Supplier selection	Yes	Maybe	No
7. Order-routine specification	Yes	Maybe	No
8. Performance review	Yes	Yes	Yes

SOURCE: Adapted from Patrick J. Robinson, Charles W. Faris, and Yoram Wind, Industrial Buying and Creative Marketing (Boston: Allyn and Bacon, 1967), p. 14.

two types of buying situations. This model is called the *buygrid* framework. We shall describe the eight steps for the typical new-task buying situation.

Problem recognition.   The buying process begins when someone in the company recognizes a problem or need that can be met by acquiring a good or a service. Problem recognition can occur as a result of internal or external stimuli. Internally, the most common events leading to problem recognition are the following:

☐ The company decides to launch a new product and needs new equipment and materials to produce this product.
☐ A machine breaks down and requires replacement or new parts.
☐ Some purchased material turns out to be unsatisfactory, and the company searches for another supplier.
☐ A purchasing manager senses an opportunity to obtain better prices or quality.

Externally, the buyer may get some new ideas at a trade show, or see an ad, or receive a call from a sales representative who offers a better product or a lower price. Industrial marketers can therefore stimulate problem recognition by developing ads, calling on prospects, and so on.

General need description.   Having recognized a need, the buyer proceeds to determine the general characteristics and quantity of the needed item. For standard items, this is not much of a problem. For complex items, the buyer will work with others—engineers, users, and so on—to define the general characteristics. They will want to rank the importance of reliability, durability, price, and other attributes desired in the item.

The industrial marketer can render assistance to the buying company in this phase. Often the buyer is not aware of the value of different product characteristics. An alert marketer can help the buyer define the company's needs.

Product specifications.   Now the buying organization proceeds to develop the item's technical specifications. A *value-analysis* engineering team will be put to work on the problem. *Value analysis*, which General Electric pioneered in the late forties, is *an approach to cost reduction in which components are carefully studied to determine if they can be redesigned or standardized or made by cheaper methods of production.* The team will examine the high-cost components in a given product—usually 20 percent of the parts account for 80 percent of the costs. The team will also look for product components that are overdesigned in that they will last longer than the product itself. Table 5–2 lists the major questions that are raised in value analysis. The team will decide on the optimal product characteristics and specify them accordingly. Tightly written specifications will allow the buyer to refuse merchandise that fails to meet the intended standards.

Sellers, too, can use value analysis as a tool for breaking into an account. By demonstrating a better way to make an object, an outside seller can turn a straight rebuy situation into a new-task situation in which the seller's company has a chance for business.

Supplier search.   The buyer now tries to identify the most appropriate vendors. The buyer can examine trade directories, do a computer search, or phone other companies for recommendations. Some of the vendors will be dropped from consideration because they are not large enough to supply the needed quantity or because they have a poor reputation for delivery and service. The buyer will end up with a small list of qualified suppliers. The newer the buying task and the more complex and expensive the item, the greater the amount of time spent in searching for, and qualifying, suppliers. The supplier's task is to get listed in major directories, develop

TABLE 5–2

QUESTIONS ASKED IN VALUE ANALYSIS
1. Does the use of the item contribute value?
2. Is its cost proportionate to its usefulness?
3. Does it need all its features?
4. Is there anything better for its intended use?
5. Can a usable part be made by a lower-cost method?
6. Can a standard product be found that will be usable?
7. Is the product made on proper tooling, considering the quantities that are used?
8. Do material, labor, overhead, and profit total its cost?
9. Will another dependable supplier provide it for less?
10. Is anyone buying it for less?

SOURCE: Albert W. Frey, *Marketing Handbook*, 2nd ed., (New York: Ronald Press, 1965), section 27, p. 21.

a strong advertising and promotion program, and strive to build a good reputation in the marketplace.

Proposal solicitation. The buyer will now invite qualified suppliers to submit proposals. Some suppliers will send only a catalog or a sales representative. Where the item is complex or expensive, the buyer will require detailed written proposals from each potential supplier. The buyer will eliminate some and ask the remaining suppliers to make formal presentations. Industrial marketers must therefore be skilled in researching, writing, and presenting proposals. Their proposals should be marketing documents, not just technical documents. Their oral presentations should inspire confidence. They should position their company's capabilities and resources so that they stand out from the competition.

Supplier selection. In this stage, the members of the buying center will review the proposals and move toward supplier selection. They will perform a *vendor analysis* to select supplier(s). They will consider not only the technical competence of the various suppliers but also their ability to deliver the item on time and provide necessary services. The buying center will often draw up a list of the desired supplier attributes and their relative importance. In selecting a chemical supplier, a buying center listed the following attributes in order of importance:

1. Technical support services
2. Prompt delivery
3. Quick response to customer needs
4. Product quality
5. Supplier reputation
6. Product price
7. Complete product line
8. Sales representatives' caliber
9. Extension of credit
10. Personal relationships
11. Literature and manuals

The members of the buying center will rate the suppliers against these attributes and will identify the most attractive suppliers. They often use a supplier evaluation model such as the one shown in Table 5–3.

Lehmann and O'Shaughnessy found that the relative importance of different attributes vary with the type of buying situation.[14] For *routine-order products*, they found that delivery reliability, price, and supplier reputation are highly important. For *procedural-problem products*, such as a dry copying machine, the three most important attributes are technical service, supplier flexibility, and product reliability. Finally, for *political-problem products* that stir rivalries in the organization, the most important attributes are price, supplier reputation, product reliability, service reliability, and supplier flexibility.

The buying center may attempt to negotiate with the preferred suppliers for better prices and terms before making the final selection. In the end, it may settle for a single supplier or a few suppliers. Many buyers prefer multiple sources of supply so that they will not be totally dependent on one supplier in case something goes

---

[14] See Donald R. Lehmann and John O'Shaughnessy, "Difference in Attribute Importance for Different Industrial Products," *Journal of Marketing*, April 1974, pp. 36–42.

TABLE 5-3

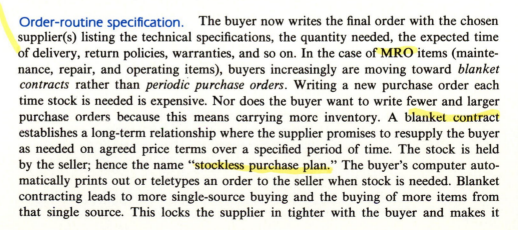

AN EXAMPLE OF VENDOR ANALYSIS

Attributes	Rating Scale				
	Unacceptable (0)	Poor (1)	Fair (2)	Good (3)	Excellent (4)
Technical and production capabilities					x
Financial strength			x		
Product reliability					x
Delivery reliability			x		
Service capability					x

Total score: 4 + 2 + 4 + 2 + 4 = 16

Average score: 16/5 = 3.2

Note: This vendor shows up as strong, except on two attributes. The purchasing agent has to decide how important the two weaknesses are. The analysis could be redone using importance weights for the five attributes.

SOURCE: Adapted from Richard Hill, Ralph Alexander, and James Cross, Industrial Marketing, 4th ed., (Homewood, IL: Richard D. Irwin, Copyright 1975), pp. 101–104.

wrong and also so that they will be able to compare the prices and performance of the various suppliers. The buyer will normally place most of the order with one supplier, and less with other suppliers. For example, a buyer using three suppliers may buy 60 percent of the needed quantity from the prime supplier and 30 and 10 percent, respectively, from the two other suppliers. The *prime supplier* will make an effort to protect its prime position, while the *secondary suppliers* will try to expand their supplier share. In the meantime, *out-suppliers* will attempt to get their foot in the door by making an especially good price offer and will then work hard to push up their share of the customer's business.

Order-routine specification. The buyer now writes the final order with the chosen supplier(s) listing the technical specifications, the quantity needed, the expected time of delivery, return policies, warranties, and so on. In the case of **MRO** items (maintenance, repair, and operating items), buyers increasingly are moving toward *blanket contracts* rather than *periodic purchase orders*. Writing a new purchase order each time stock is needed is expensive. Nor does the buyer want to write fewer and larger purchase orders because this means carrying more inventory. A blanket contract establishes a long-term relationship where the supplier promises to resupply the buyer as needed on agreed price terms over a specified period of time. The stock is held by the seller; hence the name "stockless purchase plan." The buyer's computer automatically prints out or teletypes an order to the seller when stock is needed. Blanket contracting leads to more single-source buying and the buying of more items from that single source. This locks the supplier in tighter with the buyer and makes it

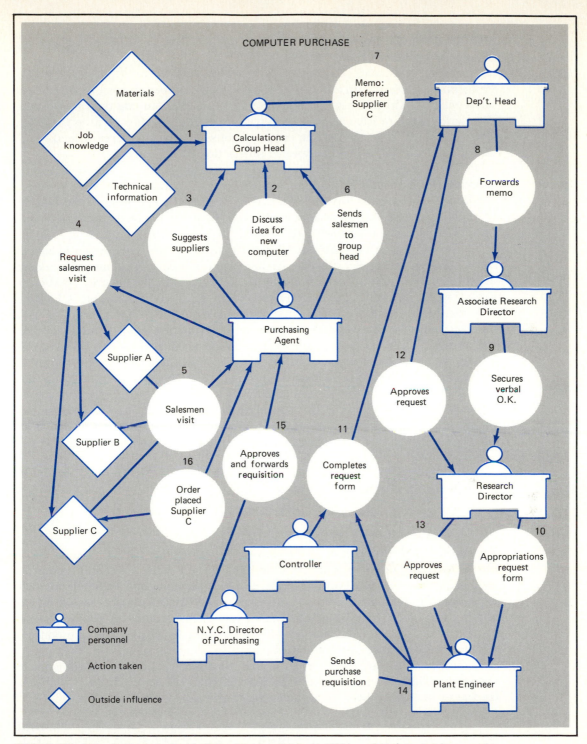

COMPUTER PURCHASE

Materials

Job knowledge

Technical information

1 Calculations Group Head

7 Memo: preferred Supplier C

Dep't. Head

8 Forwards memo

Associate Research Director

9 Secures verbal O.K.

3 Suggests suppliers

2 Discuss idea for new computer

6 Sends salesmen to group head

4 Request salesmen visit

Supplier A

5 Salesmen visit

Supplier B

16 Order placed Supplier C

Supplier C

Purchasing Agent

15 Approves and forwards requisition

11 Completes request form

12 Approves request

Research Director

Controller

13 Approves request

10 Appropriations request form

N.Y.C. Director of Purchasing

Sends purchase requisition

14 Plant Engineer

Company personnel

Action taken

Outside influence

SOURCE: "Who Makes the Purchasing Decision?" Reprinted from October 31, 1966, issue of *Marketing Insights,* copyright 1966 by Advertising Publications, Inc., Chicago, Illinois.

FIGURE 5-2
Map of Company Events in the Purchase of a Computer

difficult for out-suppliers to break in, unless the buyer becomes dissatisfied with the in-supplier's prices or service.[15]

Performance review.   In this stage the buyer reviews the performance of the particular supplier(s). The buyer may contact users and ask them to rate their satisfaction. The performance review may lead the buyer to continue, modify, or drop the seller. The seller's job is to monitor the same variables used by the buyer to make sure that the seller is delivering the expected satisfaction.

We have described the buying stages that would operate in a new-task buying situation. In the modified rebuy or straight rebuy situation, some of these stages would be compressed or bypassed. Each stage represents a narrowing of the number of supplier alternatives. A seller should try to become part of the buyer's buying process in the earliest possible stage.

The eight-stage buyphase model represents the major steps in the industrial buying process. In any real situation, further steps can occur. The industrial marketer needs to model each situation individually. Each buying situation involves a particular flow of work, and this *buyflow* can provide many clues to the marketer. A buyflow map for the purchase of a computer is shown in Figure 5–2. The map shows eight different company employees (represented by desk symbols) who were involved in this buying decision. Three suppliers were involved, as well as other outside influences (shown in the diamond-shaped figures). Finally, fifteen different events (shown as circles) led to placing the order with one of the suppliers.

Thus we see that industrial marketing is a challenging area. The key step is to know the customer's needs, who is involved in the buying decision, and the buying procedures. With this knowledge, the industrial marketer can proceed to design an effective marketing plan for selling and servicing the customer. (See Exhibit 5–1.)

THE RESELLER MARKET

Who Is in the Reseller Market?

The *reseller market* consists of all the individuals and organizations who acquire goods for the purpose of reselling or renting them to others at a profit. Instead of producing form utility, resellers produce time, place, and possession utility. The reseller market includes nearly 385,000 wholesaling firms employing 5,216,000 persons, and 1,223,000 retailing firms employing 15,000,000 persons; both sectors account for over 13 percent of the national income. Resellers are more geographically dispersed than producers but more concentrated than consumers.

Resellers purchase goods for resale and goods and services for conducting their operations. The latter are bought by resellers in their role as "producers." We shall confine the discussion here to the goods they purchase for resale.

---

[15] See Leonard Groeneveld, "The Implications of Blanket Contracting for Industrial Purchasing and Marketing," *Journal of Purchasing*, November 1972, pp. 51–58; and H. Lee Mathews, David T. Wilson, and Klaus Backhaus, "Selling to the Computer Assisted Buyer," *Industrial Marketing Management* Vol. 6, 1977, pp. 307–15.

Exhibit 5-1

ADAPTING MARKETING STRATEGY TO THE TYPE OF INDUSTRIAL BUYER: THE CASE OF MICROPROCESSORS

The market for microprocessors consists of three submarkets: military, industrial, and commercial. Each group buys quite differently.

The military buyer attaches utmost importance to the producer's quality standards and the adequacy of his plant facilities. Only after these two considerations have been realized does price become a factor.

Quality is also of great importance to industrial customers, such as computer manufacturers, for their products are used by industrial manufacturers like themselves. Loyalties can be established in this segment through high quality and good service. Price itself is not a critical factor unless it gets completely out of line.

Commercial buyers, such as pocket-radio manufacturers, are in the most competitive user market and consequently buy their components completely on price and delivery. No loyalty to suppliers exists, and quality requirements are usually minimal.

Because of these differences, marketing strategies have to be varied. In order to sell microprocessors in the military market, firms must make a considerable investment in R&D, use salesmen who know military buying procedures, and specialize in limited-line products. In order to sell in the industrial market, firms must make a modest investment in R&D, use sales people who have technical knowledge concerning the product, and offer a broad line. In order to sell to the commercial market, firms need little or no R&D effort, can use sales people who are relatively nontechnical, and should offer the most common lines that can be mass produced.

Resellers handle a vast variety of products for resale, indeed everything produced except the few classes of goods that producers sell directly to final customers. The excluded class includes heavy or complex machinery, customized products, and products sold on a direct-mail or a door-to-door basis. With these exceptions, most products are sold to final buyers through selling intermediaries.

Suppliers should view resellers as purchasing agents for their customers, not selling agents for the suppliers. Suppliers will be successful to the extent they can help the resellers serve the buyers they represent better.

What Buying Decisions Do Resellers Make?

Resellers have to make the following purchasing decisions: *What assortment to carry*? *What vendors to buy from*? and *What prices and terms to negotiate*? The assortment decision is primary and positions the reseller in the marketplace. Wholesalers and retailers can choose one of four assortment strategies:

☐ **Exclusive assortment:** carrying the line of only one manufacturer
☐ **Deep assortment:** carrying a product family in depth, drawing on many producers' outputs

☐ **Broad assortment:** carrying several product lines that fall within the normal scope of the reseller's type of business

☐ **Scrambled assortment:** carrying many unrelated product lines

Thus a camera store might carry only Kodak cameras (exclusive assortment); many brands of cameras (deep assortment); cameras, tape recorders, radios, and stereophonic equipment (broad assortment); or the last plus stoves and refrigerators (scrambled assortment). The reseller's chosen assortment will influence its customer mix, marketing mix, and supplier mix.

Resellers confront three types of buying situations.

The *new-item situation* describes the situation where the reseller is offered a new item. The reseller will give a yes-no answer, depending on how good the item looks. This differs from the new-task situation faced by producers who definitely have to purchase the needed item from someone.

The *best-vendor situation* faces the reseller who needs an item and must determine the best supplier. This occurs in two situations: (1) when the reseller does not have the space to carry all the available brands, and (2) when the reseller is seeking someone to produce a private brand. Resellers such as Sears and the A&P sell a substantial number of items under their own name; therefore much of their buying operation consists of vendor selection.

The *better-terms situation* arises when the reseller wants to obtain better terms from current suppliers. Legally, suppliers are prevented, under the Robinson-Patman Act, from granting different terms to different resellers in the same reseller class unless they reflect cost differences, distress sales, or other special conditions. Nevertheless, resellers will press their suppliers for preferential treatment, such as more service, easier credit terms, and larger-volume discounts.

Who Participates in the Reseller Buying Process?

Who does the buying for wholesale and retail organizations? In small "mom and pop" firms, the owner usually takes care of merchandise selection and buying. In large firms, buying is a specialized function and full-time job. Buying is carried out in different ways by department stores, supermarkets, drug wholesalers, and so on, and differences can even be found within each type of enterprise.

Consider supermarkets. In the corporate headquarters of a supermarket chain, specialist buyers (sometimes called merchandise managers) will have the responsibility for developing brand assortments and listening to new-brand presentations by salespersons. In some chains these buyers have the authority to accept or reject new items. In many chains, however, they are limited to screening "obvious rejects" and "obvious accepts"; otherwise they must bring new items to the chain's *buying committee* for approval. Borden found that the buyer's recommendation carries a lot of influence in the committee decision.[16]

---

[16] Neil H. Borden, Jr., *Acceptance of New Food Products by Supermarkets* (Boston: Division of Research, Graduate School of Business Administration, Harvard University, 1968).

Even when an item is accepted by a chain-store buying committee, chain-store managers may not carry it. According to one supermarket chain executive: "No matter what the sales representatives sell or buyers buy, the person who has the greatest influence on the final sale of the new item is the store manager." In the nation's chain and independent supermarkets, two-thirds of the new items accepted at the warehouse are ordered on the store manager's own decision, and only one-third represent forced distribution.[17]

Thus, producers face a major challenge trying to get new items into stores. They offer the nation's supermarkets between 150 and 250 new items each week, and store space does not permit more than 10 percent to be accepted.

Several studies have attempted to rank the acceptance criteria used by buyers, buying committees, and store managers. A. C. Nielsen Company asked store managers to rank on a three-point scale the importance of different elements in influencing their decision to accept a new item.[18] The results are shown below:

- Evidence of consumer acceptance   2.5
- Advertising/promotion   2.2
- Introductory terms and allowances   2.0
- Why item was developed   1.9
- Merchandising recommendations   1.8

Thus sellers stand the best chance when they can report strong evidence of consumer acceptance, present a well-designed advertising and sales promotion plan, and provide strong financial incentives to the retailer.[19]

The role of supermarket buyers, buying committees, and store managers characterize, with some variation, the buying organizations of other reseller enterprises. Large department-store chains use buyers who specialize by line of merchandise and have a lot of authority to select the merchandise to be featured. The buyers are aided by assistant buyers, who carry out a preliminary search and also do clerical tasks involved in ordering. The buyers may perform other functions such as demand forecasting, stock control, and merchandising. Individual store managers or their staff usually have some freedom with respect to which goods to order as well as which to display prominently.

What Are the Major Influences on Reseller Buyers?

Resellers are influenced by the same factors—environmental, organizational, interpersonal, and individual as shown in the earlier Figure 5–1. The seller has to note

---

[17] Robert W. Mueller and Franklin H. Graf, "New Items in the Food Industry, Their Problems and Opportunities" (Special report to the Annual Convention of the Supermarket Institute, Cleveland, May 20, 1968), p. 2.

[18] Ibid, p. 5.

[19] Also see David B. Montgomery, *New Product Distribution: An Analysis of Supermarket Buyer Decisions* (Cambridge, Mass.: Marketing Science Institute, March, 1973). Montgomery found the two most important variables to be company reputation and the perceived newness of the product.

these influences and develop strategies that help resellers make money or reduce their costs.

The individual buyer's buying style should be taken into account. Dickinson has distinguished seven buyer types:[20]

☐ **Loyal buyer.** This buyer remains loyal to a source year after year.
☐ **Opportunistic buyer.** This buyer selects those vendors who will further his or her long-term interests and drives the best bargain possible.
☐ **Best-deal buyer.** This buyer selects the best deal available at a given point in time.
☐ **Creative buyer.** This buyer tells the seller what he or she wants in the way of a product, services, and prices.
☐ **Advertising buyer.** This buyer attempts to obtain advertising money as part of every deal.
☐ **The chiseler.** This buyer constantly negotiates extra concessions in price. He accepts the vendor offering the greatest discount from the price he feels that other vendors might charge.
☐ **Nuts-and-bolts buyer.** This buyer selects merchandise that is the best constructed.

How Do Resellers Make Their Buying Decisions?

For new items, resellers use roughly the same buying process described for the industrial buyer. For standard items, resellers simply reorder goods when the inventory gets low. The orders are placed with the same suppliers as long as their terms, goods, and services are satisfactory. Buyers will try to renegotiate prices if their margins erode owing to rising operating costs. In many retail lines, the profit margin is so low (1 to 2 percent on sales in supermarkets, for example) that a sudden drop in demand or rise in operating costs will drive profits into the red.

Resellers are improving their buying skills over time. They are mastering the principles of demand forecasting, merchandise selection, stock control, space allocation, and display. They are learning to measure profit-per-cubic-foot rather than only profit per product.[21] They are making increased use of computers to keep current inventory figures, compute economic order quantities, prepare orders, and generate printouts of dollars spent on vendors and products. They can easily tell whether carrying a particular product is profitable.

Thus vendors are facing increasingly sophisticated buying on the part of resellers, and this accounts for some of the shifting of power from manufacturers to resellers. Vendors need to understand the resellers' changing requirements and to develop competitively attractive offers that help resellers serve their customers better. Table 5–4 lists several of the marketing tools used by vendors to improve the attractiveness of their offer to resellers.

---

[20] Roger A. Dickinson, *Buyer Decision Making* (Berkeley, Calif.: Institute of Business and Economic Research, 1967), p. 14–17.

[21] See Robert D. Buzzell, *Product Profitability Measurement and Merchandising Decisions* (Boston: Harvard University Press, 1965).

TABLE 5-4

VENDOR MARKETING TOOLS USED WITH RESELLERS

Cooperative advertising, where vendor agrees to pay a portion of the retailers advertising costs for the vendor's product.

Preticketing, where the vendor places a tag on each product listing its price, manufacturer, size, identification number, and color; these tags help the reseller reorder merchandise as it is sold.

Stockless purchasing, where the vendor carries the inventory and delivers goods to the reseller on short notice.

Automatic reordering systems, where the vendor supplies forms and computer links for the automatic reordering of merchandise by the reseller.

Advertising ads, such as glossy photos, broadcast scripts.

Special prices for storewide promotion.

Return and exchange privileges for the reseller.

Allowances for merchandise markdowns by the reseller.

Sponsorship of in-store demonstrations.

THE GOVERNMENT MARKET

Who Is in the Government Market?

The *government market* consists of *governmental units—federal, state, and local— that purchase or rent goods for carrying out the main functions of government*. In 1980 governmental units purchased $535 billion worth of products and services, or 20 percent of the gross national product, making it the nation's largest customer. The federal government accounts for approximately 35 percent of the total dollars spent by government at all levels.

What Buying Decisions Do Government Buyers Make?

Government buying is based on acquiring products and services that the voters establish as necessary to carry out public objectives. Government agencies buy an amazing range of products and services. They buy bombers, sculpture, chalkboards, furniture, toiletries, clothing, materials-handling equipment, fire engines, mobile equipment, and fuel. In 1980, federal, state, and local governmental units spent approximately $143 billion for education, $149 billion for defense, $64 billion for public welfare, $44 billion for health and hospitals, $33 billion for highways, $35 billion for natural resources, and smaller sums for postal service, space research, and housing and urban renewal. The mix of expenditures varied with the particular type of governmental unit, with defense looming large in the federal budget (33 percent) and education looming large in the state and local budgets (37 percent). No wonder the government market represents a tremendous market for any producer or reseller.

Each good that the government buys requires further decisions on how much

Exhibit 5-2

THE INSTITUTIONAL MARKET—A FOURTH TYPE OF ORGANIZATIONAL BUYING MARKET

The institutional market consists of institutions that make purchases in order to provide goods and services to those they care for and are responsible for. Schools, hospitals, nursing homes, and prisons are prime examples of institutional buyers. They are generally characterized by low budgets and captive clienteles. A hospital purchasing agent has to decide on the quality of food to buy for the patients. The buying objective is not profit since the food is provided free to the patients. The basic objective is not cost minimization either, because patients served with poor food in a hospital will complain to others and hurt the hospital's reputation. The hospital purchasing agent has to find institutional-food vendors whose quality meets a certain minimum standard and yet whose prices are low. Many food vendors set up a separate division to sell to institutional buyers because of their special buying needs and characteristics.

to buy, where to buy it, how much to pay, and what services to require. These decisions are made on the basis of trying to minimize *taxpayer cost*. Normally government buyers will favor the lowest-cost bidders that can meet the stated specifications. Parenthetically, the institutional market—which we have not described—overlaps with the government market and has many of the same buying characteristics. (See Exhibit 5–2.)

Who Participates in the Government Buying Process?

Who does the buying of the $476 billion worth of goods and services? Government buying organizations are found at the federal, state, and local levels. The federal level is the largest, and its buying units operate in the civilian and military sectors. The *federal civilian buying* establishment consists of seven categories (examples of each category are in parentheses): departments (Commerce), administration (General Services Administration), agencies (Federal Aviation Agency), boards (Railroad Retirement Board), commissions (Federal Communications Commission), the executive office (Bureau of the Budget), and miscellaneous (Tennessee Valley Authority). "No single federal agency contracts for all the government's requirements and no single buyer in any agency purchases all that agency's needs for any single item of supplies, equipment or services."[22] Many agencies control a substantial percentage of their own buying, particularly for industrial products and specialized equipment. At the same time, the General Services Administration plays a major role in centralizing the procurement of commonly used items in the civilian section (office furniture and equipment, vehicles, fuels, and so on) and in developing standardized buying procedures for the other agencies.

---

[22] Stanley E. Cohen, "Looking in the U.S. Government Market," *Industrial Marketing*, September 1964, pp. 129–38.

Federal military buying is carried out by the Defense Department, largely through the Defense Supply Agency and the army, navy, and air force. The Defense Supply Agency was set up in 1961 to procure and distribute supplies used by all military services in an effort to reduce costly duplication. It operates six supply centers, which specialize in construction, electronics, fuel, personnel support, industrial, and general supplies. The trend has been toward "single managers" for major product classifications. Each service branch procures equipment and supplies in line with its own mission; for example, the Army Department operates offices for acquiring its own material, vehicles, medical supplies and services, and weaponry.

State and local buying agencies include school districts, highway departments, hospitals, housing agencies, and many others. Each has its own buying procedures that sellers have to master.

What Are the Major Influences on Government Buyers?

Government buyers are influenced by environmental, organizational, interpersonal, and individual factors. A unique thing about government buying is that it is monitored closely by outside publics. One watchdog is Congress, and certain congressmen have made a career out of exposing government extravagance and waste. Another watchdog is the Bureau of the Budget, which checks on government spending and seeks to improve spending efficiency. Many private watchdog groups also watch government agencies to monitor how they spend the public's money.

Because spending decisions are subject to public review, government organizations get involved in considerable paper work. Elaborate forms must be filled out and signed before purchases are approved. The level of bureaucracy is high, and marketers have to find ways to "cut through the red tape."

Noneconomic criteria are playing a growing role in government buying. Government buyers are asked to favor depressed business firms and areas, small business firms, and business firms that avoid racial, sex, or age discrimination. Sellers need to keep these factors in mind when deciding whether to pursue government business.

How Do Government Buyers Make Their Buying Decisions?

Government buying practices appear complex and often frustrating to suppliers. In a recent survey, suppliers registered a variety of complaints about government purchasing procedures. These complaints included excessive paperwork, bureaucracy, needless regulations, emphasis on low bid prices, decision-making delays, frequent shifts in procurement personnel, and excessive policy changes.[23] Yet the ins and outs of selling to the government can be mastered in a short time. The government is generally helpful in diffusing information about its buying needs and procedures. Government is often as anxious to attract new suppliers as the suppliers are to find customers. For example, the Small Business Administration prints a booklet, "U.S. Government Purchasing, Specifications, and Sales Directory," listing thousands of items most fre-

---

[23] See "Out of the Maze," *Sales and Marketing Management*, April 9, 1979.

quently purchased by government and cross-referenced by the agencies most frequently buying them. The Government Printing Office prints "Commerce Business Daily," which lists current defense procurements estimated to exceed $10,000 and civilian agency procurements expected to exceed $5,000, as well as recent contract awards, which can provide leads to subcontracting markets. The General Services Administration operates business service centers in several major cities, whose staffs provide a complete education on the way government agencies buy and the steps that suppliers should follow. Various trade magazines and associations provide information on how to reach schools, hospitals, highway departments, and other government agencies.

Government buying procedures fall into two types: the *open bid* and the *negotiated contract*. Open-bid buying means that the government procuring office invites bids from qualified suppliers for carefully described items, generally awarding a contract to the lowest bidder. The supplier must consider whether it can meet the specifications and accept the terms. For commodities and standard items, such as fuel or school supplies, the specifications are not a hurdle. They may be a hurdle, however, for nonstandard items. The government procurement office is usually required to award the contract to the lowest bidder on a winner-take-all basis. In some cases allowance is made for the supplier's superior product or reputation for completing contracts.

In negotiated-contract buying, the agency works with one or more companies and directly negotiates a contract with one of them covering the project and terms. This type of buying occurs primarily in connection with complex projects, often involving major research-and-development cost and risk and/or where there is little effective competition. Contracts can have countless variations, such as *cost-plus pricing*, *fixed-pricing*, and *fixed price-and-incentive* (the supplier earns more if costs are reduced). Contract performance is open to review and renegotiation if the supplier's profits appear excessive.

Government contracts won by large companies give rise to substantial subcontracting opportunities for small companies. Thus government purchasing activity creates derived demand in the producer market. Subcontracting firms, however, must be willing to place performance bonds with the prime contractor, thereby assuming some of the risk.

Many companies that sell to the government have not manifested a marketing orientation—for a number of reasons. Total government spending is determined by elected officials rather than by marketing effort to develop this market. The government's procurement policies have emphasized price, leading the suppliers to invest all their effort in a technological orientation to bring their costs down. Where the product's characteristics are carefully specified, product differentiation is not a marketing factor. Nor are advertising and personal selling of much consequence in winning bids on an open-bid basis.

More companies are now establishing separate marketing departments to guide government-directed marketing effort. J. I. Case, Eastman Kodak, and Goodyear are examples. These companies want to coordinate bids and prepare them more scientifically, to propose projects to meet government needs rather than just to respond to government initiatives, to gather competitive intelligence, and to prepare stronger communications to describe the company's competence.

SUMMARY

The organizational market consists of all the individuals and organizations that buy goods for purposes of further production, resale, or redistribution. Organizations are a market for raw and manufactured materials and parts, installations, accessory equipment, and supplies and services.

Producers buy goods and services for the purpose of increasing sales, cutting costs, or meeting social and legal requirements. Compared with the consumer market, the producer market consists of fewer buyers, larger buyers, and more geographically concentrated buyers; the demand is derived, relatively inelastic, and more fluctuating; and the purchasing is more professional. Industrial buyers make decisions that vary with the buying situation or buyclass. Buyclasses comprise three types: straight rebuys, modified rebuys, and new tasks. The decision-making unit of a buying organization, the buying center, consists of persons who play any of five roles: users, influencers, buyers, deciders, and gatekeepers. The industrial marketer needs to know: Who are the major participants? In what decisions do they exercise influence? What is their relative degree of influence? and What evaluation criteria does each decision participant use? The industrial marketer also needs to understand the major environmental, organizational, interpersonal, and individual influences operating in the buying process. The buying process itself consists of eight stages called buyphases: problem recognition, general need description, product specification, supplier search, proposal solicitation, supplier selection, order-routine specification, and performance review. As industrial buyers become more sophisticated, industrial marketers must upgrade their marketing capabilities.

The reseller market consists of individuals and organizations that acquire and resell goods produced by others. Resellers have to decide on their assortment, suppliers, prices, and terms. They face three types of buying situations: new items, new vendors, and new terms. In small wholesale and retail organizations, buying may be carried on by one or a few individuals; in larger organizations, by a whole purchasing department. In a modern supermarket chain, the major participants include headquarters buyers, storewide buying committees, and individual store managers. With new items, the buyers go through a buying process similar to the one shown for industrial buyers; and with standard items, the buying process consists of routines for reordering and renegotiating contracts.

The government market is a vast one that annually purchases $476 billion worth of products and services—for the pursuit of defense, education, public welfare, and other public needs. Government buying practices are highly specialized and specified, with open bidding and/or negotiated contracts characterizing most of the buying. Government buyers operate under the watchful eye of Congress, the Bureau of the Budget, and several private watchdog groups. Hence they tend to fill out more forms, require more signatures, and respond more slowly in placing orders.

Questions

1. Discuss the major influences affecting how U.S. airlines buy airplane seats.

2. General Electric has begun to market a factory automation planning service along with CAD/CAM and robotic products in an attempt to sell fully automated factories-of-the-future to other manufacturers. Discuss the factors that will determine the success or failure of such a venture.

3. Farm-equipment dealers act as resellers for the products sold to them by equipment manufacturers. When International Harvester faced bankruptcy in the early 1980s, what marketing policies could they have used to prevent these resellers from abandoning them to carry a competing line of equipment?

4. How do the buying influences on the government buyer differ from those on the producer or reseller buyer?

5. Describe some of the major characteristics of commercial-services firms (finance, insurance, and real estate) as a market for goods and services.

6. There are several important institutional markets: hospitals, educational institutions, welfare organizations, and the like. Discuss the characteristic buying needs and buying organization for, say, educational institutions.

7. What types of assortment strategies are used by the following types of businesses: (a) bicycle shop, (b) sports shop, (c) pawn shop, (d) Salvation Army store, and (e) discount store?

8. A home-decorating service plans to buy a paint-mixing machine. Four machines are available:

Evoked Set	Price	Number of Speeds	Size (in Ounces)	Quietness Level*
1	$30	10	32	3
2	$22	7	30	4
3	$25	5	48	5
4	$22	5	30	4

* A score of 5 represents the least noise.

Which machine(s) would this company prefer if its decision making could be explained by: (a) a conjunctive model using cut-off points of less than $28, with at least 5 speeds, weighing 32 ounces, and with a quietness level equal to or greater than 4; (b) a disjunctive model based upon criteria of at least 8 speeds or at least 48 ounces; and (c) a lexicographic model with an importance ordering of least cost, size, speeds, and quietness. (See Exhibit 4–3 for discussion of these models.)

The Marketing Information System and Marketing Research

6

A wise man recognizes the convenience of a general statement, but he bows to the authority of a particular fact.

OLIVER WENDELL HOLMES, JR.

In order to pursue market opportunities as well as anticipate marketing problems, managers need to collect comprehensive and reliable information. Managers cannot carry out marketing analysis, planning, implementation and control without monitoring and researching customers, competitors, dealers, and their own sales and cost data. Marion Harper put it this way: "To manage a business well is to manage its future; and to manage the future is to manage information."[1]

In the long history of business enterprise, management has devoted most of its attention to managing *money*, *materials*, *machines*, and *men*. Management has paid less attention to the fifth critical resource of the firm: *information*. It is hard to find company executives who are highly satisfied with their marketing information. Their complaints include:

☐ There is not enough marketing information of the right kind.
☐ There is too much marketing information of the wrong kind.

---

[1] Marion Harper, Jr., "A New Profession to Aid Management," *Journal of Marketing*, January 1961, p. 1.

187

□ Marketing information is so dispersed throughout the company that it takes a great effort to locate simple facts.

□ Marketing information is sometimes suppressed by subordinates when they believe it will reflect unfavorably on their performance.

□ Important information often arrives too late to be useful.

□ It is difficult to know whether the information is accurate.

Many companies have not yet adapted to the intensified information requirements for effective marketing in a modern economy. Three developments render the need for marketing information stronger than at any time in the past.

□ **From local to national to international marketing.** As companies expand their geographical market coverage, their managers need more market information than ever before.

□ **From buyer needs to buyer wants.** As buyers' incomes increase, they become more selective in their choice of goods. Sellers find it harder to predict buyers' response to different features, styles, and other attributes, and they turn to formal systems of market research.

□ **From price to nonprice competition.** As sellers increase their use of branding, product differentiation, advertising, and sales promotion, they require information on the effectiveness of these marketing tools.

The explosive information requirements have been met on the supply side by impressive new information technologies. The last thirty years have witnessed the emergence of the computer, microfilming, closed-circuit television, copy machines, tape recorders, fascimile transmitters, and other devices that have revolutionized information handling. Nevertheless, many business firms lack information sophistication. Many firms do not have a marketing research department. Many other firms have small marketing research departments whose work is limited to routine forecasting, sales analysis, and occasional surveys. Only a few firms have developed advanced marketing information systems that provide company management with up-to-date marketing information and analysis.

CONCEPT AND COMPONENTS OF A MARKETING INFORMATION SYSTEM

Every firm is the scene of many information flows of interest to marketing managers. Many companies are studying their executives' information needs and designing *marketing information systems* (MIS) to meet these needs. Instead of a plethora of unrelated data, an MIS combines various inputs and presents integrated reports. We define a *marketing information system* as follows:[2]

A marketing information system is a continuing and interacting structure of people, equipment, and procedures to gather, sort, analyze, evaluate, and distribute pertinent, timely, and accurate information for use by marketing decision makers to improve their marketing planning, implementation, and control.

---

[2] This definition is adapted from "Marketing Information Systems: An Introductory Overview," in *Readings in Marketing Information Systems*, ed. Samuel V. Smith, Richard H. Brien, and James E. Stafford (Boston: Houghton Mifflin, 1968), p. 7.

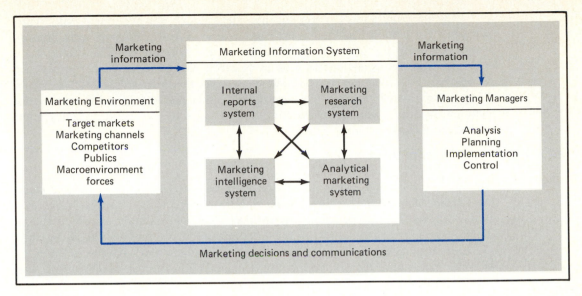

Figure 6-1
The Marketing Information System

The marketing-information-system concept is illustrated in Figure 6–1. The box on the left shows the components of the marketing environment that marketing managers must monitor. Trends in the marketing environment are picked up and analyzed through four subsystems making up the marketing information system—the *internal accounting system*, *marketing intelligence system*, *marketing research system*, and *analytical marketing system*. The information flows to marketing managers to help them in their marketing analysis planning, implementation, and control. Their marketing decisions and communications then flow back to the market.

We will now describe each of the four major subsystems of the company's MIS.

INTERNAL ACCOUNTING SYSTEM

The most basic information system used by marketing executives is the internal accounting system. It is the system that reports orders, sales, inventory levels, receivables, payables, and so on. By analyzing this information, marketing managers can spot important opportunities and problems.

The Order-Shipping-Billing Cycle

The heart of the accounting system is the order-shipping-billing cycle. Sales representatives, dealers, and customers dispatch orders to the firm. The order department prepares multicopy invoices and sends them to various departments. Out-of-stock items are back ordered. Shipped items are accompanied by shipping and billing documents that are also multicopied and sent to various departments.

The company wants to carry out these steps quickly and accurately. Sales representatives are supposed to send in their orders every evening, in some cases immediately. The order department is designed to process them quickly. The warehouse is set up to send the goods out as soon as possible. And bills should go out as soon as possible. The computer is harnessed to expedite the order-shipping-billing cycle. Ringer and Howell reported a company study that resulted in reducing the time between the receipt and execution of an order from sixty-two hours to thirty hours without any change in costs.[3]

Improving the Timeliness of Sales Reports

Marketing executives receive sales reports some time after the sales have taken place. In consumer-food companies, warehouse withdrawal reports are issued with fair regularity, but actual retail purchase reports take about two months, based on special store or consumer panel audits. In the auto industry, executives wait about ten days for their sales report; if sales are down, they will have to work harder and face ten sleepless nights until the next report. Many marketing executives complain that sales aren't reported fast enough in their company.

Here are three companies that have designed timely and comprehensive sales-reporting systems:

□ **General Mills.** Managers in the Grocery Products Division at General Mills receive sales information daily. Zone, regional, and district sales managers start their day with a teletype report on orders and shipments in their area the day before. The report also contains percentages to compare with target percentages and the previous year's percentages.

□ **Schenley.** Managers at Schenley can retrieve within seconds current and past sales and inventory figures for any brand and package size for each of four hundred distributors. They can determine all areas where sales are lagging behind targets.

□ **Mead Paper.** Mead sales representatives can obtain on-the-spot answers to customers' questions about paper availability by dialing Mead Paper's computer center. The computer determines whether paper is available at the nearest warehouse and when it can be shipped; if it is not in stock, the computer checks the inventory at other nearby warehouses until one is located. If the paper is nowhere in stock, the computer determines where and when the paper can be produced. The sales representative gets an answer in seconds and thus has an advantage over competitors.

Designing a User-Oriented Reports System

In designing an advanced sales-information system, the company should avoid certain pitfalls. First, it is possible to create a system that delivers too much information. The managers arrive at their office each morning to face voluminous sales statistics, which they either ignore or spend too much time on. Second, it is possible to create a system that delivers information that is too current! Managers may end up overreacting to minor sales declines.

With all the new information technology available, companies have to choose

---

[3] Jurgen F. Ringer and Charles D. Howell, "The Industrial Engineer and Marketing," in *Industrial Engineering Handbook*, 2nd ed., ed. Harold Bright Maynard (New York: McGraw-Hill Book Co., 1963), pp. 10, 102–3.

TABLE 6-1

QUESTIONNAIRE FOR DETERMINING MARKETING INFORMATION NEEDS

1. What types of decisions are you regularly called upon to make?
2. What types of information do you need to make these decisions?
3. What types of information do you regularly get?
4. What types of special studies do you periodically request?
5. What types of information would you like to get that you are not getting now?
6. What information would you want daily? Weekly? Monthly? Yearly?
7. What magazines and trade reports would you like to see routed to you on a regular basis?
8. What specific topics would you like to be kept informed of?
9. What types of data-analysis programs would you like to see made available?
10. What do you think would be the four most helpful improvements that could be made in the present marketing information system?

those components that its management can handle. Cox and Good see a need for system-manager balance:

> In a "steady state" . . . there usually seems to be a correspondence between management sophistication and information quality. . . . What happens when only the level of information quality is raised significantly? Our prediction is that this would not lead to better decisions. In fact, the reverse may be true, as the result of the confusion and resentment generated by the manager's inability to deal with the more sophisticated information.
>
> Information quality can be upgraded much more rapidly than management quality. It is easy to throw the management system out of balance by installing a sophisticated MIS. . . . A more positive approach is to develop a master plan for improving the system, but make the improvements gradually—say, over several years.[4]

The company's marketing information system should represent a cross between what managers think they need, what managers really need, and what is economically feasible. A useful step is the appointment of a *marketing information planning committee*, which interviews a cross-section of marketing executives—product managers, sales managers, sales representatives, and so on—to find out their information needs. A useful set of questions is shown in Table 6–1. The information planning committee will want to pay special attention to strong desires and complaints. At the same time, the committee will wisely discount some of the alleged information needs. Managers who have an appetite for information will list a great deal, failing to distinguish between *what is nice to know* and *what they need to know.* Other managers will be too busy to give the questionnaire serious thought and will omit many things they ought to know. This is why the information planning committee must take another step, that of determining what managers *should know* to be able to make responsible decisions. For example, what do brand managers need to know in order to set the

---

[4] Donald F. Cox and Robert E. Good, "How to Build a Marketing Information System," *Harvard Business Review*, May–June 1967, pp. 145–54.

size of the advertising budget? Suppose they should know the degree of market saturation, the rate of sales decay in the absence of advertising, and the spending plans
of competitors. The information system should be designed to provide the data needed
for making the key marketing decisions.

MARKETING INTELLIGENCE SYSTEM

While the internal accounting system supplies executives with *results data*, the marketing intelligence system supplies executives with *happenings* data. We define the *marketing intelligence system* as *the set of procedures and sources used by executives to obtain
their everyday information about pertinent developments in the marketing environment*.

Executives scan the environment in four ways:[5]

- ☐ **Undirected viewing:** general exposure to information where the manager has no specific
  purpose in mind.
- ☐ **Conditioned viewing:** directed exposure, not involving active search, to a more or less
  clearly identified area or type of information.
- ☐ **Informal search:** a relatively limited and unstructured effort to obtain specific information
  or information for a specific purpose.
- ☐ **Formal search:** a deliberate effort—usually following a preestablished plan, procedure,
  or methodology—to secure specific information or information relating to a specific
  issue.

Marketing executives carry on marketing intelligence mostly on their own by
reading books, newspapers, and trade publications; talking to customers, suppliers,
distributors, and other outsiders; and talking with other managers and personnel
within the company. Yet this system is quite casual, and valuable information may
be lost or come in too late. Executives may learn of a competitive move, a new-
customer need, or a dealer problem too late to make the best response.

Well-run companies take additional steps to improve the quality and quantity
of marketing intelligence. First, they train and motivate the sales force to spot and
report new developments. Sales representatives are the company's "eyes and ears."
They are in an excellent position to pick up information missed by other means.
Yet they are very busy and often fail to pass on significant information. The company
must "sell" its sales force on their importance as intelligence gatherers and must
emphasize this importance through their sales bonuses. The sales force should be
provided with easy reports to fill out. Sales representatives should know which type
of information goes to which manager in their company.

Second, the company motivates distributors, retailers, and other allies to pass
along important intelligence. Some companies appoint specialists to gather marketing
intelligence. They send out "ghost shoppers" to monitor the presentations of retail
personnel. Much can be learned about competitors through purchasing competitors'
products; attending open houses and trade shows; reading competitors' published
reports and attending stockholders' meetings; talking to competitors' former employees
and present employees, dealers, distributors, suppliers, and freight agents; collecting

[5] Francis Joseph Aguilar, *Scanning the Business Environment* (New York: Macmillan Co., 1967).

competitors' ads; and reading the *Wall Street Journal*, *New York Times*, and trade association papers.

Third, the company purchases information from outside intelligence suppliers. The A. C. Nielsen Company sells bimonthly data (based on a sample of sixteen hundred stores) on brand shares, retail prices, percentage of stores stocking the item, and percentage of stock-out stores. Market Research Corporation of America sells reports (based on the purchase diaries of a representative panel of seventy-five hundred households scattered throughout the country) on weekly movements of brand shares, sizes, prices, and deals. Clipping services are hired to report on competitors' ads, advertising expenditures, and media mixes.

Fourth, some companies have established information centers to collect and circulate marketing intelligence. The staff scans major publications, abstracts relevant news, and disseminates a news bulletin to marketing managers. It develops a file of relevant information. The staff assists managers in evaluating new information. These services greatly improve the quality of information available to marketing managers. (See Exhibit 6–1.)

Exhibit 6-1

A NEW ANSWER TO INFORMATION NEEDS—INFORMATION CENTERS

Although the concept of an *integrated management information system* was widely discussed in the 1960s, few companies did anything to centralize and coordinate their information flows. Many managers complained that needed information was somewhere in the company but that it would take too long to find. There would be no one place to find a list of the data files available in the company.

Beginning in 1979, IBM recommended that its clients establish *information centers* as adjuncts of existing data-processing departments. Many of IBM's larger clients have now done this. Travelers Insurance Company, for example, opened its information center in December 1981 with ten consultants answering 200 calls for assistance a month. A year later, Travelers had twenty consultants handling 4,000 calls a month.

Managers have found these information centers to be real time savers. In one case, an insurance manager needed to know why customers in a certain part of the country were not renewing their insurance policies. The information center quickly drew data, analyzed it, and demonstrated that the company's rates had become uncompetitive.

One of the main advantages of establishing an information center is that it leads the company for the first time to compile a list of what data files exist and where they are located, as well as what data gaps exist in terms of questions frequently asked by managers. In addition, these centers often provide a higher level of data analysis than busy executives can achieve by themselves. Montgomery and Weinberg see these centers performing many functions including data evaluation, data transformation into information, data transmission, data accumulation, data analysis, and pattern recognition.

Source: See *"Helping Decision Makers Get at Data,"* Business Week, *September 13, 1982, p. 118;* and *David B. Montgomery and Charles B. Weinberg, "Toward Strategic Intelligence Systems,"* Journal of Marketing, *Fall 1979, pp. 41–57.*

Besides internal accounting information and marketing intelligence, marketing executives often need focused studies of specific problems and opportunities. They may need a market survey, a product-preference test, a sales forecast by region, or an advertising-effectiveness study. The managers themselves normally do not have the skill or time to obtain this information. They need to commission formal marketing research. We define *marketing research* as follows:

> **Marketing research is the systematic design, collection, analysis, and reporting of data and findings relevant to a specific marketing situation facing the company.**

Suppliers of Marketing Research

A company can obtain marketing research in a number of ways. Small companies can ask students or professors at a local college to design and carry out the project, or they can hire a marketing research firm. Larger companies, in fact over 73 percent of them, have their own marketing research departments.[6] Marketing research departments consist of anywhere from one to several dozen researchers. The marketing research manager normally reports to the marketing vice-president and acts as a study director, administrator, company consultant, and advocate. The marketing research staff includes survey designers, statisticians, behavioral scientists, and model builders.

Companies normally budget marketing research at anywhere from 0.01 to 3.50 percent of company sales. Between one-half and three-quarters of this money is spent directly by the department, and the remainder is spent in buying the services of outside marketing research firms. Marketing research firms fall into three groups:

☐ **Syndicated-service research firms.** These firms gather periodic consumer and trade information, which they sell for a fee to clients. Marketing managers can purchase reports on television audiences from the A. C. Nielsen Company or the American Research Bureau (ARB); on radio audiences, from the ARB: on magazine audiences, from Simmons or the Target Group Index (TGI); on warehouse movements, from the Selling Areas-Marketing, Inc. (SAMI); and on retail shelf audits, from Nielsen. Nielsen, the largest of these firms, had estimated billings of $363 million in 1980.

☐ **Custom marketing research firms.** These firms are hired to carry out specific research projects. They participate in designing the study, and the report becomes the client's property. Market Facts is one of the leading custom marketing research firms, with annual billings of approximately $23 million.

☐ **Specialty-line marketing research firms.** These firms provide a specialized service to other marketing research firms and company marketing research departments. The best example is the field service firm, which sells field interviewing services to other firms.

----

[6] Dik Warren Twedt, ed., *1978 Survey of Marketing Research: Organization, Functions, Budget, Compensation* (Chicago: American Marketing Association, 1978).

The Scope of Marketing Research

Marketing researchers have steadily expanded their activities and techniques. Table 6–2 lists thirty-three marketing research activities and the percentage of companies carrying on each. The ten most common activities are *determination of market characteristics, measurement of market potentials, market-share analysis, sales analysis, stud-*

TABLE 6–2

RESEARCH ACTIVITIES OF 798 COMPANIES

Type of Research	Percent Doing
Advertising research:	
Motivation research	48
Copy research	49
Media research	61
Studies of ad effectiveness	67
Business economics and corporate research:	
Short-range forecasting (up to 1 year)	85
Long-range forecasting (over 1 year)	82
Studies of business trends	86
Pricing studies	81
Plant and warehouse location studies	71
Product-mix studies	51
Acquisition studies	69
Export and international studies	51
MIS (management information system)	72
Operations research	60
Internal company employees	65
Corporate responsibility research:	
Consumers "right to know" studies	26
Ecological impact studies	33
Studies of legal constraints on advertising and promotion	51
Social values and policies studies	40
Product research:	
New-product acceptance and potential	84
Competitive-product studies	85
Testing of existing products	75
Packaging research—design or physical characteristics	60
Sales and market research:	
Measurement of market potentials	93
Market-share analysis	92
Determination of market characteristics	93
Sales analysis	89
Establishment of sales quotas, territories	75
Distribution-channels studies	69
Test markets, store audits	54
Consumer-panel operations	50
Sales-compensation studies	60
Promotional studies of premiums, coupons, sampling, deals, etc.	52

SOURCE: Reprinted from Dik Warren Twedt, ed., 1978 Survey of Marketing Research (Chicago: American Marketing Association 1978), p. 41.

TABLE 6–3

EVOLVING TECHNIQUES IN MARKETING RESEARCH

Decade	Technique
Prior to 1910	Firsthand observation Elementary surveys
1910–20	Sales analysis Operating-cost analysis
1920–30	Questionnaire construction Survey technique
1930–40	Quota sampling Simple correlation analysis Distribution-cost analysis Store auditing techniques
1940–50	Probability sampling Regression methods Advanced statistical inference Consumer and store panels
1950–60	Motivation research Operations research Multiple regression and correlation Experimental design Attitude-measuring instruments
1960–70	Factor analysis and discriminant analysis Mathematical models Bayesian statistical analysis and decision theory Scaling theory Computer data processing and analysis Marketing simulation Information storage and retrieval
1970–80	Multidimensional scaling Econometric models Comprehensive marketing planning models Test-marketing laboratories Multiattribute attitude models
1980–	Conjoint analysis and tradeoff analysis Causal analysis

ies of business trends, competitive-product studies, short-range forecasting, new-produ acceptance and potential, long-range forecasting, and *pricing studies.*[7]

These studies have benefited from increasingly sophisticated techniques. Tab. 6–3 shows the approximate decade when various techniques come into consideratio.. or use in marketing research. Many of them—such as questionnaire construction and area sampling—came along early and were quickly and widely applied by marketing researchers. Others—such as motivation research and mathematical methods—came in uneasily, with prolonged and heated debates among practitioners over their practical usefulness. But they, too, settled in the corpus of marketing research methodology.

_____
[7] Twedt, *1978 Survey.*

The Marketing Research Process

Marketing research is undertaken to understand a marketing problem better. A brand manager at Procter & Gamble will commission three or four major marketing research studies annually. Marketing managers in smaller companies will order fewer marketing research studies. Nonprofit organizations increasingly find that they need marketing research. A hospital wants to know whether people in its service area have a positive attitude toward the hospital. A college wants to determine what kind of image it has among high school counselors. A political organization wants to find out what voters think of the candidates.

Managers requesting marketing research need to know enough about its potentialities and limitations so that they can get the right information at a reasonable cost. If they know nothing about marketing research, they might allow the wrong information to be collected, or collected too expensively, or interpreted incorrectly. One protection is to work with highly experienced marketing researchers because it is in their interest to produce information that leads to correct decisions. Equally important is that managers know enough about marketing research procedure to participate in its planning and subsequent interpretation. Effective marketing research involves five steps: *defining the problem and research objectives*, *developing the information sources*, *collecting the information*, *analyzing the information*, and *presenting the findings* (see Figure 6–2). We will illustrate these steps with the following situation:

> American Airlines, one of the largest U.S. air carriers, is constantly looking for new ways to serve the needs of air travelers. Management would like to offer some new service that will give it a competitive advantage. Toward this end, a few managers convened in a brainstorming session and generated a number of ideas revolving around better food service, in-flight entertainment, newspaper and magazine availability, and so on. One manager came up with the idea of offering phone service to passengers who wished to make calls while riding 30,000 feet above the earth. The other managers got excited about this idea and agreed that it should be researched further. The marketing manager who suggested the idea then volunteered to do some preliminary research. He contacted a major telecommunications company to find out if telephone service could technically be provided aboard B-747 flights between the East Coast and West Coast. He wanted to know how many calls would have to take place during an average flight, and at what price, to cover the cost of offering the service. The telecommunications company said that the system would cost the airline about $1,000 a flight. The airline could break even if it charged $25 a phone call and at least 40 passengers made calls during the flight. The marketing manager then contacted the company's marketing research manager and asked him to find out how air travelers would respond to this new service.

Defining the problem and research objectives. The first step in research calls for the marketing manager and marketing researcher to define the problem carefully and agree on the research objectives. There are hundreds of things that can be researched in any problem. Unless the problem is well defined, the cost of information gathering may well exceed the value of the findings. An old adage says "A problem well defined is half solved."

Management must steer between defining the problem too broadly and defining it too narrowly. If the marketing manager tells the marketing researcher: "Find out

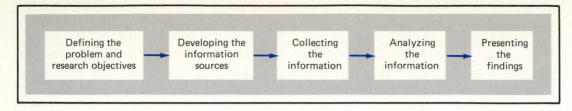

Figure 6-2
The Marketing Research Process

everything you can about air travelers' needs," the manager will get much unneeded information and may not get the information he or she really needs. On the other hand, if the marketing manager says: "Find out if enough passengers aboard a B-747 flying between the East Coast and West Coast would be willing to pay enough to call others so that American Airlines would break even on the cost of offering this service," this is too narrow a view of the problem. The marketing researcher at that point could say: "Why does American have to break even on the cost of the service itself? Advertising this service might get enough new passengers to fly American so that even if they don't make enough phone calls, American will get its money back. Many travelers might fly American just because they like to know there is a phone aboard even if they probably won't use it."

The two managers worked further on the problem, and another issue arose. If the new service was successful, how fast could other airlines copy it? The history of airline marketing competition is replete with examples of new services that are so quickly copied by competitors that no airline gains a sustainable competitive advantage. Therefore it is important to determine the value of being first and how long the lead would be sustained.

The marketing manager and marketing researcher agreed to define the problem as follows: "Will offering an in-flight phone service create enough incremental preference and profit for American airlines to justify its cost against other possible investments that American might make?" They then agreed on the following specific research objectives:

1. What are the main reasons why airline passengers might place phone calls while in flight instead of after landing?
2. What kinds of passengers would be the most likely to make phone calls during a flight?
3. How many passengers on a typical long-distance B-747 flight are likely to make phone calls, and how will this be affected by price? What would be the best price to charge?
4. How many extra passengers might choose the American flight because of this new service?
5. How much long-term goodwill will this service add to American Airlines' image?
6. What is the relative importance of other factors, such as flight frequency, food, and baggage handling, in influencing air-carrier choice, and how important will phone service be relative to these other factors?

Not all research projects can be made this specific in its objectives. Three types of research projects can be distinguished. Some research is *exploratory*; i.e., to gather

TABLE 6-4

CONSTRUCTING THE RESEARCH PLAN			
Data Sources:	Secondary data	Primary data	
Research approaches:	Observation	Surveys	Experiments
Research instruments:	Questionnaires	Mechanical instruments	
Sampling plan:	Sampling unit	Sample size	Sampling procedure
Contact methods:	Telephone	Mail	Personal

preliminary data to shed light on the real nature of the problem and possibly suggest some hypotheses or new ideas. Some research is *descriptive,* i.e., to describe certain magnitudes, such as how many people would make an in-flight phone call at $25 a call. Some research is *causal,* i.e., to test a cause-and-effect relationship, such as that a $20 charge as opposed to a $25 charge would increase the number of phone calls by at least 20 percent.

Developing the research plan. The second stage of marketing research calls for developing the most efficient plan for gathering the needed information. The marketing executive cannot simply suggest to the marketing researcher: "Find some passengers and ask them if they would make use of an in-flight phone service if it were available." The research plan should be designed professionally. At the same time, the marketing manager should know enough about marketing research to approve the research plan and know how to interpret its findings.

Table 6–4 shows that designing a research plan calls for decisions on the *data sources*, *research approaches*, *research instruments*, *sampling plan*, and *contact methods*.

Data sources. The research plan can call for gathering secondary data, primary data, or both. *Secondary data is information that already exists somewhere*, *having been collected for another purpose*. Otherwise the researcher has to gather *primary data*, *which consists of original information for the specific purpose at hand*.

SECONDARY DATA. Researchers usually start their investigation by examining secondary data to see whether their problem can be partly or wholly solved without resorting to costly primary-data collection. Table 6–5 shows the rich variety of secondary-data sources available, including *internal source*s (company profit-and-loss statements, sales-call reports, prior-research reports), and *external sources* (government publications, periodicals and books, and commercial services).[8]

In the case of the American Airlines project, the researchers will find plenty of secondary data on the air travel market. For example, U.S. Civil Aeronautics Board publications provide data on the size, growth, and market shares of the various carriers. The Air Transport Association of America has numerous studies in its library

---

[8] For an excellent annotated reference to major secondary sources of business and marketing data, see Thomas C. Kinnear and James R. Taylor, *Marketing Research*: *An Applied Approach* (New York, McGraw-Hill Book Co., 1979), pp. 128–31, 138–71.

TABLE 6-5

SECONDARY SOURCES OF DATA

A. Internal sources

Internal sources include company profit-loss statements, balance sheets, sales figures, sales-call reports, invoices, inventory records, and prior-research reports.

B. Government publications

Statistical Abstract of the U.S., updated annually, provides summary data on demographic, economic, social, and other aspects of the American economy and society.

County and City Data Book, updated every three years, presents statistical information for counties, cities, and other geographical units on population, education, employment, aggregate and median income, housing, bank deposits, retail sales, etc.

U.S. Industrial Outlook provides projections of industrial activity by industry and includes data on production, sales, shipments, employment, etc.

Marketing Information Guide provides a monthly annotated bibliography of marketing information.

Other government publications include the **Annual Survey of Manufacturers; Business Statistics; Census of Manufacturers; Census of Population; Census of Retail Trade, Wholesale Trade, and Selected Service Industries; Census of Transportation; Federal Reserve Bulletin; Monthly Labor Review; Survey of Current Business;** and **Vital Statistics Report.**

C. Periodicals and Books

Business Periodicals Index, a monthly, lists business articles appearing in a wide variety of business publications.

Standard and Poor's Industry Surveys provides updated statistics and analyses of industries.

Moody's Manuals provide financial data and names of executives in major companies.

Encyclopedia of Associations provides information on every major trade and professional association in the U.S.

Marketing journals include the **Journal of Marketing, Journal of Marketing Research,** and **Journal of Consumer Research.**

Useful trade magazines include **Advertising Age, Chain Store Age, Progressive Grocer, Sales and Marketing Management,** and **Stores.**

Useful general business magazines include **Business Week, Fortune, Forbes,** and **Harvard Business Review.**

D. Commercial Data

A. C. Nielsen Company provides data on products and brands sold through retail outlets (Retail Index Services), data on television audiences (Media Research Services), magazine circulation data (Neodata Services, Inc.), etc.

Market Research Corporation of America provides data on weekly family purchases of consumer products (National Consumer Panel), data on home food consumption (National Menu Census), and data on 6,000 retail, drug, and discount retailers in various geographical areas (Metro Trade Audits).

Selling Areas-Marketing, Inc., provides reports on warehouse withdrawals to food stores in selected market areas (SAMI reports).

Simmons Market Research Bureau provides annual reports covering television markets, sporting goods, proprietary drugs, etc., giving demographic data by sex, income, age, and brand preferences (selective markets and media reaching them).

Other commercial research houses selling data to subscribers include the **Audit Bureau of Circulation, Audits and Surveys, Dun and Bradstreet, National Family Opinion, Standard Rate and Data Service,** and **Starch.**

on the characteristics, carrier preferences, and behavior of air travelers. Similarly, various travel agencies have data that might throw light on how air travelers choose their carriers.

Secondary data provides a starting point for research and offers the advantages of lower cost and quicker availability. On the other hand, the data needed by the researcher might not exist, or the existing data might be dated, inaccurate, incomplete, or unreliable. In this case, the researcher will have to collect primary data at greater cost and longer delay, but probably with more relevance and accuracy.

PRIMARY DATA. Most marketing research projects involve some primary-data collection. Primary-data collection is more costly, but the data is usually more relevant to the issue at hand. The normal procedure is to interview some people individually and/or in groups to get a preliminary sense of how people feel about air carriers and particular services and, on the basis of the findings, develop a more formal and extensive interviewing approach and research instrument, debug it, and then carry it into the field. The various options facing the researcher for collecting primary data can be seen more clearly by examining the second element of the research plan, namely, alternative research approaches.

Research approaches.   Primary data can be collected in three broad ways: observation, surveys, and experiments.

OBSERVATIONAL RESEARCH. One way to gather fresh data is to observe the relevant actors and settings. The American Airlines researchers might linger around airports, airline offices, and travel agencies to hear how travelers talk about the different carriers and how agents handle the flight arrangement process. The researchers can fly on American and competitors' planes to observe the quality of in-flight service and hear consumer reactions. Their observations might yield some useful hypotheses about how travelers choose their air carriers.

SURVEY RESEARCH. Survey research stands midway between the casualness of observational research and the rigor of experimental research. Generally speaking, observation is best suited for exploratory research, surveys are best fitted for descriptive research, and experiments are best suited for causal research. Companies undertake surveys to learn about people's knowledge, beliefs, preferences, satisfaction, and so on, and to measure these magnitudes in the population. Thus American Airlines researchers might want to survey how many people know American, have flown it, prefer it, and so on. We will say more about survey research when we move to research instruments, sampling plan, and contact methods.

EXPERIMENTAL RESEARCH. The most formal type of research is experimental research. Experimental research calls for selecting matched groups of subjects, giving them different treatments, controlling extraneous variables, and checking on whether observed differences are statistically significant. To the extent that extraneous factors are eliminated or controlled, the observed effects can be related to the variations in the stimuli. The purpose of experimental research is to capture cause-and-effect relationships by eliminating competing explanations of the observed findings.

An example of an experimental research design would be the setting up by American of in-flight phone service on one of its regular flights from New York to Los Angeles. During the first flight, it announces the availability of this service at

Exhibit 6-2

A "QUESTIONABLE" QUESTIONNAIRE

Suppose an airline prepared the following questionnaire to use to interview passengers. What do you think of each question? (Answer before reading the comment in each box.)

1. What is your income to the nearest hundred dollars?

> People don't necessarily know their income to the nearest hundred dollars, nor do they want to reveal their income that closely. Furthermore, a questionnaire should never open with such a personal question.

2. Are you an occasional or frequent flyer?

> How do you define frequent versus occasional flying?

3. Do you like this airline?
   Yes ( ) No ( )

> *Like* is a relative term. Besides, will people answer this honestly? Furthermore, is yes-no the best way to allow a response to the question? Why is the question being asked in the first place?

4. How many airline ads did you see on television last April? This April?

> Who can remember this?

5. What are the most salient and determinant attributes in your evaluation of air carriers?

> What are "salient" and "determinant" attributes? Don't use big words on me.

6. Do you think it is right for the government to tax air tickets and deprive a lot of people of the chance to fly?

> Loaded question. How can one answer this biased question?

$25 a phone call. On the same flight the following day, it announces the availability of this service at $15 a phone call. If the plane carried the same number of passengers on each flight, and the day of the week made no difference, then any significant difference in the number of calls made could be related to the price charged. The experimental design could be elaborated further by trying other prices, replicating the same price on a number of flights, and including other routes in the experiment.

The experimental method supplies the most convincing information as to whether the proper controls are exercised. To the extent that the design and execution of the experiment eliminate alternative hypotheses that might explain the same results, the research and marketing managers can have confidence in the conclusions.[9]

Research instruments. Marketing researchers have a choice of two main research instruments in collecting primary data: the questionnaire and mechanical devices.

QUESTIONNAIRES. The questionnaire is by far the most common instrument in collecting primary data. Broadly speaking, a questionnaire consists of a set of questions presented to a respondent for his or her answers. The questionnaire is very flexible in that there are a great number of ways to ask questions. Questionnaires need to be carefully developed, tested, and debugged before they are administered on a large scale. One can usually spot several errors in a casually prepared questionnaire (see Exhibit 6–2).

In preparing a questionnaire, the marketing researcher carefully chooses the questions asked, the form of the questions, the wording of the questions, and the sequencing of the questions.

A common type of error occurs in the *questions asked*, that is, in including questions that cannot be answered or would not be answered or need not be answered and in omitting questions that should be answered. Each question should be checked to determine whether it contributes to the research objectives. Questions that are merely interesting should be dropped because they lengthen the time required and try the respondent's patience.

The *form of the question* can influence the response. Marketing researchers distinguish between closed-end and open-end questions. *Closed-end questions* include all the possible answers, and the respondent makes a choice from among them. Table 6–6A shows the most common forms of closed-end questions.

Open-end questions allow the respondent to answer in his or her own words. They take various forms; the main ones are shown in Table 6–6B. Generally speaking, open-end questions often reveal more because respondents are not constrained in their answers. Open-end questions are especially useful in the exploratory stage of research where the investigator is looking for insight into how people think rather than in measuring how many people think in a certain way. Closed-end questions, on the other hand, provide answers that are easier to interpret and tabulate.

Care should be exercised in the *wording of questions*. The researcher should use simple, direct, unbiased wording. The questions should be pretested with respondents before they are used to a wide extent.

Care should also be exercised in the *sequencing of questions*. The lead question should create interest if possible. Difficult or personal questions should be asked toward the end of the interview so that respondents do not become defensive. The questions should come up in a logical order. Classificatory data on the respondent are put last because they are more personal and less interesting to the respondent.

MECHANICAL INSTRUMENTS. Although questionnaires are the most common research instrument, mechanical devices are also used in marketing research. Galvanometers are used to measure the strength of a subject's interest or emotions aroused

---

[9] For more reading on experimental research, see Seymour Banks, *Experimentation in Marketing* (New York: McGraw-Hill Book Co., 1965).

TABLE 6-6

TYPES OF QUESTIONS

A. Closed-End Questions

Name	Description	Example
Dichotomous	A question offering two answer choices.	"In arranging this trip, did you personally phone American?" Yes ☐ No ☐
Multiple choice	A question offering three or more answer choices.	"With whom are you traveling on this flight?" No one ☐ Children only ☐ Spouse ☐ Business associates/ Spouse and friends/relatives ☐ children ☐ An organized tour group ☐
Likert scale	A statement with which the respondent shows the amount of agreement/disagreement.	"Small airlines generally give better service than large ones." Strongly Disagree Neither Agree Strongly disagree agree nor agree disagree 1 ☐ 2 ☐ 3 ☐ 4 ☐ 5 ☐
Semantic differential	A scale is inscribed between two bipolar words, and the respondent selects the point that represents the direction and intensity of his or her feelings.	**American Airlines** Large X · __ · __ · __ · __ · __ Small Experienced __ · __ · __ · __ · X · __ Inexperienced Modern __ · __ · X · __ · __ · __ Old-fashioned
Importance scale	A scale that rates the importance of some attribute from "not at all important" to "extremely important."	"Airline food service to me is" Extremely Very Somewhat Not very Not at all important important important important important 1 __ 2 __ 3 __ 4 __ 5 __
Rating scale	A scale that rates some attribute from "poor" to "excellent."	"American's food service is" Excellent Very good Good Fair Poor 1 __ 2 __ 3 __ 4 __ 5 __

B. Open-End Questions

Name	Description	Example
Completely unstructured	A question that respondents can answer in an almost unlimited number of ways.	"What is your opinion of American Airlines?"
Word association	Words are presented, one at a time, and respondents mention the first word that comes to mind.	"What is the first word that comes to your mind when you hear the following?" Airline _____ American _____ Travel _____
Sentence completion	Incomplete sentences are presented, one at a time, and respondents complete the sentence.	"When I choose an airline, the most important consideration in my decision is _____ _____
Story completion	An incomplete story is presented, and respondents are asked to complete it.	"I flew American a few days ago. I noticed that the exterior and interior of the plane had very bright colors. This aroused in me the following thoughts and feelings." **Now complete the story.**

TABLE 6–6 Continued

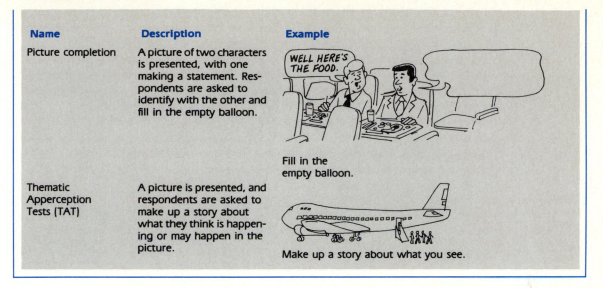

Name	Description	Example
Picture completion	A picture of two characters is presented, with one making a statement. Respondents are asked to identify with the other and fill in the empty balloon.	WELL HERE'S THE FOOD. Fill in the empty balloon.
Thematic Apperception Tests (TAT)	A picture is presented, and respondents are asked to make up a story about what they think is happening or may happen in the picture.	Make up a story about what you see.

by an exposure to a specific ad or picture. The galvanometer picks up the minute degree of sweating that accompanies emotional arousal. The tachistoscope is a device that flashes an ad to a subject with an exposure interval that may range from less than one hundredth of a second to several seconds. After each exposure, the respondent describes everything he or she recalls. Eye cameras are used to study respondent's eye movements to see at what points their eyes land first, how long they linger on a given item, and so on. The audimeter is an electronic device that is attached to television sets in participating homes to record when the set is on and to which channel it is tuned.[10]

Sampling plan. The marketing researcher must design a sampling plan, which calls for three decisions:

1. **Sampling unit.** This answers *Who is to be surveyed*? The proper sampling unit is not always obvious. In the American survey, should the sampling unit be business travelers, pleasure travelers, or both? Should travelers under twenty-one be interviewed? Should both husbands and wives be interviewed?

2. **Sample size.** This answers *How many people should be surveyed*? Large samples give more reliable results than small samples. However, it is not necessary to sample the entire target or even a substantial portion to achieve reliable results. Samples of less than 1 percent of a population can often provide good reliability, given a creditable sampling procedure.

3. **Sampling procedure.** This answers *How should the respondents be chosen*? To obtain a representative sample, a probability sample of the population should be drawn. Probability

---

[10] An overview of mechanical devices is presented in Roger D. Blackwell, James S. Hensel, Michael B. Phillips, and Brian Sternthal, *Laboratory Equipment for Marketing Research* (Dubuque, Iowa: Kendall/Hunt Publishing Co., 1970), pp. 7–8.

TABLE 6–7

A. Probability sample

Simple random sample	Every member of the population has a known and equal chance of selection.
Stratified random sample	The population is divided into mutually exclusive groups (such as age groups), and random samples are drawn from each group.
Cluster (area) sample	The population is divided into mutually exclusive groups (such as blocks), and the researcher draws a sample of the groups to interview.

B. Nonprobability sample

Convenience sample	The researcher selects the easiest population members from which to obtain information.
Judgment sample	The researcher uses his or her judgment to select population members who are good prospects for accurate information.
Quota sample	The researcher finds and interviews a prescribed number of people in each of several categories.

sampling allows the calculation of confidence limits for sampling error. Thus one could conclude after the sample is taken that "the interval 5 to 7 trips per year has 95 chances in 100 of containing the true number of trips taken annually by air travelers in the Southwest." Three types of probability sampling are described in Table 6–7A. When the cost or time involved in probability sampling is too high, marketing researchers will take nonprobability samples. Table 6–7B describes three types of nonprobability sampling. Some marketing researchers feel that nonprobability samples can be very useful in many circumstances, even though the sampling error cannot be measured.

Contact methods. This answers *How should the subject be contacted*? The choices are telephone, mail, or personal interviews.

Telephone interviewing is the best method for gathering information quickly; the interviewer is also able to clarify questions if they are not understood. The two main drawbacks are that only people with telephones can be interviewed, and the interviews have to be short and not too personal.

The *mail questionnaire* may be the best way to reach persons who would not give personal interviews or whose responses might be biased or distorted by interviewers. On the other hand, mail questionnaires require simple and clearly worded questions, and the return rate is usually low and/or slow.

Personal interviewing is the most versatile of the three methods. The interviewer can ask more questions and can supplement the interview with personal observations. Personal interviewing is the most expensive method and requires more administrative planning and supervision.

Personal interviewing takes two forms, individual and group interviewing. *Individual interviewing* involves calling on people either in their homes or their offices or stopping them on the street. The interviewer must gain their cooperation and then carry on the interview, which can last anywhere from a few minutes to several hours. Sometimes a small payment or incentive is presented to the person in appreciation of his or her time.

Group interviewing consists of inviting from six to ten persons to spend a few hours with a skilled interviewer to discuss a product, service, organization, or other marketing entity. The interviewer needs objectivity, knowledge of the subject matter and industry, and knowledge of group dynamics and consumer behavior; otherwise, the results can be misleading. The participants are normally paid a small sum for attending. The meeting is typically held in pleasant surroundings (a home, for example), and refreshments are served to increase the informality. The group interviewer starts with a broad question, such as, "How do you feel when you are about to fly on an airplane?" Questions then move to how people feel about different airlines, different services, and finally about in-flight telephone service. The interviewer encourages free and easy discussion among the participants, hoping that the group dynamics will bring out deep feelings and thoughts. At the same time, the interviewer "focuses" the discussion, and hence the name *focus-group interviewing*. The comments are recorded through note taking or on tape and subsequently studied to understand consumer attitudes and behavior. Focus-group interviewing is a useful step to take before designing a large scale survey. It provides insight into consumer perceptions, attitudes, and satisfaction that will be important in defining the issues to be researched more formally. Researchers must avoid generalizing the reported feelings of the people in the focus group(s) to the whole market, since the sample size is too small and the sample is not drawn randomly.[11]

The marketing manager should ask the marketing researcher to estimate the cost of the research plan before approving it. The purpose of the marketing research project is to help the company reduce its risks and improve its profits. Suppose the company estimates that launching the in-flight phone service without any marketing research would yield a long-term profit of $50,000. The manager also believes that the research will help him improve the promotional plan and make a long-term profit of $90,000. In this case, he should be willing to spend up to $40,000 on this research. If the research design would cost more than $40,000, he should decline it.

Collecting the information.   After developing the research design, the researcher must undertake or subcontract data collection. This phase is generally the most expensive and the most liable to error. In the case of surveys, four major problems arise. Some respondents will not be at home and must be recontacted. Other respondents may refuse to cooperate. Still others may give biased or dishonest answers. Finally some interviewers will occasionally be biased or dishonest.

In the case of experimental research, the researchers have to worry about matching the experimental and control groups, not influencing the participants by their presence, administering the treatments in a uniform way, and controlling for extraneous factors.

Data-collection methods are rapidly changing under the impact of modern telecommunications and electronics. Computers and electronic-communication hardware are bringing about a quiet revolution in marketing research. Some research firms now conduct their interviewing from a centralized location using a combination of

---

[11] Bobby J. Calder, "Focus Groups and the Nature of Qualitative Marketing Research," *Journal of Marketing Research*, August 1977, pp. 353–64.

WATS lines, cathode-ray tubes (CRT), and *data-entry terminals*. Professional telephone interviewers sit in separate booths and draw telephone numbers at random from somewhere in the nation. In dialing the person whose number has been selected, the interviewers use WATS lines, which means that the research firm has prepaid the telephone company so that it can make a certain large number of long-distance calls. When the phone is answered, the interviewer asks the person a set of questions, reading them from the cathode-ray tube. The interviewer types the respondents' answers right into a computer, using the data-entry terminal. This procedure eliminates editing and coding, reduces the number of errors, and saves time.

Other research firms have set up *interactive terminals* in shopping centers. Persons willing to be interviewed sit down at a terminal, read the questions from the CRT, and type in their answers. Most respondents enjoy this form of "robot" interviewing.

Another major marketing research breakthrough is occurring in supermarkets with the advent of *electronic cash registers*, *optical scanners*, and the *Universal Product Code*. As a customer passes through the checkout line, his or her items are read by an optical scanner, which records the brand, size, and price. The data enters a computer, where it can be analyzed for the purposes of improved inventory control and marketing decision making. Supermarket managers and consumer-goods manufacturers are able to measure the profitability of each brand and size and also the impact of different marketing variables, such as television advertisements, newspaper ads and coupons, free samples, in-store displays, shelf prices, and marketing changes.[12]

Analyzing the information. The next step in the marketing research process is to extract pertinent findings from the data. The researcher tabulates the data and develops one-way and two-way frequency distributions. Averages and measures of dispersion are computed for the major variables. The researcher will attempt to apply some of the advanced statistical techniques and decision models in the analytical marketing system in the hope of discovering additional findings. (See pp. 211–22.)

Presenting the findings. The researcher should not try to overwhelm management with lots of numbers and fancy statistical techniques—this will lose them. The researcher should present major findings that are relevant to the major marketing decisions facing management. The study is useful when it reduces management's uncertainty concerning the right move to make.

Suppose the main survey findings for the American Airlines case show that:

1. The chief reasons for using in-flight phone service are emergencies, urgent business deals, mix-ups in flight times, and so on. Making phone calls to pass the time would be rare. Most of the calls would be made by business people on expense accounts.
2. About 5 passengers out of every 200 would make in-flight phone calls at a price of $25 a call; and about 12 would make calls at $15. Thus a charge of $15 would produce more revenue ($12 \times \$15 = \$180$) than $25 a call ($5 \times \$25 = \$125$). Still, that is far below the in-flight break-even cost of $1,000.

---

[12] See "Market Research by Scanner," *Business Week*, May 5, 1980, p. 113 and "Supermarket Scanners Get Smarter," *Business Week*, August 17, 1981.

3. The promotion of in-flight phone service would win American about two extra passengers on each flight. The net revenue from these two extra passengers would be about $620, but that still would not help meet the break-even cost.
4. Offering in-flight service would strengthen the public's image of American Airlines as an innovative and progressive airline. However, it would cost American about $200 per flight to create this extra goodwill.

These findings, of course, could suffer from sampling error, and management may want to study the issue further. However, it looks like in-flight phone service would add more to cost than to long-term revenue and should not be implemented at the present time. Thus a well-defined marketing research project has helped American's managers make a better decision than would probably have come out of "seat-of-the-pants" decision making.

Characteristics of Good Marketing Research

Having examined the major steps in the marketing research process, we can highlight five characteristics of good marketing research.

Scientific method. Effective marketing research uses the principles of the scientific method: careful observation, formulation of hypotheses, prediction, and testing. An example follows.

> A mail-order house was suffering from a high rate (30 percent) of returned merchandise. Management asked the marketing research manager to investigate the causes of the high return rate. The marketing researcher examines the characteristics of returned orders, such as the geographical locations of the customers, the sizes of the returned orders, and the merchandise categories. One hypothesis was that the longer the customer waited for ordered merchandise, the greater the probability of its return. Statistical analysis confirmed this hypothesis. The researcher estimated how much the return rate would drop for a specific speed up of service. The company did this, and the prediction proved correct.[13]

Research creativity. At its best, marketing research develops innovative ways to solve a problem. A classic example of research creativity is described below:

> When instant coffee was first introduced, housewives complained that it did not taste like real coffee. Yet in blindfold tests, many of these same housewives could not distinguish between a cup of instant coffee and real coffee. This indicated that much of their resistance was psychological. The researcher decided to design two almost identical shopping lists, the only difference being that regular coffee was on one list and instant coffee on the other. The regular-coffee list was given to one group of housewives and the instant-coffee list was given to a different, but comparable, group. Both groups were asked to guess the social and personal characteristics of the woman whose shopping list they saw. The comments were pretty much the same with one significant difference; a higher proportion of the housewives whose list contained instant coffee described the subject as "lazy, a spendthrift, a poor wife, and failing to plan well for her family." These

---

[13] Horace C. Levinson, "Experiences in Commercial Operations Research," *Operations Research*, August 1953, pp. 220–39.

women obviously were imputing to the fictional housewife their own anxieties and negative images about the use of instant coffee. The instant-coffee company now knew the nature of the resistance and could develop a campaign to change the image of the housewife who serves instant coffee.[14]

Multiple methods.   Competent marketing researchers shy away from overreliance on any one method, preferring to adapt the method to the problem rather than the other way around. They also recognize the desirability of gathering information from multiple sources to give greater confidence.

Interdependence of models and data.   Competent marketing researchers recognize that the facts derive their meaning from models of the problem. These models guide the type of information sought and therefore should be made as explicit as possible.

Value and cost of information.   Competent marketing researchers show concern for measuring the value of information against its cost. Value/cost helps the marketing research department determine which research projects to conduct, which research designs to use, and whether to gather more information after the initial results are in.[15]

Management's Use of Marketing Research

In spite of the rapid growth of marketing research, many companies still fail to use it sufficiently or correctly. Several factors stand in the way of its greater utilization.

- □ **A narrow conception of marketing research.** Many executives see marketing research as only a fact-finding operation. The marketing researcher is supposed to design a questionnaire, choose a sample, carry out interviews, and report results, often without being given a careful definition of the problem or of the decision alternatives before management. As a result, some of the fact finding fails to be useful. This reinforces management's idea of the limited good that can come from marketing research.
- □ **Uneven caliber of marketing researchers.** Some executives view marketing research as little better than a clerical activity and reward it as such. Less able marketing researchers are hired, and their weak training and deficient creativity lead to unimpressive results. The disappointing results reinforce management's prejudice against expecting too much from marketing research. Management continues to pay low salaries, perpetuating the basic difficulty.
- □ **Late results.** Carefully designed marketing research can take a long time to carry out. The report may come too late in terms of when a decision has to be made.
- □ **Occasional erroneous findings by marketing research.** Many executives want conclusive information from marketing research, although marketing phenomena are often too complex to yield conclusive findings. The problem is complicated by the low budgets given to marketing researchers to get the information. Executives become disappointed, and their opinion of the value of marketing research is lowered.

---

[14] Mason Haire, "Projective Techniques in Marketing Research," *Journal of Marketing*, April 1950, pp. 649–56.

[15] See James H. Meyers and A. Coskun Samli, "Management Control of Marketing Research," *Journal of Marketing Research*, August 1969, pp. 267–77.

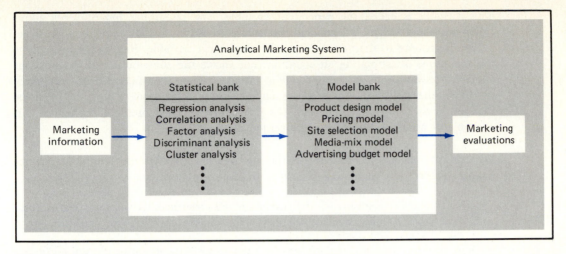

Figure 6–3
Analytical Marketing System

□ **Intellectual differences.** Intellectual divergences between the mental styles of line managers and marketing researchers often get in the way of productive relationships. The marketing researcher's report may seem abstract, complicated and tentative, while what the line manager wants is concreteness, simplicity, and certainty.

ANALYTICAL MARKETING SYSTEM

A growing number of organizations have added a fourth information service to help their marketing executives—an analytical marketing system.

An analytical marketing system consists of advanced techniques for analyzing marketing data and problems. Companies such as Lever Brothers, General Electric, and RCA make extensive use of analytical marketing systems. An analytical marketing system consists of a statistical bank and a model bank (see Figure 6–3). We will look at each of these in turn.

The Statistical Bank

The *statistical bank is a collection of statistical procedures for extracting meaningful information from data.* It contains the usual statistical routines for calculating averages, measures of dispersion, and cross-tabulations of the data. In addition, the researcher can use various *multivariate statistical techniques* to discover important relationships in the data. The most important multivariate techniques are described below.[16]

Multiple regression analysis. Every marketing problem involves a set of variables. The marketing researcher is typically interested in one of these variables, such as sales, and seeks to understand the cause(s) of its variation over time and/or space.

---

[16] For an overview, see Kinnear and Taylor, *Marketing Research*, part 8.

This variable is called the dependent variable. The researcher hypothesizes about other variables, called independent variables, whose variations over time or space might contribute to the variations in the dependent variable. Regression analysis is the technique of estimating an equation that shows the contribution of independent variables to variations in the dependent variable. When one independent variable is involved, the statistical procedure is called simple regression; when two or more independent variables are involved, the procedure is called multiple regression. An example of multiple regression is presented on page 246.

Discriminant analysis.   In many marketing situations the dependent variable is classificatory rather than numerical. Consider the following situations:

☐ An automobile company wants to explain brand preferences for Chevrolet versus Ford.
☐ A detergent company wants to determine what consumer traits are associated with heavy, medium, and light usage of its brand.
☐ A retailing chain wants to be able to discriminate between potentially successful and unsuccessful store sites.

In all these cases, the analyst visualizes two or more groups to which a person or object belongs. The challenge is to find discriminating variables that could be combined in a predictive equation to produce better-than-chance assignment of the entities to the groups. The technique for solving this problem is known as discriminant analysis.[17]

Factor analysis.   One of the problems faced in many regression and discriminant studies is a high intercorrelation among the explanatory variables, which lead to biased estimates of the effect on these variables of the dependent variables. The ideal in multiple regression is to use variables that are truly independent, both in the sense that they influence but are not influenced by the dependent variable and in the sense that each independent variable is independent of the others. The simple correlation coefficients for all pairs of variables will reveal which variables are highly intercorrelated. Factor analysis is a statistical procedure for trying to discover a few basic factors that may underlie and explain the intercorrelations among a larger number of variables. In the marketing area, factor analysis has been used to determine the basic factors underlying attitudes toward air travel, alcoholic beverages, and television programs.[18]

Cluster analysis.   Many marketing problems require the researcher to sort a set of objects into subgroups or clusters. The objects may be products, people, places, and so on. Thus the researcher might want to sort several automobile makes into major groups with as much likeness within groups and as much difference between

---

[17] See William F. Massy, "Discriminant Analysis of Audience Characteristics," *Journal of Advertising Research*, March 1965, pp. 39–48.

[18] William H. Reynolds and George T. Wofford, "A Factor Analysis of Air Traveler Attitudes," *Proceedings of the American Marketing Association* (Chicago: American Marketing Association, June 1966), pp. 640–50; Jean Stoetzel, "A Factor Analysis of the Liquor Preferences of French Consumers," *Journal of Advertising Research*, December 1960, pp. 7–11; and Arthur D. Kirsch and Seymour Banks, "Program Types Defined by Factor Analysis," *Journal of Advertising Research*, September 1962, pp. 29–32.

groups as possible; automobiles within a group can be assumed to be most competitive with each other. Or the researcher might want to cluster people into subgroups, which is essentially what we mean by market segmentation. Or the researcher might want to cluster cities into groups so that test cities could be drawn that resemble each other. In all cases, the objects are described by multidimensional data, and the chosen clustering technique operates on the data to sort the objects into a prespecified number of groups.[19]

The Model Bank

The *model bank is a collection of models that will help marketers develop better marketing decisions.* A model itself is a *set of variables and their interrelationships designed to represent some real system or process.* Models are built by management scientists (also called operations researchers), who apply scientific methodology to achieve understanding, prediction, or control over some management problem.

Although management science is a relative latecomer in marketing, it has already yielded useful models for new-product sales forecasting,[20] site selection,[21] sales-call planning,[22] media mix,[23] and marketing-mix budgeting.[24] Several models are off and running in some large companies.[25]

Although marketing executives often lack the training to understand the mathematics of some of the more complex models, they certainly can grasp the central idea behind each type of model and can judge its relevance to their work. The major types of models are listed in Table 6–8 and discussed in the following paragraphs.

Descriptive models. Descriptive models are designed to communicate, explain, or predict. They can be built at three levels of detail. A *macromodel* consists of a few variables and a set of relationships among them. An example would be a sales model

[19] See Ronald E. Frank and Paul E. Green, "Numerical Taxonomy in Marketing Research: A Review Article," *Journal of Marketing Research*, February 1968, pp. 83–98; and V. Parker Lessig and John O. Tollefson, "Market Segmentation through Numerical Taxonomy," *Journal of Marketing Research*, November 1971, pp. 480–87.

[20] Alvin J. Silk and Glen L. Urban, "Pre-Test Market Evaluation of New Packaged Goods: A Model and Measurement Methodology," *Journal of Marketing Research*, May 1978, pp. 171–91. Also see Glen L. Urban and John R. Hauser, *Design and Marketing of New Products* (Englewood Cliffs, N.J.: Prentice-Hall, 1980).

[21] T. E. Hlavac, Jr., and J. D. C. Little, "A Geographic Model of an Automobile Market," Working Paper No. 186–66 (Cambridge: Massachusetts Institute of Technology, Alfred P. Sloan School of Management, 1966).

[22] Leonard M. Lodish, "Callplan: An Interactive Salesman's Call Planning System," *Management Science*, December 1971, pp. 25–40; and Andris A. Zoltners and P. Sinha, "Integer Programming Models for Sales Resource Allocation," *Management Science*, March 1980, pp. 242–60.

[23] See John D. C. Little and Leonard M. Lodish, "A Media Planning Calculus," *Operations Research*, January-February 1969, pp. 1–35.

[24] John D. C. Little, "BRANDAID: A Marketing Mix Model, Structure, Implementation, Calibration, and Case Study," *Operations Research*, July-August 1975, pp. 628–73.

[25] The factors affecting the likelihood that a marketing model will be used are examined in Jean-Claude Lerréché and David B. Montgomery, "A Framework for the Comparison of Marketing Models: A Delphi Study," *Journal of Marketing Research*, November 1977, pp. 487–98.

TABLE 6-8

A CLASSIFICATION OF MODELS

I. According to Purpose	II. According to Techniques
A. Descriptive Models	A. Verbal Models
1. Markov-process model	B. Graphical Models
2. Queuing model	1. Logical-flow model
B. Decision Models	2. Network-planning model
1. Differential calculus	3. Causal model
2. Mathematical programming	4. Decision-tree model
3. Statistical decision theory	5. Functional-relationship model
4. Game theory	6. Feedback-systems model
	C. Mathematical Models
	1. Linear vs. nonlinear model
	2. Static vs. dynamic model
	3. Deterministic vs. stochastic model

consisting of a single equation with total sales as the dependent variable and national income, average price, and company advertising expenditures as the independent variables. They are derived by fitting the "best" possible equation to the set of variables.

A *microanalytic model* specifies more links between a dependent variable and its determinants. A good example is the DEMON model, in which the effect of advertising expenditures on sales is explained through successive linking of advertising expenditure, gross number of exposures, reach and frequency, advertising awareness, consumer trial, usage, and usage rate.[26]

A *microbehavioral model* creates hypothetical entities (consumers, dealers, and so on) who interact and produce a record of behavior, which is then analyzed. A good example is a consumer model built by Amstutz, in which a population of potential purchasers are exposed to weekly marketing stimuli, and some fraction of them purchase the product.[27]

Two descriptive models in the operations research literature are particularly germane to marketing-type problems. The first is the *Markov-process model*, which describes the probabilities of moving any current state to any new state. Suppose there are three coffee brands, A, B, and C. Of those consumers who bought brand A last time, suppose 70 percent buy it again, 20 percent buy B, and 10 percent buy C. This information is represented in row one of Figure 6–4, along with probabilities associated with brands B and C. The brand-switching matrix provides information about:

☐ The **repeat-purchase rate** for each brand, indicated by the numbers in the diagonal starting at the upper left. Under certain assumptions, the repeat-purchase rate can be interpreted as a measure of brand loyalty.

---

[26] David B. Learner, "Profit Maximization through New-Product Marketing Planning and Control," in *Applications of the Sciences to Marketing Management*, ed. Frank M. Bass et al. (New York: John Wiley & Sons, 1968), pp. 151–67.

[27] Arnold E. Amstutz, *Computer Simulation of Competitive Market Response* (Cambridge, Mass.: MIT Press, 1967).

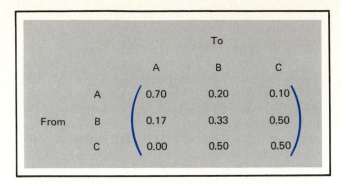

Figure 6-4
A Brand-Switching Matrix

☐ The **switching-in** and **switching-out** rate for each brand, represented by the off-diagonal numbers.

If the switching rates remain constant, the matrix can be used to forecast the magnitude and speed of change in future market shares given the market shares.[28]

Queuing models are also of interest to marketers. Queuing models describe waiting-line situations and answer two questions: What waiting time may be expected in a particular system? How will this waiting time change if the system is altered? These questions are of interest to supermarkets, gasoline stations, airline ticket offices, and so on. Wherever customers wait, there is the danger that waiting time will become excessive, leading to the loss of some customers to competitors.

If the existing system breeds long queues, the analyst can simulate the effects of different solutions. In the case of a supermarket, four possible attacks are possible. The supermarket can influence its customers to shop on less busy days. The supermarket can employ baggers to aid the cashiers and thus reduce waiting time. More service channels can be added. Finally, some of the service channels can be specialized to handle smaller orders.

Decision models.   Decision models assist managers to evaluate alternatives and find a good solution. An *optimization model* is one for which mathematical routines exist for finding the best solution. A *heuristic model* is one for which computational routines exist to find a pretty good solution. The heuristic model may involve a much more complex statement of the problem. The analyst applies heuristics, defined as rules of thumb that shorten the time required to find a reasonably good solution. For example, in a model to determine good warehouse locations, the heuristic might be, "Consider locations only in large cities." This may exclude a perfectly good location in a small city, but the savings in having to check far fewer cities may compensate for the omission.

There are four optimization-type decision models of particular relevance to marketing. The first is *differential calculus*, which is applied to well-defined mathematical functions to find the maximum or minimum value. Suppose a marketing analyst

---

[28] See John U. Farley and Alfred A. Kuehn, "Stochastic Models of Brand Switching," in *Science in Marketing*, ed. George Schwartz (New York: John Wiley & Sons, 1965), pp. 446–64.

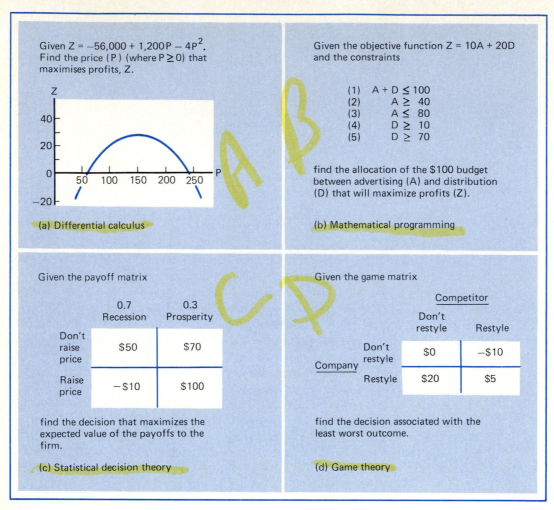

Given $Z = -56{,}000 + 1{,}200P - 4P^2$. Find the price ($P$) (where $P \geq 0$) that maximises profits, Z.

(a) Differential calculus

Given the objective function $Z = 10A + 20D$ and the constraints

(1)	$A + D \leq 100$
(2)	$A \geq 40$
(3)	$A \leq 80$
(4)	$D \geq 10$
(5)	$D \geq 70$

find the allocation of the $100 budget between advertising (A) and distribution (D) that will maximize profits (Z).

(b) Mathematical programming

Given the payoff matrix

	0.7 Recession	0.3 Prosperity
Don't raise price	$50	$70
Raise price	−$10	$100

find the decision that maximizes the expected value of the payoffs to the firm.

(c) Statistical decision theory

Given the game matrix

		Competitor Don't restyle	Restyle
Company	Don't restyle	$0	−$10
	Restyle	$20	$5

find the decision associated with the least worst outcome.

(d) Game theory

Figure 6–5
Four Decision Models

has determined the profit equation shown in Figure 6–5(a). The task is to find the best price—that is, the value of P that will maximize the value of Z. One approach is to graph the equation and examine it for the profit-maximizing price, here $150. A quicker procedure is to apply differential calculus to this equation without bothering to draw a graph.[29]

The second type of decision model is *mathematical programming*. Here the decision maker's objective is expressed as some variable to be optimized subject to

[29] The calculus reader will know that the slope of a tangent to the curve is given by the first derivative of the equation: $dZ/dP = 1{,}200 - 8P$. But the maximum (or minimum) takes place where the slope is zero: $1{,}200 - 8P = 0$. Therefore profits are a maximum when $P = \$150$. (The sign of the second derivative must be checked to be sure that $P = \$150$ establishes a maximum and not a minimum.)

a set of explicitly expressed constraints. Consider the problem in Figure 6–5(b). It shows a profit function relating profits to the amount of funds spent on advertising and distribution. A dollar of advertising contributes $10 of profit, and a dollar of distribution contributes $20. A set of policy constraints is also introduced. First the marketing budget, as divided between advertising and distribution, should not exceed $100 (constraint 1). Of this, advertising should receive at least $40 (constraint 2) and no more than $80 (constraint 3); and distribution should receive at least $10 (constraint 4) and no more than $70 (constraint 5). Because of the simplicity of this problem, the best marketing program can be found without invoking higher mathematics. Since distribution dollars are twice as effective as advertising dollars, it would make sense to spend all that is permitted within the constraints on distribution. This would be $70, leaving $30 for advertising. However, advertising must receive at least $40 according to constraint 2. Therefore, the optimal marketing-mix allocation would be $40 for advertising and $60 for distribution; and with this solution, profits will be $10($40) + $20($60) = $1,600. In larger problems, the analyst would have to use specific mathematical procedures.

The third type of decision model is called *statistical decision theory* (or Bayesian decision theory). This model calls for (1) identifying major decision alternatives facing the firm, (2) distinguishing the events (states of nature) that might, with each possible decision, bring about a distinct outcome, (3) estimating the probability of each state of nature, (4) estimating the value (payoff) of each outcome to the firm, (5) determining the expected value of each decision, and (6) choosing the decision with the highest expected value. Consider this in relation to the problem in Figure 6–5(c). Suppose a product manager is trying to decide between raising a price or leaving it alone. The outcome will be affected by whether the economy slides into a recession, of which the product manager believes there is a 0.7 chance. If a recession occurs and the price is not raised, profits will be $50; but if the price is raised, there will be a loss of $10. On the other hand, if the economy is prosperous, and prices are unchanged, the profit will be $70; and if prices had been raised, profits would have been $100. These estimates are summarized in the payoff matrix.

Statistical decision theory calls for the product manager to estimate the expected value of each decision. Expected value is the weighted mean of the payoffs, with the probabilities serving as the weights. The expected value associated with not raising the price is 0.7($50) + 0.3($70) = $56, while the expected value of raising the price is 0.7(−$10) + 0.3($100) = $23. Clearly the extra gain with the best thing happening (a raised price and prosperity) is not worth the risk, and the product manager is better off leaving the price alone. This assumes that expected value is a satisfactory criterion for the firm to maximize. This criterion is sensible for a large firm that makes repeated decisions of this kind. It makes less sense for a smaller firm facing a major one-shot decision that could ruin it if things went wrong.[30]

Game theory is a fourth approach to evaluating decision alternatives. Like statistical decision theory, it calls for an identification of the decision alternatives, uncertain

---

[30] See Frank M. Bass, "Marketing Research Expenditures: A Decision Model," *Journal of Business*, January 1963, pp. 77–90; and Rex V. Brown, "Do Managers Find Decision Theory Useful?" *Harvard Business Review*, May-June 1970, pp. 78–89.

variables, and the value of different outcomes. It differs from statistical decision theory in that the major uncertain variable is assumed to be a competitor, nature, or some other force that is malevolent. The probability is 1.00 that each actor will do what is in its best interest. Consider the example in Figure 6–5(d). An auto manufacturer is trying to decide whether to restyle its car. It knows that the competitor is also trying to make the same decision. The company estimates that if neither restyles, neither will gain anything over the normal rate of profit. If the company restyles and the competitor does not, the company will gain $20 over the competitor. (We will assume the competitor loses $20—that is, the gain to one company is a loss to the other.) If the company does not restyle and the competitor does, the company loses $10. Finally, if they both restyle, the company gains $5, and the competitor loses $5, because the company is assumed to be better at restyling.

A solution is possible if we assume that both opponents will want to take the course of action that will leave them *least worst off.* Called the *minimax criterion* (minimizing the maximum loss), it assumes that both opponents are conservative. This criterion would lead the company to prefer the restyling alternative. If it does not restyle, it might lose as much as $10; if it does restyle, it will make at least $5. The competitor would also prefer to restyle. If it does not restyle, it might lose as much as $20; if it does restyle, it cannot lose more than $5. Hence, both opponents will decide to restyle, which leads to a $5 gain for the company and a $5 loss for the competitor. Neither opponent can gain by switching unilaterally to a different strategy.[31]

Verbal models.   Models in which the variables and their relationships are described in prose are *verbal models*. Most of the great theories of individual, social, and societal behavior—theories such as those of Freud, Darwin, and Marx—are cast in verbal terms. Many models of consumer behavior are essentially in verbal-model form. Consider ". . . advertising should move people from *awareness* . . . to *knowledge* . . . to *liking* . . . to *preference* . . . to *conviction* . . . to *purchase*."[32]

Graphical models.   Graphical models represent a useful step in the process of symbolizing a verbal model. Six graphical models can be distinguished.

Figure 6–6(a) shows a *logical-flow diagram*. A logical-flow diagram is a visual representation of a logical process or operation. The boxes in the diagram are connected in a sequential flow pattern and related through two operations. One of these is *branching*. Branching takes place when a question is posed at a certain step of the process, and its possible answers are depicted as alternative branches leading away from the box. The other operation is *looping*. Looping takes place if certain answers return the flow to an earlier stage. The flow diagram in Figure 6–6(a) describes a firm's efforts to determine how many competitors will cut their prices. The firm first considers competitor *i* and asks whether it is likely to cut its price. If the answer

---

[31] See R. Duncan Luce and Howard Raiffa, *Games and Decisions* (New York: John Wiley & Sons, 1957), pp. 453–55.

[32] Robert J. Lavidge and Gary A. Steiner, "A Model for Predictive Measurements of Advertising Effectiveness," *Journal of Marketing*, October 1961, pp. 59–62.

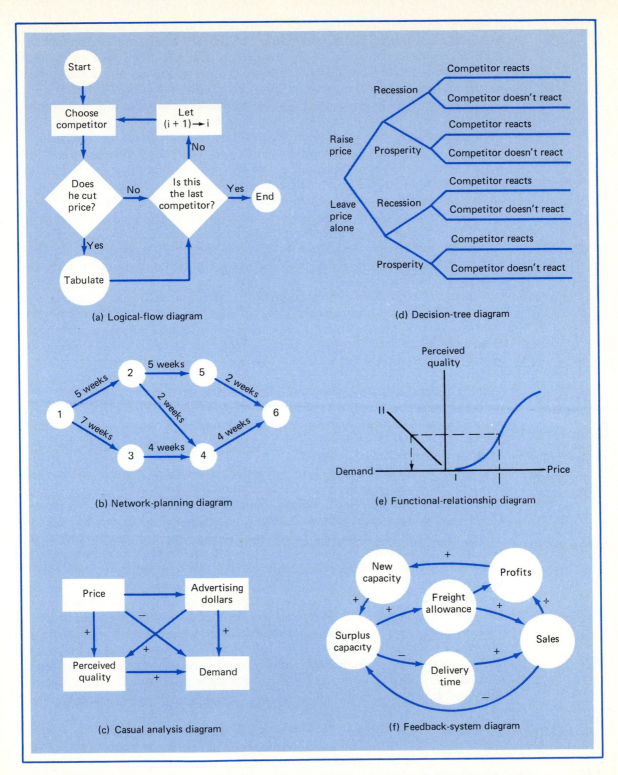

(a) Logical-flow diagram

(d) Decision-tree diagram

(b) Network-planning diagram

(e) Functional-relationship diagram

(c) Casual analysis diagram

(f) Feedback-system diagram

Figure 6-6
Six Graphical Models for Marketing Analysis

is yes, this result is tabulated, and then the firm asks whether there are any additional competitors to consider. If the answer is no, the firm goes directly to the next question. If there are more competitors to consider, the logical flow loops back to the first box; otherwise the flow ends. Logical-flow diagrams are coming into increasing use in marketing because of the clarity with which they illustrate a logical process.

Figure 6–6(b) shows a *network-planning diagram* (also called a critical-path diagram), which portrays the events that must occur to complete a project. The events, shown as circles, are connected by arrows indicating precedent relationships. In Figure 6–6(b), event 6 cannot occur until events 4 and 5 are completed; event 5 cannot occur until event 2 is completed; event 4 cannot occur until events 2 and 3 are completed; and so on. By estimating the completion time of each task (and sometimes the optimistic and pessimistic completion times), the analyst can find the earliest date to completion of the entire project. The network will contain a critical path that defines the earliest possible completion time; here it is fifteen weeks. Unless this critical path is shortened, there is no way to complete the project earlier. This diagram is the basis of planning, scheduling, and controlling projects, such as the development of a new product.

Figure 6–6(c) shows a *causal-analysis diagram*, which is used to portray the directions of influence of specific variables on each other. This diagram shows that price has a direct (negative) influence on demand and an indirect influence also through its positive effects on advertising dollars and perceived quality. A high price leads to high perceived quality and leads the company to spend more on advertising. Both of these in turn have a positive effect on demand. (Not shown is the fact that the resulting demand will have a feedback influence on advertising expenditures as well as on the perceived quality.) The value of causal-analysis diagrams is in exposing the complex relationships that the analyst should take into account. They remind us that single-equation relationships between variables may fail to capture the true influence structure of the phenomena.

Figure 6–6(d) shows a *decision-tree diagram*, which portrays the decision alternatives and consequences found in a decision situation. A manager is trying to decide between raising the price and leaving it alone. The outcome will be influenced by whether the economy moves toward recession or prosperity and further by whether competitors react. The tree could be extended to show other contingencies related to buyer reactions, inventory situations, and so on. By adding payoffs and probabilities to the various branches of the tree, the best decision can be found by using statistical decision theory.

Figure 6–6(e) is a *functional-relationship diagram*, which portrays functional relationship(s) between two or more variables. Quadrant I shows a positive relationship between price and perceived quality. Quadrant II shows a positive relationship between perceived quality and demand. The two quadrants enable the analyst to trace the effect of a *particular* price, through perceived quality, on a *particular* demand level. Thus one can generate a demand function from knowledge of two other functions. Functional graphs can be used to portray sales-response functions, probability distributions, and many other relationships.

Figure 6–6(f) shows a *feedback-system diagram*, which portrays any system whose outputs return and influence subsequent outputs. This process should not be confused with looping in logical-flow diagrams, which merely returns the procedure to an earlier point without implying any influence on that point. The example shows the interactions among sales, profits, capacity, and marketing variables. Surplus capacity leads the company to offer higher freight allowances to customers and faster delivery time. These lead to higher sales. Increased sales lead to increased profits while drawing down surplus capacity. In the meantime, the higher freight allowances reduce profits. If the net effect is a gain in profits, that leads to additional investment in capacity; and the cycle continues. Thus feedback-system diagrams are useful devices for representing variables that have interactive properties and feedbacks.[33]

Graphical models have all the virtues that are found in "pictures." A graph strips the phenomenon of inessentials; it allows a viewer to grasp the whole and select which relationships to examine. For marketing analysts, graphs improve exposition, facilitate discussion, and guide analysis.

Mathematical models.   Mathematical models can be subclassified in many ways. One distinction is between *linear* and *nonlinear models*. In a *linear model* all the relationships between variables are expressed as straight lines. This means that a unit change in one variable has a *constant* marginal impact on a related variable. The advertising-sales relationship would be linear if every $100 increase in advertising created a $1,000 increase in sales, no matter how much had already been spent. This kind of increase is unlikely, however, because increasing or diminishing returns to advertising can be expected. It is also likely that other marketing inputs, such as price and sales-call time, do not relate to sales in a thoroughly linear way. The assumption of linearity is useful as a first approximation for mathematical convenience.

A second distinction can be drawn between *static* and *dynamic models*. A *static model* centers on the ultimate state (or solution) of a system, independent of time. A *dynamic model* brings time explicitly into its framework and allows the state of the system to be observed over time. The demand-supply diagram in beginning economics courses represents a static model of price determination in that it indicates where price and output will be in equilibrium without indicating the path of adjustment through time. Brand-switching models are dynamic in that they predict period-to-period changes in customer brand choices.

A third distinction can be drawn between *deterministic* and *stochastic models*. A *deterministic* model is one in which chance plays no role. The solution is determined by a set of exact relationships. The linear-programming model for determining blends (oils, animal feeds, candies) is deterministic, because the relationships are exact and the cost data are known. A *stochastic model*, on the other hand, is one where chance or random variables are introduced explicitly. Brand-switching models are stochastic in that customer's brand choices are regulated by probabilities.

As management scientists gain acceptance in companies, they will provide a set of statistical procedures and decision models that will greatly enhance the marketing manager's skill to make better-informed decisions. The main need is that marketing

---

[33] See Jay W. Forrester, "Modeling of Market and Company Interactions," in *Marketing and Economic Development*, ed. Peter D. Bennett (Chicago: American Marketing Association, 1965), pp. 353–64.

managers and management scientists move rapidly toward understanding each other's needs and capacities.[34]

SUMMARY

Marketing information is a critical element in effective marketing as a result of the trend toward national and international marketing, the transition from buyer needs to buyer wants, and the transition from price to nonprice competition. All firms have a marketing information system connecting the external environment with its executives, but the systems vary greatly in the level of sophistication. In too many cases, information is not available or comes too late or cannot be trusted. An increasing number of companies are not taking steps to improve their marketing information systems.

A well-designed market information system consists of four subsystems. The first is the internal reports system, which provides current data on sales, costs, inventories, cash flows, and accounts receivable and payable. Many companies have developed advanced computer-based internal reports systems to allow for speedier and more comprehensive information.

The second is the marketing intelligence system, which supplies marketing executives with everyday information about developments in the external marketing environment. Here a well-trained sales force, special intelligence personnel, purchased data from syndicated sources, and an intelligence office can improve the marketing intelligence available to company executives.

The third system is marketing research, which involves collecting information that is relevant to a specific marketing problem facing the company. The marketing research process consists of five steps: defining the problem and research objectives; developing the research plan; collecting the information; analyzing the information; and presenting the findings.

Good marketing research is characterized by the scientific method, creativity, multiple methodologies, model building, and cost/benefit measures of the value of information.

The analytical marketing system is responsible for building models to explain, predict, and/or control marketing processes. Marketing management scientists may build or use descriptive or decision models and verbal, graphical, or mathematical models to come to grips with marketing problems.

The fourth system is the analytical marketing system, which consists of advanced statistical procedures and models to develop more rigorous findings from information. A growing number of companies are building statistical and model banks to improve their analytical capabilities.

QUESTIONS

1. The uses of the computer for *analyzing* market research data are well known. What are some ways the computer can be helpful in *collecting* marketing research information?

---

[34] For an overview of statistical and decision models in marketing, see Gary L. Lilien and Philip Kotler, *Marketing Decision Making: A Model-Building Approach*, 2nd ed. (New York: Harper & Row, 1983).

2. In several communities in the U.S. it is possible to scan a consumer's purchases at a grocery checkout counter with optical scanning devices, register these purchases for a particular consumer by a special card he or she presents at the time of purchase, beam customer-tailored commercials into that consumer's home via split cable TV, and determine if the consumer changed his or her purchasing patterns after having seen the ads. Consumers volunteer for participation in this test. The ACLU claims this is an invasion of privacy; marketers claim it will revolutionize the marketing research business. What do you think?

3. What might some research tasks be for the following areas: distribution decisions, product decisions, advertising decisions, personal-selling decisions, pricing decisions?

4. You are a marketing director. Your boss wants to know how many stores carry your dry cereal. Since you sell through food brokers, you don't know the answer. She wants the answer in two days. What would you do?

5. (a) Suggest how a liquor company might estimate liquor consumption in a legally dry town. (b) Suggest how a research organization might estimate the number of people who read a specific magazine in doctors' offices. (c) Suggest six ways in which male respondents can be interviewed on their usage of hair tonics.

6. A manufacturer of automobiles is testing a new direct-mail approach B versus a standard approach A. An experiment is conducted in which each approach is tried out on random samples of size n (sample size $2n$ in total) from a large national mailing list. Suppose that $n = 100,000$, so that 200,000 is the total sample size of the experiment. During a three-month period, approach B has 761 sales and A has 753. What decision should be made? List the alternatives and the rationale of each.

7. Evaluate the following questions found in a consumer survey: (a) What is your husband's favorite brand of golf balls? (b) What TV programs did you watch last Monday? (c) How many pancakes did you make for your family last year? (d) Tell me your exact income. (e) Can you supply a list of your grocery purchases this month?

8. In obtaining estimates from company sales people, product managers, and other personnel, one must discourage estimates that are self-serving. Give some examples of self-serving estimates, and suggest how to combat this problem.

9. Some marketers are hostile toward mathematical model building in marketing. They will make the following statements: (a) We don't use models. (b) Models are unrealistic. (c) Anyone can build a model. (d) A model is useless unless you can get the data. How would you answer each objection?

10. Large companies are trying to determine the proper organizational relationships between marketing research activities (MR) and marketing operations research (MOR). Describe five possibilities.

Market Measurement and Forecasting

7

Forecasting is hard, particularly of the future.

ANONYMOUS

Forecasting is like trying to drive a car blindfolded and following directions given by a person who is looking out of the back window.

ANONYMOUS

One of the major tasks in researching a market is to estimate its current and future size. Many company decisions hang on these estimates. Whether a company should enter a particular market depends upon whether the market is large enough and/or will grow fast enough in the future to justify market entry. Once a company enters a market, it has to estimate the market potential of different geographical areas and market segments in order to allocate its resources effectively. Company marketers then have to watch the sales results and see if they measure up to the rated market potentials. Thus we can see that demand estimates are essential in carrying out three important management functions—the *analysis* of market opportunities, the *planning* of marketing effort, and the *control* of marketing performance.

The first part of this chapter will look at major concepts in demand measurement. The second and third parts will describe major methods for estimating current and future demand, respectively.

MAJOR CONCEPTS IN DEMAND MEASUREMENT

Managers need to define carefully what they mean by market demand. We will present several distinctions that will help managers talk more precisely about market demand.

A Multitude of Measures of Market Demand

As part of their ongoing planning, companies prepare a great number of market-size estimates. Figure 7–1 shows *ninety* different types of demand estimates that a company can make. Demand can be measured for six different *product levels* (product item, product form, product line, company sales, industry sales, national sales), five different *space levels* (customer, territory, region, U.S.A., world), and three different *time levels* (short-range, medium-range, and long-range).

Each type of demand measurement serves a specific purpose. Thus a company might make a short-range forecast of the total demand for a particular product item to provide a basis for ordering raw materials, planning production, and scheduling short-run financing. Or it might make a long-range forecast of regional demand for its major product line to provide a basis for considering market expansion.

Which Market to Measure?

Marketers talk about *potential markets*, *available markets*, *served markets*, and *penetrated markets*. To clarify these terms, let us start with the notion that a market is

FIGURE 7–1
Ninety Types of Demand Measurement (6x5x3)

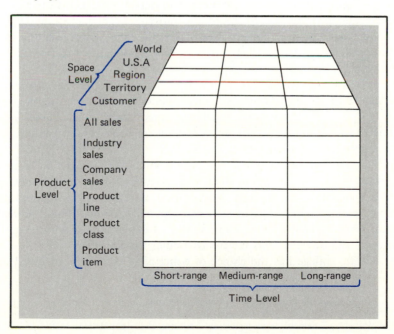

the set of all actual and potential buyers of a product. The *size* of a market then hinges on the number of buyers who might exist for a particular market offer. Those who are in the market would have three characteristics: *interest*, *income*, and *access*. As an illustration, consider the following situation:

> The chairman of the French department at a small college is concerned with the declining number of students signing up for French. One faculty member has already been dismissed, and another will be dismissed if the market for teaching French continues to shrink. The French-department chairman is thinking of offering an evening noncredit course on French culture to adults in the community. She is interested in estimating whether enough adults in the community would be in the "market" for this course.

The first thing to estimate is the number of adults in the community with a potential interest in a course on French culture. There are a number of ways to do this. The chairman could contact other colleges offering this course and find out their enrollment levels. A more direct approach would be to phone a random sample of adults in the community and ask about their level of interest in a French-culture course. The question could be asked: "If a noncredit French-culture course were offered in the evening at our college, would you definitely take it, probably take it, or not be interested in taking it?" Suppose 4 out of 100 say they would definitely take the course, 6 say they might take it, and 90 say they would not take it. At the most it appears that 10 percent have an interest in this course.[1] This percentage can be multiplied by the adult population in the community to estimate the potential market for this course. The *potential market* is the set of consumers who profess some level of interest in a defined market offer.

Consumer interest is not enough to define a market. Potential consumers must have adequate *income* to afford the purchase. They must be *able to buy* besides having *an interest in buying*. The higher the price, the fewer the number of people who will stay in the market. The size of a market is a function of both interest and income.

Market size is further reduced by personal *access* barriers that might prevent response to the offer. Interested consumers may not be able to take the French course at the place or at the time it is offered. Access factors will make the market smaller. The *available market* is the set of consumers who have interest, income, and access to a particular market offer.

In some market offers, the organization may restrict sales to certain groups. Although a college sells football tickets to everyone, it may not accept everyone who wants to study French. The college may accept only adults who are twenty-four years or older and have a high school diploma. These adults constitute the *qualified available market*, namely, the set of consumers who have interest, income, access, and qualifications for the particular market offer.

The college has the choice of going after the whole qualified available market

---

[1] Some analysts use all the "definites" and some arbitrary fraction of the "probablys" to estimate the demand level. Thus, they may say that the demand is made up of four "definites" and half of the six "probablys," namely, seven people, or 7 percent of the population.

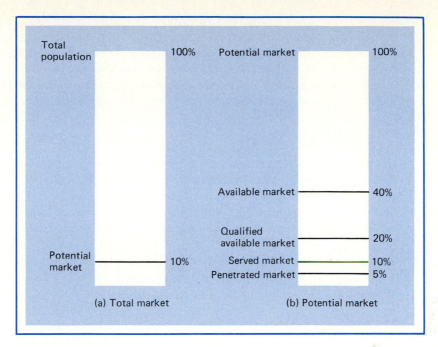

FIGURE 7–2
Levels of Market Definition

or concentrating its efforts on certain segments. The *served market* is the part of the qualified available market that the organization decides to pursue. Suppose the college prefers to attract primarily middle- and upper-class adults to its evening classes and, as a result, promotes the French-culture course primarily in certain sections of the city. Here the served market is somewhat smaller than the qualified market.

Once the course is advertised, it will attract some number of adult learners. The *penetrated market* is the set of consumers who actually buy the product.

Figure 7–2 brings the preceding concepts together with some hypothetical numbers. The bar on the left illustrates the ratio of the potential market to the total population, here 10 percent. The bar on the right illustrates several breakdowns of the potential market. The available market—those who have interest, income, and access—is 40 percent of the potential customers. The qualified available market—those who would meet the college's admissions requirements—is 20 percent of the potential market (or 50 percent of the available market). The college is actively trying to attract half of the qualified available market, or 10 percent of the potential market. Finally, the college is shown as enrolling 5 percent of the potential market in the course.

These definitions of a market are a useful tool for marketing planning. If the organization is not satisfied with current sales, it can consider a number of actions. It could try to attract a larger percentage of people from its served market. If it finds that the nonenrolling part of the served market has chosen to study French culture at another college, this college might try to widen its served market by promoting the course in other parts of the city. The college could relax the qualifications for admission, thus expanding the qualified available market. The next step would be to consider expanding the available market by lowering the tuition, improving the location and time of the course offering, and doing other things to reduce cost and increase access. Ultimately, the college could try to expand the potential market by launching a campaign to convert uninterested consumers into interested consumers.

A Vocabulary for Demand Management

The field of demand measurement is filled with a confusing number of terms. Company executives talk of forecasts, predictions, potentials, estimates, projections, goals, targets, quotas, and budgets. Many of these terms are redundant. The major concepts in demand measurement are *market demand* and *company demand*. Within each, we distinguish between a *demand function*, a *forecast*, and a *potential*.

Market demand. In evaluating marketing opportunities, the first step is to estimate total market demand. It is not a simple concept, however, as the following definition makes clear:

> Market demand for a *product* is the *total volume* that would be *bought* by a defined *customer group* in a defined *geographical area* in a defined *time period* in a defined *marketing environment* under a defined *marketing program*.

There are eight elements in this definition.

- [ ] **Product.** Market demand measurement requires defining the scope of the product class. A tin-can manufacturer has to define whether its market is all metal-can users or all container users. It depends on how the manufacturer views its opportunities for penetrating adjacent markets.
- [ ] **Total volume.** Market demand can be measured in terms of physical volume, dollar volume, or relative volume. The U.S. market demand for automobiles may be described as 10 million cars or $100 billion. The market demand for automobiles in the Greater Chicago area can be expressed as 3 percent of the nation's total demand.
- [ ] **Bought.** In measuring market demand, it is important to define whether "bought" means the volume ordered, shipped, paid for, received, or consumed. For example, a forecast of new housing for the next year usually means the number of units that will be ordered, not the number that will be completed (called housing starts).
- [ ] **Customer group.** Market demand may be measured for the whole market or for any segment(s). Thus a steel producer may make separate estimates of the volume to be bought by the construction industry and by the transportation industry.
- [ ] **Geographical area.** Market demand should be measured with reference to well-defined geographical boundaries. A forecast of next year's passenger automobile sales will vary depending upon whether the boundaries are limited to the United States or include Canada and/or Mexico.
- [ ] **Time period.** Market demand should be measured with reference to a stated period of time. One can talk about the market demand for the next calendar year, for the coming five years, or for the year 2000. The longer the forecasting interval, the more tenuous the forecast. Every forecast is based on a set of assumptions about environmental and marketing conditions, and the chance that some of these assumptions will not be fulfilled increases with the length of the forecast period.

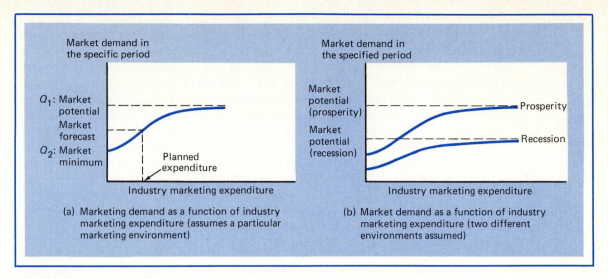

FIGURE 7–3
Market Demand

☐ **Marketing environment.** Market demand is affected by a host of uncontrollable factors. Every forecast of demand should explicitly list the assumptions made about the demographic, economic, technological, political, and cultural environment. Demographic and economic forecasting are well developed, technological forecasting is coming into its own, but political and cultural forecasting are still in their infancy. Much interest in the whole subject of predicting future environments is being stimulated by futurists. At the same time, Levitt has cautioned: "The easiest kind of expert to be is the specialist who predicts the future. It takes only two things: imagination and a good command of the active verb."[2]

☐ **Marketing program.** Market demand is also affected by controllable factors, particularly marketing programs developed by the sellers. Demand in most markets will show some elasticity with respect to industry price, promotion, product improvements, and distribution effort. Thus a market demand forecast requires assumptions about future industry prices, product features, and marketing expenditures.

The most important thing to realize about total market demand is that it is not a fixed number but a function. For this reason it is also called the *market demand function* or *market response function*. The dependence of total market demand on these conditions is illustrated in Figure 7–3(a). The horizontal axis shows different possible levels of industry marketing expenditure in a given time period. The vertical axis shows the resulting demand level. The curve represents the estimated level of market demand associated with varying levels of industry marketing expenditure. Some base sales (called the *market minimum*) would take place without any demand-stimulating expenditures. Higher levels of industry marketing expenditures would yield higher levels of demand, first at an increasing rate, then at a decreasing rate. Marketing expenditures beyond a certain level would not stimulate much further

---

[2] Theodore Levitt, "The New Markets—Think Before You Leap," *Harvard Business Review,* May-June 1969, pp. 53–68, here p. 53.

demand, thus suggesting an upper limit to market demand called the *market potential*.

The distance between the market minimum and the market potential shows the overall *marketing sensitivity of demand*. We can think of two extreme types of markets, the *expansible* and the *nonexpansible*. An expansible market, such as the market for racquetball, is quite affected in its total size by the level of industry marketing expenditures. In terms of Figure 7–3(a), the distance between Q_0 and Q_1 is relatively large. A nonexpansible market, such as the market for opera, is not much affected by the level of marketing expenditures; the distance between Q_0 and Q_1 is relatively small. Organizations selling in a nonexpansible market can take the market's size (the level of *primary demand*) for granted and concentrate their marketing resources on getting a desired market share (the level of *selective demand*).

It is important to emphasize that the *market demand function* is *not* a picture of market demand *over time*. Rather, the curve shows alternative current forecasts of market demand associated with alternative possible levels of industry marketing effort in the current period.

Market forecast.   Only one of the many possible levels of industry marketing effort will actually occur. The market demand corresponding to the expected effort is called the *market forecast*. The market forecast shows the level of market demand corresponding to the actual level of industry marketing expenditure in the given environment.

Market potential.   The market forecast shows expected market demand, not maximum market demand. For the latter, we have to visualize the level of market demand for a very "high" level of industry marketing effort, where further increases in marketing effort would have little effect in stimulating further demand. *Market potential is the limit approached by market demand as industry marketing effort goes to infinity, for a given environment.*

The phrase "for a given environment" is crucial in the concept of market potential. Consider the market potential for automobiles in a period of recession versus a period of prosperity. The market potential is higher during prosperity. In other words, market demand is income-elastic. The dependence of market potential on the environment is illustrated in Figure 7–3(b). Thus the analyst distinguishes between the position of the market demand function and movement along it. The sellers cannot do anything about the position of the market demand function; that is determined by the marketing environment. The sellers influence their particular location on the function, however, in deciding how much to spend on marketing.

Company demand.   We are now ready to define company demand. *Company demand* is the company's *share of market demand*. In symbols:

$$Q_i = s_i Q \tag{7–1}$$

where:

Q_i = company i's demand
s_i = company i's market share
Q = total market demand

Company demand, like market demand, is a function—called the *company demand function* or *sales-response function*—and is subject to all the determinants of market demand *plus whatever influences company market share*.

But what influences company market share? The most popular theory is that the *market shares* of various competitors will be proportional to their *marketing-effort shares*. This normal expectation can be called *the fundamental theorem of market-share determination* and is expressed:

$$s_i = \frac{M_i}{\Sigma M_i} \qquad (7\text{--}2)$$

where:

$$M_i = \text{company } i\text{'s marketing effort}$$

Consider the simple case where two identical firms are selling the same product but spending different amounts on marketing: $60,000 and $40,000 respectively. Using equation (7–2), company one's market share is predicted to be 60 percent:

$$s_1 = \frac{\$60,000}{\$60,000 + \$40,000} = 0.60$$

If company one is not enjoying a 0.60 market share, additional factors must be operating. Suppose the companies differ in the *effectiveness* with which they spend marketing dollars. Then equation (7–2) can be revised to read:

$$s_i = \frac{\alpha_i M_i}{\Sigma \alpha_i M_i} \qquad (7\text{--}3)$$

where:

$$\alpha_i = \text{marketing effectiveness of a dollar spent by company } i$$
$$(\text{with } \alpha = 1.00 \text{ for average effectiveness})$$
$$\alpha_i M_i = \text{company } i\text{'s effective marketing effort}$$

Suppose that company one spends its marketing funds less effectively than company two, with $\alpha_i = 0.90$ and $\alpha_2 = 1.20$. Then company one's market share would be 53 percent:

$$s_1 = \frac{0.90(\$60,000)}{0.90(\$60,000) + 1.20(\$40,000)} \cong 53$$

Equation (7–3) assumes a strict proportionality between market share and effective effort share. Yet if there are grounds for expecting diminishing returns as one firm's effective effort increases relative to the industry's effective effort, equation (7–3) should be modified to reflect this expectation. One way to reflect diminishing returns is through the use of a marketing-effort elasticity exponent that is less than unity:

$$s_i = \frac{(\alpha_i M_i)^{e_{m_i}}}{\Sigma(\alpha_i M_i)^{e_{m_i}}}, \qquad \text{where } 0 < e_{m_i} < 1 \qquad\qquad (7\text{--}4)$$

where:

e_{m_i} = elasticity of market share with respect to company i's effective marketing effort

Assume that the marketing-effort elasticity is 0.8 for all companies. As a result, company one's market share would be

$$s_1 = \frac{[(0.90)(\$60,000)]^{0.8}}{[(0.90)(\$60,000)]^{0.8} + [(1.20)(\$40,000)]^{0.8}} \cong 0.50$$

Thus company one's estimated market share is revised to reflect diminishing returns. Although company one is spending 60 percent of the marketing funds in the industry, its market share is only 50 percent, because of lower spending efficiency and diminishing returns.

A further improvement can be introduced by breaking up each company's marketing effort into its major components and separately expressing the effectiveness and elasticity of each marketing component. The equation becomes:

$$s_{it} = \frac{R_{it}{}^{e_{Ri}} P_{it}{}^{-e_{Pi}} (a_{it} A_{it})^{e_{Ai}} (d_{it} D_{it})^{e_{Di}}}{\Sigma [R_{it}{}^{e_{Ri}} P_{it}{}^{-e_{Pi}} (a_{it} A_{it})^{e_{Ai}} (d_{it} D_{it})^{e_{Di}}]} \qquad\qquad (7\text{--}5)$$

where:

s_{it} = company i's estimated market share at time t
R_{it} = quality rating of company i's product in year t
P_{it} = price of company i's product in year t
A_{it} = advertising and promotion costs of company i in year t
D_{it} = distribution and sales-force costs of company i in year t
a_{it} = advertising-effectiveness index for company i at time t
d_{it} = distribution-effectiveness index for company i at time t

$\left.\begin{array}{l} e_{Ri}, e_{Pi}, \\ e_{Ai}, e_{Di} \end{array}\right\}$ = elasticities of quality, price, advertising, and distribution, respectively, of company i

Thus equation (7–5) reflects four major influences on a company's market share: *marketing expenditures, marketing mix, marketing effectiveness,* and *marketing elasticity.* Although this would seem to be a great deal, the expression could be further refined (we shall not do this here) to take into account (1) *geographical allocation of marketing expenditures,* (2) *carry-over effects of past marketing expenditures,* and (3) *synergistic effects of marketing-mix variables.*[3]

---

[3] See Gary Lilien and Philip Kotler, *Marketing Decision Making: A Model-Building Approach* (New York: Harper & Row, 1983). Also see David E. Bell, Ralph L. Keeney, and John D. C. Little, "A Market Share Theorem," *Journal of Marketing Research,* May 1975, pp. 136–41.

Company forecast.   Company demand describes estimated company sales at alternative levels of company marketing effort. It remains for management to choose one of the levels.[4] The chosen level of marketing effort implies a particular level of sales, which may be called the company sales forecast:

> The *company sales forecast* is the expected level of company sales based on a chosen marketing plan and an assumed marketing environment.

The company sales forecast is represented graphically in the same way as the market forecast was in Figure 7–3(a); substitute company sales for the vertical axis and company marketing effort for the horizontal axis.

Too often the sequential relationship between the company forecast and the company marketing plan is confused. One frequently hears that the company should develop its marketing plan on the basis of its sales forecast. The forecast-to-plan sequence is valid if *forecast* means an estimate of national economic activity or if company demand is minimally expansible. The sequence is not valid, however, where market demand is expansible, nor where *forecast* means an estimate of company sales. The company sales forecast does not establish a basis for deciding on the amount and composition of marketing effort; quite the contrary, it is the *result* of an assumed marketing plan.

Two other concepts are worth mentioning in relation to the company forecast.

> A *sales quota* is the sales goal set for a product line, company division, or sales representative. It is primarily a managerial device for defining and stimulating sales effort.

Management sets sales quotas on the basis of the company forecast and the psychology of stimulating its achievement. Generally sales quotas are set slightly higher than estimated sales to stretch the sales force's effort.

The other concept is a *sales budget.*

> A *sales budget* is a conservative estimate of the expected volume of sales and is used primarily for making current purchasing, production, and cash-flow decisions.

The sales budget considers the sales forecast and the need to avoid excessive risk. Sales budgets are generally set slightly lower than the company forecast.

Company potential.   Company sales potential is *the limit approached by company demand as company marketing effort increases relative to competitors*. The absolute limit of company demand is, of course, the market potential. The two would be equal if the company achieved 100 percent of the market—that is, if the company became a monopolist. In most cases, company sales potential is less than market potential, even when company marketing expenditures increase considerably relative to competitors. The reason is that each competitor has a hard core of loyal buyers who are not very responsive to other companies' efforts to woo them away.

---

[4] The theory of choosing the best level of marketing effort is described in Chapter 9.

ESTIMATING CURRENT DEMAND

We will now examine practical methods for estimating current market demand. Marketing executives will want to estimate *total market potential*, *area market potential*, and *actual sales and market shares*.

Total Market Potential

Total market potential is the maximum amount of sales (in units or dollars) that might be available to all the firms in an industry during a given period under a given level of industry marketing effort and given environmental conditions. A common way to estimate it is as follows:

$$Q = nqp \tag{7-6}$$

where:

> Q = total market potential
> n = number of buyers in the specific product/market under the given assumptions
> q = quantity purchased by an average buyer
> p = price of an average unit

Thus if there are 100 million buyers of books each year, and the average book buyer buys three books a year, and the average price is $4, then the total market potential for books is $1.2 billion (= $100,000,000 \times 3 \times \$4$).

The most difficult component to estimate in (7–6) is n, the number of buyers in the specific product/market. One can always start with the total population in the nation, say 233,000,000 people. This can be called the *suspect pool*. The next step is to eliminate groups that obviously would not buy the product. Let us assume that illiterate people, children under twelve, and persons with poor eyesight do not buy books, and they constitute 20 percent of the population. Then only 80 percent of the population, or 186,400,000 people, would be in the *prospect pool*. We might do further research and find that persons of low income and low education do not read books, and they are over 30 percent of the prospect pool. Eliminating them, we arrive at a *hot prospect pool* of approximately 130,480,000 book buyers. We would use this number of potential buyers in formula (7–6) for calculating total market potential.

A variation on formula (7–6) is known as the *chain ratio method*. The chain ratio method involves multiplying a base number by several adjusting percentages. Suppose a brewery is interested in estimating the market potential for a new dietetic beer. An estimate can be made by the following calculation:[5]

---

[5] See Russell L. Ackoff, *A Concept of Corporate Planning* (New York: Wiley-Interscience, 1970), pp. 36–37.

$$
\left.\begin{array}{c}
\text{Demand} \\
\text{for the} \\
\text{new} \\
\text{dietetic} \\
\text{beer}
\end{array}\right\} = \left\{\begin{array}{l}
\text{Population} \times \text{personal discretionary income per capita} \times \text{average per-} \\
\text{centage of discretionary income spent on food} \times \text{average percentage} \\
\text{of amount spent on food that is spent on beverages} \times \text{average percent-} \\
\text{age of amount spent on beverages that is spent on alcoholic beverages} \\
\times \text{ average percentage of amount spent on alcoholic beverages that} \\
\text{is spent on beer} \times \text{expected percentage of amount spent on beer that} \\
\text{will be spent on dietetic beer.}
\end{array}\right.
$$

Area Market Potential

Companies face the problem of selecting the best territories and allocating their marketing budget optimally among these territories. Therefore, they need to estimate the market potential of different territories. Two major methods are available: the *market-buildup method*, which is used primarily by industrial-goods firms, and the *multiple-factor index method*, which is used primarily by consumer-goods firms.

Market-buildup method.   The market-buildup method calls for identifying all the potential buyers in each market and estimating their potential purchases. The market-buildup method is straightforward if one has a list of all potential buyers *and* a good estimate of what each will buy. Unfortunately one or both are usually lacking.

Consider a machine-tool company that wants to estimate the area market potential for its wood lathe in the Greater Boston area.

The first step is to identify all potential buyers of lathes in the Boston area. The lathe is of no purchase interest to households and many other types of buyers, such as hospitals, retailers, and farmers. The market consists primarily of manufacturing establishments, specifically, those that have to shape or ream wood as part of their operation.

The company could compile a list from a directory of all manufacturing establishments in the Greater Boston area. Then it might estimate the number of lathes each industry might purchase based on the number of lathes per thousand employees or per $1 million of sales in that industry.

An efficient method of estimating area market potentials makes use of the Standard Industrial Classification System (S.I.C.) developed by the U.S. Bureau of the Census. The S.I.C. classifies all manufacturing into 20 major industry groups, each having a two-digit code. Thus, #25 is furniture and fixtures, and #35 is machinery, except electrical. Each major industry group is further subdivided into about 150 industry groups designated by a three-digit code (#251 is household furniture, and #252 is office furniture). Each industry is further subdivided into approximately 450 product categories designated by a four-digit code (#2521 is wood office furniture, and #2522 is metal office furniture).

For each four-digit S.I.C. number, the Census of Manufacturers provides the number of establishments subclassified by location, number of employees, annual sales, and net worth.

To use the S.I.C., the lathe manufacturer first must determine the four-digit S.I.C. codes that represent products whose manufacturers are likely to require lathe machines. For example, lathes will be used by manufacturers in S.I.C. #2511 (wood

TABLE 7–1

	MARKET-BUILDUP METHOD USING S.I.C. CODES (HYPOTHETICAL LATHE MANUFACTURER—BOSTON AREA)			
	1	**2**	**3**	**4**
S.I.C.	**Annual Sales (in Millions $)**	**Number of Establishments**	**Potential Number of Lathe Sales per $1 Million Customer Sales**	**Market Potential (1 × 2 × 3)**
2511	$1	6	10	60
	5	2	10	100
2521	1	3	5	15
	5	1	5	25
				200

household furniture), #2521 (wood office furniture), and so on. To get a full picture of all four-digit S.I.C. industries that might use lathes, the company can use three methods. It can determine the S.I.C. codes of past customers. It can go through the S.I.C. manual and check off all the four-digit industries that in its judgment would have an interest in lathes. It can mail questionnaires to a wide range of companies inquiring about their interest in wood lathes.

The company's next task is to determine an appropriate base for estimating the number of lathes that will be used in each industry. Suppose customer industry sales are the most appropriate base. For example, in S.I.C. #2511, ten lathes may be used for every $1 million worth of sales. Once the company estimates the rate of lathe ownership relative to the customer industry's sales, it can compute the market potential.

Table 7–1 shows a hypothetical computation for the Boston area involving two S.I.C. codes. In #2511 (wood household furniture) there are six establishments with annual sales of $1 million and two establishments with annual sales of $5 million. It is estimated that ten lathes can be sold in this S.I.C. code for every $1 million in customer sales. Since there are six establishments with annual sales of $1 million, they account for $6 million in sales, which is a potential of 60 lathes (6 × 10). The other figures in the table are similarly computed. Altogether, it appears that the Greater Boston area has a market potential for 200 lathes.

The company can use the same method to estimate the market potential for other areas in the country. Suppose the market potentials for all the markets add to 2,000 lathes. Then the Boston market contains 10 percent of the total market potential. This might warrant the company's allocating 10 percent of its marketing expenditures to the Boston market. In practice, the lathe manufacturer needs additional information about each market, such as the extent of market saturation, the number of competitors, the market growth rate, and the average age of existing equipment.

If the company decides to sell lathes in Boston, it must know how to identify the best-prospect companies. In the old days, sales reps called on companies door to door; this was called *bird-dogging* or *smokestacking*. "Cold calls" are far too costly today. The company should get a list of the companies in Boston, qualify them, and then use direct mail or phone calls to reach the best prospects. The lathe manufacturer can use *Dun's Market Identifiers*, which lists twenty-seven key facts for over 3,250,000 establishments in the U.S. and Canada.[6]

Multiple-factor index method. Consumer companies also have to estimate area market potentials. Because their customers are so numerous, they cannot list them. The method most commonly used is a straightforward *index method*. A drug manufacturer, for example, might assume that the market potential for drugs is directly related to population. If the state of Virginia has 2.28 percent of the U.S. population, the company might assume that Virginia would be a market for 2.28 percent of total drugs sold.

A single factor, however, is rarely a complete indicator of sales opportunity. Regional drug sales are also influenced by per capita income and the number of physicians per 10,000 people. This makes it desirable to develop a multiple-factor index with each factor assigned a specific weight.

One of the best-known multiple-factor indices of area demand is the "Annual Survey of Buying Power" published by *Sales and Marketing Management*.[7] The index reflects the relative consumer buying power in the different regions, states, and metropolitan areas of the nation. *Sales and Marketing Management's* index of the relative buying power of an area is given

$$B_i = 0.5y_i + 0.3r_i + 0.2p_i \qquad (7\text{--}7)$$

where:

B_i = percentage of total national buying power found in area i
y_i = percentage of national *disposable personal income* originating in area i
r_i = percentage of national *retail sales* in area i
p_i = percentage of national *population* located in area i

For example, suppose Virginia has 2.00 percent of the U.S. disposable personal income, 1.96 percent of U.S. retail sales, and 2.28 percent of U.S. population. The buying-power index for Virginia would be:

$$0.5(2.00) + 0.3(1.96) + 0.2(2.28) = 2.04$$

Thus 2.04 percent of the nation's drug sales might be expected to take place in Virginia.

The manufacturer recognizes that the weights used in the buying-power index are somewhat arbitrary. They apply mainly to consumer goods that are neither low-

---

[6] *Dun's Market Identifiers* (DMI), Dun & Bradstreet, New York, 1982.

[7] For a helpful exposition on using this survey and three other surveys published by *Sales and Marketing Management*, see "Putting the Four to Work," *Sales Management*, October 28, 1974, pp. 13 ff.

TABLE 7-2

	INDICES OF CATEGORY DEVELOPMENT, BRAND DEVELOPMENT, AND MARKET OPPORTUNITY					
Territory	Percent of Total U.S. Population (1)	Percent of Total Sales of Product Category (2)	Percent of Total Sales of Brand A (3)	Category Development Index (4) = (2 ÷ 1)	Brand Development Index (5) = (3 ÷ 1)	Market Opportunity Index (6) = (4 ÷ 5)
Seattle	1.23	2.71	3.09	221	252	0.88
Portland	1.02	2.17	2.48	212	242	0.88
Los Angeles	5.54	10.41	6.74	188	122	1.54
Boston	2.18	3.85	3.49	177	160	1.11
San Francisco	3.66	6.41	7.22	175	198	0.88
Toledo	0.79	0.81	0.97	102	123	0.83
Albuquerque	0.79	0.81	1.13	102	143	0.71
Baltimore	2.67	3.00	3.12	113	117	0.97

priced staples nor high-priced luxury goods. Other weights can be assigned if more appropriate. Furthermore, the manufacturer would want to adjust the market potential for additional factors, such as competitors' presence in that market, local promotional costs, seasonal factors, and local market idiosyncrasies.

Many companies will compute additional area indices as a guide to allocating marketing resources. Suppose the company is reviewing the eight cities listed in Table 7–2. The first three columns show the percentage of total U.S. population, category sales, and brand A sales, respectively, in these eight cities. Column 4 shows the *category development index*, which is the ratio of consumption intensity to population intensity. Seattle, for example, has a category development index of 221 because it accounts for 2.71 percent of the nation's consumption of this category, while it has only 1.23 percent of the nation's population. Column 5 shows the *brand development index,* which is the ratio of brand consumption intensity to population intensity. For Seattle, the brand development index is 252 because Seattle consumes 3.09 percent of this brand and has only 1.23 percent of the nation's population. Column 6 shows the *market opportunity index*, which is the ratio of category development to brand development. This ratio is .88 for Seattle, indicating that the company's brand is more developed in Seattle than in other cities. Seattle is an area of low (incremental) opportunity in that the company brand is highly developed in Seattle. In Los Angeles, the market opportunity index stands at 1.54, indicating a high opportunity in that area. Companies do not necessarily put all of their money in the high market opportunity areas.

After the company decides on the city-by-city allocation of its budget, it can refine each city allocation down to *census tracts* or *ZIP-code centers*. Census tracts are small areas about the size of a neighborhood, and ZIP-code centers (which were designed by the U.S. Post Office Department) are larger areas, often the size of small towns. Information on population size, median family income, and other characteristics is available for each type of unit. Marketers have found this data extremely useful for identifying high-potential retail areas within large cities or for buying mailing lists to use in direct-mail campaigns.[8]

Estimating Actual Sales and Market Shares

Besides estimating total potential and area potential, a company needs to know the actual industry sales taking place in its market. This means that it must identify its competitors and estimate their sales.

The industry's trade association will often collect and publish total industry sales, although not listing individual company sales separately. In this way, each company can evaluate its performance against the whole industry. Suppose a company's sales are increasing 5 percent a year, and industry sales are increasing 10 percent. This company is actually losing its relative standing in the industry.

Another way to estimate sales is to buy reports from a marketing research firm that audits total sales and brand sales. For example, A. C. Nielsen Company audits retail sales in various product categories in supermarkets and drug stores and sells this information to interested companies. In this way, a company learns total product-category sales as well as brand sales. It can compare its performance to the total industry and/or any particular competitor to see whether it is gaining or losing.

ESTIMATING FUTURE DEMAND

Having looked at ways to estimate current demand, we are now ready to examine ways to estimate future demand. Very few products or services lend themselves to easy forecasting. Cases of easy forecasting generally involve a product whose absolute level or trend is fairly constant and a situation where competitive relations are nonexistent (public utilities) or stable (pure oligopolies). In most markets, total demand and company demand are not stable, and good forecasting becomes a key factor in company success. Poor forecasting can lead to overly large inventories, costly price markdowns, or lost sales due to being out of stock. The more unstable the demand, the more critical is forecast accuracy, and the more elaborate is forecasting procedure.

Forecasting methods range from the crude to the highly sophisticated. Many technical aspects fall within the province of experts. Yet marketing managers need to be familiar with the major forecasting methods. They need to understand each method's advantages and limitations.

Companies commonly use a three-stage procedure to arrive at a sales forecast. They make an *environmental forecast*, followed by an *industry forecast*, followed by a *company sales forecast*. The environmental forecast calls for projecting inflation, unemployment, interest rates, consumer spending and saving, business investment,

---

[8] See Bob Stone, *Successful Direct Marketing Methods*, 2nd ed. (Chicago: Crain Books, 1979).

government expenditures, net exports, and other environmental magnitudes and events of importance to the company. (See Exhibit 7–1.) The end result is a forecast of gross national product, which is used, along with other environmental indicators, to forecast industry sales. Then the company bases its sales forecast on the assumption of achieving a certain share of industry sales. Forecasts are built on one of three information bases: *what people say*, *what people do*, or *what people have done*.

The first basis—*what people say*—involves surveying the opinions of buyers or those close to them, such as salesmen or outside experts. It encompasses three methods: surveys of buyer intentions, composites of sales-force opinions, and expert opinion. Building a forecast on *what people do* involves another method, that of putting the product into a market test to indicate buyer response. The final basis—*what people have done*—involves analyzing records of past buying behavior or using time-series analysis or statistical demand analysis.

Exhibit 7–1

METHODS OF ENVIRONMENTAL FORECASTING

The key to organizational survival and growth is the firm's ability to adapt its strategies to a rapidly changing environment. This puts a large burden on management to correctly anticipate future events. The price can be enormous when a mistake is made. For example, Montgomery Ward lost its leadership in the chain-store retailing field after the Second World War because its chairman, Sewell Avery, bet on a stagnant economy, while its major competitor, Sears, bet on an expanding economy. That is why a growing number of companies carry out *environmental forecasting*.

How do firms develop environmental forecasts? Large firms have planning departments that develop long-run forecasts of key environmental factors affecting their markets. General Electric, for example, has a large staff of forecasters, who study worldwide forces that affect its operations. GE makes its forecasts available to GE divisions and also sells certain forecasts to other firms.

Smaller firms can buy forecasts from several types of suppliers. *Marketing research firms* can develop a forecast by interviewing customers, distributors, and other knowledgeable parties. *Specialized forecasting firms* will produce long-range forecasts of particular macroenvironmental components, such as the economy, the population, natural resources, or technology. Finally, there are *futurist research firms* that produce future scenarios that are rich in speculation and creative ideas. Among the latter are the Hudson Institute, the Futures Group, and the Institute for the Future.

Here are some methodologies used to produce environmental forecasts:

☐ **Expert opinion.** Knowledgeable people are selected and asked to assign importance and probability ratings to various possible future developments. The most refined version, the Delphi method, puts experts through several rounds of event assessment, where they keep refining their assumptions and judgments.

☐ **Trend extrapolation.** Researchers fit best-fitting curves (linear, quadratic, or S-shaped growth curves) through past time series to use for extrapolation. This method can be very unreliable in that new developments can completely alter the future direction.

- ☐ **Trend correlation.** Researchers correlate various time series in the hope of identifying leading and lagging indicators that can be used for forecasting. The National Bureau of Economic Research has identified twelve of the best-looking economic indicators, and their values are published monthly in the *Survey of Current Business.*
- ☐ **Dynamic modeling.** Researchers build sets of equations that attempt to describe the underlying system. The coefficients in the equations are fitted through statistical means. Econometric models of more than three hundred equations, for example, are used to forecast changes in the U.S. economy.
- ☐ **Cross-impact analysis.** Researchers identify a set of key trends (those high in importance and/or probability). The question is then put: "If event A occurs, what will be the impact on all other trends?" The results are then used to build sets of "domino chains," with one event triggering others.
- ☐ **Multiple scenarios.** Researchers build pictures of alternative futures, each internally consistent and having a certain probability of occurring. The major purpose of the scenarios is to stimulate contingency planning.
- ☐ **Demand/hazard forecasting.** Researchers identify major events that would affect the firm greatly. Each event is rated for its *convergence* with several major trends taking place in society. It is also rated for its *appeal* to each major public in the society. The higher the event's convergence and appeal, the higher its probability of occurring. The highest scoring events are then researched further.

Survey of Buyers' Intentions

Forecasting is the art of anticipating what buyers are likely to do under a given set of conditions. That suggests that the buyers should be surveyed. Surveys are especially valuable if the buyers have clearly formulated intentions, will carry them out, and will describe them to interviewers.

In regard to *major consumer durables*, several research organizations conduct periodic surveys of consumer buying intentions. These organizations ask questions like the following:

Do you intend to buy an automobile within the next six months?										
0.00	0.10	0.20	0.30	0.40	0.50	0.60	0.70	0.80	0.90	1.00
No chance	Very slight possibility	Slight possibility	Some possibility	Fair possibility	Fairly good possibility	Good possibility	Probably	Very probably	Almost sure	Certain

This is called a *purchase probability scale.* In addition, the various surveys inquire into the consumer's present and future personal finances and expectations about the economy. The various bits of information are combined into a *consumer sentiment measure* (Survey Research Center of the University of Michigan) or a *consumer confidence measure* (Sindlinger and Company). Consumer durable-goods producers subscribe to these indices in the hope of anticipating major shifts in consumer buying intentions so that they can adjust their production and marketing plans accordingly.[9]

In the realm of *industrial buying*, various agencies carry out buyer intention surveys regarding plant, equipment, and materials. The better known among these are McGraw-Hill Research of New York and Opinion Research Corporation of Princeton. Most of the estimates have been within a 10 percent error band of the actual outcomes.

Various industrial firms carry on their own surveys of customer buying intentions:

> National Lead's marketing research personnel periodically visit a carefully selected sample of 100 companies and interview the manufacturer's technical research director, sales manager, and purchasing director, in that order. The technical research director is asked about the rate of incorporation of titanium in the manufacturer's various products: the sales manager is questioned about the sales outlook for the company's products that incorporate titanium: and the purchasing director is queried about the total amount of titanium his company plans to purchase in relation to past purchases. On the basis of these interviews and supplementary information, National's marketing research department estimates the market demand for titanium and prepares a "most favorable" forecast and a "least favorable" forecast. There are also indirect benefits. National Lead's analysts learn of new developments and modes of thinking that would not be apparent through secondary data. Their visits also promote National's image as a company that is concerned about buyers' need. Another advantage of this method is that it yields subestimates for various industries and territories in the process of building an aggregate estimate.[10]

In summary, the value of a buyers' intentions survey increases to the extent that the buyers are few, the cost of effectively reaching them is small, they have clear intentions, they follow out their original intentions, and they are willing to disclose their intentions. As a result, it is of value for industrial products, for consumer durables, for product purchases where advanced planning is required, and for new products where past data does not exist.

Composite of Sales-Force Opinions

Where buyer interviewing is impractical, the company may ask its sales representatives for estimates. An example is the Pennwalt Corporation.

---

[9] The consumer pollsters include the Survey Research Center at the University of Michigan; Sindlinger & Company of Norwood, Pa.; The Conference Board, Inc., and the Commercial Credit Corporation. For a discussion, see "How Good are Consumer Pollsters?" *Business Week*, November 9, 1969, pp. 108–10.

[10] Adapted from *Forecasting Sales*, Business Policy Study No. 106 (New York: National Conference Board, 1963), pp. 31–32.

In August, the field sales personnel are provided with tabulating cards to prepare their sales forecasts for the upcoming year. Individual cards are prepared for each product sold to each major customer, showing the quantity shipped to the customer in the previous six months. Each card also provides space in which the field salesmen post their forecasts for the coming year. Additional tab cards are also supplied for those customers who were not sold in the current six-month period but who were customers in the prior year; and finally, blank cards are provided for submitting forecasts of sales to new customers. Salesmen fill in their forecasts (on the basis of current prices) using informed judgment; in some divisions, they are in a position to substantiate their forecasts by obtaining purchase estimates from their customers.[11]

Few companies use their sales force's estimates without some adjustments. Sales representatives are biased observers. They may be congenitally pessimistic or optimistic, or they may go to one extreme or another because of a recent sales setback or success. Furthermore, they are often unaware of larger economic developments and do not know whether their company's marketing plans will influence future sales in their territory. They may understate demand so that the company will set a low sales quota. They may not have the time to prepare careful estimates or may not consider it worthwhile.

In the light of these contaminating factors, why are sales-force estimates used at all? There is the possibility that the over-and-under errors may cancel out. Or a consistent bias in the forecast of individual sales representatives may be recognized and adjustments made before aggregating the individual sales forecasts.

The company may supply certain aids or incentives to the sales force to encourage better estimating. The sales representatives may receive a record of their past forecasts compared with their actual sales, and also a set of company assumptions on the business outlook. Some companies will summarize individual forecasting records and distribute them to the sales force. A tendency for sales representatives to produce ultraconservative estimates to keep down their sales quota can be countered by basing territorial advertising and promotional expenditures on each sales representative's estimate.

Assuming these biases can be countered, a number of benefits can be gained by involving the sales force in forecasting. Sales representatives may have better insight into developing trends than any other single group. Through participating in the forecasting process, the sales representatives may have greater confidence in their sales quotas and more incentive to achieve them.[12] Also, a "grassroots" forecasting procedure provides estimates broken down by product, territory, customer, and sales representatives.

Expert Opinion

Companies can also obtain forecasts by turning to experts. Experts include dealers, distributors, suppliers, marketing consultants, and trade associations. Thus auto companies survey their dealers periodically for their forecasts of short-term demand.

---

[11] Ibid., p. 25.

[12] See Jacob Gonik, "Tie Salesmen's Bonuses to Their Forecasts," *Harvard Business Review*, May-June 1978, pp. 116–23.

Dealer estimates, however, are subject to the same strengths and weaknesses as sales-force estimates.

Many companies buy economic and industry forecasts from well-known economic forecasting firms, such as Data Resources, Wharton Econometric, and Chase Econometric. These forecasting specialists are in a better position than the company to prepare economic forecasts because they have more data available and more forecasting expertise.

Occasionally companies will put together a special group of experts to make a particular kind of forecast. The experts are asked to exchange views and come up with a group estimate (*group-discussion methods*). Or they may be asked to supply their estimates individually, and the analyst combines them in a single estimate (*pooling of individual estimates*). Or they may supply individual estimates and assumptions that are reviewed by a company analyst, revised, and followed by further rounds of estimating (*Delphi method*).[13]

An interesting variant of the expert-opinion method has been used by Lockheed Aircraft Corporation.[14] A group of Lockheed executives pose as different major customers. In a hardheaded way, they evaluate Lockheed's offer in relation to competitors' offers. A decision on what and where to buy is made for each customer. The purchases from Lockheed are totaled and reconciled with an independent statistical forecast to become Lockheed's sales forecast.

Market-Test Method

Where buyers do not plan their purchases carefully or are very erratic in carrying out their intentions or where experts are not very good guessers, a direct market test is desirable. A direct market test is especially desirable in forecasting the sales of a new product or of an established product in a new channel of distribution or territory. Market testing is discussed in Chapter 10.

Time-Series Analysis

Many firms prepare their forecasts on the basis of past sales. The assumption is that past data captures causal relations that can be uncovered through statistical analysis. These causal relations can be used to predict future sales.

A time series of a product's past sales (Y) can be analyzed into four major components.

The first component, *trend* (T), is the result of basic developments in population, capital formation, and technology. It is found by fitting a straight or curved line through past sales.

---

[13] See Normal Dalkey and Olaf Helmer, "An Experimental Application of the Delphi Method to the Use of Experts," *Management Science*, April 1963, pp. 458–67. Also see Roger J. Best, "An Experiment in Delphi Estimation in Marketing Decision Making," *Journal of Marketing Research*, November 1974, pp. 447–52.

[14] See Gerald A. Busch, "Prudent Manager Forecasting," *Harvard Business Review*, May-June 1961, pp. 57–64.

The second component, *cycle* (*C*), captures the wavelike movement of sales. Many sales are affected by swings in general economic activity, which tends to be somewhat periodic. The cyclical component can be useful in intermediate-range forecasting.

The third component, *season* (*S*), refers to a consistent pattern of sales movements within the year. The term *season* describes any recurrent hourly, weekly, monthly, or quarterly sales pattern. The seasonal component may be related to weather factors, holidays, and trade customs. The seasonal pattern provides a norm for forecasting short-range sales.

The fourth component, *erratic events* (*E*), includes strikes, blizzards, fads, riots, fires, war scares, and other disturbances. These erratic components are by definition unpredictable and should be removed from past data to see the more normal behavior of sales.

Time-series analysis consists of decomposing the original sales series, *Y*, into the components, *T*, *C*, *S*, and *E*. Then these components are recombined to produce the sales forecast.[15] Here is an example:

> An insurance company sold 12,000 new ordinary life insurance policies this year. It would like to predict next year's December sales. The long-term trend shows a 5 percent sales growth rate per year. This alone suggests sales next year of 12,600 (= 12,000 × 1.05). However, a business recession is expected next year and will probably result in total sales achieving only 90 percent of the expected trend-adjusted sales. Sales next year will more likely be 11,340 (= 12,600 × 0.90). If sales were the same each month, monthly sales would be 945 (= 11,340/12). However, December is an above-average month for insurance-policy sales, with a seasonal index standing at 1.30. Therefore December sales may be as high as 1,228.5 (= 0.945 × 1.3). No erratic events, such as strikes or new insurance regulations, are expected. Therefore the best estimate of new policy sales next December is 1,228.5.

For a company with hundreds of items in its product line that wants to produce efficient and economical short-run forecasts, a newer time-series technique called *exponential smoothing* is available. In its simplest form, exponential smoothing requires only three pieces of information: this period's actual sales, Q_t; this period's smoothed sales, $\bar{Q}_t$; and a smoothing parameter, *a*. The sales forecast for next period's sales is given by

$$\bar{Q}_{t+1} = aQ_t + (1 - a)\bar{Q}_t \qquad (7\text{--}8)$$

where:

$\bar{Q}_{t+1}$ = sales forecast for next period
a = the smoothing constant, where $0 \leq a \leq 1$
Q_t = current sales in period *t*
$\bar{Q}_t$ = smoothed sales in period *t*

[15] See Ya-Lun Chou, *Statistical Analysis with Business and Economic Applications*, 2nd ed., (New York: Holt, Rinehart and Winston, 1975), chap. 2. For computer programs, see Julius Shiskin, *Electronic Computers and Business Indicators* (New York: National Bureau of Economics Research, 1957). For an application, see Robert L. McLaughlin, "The Breakthrough in Sales Forecasting," *Journal of Marketing*, April 1963, pp. 46–54.

Suppose the smoothing constant is 0.4, current sales are $50,000, and smoothed sales are $40,000. Then the sales forecast is

$$\bar{Q}_{t+1} = 0.4(\$50{,}000) + 0.6(\$40{,}000) = \$44{,}000$$

In other words, the sales forecast is always between (or at an extreme of) current sales and smoothed sales. The relative influence of current and smoothed sales depends on the smoothing constant, here 0.4. Thus the sales forecast "tracks" actual sales.

For each of its products, the company determines an initial level of smoothed sales and a smoothing constant. The initial level of smoothed sales can be simply average sales for the last few periods. The smoothing constant is derived by trial-and-error testing of different smoothing constants between zero and one to find the one that produces the best fit of past sales. The method can be refined to reflect seasonal and trend factors by adding two more constants.[16]

Statistical Demand Analysis

Time-series analysis treats past and future sales as a function of time, rather than of any real demand factors. Numerous real factors affect the sales of any product. *Statistical demand analysis* is a set of statistical procedures designed to discover the most important real factors affecting sales and their relative influence. The factors most commonly analyzed are price income, population, and promotion.

Statistical demand analysis consists of expressing sales (Q) as a dependent variable and trying to explain sales as a function of a number of independent demand variables $X_1, X_2, \ldots, X_n$; that is,

$$Q = f(X_1, X_2, \ldots, X_n) \tag{7–9}$$

Using a technique called multiple-regression analysis, various equation forms can be statistically fitted to the data in the search for the best predicting factors and equation.

For example, Palda found that the following demand equation gave a fairly good fit to the historical sales of Lydia Pinkham's Vegetable Compound between the years 1908 and 1960:[17]

$$Y = -3649 + 0.665X_1 + 1180 \log X_2 + 774X_3 + 32X_4 - 2.83X_5 \tag{7–10}$$

where:

Y = yearly sales in thousands of dollars
X_1 = yearly sales (lagged one year) in thousands of dollars
X_2 = yearly advertising expenditures in thousands of dollars

---

[16] See Nick T. Thomopoulos, *Applied Forecasting Methods for Management* (Englewood Cliffs, N.J.: Prentice-Hall, 1980), pp. 186–93. For another interesting method, the *Box-Jenkins method*, also see pp. 214–44.

[17] Kristian S. Palda, *The Measurement of Cumulative Advertising Effects* (Englewood Cliffs, N.J.: Prentice-Hall, 1964), pp. 67–68.

$X_3 =$ a dummy variable, taking on the value 1 between 1908 and 1925 and 0 from 1926 on

$X_4 =$ year (1908 = 0, 1909 = 1, and so on)

$X_5 =$ disposable personal income in billions of current dollars

The five independent variables on the right account for 94 percent of the yearly variation in the sale of Lydia Pinkham's Vegetable Compound between 1908 and 1960. To use it as a sales-forecasting equation for 1961, it would be necessary to insert figures for the five independent variables. Sales in 1960 should be put in X_1; the log of the company's planned advertising expenditures for 1961 should be put in X_2; 0 should be put in X_3; the numbered year corresponding to 1961 should be put in X_4; and estimated 1961 disposable personal income should be put in X_5. The result of multiplying these numbers by the respective coefficients and summing them gives a sales forecast (Y) for 1961.

Basically, demand equations are derived by fitting the "best" equation to historical or cross-sectional data. The coefficients of the equation are estimated according to the *least squares* criterion. According to this criterion, the best equation is one that *minimizes the sum of the squared deviations of the actual from the predicted observations*. The equation can be derived through the use of standard formulas. The closer the fit, the more useful the equation, all other things being equal.

Computers have rendered statistical demand analysis an increasingly popular approach to forecasting. The user, however, should be wary of five problems that might diminish the validity or usefulness of a statistical demand equation: too few observations, too much correlation among the independent variables, violation of normal distribution assumptions, two-way causation, and emergence of new variables not accounted for.[18]

SUMMARY

In order to carry out their responsibilities, marketing managers need various estimates of current and future demand. Quantitative measurements are essential for the analysis of market opportunity, the planning of marketing programs, and the control of marketing effort. The firm may prepare several estimates of demand, varying in the level of product aggregation, the time dimension, and the space dimension.

A market consists of the set of actual and potential consumers of a market offer. The size of the market depends on how many people have interest, income, and access to the market offer. Marketers must know how to distinguish between the potential market, available market, qualified available market, served market, and penetrated market.

Marketers must also distinguish between market demand and company demand, and within these, between potentials and forecasts. Market demand is a function, not a single number, and as such is highly dependent on the level of other variables.

A major task is estimating current demand. Total demand can be estimated through

---

[18] For further reading on contemporary methods of demand analysis, see G. David Hughes, *Demand Analysis for Marketing Decisions* (Homewood, Ill., Richard D. Irwin, 1973).

the chain ratio method, which involves multiplying a base number by successive percentages. Area market demand can be estimated by the market-buildup and/or a **multiple-factor index** method. Actual industry sales require identifying the relevant competitors and using some method of estimating the sales of each. Finally, companies are interested in estimating the market shares of competitors to judge their relative performance.

For estimating future demand, the company can use six major forecasting methods: buyer intentions surveys, composite of sales-force opinion, expert opinion, market tests, time-series analysis, leading indicators, and statistical demand analysis. These methods vary in their appropriateness with the purpose of the forecast, the type of product, and the availability and reliability of data.

QUESTIONS

1. Describe the difference between the potential market, available market, served market, and penetrated market for a Rolls Royce Silver Spirit.

2. List some expansible and nonexpansible markets. Can you think of any markets that may have been previously considered nonexpansible but have been expanded? What caused the unexpected expansion to occur?

3. The market for home-entertainment electronic equipment has grown tremendously in the 1980s. How might this growth have influenced the forecasting of sales by LP record manufacturers?

4. A beverage company wants to use multiple regression to explain state-to-state variations in the consumption of soft drinks. (a) What independent variable should be tested? (b) If the fitted regression equation "explains" most of the state-to-state variation in sales, does it follow that it indicates relative market potential by state?

5. A manufacturer of women's hair products (home permanents, hair rinses, shampoos, and so on) wants to determine the relative market potential for its products in each county of the United States. What factors are most likely to belong in a weighted index of potential?

6. A marketing researcher sought a multiple-regression equation to explain past sales in an industry. Industry data on the dependent and independent variables went back only five years. The following equation was fitted:

$$Y = 5,241 + 31X_1 + 12X_2 + 50X_3$$

where:

Y = yearly sales in thousands of dollars
X_1 = U.S. disposable personal income in billions of dollars
X_2 = U.S. population in millions of households
X_3 = time, in years (1979 = 0)

The marketing researcher was pleased that this equation accounted for 98 percent of the yearly variations in industry sales. List any reservations you have about using this equation to forecast future industry sales.

7. A chemical company wants to estimate the demand for sulphur next year. One use of sulphur is to manufacture sulphuric acid. Another use of sulphur is in polishing new cars. Auto maker C is a customer of this manufacturer. What ratios have to be linked to go from auto maker C's new-car production to its impact on the company's sulphur sales?

8. Suppose a company's past sales are: 10, 12, 15, 12, 11, 13, 18, 20. The company forecaster uses an exponential smoothing equation with $a = 0.4$ and initial $\bar{Q}_t = 10$. Estimate the exponentially smoothed sales that would be predicted for the third period on.

9. An automotive manufacturer is developing its sales forecast for next year. The company forecaster has estimated sales for six different environment-strategy combinations:

Sales Forecasts			
	High Marketing Budget	Medium Marketing Budget	Low Marketing Budget
Recession	15	12	10
Normal	20	16	14

He believes that there is a 0.20 probability of recession and an 0.80 probability of normal times. He also believes the probabilities of a high, medium, and low company marketing budget are 0.30, 0.50, and 0.20, respectively. How might he arrive at a single point forecast? What assumptions are being made?

10. A motorboat company located in Washington state plans to open additional retail outlets in several counties on the Columbia River and Puget Sound. Using market opportunity indexes, recommend in which counties the outlets should be located.

County	Population	Sales of Motorboats (in Dollars)	Sales of Company's Boats (in Dollars)
Clark	161,300	2,800,000	186,200
Klickitat	13,400	140,000	38,000
Cowlitz	72,000	455,000	72,000
Snohomish	261,700	2,835,000	361,000
Pacific	16,200	1,750,000	836,000
Skagit	56,200	2,310,000	155,000
Total in Counties	580,000	10,290,000	1,649,000
Total in State	3,583,400	3,500,000	3,800,000

Market Segmentation, Targeting, and Positioning

8

Never follow the crowd.

BERNARD M. BARUCH

An organization that decides to operate in some market—whether consumer, industrial, reseller, or government—recognizes that it normally cannot serve all the customers in that market. The customers are too numerous, widely scattered, and heterogeneous in their buying requirements. Some competitors will be in a better position to serve particular customer segments of that market. The firm, instead of competing everywhere, often against superior odds, should identify the most attractive parts of the market that it could serve effectively.

Sellers have not always held this view. Their thinking passed through three stages:

☐ **Mass marketing.** In mass marketing, the seller mass produces, mass distributes, and mass promotes one product to all buyers. At one time Coca-Cola produced only one drink for the whole market, hoping it would appeal to everyone. The argument for mass marketing is that it should lead to the lowest costs and prices and create the largest potential market.

☐ **Product-differentiated marketing.** Here the seller produces two or more products that exhibit different features, styles, quality, sizes, and so on. Today Coca-Cola produces

Market Segmentation	Market Targeting	Product Positioning
1. Identify bases for segmenting the market 2. Develop profiles of resulting segments	3. Develop measures of segment attractiveness 4. Select the target segment(s)	5. Develop product positioning for each target segment 6. Develop marketing mix for each target segment

FIGURE 8-1
Steps in Market Segmentation, Targeting, and Positioning

several soft drinks packaged in different sizes and containers. They are designed to offer variety to buyers rather than to appeal to different market segments.

☐ **Target marketing.** Here the seller distinguishes among many market segments, selects one or more of these segments, and develops products and marketing mixes tailored to each segment. For example, Coca-Cola developed Tab to meet the needs of diet-conscious drinkers.

Today's companies are finding it increasingly hard to practice mass marketing. Mass markets are undergoing "de-massification." Consumers no longer watch only three network TV stations; many enjoy cable service and can view any of thirty to sixty stations. Nor do consumers buy from a few large supermarket chains and department stores; they can shop for products in hundreds of stores. According to Arbeit:

> All advertisers will be forced to design products that fit with the multiplicity of channels, with a multiplicity of retail outlets, and with a multiplicity of discrete consumer target audiences.[1]

He goes on to observe:

> McDonald's understands the great lesson of the 1980's—that marketing in the 80's is guerrilla warfare. You can no longer fly over in your network B-52's and drop coherent, heavy messages, saturating communities with what you want to say, and hope for a response. Guerrilla warfare marketing in the 80's means that the battles for the heart and mind and pocketbook of the consumer will be won on a block-by-block, store-by-store, purchase-by-purchase basis.[2]

Companies are increasingly embracing target marketing. Target marketing helps sellers identify marketing opportunities better. The sellers can develop the right product for each target market. They can adjust their prices, distribution channels, and advertising to reach the target market efficiently. Instead of scattering their marketing effort ("shotgun" approach), they can focus it on the buyers who have the greatest purchase interest ("rifle" approach).

Target marketing calls for three major steps (Figure 8–1). The first is *market*

---

[1] Stephen P. Arbeit, "Confronting the Crisis in Mass Marketing," *Viewpoint*, Vol. 2 1982, p. 2.

[2] Ibid., p. 9.

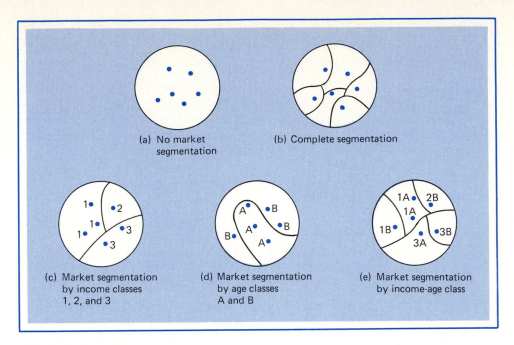

FIGURE 8–2
Different Segmentations of a Market

segmentation, the act of dividing a market into distinct groups of buyers who might require separate products and/or marketing mixes. The company identifies different ways to segment the market, develops profiles of the resulting market segments, and evaluates each segment's attractiveness. The second step is market targeting, the act of evaluating and selecting one or more of the market segments to enter. The third step is product positioning, the act of formulating a competitive positioning for the product and a detailed marketing mix. This chapter will describe the principles of market segmentation, market targeting, and product positioning.

MARKET SEGMENTATION

Markets consist of buyers, and buyers differ in one or more respects. They may differ in their wants, resources, geographical locations, buying attitudes, and buying practices. Any of these variables can be used to segment a market.

The General Approach to Segmenting a Market

Figure 8–2(a) shows a market of six buyers. Each buyer is potentially a separate market because of unique needs and wants. Ideally, a seller might design a separate marketing program for each buyer. For example, airframe producers such as Boeing and McDonnell-Douglas face only a few buyers and treat them as separate markets. This ultimate degree of market segmentation is illustrated in Figure 8–2(b).

Most sellers will not find it worthwhile to "customize" their product to satisfy each specific buyer. Instead, the seller identifies broad classes of buyers who differ in their product requirements and/or marketing responses. For example, the seller may discover that income groups differ in their wants. In Figure 8–2(c), a number (1, 2, or 3) is used to identify each buyer's income class. Lines are drawn around buyers in the same income class. Segmentation by income results in three segments, the most numerous segment being income class 1.

On the other hand, the seller may find pronounced differences between younger and older buyers. In Figure 8–2(d), a letter (A or B) is used to indicate each buyer's age. Segmentation by age class results in two segments, each with three buyers.

Now income and age may both count heavily in influencing the buyer's behavior toward the product. In this case, the market can be divided into five segments: 1A, 1B, 2B, 3A, and 3B. Figure 8–2(e) shows that segment 1A contains two buyers, and the other segments contain one buyer. As a market is segmented using more characteristics, the seller achieves finer precision but at the price of multiplying the number of segments and thinning out the populations in the segments.

Patterns of Market Segmentation

In the preceding illustration, the market was segmented by income and age, resulting in different *demographic segments*. Suppose, instead, buyers are asked how much they want of two product attributes (say *sweetness* and *creaminess* in the case of ice cream). The result is the identification of different *preference segments* in the market. Three different patterns can emerge.

☐ **Homogeneous preferences.** Figure 8–3(a) shows a market where all the consumers have roughly the same preference. The market shows no *natural segments*, at least as far as the two attributes are concerned. We would predict that existing brands would be similar and located in the center of the preferences.

FIGURE 8–3
Basic Market-Preference Patterns

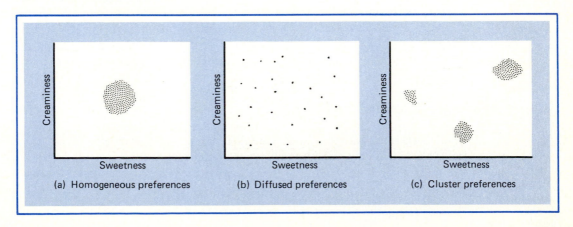

(a) Homogeneous preferences   (b) Diffused preferences   (c) Cluster preferences

□ **Diffused preferences.** At the other extreme, consumer preferences may be scattered throughout the space (Figure 8–3(b)), showing that consumers differ in what they want from the product. If one brand exists in the market, it is likely to be positioned in the center to appeal to the most people. A brand in the center minimizes the sum of total consumer dissatisfaction. A new competitor could locate next to the first brand and fight for market share. Or the competitor can locate in a corner to win over a customer group that is not satisfied with the center brand. If several brands are in the market, they are likely to be positioned throughout the space and show real differences to match consumer-preference differences.

□ **Clustered preferences.** The market might reveal distinct preference clusters, called *natural market segments* (Figure 8–3(c)). The first firm in this market has three options. It might position itself in the center hoping to appeal to all the groups (undifferentiated marketing). It might position itself in the largest market segment (concentrated marketing). It might develop several brands, each positioned in a different segment (differentiated marketing). Clearly, if it developed only one brand, competition would enter and introduce brands in the other segments.

Market Segmentation Procedure

We have seen that market segments can be identified by applying successive variables to subdivide a market. As an illustration: An airline is interested in attracting nonflyers (segmentation variable: *user status*). Nonflyers consist of those who fear flying, those who are indifferent, and those who are positive toward flying (segmentation variable: *attitude*). Among those who feel positive are people with higher incomes who can afford to fly (segmentation variable: *income*). The airline may decide to target higher-income people who have a positive attitude toward flying but simply have not flown.

How does the seller know which segmentation variables to use? One approach is to interview a sample of consumers and discover the *hierarchy of variables* that these consumers use on their way to a purchase decision. Consider the purchase of an automobile. Years ago, many car buyers were primarily brand loyal and would first decide the brand they wanted and then on the car form. If most buyers buy this way, we call it a *brand-form market*. On the other hand, a buyer might decide to buy high-performance, an intermediate-size, a four-door, and a Cadillac, in that order. If most car buyers buy this way, we call it a *need-size-form-brand market*. In this kind of market, most of the brands do not compete against each other. The competitive brands are those that satisfy the need-size-form prerequisites. The Hendry Corporation of New York has built a successful brand-forecasting system based on the primary partitioning variables used by buyers. They have used *market partitioning theory* to help a number of companies understand their market segments and major competitors.[3]

Bases for Segmenting Consumer Markets

There is no single way to segment a market. A marketer has to try different segmentation variables, singly and in combination, hoping to find an insightful way to view the market structure. Here we will examine the major geographic, demographic,

---

[3] See Manohar U. Kalwani and Donald G. Morrison, "A Parsimonious Description of the Hendry System," *Management Science*, January 1977, pp. 467–77.

psychographic, and behavioristic variables used in segmenting consumer markets (see Table 8–1).

Geographic segmentation.
Geographic segmentation calls for dividing the market into different geographical units such as nations, states, regions, counties, cities, or neighborhoods. The company can decide to operate in one or a few geographic areas or operate in all but pay attention to variations in geographic needs and preferences. For example, General Foods' Maxwell House ground coffee is sold nationally but is flavored regionally. People in the West prefer stronger coffee than people in the East.

Some companies even subdivide major cities into smaller geographical areas. R. J. Reynolds Company has subdivided Chicago into three distinct submarkets.[4] In the North Shore area, Reynolds promotes its low-tar brands because residents are better educated and concerned about health. In the blue-collar Southeast area, Reynolds promotes Winston because this area is conservative. In the black South side, Reynolds promotes the high menthol content of Salem, using the black press and billboards heavily.

Demographic segmentation.
Demographic segmentation consists of dividing the market into groups on the basis of demographic variables such as age, sex, family size, family life cycle, income, occupation, education, religion, race, and nationality. Demographic variables are the most popular bases for distinguishing customer groups. One reason is that consumer wants, preferences, and usage rates are often highly associated with demographic variables. Another is that demographic variables are easier to measure than most other types of variables. Even when the target market is described in nondemographic terms (say, a personality type), the link back to demographic characteristics is necessary in order to know the size of the target market and how to reach it efficiently.

Here we will illustrate how certain demographic variables have been applied to market segmentation.

Age and life-cycle stage. Consumer wants and capacities change with age. Even six-month-old infants differ from three-month-old infants in their consumption potential. Alabe Products, a toy manufacturer, realized this and designed different toys for babies as they move through various stages from three months to one year. Crib Jiminy is to be used when babies begin to reach for things, Talky Rattle when they first grasp things, and so on.[5] This segmentation strategy means that parents and gift givers can more easily find the appropriate toy by considering the baby's age.

Recently General Foods applied the same strategy to dog food. Many dog owners know that their dog's food needs change with age. So General Foods formulated four types of canned dog food: Cycle 1 for puppies, Cycle 2 for adult dogs, Cycle 3

---

[4] See "R. J. Reynolds Stops a Slide in Market Share," *Business Week*, January 26, 1976, p. 92.

[5] "Can the Baby Toy Market Be Segmented 12 Ways?" *Business Week*, February 14, 1977, p. 62.

TABLE 8-1

MAJOR SEGMENTATION VARIABLES FOR CONSUMER MARKETS

Variable	Typical Breakdowns
Geographic	
Region	Pacific, Mountain, West North Central, West South Central, East North Central, East South Central, South Atlantic, Middle Atlantic, New England
County size	A, B, C, D
City or SMSA size	Under 5,000; 5,000–20,000; 20,000–50,000; 50,000–100,000; 100,000–250,000; 250,000–500,000; 500,000–1,000,000; 1,000,000–4,000,000; 4,000,000 or over
Density	Urban, suburban, rural
Climate	Northern, southern
Demographic	
Age	Under 6, 6–11, 12–19, 20–34, 35–49, 50–64, 65+
Sex	Male, female
Family size	1–2, 3–4, 5+
Family life cycle	Young, single; young, married, no children; young, married, youngest child under 6; young, married, youngest child 6 or over; older, married, with children; older, married, no children under 18; older, single; other
Income	Under $2,500; $2,500–$5,000; $5,000–$7,500; $7,500–$10,000; $10,000–$15,000; $15,000–$20,000; $20,000–$30,000; $30,000–$50,000; $50,000 and over
Occupation	Professional and technical; managers, officials, and proprietors; clerical, sales; craftsmen, foremen; operatives; farmers; retired; students; housewives; unemployed
Education	Grade school or less; some high school; high school graduate; some college; college graduate
Religion	Catholic, Protestant, Jewish, other
Race	White, black, Oriental
Nationality	American, British, French, German, Scandinavian, Italian, Latin American, Middle Eastern, Japanese
Psychographic	
Social class	Lower lowers, upper lowers, lower middles, upper middles, lower uppers, upper uppers
Lifestyle	Straights, swingers, longhairs
Personality	Compulsive, gregarious, authoritarian, ambitious
Behavioral	
Use occasion	Regular occasion, special occasion
Benefits sought	Quality, service, economy
User status	Nonuser, ex-user, potential user, first-time user, regular user
Usage rate	Light user, medium user, heavy user
Loyalty status	None, medium, strong, absolute
Readiness stage	Unaware, aware, informed, interested, desirous, intending to buy
Attitude toward product	Enthusiastic, positive, indifferent, negative, hostile

for overweight dogs, and Cycle 4 for older dogs. General Foods managed to grab a large market share through this creative segmentation strategy.[6]

Nevertheless, age and life cycle can be tricky variables. For example, the Ford Motor Company used buyers' ages in developing its target market for its Mustang automobile; the car was designed to appeal to young people who wanted an inexpensive sporty automobile. But Ford found that the car was being purchased by all age groups. It then realized that its target market was not the chronologically young but the psychologically young.

Sex. Sex segmentation has long been applied in clothing, hairdressing, cosmetics, and magazines. Occasionally other marketers will notice an opportunity for sex segmentation. The cigarette market provides an excellent example. Most cigarette brands are smoked by men and women alike. Increasingly, however, feminine brands like Eve and Virginia Slims have been introduced, accompanied by appropriate flavor, packaging, and advertising cues to reinforce the female image. Today it is as unlikely that men will smoke Eve as it is that women will smoke Marlboros. Another industry that is beginning to recognize the potential for sex segmentation is the automobile industry. In the past, cars were designed to appeal primarily to males. With more women car owners, however, some manufacturers are studying the opportunity to design cars with features appealing to women.

Income. Income segmentation is another longstanding practice in such product and service categories as automobiles, boats, clothing, cosmetics, and travel. Other industries occasionally recognize its possibilities. For example, Suntory, the Japanese liquor company, introduced a scotch selling for $75 to attract drinkers who want the very best.

At the same time, income does not always predict the best customers for a given product. One would think that manual workers would buy Chevrolets and managers would buy Cadillacs. Yet many Chevrolets are bought by managers (often as a second car), and some Cadillacs are bought by manual workers (such as highly paid plumbers and carpenters). Manual workers were among the first purchasers of color television sets; it was cheaper for them to buy these sets than to go to movies and restaurants. Coleman drew a distinction between the "underprivileged" segments and the "overprivileged" segments of each social class.[7] The most economical cars are not bought by the really poor, Coleman pointed out, but rather by "those who think of themselves as poor relative to their status aspirations and to their needs for a certain level of clothing, furniture, and housing which they could not afford if they bought a more expensive car." On the other hand, medium-priced and expensive cars tend to be purchased by the overprivileged segments of each social class.

Multivariable demographic segmentation. Most companies will segment a market by combining two or more demographic variables. For example, a furniture company

---

[6] "Dog Food Concept Turns into a Scrap," *Business Week*, April 19, 1976, pp. 137–38.

[7] Richard P. Coleman, "The Significance of Social Stratification in Selling," in *Marketing: A Maturing Discipline*, ed. Martin L. Bell (Chicago: American Marketing Association, 1961), pp. 171–84.

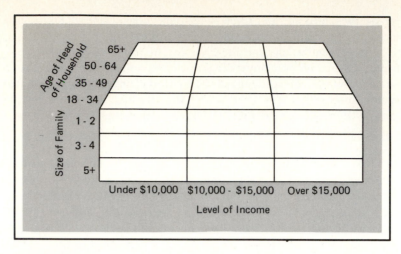

FIGURE 8–4
Segmentation of the Furniture Market by Three Demographic Variables

may segment its market by three demographic variables: age of head of household, size of family, and level of income. Figure 8–4 shows a joint segmentation of the market according to these variables. Each variable is subdivided into a number of levels; the result is 36 (4 × 3 × 3) distinct segments. Every family belongs to one of these 36 segments. Having segmented the market in this way, management can proceed to estimate for each segment the number of families, the average purchase rate, and the extent of competition. These pieces of information can be combined to estimate the profit potential of each segment.

Psychographic segmentation. In psychographic segmentation, buyers are divided into different groups on the basis of their social class, life style, and/or personality characteristics. People within the same demographic group can exhibit very different psychographic profiles.

Social class. We described the six American social classes in Chapter 4, pp. 126–27, and showed that social class has a strong influence on the person's preferences in cars, clothing, home furnishings, leisure activities, reading habits, retailers, and so on. Many companies design products and/or services for specific social classes, building in those features that appeal to the target social class.

Lifestyle. We also saw in Chapter 4 that people's interest in various goods is influenced by their lifestyles, and in fact the goods they consume express their lifestyle. Marketers of various products and brands are increasingly segmenting their markets by consumer lifestyles. Volkswagen, for example, has designed lifestyle automobiles: a car for "the good citizen" emphasizing economy, safety, and ecology; and a car for the "car freak" emphasizing handling, maneuverability, and sportiness. Manufacturers of women's clothing have followed Du Pont's advice to design different clothes for the "plain woman," the "fashionable woman," and the "manly woman." Cigarette companies develop brands for the "defiant smoker," the "casual smoker," and the "careful smoker." Companies making cosmetics, alcoholic beverages, and furniture are seeking opportunities in lifestyle segmentation. At the same time, lifestyle segmentation does not always work; Nestlé introduced a special brand of decaffeinated coffee for "late nighters," and it failed.[8]

Personality. Marketers have also used personality variables to segment markets. They endow their products with *brand personalities* that correspond to *consumer personalities.* In the late fifties, Fords and Chevrolets were promoted as having different personalities. Ford buyers were identified as "independent, impulsive, masculine, alert to change, and self-confident, while Chevrolet owners were conservative, thrifty, prestige-conscious, less masculine, and seeking to avoid extremes.[9] Evans investigated the validity of these descriptions by subjecting Ford and Chevrolet owners to the Edwards Personal Preference test, which measured needs for achievement, dominance, change, aggression, and so on. Except for a slightly higher score on dominance, Ford owners did not score significantly differently from Chevrolet owners. Evans concluded that "the distributions of scores for all needs overlap to such an extent that [personality] discrimination is virtually impossible." Work subsequent to Evans on a wide variety of products and brands has occasionally turned up personality differences. Westfall found some evidence of personality differences between the owners of convertibles and nonconvertibles, owners of the former appearing to be more active, impulsive, and sociable.[10] Shirley Young, the director of research for a leading advertising agency, reported developing successful market segmentation strategies based on personality traits in such product categories as women's cosmetics, cigarettes, insurance, and liquor.[11]

Behavioral segmentation. In behavioral segmentation, buyers are divided into groups on the basis of their knowledge, attitude, use, or response to a product. Many marketers believe that behavioral variables are the best starting point for constructing market segments.

Occasions. Buyers can be distinguished according to occasions when they develop a need, purchase, or use a product. For example, air travel is triggered by occasions related to business, vacation, or family. An airline can specialize in serving people for whom one of these occasions dominates. Thus charter airlines serve people who fly for a vacation.

Occasion segmentation can help firms expand product usage. For example, orange juice is most commonly consumed at breakfast. An orange juice company can

---

[8] Joseph T. Plummer, "Life Style Patterns: New Constraint for Mass Communications Research," *Journal of Broadcasting*, winter 1971–72, pp. 79–89.

[9] Quoted in Franklin B. Evans, "Psychological and Objective Factors in the Prediction of Brand Choice; Ford versus Chevrolet," *Journal of Business*, October 1959, pp. 340–69.

[10] Ralph Westfall, "Psychological Factors in Predicting Product Choice," *Journal of Marketing*, April 1962, pp. 34–40.

[11] Shirley Young, "The Dynamics of Measuring Unchange," in Russell I. Haley, ed., *Attitude Research in Transition* (Chicago: American Marketing Association, 1972), pp. 61–82.

TABLE 8-2

BENEFIT SEGMENTATION OF THE TOOTHPASTE MARKET				
Benefit Segments	**Demographics**	**Behavioristics**	**Psychographics**	**Favored Brands**
Economy (low price)	Men	Heavy users	High autonomy, value oriented	Brands on sale
Medicinal (decay prevention)	Large families	Heavy users	Hypochondriac, conservative	Crest
Cosmetic (bright teeth)	Teens, young adults	Smokers	High sociability, active	Macleans, Ultra Brite
Taste (good tasting)	Children	Spearmint lovers	High self-involvement, hedonistic	Colgate, Aim

SOURCE: Adapted from Russell J. Haley, "Benefit Segmentation: A Decision Oriented Research Tool," *Journal of Marketing*, July 1963, pp. 30–35.

try to promote drinking orange juice at lunch or dinner. Certain holidays—Mother's Day and Father's Day for example—were promoted partly to increase the sale of candy and flowers. The Curtis Candy Company promoted the "trick-or-treat" custom at Halloween, with every home ready to dispense candy to eager little callers knocking at their doors.

Benefits sought. A powerful form of segmentation is the classification of buyers according to the different benefits that they seek from the product. Yankelovich applied benefit segmentation to the purchase of watches. He found that "approximately 23 percent of the buyers bought for lowest price, another 46 percent bought for durability and general product quality, and 31 percent bought watches as symbols of some important occasion."[12] The better-known watch companies at the time focused almost exclusively on the third segment by producing expensive watches, stressing prestige, and selling through jewelry stores. The U.S. Time Company decided to focus on the first two segments by creating Timex watches and selling them through mass merchandisers. This segmentation strategy led to its becoming one of the world's largest watch companies.

Benefit segmentation requires determining the major benefits that people look for in the product class, the kinds of people who look for each benefit, and the major brands that deliver each benefit. One of the most successful benefit segmentations was reported by Haley, who studied the toothpaste market (see Table 8–2). Haley's research uncovered four benefit segments, seeking economy, protection, cosmetic, and taste benefits, respectively. Each benefit-seeking group had particular demographic, behavioristic, and psychographic characteristics. For example, decay-prevention seekers had large families, were heavy toothpaste users, and were conservative. Each segment also favored certain brands. A toothpaste company can use these findings

---

[12] See Daniel Yankelovich, "New Criteria for Market Segmentation," *Harvard Business Review*, March-April 1964, pp. 83–90, here p. 85.

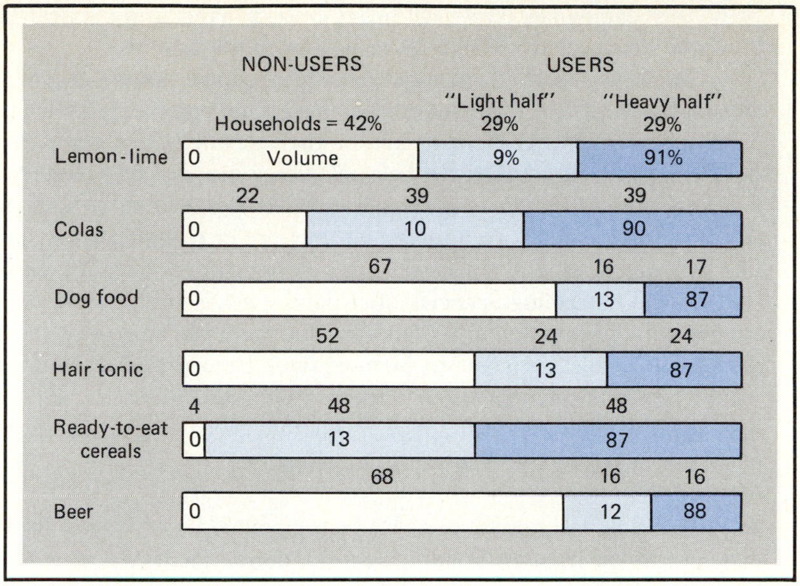

NON-USERS   USERS

	Non-users Households = 42%	"Light half" 29%	"Heavy half" 29%
Lemon-lime	0 Volume	9%	91%
	22	39	39
Colas	0	10	90
	67	16	17
Dog food	0	13	87
	52	24	24
Hair tonic	0	13	87
	4 48	48	
Ready-to-eat cereals	0	13	87
	68	16	16
Beer	0	12	88

Source: Dik Warren Twedt, "How Important to Marketing Strategy is the 'Heavy User'?" *Journal of Marketing,* January 1974, p. 72.

FIGURE 8–5
Annual Purchase Concentration in Several Product Categories

to clarify which benefit segment it is appealing to, the characteristics of that segment, and the major competitive brands. The company can also search for a new benefit and launch a brand that delivers it.

User status. Many markets can be segmented into nonusers, ex-users, potential users, first-time users, and regular users of a product. High-market-share companies are particularly interested in converting potential users into actual users, while smaller firms will try to get users of competitive brands to switch to their brand. Potential users and regular users require different marketing approaches.

Social marketing agencies pay close attention to user status. Drug rehabilitation agencies sponsor rehabilitation programs to help regular users quit the habit. They sponsor talks by ex-users to discourage young people from trying drugs.

Usage rate. Markets can also be segmented into light-, medium-, and heavy-user groups of the product (called *volume segmentation*). Heavy users are often a small percentage of the market but account for a high percentage of total consumption. Some data on usage rates for popular consumer products are shown in Figure 8–5. Using beer as an example, the chart shows that 68 percent of the panel members did not drink beer. The 32 percent who did were divided into two groups. The lower 16 percent were light users and accounted for only 12 percent of total beer consumption. The heavy half accounted for 88 percent of the total consumption— that is, for over seven times as much consumption as the light users. Clearly a beer company would prefer to attract one heavy user to its brand over several light users.

Most beer companies target the heavy beer drinker, using appeals such as Schaefer's "the one beer to have when you're having more than one."

The heavy users of a product often have common demographics, psychographics, and media habits. In the case of heavy beer drinkers, their profile shows the following characteristics: More of them are in the working class compared with light beer drinkers; they fall between the ages of twenty-five and fifty (instead of under twenty-five and over fifty); they watch television more than three and one-half hours per day (instead of under two hours); and they prefer to watch sports programs.[13] Profiles like this one assist the marketer in developing price, message, and media strategies.

Social marketing agencies often face a heavy-user dilemma. A family-planning agency would normally target families who have the most children; but these families are also the most resistant to birth-control messages. The National Safety Council would target unsafe drivers; but these drivers are the most resistant to safe-driving appeals. The agencies must consider whether to go after a few highly resistant heavy offenders or many less resistant light offenders.

Loyalty status. A market can also be segmented by consumer loyalty patterns. Consumers can be loyal to brands (Schlitz), stores (Sears), and other entities. We will deal here with brand loyalty. Suppose there are five brands: A, B, C, D, and E. Buyers can be divided into four groups according to their loyalty status:[14]

☐ **Hard-core loyals.** Consumers who buy one brand all the time. Thus a buying pattern of A, A, A, A, A, A, represents a consumer with undivided loyalty to brand A.
☐ **Soft-core loyals.** Consumers who are loyal to two or three brands. The buying pattern A, A, B, B, A, B represents a consumer with a divided loyalty between A and B.
☐ **Shifting loyals.** Consumers who shift from favoring one brand to another. The buying pattern A, A, A, B, B, B would suggest a consumer who is shifting brand loyalty from A to B.
☐ **Switchers.** Consumers who show no loyalty to any brand. The buying pattern A, C, E, B, D, B would suggest a nonloyal consumer who is either *deal prone* (buys the brand on sale) or *variety prone* (wants something different).

Each market is made up of different numbers of the four types of buyers. A brand-loyal market is one with a high percentage of the buyers showing hard-core brand loyalty. Thus the toothpaste market and the beer market seem to be fairly high brand-loyal markets. Companies selling in a brand-loyal market have a hard time gaining more market share, and companies that enter such a market have a hard time getting in.

A company can learn a great deal by analyzing loyalty patterns in its market. It should study the characteristics of its own hard-core loyals. Colgate finds that its hard-core loyals are more middle class, have larger families, and are more health conscious. This pinpoints the target market for Colgate.

---

[13] Frank M. Bass, Douglas J. Tigert, and Ronald T. Lonsdale, "Market Segmentation: Group versus Individual Behavior," *Journal of Marketing Research*, August 1968, p. 276.

[14] This classification was adapted from George H. Brown, "Brand Loyalty—Fact or Fiction?" *Advertising Age*, June 1952–January 1953, a series.

By studying its soft-core loyals, the company can pinpoint which brands are most competitive with its own. If many Colgate buyers also buy Crest, Colgate can attempt to improve its positioning against Crest, possibly using direct-comparison advertising.

By looking at customers who are shifting away from its brand, the company can learn about its marketing weaknesses. As for nonloyals, the company can attract them by putting its brand on sale.

The company should be aware that what appear to be brand-loyal purchase patterns may reflect *habit*, *indifference*, a *low price*, or the *nonavailability* of other brands. The concept of brand loyalty has some ambiguities and must be used carefully.

Buyer readiness stage. At any time, people are in different stages of readiness to buy a product. Some people are unaware of the product; some are aware; some are informed; some are interested; some are desirous of buying; and some intend to buy. The relative numbers make a big difference in designing the marketing program. Suppose a health agency wants women to take an annual Pap test to detect cervical cancer. At the beginning, most women are unaware of the Pap test. The marketing effort should go into high-awareness-building advertising using a simple message. If successful, the advertising should then dramatize the benefits of the Pap test and the risks of not taking it, in order to move more women into the stage of desire. Facilities should be readied for handling the large number of women who may be motivated to take the examination. In general, the marketing program must be adjusted to the changing distribution of buyer readiness.

Attitude. People in a market can be classified by their degree of enthusiasm for the product. Five attitude classes can be distinguished: enthusiastic, positive, indifferent, negative, and hostile. Door-to-door workers in a political campaign use the voter's attitude to determine how much time to spend with the voter. They thank enthusiastic voters and remind them to vote; they reinforce those who are positively disposed; they try to win the votes of indifferent voters; they spend no time trying to change the attitudes of negative and hostile voters. To the extent that attitudes are correlated with demographic descriptors, the organization can increase its efficiency in reaching the best prospects.[15]

Bases for Segmenting Industrial Markets

Industrial markets can be segmented with many of the same variables used in consumer market segmentation. Industrial buyers can be segmented geographically and by several behavioristic variables: benefits sought, user status, usage rate, loyalty status, readiness stage, and attitudes.

A common way to segment industrial markets is by *end users*. Different end users often seek different benefits and can be approached with different marketing mixes. Consider the rubber tire market:

---

[15] For more on consumer segmentation variables, see Ronald Frank, William Massy, and Yoram Wind, *Market Segmentation* (Englewood Cliffs, N.J.: Prentice-Hall, 1972).

> Automobile manufacturers seeking original equipment tires vary in their requirements, with luxury car manufacturers wanting a much higher grade tire than standard car manufacturers. And the tires needed by aircraft manufacturers have to meet much higher safety standards than tires needed by farm tractor manufacturers.

Customer size is another industrial segmentation variable. Many companies set up separate systems for dealing with major and minor customers. For example, Steelcase, a major manufacturer of office furniture, divides its customers into two groups:

☐ **Major accounts.** Accounts such as IBM, Prudential, and Standard Oil are handled by national account managers working with field district managers.

☐ **Dealer accounts.** Smaller accounts are handled through field sales personnel working with franchised dealers who sell Steelcase products.

Industrial companies typically define their target market opportunities by applying several segmentation variables. This is illustrated in Figure 8–6 for an aluminum company:

> The aluminum company first undertook **macrosegmentation** consisting of three steps.[16] It looked at which end-use market to serve: automobile, residential, or beverage containers. Choosing the residential market, it determined the most attractive product application: semifinished material, building components, or aluminum mobile homes. Deciding to focus on building components, it next considered the best customer size to serve and chose large customers.
>
> The second stage consisted of **microsegmentation** within the large-customer building-components market. The company saw customers falling into three groups—those who bought on price, those who bought on service, and those who bought on quality. Because the aluminum company had a high-service profile, it decided to concentrate on the service-motivated segment of the market.

Requirements for Effective Segmentation

Clearly, there are many ways to segment a market. Not all segmentations, however, are effective. For example, buyers of table salt could be divided into blond and brunet customers. But hair color is not relevant to the purchase of salt. Furthermore, if all salt buyers buy the same amount of salt each month, believe all salt is the same, and want to pay the same price, this market would be minimally segmentable from a marketing point of view.

To be maximally useful, market segments must exhibit the following characteristics:

☐ Measurability, the degree to which the size and purchasing power of the segments can be measured. Certain segmentation variables are difficult to measure. An illustration

---

[16] Wind and Cardozo suggest that industrial segmentation should proceed by first developing macrosegments and then microsegments. See Yoram Wind and Richard Cardozo, "Industrial Market Segmentation," *Industrial Marketing Management* Vol. 3, 1974, pp. 153–66. For another view, see Thomas V. Bonoma and Benson P. Shapiro, *Segmenting the Industrial Market* (Lexington, Mass.: Lexington Books, 1983).

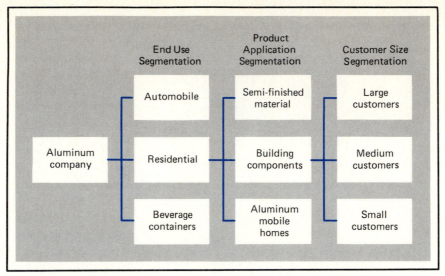

Source: Based on an example in E. Raymond Corey, "Key Options in Market Selection and Product Planning," *Harvard Business Review,* September-October 1975, pp. 119–28.

FIGURE 8–6
Three-Step Segmentation of the Aluminum Market

would be the size of the segment of teenage smokers who smoke primarily to rebel against their parents.

☐ Accessibility, the degree to which the segments can be effectively reached and served. Suppose a perfume company finds that heavy users of its brand are single women who are out late at night and frequent bars. Unless this group lives or shops at certain places and is exposed to certain media, they will be difficult to reach.

☐ Substantiality, the degree to which the segments are large and/or profitable enough. A segment should be the largest possible homogeneous group worth going after with a tailored marketing program. It would not pay, for example, for an automobile manufacturer to develop cars for persons who are shorter than four feet.

☐ Actionability, the degree to which effective programs can be formulated for attracting and serving the segments. A small airline, for example, identified seven market segments, but its staff was too small to develop separate marketing programs for each segment.

MARKET TARGETING

Market segmentation reveals the market segment opportunities facing the firm. The firm now has to evaluate the various segments and decide how many to serve. We shall look at each decision in turn.

Evaluating the Market Segments

Suppose the firm has identified several market segments. In order to choose market targets, it has to first evaluate the profit potential of the various segments. A useful analytical approach is illustrated in Figure 8–7, which shows the market for the

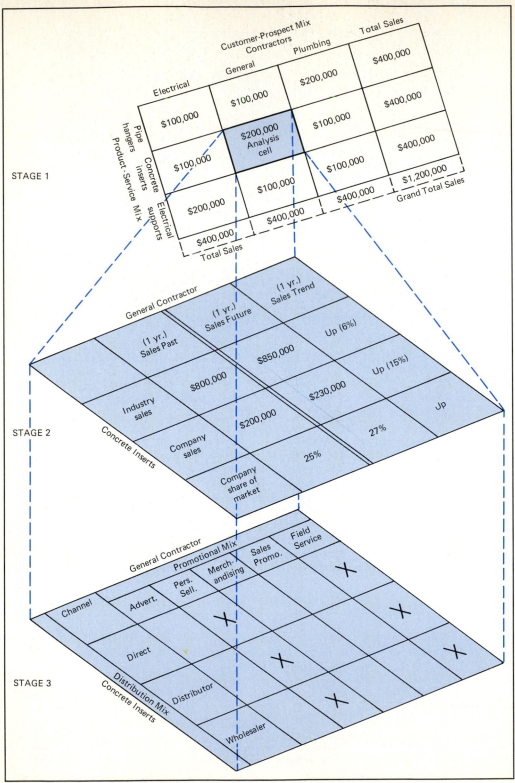

STAGE 1

STAGE 2

STAGE 3

Source: From an unpublished paper by Rhett W. Butler, Northwestern University, 1964.

FIGURE 8-7
Analyzing the Worth of Different Market Segments for Steel-Fabricated Products

product line of a steel-fabricating company. Stage 1 shows a segmentation of this market, using the customer-prospect mix and the product-service mix. The customer-prospect mix consists of contractors in electrical, general, and plumbing lines. The product-service mix consists of three products sold to contractors: pipe hangers, concrete inserts, and electrical supports. This joint segmentation results in nine market segments. A dollar figure in each cell represents the company's sales in that segment.

Company sales in the nine segments provide no indication of their relative profit potential. The latter depends upon market demand, company costs, and competitive trends in each submarket. Stages 2 and 3 show how one product submarket, the general-contractor market for concrete inserts, can be analyzed in depth.

Stage 2 estimates present and future sales in the submarket. The vertical axis accommodates estimates of industry sales, company sales, and company market share. The horizontal axis is used to project future sales and market shares. Last year the company sold in this submarket $200,000 worth of goods, or one-fourth of total estimated industry sales. Looking ahead, the company expects industry sales in this submarket to rise by 6 percent and its own sales to rise by 15 percent.

Stage 3 probes deeper into the marketing thinking behind the sales forecasts of stage 2. The horizontal axis shows the promotional mix that the company is using or plans to use to stimulate the sale of concrete inserts to general contractors. The vertical axis shows the distribution mix that the company is using or plans to use to move concrete inserts into the hands of general contractors. The actual promotion-distribution mix could be detailed by placing budget figures (funds and personnel) in the relevant cells. The company will use all three types of distribution and rely mainly on personal selling and field service for stimulating sales to general contractors.

This analysis allows the marketer to evaluate the long-run profit potential of each segment as an aid to deciding how many and which segments to choose.[17]

Distinguishing Among Possible Market Coverage Strategies

Now the firm has to decide on its market coverage strategy, namely how many markets it will serve. The firm can adopt one of three market coverage strategies, known as undifferentiated marketing, differentiated marketing, and concentrated marketing. They are illustrated in Figure 8–8 and discussed below.

Undifferentiated marketing.   The firm might decide to ignore market segment differences and go after the whole market with one market offer.[18] It focuses on what is common in the needs of consumers rather than on what is different. It designs a product and a marketing program that will appeal to the broadest number of buyers. It relies on mass distribution and mass advertising. It aims to endow the product

---

[17] For further discussion of this approach, see William J. Crissy and Frank H. Mossman, "Matrix Models for Marketing Planning: An Update and Expansion," *MSU Business Topics*, autumn 1977, pp. 17–26.

[18] See Wendell R. Smith, "Product Differentiation and Market Segmentation as Alternative Marketing Strategies," *Journal of Marketing*, July 1956, pp. 3–8; and Alan A. Roberts, "Applying the Strategy of Market Segmentation," *Business Horizons*, fall 1961, pp. 65–72.

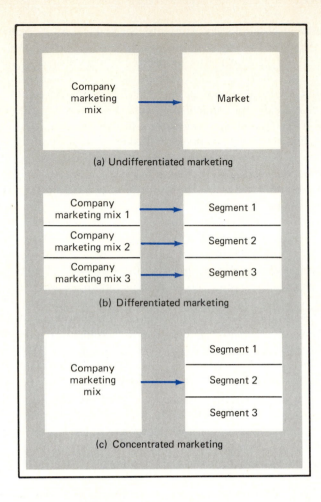

(a) Undifferentiated marketing

(b) Differentiated marketing

(c) Concentrated marketing

FIGURE 8-8
Three Alternative Market
Selection Strategies

with a superior image in people's minds. An example of undifferentiated marketing is the Coca-Cola Company's early marketing of only one drink in one bottle size in one taste to suit all.

Undifferentiated marketing is defended on the grounds of cost economies. It is seen as "the marketing counterpart to standardization and mass production in manufacturing."[19] The narrow product line keeps down production, inventory, and transportation costs. The undifferentiated advertising program keeps down advertising costs. The absence of segment marketing research and planning lowers the costs of marketing research and product management.

Nevertheless, a growing number of marketers have expressed strong doubts about this strategy. Gardner and Levy, while acknowledging that "some brands have very skillfully built up reputations of being suitable for a wide variety of people," noted that:

[19] Smith, "Product Differentiation," p. 4.

In most areas audience groupings will differ, if only because there are deviants who refuse to consume the same way other people do. . . . It is not easy for a brand to appeal to stable lower-middle-class people and at the same time to be interesting to sophisticated, intellectual upper-middle-class buyers. . . . It is rarely possible for a product or brand to be all things to all people.[20]

The firm practicing undifferentiated marketing typically develops an offer aimed at the largest segments in the market. When several firms do this, the result is intense competition for the largest segments and undersatisfaction of the smaller ones. Thus the American auto industry for a long time produced only large automobiles. The further result is that the larger segments may be less profitable because they attract disproportionately heavy competition. Kuehn and Day have called this tendency to go after the largest market segment the "majority fallacy."[21] The recognition of this fallacy has led firms into increased interest in the smaller segments of the market.

Differentiated marketing. Here the firm decides to operate in several segments of the market and designs separate offers to each. Thus General Motors tries to produce a car for every "purse, purpose, and personality." By offering product and marketing variations, it hopes to attain higher sales and a deeper position within each market segment. It hopes that obtaining a deep position in several segments strengthens the consumers' overall identification of the company with the product category. Furthermore, it hopes for greater repeat purchasing because the firm's offer matches the customer's desire rather than the other way around.

A growing number of firms have adopted differentiated marketing. Here is an excellent example:[22]

> Edison Brothers operates nine hundred shoe stores that fall into four different chain categories, each appealing to a different market segment. Chandler's sells higher-priced shoes. Baker's sells moderate-priced shoes. Burt's sells shoes for budget shoppers, and Wild Pair is oriented to the shopper who wants very stylized shoes. Within three blocks on State Street in Chicago are found Burt's, Chandler's, and Baker's. Putting the stores near each other does not hurt them because they are aimed at different segments of the women's shoe market. This strategy has made Edison Brothers the country's largest retailer of women's shoes.

Differentiated marketing typically creates more total sales than undifferentiated marketing. "It is ordinarily demonstrable that total sales may be increased with a more diversified product line sold through more diversified channels."[23] However, it also increases the costs of doing business. The following costs are likely to be higher:

---

[20] Burleigh Gardner and Sidney Levy, "The Product and the Brand," *Harvard Business Review*, March–April 1955, p. 37.

[21] Alfred A. Kuehn and Ralph L. Day, "Strategy of Product Quality," *Harvard Business Review*, November–December 1962, pp. 101–2.

[22] Natalie Mckelvy, "Shoes Make Edison Brothers a Big Name," *Chicago Tribune*, February 23, 1979.

[23] Roberts, "Applying the Strategy of Market Segmentation," p. 66.

- □ **Product modification costs.** Modifying a product to meet different market segment requirements usually involves some R&D, engineering, and/or special tooling costs.
- □ **Production costs.** It is usually more expensive to produce, say, ten units of ten different products than one hundred units of one product. The longer the production setup time for each product and the smaller the sales volume of each product, the more expensive it becomes. On the other hand, if each model is sold in sufficiently large volume, the higher costs of setup time may be quite small per unit.
- □ **Administrative costs.** The company has to develop separate marketing plans for the separate segments of the market. This requires extra marketing research, forecasting, sales analysis, promotion, planning, and channel management.
- □ **Inventory costs.** It is generally more costly to manage inventories of differentiated products than an inventory of only one product. The extra costs arise because more records must be kept and more auditing must be done. Furthermore, each product must be carried at a level that reflects basic demand plus a safety factor to cover unexpected variations in demand. The sum of the safety stocks for several products will exceed the safety stock required for one product.
- □ **Promotion costs.** Differentiated marketing involves trying to reach different market segments with different advertising. This leads to lower usage rates of individual media and the loss of quantity discounts. Furthermore, since each segment may require separate creative advertising planning, promotion costs are increased.

Since differentiated marketing leads to higher sales and costs, nothing can be said in advance regarding the profitability of this strategy. Some firms find that they have *oversegmented* their market and offer too many brands. They would like to manage fewer brands, with each appealing to a broader customer group. Called "countersegmentation" or "broadening the base," they seek a larger volume for each brand.[24] Johnson & Johnson, for example, as we mentioned in an earlier chapter, broadened its target market for its baby shampoo to include adults. And Beecham launched its Aquafresh toothpaste to attract two benefit segments, those seeking fresh breath and those seeking cavity protection.

Concentrated marketing. Many firms see a third possibility that is especially appealing when company resources are limited. Instead of going after a small share of a large market, the firm goes after a large share of one or a few submarkets.

Several examples of concentrated marketing can be cited. Volkswagen has concentrated on the small-car market, Hewlett-Packard on the high-price calculator market, and Richard D. Irwin on the economics and business texts market. Through concentrated marketing the firm achieves a strong market position in the segments it serves, owing to its greater knowledge of the segments' needs and the special reputation it acquires. Furthermore, it enjoys many operating economies because of specialization in production, distribution, and promotion. If the segment is chosen well, the firm can earn a high rate of return on its investment.

At the same time, concentrated marketing involves higher than normal risks. The particular market segment can turn sour; for example, when young women sud-

---

[24] Alan J. Resnik, Peter B. B. Turney, and J. Barry Mason, "Marketers Turn to 'Countersegmentation,'" *Harvard Business Review*, September–October, 1979, pp. 100–106.

denly stopped buying sportswear, it caused Bobbie Brooks's earnings to go deeply into the red. Or a competitor may decide to enter the same segment. For these reasons, many companies prefer to diversify in several market segments.

Choosing A Market Coverage Strategy

In choosing one of the three preceding market coverage strategies, the following factors should be considered.[25]

☐ **Company resources.** When the firm's resources are limited, concentrated marketing makes the most sense.

☐ **Product homogeneity.** Undifferentiated marketing is more suited for homogeneous products, such as grapefruit or steel. Products that are capable of design variation, such as cameras and automobiles, are more suited to differentiation or concentration.

☐ **Product stage in the life cycle.** When a firm introduces a new product, it is practical to launch only one version, and undifferentiated marketing or concentrated marketing makes the most sense. In the mature stage of the product life cycle, differentiated marketing starts making more sense.

☐ **Market homogeneity.** If buyers have the same tastes, buy the same amounts per periods, and react the same way to marketing stimuli, a strategy of undifferentiated marketing is appropriate.

☐ **Competitive marketing strategies.** When competitors practice active segmentation, undifferentiated marketing can be suicidal. Conversely, when competitors practice undifferentiated marketing, a firm can gain by pursuing differentiated or concentrated marketing.

We have assumed that individual segments or combinations of segments could be independently chosen, but this assumption ignores synergies that might exist between various market segments. Figure 8–9(a) shows a market consisting of twelve

FIGURE 8-9
Segments and Supersegments

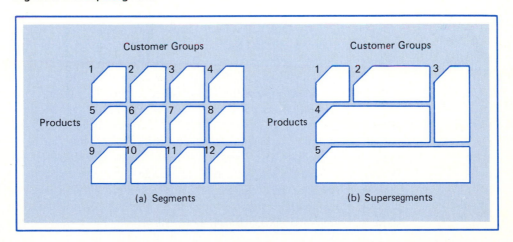

(a) Segments   (b) Supersegments

[25] R. William Kotrba, "The Strategy Selection Chart," *Journal of Marketing*, July 1966, pp. 22–25.

segments. A closer examination of these segments shows, however, that they group into five *supersegments* based on certain synergies, such as using the same raw materials, manufacturing facilities, or distribution channels [see Figure 8–9(b)]. Even if the firm favored market concentration, it would be wise to focus on one of the five supersegments instead of one of the twelve smaller segments. Otherwise it might be at a competitive disadvantage with those firms that have taken advantage of market segment synergies.

PRODUCT POSITIONING

For each segment a company pursues, it needs to develop and communicate a product-positioning strategy. Presumably each competitive product currently occupies a given place in the market segment. What is important is the consumer perception of the place each product occupies in the market. *Positioning* is *the act of designing the company's product and marketing mix to fit a given place in the consumer's mind.* (See Exhibit 8–1.)

Here is an example of product positioning using perceptual maps. A theme park company wants to build a new theme park in the Los Angeles area to take advantage of the substantial number of tourists who come to Los Angeles with the idea of seeing Disneyland and other tourist attractions in the area. At least seven theme parks presently operate in the Los Angeles area. Management feels that the existing theme parks are quite expensive: A family of four will pay $50 for a day at Disneyland. Management believes they could develop a less expensive theme park that would appeal to the segment of cost-conscious tourists. Management, however, needs to know how consumers view the seven existing theme parks in terms of the various satisfactions they seek in a theme park, including low cost.

The company's marketing researcher used the following procedure to develop a perceptual map of Los Angeles's seven major tourist attractions.[26] The marketing researcher presented consumers with a series of triads (such as the triad "Busch Gardens, Japanese Deer Park, and Disneyland") and asked them to choose the two most similar attractions and the two least similar attractions in each triad. A statistical analysis led to the perceptual map shown in Figure 8–10.

This map contains two features. There are seven dots representing the seven major tourist attractions in the Los Angeles area. The closer any two attractions are, the more similar they are; thus Disneyland and Magic Mountain are perceived as similar, whereas Disneyland and Lion Country Safari are perceived as very dissimilar. The map also contains nine satisfactions that people look for in tourist attractions, indicated by arrows. The standing of each tourist attraction on each attribute can be read. For example, Marineland of the Pacific is perceived by consumers as involving the "least waiting time" because it is furthest along the imaginary line of the "little waiting" arrow, while Magic Mountain is perceived as involving the most waiting time. Consumers think of Busch Gardens as the most economical attraction and

---

[26] See Robert V. Stumpf, "The Market Structure of the Major Tourist Attractions in Southern California." *Proceedings* of the 1976 Sperry Business Conference (Chicago: American Marketing Association, pp. 101–6).

Exhibit 8-1

"POSITIONING" ACCORDING TO RIES AND TROUT

The word *positioning* was popularized in 1972 by two advertising executives, Al Ries and Jack Trout, in a series of articles in *Advertising Age* called "The Positioning Era." Later they wrote a book called *Positioning: The Battle For Your Mind*. Ries and Trout see positioning as a creative exercise done with an existing product. Here is their definition:

Positioning starts with a product. A piece of merchandise, a service, a company, an institution, or even a person. . . . But positioning is not what you do to a product. Positioning is what you do to the mind of the prospect. That is, you position the product in the mind of the prospect.

They go on to say that positioning might lead to changes in the product's name, price, and packaging, but these are "cosmetic changes done for the purpose of securing a worthwhile position in the prospect's mind." Thus they are more interested in the *psychological positioning or repositioning* of existing products than in the *product positioning* of potential products. In the latter case, the marketer has to develop all the 4 Ps from scratch so that the product characteristics appeal exactly to a chosen target market. The product positioner is as much interested in what is done to the product as in what is done to the mind.

Ries and Trout offer some sage advice about psychological positioning. They start with the observation that many markets consist of similar products that fail to achieve any distinctiveness in the consumer's mind. In an "overcommunicated society," the marketer's task is to create product distinctiveness. Their key idea is that consumers mentally rank products along one or more dimensions. Thus consumers think of Hertz, Avis, and National in that order when thinking about which car-rental agency has the most cars or services. The marketer's task is to get the product to be ranked *first* along some significant dimension of purchase. This is because consumers remember number one better. For example, everyone knows that Lindbergh was the first person to fly across the Atlantic; people rarely know who was the second person. Also consumers tend to prefer to go with number one.

If a market contains a strong number one brand, a challenger can play one of two games. One is the underdog game, claiming to be as good or better than the leader, as Avis did in its classic campaign, "We're number two. We try harder." The other is to find another dimension along which the brand can be positioned as the clear leader. The marketer searches for a *creneau*, or hole, in the consumer's mind not occupied by someone else. Thus Seven-up advertises itself as The Uncola so that consumers will think of it first when they want a noncola drink.

See Al Ries and Jack Trout, Positioning: The Battle for Your Mind *(New York: Warner Books, 1982).*

Knott's Berry Farm as the most expensive attraction. Clearly the theme park company will face Busch Gardens as a major competitor if it decides to build a theme park to appeal to cost-conscious tourists. At the same time, management will pay attention to all the other satisfactions consumers seek as it figures out a product concept for the theme park and its positioning strategy in relation to the other theme parks in the Los Angeles area.

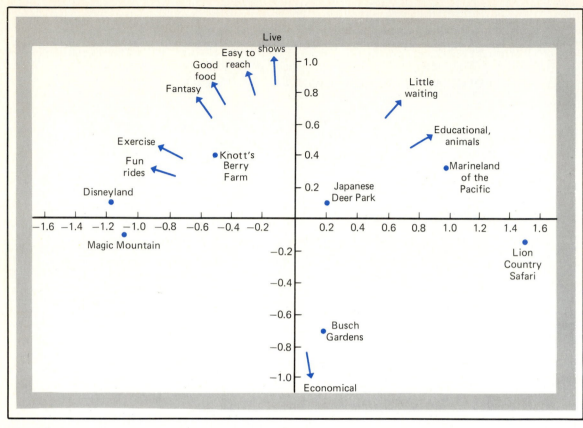

Adapted from Robert V. Stumpf, "The Market Structure of the Major Tourist Attractions in Southern California," *Proceedings* of the 1976 Sperry Business Conference (Chicago: American Marketing Association), pp. 101–6.

FIGURE 8-10
Perceptual Map Showing the Positioning of Theme Parks in the Los Angeles Area

The analysis can be improved further by preparing a separate perceptual map for each market segment, instead of one map for the total market. Each market segment is likely to perceive the products and benefits somewhat differently. The marketer really wants to know how its target market(s) perceive the product alternatives.

Clearly every product offered to a market needs a positioning strategy so that its place in the total market can be communicated to the target market. Professor Wind has identified six alternative bases for constructing a product-positioning strategy.[27] They are listed below and hypothetically illustrated for the case of theme parks:

---

[27] Yoram J. Wind, *Product Policy: Concepts, Methods, and Strategy* (Reading, Mass.: Addison-Wesley Publishing Co., 1982), pp. 79–81.

□ **Positioning on specific product features.** Disneyland can advertise itself as the largest theme park in the world. Largeness is a product feature that indirectly implies a benefit, namely, the most entertainment options.

□ **Positioning on benefits, problem solution, or needs.** Knott's Berry Farm can position itself as a theme park for people seeking a fantasy experience.

□ **Positioning for specific usage occasions.** Japanese Deer Park can position itself for the tourist who can spend only an hour and wants to catch some quick entertainment.

□ **Positioning for user category.** Magic Mountain can advertise itself as the theme park for "thrill seekers," thus defining itself through a user category.

□ **Positioning against another product.** Lion Country Safari can advertise that it has a greater variety of animals than the Japanese Deer Park.

□ **Product class dissociation.** Marineland of the Pacific can position itself not as a "recreational theme park" but as an "educational institution," thus putting itself into another product class than the expected one.

All said, the company's fundamental decision on which market segment(s) to target determines its customers and set of competitors. The company's product-positioning decision further defines its customers and competitors. At this point the company is ready to start planning the details of its marketing mix.

SUMMARY

Sellers can take three approaches to a market. **Mass marketing** is the decision to mass produce and mass distribute one product and attempt to attract all kinds of buyers. **Product differentiation** is the decision to produce two or more market offers differentiated in style, features, quality, sizes, and so on and designed to offer variety to the market and distinguish the seller's products from competitors' products. **Target marketing** is the decision to distinguish the different groups that make up a market and to develop corresponding products and marketing mixes for each target market. Sellers today are moving away from mass marketing and product differentiation toward target marketing because the latter is more helpful in spotting market opportunities and developing effective products and marketing mixes.

The key steps in target marketing are market segmentation, market targeting, and product positioning. Market segmentation is the act of dividing a market into distinct groups of buyers who might merit separate products and/or marketing mixes. The marketer tries different variables to see which reveal the best segmentation opportunities. For consumer marketing, the major segmentation variables are geographic, demographic, psychographic, and behavioral. Industrial markets can be segmented by end use, customer size, geographical location, and product application. The effectiveness of the segmentation analysis depends upon arriving at segments that are measurable, accessible, substantial, and actionable.

Next, the seller has to target the best market segment(s). To do this, the seller must first evaluate the profit potential of each segment. Then the seller must decide how many segments to cover. The seller can ignore segment differences (undifferentiated marketing), develop different market offers for several segments (differentiated marketing), or go after one or a few market segments (concentrated marketing). The market coverage decision will be influenced by such factors as company resources, product and market homogeneity, product life-cycle stage, and competitive marketing strategies.

Market targeting then defines the company's competitors. The company researches the competitors' positions and decides whether to position its offer next to some competitor or go after a hole in the market. If the company positions its basic offer next to a competitor, it must seek further differentiation through other marketing variables. Its product-positioning strategy will then enable it to take the next step, namely, planning the details of the marketing mix.

QUESTIONS

1. The choice of a base for segmenting consumer markets depends on its relevance for differentiating the buying patterns of consumer groups in a particular market. What might be a relevant base(s) for segmenting the market for banking and other financial services?

2. By making slight changes in the product and its packaging, cigarette manufacturers have been able to make what is essentially the same product appeal to a wide variety of consumer segments. In what ways has the smoking public been segmented, and how have cigarette makers positioned their products to these markets via product and package design and advertising messages?

3. Choose a consumer service and discuss how the market for such a service is segmented.

4. Market segments can be developed by cross-classifying pertinent variables. What problems arise in trying to cross-classify more than a few variables?

5. Suggest a useful way to segment the markets for the following products: (a) household detergents, (b) animal feeds, (c) household coffee, (d) automobile tires.

6. A camera manufacturer wants to develop a benefit segmentation of the camera market. Suggest some major benefit segments.

7. The Quaker Oats Company produces a dry breakfast cereal called Life. Life's brand manager wants to identify different market segments for the cereal. The segments are formed by using wife's age, family size, and city size. Rank the segments from the most important to the least important.

8. A clock manufacturer recognizes that it is basically in the time-measurement business. It wants to segment the time-measurement market in order to identify new opportunities. Identify the major segments in this market.

The Marketing Planning Process

Plans are nothing; planning is everything.

DWIGHT D. EISENHOWER

We are now ready to examine how an organization can develop marketing plans and strategies for serving its markets. Organizations cannot survive by simply reacting to new developments as they occur. Ad hoc marketing will result in inconsistent actions and expenditures, leaving the organization vulnerable to more forward-planning competitors. Each organization must take a planned approach to the marketplace.

Several questions arise in connection with marketing planning. What are the stages through which business- and marketing-planning systems evolve? What is a marketing plan and what are its components? What are the theoretical underpinnings of effective marketing planning? We shall address these questions in this chapter.

EVOLUTION OF BUSINESS PLANNING

Business planning is a relatively new development in the corporate world. Businesses pass through four stages on their way to sophisticated planning. Today various companies can be found in each of these stages.

Unplanned Stage

When companies are first organized, their managers are so busy hunting for funds, customers, equipment, and materials that they have little time to plan. Management is engrossed in the day-to-day operations required to survive.

Budgeting-System Stage

The company eventually installs a budgeting system to improve its control of cash flow. Management estimates total sales for the coming year and the associated costs and cash flows. Department managers prepare budgets for their departments. These budgets are financial and do not require the level of thought that goes into real planning. Budgets should not be confused with full-scale plans.

Annual-Planning Stage

Management eventually recognizes the advantages of developing annual plans. It adopts one of three possible approaches to planning.

The first, *top-down planning*, involves the setting of goals and *plans* by top management for all the lower levels of management. This model is used in military organizations, where the generals prepare the plans and the troops carry them out. In business firms, it goes along with a theory X view of employees, that they dislike responsibility and prefer to be directed.[1]

In the opposite system, *bottom-up planning*, the various units of the organization prepare their own goals and plans based on the best they think they can do and send them to higher levels of management for approval. This approach is based on theory Y, that employees like responsibility and are more creative and committed if they participate in the planning of the enterprise.

Most companies use a third system, known as *goals-down–plans-up planning*. Here top management looks at the company's opportunities and requirements and sets corporate goals for the year. The various units of the company are responsible for developing plans to help the company reach these goals. These plans, when approved by top management, become the official annual plan. A typical example is afforded by the Celanese Company:

> The annual-planning process starts in late August, with top management receiving marketing research reports and sending out a guidance letter stating overall volume and profit goals. During September and October, product-planning managers develop overall marketing plans in consultation with the field sales manager and the marketing vice-president. In the middle of October, the marketing vice-president reviews and approves the plans and submits them to the president for final approval. In the meantime, the field sales manager works with his regional sales managers and sales people to develop field sales plans. Finally, in the fourth week in October, the controller prepares an operating budget: in early November, it goes to top management for final approval. Thus, three months after the planning process started, a completed plan and a budget are ready to be put into operation.[2]

---

[1] Douglas McGregor, *The Human Side of Enterprise* (New York: McGraw-Hill Book Co., 1960).

[2] *The Development of Marketing Objectives and Plans: A Symposium* (New York: Conference Board, 1963), p. 38.

Annual-planning systems may take some years to work successfully. Some executives will resist having to prepare plans for their operations. They may not want to commit themselves to goals and strategies in a rapidly changing environment. They resent the time required to prepare plans when they can be out selling. They may think of planning as something to satisfy their superiors rather than a tool for improving their own performance. Therefore top management must give thought to how to introduce a *planning culture* into the organization. Top management needs a plan for selling its managers on the benefits of planning. The main benefits of planning are:

☐ Encourages systematic thinking ahead by management.
☐ Leads to a better coordination of company efforts.
☐ Leads to the development of performance standards for control.
☐ Causes the company to sharpen its guiding objectives and policies.
☐ Results in better preparedness for sudden developments.
☐ Brings about a more vivid sense in the participating executives of their interacting responsibilities.[3]

Given that the president is fully committed to planning, the president should hire a planning officer. The planning officer would meet with various managers to get their ideas, design a planning methodology, and test it with some managers until it is ready to launch companywide. When the calendar for planning is approved, this officer assists the managers in gathering information and writing their plans. The initial plans should be short and practical. Over the years, more sections should be added to the plan format as the managers become more willing and able to plan.

Long-Range-Planning Stage

Management eventually realizes that annual planning should be preceded by long-range planning. The annual plan should be a detailed version of the first year of a long-range plan. For example, managers at the American Hospital Supply Company prepare a five-year plan for each product early in the year and an annual plan later in the year. The five-year plan is reworked each year (called *rolling planning*) because the environment changes and the long-run planning assumptions need to be reviewed.

Strategic-Planning Stage

Finally the company realizes that most of its planning deals with its existing businesses and how to keep them going, when in fact, the company should reexamine which businesses it should grow, maintain, harvest, and terminate and which new businesses it should enter. The environment is so full of surprises that the company needs to develop a portfolio of businesses that can withstand shocks. Strategic planning deals with efforts to keep the whole corporation optimally adapted to its best opportunities in the face of a constantly changing environment.

---

[3] Melville C. Branch, *The Corporate Planning Process* (New York: American Management Association, 1962), pp. 48–49.

As the company gains further experience with planning, the plan formats are standardized. It is important that the plans for divisions, product lines, products, or brands follow the same format, to permit intelligent comparison by higher management. Managers also receive training in *financial analysis* so they can defend their plan not in sales-volume terms but in terms of contribution margin, cash flow, and rate of return on manageable assets. *Computer programs* are developed to help marketing managers examine the effects of alternative marketing plans and environmental assumptions on sales and profit. Managers are asked to develop *contingency plans* alongside main plans showing how they would respond to critical events. These and other refinements mark the emergence of a true strategic-planning culture in the firm.

THE NATURE AND CONTENTS OF A MARKETING PLAN

As part of the company planning process, one hears talk about "marketing plans," "business plans," "financial plans," and so on. Often these are used loosely and differently by different companies. Sometimes the marketing plan means the business plan; sometimes it is only a component of a business plan. The fact is that companies produce a large number of plans, each of which has a heavy marketing component. There are at least eight different plans that require marketing input:

1. **Corporate plan.** The corporate plan describes the overall business plan for the corporation. It might be an annual, intermediate, or long-range plan. The corporate plan deals with company missions, growth strategies, portfolio decisions, investment decisions, and current objectives and goals. It does not contain details on the activities of individual business units.
2. **Divisional plan.** The divisional plan is similar to the corporate plan and describes the division's plan for growth and profitability. It describes marketing, financial, manufacturing, and personnel strategies and may use a short, intermediate or long-run planning horizon. In some cases, the divisional plan is the sum of all the separate plans prepared within the division.
3. **Product-line plan.** A product-line plan describes objectives, strategies, and tactics for a specific product line. Each product-line manager prepares this plan.
4. **Product plan.** A product plan describes objectives, strategies, and tactics for a particular product or product category. Each product manager prepares a product plan.
5. **Brand plan.** A brand plan describes objectives, strategies, and tactics for a specific brand within the product category. Each brand manager prepares a brand plan.
6. **Market plan.** A market plan is a plan for developing and serving a particular industrial or geographical market. Each market manager would prepare this plan. Related to this would be *customer plans* prepared for important customers.
7. **Product/market plan.** A product/market plan is a plan for marketing a particular product or product line of the company in a particular industrial or geographical market. An example would be a bank's plan to market its lending services to the real estate industry in the eastern part of the U.S.
8. **Functional plan.** A functional plan is a plan for one of the major functions, such as marketing, manufacturing, manpower, finance, or research and development. It also describes plans for subfunctions within a major function, such as, in the case of marketing, an advertising plan, a sales promotion plan, a sales-force plan, and a marketing research plan.

TABLE 9–1

CONTENTS OF A MARKETING PLAN	
Section	**Purpose**
I. Executive Summary	This presents an abbreviated overview of the proposed plan for quick management skimming.
II. Current Marketing Situation	This presents relevant background data on the market, product, competition, distribution, and macroenvironment.
III. Opportunity and Issue Analysis	This summarizes the main opportunities/threats, strengths/weaknesses, and issues facing the product that the plan must deal with.
IV. Objectives	This defines the goals the plan wants to reach in the areas of sales volume, market share, and profit.
V. Marketing Strategies	This presents the broad marketing approach that will be used to meet the plan's objectives.
VI. Action Programs	This answers **What** will be done? **Who** will do it? **When** will it be done? and **How much** will it cost?
VII. Projected Profit-and-Loss Statement	This summarizes the expected financial payoff from the plan.
VIII. Controls	This tells how the plan will be monitored.

As noted earlier, these plans require marketing input. In fact, marketing input is not only essential but usually takes priority in the plan's development. Planning often starts with the question, How great a sales volume can we hope to obtain at a profit? This is answered by marketing analysis and the development of a marketing plan. After this plan is approved, nonmarketing executives start working on their manufacturing, financial, and personnel plans to support the marketing plan. Thus the marketing plan is the starting point for the planning of the other activities of the company.

How does a marketing plan look? Marketing plans will have several sections, varying with how much detail top management wants from its managers. Most marketing plans, particularly product and brand plans, will have the following sections: *executive summary*, *current marketing situation*, *opportunity and issue analysis*, *objectives*, *marketing strategy*, *action programs*, *projected profit-and-loss statement*, and *controls*. These sections and their purposes are listed in Table 9–1 and discussed in the following paragraphs. The plan sections will be illustrated with the following case:[4]

---

[4] This example is adapted with several changes and additions from "Zenith Radio Corporation; Allegro," a Harvard Business School case 9–575–062 prepared by Ed Popper under the supervision of Scott Ward, 1975.

> Zenith Corporation is a major producer of electronic consumer products, including television receivers, radios, and stereo equipment. Each product line is the responsibility of a product manager, who must prepare a long-range plan and an annual plan that would meet the financial objectives of the Zenith Corporation.
>
> Currently Jane Melody is the product manager of Zenith's line of modular stereo systems, called the Allegro line. Each system consists of an AM-FM tuner/amplifier plus phonograph plus tape deck and separate speakers. Zenith offers thirteen different models that sell in the $150–$400 range. A modular stereo system differs on the one hand from **stereo consoles**, in which all of the components are built into one cabinet, and on the other hand from **audio component systems**, where consumers select unrelated but compatible components to make up the systems they want. Zenith also produces a line of stereo console units, but the console market is in a state of decline as consumers switch to smaller sound systems. Zenith does not produce audio components but has considered it from time to time. Zenith's main goal is to increase its market share and profitability in the modular-stereo-system market. As product manager, Jane Melody has to prepare a marketing plan to improve the performance of the Allegro line.

Executive Summary

The planning document should open with a short summary of the main goals and recommendations to be found in the body of the plan. Here is an abbreviated example:

> The 1984 Allegro marketing plan seeks to generate a significant increase in company sales and profits over the preceding year. The profit target is set at $1.8 million. The sales-revenue target is set at $18 million, which represents a planned 9 percent sales gain over last year. This increase is seen as attainable through improved pricing, advertising, and distribution effort. The required marketing budget will be $2,290,000, a 14 percent increase over last year. . . . [More details follow]

The executive summary permits higher management to quickly grasp the major thrust of the plan. A table of contents should follow the executive summary.

Current Marketing Situation

This section of the plan presents relevant background data on the market, product, competition, distribution, and macroenvironment.

Market situation.   Here data is presented on the served market. The size and growth of the market (in units and/or dollars) is shown for several past years in total and by market and geographical segments. Data is also presented on customer needs, perceptions, and buying behavior trends.

> The modular stereo market accounts for approximately $400 million or 20 percent of the home stereo market. Sales are expected to be stable or declining over the next few years. . . . The primary buyers are upscale people who want to listen to good music but do not want to invest in expensive component equipment. They want to buy a complete system produced by a name they can trust. They want a system with good sound and whose looks fit the decor primarily of dens or living rooms.

Product situation. Here the sales, prices, contribution margins and net profits are shown for each major product in the line for several past years.

Table 9–2 shows an example of how product data might be presented for the modular stereo line. Row 1 shows the total industry sales in units growing at 5 percent annually until 1983, when demand declined slightly. Row 2 shows Zenith's market share hovering around 3 percent, although it reached 4 percent in 1982. Row 3 shows the average price for an Allegro stereo rising about 10 percent a year except the last year, when it rose 4 percent. Row 4 shows variable costs—materials, labor, energy—rising each year. Row 5 shows that the gross contribution margin per unit—the difference between price (row 3) and unit variable cost (row 4)—rose the first few years and remained at $100 in the latest year. Rows 6 and 7 show sales volume in units and dollars, and row 8 shows the total gross contribution margin, which rose until the latest year, when it fell. Row 9 shows that overhead remained constant during 1980 and 1981 and increased to a higher level during 1982 and 1983, due to an explosion of manufacturing capacity. Row 10 shows net contribution margin, that is, gross contribution margin less overhead. Rows 11, 12, and 13 show marketing expenditures on advertising and promotion, sales force and distribution, and marketing research. Finally, row 14 shows net operating profit after marketing expenses. The picture is one of increasing profits until 1983, when they fell to about one-third of the 1982 level. Clearly Zenith's product manager needs to find a strategy for 1984 that will once again restore healthy growth in sales and profits to the product line.

Competitive situation. Here the major competitors are identified and are described in terms of their size, goals, market share, product quality, marketing strategies,

TABLE 9-2

HISTORICAL PRODUCT DATA

Variable	Columns	1980	1981	1982	1983
1. Industry sales—in units		2,000,000	2,100,000	2,205,000	2,200,000
2. Company market share		0.03	0.03	0.04	0.03
3. Average price per unit $		200	220	240	250
4. Variable cost per unit $		120	125	140	150
5. Gross contribution margin per unit $	$(3-4)$	80	95	100	100
6. Sales volume in units	(1×2)	60,000	63,000	88,200	66,000
7. Sales revenue $	(3×6)	12,000,000	13,860,000	21,168,000	16,500,000
8. Gross contribution margin $	(5×6)	4,800,000	5,985,000	8,820,000	6,600,000
9. Overhead $		2,000,000	2,000,000	3,500,000	3,500,000
10. Net contribution margin $	$(8-9)$	2,800,000	3,985,000	5,320,000	3,100,000
11. Advertising and promotion $		800,000	1,000,000	1,000,000	900,000
12. Sales force and distribution $		700,000	1,000,000	1,100,000	1,000,000
13. Marketing research $		100,000	120,000	150,000	100,000
14. Net operating profit $	$(10-11-12-13)$	1,200,000	1,865,000	3,070,000	1,100,000

and any other characteristics that are appropriate to understanding their intentions and behavior.

> Zenith's major competitors in the modular stereo system market are Panasonic, Sony, Magnovox, General Electric, and Electrophonic. Each competitor has a specific strategy and niche in the market. Panasonic, for example, offers thirty-three models covering the whole price range, sells primarily in department stores and discount stores, is a heavy advertising spender, and so on. It is out to dominate the market through product proliferation and price discounting. . . . [Similar descriptions are prepared for each of the other competitors.]

Distribution situation. This section presents data on the number of stereo units sold in each distribution channel and the changing importance of each channel. Changes are noted in the power of distributors and dealers as well as in the prices and trade terms necessary to motivate them.

> Modular stereo sets are sold through a variety of distribution channels: department stores, radio/TV stores, appliance stores, discount stores, furniture stores, music stores, audio specialty stores, and mail order. Zenith sells 37 percent of its sets through appliance stores, 23 percent through radio/TV stores, 10 percent through furniture stores, 3 percent through department stores, and the remainder through other channels. Zenith dominates in all those channels, which unfortunately are declining in importance, while it is a weak competitor in the faster growing channels, such as discount stores. Zenith gives about a 30 percent margin to its dealers, which is similar to what other competitors give.

Macroenvironment situation. This section describes broad macroenvironment trends—demographic, economic, technological, political/legal, social/cultural—that have a bearing on the future of this product line.

> About 50 percent of U.S. households now have stereo equipment. As the market approaches saturation, effort must be turned to convincing consumers to upgrade their equipment. . . . The economy is expected to remain in a weak state, which means people will postpone consumer-durables purchases. . . . The Japanese are designing more-compact audio systems and working on a new and better sound system.

Opportunity and Issue Analysis

On the basis of the data describing the current marketing situation, the product manager needs to identify the major *opportunities/threats*, *strengths/weaknesses*, and *issues* the company faces with this product over the term of the plan.

Opportunities/threats analysis (O/T analysis). Here the manager identifies the main opportunities and threats facing the business. Opportunities and threats refer to *outside* factors that can affect the future of the business. They are written so as to suggest some possible actions that might be taken. The manager should rank the opportunities and threats so that the more important ones can be given special attention.

The main *opportunities* facing Zenith's Allegro line are:

☐ Consumers are showing increased interest in more-compact modular stereo systems, and Zenith should consider designing one or more compact models.
☐ Two major national department store chains are willing to carry the Allegro line if we will give them extra advertising support.
☐ A major national discount chain is willing to carry the Allegro line if we will offer a special discount for higher volume.

The main *threats* facing Zenith's Allegro line are:

☐ An increasing number of consumers who choose modular stereo systems are buying them in mass-merchandise and discount stores, in which we have weak representation.
☐ An increasing number of upscale consumers are showing a preference for component systems, and we do not have an audio component line.
☐ Some of our competitors have introduced smaller speakers with good-quality sound, and consumers seem to favor smaller speakers.
☐ The federal government may pass a more stringent product-safety law, which would entail some product redesign work on our part.

Strengths/weaknesses analysis (S/W analysis). The manager should also identify company strengths and weaknesses. Strengths and weaknesses are inside factors, in contrast to opportunities and threats, which are outside factors. Company strengths point to certain strategies the company might be successful in using, while company weaknesses point to certain things the company needs to correct.

The main *strengths* of Zenith's Allegro line are:

☐ Zenith's name has excellent brand awareness and an image of high quality.
☐ Dealers who sell the Allegro line are knowledgeable and well trained in selling.
☐ Zenith has an excellent service network, and consumers know they will get quick repair service if needed.

The main *weaknesses* of Zenith's Allegro line are:

☐ The sound quality of Allegro is not demonstrably better than the sound quality of competing sets, and yet sound quality can make a big difference in brand choice.
☐ Zenith is budgeting only 5 percent of its sales revenue for advertising and promotion, while some major competitors are spending at twice that level.
☐ Zenith's Allegro line is not clearly positioned compared to Magnavox ("quality") and Sony ("innovation"). Zenith needs a unique selling proposition. The current advertising campaign is not particularly creative or exciting.
☐ Zenith's brand is priced higher relative to other brands without being supported by a real perceived difference in quality. The brand loses the price-conscious buyer. The pricing strategy should be reevaluated.

Issues analysis. In this section, the company uses the findings of the O/T and S/W analysis to define the main issues that must be addressed in the plan. Decisions on these issues will lead to the subsequent setting of objectives, strategies, and tactics.

Zenith must consider the following basic *issues* with respect to the Allegro line:

☐ Should Zenith stay in the stereo-equipment business? Can it compete effectively? Or should it harvest or divest this product line?

☐ If Zenith stays in, should it continue with its present products, channels of distribution, price and promotion policies, just making further refinements where possible?

☐ Or should Zenith switch to high-growth channels (such as discount stores), and can it do this and yet keep the loyalty of its traditional channels?

☐ Should Zenith go into more-intensive advertising and promotion to match competitors' expenditures, and will that lead to sufficient increases in market share and profitability?

☐ Or should Zenith pour money into R&D to develop advanced features, sound, and styling?

Objectives

At this point, management knows the issues and is faced with making some basic decisions about the objectives. These objectives will guide the subsequent search for strategies and action programs.

Two types of objectives must be set: financial and marketing.

Financial objectives.   Every company seeks certain financial objectives. The owners will be looking for a certain long-run rate of return on investment and know the profits they would like in the current year.

Zenith's management wants each business unit to deliver a certain rate of profit and return on investment. Furthermore they want the Allegro line to grow stronger. The product manager sets the following *financial objectives* for the Allegro line:

☐ Earn an average rate of return on investment over the next five years of 20 percent after taxes.

☐ Produce net profits of $1,800,000 in 1984.

☐ Produce a cash flow of $2,000,000 in 1984.

Marketing objectives.   The financial objectives must be converted into marketing objectives. For example, if the company wants to earn $1,800,000 profit, and its target profit margin is 10 percent on sales, then it must set a goal of $18 million in sales revenue. If the company sets an average price of $260, it must sell 69,230 units. If it expects total industry sales to reach 2.3 million units, that is a 3 percent market share. To maintain this market share, the company will have to set certain goals for consumer awareness, distribution coverage, and so on. Thus the *marketing objectives* might read:

☐ Achieve total sales revenue of $18,000,000 in 1984, which represents a 9 percent increase from last year.

☐ Therefore achieve a sales volume in units of 69,230, which represents an expected market share of 3 percent.

☐ Expand consumer awareness of the Allegro brand from 15 percent to 30 percent over the planning period.

☐ Expand the number of distribution outlets by 10 percent.

☐ Aim for an average realized price of $260.

The set of objectives should meet certain criteria. First, each objective should be stated in an unambiguous and measurable form with a stated time period for accomplishment. Second, the various objectives should be internally consistent. Third, the objectives should be stated hierarchically, if possible, with lower objectives being clearly derived from higher objectives. Fourth, the objectives should be attainable but sufficiently challenging to stimulate maximum effort.

Marketing Strategy

In this section, the manager outlines the broad marketing strategy, or "game plan," that will be used. We define marketing strategy as follows:

Marketing strategy is the basic approach that the business unit will use to achieve its objectives, and it consists of broad decisions on target markets, marketing positioning and mix, and marketing expenditure levels.

In developing a marketing strategy, a manager faces a great number of possible choices. Each objective can be achieved in a number of ways. For example, the objective *increase the sales revenue by 9 percent* can be achieved by increasing the average price on all units, increasing the overall sales volume, and/or selling more of the higher-price units. Each of these objectives can in turn be achieved in a number of ways. The *overall sales volume* can be increased by increasing market growth and/or increasing market share. In turn, *increased market growth* can come about by convincing people to own more stereo systems per household or to replace their old systems more frequently. By going down the path of each objective, the manager can identify the major strategy options facing the product line.

Strategy formulation calls for making basic choices among these strategy options. The manager can write up a basic strategy statement in verbal form, such as:

Zenith's basic strategy for Allegro is to aim at the upscale family, with particular emphasis on the woman buyer. The product line will be expanded by adding lower-price and higher-price units. The average price of the line will be raised 4 percent. A new and intensified advertising campaign will be developed to increase the perceived reliability of our brand in the consumer's mind. We will schedule a strong sales promotion program to attract increased consumer and dealer attention to our line. We will expand distribution to cover department stores but will avoid discount stores. We will put more funds into restyling the Allegro line so that it shouts high-quality sound and reliability.

Alternatively, the strategy statement can be presented in list form covering the major marketing tools:

STRATEGY STATEMENT

Target market:	Upscale households, with particular emphasis on female buyer.
Positioning:	The best sounding and most reliable modular stereo system.

Product line:	Add one lower-price model and two higher-price models.
Price:	Price somewhat above competitive brands.
Distribution outlets:	Heavy in radio/TV stores and appliance stores; increased effort to penetrate department stores.
Sales force:	Expand by 10 percent and introduce a national account-management system.
Service:	Widely available and quick service.
Advertising:	Develop a new advertising campaign, directed at the target market, that supports the positioning strategy; emphasize higher-price units in the ads; increase the advertising budget by 20 percent.
Sales promotion:	Increase the sales promotion budget by 15 percent to develop a point-of-purchase display and to participate to a greater extent in dealer trade shows.
Research and development:	Increase expenditures by 25 percent to develop better styling of Allegro line.
Marketing research:	Increase expenditures by 10 percent to improve knowledge of consumer-choice process and to monitor competitor moves.

In developing the strategy, the manager needs to discuss it with others whose cooperation will make the difference between failure and success. The product manager will see the purchasing and manufacturing people to make sure they are able to buy enough material and produce enough units to meet the planned sales-volume levels, the sales manager to obtain the planned sales-force support, and the financial officer to make sure enough funds will be available.

Action Programs

The strategy statement represents the broad marketing thrusts that the manager will use to achieve the business objectives. Each element of the marketing strategy must now be elaborated in a separate section to answer: *What* will be done? *When* will it be done? *Who* will do it? *How much* will it cost? Here is an example:

Zenith's sales promotion program will be divided into two parts, one directed at dealers and the other at consumers. The dealer promotion program will consist of:

April. Zenith will participate in the Consumer Electronics Trade Show in Chicago. John Smith, dealer promotion director, will make the arrangements. The expected cost is $14,000.

August. A sales contest will be conducted, which will award three Hawaiian vacations to the three dealers producing the greatest percentage increase in sales of Allegro units. The contest will be handled by John Smith at a planned cost of $13,000.

The consumer promotion program will consist of:

February. Zenith will advertise in the newspapers that a free Anne Murray record album will be given to everyone buying an Allegro unit this month. Ann Morris, consumer promotion director, will handle this project at a planned cost of $5,000.

September. A newspaper advertisement will announce that consumers who listen to an Allegro store demonstration in the second week of September will have their names entered in a sweepstakes, the grand prizes to be ten Allegros. Ann Morris will handle this project at a planned cost of $4,000.

Projected Profit-and-Loss Statement

The action plans allow the product manager to assemble a supporting budget that is essentially a projected profit-and-loss statement. On the revenue side, it shows the forecasted sales volume in units and the average realized price. On the expense side, it shows the cost of production, physical distribution, and marketing, broken down into finer categories. The difference is projected profit. Higher management will review the budget and approve or modify it. If the requested budget is too high, the product manager will have to make some cuts. Once approved, the budget is the basis for developing plans and schedules for material procurement, production scheduling, manpower recruitment, and marketing operations.

Controls

The last section of the plan outlines the controls that will be applied to monitor the plan's progress. Typically the goals and budget are spelled out for each month or quarter. Higher management can review the results each period and spot businesses that are not attaining their goals. Managers of lagging businesses must explain what's happening and the actions they are taking to improve plan fulfillment.

Some control sections include contingency plans. A contingency plan outlines the steps that management would implement for specific adverse developments that might occur, such as a price war or a strike. The purpose of contingency planning is to encourage managers to give prior thought to some difficulties that might be ahead.

THE THEORY OF EFFECTIVE MARKETING-RESOURCE ALLOCATION

Having examined how actual marketing plans are constructed, we will now describe some important tools and concepts that managers can use to improve their marketing planning. Much planning can be done on microcomputers using tailored computer programs. At companies such as Quaker Oats and General Mills brand managers develop and cost different marketing strategies, using computer programs, in the search for the best plan. These computer programs utilize simple sales-and-profit equations and model how sales and profits would respond to different marketing-mix expenditures. We will illustrate these concepts in the following paragraphs.

The Profit Equation

Every marketing-mix strategy will lead to a certain level of profit. The profit can be estimated through a profit equation.

Profits (Z) by definition are equal to the product's revenue (R) less its costs (C):

$$Z = R - C \qquad (9\text{--}1)$$

Revenue is equal to the product's net price (P') times its unit sales (Q):

$$R = P'Q \qquad (9\text{--}2)$$

But the product's net price (P') is equal to its list price (P) less any allowance per unit (k) representing freight allowances, commissions, and discounts:

$$P' = P - k \qquad (9\text{--}3)$$

The product's costs can be conveniently classified into unit variable nonmarketing costs (c), fixed costs (F), and marketing costs (M):

$$C = cQ + F + M \qquad (9\text{--}4)$$

Substituting equations (9–2), (9–3), and (9–4) into (9–1) and simplifying,

$$Z = [(P - k) - c]Q - F - M \qquad (9\text{--}5)$$

where:

Z = total profits
P = list price
k = allowance per unit (such as freight allowances, commissions, discounts)
c = production and distribution variable cost (such as labor costs, delivery costs)
Q = number of units sold
F = fixed costs (such as salaries, rent, electricity)
M = discretionary marketing costs

The expression $[(P - k) - c]$ is the *gross contribution margin per unit*—the amount the company realizes on the average unit after deducting allowances and the variable costs of producing and distributing the average unit. The expression $[(P - k) - c]Q$ is the *gross contribution margin*—the net revenue available to cover the fixed costs, profits, and discretionary marketing expenditures.

The Sales Equation

In order to use the profit equation for planning purposes, the product manager needs to model the determinants of sales volume (Q). The relation of sales volume to its determinants is specified in a sales equation (also called the *sales-response function*):

$$Q = f(X_1, X_2 \ldots, X_n, Y_1, Y_2, \ldots, Y_m) \qquad (9\text{--}6)$$

where:

$(X_1, X_2, \ldots, X_n)$ = sales variables under the control of the firm
$(Y_1, Y_2, \ldots, Y_m)$ = sales variables not under the control of the firm

Y variables include such things as the cost-of-living index, the size and income of the served market, and so on. As these variables change, so does the market's buying rate. The manager has no influence over the Y variables but needs to estimate them for use in forecasting. We will assume that the manager has estimated the Y variables and their effect on sales volume, which is conveyed by:

$$Q = f(X_1, X_2, \ldots, X_n / Y_1, Y_2, \ldots, Y_m) \qquad (9\text{–}7)$$

which says that sales volume is a function of the X variables, for given levels of the Y variables.

The X variables are the variables that the manager can use to influence the sales level. The X variables include the list price (P), allowances (k), variable cost (c) (to the extent that high variable costs reflect improved product quality, delivery time, and customer service), and marketing expenditures (M). Thus sales, as a function of the manager's controllable variables, is described by:

$$Q = f(P, k, c, M) \qquad (9\text{–}8)$$

We can make one additional refinement. The marketing budget, M, can be spent in several ways, such as advertising (A), sales promotion (S), sales force (D), and marketing research (R).

The sales equation is now:

$$Q = f(P, k, c, A, S, D, R) \qquad (9\text{–}9)$$

where the elements in the parentheses represent the marketing mix.

Profit-Optimization Planning

Suppose the manager wants to find a marketing mix that will maximize profits in the coming year. This requires having some idea of how each element in the marketing mix will affect sales. We shall use the term *sales-response function* to describe the relationship between sales volume and a particular element of the marketing mix. Specifically, *the sales-response function forecasts the likely sales volume during a specified time period associated with different possible levels of a marketing-mix element, holding constant the other marketing-mix elements.* It should not be thought of as describing a relationship over time between the two variables. To the extent that managers have a good feel for the relevant sales-response functions, they are in a position to formulate more effective marketing plans.

What are the possible shapes of sales-response functions? Figure 9–1 shows several possibilities. Part (a) shows the well-known relationship between price and sales volume, known as the law of demand. The relationship states that more sales will occur, other things being equal, at lower prices. The illustration shows a curvilinear relationship, although a linear relationship is also possible.

Figure 9–1(b) shows four possible functional relationships between sales volume and marketing expenditures. Marketing expenditure function (A) is the least plausible: It states that sales volume is not affected by the level of marketing expenditures. It would mean that the number of customers and their purchasing rates are not affected

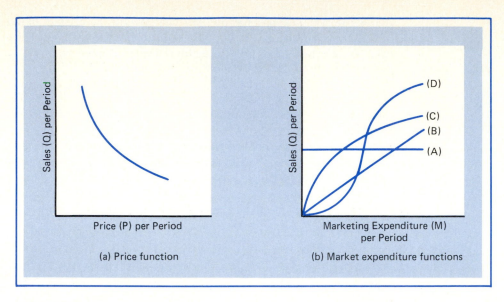

FIGURE 9-1
Sales-Response Functions

by sales calls, advertising, sales promotion, or marketing research. Marketing expenditure function (*B*) states that sales volume grows linearly with marketing expenditures. In the illustration, the intercept is 0, but this is inaccurate if some sales would take place even in the absence of marketing expenditures.

Marketing expenditure function (*C*) is a concave function showing sales volume increasing throughout at a decreasing rate. It is a plausible description of sales response to sales-force-size increases. The rationale is as follows: If a field sales force consisted of one sales representative, that representative would call on the best prospects, and the marginal rate of sales response would be highest. A second sales rep would call on the next best prospects, and the marginal rate of sales response would be somewhat less. Successively hired sales reps would call on successively less responsive prospects, resulting in a diminishing rate of sales increase.

Marketing expenditure function (*D*) is an S-shaped function showing sales volume initially increasing at an increasing rate and then increasing at a decreasing rate. It is a plausible description of sales response to increasing levels of advertising expenditure. The rationale is as follows: Small advertising budgets do not buy enough advertising to create more than minimal brand awareness. Larger budgets can produce high brand awareness, interest, and preference, all of which might lead to increased purchase response. Very large budgets, however, may not produce much additional response because the target market is already highly familiar with the brand.

The occurrence of eventually diminishing returns to increases in marketing expenditures is plausible for the following reasons. First, there is an upper limit to the total potential demand for any particular product. The easier sales prospects buy almost immediately, leaving the more recalcitrant sales prospects. As the upper limit is approached, it becomes increasingly expensive to attract the remaining buyers. Second, as a company steps up its marketing effort, its competitors are likely to do the same, with the net result that each company experiences increasing sales resistance. And third, if sales were to increase at an increasing rate throughout, natural monopolies would result. A single firm would take over each industry. Yet we do not observe this happening.

How can marketing managers estimate the sales-response functions that apply to their business? Three methods are available. The first is the *statistical method*, where the manager gathers data on past sales and levels of marketing-mix variables and estimates the sales-response functions through statistical techniques. Several researchers have used this method with varying degrees of success, depending on the quantity and quality of available data and the stability of the underlying relationships.[5] The second is the *experimental method*, which calls for varying the marketing expenditure and mix levels in matched samples of geographical or other units and noting the resulting sales volume.[6] The experimental method produces the most reliable results but is not used extensively because of its complex requirements, high cost, and inordinate level of management resistance. The third is the *judgmental method*, where experts are asked to make intelligent guesses about the needed magnitudes. This method requires a careful selection of the experts and a defined procedure for gathering and combining their estimates, such as the Delphi method.[7] The judgmental method is often the only feasible one and can be quite useful. We believe that using the estimates of experts is better than foregoing formal analysis of profit optimization.

In estimating sales-response functions, some cautions have to be observed. The sales-response function assumes that other variables remain constant over the range of the function. Thus the company's price and competitors' prices are assumed to remain unchanged no matter what the company spends on marketing. Since this assumption is unrealistic, the sales-response function has to be modified to reflect competitors' probable responses. The sales-response function also assumes a certain level of company efficiency in spending marketing dollars. If the spending efficiency rises or falls, the sales-response function has to be modified. Also, the sales-response function has to be modified to reflect delayed impacts of expenditures on sales beyond one year. These and other characteristics of sales-response functions are spelled out in more detail elsewhere.[8]

[5] For examples of empirical studies using fitted sales-response functions, see Doyle L. Weiss, "Determinants of Market Share," *Journal of Marketing Research*, August 1968, pp. 290–95; Donald E. Sexton, Jr., "Estimating Marketing Policy Effects on Sales of a Frequently Purchased Product," *Journal of Marketing Research*, August 1970, pp. 338–47; and Jean-Jacques Lambin, "A Computer On-Line Marketing Mix Model," *Journal of Marketing Research*, May 1972, pp. 119–26.

[6] See Russell Ackoff and James R. Emshoff, "Advertising Research at Anheuser-Busch," *Sloan Management Review*, winter 1975, pp. 1–15.

[7] See Philip Kotler, "A Guide to Gathering Expert Estimates," *Business Horizons*, October 1970, pp. 79–87.

[8] See Gary L. Lilien and Philip Kotler, *Marketing Decision Making: A Model Building Approach*, 2nd ed. (New York: Harper & Row, 1983).

Profit Optimization

Once the sales-response functions are estimated, how are they used in profit optimization? Graphically, we introduce some further curves to find the point of optimal marketing expenditure. The analysis is shown in Figure 9–2. The sales-response function shown here is S-shaped, although the same analysis applies to any shape. First the manager subtracts all nonmarketing costs from the *sales-response function* to derive the *gross profit function*. Next, the marketing expenditure function is represented as a straight line starting at the origin and rising at the rate of one dollar of marketing expenditure for every ten dollars of the vertical axes. The marketing expenditure function is then subtracted from the *gross profit curve* to derive the *net profit curve*. The net profit curve shows positive net profits with marketing expenditures between M_L and M_U, which could be defined as the rational range of marketing expenditure. The net profit curve reaches a maximum of M. Therefore the marketing expenditure that would maximize net profit is $M.

The graphical solution can also be carried out numerically or algebraically; indeed it has to be, if sales volume is a function of more than one marketing-mix variable. Here we will present a numerical example of how it is done.

A numerical example. Jane Melody, the Allegro product manager at Zenith, also handles a small phonograph-record-cleaning machine that sells for $16. For some years, she has been using a low-price, low-promotion strategy. Last year she spent $10,000 on advertising and another $10,000 on sales promotion. Sales were 12,000 units, and profits were $14,000. Her boss thinks more profits could be made on this item. Ms. Melody is anxious to find a better strategy to increase profits.

Her first step is to visualize some alternative marketing-mix strategies. She imagines the eight strategies shown in the first three columns of Table 9–3 (the first strategy is the current one). They were formed by assuming a high and a low level for each of three marketing variables and elaborating all the combinations ($2^3 = 8$).

Her next step is to estimate the likely sales that would be attained with each marketing mix. She feels that the needed estimates are unlikely to be found through fitting historical data or through conducting experiments. She decides to ask the sales manager for his estimates since he has shown an uncanny ability to be on target. Suppose he provides the sales estimates shown in the last column in Table 9–3.

The final step calls for determining which marketing mix maximizes profits, assuming the sales estimates are reliable. This calls for introducing a profit equation and inserting the different marketing mixes into this equation to see which maximizes profits.

Suppose fixed costs, F, are $38,000; unit variable costs, c, are $10; and the contemplated allowance off list price, k, is $0. Then profit equation (9–5) reads:

$$Z = (P - 10)Q - 38,000 - A - S \qquad (9-11)$$

Thus profits are a function of the chosen price and the advertising and sales promotion budgets.

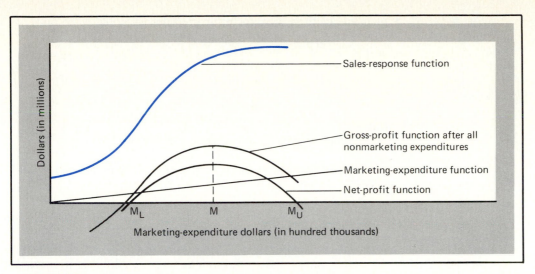

FIGURE 9-2
Relationship between Sales Volume, Marketing Expenditures, and Profits

At this point the manager can insert each marketing mix and estimated sales level (from Table 9–3) into this equation. The resulting profits are #1($16,400), #2($13,000), #3(−$7,400), #4(−$2,400), #5($19,000), #6($16,800), #7(−$4,200), and #8($2,000). Marketing mix #5, calling for a price of $24, advertising of $10,000, and promotion of $10,000, yields the highest expected profits ($19,000).

The manager can take one more step. Some marketing mix not shown might yield a still higher profit. To check that possibility, the product manager can fit a sales equation to the data shown in Table 9–3. The sales estimates can be viewed as a sample from a larger universe of expert judgments concerning the sales equation

TABLE 9-3

MARKETING MIXES AND ESTIMATED SALES			
Marketing Mix No.	Price (P)	Advertising (A)	Promotion (S)	Sales (Q)
1	$16	$10,000	$10,000	12,400
2	16	10,000	50,000	18,500
3	16	50,000	10,000	15,100
4	16	50,000	50,000	22,600
5	24	10,000	10,000	5,500
6	24	10,000	50,000	8,200
7	24	50,000	10,000	6,700
8	24	50,000	50,000	10,000

$Q = f(P,A,S)$. A plausible mathematical form for the sales equation is the multiple exponential:

$$Q = bP^p A^a S^s \qquad (9\text{--}12)$$

where:

$b =$ a scale factor
$p,a,s =$ price, advertising, and promotion elasticity, respectively

Using least-squares regression estimation (not shown), the manager finds the fitted sales equation to be:

$$Q = 100{,}000P^{-2}A^{1/8}S^{1/4} \qquad (9\text{--}13)$$

This fits the sales estimates in Table 9–3 extremely well. Price has an elasticity of -2, that is, a 1 percent reduction in price, other things being equal, tends to increase unit sales by 2 percent. Advertising has an elasticity of $\frac{1}{8}$, and promotion has an elasticity of $\frac{1}{4}$. The coefficient 100,000 is a scale factor that translates the dollar magnitudes into sales-volume units.

The product manager now substitutes this sales equation for Q in the profit equation (9–11). This yields, when simplified:

$$Z = 100{,}000\, A^{1/8}S^{1/4}[P^{-1} - 10P^{-2}] - 38{,}000 - A - S \qquad (9\text{--}14)$$

Profits are shown to be strictly a function of the chosen marketing mix. The manager can insert any marketing mix (including those not shown in Table 9–3) and derive an estimate of profits. To find the profit-maximizing marketing mix, she applies standard calculus. The optimal marketing mix (P,A,S) is ($20, $12,947, $25,894). Twice as much is spent on promotion as on advertising because its elasticity is twice as great. The product manager would forecast a sales volume of 10,358 units and profits of $26,735. While other marketing mixes can produce higher sales, no other marketing mix can produce higher profits. Using this equation, the product manager has solved not only the optimum marketing mix but also the optimum marketing budget $(A + S = \$38{,}841)$.

To facilitate profit-optimization planning, several companies have designed computer programs for use by marketing managers to identify and assess the impact of alternative marketing plans on profits and sales. The marketing manager sits at a computer terminal, requests the particular program, and proceeds to build and test a marketing expenditure plan. One computer program consists of four subprograms.[9] First the marketing manager retrieves the major statistics on the product for the last several years. This material is called the *historical base* and is similar to Table 9–2. He then instructs the computer to produce a *straightforward projection* of the major statistics for the next several years, using extrapolation. He then modifies any

---

[9] See "Concorn Kitchens," in Harper W. Boyd, Jr., and Robert T. Davis, *Marketing Management Casebook* (Homewood, Ill.: Richard D. Irwin, 1971), pp. 125–36.

projections based on his own knowledge, and the result is called the *profit-and-loss planning base*. This shows a normal "extrapolated" level of marketing expenditures, price, and sales, and the resulting profits. If the projected profits are satisfactory, the marketing manager can stop here. However, a fourth subprogram called a *marketing plan simulator* is available for trying out alternative marketing plans and estimating their sales and profits. The simulator incorporates an estimated sales equation. The marketing manager tests alternative marketing plans until he finds a satisfactory one.

Long-run Profit Projection

Computer programs have also been designed to help marketing managers build and test long-run strategies for the development of a product or market. The marketing manager may want to forecast, for a given product, the expected costs, prices, sales, profits, cash flow, and return on investment for the next several years as an indication of whether the particular product business should be built, maintained, harvested, or terminated. Table 9–4 shows the printout from one computer program for a ready-to-eat cereal product.

The first line shows that this projection is for a seven-year period. Details then appear on the undepreciated value of plant and equipment devoted to this product, current opportunity cost, working capital, and expected terminal salvage value.

The rest of the printout shows the expected or planned year-to-year levels of important variables that will affect the internal rate of return. Column 1 shows the retail price per unit, which is expected to rise from $.58 to $.70 in the course of seven years. Column 2 shows that the retail margin for this product (18 percent) is not expected to change. Column 3 shows the resulting wholesale prices. Since this company will sell direct to the retailers, there is no wholesale margin (column 4), and the factory price (column 5) is the same as the wholesale price.

Column 6 shows estimated variable manufacturing costs, and they too are expected to rise over the period, from a present level of $.19 to $.23 in 1982. The ratio of variable manufacturing costs to factory prices is shown in column 7, followed by the planned ratio of variable marketing costs to factory prices (column 8). Subtracting variable manufacturing and marketing costs per unit from the price, the result is the contribution to fixed costs and profits, which is shown in dollar and percentage form in columns 9 and 10 respectively.

The next step calls for estimating fixed manufacturing costs and fixed marketing costs over the next seven years, which are shown in columns 11 and 12. The symbol $E + 06$ is computer printout shorthand and means that the reader should move the decimal place, in the associated number, six places to the right. Thus $1.028E + 06$ means $1,028,000. Columns 13 and 14 show the anticipated investments in plant, equipment, and building over the next seven years, and column 15 shows the estimated total depreciation expense.

We now arrive at the estimated sales and profits. Columns 16 and 17 show management's estimates of sales (in percentage and in unit terms, respectively) over the next seven years. The figures indicate that management expects company sales (in units) to rise at the rate of about 10 percent a year, on the basis of its planned

TABLE 9-4

SAMPLE PRINTOUT FROM COMPUTER SYSTEM

```
                    TIME HORIZON = 7                              YEARS
        REMAINING UNDEPR. P&E INVEST. AT BEGIN. YR. 1 = 900000   DOLLARS
        REMAINING NO. OF YEARS OF P&E DEPRECIATION    = 3         YEARS
        REMAINING UNDEP. BLDG. INVEST. AT BEGIN. YR. 1 = 210000  DOLLARS
        REMAINING NO. OF YEARS OF BLDG. DEPRECIATION  = 21        YEARS

         DEPRECIATION HORIZON FOR P&E INVESTMENTS     = 10        YEARS
         DEPRECIATION HORIZON FOR BLDG. INVESTMENTS   = 30        YEARS
         OPPORTUNITY COST (AT BEGINNING OF PERIOD) = 2.E+06       DOLLARS
                              WORKING CAPITAL = 13                PCNT SALES
                 SALVAGE VALUE (AT END OF PERIOD) = 10            X EARNINGS
```

	1	2	3	4
YEAR	RET.PRICE($)	RET.MAR.(PCNT)	WHOLE.PRICE($)	WHOLE.MAR.(PCNT)
1984	.577	18	.473	0
1985	.602	18	.494	0
1986	.621	18	.509	0
1987	.639	18	.524	0
1988	.659	18	.54	0
1989	.675	18	.554	0
1990	.698	18	.572	0

	5	6	7	8
YEAR	FACTORY PRICE($)	VARIABLE MAN. COST($)	VARIABLE MAN. COST(PCNT)	VARIABLE MKTG COST(PCNT)
1984	.473	.191	40.4	5
1985	.494	.196	39.7	5
1986	.509	.202	39.7	5
1987	.524	.208	39.7	5
1988	.54	.214	39.6	5
1989	.554	.221	39.9	5
1990	.572	.227	39.7	5

	9	10	11	12
YEAR	CONTRIB. TO FIXED COSTS AND PROFIT ($)	(PCNT)	FIXED MAN.COST ($)	FIXED MKTG. COST ($)
1984	.258	54.6	915000	4.25E+06
1985	.273	55.3	971000	4.9E+06
1986	.282	55.3	1.028E+06	5.5E+06
1987	.29	55.3	1.31E+06	5.75E+06
1988	.299	55.4	1.386E+06	6.25E+06
1989	.305	55.1	1.471E+06	6.85E+06
1990	.317	55.3	1.824E+06	7.6E+06

	13	14	15
YEAR	P&E INVEST.	BLDG. INVEST.	DEPREC. EXPENSE
1983	850000	0	
1984	0	0	395000
1985	0	0	395000
1986	850000	1.E+06	395000
1987	0	0	213333
1988	0	0	213333
1989	850000	1.E+06	213333
1990	0	0	331666

	16	17	18	19
YEAR	INDEX OF COMPANY SALES	COMPANY SLS(UNITS)	INDUSTRY SLS (UNITS)	MARKET SHARE
1984	1	3.E+07	1.166E+09	2.6
1985	1.1	3.3E+07	1.182E+09	2.8
1986	1.2	3.6E+07	1.198E+09	3
1987	1.3	3.9E+07	1.215E+09	3.2
1988	1.4	4.2E+07	1.23E+09	3.4
1989	1.5	4.5E+07	1.247E+09	3.6
1990	1.6	4.8E+07	1.265E+09	3.8

	20	21	22	23
YEAR	MKTG. EXP. (PCNT SLS)	P.A.T.(PCNT SLS)	P.A.T.($)	CSH FLOW(A.T.)
1983				-2.85E+06
1984	34.9	7.7	1.097245E+06	-353001
1985	35.1	8.4	1.370807E+06	1.493337E+06
1986	35	8.8	1.610162E+06	-110272
1987	33.1	9.9	2.014062E+06	1.953967E+06
1988	32.5	10.4	2.361914E+06	2.281351E+06
1989	32.5	10.4	2.591395E+06	667228
1990	32.7	9.9	2.723974E+06	2.722089E+06

```
        CALCULATED INTERNAL RATE OF RETURN (AFTER TAXES) = 45    PCNT
```

SOURCE: Case material of the Harvard University Graduate School of Business Administration, prepared by Professors Derek Abell and Ralph Sultan, used by permission.

levels of marketing expenditures. Column 18 presents management's estimates of industry sales for the next seven years.

The figures in column 19, market share, are derived by dividing estimated company sales (column 17) by estimated industry sales (column 18). We see that management expects market share to grow from 2.6 percent to 3.8 percent over a seven-year period. Column 20 expresses total marketing expenditures (columns 8 and 12) as a percent of sales, and this percentage is expected to fall. Examining this more closely, we see that management expects sales to rise faster than marketing expenditures; hence it is expecting increased marketing productivity.

Columns 21 and 22 show yearly profits after taxes in percentage and dollar terms. The computer program uses the following formula to calculate dollar profits after taxes:

$$Z = (1 - t)(mQ - F - D) \qquad (9\text{--}15)$$

where:

Z = profits after taxes
t = tax rate
m = contribution margin to fixed costs and profit
Q = sales in units
F = fixed manufacturing and marketing costs
D = depreciation

For example, the profits after taxes for 1984 are

$$(1 - .4967)[(\$.258)(30{,}000{,}000) - \$5{,}165{,}000 - \$395{,}000] = \$1{,}097{,}245$$

Column 23 shows the results of the conversion of *profits after taxes to cash flow after taxes*. The formula for cash flow is

$$L = Z + D - W - I \qquad (9\text{--}16)$$

where:

L = cash flow after taxes
Z = profits after taxes
D = depreciation
W = working capital in dollars (that is, working capital as a percent of sales, times wholesale price, times sales in units)
I = new investment expenditure

For example, the cash flow after taxes for 1984 is

$$\$1,097,245 + \$395,000 - [.13(\$.473)(30,000,000)] - 0 = -\$353,001$$

The computer now calculates the internal rate of return corresponding to the cash flow in column 23. This is found by taking the opportunity cost at the beginning of the period and searching for the interest rate that would discount the future cash flows so that the sum of the discounted cash flows is equal to the initial opportunity cost; this rate turns out to be 45 percent.

Thus a computer program enables the product manager to estimate the financial consequences of a particular strategy, environment, and set of costs. The manager can easily recalculate the profit impact of any alterations in the data or assumptions.

Marketing-Mix Optimization

The theory of profit optimization leads to finding the optimal total marketing expenditure level. Now we want to examine the issue of optimally dividing the marketing budget over the elements of the marketing mix. Clearly the elements of the mix are partially substitutable for each other. A company that is seeking increased sales can achieve them by lowering the price or increasing the sales force, advertising budget, or promotion budget. The challenge is to find the optimal mix.

Assume that a product manager has identified advertising and promotion dollars as the two major elements of the marketing budget. In principle, the marketing budget can be divided in an infinite number of ways on these two items. That is shown in Figure 9–3(a). If there are no constraints on the level of advertising and promotion, then every point in the A-S plane shown in Figure 9–3(a) is a possible marketing mix. An arbitrary line drawn from the origin, called a *constant-mix line*, shows the set of all marketing mixes where the two tools are in a fixed ratio but where the budget varies. Another arbitrary line, called a *constant-budget line*, shows a set of varying mixes that would be affordable with a fixed marketing budget.

Associated with every possible marketing mix is a resulting sales level. Three sales levels are shown in Figure 9–3(a). The marketing mix $(A_1 S_2)$—calling for a small budget and a rough equality between advertising and promotion—is expected to produce sales of Q_1. The marketing mix $(A_2 S_1)$ involves the same budget with more expenditure on advertising than on promotion; this is expected to produce slightly higher sales, Q_2. The mix $(A_3 S_3)$ calls for a larger budget but a relatively equal splitting between advertising and promotion and is expected to yield Q_3. Given the many possibilities, the marketer's job is to find the sales equation that predicts the Qs.

For a given marketing budget, the money should be divided among the various marketing tools in a way that gives the same marginal profit on the marginal dollar spent on each tool. A geometrical version of the solution is shown in Figure 9–3(b). Here we are looking down at the A-S plane shown in Figure 9–3(a). A constant-budget line is shown, indicating all the alternative marketing mixes that could be achieved with this budget. The curved lines are called *iso-sales curves*. An iso-sales

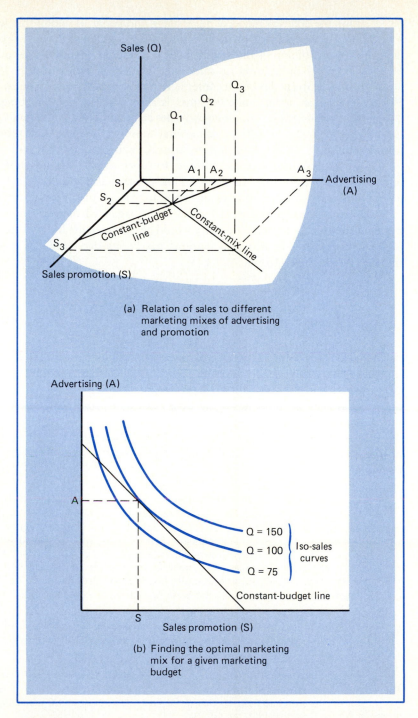

(a) Relation of sales to different
    marketing mixes of advertising
    and promotion

(b) Finding the optimal marketing
    mix for a given marketing
    budget

FIGURE 9–3
The Sales Function Associated with Two Marketing-Mix Elements

curve shows the different mixes of advertising and personal selling that would produce a given level of sales. It is a projection into the A-S plane of the set of points resulting from horizontal slicing of the sales function shown in Figure 9–3(a) at a given level of sales. Figure 9–3(b) shows iso-sales curves for three different sales levels: 75, 100, and 150 units. Given the budget line, it is not possible to attain sales of more than 100 units. The optimum marketing mix is shown at the point of tangency between the budget line and the last-touching iso-sales curve above it. Consequently, the marketing mix (A^*S^*), which calls for somewhat more advertising than promotion, is the sales-maximizing (and in this case profit-maximizing) marketing mix.

This analysis could be generalized to more than two marketing tools. Ferber and Verdoorn stated that "In an optimum position the additional sales obtained by a small increase in unit costs are the same for all nonprice instruments . . ."[10]

Dorfman and Steiner went further and formalized the conditions under which price, promotion, and product quality would be optimized.[11] More recently, marketing scientists have investigated how various marketing-mix variables interact in their impact on sales. (See Exhibit 9–1.)

Marketing Allocation Optimization

A final issue facing the marketing planner is to optimally allocate a given marketing budget to the various *target markets* (TMs). The TMs could be different sales territories, customer groups, or other market segments. With a given marketing budget and mix, it may be possible to increase sales and profits by shifting funds among different markets.

Most marketing managers allocate their marketing budgets to the various TMs on the basis of some percentage of actual or expected sales. Consider the following example:

> The marketing manager at the Guardian Oil Company (name disguised) estimates total gasoline sales volume (which combines regular and premium gasoline) and adds premium sales volume back to this figure to yield "profit gallons" (thus giving double weight to premium gasoline sales). The manager then takes the ratio of the advertising budget to the profit gallons to establish a figure for advertising dollars per profit gallon. This is called the prime multiplier. Each market receives an advertising budget equal to its previous year's profit gallons sold multiplied by the prime multiplier. Thus the advertising budget is allocated largely on the basis of last year's company sales in the territory.[12]

Unfortunately, size rules for allocating funds lead to inefficient allocations. They confuse "average" and "marginal" sales response. Figure 9–4(a) on page 304 illustrates

---

[10] Robert Ferber and P. J. Verdoorn, *Research Methods in Economics and Business* (New York: Macmillan Co., 1962), p. 535.

[11] Robert Dorfman and Peter O. Steiner, "Optimal Advertising and Optimal Quality," *American Economic Review*, December 1954, pp. 826–36.

[12] Donald C. Marschner, "Theory versus Practice in Allocating Advertising Money," *Journal of Business*, July 1967, pp. 286–302.

Exhibit 9-1

MARKETING-MIX INTERACTIONS NEED TO BE WATCHED

Marketing managers carry beliefs in their head about how specific pairs of marketing variables interact. Here are some of the more popular beliefs:

☐ Higher advertising expenditures reduce buyers' price sensitivity. Thus a company wishing to charge a higher price should spend more on advertising.

☐ Advertising expenditures have a greater sales impact on low price products than high price products.

☐ Better advertising copy positioning of a product reduces buyers' price sensitivity.

☐ Higher advertising expenditures reduce the total cost of selling. The advertising expenditures presell the customer and sales representatives can spend their time answering objections and closing the sale.

☐ Higher product quality allows a disproportionately higher price to be charged.

☐ Higher prices lead buyers to impute higher product quality.

☐ Price cuts or increased sales effort place a strain on the distribution system and may require its enlargement or revision.

☐ Tighter credit terms require much greater selling and advertising effort to move the same volume of goods.

While many of these relationships hold true for many products, managers of particular products should be cautious. For example, Sasieni showed data on advertising elasticities for a number of brands and found that while some showed a more sensitive response at high prices, others were more sensitive at lower prices. He concluded that without a clear understanding of the nature of the advertising appeal and the structure of the market, a clear direction for such interactions could not be predicted a priori (Maurice Sasieni, "Pricing and Advertising for Profit," paper presented at Pennsylvania State University, October 1981).

Marketing-mix variables not only interact with each other but also with nonmarketing variables in the firm. A manager cannot set the product's price and quality at any level he or she wishes. The chart below shows that the product's price and product quality are dependent upon nonmarketing variables.

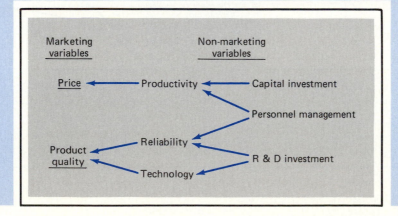

Japanese companies are especially sensitive to the dependence of marketing variables on non-marketing variables. The price they can charge depends upon the company's productivity, which is influenced by personnel policies as well as investment decisions. Similarly, product quality is influenced by production reliability and technology, which in turn are influenced by personnel management and R&D investment. Thus marketers must not take price and product for granted but influence those nonmarketing variables that will enable the company to drive down costs and produce higher quality products.

the difference between the two and makes it clear that there is no reason to assume they are correlated. The two dots in the figure show current marketing expenditures and company sales in two TMs. The company spends $3 million on marketing in both TMs. Company sales are $40 million in TM 1 and $20 million in TM 2. The average sales response to a dollar of marketing effort is thus greater in TM 1 than in TM 2; it is $\frac{40}{3}$ as opposed to $\frac{20}{3}$, respectively. It might seem desirable to shift funds from TM 2 to TM 1, where the average response is greater. Yet the real issue is one of the marginal response. The marginal response is represented by the *slope* of the sales function through the points. A higher slope has been drawn for TM 2 than for TM 1. The respective slopes show that another $1 million in marketing expenditure would produce a $10 million sales increase in TM 2 and only a $2 million sales increase in TM 1. Clearly marginal response, not average response, should guide the allocation of marketing funds.

Marginal response is indicated along the sales-response function for each territory. Assume that a company is able to estimate TM sales-response functions. Suppose

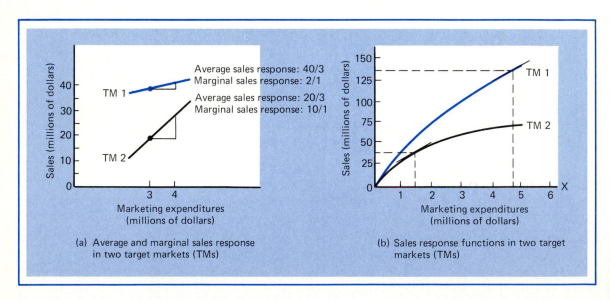

(a) Average and marginal sales response in two target markets (TMs)

(b) Sales response functions in two target markets (TMs)

FIGURE 9–4
Sales-Response Functions in Two Target Markets (TMs)

the sales response functions for two TMs are those shown in Figure 9–4(b). The company wishes to allocate a budget of B dollars between the two TMs to maximize profits. When costs are identical for the two TMs, then the allocation that will maximize profits is the one that will maximize sales. The funds are optimally allocated when they exhaust the budget, and the marginal sales response is the same in both TMs. Geometrically, this means that the slopes of the tangents to the two sales-response functions at the optimal allocations will be equal. Figure 9–4(b) shows that a budget of $6 million would be allocated in the amounts of approximately $4.6 million to TM 1 and $1.4 million to TM 2 to produce maximum sales of approximately $180 million. The marginal sales response would be the same in both TMs.

The principle of allocating funds to TMs to equalize the marginal response is used in the planning technique called *zero-based budgeting*.[13] The manager of each TM is asked to formulate a marketing plan and estimate the expected sales for (say) three levels of marketing expenditure, such as 30 percent below the normal level, the normal level, and 30 percent above the normal level. An example is shown in Table 9–5, outlining what the Zenith marketing manager would do with each budget level and her estimate of Allegro sales volume. Then higher management reviews this response function against those of other product managers and gives serious consideration to shifting funds from TMs with low marginal responses to TMs with higher marginal responses.

TABLE 9–5

ILLUSTRATION OF ZERO-BASED MARKETING BUDGETING

Budget (M)	Marketing Plan	Sales Forecast (Q)
$1,400,000	Maintain sales and market share in the short term by concentrating sales effort on largest chain stores, advertising only on TV, sponsoring two promotions a year, and carrying on only limited marketing research.	60,000 units
$2,000,000	Implement a coordinated effort to expand market share by contacting 80 percent of all retailers, adding magazine advertising, adding point-of-purchase displays, and sponsoring three promotions during the year.	70,000 units
$2,600,000	Seek to expand market size and share by adding two new product sizes, enlarging the sales force, increasing marketing research, and expanding the advertising budget.	90,000 units

[13] See Paul J. Stonich, *Zero-Base Planning and Budgeting: Improved Cost Control and Resource Allocation* (Homewood, Ill.: Dow-Jones-Irwin, 1977).

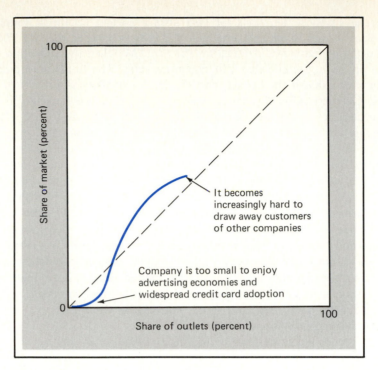

FIGURE 9–5
Share of Market as a Function of Share of Outlets

Measuring sales-response functions can lead to substantial shifts in company marketing strategy. A major oil company had located its service stations in every major U.S. city.[14] In many markets, it operated only a small percentage of the total stations. Company management began to question this broad location strategy. It decided to estimate how the company's market share in each city varied with its percentage share of marketing expenditures in each city (as measured by the share of outlets). A curve was fitted showing the share of outlets and share of markets in different cities. The resulting curve was S-shaped (see Figure 9–5). This showed that having a low percentage of stations in a city yielded an even lower percentage of market volume. The practical implication was clear: The company should either withdraw from its weak markets or build them up to, say, 15 percent of the competitive outlets. Instead of establishing a few outlets in each of many cities, the oil company should establish a large number of outlets in a smaller number of cities.

SUMMARY

Not all companies use formal planning, and not all companies that use it use it well. Yet formal planning can confer several benefits, including more systematic thinking, better

---

[14] See John J. Cardwell, "Marketing and Management Science–A Marriage on the Rocks?" *California Management Review*, Summer 1968, pp. 3–12.

coordination of company efforts, sharper objectives, and improved performance measurement, all of which hopefully lead to improved sales and profits. Planning in companies seems to evolve through a budgeting-system stage, annual planning stage, long-range planning stage, and strategic planning stage. Even the term **marketing plan** has several usages. It turns out that marketing input is necessary in formulating various company plans, including the corporate plan, divisional plans, product-line plans, brand plans, market plans, product/market plans, and functional plans. The contents of marketing plans vary from company to company but at a minimum should contain an executive summary, current marketing situation, opportunity and issue analysis, objectives, marketing strategy, action programs, projected profit-and-loss statement, and controls.

In order to plan effectively, marketing managers must understand the key relationship between types of marketing-mix expenditures and their sales and profit consequences. These relationships are captured in a profit equation and a sales equation. Profit-optimization planning calls for finding the profit-maximizing plan. It involves determining the optimal marketing expenditure level, marketing mix, and marketing allocation.

QUESTIONS

1. Opportunities/threats analysis is an important part of the marketing plan, designed to let management see what external factors they are facing and the possible action they might take. Develop an O/T analysis for the cigarette line of Philip Morris.

2. One marketing theorist maintains that "value rigidity" on the part of marketing managers poses a serious problem in the development of marketing plans. What might he mean by this assertion?

3. Conduct an "issue analysis" for Apple Computer's entry into the corporate computer market with the introduction of the $10,000 "Lisa" and $2,000 "Macintosh" computers.

4. A marketer evaluates two marketing strategies and estimates their expected rates of return to be 8 percent and 12 percent, respectively. Which strategy should be chosen if this decision is to be made many times? Which strategy should be chosen if this decision is to be made only once?

5. Suppose the quantity sold (Q) of an item depends upon the price charged (P), the level of advertising expenditure (A), and the level of distribution expenditure (D). Develop a sales-response equation (a) where the marginal effect of each marketing variable is uninfluenced by the levels of the other marketing variables; (b) where the marginal effect of each marketing variable is influenced by the levels of the other variables.

6. A firm wants to decide how much quality to build into a new machine tool. Illustrate diagrammatically the logic of determining the optimal quality level.

7. Suggest four improvements in the computer program shown in Table 9–4 for projecting sales and profits.

8. Suggest some equation forms that might be used to represent (a) a sales-response function when sales increase at a decreasing rate with marketing expenditures; (b) a sales-response function where sales increase at an increasing and then decreasing rate.

9. The brand manager in charge of a dry breakfast cereal has the following sales and expense statement:

Net Sales		100%
Manufacturing and shipping costs		
Fixed	12.9	
Variable	39.6	
Total		52.5
All other expenses (excluding advertising and merchandising expenses)		
Distribution and delivery expenses	5.4	
Administrative and general expenses	4.0	
Sales people's expenses	3.5	
Market research	0.5	
Total		13.4
Available for advertising and merchandising and profit		34.1

Name several ways the brand manager can try to increase profit.

The New Product Development Process

10

Nothing in this world is so powerful as an idea whose time has come.

VICTOR HUGO

One of the major challenges in marketing planning is to develop ideas for new products and to launch them successfully. The company will have to find replacements for its products that have entered the decline stage. Customers want new products, and competitors will do their best to supply them. A recent Booz, Allen & Hamilton survey of 700 companies reported that these companies expect that 31 percent of their profits over the next five years will come from new products.[1]

The new-product-planning gap can be filled in two ways: *acquisition* or *new product development*. The acquisition route can take three forms. First the company can pursue a *corporate-acquisition* program involving the search for smaller companies that have attractive product lines. Companies such as Beatrice Food and Litton Industries have much experience in spotting and buying companies. Second, the company can pursue a *patent-acquisition* program in which it buys the rights to new products from their patent holders. Third, the company can pursue a *license-acquisition* program

---

[1] *New Products Management for the 1980s* (New York: Booz, Allen & Hamilton, 1982).

for manufacturing various products. In all three cases, the company does not develop any new products but simply acquires the rights to existing ones.

The new product route can take two basic forms. The company can pursue *internal new product development* by operating its own research-and-development department. Or it can pursue *contract new product development*, which involves hiring independent researchers or new-product-development agencies to develop specific products for the firm.

Many companies combine several of these strategies for growth. General Mills bases its growth on a fifty-fifty mix of acquisition and new product development. Its management feels that the economy may favor acquisition at certain times and new product development at other times, and they want to be skilled at both.

This chapter will focus on new product development as a growth strategy, because of the heavy role that marketing plays in finding, developing, and launching successful new products. "New products" for our purposes will include *original products*, *product improvements*, *product modifications*, and *new brands* that the firm develops through its own R&D efforts. We will also be concerned with whether the consumer sees them as "new." Booz, Allen & Hamilton recently identified six categories of new products in terms of their newness to the company and to the marketplace.[2] Figure 10–1 shows these categories and the percentage of products appearing in each category over the last five years. The categories are:

- ☐ **New-to-the-world products**: new products that create an entirely new market
- ☐ **New-product lines**: new products that allow a company to enter an established market for the first time
- ☐ **Additions to existing product lines**: new products that supplement a company's established product lines
- ☐ **Improvements in/revisions to existing products**: new products that provide improved performance or greater perceived value and replace existing products
- ☐ **Repositionings**: existing products that are targeted to new markets or market segments
- ☐ **Cost reductions**: new products that provide similar performance at lower cost

A company usually pursues a mix of these new products. An important finding is that only 10 percent of all new products are truly innovative or new to the world. These products involve the most cost and risk because they are new to both the company and the marketplace.

THE NEW-PRODUCT-DEVELOPMENT DILEMMA

Under modern conditions of competition, companies that do not develop new products risk much. Such companies will find their products falling victim to changing consumer needs and tastes, new technologies, shortened product life cycles, and increased domestic and foreign competition.

At the same time, new product development can be very risky. Ford lost an estimated $350 million on its ill-fated Edsel; Du Pont lost an estimated $100 million

---

[2] Ibid.

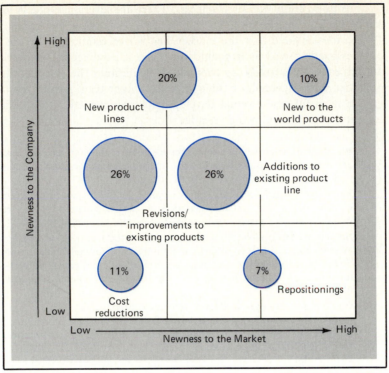

Source: *New Products Management for the 1980s* (New York: Booz, Allen & Hamilton, 1982).

FIGURE 10-1
Types of New Products

on its synthetic leather called Corfam; Xerox's venture into computers was a disaster; and the French Concorde aircraft will probably never recover its investment. Here are several consumer-packaged-goods products, launched by sophisticated companies, that failed in the marketplace:

- ☐ Red Kettle soup (Campbell)
- ☐ Knorr soup (Best)
- ☐ Cut toothpaste (Colgate)
- ☐ Flavored ketchups (Hunts)
- ☐ Babyscott diapers (Scott)
- ☐ Nine Flags men's cologne (Gillette)

- ☐ Vim tablet detergent (Lever)
- ☐ Post dried fruit cereal (General Foods)
- ☐ Gablinger's beer (Rheingold)
- ☐ Resolve analgesic (Bristol-Myers)
- ☐ Mennen E deodorant (Mennen)

One study found that the new-product failure rate was 40 percent for consumer products, 20 percent for industrial products, and 18 percent for services.[3] The failure rate for new consumer products is especially disturbing.

---

[3] David S. Hopkins and Earl L. Bailey, "New Product Pressures, *Conference Board Record*, June 1971, pp. 16–24.

Why do many new products fail? There are several factors. A high-level executive might push a favorite idea through in spite of negative marketing research findings. Or the idea is good, but the market size is overestimated. Or the actual product is not designed as well as it should be. Or it is incorrectly positioned in the market, not advertised effectively, or overpriced. Sometimes the cost of product development is higher than expected, or the competitors fight back harder than expected.

Successful new-product development may even be more difficult to achieve in the future for the following reasons:

☐ **Shortage of important new-product ideas in certain areas**. Some scientists think there are too few new technologies of the investment magnitude of the automobile, television, computers, xerography, and wonder drugs.

☐ **Fragmented markets**. Keen competition is leading to increasingly fragmented markets. Companies have to aim new products at smaller market segments rather than the mass market, and this means lower sales and profits for each product.

☐ **Social and governmental constraints**. New products have to satisfy public criteria such as consumer safety and ecological compatibility. Government requirements have slowed down innovation in the drug industry and have complicated product-design and advertising decisions in such industries as industrial equipment, chemicals, automobiles, and toys.

☐ **Costliness of the new-product-development process**. A company typically has to generate many new-product ideas in order to finish with a few good ones. Each product costs more to develop and launch due to the effect of the recent inflation on manufacturing, media, and distribution costs.

☐ **Capital shortage**. Many companies cannot afford or raise the funds needed to research true innovations. They emphasize new product modifications and imitations instead of true innovation.

☐ **Shorter growth periods for successful products**. When a new product is successful, rivals are so quick to imitate it that the new product's growth stage is shortened. Alberto-Culver was so eager to follow P&G into the shampoo market that it devised a name and filmed a TV commercial before it had even developed its own product.

The answer to successful new-product introductions lies in two directions. First the organization must improve its organizational arrangements for handling the new-product-development process. Second it must handle each step of the process with the best available techniques. We shall look at each in turn.

EFFECTIVE ORGANIZATIONAL ARRANGEMENTS

Top management bears the ultimate responsibility for the quality of the new-product-development work at the company. It cannot simply hire some new-product specialists and leave them to come up with useful new ideas. Effective new-product-development work must start with a clear definition of company growth strategy that specifies the business domains and product categories in which the company wants to do business. In one food company, the new-product manager spent thousands of dollars researching a new snack idea only to hear the president say, "Drop it. We don't want to be in the snack business."

Top management should set specific criteria for new-product-idea acceptance, especially in large multidivisional companies where all kinds of projects bubble up as favorites of specific managers. The criteria can vary with the specific *strategic role* the product is expected to play. Booz, Allen & Hamilton identified six major strategic roles that companies set for their new products (percentages show the percent of recent products playing each role):

☐ Maintain position as a product innovator (46 percent)
☐ Defend a market-share position (44 percent)
☐ Establish a foothold in a future new market (37 percent)
☐ Preempt a market segment (33 percent)
☐ Exploit technology in a new way (27 percent)
☐ Capitalize on distribution strengths (24 percent)[4]

Thus the Gould Corporation established the following acceptance criteria for new products aimed at exploiting a technology in a new way: (1) the product can be introduced within five years; (2) the product has a market potential of at least $50 million and a 15 percent growth rate; (3) the product will provide at least 30 percent return on sales and 40 percent on investment; and (4) the product will achieve technical or market leadership.

Top management must decide how much to budget for new-product development. Research and development outcomes are so uncertain that it is difficult to use normal investment criteria for budgeting. Some companies solve this problem by encouraging and financing as many project proposals as possible, hoping to hit a few winners. Other companies set their R&D budget by applying a conventional percentage-to-sales figure or by spending what competition spends. Still other companies decide how many successful new products they need and work backwards to estimate the required R&D investment.

Booz, Allen & Hamilton has conducted several studies of how many new-product ideas it takes to yield one successful product. (See Exhibit 10–1 for a summary of their latest findings.) Fifteen years ago it took fifty-eight new-product ideas to yield one good one. Their latest study shows that companies are now able to turn one out of seven new-product ideas into a successful new product. Figure 10–2 on page 315 shows the decay curve for new-product ideas. Booz, Allen & Hamilton concluded that many companies have learned to handle prescreening and planning more effectively and are putting money only on the best ideas instead of using a shotgun approach.

Table 10–1 on page 316 shows how a company can work out the investment cost of new-product development. The new-products manager at a large consumer-packaged-goods company reviewed the results of sixty-four new-product ideas his company considered. Only one in four ideas, or sixteen, passed the idea-screening stage, and it cost $1,000 per idea reviewed at this stage. Half of these ideas, or eight, survived the concept-testing stage, at a cost of $20,000 each. Half of these, or four, survived the product-development stage. Half of these, or two, did well in

---

[4] *New Products Management for the 1980s.*

Exhibit 10–1

BOOZ, ALLEN & HAMILTON'S LATEST STUDY OF NEW-PRODUCT-MANAGEMENT ACTIVITY

The international management and technology consulting firm of Booz, Allen & Hamilton released in 1982 an updated study of new-product-management activity. Their study consisted of a mail survey of 700 consumer and industrial companies and lengthy interviews with 150 new-product executives. Here are some of their key findings:

1. Management reported an average new-product-success rate of 65 percent.
2. Companies were able to develop one successful product out of every seven they researched, which is a substantial improvement over the 1968 rate of one out of every fifty-eight ideas.
3. Only 10 percent of the new products were "new to the world," and only 20 percent were "new-product lines," but these highest-risk products represented 60 percent of the "most successful" new products.
4. New-product spending has become more efficient, in that successful entries accounted for 54 percent of total new-product expenditures, up from 30 percent in 1968.
5. Successful new-product companies don't spend more on R&D and marketing, as a percentage of sales, than unsuccessful ones.
6. The median number of new products introduced between 1976 and 1981 was five; that number is expected to double over the next five years.
7. Managers expect new products to increase company sales growth by one-third over the next five years, while the portion of total company profits generated by new products is expected to be 40 percent.

Source: New Products Management for the 1980s (*New York: Booz, Allen & Hamilton, 1982*).

---

the test market, at a cost of $500,000 each.[5] When these two ideas were launched, at a cost of $500,000 each, only one was highly successful. Thus the one successful idea had cost the company $5,721,000 to develop. In the process, sixty-three other ideas fell by the wayside. Therefore the total cost for developing one successful new product was $13,984,400. Unless the company can improve the pass ratios and reduce the costs at each stage, it will have to budget nearly $14,000,000 for each successful new idea it hopes to find. If top management wants four successful new products in the next few years, it will have to budget $56,000,000 (= 4 × $14,000,000) for new-product development—even more, to allow for inflation.

A key factor in effective new-product-development work is to establish workable

---

[5] In a sample of 228 frequently purchased consumer products that were test marketed in 1977, 64.5 percent were not launched nationally. See Nielsen Marketing Service, "New Product Success Ratios," *The Nielsen Researcher*, 1979, pp. 2–9.

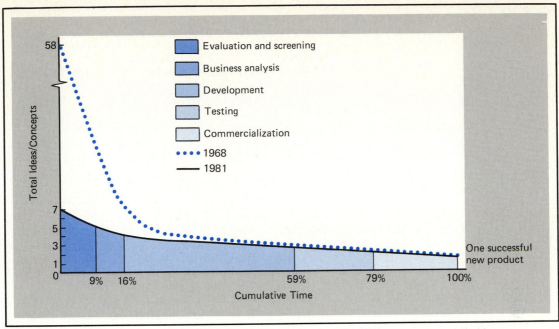

Source: *New Products Management for the 1980s* (New York: Booz, Allen & Hamilton, 1982).

FIGURE 10–2
Mortality of New-Product Ideas

organizational structures. Companies handle new-product development in several ways:[6]

☐ **Product managers**. Many companies leave new-product development to their product managers. In practice, this system has several faults. Product managers are usually so busy managing their product lines that they give little thought to new products other than brand modifications or extensions; they also lack the specific skills and knowledge needed to develop new products.

☐ **New-product managers**. General Foods and Johnson & Johnson have new-product managers, who report to group product managers. This position professionalizes the new-product function; on the other hand, new-product managers tend to think in terms of product modifications and line extensions limited to their product market.

☐ **New-product committees**. Most companies have a high-level management committee charged with reviewing new-product proposals. Consisting of representatives from marketing, manufacturing, finance, engineering, and other departments, its function is not development of coordination so much as reviewing and approving new-product plans.

☐ **New-product departments**. Large companies often establish a new-product department headed by a manager who has substantial authority and access to top management. The department's major responsibilities include generating and screening new ideas, directing and coordinating research and development work, and carrying out field testing and precommercialization work.

[6] See *Organization for New-Product Development* (New York: Conference Board, 1966) and David S. Hopkins, *Options in New-Product Organization* (New York: Conference Board, 1974).

TABLE 10-1

ESTIMATED COST OF FINDING ONE SUCCESSFUL NEW PRODUCT (STARTING WITH SIXTY-FOUR NEW IDEAS)				
Stage	Number of Ideas	Pass Ratio	Cost per Product Idea	Total Cost
1. Idea screening	64	1:4	$ 1,000	$ 64,000
2. Concept test	16	1:2	20,000	320,000
3. Product development	8	1:2	200,000	1,600,000
4. Test marketing	4	1:2	500,000	2,000,000
5. National launch	2	1:2	5,000,000	10,000,000
			$5,721,000	$13,984,000

□ **New-product venture teams**. Dow, Westinghouse, Monsanto, and General Mills assign major new-product-development work to venture teams. A venture team is a group brought together from various operating departments and charged with bringing a specific product or business into being.

According to Booz, Allen & Hamilton, the most successful companies have made a consistent commitment of resources to new-product development, have designed a new-product strategy that is linked to their strategic planning process, and have established formal and sophisticated mechanisms for managing the new-product-development process.

We are now ready to look at the stages of the new-product-development process. Eight stages are involved: *idea generation*, *screening*, *concept development and testing*, *marketing strategy*, *business analysis*, *product development*, *market testing*, and *commercialization*.

IDEA GENERATION

The new-product-development process starts with the search for ideas. The search should not be casual or open-ended. Top management should define the products and markets to emphasize. It should state the new-product objectives, whether it is high cash flow, market-share domination, or some other objective. It should state how much effort should be devoted to developing original products, modifying existing products, and imitating competitors' products.

Sources of New-Product Ideas

New-product ideas can be derived from many sources: customers, scientists, competitors, company sales people and dealers, and top management.

The marketing concept suggests that *customers' needs and wants* are the logical places to start in the search for new-product ideas. Hippel has shown that a great number of ideas for new industrial products originated with customers.[7] Companies

---

[7] Eric A. von Hippel, "Users as Innovators," *Technology Review*, January 1978, pp. 3–11.

can identify customers' needs and wants through direct customer surveys, projective tests, focused group discussion, and suggestion and complaint letters from customers. Many idea hunters claim to find the best ideas by asking customers to describe their *problems* with current products rather than by asking them for new-product ideas directly.

Many companies rely on their *scientists* for new product ideas. Companies in the chemical, electronics, and pharmaceutical industries, such as Du Pont, Bell Laboratories, and Merck, rely on scientists for new ideas.

Companies can find new ideas by monitoring their *competitors'* products. They can listen to distributors, suppliers, and sales representatives as to what is in the works. The company should assess who is buying competitors' new products and why. Many companies buy competitors' products, take them apart, and build better ones. Their competitive strategy is one of *product imitation and improvement* rather than *product innovation*.

Company *sales representatives* and *dealers* are a particularly good source of new-product ideas. They have firsthand exposure to customers' needs and complaints. They are often the first to learn of competitive developments. An increasing number of companies are training and rewarding their sales representatives and dealers for producing new ideas.

Top management is another major source of new-product ideas. Some company leaders, such as Edwin H. Land, former CEO of Polaroid, take personal responsibility for technological innovation in their companies. This isn't always constructive, as when a top executive pushes through a pet idea without thoroughly researching market size or interest. This happened when Land pushed forward his Polavision project (instant-developed movies) which ended as a product failure because the market had grown more interested in video tapes as a way to capture action.

Finally, new-product ideas can come from a variety of other sources, including inventors, patent attorneys, university and commercial laboratories, industrial consultants, advertising agencies, marketing research firms, and industrial publications.

While ideas will come in from many sources, their chance of receiving serious attention often depends on someone in the organization taking the role of *product champion*. Unless someone is personally enthusiastic about the product idea and willing to make a personal commitment to carry it all the way to fruition, the idea is not likely to receive serious consideration.

Idea-Generating Techniques

Really good ideas come out of inspiration, perspiration, and techniques. A number of "creativity" techniques are available to help individuals and groups generate better ideas.

Attribute listing. The major attributes of an existing product are listed, and then each attribute is modified in the search for an improved product. Consider a screwdriver.[8] Its attributes: a round, steel shank, a wooden handle, manually operated,

---

[8] See John E. Arnold, "Useful Creative Techniques," in *Source Book for Creative Thinking*, ed. Sidney J. Parnes and Harold F. Harding (New York: Charles Scribner's Sons, 1962), p. 255.

and torque provided by twisting action. Now a group is asked to propose attribute modifications to improve product performance or appeal. The round shank could be made to be hexagonal so that a wrench could be applied to increase the torque; electric power could replace manual power; the torque could be produced by pushing. Osborn suggested that useful ideas can be stimulated by putting the following questions to an object and its attributes: put to other uses? adapt? magnify? minify? substitute? rearrange? reverse? combine?[9]

Forced relationships.   Here several objects are listed, and each object is considered in relation to every other object. Recently an office-equipment manufacturer wanted to design a new desk for executives. Several objects were listed—a desk, television set, clock, computer, copying machine, bookcase, and so on. The result was a fully electronic desk with a console resembling that found in a pilot cockpit.

Morphological analysis.   Morphology means structure and this method calls for identifying the structural dimensions of a problem and examining the relationships among them. Suppose the problem is described as that of "getting something from one place to another via a powered vehicle." The important dimensions are the type of vehicle (cart, chair, sling, bed); the medium in which the vehicle operates (air, water, oil, hard surface, rollers, rails); the power source (pressed air, internal-combustion engine, electric motor, steam, magnetic fields, moving cables, moving belt). Then the imagination is let loose on every combination. A cart-type vehicle powered by an internal-combustion engine and moving over hard surfaces is the automobile. The hope is to find some novel combinations.[10]

Problem analysis.   The preceding creativity techniques do not require consumer input to generate ideas. Problem analysis, on the other hand, starts with the consumer. Consumers are asked for problems they encounter in using a particular product or product category. Thus Kodak might ask consumers about problems they have with their movie projectors. Each problem can be the source of a new idea. "It is time consuming to rewind the film" suggests automatic rewinding. "The scene is too small to see on the screen" suggests a zoom lens. "Some of the film is boring" suggests a fast-forward mechanism. Not all of these ideas will be worth developing. The problems have to be rated by their *seriousness*, *incidence*, and *cost of remedying*, in order to choose the ones to work on.

The technique can be used in reverse. Consumers receive a list of problems and tell which products come to mind as having each problem.[11] Thus the question: "The package of _____ doesn't fit well on the shelf" might lead consumers to name

---

[9] See Alex F. Osborn, *Applied Imagination*, 3rd ed. (New York: Charles Scribner's Sons, 1963), pp. 286–87.

[10] See Edward M. Tauber, "HIT: Heuristic Ideation Technique-A Systematic Procedure for New Product Search," *Journal of Marketing*, January 1972, pp. 58–70; and Charles L. Alford and Joseph Barry Mason, "Generating New Product Ideas," *Journal of Advertising Research*, December 1975, pp. 27–32.

[11] See Edward M. Tauber, "Discovering New Product Opportunities with Problem Inventory Analysis," *Journal of Marketing*, January 1975, pp. 67–70.

dog foods and dry breakfast cereals. A food marketer might think of entering these markets with a smaller-size package.

Brainstorming. Groups can be stimulated to greater creativity through the technique called *brainstorming*, whose principles were developed by Alex Osborn. A brainstorming session is held to produce a lot of ideas. Generally the group size ranges between six and ten. It is not a good idea to include too many experts in the group, because they tend to look at a problem in a rigid way. The problem should be specific, and there should be no more than one problem. The sessions, preferably held in the morning, should last about an hour. The chairman starts with, "Remember, we want as many ideas as possible—the wilder the better, and remember, no *evaluation*." The ideas start flowing, one idea sparks another, and within an hour over a hundred or more new ideas may find their way into the tape recorder. For the conference to be maximally effective, Osborn laid down four guidelines:

- ☐ **Criticism is ruled out**. Negative comments on ideas must be withheld until later.
- ☐ **Freewheeling is welcomed**. The wilder the idea, the better; it is easier to tame down than to think up.
- ☐ **Quantity is encouraged**. The greater the number of ideas, the more the likelihood of useful ideas.
- ☐ **Combining and improving ideas is encouraged**. Participants should suggest how ideas of others can be joined into still newer ideas.[12]

Synectics. William J. J. Gordon felt that Osborn's brainstorming session produced solutions too quickly, before a sufficient number of perspectives had been developed. Gordon decided to define the problem so broadly that the group would have no inkling of the specific problem.

One of the problems was to design a vapor-proof method of closing vapor-proof suits worn by workers who handled high-powered fuels.[13] Gordon kept the specific problem a secret and sparked a discussion of the general notion of "closure," which led to images of different closure mechanisms, such as birds' nests, mouths, or thread. As the group exhausted the initial perspectives, Gordon gradually introduced facts that defined the problem further. When the group was getting close to a good solution, Gordon described the problem. Then the group started to refine the solution. These sessions would last a minimum of three hours, for Gordon believed that fatigue played an important role in unlocking ideas. Gordon described five principles underlying the synectics method:

- ☐ **Deferment**. Look first for viewpoint rather than solutions.
- ☐ **Autonomy of object**. Let the problem take on a life of its own.
- ☐ **Use of the commonplace**. Take advantage of the familiar as a springboard to the strange.
- ☐ **Involvement/detachment**. Alternate between entering into the particulars of the problem and standing back from them, in order to see them as instances of a universal.

---

[12] Osborn, *Applied Imagination*, p. 156.

[13] John W. Lincoln, "Defining a Creativeness in People," in *Source Book for Creative Thinking*, Parnes and Harding, pp. 274–75.

☐ **Use of metaphor**. Let apparently irrelevant, accidental things suggest analogies that are sources of new viewpoints.[14]

IDEA SCREENING

The purpose of idea generation is to create a large number of ideas. The purpose of the succeeding stages is to *reduce* the number of ideas. The first idea-pruning stage is screening.

In the screening state, the company must avoid two types of errors. A DROP-*error* occurs when the company dismisses an otherwise good idea. Some companies shudder when they think of some of the ideas they dismissed:

> Xerox saw the novel promise of Chester Carlson's copying machine; IBM and Eastman Kodak did not see it at all. RCA was able to envision the innovative opportunity of radio; the Victor Talking Machine Company could not. Henry Ford recognized the promise of the automobile; yet only General Motors realized the need to segment the automobile market into price and performance categories, with a model for every classification, if the promise was to be fully achieved. Marshall Field understood the unique market development possibilities of installment buying; Endicott Johnson did not, calling it "the vilest system yet devised to create trouble." And so it has gone.[15]

If a company makes too many DROP-errors, its standards are too conservative.

A GO-*error* occurs when the company permits a poor idea to move into development and commercialization. We can distinguish three types of product failures that ensue. An *absolute product failure* loses money, and its sales do not cover variable costs; a *partial* product failure loses money, but its sales cover all the variable costs and some of the fixed costs; and a *relative* product failure yields a profit that is less than the company's normal rate of return.

The purpose of screening is to spot and drop poor ideas as early as possible. The rationale is that product-development costs rise substantially at each successive development stage. When products reach later stages, management often feels that they have invested so much in developing the product that it should be launched to recoup some of the investment. But this is letting good money chase bad money, and the real solution is to not let poor product ideas get this far.

Product-Idea Rating Devices

Most companies require their executives to write up new-product ideas on a standard form that can be reviewed by a new-product committee. They describe the product, the target market, and the competition and make some rough guesses as to market size, product price, development time and costs, manufacturing costs, and rate of return.

Even if the idea looks good, the question arises, Is it appropriate for the particular

---

[14] Ibid., p. 274.

[15] Mark Hanan, "Corporate Growth through Venture Management," *Harvard Business Review*, January-February 1969, p. 44.

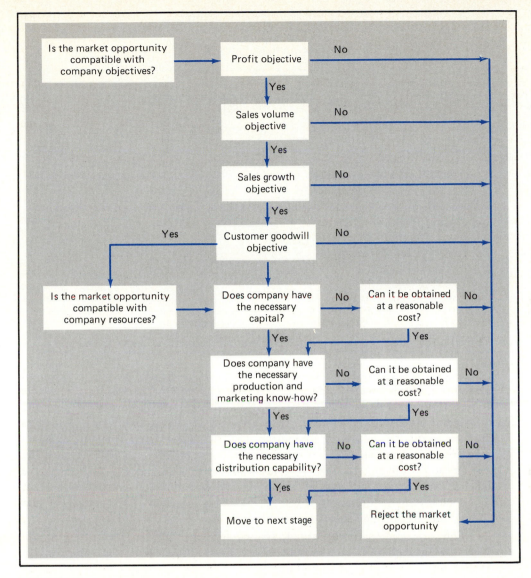

FIGURE 10–3
Evaluating a Market Opportunity in Terms of the Company's Objectives and Resources

company? Does it mesh well with the company's objectives, strategies, and resources? Figure 10–3 shows a set of questions that should be put to every new-product idea. Ideas that do not satisfy one or more of these questions are dropped.

The remaining ideas can be rated using the weighted index method shown in Table 10–2. The first column lists factors required for the successful launching of the product in the marketplace. In the next column, management assigns weights to these factors to reflect their relative importance. Thus management believes market-

TABLE 10-2

PRODUCT-IDEA-RATING DEVICE

Product Success Requirements	Relative Weight (A)	Company Competence Level (B)											Rating (A × B)
		0.0	0.1	0.2	0.3	0.4	0.5	0.6	0.7	0.8	0.9	1.0	
Company personality and goodwill	0.20							✓					0.120
Marketing	0.20										✓		0.180
Research and development	0.20								✓				0.140
Personnel	0.15							✓					0.090
Finance	0.10										✓		0.090
Production	0.05									✓			0.040
Location and facilities	0.05				✓								0.015
Purchasing and supplies	0.05										✓		0.045
Total	1.00												0.720*

* Rating scale: 0.00–0.40 poor: 0.41–0.75 fair: 0.76–1.00 good. Present minimum acceptance rate: 0.70.

SOURCE: Adapted with modifications from Barry M. Richman, "A Rating Scale for Product Innovation," *Business Horizons,* summer 1962, pp. 37–44.

ing competence will be very important (0.20) and purchasing and supplies competence to be of minor importance (0.05). The next task is to rate the company's competence on each factor on a scale from 0.0 to 1.0. Here management feels that its marketing competence is very high (0.9) and its location and facilities competence low (0.3). The final step is to multiply the importance of each success factor by the company competence level to obtain an overall rating of the company's ability to launch this product successfully into the market. Thus if marketing is an important success factor, and this company is very good at marketing, the overall rating of the product idea will be increased. In the example the product idea scored 0.72, which places it at the high end of the "fair idea" level.

This basic rating device can be refined further.[16] Its purpose is to promote more systematic product-idea evaluation—it is not designed to make the decision for management.

CONCEPT DEVELOPMENT AND TESTING

Surviving ideas must now be developed into product concepts. It is important to distinguish between a product idea, a product concept, and a product image. A *product idea* is an idea for a possible product that the company can see itself offering to the market. A *product concept* is an elaborated version of the idea expressed in mean-

---

[16] See John T. O'Meara, Jr., "Selecting Profitable Products," *Harvard Business Review*, January-February 1961, pp. 110–18.

ingful consumer terms. A *product image* is the particular picture that consumers acquire of an actual or potential product.

Concept Development

We shall illustrate concept development with the following situation. A large food processor gets the idea of producing a powder to add to milk to increase its nutritional level and taste. This is a product idea. Consumers, however, do not buy product ideas; they buy product concepts.

Any product idea can be turned into several product concepts. First, the question can be asked, Who is to use this product? The powder can be aimed at infants, children, teenagers, young or middle-aged adults, or senior citizens. Second, What primary benefit should be built into this product? Taste, nutrition, refreshment, energy? Third, What is the primary occasion for this drink? Breakfast, midmorning, lunch, midafternoon, dinner, late evening? By asking these questions, a company can form several product concepts:

- ☐ **Concept 1:** An *instant breakfast drink* for adults who want a quick nutritional breakfast without preparing a breakfast.
- ☐ **Concept 2:** A *tasty snack drink* for children to drink as a midday refreshment.
- ☐ **Concept 3:** A *health supplement* for senior citizens to drink in the late evening before retiring.

Concept Positioning

Each concept requires positioning so that its real competition would be understood. An *instant breakfast drink* would compete against bacon and eggs, breakfast cereals, coffee and pastry, and other breakfast alternatives. A *tasty snack drink* would compete against soft drinks, fruit juices, and other tasty thirst quenchers. The product concept, and not the product idea, defines the product's competition.

Let us look at the instant breakfast drink concept further. Figure 10–4(a) is a *product-positioning map* showing where an instant breakfast drink stands in relation to other breakfast products, using the two dimensions of cost and preparation time. An instant breakfast drink offers the buyer low cost and quick preparation. Its nearest competitor is cold cereal; its most distant competitor is bacon and eggs. These contrasts can be utilized in communicating the concept to the market.

The concept also has to be positioned against existing brands in the product category. Figure 10–4(b) shows the positions of three other instant breakfast drinks. The company needs to decide how much to charge and how calorific to make its drink, if these are salient attributes to buyers. The new brand could be positioned in the medium-price, medium-calorie market or in the low-price, low-calorie market. The new brand would gain distinctiveness in either position, as opposed to positioning next to another brand and fighting for share-of-market. This decision requires researching the size of alternative preference segments of the market.

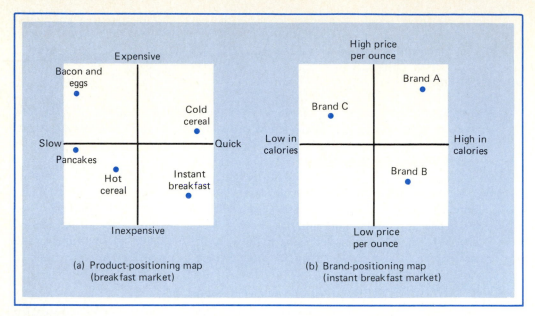

FIGURE 10-4
Product and Brand Positioning

Concept Testing

Concept testing calls for testing these concepts with an appropriate group of target consumers. The concepts may be presented symbolically or physically. At this stage a word and/or picture description suffices, although the reliability of a concept test increases, the more concrete and physical the stimulus. The consumers are presented with an elaborated version of each concept. Here is concept 1:

> A powdered product that is added to milk to make an instant breakfast that gives the person all the breakfast nutrition needed along with good taste and high convenience. The product would be offered in three flavors, chocolate, vanilla, and strawberry, and would come in individual packets, six to a box, at 79¢ a box.

Consumers are asked to react to each concept with questions shown in Table 10–3. The consumers' responses will help the company determine which concept has the strongest appeal. For example, question 5 goes after the consumer's *intention to buy* and usually reads: "Would you *definitely, probably, probably not, definitely not* buy this product?" Suppose 40 percent of the consumers said "definitely" and another 30 percent said "probably." Most companies have developed norms to judge how well these intention-to-buy results predict actual buying. One food manufacturer rejects any product idea that does not draw a definite intention-to-buy score above

TABLE 10–3

MAJOR QUESTIONS IN A CONCEPT TEST

1. **Is the concept clear and easy to understand?** (Often the concept test reveals that people are not really grasping the concept.)
2. **Do you see some distinct benefits of this product over competing offerings?** (The respondents must recognize distinct benefits of this product over its near substitutes.)
3. **Do you find the concept and claims believable?** (The respondents may have strong doubts about the product claims, which the manufacturer will have to overcome.)
4. **Do you like this product better than its major competitors?** (The respondents report whether they really prefer this product.)
5. **Would you buy this product?** (The company must find out if there is a sufficient percentage of respondents with an actual intention to buy this product.)
6. **Would you replace your current product with this new product?** (The company must find out if the consumer envisions not only trying this product but also substituting it permanently for the current product.)
7. **Does this product meet a real need of yours?** (If consumers do not feel a real need for the product, they may buy it only once out of curiosity.)
8. **What improvements can you suggest in various attributes of the product?** (This question enables the company to bring about further improvements in form, features, pricing, quality, and so on.)
9. **How frequently would you buy this product?** (The answer indicates whether the consumer sees it as an everday product or a specialty product.)
10. **Who would use the product?** (This question helps the marketer define the target user.)
11. **What do you think the price of this product should be?** (This question helps the marketer know the consumer's value perception of the product.)

50 percent. Another food manufacturer takes the "definite" score plus half of the "probable" score and requires the sum to exceed 50 percent.

Concept development and testing methodology applies to any product, service, or idea, such as an electric car, a new banking service, a new type of museum, or a new health plan. Too many managers think their job is done when they get a product idea. They do not develop it into some alternative concepts and test them adequately. Later the product encounters all kinds of problems in the marketplace that would have been avoided if the company had done a good job of concept development and testing. (For some advanced methods of concept development and testing, see Exhibit 10–2.)

MARKETING-STRATEGY DEVELOPMENT

The new-product manager will have to develop a preliminary marketing-strategy statement for introducing this product into the market. The marketing strategy will be refined in subsequent stages.

The marketing-strategy statement consists of three parts. The first part describes the size, structure, and behavior of the target market, the planned product positioning and the sales, market share, and profit goals sought in the first few years. Thus:

> The target market for the instant breakfast drink is families with children who are receptive to a new, convenient, nutritious, and inexpensive form of breakfast. The company's brand will be positioned at the higher-price, higher-quality end of the market. The company will aim initially to sell 500,000 cases or 10 percent of the market, with a loss in the first year not exceeding $1.3 million dollars. The second year will aim for 700,000 cases or 14 percent of the market, with a planned profit of $2.2 million dollars.

The second part of the marketing-strategy statement outlines the product's planned price, distribution strategy, and marketing budget for the first year:

> The product will be offered in a chocolate flavor in individual packets of six to a box at a retail price of 79¢ a box. There will be forty-eight boxes per case, and the case's price to distributors will be $24. For the first two months, dealers will be offered one case free for every four cases bought, plus cooperative-advertising allowances. Free samples will be distributed door to door. Coupons with 10¢ off will be advertised in newspapers. The total sales promotion budget will be $2,900,000. An advertising budget of $6,000,000 will be split between national and local 50:50. Two-thirds will go into television and one third into newspapers. Advertising copy will emphasize the benefit concepts of nutrition and convenience. The advertising-execution concept will revolve around a little boy who drinks instant breakfast and grows strong. During the first year, $100,000 will be spent on marketing research to buy store audits and consumer panel information to monitor the market's reaction and buying rates.

The third part of the marketing-strategy statement describes the planned long-run sales and profit goals and marketing-mix strategy over time:

> The company intends to ultimately capture 25 percent market share and realize an after-tax return on investment of 12 percent. To achieve this, product quality will start high and be further improved over time through technical research. Price will initially be set at a skimming level and lowered gradually to expand the market and meet competition. The total promotion budget will be boosted each year about 20 percent, with the initial advertising/sales promotion split of 63:37 evolving eventually to 50:50. Marketing research will be reduced to $60,000 per year after the first year.

Exhibit 10-2

NEW WAYS TO MEASURE CONSUMER PREFERENCES FOR ALTERNATIVE PRODUCT CONCEPTS

Among the ways to measure consumer preferences for alternative product concepts are two advanced methods, namely, *conjoint measurement* and *trade-off analysis*. We will illustrate these methods below.

Conjoint Measurement

Green and Wind have illustrated the technique of conjoint measurement in connection with developing a new carpet-cleaning agent for home use. Suppose the new-product marketer is considering the following five design elements:

- ☐ Three package designs (a, b, c—see figure below)
- ☐ Three brand names (K2R, Glory, Bissell)
- ☐ Three prices ($1.19, $1.39, $1.59)
- ☐ A possible Good Housekeeping seal (Yes, No)
- ☐ A possible money-back guarantee (Yes, No)

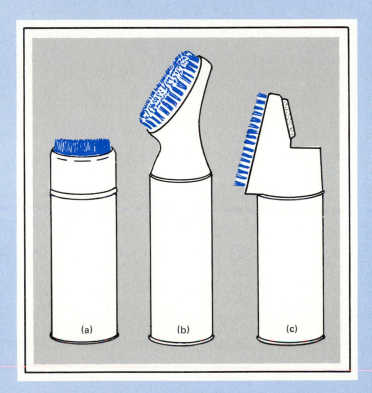

(a)   (b)   (c)

Experimental Design Used in Spot-Remover Product Evaluation

Altogether, the marketer can form 108 possible product concepts (3 × 3 × 3 × 2 × 2). It would be too much to ask consumers to rank or rate all of these concepts. A sample of, say, 18 contrasting product concepts can be chosen, and consumers would find it easy enough to rank them from the most preferred to the least preferred. The chart on the next page shows how one consumer ranked the eighteen product concepts.

STIMULUS COMBINATIONS

Card	Package Design	Brand Name	Price	Good Housekeeping Seal?	Money-Back Guarantee?	Respondent's Evaluation (rank number)
1	A	K2R	$1.19	No	No	13
2	A	Glory	1.39	No	Yes	11
3	A	Bissell	1.59	Yes	No	17
4	B	K2R	1.39	Yes	Yes	2
5	B	Glory	1.59	No	No	14
6	B	Bissell	1.19	No	No	3
7	C	K2R	1.59	No	Yes	12
8	C	Glory	1.19	Yes	No	7
9	C	Bissell	1.39	No	No	9
10	A	K2R	1.59	Yes	No	18
11	A	Glory	1.19	No	Yes	8
12	A	Bissell	1.39	No	No	15
13	B	K2R	1.19	No	No	4
14	B	Glory	1.39	Yes	No	6
15	B	Bissell	1.59	No	Yes	5
16	C	K2R	1.39	No	No	10
17	C	Glory	1.59	No	No	16
18	C	Bissell	1.19	Yes	Yes	1*

* Highest ranked

This consumer ranked row 18 the highest, thus preferring package design C, the name Bissell, a price of $1.19, a Good Housekeeping seal, and a money-back guarantee.

Now suppose 100 consumers provided their rankings. A statistical program will allow these rankings to be analyzed and a utility function measured for each attribute. Suppose the derived utility functions are those shown in the following illustration.

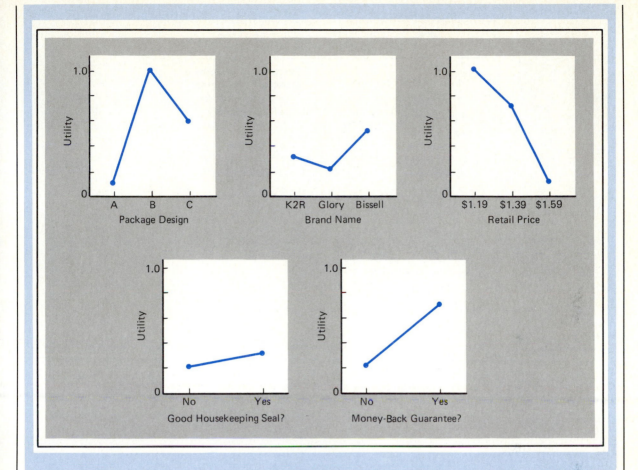

Results of Computer Analysis of Experimental Data

From these utility functions, we can derive a number of conclusions. Package B is the most favored, followed by C and then A; in fact, A has hardly any utility. The preferred names are Bissell, K2R, and Glory, in that order. The consumer's utility varies inversely with price. A Good Housekeeping seal is preferred, but it does not add that much utility and may not be worth the bother of obtaining it. A money-back guarantee is strongly preferred. Putting these results together, we can see that the most desirable offer would be package design B, with the brand name Bissell, selling at the price of $1.19, with a Good Housekeeping seal and a money-back guarantee. Thus we see how conjoint measurement can help the new-product researcher develop and test the attractiveness of alternative product concepts.

Trade-Off Analysis

An alternative technique is called *trade-off analysis*. In trade-off analysis consumers are asked to indicate their preferences for attributes levels, with two attributes taken at a time. The table on the next page shows how a consumer filled in six trade-off matrices:

ONE RESPONDENT'S TRADE-OFF DATA
(RANK ORDERS OF PREFERENCE)

	Top speed			Seating capacity			Months of warranty		
	130	100	70	2	4	6	60	12	3
Price									
$2,500	1	2	5	2	1	3	1	3	4
$4,000	3	4	6	5	4	6	2	5	6
$6,000	7	8	9	8	7	9	7	8	9
Top speed									
130 MPH				2	1	3	1	2	5
100 MPH				5	4	6	3	4	6
70 MPH				8	7	9	7	8	9
Seating capacity									
2							2	5	8
4							1	4	7
6							3	6	9

Look at the upper left matrix, which shows three car prices and three top car speeds. The consumer placed a *1* in the most preferred cell; here it is for a car priced at $2,500 with a top speed of 130 miles. The consumer placed a *2* in the next preferred cell, showing that he would prefer to pay $2,500 and give up some top speed. The consumer placed the remaining numbers, each time showing the trade-off he would make. The other matrices were similarly filled in by the consumer. By collecting the numbers from many consumers, the researcher can derive the utility functions for each attribute: price, top speed, seating capacity, and months of warranty. These utility functions will help the researcher figure out the most ideal car to design.

Sources: The conjoint measurement example was taken from Paul E. Green and Yoram Wind, "New Ways to Measure Consumers' Judgments," Harvard Business Review (July-August, 1975), pp. 107–17. Copyright © 1975 by the President and Fellows of Harvard College; all rights reserved. The trade-off example was taken from Richard M. Johnson, "Trade-off Analysis of Consumer Values," Journal of Marketing Research, May 1974, pp. 121–27. For technical details on these techniques, see Paul E. Green and Donald S. Tull, Research for Marketing Decisions, *4th ed., (Englewood Cliffs, N.J.: Prentice-Hall, 1978), chap. 14.*

BUSINESS ANALYSIS

Once management develops the product concept and a marketing strategy, it can evaluate the business attractiveness of the proposal. Management must review the sales, cost, and profit projections to determine whether they satisfy the company's objectives. If they do, the product concept can move to the product-development stage. As new information comes in, there will be further revision of the business analysis.

Estimating Sales

Management needs to estimate whether sales will be high enough to return a satisfactory profit to the firm. Management should examine the sales history of similar products and should survey market opinion. Management should prepare estimates of minimum and maximum sales to learn the range of risk.

Sales-estimation methods depend upon whether they deal with a one-time purchase product, an infrequently purchased product, or a frequently purchased product. Figure 10–5(a) illustrates the product life-cycle sales that can be expected for one-time purchased products. Sales rise at the beginning, peak, and later approach zero as the number of potential buyers is exhausted. If new buyers keep entering the market, the curve will not go down to zero.

Infrequently purchased products, such as automobiles, toasters, and industrial equipment, exhibit replacement cycles, dictated either by their physical wearing out or their obsolescence associated with changing styles, features, and tastes. Sales forecasting for this product category calls for separately estimating first-time sales and replacement sales. [See Figure 10–5(b).]

Frequently purchased products, such as consumer and industrial nondurables, have product life-cycle sales resembling Figure 10–5(c). The number of first-time buyers initially increases and then decreases as fewer are left (assuming a fixed population). Repeat purchases occur soon, providing that the product satisfies some fraction of people who become steady customers. The sales curve eventually falls to a plateau representing a level of steady repeat-purchase volume; by this time the product is no longer in the class of new products.

Estimating first-time sales. The first task, regardless of the type of product, is to estimate first-time purchases of the new product in each period. Three examples of methods for estimating first-time purchases are shown in Exhibit 10–3.

FIGURE 10–5
Product Life-Cycle Sales for Three Types of Products

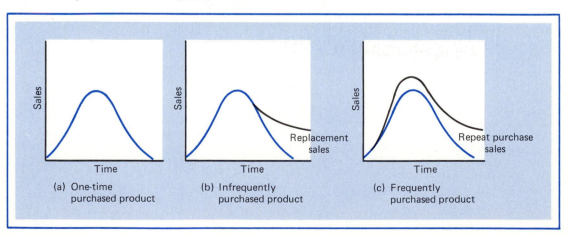

(a) One-time purchased product

(b) Infrequently purchased product

(c) Frequently purchased product

Exhibit 10-3

ESTIMATING FIRST-TIME PURCHASES OF NEW PRODUCTS— THREE EXAMPLES

Medical equipment. A medical-equipment manufacturer developed a new instrument for analyzing blood specimens. The company identified three market segments—hospitals, clinics, and unaffiliated laboratories. For each segment, management defined the minimum-size facility that would buy this instrument. Then it estimated the number of facilities in each segment. It reduced the number by the estimated purchase probability, which varied from segment to segment. It then summed the remaining number of potential customers and called this the *market potential*. *Market penetration* was then estimated, based on the planned advertising and personal selling per period, the rate of favorable word of mouth, the price of the machine, and the activity of competitors. These two estimates were multiplied to estimate new-product sales.

Room air conditioners. Models of epidemics (sometimes called contagion models) provide a useful analogy to the new-product diffusion process. Bass has used an epidemic equation to forecast sales of appliances when they were first introduced, including room air conditioners, refrigerators, home freezers, black-and-white television, and power lawn mowers.* He used sales data for the first few years of product introduction to estimate sales for the subsequent years, until replacement demand became a major factor. His sales projection for room air conditioners fit the pattern of actual sales with a coefficient of determination, $R^2 = 0.92$. The predicted time of peak was 8.6 years as against an actual time of peak of 7.0 years. The predicted magnitude of peak was 1.9 million as against an actual peak of 1.8 million.

Consumer nondurables. Fourt and Woodlock developed a first-time sales model that they tested with several new consumer-nondurable products.† Their observation of new-product market-penetration rates showed that (1) cumulative sales approached a limiting penetration level of less than 100 percent of all households and (2) the successive increments of gain declined. Their equation is

$$q_t = r\bar{q}(1 - r)^{t-1} \qquad (10\text{--}1)$$

where:

q_t = percentage of total U.S. households expected to try the product in period t
r = rate of penetration of untapped potential
$\bar{q}$ = percentage of total U.S. households expected to eventually try the new product
t = time period

Assume that it is estimated that 40 percent of all households will eventually try a new product ($\bar{q} = 0.4$). Furthermore, in each period 30 percent of the remaining new-buyer potential is penetrated ($r = 0.3$) The percentages of U.S. households trying the product in the first four periods are:

$q_1 = r\bar{q}(1 - r)^{1-1} = (0.3)(0.4)(0.7^0) = 0.120$
$q_2 = r\bar{q}(1 - r)^{2-1} = (0.3)(0.4)(0.7^1) = 0.084$
$q_3 = r\bar{q}(1 - r)^{3-1} = (0.3)(0.4)(0.7^2) = 0.059$
$q_4 = r\bar{q}(1 - r)^{4-1} = (0.3)(0.4)(0.7^3) = 0.041$

As time moves on, the incremental trial percentage moves toward zero. To estimate dollar sales from new buyers in any period, the estimated trial rate for any period is multiplied by the total number of U.S. households times the expected first-purchase expenditure per household of the product.

* Frank M. Bass, "A New Product Growth Model for Consumer Durables," *Management Science*, January 1969, pp. 215–17.
† Louis A. Fourt and Joseph N. Woodlock, "Early Prediction of Market Success for New Grocery Products," *Journal of Marketing*, October 1960, pp. 31–38.

Estimating replacement sales. To estimate replacement sales, management has to research the *survival-age distribution* of its product. The low end of the distribution indicates when the first replacement sales will take place. The actual timing of replacement will be influenced by the customer's economic outlook, cash flow, and product alternatives as well as the company's prices, financing terms, and sales effort. Since replacement sales are difficult to estimate before the product is in actual use, some manufacturers rest the case for launching the new product solely on their estimate of first-time sales.

Estimating repeat sales. For a frequently purchased new product, the seller has to estimate repeat sales as well as first-time sales. That is because the unit value of frequently purchased products is low, and repeat purchases take place soon after the introduction. A high rate of repeat purchasing means that customers are satisfied; sales are likely to stay high even after all first-time purchases take place. The seller should note the percentage of repeat purchases that take place in each *repeat-purchase class*: those who buy once, twice, three times, and so on. Some products and brands are bought a few times and dropped. It is important to estimate whether the repeat-purchase ratio is likely to rise or fall, and at what rate, with deeper repeat-purchase classes.[17]

Estimating Costs and Profits

After preparing the sales forecast, management can estimate the expected costs and profits of this venture. The costs are estimated by the R&D, manufacturing, marketing and finance departments. Table 10–4 illustrates a five-year projection of sales, costs, and profits for the instant breakfast drink product.

Row 1 shows the projected sales revenue over the five-year period. The company expects to sell $11,889,000 (approximately 500,000 cases at $24 per case) in the first year. Sales are expected to rise around 28 percent in each of the next two years, increase by 47 percent in the fourth year, and then slow down to 15 percent growth in the fifth year. Behind this sales projection is a set of assumptions about the rate of market growth, the company's market share, and the factory-realized price.

[17] See Robert Blattberg and John Golanty, "Tracker: An Early Test Market Forecasting and Diagnostic Model for New Product Planning," *Journal of Marketing Research*, May 1978, pp. 192–202.

TABLE 10–4

PROJECTED FIVE-YEAR CASH-FLOW STATEMENT (IN THOUSANDS OF DOLLARS)						
	Year 0	Year 1	Year 2	Year 3	Year 4	Year 5
1. Sales revenue	0	11,889	15,381	19,654	28,253	32,491
2. Cost of goods sold	0	3,981	5,150	6,581	9,461	10,880
3. Gross margin	0	7,908	10,231	13,073	18,792	21,611
4. Development costs	−3,500	0	0	0	0	0
5. Marketing costs	0	8,000	6,460	8,255	11,866	13,646
6. Allocated overhead	0	1,189	1,538	1,965	2,825	3,249
7. Gross contribution	−3,500	−1,281	2,233	2,853	4,101	4,716
8. Supplementary contribution	0	0	0	0	0	0
9. Net contribution	−3,500	−1,281	2,233	2,853	4,101	4,716
10. Discounted contribution (15%)	−3,500	−1,113	1,691	1,877	2,343	2,346
11. Cumulative discounted cash flow	−3,500	−4,614	−2,922	−1,045	1,298	3,644

Row 2 shows the *cost of goods sold*, which hovers around 33 percent of sales revenue. This cost is found by estimating the average cost of labor, ingredients, and packaging per case.

Row 3 shows the expected *gross margin*, which is the difference between sales revenue and cost of goods sold.

Row 4 shows anticipated *development costs* of $3.5 million. The development costs are made up of three components. The first is the *product-development cost* of researching, developing, and testing the physical product. The second is the *marketing research costs* of fine tuning the marketing program and assessing the market's likely response. It covers the estimated costs of package testing, in-home placement testing, name testing, and test marketing. The third is the *manufacturing-development costs* of new equipment, new or renovated plant, and inventory investment.

Row 5 shows the estimated *marketing costs* over the five-year period to cover advertising, sales promotion, and marketing research and an amount allocated for sales-force coverage and marketing administration. In the first year, marketing costs stand at 67 percent of sales and by the fifth year are estimated to run at 42 percent of sales.

Row 6 shows the *allocated overhead* to this new product to cover its share of the cost of executive salaries, heat, light, and so on.

Row 7, the *gross contribution*, is found by subtracting the preceding three costs from the gross margin. Years 0 and 1 involve losses, and thereafter the gross contribution becomes positive and is expected to run as high as 15 percent of sales by the fifth year.

Row 8, *supplementary contribution*, is used to list any change in income from other company products caused by the introduction of the new product. It has two components. *Dragalong income* is additional income on other company products resulting from adding this product to the line. *Cannibalized income* is the reduced income on other company products resulting from adding this product to the line.[18]

Row 9 shows the *net contribution*, which in this case is the same as the gross contribution.

Row 10 shows the *discounted contribution*, namely the present value of each future contribution discounted at 15 percent per annum. For example, the company will not receive $4,716,000 until the fifth year, which means that it is worth only $2,346,000 today if the company can earn 15 percent on its money.[19]

Finally, row 11 shows the *cumulative discounted cash flow*, which is the cumulation of the annual contributions in row 10. This cash flow is the key series on which management bases its decision on whether to go forward into product development or drop the project. Two things are of central interest. The first is the *maximum investment exposure*, which is the highest loss that the project can create. We see that the company will be in the hole for a maximum of $4,614,000 in year 1; this will be the company's loss if it terminates the project. The second is the *payback period*, which is the time when the company recovers all of its investment including the built-in return of 15 percent. The payback period here is approximately three and a half years. Management therefore has to decide whether it can expose itself to a maximum investment loss of $4.6 million and wait three and a half years for payback.[20]

PRODUCT DEVELOPMENT

If the product concept passes the business test, it moves to R&D and/or engineering to be developed into a physical product. Up to now it has existed only as a word description, a drawing, or a very crude mock-up. This step calls for a large jump in investment, which dwarfs the idea-evaluation costs incurred in the earlier stages. This stage will answer whether the product idea can be translated into a technically and commercially feasible product. If not, the company's accumulated investment will be lost except for any useful information gained in the process.

The R&D department will develop one or more physical versions of the product concept. It hopes to find a prototype that satisfies the following criteria: (1) Consumers see it as embodying the key attributes described in the product-concept statement;

---

[18] See Roger A. Kerin, Michael G. Harvey and James T. Rothe, "Cannibalism and New Product Development," *Business Horizons*, October 1978, pp. 25–31.

[19] The *present value* (V) of a future sum (I) to be received t years from today and discounted at the interest rate (r) is given by $V = I_t /(1 + r)^t$. Thus $\$4,716/(1.15)^5 = \$2,346$.

[20] Companies use other financial measures to evaluate the merit of a new-product proposal. The simplest is *break-even analysis*, where management estimates how many cases of the product the company would have to sell to break even with the given price and cost structure. If management believes that the company can sell at least the break-even number of cases; then it would normally move the project into product development. The most complex method is *risk analysis*. Here three estimates (optimistic, pessimistic, and most likely) are obtained for each uncertain variable affecting profitability under an assumed marketing environment and marketing strategy for the planning period. The computer simulates possible outcomes and computes a rate-of-return probability distribution, showing the range of possible rates of returns and their probabilities. See David B. Hertz, "Risk Analysis in Capital Investment," *Harvard Business Review*, January-February 1964, pp. 96–106.

(2) the prototype performs safely under normal use and conditions; (3) the prototype can be produced for the budgeted manufacturing costs.

Developing a successful prototype can take days, weeks, months, or even years. Designing a new commercial aircraft, for example, will take several years of development work. Even developing a new taste formula can take time. For example, the Maxwell House Division of General Foods discovered that consumers wanted a brand of coffee that was "bold, vigorous, deep tasting."[21] Its laboratory technicians spent over four months working with various coffee blends and flavors to formulate a corresponding taste. It turned out to be too expensive to produce, and the company "cost reduced" the blend to meet the target manufacturing cost. This compromised the taste, however, and the new coffee brand did not do well in the market.

The lab scientists must not only design the required functional characteristics but also know how to communicate the psychological aspects through *physical cues*. This requires knowing how consumers react to different colors, sizes, weights, and other physical cues. In the case of a mouthwash, a yellow color supports an "antiseptic" claim (Listerine), a red color supports a "refreshing" claim (Lavoris), and a green color supports a "cool" claim (Micrin). Or to support the claim that a lawnmower is powerful, the lab people have to design a heavy frame and a fairly noisy engine. Marketers need to work with lab people to fill them in on how consumers judge product qualities they are seeking.

When the prototypes are ready, they must be put through rigorous functional and consumer tests. The *functional tests* are conducted under laboratory and field conditions to make sure that the product performs safely and effectively. The new aircraft must fly; the new snack food must be shelf stable; the new drug must not create dangerous side effects. Functional product testing of new drugs now takes years of laboratory work with animal subjects and then human subjects before they obtain Federal Drug Administration approval. In the case of equipment testing, consider the Bissell Company's experience testing a combination electric vacuum and floor scrubber:

> . . . four were left with the research and development department for continued tests on such things as water lift, motor lift, effectiveness in cleaning, and dust bag design. The other eight were sent to the company's advertising agency for tests by a panel of fifty housewives. The research and development department found some serious problems in their further tests of the product. The life of the motor was not sufficiently long, the filter bag did not fit properly, and the scrubber foot was not correct. Similarly, the consumer tests brought in many consumer dissatisfactions that had not been anticipated; the unit was too heavy, the vacuum did not glide easily enough, and the scrubber left some residue on the floor after use.[22]

Consumer testing can take a variety of forms, from bringing consumers into a lab to test the product versions to giving them samples to use in their homes. *In-home product-placement tests* are common with products ranging from ice cream flavors to new appliances. When Du Pont developed its new synthetic carpeting, it

---

[21] See "Maxwell House Division (A)" (Boston: Intercollegiate Case Clearing House, ICH 13M83, 1970).

[22] Ralph Westfall and Harper W. Boyd, Jr., *Cases in Marketing Management* (Homewood, Ill.: Richard D. Irwin, 1961), p. 365.

Exhibit 10-4

METHODS FOR MEASURING CONSUMER PREFERENCES

Suppose a consumer is shown three items—A, B, and C. They might be three automobiles or advertisements or names of political candidates. There are three methods—simple rank ordering, paired comparison, and monadic rating—for measuring an individual's preferences for these items.

The *simple rank order* method asks the consumer to rank the three items in order of preference. The consumer might respond with $A > B > C$. This method does not reveal how intensely the consumer feels about each item. He may not like any one of them very much. Nor does it indicate how much he prefers one object to another. Also, this method is difficult to use when the set of objects is large.

The *paired comparison* method calls for presenting a set of items to the consumer, two at a time, asking which one is preferred in each pair. Thus the consumer could be presented with the pairs, AB, AC, and BC and say that he or she prefers A to B, A to C, and B to C. Then we could conclude that $A > B > C$. Paired comparisons offer two major advantages. First people find it easy to state their preference between items taken two at a time. The second advantage is that the paired comparison method allows the consumer to concentrate intensely on the two items, noting their differences and similarities.

The *monadic rating* method asks the consumer to rate his or her liking of each product on a scale. Suppose the following seven-point scale is used:

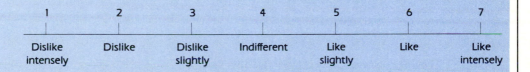

1	2	3	4	5	6	7
Dislike intensely	Dislike	Dislike slightly	Indifferent	Like slightly	Like	Like intensely

Suppose the consumer returns the following ratings: $A = 6$, $B = 5$, $C = 3$. This yields more information than the previous methods. We can derive the individual's preference order (i.e., $A > B > C$) and even know the qualitative levels of his preference for each and the rough distance between preferences. This method is also easy for respondents to use, especially when there is a large set of objects to evaluate.

installed free carpeting in several homes in exchange for the homeowners' willingness to report their likes and dislikes about the new carpeting in relation to conventional carpeting. Consumer-preference testing draws on a variety of techniques, such as simple ranking, paired comparisons, and rating scales, each with its own advantages and biases (see Exhibit 10–4).

MARKET TESTING

After management is satisfied with the product's functional performance, the product is ready to be dressed up with a brand name, packaging, and a preliminary marketing program, to test it in more authentic consumer settings. (Branding and packaging decisions are discussed in Chapter 15.) The purpose of market testing is to learn how consumers and dealers react to handling, using, and repurchasing the actual product and how large the market is.

Not all companies choose the route of market testing. A company officer of Revlon, Inc., stated:

> In our field—primarily higher-priced cosmetics not geared for mass distribution—it would be unnecessary for us to market test. When we develop a new product, say an improved liquid makeup, we know it's going to sell because we're familiar with the field. And we've got 1,500 demonstrators in department stores to promote it.[23]

Most companies, however, know market testing can yield valuable information about buyers, dealers, marketing program effectiveness, market potential, and other matters. The main issues are, How much market testing and what kind?

The amount of market testing is influenced by the *investment cost and risk* on the one hand, and the *time pressure* and *research cost* on the other. High investment/risk products deserve to be market tested so as not to make a mistake; the cost of the market tests will be an insignificant percentage of the cost of the project itself. High-risk products—those that create new-product categories (first instant breakfast) or have novel features (first fluoride toothpaste)—warrant more market testing than modified products (another toothpaste brand). But the amount of market testing may be severely limited if the company is under great pressure to introduce its brand because the season is just starting, or competitors are about to launch their brands. The company may prefer the risk of a product failure to the risk of losing distribution or market penetration on a highly successful product. The cost of market testing will also affect how much is done and what kind.

Market-testing methods differ in the testing of consumer versus industrial products.

Consumer-Goods Market Testing

In testing consumers, the company wants to estimate the main determinants of sales, namely, *trial*, *first repeat*, *adoption*, and *purchase frequency*. The company hopes to find all of these at high levels. In some cases, it will find many consumers trying the product but not rebuying it, showing a lack of product satisfaction. Or it might find high first-time repurchase but then a rapid wear-out effect. Or it might find high permanent adoption but low frequency of purchase (with gourmet frozen foods) because the buyers use the product only on special occasions.

In testing the trade, the company wants to learn how many and what types of dealers will handle the product, under what terms, and with what shelf-position commitments.

---

[23] "Product Tryouts: Sales Tests in Selected Cities Help Trim Risks of National Marketings," *Wall Street Journal*, August 10, 1962, p. 1.

The major methods of consumer-goods market testing, from the least to the most costly, are described in the following paragraphs.[24]

Sales-wave research.

Sales-wave research is an extension of the ordinary home-use testing in which consumers who initially try the product at no cost are reoffered the product, or a competitor's products, at slightly reduced prices. They may be reoffered the product as many as three to five times (sales waves), the company noting how many consumers selected that company's product again and their reported level of satisfaction. Sales-wave research can also include exposing consumers to one or more advertising concepts in rough form to see what impact the advertising has on repeat purchase.

Sales-wave research enables the company to estimate the repeat-purchase rate under conditions where consumers spend their own money and choose among competing brands. The company can also gauge the impact of alternative advertising concepts on producing repeat purchases. Finally, sales-wave research can be implemented quickly, conducted under relative competitive security, and carried out without needing to develop final packaging and advertising.

On the other hand, sales-wave research does not indicate the trial rates that would be achieved with different sales promotion incentives, since the consumers are preselected to try the product. Nor does it indicate the brand's power to gain distribution and favorable shelf position from the trade.

Simulated store technique.

The simulated store technique (also called "laboratory test markets," "purchase laboratories," or "accelerated test marketing") calls for finding thirty to forty shoppers (at a shopping center or elsewhere) and inviting them to a brief screening of some television commercials. Included are a number of well-known commercials and some new ones, and they cover a range of products. One commercial advertises the new product, but it is not singled out for attention. The consumers are given a small amount of money and invited into a store where they may use the money to buy any items or keep the money. The company notes how many consumers buy the new product and competing brands. This provides a measure of trial of the commercial's effectiveness against competing commercials. The consumers reconvene and are asked the reasons for their purchases or nonpurchases. Some weeks later they are reinterviewed by phone to determine product attitudes, usage, satisfaction, and repurchase intention and are offered an opportunity to repurchase any products.

This method has several advantages, including the measuring of trial rates (and repeat rates if extended), advertising effectiveness, speedy results, and competitive security. The results are usually incorporated into mathematical models to project ultimate sales levels. Marketing research firms that offer this service report surprisingly

---

[24] See Edward M. Tauber, "Forecasting Sales Prior to Test Market," *Journal of Marketing*, January 1977, pp. 80–84.

accurate prediction of sales levels of products that are subsequently launched in the market.[25]

Controlled test marketing.   Several research firms have arranged a controlled panel of stores that have agreed to carry new products for a certain fee. The company with the new product specifies the number of stores and geographical locations it wants. The research firm delivers the product to the participating stores and controls shelf location, number of facings, displays and point-of-purchase promotions, and pricing, according to prespecified plans. Sales results can be audited both from shelf movement and from consumer diaries. The company can also test small-scale advertising in local newspapers during the test.

Controlled testing (also called "minimarket testing") allows the company to test the impact of in-store factors and limited advertising on consumers' buying behavior without involving consumers directly. A sample of consumers can be interviewed later to gather their impressions of the product. The company does not have to use its own sales force, give trade allowances, or take the time to buy into distribution. On the other hand, controlled test marketing does not provide experience in trying to sell the trade on carrying the new product. This technique also exposes the product to competitors.

Test markets.   Test markets are the ultimate way to test a new consumer product in a situation resembling the one that would be faced in a full-scale launching of the product. The company usually works with an outside research firm to locate a small number of representative test cities in which the company's sales force will try to sell the trade on carrying the product and giving it good shelf exposure. The company will put on a full advertising and promotion campaign in these markets similar to the one that would be used in national marketing. It is a chance to do a dress rehearsal of the total plan. Test marketing can cost the company several hundred thousand dollars, depending upon the number of cities tested, the duration of the test, and the amount of data the company wants to collect. Exhibit 10–5 shows the major decisions called for in test marketing.

Test marketing can yield several benefits. Its primary benefit is to yield *a more reliable forecast of future sales*. If product sales fall below target levels in the test market, the company will drop or modify the product.

A second benefit is the *pretesting alternative marketing plans*. Some years ago Colgate-Palmolive used a different marketing mix in each of four cities to market a new soap product. The four approaches were (1) an average amount of advertising coupled with free samples distributed door to door, (2) heavy advertising plus samples, (3) an average amount of advertising linked with mailed redeemable coupons, and (4) an average amount of advertising with no special introductory offer. The third alternative generated the best profit level.

Through test marketing, the company may discover a product fault that escaped

---

[25] The best-known systems are Yankelovich's "Laboratory Test Market," Elrick and Lavidge's "Comp," and Management Decision Systems's "Assessor." For a description of "Assessor," see Alvin J. Silk and Glen L. Urban, "Pre-Test Marketing Evaluation of New Packaged Goods: A Model and Measurement Methodology," *Journal of Marketing Research*, May 1978, pp. 171–91.

Exhibit 10-5

DECISIONS FACING MANAGEMENT IN SETTING UP TEST MARKETS

1. **How many test cities**? Most tests use between two and six cities, with an average of four. A larger number of cities should be used, (1) the greater the maximum possible loss and/or the probability of loss from going national, (2) the greater the number of contending/marketing strategies and/or the greater the uncertainty surrounding which is best, (3) the greater the regional differences, and (4) the greater the chance of calculated test-market interference by competitors.

2. **Which cities**? No city is a perfect microcosm of the nation as a whole. Some cities, however, typify aggregate national or regional characteristics better than other, such as Syracuse, Dayton, Peoria, and Des Moines. Each company develops its own test-city selection criteria. One company looks for test cities that have diversified industry, good media coverage, cooperative chain stores, average competitive activity, and no evidence of being overtested. Additional test-city selection criteria may be introduced because of the special characteristics of the product. Patio Foods, in testing a new line of frozen Mexican dinners, selected cities according to the incidence of travel to Mexico, the existence of a Spanish-language press, and good retail sales of prepared chili and frozen Chinese food.

3. **Length of test**? Test markets last anywhere from a few months to several years. The longer the product's *average repurchase period*, the longer the test period necessary to observe repeat-purchase rates. On the other hand, the period should be cut down if competitors are rushing to the market.

4. **What information**? Management must decide on the type of information to collect in relation to its value and cost. *Warehouse shipment data* will show gross inventory buying but will not indicate weekly sales at retail. *Store audits* will show actual retail sales and competitors' market shares but will not reveal the characteristics of the buyers of the different brands. *Consumer panels* will indicate which people are buying which brands and their loyalty and switching rates. *Buyer surveys* will yield in-depth information about consumer attitudes, usage, and satisfaction. Among other things that can be researched are trade attitudes, retail distribution, and the effectiveness of advertising, promotion, and point-of-sale material.

5. **What action to take**? If the test markets show a high trial and high repurchase rate, this indicates a GO-decision. If the test markets show a high trial and a low repurchase rate, the customers are not satisfied, and the product should be redesigned or dropped. If the test markets show a low trial and a high repurchase rate, the product is satisfying, but more people have to try it: This means increasing advertising and sales promotion. Finally, if the trial and repurchase rates are both low, then the product should be dropped.

its attention in the product-development stage. It may pick up valuable clues to distribution-level problems. And the company may gain better insight into the behavior of different market segments.

In spite of the benefits of test marketing, some experts question its value. Achenbaum lists the following concerns:

- ☐ There is the problem of obtaining a set of markets that is reasonably representative of the country as a whole.
- ☐ There is the problem of translating national media plans into local equivalents.
- ☐ There is the problem of estimating what is going to happen next year based on what has happened in this year's competitive environment.
- ☐ There is the problem of competitive knowledge of your test and of deciding whether any local counteractivities are representative of what competition will do nationally at a later date.
- ☐ There is the problem of extraneous and uncontrollable factors such as economic conditions and weather.[26]

Achenbaum contends that test marketing's main value lies not in sales forecasting but in learning about unsuspected problems and opportunities connected with the new product. He points to the large number of products that failed after successful test-market results. Some large companies are skipping the test-marketing stage and relying on the earlier market-testing methods.[27]

Industrial-Goods Market Testing

New industrial goods typically undergo extensive *product testing* in the labs to measure performance, reliability, design, and operating cost. Following satisfactory results, many companies will commercialize the product by listing it in the catalog and turning it over to the sales force. Today, however, an increasing number of companies are turning to *market testing* as an intermediate step. Market testing can indicate: the product's performance under actual operating conditions; the key buying influences; how different buying influences react to alternative prices and sales approaches; the market potential; and the best market segments.

Test marketing is not typically used in the case of industrial products. It is too expensive to produce a sample of Concordes or new computers, let alone put them up for sale in a select market to see how well they sell. Industrial buyers won't buy durable goods without assurances of service and parts. Furthermore, marketing research firms have not built the test-market systems that are found in consumer markets. Therefore, industrial-goods manufacturers have to use other methods to research the market's interest in a new industrial product.

The most common method is a *product-use test*, similar to the in-home use test for consumer products.[28] The manufacturer selects some potential customers, who agree to use the new product for a limited period. The manufacturer's technical people observe how these customers use the product, a practice that often exposes unanticipated problems of safety and servicing and clues the manufacturer about

---

[26] Alvin A. Achenbaum, "The Purpose of Test Marketing," in *The Marketing Concept in Action*, ed. Robert M. Kaplan (Chicago: American Marketing Association, 1964), p. 582.

[27] For further discussion, see N. D. Cadbury, "When, Where and How to Test Market," *Harvard Business Review*, May-June 1975, pp. 96–105; and Jay E. Klompmaker, G. David Hughes, and Russell I. Haley, "Test Marketing in New Product Development," *Harvard Business Review*, May-June 1976, pp. 128–38.

[28] The discussion of this and other methods draws heavily on Morgan B. MacDonald, Jr., *Appraising the Market for New Industrial Products* (New York: Conference Board, 1967), chap. 2.

customer training and servicing requirements. After the test, the customer is asked to express purchase intent and other reactions.

A second common market-test method is to introduce the new industrial product at *trade shows*. Trade shows draw a large number of buyers, who view new products in a few concentrated days. The manufacturer can see how much interest buyers show in the new product, how they react to various features and terms, and how many express purchase intentions or place orders. The disadvantage is that trade shows reveal the product to competitors; therefore the manufacturer should be ready to launch the product at that point.

The new industrial product can also be tested in *distributor and dealer display rooms*, where it may stand next to the manufacturer's other products and possibly competitors' products. This method yields preference and pricing information in the normal selling atmosphere for the product. The disadvantages are that the customers may want to place orders that cannot be filled, and those customers who come in might not be representative of the target market.

Controlled or test marketing has been used by some manufacturers. They produce a limited supply of the product and give it to the sales force to sell in a limited set of geographical areas that will be given promotional support, printed catalogue sheets, and so on. In this way, management can learn what might happen under full-scale marketing and make a more informed decision about launching.

COMMERCIALIZATION

Market testing presumably gives management enough information to make a final decision about whether to launch the new product. If the company goes ahead with commercialization, it will face its largest costs to date. The company will have to build or rent a full-scale manufacturing facility. The size of the plant will be a critical decision variable. The company can build a smaller plant than called for by the sales forecast, to be on the safe side. That is what Quaker Oats did when it launched its 100% Natural breakfast cereal. The demand so exceeded their sales forecast that for about a year they could not supply enough product to the stores. Although they were gratified with the response, the low forecast cost them a considerable amount of lost profits.

Another major cost is marketing. To introduce a major new consumer packaged good into the national market, the company may have to spend between $10 and $50 million in advertising and promotion in the first year. In the introduction of new food products, marketing expenditures typically represent 57 percent of sales during the first year.

When (Timing)

In launching a new product, the company must make four decisions. The first decision is whether it is the right time to introduce the new product. If the new product replaces another product, its introduction might be delayed until the old product's stock is drawn down, through normal sales. If the demand is highly seasonal, the new product should not be introduced until the right season arrives. If the new product could be improved further, the company may prefer to miss the selling season in order to come out with a better product.

Where (Geographical Strategy)

The company must decide whether to launch the new product in a *single locality*, a *region*, *several regions*, the *national market*, or the *international market*. Few companies have the confidence, capital, and capacity to launch new products into full national distribution. They will develop a *planned market rollout* over time. Small companies, in particular, will select an attractive city and put on a blitz campaign to enter the market. They will enter other cities one at a time. Large companies will introduce their product into a whole region and then move to the next region. Companies with national distribution networks, such as auto companies, will launch their new models in the national market unless there are production shortages.

In rollout marketing, the company has to rate the alternative markets for their attractiveness. The candidate markets can be listed as rows, and rollout attractiveness criteria can be listed as columns. The major rating criteria are *market potential*, *company's local reputation*, *cost of filling the pipeline*, *quality of research data in that area*, *influence of area on other areas*, and *competitive penetration*. In this way the company determines the prime markets and develops a geographical rollout plan.

The factor of competitive presence is very important. Suppose McDonald's wants to launch a new chain of fast-food pizza parlors. Suppose Shakey's, a formidable competitor, is strongly entrenched on the East Coast. Another pizza chain is entrenched on the East Coast but is weak. The Midwest is the battleground between two other chains. The South is open, but Shakey's is planning to move in. We can see that McDonald's faces quite a complex decision in choosing a rollout strategy.

To Whom (Target-Market Prospects)

Within the rollout markets, the company must target its distribution and promotion to the best prospect groups. Presumably the company has already profiled the prime prospects on the basis of earlier market testing. Prime prospects for a new consumer product would ideally have the following characteristics: They would be early adopters; they would be heavy users; they would be opinion leaders and would talk favorably about the product; they could be reached at a low cost.[29] Few groups have all of these characteristics. The company can rate the various prospect groups on these characteristics and target to the best prospect group. The aim is to generate high sales as soon as possible to motivate the sales force and attract other new prospects.

How (Introductory Market Strategy)

The company must develop an action plan for introducing the new product into the rollout markets. It must allocate the marketing budget among the marketing-

---

[29] Philip Kotler and Gerald Zaltman, "Targeting Prospects for a New Product," *Journal of Advertising Research*, February 1976, pp. 7–20.

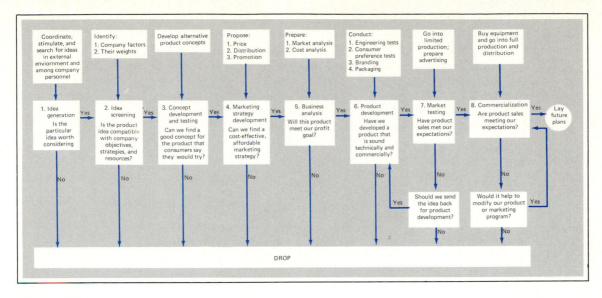

FIGURE 10-6
Summary of the New-Product-Development Decision Process

mix elements and sequence the various activities. Thus a new-car launch might be preceded by a teaser publicity campaign after the car arrives in the showrooms and then by offers of gifts, to draw more people to the showrooms. The company must prepare a separate marketing plan for each new market. To sequence and coordinate the many activities involved in launching a new product, management makes use of various network-planning techniques such as critical path scheduling.

The various steps and decisions in the new-product-development process are summarized in Figure 10–6.

THE CONSUMER-ADOPTION PROCESS

The *consumer-adoption process* begins where the *firm's innovation process* leaves off. It describes how potential customers learn about new products, try them, and adopt or reject them. Management must understand this process in order to build an effective strategy for early market penetration. The *consumer-adoption process* is later followed by the *consumer-loyalty process,* which is the concern of the established producer.

Years ago, new-product marketers used a *mass-market approach* in launching their product. They would distribute the product everywhere and advertise it to everyone on the notion that most people are potential buyers. The *mass-market approach*, however, has two drawbacks: It calls for heavy marketing expenditures, and it involves many wasted exposures to people who are not potential consumers. These drawbacks led to a second approach, *heavy-user target marketing*, where the product is aimed initially at the heavy users. This approach makes sense, provided heavy users are identifiable and among the first to try the new product. But even within the heavy-user group, consumers differ in their interest in new products and brands; many heavy users are quite loyal to their existing brands. Certain heavy users are earlier adopters than others. New-product marketers then decided to aim at those consumers who are likely to be the earlier adopters. *Early-adopter theory* holds that:

- ☐ Persons within a target market differ in the amount of time between their exposure to a new product and their trial of the new product.
- ☐ Early adopters share some traits that differentiate them from late adopters.
- ☐ Efficient media exist for reaching early-adopter types.
- ☐ Early-adopters tend to be opinion leaders and helpful in "advertising" the new product to other potential buyers.

We now turn to the theory of innovation diffusion and consumer adoption, which provides clues to identifying early adopters.

Concepts in Innovation Diffusion and Adoption

An *innovation* refers to any good, service, or idea that is *perceived* by someone as new. The idea may have a long history, but it is an innovation to the person who sees it as new.

Innovations take time to spread through the social system. The *diffusion process* is defined by Rogers as "the spread of a new idea from its source of invention or creation to its ultimate users or adopters."[30] The *adoption process*, on the other hand, focuses on "the mental process through which an individual passes from first hearing about an innovation to final adoption." *Adoption* is the decision of an individual to become a regular user of a product.

We will now examine the main generalizations drawn from hundreds of studies of how people accept new ideas.

Stages in the Adoption Process

Adopters of new products have been observed to move through the following five stages:

- ☐ **Awareness.** The consumer becomes aware of the innovation but lacks information about it.
- ☐ **Interest.** The consumer is stimulated to seek information about the innovation.
- ☐ **Evaluation.** The consumer considers whether it would make sense to try the innovation.
- ☐ **Trial.** The consumer tries the innovation on a small scale to improve his or her estimate of its value.
- ☐ **Adoption.** The consumer decides to make full and regular use of the innovation.

This progression suggests that the new-product marketer should think about how to facilitate consumer movement through these stages. An electric-dishwasher manufacturer might discover that many consumers are stuck in the interest stage;

---

[30] The following discussion leans heavily on Everett M. Rogers, *Diffusion of Innovations* (New York: Free Press, 1962).

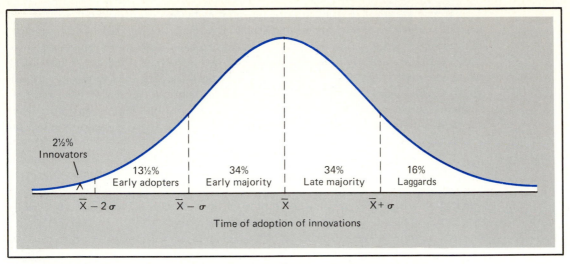

2½%
Innovators

13½%
Early adopters

34%
Early majority

34%
Late majority

16%
Laggards

$\overline{X} - 2\sigma$ $\overline{X} - \sigma$ $\overline{X}$ $\overline{X} + \sigma$

Time of adoption of innovations

Source: Redrawn from Everett M. Rogers, *Diffusion of Innovations* (New York: Free Press, 1962), p. 162.

FIGURE 10-7
Adopter Categorization on the Basis of Relative Time of Adoption of Innovations

they do not move to the trial stage because of their uncertainty and the large investment cost. But these same consumers would be willing to use an electric dishwasher on a trial basis for a small monthly fee. The manufacturer should consider offering a trial-use plan with option to buy.

Individual Difference in Innovativeness

People differ markedly in their readiness to try new products. Rogers defines a person's *innovativeness* as "the degree to which an individual is relatively earlier in adopting new ideas than the other members of his social system." In each product area, there are apt to be "consumption pioneers" and early adopters. Some women are the first to adopt new clothing fashions or new appliances, such as the microwave oven; some doctors are the first to prescribe new medicines;[31] and some farmers are the first to adopt new farming methods.[32]

And other individuals adopt new products much later. People can be classified into the adopter categories shown in Figure 10–7. The adoption process is represented as a normal distribution when plotted over time. After a slow start, an increasing number of people adopt the innovation, the number reaches a peak, and then it diminishes as fewer nonadopters remain. Innovators are defined as the first 2½ percent of the buyers to adopt a new idea; the early adopters are the next 13½ percent who adopt the new idea; and so forth.

[31] See James Coleman, Elihu Katz, and Herbert Menzel, "The Diffusion of an Innovation among Physicians," *Sociometry*, December 1957, pp. 253–70.

[32] See J. Bohlen and G. Beal, *How Farm People Accept New Ideas*, Special Report No. 15 (Ames: Iowa State College Agricultural Extension Service, November 1955).

Rogers sees the five adopter groups as differing in their value orientations. Innovators are *venturesome*; they are willing to try new ideas at some risk. Early adopters are guided by *respect*; they are opinion leaders in their community and adopt new ideas early but carefully. The early majority are *deliberate*; they adopt new ideas before the average person, although they are rarely leaders. The late majority are *skeptical*; they adopt an innovation only after a majority of people have tried it. Finally, laggards are *tradition bound*; they are suspicious of changes, mix with other tradition-bound people, and adopt the innovation only because it has now taken on a measure of tradition itself.

This adopter classification suggests that an innovating firm should research the demographic, psychographic, and media characteristics of innovators and early adopters and direct communications specifically to them. Identifying early adopters is not always easy. No one has demonstrated the existence of a general personality trait called innovativeness. Individuals tend to be innovators in certain areas and laggards in others. We can think of a businessman who dresses conservatively but who delights in trying unfamiliar cuisines. The marketer's challenge is to identify the characteristics of likely early adopters in its product area. For example, studies show that innovative farmers are likely to be better educated and more efficient than noninnovative farmers. Innovative housewives are more gregarious and usually higher in social status than noninnovative housewives. Certain communities tend to have more people who are early adopters. Rogers offered the following hypotheses about early adopters:

> The relatively earlier adopters in a social system tend to be younger in age, have higher social status, a more favorable financial position, more specialized operations, and a different type of mental ability from later adopters. Earlier adopters utilize information sources that are more impersonal and cosmopolite than later adopters and that are in closer contact with the origin of new ideas. Earlier adopters utilize a greater number of different information sources than do later adopters. The social relationships of earlier adopters are more cosmopolite than for later adopters, and earlier adopters have more opinion leadership.[33]

Role of Personal Influence

Personal influence plays a large role in the adoption of new products. Personal influence describes the effect of product statements made by one person on another's attitude or probability of purchase. According to Katz and Lazarsfeld:

> About half of the women in our sample reported that they had recently made some change from a product or brand to which they were accustomed to something new. The fact that one third of these changes involved personal influences indicates that there is also considerable traffic in marketing advice. Women consult each other for opinions about new products, about the quality of different brands, about shopping economies and the like.[34]

---

[33] Rogers, *Diffusion of Innovations*, p. 192.

[34] Elihu Katz and Paul F. Lazarsfeld, *Personal Influence* (New York: Free Press, 1955), p. 234.

Although personal influence is an important factor, its significance is greater in some situations and for some individuals than for others. Personal influence is more important in the evaluation stage of the adoption process than in the other stages. It has more influence on late adopters than early adopters. And it is more important in risky situations than in safe situations.

Influence of Product Characteristics on the Rate of Adoption

The characteristics of the innovation affects its rate of adoption. Some products catch on almost overnight (e.g., frisbees), whereas others take a long time to gain acceptance (e.g., diesel-engine autos). Five characteristics are especially important in influencing the rate of adoption of an innovation. We will consider these characteristics in relation to the rate of adoption of personal computers for home use.

The first is the innovation's *relative advantage*—the degree to which it appears superior to existing products. The greater the perceived relative advantage of using a personal computer, say, in preparing income taxes and keeping financial records, the more quickly personal computers will be adopted.

The second characteristic is the innovation's *compatibility*—the degree to which it matches the values and experiences of the individuals in the community. Personal computers, for example, are highly compatible with the lifestyles found in upper-middle-class homes.

Third is the innovation's *complexity*—the degree to which it is relatively difficult to understand or use. Personal computers are complex and therefore will take a longer time to penetrate U.S. homes.

Fourth is the innovation's *divisibility*—the degree to which it may be tried on a limited basis. The availability of rentals of personal computers with an option to buy increases their rate of adoption.

The fifth characteristic is the innovation's *communicability*—the degree to which the results of its use are observable or describable to others. The fact that personal computers lend themselves to demonstration and description helps them diffuse faster in the social system.

Other characteristics influence the rate of adoption, such as initial costs, ongoing costs, risk and uncertainty, scientific credibility, and social approval. The new-product marketer has to research all these factors and give the key ones maximum attention in designing the new-product and marketing program.

Influence of Organizational Buyers' Characteristics on the Rate of Adoption

Organizations can also be classified as to their readiness to try and adopt a new product. Thus the producer of a new teaching method would want to identify the schools that have a high adoption probability. The producer of a new piece of medical equipment would want to identify hospitals that rank high in adoption probability. Adoption is associated with variables in the organization's environment (community progressiveness, community income), the organization itself (size, profits, pressure to change), and the administrators (education level, age, cosmopoliteness). Once a set of useful indicators are found, they can be used to identify the best target organizations.

SUMMARY

Organizations are increasingly recognizing the necessity and advantages of developing new products and services. Their current offerings face the end of their life spans and must be replaced by newer products.

New products, however, can fail. The risks of innovation are as great as the rewards. The key to successful innovation lies in developing better organizational arrangements for handling new-product ideas and developing sound research and decision procedures at each stage of the new-product-development process.

The new-product-development process consists of eight stages: idea generation, idea screening, concept development and testing, marketing strategy development, business analysis, product development, market testing, and commercialization. The purpose of each stage is to decide whether the idea should be further developed or dropped. The company wants to minimize the chances that poor ideas will move forward and good ideas will be rejected.

With regard to new products, consumers respond at different rates, depending on the consumer's characteristics and the product's characteristics. Manufacturers try to bring their new products to the attention of potential early adopters, particularly those with opinion-leader characteristics.

QUESTIONS

1. Devise a list of questions management should answer prior to developing a new product. Organize the questions according to the following areas: market opportunity, competition, production, patents, distribution, finance.

2. A food company develops a new salad dressing powder that is mixed with water. The company is trying to compete against another company that has a powdered dressing that is mixed with oil and vinegar. Discuss different methods of concept testing this new product.

3. Polaroid, an acknowledged leader in photographic technology, introduced an "instant movie" system, Polavision, with substantial promotional expenditures to retailers and consumers. Polaroid spent $60 million in the first two years after introduction of the product, yet the product never gained wide acceptance. Given Polaroid's previous record of new product successes, how can you explain Polavision's failure?

4. A candy-store chain is seeking ideas for a new sales promotion campaign. Show how morphological analysis might be used to generate a large number of ideas for a campaign.

5. (a) Expected profit and risk are two dimensions for determining whether to introduce a new product nationally. Can you develop a diagram using these two dimensions to show how critical limits might be set up by a firm before a market test to guide its decision after the test? (b) Suppose a firm finds that test-market results are borderline and concludes that the product would probably yield a below-average return. It has sunk a lot of money into the development of the product. Should it introduce the product nationally or drop it? (c) State the two opposing risks that a firm faces when it bases its new-product decision on test-market results. How can it reduce these risks? (d) In the test marketing of Colgate's new soap (described in the text), the third marketing mix yielded the highest sales. Does this mean that it should be adopted when the product is launched nationally?

6. A school-furniture manufacturer wants to develop a line of lightweight chairs for elementary school classrooms. Recommend steps for researching, developing, and testing these chairs.

7. A company president asked the new-product manager what a proposed new product would earn if launched. "Profits of three million dollars in five years." Then the president asked whether the product might fail. "Yes." "What would we lose if the product fails?" "One million dollars." "Forget it," said the president. Do you agree with the president's decision?

Marketing Strategies in Different Stages of the Product Life Cycle

This is one of the saddest days of my life, a sad one for me, for our employees, officers, and directors; indeed, it is sad for the American public. Apparently, there is just not the need for our product in today's scheme of living.

MARTIN ACKERMAN, **president of** *The Saturday Evening Post*

After launching the new product, management prays that the product will enjoy a long and happy life. Although under no illusion that the product will sell forever, management wants to earn a decent profit to cover all the effort and risk that went into it. Management hopes that sales will be high and long lasting. Management is aware that each product will exhibit a life cycle, although the exact shape and duration is not easily known in advance.

During the product's life, the company will need to reformulate the marketing strategy several times in response to changing marketing conditions. Several factors can call for a major overhaul of marketing strategy. We shall look at three major factors in this and the next two chapters:

☐ **Product life cycle stage.** Marketing strategy must be adapted to the product's stage in its life cycle—introduction, growth, maturity, or decline (Chapter 11).

☐ **Company's competitive position in the market.** Marketing strategy must be adapted to the company's position in its market—whether it is a leader, challenger, follower, or nicher (Chapter 12).

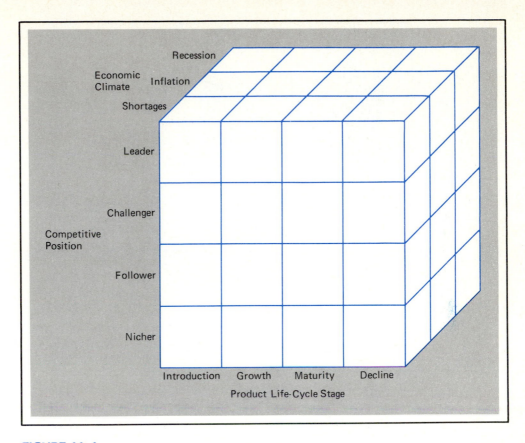

FIGURE 11-1
Marketing Strategy as a Function of Product Life Cycle Stage, Competitive Position, and Economic Climate

□ **The economic climate.** Marketing strategy must be adapted to the economic climate and outlook—whether the economy is in a state of shortages, inflation, or recession (Chapter 13).

These three factors are illustrated in Figure 11–1. Each cell represents the convergence of three conditions, and marketing management must formulate an appropriate strategy for any cell in which it might find itself at the time. In this chapter, we will focus on appropriate marketing strategies as the company's product passes through different stages of its life cycle.

THE CONCEPT OF PRODUCT LIFE CYCLE

A product's sales potential and profitability will change over time. The product life cycle is an attempt to recognize *distinct stages* in the *sales history* of the product. Corresponding to these stages are distinct opportunities and problems with respect

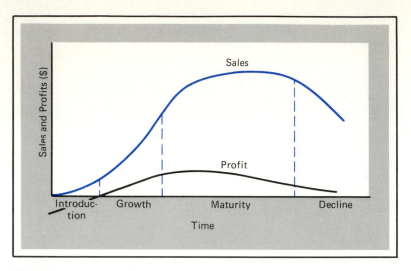

FIGURE 11–2
Sales and Profit Life Cycles

to marketing strategy and profit potential. By identifying the stage that a produ is in, or may be headed toward, companies can formulate better marketing plans. To say that a product has a life cycle is to assert four things:

☐ Products have a limited life.
☐ Product sales pass through distinct stages, each posing different challenges to the seller.
☐ Product profits rise and fall at different stages of the product life cycle.
☐ Products require different marketing, financial, manufacturing, purchasing, and personnel strategies in the different stages of their life cycle.

Major Stages of the S-Shaped Product Life Cycle

Most discussions of product life cycle (PLC) portray the sales history of a typical product as following an S-shaped curve. (See Figure 11–2.) This curve is typically divided into four stages, known as *introduction*, *growth*, *maturity*, and *decline*:[1]

☐ **Introduction:** a period of slow sales growth as the product is introduced in the market. Profits are nonexistent in this stage because of the heavy expenses of product introduction.
☐ **Growth:** a period of rapid market acceptance and substantial profit improvement.

---

[1] Some authors distinguish additional stages. Wasson suggested a stage of *competitive turbulence* between growth and maturity. (See Chester R. Wasson, *Dynamic Competitive Strategy and Product Life Cycles* (Austin, Texas: Austin Press, 1978.) *Maturity* describes a stage of sales growth slowdown and *saturation* a stage of flat sales after sales have peaked. A stage of *petrification* follows decline if sales stabilize at some low but positive level. (See George C. Michael, "Product Petrification: A New Stage in the Life Cycle Theory," *California Management Review*, fall 1971, pp. 88–91.)

☐ **Maturity:** a period of a slowdown in sales growth because the product has achieved acceptance by most of the potential buyers. Profits stabilize or decline because of increased marketing outlays to defend the product against competition.

☐ **Decline:** the period when sales show a strong downward drift and profits erode.

Designating where each stage begins and ends is somewhat arbitrary. Usually the stages are marked where the rates of sales growth or decline become pronounced. Polli and Cook proposed an operational measure based on a normal distribution of percentage changes in real sales from year to year.[2]

Studies by Buzzell[3] of grocery food products and Polli and Cook[4] of consumer nondurables showed that the S-shaped PLC concept holds up well for many product categories. Those planning to use this concept must investigate the extent to which the PLC concept describes product histories in their industry. They should check the normal sequence of stages and the average duration of each stage. Cox found that a typical ethical drug spanned an introductory period of one month, a growth stage of six months, a maturity stage of fifteen months, and a very long decline stage—the last because of manufacturers' reluctance to drop drugs from their catalogs. These stage lengths must be reviewed periodically. Intensifying competition is leading to shortening PLCs over time, which means that products must make their profits in a shorter period.

Product-Category, Product-Form, and Brand Life Cycles

The PLC concept can be used to analyze a product category (cigarettes), a product form (plain filter cigarettes), or a brand (Philip Morris regular nonfilter). (See Figure 11–3.) The PLC concept has a different degree of applicability in each case.

☐ **Product categories** have the longest life cycles. The sales of many product categories stay in the mature stage for an indefinite duration, since they are highly population related. Some major product categories—cigars, newspapers, coffee, movies—seem to have entered the decline stage of the PLC.[5] Meanwhile some others—microcomputers, videocassettes, cordless telephones—are clearly in the introductory or growth stage.

☐ **Product forms** tend to exhibit the standard PLC histories more faithfully than do product categories. Thus manual typewriters went through the stages of introduction, growth, maturity, and decline; now electric typewriters are showing a similar history as electronic typewriters start replacing them.

☐ **Brands** tend to show the shortest PLC history. A Nielsen study found that in the past the life expectancy of a new brand was approximately three years, and the signs were that it was growing shorter.[6] At the same time, some very old brands—such as Arm & Hammer Baking Soda, Ivory Soap, Jell-O—are still going strong.

---

[2] Rolando Polli and Victor Cook, "Validity of the Product Life Cycle," *Journal of Business*, October 1969, pp. 385–400.

[3] Robert D. Buzzell, "Competitive Behavior and Product Life Cycles," in *New Ideas for Successful Marketing*, ed. John S. Wright and Jac L. Goldstucker (Chicago: American Marketing Association, 1966), pp. 46–68.

[4] Polli and Cook, "Product Life Cycle."

[5] For some prescriptions, see Richard G. Hamermesh and Steven B. Silk, "How to Compete in Stagnant Industries," *Harvard Business Review*, September-October 1979, pp. 161–68.

[6] *The Nielsen Researcher*, no. 1, (Chicago: A. G. Nielsen Co., 1968).

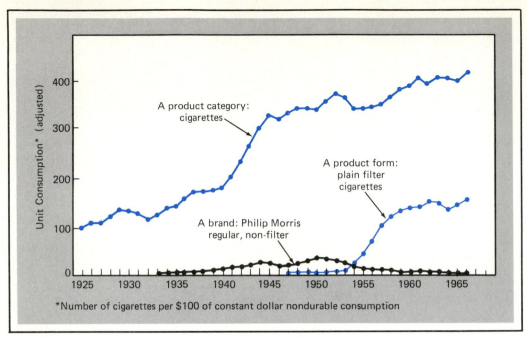

*Number of cigarettes per $100 of constant dollar nondurable consumption

Source: Rolando Polli and Victor Cook, "Validity of the Product Life Cycle," *Journal of Business*, October 1969, p. 389. The University of Chicago Press. Copyright © 1969 by The University of Chicago Press.

FIGURE 11–3
PLCs for a Product Category, Product Form, and Brand

Other Shapes of the Product Life Cycle

Not all products exhibit an S-shaped product life cycle. Cox studied the sales histories of 754 ethical-drug products and found six different product life-cycle patterns.[7] A typical form is a "cycle-recycle" pattern, with the recycle normally having a smaller magnitude and duration than the primary cycle. [See Figure 11–4(a).] The second "hump" in sales is caused by a promotional push in the decline stage.[8] Another common pattern is "scalloped" [Figure 11–4(b)], consisting of a succession of life cycles based on the discovery of new-product characteristics, uses, or users. Nylon's sales, for example, show a scalloped pattern because of the many new uses—parachutes, hosiery, shirts, carpeting—discovered over time.[9] Swan and Rink found eleven different PLC patterns and argue that the key challenge for the marketer is to forecast correctly the PLC pattern that applies to the company's product.[10] Wind also identified eleven

---

[7] William E. Cox, Jr., "Product Life Cycles as Marketing Models," *Journal of Business*, October 1967, pp. 375–84.

[8] This cycle-recycle pattern is also descriptive of many consumer packaged goods. See *The Nielsen Researcher*.

[9] Jordan P. Yale, "The Strategy of Nylon's Growth," *Modern Textiles Magazine*, February 1964, pp. 32 ff. Also see Theodore Levitt, "Exploit the Product Life Cycle," *Harvard Business Review*, November-December 1965, pp. 81–94.

[10] See John E. Swan and David R. Rink, "Fitting Market Strategy to Varying Product Life Cycles," *Business Horizons*, January-February 1982, pp. 72–76.

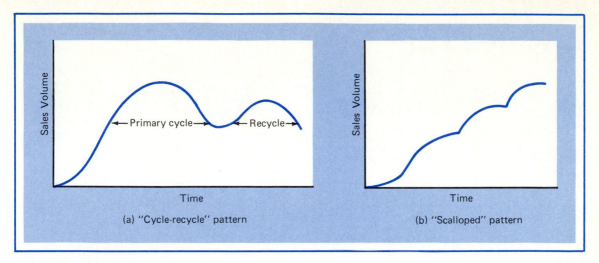

FIGURE 11-4
Some Anomalous Product Life Cycle Patterns

PLC patterns,[11] while Tellis and Crawford identified seventeen patterns.[12] Exhibit 11–1 describes some of the major factors that shape the PLC for a specific product. Here we will discuss the shapes of the special cycles describing styles, fashions, and fads as well as the international product life cycle.

Style, fashion, and fad life cycles.   There are three categories of product life cycles that should be distinguished from the others, those pertaining to styles, fashions, and fads. (See Figure 11–5.)

A *style* is a basic and distinctive mode of expression appearing in a field of human endeavor. For example, styles appear in homes (colonial, ranch, Cape Cod); clothing (formal, casual, funky); and art (realistic, surrealistic, abstract). Once a style is invented, it may last for generations, going in and out of vogue. A style exhibits a cycle showing several periods of renewed interest.

A *fashion* is a currently accepted or popular style in a given field. For example, jeans are a fashion in today's clothing, and "country western" is a fashion in today's popular music. Fashions pass through four stages.[13] In the *distinctiveness stage*, some consumers take an interest in something new to set themselves apart from other consumers. The products may be custom-made or produced in small quantities by some manufacturer. In the *emulation stage*, other consumers take an interest out of a desire to emulate the fashion leaders, and additional manufacturers begin to produce larger quantities of the product. In the *mass-fashion stage*, the fashion has become

---

[11] Yoram J. Wind, *Product Policy: Concepts, Methods, and Strategy* (Reading, Mass.: Addison Wesley Publishing Co., 1982).

[12] Gerald J. Tellis and C. Merle Crawford, "An Evolutionary Approach to Product Growth Theory," *Journal of Marketing*, fall 1981, pp. 125–34.

[13] Chester R. Wasson, "How Predictable Are Fashion and Other Product Life Cycles?" *Journal of Marketing*, July 1968, pp. 36–43.

Exhibit 11–1

AN APPROACH TO FORECASTING THE GENERAL SHAPE AND DURATION OF THE PRODUCT LIFE CYCLE FOR A NEW PRODUCT

Goldman and Muller have presented some interesting observations on factors influencing the shape and duration of product-specific life cycles. First consider the shape that an ideal product life cycle would exhibit. It is shown below:

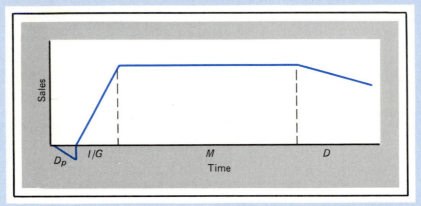

This shape is ideal for the following reasons:

- The product development period (D_p) is short, and therefore the company's product development costs are low.
- The introduction/growth period (*IG*) is short, and therefore sales reach their peak quite soon, which means early maximum revenue.
- The maturity period (*M*) lasts quite long, which means the company enjoys an extended period of profits.
- The decline (*D*) is very slow, which means that profits fall gradually rather than suddenly.

A firm that is considering launching a new product should forecast the PLC shape based on factors that influence the length of each stage:

- **Development time** is shorter and less costly for routine products than for high-tech products. Thus new perfumes, new snacks, and so on do not involve much development time, whereas high-tech products require much R&D and engineering time and cost.
- **Introduction and growth time** will be short under the following conditions:
  - The product does not require setting up a new infrastructure of channel institutions, transportation, services, or communication.
  - The dealers will readily accept and promote the new product.
  - Consumers have an interest in the product, will adopt it early, and give it favorable word of mouth.

  These conditions apply to many familiar consumer products. They are less valid for many high-tech products, which therefore require longer introduction/growth periods.

□ **Maturity time** will last long to the extent that consumer tastes and product technology are fairly stable and the company maintains leadership in the market. Companies make the most money by riding out a long maturity period. If the maturity period is short, the company may not recover its full investment.

□ The **decline time** is long if consumer tastes and product technology change only slowly. The more brand loyal the consumers, the slower the rate of decline. The lower the exit barriers, the faster some firms will exit, and this will slow down the rate of decline for the firms remaining in the industry.

Given these factors, we can see why many high-tech firms fail. They face highly unattractive PLCs. The worst type of PLC would look like this:

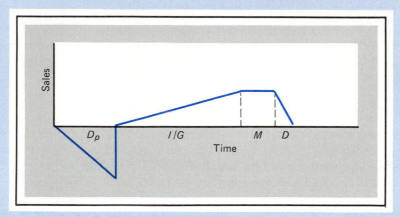

The development time is long, and the development cost is steep; the introduction/growth time is long; the maturity period is short; and the decline is fast. Many high-tech firms must invest a great amount of time and cost to develop their product; they find that it takes a long time to introduce it to the market; the market does not last long; and the decline is steep, due to the rapid technological change.

Source: Arieh Goldman and Eitan Muller, "Measuring Shape Patterns of Product Life Cycles: Implications for Marketing Strategy," an unpublished paper, August 1982.

extremely popular and manufacturers have geared up for mass production. Finally, in the *decline stage*, consumers start moving toward other fashions that are beginning to catch their eye.

Thus fashions tend to grow slowly, remain popular for a while, and decline slowly. The length of a fashion cycle is hard to predict. Wasson believes that fashions come to an end because they represent a purchase compromise, and consumers start looking for missing attributes. For example, as automobiles get shorter, they get less comfortable, and then a growing number of buyers start wanting longer cars. Furthermore, too many consumers adopt the fashion, thus turning others away. Reynolds suggests that the length of a particular fashion cycle depends on the extent to which the fashion meets a genuine need, is consistent with other trends in the

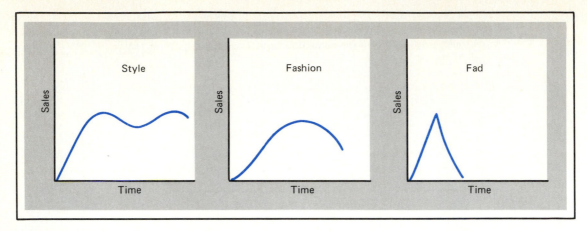

FIGURE 11–5
Style, Fashion, and Fad Life Cycles

society, satisfies societal norms and values, and does not meet technological limits as it develops.[14] Robinson, however, sees fashions as living out inexorable cycles regardless of economic, functional, or technological changes in society.[15] Sproles has recently reviewed and compared several theories of fashion cycles.[16]

Fads are fashions that come quickly into the public eye, are adopted with great zeal, peak early, and decline very fast. Their acceptance cycle is short, and they tend to attract only a limited following. They often have a novel or capricious aspect, as when people start buying "pet rocks" or run naked and "streak." Fads appeal to people who are searching for excitement or who want to distinguish themselves from others or have something to talk about to others. Fads do not survive because they do not normally satisfy a strong need or at least do not satisfy it well. It is difficult to predict whether something will be only a fad, and if so, how long it will last—a few days, weeks, or months. The amount of media attention it receives, along with other factors, will influence its duration.

International product life cycle.   Marketers have a special interest in a cycle called the international product life cycle. The international product life cycle allows companies to extend the life of their products by taking them abroad. It also means that foreign companies will eventually learn to make the same products and bring them into the domestic market. As described by Wells, "Many products go through a trade cycle, during which the United States is initially an exporter, then loses its

[14] William H. Reynolds, "Cars and Clothing: Understanding Fashion Trends," *Journal of Marketing*, July 1968, pp. 44–49.

[15] Dwight E. Robinson, "Style Changes: Cyclical, Inexorable and Foreseeable," *Harvard Business Review*, November-December 1975, pp. 121–31.

[16] George B. Sproles, "Analyzing Fashion Life Cycles—Principles and Perspective," *Journal of Marketing*, fall 1981, pp. 116–24.

export markets and may finally become an importer of the product."[17] The four stages are:

- ☐ **U.S. export strength.** An innovation is launched in the U.S. and succeeds because of the huge market and the highly developed infrastructure. Eventually U.S. producers start exporting the product to other countries.
- ☐ **Foreign production starts.** As foreign manufacturers become familiar with the product, some of them start producing it for their market. They do this under licensing or joint venture arrangement or simply by copying the product. The government may abet their efforts by imposing tariffs or quotas on imports of the product.
- ☐ **Foreign production becomes competitive in export markets.** By now, foreign manufacturers have gained production experience, and with their lower costs, they start exporting the product to other countries.
- ☐ **Import competition begins.** The foreign manufacturers' growing volume and lower costs lead them to start exporting the product to the U.S. in direct competition with U.S. producers.

Thus the product has moved from a *new product* (stage 1) to a *mature product* (stage 2) to a *standardized product* (stages 3 and 4). The implication is that a U.S. manufacturer's sales in the home market will eventually decline as foreign markets start producing the product and ultimately exporting it to the U.S. The U.S. manufacturers' best defense is to become global marketers. U.S. firms should open production and distribution facilities in other countries with large markets and/or lower costs. Global marketers are able to stretch out the product life cycle of any product form by taking it to the countries that are getting ready to use it.

The international product life cycle describes past developments in such markets as office machinery, consumer durables, and synthetic materials. Some critics feel that it has less validity today because multinational enterprises now operate vast global networks through which they may innovate new products anywhere in the world and move them through various countries not necessarily in the sequence predicted by the original formulation of the international PLC.[18]

Rationale for the Product Life Cycle

We described earlier the S-shaped PLC concept without providing a rationale in marketing terms. The theory of the diffusion and adoption of innovations provides the underlying rationale. (See pp. 345–49.) When a new product is launched, the company has to stimulate awareness, interest, trial, and purchase. This takes time, and in the introductory stage only a few persons ("innovators") will buy it. If the

---

[17] Louis T. Wells, Jr., "A Product Life Cycle for International Trade?" *Journal of Marketing*, July 1968, p. 1–6. The original formulation was stated in Raymond Vernon, "International Investment and International Trade in the Product Cycle," *Quarterly Journal of Economics*, May 1966, pp. 190–207.

[18] See Ian H. Giddy, "The Demise of the Product Cycle Model in International Business Theory," *Columbia Journal of World Business*, spring 1978, p. 92; and Raymond Vernon, "The Product Cycle Hypothesis in a New International Environment," *Oxford Bulletin of Economics and Statistics*, November 1979, pp. 255–67.

product is satisfying, larger numbers of buyers ("early adopters") are drawn in. The entry of competitors into the market speeds up the adoption process by increasing the market's awareness and by causing prices to fall. More buyers come in ("early majority") as the product is legitimized. Eventually the growth rate decreases as the number of potential new buyers approaches zero. Sales become steady at the replacement purchase rate. Eventually sales decline as new-product classes, forms, and brands appear and divert buyer interest from the existing product. Thus the product life cycle is explained by normal developments in the diffusion and adoption of new products.

The PLC concept provides a useful framework for developing effective marketing strategies in different stages of the product life cycle. We now turn to these stages and consider the appropriate marketing strategies.

INTRODUCTION STAGE

The introduction stage starts when the new product is first distributed and made available for purchase. It takes time to fill the dealer pipelines and roll out the product in several markets; so sales growth is apt to be slow. Such well-known products as instant coffee, frozen orange juice, and powdered coffee creamers lingered for many years before they entered a stage of rapid growth. Buzzell identified several causes for the slow growth of many processed food products: delays in the expansion of production capacity; technical problems ("working out the bugs"); delays in making the product available to customers, especially in obtaining adequate distribution through retail outlets; and customer reluctance to change established behavior patterns.[19] In the case of expensive new products, sales growth is retarded by additional factors, such as the small number of buyers who can afford the new product.

In this stage, profits are negative or low because of the low sales and heavy distribution and promotion expenses. Much money is needed to attract distributors and "fill the pipelines." Promotional expenditures are at their highest ratio to sales "because of the need for a high level of promotional effort to (1) inform potential consumers of the new and unknown product, (2) induce trial of the product, and (3) secure distribution in retail outlets."[20]

There are only a few competitors, and they produce basic versions of the product, since the market is not ready for product refinements. The firms focus their selling on those buyers who are the readiest to buy, usually higher-income groups. Prices tend to be on the high side because "(1) costs are high due to relatively low output rates, (2) technological problems in production may have not yet been fully mastered, and (3) high margins are required to support the heavy promotional expenditures which are necessary to achieve growth."[21]

---

[19] Buzzell, "Competitive Behavior," p. 51.
[20] Ibid.
[21] Ibid., p. 52.

Marketing Strategies in the Introduction Stage

In launching a new product, marketing management can set a high or a low level for each marketing variable, such as price, promotion, distribution, and product quality. Considering only price and promotion, management can pursue one of the four strategies shown in Figure 11–6.

A *rapid-skimming strategy* consists of launching the new product at a high price and a high promotion level. The firm charges a high price in order to recover as much gross profit per unit as possible. It spends heavily on promotion to convince the market of the product's merits even at the high price level. The high promotion acts to accelerate the rate of market penetration. This strategy makes sense under the following assumptions: (1) a large part of the potential market is unaware of the product; (2) those who become aware are eager to have the product and able to pay the asking price; (3) the firm faces potential competition and wants to build up brand preference.

A *slow-skimming strategy* consists of launching the new product at a high price and low promotion. The purpose of the high price is to recover as much gross profit per unit as possible; and the low level of promotion keeps marketing expenses down. This combination is expected to skim a lot of profit from the market. This strategy makes sense when: (1) the market is limited in size; (2) most of the market is aware of the product; (3) buyers are willing to pay a high price; and (4) potential competition is not imminent.

A *rapid-penetration strategy* consists of launching the product at a low price and spending heavily on promotion. This strategy promises to bring about the fastest market penetration and the largest market share. This strategy makes sense when: (1) the market is large; (2) the market is unaware of the product; (3) most buyers are price sensitive; (4) there is strong potential competition; and (5) the company's unit manufacturing costs fall with the scale of production and accumulated manufacturing experience.

FIGURE 11–6
Four Introductory Marketing Strategies

		Promotion: High	Promotion: Low
Price	High	Rapid-skimming strategy	Slow-skimming strategy
	Low	Rapid-penetration strategy	Slow-penetration strategy

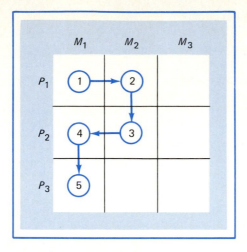

FIGURE 11–7
Long-Range Product/Market Expansion Strategy
(P_i = product i; M_j = market j)

A *slow-penetration strategy* consists of launching the new product at a low price and low level of promotion. The low price will encourage rapid product acceptance; and the company keeps its promotion costs down in order to realize more net profit. The company believes that market demand is highly price elastic but minimally promotion elastic. This strategy makes sense when (1) the market is large; (2) the market is highly aware of the product; (3) the market is price sensitive; and (4) there is some potential competition.

A company, especially the market pioneer, must not choose one of these strategies arbitrarily; rather the strategy must be the carefully chosen first step in a grand plan for life-cycle marketing. If the pioneer chooses its initial strategy to make a "killing," it will sacrifice long-run revenue for short-run gain. Market pioneers have the best chance of retaining market leadership, if they play their cards right. The pioneer should visualize the various product markets that it could initially enter, knowing that it cannot enter all of them. Suppose market segmentation analysis reveals the product market segments shown in Figure 11–7. The pioneer should analyze the profit potential of each market singly and in combination and decide on a market expansion strategy. Thus the pioneer in Figure 11–7 plans to launch its initial product in product market P_1M_1, then take the same product into a second market (P_1M_2), then surprise competition by developing a second product for the second market (P_2M_2), then take the second product back into the first market (P_2M_1), and then launch a third product for the first market (P_3M_1). If this battle plan works, the market-pioneer firm will own a good part of the first two market segments and serve them with two or three products. Naturally this battle plan may be altered as time passes and new factors emerge. But at least the firm has thought ahead how it wants to evolve in this new market. Pepsi-Cola had thought this through when it launched its ten-year plan to catch up to Coca-Cola, attacking first the grocery segment, then the vending-machine segment, and then the restaurant segment.

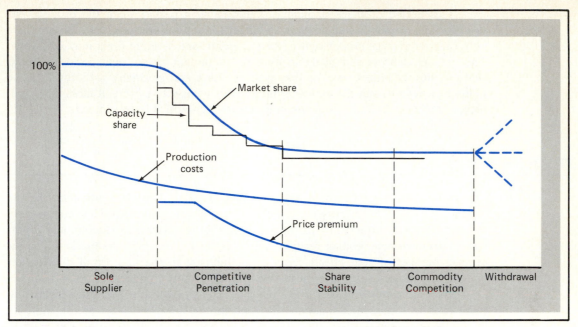

Source: John B. Frey, "Pricing Over the Competitive Cycle," speech presented at the 1982 Marketing Conference, © 1982, The Conference Board, New York.

FIGURE 11–8
Stages of the Competitive Cycle

By looking ahead, the pioneer knows that competition will enter sooner or later and cause both prices and its market share to fall. The questions are, When will this happen? and What should the pioneer do at each stage? Frey has described the stages of the competitive cycle that the pioneer has to look forward to. (See Figure 11–8.)[22] Initially, the pioneer is the sole supplier, having 100 percent of the production capacity and, of course, all of the sales of the product. The second stage, competitive penetration, starts when a new competitor has built production capacity and begins commercial sales. Other competitors enter as well and the leader's share of production capacity and of sales fall.

Subsequent competitors often enter the market at a lower price than the leader's due to perceived risks and uncertainties in their quality. As time goes on, the perceived relative values associated with the leader decline, causing a decline in the leader's price premium.

Capacity tends to be overbuilt during the rapid growth stages, so that when a cyclical slowdown occurs, industry overcapacity drives down margins to more "normal" levels. New competitors become reluctant to enter, and those already in try to solidify their positions. This leads to the third stage, share stability, in which capacity shares and market shares tend to stabilize.

---

[22] John B. Frey, "Pricing Over the Competitive Cycle," speech presented at the 1982 Marketing Conference, The Conference Board, New York.

Strategies in Different Stages of the Product Life Cycle **365**

This period of share stability is followed by a period when the product has turned into a commodity and buyers no longer pay a price premium, and the suppliers only earn an average rate of return. At this point, one or more firms may withdraw. The pioneer, who is still likely to own the dominant share, may decide to build share further as others leave or may give up share and gradually withdraw. As the pioneer passes through the various stages of this competitive cycle, it faces new challenges and must formulate new pricing and marketing if it is to succeed.

GROWTH STAGE

The growth stage is marked by a rapid climb in sales. The early adopters like the product, and middle-majority consumers start following their lead. New competitors enter the market, attracted by the opportunities for large-scale production and profit. They introduce new-product features, and this further expands the market. The increased number of competitors leads to an increase in the number of distribution outlets, and factory sales jump just to fill the distribution pipeline.

Prices remain where they are or fall only slightly insofar as demand is increasing quite rapidly. Companies maintain their promotional expenditures at the same or at a slightly raised level to meet competition and continue educating the market. Sales rise much faster, causing a decline in the promotion-sales ratio.

Profits increase during this stage as promotion costs are spread over a larger volume, and unit manufacturing costs fall faster than price declines owing to the "experience-curve" effect.

Marketing Strategies in the Growth Stage

During this stage, the firm uses several strategies to sustain market growth as long as possible:

- ☐ The firm improves product quality and adds new-product features and models.
- ☐ It enters new market segments.
- ☐ It enters new distribution channels.
- ☐ It shifts some advertising from building product awareness to bringing about product conviction and purchase.
- ☐ It lowers prices at the right time to attract the next layer of price-sensitive buyers.

The firm that pursues these market-expanding strategies will increase its competitive position. But this improvement comes at additional cost. The firm in the growth stage faces a trade-off between high market share and high current profit. By spending a lot of money on product improvement, promotion, and distribution, it can capture a dominant position. It foregoes maximum current profit in the hope of making it up in the next stage.

MATURITY STAGE

At some point a product's rate of sales growth will slow down, and the product will enter a stage of relative maturity. This stage normally lasts longer than the previous stages, and it poses formidable challenges to marketing management. *Most products are in the maturity stage of the life cycle, and therefore most of marketing management deals with the mature product.*

The maturity stage can be divided into three phases. In the first phase, *growth maturity*, the sales-growth rate starts to decline because of distribution saturation. There are no new distribution channels to fill, although some laggard buyers still enter the market. In the second phase, *stable maturity*, sales become level on a per capita basis because of market saturation. Most potential consumers have tried the product, and future sales are governed by population growth and replacement demand. In the third phase, *decaying maturity*, the absolute level of sales now starts to decline, and customers start moving toward other products and substitutes.

The slowdown in the rate of sales growth creates overcapacity in the industry. This overcapacity leads to intensified competition. Competitors engage more frequently in markdowns and off-list pricing. They increase their advertising and trade and consumer deals. They increase their R&D budgets to find better versions of the product. These steps mean some profit erosion. Some of the weaker competitors start dropping out. The industry eventually consists of well-entrenched competitors whose basic drive is to gain competitive advantage.

Marketing Strategies in the Mature Stage

Many companies give up on mature products, feeling there is little they can do. They think the best thing is to conserve their money and spend it on newer products in the development pipeline. This ignores the low success rate of new products and the high potential that many old products still have. Seemingly moribund brands like Jell-O, Ovaltine, Arm & Hammer Baking Soda, have had major sales revivals several times, through the exercise of marketing imagination. Marketing managers should not ignore or passively defend aging or "dog-eared" products. A good offense is the best defense. Marketers should systematically consider strategies of market, product, and marketing-mix modification.

Market modification. The company should seek to expand the market for its brand by working with the two factors that make up sales volume:

$$\text{Volume} = \text{Number of brand users} \times \text{Usage rate per user}$$

We will examine each factor in turn.

The company can try to expand the number of brand users in three ways:

☐ **Convert nonusers.** The company can try to convert nonusers into users of the product category. For example, the key to the growth of air freight service is the constant search for new users to whom air carriers can demonstrate the benefits of using air freight over ground transportation.

□ **Enter new market segments.** The company can try to enter new market segments— geographic, demographic, and so on—that use the product but not the brand. For example, Johnson & Johnson successfully promoted its baby shampoo to adult users.

□ **Win competitors' customers.** The company can work to attract competitors' customers to try or adopt the brand. For example, Pepsi-Cola is constantly coaxing Coca-Cola users to switch to Pepsi-Cola, throwing out one challenge after another.

Volume can also be increased by getting current brand users to increase their annual usage of the brand. Here there are three strategies:

□ **More frequent use.** The company can try to get customers to use the product more frequently. For example, orange juice marketers try to get people to drink orange juice on occasions other than breakfast time.

□ **More usage per occasion.** The company can try to interest users in using more of the product each time it is used. Thus a shampoo manufacturer might indicate that the shampoo is more effective with two rinsings than one.

□ **New and more varied uses.** The company can try to discover new uses for the product and convince people to make more varied use of it. A common practice of food manufacturers, for example, is to list several recipes on their packages to broaden the consumers' awareness of all the uses of the product.

Product modification.   Managers also try to turn sales around by modifying the product's characteristics in a way that will attract new users and/or more usage from current users. The *product relaunch* can take several forms.

A strategy of *quality improvement* aims at increasing the functional performance of the product—its durability, reliability, speed, taste. A manufacturer can often overtake its competition by launching the "new and improved" automobile, television set, coffee, or cigarette. Grocery manufacturers call this a "plus" launch and promote a new additive or advertise something as "stronger," "bigger," or "better." This strategy is effective to the extent that the quality can be improved, buyers believe the claim of improved quality, and a sufficient number of buyers want higher quality.

A strategy of *feature improvement* aims at adding new features (e.g., size, weight, materials, additives, accessories) that expand the product's versatility, safety, or convenience. For example, the addition of power to hand lawn mowers increased the speed and ease of cutting grass. Manufacturers then worked on engineering better safety features. Some manufacturers have added conversion features so that a power lawn mower doubles as a snow plow. Stewart outlined five advantages of feature improvement:

□ New features build a company image of progressiveness and leadership.
□ New features can be adapted quickly, dropped quickly, and often made optional at very little expense.
□ New features can win the loyalty of certain market segments.
□ New features can bring the company free publicity.
□ New features generate sales-force and distributors' enthusiasm.[23]

---

[23] John B. Stewart, "Functional Features in Product Strategy," *Harvard Business Review*, March-April 1959, pp. 65–78.

The chief disadvantage is that feature improvements are highly imitable; unless there is a permanent gain from being first, the feature improvement may not pay.

A strategy of *style improvement* aims at increasing the aesthetic appeal of the product. The periodic introduction of new car models amounts to style competition rather than quality or feature competition. In the case of packaged-food and household products, companies introduce color and texture variations and often restyle the package, treating it as an extension of the product. The advantage of a style strategy is that it might confer a unique market identity and secure a loyal following. Yet style competition has some problems. First, it is difficult to predict whether people—and which people—will like a new style. Second, style changes usually mean discontinuing the old style, and the company risks losing some customers who liked the old style.

Marketing-mix modification. The product manager should also try to stimulate sales through modifying one or more marketing-mix elements. Here is a list of key questions that marketing managers should ask about the nonproduct elements of the marketing mix in their search for ways to stimulate the sales of a mature product.

- ☐ **Prices.** Would a price cut attract new triers and users? If so, should the list price be lowered, or should prices be lowered through price specials, volume or early-purchase discounts, freight absorption, or easier credit terms? Or would it be better to raise the price to suggest more quality?
- ☐ **Distribution.** Can the company obtain more product support and display in the existing outlets? Can more outlets be penetrated? Can the company get the product into some new types of distribution channels?
- ☐ **Advertising.** Should advertising expenditures be increased? Should the advertising message or copy be changed? Should the media vehicle mix be changed? Should the timing, frequency, or size of ads be changed?
- ☐ **Sales promotion.** Should the company step up sales promotion—trade deals, cents-off, rebates, warranties, gifts, and contests?
- ☐ **Personal selling.** Should the number or quality of sales people be increased? Should the basis for sales-force specialization be changed? Should sales territories be revised? Should sales-force incentives be revised? Can sales-call planning be improved?
- ☐ **Services.** Can the company speed up delivery? Can it extend more technical assistance to customers? Can it extend more credit?

Years ago, Gòsta Mickwitz speculated on the elasticity of different marketing-mix tools at different stages of the product life cycle.[24] For mature products, he held that the impact of marketing-mix tools ranked in this order (from high to low): price, advertising and sales promotion, product quality, and service. His distinctions, however, were not fine enough. For example, what is the relative effectiveness of advertising versus sales promotion in the case of mature products? Many marketers argue that sales promotion has more impact than advertising because consumers have reached an equilibrium in their buying habits and preferences, and psychological persuasion (advertising) is not as effective as financial persuasion (sales promotion deals) in breaking this equilibrium. Hence, many consumer-packaged-goods companies spend over 50 percent of their total promotion budget on sales promotion to support

---

[24] Gòsta Mickwitz, *Marketing and Competition* (Finland: Centraltryckeriet, Kelsing & Fors, 1959).

mature products. Yet there are also voices taking exception to this. Seymour Banks, a former vice-president at Leo Burnett, says that brands should be managed as capital assets. Advertising is wrongly treated as an expense rather than a capital investment. Brand managers like to use sales promotion because its effects are more currently visible to their superiors, but they are actually hurting the brand's long-run profit performance.

A major problem with marketing-mix modifications is that they are highly imitable by competition, especially price reductions, additional services, and mass-distribution penetration. The firm may not gain as much as expected, and in fact, all firms may experience profit erosion as they step up their marketing attacks on each other.

DECLINE STAGE

The sales of most product forms and brands eventually decline. The sales decline may be slow, as in the case of oatmeal cereal; or rapid, as in the case of the Edsel automobile. Sales may plunge to zero, or they may petrify at a low level and continue for many years at that level.

Sales decline for a number of reasons, including technological advances, consumer shifts in tastes, and increased domestic and foreign competition. All of these lead to overcapacity, increased price cutting, and profit erosion.

As sales and profits decline, some firms withdraw from the market. Those remaining may reduce the number of product offerings. They may drop smaller market segments and marginal trade channels. They may cut the promotion budget and reduce their prices further.

Unfortunately, most companies have not developed a well-thought-out policy for handling their aging products. Sentiment plays a role:

> But putting products to death—or letting them die—is a drab business, and often engenders much of the sadness of a final parting with old and tried friends. The portable, six-sided pretzel was the first product The Company ever made. Our line will no longer be our line without it.[25]

Logic also plays a role. Management believes that product sales will improve when the economy improves, or when the marketing strategy is revised, or when the product is improved. Or the weak product may be retained because of its alleged contribution to the sales of the company's other products. Or it may be that its revenue covers out-of-pocket costs, and the company has no better way of using the money.

Unless strong reasons for retention exist, carrying a weak product is very costly to the firm. The cost is not just the amount of uncovered overhead and profit. Financial accounting cannot adequately convey all the hidden costs: The weak product may consume a disproportionate amount of management's time; it often requires frequent

---

[25] R. S. Alexander, "The Death and Burial of 'Sick Products'," *Journal of Marketing*, April 1964, p. 1.

price and inventory adjustment; it generally involves short production runs in spite of expensive setup times; it requires both advertising and sales-force attention that might better be diverted to making the "healthy" products more profitable; its very unfitness can cause customer misgivings and cast a shadow on the company's image. The biggest cost may well lie in the future. By not being eliminated at the proper time, weak products delay the aggressive search for replacement products; they create a lopsided product mix, long on "yesterday's breadwinners" and short on "tomorrow's breadwinners"; they depress current profitability and weaken the company's foothold on the future.

Marketing Strategies During the Decline Stage

A company faces a number of tasks and decisions to handle its aging products.

Identifying the weak products. The first task is to establish a system for identifying weak products. Six steps are involved:[26]

- ☐ The company appoints a product-review committee with representatives from marketing, manufacturing, and finance.
- ☐ This committee develops a system for identifying weak products.
- ☐ The controller's office supplies data for each product showing trends in market size, market share, prices, costs, and profits.
- ☐ This information is analyzed by a computer program that identifies dubious products. The criteria include the number of years of sales decline, market-share trends, gross profit margin, and return on investment.
- ☐ Products put on the dubious list are reported to those managers responsible for them. The managers fill out rating forms showing where they think sales and profits will go, with and without any changes in marketing strategy.
- ☐ The product-review committee examines this information and makes a recommendation for each dubious product—leave it alone, modify its marketing strategy, or drop it.

Determining marketing strategies. Some firms will abandon declining markets earlier than others. Much depends on the level of the *exit barriers*.[27] The lower the exit barriers, the easier it is for firms to leave the industry, and the more tempting it is for the remaining firms to remain and attract the customers of the withdrawing firms. The remaining firms will enjoy an increase in sales and profits. Thus a firm must decide whether to stay in the market until the end. For example, Procter & Gamble remained in the declining liquid-soap business until the end and made good profits as the others withdrew.

In a study of company strategies in declining industries, Harrigan distinguished five decline strategies open to the firm:

---

[26] See Philip Kotler, "Phasing Out Weak Products," *Harvard Business Review*, March-April 1965, pp. 107–18; and Paul W. Hamelman and Edward M. Mazze, "Improving Product Abandonment Decisions," *Journal of Marketing*, April 1972, pp. 20–26.

[27] See Kathryn Rudie Harrigan, "The Effect of Exit Barriers Upon Strategic Flexibility," *Strategic Management Journal*, vol. 1, 1980, pp. 165–76.

- □ Increasing the firm's investment (to dominate or get a good competitive position).
- □ Holding the firm's investment level until the uncertainties about the industry are resolved.
- □ Decreasing the firm's investment posture selectively, by sloughing off the unpromising customer groups, while simultaneously strengthening the firm's investment posture within the lucrative niches of enduring customer demands.
- □ Harvesting (or milking) the firm's investment to recover cash quickly, regardless of the resulting investment posture.
- □ Divesting the business quickly by disposing of its assets as advantageously as possible.[28]

The appropriate decline strategy is a function of the industry's relative attractiveness and the company's competitive strength in that industry. For example, a company that finds itself in an unattractive industry and yet has competitive strength should consider shrinking selectively; however, if it finds itself in an attractive industry and has competitive strength, it should consider increasing or holding its investment level.

If a company with high brand loyalty chooses a harvesting strategy, its sales may continue for a long time although it is putting little into the business. An interesting example is afforded by Ipana toothpaste:[29]

> Bristol-Myers marketed Ipana toothpaste until 1968. In early 1969, two Minnesota businessmen bought the Ipana name and formula from Bristol-Myers, and produced it in a garage. With no promotion, they sold $250,000 in the first seven months of operation.

The drop decision. When a company decides to drop a product, the firm faces further decisions. First, it can sell or transfer the product to someone else or drop it completely. Second, it must decide whether to drop the product quickly or slowly. Third, it must decide on how much parts inventory and service to maintain to service past customers.

SUMMARY AND CRITIQUE OF THE PRODUCT LIFE-CYCLE CONCEPT

Table 11–1 summarizes the characteristics, marketing objectives, and marketing strategies of the four stages of the PLC. Not all marketers would agree with all strategies, but they represent a consensus of what a number of marketers would advise.

Some marketers have prescribed more specific strategies during each stage of the PLC. Figure 11–9 shows a more elaborate analysis for grocery-product marketing, based on the assumption that many brands exhibit a cycle-recycle PLC.[30]

The PLC concept is used by many managers to interpret product and market dynamics. Its real usefulness varies in different decision-making situations. As a *planning* tool, the PLC concept characterizes the main marketing challenges in each stage and suggests major alternative marketing strategies the firm might pursue. As

---

[28] Kathryn Rudie Harrigan, "Strategies For Declining Industries," *The Journal of Business Strategy*, fall 1980, p. 27.

[29] "Abandoned Trademark Turns a Tidy Profit for Two Minnesotans," *Wall Street Journal*, October 27, 1969, p. 1.

[30] See *The Nielsen Researcher*.

TABLE 11-1

CHARACTERISTICS	Introduction	Growth	Maturity	Decline
Sales	Low sales	Rapidly rising sales	Peak sales	Declining sales
Costs	High cost per customer	Average cost per customer	Low cost per customer	Low cost per customer
Profits	Negative	Rising profits	High profits	Declining profits
Customers	Innovators	Early adopters	Middle majority	Laggards
Competitors	Few	Growing number	Stable number beginning to decline	Declining number

MARKETING OBJECTIVES				
	Create product awareness and trial	Maximize market share	Maximize profit while defending market share	Reduce expenditure and milk the brand

STRATEGIES				
Product	Offer a basic product	Offer product extensions, service, warranty	Diversity brands and models	Phase out weak items
Price	Use cost-plus	Price to penetrate market	Price to match or beat competitors	Cut price
Distribution	Build selective distribution	Build intensive distribution	Build more intensive distribution	Go selective: phase out unprofitable outlets
Advertising	Build product awareness among early adopters and dealers	Build awareness and interest in the mass market	Stress brand differences and benefits	Reduce to level needed to retain hardcore loyals
Sales Promotion	Use heavy sales promotion to entice trial	Reduce to take advantage of heavy consumer demand	Increase to encourage brand switching	Reduce to minimal level

SOURCES: This table was assembled by the author from several sources: Chester R. Wasson, Dynamic Competitive Strategy and Product Life Cycles (Austin, Texas: Austin Press, 1978); John A. Weber, "Planning Corporate Growth With Inverted Product Life Cycles," Long Range Planning, October 1976, pp. 12–29; and Peter Doyle, "The Realities of the Product Life Cycle," Quarterly Review of Marketing, summer 1976, pp. 1–6.

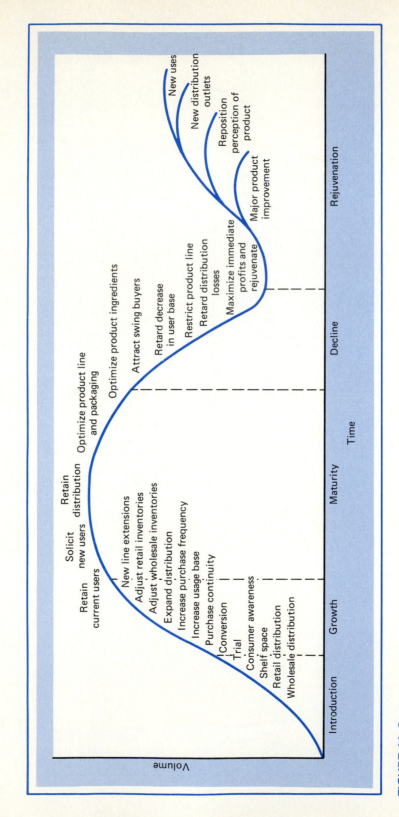

FIGURE 11-9
PLC Marketing for Grocery Products

a *control* tool, the PLC concept allows the company to compare product performance against similar products in the past. As a *forecasting* tool, the PLC concept is less useful because sales histories exhibit diverse patterns, and the stages are of varying duration.

PLC theory has its share of critics. Critics claim that life-cycle patterns are too variable, as evidenced by the several shapes that the PLCs of different products have shown. They charge that the stages don't have predictable durations. In other words, PLCs lack what living organisms have, namely, a fixed sequence of stages and a fixed length of each stage. They even charge that the marketer can't often tell what stage the product is in. A product may appear to be mature when actually it has only reached a temporary plateau in the growth stage prior to another upsurge. Finally they charge that the PLC pattern is an artifact of the marketing strategies used rather than an inevitable course that sales have to follow:

> Suppose a brand is acceptable to consumers but has a few bad years because of other factors—for instance, poor advertising, delisting by a major chain, or entry of a "me-too" competitive product backed by massive sampling. Instead of thinking in terms of corrective measures, management begins to feel that its brand has entered a declining stage. It therefore withdraws funds from the promotion budget to finance R&D on new items. The next year the brand does even worse, panic increases. . . . Clearly, the PLC is a *dependent* variable which is determined by marketing actions; it is not an *independent* variable to which companies should adapt their marketing programs.[31]

In other words, product sales do not follow a natural and inevitable cycle, as living organisms do. The PLC is the result, not the cause, of the marketing strategies chosen by the firm.

Thus if a brand's sales are declining, management should not conclude that the brand is inevitably in the decline stage of its life cycle. If it starts withdrawing funds from the brand, it will create a self-fulfilling prophecy that the brand is at the end of its life. Instead, management should examine all the ways it could try to stimulate sales: modifying the customer mix, the brand's positioning, or the marketing mix. Only when management cannot identify a promising turnaround strategy might it draw the conclusion that the brand is in the decline stage of its life cycle. Then it must decide what to do given this conclusion.

Furthermore the best marketing strategy to follow in a given stage of the PLC is not necessarily the one prescribed in the PLC charts. Each company needs to develop a distinctive strategy at each stage, not the one everyone else is using.

THE CONCEPT OF MARKET EVOLUTION

The PLC focuses on what is happening to a particular product or brand rather than on what is happening to the overall market. It yields a product-oriented picture rather than a market-oriented picture. It needs to be complemented by a theory

---

[31] Nariman K. Dhalla and Sonia Yuspeh, "Forget the Product Life Cycle Concept!" *Harvard Business Review*, January-February 1976, pp. 102–12, here p. 105.

that analyzes the evolution of the market itself and the emerging opportunities. Firms need a way to anticipate the evolutionary path of a market as it is affected by new needs, competitors, technology, channels, and other developments.

Stages in Market Evolution

A market evolves through five stages: market crystallization, expansion, fragmentation, reconsolidation, and termination. We will describe and illustrate these stages below.

Market-crystallization stage.   Before a market materializes, it exists as a *latent market*. A latent market consists of people who share a similar need or want for something that does not yet exist. For example, people want a means of more rapid calculation than can be achieved by mental calculation or by using a paper and pencil. Until recently, this need was imperfectly satisfied through abacuses, slide rules, and large desk calculators.

Suppose John Smith, an entrepreneur, recognizes people's latent need for a more rapid means of calculation. Suppose he imagines a solution in the form of a small, hand-size electronic calculator. He works hard and develops a working proto-type. John Smith now turns to the marketing problem. He has to determine target markets, product attributes, prices, distribution channels, and promotion for this new product. Here we will consider only one problem, that of determining the product attributes. Suppose he has to decide on two product attributes: *physical size* and *number of arithmetic functions*. Being market oriented, he decides to interview poten-tial buyers. He asks them to state their preferred levels for each attribute. Each person's ideal product can be represented by a point (called ideal point) in a diagram showing the two attributes.

Suppose consumer preferences are those shown in Figure 11-10(a). Evidently target customers differ greatly in their attribute preferences. Some want a four-function calculator (adding, subtracting, multiplying, and dividing) and others want more func-tions (calculating percentages, square roots, logs, and so forth). Some want a small hand calculator and others want a large one. When buyer preferences scatter evenly in a market, it is called a *diffused-preference market*.

The entrepreneur's problem is to design an optimal product for this market.[32] He has three options:

☐ The new product can be designed to meet the preferences of one of the corners of the market (*a single-niche strategy*).

☐ Two or more products can be simultaneously launched to capture two or more parts of the market (*a multiple-niche strategy*).

☐ The new product can be designed for the middle of the market (*a mass-market strategy*).

For small firms, a single-niche market strategy makes the most sense. A small firm has insufficient resources for capturing and holding the mass market. Larger

---

[32] This problem is trivial if consumers' preferences are concentrated at one point. If there are distinct clusters of preference, the entrepreneur can design a product for the largest cluster or for the cluster that the company can serve best.

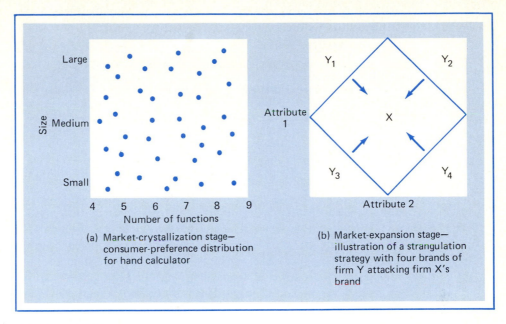

FIGURE 11–10
Market-Space Diagrams

firms would enter and clobber the small firm. Its best bet is to develop a specialized product and capture a corner of the market that won't attract competitors for a long time.

If the firm is large, it makes sense to go after the mass market by designing a product that is "medium" in size and number of functions. A product in the center minimizes the sum of the distances of existing preferences from the actual product. An electronic hand calculator designed for the mass market will minimize total dissatisfaction.

We will assume that the pioneer firm is large and designs its product for the mass market. It launches the product and sales start to climb. The stage of *market crystallization* has begun.

Market-expansion stage.   An interesting question now arises. Where will a second firm enter the market, assuming that the first firm established itself in the center? This begins the *market-expansion* stage. The second firm has three options:

☐ It can locate its brand in one of the corners (*a single-niche strategy*).
☐ It can locate its brand next to the first competitor (*a mass-market strategy*).
☐ It can launch two or more products in different unoccupied corners (*a multiple-niche strategy*).

If the second firm is small, it will avoid head-on competition with the pioneer and launch a product in one of the market corners. If the second firm is large, it might launch its brand in the center against the pioneer firm. The two firms can easily end up sharing the mass market almost equally. Or a large second firm can implement a multiniche strategy.

> Procter & Gamble will occasionally enter a market containing a large, entrenched competitor, and instead of launching a me-too product or single-segment product, it introduces a succession of products aimed at different segments. Each entry creates a loyal following and takes some business away from the major competitor. Soon the major competitor is surrounded, its revenue is weakened, and it is too late to launch new brands in outlying segments. P&G, in a moment of triumph, then launches a brand against the major segment. This is called a strangulation strategy and is illustrated in Figure 11–10(b).

Market-fragmentation stage. Each firm entering the market will go after some position, either locating next to a competitor or in some unoccupied segment. Eventually the competitors cover and serve all the major market segments. In fact, they go further and invade each other's segments, reducing everyone's profits in the process. The market splits into finer and finer fragments. This is called the *market-fragmentation stage*. The few uncovered segments whose needs are not met by existing products are too small to serve economically. The market reaches maturity, with few new products emerging at this stage. This is illustrated in Figure 11–11(a), with the letters representing different companies supplying various segments. Note that two segments are unserved.[33]

Market-reconsolidation stage. This, however, is not the end of the evolution of a market. The stage of fragmentation is often followed by a stage of *market-reconsolidation*, caused by the emergence of a new attribute that has cogent market appeal. Market reconsolidation took place in the toothpaste market when P&G introduced its new fluoride toothpaste, Crest, which effectively retarded dental decay. Suddenly other toothpaste brands that claimed whitening power, cleaning power, sex appeal, taste, and mouthwash effectiveness were pushed into the corners because consumers primarily wanted a dental-protection toothpaste. P&G's Crest won a lion's share of the market, as shown by the X territory in Figure 11–11(b).

But even a reconsolidated market is not the last stage in the evolution of a market. Other companies will copy the successful brand, and the market will eventually become fragmented again. Markets swing between market fragmentation and market reconsolidation. The fragmentation is brought about by competition, and the reconsolidation is brought about by innovation.

Market-termination stage. Termination of this "see-saw" process occurs when a radically new innovation destroys the old market. If an entrepreneur discovers an effective mouth-spray substitute for toothpaste, the new product will eventually destroy the toothpaste market. That is an example of the *market-termination stage*. Thus a product form ends when a new form emerges that meets consumer needs in a superior way.

---

[33] The product space is drawn with two attributes for simplicity. Actually, more attributes come into being as the market evolves. The product space grows from a two-dimensional to an n-dimensional space, which unfortunately cannot be drawn.

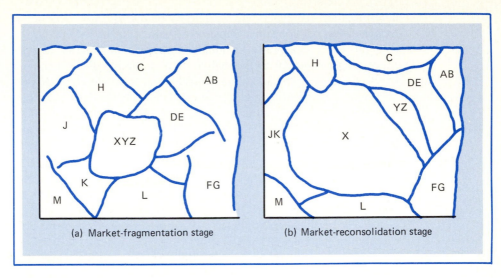

(a) Market-fragmentation stage   (b) Market-reconsolidation stage

FIGURE 11-11
Market-Fragmentation and Market-Reconsolidation Stages

Dynamics of Attribute Competition

Thus markets move through the stages of *market crystallization*, *market expansion*, *market fragmentation*, *market reconsolidation*, and eventually *market termination*. In the long run, profit levels will deteriorate because of free entry and competition. The process is temporarily reversed through *innovation*, that is, the development of new customer benefits. The evolution of markets is very much the history of competitors coming out with new benefits to offer to buyers.

Consider the evolution of the paper towel market. Originally, homemakers used only cotton and linen dish cloths and towels in their kitchens. A paper company, looking for new markets, developed paper towels to compete with cloth towels. This development crystallized a new market. Other paper manufacturers entered and expanded the market. The number of brands proliferated and created market fragmentation. Industry overcapacity led manufacturers to search for new features. One manufacturer, hearing consumers complain that paper towels were not absorbent, introduced "absorbent" paper towels and increased its market share. This stage of market reconsolidation did not last long because competitors came out with their versions of absorbent paper towels. The market became fragmented again. Then another manufacturer heard consumers express a wish for a "superstrength" paper towel, and proceeded to introduce one. It was soon copied by other manufacturers. Another manufacturer introduced a "lint-free" paper towel, which was subsequently copied. Thus paper towels evolved from a simple product to one with various absorbencies, strengths, and applications. Market evolution was driven by the forces of innovation and competition.

Competition in a market produces a continuous round of new-product attributes. If a new attribute succeeds, then several competitors soon offer it, and it loses its determinance. To the extent that most banks are now "friendly," friendliness no longer influences consumer choice of a bank. To the extent that most airlines serve in-flight meals, meals are no longer a basis for air-carrier choice. This underlines the strategic importance of a company's maintaining the lead in innovating new attributes. Each new attribute, if successful, creates a differential advantage for the firm, leading to temporarily higher-than-average market share and profits. The market leader must learn to routinize the innovation process.

A crucial question is, Can a firm look ahead and anticipate the sequence of attributes that are likely to be high in demand and technologically feasible over time? How can the firm search for new attributes? There are four possible approaches.

The first approach employs an *empirical process* to identify new attributes. The company asks consumers what attributes they would like added to the product and their desire level for each. The firm also examines the cost of developing each attribute and likely competitive responses. It decides to develop those attributes promising the highest incremental profit.

The second approach sees attribute search as an *intuitive process*. Entrepreneurs get hunches and go into product development without much marketing research. Natural selection determines the winners and the losers. If a manufacturer has intuited an attribute that the market wants, that manufacturer is considered smart, although from another perspective, it was only luck. This theory offers no guidance as to how to visualize new attributes.

A third approach says that new attributes emerge through a *dialectical process*. Any valued attribute gets pushed to an extreme form through the competitive process. Thus blue jeans, starting out as an inexpensive clothing article, over time became fashionable and more expensive. This unidirectional movement, however, contains the seeds of its own destruction. Eventually some manufacturer will discover a new cheap material for pants, and consumers will flock to buy it. The message of dialectical theory is that innovators should not march with the crowd but rather head in the opposite direction toward market segments that are suffering from increasing neglect.

A fourth approach holds that new attributes emerge through a *needs-hierarchy process* (see Maslow's theory, pp. 138–39). On this theory, we would predict that the first automobiles would provide basic transportation and be designed for safety. At a later time, automobiles would start appealing to social acceptance and status needs. Still later, automobiles would be designed to help people "fulfill" themselves. The innovator's task is to assess when the market is ready to satisfy a higher-order need.

The actual unfolding of new attributes in a market is more complex than any simple theories would suggest. We should not underestimate the role of technological and societal processes in influencing the emergence of new attributes. For example, the strong consumer interest in compact-size television sets remained unmet until miniaturization technology was sufficiently developed. Technological forecasting attempts to predict the timing of future technological development that will permit new-attribute offers to consumers. The societal factor also plays a major role in shaping attribute evolution. Developments such as inflation, shortages, environmentalism, consumerism, and new lifestyles create consumer disequilibrium and lead consumers to reevaluate product attributes. For example, inflation increases the desire for a smaller car, and car safety increases the desire for a heavier car. The innovator must use marketing research to gauge the demand potency of different attributes in order to determine the company's best move vis-à-vis competition.

SUMMARY

Every new product when launched goes through a product life-cycle market with changing problems and opportunities. The sales history of many products follow an S-shaped curve made up of four stages. The **introduction** stage is marked by slow growth and minimal profits as the product is pushed into distribution. The company has to decide during this stage between the four strategies of rapid skimming, slow skimming, rapid penetration, or slow penetration. If successful, the product enters a **growth** stage marked by rapid sales growth and increasing profits. During this stage, the company attempts to improve the product, enter new market segments and distribution channels, and reduce its prices slightly. There follows a **maturity** stage in which sales growth slows down and profits stabilize. The company seeks innovative strategies to renew sales growth, including market, product and marketing-mix modification. Finally, the product enters a **decline** stage in which little can be done to halt the deterioration of sales and profits. The company's task during this period is to identify the truly weak products, develop for each one a strategy of continuation, focusing, or milking, and finally phase out weak products in a way that minimizes the hardship to company profits, employees, and customers.

Not all products pass through an S-shaped PLC. Some products show a cycle-recycle shape, others a scalloped shape. Some investigators have discovered over a dozen PLC shapes, including those describing styles, fashions, and fads, as well as the international product life cycle. PLC theory has been criticized on the grounds that companies cannot predict the shapes in advance, or know what stage they are in within a given shape, or predict the duration of the stages. Also, PLCs are the result of chosen marketing strategies rather than of an inevitable sales history that is independent of the chosen marketing strategies.

Product life-cycle theory must be complemented by a theory of market evolution. The theory of market evolution holds that new markets **crystallize** when a product is created to satisfy an unmet need. The innovator usually designs a product for the mass market. Competitors enter the market with similar products leading to **market expansion**. The market undergoes increasing **fragmentation** until some firm introduces a powerful new attribute that **reconsolidates** the market into fewer and larger parts. This stage does not last, because competitors copy the new attributes. There is a cycling back and forth between market reconsolidation based on innovation and fragmentation based on competition. The market may ultimately **terminate** upon the discovery of a superior new product form.

Companies must try to anticipate new attributes that the market wants. Profits go to those who introduce new and valued benefits early. The search for new attributes can be based on empirical work, intuition, dialectical reasoning, or needs-hierarchy reasoning.

Market-evolution theory shifts marketers' attention from specific brand PLCs to the evolution of the overall market. Each brand tells only a limited story about the opportunities and evolution of the market. Successful marketing comes through creatively visualizing the market's evolutionary potential.

QUESTIONS

1. After eight consecutive years of record earnings, Levi Strauss experienced income decline in 1981 and 1982. Some analysts believe that the denim jean market has reached the decline stage of its PLC. If this is true, what strategies could Levi Strauss pursue to increase profits?

2. The American Motors/Renault Alliance was introduced in late 1982 into a depressed U.S. new-car market. What introductory-stage marketing strategies did they pursue? What marketing strategies would you suggest for the Alliance in the introductory and growth stages of the PLC?

3. What should be the focus for marketing research studies at each stage of the PLC?

4. Develop a long-range marketing plan for a new line of electric can openers, indicating for each stage in the product life cycle the major objective and the likely policy on price, quality, advertising, personal selling, and channels.

5. As a product passes through the successive stages of its product life cycle, both its rate of sales growth and its rate of return on investment change. Using these two variables as axes, develop a diagram showing the typical trajectory of these variables over the product life cycle.

6. Discuss the changes in the promotion level and mix in the different stages of the product life cycle.

7. Select an actual fad and a fashion product and plot their respective product life-cycle patterns on one graph. How do they differ from each other?

8. What is the difference between a product life-cycle analysis of the product class "paper towels" and the market-evolution analysis of them found in the chapter?

Marketing Strategies for Market Leaders, Challengers, Followers, and Nichers

"Cheshire Puss," she [Alice] began . . . "would you please tell me which way I ought to go from here?" "That depends on where you want to get to," said the cat.

LEWIS CARROLL

In this chapter, we will look at how marketing strategy must be adapted not only to the target customers but also to the competitors who are serving the same target customers. In the fast-growth economy of the 1960s, companies paid less attention than today to their competitors. The economic pie was growing fast enough for everyone to succeed. In the seventies and eighties, lackluster economic growth brought about intensified competition. Companies specifically studied competitors' weaknesses and often launched surprise attacks on competitors' positions. Companies increasingly based their marketing strategies on the logic of both consumer wants and competitors' positions.[1]

Marketing strategy is dependent on each firm's size and position in its industry. Large firms can practice certain strategies not affordable by small firms. Being large, however, is not enough, and as there are some winning strategies for large firms, there are also some losing strategies for large firms. And small firms can often find

---

[1] See Alfred R. Oxenfeldt and William L. Moore, "Customer or Competitor: Which Guidelines for Marketing?" *Management Review*, August 1978, pp. 43–48.

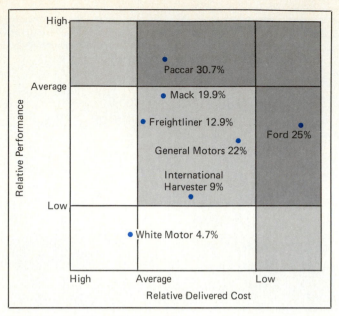

FIGURE 12–1
Profiles of Competitive Images in the U.S. Heavy-Duty Truck Manufacturing Industry

strategies to achieve as good or better a rate of return as large firms.

Michael Porter, in his *Competitive Strategy*, distinguished four generic strategies that companies could follow, three winning strategies and one losing one.[2] Companies could enjoy a high rate of return if they achieved cost-leadership, high product differentiation, or market focusing. They would show only average or below average returns if they pursued a middle-of-the-road strategy of doing a little of everything but nothing particularly well. The role of the generic strategies can be illustrated by some research of William Hall in the truck manufacturing industry.[3] Figure 12–1 shows how seven truck manufacturers are positioned according to their *relative delivered cost* (i.e., being a low-cost firm) and their *relative performance* (i.e., offering the most differentiated or desirable product and service). The percentages in the figure represent each manufacturer's rate of return on investment (ROI) in this industry.

Ford leads the other manufacturers in having the lowest relative delivered cost. Its trucks show average performance, but the fact that Ford is the low-cost leader gives it a higher profit margin and accounts for its high 25 percent ROI. Paccar is the industry leader in high-performance trucks (its Peterbilt and Kenworth trucks are considered the Cadillacs of the industry) and commands a 31 percent ROI.

---

[2] Michael E. Porter, *Competitive Strategy: Techniques for Analyzing Industries and Competitors* (New York: Free Press, 1980), chap. 2.

[3] William K. Hall, "Survival Strategies in a Hostile Environment," *Harvard Business Review*, September-October 1980, p. 81.

At the other extreme is White Motor, whose trucks were below average in performance and high in manufactured cost. Not surprisingly, its rate of return was 4.7 percent, and White was subsequently purchased by Volvo in the hope of improving its competitive effectiveness.

The four companies in the middle box are "middle-of-the-roaders" that try to be good at performance and cost but are not especially good at either. Their rates of return are lower than the leading two firms. As it turns out, Freightliner was subsequently purchased by Mercedes, and International Harvester's truck line is in deep trouble.

In order for a middle-of-the-roader to improve its ROI, the company must make a clearer commitment to one of the three winning strategies. For example, International Harvester (IH) has three options. IH can invest in a more modern plant in a drive to become the low-cost firm. In this case, its major competitors would be Ford and General Motors, both of whom make up the *strategic group* pursuing cost leadership. (A strategic group is the set of firms pursuing the particular generic strategy.) Alternatively, IH could try to improve the quality of its trucks and services so that it competes with Paccar and Mack, the strategic group pursuing profitability through product differentiation. This would be harder for IH because it takes years to build a better product and reputation, and Paccar is too well entrenched. Finally, IH might choose to go after multiple niches within the trucking industry (this cannot be shown in Figure 12–1), becoming a leader in each niche through either low costs or product differentiation or through both. But if IH stays where it is, trying to be a little of everything, its future is precarious.

Thus we see that the firms in an industry pursue different competitive strategies and enjoy different competitive positions. The competitive positions of firms in a given industry can be described in different ways. Arthur D. Little, a leading management consulting firm, sees firms as occupying one of six competitive positions in their industry:[4]

- ☐ **Dominant.** This firm controls the behavior of other competitors and has a wide choice of strategic options.
- ☐ **Strong.** This firm can take independent action without endangering its long-term position and can maintain its long-term position regardless of competitors' actions.
- ☐ **Favorable.** This firm has a strength that is exploitable in particular strategies and has more than average opportunity to improve its position.
- ☐ **Tenable.** This firm is performing at a sufficiently satisfactory level to warrant continuing in business, but it exists at the sufferance of the dominant company and has a less-than-average opportunity to improve its position.
- ☐ **Weak.** This firm has unsatisfactory performance but an opportunity exists for improvement and it must change or else exit.
- ☐ **Non-viable.** This firm has unsatisfactory performance and no opportunity for improvement.

Every firm or business unit can recognize itself in one of these competitive positions. The business unit's competitive position, along with its stage in the product life cycle, will help it decide whether to invest, maintain, shrink, or exit from the industry.

---

[4] See Robert V. L. Wright, *A System for Managing Diversity* (Cambridge, Mass: Arthur D. Little, December 1974).

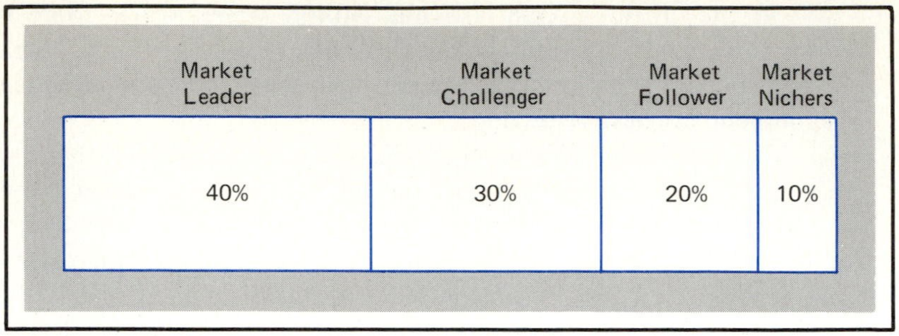

Market Leader	Market Challenger	Market Follower	Market Nichers
40%	30%	20%	10%

FIGURE 12–2
Hypothetical Market Structure

We will develop a different classification of competitive positions in this chapter. Much can be gained by classifying firms by their behavior in an industry, that of leading, challenging, following, or niching. Suppose an industry consists of the firms shown in Figure 12–2. Forty percent of the market is in the hands of a *market leader*, the firm with the largest market share. Another 30 percent is in the hands of a *market challenger*, a runner-up firm that is fighting hard for an increased market share. Another 20 percent is in the hands of a *market follower*, another runner-up firm that is willing to maintain its market share and not rock the boat. The remaining 10 percent is in the hands of *market nichers*, firms that serve small market segments not being pursued by larger firms.

We will now examine specific marketing strategies that are available to market leaders, challengers, followers, and nichers.

MARKET-LEADER STRATEGIES

Most industries contain one firm that is acknowledged as the market leader. This firm has the largest market share in the relevant product market. It usually leads the other firms in price changes, new-product introductions, distribution coverage, and promotional intensity. The leader may or may not be admired or respected, but other firms acknowledge its dominance. The leader is an orientation point for competitors, a company to either challenge, imitate, or avoid. Some of the best-known market leaders are General Motors (autos), Kodak (photography), U.S. Steel (steel), IBM (computers), Xerox (copying), Procter & Gamble (consumer packaged goods), Caterpillar (earth-moving equipment), Coca-Cola (soft drinks), Sears (retailing), McDonald's (fast food), and Gillette (razor blades).

Unless a dominant firm enjoys a legal monopoly, its life is not altogether easy. It must maintain a constant vigilance. Other firms keep challenging its strengths or trying to take advantage of its weaknesses. The market leader can easily miss a turn in the road and plunge into second or third place. A product innovation may come along and hurt the leader (e.g., Tylenol's nonaspirin painkiller taking over the lead from Bayer Aspirin). The leader might spend conservatively, expecting hard times, while a challenger spends liberally (Montgomery Ward's loss of its retail dominance to Sears after World War II). The dominant firm might look old-fashioned against new and peppier rivals (*Playboy* magazine's fall to second place in newsstand circulation after *Penthouse*). The dominant firm's costs might rise excessively and hurt its profits (Food Fair's decline, resulting from poor cost control).

Dominant firms want to remain number one. This calls for action on three fronts. First, the firm must find ways to expand total demand. Second, the firm must protect its current market share through good defensive and offensive actions. Third, the firm can try to expand its market share further, even if market size remains constant.

Expanding the Total Market

The dominant firm normally gains the most when the total market is expanded. If Americans buy ten million cars instead of eight million, General Motors stands to gain the most because they produce over half of the domestic cars sold in the U.S. If General Motors can convince more Americans to own cars, or own more cars per household, or replace them more often, they will benefit. In general, the leader should look for *new users*, *new uses*, and *more usage* of its products.

New users.   Every product class has the potential of attracting buyers who are unaware of the product or who are resisting it because of its price or lack of certain features. A manufacturer can search for new users among three groups. For example, a perfume manufacturer can try to convince women who do not use perfume to use perfume (*market-penetration strategy*), or convince men to start using perfume (*new-market strategy*), or sell perfume in other countries (*geographical-expansion strategy*).

One of the great success stories in developing a new class of users is that of Johnson & Johnson's baby shampoo, the leading brand of baby shampoo. The company became concerned about future sales growth when the birthrate slowed down. Their marketers noticed that other family members occasionally used the baby shampoo for their own hair. Management decided to develop an advertising campaign aimed at adults. In a short time, Johnson & Johnson baby shampoo became the leading brand in the total shampoo market.

In another case, Boeing faced a sharp decline in orders for B-747 jumbo jets when the airlines had acquired enough aircraft to serve existing demand. Boeing concluded that the key to more B-747 sales was to help the airlines attract more people to flying. Most airlines were competing with each other for existing flyers rather than trying to attract new people to flying. Boeing analyzed potential flying segments and concluded that the working class did not fly much, although the cost was within their reach. Boeing encouraged the airlines and the travel industry to create and sell charter travel packages to unions, churches, and lodges. This strategy had worked in Europe and seemed like a promising way to expand the American flying market.

New uses.   Markets can be expanded through discovering and promoting new uses for the product. For example, the average American eats dry breakfast cereal three mornings a week. Cereal manufacturers would gain if they could promote cereal eating on other occasions during the day. Thus some cereals are promoted as snacks to increase their use frequency.

Du Pont's nylon provides a classic story of new-use expansion. Every time nylon became a mature product, some new use was discovered. Nylon was first used as a synthetic fiber for parachutes; then as a fiber for women's stockings; later, a major material in women's blouses and men's shirts; still later, it entered automobile tires, seat upholstery, and carpeting.[5] Each new use started the product on a new life cycle. Credit goes to Du Pont's continuous R&D program to find new uses.

In even more cases, customers deserve credit for discovering new uses. Vaseline petroleum jelly started out as a simple machine lubricant, and over the years users have reported many new uses for the product, including use as a skin ointment, a healing agent, and a hair dressing.

Arm & Hammer, the baking-soda manufacturer, had a product whose sales were on a plateau for 125 years. Baking soda had a number of uses, but no single use was advertised. Then the company discovered some consumers were using it as a refrigerator deodorant. It launched a heavy advertising and publicity campaign focusing on this single use and succeeded in getting half of the homes in America to place an open box of baking soda in their refrigerator. A few years later, Arm & Hammer discovered consumers who used it to quell kitchen grease fires, and they promoted this use with great results.

The company's task is to monitor customers' uses of the product. This applies to industrial products as well as consumer products. Von Hippel's studies show that most new industrial products were originally suggested by customers rather than by company R&D laboratories.[6] This highlights the importance of *marketing research* as a contributor to company growth and profits.

More usage.   A third market-expansion strategy is to convince people to *use more of the product per use occasion*. If a cereal manufacturer convinces consumers to eat a full bowl of cereal instead of half a bowl, total sales will increase. Procter & Gamble advises users that its Head and Shoulders shampoo is more effective with two applications instead of one per shampoo.

A creative example of a company stimulating higher usage per occasion is the Michelin Tire Company (French). Michelin wanted French car owners to drive their cars more miles per year—thus leading to more tire replacement. They conceived the idea of rating French restaurants on a three-star system. They reported that many of the best restaurants were in the south of France, leading many Parisians to consider weekend drives to the south of France. Michelin also published guidebooks with maps and sights along the way to further entice travel.

---

[5] See Jordan P. Yale, "The Strategy of Nylon's Growth," *Modern Textiles Magazine*, February 1964, pp. 32 ff. Also see Theodore Levitt, "Exploit the Product Life Cycle," *Harvard Business Review*, November-December 1965, pp. 81–94.

[6] See Eric von Hippel, *A Customer-Active Paradigm for Industrial Product Idea Generation*, unpublished working paper, Sloan School of Management, MIT, Cambridge, Mass., May 1977.

Protecting Market Share

While trying to expand total market size, the dominant firm must continuously protect its current business against enemy attacks. The leader is like the largest elephant in a herd of elephants being bothered by bees. The largest and nastiest bee keeps buzzing around the leader. Coca-Cola must constantly maintain its guard against Pepsi-Cola; Gillette against Bic; Kodak against Fuji; Hertz against Avis; McDonald's against Burger King; General Motors against Ford.

What can the market leader do to protect its terrain? The most constructive response is *continuous innovation*. The leader refuses to be content with the way things are and leads the industry in new-product ideas, customer services, distribution effectiveness, and cost cutting. It keeps increasing its competitive effectiveness and value to customers. The leader applies the "military principle of the offensive": the commander exercises initiative, sets the pace, and exploits enemy weaknesses. The best defense is a good offense.

The dominant firm, even when it does not launch offensives, must at least guard all of its fronts and not leave any exposed flanks. It must keep its costs down, and its prices must be consonant with the value the customers see in the brand. The leader must "plug holes" so that attackers don't jump in. Thus a consumer-packaged-goods leader will produce its brands in several sizes and forms to meet varying consumer preferences and hold on to as much scarce dealer shelf space as possible.

The intensified competition that has taken place worldwide in recent years has sparked management's interest in models of military warfare, particularly as described in the writings of Sun-Tsu, Mushashi, von Clausewitz, and Liddell Hart.[7] Leader companies, like leader nations, have been advised to protect their interests with such strategies as "brinkmanship," "massive retaliation," "limited warfare," "graduated response," "diplomacy of violence," and "threat systems." There are, in fact, six military defense strategies that a dominant firm can use. They are illustrated in Figure 12–3 and described below.[8]

Position defense. The most basic idea of defense is to build an impregnable fortification around one's territory. The French built the famous Maginot Line in peacetime to protect its territory against possible future German invasion. But this fortification, like all static defense maneuvers, failed. Simply defending one's current position or products is a form of *marketing myopia*. Henry Ford's myopia about his Model-T brought an enviably healthy company with $1 billion in cash reserves at its zenith to the brink of financial ruin. Even such death-defying brands as Coca-Cola and Bayer Aspirin cannot be relied upon by their companies as the main sources of future growth and profitability. Coca-Cola today, in spite of producing nearly half

---

[7] Sun Tsu, *The Art of War* (London: Oxford University Press, 1963); Miyamoto Mushashi, *A Book of Five Rings* (Woodstock, N.Y., Overlook Press, 1974); Carl von Clausewitz, *On War* (London: Routledge & Kegan Paul, 1908); and B. H. Liddell Hart, *Strategy* (New York: Praeger, 1967).

[8] These six defense strategies, as well as the five attack strategies described on pp. 401–06, are taken from Philip Kotler and Ravi Singh, "Marketing Warfare in the 1980s," *Journal of Business Strategy*, winter 1981, pp. 30–41.

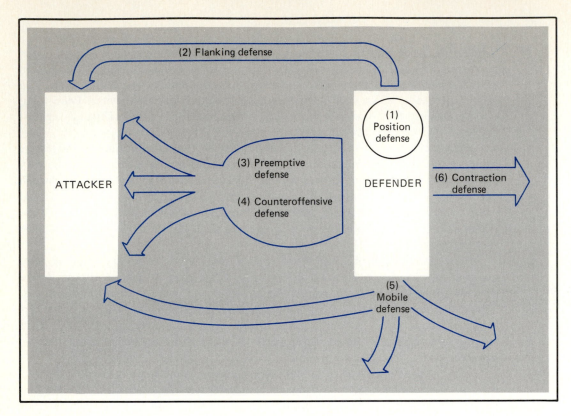

FIGURE 12–3
Defense Strategies

the soft drinks of the world, has aggressively moved into the wine market, has acquired fruit-drink companies, and has diversified into desalinization equipment and plastics. Clearly leaders under attack would be foolish to put all their resources into building fortifications around their current product.

Flanking defense.   The market leader should not only guard its territory but also erect some flanks or outposts to serve as a defensive corner to protect a weak front or possibly as an invasion base for counterattacking if necessary. The flanking position is of little value if it is so lightly held that an enemy could pin it down with a small force while its main formations swing past unmolested. A careful assessment of any potential threat must be made, and if indicated, a relatively serious commitment should be made to flanking the threat.

Many instances of flank positions are to be found in the business world.

Preemptive defense.   A more agressive defense maneuver is to actually launch an offense against the enemy *before* he starts his offense against the company. The company cuts down the enemy before he strikes and thus engages in the paradox of an offensive defense. Preemptive defense assumes that an ounce of prevention is worth

The defensive stance taken by Chicago-based Jewel Food Stores is instructive. The company believes that the supermarket will continue to remain a dominant force but is flanking its position by strengthening its food-retailing-assortment mix to meet new challenges. The fast-food boom has been met by offering a wide assortment of instant and frozen meals and the discount-food challenge by promoting generic lines: Jewel's various supermarkets are being tailored to suit local demands for such items as fresh bakery products and ethnic foods. And the company is taking no chances with some institutional developments. It has set up the Jewel-T division, which is a network of "box" discount stores patterned after pioneer Aldi. Watching a sudden turnaround in the competitive position of "independents" in 1977, Jewel's Star Market division in New England promptly began moving into franchising the following year. To hedge the "combination store" challenge, it integrated a large number of its supermarkets with its Osco Drug stores, using both side-by-side and fully integrated designs.

more than a pound of cure. For example, a company could launch an attack against a competitor whose market share is approaching some dangerous level. When Chrysler's market share began rising from 12 to 18 percent some years ago, one rival marketing executive was overheard to say, "If they [Chrysler] go to 20 percent, it will be over our dead bodies."

Or a company could wage guerrilla action across the market—hitting one competitor here, another there—and keep everyone off balance. Or the offensive defense could assume the proportions of a grand market envelopment, as practiced by Seiko with its 2,300 watch models distributed worldwide.[9] Or it could resemble the sustained frontal barrage of the Texas Instruments type. Sustained high-pressure strategies aim at retaining the initiative at all times and keeping the competition always on the defensive.

Sometimes the preemptive strike is waged psychologically rather than actually carried out. The market leader sends out market signals to dissuade competitors from attacking.[10] A major U.S. pharmaceutical firm is the leader in a certain drug category. Every time it learns that a competitor is about to build a factory to produce that drug, the company leaks the news that it is considering cutting the drug price and building another plant. This intimidates the competitor, who decides against entering that product arena. Meanwhile the leader never gets to cutting its price or adding another plant. Of course, this *bluff* can work only a few times.

Companies fortunate enough to enjoy high market assets—high brand loyalty, technological leadership, and so on—would probably find it disadvantageous to pursue too broad a preemptive strategy. They have the capacity to weather some punishment, and some may even prefer to entice the opponents into expensive and costly attacks that will not pay off (they hope) in the long run. Heinz let Hunt's carry out its massive attack in the ketchup market without much counteroffensive; and in the end, this proved very costly to Hunt's.[11] Standing firm in the face of an attack, however, calls for great confidence in the ultimate superiority of the company's market offer.

---

[9] See "Japanese Heat on the Watch Industry," *Business Week*, May 5, 1980, pp. 92–103.

[10] See Porter, *Competitive Strategy*, chap. 4.

[11] See "The H. J. Heinz Company (A)," Harvard Business School Case 9–569–011 M-357. Also see page 404 of this text.

Counteroffensive defense.   When a market leader is attacked in spite of its flanking and even preemptive maneuvers, it must respond with a counterattack on the opponent. The leader cannot remain passive in the face of a competitor's price cut, promotion blitz, product improvement, or sales-territory invasion. The leader has the strategic choice of meeting the attacker's spearhead head on, or maneuvering against the attacker's flank, or launching a pincer movement to cut off the attacking formations from their base of operation.

> Clearasil, the market leader in the acne medications market, suddenly found itself under a powerful promotional attack by Oxy-5. Clearasil retaliated with a stepped-up counterpromotion of its own.

Sometimes market-share erosion is so rapid that a head-on counterattack is necessary. But a defender enjoying some strategic depth can often weather the initial attack and riposte effectively at the opportune moment. In many situations, it may be worth some minor setbacks to allow the offensive to develop fully (and be understood) before countering. This may seem a dangerous strategy of "wait and see," but there are sound reasons for not barreling into a counteroffensive.

A better retort to an offensive is for the defender to pause and identify a chink in the attacker's armor, namely, a segment gap in which a viable counteroffensive can be launched. Cadillac designed its Seville as an alternative to the Mercedes and pinned its hope on offering a smoother ride and more creature comforts than Mercedes was willing to design.

An example of pincering out the opponent's attack is Heublein's strategy in defending its Smirnoff vodka against an attack from Wolfschmidt in the 1960s. Wolfschmidt priced its vodka at a dollar less a bottle and claimed it to be of the same quality as Smirnoff. Heublein responded by raising Smirnoff's price by one dollar and strengthened two other brands, one to meet Wolfschmidt head on (same price) and the other to flank Wolfschmidt (lower price).

When a market leader's territory is attacked, an effective counterattack is to invade the attacker's main territory so that it will have to pull back some of its troops to defend its territory. One of Northwest Airlines's most profitable routes is Minneapolis to Atlanta. A small carrier launched a deep fare cut and advertised it heavily, to expand its share in this market. Northwest retaliated by cutting its fares on the Minneapolis/Chicago route, which the other airline depended upon for its major revenue. With its major revenue source hurting, the other airline restored its Minneapolis/Atlanta fare to a normal level.

Mobile defense.   Mobile defense involves more than the leader's aggressively defending its current territory. Mobile defense consists of the leader's stretching its domain over new territories that can serve as future centers for defense and offense. It spreads to these new territories not so much through normal brand proliferation as through innovation activity on two fronts, namely, market broadening and market diversification. These moves generate "strategic depth" for the firm, which enables it to weather continual attacks and to launch retaliatory strikes.

Market broadening calls upon a company to shift its focus from the current product to the underlying generic need and to get involved in R&D across the whole range of technology associated with that need. Thus "petroleum" companies are asked to recast themselves into "energy" companies. Implicitly, this demands that they dip their research fingers into the oil, coal, nuclear, hydroelectric, and chemical industries. But this market-broadening strategy should not be carried too far, or it would fault two fundamental military principles—the *principle of the objective* ("pursue a clearly defined and attainable objective") and the *principle of mass* ("concentrate your efforts at a point of the enemy's weakness"). The objective of being in the energy business is too broad. The energy business is not a single need but a whole range of needs (heating, lighting, propelling, and so on). That leaves very little in the world that is not potentially the energy business. Furthermore, too much broadening would dilute the company's mass in the competitive theater today, and survival today surely must take precedence over the grand battles imagined for some tomorrow. The error of *marketing myopia* would be replaced by *marketing hyperopia*, a condition where vision is better for distant than for near objects.

Reasonable broadening, however, makes sense. Armstrong Cork exemplified a successful market-broadening strategy by redefining its domain from "floor covering" to "decorative room covering" (including walls and ceilings). By recognizing the customer's need to create a pleasant interior through various covering materials, Armstrong Cork expanded into neighboring businesses that were synergistically balanced for growth and defense.

Market diversification into unrelated industries is the other alternative to generating "strategic depth." When U.S. tobacco companies like Reynolds and Philip Morris acknowledged the growing curbs on cigarette smoking, they were not content with position defense or even with looking for new substitutes for the cigarette; instead they moved quickly into new industries such as beer, liquor, soft drinks, and frozen food.

Contraction defense.   Large companies sometimes recognize that they can no longer defend all of their territory. Their forces are spread too thin, and competitors are nibbling away on several fronts. The best course of action then appears to be planned contraction (also called strategic withdrawal). Planned contraction is not market abandonment but rather giving up the weaker territories and reassigning forces to stronger territories. Planned contraction is a move to consolidate one's competitive strength in the market and concentrate mass at pivotal positions.

In the slow-growth 1980s, an increasing opportunity seems to be emerging for profitable strategy in either eliminating or fusing fragmented market segments. Westinghouse cut its number of refrigerator models from forty to the thirty that accounted for 85 percent of sales. General Motors standardized its auto engines and now offers fewer options. Campell's Soup, Heinz, General Mills, Del Monte, and Georgia-Pacific are among those companies that have significantly pruned their product lines in recent years. Once again we find the underlying principle is concentration of mass if the desegmentation opportunity permits.

Market leaders can also grow through increasing their market share further. The well-publicized Profit Impact of Management Strategies (PIMS) studies indicate that *profitability* (measured by pretax ROI) rises linearly with *market share*.[12] The empirical relationship is shown in Figure 12–4(a).[13]

According to a PIMS report, "The average ROI for business with under 10 percent market share was about 9 percent. . . . On the average, a difference of 10 percentage points in market share is accompanied by a difference of about 5 points in pretax ROI." The PIMS study shows that businesses with market shares above 40 percent earn an average ROI of 30 percent, or three times that of those with shares under 10 percent.

These findings have led many companies to adopt the objective of expanding their market share since this would produce not only more *profit dollars* but also more *profitability* (return on investment). General Electric, for example, has decided that it wants to be at least number one or two in each of its markets or else get out. GE divested its computer business and its air-conditioning business because it could not achieve top-dog position in these industries.

Other studies have yielded a V-shaped relationship between market share and profitability in many industries. [See Figure 12–4(b).][14] Such industries have one or a few highly profitable leaders, several profitable small and more-focused firms, and a large number of medium-sized firms with poorer profit performance. According to Roach:

> The large firms on the V-curve tend to address the entire market, achieving cost advantages and high market share by realizing economies of scale. The small competitors reap high profits by focusing on some narrower segment of the business and by developing specialized approaches to production, marketing, and distribution for that segment. Ironically, the medium-sized competitors at the trough of the V-curve are unable to realize any competitive advantage and often show the poorest profit performance. Trapped in a strategic "No Man's Land," they are too large to reap the benefits of more focused competition, yet too small to benefit from the economies of scale that their larger competitors enjoy.[15]

As an example, many medium-sized management consulting firms don't do as well as smaller specialized firms or the large leaders who are preferred for their reputations

[12] Sidney Schoeffler, Robert D. Buzzell, and Donald F. Heany, "Impact of Strategic Planning on Profit Performance," *Harvard Business Review*, March-April 1974, pp. 137–45; and Robert D. Buzzell, Bradley T. Gale, and Ralph G. M. Sultan, "Market Share—A Key to Profitability," *Harvard Business Review*, January-February 1975, pp. 97–106.

[13] See Buzzell et al., "Market Share," pp. 97, 100. The results should be interpreted cautiously because the data came from a limited number of industries and there was some variance around the main line of relationship.

[14] John D. C. Roach, "From Strategic Planning to Strategic Performance: Closing the Achievement Gap," *Outlook* published by Booz, Allen & Hamilton, New York, spring 1981, p. 22. This curve assumes that pretax return on sales is highly correlated with profitability and that company revenue is a surrogate for market share. Michael Porter, in his *Competitive Strategy*, p. 43, shows a similar V-shaped curve that makes the same point.

[15] Roach, "Strategic Planning," p. 21.

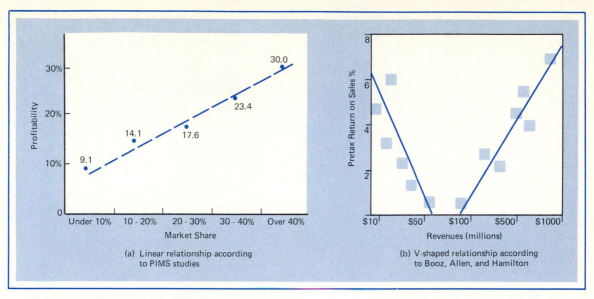

Source: Strategic Planning Institute (The PIMS Program), 1033 Massachusetts Avenue, Cambridge, Mass. 02138.

Source: John D. C. Roach, "From Strategic Planning to Strategic Performance: Closing the Achievement Gap," *Outlook* published by Booz, Allen & Hamilton, New York, spring 1981, p. 22.

FIGURE 12–4
Relationships between Market Share and Profitability

and resources. The message is that medium-sized firms need to figure out how to break into the big league or else settle in some specialized niches where they can do outstanding work.

Medium-sized companies must not think, however, that gaining increased market share will automatically improve their profitability. Much depends on their strategy for gaining increased market share. Business analysts have cited many high-market-share companies with low profitability, and many low-market-share companies with high profitability. The cost of buying higher market share may far exceed its revenue value. There are three factors the company should consider before blindly pursuing increased market share.

The first factor is the possibility of provoking antitrust action. Jealous competitors are likely to cry "monopolization" if a dominant firm makes further inroads on market share. This rise in risk would cut down the attractiveness of pushing market-share gains too far.

The second factor is economic cost. The cost of making further gains in market share after a large market share has been achieved may rise fast and reduce the profit margin. A company that has (say) 60 percent of the market must recognize that the "holdout" customers may dislike the company, be loyal to competitive suppliers, have unique needs, or prefer dealing with smaller suppliers. Furthermore the competitors are likely to fight harder to defend their falling market share. The cost of legal work, public relations, and lobbying rises with market share. The leader may prefer to concentrate on expanding the size of the total market rather than

Strategies For Leaders, Challengers, Followers, and Nichers **395**

Exhibit 12–1

THE IMPACT OF DIFFERENT MARKETING-MIX VARIABLES ON MARKET SHARE

Some light on the impact of different marketing variables on market share was shed by Buzzell and Wiersema, drawing on the PIMS (Profit Impact of Management Strategies) data base. They found that companies showing market-share gains typically outperformed their competitors in three areas: new-product activity, relative product quality, and marketing expenditures. Specifically:

1. Share-gaining companies typically developed and added more new products to their line.
2. Companies that increased their product quality relative to competitors' enjoyed greater share gains than those whose quality ratings remained constant or declined.
3. Companies that increased their marketing expenditures faster than the rate of market growth typically achieved share gains. Increases in sales-force expenditures were effective in producing share gains for both industrial and consumer markets. Increased advertising expenditures produced share gains mainly for consumer-goods companies. Increased sales promotion expenditures were effective in producing share gains for all kinds of companies.
4. Companies that cut their prices more deeply than competitors did not achieve significant market-share gains, contrary to expectations. Presumably enough rivals met the price cuts partly, and others offered other values to the buyers, so that buyers did not switch as much to the price cutter.

The reported study did not investigate whether the market-share gains were worth the cost of achieving them. Clearly companies are able to "buy" a higher market share, but the real issue is whether it will lead to higher profits sooner or later.

Source: Based on Robert D. Buzzell and Frederik D. Wiersema, "Successful Share-Building Strategies," Harvard Business Review, January-February, 1981, pp. 135–44.

fight for further increases in market share. Some dominant markets have even gained by selectively decreasing their market share in weaker areas.[16]

The third factor is that companies may pursue the wrong marketing-mix strategy in their bid for higher market share and therefore not increase their profit. While certain marketing-mix variables are more effective in building market share, their use does not necessarily lead to higher profits. (See Exhibit 12–1.) Higher shares tend to produce higher profits under two conditions:

☐ **Unit costs fall with increased market share.** Unit costs fall both because the leader enjoys cost economies of scale by running larger plants and because he goes down the cost experience curve faster. This means that one effective marketing strategy for gaining

---

[16] Philip Kotler and Paul N. Bloom, "Strategies for High Market-Share Companies," *Harvard Business Review*, November-December 1975, pp. 63–72.

profitable increases in market share is to fanatically pursue the lowest costs in the industry and pass the cost savings on to customers through lower prices. That was Henry Ford's strategy for selling autos in the 1920s and Texas Instruments' strategy for selling transistors in the 1960s.

☐ **The company offers a superior-quality product and charges a premium price that more than covers the cost of offering higher quality.** Crosby, in his book *Quality Is Free*, claims that building more quality into a product does not cost the company much more because the company saves in less scrappage, after-sales servicing, and so on.[17] But its products are so desired that consumers pay a large premium that is the basis of the higher profit margin. This strategy for profitable market share growth is pursued by IBM, Caterpillar, and Michelin, among others.

All said, market leaders who stay on top have learned the art of expanding the total market, defending their current territory, and increasing their market share profitably. Exhibit 12–2 details the specific principles that two great companies—Procter & Gamble and Caterpillar—use to maintain and expand their leadership in their respective markets.

MARKET-CHALLENGER STRATEGIES

The firms that occupy second, third, and lower ranks in an industry can be called runner-up or trailing firms. Some are quite large in their own right, such as Colgate, Ford, Montgomery Ward, Avis, Westinghouse, Schlitz, and Pepsi-Cola. These runner-up firms can adopt one of two postures. They can attack the leader and other competitors in an aggressive bid for further market share (market challengers). Or they can play ball and not rock the boat (market followers). Dolan found that competitive rivalry is most intense in industries with high fixed costs, high inventory costs, and stagnant primary demand.[18] We shall examine below the competitive attack strategies available to market challengers.[19]

Defining the Strategic Objective and Opponent(s)

A market challenger must first define its strategic objective. The military "principle of objective" holds that "every military operation must be directed toward a clearly defined, decisive, and attainable objective." The strategic objective of most market challengers is to increase their market shares, thinking that this will lead to greater profitability (subject to the preceding caveats on pp. 394–96). Deciding on the objective, whether it is to crush the competitor or reduce its share, interacts with the question of who the competitor is. Unlike war, where the enemy is "given," the

---

[17] Philip B. Crosby, *Quality is Free* (New York: McGraw-Hill Book Co., 1979).

[18] See Robert J. Dolan, "Models of Competition: A Review of Theory and Empirical Evidence" in Ben M. Enis and Kenneth J. Roering, eds., *Review of Marketing* (Chicago: American Marketing Association, 1981), pp. 224–34.

[19] For additional reading, see C. David Fogg, "Planning Gains in Market Share," *Journal of Marketing*, July 1974, pp. 30–38; and Bernard Catry and Michel Chevalier, "Market Share Strategy and the Product Life Cycle," *Journal of Marketing*, October 1974, pp. 29–34.

Exhibit 12-2

HOW TWO GREAT COMPANIES—PROCTER & GAMBLE AND CATERPILLAR—MAINTAIN THEIR MARKET LEADERSHIP

The principles of maintaining market leadership are admirably illustrated by companies such as Procter & Gamble, Caterpillar, IBM, McDonald's, and Hertz, all of whom have shown a remarkable ability to protect their market shares against repeated attacks by able challengers. Their success is based not on doing one thing well but on doing everything well. They don't allow any weaknesses to develop. We shall examine the basics behind Procter & Gamble's and Caterpillar's success.

Procter & Gamble. P&G is widely regarded as the nation's most skilled marketer of consumer packaged goods. It sells the number one brand in each of eight important categories: disposable diapers (Pampers), detergents (Tide), toilet tissue (Charmin), paper towels (Bounty), fabric softeners (Downy), toothpaste (Crest), shampoo (Head & Shoulders), and mouthwash (Scope). (See "P&G Up Against Its Wall," *Fortune*, February 23, 1981, pp. 49–54). Its market leadership rests on several principles.

☐ **Product innovation.** P&G is an active product innovator and benefit segmentor. It launches brands offering new consumer benefits rather than me-too brands backed by heavy advertising. P&G spent ten years researching and developing the first effective anticavity toothpaste, Crest. It spent several years researching the first effective over-the-counter antidandruff shampoo, Head & Shoulders. The company thoroughly tests its new products with consumers, and only when real preference is indicated does it launch them in the national market.

☐ **Quality strategy.** P&G designs products of above-average quality. Once launched, it makes a continuous effort to improve the product's quality over time. When they announce "new and improved," they mean it. This is in contrast to some companies that, after establishing the quality level, rarely improve it, and to other companies that deliberately reduce the quality in an effort to squeeze out more profit.

☐ **Product flanking.** P&G produces its brands in several sizes and forms to satisfy varying consumer preferences. This gives its brand more shelf space and prevents competitors from moving in to satisfy unmet needs in the market.

☐ **Multibrand strategy.** P&G is the originator of the art of marketing several brands in the same product category. For example, it produces ten brands of laundry detergents, each positioned somewhat differently in the consumer's mind. The trick is to design brands that meet different consumer wants and that compete against specific competitors' brands. Each brand manager runs the brand independently of the other brand managers and competes for company resources. Having several brands on the shelf, the company "locks up" shelf space and gains more clout with distributors.

☐ **Brand-extension strategy.** P&G will often use its strong brand names to launch new products. For example, the Ivory brand has been extended from a soap to include liquid soap and a detergent. Launching a new product under a strong existing brand name gives it more instant recognition and credibility with much less advertising outlay.

☐ **Heavy advertising.** P&G is the nation's largest consumer-packaged-goods advertiser, spending over $672 million per year. It never stints on spending money to create strong consumer awareness and preference.

- ☐ **Aggressive sales force.** P&G has a top-flight field sales force, which is very effective in gaining shelf space and retailer cooperation in point-of-purchase displays and promotions.
- ☐ **Effective sales promotion.** P&G has a sales promotion department to counsel its brand managers on the most effective promotions to achieve particular objectives. The department studies the results of consumer and trade deals and develops an expert sense of their effectiveness under varying circumstances. At the same time, P&G prefers to minimize the use of sales promotion, preferring to rely on advertising to build long-term consumer preference.
- ☐ **Competitive toughness.** P&G carries a big stick when it comes to constraining aggressors. P&G is willing to spend large sums of money to outpromote new competitive brands and prevent them from getting a foothold in the market.
- ☐ **Manufacturing efficiency.** P&G's reputation as a great marketing company is matched by its greatness as a manufacturing company. P&G spends large sums of money developing and improving production operations to keep its costs among the lowest in the industry.
- ☐ **Brand-management system.** P&G originated the brand-management system, in which one executive is responsible for each brand. The system has been copied by many competitors but frequently without the success that P&G has achieved through perfecting its system over the years.

Thus P&G's market leadership is not based on doing one thing well but on the successful orchestration of all the factors that count in market leadership.

Caterpillar. Since the 1940s, Caterpillar has dominated the construction-equipment industry. Its tractors, crawlers, and loaders, painted in familiar yellow, are a common sight at any construction area and account for 50 percent of the world's sales of heavy construction equipment. Caterpillar has managed to retain leadership in spite of charging a premium price for its equipment and being challenged by a number of able competitors, including John Deere, Massey-Ferguson, J. I. Case, and Komatsu. Several principles combine to explain their success:

- ☐ **Premium-product quality.** Caterpillar produces high-quality equipment known for its reliability. Reliability is a key buyer consideration in the purchase of heavy industrial equipment. Caterpillar designs its equipment with a heavier gauge of steel than necessary, to convince buyers of its superior quality.
- ☐ **Extensive-and-efficient-dealership system.** Caterpillar maintains the largest number of independent construction-equipment dealers in the industry. Its 260 dealers are located throughout the world and carry a complete line of Caterpillar equipment. Caterpillar dealers can focus all of their attention on Caterpillar equipment and don't need to carry other lines. Competitors' dealers, on the other hand, normally lack a full line and have to carry complementary, noncompeting lines. Caterpillar can choose the best dealers among those applying (a new Caterpillar dealership costs the franchisee $5 million) and spends the most money in training, servicing, and motivating them.
- ☐ **Superior service.** Caterpillar has built a worldwide parts and service system second to none in the industry. Caterpillar can deliver replacement parts and service anywhere in the world within a few hours of equipment breakdown. This service level is hard for competitors to match without a substantial investment. Any competitor duplicating the service level would only neutralize Caterpillar's advantage rather than gaining any net advantage.
- ☐ **Superior parts management.** Thirty percent of Caterpillar's sales volume and over 50 percent of its profit come from the sale of replacement parts. Caterpillar has developed a superior parts-management system to keep margins high in this end of the business.

business firm in most cases is able to choose its opponent. Basically, an aggressor can choose to attack one of three types of firms:

☐ **It can attack the market leader.** This is a high-risk but potentially high-payoff strategy and makes good sense if the leader is not a "true leader" and is not serving the market well. The "terrain" to examine closely is consumer need or dissatisfaction. If a substantial area is unserved or poorly served, it offers a great strategic target. Miller's campaign in the beer market was successful because it pivoted initially on discovering many consumers who wanted a "lighter" beer. The alternative strategy is to out-innovate the leader across the whole segment. Thus Xerox took the copy market away from 3M by developing a better copying process (dry copying instead of wet copying).

☐ **It could attack firms of its own size that are not doing the job and that are underfinanced.** Both consumer satisfaction and innovation potential need to be examined minutely. Even a frontal attack might work if the other firm's resources are limited.

☐ **It could attack small local and regional firms that are not doing the job and are underfinanced.** Several of the major beer companies grew to their present size not by stealing each other's customers so much as by gobbling up the "small fry," or "guppies."

Thus the issue of choosing the opponent and choosing the objective interact. If the attacking company goes after the market leader, its objective may be to wrest a certain share. Thus Bic is under no illusion that it could topple Gillette in the razor market—it is simply seeking a larger share. If the attacking company goes after a small local company, its objective may be to drive that company out of existence. The important principle remains: "Every military operation must be directed toward a clearly defined, decisive, and attainable objective."

Critical to choosing opponents and objectives is the need for systematic competitive analysis. Each company must collect up-to-date information on competitors. Its competitive information and analysis system must allow it to answer the following questions:[20]

☐ Who are our competitors?

☐ What is each competitor's sales, market share, and financial standing?

☐ What is each competitor's goals and assumptions?

☐ What is each competitor's strategy?

☐ What is each competitor's strengths and weaknesses?

☐ What changes is each competitor likely to make in its future strategy in response to environmental, competitive, and internal developments?

---

[20] For further discussion of competitive analysis, see chap. 3 in Michael E. Porter, *Competitive Strategy*.

Choosing an Attack Strategy

Given clear opponents and objectives, how do military strategists view their major options in attacking an enemy? The starting point is known as the "principle of mass," which holds that "superior combat power must be concentrated at the critical time and place for a decisive purpose." We can make progress by imagining an opponent who occupies a certain market territory. We distinguish the five possible attack strategies shown in Figure 12–5 and discussed below.

Frontal attack. An aggressor is said to launch a frontal (or "head-on") attack when it masses its forces right up against those of its opponent. It attacks the opponent's strengths rather than its weaknesses. The outcome depends on who has the greater strength and endurance. In a pure frontal attack, the attacker matches its opponent's product, advertising, price, and so on. Recently the second-place razor-blade manufacturer in Brazil decided to go after Gillette, the market leader. Management was

FIGURE 12–5
Attack Strategies

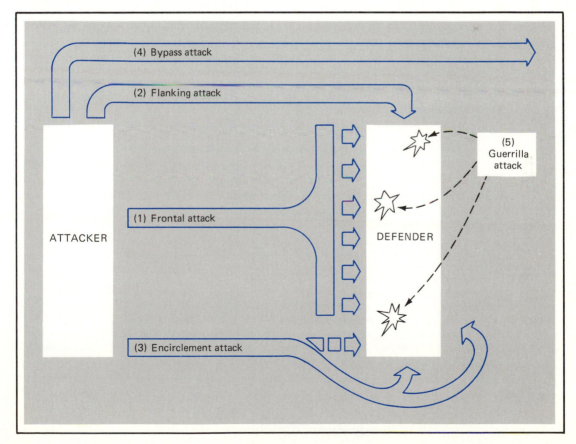

asked if it was offering the consumer a better blade. "No," was the reply. "A lower price?" "No." "A better package?" "No." "A cleverer advertising campaign?" "No." "Better allowances to the trade?" "No." "Then how do you expect to take share away from Gillette?" "Sheer determination" was the reply. Needless to say, its offensive failed.

For a pure frontal attack to succeed, the aggressor needs a strength advantage over the competitor. The "principle of force" says that the side with the greater manpower (resources) will win the engagement. This rule is modified if the defender has greater firing efficiency through enjoying a terrain advantage (such as holding a mountain top). The military dogma is that for a frontal attack to succeed against a well-entrenched opponent or one controlling the "high ground," the attacking forces must deploy at least a 3:1 advantage in combat firepower. If the aggressor has a smaller force or poorer firepower than the defender, a frontal attack amounts to a suicide mission and makes no sense. RCA, GE, and Xerox learned this the hard way when they launched frontal attacks on IBM, overlooking its superior defensive position.[21]

> As an example of a successful pure frontal attack and the resources it required, consider S. C. Johnson & Son's entry into the shampoo market with its new Agree brand.[22] In 1977, with what **Forbes** described as "almost Japanese-like thoroughness," S. C. Johnson first raided Colgate and others for experienced executives. Then it blitzed the market with a $14 million promotion that included 30 million sample bottles of its new hair conditioner, Agree. That about equaled the industry's total promotion on hair conditioners. It grabbed 15 percent of the market in its first year, wrested from such giants as Gillette's Toni, Breck, and Clairol. (By 1979, its share was 20 percent.) Then, in 1978, it invaded the shampoo market, reportedly spending $30 million in marketing costs in the summer of that year. It ended up with a 6 percent share of that market.

As an alternative to a pure frontal attack, the aggressor may launch a modified frontal attack, the most common being to cut its price vis-à-vis the opponent's. Such attacks can take two forms. The more usual ploy is to match the leader's offer on other counts and beat it on price. This can work if the market leader does not retaliate by cutting price, too, and if the competitor convinces the market that its product is equal to the competitor's or, that at a lower price, it is a real value.

> Helene Curtis is a master practitioner of the somewhat risky strategy of convincing the market that its product is equal in quality to the higher-priced products of competitors.[23] Curtis makes no bones about its approach—making budget imitations of leading high-priced brands and promoting them with blatant comparative advertising campaigns: "We do what theirs does for less than half the price," is the message. In 1972 Curtis had a meager 1 percent share of the shampoo market for its five Suave shampoos. Its new strategy was launched in 1973. By 1976, it had overtaken Procter & Gamble's Head & Shoulders and Johnson & Johnson's Baby Shampoo to lead the market in volume. Its share hit 16 percent in 1979.

---

[21] "The 250 Million Dollar Disaster That Hit RCA," *Business Week*, Sept. 25, 1971.

[22] See "Stopping the Greasies," *Forbes*, July 9, 1979, p. 121.

[23] "A 'Me-Too' Strategy That Paid Off," *Fortune*, August 27, 1979, p. 86.

The other form of price-aggressive strategy is one in which the attacker invests heavily in research to achieve lower production costs and then attacks competitors on a price basis. Texas Instruments has had brilliant success in using the price weapon strategically. It invests heavily in R&D and moves very rapidly down the experience curve. The Japanese, too, launch frontal attacks on the basis of cost-related price cutting, and this is one of the most viable bases upon which a sustained frontal-attack strategy can be founded.

Flank attack. An enemy's army is strongest where it expects to be attacked. It is necessarily less secure in its flanks and rear. Its weak spots (blind sides), therefore, are natural points of attack for the enemy. The major principle of modern offensive warfare is "concentration of strength against weakness." The aggressor will act as if he will attack the strong side to tie up the defender's troops but will launch the real attack at the side or rear. This "turning" maneuver catches the defending army off guard. Flank attacks make excellent marketing sense and are particularly attractive to the aggressor possessing fewer resources than the opponent. If he cannot overwhelm the defender with brute strength, he can outmaneuver him with subterfuge.

A flank attack can be directed against a competitor along two strategic dimensions—geographical and segmental. A geographical attack consists of the aggressor's spotting areas in the country or the world in which the opponent is not performing at high levels. For example, some of IBM's rivals chose to set up strong branches in medium- and smaller-sized cities, which are relatively neglected by IBM. According to a Honeywell field sales manager:

> Out in the rural areas, we are relatively better off than in the cities. We have been quite successful in these areas because our sales force does not meet the ten plus to one ratio it hits in the cities where IBM concentrates its people. Thus, ours must be a concentration game.[24]

The other, and potentially more powerful, flanking strategy is to spot uncovered market needs not being served by the leaders:

> German and Japanese auto makers chose not to compete with American auto makers by producing large, flashy, gas-guzzling automobiles, even though these were supposedly the preference of American buyers. Instead they recognized an unserved consumer segment that wanted small, fuel-efficient cars. They moved vigorously to fill this hole in the market, and to their satisfaction and Detroit's surprise, American taste for smaller, fuel-efficient cars grew to be a substantial part of the market.
>
> "Discovering," so to speak, the "light" beer segment, Miller Brewing Company pivoted on this unserved gap in the market and vigorously developed it into a huge breach across the whole industry's front and propelled itself from seventh place in the industry to a very close second in five years.

A flanking strategy is another name for identifying shifts in market segments—which are causing gaps to develop that are not being served by the industry's product

---

[24] Quoted in "Honeywell Information Systems (case available from the Intercollegiate Case Clearing House, Soldiers Field, Boston, 1975), pp. 7–8.

profile—and rushing in to fill the gaps and develop them into strong segments. Instead of a bloody battle between two or more companies trying to serve the same market, flanking leads to a fuller coverage of the varied needs of the whole market. Flanking is in the best tradition of the modern marketing philosophy, which holds that the purpose of marketing is to "discover needs and serve them." Flank attacks have a higher probability of being successful than frontal attacks. This is also borne out in military history. In his penetrating analysis of the thirty most important conflicts of the world from the Greek wars up to World War I (which embraced more than 280 campaigns), Liddell Hart concluded that in only six campaigns did decisive results follow strategies of direct head-on assault.[25] The strategy of "the indirect approach" has overwhelming support from history as the most effective and economic form of strategy.

Encirclement attack. The pure flanking maneuver was defined as pivoting on a gap in the existing market coverage of the competitors. The encirclement maneuver, on the other hand, is an attempt to pierce the enemy's territory. Encirclement involves launching a grand offensive on several fronts, so that the enemy must protect its front, sides, and rear simultaneously. The aggressor may offer the market everything the opponent offers and more, so that the offer is unrefusable. Encirclement makes sense as a strategy where the aggressor commands superior resources to those of the opponent and believes that the encirclement will be complete and swift enough to break the opponent's will to resist. Here are two examples:

Seiko's attack on the watch market illustrates an encirclement strategy.[26] For several years, Seiko has been acquiring distribution in every major watch outlet and overwhelming its competitors and consumers with an enormous variety of constantly changing models. In the United States, it offers some four hundred models, but its marketing clout is backed by the some twenty-three hundred models it makes and sells worldwide. "They hit the mark on fashion, features, user preferences, and everything else that might motivate the consumer," says an admiring vice-president of a U.S. competitor.

An encirclement attack does not always work, as Hunt's found out when it tried to blitz Heinz's brand of ketchup in a grab for increased market share. In 1963 Hunt's, with a 19 percent share of the ketchup market, launched a major encirclement attack on Heinz to go after Heinz's 27 percent market share. Hunt's rolled out a number of marketing attacks simultaneously. It introduced two new flavors of ketchup (pizza and hickory) to disrupt the consumers' traditional taste preference for Heinz and also to capture more retail shelf space. It lowered its price to 70 percent of Heinz's price. It offered heavy trade allowances to the retailers. It raised its advertising budget to over twice the level of Heinz's. This marketing program meant that Hunt's would lose money while the battle raged but would make it up if it attracted enough brand switchers. The strategy failed to work. The Heinz brand continued to enjoy consumer preference: as a result, not enough Heinz users tried the Hunt's brand, and most of those who did returned to the Heinz brand. By the mid-1970s, Heinz had increased its share to over 40 percent.

---

[25] Liddell-Hart, *Strategy*, p. 161.
[26] See "Seiko's Smash," *Business Week*, June 5, 1978, p. 89.

Hunt's debacle underscores our core proposition that segmentation opportunity is fundamental to choosing the axis for an indirect approach. If empty niches do not now exist or cannot be created by segment diffusion tactics, then what is a flank attack in the mind of the aggressor peters out into a plain frontal attack in the marketplace. As such, it would require the 3:1 advantage in combat firepower to succeed.

Bypass attack.   The bypass is the most indirect of assault strategies and eschews any belligerent move directed against the enemy's existing territory. It means bypassing the enemy and attacking easier markets to broaden one's resources base. This offers three lines of approach: diversifying into *unrelated products*, diversifying into *new geographical markets* for existing products, and leapfrogging into *new technologies* to supplant existing products.

> Colgate's impressive turnaround utilized the first two principles.[27] In the United States, Colgate has always struggled in Procter & Gamble's shadow. In heavy-duty detergents, P&G's Tide routed Colgate's Fab by almost 5:1. In dishwashing liquids, P&G had almost twice Colgate's share. In soaps, too, Colgate trailed far behind. When David Foster took over as CEO in 1971, despite it's $1.3 billion in sales, Colgate still had the reputation as a stodgy marketer of soap and detergent. By 1979 Foster had transformed the company into a $4.3 billion conglomerate, capable of challenging P&G if necessary. Foster's real achievement was in recognizing that any head-on battle with P&G was futile. "They outgunned us 3 to 1 at the store level," said Foster, "and had three research people to our one." Foster's strategy was simple—increase Colgate's lead abroad and bypass P&G at home by diversifying into non-P&G markets. A string of acquisitions followed in textiles and hospital products, cosmetics, and a range of sporting goods and food products. The outcome: In 1971, Colgate was underdog to P&G in about half of its business. By 1976, in three-fourths of its business, it was either comfortably placed against P&G or didn't face it at all.

Technological leapfrogging is a bypass strategy used often in high-tech industries. Instead of imitating the competitor's product and engaging in a costly frontal attack, the challenger patiently researches and develops the next technology and, when satisfied about its superiority, launches an attack, thus shifting the battleground to its territory, where it has an advantage. Intellevision's attack strategy on Atari in the videogame market was precisely to bypass Atari's state-of-the-art and attack when it had discovered a superior technology.

Guerrilla attack.   Guerrilla attack is another option available to market aggressors, especially smaller undercapitalized ones. Guerrilla warfare consists of making small, intermittent attacks on different territories of the opponent, with the aim of harassing and demoralizing the opponent and eventually securing permanent footholds. The military rationale was stated by Liddell Hart:

> The more usual reason for adopting a strategy of limited aim is that of awaiting a change in the balance of force—a change often sought and achieved by draining the

---

[27] See "The Changing of the Guard," *Fortune*, Sept. 24, 1979; "How to Be Happy Though No. Two," *Forbes*, July 15, 1976, p. 36.

enemy's force, weakening him by pricks instead of risking blows. The essential condition of such a strategy is that the drain on him should be disproportionately greater than on oneself. The object may be sought by raiding his supplies; by local attacks which annihilate or inflict disproportionate loss on parts of his force: by bringing him into unprofitable attacks; by causing an excessively wide distribution of his force; and, not least, by exhausting his moral and physical energy.[28]

The guerrilla attacker will use both conventional and unconventional means to harass the opponent. In the business world, these would include selective price cuts, supply interferences, executive raids, intense promotional bursts, and assorted legal actions against the opponent. The last, legal action, is becoming one of the most common ways to harass the other side.

> A Seattle-based beer distributor who had been supplying beer to Alaska by ship was upset when the Oetker Group of West Germany obtained a 75 percent tax credit for ten years from the Alaska legislature to establish beer production in Alaska. The Seattle distributor slapped a lawsuit on Oetker, charging the tax incentive was unconstitutional. Oetker eventually won in the courts, but four years of delay crippled its hope of capitalizing on the oil pipeline construction boom. After operating just thirty months, Oetker closed its Anchorage brewery.[29]

Normally guerrilla warfare is practiced by a smaller firm against a larger one. Not able to mount a frontal or even an effective flanking attack, the smaller firm launches a barrage of short promotional and price attacks in random corners of the larger opponent's market in a manner calculated to gradually weaken the opponent's market power. Even here, the attacker has to decide between launching a few major attacks or a continual stream of minor attacks. Military dogma holds that a continual stream of minor attacks usually creates more cumulative impact, disorganization, and confusion in the enemy than a few major ones. In line with this, the guerrilla attacker would find it more effective to attack small, isolated, weakly defended markets rather than major stronghold markets like New York, Chicago, and Los Angeles, where the defender is better entrenched and more willing to retaliate quickly and decisively.

It would be a mistake to think of a guerrilla campaign as only a "low-resource" strategy alternative available to financially weak challengers. Conducting a continual guerrilla campaign can be expensive, although admittedly less expensive than a frontal, encirclement, or even flanking attack. Furthermore guerrilla war is more a preparation for war than a war itself. Ultimately it must be backed by a stronger attack if the aggressor hopes to "beat" the opponent. Hence in terms of resources, guerrilla warfare is not necessarily a cheap operation.

The preceding attack strategies are very broad. The challenger must put together a total strategy consisting of several specific strategies. Exhibit 12–3 lists several specific marketing strategies for attacking competitive positions. Exhibit 12–4 details how two well-known challenger companies, Pepsi-Cola and Yamaha, attacked the leaders in their respective industries.

---

[28] Liddell-Hart, *Strategy*, p. 335.

[29] "Alaska Chills a German Beer," *Business Week*, April 23, 1979, p. 42.

Exhibit 12–3

SOME SPECIFIC ATTACK STRATEGIES AVAILABLE TO CHALLENGERS

Several specific attack strategies are available to the market challenger who is seeking an advantage vis-à-vis competition:

1. **Price-discount strategy.** A major attack strategy for challengers is to offer buyers a product comparable to the leader's at a lower price. (See Figure 16–7, p. 528. Leader in cell 1, challenger in cell 2.) The Fuji Corporation used this strategy to attack Kodak's preeminence in the photographic-paper field. Its paper is of comparable quality and is priced 10 percent lower than Kodak's. Kodak chose not to lower its price, with the result that Fuji achieved strong market-share inroads. Texas Instruments is the prime practitioner of price cutting. It will offer a comparable-quality product and cut its price progressively to gain market share and still lower costs of production. Texas Instruments willingly foregoes profits in the first few years in a drive to gain unchallenged market leadership. They did this with transistors and hand calculators and now seem bent on doing it in the personal computer market. For a price-discount strategy to work, three assumptions must be fulfilled. First, the challenger must convince buyers that its product and service are comparable to the leader's. Second, the buyers must be sensitive to the price difference and feel comfortable about turning their back on existing suppliers. Third, the market leader must refuse to cut its price in spite of the competitor's attack.

2. **Cheaper-goods strategy.** Another strategy is to offer the market an average- or low-quality product at a much lower price. (See Figure 16–7, p. 528. Leader in cell 1, challenger in cell 5 or 9.) This works when there is a sufficient segment of buyers who are interested only in price. Firms that get established through this strategy, however, may be attacked by "cheaper-goods" firms whose prices are even lower. In defense, they try to upgrade their quality gradually over time.

3. **Prestige-goods strategy.** A market challenger can launch a higher-quality product and charge a higher price than the leader. (See Figure 16–7, p. 528. Leader in cell 1, challenger goes to northwest of cell 1.) Mercedes gained on Cadillac in the American market by offering a car of even higher quality and higher price. Some prestige-goods firms later roll out lower-price products to take advantage of their charisma.

4. **Product-proliferation strategy.** The challenger can go after the leader by launching a large number of product versions thus giving buyers more options. Hunt went after Heinz's leadership in the ketchup market by creating several new ketchup flavors and bottle sizes in contrast to Heinz's reliance on one flavor of ketchup, sold in a limited number of bottle sizes.

5. **Product-innovation strategy.** The challenger may pursue product innovation to attack the leader's position. Polaroid and Xerox are companies whose success is based on continuously introducing outstanding innovations in the camera and copying fields, respectively. Miller rose to second place in the beer industry by successfully launching a light beer and introducing "pony-sized" bottles for lighter beer drinkers. The public often gains most from challenger strategies oriented toward product innovation.

6. **Improved-services strategy.** The challenger might find ways to offer new or better services to customers. IBM achieved its success by recognizing that customers were more interested in the software and the service than in the hardware. Avis's famous attack on Hertz, "We're only second. We try harder," was based on promising and delivering cleaner cars and faster service than Hertz.

7. **Distribution-innovation strategy.** A challenger might discover or develop a new channel of distribution. Avon became a major cosmetics company by perfecting door-to-door selling instead of battling other cosmetic firms in conventional stores. U.S. Time Company achieved great success by selling its low-price Timex watches through mass-merchandise channels instead of jewelry stores.

8. **Manufacturing-cost-reduction strategy.** The challenger might seek to achieve lower manufacturing costs than its competitors', through more efficient purchasing, lower labor costs, and more modern production equipment. The company can use its lower costs to price more aggressively in order to gain market share. This strategy has been the key to the successful Japanese invasion of various world markets.

9. **Intensive advertising promotion.** Some challengers attack the leader by increasing their expenditures on advertising and promotion. When Hunt went after Heinz in the ketchup market, it built its annual spending level to $6.4 million as against Heinz's $3.4 million. Miller Beer similarly outspent Budweiser in its attempt to achieve first place in the U.S. beer market. Substantial promotional spending, however, is usually not a sensible strategy unless the challenger's product or advertising message exhibits some superiority over competition.

A challenger rarely succeeds in improving its market share by relying on only one strategy element. Its success depends on designing a total strategy that will improve its position over time.

Exhibit 12–4

HOW TWO CHALLENGERS—PEPSI-COLA AND YAMAHA— GAINED SHARE ON THEIR RESPECTIVE MARKET LEADERS

Pepsi-Cola attacks Coca-Cola Before the Second World War, Coca-Cola dominated the American soft-drink industry. There was no second-place firm worth mentioning. "Pepsi raised hardly a flicker of recognition in Coke's consciousness." Pepsi-Cola was a newer drink, costing less to manufacture and with a less satisfactory taste than Coke's. Its major selling point was more drink for the same price. Pepsi emphasized this in its advertising, "Twice as much for a nickel, too." Its plain bottle carried a paper label that often got dirty in transit, adding to the impression that it was a second-class soft drink.

During the Second World War, Pepsi and Coke both enjoyed increased sales, as they followed the flag around the world. After the war, Pepsi's sales started to fall relative to Coke's. A number of factors contributed to Pepsi's problems, including poor image, poor taste, poor packaging, and poor quality control. Furthermore Pepsi had to raise its prices to cover rising costs, and it became less of a bargain than before. Morale was quite low at Pepsi toward the end of the 1940s.

At this point, Alfred N. Steele came to the presidency of Pepsi-Cola with a great reputation for merchandising. He and his staff recognized that the main hope lay in transforming Pepsi from a cheap imitation of Coke into a first-class soft drink. They recognized that this turnaround would take several years. They conceived of a *grand offensive* against Coke that would take place in two phases. In the first phase, which lasted from 1950 to 1955, the following steps were taken: First, Pepsi's taste was improved. Second, the bottle and other corporate symbols were redesigned and unified. Third, the advertising campaign was redesigned to upgrade Pepsi's image. Fourth, Steele decided to concentrate on the take-home market, which Coke had neglected. Finally, Steele singled out twenty-five cities for a special push for market share.

By 1955, all of Pepsi's major weaknesses had been overcome, sales had climbed substantially, and Steele was ready for the next phase. The second phase consisted of mounting a direct attack on Coke's "on-premise" market, particularly the vending machine and cold-bottle segments, which were growing fast. Another decision was to introduce new-size bottles that offered convenience to customers in the take-home and cold-bottle markets. Finally, Pepsi offered to finance its bottlers who were willing to buy and install Pepsi vending machines. These actions during 1955 to 1960 led to considerable sales growth for Pepsi. Within one decade, Pepsi's sales had grown fourfold.

Yamaha attacks Honda In the early 1960s, Honda had established itself as the number one motorcycle brand in the United States. Its lightweight machines with their great eye appeal, the slogan, "You Meet the Nicest People on a Honda," and an aggressive sales organization and distribution network combined to greatly expand the total motorcycle market. Yamaha, another Japanese manufacturer, decided to enter the market against Honda. Its first step was to study Honda's major weaknesses, which included several dealers who had grown rich and lazy, abrupt management changes, discouragement of franchise-seeking dealers, and failure to promote the mechanical features of their motorcycles. Yamaha offered franchises to the best of the Honda-rejected franchises and used an enthusiastic sales force to train and motivate these dealers. They improved their motorcycle to the point that they could claim and demonstrate its mechanical superiority. They spent liberally on advertising and sales promotion programs to build buyer awareness and dealer enthusiasm. When motorcycle safety became a big issue, they designed superior safety features and advertised them extensively. These strategies propelled Yamaha into a clear second position in an industry swarming with over fifty manufacturers.

Source: Alvin Toffler, "The Competition that Refreshes," Fortune, May 1961. Also see "Pepsi Takes on the Champ," Business Week, June 12, 1978, pp. 88–97.

MARKET-FOLLOWER STRATEGIES

Not all runner-up companies will challenge the market leader. The effort to draw away the leader's customers is never taken lightly by the leader. If the challenger's lure is lower prices, improved service, or additional product features, the leader can quickly match these to diffuse the attack. The leader probably has more staying power in an all-out battle. A hard fight might leave both firms worse off, and this means the challenger must think twice before attacking. Unless the challenger can launch a preemptive strike—in the form of a substantial product innovation or distribution breakthrough—he often prefers to follow rather than attack the leader.

Patterns of "conscious parallelism" are common in capital-intensive homogeneous-product industries, such as steel, fertilizers, and chemicals. The opportunities for product differentiation and image differentiation are low; service quality is often comparable; price sensitivity runs high. Price wars can erupt at any time. The mood in these industries is against short-run grabs for market share because that strategy only provokes retaliation. Most firms decide against stealing each other's customers.

Instead they present similar offers to buyers, usually by copying the leader. Market shares show a high stability.

This is not to say that market followers are without strategies. A market follower must know how to hold current customers and win a fair share of new customers. Each follower tries to bring distinctive advantages to its target market—location, services, financing. The follower is a major target of attack by challengers. Therefore the market follower must keep its manufacturing costs low and its product quality and services high. It must also enter new markets as they open up. Followship is not the same as being passive or a carbon copy of the leader. The follower has to define a growth path but one that does not create competitive retaliation. Three broad followership strategies can be distinguished:

☐ **Following closely.** Here the follower emulates the leader in as many market-segmentation and marketing-mix areas as possible. The follower almost appears to be a challenger, but if it does not radically block the leader, no direct conflict will occur. Some followers may even be described as parasitic, in that they put very little into stimulating the market, hoping to live off the market leader's investments.

☐ **Following at a distance.** Here the follower maintains some differentiation but follows the leader in terms of major market and product innovations, general price levels, and distribution. This follower is quite acceptable to the market leader, who may see little interference with its market plans and may be pleased that the follower's market share helps the leader avoid charges of monopolization. The distant follower may achieve its growth through acquiring smaller firms in the industry.

☐ **Following selectively.** This company follows the leader quite closely in some ways and sometimes goes its own way. The company may be quite innovative, and yet it avoids direct competition and follows many strategies of the leader where advantages are apparent. This company often grows into the future challenger.

Market followers, although they have lower market shares than the leader, may be as profitable or even more profitable. A recent study reported that many companies with less than half the market share of the leader had a five-year average return on equity that surpassed the industry median.[30] Burroughs (computers), Crown Cork & Seal (metal containers), and Union Camp Corporation (paper) were among the successful market followers. The keys to their success were conscious market segmentation and concentration, effective research and development, profit emphasis rather than market-share emphasis, and strong top management.

MARKET-NICHER STRATEGIES

Almost every industry includes minor firms that specialize in parts of the market where they avoid clashes with the majors. These smaller firms occupy market niches that they serve effectively through specialization and which the majors are likely to overlook or ignore. These firms go by various names: market nichers, market specialists, threshold firms, or foothold firms. Market niching is of interest not only to small

---

[30] R. G. Hamermesh, M. J. Anderson, Jr., and J. E. Harris, "Strategies for Low Market Share Businesses," *Harvard Business Review*, May-June 1978, pp. 95–102.

companies but also to smaller divisions of larger companies that are not able to achieve major standing in that industry.

These firms try to find one or more market niches that are safe and profitable. An ideal market niche would have the following characteristics:

☐ The niche is of sufficient size and purchasing power to be profitable.
☐ The niche has growth potential.
☐ The niche is of negligible interest to major competitors.
☐ The firm has the required skills and resources to serve the niche effectively.
☐ The firm can defend itself against an attacking major competitor through the customer goodwill it has built up.

The key idea in nichemanship is specialization. The firm has to specialize along market, customer, product, or marketing-mix lines. Here are several specialist roles open to a market nicher:

☐ **End-use specialist.** The firm specializes in serving one type of end-use customer. For example, a law firm can specialize in the criminal, civil, or business law markets.
☐ **Vertical-level specialist.** The firm specializes at some vertical level of the production-distribution cycle. For example, a copper firm may concentrate on producing raw copper, copper components, or finished copper products.
☐ **Customer-size specialist.** The firm concentrates on selling to either small-, medium- or large-size customers. Many nichers specialize in serving small customers who are neglected by the majors.
☐ **Specific-customer specialist.** The firm limits its selling to one or a few major customers. Many firms sell their entire output to a single company, such as Sears or General Motors.
☐ **Geographic specialist.** The firm sells only in a certain locality, region, or area of the world.
☐ **Product or product-line specialist.** The firm produces only one product line or product. Within the laboratory-equipment industry are firms that produce only microscopes, or even more narrowly, only lenses for microscopes.
☐ **Product-feature specialist.** The firm specializes in producing a certain type of product or product feature. Rent-a-Wreck, for example, is a California car-rental agency that rents only "beat-up" cars.
☐ **Job-shop specialist.** The firm manufactures customized products as ordered by the customer.
☐ **Quality/price specialist.** The firm operates at the low or high end of the market. For example, Hewlett-Packard specializes in the high-quality, high-price end of the hand-calculator market.
☐ **Service specialist.** The firm offers one or more services not available from other firms. An example would be a bank that takes loan requests over the phone and hand delivers the money to the customer.

Niching carries a major risk in that the market niche may dry up or be attacked. That is why *multiple niching* is preferable to *single niching*. By developing strength in two or more niches, the company increases its chances for survival. Even some large firms prefer a multiple-niche strategy to serving the total market. One large law firm has developed a national reputation in the three areas of mergers and acquisitions, bankruptcies, and prospectus development, and does little else.

The main point is that low-share firms can be profitable too, and smart niching is one of the main answers. It is not all that is involved, however. Woo and Cooper studied the strategies of high-performing versus low-performing, low-share businesses to see what made the former do so well. They found that:[31]

☐ Many profitable low-share businesses are found in low-growth markets that are fairly stable. Most of them make industrial components or supplies that are purchased frequently. These firms don't change their products often. Most of their products are standardized, and the companies provide few extra services. The businesses tend to be found in high-value-added industries.

☐ These firms are strongly focused, not trying to do everything.

☐ They normally have a reputation for high quality and medium-to-low prices relative to high quality.

☐ They often have lower unit costs because they concentrate on a narrower product line and spend less on product R&D, new-product introduction, advertising, sales promotion, and sales-force support.

We can see that small firms have many opportunities to serve customers in profitable ways. Many small firms discover good niches through blind luck, although good opportunities can be detected and developed in a more systematic manner. Exhibit 12–5 describes the major entry strategies used by a sampling of companies that entered markets occupied by incumbents. Most of the companies chose a niching strategy.

SUMMARY

One of the key influences in formulating marketing strategy is the company's role and size in the industry. Marketing strategies are dependent on whether the company is a market leader, challenger, follower, or nicher.

A market leader faces three challenges: expanding the total market, protecting market share, and expanding market share. The market leader is interested in finding ways to expand the total market because it is the chief beneficiary of any increased sales. To expand market size the leader looks for new users of the product, new uses, and more usage. To protect its existing market share, the market leader has several defenses: position defense, flanking defense, preemptive defense, counteroffensive defense, mobile defense, and contraction defense. The most sophisticated leaders cover themselves by doing everything right, leaving no openings for competitive attack. Leaders can also try to increase their market share. This makes sense if profitability increases at higher market-share levels and the company's tactics won't invite antitrust action.

A market challenger is a firm that aggressively tries to expand its market share by attacking the leader, other runner-up firms, or smaller firms in the industry. The challenger can choose from a variety of attack strategies, including a frontal attack, flanking attack, encirclement attack, bypass attack, and guerrilla attack.

A market follower is a runner-up firm that chooses not to rock the boat, usually out of fear that it stands to lose more than it might gain. The follower is not without a

[31] Carolyn Y. Woo and Arnold C. Cooper, "The Surprising Case for Low Market Share," *Harvard Business Review*, November-December 1982, pp. 106–13.

Exhibit 12-5

STRATEGIES USED BY FIRMS ENTERING MARKETS HELD BY INCUMBENT FIRMS

What marketing strategies do companies use to enter a market that is already occupied by incumbent firms? Biggadike examined the strategies of forty firms that had recently entered a market occupied by incumbents. He found that ten market entrants came in at a lower price, nine matched the incumbents' prices, and twenty-one entered at a higher price. He also found that twenty-eight claimed superior quality, five matched incumbents' quality, and seven reported inferior product quality. Most of the entrants offered a specialist product line and served a narrower market segment. Less than 20 percent managed to innovate a new channel of distribution. Over half of the entrants claimed to offer a higher level of customer service. And over half of the entrants spent less than incumbents on sales force, advertising, and promotion. Thus the modal marketing mix of entrants was:

- ☐ Higher prices and higher quality
- ☐ Narrower product line
- ☐ Narrower market segment
- ☐ Similar distribution channels
- ☐ Superior service
- ☐ Lower expenditure on sales force, advertising, and promotion

Source: *Ralph Biggadike*, Entering New Markets: Strategies and Performance (*Cambridge, Mass:* Marketing Science Institute, September 1977), pp. 12–20.

strategy, however, and seeks to use its particular competences to participate actively in the growth of the market. Some followers enjoy a higher rate of return on equity than the leaders in their industry do.

A market nicher is a smaller firm that chooses to operate in some part of the market that is specialized and not likely to attract the larger firms. Market nichers often become specialists in some end use, vertical level, customer size, specific customer, geographic area, product or product line, product feature, or service.

QUESTIONS

1. Suggest a strategy for a new small firm entering the photocopying market.

2. What might a "harassment" strategy look like for a dominant firm trying to protect its market share from challengers?

3. Hewlett-Packard, a market leader in the top end of the hand-held calculator market, has found itself in a squeeze between agressively promoted portable computers and less expensive calculators with increasingly sophisticated features. What market-leader strategy would you recommend for Hewlett-Packard?

4. Comment on the following statements made about the appropriate marketing strategy of smaller firms: (a) "The smaller firm should concentrate on pulling away the larger firm's customers, while the larger firm should concentrate on stimulating new customers to enter the market." (b) "Larger firms should pioneer new products, and smaller ones should copy them."

5. Although Caterpillar is an extremely strong company, it has some vulnerabilities. Name some potential threats to Caterpillar.

6. What are some of the marketing principles that General Motors used to maintain its four decades of leadership in the U.S. auto industry?

7. Briefly critique the following marketing strategy statement: "The company will offer the best product and best service at the lowest price."

Marketing Strategies During Periods of Shortages, Inflation, and Recession

13

We are all continually faced with a series of great opportunities brilliantly disguised as insoluble problems.

JOHN W. GARDNER

Ever since the oil crisis in 1973, "normal" times have not been seen in the U.S. or abroad. From the end of World War II to 1973, the world economy enjoyed rising incomes, and the rates of inflation and unemployment held below 5 percent annually in many countries. The world's population got lulled into expectations of ever rising incomes and standards of living. Business firms became accustomed to sales growth and supported this pattern with growing investment in plant, equipment, and R&D. Aside from minor recessions every three or four years, every recovery led to higher levels than before. Business could make investments with confidence that sheer economic growth would provide them with a good return. Their mood, as well as the mood of consumers, was "upward and onward."

Following the Mideast war of 1972, the Arab countries expropriated foreign oil properties and started restricting the supply of oil. The price of oil, which had been $2.18 a barrel before the war, was raised by the OPEC cartel to $5 in 1973, $11 in 1974, $15 in 1979, and as high as $35 in 1981. The world was plunged into an oil and energy crisis. The restricted oil supply led to worldwide shortages not only of oil but of many oil-derived products, such as plastics and synthetics. Business customers and consumers had to get used to a *shortage economy*. Suppliers of scarce products, who had worked hard to market them in the previous period, were now wondering whether they needed marketing at all, given the almost unlimited demand for their products. Oil and its derivative products jumped in price, and these higher costs were passed on to consumers through price increases. Double-digit inflation took over the world economy, and business firms had to learn how to market and price in an *inflation economy*. Governments adopted various antiinflationary measures—higher taxes, restricted money supply, price controls—and succeeded in curbing inflation at the cost of increased unemployment. For a while companies operated in a paradoxical economy of high inflation and high stagnation, appropriately called a *stagflation economy*. Many households and business customers were changing the way they bought things, and sellers had to formulate effective marketing strategies for the new stagflation economy. As government policies started to bring down the inflation rate, the world economy drifted into a *recession economy*. Business firms now faced the challenge of selling their products in the face of increased consumer pessimism and lowered incomes.

Clearly companies need to know how to adjust their marketing strategies to different economic climates, both current and expected. In this chapter we will to look at three types of economic climates—shortages, inflation, and recession—and ask about their characteristics and the appropriate marketing strategies.[1]

SHORTAGES

Nature and Characteristics of Shortages

Specific industries experience overdemand from time to time, when companies cannot supply all their customer needs. When many industries get into a short-supply position at the same time, we say that a *shortage economy* exists. Many less developed countries can be characterized as shortage economies. The U.S. experienced a shortage economy in each major war and in peacetime during 1973–76, following the oil crisis. Starting in 1973 there were shortages of oil, chemicals, electricity, natural gas, cement, aluminum, copper, textiles, paper, glass, and furniture. Ironically, as late as 1972 most of these firms were spending the greater part of their time trying to dispose of surpluses.

Companies suddenly found it necessary to learn how to allocate scarce supplies to their customers and how to obtain scarce materials needed for their operations. Many articles were written on how to manage firms in a shortage economy, and

---

[1] When an economy is plagued by a combination of problems at the same time, such as inflation-shortage, inflation-recession, or recession-shortage, marketing management faces an even greater challenge. See Avraham Shama, "Management and Consumers in an Era of Stagflation," *Journal of Marketing*, July 1978, pp. 43–52; and his *Marketing in a Slow-Growth Economy* (New York: Praeger, 1980).

many articles tendered advice on the marketing aspects of the problem.[2] Too many companies were taking actions that ran counter to the marketing concept: raising prices to the maximum, cutting customer supplies in an arbitrary fashion, reducing advertising, dismissing sales representatives. One business columnist expressed the new thinking:

> There is little doubt that the energy crisis will force an alteration in the role of the marketing man. In some industries, it may alter him out of existence. . . . When demand exceeds supply, marketing men can be replaced by order-takers. The art of selling is unnecessary. There also is no need for advertising, sales promotion, incentives, sweepstakes, trading stamps, free road maps or even windshield cleaning.[3]

The truth is that a shortage period is not a time to abandon good marketing practice. Marketing is not a fair-weather concept, to be used only when customers are scarce. Marketing adjustments are required in a period of shortages, but they should be directed to preserving and deepening the company's relation to its valued customers.

Some marketers might feel that shortages is a past problem and does not warrant much attention. This view, however, is in error for the following reasons:

☐ Certain industries pass through a shortage-surplus cycle every few years. For example, the paper industry is not investing in new plant capacity because current prices and costs yield a poor return on further investment. As a result, a future shortage is inevitable as demand grows while capacity stands still. Paper companies will have to know how to handle the shortage when it occurs.

☐ Certain industries decide to underproduce in order to extract higher prices. For example, chemical companies, in the face of declining demand, have reduced production and raised prices rather than produce at capacity and cut prices. Through "controlled production" they maintain artificially high prices.[4]

☐ Various raw-material-exporting countries have combined in cartels to limit production and raise prices. They are also resorting to more internal processing of their own raw materials, thus reducing supplies abroad. They can cut off exports and plunge the world into a new round of shortages.

☐ Some analysts forecast shortages of key resources resulting from the sheer growth of population and industrialization. The book *The Limits to Growth* caused a sensation by presenting scenarios of increasing food and material shortages resulting from exponential demand growth against fixed levels of supply.[5] Shortages may become a generalized state for the world economy.

---

[2] Many articles appeared during the shortage economy of 1973–75. They include George S. Dominguez, *Marketing in a Shortage Economy* (New York: AMACOM, 1974); A. B. Blankenship and John H. Holmes, "Will Shortages Bankrupt the Marketing Concept?" *Business Topics*, spring 1974, pp. 13–18; Charles A. Nekvasil, "Marketing in Time of Shortages," *Industry Week*, March 18, 1974, pp. 23–28; David W. Cravens, "Marketing Management in an Era of Shortages," *Business Horizons*, February 1974, pp. 79–85; Philip Kotler, "Marketing During Periods of Shortage," *Journal of Marketing*, July 1974, pp. 20–29; and Philip Kotler and V. Balachandran, "Strategic Remarketing: The Preferred Response to Shortages and Inflation," *Sloan Management Review*, fall 1975, pp. 1–17.

[3] Joe Cappo, "Will Marketing Run Out of Energy?" *Chicago Daily News*, November 27, 1973.

[4] "Prices Rise in Spite of Spare Capacity," *Business Week*, March 21, 1977, pp. 120–26.

[5] Donnella H. Meadows, Dennis L. Meadows, Jorgen Randers, and William W. Behrens III, *The Limits to Growth* (New York: New American Library, 1972), p. 41.

These factors suggest that businesses will have to learn the theory and art of managing their resources in periods of shortages.

A Shortage Economy's Impact on Consumers

The years 1973–76 were difficult ones for consumers: They waited in long lines for their gasoline; they had to reduce their driving; they had to reschedule their vacations because airline space was at a premium; they waited longer for purchased furniture; and those who were building homes saw the building time stretch out as deliveries on glass, cement, and other materials were delayed. In addition, prices kept rising fast.

In the face of deep and prolonged shortages, consumers go through a number of stages:

☐ In the first stage, consumers convince themselves that shortages are a temporary fluke.
☐ In the second stage, they start to hoard or bargain for scarce goods. Some people can do this successfully, but most can't or won't.
☐ In the third stage, consumers become hostile and blame government, business, ecologists, foreign countries, or other groups linked in their minds directly or indirectly to the shortage.
☐ In the fourth stage, consumers realize that they are relatively helpless to cope with shortages, and this realization brings on deep psychological depression.
☐ In the fifth stage, consumers begin to accept their situation and start reshaping their goals, values, and activities.[6]

Fortunately, most shortages end before consumers get to the fourth or fifth stage.

A Shortage Economy's Impact on Organizational Buyers

When companies anticipate or experience shortages of needed key resources, they act fast to find new sources of supply. The last thing they want to do is close their plant and lay off workers, especially when their end product is in strong demand. Purchasing agents get on the phone and call suppliers whom they have never dealt with and in some cases refused to see in the past. They offer more than the "list" price, officially or unofficially, to insure a flow of supply. They develop a plan to market themselves to new suppliers.[7] They often promise new suppliers to continue buying from them after availability returns. If they still can't get enough fuel, raw materials, and components, they start searching for near substitutes, such as aluminum for steel, or electric energy for oil. They give serious thought to acquiring suppliers so that in the future they are less dependent. In the meantime, they are not able to produce enough to meet their customer needs. They must wrestle with the problem of allocating their limited supply so as to maintain as much customer goodwill as possible through the shortage period.

---

[6] Stages suggested by Professor Joseph M. Kamen, in private correspondence.
[7] See "Purchasing Becomes a 'Selling' Operation," *Industry Week*, December 10, 1973, pp. 46–47.

Company Marketing Strategies During Shortages

What marketing adjustments should a company make in the face of widening shortages? The two most common responses to shortages are both shortsighted.

The first is an *aggressive demarketing response*. The company raises its prices sharply, cuts product quality and new-product development, eliminates weaker customers, reduces customer services, allocates supplies to customers according to their ability to pay, cuts marketing budgets for research, advertising, and sales calls, and drops low-profit items. All of these steps admittedly will increase current profits. But the company is playing dangerously with its only asset, its customers. Their goodwill will be taxed, and when normal times return, many customers will prefer dealing with other vendors.

The second is a *marketing-as-usual approach*. Here the company expects shortages to be temporary. The company produces the same products and sells to the same customers. It raises prices to cover cost increases but not excessively. It spends the same amount on advertising, sales force and marketing research, with minor changes in its messages. These steps will maintain the company's profit margins and customer goodwill. On the other hand, they may be too weak to improve the company's position in the long run.

A period of deep shortages calls for a third response, that of *strategic remarketing*. Top management should appoint a committee to evaluate the shortage outlook and make recommendations concerning appropriate changes in the customer mix and marketing mix.

The committee's first task is to develop some assumptions about the shortage outlook. Specifically, the committee needs to estimate the likely *depth* and *duration* of the shortage and the *availability* of substitutes. Strategic remarketing is most warranted where shortages are expected to be severe, long lasting, and with no relief in sight from near substitutes.

The committee then must address the following questions:

☐ Which markets and customers will be the best ones to serve in the coming years? How should the scarce supplies be allocated to current customers? What new customers can be cultivated without hurting the supply needs of current customers?

☐ What products might the company drop from its line, and what products should it add?

☐ How much price increase can the company safely and fairly pass on to its customers?

☐ What should the company communicate to its customers, and how much should it spend on advertising and public relations?

☐ How many sales representatives does the company need, and what kind of restraining should they receive? How can they assist customers to solve their shortage problems?

Their recommendations will take the form of suggested adjustments in the customer mix and the marketing mix. We will now consider these possible adjustments.

Customer mix.   As a rule, a small percentage of a company's customers account for a large percentage of its sales (the so-called 20–80 rule). Companies respond by directing different levels of sales effort to different size customers. When a shortage occurs, the company will find it tempting to cut off weak customers or substantially reduce their supplies. That would free up more supplies for important customers and increase their loyalty to the firm. This approach is the philosophy of "key account concentration."

Some companies, however, prefer making "across-the-board" cuts to customers because it is simpler and fairer. In fact, the government required equitable cuts during the oil shortage of 1973–74.

Companies that choose to practice disproportional allocation should be guided by *long-run customer profitability*. Most companies classify their customers into A-B-C-D type accounts that reflect such factors as sales volume, sales growth, profit margin and expenses of serving the account. These factors can be combined into a measure of long-run customer profitability, defined as the *present value of the future income stream expected over a given time horizon of transacting with the customer*. (See Exhibit 22–4 in Chapter 22.) Using this measure, the company can establish boundaries between key accounts (A), good accounts (B), fair accounts (C), and poor accounts (D). The company can then formulate an allocation rule such as:

> Supply 100 percent of the requirements of class A accounts as long as their requirements are not substantially greater than preshortage order levels: 80 percent of the preshortage order levels of class B accounts: 50 percent of the preshortage order levels of class C accounts: and 20 percent of the preshortage order levels of class D accounts. In addition, go after five new class A accounts offering them 50 percent of their total requirements.

The specific percentages are illustrative only. The analytical challenge is to find the set of percentages that maximizes the company's long-run profitability without overcommitting the company's available supply.

Some companies establish generous allotments for key customers and leave it to their sales people to allocate the remaining supply as they see fit. This has two benefits. It boosts the morale of the sales force, who are on the receiving end of customer criticism and hostility. Giving them some control in allocating the available supply strengthens their sense of authority and responsibility. In addition they know the customers best and they know how they would react to different allocations. Consider the following two types of customers:

☐ **Nonforgivers:** customers who expect special treatment during the shortage; if they receive much less than they want, they will switch to another supplier when supply becomes abundant. They do not forgive or forget.

☐ **Tolerants:** customers who are grateful for what they receive as long as it appears that the suppliers are doing their best.

If the sales people know their customers in this way, they should make higher allocations to the *nonforgivers* and smaller allocations to the *tolerants*. This will minimize the amount of lost goodwill.

During this period, sales people need to know the art of saying no in a way that preserves customer goodwill. They must convince their customers that they are doing their best and not playing favorites.

A shortage period is, paradoxically, a good time to pursue new customers, especially high-potential ones who are not getting enough satisfaction from the main suppliers. The firm suddenly hears from prospect accounts who refused to see them in the past but who now want supplies. To refuse their overtures is to hurt any chance of attracting their business when demand returns to normal. The firm should welcome, even solicit, certain accounts during this period.

Product mix and design. The occurrence of resource shortages and rising input prices will change the profitability of different items in the company product mix. Companies will channel scarce raw materials and fuels into their more profitable products.

Companies need to undertake a review of their most potentially profitable products. Management will identify some products that are no longer worth carrying. *Sales Management* polled ninety-three industrial companies about product pruning intentions: 63 percent of these companies said they intended to eliminate slow-moving items, and 23 percent said they would reduce the number of sizes and colors.[8] These words were followed by actions:

> In its pursuit of higher profits, General Electric Co. has dropped blenders, fans, heaters, humidifiers, and vacuum cleaners. Shell Chemical Co. is ending production of styrene butadiene rubber, isoprene rubber, and fertilizer (ammonia, urea, and ammonium sulfate). Philco-Ford Corp. has eliminated 50 percent of its color-TV screen sizes and 40 percent of its refrigerator models. Crown Zellerbach Corp. and other papermakers have cut their lines by as much as 60 percent.[9]

In addition to eliminating weak products, a shortage period paradoxically warrants adding new products and redesigning existing products. *Shortage periods are an opportunity to the enterprising firm.* The very definition of a shortage is that customers' needs are not being met. The resourceful firm will try to find new ways to meet these customer needs. Many large companies redesigned their products to be energy efficient. For example, Philco-Ford advertised that its Cold Guard refrigerators would save "about one-third (or more)" in electricity, compared with competitive brands. U.S. auto companies started to downsize their cars to offer customers more fuel economy.

Management faces the problem of how to allocate its scarce resources over the products it wants to produce. The various products in the line consume scarce resources in different degrees. Further, demand can be estimated for each product as a function of its price, marketing budget, and key environmental factors. The optimization task is to find the prices and marketing budgets that will maximize total profits and involve production levels that will not exceed the scarce supplies. A linear programming analysis will yield the optimal marketing mix for the products and the prices that are worth paying to acquire additional scarce resources if they happen to be available at higher prices.

---

[8] See *Sales Management*, January 21, 1974, p. 27.

[9] "The Squeeze on Product Mix," *Business Week*, January 5, 1974, pp. 50–55.

Pricing.   Companies that have scarce supplies face the problem of allocating them to customers. One effective allocation device is to raise prices. Those customers with the most intense need for the product will pay the higher prices, and this will bring demand down to the level of supply.

The company must be discreet about how high to raise its prices on goods in short supply. It must consider at least three parties. One is *government*, which may have established regulations or exhortations against price increases. A second is *competitors*, whose price behavior limits the company's price behavior. The company cannot raise its prices by much more than competitors raise their prices. The third is *customers*, who will form an impression about whether the company's repricing is fair or exorbitant. Customers who believe the supplier is "price gouging" will drop the supplier when normal times return.[10]

The company might decide to raise prices and limit purchasing of each customer so that everyone can be supplied. During the 1973 gasoline shortage, individual gas stations had to decide whether to raise prices and/or limit the amount of gasoline per customer. Some stations raised the price and limited each customer to five gallons; other stations raised the price and placed no limit on the amount sold; and so on. Each strategy had to be evaluated for its impact on the number of customers served, customer attitudes, and short-run profits.

Sometimes the issue is how to reprice the whole product line, consisting as it does of some products in short supply and others in oversupply. Furthermore the products will have various demand and cost cross-elasticities. Management scientists have built some useful models for pricing the product line under these circumstances.[11]

When the company decides to raise certain prices, it can proceed in several ways, each with a slightly different effect on the perception of price increase. It can eliminate volume discounts or freight-absorption allowances. It can concentrate on producing higher-priced models without raising list prices. It can reduce the size of the product while preserving price. It can require customers to buy some oversupplied product along with the scarce product. Whichever repricing method is chosen, the company should explain the higher price to its close customers rather than just levy higher prices. The higher prices can be justified in terms of the sellers' higher costs or their needs for additional funds to support research into new sources of supply. Here the company sales force plays an important role. The company's sales people should continue to give customers attention and assistance during the shortage period so as to maintain their goodwill into the next period.

Distribution.   A company often uses more than one trade channel to reach its customers. The eruption of shortages makes it desirable to examine trade-channel profitability. The company may want to drop or alter trade channels of marginal profitability. Thus outlets selling only a few units of the company's product may no longer be worth supplying. The company also has to decide how much to supply to each of

---

[10] "Pricing Gouging Spreads as Suppliers Seek Ways to Profit on Shortages," *Wall Street Journal*, November 2, 1973.

[11] See Kent B. Monroe and Andris A. Zoltners, "Pricing the Product Line during Periods of Scarcity," *Journal of Marketing*, summer 1979, pp. 49–59.

its viable outlets. The company will be tempted to favor the high-margined outlets (traditional retailers) over the low-margined outlets (mass merchandisers) because that means more profits to the company. But the low-margined outlets are where the firm's future lies, and the company will need to heed their requirements.

Advertising and sales promotion. Companies are tempted during shortages to reduce their advertising, on the theory that nothing is to be gained by keeping a high flame under a boiling pot. Yet there are four viable alternatives to a drastic cut in advertising.

First, the company can redirect its advertising budget to build up demand for its oversupplied products. For example, Sun Oil ran an ad campaign to get consumers to think of Sunoco stations as "tire stores." This strategy makes sense for products that have a good unexploited potential. However, if these items are in the declining stage of their life cycle, advertising might be a waste of money.

Second, the company can redirect its advertising budget to building the demand for new products it is launching. When normal times return, these new products will be well into their growth stage.

Third, advertising can be redesigned to help users understand how to use the scarce product more effectively. Standard Oil Company of Ohio sponsored full-page newspaper ads listing ten tips on how motorists could make their gas go further, including "Have your car tuned regularly," "Slow down," "Avoid jack-rabbit starts," and "Keep your tires properly inflated." This public-service advertising will lower the demand pressure and build customer goodwill. Some companies have used advertising to inform their consuming publics about company efforts to solve the shortages.

Fourth, the company can sponsor corporate messages justifying its corporate profits. Some oil companies placed full-page ads explaining that their increased profits were needed to finance new explorations and refinery construction. Others stated that their current high profits were making up for low profits in the past. One company showed how much it contributed to American charities. The effectiveness of this type of advertising is questionable. The companies would gain more credence with advertising directed at helping customers solve their problems.

Sales-force and customer service. A sales force does not become superfluous when a company cannot keep up with customer demand. Sales people perform several functions for the company that continue to be needed in periods of shortages as well as surpluses.

With regard to *selling*, sales people are needed to call attention to other company products that are in surplus. They can show customers how an available product can serve the same need as the one that is in short supply. Auto sales people pointed out the merits of large cars when small cars were out of stock. Sales people can sell minor products that have not received much sales attention in the past. They can try to sell key customers on lengthening their supply contracts beyond the current period.

Sales people's *counseling role* becomes critically important during periods of shortages. Sales people can study customer problems and counsel them on possible solutions. Paper sales reps can counsel industrial users on other grades of paper serving the same purpose, on ways to conserve on paper, and on alternative supply sources for the same grade of paper. By applying value analysis, suggesting substitutes, and helping find other temporary sources of supply, sales people can show their concern for their customers' well-being.

Sales people can provide other *services* to the customer. They can advise on delivery dates and keep customers informed about the future supply outlook. They can handle problems of bad merchandise, make credit adjustments, supervise installation service, and so on. Sales people are the customers' chief link with the company, and their helpfulness during a trying period may stand out as the most important investment the company has made to ensure a future market for its products.

Sales people also have an important role to play in *gathering intelligence* on customers, prospects, and competitors. This is a period when customers are being exposed to new sources of supply, trying out different substitutes, and possibly evolving new forms of purchasing behavior. They might be moving toward tighter purchasing relations with competitors, such as long-term supply contracts and programmed merchandising. Sales people must observe these developments and report them quickly to their superiors.

At the same time, the company can use the shortage period to terminate some of its poorer sales people. Every company has some weak sales people who just managed to pay their way when there were not enough customers. Now the company has an opportunity to trim and upgrade its sales force. The company should not trim its sales force too deeply, however. Should surpluses emerge, the company will need a good-sized sales force to serve existing customers and win new ones. It can be sure that its competitors will try to build new relationships as fast as their sales-force size permits.

INFLATION

A period of shortages is almost always accompanied or followed by a period of inflation. Inflation throws out several new challenges to the marketing management group.

Nature and Characteristics of Inflation

Inflation is an economic climate in which the general price level—reflecting prices of raw materials and final products—rises faster than a few percent annually (normal inflation). No one is disturbed by an inflation rate of a few percent a year, because wages normally rise enough to cover the increased cost of living. An inflation rate that runs between 4 and 9 percent is called *creeping inflation*. It needs more attention but is not as serious as when inflation rises to a double-digit level, which is called *strong inflation*. For example, the U.S. inflation rate hit 13 percent in the late 1970s. Even this rate is low compared to *runaway inflation* of 100 percent, which has hit such countries as Argentina, Brazil, Mexico, and Israel at various times. Even in these countries, companies and consumers have adjusted through adopting a variety of measures, including the indexing of wages and prices. The worst case is *hyperinfla-*

tion. One of the world's worst inflations occurred in Germany during 1920–23; it was so severe that people received a daily paycheck and ran to buy groceries and hard goods during their lunch break. Clearly inflation, if unchecked, hurts everyone and threatens to topple a country's political and business institutions.

Periods of rapid inflation can be triggered by different factors. Economists have recently debated about the relative role of *demand-pull* versus *cost-push* factors in fanning the inflation. Demand-pull economists see inflation as caused by too much money chasing too few goods. Their recommendation is therefore to reduce demand by reducing the money supply, raising interest rates and imposing higher taxes. Cost-push economists see inflation as caused by insufficient productivity, excessive wage demands by unions, and decisions by the company in an industry to raise prices rather than compete. The key to breaking up a cost-push inflation is to apply antitrust laws more vigorously against companies and unions and to provide greater incentives for companies to invest in more productive facilities.

Governments have not found easy remedies to combat inflation without hurting employment. The famous Phillips curve holds that inflation can be brought down only by pushing up unemployment. As various antiinflationary measures in the U.S. brought down the inflation rate to single-digit inflation in the early 1980s, the U.S. unemployment rate shot up to approximately 10 percent. The main way out of this seemingly inexorable Phillips curve is productivity increases. Yet productivity increases come about slowly and require major new business investment—something less likely to happen during periods of high unutilized capacity.

Although inflation can be tamed, several forces make it likely that inflation will continue to be a major recurring economic and social problem. These forces include:

- Raw-material-exporting countries are engaging in more price fixing of oil, coffee, cocoa, and various minerals and metals.
- Wage settlements are exceeding productivity gains in most industrial countries.
- Affluent economies with a growing service sector are subject to more inflationary pressure because of the greater difficulty of achieving productivity gains in service industries.
- Increased government legislation and regulation covering antipollution investment, product liability, consumerism, and environmentalism raise the costs of doing business and are passed on to consumers in the form of higher prices.
- The lengthening of the educational span and the life span tends to increase the proportion of nonproductive workers in an economy.
- The deep indebtedness of many foreign governments—Mexico, Poland, Rumania, Brasil and so on—will lead those governments to print money which will increase the inflation rate in their countries.

Inflation's Impact on Consumers

A period of rapid inflation typically causes consumer incomes to start shrinking in real terms and leads to changes in consumer attitudes and behavior.

In the years before 1973, real disposable income per person was rising about 3 percent a year; between 1973 to 1979, the gain was less than 1 percent a year; and after 1979, average consumer disposable income actually fell each year. With the consumer price index rising at 13 percent toward the end of the 1970s, and wages rising at only 4–6 percent, consumers experienced declines in their real income.[12]

The high inflation rate had the effect of undermining consumer expectations of ever rising standards of living. Making money, borrowing money, and spending money had been a way of life and a real spur to economic growth. But now consumers began to make adjustments in their spending patterns. Consumers adopted various forms of *economizing behavior*. The main consumer adjustments to inflation are the following:

☐ Consumers postpone expensive discretionary purchases. They delay buying new cars, refrigerators, and other durables; they go for lower-price vacations or skip vacations altogether. They put their money into savings instruments that pay attractive interest rates.

☐ Consumers engage in more comparison shopping to find the best prices on their preferred brands. They switch more of their purchasing to lower-price outlets. They watch for coupon ads offering price savings on their favorite brands of coffee, soft drinks, and so on.

☐ Consumers "trade down" from preferred brands and products to acceptable brands and products. They buy private labels and generic labels in product categories that are not important to them. They do more bargain hunting at used-clothing stores, flea markets, and garage sales. They do less impulse buying. They reduce their purchases of red meat and increase their purchases of chicken, peanut butter, and powdered drink mixes. Consumers pay more for products that have more quality or durability.

☐ Consumers move into more self-production to save money. They do more of their own painting, food growing, and clothes making.

Not all consumers change their behavior in these directions. Those with high incomes and secure outlooks operate with "business as usual." At the other extreme are "conspicuous conservors" who practice "less is more." Marketers must be aware that consumers will show different response patterns in the face of rapid inflation.

Inflation's Impact on Organizational Buyers

Industrial buyers undertake a reexamination of long-standing supplier relations. Purchasing agents are under pressure to search for alternative and cheaper sources of supply. They place increased emphasis on price and reduced emphasis on services. They become interested in suppliers who will offer long-term contracts at controlled prices. They become angry at suppliers who raise their prices excessively. They will finance the higher cost of inventory by slowing down their invoice payment time.

Company Marketing Strategies During Inflation

Business firms need to make a number of adjustments as their costs of materials, energy, equipment, and labor rise. When they can't pass along commensurate price increases, either because of weak market demand or because of price controls, their profits fall. They reduce their planned capital investments and thus slow down any

---

[12] See "The Shrinking Standard of Living," *Business Week*, January 28, 1980, pp. 72–78.

productivity improvements. During inflation, company accounting practices lead to an overstatement of profits because the depreciation levels are inadequate to provide capital replacement funds at the higher prices. Companies have to go into heavier borrowing when they modernize, and this borrowing reduces their net-worth-to-assets ratio.

GE introduced inflation-adjusted accounting to revise its picture of the relative attractiveness of the different businesses it is in.[13] One GE strategic business unit that ranked 8 (out of 35) using normal accounting fell to a ranking of 31 out of 35 when its inflation-adjusted standing was calculated. Obviously this business deserves less resource allocation than formerly because the cost of maintaining the business is higher than expected.

Clearly companies need to adjust their marketing strategies during periods of high inflation. The amount and types of adjustment depend on the company's view of how steep the inflation will be, how long it will last, and how sensitive buyers will be. A company expecting a low-rate, short-lived inflation with little buyer resistance will make few changes in its marketing strategy. A company expecting a steep, prolonged inflation with strong consumer resistance will have to modify its marketing program substantially.

Customer mix.   During a period of rapid inflation, companies will have to pass on some price increases to customers. Customers will vary in their ability to absorb price increases, and the company will lose some accounts. The company should review its major markets and customers to see which are central and which are peripheral. The company needs to be circumspect about its price increases to important markets and customers. It must consider its competitors' pricing to these markets, the availability of substitutes, and the customer-goodwill implications of raising its prices.

A period of rising prices affords the company an opportunity to pursue new accounts that were inaccessible during normal times. Prospects are willing to receive sales representatives who can show them how to contain costs or improve profitability. Smart marketing during inflation would include identifying excellent prospects and laying marketing plans to gain some of their business.

Product mix and design.   The company will need to review how inflation has affected the profitability of its different products. Products with a high content of the more cost-inflating inputs will fall in their profitability. If their prices cannot be raised sufficiently, and they are not essential to the product mix, the company might consider eliminating some of them.

> Sun Oil's division of Lubrication and Metalworking materials has cut its metalworking oils from 1,150 grades to 92, its lubes from 1,000 grades to 200, and its greases from 225 grades to 29. This product-line pruning has increased productivity by 20–30 percent. . . .[14]

---

[13] See "How GE Manages Inflation," *Fortune*, May 4, 1981, pp. 121–24.

[14] "The Squeeze on the Product Mix," *Business Week*, January 5, 1974, pp. 50–55.

The company needs to find ways to keep costs down on individual products. The possibilities include:

☐ Shrinking the amount of product instead of raising the price. (For example, Hershey Foods maintained its fifteen-cent candy bar but trimmed its size. Nestlé, on the other hand, maintained the old size but raised the price to twenty cents.)[15]

☐ Substituting less expensive materials or ingredients. (For example, many candy bar companies substituted synthetic chocolate for real chocolate to fight the price increases in cocoa. Auto manufacturers have replaced metal with plastic wherever possible.)

☐ Reducing or removing product features to reduce cost. (For example, Sears engineered down a number of its appliances so they could be priced competitively with those sold in discount stores.)

☐ Removing or reducing product services, such as installation, free delivery, or long warranties.

☐ Using less expensive packaging material or promoting larger units to keep down the relative cost of packaging.

☐ Reducing the number of sizes and models offered.

☐ Creating new economy brands or generic brands. (For example, the Jewel Food Stores introduced 170 generic items selling at 10 to 30 percent less than national brands to offer to price-conscious consumers.)

The best action to take is not always obvious. Quaker Oats produces the successful breakfast cereal called Quaker Oats Natural, which contains several ingredients, such as almonds and raisins, whose prices jumped during the inflation. Quaker Oats saw two choices, namely, raising the price or cost-reducing the contents by including fewer almonds and raisins or finding cheaper substitutes. They wanted to avoid tampering with the product and raised the price. But the price elasticity was high, and sales fell. This forced them to reconsider ways to cost-reduce the contents, knowing that it would involve a great risk.

Management will want to add some new products to its line in response to inflation. Some will be economy versions of existing products, to catch buyers who are trading down. Some will be introduced to get around price control, since new products can be priced freely at the time of introduction.

Pricing. Price adjustments are the most common response to inflation. Price adjustments can be instituted rapidly, and if successful, they will preserve the company's profit margins.

Assuming no price control, the company must decide on the amount of the price increase and the method of effecting it. As for the amount, many companies seek to raise their price to cover the cost increase so as to leave the margin unchanged. This is cost-oriented reasoning and does not make good marketing sense, in that it ignores the state of demand and competition. If demand elasticity is low and further cost increases are anticipated, prices should be raised by more than cost, if competition permits. But if demand elasticity is high, the company should refrain from raising its price to cover the cost increase, lest it incur a sharp drop in market share. The

---

[15] "Consumers Find Firms Are Paring Quantities to Avoid Price Rises," *Wall Street Journal*, February 15, 1977.

appropriate price increase requires a thorough analysis of demand, cost, and competition. The company should determine the perceived value of its offer relative to competitors. If the perceived value is high and there is high customer loyalty, the company can pass on a higher price increase. If the offer does not have high value perception in the minds of the buyers, any price increase can hurt market share. The company must also estimate competitors' probable responses to its planned price increases.

Many companies expecting the government to impose price controls will choose to raise their prices by more than their increased costs, so that they are not stymied later. For example, the steel industry will put through higher prices during an inflation in spite of operating at less than half capacity. This practice has been called anticipatory pricing, hedge pricing, or inflation premium pricing.[16] This advice ironically increases the government's determination to impose price controls.

Besides the amount of price increase, companies have to decide on the best form of the price increase. The "real" price can be increased in several ways, each with a different perceived impact on buyers. The most common price adjustments are:

☐ **Adoption of delayed quotation pricing.** The company decides not to set its final price until the product is finished or delivered. Delayed quotation pricing is prevalent in industries with long production lead times, such as industrial construction and heavy-equipment manufacture.

☐ **Use of escalator clauses.** The company requires the customer to pay today's price and all or part of any inflation increase that takes place before delivery. An escalator clause in the contract bases price increases on some specified price index, such as the cost-of-living index. Escalator clauses are found in many contracts involving industrial projects of long duration.

☐ **Unbundling of goods and services.** The company maintains its price but removes or prices separately one or more elements that were part of the former offer, such as free delivery or installation. IBM, for example, now offers training as a separately priced service. Many restaurants have shifted from dinner pricing to à la carte pricing. A joke in Argentina is that the current price of a car no longer includes the tires and steering wheel.

☐ **Reduction of discounts.** The company reduces its normal cash and quantity discounts and instructs its sales force not to offer off-list pricing to get the business.

If price controls have been installed, some of the preceding pricing tactics are no longer possible. Some companies will hold back stock, hoping to increase the pressure on government to permit a price increase. They may take existing models, change their features, and launch them as new models at higher prices. They may reduce their product quality or quantity per unit. In taking these steps, companies may risk legal action and, what is worse, losing customer goodwill.[17]

---

[16] "How Price Tactics Feed Inflation," *Business Week*, March 10, 1980, pp. 36–37; and "Fear of New Controls Causes Many Concerns to Keep Prices High," *Wall Street Journal*, January 8, 1975.

[17] For additional readings, see "Pricing Strategy in an Inflation Economy," *Business Week*, April 6, 1974, pp. 43–49; Norman H. Fuss, Jr., "How to Raise Prices—Judiciously—to Meet Today's Conditions," *Harvard Business Review*, May-June 1975, pp. 10ff; Judith Bauer, "Coping With Inflationary Costs—by Hiking Product Prices," *The Conference Board Record*, September 1974, pp. 52–57; and Mary Louise Hatten, "Don't Get Caught With Your Prices Down: Pricing in Inflationary Times," *Business Horizons*, March-April 1982, pp. 23–28.

Distribution. During inflation, customers will do more price-comparison shopping and buy more often from lower-cost outlets and suppliers. Companies therefore need to review their distribution channels and put more emphasis on lower-cost channels, such as mass-merchandising and discount operations. Companies sticking only to high-cost channels will find their market share shrinking.

Advertising and sales promotion. Companies need to review their advertising budget, message, and media during a period of rapid inflation. Some companies cut their advertising expenditures to reduce their costs. Usually sales will hold up for a while because of customer habit. But eventually, customers will forget the company brand or try brands that are more heavily promoted.

Other companies maintain their advertising expenditures during inflation to avoid losing share-of-mind. In fact, maintaining the current rate of advertising expenditure in the face of rising media costs means reduced advertising impact in real terms. This can be an argument for *increasing* the advertising budget during rapid inflation.

The appropriate advertising budget depends on whether the company has an effective message for buyers during the period. If the company sells a low-priced unit of comparable quality to higher-priced units, advertising will pay because buyers are looking for price breaks. The company can advertise "an inflation-fighting brand." If the company sells a high-priced unit of superior quality, it can advertise "the most value for the price," since buyers are value conscious. During rapid inflation, marketers have also used the appeal "Buy now and save." Pan American's overseas-travel campaign said "Live today. Tomorrow may cost more."

Companies should also observe the inflation rates of the different media. During the high inflation of the late 1970s, the cost of television rose faster than other media costs, leading many companies to switch money from broadcast to print media, where they expected more results per dollar.

Sales promotion as a marketing tool increases in importance during inflation. Consumers are much more responsive to price deals and premiums. They are constantly looking for bargains. Some companies raise their list prices and then engage in aggressive price dealing to give consumers a sense of savings. Companies should avoid too much price dealing, however, for it can depreciate the brand image and/or lead consumers to postpone purchase until the next deal.

Sales-force and customer service. Sales people bear the brunt of customer antagonism when price increases are put into effect. They must understand the basis for the company's price increases and know the competitors' price increases. They must be able to argue value-for-the-price to customers who are balking at the price increases. They must be able to show customers ways to economize on the use of the product. They must be able to offer more economical versions of products where customer resistance is high.

Exhibit 13–1 shows marketing-mix alternatives a company faces when it must readjust its value/price relationship as seen by the market.

Because high rates of inflation can damage an economy, most governments will introduce antiinflationary measures to curb demand. To the extent that government succeeds, some factories will lay off workers, and unemployment will rise. The economy

Exhibit 13-1

ANALYZING THE MARKETING-MIX ALTERNATIVES FACING A FIRM DURING INFLATION

Here we will describe an actual but disguised situation involving two competing appliance manufacturers. Company A's appliances are perceived to be of higher quality and higher prices than company B's appliances. The perceived positions of the two brands are shown in Figure (a) along the dimensions of *perceived value* and *price*. Note that the two brands lie on the same value-to-price line. This means that consumers feel they would get approximately the same value per dollar whether they bought brand A or B. Those who want more total value would buy A if they could afford it. Those who want to spend less would buy B.

The dots in Figure (a) represent the preferences of potential buyers for value/price combinations. Buyers whose preferences are nearest to A will buy A; the same goes for B. Clearly each brand has a substantial market, and both are likely to enjoy good market shares.

Now double-digit inflation enters the picture. The effect of inflation is to shift buyer preferences toward the cheaper appliance B. [See Figure (b).] The number of buyers who are willing to buy the higher-price appliance diminishes. If company A does nothing about this, its market share will shrink.

Company A must identify its marketing alternatives and choose among them. At least seven marketing alternatives exist. They are illustrated in Figure (c) and described on the next page.

Strategic Options	Reasoning	Consequences
1. Maintain price and perceived value. Engage in selective customer pruning.	Firm has high customer loyalty. It is willing to lose poorer customers to competitors.	Smaller market share. Lower profitability.
2. Raise price and perceived value.	Raise price to cover rising costs. Improve offer quality to justify higher prices.	Smaller market share. Maintained profitability.
3. Maintain price and raise perceived value.	It is cheaper to maintain price and raise perceived value.	Smaller market share. Short-term decline in profitability. Long-term increase in profitability.
4. Cut price partly and raise perceived value.	Must give customers some price reduction but stress higher value of offer.	Maintained market share. Short-term decline in profitability. Long-term maintained profitability.
5. Cut price fully and maintain perceived value.	Discipline and discourage price competition.	Maintained market share. Short-term decline in profitability.
6. Cut price fully and reduce perceived value.	Discipline and discourage price competition and maintain profit margin.	Maintained market share. Maintained margin. Reduce long-term profitability.
7. Maintain price and reduce perceived value.	Cut marketing expenses to combat rising costs.	Smaller market share. Maintained margin. Reduce long-term profitability.

Here we want to make a few observations:

☐ Company A should think seriously about launching an economy model located close to company B's model so that it can capture the increased number of economy-minded customers (a modification of alternative 6). By offering both a prestige and an economy model, company A can hold or increase its market share.

☐ If company A is forced to raise its prices, it should try to raise its perceived value at the same time (alternative 2). Perceived value can be increased by quality, feature and style improvements, better customer service, and more effective advertising.

☐ The choice of a marketing strategy should hinge on a number of considerations, including company A's current market share, current and planned capacity, market-growth rate, customer price sensitivity and perceived value sensitivity, market share/profitability relationship, and competitors' probable strategic responses and initiatives. The company should try to forecast the impact of each marketing strategy on its sales, market share, costs, profit, and long-run investment.

will move into a recession, marked by a further decline in real income. In the early 1980s, 10 percent of the U.S. labor force was out of work, and in some depressed industrial areas and among some depressed groups, the figure was higher. Whereas an inflationary period is one where people have jobs and a fairly optimistic attitude toward the future, a recession is a period of increasing pessimism. People have less money and become very careful in spending their money. A period of recession throws out new challenges to marketing management.

Nature and Characteristics of Recession

A recession is a period of slowed-down economic growth, marked by a decline in orders, a rise in inventories, a low utilization of capacity, and a rise in unemployment. At one extreme are the light cyclical recessions that have recurred in the U.S. economy every three to four years, lasting an average of ten months and always followed by an upsurge of demand and employment. At the other extreme are deep and long recessions—called depressions—such as occurred in the 1930s, which amount to a long period of secular stagnation awaiting some basic shifts to take place in the economy.

The recession starting in the late 1970s and stretching into the early 1980s falls somewhere between the classic short-cycle recession and the long, 1930s-type depression. This 1980s recession is marked by a deep malaise in such basic industries as automobiles, steel, and housing, whose depressed economic conditions have reverberated through the rest of the economy. Pessimists feel that a number of major U.S. manufacturing industries that used to be the economy's mainstay have lost their global economic advantage and have turned into "sunset" industries. Until strong new industries with global competitive advantages emerge in the U.S., the American economy will continue to show basic weaknesses in consumer demand and employment.

Geoffrey Moore rates recessions by three characteristics—their *duration*, their *depth*, and their *diffusion*.[18] Duration describes how long the recession lasts; depth, how deep the recession goes; and diffusion, how wide it spreads. This last dimension is important because recessions don't affect all consumers or all industries, although deep and enduring ones eventually will. Business executives, in facing a period of slower economic growth, must forecast these three Ds before they can decide what action to take. If they expect a short, light, and highly confined recession, then less marketing adjustment is warranted than in the opposite case.

Recession's Impact on Consumers

As a recession starts and deepens, consumers become more careful and cautious in their spending. The degree to which they make spending adjustments varies with their situation. We can distinguish four groups:

☐ **The underclass poor.** These people were below the poverty line even before the recession. About 20 percent of U.S. citizens are thought to live below the poverty line. Since their incomes are low all the time, their spending habits don't change much.

☐ **The job losers.** People who have lost their jobs normally receive unemployment insurance, which cushions the income contraction. But their outlook is gloomy, and they make several downward adjustments in their spending. These adjustments include "trad-

---

[18] See "This Unusual Recession: Some Prosper While Others Suffer," *Wall Street Journal*, April 20, 1982.

ing down," shifting to discount stores, postponing expensive purchases, hunting for bargains, and becoming "do-it-yourselfers." (See p. 426.)

☐ **The job holders.** Job holders continue to receive their full income. At the same time, they get more cautious with all the bad news and adopt more efficient spending techniques, such as looking harder at values and prices.

☐ **The affluents.** Affluent adults, those earning $40,000 or more, constitute 20 percent of all adults, or 30 million people.[19] Households at the higher end of the income scale are relatively immune from the recession and continue living their normal lifestyles. Residents in Bronxville, N.Y., an upper-income suburb fifteen miles from Manhattan, have continued to buy expensive cars and vacations as if nothing had happened. The existence of an affluent market segment explains the paradox of both low-priced and high-priced goods selling in the same depressed economy. While the sales of automobiles and refrigerators fall, sales sizzle in such categories as videogames, videorecorders, personal computers, and fashion goods.[20]

Those consumers whose incomes fall go through several stages in adjusting their spending pattern:

☐ At first they maintain their old spending pattern, refusing to take their real-income loss seriously.

☐ As things get worse, they cut certain items from their budget and search for less expensive goods.

☐ At a further point, they get angry and blame certain forces for the economic downturn—big business, unions, government.

☐ Still later they start despairing because the situation continues to worsen, and no remedies seem to work.

☐ Finally, consumers take stock of their new situation and resign themselves to their lower standard of living.

Thus this group adopts a prudent lifestyle, leading them to shop more efficiently. Some consumers adopt an austere lifestyle, living with fewer appliances, making some of their own clothes and furniture, growing some of their own food, and eating less.[21]

Recession's Impact on Organizational Buyers

During a recession, business firms experience declining sales, falling productivity, underutilized capacity, and a demoralized work force. These firms are under terrific pressure to lower their break-even point by increasing efficiency and reducing fixed

---

[19] See "More Affluence," *Wall Street Journal*, March 24, 1983.

[20] See "Recession Causes Hardly a Ripple in this Wealthy New York Suburb," *Wall Street Journal*, April 20, 1982; and "Games, Other Luxuries Sell Well as Slump Slows Sales of Durables," *Wall Street Journal*, May 6, 1982.

[21] For quite different reports on consumer behavior during hard times, see "The Squeeze on the Middle Class," *Business Week*, March 10, 1975, p. 52–60; Zoher E. Shipchandler, "Keeping Down with the Joneses: Stagflation and Buyer Behavior," *Business Horizons*, November-December 1982, pp. 32–37; and Avraham Shama, "Coping with Stagflation: Voluntary Simplicity," *Journal of Marketing*, summer 1981, pp. 120–34.

costs.[22] Top management puts pressure on their purchasing department to search for ways to do with less or to trade down in what they buy. The purchasing agents start searching for additional suppliers and lower prices. They get tough with their existing suppliers, trying to wrest lower prices and threatening to switch to other suppliers. They want sales people "to show why we should pay more to you than the other feller."

Thus sellers have to think hard about price and value positioning as they try to maintain their business with existing customers. It is also a time of new opportunities. Sellers who can innovate products that will save companies money will find a welcome mat at the buyer's door.

Company Marketing Strategies During Recession

During a recession, companies normally experience a decline in sales volume. If, in addition, their prices fall and their costs rise, their profits will shrink considerably. The company's task is to figure out how to keep prices and volume up and costs down.

The extent and speed of management's response will depend on how much company profits have shrunk and their estimate of how deep the recession will be, how long it will last, and how price sensitive the target market is.

At one extreme are companies that do well in spite of the recession. They don't have much of a need to shift marketing strategies. *Forbes* described some of the "recession beaters":

> To begin with, there is a sprinkling of high-tech innovators, like Tandem Computers and Wang Labs, and some movers in hot new markets, like Federal Express and Warner Communications. Then there are classic situations, where profits actually pick up as pockets get empty. Examples include such brewers as Anheuser-Busch, which makes Budweiser, and Philip Morris, which makes Miller. It's something called "trading down." People don't have enough money for whiskey, so they buy beer. Philip Morris is also getting another boost from the recession: When people worry about the economy they smoke more. . . . Other companies on the honor roll are in those industries that are often considered recession-proof—where demand doesn't react directly to the economy's ups and downs. The food industry meets this criterion perfectly. After all, people have to eat. Refuse also has to be disposed of, so Browning-Ferris and Waste Management are doing well as a result.[23]

At the other extreme are the hard-hit companies—autos, steel, construction—which must make quick and sometimes radical adjustments. On the nonmarketing front, general management normally takes the following actions during downturns: They reduce general overhead, lay off some personnel, appoint cost-reduction task forces, initiate a strong working-capital-control program, increase liquidity, move toward more buy than make, and purchase more carefully.[24] This effort is directed

---

[22] See "Slump Forcing Firms to Cut Costs So Lower Sales Still Bring a Profit," *Wall Street Journal*, March 3, 1982.

[23] "Strong-Arming the Recession," *Forbes*, July 5, 1982, p. 99.

[24] See Eugene H. Fram and Herbert J. Mossien, *Before the Economy Dips: Planning Protective Action*, Special Study No. 66, prepared for the Presidents Association, 1977.

at cutting the break-even point so that the company can operate at a much lower capacity and still earn money. On the marketing front, management must consider a whole set of possible adjustments in their customer mix and marketing mix.

Customer mix.　In times of economic downturn, companies must reexamine their markets and consider which ones have the best potential for expansion and which lose money year after year. By withdrawing from losing markets and redirecting resources into building up or entering more promising markets, the company will be securing its long-run future. For example:

> Restaurants are closing marginal units, and oil companies are pulling out of areas where they have only a few service stations. Marshall Field & Co. sold the Halle Bros. department store operation in Ohio, and the new owner is cutting it back to six stores from sixteen.[25]

In recessions, business firms are anxious to find new customers to make up for the slackened buying of their current customers. They can search for hidden customers in less visible market segments and geographical areas. The company should consider adding or increasing export sales at this time if the opportunities look better abroad than at home. To attract new customers, the firm can do a number of things, including offering better credit terms and new or improved customer services.

A sound objective for a company during a recession is to try to increase its market share. A recession is the easiest time to do this because weaker competitors are dropping out. According to the Strategic Planning Institute:

> During recessions . . . the average surviving business picks up 0.63 of a percentage point of market share. . . . Significant market-share gainers during recessions were companies that increased their advertising by 28 percent or more. Those concerns . . . picked up an average of 1.5 points of market share.[26]

Product mix and design.　During prosperous times, companies will proliferate new products until every segment is covered. From 1960 to 1970, "the number of breakfast cereals jumped 125 percent, cigarette brands 130 percent, car models 54 percent, general-purpose computers 285 percent, electric toasters 250 percent, and refrigerators 52 percent."[27] The arrival of an economic downturn is a good time to analyze product-line profitability and prune out losing products and build more strength in winning products. General Foods has deemphasized its slowest-selling products and switched the money to support its best sellers. A company should give serious thought to introducing economy models of their products to meet the market's need for lower prices and more value per dollar.

---

[25] "Slump Forcing Firms to Cut Costs So Lower Sales Still Bring a Profit," *Wall Street Journal*, March 3, 1982.

[26] See "Ad Spending Rise Isn't Likely . . . When to Gain Market Share," *Wall Street Journal*, July 8, 1982.

[27] "Marketing When the Growth Slows," *Business Week*, April 14, 1975, p. 46.

General Motors . . . stripped down nine of its small car models—eliminating, among other things, four-speed transmissions and steel-belted tires from the list of standard equipment. These product changes made it possible for GM to chop as much as 8 percent off the list price.[28]

Of course, the company should not make cheap models that fall apart but rather models where nonessential features are removed or products that have improved value engineering. The company should also search for new markets to enter, particularly high-growth markets (there are always some high-growth markets during a recession) and more recession-proof markets. Some companies see their salvation in launching new, exciting products in their product category. Jovan, the Chicago-based fragrance firm, launched ten new products in the recession year 1980, feeling that consumers are looking for "little pleasures" in dismal times. Jovan's management is increasing rather than cutting its advertising budget, hoping to increase its market share against those competitors that are tightening their belts.[29]

Pricing.   During recessions, competitors will engage in aggressive pricing to lure customers into their camp. Every company has to review, and many will have to revise, their pricing strategy. Each company will have to decide whether to emphasize price or value in its marketing strategy. Companies with a good image and superior product will want to emphasize value and avoid aggressive price tactics that might cheapen its image. If the company's product range stretches from economy to expensive models, management has to decide which to advertise. Some marketers prefer to advertise the economy models to attract customers to look at their line, hoping customers will trade up. Other manufacturers would stress the more expensive models to convey an image of high quality.

Companies resorting to aggressive price tactics can lower their list price or offer a lower "real price" in other ways. Manufacturers resist list price reductions because consumers may view them as permanent, and they may cheapen the brand image. More manufacturers prefer offering *rebates* to customers. Rebates emerged as a major pricing tool used by auto manufacturers in 1974, and appliance manufacturers followed. In 1982 General Electric offered rebates on sixty-two small appliances and twenty-three refrigerators and ovens and on lighting fixtures and certain television sets.[30] Customers would get $4 back on a $25 General Electric iron, $5 back on a $110 Sunbeam food processor, or $100 back on a $300 Texas Instruments home computer. Yet many manufacturers dislike using rebates. Consumers are not responding as much to rebates as in the past, and retailers don't like the paper work. Many manufacturers offer them mainly in self-defense rather than in any expectation that rebates will give them any permanent share advance.

Companies are always searching for effective alternatives to rebates. Auto makers

---

[28] Ibid, pp. 44–50.

[29] "Jovan Smells Profit," *Chicago Tribune*, April 20, 1980.

[30] See "Rebating Rises, but Unhappy Firms Can't Think of a Good Alternative," *Wall Street Journal*, December 6, 1982.

have come up with *low-interest financing*,[31] *free maintenance*, and *longer product warranties* as alternative appeals. Airlines offer *free airline tickets* to travelers accumulating certain mileage records on their routes. The difficulty with promotional pricing tactics is that if they work, competitors copy them rapidly, and they lose their effectiveness for the individual company; if they don't work, they waste company money that could have been put into longer-impact marketing tools, such as building up product quality and service and improving the product image through advertising.

Distribution.   Lower incomes will lead consumers to reshape their shopping habits and patronize low-price retail outlets. High-price department stores will lose out to mass merchandisers and discount stores. The recession has already spawned new discount stores in such fields as food, books, sports equipment, and even computers. Low-income consumers will also pay more attention to used-goods stores, factory sales outlets, and garage sales. All this poses a major problem for the company that is locked into high-cost distribution. The company will watch its volume shrink and yet hesitate to court the lower-price retailers because it would lower the profit margins, cheapen the brand image, and alienate higher-price retailers' goodwill. The company prays for a short-lived recession so that it does not have to shift to lower-price retailers. But the company forgets that lower-price retailing will endure and even grow when good times return.

Advertising and sales promotion.   In the face of an economic downturn, companies have to reassess their advertising budgets, message, and media as well as their sales promotion. During the 1973–75 recession, many companies cut back on their advertising budgets, advertising being a traditional target of corporate cost cutters. According to a study by Meldrum & Fewsmith, Inc.:

> Such spending was cut by 15 percent to 23 percent in that earlier recession by more than half the 143 companies. . . . The research found . . . that companies cutting ad spending generally lost sales and market share, and they took longer to recover than did companies that maintained their spending levels. Companies that didn't curtail advertising increased profits by an average of 27 percent a year from 1974 to 1976, compared with gains of between 8 percent and 16 percent by those that reduced ad budgets. . . .[32]

In the recent recession, many companies maintained their advertising budget, and a few adopted aggressive countercyclical spending.

Companies also seek new messages that are more attuned to the buyer's economizing state of mind. Michelin ads talked about how "surprisingly affordable" Michelin tires are; Xerox for the first time takes full-page newspaper ads advertising "SALE!"; and IBM touts some of its equipment as much less expensive than its competitors'.

---

[31] Low-interest financing attracts customers to auto showrooms, but many don't buy when they learn that a large down payment is required; the loan must be paid back in thirty months instead of sixty months; the car price is not discounted much with this kind of loan; and the loan may apply only to expensive cars. See "Finance Deals Aren't Helping Sales of Autos," *Wall Street Journal*, March 17, 1983.

[32] See "Many Advertisers Alter Campaigns to Account for Recession Strategy," *Wall Street Journal*, August 10, 1982.

Some companies emphasize how their product helps consumers save money. Campbell and Lipton try to show consumers that soups are cheap and quick to prepare, and Quaker Oats advertises its products as an inexpensive source of protein. During a recession, companies cut their budgets on image advertising because these ads don't speak to what is on the consumer's mind.

Advertisers are very sensitive to media costs and move their money into more-cost-effective media. Money tends to move from television toward the use of more radio and newspapers.

Sales promotion increases markedly during recessions, taking the form of cents-off coupons, two-for-the-price-of-one sales, contests, and sweepstakes. Consumers are highly deal prone, and companies therefore shift some of their funds from advertising into sales promotion.

Sales-force and customer service. During a recession, the sales force finds it harder to sell, and their spirits sag. Companies then have to find ways to incite their sales force to try harder. Some companies add bonuses for selling the higher-profit products and excess-inventory products. Management introduces sales contests with larger prizes. Companies train their sales people to use the telephone more effectively. They increase their use of direct mail to find customer leads. Top management starts pitching in to help drum up sales. Lee Iacocca, the president of Chrysler, goes on television to tout the Chrysler product line and challenge consumers to find a better-built car.

Companies are tempted to eliminate some customer services to save money, but this must be done carefully. It might be better to unbundle the services and price them separately than to eliminate them. A company should maintain its service image during poor as well as good times, or else it will soon be indistinguishable from its competitors.

All these economic climates—shortages, inflation, recession—pose major challenges to the firm. Firms are sorely tempted to substitute short-run strategy for long-run strategy. They are tempted to raise their prices high during shortages or inflations to make a quick killing. They are tempted to cut out important investments or expenditures during recessions to preserve their profit margin. If they do this, they will pay a price when the recovery starts. They will have hurt customer goodwill and also lack the most modern products to offer the market.

Some companies that go through hard times manage to keep their eyes on the future and invest in building up their long-term position. John Deere & Company has kept investing in product improvements and improved productivity in farm-equipment manufacture all through the recession and in the face of falling earnings.[33] Cummins Engine likewise continued to improve its product lines and production facilities at great cost during the recession in order to be in a strong position when the recovery returned.[34] The key idea is that companies must make a long-run commitment to certain markets and marketing strategies and should not junk them at the first surprise downturn of the economy.

---

[33] "Planting Deep and Wide at John Deere," *Forbes*, March 14, 1983, pp. 119–23.

[34] "Minding its Own Business," *Forbes*, March 14, 1983, pp. 55–56.

SUMMARY

Companies must revise their marketing strategy as the economy shifts through different economic climates such as shortages, inflation, and recession.

Shortages will hit different industries at different times. Sometimes the whole economy enters a shortage phase caused by a major war or by a cartel action by suppliers of certain essential goods. During this period, buyers will search hard for new sources of supply and offer over-the-list prices for scarce supplies. Companies will reexamine their customer mix and decide which customers are the most important ones to supply and how much to allocate to each. Companies will want to strategically reprogram their marketing mix. They will concentrate on producing their highest-profit products and not waste scarce supplies producing their weaker products. Prices will undoubtedly be raised, to ration supply. Companies will concentrate on their strongest distribution channels and pay less attention to weaker channels. They will reduce their advertising budget but still use advertising to draw attention to other products in their line and to show customers how they can use the scarce supplies more efficiently. Sales personnel will have the difficult task of allocating supplies to disgruntled customers in a way that is profitable to the company and yet is fair to the customers. The key marketing platform during this period is to help customers get through the shortage so they will be loyal to the company in the post-shortage period. The company must avoid acquiring the image of a price gouger.

A period of rapid inflation will accompany or follow the shortage period. Consumers will become highly price sensitive and respond with economizing behavior which will take many forms, including purchase postponement, more comparison shopping, shifting to discount stores, trading down, and so on. Purchasing agents will bargain harder and search for new and cheaper sources of supply. Companies will review their customer mix and concentrate on customers who are willing and able to pay the higher prices. They will review product-line profitability and focus on selling the more profitable products. This will be a good time to introduce economy models because customers will be looking for ways to save money. The company must decide by how much to raise prices and in what form, such as delayed quotation pricing, escalator clauses, unbundling, and elimination of discounts. The company may want to increase its use of low-price distribution channels because customers will start favoring them. The company will need to revise its advertising budget, message, and media during this period. Sales people will have to explain company pricing policies to buyers and help them contend with the inflation.

A recession usually follows a period of rapid inflation because government policies will be directed at restricting demand. The effect will be excess inventories, worker layoffs, and reduced purchasing power. Buyers will respond to the income squeeze by buying less and buying more efficiently. Companies will want to hold on to their current customers and search hard for new customers. Companies will find it an opportune time to introduce economy models. Lower prices will come about through competitive price cutting. Companies will want to enlarge their role in lower-price channels of distribution where the action is. Companies will decide whether to advertise price or value in trying to hold their markets. Companies will shift some promotion money from advertising to sales promotion. Sales management will encourage the sales force to work harder through sales contests and offers of bonuses for selling certain products.

QUESTIONS

1. Distinguish four alternative advertising strategies to be used by an oil company in the event of another major fuel shortage.

2. Two companies, A and B, account for virtually 100 percent of the sales in a certain industry. Company A is the high-price, high-quality company, and company B is the low-price, low-quality company. During the period of rising real incomes, company A enjoyed a 60 percent market share, and company B had the rest. In the subsequent period of high inflation and recession, several buyers switched to company B because of their need to economize. What are some of the strategies available to company A to avoid losing further market share?

3. Stagflation—concurrent inflation, shortages, and recession—is an economic phenomenon that has occurred in the 1970s and 1980s. Should marketers' response to stagflation be any different from their separate responses to inflation, shortages, and recession?

4. The Conference Board publishes an index of consumer confidence that reflects the extent to which consumers believe the economy is improving. How might a department-store chain use such an index in planning its purchasing patterns?

5. After years of double-digit or near double-digit inflation during 1973–81, the United States entered a period of "disinflation" beginning in 1982–83. What are the consequences to marketers of a disinflation economy?

6. Canteen Corporation, a food-service company specializing in catering to smokestack industries, suffers declining sales when a recessionary economy causes layoffs in heavy industry. What marketing strategy would you recommend for Canteen?

7. In September of 1979 the Financial Accounting Standards Board issued Statement 33, which requires many corporations to compute inflation's effects on profit-and-loss figures. What are some of the ways inflation-adjusted accounting will influence measures of marketing performance?

Marketing Strategies for the Global Marketplace

14

A traveller without knowledge is a bird without wings.

SA'DI, GULISTAN (1258)

Because of the large size of the U.S. market and some disappointing marketing experiences abroad, many American companies have avoided aggressive international marketing. Most American firms prefer domestic to foreign marketing. Domestic marketing is simpler and safer. Managers do not have to learn another language, deal with a different currency, face political and legal uncertainties, or adapt the product to different customer needs and expectations.

Two factors, however, draw American companies into international marketing. First, they might be *pushed* by a weakening of marketing opportunities at home. GNP growth may slow down; R&D and manufacturing costs might escalate and be recovered only by "going global"; government might become antibusiness; the tax burden might become too heavy; the government might push business into expanding abroad in order to earn more foreign exchange and reduce the U.S. trade deficit.[1] Second, American companies might be *pulled* into foreign trade by growing opportunities for their product in other countries. Without abandoning the domestic market,

---

[1] See "The Reluctant Exporter," *Business Week*, April 10, 1978, pp. 54–66.

they might find other markets attractive even allowing for the extra costs and encumbrances they face in operating abroad.

American exports accounted for 11 percent of the U.S. gross national product in 1979. This makes the United States the world's largest exporting nation in absolute dollars. Other countries, however, are more involved in world trade in relation to their gross national product. The United Kingdom, Belgium, the Netherlands, and New Zealand have to sell more than half their output abroad in order to have high employment and pay for imported goods. International marketing is second nature to the companies in these countries.

Some countries here and abroad have gone into world marketing on such a large scale that they can be called *multinational companies*. Among American companies deriving more than 60 percent of their revenue from abroad in 1981 are Pan Am World Airways (92 percent), Exxon (72 percent), Citicorp (67 percent), Texaco (62 percent), Mobil (60 percent), and Colgate-Palmolive (60 percent).[2] Caterpillar, Coca-Cola, Dow Chemical, Ford, Gillette, Gulf Oil, IBM, ITT, Kodak, Pfizer, and Xerox earn about half of their profits abroad, and their foreign operations are growing faster than their domestic operations. American companies face formidable multinational competitors such as Royal Dutch/Shell, British Petroleum, Unilever, Philips, Volkswagenwerk, Nippon Steel, Siemens, Toyota Motors, and Nestlé.

While some American companies have aggressively expanded abroad, many foreign companies have entered the American market. Their names and brands have become household words, such as Sony, Honda, Datsun, Nestlé, Perrier, Norelco, Mercedes-Benz, and Volkswagen, with many Americans showing a preference for these brands over domestic brands. There are many other products that appear to be produced by American firms but are really produced by foreign multinationals. This group includes Bantam Books, Baskin-Robbins Ice Cream, Capitol Records, Kiwi Shoe Polish, Lipton Tea, and Saks Fifth Avenue. America is also attracting huge foreign investments in tourist and real estate ventures, notably Japanese land purchases in Hawaii, Kuwait's resort development off the South Carolina coast, and Arab purchases of Manhattan office buildings—and one offer by a Saudi Arabian sheik to buy the Alamo for his son.

Thus we see that international trade is both an opportunity and a threat. It is an opportunity in that it provides U.S. companies with an additional outlet for their goods. Through international trade, U.S. companies can extend the life cycle of their products by bringing them to other countries as those countries become ready to use them. International trade is also a threat in that eventually other countries learn to make the same or better goods at lower costs and invade the U.S. market. All said, the international product life cycle requires companies to take a global view of their business. (See the earlier discussion of the international product life cycle in Chapter 11, pp. 360–61.)

As international competition intensifies, American companies have to increase their sophistication in handling international marketing operations. Some of America's most successful marketers fumbled when they went abroad. Kentucky Fried Chicken opened eleven outlets in Hong Kong, and all failed within two years. McDonald's

---

[2] See "The Top 1500 Companies," published by Economic Information Systems, New York, 1982.

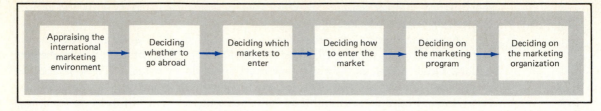

FIGURE 14-1
Major Decisions in International Marketing

located its first European outlet in an Amsterdam suburb, but sales were disappointing. Marketing blunders abroad were committed by some of the United States's strongest domestic marketers—Campbell's, Procter & Gamble, General Motors, and so on.

One might ask whether global marketing involves any new principles. Obviously the principles of setting marketing objectives, choosing target markets, developing marketing positions and mixes, and carrying out marketing control apply. The principles are not new, but the differences between nations can be so great that the international marketer needs to understand foreign environments and institutions and be prepared to revise the most basic assumptions about how people respond to marketing stimuli.

We will now examine the six basic decisions that a company faces in considering international marketing. (See Figure 14-1.)

APPRAISING THE INTERNATIONAL MARKETING ENVIRONMENT

A company has to learn many things before deciding whether to sell abroad. The company has to acquire a thorough understanding of the international marketing environment. The international marketing environment has undergone significant changes since 1945, creating both new opportunities and new problems. The most significant changes are:[3]

☐ The internationalization of the world economy reflected in the rapid growth of world trade and investment

☐ The gradual erosion of the U.S.'s dominant position and its attendant problems of an unfavorable balance of trade (a $43 billion foreign trade deficit in 1982) and a strong dollar in world markets, causing U.S. prices to be too high

☐ The rising economic power of Japan in world markets (see Exhibit 14-1.)

☐ The establishment of an international financial system offering improved currency convertibility

☐ The shift in world income since 1973 to the oil-producing countries

☐ The increasing trade barriers put up to protect domestic markets against foreign competition

☐ The gradual opening up of major new markets, namely, China, the USSR, and the Arab countries

---

[3] See Warren J. Keegan, "Multinational Product Planning: New Myths and Old Realities," in *Multinational Product Management* (Cambridge, Mass.: Marketing Science Institute, 1976), pp. 1–8.

Exhibit 14-1

THE WORLD'S CHAMPION MARKETERS: THE JAPANESE?

Few dispute that the Japanese have performed an economic miracle since World War II. In a relatively short time, they have achieved global market leadership in industries thought to be dominated by impregnable giants: autos, motorcycles, watches, cameras, optical instruments, steel, shipbuilding, pianos, zippers, radios, television, video recorders, hand calculators, and so on. Japanese firms are currently moving into the number-two position in computers and construction equipment and making strong inroads into the chemical, pharmaceutical, and machine-tool industries.

Many theories have been offered to explain Japan's global successes. Some point to their unique business practices, such as lifetime employment, quality circles, consensus management, and just-in-time delivery. Others point to the supportive role of government policies and subsidies, the existence of powerful trading companies, and businesses' easy access to bank financing. Still others view Japan's success as based on low wage rates and unfair dumping policies.

One of the main keys to Japan's performance is its skill in marketing-strategy formulation and implementation. The Japanese came to the U.S. to study marketing and went home understanding its principles better than many U.S. companies did. The Japanese know how to select a market, enter it in the right way, build their market share, and protect their leadership position against competitors' attacks.

Selecting Markets

The Japanese government and companies work hard to identify attractive global markets. They favor industries that require high skills, high labor intensity, and only small quantities of natural resources: candidates include consumer electronics, cameras, watches, motorcycles, and pharmaceuticals. They prefer product markets that are in a state of technological evolution. They like product markets where consumers around the world would be willing to buy the same product designs. They look for industries where the market leaders are complacent or underfinanced.

Entering Markets

The Japanese send study teams into the target country to spend several months evaluating the market and figuring out a strategy. The teams search for niches to enter that are not being satisfied by any current offerings. Sometimes they establish their beachhead with a low-price stripped-down version of a product, sometimes with a product that is as good as the competitions' but priced lower, sometimes with a product exhibiting higher quality or new features or designs. The Japanese proceed to line up good distribution in order to provide quick service to their customers. They rely on advertising to bring their products to the public's attention. A key characteristic of their entry strategy is to build market share rather than early profits. The Japanese are patient capitalists who are willing to wait even a decade before realizing their profits.

Building Market Share

Once Japanese firms gain a market foothold, they direct their energies toward expanding their market share. They rely on product-development strategies and market-development strategies.

They pour money into product improvement, product upgrading, and product proliferation, so that they can offer more and better things than the competition. They spot new opportunities through market segmentation, and sequence market development across a number of countries, pushing toward building a network of world markets and production locations.

Protecting Market Share

Once the Japanese achieve market domination, they find themselves in the role of defenders rather than attackers. U.S. firms such as IBM, Xerox, Motorola, and Texas Instruments are mounting counterattacks. The Japanese defense strategy is a good offense through continuous product development and refined market segmentation. Their aim is to fill holes in the market before their competition can.

Source: For further discussion, see Philip Kotler and Liam Fahey, "The World's Champion Marketers: The Japanese," Journal of Business Strategy, *summer 1982, pp. 3–13.*

☐ The severe debt problems of several countries, such as Mexico and Poland, along with the growing stress on the international financial system

The International Trade System

The American company looking abroad must start with an appreciation of the international trade system. In attempting to sell to another country, the American firm will face various trade restrictions. The most common is the *tariff*, which is a tax levied by the foreign government against designated imported products. The tariff may be designed to raise revenue (revenue tariff) or to protect domestic firms (protective tariff). The exporter may also face a *quota*, which sets limits on the amount of goods that the importing country will accept in certain product categories. The purpose of the quota is to conserve on foreign exchange and protect local industry and employment. An *embargo* is the ultimate form of quota in that imports in prescribed categories are totally banned. Trade is also discouraged by *exchange control*, which regulates the amount of available foreign exchange and its exchange rate against other currencies. The American company may also confront a set of *nontariff barriers*, such as discrimination against American company bids, and product standards that discriminate against American product features. For example, the Dutch government bars tractors that run faster than ten miles an hour, which means that most American-made tractors are barred.

At the same time, certain forces seek to liberalize and foster trade between nations, or at least between some nations. The General Agreement on Tariffs and Trade (GATT) is an international agreement that has reduced the level of tariffs throughout the world on six different occasions. Certain countries have formed *economic communities,* the most important of which is the European Economic Community (EEC, also known as the Common Market). The EEC's members are the major Western European nations, and they are striving to reduce tariffs within the community, reduce prices, and expand employment and investment. EEC has taken the form of a *customs union*, which is a *free-trade area* (no tariffs facing the members) that imposes a uniform tariff for trade with nonmember nations. The next move would be an *economic union* in which all members would operate under the same trade policies. Since EEC's formation, other economic communities have been formed, notably the Latin American Free Trade Association (LAFTA), the Central American Common Market (CACM), and the Council for Mutual Economic Assistance (CMEA) (Eastern European countries).

Each nation has unique features that must be grasped. A nation's readiness for different products and services and its attractiveness as a market to foreign firms depend on its economic, political-legal, cultural, and business environment.

Economic Environment

In considering foreign markets, the international marketer must study each country's economy. Two economic characteristics reflect the country's attractiveness as an export market.

The first is the country's *industrial structure*. The country's industrial structure shapes its product and service requirements, income levels, employment levels, and so on. Four types of industrial structure can be distinguished:

1. **Subsistence economies.** In a subsistence economy the vast majority of people engage in simple agriculture. They consume most of their output and barter the rest for simple goods and services. They offer few opportunities for exporters.

2. **Raw-material-exporting economies.** These economies are rich in one or more natural resources but poor in other respects. Much of their revenue comes from exporting these resources. Examples are Chile (tin and copper), Congo (rubber), and Saudi Arabia (oil). These countries are good markets for extractive equipment, tools and supplies, materials-handling equipment, and trucks. Depending on the number of foreign residents and wealthy native rulers and landholders, they are also a market for Western-style commodities and luxury goods.

3. **Industrializing economies.** In an industrializing economy, manufacturing is beginning to account for between 10 and 20 percent of the country's gross national product. Examples include Egypt, the Philippines, India, and Brazil. As manufacturing increases, the country relies more on imports of textile raw materials, steel, and heavy machinery and less on imports of finished textiles, paper products, and automobiles. The industrialization creates a new rich class and a small but growing middle class, both demanding new types of goods, some of which can be satisfied only by imports.

4. **Industrial economies.** Industrial economies are major exporters of manufactured goods and investment funds. They trade manufactured goods among themselves and also export them to other types of economies in exchange for raw materials and semifinished goods. The large and varied manufacturing activities of these industrial nations and their sizable middle class make them rich markets for all sorts of goods.

These four structural types are not necessarily chronological. Many developing countries are characterized by a *dual economy* where a subsistence sector coexists with a type 2 or 3 modern sector. In these, opportunities for exporters may be significantly increased if marketing efforts are aimed at integrating the two sectors.

The second economic characteristic is the country's *income distribution*. Income distribution is related to a country's industrial structure but is also affected by the political system. The international marketer distinguishes countries with five different income-distribution patterns: (1) very low family incomes, (2) mostly low family incomes, (3) very low, very high family incomes, (4) low, medium, high family incomes, and (5) mostly medium family incomes. Consider the market for Lamborghinis, an automobile costing more than $50,000. The market would be very small in countries with type (1) or (2) income patterns. The largest single market for Lamborghinis turns out to be Portugal (income pattern 3), the poorest country in Europe but one with enough wealthy status-conscious families to afford them.

Income distribution is not an accurate indicator of development in countries where an important subsistence sector has a noncash income that is not easily quantifiable in standard terms. Other measurements used increasingly are the energy and food consumption indices and the percentage of labor force in industrial employment.

Political-Legal Environment

Nations differ greatly in their political-legal environment. A company should consider four factors in deciding whether to do business in a particular country.

Attitudes toward international buying. Some nations are very receptive, indeed encouraging, to foreign firms, and others are very hostile. As an example of the former, Mexico for a number of years has been attracting foreign investment by offering investment incentives and site-location services. On the other hand, India has required the exporter to deal with import quotas, blocked currencies, stipulations that a high percentage of the management team be nationals, and so on. IBM and Coca-Cola made the decision to leave India because of all the "hassles."

Political stability. The country's future stability is another issue. Governments change hands, sometimes quite violently. Even without a change, a regime may decide to respond to new popular feelings. The foreign company's property may be expropriated; or its currency holdings may be blocked; or import quotas or new duties may be imposed. Where political instability is high, international marketers may still find it profitable to do business in that country, but the situation will affect their mode of entry. They will favor export marketing to direct foreign investment. They will keep their foreign stocks low. They will convert their currency rapidly. As a result, the people in the host country pay higher prices, have fewer jobs, and get less satisfactory products.[4]

Monetary regulations. Sellers want to realize profits in a currency of value to them. In the best situation the importer can pay either in the seller's currency or in hard world currencies. Short of this, sellers might accept a blocked currency if they can buy other goods in that country that they need or that they can sell elsewhere for a needed currency. In the worst case they have to take their money out of the host country in the form of relatively unmarketable products that they can sell else-

---

[4] For a system of rating the political stability of different nations, see F. T. Haner, "Rating Investment Risks Abroad," *Business Horizons*, April 1979, pp. 18–23.

where only at a loss. (For a description of various countertrade practices, see Exhibit 1–1, p. 9.) Besides currency restrictions, a fluctuating exchange rate also creates high risks for the exporter.

Government bureaucracy.   A fourth factor is the extent to which the host government runs an efficient system for assisting foreign companies: efficient customs handling, adequate market information, and other factors conducive to doing business. A common shock to Americans is the extent to which impediments to trade disappear if a suitable payment (bribe) is made to some official(s).

Cultural Environment

Each country has its own folkways, norms, and taboos. The way foreign consumers think about and use certain products must be checked out by the seller before planning the marketing program. Here is a sampling of some of the surprises in the consumer market:

- ☐ The average Frenchman uses almost twice as many cosmetics and beauty aids as does his wife.
- ☐ The Germans and the French eat more packaged, branded spaghetti than the Italians.
- ☐ Italian children like to eat a bar of chocolate between two slices of bread as a snack.
- ☐ Women in Tanzania will not give their children eggs for fear of making them bald or impotent.

Business norms and behavior also vary from country to country. U.S. business executives need to be briefed on these before negotiating in another country. Here are some examples of business behavior at variance with U.S. business behavior:

- ☐ South Americans are accustomed to talking business in close physical proximity with other persons—in fact, almost nose to nose. The American business executive retreats, and the South American pursues. And both end up being offended.
- ☐ In face-to-face communications Japanese business executives rarely say no to an American business executive. Americans are frustrated and don't know where they stand. Americans come to the point quickly. Japanese business executives find this offensive.
- ☐ In France, wholesalers don't care to promote a product. They ask their retailers what they want and deliver it. If an American company builds its strategy around the French wholesaler cooperating in promotions, it is likely to fail.

Each country (and even regional groups within each country) has cultural traditions, preferences, and taboos that the marketer must study.[5]

DECIDING WHETHER TO GO ABROAD

Companies get involved in international marketing in one of two ways. Someone— a domestic exporter, a foreign importer, a foreign government—solicits the company

---

[5] For further examples, see David A. Ricks, Marilyn Y. C. Fu, and Jeffery S. Arpan, *International Business Blunders* (Columbus, Ohio: Grid, 1974).

to sell abroad. Or the company starts to think on its own about going abroad. It might face overcapacity or see better marketing opportunities in other countries than at home.

Before going abroad, the company should try to define its *international marketing objectives and policies*. First, it should decide *what proportion* of foreign to total sales it will seek. Most companies start small when they venture abroad. Some plan to stay small, seeing foreign operations as a small part of their business. Other companies will have more grandiose plans, seeing foreign business as ultimately equal to, or even more important than, their domestic business.

Second, the company must choose between marketing in a *few countries* or *many countries*. The Bulova Watch Company made the latter choice and expanded into over one hundred countries. It spread itself too thin, made profits in only two countries, and lost around $40 million.[6]

Third, the company must decide on the *types of countries* to consider. The countries that are attractive will depend on the product, geographical factors, income and population, political climate, and other factors. The seller may have a predilection for certain groups of countries or parts of the world.

DECIDING WHICH MARKETS TO ENTER

After developing a list of possible export markets, the company will have to screen and rank them. Consider the following example:

> CMC's market research in the computer field revealed that England, France, West Germany, and Italy offer us significant markets. England, France, and Germany are about equal-size markets, while Italy represents about two thirds the potential of any one of those countries. . . . Taking everything into consideration, we decided to set up first in England because its market for our products is as large as any and its language and laws are similar to ours. England is different enough to get your feet wet, yet similar enough to the familiar U.S. business environment so that you do not get in over your head.[7]

The market choice seems relatively simple and straightforward. Yet one can question whether the reason for selecting England—the compatibility of its language and culture—should have been given this prominence. The candidate countries should be ranked on several criteria, such as market size, market growth, cost of doing business, competitive advantage, and risk level.

The goal is to estimate the probable rate of return on investment in each market. Five steps are involved.[8]

---

[6] Igal Ayal and Jehiel Zif, "Market Expansion Strategies in Multinational Marketing," *Journal of Marketing*, spring 1979, pp. 84–94.

[7] James K. Sweeney, "A Small Company Enters the European Market," *Harvard Business Review*, September-October 1970, pp. 127–28.

[8] See David S. R. Leighton, "Deciding When to Enter International Markets," in *Handbook of Modern Marketing*, ed. Victor P. Buell (New York: McGraw-Hill Book Co., 1970), sec. 20, pp. 23–28.

1. **Estimate of current market potential.** The first step is to estimate current market potential in each market. This task calls for using published data and primary data collected through company surveys.

2. **Forecast of future market potential and risk.** The firm also needs to forecast future market potential, a difficult task. It includes predictions of economic performance, such as projected annual growth rate of GNP/capita, and measurements of elite, communal, and mass political instability, based on variables such as reported strikes, demonstrations, riots, and terrorist events over a given period of time.

3. **Forecast of sales potential.** Estimating the company's sales potential requires forecasting its probable market share, another difficult task.

4. **Forecast of costs and profits.** Costs will depend on the company's contemplated entry strategy. If it exports or licenses, its costs will be spelled out in the contracts. If it locates manufacturing facilities abroad, its costs estimation will require understanding local labor conditions, taxes, trade practices, and so on. The company subtracts estimated costs from estimated sales to find company profits for each year of the planning horizon.

5. **Estimate of rate of return on investment.** The forecasted income stream should be related to the investment stream to derive the implicit rate of return. This should be high enough to cover (1) the company's normal target return on its investment and (2) the risk of uncertainty of marketing in that country.

DECIDING HOW TO ENTER THE MARKET

Once a company decides to sell to a particular country, it has to determine the best mode of entry. Its choice are *exporting, joint venturing, and direct investment abroad*.[9] Each succeeding strategy involves more commitment, risk, and possible profits. The three market entry strategies are shown in Figure 14–2, along with the various options under each.

Export

The simplest way to get involved in a foreign market is through export. *Occasional exporting* is a passive level of involvement where the company exports surpluses from time to time and sells goods to resident buyers representing foreign countries. *Active* exporting takes place when the company makes a commitment to expand exports to a particular market. In either case the company produces all of its goods in the home country. It may or may not modify them for the export market. Exporting involves the least change in the company's product lines, organization, investments, or mission.

A company can export its product in two ways. It can hire independent international marketing middlemen (indirect export) or handle its own exporting (direct export).

Indirect export.   Indirect export is more common in companies just beginning their exporting. First, it involves less investment. The firm does not have to develop an

---

[9] The discussion of entry strategies in this section is based on the discussion in Gordon E. Miracle and Gerald S. Albaum, *International Management* (Homewood, Ill.: Richard D. Irwin, 1970), chaps. 14–16.

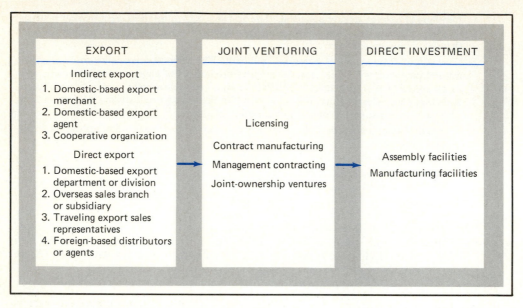

FIGURE 14-2
Market Entry Strategies

overseas sales force or a set of contracts. Second, it involves less risk. International-marketing middlemen bring know-how and services to the relationship, and the seller will normally make fewer mistakes.

Four types of domestic middlemen are available to the exporting company:

☐ **Domestic-based export merchant.** This middleman buys the manufacturer's product and sells it abroad on its own account.

☐ **Domestic-based export agent.** This agent seeks and negotiates foreign purchases for a commission. Included in the group are trading companies.

☐ **Cooperative organization.** A cooperative organization carries on exporting activities on behalf of several producers and is partly under their administrative control. This form is often used by producers of primary products—fruits, nuts, and so on.

☐ **Export-management company.** This middleman agrees to manage a company's export activities for a fee.

Direct export.   Sellers who are approached by foreign buyers are likely to use direct export. So will sellers whose exporters have grown sufficiently large to undertake their own exporting. The investment and risk are somewhat greater, but so is the potential return.

The company can carry on direct exporting in several ways:

☐ **Domestic-based export department or division.** An export sales manager with some clerical assistants carry on the actual selling and draw on market assistance as needed. It might evolve into a self-contained export department or sales subsidiary carrying out all the activities involved in export and possibly operating as a profit center.

- ☐ **Overseas sales branch or subsidiary.** An overseas sales branch allows the manufacturer to achieve greater presence and program control in the foreign market. The sales branch handles sales distribution and may handle warehousing and promotion as well. It often serves as a display center and customer-service center.
- ☐ **Traveling export sales representatives.** The company can send home-based sales representatives abroad at certain times to find business.
- ☐ **Foreign-based distributors or agents.** Foreign-based distributors would buy and own the goods; foreign-based agents would sell the goods on behalf of the company. They may be given exclusive rights to represent the manufacturer in that country or only general rights.

Joint Venturing

A second broad method of entering a foreign market is to join with foreign nationals to set up production and marketing facilities. Joint venturing differs from exporting in that a partnership is formed that leads to some production facilities abroad, and it differs from direct investment in that an association is formed with someone in that country. Four types of joint venture can be distinguished.

Licensing. Licensing represents a simple way for a manufacturer to become involved in international marketing. The licensor enters an agreement with a licensee in the foreign market, offering the right to use a manufacturing process, trademark, patent, trade secret, or other item of value for a fee or royalty. The licensor gains entry into the market at little risk; the licensee gains production expertise or a well-known product or name, without having to start from scratch. Gerber introduced its baby foods in the Japanese market through a licensing arrangement. Coca-Cola carried out its international marketing by licensing bottlers around the world—or, more technically, *franchising* bottlers—and supplies them with the syrup needed to produce the product.

Licensing has potential disadvantages in that the firm has less control over the licensee than if it had set up its own production facilities. Furthermore, if the licensee is very successful, the firm has foregone profits, and if and when the contract ends, it may find it has created a competitor. To avoid these dangers the licensor must establish a mutual advantage in working together, and a key to doing this is to remain innovative so that the licensee continues to depend on the licensor.

Contract manufacturing. Another option is to contract with local manufacturers to produce the product. Sears used this method in opening up department stores in Mexico and Spain. Sears found qualified local manufacturers to produce many of the products it sells.

Contract manufacturing has the drawback of less control over the manufacturing process and the loss of potential profits on manufacturing. On the other hand, it offers the company a chance to start faster, with less risk, and with the opportunity to form a partnership or buy out the local manufacturer later.

Management contracting. Here the domestic firm supplies the management know-how to a foreign company that supplies the capital. The domestic firm is exporting management services rather than products. This arrangement is used by Hilton in managing hotels around the world.

Management contracting is a low-risk method of getting into a foreign market, and it yields income from the beginning. The arrangement is especially attractive if the contracting firm is given an option to purchase some share in the managed company within a stated period. On the other hand, the arrangement is not sensible if the company can put its scarce management talent to better uses or if there are greater profits to be made by undertaking the whole venture. Management contracting prevents the company from setting up its own operations for a period of time.

Joint-ownership ventures. In joint-ownership ventures foreign investors joining with local investors to create a local business in which they share joint ownership and control. The foreign investor may buy an interest in a local company, a local company may buy an interest in an existing operation of a foreign company, or the two parties may form a new business venture.

A jointly owned venture may be necessary or desirable for economic or political reasons. The firm may lack the financial, physical, or managerial resources to undertake the venture alone. Or the foreign government may require joint ownership as a condition for entry.

Joint ownership has certain drawbacks. The partners may disagree over investment, marketing, or other policies. Where many American firms like to reinvest earnings for growth, local firms often like to take out these earnings. Where American firms accord a large role to marketing, local investors may rely only on selling. Furthermore, joint ownership can hamper a multinational company from carrying out specific manufacturing and marketing policies on a worldwide basis.

Direct Investment

The ultimate involvement in a foreign market is investment in foreign-based assembly or manufacturing facilities. As a company gains experience in export, and if the foreign market appears large enough, foreign production facilities offer distinct advantages. First, the firm may secure cost economies in the form of cheaper labor or raw materials, foreign-government investment incentives, freight savings, and so on. Second, the firm will gain a better image in the host country because it creates jobs. Third, the firm develops a deeper relationship with government, customers, local suppliers, and distributors, enabling it to adapt its products better to the local marketing environment. Fourth, the firm retains full control over the investment and therefore can develop manufacturing and marketing policies that serve its long-term international objectives.

The main disadvantage is that the firm exposes a large investment to risks, such as blocked or devalued currencies, worsening markets, or expropriation. In some cases, the firm has no choice but to accept these risks if it wants to operate in the host country.

Companies that operate in one or more foreign markets must decide how much, if at all, to adapt their marketing mix to local conditions. At one extreme are companies that use a *standardized marketing mix* worldwide. Standardization of the product, advertising, distribution channels, and other elements of the marketing mix promises the lowest costs because no major changes have been introduced. This thinking is behind the idea that Coca-Cola should taste the same around the world and General Motors should produce a "world car" that suits the needs of most consumers in most countries. At the other extreme is the idea of a *customized marketing mix,* where the producer adjusts the marketing-mix elements to each target market, bearing more costs but hoping for a larger market share and return. Nestlé, for example, varies its product line and its advertising in different countries. Between these two extremes, many possibilities exist. Thus Levi Strauss can sell the same jeans worldwide but vary the advertising theme in each country.

A recent survey of leading consumer-packaged-goods multinationals concluded: "To the successful multinational, it is not really important whether marketing programs are internationally standardized or differentiated; the important thing is that the *process* through which these programs are developed is standardized."[10]

Here we will examine possible company adaptations of their product, promotion, price, and distribution as they go abroad.

Product

Keegan distinguished five adaptation strategies of product and promotion to a foreign market (Figure 14–3).[11] Here we will examine the three product strategies, and later we will look at the two promotion strategies.

Straight extension means introducing the product in the foreign market without any change. Top management instructs its marketing people: "Take the product as it is and find customers for it." The first step, however, should be to determine whether the foreign consumers use that product. Deodorant usage among men ranges from 80 percent in the United States to 55 percent in Sweden to 28 percent in Italy to 8 percent in the Philippines. Many Spaniards do not use such common products as butter and cheese.

Straight extension has been successful in some cases but a disaster in others. General Foods introduced its standard powdered Jell-O in the British market only to find that British consumers prefer the solid wafer or cake form. Campbell Soup lost an estimated $30 million in introducing its condensed soups in England by failing to explain that consumers should add water; the consumers saw the small-size cans and thought they were expensive. Straight extension is tempting because it involves

---

[10] Ralph Z. Sorenson and Ulrich E. Wiechmann, "How Multinationals View Marketing Standardization," *Harvard Business Review*, May-June 1975, pp. 38–54.

[11] Warren J. Keegan, "Multinational Product Planning: Strategic Alternatives," *Journal of Marketing*, January 1969, pp. 58–62.

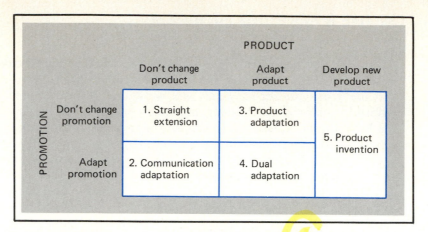

FIGURE 14–3
Five International Product and Promotion Strategies

no additional R&D expense, manufacturing retooling, or promotional modification. But it can be costly in the long run.

One way to increase its utility is to use market research to discover possible new applications for the product in foreign markets. Variations in product use are common in developing countries. In Nigeria, for instance, Swiss-made embroidered fabrics are purchased for both male and female clothing, whereas the European market is restricted to the female segment.

Product adaptation involves altering the product to meet local conditions or preferences. Heinz varies its baby-food products: In Australia it sells a baby food made from strained lamb brains; and in the Netherlands, a baby food made from strained brown beans. General Foods blends different coffees for the British (who drink their coffee with milk), the French (who drink their coffee black), and Latin Americans (who want a chicory taste).

An important variant of product adaptation responds to the *basic-needs* concept in developing economies. Pharmaceutical companies such as Ciba-Geigy have set up a specific product line for these markets, distinguished by a narrower and more focused range (stressing, for example, antibiotics) and by "no-frills" packaging, allowing a reduced price. This concept, close to a branded generics line, is equally applicable to other areas, such as the food and beverage industry.

Product invention consists of creating something new. This can take two forms. *Backward invention* is the reintroducing of earlier product forms that happen to be well adapted to the needs of a country. The National Cash Register Company reintroduced its crank-operated cash register, which could sell at half the cost of a modern cash register and sold substantial numbers in the Orient, Latin America, and Spain. This illustrates the existence of *international product life cycles* where countries stand at different stages of readiness to accept a particular product. (See Exhibit 11–1, pp. 360–61.) *Forward invention* is creating a brand new product to meet a need in another country. There is an enormous need in less-developed countries for low-cost, high-protein foods. Companies such as Quaker Oats, Swift, and Monsanto are researching the nutrition needs of these countries, formulating new foods, and developing advertising campaigns to gain product trial and acceptance. Product invention appears to be a costly strategy, but the payoffs might also be great.

Promotion

Companies can either adopt the same promotion strategy they used in the home market or change it for each local market.

Consider the message. Many multinational companies use a standardized advertising theme around the world. Exxon used "Put a tiger in your tank" and gained international recognition. The copy is varied in a minor way, such as changing the colors to avoid taboos in other countries. Purple is associated with death in most of Latin America; white is a mourning color in Japan; and green is associated with jungle sickness in Malaysia. Even names have to be modified. In Germany, *mist* means "manure," and *scotch* (scotch tape) means "schmuck"; in Spain, Chevrolet's *Nova* translates as *no va*, which means "it doesn't go"! In Sweden, Helene Curtis renamed Every Night Shampoo to Every Day because Swedes wash their hair in the morning.

Other companies encourage their international divisions to develop their own ads. The Schwinn Bicycle Company might use a pleasure theme in the United States and a safety theme in Scandinavia.

The use of media also requires international adaptation because media availability varies from country to country. Time for TV commercials is available for one hour each evening in Germany, and advertisers must buy time months in advance. In Sweden, commercial TV and radio is nonexistent. Magazines are a major medium in Italy and a minor one in Austria. Newspapers are national in the United Kingdom and local in Spain.

Price

Manufacturers often price their products lower in foreign markets. Incomes may be low, and a low price is necessary to sell the goods. The manufacturer may set low prices to build market share. Or the manufacturer may want to dump goods that have no market at home. When the manufacturer charges less in the foreign market than in the home market, the practice is called *dumping*. The Zenith Company accused Japanese television manufacturers of dumping their TV sets on the U.S. market. If the U.S. Customs Bureau finds dumping, it can levy a dumping tariff.

Manufacturers have little control over the retail prices charged by foreign middlemen who carry their products. Many foreign middlemen use high markups, even though this means selling fewer units. They also like to buy on credit and this increases the manufacturer's cost and risk.

Distribution Channels

The international company must take a *whole-channel* view of the problem of distributing product to the final consumers.[12] Figure 14–4 shows the three major links between

---

[12] See Miracle and Albaum, *International Marketing Management*, pp. 317–19.

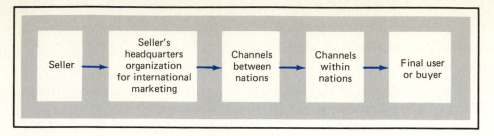

FIGURE 14–4
Whole-Channel Concept for International Marketing

the seller and ultimate buyer. The first link, *seller's headquarters organization*, supervises the channels and is part of the channel itself. The second link, *channels between nations,* gets the products to the borders of the foreign nations. The third link, *channels within nations*, gets the products from their foreign entry point to the ultimate consumers. Too many American manufacturers think their job is done once the product leaves their hands and should pay more attention to how it is handled within the foreign country.

Within-country channels of distribution vary considerably from country to country. There are striking differences in the *number and types of middlemen* serving each foreign market. To get soap into Japan, Procter & Gamble has to work through what is probably the most complicated distribution system in the world. It must sell to a *general wholesaler*, who sells to a *basic product specialty wholesaler*, who sells to a *specialty wholesaler*, who sells to a *regional wholesaler*, who sells to a *local wholesaler*, who finally sells to *retailers*. All of these distribution levels may result in the doubling or tripling of the consumers' price over the importer's price.[13] If P&G takes the same soap to tropical Africa, the company might sell to an *import wholesaler*, who sells to one or several middlemen, who in turn sell to petty traders (mostly women) established in local markets.

Another difference lies in the *size and character of retail units* abroad. Where large-scale retail chains dominate the U.S. scene, most foreign retailing is in the hands of many small independent retailers. In India, millions of retailers operate tiny shops or sell in open markets. Their markups are high, but the real price is brought down through price haggling. Supermarkets could conceivably bring down prices, but they are difficult to start because of many economic and cultural barriers.[14] People's incomes are low, and they must shop daily for small amounts, which are also limited to whatever quantity may be carried home on foot or on a bicycle. Also, there is a lack of storage and refrigeration space to keep food for several days. Packaging is not well developed because it would add to the cost and detract from

---

[13] See William D. Hartley, "How Not to Do It: Cumbersome Japanese Distribution System Stumps U.S. Concerns," *Wall Street Journal*, March 2, 1972.

[14] See Arieh Goldman, "Outreach of Consumers and the Modernization of Urban Food Retailing in Developing Countries," *Journal of Marketing*, October 1974, pp. 8–16.

sales—often conducted in fractions of Western units (such as cigarettes sold singly instead of in packs). Breaking bulk remains an important function of middlemen and petty traders and helps perpetuate the long channels of distribution that are a major obstacle to the expansion of large-scale retailing in developing countries.

DECIDING ON THE MARKETING ORGANIZATION

Companies manage their international marketing activities in at least three different ways.

Export Department

A firm normally gets into international marketing by simply shipping out the goods. If its international sales expand, the company organizes an export department consisting of a sales manager and a few assistants. As sales increase further, the export department is expanded to include various marketing services so that it can go after business more aggressively. If the firm moves into joint ventures or direct investment, the export department will no longer be adequate.

International Division

Many companies get involved in several international markets and ventures. A company may export to one country, license to another, have a joint-ownership venture in a third, and own a subsidiary in a fourth. Sooner or later it will create an international division or subsidiary to handle all its international activity. The international division is headed by an international-division president, who sets goals and budgets and is responsible for the company's growth in the international market.

International divisions are organized in a variety of ways. The international division's corporate staff consists of specialists in marketing, manufacturing, research, finance, planning, and personnel; they will plan for, and provide services to, various operating units. The operating units may be organized according to one or more of three principles. They may be *geographical organizations*. Reporting to the international-division president may be vice-presidents for North America, Latin America, Europe, Africa, and the Far East. These area vice-presidents are responsible for a sales force, sales branches, distributors, and licensees in their respective areas. Or the operating units may be *product-group organizations*, with a vice-president responsible for worldwide sales of each product group. The vice-presidents may draw on corporate-staff area specialists for expertise on different geographical areas. Finally, the operating units may be *international subsidiaries*, each headed by a president. The various subsidiary presidents report to the president of the international division.

A major disadvantage of the international-division concept is that the corporation's top management may think of it as just another division and never get involved enough to appreciate and plan for global marketing.

Multinational Organization

Several firms have passed beyond the international-division stage and become truly multinational organizations. They stop thinking of themselves as national marketers who venture abroad and start thinking of themselves as global marketers. The top corporate management and staff are involved in the planning of worldwide manufacturing facilities, marketing policies, financial flows, and logistical systems. The global operating units report directly to the chief executive or executive committee, not to the head of an international division. Executives are trained in worldwide operations, not just domestic *or* international. Management is recruited from many countries; components and supplies are purchased where they can be obtained at the least cost; and investments are made where the anticipated returns are greatest.

Major companies must go more multinational in the 1980s if they are going to grow. As foreign companies successfully invade the domestic market, U.S. companies will have to move more aggressively into foreign markets. Their European-based counterparts have already largely evolved from *ethnocentric* companies treating their foreign operations as secondary to *polycentric* organizations and finally to *geocentric* companies that view the entire world as a single market. This latter stage, however, is not without its drawbacks. A geocentric policy is often linked to a highly decentralized structure, and many companies who "went global" are now seeking to regain a certain degree of centralized control.[15]

SUMMARY

Companies undertake international marketing for a variety of reasons. Some are pushed by poor opportunities in the home market, and some are pulled by superior opportunities abroad. Given the risk of international marketing, companies need a systematic way to make their international marketing decisions.

The first step is to understand the international marketing environment, particularly the international trade system. In considering a particular foreign market, its economic, political-legal, and cultural characteristics must be assessed. Second, the company must consider what proportion of foreign to total sales it will seek, whether it will do business in a few or many countries, and what types of countries it wants to market in. The third step is to decide which particular markets to enter, and this calls for evaluating the probable rate of return on investment against the level of risk. Fourth, the company has to decide how to enter each attractive market, whether through exporting, joint venturing, or direct investment. Many companies start as exporters, move to joint venturing, and finally undertake direct investment. Companies must next decide on the extent to which their products, promotion, price, and distribution should be adapted to individual foreign markets. Finally, the company must develop an effective organization for pursuing international marketing. Most firms start with an export department and graduate to an international division. A few pass to a multinational organization, which means that worldwide marketing is planned and managed by the top officers of the company.

---

[15] See Yoram Wind, Susan P. Douglas, and Howard V. Perlmutter, "Guidelines for Developing International Marketing Strategies," *Journal of Marketing*, April 1973, pp. 14–23.

QUESTIONS

1. In 1977 the U.S. Congress passed the Foreign Corrupt Practices Act, which attempts to curb bribery by prohibiting firms from making or authorizing payments, offers, promises, or gifts for the purpose of "corruptly" influencing actions by governments or their officials in order to obtain or retain business for a company. The act has been criticized as an expression of cultural/moral ethnocentrism and as a deterrent to effective marketing practices overseas. What do you think is the proper stance for the U.S. government to take?

2. Discuss the relevant aspects of the political-legal environment that might affect K-Mart's decision to open retail outlets in Italy.

3. What product-strategy possibilities might Hershey's consider in marketing its chocolate bars in South American countries?

4. Which type of international marketing organization would you suggest for the following companies? (a) Huffy bicycles in planning to sell three models in the Far East; (b) a small manufacturer of toys about to market its products in Europe; and (c) Dodge in contemplating selling its full line of cars and trucks in Kuwait.

5. A U.S. heavy-equipment manufacturer operating in Western Europe has been using Americans as sales people. The company feels that it could reduce its costs by hiring and training nationals for sales people. What are the advantages and disadvantages of using Americans versus nationals for selling abroad?

6. A large American company decided to enter the French tire market some years ago. The company produced tires for medium-sized trucks designed to meet the official rear-axle weight. Its subsequent experience was bad, many of its tires blowing out. The company acquired a poor image in France as a result. What went wrong?

7. Select one of the following nations—Italy, Japan, or the USSR—and describe its marketing institutions and practices.

Product, Brand, Packaging, and Services Decisions

15

In the factory, we make cosmetics; in the store we sell hope.

CHARLES REVSON

We are now ready to examine in Part Five, each of the major marketing-mix elements. It is appropriate to begin with product, the most important marketing-mix element. First we ask, *What is a product*? It turns out that *product* is a complex concept, which has to be carefully defined. We will then look at ways to *classify the multitude of products* found in consumer and industrial markets, hoping to find links between appropriate marketing strategies and types of products. Next, we will look at the major decisions involved in managing the *product mix*, a *product line* within the product mix, an *individual product* within the product line, and a *service product*.

WHAT IS A PRODUCT?

A pair of skis, a haircut, a Rolling Stone concert, and a Hawaiian vacation are all products. We define *product* as follows:

> A *product* is anything that can be offered to a market for attention, acquisition, use, or consumption that might satisfy a want or need. It includes physical objects, services, persons, places, organizations, and ideas.

Core, Tangible, and Augmented Product

In developing a product, the product planner needs to think about the product on three levels. The most fundamental level is the *core product*, which answers the question, What is the buyer really buying? Every product is really the packaging of a problem-solving service. A woman buying lipstick is not simply buying lip color. Charles Revson of Revlon, Inc., recognized this early: "In the factory, we make cosmetics; in the store we sell hope." Theodore Levitt pointed out that "purchasing agents do not buy quarter-inch drills; they buy quarter-inch holes." And supersalesman Elmer Wheeler would say: "Don't sell the steak—sell the sizzle." The marketer's job is to uncover the needs hiding under every product and to sell *benefits*, not *features*. The core product stands at the center of the total product, as illustrated in Figure 15–1.

The product planner has to turn the core product into a *tangible product*. Lipsticks, computers, educational seminars, political candidates are all tangible products. Tangible products may have as many as five characteristics: *a quality level*, *features*, *styling*, a *brand name*, and *packaging*.

FIGURE 15–1
Three Levels of Product

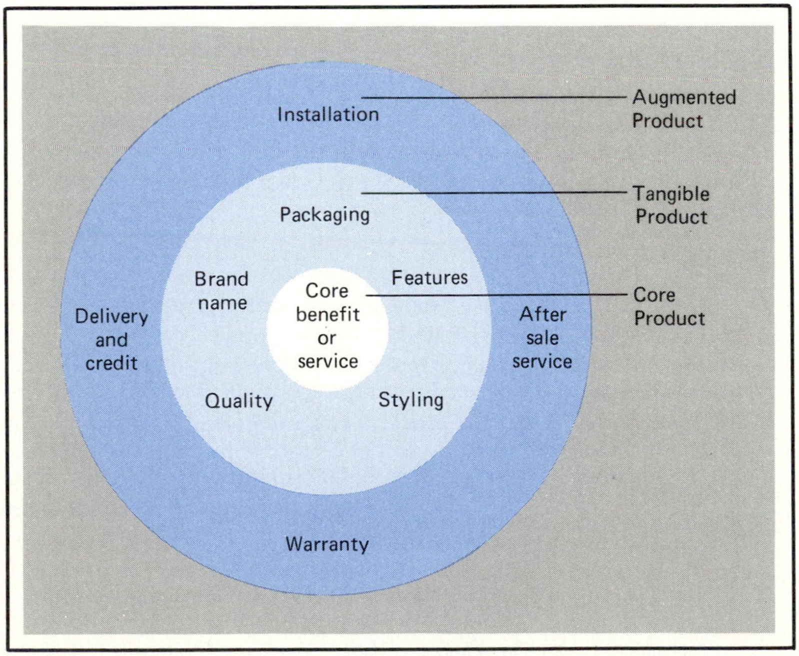

Even a service may have all five characteristics. The U.S. Income Tax Advisory Service exhibits a certain quality level in that government tax advisers have a certain level of competence. The service has certain features, such as being available at no charge and usually requiring some waiting time. The service has a certain style, such as being brief, cursory, and impersonal. The service has a formal name, that of Federal Income Tax Advisory Service. Finally, the service is packaged within branch offices located in various cities.

Finally, the product planner may offer additional services and benefits that make up an *augmented product*. IBM's success is partly traceable to its skillful augmentation of its tangible product—the computer. While its competitors were busy selling computer features to buyers, IBM recognized that customers were more interested in solutions, not hardware. Customers wanted instruction, canned software programs, programming services, quick repairs, guarantees, and so on. IBM sold a system, not just a computer.

Product augmentation leads the marketer to look at the buyer's total *consumption system*: "The way a purchaser of a product performs the total task of whatever it is that he or she is trying to accomplish when using the product."[1] In this way, the marketer will recognize many opportunities for augmenting its offer in a competitively effective way. According to Levitt:

> The *new competition* is not between what companies produce in their factories, but between what they add to their factory output in the form of packaging, services, advertising, customer advice, financing, delivery arrangements, warehousing, and other things that people value.[2]

A firm should search for meaningful ways to augment its product offer.

Product Hierarchy
— See Also 10/29 NOTES

Each product is related hierarchically to certain other products. Product hierarchies stretch from basic needs down to particular items that might satisfy those needs. We can identify seven levels of the product hierarchy. Here they are defined and illustrated for life insurance:

1. **Need family.** The core need that actualizes the product family. Example: security.
2. **Product family.** All the product classes that can satisfy a core need with more or less effectiveness. Example: savings and income.
3. **Product class.** A group of products within the product family that are recognized as having a certain functional coherence. Example: financial instruments.
4. **Product line.** A group of products within a product class that are closely related, because they function in a similar manner or are sold to the same customer groups or are marketed through the same types of outlets or fall within given price ranges. Example: life insurance.
5. **Product type.** Those items within a product line that share one of several possible forms of the product. Example: term life.

---

[1] See Harper W. Boyd, Jr., and Sidney J. Levy, "New Dimensions in Consumer Analysis," *Harvard Business Review*, November-December 1963, pp. 129–40.

[2] Theodore Levitt, *The Marketing Mode* (New York: McGraw-Hill Book Co., 1969), p. 2.

6. **Brand.** The name associated with one or more items in the product line that is used to identify the source or character of the item(s). Example: Prudential.

7. **Item. A** distinct unit within a brand or product line that is distinguishable by size, price, appearance, or some other attribute. The item is called a *stockkeeping unit*, a product variant, or subvariant. Example: renewable.

Another example: the need "hope" gives rise to a product family called toiletries and a product class within that family called cosmetics, of which one line is lipstick, which has different product forms, such as tube lipstick, which is offered as a brand called Revlon in a particular type, such as "frosted."

Two other terms frequently arise. A *product system* is a group of diverse but related items that function in a compatible manner. For example, the Nikon Company sells a basic 35mm camera along with an extensive set of lenses, filters, and other options that constitute a product system. A *product mix* (or *product assortment*) is the set of all products and items that a particular seller makes available to the buyers.

PRODUCT-CLASSIFICATION SCHEMES

Marketers have developed several product-classification schemes based on product characteristics as an aid to developing appropriate marketing strategies.

Durable Goods, Nondurable Goods, and Services

Products can be classified into three groups according to their durability or tangibility.[3]

☐ **Nondurable goods. Nondurable goods are tangible goods that normally are consumed in one or a few uses.** Examples include beer, soap, and salt. Since these goods are consumed fast and purchased frequently, the appropriate strategy is to make them available in many locations, charge only a small markup, and advertise heavily to induce trial and build preference.

☐ **Durable goods. Durable goods are tangible goods that normally survive many uses.** Examples include refrigerators, machine tools and clothing. Durable products normally require more personal selling and service, command a higher margin, and require more seller guarantees.

☐ **Services. Services are activities, benefits, or satisfactions that are offered for sale.** Examples include haircuts and repairs. Services are intangible, inseparable, variable, and perishable. As a result, they normally require more quality control, supplier credibility, and adaptability. (For further discussion of services, see pp. 496–502.)

Consumer-Goods Classification

Consumers buy a vast number of goods. A useful way to classify these goods is on the basis of *consumer shopping habits* because they have implications for marketing

_____

[3] See *Marketing Definitions: A Glossary of Marketing Terms*, compiled by the Committee on Definitions of the American Marketing Association (Chicago: American Marketing Association, 1960).

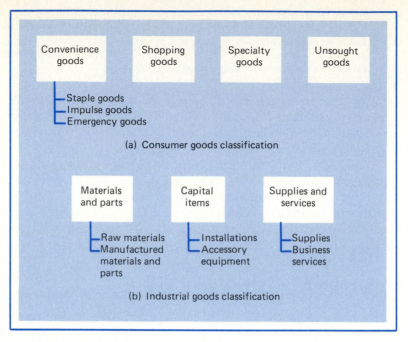

FIGURE 15–2
Classification of Consumer and Industrial Goods

strategy. We can distinguish among convenience, shopping, specialty, and unsought goods. [See Figure 15–2(a)].[4]

☐ **Convenience goods. Goods that the customer usually purchases frequently, immediately, and with the minimum of effort in comparison and buying.** Examples include tobacco products, soap, and newspapers.

Convenience goods can be further divided into staples, impulse goods, and emergency goods. *Staples* are goods that consumers purchase on a regular basis. For example, one buyer might routinely purchase Heinz ketchup, Crest toothpaste, and Ritz crackers. *Impulse goods* are purchased without any planning or search effort. These goods are normally available in many places because consumers do not normally look for them. Thus candy bars and magazines are placed next to checkout counters because shoppers may not have thought of buying them. *Emergency goods* are purchased when a need is urgent—umbrellas during a rainstorm, boots and shovels during the first winter snowstorm. Manufacturers of emergency goods will place them in many outlets so they will not lose the sale when the customer needs these goods.

---

[4] The first three definitions are found in *Marketing Definitions*. For further readings on this classification of goods, see Richard H. Holton, "The Distinction between Convenience Goods, Shopping Goods, and Specialty Goods," *Journal of Marketing*, July 1958, pp. 53–56; and Gordon E. Miracle, "Product Characteristics and Marketing Strategy," *Journal of Marketing*, January 1965, pp. 18–24.

☐ **Shopping goods. Goods that the customer, in the process of selection and purchase, characteristically compares on such bases as suitability, quality, price, and style.** Examples include furniture, clothing, used cars, and major appliances.

Shopping goods can be divided into homogeneous and heterogeneous goods. The buyer sees homogeneous shopping goods as similar in quality but different enough in price to justify shopping comparisons. The seller has to "talk price" to the buyer. But in shopping for clothing, furniture, and more heterogeneous goods, product features are often more important to the consumer than the price. If the buyer wants a pin-striped suit, the cut, fit and look are likely to be more important than small price differences. The seller of heterogeneous shopping goods must therefore carry a wide assortment to satisfy individual tastes and must have well-trained sales personnel to provide information and advice to customers.

☐ **Specialty goods. Goods with unique characteristics and/or brand identification for which a significant group of buyers are habitually willing to make a special purchasing effort.** Examples would include specific brands and types of fancy goods, cars, hi-fi components, photographic equipment, and men's suits.

A Mercedes, for example, is a specialty good because buyers are willing to travel far to buy a Mercedes. Specialty goods do not involve the buyer's making comparisons; the buyer only invests time to reach the dealers carrying the wanted products. The dealers do not need convenient locations; however, they must let prospective buyers know their locations.

☐ **Unsought goods. Goods that the consumer does not know about or knows about but does not normally think of buying.** New products, such as smoke detectors and food processors, are unsought goods until the consumer is made aware of them through advertising. The classic examples of known but unsought goods are life insurance, cemetery plots, gravestones, and encyclopedias.

By their very nature, unsought goods require a lot of marketing effort in the form of advertising and personal selling. Some of the most sophisticated personal-selling techniques have developed out of the challenge of selling unsought goods.

Industrial-Goods Classification

Organizations buy a vast variety of goods and services. A useful industrial-goods classification would suggest appropriate marketing strategies in the industrial market. Industrial goods can be classified in terms of *how they enter the production process and their relative costliness*. We can distinguish three groups: materials and parts, capital items, and supplies and services. [See Figure 15–2(b)].

☐ **Materials and parts. Goods that enter the manufacturer's product completely.** They fall into two classes: raw materials, and manufactured materials and parts.

Raw materials in turn fall into two major classes: *farm products* (e.g., wheat, cotton, livestock, fruits and vegetables) and *natural products* (e.g., fish, lumber, crude petroleum, iron ore). Each is marketed somewhat differently. *Farm products* are supplied by many small producers, who turn them over to marketing intermediaries, who provide assembly, grading, storage, transportation, and selling services. Farm products are somewhat expandable in the long run, but not in the short run. Farm products' perishable and seasonal nature gives rise to special marketing practices. Their commodity character results in relatively little advertising and promotional activity, with some exceptions. From time to time, commodity groups will launch campaigns to promote the consumption of their product—such as potatoes, prunes, or milk. And some producers even brand their product—such as Sunkist oranges and Chiquita bananas.

Natural products are highly limited in supply. They usually have great bulk and low unit value and require substantial transportation to move them from producer to user. There are fewer and larger producers, who tend to market them directly to industrial users. Because the users depend on these materials, long-term supply contracts are common. The homogeneity of natural materials limits the amount of demand-creation activity. Price and delivery reliability are the major factors influencing the selection of suppliers.

Manufactured materials and parts are exemplified by *component materials* (e.g., iron, yarn, cement, wires) and *component parts* (e.g., small motors, tires, castings). *Component materials* are usually fabricated further—for example, pig iron is made into steel, and yarn is woven into cloth. The standardized nature of component materials usually means that price and supplier reliability are the most important purchase factors. *Component parts* enter the finished product completely with no further change in form, as when small motors are put into vacuum cleaners and tires are added on automobiles. Most manufactured materials and parts are sold directly to industrial users, with orders often placed a year or more in advance. Price and service are the major marketing considerations, and branding and advertising tend to be less important.

☐ **Capital items.** Goods that enter the finished product partly. They include two groups: installations and accessory equipment.

Installations consist of *buildings* (e.g., factories and offices) and *fixed equipment* (e.g., generators, drill presses, computers, elevators). Installations are major purchases. They are usually bought directly from the producer, with the typical sale being preceded by a long negotiation period. The producers use a top-notch sales force, which often includes sales engineers. The producers have to be willing to design to specification and to supply postsale services. Advertising is used but is much less important than personal selling.

Accessory equipment comprises *portable factory equipment and tools* (e.g., hand tools, lift trucks) and *office equipment* (e.g., typewriters, desks). These types of equipment do not become part of the finished product. They simply aid in the production process. They have a shorter life than installations but a longer life than operating supplies. Although some accessory-equipment manufacturers sell direct, more often they use middlemen because the market is geographically dispersed, the buyers are numerous, and the orders are small. Quality, features, price, and service are major considerations in vendor selection. The sales force tends to be more important than advertising, although the latter can be used effectively.

□ **Supplies and services. Items that do not enter the finished product at all.**

Supplies are of two kinds: *operating supplies* (e.g., lubricants, coal, typing paper, pencils) and *maintenance and repair items* (paint, nails, brooms). Supplies are the equivalent of convenience goods in the industrial field because they are usually purchased with a minimum effort on a straight rebuy basis. They are normally marketed through intermediaries because of the great number of customers, their geographical dispersion, and the low unit value of these goods. Price and service are important considerations because suppliers are quite standardized, and brand preference is not high.

Business services include *maintenance and repair services* (e.g., window cleaning, typewriter repair) and *business advisory services* (e.g., legal, management consulting, advertising). Maintenance and repair services are usually supplied under contract. Maintenance services are often provided by small producers, and repair services are often available from the manufacturers of the original equipment. Business advisory services are normally new task-buying situations, and the industrial buyer will choose the supplier on the basis of the supplier's reputation and personnel.

Thus we see that a product's characteristics will have a major influence on marketing strategy (see Exhibit 15–1). At the same time, marketing strategy will also depend on other factors, such as the product's stage of the life cycle, the number and strategies of competitors, and the economic climate.

PRODUCT-MIX DECISIONS

We will now examine concepts and tools for making product-mix decisions. A company's product mix is defined as follows:

> *A product mix* (also called *product assortment*) is the set of all product lines and items that a particular seller offers for sale to buyers.[5]

Avon's product mix consists of three major product lines: cosmetics, jewelry, and household items. Each product line consists of several sub-lines: for example, cosmetics breaks down into lipstick, rouge, powder, and so on. Each line and sub-line has many individual items.

Altogether, Avon's product mix includes 1,300 items. A large supermarket handles as many as 10,000 items; a typical K-Mart stocks 15,000 items; and General Electric manufactures as many as 250,000 items.

A company's product mix can be described as having a certain width, length, depth, and consistency. These concepts are illustrated in Table 15–1 in connection with selected Procter & Gamble consumer products.

---

[5] *Marketing Definitions.*

Exhibit 15–1

HOW PRODUCT CHARACTERISTICS INFLUENCE MARKETING STRATEGY—THE CASE OF STEEL AND ELECTRIC FORKLIFT TRUCKS

Here are two examples of how a product's physical characteristics and use pattern influences its marketing strategy.

Steel. Steel is an important component material in durable-goods manufacture and construction. There are different grades and alloys of steel, but within any category most steel is identical. Therefore steel is basically a commodity, and the major product variables that matter to the buyer are consistency of quality and the width of the steel maker's product line. The buyer's main concern is price, and a seller who offers his product at the lowest price has the best chance of getting the order. Price reductions can be effected through volume discounts, freight absorption allowances, or generous credit terms.

Because most sellers offer similar terms, competition also takes place on a nonprice front. An important variable is the seller's delivery reliability, because the buyer's production operation is geared to the continual delivery of steel or its emergency ordering. The steel marketer who is located nearest to the buyer, or who reliably meets promised delivery dates, has a differential advantage. Company sales people cannot make much of a difference if their company's price or delivery reliability is not right, but they can make a contribution by making contacts and being in the right place at the right time. Advertising plays only a small role, usually taking the form of either corporate-image advertising or new-product advertising to promote a new steel alloy. In this kind of business it is hard for a company to discover a marketing angle that helps it substantially increase its market share without competitors' retaliating effectively with the same or an offsetting tactic.

Electric forklift trucks. The marketing mix for forklift trucks differs from that for steel because the trucks can be engineered in many variations to perform different tasks. The buyer seeks a truck that satisfies certain criteria of size, lifting capacity, operating cost, features, and price. The seller's product-design capability is an important factor in getting business. A higher price can be charged for trucks with better performance or extra features, styling, or comfort.

Another important marketing variable is the seller's backup for the purchase—particularly delivery times, parts availability, and service. Some of these things are in the hands of channel middlemen through whom the manufacturer sells. Trade journal advertising plays a useful role in creating buyer awareness and interest in the company's product line. The promotional budget also goes into specification sheets, catalogs, training films, trade shows, and sales-force contests.

The *width* of P&G's product mix refers to how many different product lines the company carries. Table 15–1 shows a product-mix width of six lines. (In fact, P&G produces many additional lines—mouthwashes, toilet tissue, and so on.)

The *length* of P&G's product mix refers to the total number of items in its product mix. In Table 15–1, it is thirty-one. We can also talk about the average

TABLE 15-1

PRODUCT-MIX WIDTH AND PRODUCT-LINE LENGTH SHOWN FOR PROCTER & GAMBLE PRODUCTS

←——— **Product-Mix Width** ———→

Detergents	Toothpaste	Bar Soap	Deodorants	Disposable Diapers	Coffee
Ivory Snow 1930	Gleem 1952	Ivory 1879	Secret 1956	Pampers 1961	Folger's 1963
Dreft 1933	Crest 1955	Camay 1927	Sure 1972	Luvs 1976	Instant Folger's 1963
Tide 1946		Lava 1928			High Point Instant 1975
Joy 1949		Kirk's 1930			Folger's Flaked Coffee 1977
Cheer 1950		Zest 1952			
Oxydol 1952		Safeguard 1963			
Dash 1954		Coast 1974			
Cascade 1955					
Duz 1956					
Ivory Liquid 1957					
Gain 1966					
Dawn 1972					
Era 1972					
Bold 3 1976					

Product-Line-Length

length of a line at P&G. This is obtained by dividing the total length (here 31) by the number of lines (here 6), or 5.2. The average product line at P&G, as represented in Table 15–1, consists of 5.2 brands.

The *depth* of P&G's product mix refers to how many variants are offered of each product in the line. Thus if Crest comes in three sizes and two formulations (regular and mint), Crest has a depth of six. By counting the number of variants within each brand, the average depth of P&G's product mix can be calculated.

The *consistency* of the product mix refers to how closely related the various product lines are in end use, production requirements, distribution channels or some other way. P&G's product lines are consistent insofar as they are consumer goods that go through the same distribution channels. The lines are less consistent insofar as they perform different functions for the buyers.

These four dimensions of the product mix provide the handles for defining the company's product strategy. The company can grow its business in four ways. The company can add new product lines, thus widening its product mix. In this way, its new lines capitalize on the company's reputation in its other lines. Or the company can lengthen its existing product lines to become a more full-line company. Or the company can add more product variants to each product and thus deepen its product mix. Finally, the company can pursue more product-line consistency or less, depending upon whether it wants to acquire a strong reputation in a single field or participate in several fields.

Product-mix planning is largely the responsibility of the company's strategic planners. They must assess, with information supplied by the company marketers, which product lines to grow, maintain, harvest, and divest. We have already reviewed the various analytical approaches to this task in Chapter 2.

PRODUCT-LINE DECISIONS

A product mix is made up of various product lines. We define a product line as follows:

> A *product line* is a group of products that are closely related, because they function in a similar manner, are sold to the same customer groups, are marketed through the same types of outlets, or fall within given price ranges.

Each product line within a company is usually managed by some executive. In General Electric's Consumer Appliance Division, there are product-line managers for refrigerators, stoves, washing machines, dryers, and other appliances. At Northwestern University, there are separate academic deans for the medical school, law school, business school, music school, speech school, journalism school, and the college of liberal arts.

Product-Line Analysis

Product-line managers have two important information needs. First, they must know the sales and profits of each item in the line. Second, they must know how their product line compares to competitors' product lines in the same markets.

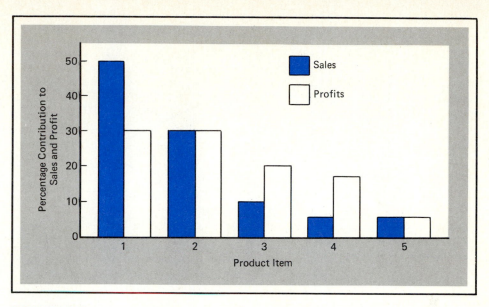

FIGURE 15–3
Product-Item Contributions to a Product Line's Total Sales and Profits

Product-line sales and profits. Each item in a product line contributes differently to total sales and profits. The product-line manager needs to know the percentage of total sales and profits contributed by each item in the line. An example of a five-item product line is shown in Figure 15–3.

The first item in the product line accounts for 50 percent of total sales and 30 percent of total profits. The first two items account for 80 percent of total sales and 60 percent of total profits. If these two items were suddenly hurt by a competitor, the product line's sales and profitability would collapse. A high concentration of sales in a few items means line vulnerability. These items must be carefully monitored and protected. At the other end, the last item constitutes only 5 percent of the product line's sales and profits. The product-line manager may even want to consider dropping this slow seller from the line.

Product-line market profile. The product-line manager must also review how the product line is positioned against competitors' product lines. Consider a paper company with a product line consisting of paper board.[6] Two of the major attributes of paper board are paper weight and finish quality. Paper weight is usually offered at standard levels of 90, 120, 150, and 180 weight. Finish quality is offered at three standard levels: Figure 15–4 is a product map showing the location of the various product-line items of company X and four competitors, A, B, C, and D. Competitor A sells two product items in the extra-high weight class ranging from medium to low finish quality. Competitor B sells four items that vary in weight and finish quality. Competitor C sells three items in which the greater their weight, the greater their finish quality.

---

[6] This illustration is found in Benson P. Shapiro, *Industrial Product Policy: Managing the Existing Product Line* (Cambridge, Mass.: Marketing Science Institute, September 1977), pp. 3–5, 98–101.

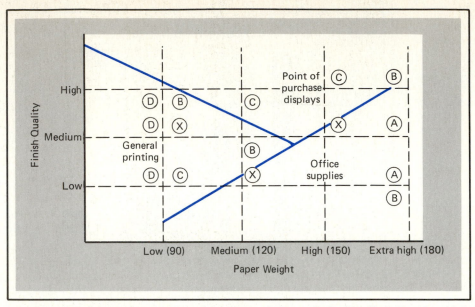

Source: Benson P. Shapiro, *Industrial Product Policy: Managing the Existing Product Line* (Cambridge, Mass.: Marketing Science Institute, September 1977), p. 101.

FIGURE 15–4
Product Map for a Paper-Product Line

Competitor D sells three items, all lightweight but varying in finish quality. Finally, company X offers three items that vary in weight and vary between low and medium finish quality.

This product-item mapping is useful for designing product-line marketing strategy. It shows which competitors' items are competing against company X's items. For example, company X's low-weight/medium-quality paper competes against competitor D's paper. But its high-weight/medium-quality paper has no direct competitor. The map reveals locations for possible new-product items. For example, no manufacturer offers a high-weight/low-quality paper. If company X determines there is a strong unmet demand and can produce this paper and price it right, it should add this item to its line.

Another benefit of product mapping is that it identifies market segments according to their paper-buying preferences. Figure 15–4 shows the types of paper, by weight and quality, preferred by the general printing industry, the point-of-purchase display industry, and the office-supply industry, respectively. The map shows that company X is well positioned to serve the needs of the general printing industry but is less effective in serving the other two industries and should consider bringing out more paper types that meet these needs.

Product-Line Length

One of the major issues facing product-line managers is the optimal length (the number of items) of the product line. The line is too short if the manager can increase profits by adding items; the line is too long if the manager can increase profits by dropping items.

The issue of product-line length is influenced by company objectives. Companies that want to be positioned as full-line companies and/or are seeking high market share and market growth will carry longer lines. They are less concerned when some items fail to contribute to profits. Companies that are keen on high profitability will carry shorter lines consisting of "cherry-picked" items.

Product lines tend to lengthen over time.[7] Excess manufacturing capacity will put pressure on the product-line manager to develop new items. The sales force and distributors will also pressure for a more complete product line to satisfy their customers. The product-line manager will want to add items to the product line in pursuit of greater sales and profits.

But as items are added, several costs rise: design and engineering costs, inventory-carrying costs, manufacturing-changeover costs, order-processing costs, transportation costs, and new-item promotional costs. Eventually someone calls a halt to the mushrooming product line. Top management may freeze things because of insufficient funds or manufacturing capacity. Or the controller may question the line's profitability and call for a study. The study will probably show a large number of money-losing items, and they will be pruned from the line in a major effort to increase profitability. A pattern of undisciplined product-line growth followed by massive product pruning will repeat itself many times.

A company can systematically enlarge the length of its product line in two ways: by stretching its line and by filling its line.

Line-stretching decision. Every company's product line covers a certain part of the total range offered by the industry as a whole. For example, BMW automobiles are located in the medium-high price range of the automobile market. *Line stretching* occurs when a company lengthens its product line beyond its current range. The company can stretch its line downward, upward, or both ways.

Downward stretch. Many companies initially locate at the high end of the market and subsequently stretch their line downward. Here are two examples:

> **Caterpillar**. For years, Caterpillar has been the dominant supplier of tractors above 100 horse-power (with five models), while John Deere has dominated the lower-horsepower end of the market (with three models). In the early 1970s, each company invaded the other's market segment. Caterpillar teamed up with a Japanese supplier to build a lighter tractor. Deere went for a high-end stretch by designing its first large tractor. Caterpillar moved toward the low end to participate in a growing market segment that it had been neglecting.
>
> **IBM**. IBM historically operated in the large main-frame end of the computer market, leaving minicomputer manufacture to other firms, such as Digital Equipment and Data General. However, the slowdown in growth of the large-batch-oriented data-processing units had led IBM to enter minicomputer manufacture as an avenue to further growth. IBM's interest in minicomputers is further stimulated by its growing interest in computer networks and distributed data-processing systems.

---

[7] See Shapiro, *op. cit.*, pp. 9–10.

A company may stretch downward for any of the following reasons:

- ☐ The company is attacked at the high end and decides to counterattack by invading the low end.
- ☐ The company finds that slower growth is taking place at the high end.
- ☐ The company initially entered the high end to establish a quality image and intended to roll downward.
- ☐ The company adds a low-end unit to plug a market hole that would otherwise attract a new competitor.

In making a downward stretch, the company faces some risks. The new low-end item might *cannibalize* higher-end items, leaving the company worse off. Consider the following:[8]

> Ford introduced the small-size Falcon in 1959 to attract economy-car buyers. But many of its buyers were those who would have bought the standard-size Ford. In effect, Ford reduced its own profit margin by failing to design its car for a really different segment from loyal Ford buyers.

Or the low-end item might provoke competitors to counteract by moving into the higher end. Or the company's dealers may not be willing or able to handle the lower-end products because they are less profitable or dilute their image. Harley Davidson's dealers neglected the small motorcycles Harley finally designed to compete with the Japanese.

One of the great miscalculations of several American companies has been their unwillingness to plug holes in the lower end of their markets. General Motors resisted building smaller cars, and Xerox resisted building smaller copying machines. Japanese companies spotted a major opening and moved in quickly.

Upward stretch. Companies in the lower end of the market might contemplate entering the higher end. They may be attracted by a higher growth rate, higher margins, or simply the chance to position themselves as full-line manufacturers.

An upward-stretch decision can be risky. Not only are the higher-end competitors well entrenched but they may counterattack by entering the lower end of the market. Prospective customers may not believe that the newcomer can produce quality products. Finally, the company's sales representatives and distributors may lack the talent and training to serve the higher end of the market.

Two-way stretch. Companies in the middle range of the market may decide to stretch their line in both directions. Texas Instruments' strategy in the hand-calculator market illustrates this. Before Texas Instruments (TI) entered this market, the market was dominated primarily by Bowmar at the low-price/low-quality end and Hewlett-Packard at the high-price/high-quality end. (See Figure 15–5.) TI introduced its first calculators in the medium-price/medium-quality end of the market. Gradually it

---

[8] Mark Hanan, *Market Segmentation* (New York: American Management Association, 1968), pp. 24–26.

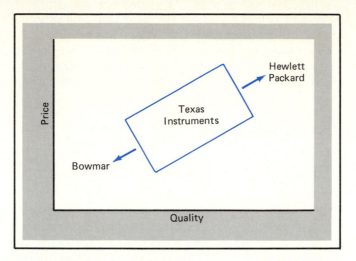

FIGURE 15-5
Two-Way Product-Line Stretch in the Hand-Calculator Market

added more machines at each end. It offered better calculators at the same price as, or at lower prices than, Bowmar, ultimately destroying it; and it designed high-quality calculators selling at lower prices than Hewlett-Packard calculators, taking away a good share of HP's sales at the high end. This two-way stretch won TI the market leadership in the hand-calculator market.

Line-filling decision.   A product line can also be lengthened by adding more items within the present range of the line. There are several motives for line filling: reaching for incremental profits; trying to satisfy dealers who complain about lost sales because of missing items in the line; trying to utilize excess capacity; trying to be the leading full-line company; and trying to plug holes to keep out competitors.

Line filling is overdone if it results in cannibalization and customer confusion. The company needs to differentiate each item in the consumer's mind. Each item should possess a *just noticeable difference*. According to Weber's law, customers are more attuned to relative than to absolute difference.[9] They will perceive the difference between boards two and three feet long and boards twenty and thirty feet long but not between boards twenty-nine and thirty feet long. The company should make sure that new product items have a noticeable difference.

The company should check that the proposed item enjoys some market demand and is not being added simply to satisfy an internal need. The famous Edsel automobile, on which Ford lost $350 million, met Ford's internal positioning needs but not the market's needs. Ford noticed that owners of Fords would trade up to General Motors products like Oldsmobile or Buick rather than step up to Ford's Mercury or Lincoln. Ford decided to create a stepping-stone car to fill its line. The Edsel was created,

---

[9] See Steuart Henderson Britt, "How Weber's Law Can Be Applied to Marketing," *Business Horizons*, February 1975, pp. 21–29.

but it failed to meet a market need since many similar cars were available to the same buyers, and many buyers were beginning to buy smaller cars.

Once the product-line manager decides to add another item to sell at a certain price, the design task is turned over to the company engineers. The planned price will dictate how the item is designed, rather than the design dictating the price that will be charged.

Line-Modernization Decision

In some cases, product-line length is adequate, but the line needs to be modernized. For example, a company's machine tools may have a 1920s look and lose out to better-styled competitors' lines.

The issue is whether to overhaul the line piecemeal or all at once. A piecemeal approach allows the company to see how customers and dealers take to the new style before changing the whole line. Piecemeal modernization is less draining on the company's cash flow. A major disadvantage of piecemeal modernization is that it allows competitors to see changes and start designing their own line.

In rapidly changing hi-tech products, product modernization is a must. Although Apple personal computers are only a few years old, the line has already migrated from Apple 1 to Apple 2 and Apple 3. Competitors are constantly upgrading the equipment, and each company must defend itself by designing a new generation of equipment to replace the current line. Companies plan product improvements to induce *customer migration* to higher-priced replacement lines. A major issue is timing the product improvements so they don't come out too early (thus damaging sales of the current product line) or too late (after competition has established a strong reputation for more advanced equipment).

Line-Featuring Decision

The product-line manager typically selects one or a few items in the line to feature. Sometimes managers feature promotional models at the low end of the line to serve as "traffic builders." Thus Sears will announce a special low-priced sewing machine to attract people. And Rolls Royce announced an economy model selling for only $49,000—in contrast to its high-end model selling for $108,000—to bring people into its showrooms. Once the customers arrive, sales people may try to influence them to buy at the high end of the line.

At other times, managers will feature a high-end item to lend class to the product line. Stetson promotes a man's hat selling for $150, which few people buy but which acts as a "flagship" or "crown jewel" to enhance the whole line.

Sometimes a company finds one end of its line selling well and the other end poorly. The company may try to boost demand for the slower sellers, especially if the slower sellers are produced in a separate factory that is idled by the lack of demand. This situation faced Honeywell when its medium-size computers were not selling as well as its large computers. But things are not this simple. It could be argued that the company should promote the items that sell well rather than try to prop up weak demand. Recently a textbook author complained to his publisher that not enough money was being spent promoting his successful textbook, only to hear the editor say that promotion money should be used for the books that were not selling!

Line-Pruning Decision

Product-line managers must periodically review items for pruning. There are two occasions for pruning. One is when the product line includes deadwood that is depressing profits. The weak items can be identified through sales and cost analysis. RCA cut down its color television sets from 69 to 44 models, and a chemical company cut down its products from 217 to the 93 with the largest volume, the largest contribution to profits, and the greatest long-term potential. Many companies that have implemented major prunings have achieved stronger long-term profits.

The other occasion for product pruning is when the company lacks production capacity to produce all of the items demanded in their desired quantities. The manager should examine the profit margins and concentrate on producing the higher-margin items, dropping some of the low-margin or losing items. Companies typically shorten their lines in periods of tight demand and lengthen their lines in periods of slow demand.

INDIVIDUAL PRODUCT DECISIONS

We will now look at decisions pertaining to developing and marketing the individual product. We will look at the following product variables: *product attributes*, *branding*, *packaging and labeling*, and *customer service*. Nonproduct marketing variables, such as pricing, distribution, advertising and promotion, will be examined in the following chapters.

Product-Attribute Decisions

Every product will have tangible attributes, such as a quality level, features, and styling. These attributes are established in the process of refining the product concept and later the product prototype. After the company introduces the product into the market, it will modify the product's attributes to meet challenges in each new stage in the product's life cycle. To improve sales or profits, the quality might be raised or lowered, features might be added or withdrawn, and the styling might be changed. We want to look at the decision issues posed by each attribute.

Product quality.   In developing a product, the manufacturer has to choose a quality level that will support the product's intended position in the target market. Quality is one of the major product-positioning tools. *Quality* stands for *the rated ability of the brand to perform its functions*. Quality is a summary term for the product's durability, reliability, precision, ease of operation and repair, and other valued attributes. Some of these attributes can be measured objectively. From a marketing point of view, quality should be measured in terms of buyers' perceptions of quality.

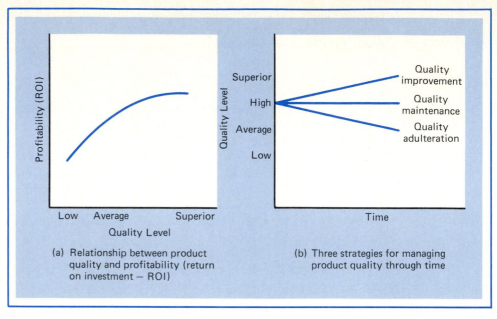

FIGURE 15–6
Brand-Quality Strategies and Profitability

Most products are established initially at one of four quality levels: low, average, high, and superior.[10] In one study, investigators found that profitability rose with product quality. [See Figure 15–6(a).[11] Higher quality allows the firm to charge a higher price, while providing the higher quality doesn't cost the firm that much more. Going from high to superior quality, however, doesn't add much to profitability. The curve suggests that a company should aim at delivering high quality; inferior quality hurts profitability substantially. At the same time, if all competitors delivered high quality, this strategy would be less effective. Quality must be chosen with a target market segment in mind.

A company must also decide how to manage product quality through time. Three strategies are illustrated in Figure 15–6(b). The first, where the manufacturer invests in continuous research and development to improve the product, usually produces the highest return and market share. Procter & Gamble is a major practitioner of product-improvement strategy which, combined with the high initial product quality, helps explain its leading position in many markets. The second strategy is to maintain product quality. Many companies leave their quality unaltered after its initial formulation unless glaring faults or opportunities occur. The third strategy is to reduce product quality through time. Some companies cut the quality to offset rising costs, hoping the buyers don't notice any difference. Others adulterate their

---

[10] Or six levels could be used: shoddy quality, below-average quality, average quality, plus quality, double-plus quality, finest quality.

[11] Sidney Schoeffler, Robert D. Buzzell, and Donald F. Heany, "Impact of Strategic Planning on Profit Performance," *Harvard Business Review*, March-April 1974, pp. 137–45.

products deliberately in order to increase their current profits, although often this hurts their long-run profitability.

The theme of quality is attracting stronger interest among consumers and companies in the 1980s. American consumers have been impressed with the product quality found in Japanese autos and electronics and in European autos, apparel, and food. Many consumers are favoring apparel that lasts and stays in style longer, instead of trendy apparel. They are showing a growing interest in fresh and nutritious foods, gourmet items, and natural cheeses and less interest in soft drinks, sweets, and TV dinners. A number of companies are catering to this growing interest in quality, and much more can be done to build in more quality and communicate it to target buyers.[12]

Product features. Any product can be offered with varying features. A "stripped-down" or "bare-bones" model is the starting point, one without any "extras." The company can create higher-level models by adding one or more features. In the case of an automobile, the buyer can order electric windows, automatic transmission, air conditioning, stereo radio, and so on. The automobile manufacturer needs to decide which features to build in and which to make optional. Each feature has a chance of capturing the fancy of additional buyers.

Features are a competitive tool for differentiating the company's product from competitors' products. Some companies are extremely innovative in finding new features to add to their product. The Japanese have an excellent record of improving 35mm cameras through new features such as autofocusing and built-in flash. Their calculators and wrist watches in some cases allow owners to play music or games in addition to calculating or telling time. Their videorecorders come in several models with new features available at each higher level, for which the consumer pays a premium. Being the first producer to introduce a needed and valued new feature is one of the most effective ways to compete.

Product style. Another way to add product distinctiveness is through style or design. Some companies stand out for their design distinctiveness, such as IBM in computers, Herman Miller in modern furniture, Olivetti in office machines, Bang & Olufsen in home stereo equipment, and Datsun and Mazda in the design of sports cars. These are the exceptions rather than the rule, since most companies lack a "design touch." Their products are prosaically styled. Many cars look the same, many toasters look the same, many television sets look the same.

Good design offers several benefits. It can create a personality for a newly launched product so that it stands out from its more prosaic competitors. It can create product-replacement cycles for products in the mature stage of their product life cycle. It can communicate value to the consumer and make selection easier. Companies need to make sure their engineering staff contains good product designers who work well with the product managers.

---

[12] "Research Suggests Consumers Will Increasingly Seek Quality," *Wall Street Journal*, October 15, 1981.

Brand Decisions

In developing a marketing strategy for individual products, the seller has to confront the issue of branding. Branding can add value to a product and is therefore an intrinsic aspect of product strategy.

First, we should become familiar with the language of branding. Here are some key definitions:[13]

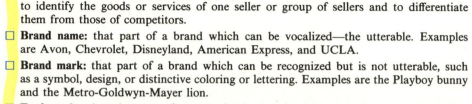

- ☐ **Brand:** a name, term, sign, symbol, or design, or a combination of them, which is intended to identify the goods or services of one seller or group of sellers and to differentiate them from those of competitors.
- ☐ **Brand name:** that part of a brand which can be vocalized—the utterable. Examples are Avon, Chevrolet, Disneyland, American Express, and UCLA.
- ☐ **Brand mark:** that part of a brand which can be recognized but is not utterable, such as a symbol, design, or distinctive coloring or lettering. Examples are the Playboy bunny and the Metro-Goldwyn-Mayer lion.
- ☐ **Trademark:** a brand or part of a brand that is given legal protection because it is capable of exclusive appropriation. A trademark protects the seller's exclusive rights to use the brand name and/or brand mark.
- ☐ **Copyright:** the exclusive legal right to reproduce, publish, and sell the matter and form of a literary, musical, or artistic work.

Branding poses challenging decisions to the marketer. The key decisions are shown in Figure 15–7 and discussed below.

Branding decision.   The first decision is whether the company should put a brand name on its product. Historically, most products went unbranded. Producers and middlemen sold their goods directly out of barrels, bins, and cases, without any supplier identification. The earliest signs of branding were in the efforts of medieval guilds to require craftsmen to put trade marks on their products to protect themselves and consumers against inferior quality. In the fine arts, too, branding began with artists signing their works.

In the United States the earliest brand promoters were the patent-medicine makers. Branding's real growth occurred after the Civil War with the growth of national firms and national advertising media. Some of the early brands still survive, such as Borden's Condensed Milk, Quaker Oats, Vaseline, and Ivory Soap.

Branding has grown so strong that today hardly anything goes unbranded. Salt is packaged in distinctive manufacturers' containers, oranges are stamped with growers' names, common nuts and bolts are packaged in cellophane with a distributor's label, and automobile components—spark plugs, tires, filters—bear separate brand names from the auto makers. Even chicken has been branded successfully:[14]

---

[13] The first four definitions can be found in *Marketing Definitions*.

[14] See Bill Paul, "It isn't Chicken Feed to Put Your Brand on 78 Million Birds," *Wall Street Journal*, May 13, 1974.

Frank Perdue of Perdue Farms, Salisbury, Maryland, has converted a basic agricultural commodity into a branded product. Many consumers on the East Coast insist on a Perdue chicken. Perdue spends about $1 million annually on television and radio commercials in which he touts the merits of his chickens. His theme is, "It takes a tough man to make a tender chicken," and he offers a money-back guarantee to dissatisfied customers.

Recently, there has been some return to "no branding" of certain staple consumer goods and pharmaceuticals. In 1977 the Jewel Food Stores, a large Chicago-based supermarket chain, introduced a forty-item "generic" line. *Generics* are unbranded,

FIGURE 15-7
An Overview of Branding Decisions

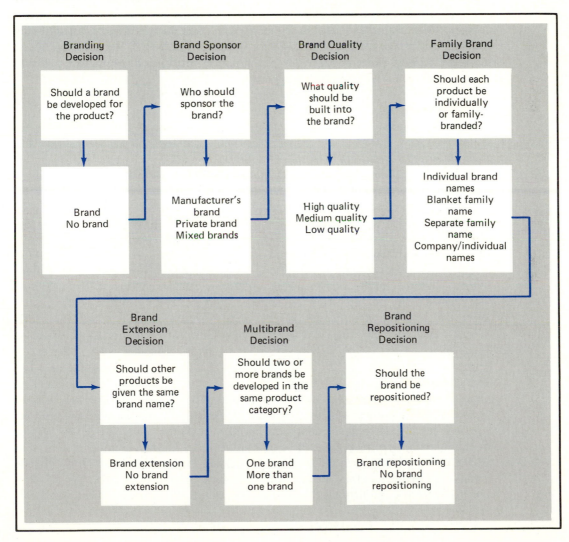

plainly packaged, less-expensive versions of common products purchased in supermarkets, such as spaghetti, paper towels, and canned peaches. They offer standard or lower quality at a price that may be as much as 30 percent lower than that of nationally advertised brands and 15 percent lower than that of private labels. The lower price is made possible by lower-quality ingredients, lower-cost labeling and packaging, and minimal advertising. Nevertheless, they are sufficiently satisfying so that over 70 percent of those who have purchased generics said they would buy them again. Generic products in the food, household goods, and pharmaceutical industries offer a major threat to the higher-priced branded goods and are putting branding itself to a real test.[15]

Indeed, why should sellers resort to branding when it clearly involves a cost—packaging, labeling, legal protection—and a risk if the product should prove unsatisfying to the user? It turns out that branding gives the seller several advantages.

First, the brand name makes it easier for the seller to process orders and track down problems. Thus Anheuser-Busch receives an order for a hundred cases of Michelob eight-ounce beer instead of an order for "some of your better beer." Furthermore, the seller finds it easier to trace the order if it is misshipped, or to find out why the beer was rancid if consumers complain.

Second, the seller's brand name and trademark provide legal protection of unique product features, which would otherwise be copied by competitors.

Third, branding gives the seller the opportunity to attract a loyal and profitable set of customers. Brand loyalty gives sellers some protection from competition and greater control in planning their marketing mix.

Fourth, branding helps the seller segment markets. Instead of P&G's selling a simple detergent, it can offer eight detergent brands, each formulated somewhat differently and aimed at specific benefit-seeking segments.

Fifth, good brands help build the corporate image. By carrying the company's name, they help advertise the quality and size of the company.

There is evidence that distributors want brand names as a means of making the product easier to handle, identifying suppliers, holding production to certain quality standards, and increasing buyer preference. Consumers want brand names to help them identify quality differences and shop more efficiently. In the Soviet Union, consumers look for identification marks on television receivers to find out which factory produced them, since the factories have different reputations for reliability.

Brand-sponsor decision. In deciding to brand a product, the manufacturer has several options with respect to brand sponsorship. The product may be launched as a *manufacturer-owned brand*. Or it may be launched by the manufacturer as a *licensed name brand*. Or the manufacturer may sell the product to middlemen, who put on a *private brand* (also called middlemen brand, distributor brand, or dealer brand). Or the manufacturer may produce some output under its own name and some that is sold under private labels. Kellogg's, John Deere & Company, and IBM produce virtually all of their output under their own brand names. Hart Schaffner & Marx sells a lot of its manufactured clothes under licensed names such as Christian Dior,

---

[15] See "Buyers Mix Generics, Quality," *Advertising Age*, August 20, 1979, p. 3.

Pierre Cardin, and Johnny Carson. Warwick Electronics produces virtually all of its output under various distributors' names such as Sears. Whirlpool produces output both under its own name and under distributors' names.

Manufacturers' brands tend to dominate the American scene. Consider such well-known brands as Campbell's Soup and Heinz Tomato Ketchup. In recent times, however, large retailers and wholesalers have developed their own brands. The private-label tires of Sears and J. C. Penney are as well known today as the manufacturers' brands of Goodyear, Goodrich, and Firestone. Sears has created several names—Diehard batteries, Craftsman tools, Kenmore appliances—that command brand preference and even brand insistence. Over 90 percent of Sears's products are sold under its own labels. The A&P has created different private labels for its canned goods, and they account for over 25 percent of its sales. An increasing number of department stores, service stations, clothiers, drugstores, and appliance dealers are launching private labels.

Why do middlemen bother with sponsoring their own brands? They have to hunt down qualified suppliers who can deliver consistent quality. They have to order large quantities and tie up their capital in inventories. They have to spend money promoting their private label; Sears spent $600 million on major advertising in 1980. They have to take the chance that if their private-label product is not good, the customer will develop a negative attitude toward their other products.

In spite of these potential disadvantages, middlemen develop private brands because they can be profitable. They can often locate manufacturers with excess capacity who will produce the private label at a low cost. Other costs, such as advertising and physical distribution, may also be low. This means that the private brander is able to charge a lower price and often make a higher profit margin. The private brander may be able to develop some strong store brands that draw traffic into its stores.

The competition between manufacturers' and middlemen's brands is called *the battle of the brands*. In this confrontation, middlemen have many advantages. Retail shelf space is scarce, and many manufacturers, especially newer and smaller ones, cannot introduce products into distribution under their own name. Middlemen take special care to maintain the quality of their brands, thus building consumers' confidence. Many shoppers know that the private-label brand is often manufactured by one of the larger manufacturers anyway. Middlemen's brands are often priced lower than comparable manufacturers' brands, thus appealing to budget-conscious shoppers, especially in times of inflation. Middlemen give more prominent display to their own brands and make sure they are better stocked. As a result, the former dominance of manufacturers' brands is weakening. Some marketing commentators predict that middlemen's brands will eventually knock out all but the strongest manufacturers' brands.

Manufacturers of national brands are very frustrated. Their inclination is to spend a lot of money on consumer-directed advertising and promotion to maintain strong brand preference. Their price has to be somewhat higher to cover this promotion. At the same time, the mass distributors put considerable pressure on them to put more of their promotional money into trade allowances and deals if they want adequate shelf space. Once manufacturers start giving in, they have less to spend on consumer promotion, and their brand leadership starts slipping. This is the national brand manufacturers' dilemma.[16]

Family-brand decision. Manufacturers who brand their products face several further choices. At least four brand-name strategies can be distinguished:

1. **Individual brand names.** This policy is followed by Procter and Gamble (Tide, Bold, Dash, Cheer, Gain, Oxydol, Duz) and Genesco, Inc. (Jarman, Mademoiselle, Johnson & Murphy, and Cover Girl).
2. **A blanket family name for all products.** This policy is followed by Heinz and General Electric.
3. **Separate family names for all products.** This policy is followed by Sears (Kenmore for appliances, Kerrybrook for women's clothing, and Homart for major home installations).
4. **Company trade name combined with individual product names.** This policy is followed by Kellogg's (Kellogg's Rice Krispies and Kellogg's Raisin Bran).

Competitors within the same industry will often adopt different brand-name strategies. In the soap industry, Procter & Gamble favors individual brand names. P&G will use its name with new products during the first six weeks of television promotion and then deemphasize it. P&G wants each product to make it on its own. Colgate, on the other hand, makes much use of the phrase "the Colgate family" to help its individual products along.

What are the advantages of an individual brand-names strategy? A major advantage is that the company does not tie its reputation to the product's acceptance. If the product fails or comes across as having lower quality, it does not compromise the manufacturer's name. A manufacturer of expensive watches or high-quality foods can introduce lower-quality lines without diluting its high-quality brand names. The individual-brand-names strategy permits the firm to search for the best name for each new product. A new name permits the building of new excitement and conviction.

Using a blanket family name for all products also has some advantages. The cost of introducing the product will be less, because there is no need for "name" research or for heavy advertising expenditures to create brand-name recognition and preference. Furthermore sales will be strong if the manufacturer's name is good. Thus Campbell's introduces new soups under its brand name with extreme simplicity and instant recognition. On the other hand, Phillips in Europe uses its name on all of its products, but since its products differ greatly in quality, most people expect only average quality in a Phillips product. That hurts the sales of its superior products; here is a case where individual branding might be better, or the company might avoid putting its own name on its weaker products.

Where a company produces quite different products, it may not be appropriate to use one blanket family name. Swift and Company developed separate family names for its hams (Premium) and fertilizers (Vigoro). When Mead Johnson developed a diet supplement for *gaining* weight, it created a new family name, Nutriment, to avoid confusion with its family-brand weight-*reducing* products, Metrecal. Companies

---

[16] See E. B. Weiss, "Private Label?" *Advertising Age*, September 30, 1974, pp. 27ff.

will often invent different family brand names for different quality lines within the same product class. Thus A&P sells a first grade, second grade, and third grade set of brands—Ann Page, Sultana, and Iona, respectively.

Finally, some manufacturers want to associate their company name along with an individual brand name for each product. The company name legitimizes, and the individual name individualizes, the new product. Thus Quaker Oats in *Quaker Oats Cap'n Crunch* taps the company's reputation in the breakfast-cereal field and Cap'n Crunch individualizes and dramatizes the new product.

The brand name should not be a casual afterthought but an integral reinforcer of the product concept. Among the desirable qualities for a brand name are the following: (1) *It should suggest something about the product's benefits*. Examples: Coldspot, Beautyrest, Craftsman, Accutron; (2) *It should suggest product qualities such as action or color*. Examples: Duz, Sunkist, Spic and Span, Firebird. (3) *It should be easy to pronounce, recognize, and remember.* Short names help. Examples: Tide, Crest, Puffs; (4) *It should be distinctive*. Examples: Mustang, Kodak, Exxon.

Marketing research firms have developed elaborate name-research procedures including *association tests* (what images come to mind?), *learning tests* (how easily is the name pronounced?), *memory tests* (how well is the name remembered?), and *preference tests* (which names are preferred?).

Many firms strive to build a unique brand name that will eventually become identified with the product category. Such brand names as Frigidaire, Kleenex, Levis, Jell-O, Scotch Tape, and Fiberglas have succeeded in this way. However, their very success may threaten the exclusive rights to the name. Cellophane and shredded wheat are now names in the common domain.

Brand-extension decision. *A brand-extension strategy is any effort to use a successful brand name to launch product modifications or new products*. In the case of product modifications, the detergent industry will launch brand X, then the new, improved brand X, then the new brand X with additives. Brand extension also covers the introduction of new package sizes, flavors, and models. More interesting is the use of a successful brand name to launch new products. After Quaker Oats's success with Cap'n Crunch dry breakfast cereal, the company used the brand name and cartoon character to launch a line of ice cream bars, T-shirts, and other products. Armour used its Dial brand name to launch a variety of new products that would not easily have obtained distribution without the strength of the Dial name. Honda Motor Company used its name to launch its new power lawnmower. Another kind of brand extension occurs when durable-goods manufacturers add stripped-down models to the lower end of their line in order to advertise their brand as starting at a low price. Thus Sears may advertise room air conditioners "starting at $240," and General Motors may advertise a new Chevrolet at $6,000. These "fighter" or "promotional" models are used to draw in customers on a price basis who, upon seeing the better models, often decide to trade up. This strategy must be used carefully. The "promotional" brand, although stripped, must be up to the brand's quality image. The seller must be sure to have the promotional model in stock when it is advertised. Consumers must not feel they were "baited and then switched."

Brand extension saves the manufacturer the high cost of promoting new names and creates instant brand recognition of the new product. At the same time, if the new product fails to satisfy, it might hurt consumers' attitudes toward the other products carrying the same brand name.[17]

Multibrand decision. In multibrand strategy, the seller develops two or more brands in the same product category. This marketing practice was pioneered by P&G when it introduced Cheer detergent as a competitor for its already successful Tide. Although Tide's sales dropped slightly, the combined sales of Cheer and Tide were higher. P&G now produces eight detergent brands.

Manufacturers adopt multibrand strategies for several reasons. First, manufacturers can gain more shelf space, thus increasing the retailer's dependence on their brands. Second, few consumers are so loyal to a brand that they will not try another. The only way to capture the "brand switchers" is to offer several brands. Third, creating new brands develops excitement and efficiency within the manufacturer's organization. Managers in P&G and General Motors compete to outperform each other. Fourth, a multibrand strategy positions the different benefits and appeals, and each brand can attract a separate following.

In deciding whether to introduce another brand, the manufacturer should consider such questions as

- ☐ Can a unique story be built for the new brand?
- ☐ Will the unique story be believable?
- ☐ How much will the new brand cannibalize the manufacturer's other brands versus competitors' brands?
- ☐ Will the cost of product development and promotion be covered by the sales of the new brand?

A major pitfall in introducing a number of multibrand entries is that each may obtain only a small share of the market, and none may be particularly profitable. The company will have dissipated its resources over several brands instead of building a few brands to a highly profitable level. These companies should weed out the weaker brands and establish tighter screening procedures for choosing new brands. Ideally, a company's brands should cannibalize the competitors' brands and not each other.[18]

Brand-repositioning decision. However well a brand is initially positioned in a market, the company may have to reposition it later. A competitor may have launched a brand next to the company's brand and cut into its market share. Or customer preferences may have shifted, leaving the company's brand with less demand.

A classic story of successful brand repositioning is the campaign developed by Seven-Up. Seven-Up was one of many soft drinks and bought primarily by older

---

[17] See Theodore R. Gamble, "Brand Extension," in *Plotting Marketing Strategy*, ed. Lee Adler (New York: Simon & Schuster, 1967), pp. 170–71. For several recent examples, see "Name Game," *Time*, August 31, 1981, pp. 41–42.

[18] See Robert W. Young, "Multibrand Entries," in Adler, *Plotting Marketing Strategy*, pp. 143–64.

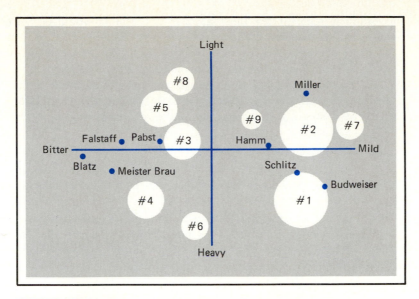

FIGURE 15–8
Distribution of Perceptions and Preferences in the Beer Market

people who wanted a bland, lemon-flavored drink. Research indicated that while a majority of soft-drink consumers preferred a cola, they did not prefer it all the time, and many other consumers were noncola drinkers. Seven-Up went for leadership in the noncola market by executing a brilliant campaign, calling itself the Uncola. The Uncola was featured as a youthful and refreshing drink, the one to reach for instead of a cola. Seven-Up created a new way for consumers to view the soft-drink market, as consisting of colas and uncolas, with Seven-Up leading the uncolas.

The problem of repositioning a brand can be illustrated for Hamm's beer. Figure 15–8 shows beer brand perceptions and taste preferences on two attributes: lightness and mildness. The dots show the perceived positions of the brands, and the circles represent locations of consumer preference. The larger circles represent more-intense preference. This map reveals that Hamm is not meeting the preferences of any distinct segment.

To remedy this problem, Hamm needs to identify the best preference cluster in which to reposition. Preference cluster #1 would be a poor choice because Schlitz and Budweiser are serving this segment. Preference cluster #2 seems like a good choice because of its size and the presence of only one competitor, Miller. Preference cluster #9 would be another possibility, although it is relatively small. Hamm can also think about a long-shot repositioning toward the supercluster #3, #5, and #8 or the supercluster #4 and #6.

Management must weigh two factors in making its choice. The first is the *cost* of shifting the brand to that segment. The cost includes changing the product's qualities, packaging, advertising, and so on. In general, the repositioning cost rises with the repositioning distance. The more radically the brand image has to be modified, the greater the required investment. Hamm would need more money to reposition its brand in segment #8 than segment #2. Hamm would be better off creating a new brand for segment #8 than repositioning its present brand.

The other factor is the *revenue* that would be earned by the brand in the new position. The revenue depends upon the number of consumers in the preference segment, their average purchase rate, the number and strength of competitors in that segment, and the price charged by brands in that segment. Hamm must make its choice by comparing likely revenues and costs of each repositioning alternative.

Packaging and Labeling Decisions

Many physical products going to the market have to be *packaged* and *labeled*.

Packaging.   Packaging can play a minor role (e.g., inexpensive hardware items) or a major role (e.g., cosmetics). Some packages—such as the Coke bottle and the L'eggs container—are world famous. Many marketers have called packaging a fifth P, along with price, product, place, and promotion. Most marketers, however, treat packaging as an element of product strategy.

We define *packaging as the activities of designing and producing the container or wrapper for a product*. The container or wrapper is called the *package*. The package may include up to three levels of material. The *primary package* is the product's immediate container. Thus the bottle holding Old Spice After-Shave Lotion is the primary package. The *secondary package* refers to material that protects the primary package and which is discarded when the product is about to be used. The cardboard box containing the bottle of after-shave lotion is a secondary package and provides additional protection and promotion opportunity. The *shipping package* refers to packaging necessary for storage, identification, or transportation. Thus a corrugated box carrying six dozen of Old Spice After-Shave Lotion is a shipping package. Finally, *labeling* is part of packaging and consists of printed information that describes the product, appearing on or with the package.

In recent times, packaging has become a potent marketing tool. Well-designed packages can create convenience value for the consumer and promotional value for the producer. Various factors have contributed to packaging's growing use as a marketing tool:

☐ **Self-service.** An increasing number of products are sold on a self-service basis at supermarkets and discount houses. The package must now perform many of the sales tasks. It must attract attention, describe the product's features, give the consumer confidence, and make a favorable overall impression.

☐ **Consumer affluence.** Rising consumer affluence means consumers are willing to pay a little more for the convenience, appearance, dependability, and prestige of better packages.

☐ **Company and brand image.** Companies are recognizing the power of well-designed packages to contribute to instant consumer recognition of the company or brand. Every film buyer immediately recognizes the familiar yellow packaging of Kodak Film.

☐ **Innovational opportunity.** Innovative packaging can bring large benefits to consumers and profits to producers. Uneeda Biscuit's innovation in 1899 of a stay-fresh unit package (paperboard, inner paper wrap, and paper overwrap) managed to prolong the shelf life of crackers better than the old cracker boxes, bins, and barrels could. Kraft's development of processed cheese in tins extended the shelf life of cheese and earned Kraft a reputation for reliability. Today Kraft is testing retort pouches, which are foil-and-plastic containers, as a successor to cans. The first companies to put their soft drinks in pop-top cans and their liquid sprays in aerosol cans attracted many new customers. Now wine makers are experimenting with pop-top cans and bag-in-the-carton forms of packaging.

Developing an effective package for a new product requires a large number of decisions. The first task is to establish the *packaging concept*. The packaging concept is a definition of what the package should basically *be* or *do* for the particular product. Should the main function(s) of the package be to offer superior product protection, introduce a novel dispensing method, suggest certain qualities about the product or the company, or something else?

General Foods developed a new dog-food product in the form of meatlike patties. Management decided that the unique and palatable appearance of these patties demanded maximum visibility. Visibility was defined as the basic packaging concept, and management considered alternatives in this light. It finally narrowed down the choice to a tray with a film covering.[19]

Decisions must be made on further elements of package design—*size, shape, materials, color, text*, and *brand mark*. Decisions must be made on much text or little text, cellophane or other transparent films, a plastic or a laminate tray, and so on. The various packaging elements must be harmonized. Size suggests certain things about materials, colors, and so forth. The packaging elements must also be harmonized with decisions on pricing, advertising, and other marketing elements.

After the packaging is designed, it must be put through a number of tests. *Engineering tests* are conducted to ensure that the package stands up under normal conditions; *visual tests*, to ensure that the script is legible and the colors harmonious; *dealer tests*, to ensure that dealers find the packages attractive and easy to handle; and *consumer tests*, to ensure favorable consumer response.

In spite of these precautions, a packaging design occasionally gets through with some basic flaw:

Sizzl-Spray, a pressurized can of barbeque sauce developed by Heublein, . . . had a potential packaging disaster that was discovered in the market tests. . . . "We thought we had a good can, but fortunately we first test marketed the product in stores in Texas and California. It appears as soon as the cans got warm they began to explode. Because we hadn't gotten into national distribution, our loss was only $150,000 instead of a couple of million."[20]

Developing effective packaging for a new product may cost a few hundred thousand dollars and take from a few months to a year. The importance of packaging cannot be overemphasized, considering the several functions it performs in attracting and satisfying customers. Companies must pay attention, however, to the growing

---

[19] "General Foods—Post Division (B)," Case M-102, Harvard Business School, 1964.

[20] "Product Tryouts: Sales Tests in Selected Cities Help Trim Risks of National Marketing," *Wall Street Journal*, August 10, 1962.

societal concerns about packaging and make decisions that serve society's interests as well as immediate customer and company objectives.

Labeling. Sellers will also design labels for their products. The label may be a simple tag attached to the product or an elaborately designed graphic that is part of the package. The label might carry only the brand name or a great deal of information. Even if the seller prefers a simple label, the law may require additional information.

Labels perform several functions, and the seller has to decide which ones to use. At the very least, the label *identifies* the product or brand, such as the name Sunkist stamped on oranges. The label might also *grade* the product; thus canned peaches are grade-labeled A, B, and C. The label might *describe* several things about the product: who made it, where it was made, when it was made, its contents, how it is to be used, and how to use it safely. Finally, the label might *promote* the product through its attractive graphics. Some writers distinguish between identification labels, grade labels, descriptive labels, and promotional labels.

Labels of well-known brands grow old-fashioned looking after a while and need freshening up. The label on Ivory soap has been redone eighteen times since the 1890s, with gradual changes in the size and design of the letters. The label on Orange Crush soft drink was substantially changed when its competitors' labels began to picture fresh fruits, thereby pulling in more sales. Orange Crush developed a label with new symbols to suggest freshness and much stronger and deeper colors.

There has been a long history of legal concerns surrounding labels. Formerly labels could mislead customers or fail to describe important ingredients or fail to include sufficient safety warnings. As a result, several federal and state laws were enacted to regulate labeling, the most prominent being the Fair Packaging and Labeling Act of 1966. Labeling practices have been affected in recent times by *unit pricing* (stating the price per unit of standard measure), *open dating* (stating the expected shelf life of the product), and *nutritional labeling* (stating the nutritional values in the product). Sellers should make sure that their labels contain all the required information before launching new products.

Customer-Service Decisions

Customer service is another element of product strategy. A company's offer to the marketplace usually includes some services. The service component can be a minor or a major part of the total offer. In fact, the offer can range from a pure good on the one hand to a pure service on the other. Four categories of offer can be distinguished:

1. **A pure tangible good.** Here the offer consists primarily of a tangible good such as soap, toothpaste, or salt. No services accompany the product.

2. **A tangible good with accompanying services.** Here the offer consists of a tangible good accompanied by one or more services to enhance its consumer appeal. For example, an automobile manufacturer sells an automobile with a warranty, service and maintenance instructions, and so on. Levitt observes that "the more technologically sophisticated the generic product (e.g., cars and computers), the more dependent are its sales on the

quality and availability of its accompanying customer services (e.g., display rooms, delivery, repairs and maintenance, application aids, operator training, installation advice, warranty fulfillment). In this sense, General Motors is probably more service intensive than manufacturing intensive. Without its services, its sales would shrivel."[21]

3. **A major service with accompanying minor goods and services.** Here the offer consists of a major service along with some additional services and/or supporting goods. For example, airline passengers are buying transportation service. They arrive at their destinations without anything tangible to show for their expenditure. However, the trip includes some tangibles, such as food and drinks, a ticket stub, and an airline magazine. The service requires a capital-intensive good called an airplane for its realization, but the primary item is a service.

4. **A pure service.** Here the offer consists primarily of a service. Examples include psychotherapy and massages. The psychoanalyst gives a pure service, with the only tangible elements consisting of an office and couch.

Thus the company's product can be a good or a service, and additional services might be included. Here we shall focus on customer services accompanying the main offer. Service products themselves are discussed in the final section of this chapter.

The marketer faces three decisions with respect to customer service. What customer services should be included in the customer-services mix? What level of service should be offered? In what forms should the services be provided?

The service-mix decision.   The marketer needs to survey customers to identify the main services that might be offered and their relative importance. For example, Canadian buyers of industrial equipment ranked thirteen service elements in the following order of importance: (1) delivery reliability, (2) prompt quotation, (3) technical advice, (4) discounts, (5) after-sales service, (6) sales representation, (7) ease of contact, (8) replacement guarantee, (9) wide range of manufacturer, (10) pattern design, (11) credit, (12) test facilities, and (13) machining facilities.[22] These importance rankings suggest that the seller should at least match competition on delivery reliability, prompt quotation, technical advice, and other services deemed most important by the customers.

But the issue of which services to offer is more subtle than this. A service can be highly important to customers and yet not determine supplier selection if all the suppliers offer the service at the same level. Consider the following example:

> The Monsanto Company was seeking a way to improve its customer-services mix. Customers were asked to rate Monsanto, Du Pont, and Union Carbide on several attributes. All three companies were seen by customers as offering high delivery reliability and having good sales representatives. However, none were viewed as rendering sufficient technical service. Monsanto carried out a study to determine how important technical service is to chemical buyers and found out it had high importance. Monsanto then hired and trained additional technical people and launched a campaign describing itself as the leader in technical service. This gave Monsanto a different advantage in the minds of buyers seeking technical service.

---

[21] Theodore Levitt, "Production-Line Approach to Service," *Harvard Business Review*, September-October 1972, pp. 41–42.

[22] Peter G. Banting, "Customer Service in Industrial Marketing: A Comparative Study," *European Journal of Marketing*, 10, No. 3 (1976), 140.

The service-level decision.   Customers not only want certain services but also want them in the right amount and quality. If bank customers have to stand in long lines or confront frowning bank tellers, they might switch their bank.

Companies need to check on their own and competitors' service levels in relation to customers' expectations. The company can spot service deficiencies through a number of devices: *comparison shopping, periodic customer surveys, suggestion boxes,* and *complaint-handling systems.* The task is not to *minimize* complaining behavior but to *maximize* the customer's opportunity to complain so that the company can know how it is doing and disappointed customers can obtain satisfaction.

A useful device is to survey customers periodically to find out how they feel about each service. Figure 15–9(a) shows how customers rated fourteen service elements (attributes) of an automobile dealer's service department on importance and performance. Importance was rated on a four-point scale of "extremely important," "important," "slightly important," and "not important." Dealer performance was rated on a four-point scale of "excellent," "good," "fair," and "poor." For example, "Job done right the first time," received a mean importance rating of 3.83 and a mean performance rating of 2.63, indicating that customers felt it was highly important, but not being performed that well. The ratings of the fourteen elements are displayed in Figure 15–9(b). The figure is divided into four sections. Quadrant A shows important

FIGURE 15–9
Importance and Performance Ratings for Automobile Dealer's Service Department

Source: John A. Martilla and John C. James, "Importance-Performance Analysis," *Journal of Marketing,* January 1977, pp. 77–79.

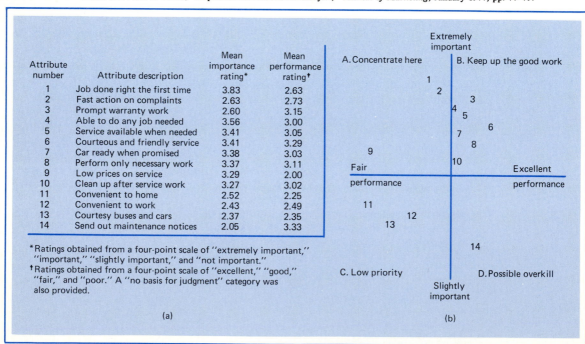

Attribute number	Attribute description	Mean importance rating*	Mean performance rating†
1	Job done right the first time	3.83	2.63
2	Fast action on complaints	2.63	2.73
3	Prompt warranty work	2.60	3.15
4	Able to do any job needed	3.56	3.00
5	Service available when needed	3.41	3.05
6	Courteous and friendly service	3.41	3.29
7	Car ready when promised	3.38	3.03
8	Perform only necessary work	3.37	3.11
9	Low prices on service	3.29	2.00
10	Clean up after service work	3.27	3.02
11	Convenient to home	2.52	2.25
12	Convenient to work	2.43	2.49
13	Courtesy buses and cars	2.37	2.35
14	Send out maintenance notices	2.05	3.33

*Ratings obtained from a four-point scale of "extremely important," "important," "slightly important," and "not important."
†Ratings obtained from a four-point scale of "excellent," "good," "fair," and "poor." A "no basis for judgment" category was also provided.

(a)

(b)

service elements that are not being performed at the desired levels; they include elements 1, 2, and 9. The dealer should concentrate on improving the service department's performance on these elements. Quadrant B shows important service elements where the department is performing well; its job is to maintain the high performance. Quadrant C shows minor service elements that are being delivered in a mediocre way, but which do not need any attention since they are not very important. Quadrant D shows that a minor service element, "Send out maintenance notices," is being performed in an excellent manner, a case of possible overkill. Measuring service elements according to their importance and performance tells marketers where to focus their efforts.

The service-form decision. Marketers must also decide on the forms in which to offer various services. The first question is how to price each service element. Consider, for example, what Zenith should offer in repair services on its television sets. Zenith has three options:

☐ It could offer free television-repair service for a year with the sale of its set.
☐ It could sell a service contract.
☐ It could offer no repair service, leaving this to television-repair specialists.

Furthermore, Zenith can visualize providing repair service in three ways:

☐ It could hire and train its own service specialists and locate them throughout the country.
☐ It could make arrangements with distributors and dealers to provide the repair services.
☐ It could leave it to independent companies to provide the necessary repair services.

For each service, various options exist. The company's decision depends on customers' preferences as well as competitors' strategies.

The customer-service department. Given the importance of customer service as a competitive tool, many companies have established strong customer-service departments, handling the following customer services:[23]

☐ **Complaints and adjustments.** Procedures are established for handling complaints. Whirlpool, for example, has set up hot lines to facilitate consumer complaining. By keeping statistics on the types of complaints, the customer-service department can press for desired changes in product design, quality control, high-pressure selling, and so on. It is less expensive to preserve the goodwill of existing customers than to attract new customers or woo back lost customers.
☐ **Credit service.** Companies can offer customers a number of credit options, including installment credit contracts, open-book credit, loans, and leasing options. The costs of extending credit are usually more than covered by the gross profit on the additional sales and the reduced cost of marketing expenditures to overcome the customers' feeling that they can't afford the purchase.

---

[23] See Ralph S. Alexander and Thomas L. Berg, *Dynamic Management in Marketing* (Homewood, Ill.: Richard D. Irwin, 1965), pp. 419–28.

□ **Maintenance service.** Well-managed companies run a parts and service department that is effective, speedy, and reasonable in cost. While maintenance service is often run by the production department, marketing should monitor customers' satisfaction with this service.

□ **Technical service.** Companies can provide customers who buy complex equipment with technical services such as custom design work, installation, customer training, applications research, and process-improvement research.

□ **Information service.** The companies can set up an information unit that answers customer inquiries and disseminates information on new products, features, processes, expected price changes, order-backlog status, and new company policies.

All of these services should be coordinated and used as tools in creating customer satisfaction and loyalty.

SERVICE-PRODUCT DECISIONS

Marketing as a discipline developed initially in connection with selling physical products such as toothpaste, cars, steel, and equipment. One of the major developments in America has been the phenomenal growth of service industries. Service businesses now provide 73 percent of the payroll jobs of the U.S. nonfarm work force. In contrast, Germany has 41 percent of its work force in the service sector and Italy 35 percent. As a result of rising affluence, more leisure, and the growing complexity of products that require servicing, the United States has become the world's first service economy. There is understandably a growing interest in how services should be marketed, in contrast to physical products.[24] We shall look at the issues here.

Service industries are quite varied. The government sector, with its courts, employment services, hospitals, loan agencies, military services, police and fire departments, post office, regulatory agencies, and schools, is in the service business. The private nonprofit sector, with its museums, charities, churches, colleges, foundations, and hospitals, is in the service business. A good part of the business sector, with its airlines, banks, computer service bureaus, hotels, insurance companies, law firms, management consulting firms, medical practices, motion picture companies, plumbing-repair companies, and real estate firms, is in the service business.

Not only are there traditional service industries, but new types keep popping up all the time:

For a fee, there are now companies that will balance your budget, babysit your philodendron, wake you up in the morning, drive you to work, or find you a new home, job, car, wife, clairvoyant, cat feeder, or gypsy violinist. Or perhaps you want to rent a garden tractor? A few cattle? Some original paintings? Or maybe some hippies to decorate your next cocktail party? If it is business services you need, other companies will plan

---

[24] See G. Lynn Shostack, "Breaking Free from Product Marketing," *Journal of Marketing*, April 1977, pp. 73–80; Leonard L. Berry, "Services Marketing is Different," *Business*, May-June 1980, pp. 24–30; and Eric Langeard, John E. G. Bateson, Christopher H. Lovelock, and Pierre Eiglier, *Services Marketing: New Insights from Consumers and Managers* (Cambridge, Mass.: Marketing Science Institute, 1981).

your conventions and sales meetings, design your products, handle your data processing, or supply temporary secretaries or even executives.[25]

Nature and Characteristics of a Service

We define a *service* as follows:

> A *service* is any activity or benefit that one party can offer to another that is essentially intangible and does not result in the ownership of anything. Its production may or may not be tied to a physical product.

Renting a hotel room, depositing money in a bank, traveling on an airplane, visiting a psychiatrist, having a haircut, having a car repaired, watching a professional sport, seeing a movie, having clothes cleaned in a dry-cleaning establishment, getting advice from a lawyer—all involve buying a service.

Services have four characteristics that must be considered when designing marketing programs.

Intangibility. Services are intangible. They cannot be seen, tasted, felt, heard, or smelled before they are bought. The person getting a "face lift" cannot see the result before the purchase, and the patient in the psychiatrist's office cannot know the outcome in advance. The buyer has to have faith in the service provider.

Service providers can do certain things to improve the client's confidence. First, they can increase the service's tangibility. A plastic surgeon can make a drawing showing how the patient will look after the surgery. Second, service providers can emphasize the benefits of the service rather than just describing its features. Thus a college admissions officer can talk to prospective students about the great jobs its alumni have found instead of only describing life on the campus. Third, service providers can develop brand names for their service to increase confidence, such as Magikist cleaning, the United Airlines Red Carpet Service, and Transcendental Meditation. Fourth, service providers can use a celebrity to create confidence in the service, as Hertz has done with O. J. Simpson.

Inseparability. A service is inseparable from its source whether the source is a person or machine. But a physical product exists whether or not its source is present. Consider going to a Rolling Stones concert. The entertainment value is inseparable from the performer. It is not the same service if an announcer tells the audience that Mick Jagger is indisposed and Donny and Marie Osmond will substitute. This means that the number of people who can buy this service—watching Mick Jagger perform live—is limited to the amount of time that Mick Jagger gives to concerts.

Several strategies exist for getting around this limitation. The service provider can learn to work with larger groups. Psychotherapists have moved from one-on-one therapy to small-group therapy to groups of over three hundred people in a large hotel ballroom getting "therapized." The service provider can learn to work faster—the psychotherapist can spend thirty minutes with each patient instead of

---

[25] "Services Grow While the Quality Shrinks," *Business Week*, October 30, 1971, p. 50.

fifty minutes and see more patients. The service organization can train more service providers and build up client confidence, as H&R Block has done with its national network of trained tax consultants.

Variability. Services are highly variable, as they depend on who provides them and when and where they are provided. A Dr. Christiaan Barnard heart transplant is likely to be of higher quality than one performed by a recent M.D. And Dr. Barnard's heart transplants will vary with his energy and mental set at the time of each operation. Service buyers are aware of this high variability and frequently talk to others before selecting a service provider.

Service firms can take two steps toward quality control. The first is investing in good personnel selection and training. Airlines, banks, and hotels spend substantial sums to train their employees in providing good service. One should find the same friendly and helpful personnel in every Marriott Hotel. The second step is monitoring customer satisfaction through suggestion and complaint systems, customer surveys, and comparison shopping, so that poor service can be detected and corrected.[26]

Perishability. Services cannot be stored. The reason many doctors charge patients for missed appointments is that the service value existed only at that point when the patient did not show up. The perishability of services is not a problem when demand is steady because it is easy to staff the services in advance. When demand fluctuates, service firms have difficult problems. For example, public transportation companies have to own much more equipment because of rush-hour demand than they would if demand were even throughout the day.

Sasser has described several strategies for producing a better match between demand and supply in a service business.[27]

On the demand side:

☐ **Differential pricing** will shift some demand from peak to off-peak periods. Examples include low early-evening movie prices and weekend discount prices for car rentals.
☐ **Nonpeak demand can be cultivated.** McDonald's opened its Egg McMuffin breakfast service, and hotels developed their minivacation weekends.
☐ **Complementary services** can be developed during peak time to provide alternatives to waiting customers, such as cocktail lounges to sit in while waiting for a table and automatic tellers in banks.
☐ **Reservation systems** are a way to manage the demand level, and airlines, hotels, and physicians employ them extensively.

On the supply side:

☐ **Part-time employees** can be hired to serve peak demand. Colleges add part-time teachers when enrollment goes up, and restaurants call in part-time waitresses when needed.
☐ **Peak-time efficiency routines** can be introduced. Employees perform only essential tasks during peak periods. Paramedics assist physicians during busy periods.

---

[26] For a good discussion of quality-control systems at the Marriott Hotel chain, see G. M. Hostage, "Quality Control in a Service Business," *Harvard Business Review*, July-August 1975, pp. 98–106.

[27] See W. Earl Sasser, "Match Supply and Demand in Service Industries," *Harvard Business Review*, November-December 1976, pp. 133–40.

- ☐ **Increased consumer participation** in the tasks can be encouraged, as when consumers fill out their own medical records or bag their own groceries.
- ☐ **Shared services** can be developed, as when several hospitals share medical-equipment purchases.
- ☐ **Facilities for future expansion** can be developed, as when an amusement park buys surrounding land for later development.

Classification of Services

It is difficult to generalize about services marketing because services vary considerably. Services can be classified in a number of ways. First, is the service *people based* or *equipment based*? A psychiatrist needs virtually no equipment, but a pilot needs an airplane. With people-based services, we can distinguish among those involving professionals (accounting, management consulting), skilled labor (plumbing, car repair), and unskilled labor (janitorial service, lawn care). In equipment-based services, we can distinguish between those involving automated equipment (automated car washes, vending machines), equipment operated by relatively unskilled labor (taxis, motion picture theatres), and equipment operated by skilled labor (airplanes, computers).[28] Even within a specific service industry, different service providers vary in the amount of equipment they use—contrast James Taylor with his single guitar and the Rolling Stones with their tons of audio equipment. Sometimes the equipment adds value to the service (stereo amplification), and sometimes it exists to reduce the amount of labor needed (automated car washes).

Second, is the *client's presence* necessary to the service? Thus brain surgery involves the client's presence, but a car repair does not. If the client must be present, the service provider has to be considerate of his or her needs. Thus beauty shop operators will invest in their shop's decor, play background music, and engage in light conversation with the client.

Third, what about the *client's purchase motive*? Does the service meet a *personal* need (personal services) or a *business* need (business services)? Physicians will price physical examinations differently for private patients versus company employees on a retainer. Service providers typically develop different marketing programs for personal and business markets.

Fourth, what about the *service provider's motives* (*profit* or *nonprofit*) and *form* (*private* or *public*)? These two characteristics, when crossed, produce four quite different types of service organizations. Clearly the marketing programs of a private investor hospital will differ from those of a private charity hospital or a Veterans' Administration hospital.

The Extent and Importance of Marketing in the Service Sector

Service firms typically lag behind manufacturing firms in their use of marketing. George and Barksdale surveyed 400 service and manufacturing firms and concluded that:

---

[28] See Dan R. E. Thomas, "Strategy Is Different in Service Businesses," *Harvard Business Review*, July-August 1978, p. 161.

In comparison to manufacturing firms, service firms appear to be: (1) generally less likely to have marketing-mix activities carried out in the marketing department, (2) less likely to perform analysis in the offering area, (3) more likely to handle their advertising internally rather than go to outside agencies, (4) less likely to have an overall sales plan, (5) less likely to develop sales training programs, (6) less likely to use marketing research firms and marketing consultants, and (7) less likely to spend as much on marketing when expressed as a percentage of gross sales.[29]

There are several reasons why service firms have neglected marketing. Many service businesses are small (shoe repair, barbershops) and do not use management techniques, such as marketing that they think would be expensive or irrelevant. There are also service businesses (law and accounting firms) that formerly believed it was unprofessional to use marketing. Other service businesses (colleges, hospitals) had so much former demand that they had no need for marketing until recently.

Today, as competition intensifies, as costs rise, as productivity stagnates, and as service quality deteriorates, more service firms are taking an interest in marketing. Airlines were one of the first service industries to study their customers and competition and take positive steps to make travelers' trips easier and more pleasant. Banks are another industry that moved toward more active use of marketing in a relatively short period of time. In stock brokerage, insurance, and lodging, the marketing concept has come in unevenly, with some leaders taking major marketing steps (Merrill Lynch, Marriott) and most firms lagging behind.

As services competition intensifies, more marketing sophistication will be needed. One of the main agents of change will be product marketers who move into service industries. Sears moved into services marketing years ago—insurance, banking, income tax consulting, car rentals. Xerox Corporation operates a major sales-training business (Xerox Learning), and Gerber Products runs nursery schools and insurance companies.

Service firms are under great pressure to increase productivity. Since the service business is highly labor intensive, costs have been rising rapidly. There are five approaches to improving service productivity. The first is to have service providers work harder or more skillfully for the same pay. Working harder is not a likely solution, but working more skillfully can occur through better selection and training procedures. The second is to increase the quantity of service by surrendering some quality. Doctors, for example, could give less time to each patient. The third is to add equipment to increase service capabilities. Levitt recommended that companies adopt a "manufacturing attitude" toward producing services as represented by McDonald's assembly-line approach to fast-food retailing, culminating in the "technological hamburger."[30] Commercial dishwashing, jumbo jets, multiple-unit motion picture theatres—all represent technological expansions of service. The fourth is to reduce or make obsolete the need for a service by inventing a product solution, the way television substituted for out-of-home entertainment, the wash-and-wear shirt reduced the need for commercial laundry, and penicillin reduced the need for tuberculosis

---

[29] William R. George and Hiram C. Barksdale, "Marketing Activities in the Service Industries," *Journal of Marketing*, October 1974, p. 65.

[30] Theodore Levitt, "Product-Line Approach to Service," *Harvard Business Review*, September-October 1972, pp. 41–52; also see his "The Industrialization of Service," *Harvard Business Review*, September-October 1976, pp. 63–74.

sanitariums. The fifth is to design a more effective service. How-to-quit-smoking clinics and jogging may reduce the need for expensive medical services later on. Hiring paralegal workers reduces the need for expensive legal professionals.

Service products represent one of the main areas of future marketing management and research. A few companies—Disney, Marriott Hotels, Delta Airlines, McDonald's—are widely acknowledged to be leaders in service marketing (see Exhibit 15–2). Hopefully, further research will uncover additional principles for successfully managing and marketing service businesses.

Exhibit 15-2

WALT DISNEY ENTERPRISES—A HIGHLY RESPONSIVE ORGANIZATION

Service organizations—colleges, hospitals, social agencies, and others—are increasingly recognizing that their marketing mix consists of five Ps—product, price, place, promotion, people. And people may be the most important P! The organization's employees are in constant contact with consumers and can create good or bad impressions.

Organizations are eager to figure out how to "turn on" their inside people (employees) to serve their outside people (customers). Here is what the Disney organization does to market "positive customer attitudes" to its employees:

1. The personnel staff at Disney extends a special welcome to new applicants. Those who are hired are given written instructions on what to expect—where to report, what to wear, and how long each training phase will be.

2. On the first day, new employees report to Disney University for an all-day orientation session. They sit four to a table, receive name tags, and enjoy coffee, juice, and pastry while they introduce themselves and get acquainted. The result is that each new employee immediately knows three other people and feels part of a group.

3. The employees are introduced to the Disney philosophy and operations through the latest audiovisual presentations. They learn that they are in the entertainment business. They are "cast members" whose job it is to be enthusiastic, knowledgeable, and professional in serving Disney's "guests." Each division is described, and the new employees learn how they will each play a role in producing the "show." Then they are treated to lunch, tour the park, and are shown the recreational area set aside for the employees' exclusive use. That area consists of a lake, recreation hall, picnic area, boating and fishing facilities, and a large library.

4. The next day, the new employees report to their assigned jobs, such as security hosts (police), transportation hosts (drivers), custodial hosts (street cleaners), or food and beverage hosts (restaurant workers). They will receive a few days of additional training before they go "on stage." When they have learned their function, they receive their "theme costumes" and are ready to go on stage.

5. The new employees receive additional training on how to answer questions guests frequently ask about the park. When they don't have the answer, they can dial switchboard operators armed with thick fact books, who stand ready to answer any question.

6. The employees receive a Disney newspaper called *Eyes and Ears*, which features news of activities, employment opportunities, special benefits, educational offerings, and so on. Each issue contains a generous number of pictures of smiling employees.

7. Each Disney manager spends a week each year in "cross-utilization," namely, giving up the desk and heading for the front line, such as taking tickets, selling popcorn, or loading or unloading rides. In this way, management stays in touch with running the park and maintaining quality service to satisfy the millions of visitors. All managers and employees wear name badges and address each other on a first-name basis, regardless of rank.

8. All exiting employees answer a questionnaire on how they felt about working for Disney and any dissatisfactions they might have. In this way, Disney's management can measure their success in producing employee satisfaction and ultimately customer satisfaction.

No wonder the Disney people are so successful in satisfying their "guests." Their exchange with employees helps the latter feel important and personally responsible for the "show." The employees' sense of "owning this organization" spills over to the millions of visitors with whom they come in contact.

Source: This is a summary of the major points found in N. W. Pope, "Mickey Mouse Marketing," American Banker, *July 25, 1979; and "More Mickey Mouse Marketing,"* American Banker, *September 12, 1979.*

SUMMARY

Product is the first and most important element of the marketing mix. Product strategy calls for making coordinated decisions on product mixes, product lines, individual products, and service products.

Each product offered to customers can be looked at on three levels. The core product is the essential service that the buyer is really buying. The tangible product is the features, styling, quality, brand name, and packaging that constitute the tangible product. The augmented product is the tangible product plus the various services accompanying it, such as warranty, installation, service maintenance, and free delivery.

Several schemes have been proposed for classifying products. For example, all products can be classified according to their durability (nondurable goods, durable goods, and services). Consumer goods are usually classified according to consumer shopping habits (convenience, shopping, specialty, and unsought goods). Industrial goods are classified according to how they enter the production process (materials and parts, capital items, and supplies and services).

Most companies handle more than one product, and then product mix can be described as having a certain width, length, depth, and consistency. The four dimensions of the product mix are the tools for developing the company's product strategy. The various lines making up the product mix have to be periodically evaluated for profitability and growth potential. The company's better lines should receive disproportionate support; weaker lines should be phased down or out; and new lines should be added to fill the profit gap.

Each product line consists of product items, which should be evaluated. The product-line manager should study the sales and profit contributions of each item in the product line as well as how the items are positioned against competitors' items. This provides information needed for making several product-line decisions. Line stretching involves the question of whether a particular line should be extended downward, upward, or both ways. Line filling raises the question of whether additional items should be added within the present range of the line. Line modernization raises the question of whether the line needs a new look and whether the new look should be installed piecemeal or all at once. Line featuring raises the question of which items to feature in promoting the line. Line pruning raises the question of how to detect and remove weaker product items from the line.

Companies have to develop brand policies for the individual product items in their lines. They must decide whether to brand at all, whether to do manufacturing or private branding, what quality they should build into the brand, whether to use family brand names or individual brand names, whether to extend the brand name to new products, whether to put out several competing brands, and whether to reposition any of the brands.

Physical products require packaging decisions to create such benefits as protection, economy, convenience, and promotion. Marketers have to develop a packaging concept and test it functionally and psychologically to make sure it achieves the desired objectives and is compatible with public policy. Physical products also require labeling for identification and possible grading, description, and promotion of the product. U.S. laws require sellers to present certain minimum information on the label to inform and protect consumers.

Companies have to develop customer services that are desired by customers and effective against competitors. The company has to decide on the most important services to offer, the level at which each service should be provided, and the form of each service. The service mix can be coordinated by a customer-service department that handles complaints and adjustments, credit, maintenance, technical service, and customer information.

As the United States moves increasingly toward a service economy, marketers need to know more about marketing service products. Services are activities or benefits that one party can offer to another that are essentially intangible and do not result in the ownership of anything. Services are intangible, inseparable, variable, and perishable. Service industries lag behind manufacturing firms in adopting and using marketing concepts, but a strong interest is now emerging.

QUESTIONS

1. In 1983, by refusing to review a lower-court decision, the U.S. Supreme Court said, in effect, that Parker Bros.'s game "Monopoly" was a generic trademark. The ruling was based on a market survey of buyers' motivations submitted by the makers of another board game, "Antimonopoly," which revealed that 65 percent of the people surveyed would buy Monopoly if it were produced by any manufacturer. What implications does this ruling have for trademark protection by marketers?

2. Both North American Watch (marketers of Piaget, Corum, and Concord brands) and Timex have changed from advertising their products as accurate timepieces to promoting them as jewelry that tells time. What changes have taken place in the core, tangible, and augmented product, and what are the respective companies' chances for success with the new strategy?

3. Describe some of the service decisions that the following marketers must make: (a) women's dress shop, (b) savings and loan, (c) sporting goods store.

4. Define the primary want-satisfying purpose(s) of the following goods: (a) cars; (b) bread; (c) oil; (d) pillows; (e) pens; (f) novels; (g) textbooks; (h) uniforms; (i) detergents.

5. Offer a definition of the basic business of each of the following large companies: (a) General Motors; (b) Bayer's (maker of aspirin); (c) Massachusetts Investors Trust (a mutual fund); (d) Sears; and (e) *Time* magazine.

6. Most firms prefer to develop a diversified product line to avoid overdependence on a single product. Yet there are certain advantages that accrue to the firm that produces and sells one product. Name them.

7. "As a firm increases the number of its products arithmetically, management's problems tend to increase geometrically." Do you agree?

8. Does the ranking of a company's products according to their relative profit contribution indicate the best way to allocate the marketing budget to these products? If yes, how should the budget be allocated to the products? If no, why?

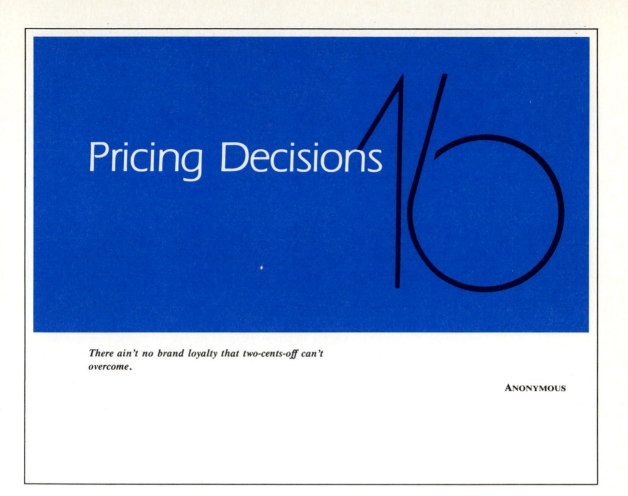

Pricing Decisions 16

There ain't no brand loyalty that two-cents-off can't overcome.

ANONYMOUS

All profit organizations and many nonprofit organizations face the task of setting a price on their products or services. Price goes by many names:

> Price is all around us. You pay *rent* for your apartment, *tuition* for your education, and a *fee* to your physician or dentist. The airline, railway, taxi, and bus companies charge you a *fare*; the local utilities call their price a *rate*; and the local bank charges you *interest* for the money you borrow. The price for driving your car on Florida's Sunshine Parkway is a *toll*, and the company that insures your car charges you a *premium*. The guest lecturer charges an *honorarium* to tell you about a government official who took a *bribe* to help a shady character steal *dues* collected by a trade association. Clubs or societies to which you belong may make a special *assessment* to pay unusual expenses. Your regular lawyer may ask for a *retainer* to cover her services. The "price" of an executive is a *salary*, the price of a salesperson may be a *commission*, and the price of a worker is a *wage*. Finally, although economists would disagree, many of us feel that *income taxes* are the price we pay for the privilege of making money.[1]

---

[1] David J. Schwartz, *Marketing Today: A Basic Approach*, 3rd ed. (New York: Harcourt Brace Jovanovich, 1981), p. 271.

How are prices set? Through most of history, prices were set by buyers and sellers negotiating with each other. Sellers would ask for a higher price than they expected to receive, and buyers would offer less than they expected to pay. Through bargaining, they would arrive at an acceptable price.

Setting one price for all buyers is a relatively modern idea. It was given impetus by the development of large-scale retailing at the end of the nineteenth century. F. W. Woolworth, Tiffany and Co., John Wanamaker, J. L. Hudson, and others advertised a "strictly one-price policy" because they carried so many items and supervised so many employees.

Through most of history, price has operated as the major determinant of buyer choice. This is still true in poorer nations, among poorer groups, and with commodity-type products. However, nonprice factors have become relatively more important in buyer-choice behavior in recent decades. Yet price still remains one of the most important elements determining company market share and profitability.

Price is the only element in the marketing mix that produces revenue; the other elements represent costs. Yet many companies do not handle pricing well. The most common mistakes are: pricing is too cost oriented; price is not revised often enough to capitalize on market changes; price is set independently of the rest of the marketing mix rather than as an intrinsic element of market-positioning strategy; and price is not varied enough for different product items and market segments.

Companies handle pricing in a variety of ways. In small companies, prices are often set by top management rather than by the marketing or sales department. In large companies, pricing is typically handled by divisional and product-line managers. Even here, top management sets the general pricing objectives and policies and often approves the prices proposed by lower levels of management. In industries where pricing is a key factor (aerospace, railroads, oil companies), companies will often establish a pricing department to set prices or assist others in determining appropriate prices. This department reports either to the marketing department or top management. Others who exert an influence on pricing include sales managers, production managers, finance managers, and accountants.

In this chapter, we will look at three major pricing-decision problems facing sellers. The first is how to set prices on a product for the first time. The second is how to modify a product's price over time and space to meet varying circumstances and opportunities. The third is how to initiate and respond to price changes.

SETTING THE PRICE

Pricing is a problem when a firm has to set a price for the first time. This happens when the firm develops or acquires a new product, when it introduces its regular product into a new distribution channel or geographical area, and when it regularly enters bids on new contract work. The firm has to consider a large number of factors in setting a price for the first time. In the following paragraphs, we will describe a six-step procedure for price setting: (1) selecting the pricing objective, (2) determining demand, (3) estimating costs, (4) analyzing competitors' prices and offers, (5) selecting a pricing method, and (6) selecting the final price.

Selecting the Pricing Objective

The company first has to decide what it wants to accomplish with the particular product. If the company has selected its target market and market positioning carefully, then its marketing-mix strategy, including price, will be fairly straightforward. For example, if a recreational-vehicle company wants to produce a luxurious truck camper for the affluent-customer segment, this implies charging a high price. Thus pricing strategy is largely determined by the prior decision on market positioning.

At the same time, the company may pursue additional objectives. The clearer a firm is about its objectives, the easier it is to set price. Each possible price will have a different impact on such objectives as profits, sales revenue, and market share. This is shown in Figure 16–1 for a hypothetical product. If the company wants to maximize pretax profits, it should charge $97. If it wants to maximize sales revenue, it should charge $86. If it wants to maximize market share, it should set an even lower price.

We will examine four major business objectives that a company can pursue through its pricing, namely: survival, current profit maximization, market-share leadership, and product-quality leadership.

FIGURE 16–1
Relation Between Price, Revenue, Market Share, and Profits

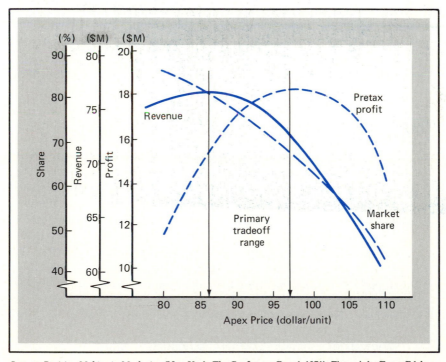

Source: *Decision Making in Marketing* (New York: The Conference Board, 1971). Figure is by Franz Edelman.

Survival. Companies set survival as their major objective if plagued with overcapacity, intense competition, or changing consumer wants. To keep the plant going and the inventories turning over, they must set a low price, hoping that the market is price sensitive. Profits are less important than survival. Troubled companies such as Chrysler and International Harvester recently resorted to large price-rebate programs in order to stay alive. As long as their prices covered variable costs and some fixed costs, they were able to stay in business.

Current profit maximization. Many companies want to set a price that will maximize current profits. They estimate the demand and costs associated with alternative prices and choose the price that will produce the maximum current profit, cash flow, or rate of return on investment. In all cases, the company is emphasizing current financial performance rather than long-run performance. (See Exhibit 16–1 for the theory of profit-maximization pricing.)

Market-share leadership. Other companies want to achieve the dominant market share. They believe that the company owning the largest market share will enjoy the lowest costs and highest long-run profit. They go after market-share leadership by setting prices as low as possible. A variation of this objective is to pursue a specific market-share gain: Say the company wants to increase its market share from 10 percent to 15 percent in one year. It will search for the price and marketing program to achieve this.

Product-quality leadership. A company might adopt the objective of being the product-quality leader in the market. This normally calls for charging a high price to cover the high product quality and high cost of R&D. Caterpillar is a prime example of a firm pursuing product-quality leadership. It builds high-quality construction equipment and offers excellent service, with the result that it is able to price its equipment at a premium.

Determining Demand

Each price that the company might charge will lead to a different level of demand and therefore have a different effect on its marketing objectives. The relation between the price charged and the resulting demand level is captured in the familiar *demand schedule*. (See Figure 16–2a.) The demand schedule shows the number of units the market will buy in a given time period at alternative prices that might be charged during the period. In the normal case, demand and price are inversely related, that is, the higher the price, the lower the demand (and conversely).

In the case of prestige goods, the demand curve is sometimes positively sloped. A perfume company found that by raising its price, it sold more perfume rather than less! Consumers take the higher price to signify a better or more expensive perfume. However, if too high a price is charged, the level of demand will be lower.

Methods of estimating demand schedules. Most companies make some attempt to measure their demand schedules. In researching the demand schedule, the investiga-

Exhibit 16-1

FINDING THE PRICE THAT WILL MAXIMIZE CURRENT PROFITS

Economists have worked out a simple model for pricing to maximize current profits. The model assumes that the firm has knowledge of its demand and cost functions for the product in question. The demand function describes the estimated quantity (Q) that would be purchased per period at various prices (P) that might be charged. Suppose the firm determines through statistical demand analysis that its *demand equation* is

$$Q = 1,000 - 4P \qquad (16-1)$$

This equation expresses the law of demand—less will be bought per period at higher prices.

The cost function describes the total cost (C) of producing any quantity per period (Q). In the simplest case, the total cost function is described by the linear equation $C = F + cQ$ where F is total fixed cost and c is unit variable cost. Suppose the company estimated the following *cost equation* for its product:

$$C = 6,000 + 50Q \qquad (16-2)$$

Management is almost in a position to determine the current profit-maximizing price. It needs only two more equations, both definitional. First, *total revenue* (R) is equal to price times quantity sold—that is,

$$R = PQ \qquad (16-3)$$

Second, *total profits* (Z) is the difference between total revenue and total cost—that is,

$$Z = R - C \qquad (16-4)$$

The company can now determine the relationship between profits (Z) and price (P) by starting with the profit equation (16-4) and going through the following derivation:

$$Z = R - C$$
$$Z = PQ - C$$
$$Z = PQ - (6,000 + 50Q)$$
$$Z = P(1,000 - 4P) - 6,000 - 50(1,000 - 4P)$$
$$Z = 1,000P - 4P^2 - 6,000 - 50,000 + 200P$$
$$Z = -56,000 + 1,200P - 4P^2$$

Total profits turn out to be a second-degree function of price. It is a hatlike figure (a parabola), and profits reach their highest point ($34,000) at a price of $150. The optimal price of $150 can be found by drawing the parabola with some sample prices and locating the high point, or by using calculus.

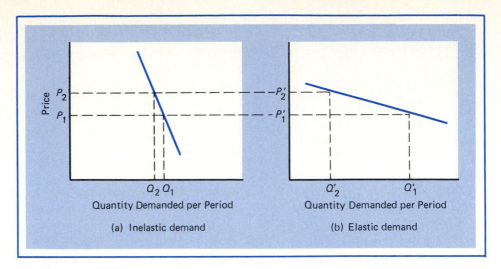

FIGURE 16–2
Inelastic and Elastic Demand

tor should make the assumptions about competition explicit. There is no problem when a monopolist is selling to the market. The demand schedule shows the total market demand resulting from different prices. However, if the company faces competition, there are two ways to estimate demand. One is to assume that competitors' prices remain constant regardless of the price charged by the company. The other is to assume that competitors charge a different price for each price the company chooses. We will assume the former and defer the question of competitors' prices until step four.

To measure a demand schedule requires varying the price. Pessemier developed a laboratory method of finding out how many units of a good people will buy at different possible prices.[2] Bennett and Wilkinson used an in-store method of estimating the demand schedule: They systematically varied the prices of several products sold in a discount store and observed the results.[3]

In measuring the price/demand relationship, the market researcher must control or allow for other factors that might affect demand. If a company raised its advertising budget at the same time that it lowered its price, we would not know how much of the increased demand was due to the lower price and how much to the increased advertising. Economists show the impact of nonprice factors on demand by shifts of the demand curve rather than movements along the demand curve.

Price elasticity of demand.   Marketers need to know how responsive demand would be to a change in price. Consider the two demand curves in Figure 16–2. In (a), a

[2] Edgar A. Pessemier, "An Experimental Method For Estimating Demand," *Journal of Business*, October 1960, pp. 373–83.

[3] See Sidney Bennett and J. B. Wilkinson, "Price-Quantity Relationships and Price Elasticity Under In-Store Experimentation," *Journal of Business Research*, January 1974, pp. 30–34.

price increase from P_1 to P_2 leads to a relatively small decline in demand from Q_1 to Q_2. In (b), the same price increase leads to a substantial drop in demand from Q_1' to Q_2'. If demand hardly changes with a small change in price, we say the demand is inelastic. If demand changes greatly, we say demand is elastic. Specifically, the price elasticity of demand is given by the following formula:[4]

$$\text{Price elasticity of demand} = \frac{\% \text{ change in quantity demanded}}{\% \text{ change in price}}$$

Suppose demand falls by 10 percent when a seller raises the price by 2 percent. Price elasticity of demand is therefore −5 (the minus sign confirms the inverse relation between price and demand). If demand fell by 2 percent with a 2 percent increase in price, then elasticity is −1. In this case, the seller's total revenue stays the same: The seller sells fewer items but at a higher price that preserves the same total revenue. If demand fell by 1 percent when price increased by 2 percent, then elasticity is −½. The less elastic the demand, the more it pays for the seller to raise the price.

What determines the price elasticity of demand? Demand is likely to be less elastic under the following conditions: (1) There are few or no substitutes or competitors; (2) buyers don't readily notice the higher price; (3) buyers are slow to change their buying habits and search for lower prices; (4) buyers think the higher prices are justified by quality improvements, normal inflation, and so on.

If demand is elastic rather than inelastic, sellers will consider lowering their price. A lower price will produce more total revenue. This makes sense as long as the costs of producing and selling more do not increase disproportionately.

Various studies of price elasticity have been reported. For example, the price elasticity of housing, 0.5; refrigerators, −1.07 to −2.06; and automobiles, −0.6 to −1.1.[5] But one must be careful in using these estimates. Price elasticity depends on the magnitude and direction of the contemplated price change. It may be negligible with a small price change and substantial with a large price change. It may differ for a price cut versus a price increase. Finally, long-run price elasticity is apt to differ from short-run elasticity. Buyers may continue with their current supplier after a price increase because choosing a new supplier takes time, but they may eventually

---

[4] In symbols:

$$Eqp = \frac{(Q_1 - Q_0)/\frac{1}{2}(Q_0 + Q_1)}{(P_1 - P_0)/\frac{1}{2}(P_0 + P_1)}$$

where:

Eqp = elasticity of quantity sold with respect to a change in price
Q_0, Q_1 = quantity sold per period before and after price change
P_0, P_1 = old and new price

Suppose a company lowers its price from $10 to $5, and its sales rise from 100 units to 150 units.

$$\frac{(150 - 100)/\frac{1}{2}(100 + 150)}{(\$5 - \$10)/\frac{1}{2}(\$10 + \$5)} = \frac{.40}{-.67} = -.60$$

Thus the demand elasticity is less than −1, or inelastic, and we know that total revenue will fall. Checking this, we note that the total revenue fell from $1,000 to $750.

[5] Arnold C. Harberger, *The Demand For Durable Goods* (Chicago: University of Chicago Press, 1960), pp. 3–14.

switch suppliers. In this case, demand is more elastic in the long run than in the short run.[6] Or the reverse may happen: Buyers drop a supplier after being notified of a price increase but return later. The distinction between short-run and long-run elasticity means that sellers will not know for a while the total effect of their price change. (Exhibit 16–2 illustrates some methods of estimating price elasticity.)[7]

Estimating Costs

Demand largely sets a ceiling to the price that the company can charge for its product. And company costs set the floor. The company wants to charge a price that covers all of its costs of producing, distributing, and selling the product, including a fair return for its effort and risk.

Types of costs.　A company's costs take two forms, fixed and variable. *Fixed costs* (also known as overhead) are costs that do not vary with production or sales revenue. Thus a company must pay bills each month for rent, heat, interest, executive salaries, and so on, whatever the company's output. Fixed costs go on irrespective of the production level.

Variable costs vary directly with the level of production. For example, each hand calculator produced by Texas Instruments (TI) involves a cost of plastic, wires, packaging, and the like. These costs tend to be constant per unit produced. They are called variable because their total varies with the number of units produced.

Total costs is the sum of the fixed and variable costs for any given level of production. Management wants to charge a price that will at least cover the total production costs at a given level of production.

Cost behavior at different levels of production per period.　In order to price intelligently, management needs to know how its costs vary with different levels of production.

First take the case where a company such as TI has built a fixed-size plant to produce 1,000 hand calculators a day. Figure 16–3 shows the typical U-shaped behavior of the short-run average cost curve (SRAC). The cost per unit is high if few units are produced per day. As production approaches 1,000 units per day, average cost falls. The reason is that the fixed costs are spread over more units, with each one bearing a smaller fixed cost. TI can try to produce more than 1,000 units per day but at increasing costs. Average cost increases after 1,000 units because the plant becomes inefficient: Workers have to queue for machines, machines break down more often, and workers get in each other's way.

If TI believes that it could sell 2,000 units a day, it should consider building a larger plant. The plant will use more efficient machinery and work arrangements,

---

[6] Stigler suggests that demand is generally more elastic in the long run because the short run is marked by the difficulty of rapid adjustment, the existence of market imperfections, and the presence of habit. See George Stigler, *Theory of Price*, rev. ed. (New York: Macmillan Co., 1952), pp. 45–47.

[7] Also see Leonard J. Parsons and Randall L. Schultz, *Marketing Models and Econometric Research* (New York: North-Holland, 1976).

Exhibit 16-2

DIFFERENT METHODS OF ESTIMATING PRICE ELASTICITY —AN ILLUSTRATION

Different techniques have evolved for estimating price elasticity. Consider the following case:

> A Bell telephone company was considering offering a rate reduction on second phones, which it installed for an extra monthly charge of seventy-five cents. The company had been using heavy advertising to sell families on second phones, but the advertising was beginning to show diminishing returns. The company wondered how many additional extension phones would be ordered if the monthly charge was lowered to fifty cents.

The company could estimate the likely reactions of the ultimate customers, using one of four methods.

☐ **Direct-attitude survey.** The company could ask potential users whether they would add another phone if the monthly service charge was lowered to fifty cents. The percentage saying yes could be applied against the number of potential users to calculate the number of extra extensions.

☐ **Statistical analysis.** This could take the form of a historical or a cross-sectional analysis of the relationship between price and quantity. A historical analysis consists in observing how extension usage was affected by past rate reductions. A cross-sectional analysis consists in observing how extension usage varies with the rates charged by different Bell companies.

☐ **Market test.** The company could offer potential users a chance to have an extension phone for fifty cents a month if they acted within a specified time period. The percentage who took advantage of the offer could then be multiplied by the number of potential users.

☐ **Analytic inference.** The company could conjecture how many additional families would find a second phone worthwhile at the lower price. A second phone adds convenience at a cost. The company could segment the market into different-size dwelling units and income levels. A high-income family in a large home would be highly interested in a second phone. The company could estimate how many families in this segment lacked second phones and apply the probability that they would acquire the phone at the reduced rate. This could be done for all the segments, to build up an estimate.

As an interesting side note, potential users were asked what they thought the extension service cost. Over 80 percent named a price above seventy-five cents a month, in some cases as high as two dollars. The amount of price misinformation was profound. The strategy implication is that *bringing people closer to an understanding of the correct price would be tantamount to a price reduction*. If a homemaker thought the monthly charge was one dollar and learned that it was only seventy-five cents, this is equivalent to a price reduction *in her mind* of 25 percent. Rather than reducing the monthly rate to fifty cents, the company might gain more by advertising heavily the current price.

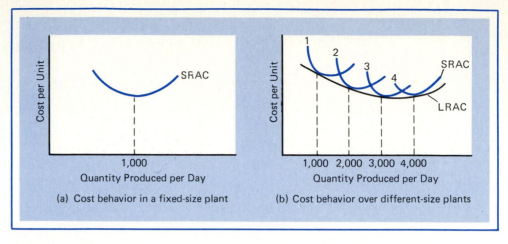

FIGURE 16–3
Cost per Unit at Different Levels of Production per Period

and the unit cost of producing 2,000 units per day will be less than the unit cost of producing 1,000 units per day. This is shown in the long-run average cost curve. [See Figure 16–3(b).] In fact, a 3,000-capacity plant would be even more efficient according to Figure 16–3(b). But a 4,000-daily production plant would be less efficient because of increasing diseconomies of scale: There are too many workers to manage, paperwork slows things down, and so on. Figure 16–3(b) indicates that a 3,000-daily production plant is the optimal size to build, if demand is strong enough to support this level of production.[8]

Cost behavior as a function of accumulated production. Suppose TI runs a plant that produces 3,000 hand calculators a day. As TI gains experience producing hand calculators, it learns how to do it better. The workers learn short cuts, the flow of materials is improved, procurement costs are cut, and so on. The result is that average cost tends to fall with accumulated production experience. This is shown in Figure 16–4. Thus the average cost of producing the first 100,000 calculators is $10 per calculator. When the company has produced the first 200,000 calculators, the average cost has fallen to $9. After its accumulated production experience doubles again to 400,000, the average cost is $8. This decline in the average cost with accumulated production experience is called the *experience curve* (sometimes *learning curve*).

If a downward sloping experience curve exists, that is highly significant for the company. Not only will the company's unit production cost fall, it will fall faster if the company makes and sells more during a given time period. But the market has to stand ready to buy the higher output. This suggests the following pricing strategy. TI should price its calculators low; its sales will increase, its costs will fall as the company gains experience; then it can lower its prices further. This logic is

---

[8] For measuring cost functions, see Jack Johnston, *Statistical Cost Functions*, (New York: McGraw-Hill Book Co., 1960).

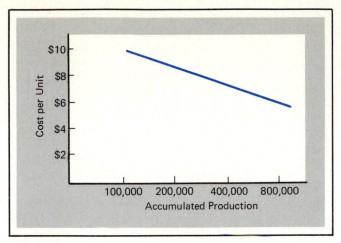

FIGURE 16-4
Cost per Unit as a Function of Accumulated Production: The Experience Curve

used by Texas Instruments in its pricing. It prices very aggressively, gets a lion's share of the market, and finds its costs falling further.

Analyzing Competitors' Prices and Offers

While market demand might set a ceiling and costs set a floor to pricing, competitors' prices and possible price reactions help the firm establish where its prices might be set. The company needs to learn the price and quality of each competitor's offer. This can be done in several ways. The firm can send out comparison shoppers to price and compare competitors' offers. The firm can acquire competitors' price lists and buy competitors' equipment and take it apart. The firm can ask buyers how they perceive the price and quality of each competitor's offer.

Once the company is aware of competitors' prices and offers, it can use them as an orienting point for its own pricing. If the firm's offer is similar to a major competitor's offer, then the firm will have to price close to the competitor or lose sales. If the firm's offer is inferior, the firm will not be able to charge as much as the competitor does. If the firm's offer is superior, the firm can charge more than the competitor. The firm must be aware, however, that competitors might change their prices in response to the firm's price. Basically, the firm will use price to position its offer vis à vis competitors.

Selecting a Pricing Method

Given the demand schedule, the cost function, and competitors' prices, the company is now ready to select a price. The price will be somewhere between one that is too low to produce a profit and one that is too high to produce any demand. Figure

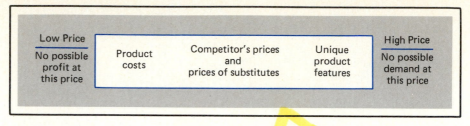

FIGURE 16–5
Major Considerations in Setting a Price

16–5 summarizes the three major considerations in price setting. Product costs set a floor to the price. Competitors' prices and the price of substitutes provide an orienting point that the company has to consider in setting its price. Unique product features in the company's offer establish the ceiling on its price.

Companies resolve the pricing issue by selecting a pricing method that includes one or more of these three considerations. The pricing method will then hopefully lead to a specific price. We shall examine the following price-setting methods: cost-plus pricing, break-even analysis and target-profit pricing, perceived-value pricing, going-rate pricing, and sealed-bid pricing.

Cost-plus pricing. The most elementary pricing method is to add a standard markup to the cost of the product. Thus an appliance retailer might pay a manufacturer $20 for a toaster and mark it up to sell at $30, which is a 50 percent markup on cost (or alternatively, a 33⅓ percent markup on the retail price). His gross margin is $10. If his store's operating costs amount to $8 per toaster sold, his profit margin will be $2.

The manufacturer who made the toaster also probably used cost-plus pricing. If the manufacturer's standard cost of producing the toaster was $16, he might have added a 25 percent markup, setting the price to the retailer at $20. Construction companies submit job bids by estimating the total project cost and adding a standard markup for profit. Lawyers and other professionals typically price by adding a standard markup to their costs. Some sellers tell their customers they will charge their cost plus a specified markup; for example, aerospace companies price this way to the government.

Markups vary considerably among different goods. Some common markups (on price, not cost) in department stores are 20 percent for tobacco goods, 28 percent for cameras, 34 percent for books, 41 percent for dresses, 46 percent for costume jewelry, and 50 percent for millinery.[9] In the retail grocery industry, coffee, canned milk, and sugar tend to have low markups, while frozen foods, jellies, and some canned products have high markups. Quite a lot of dispersion is found around the averages. Within the frozen-foods category, for example, markups on retail price

---

[9] *Departmental Merchandising and Operating Results of 1965* (New York: National Retail Merchants Association, 1965).

range from a low of 13 percent to a high of 53 percent.[10] Preston found that varying markups reflected differences in unit costs, sales, turnover, and manufacturers' versus private brands, but still a lot remained unexplained.[11]

Does the use of standard markups to set prices make logical sense? Generally, no. Any pricing method that ignores current demand and competition is not likely to lead to the optimal price. The retail graveyard is full of merchants who insisted on using standard markups in the face of competitors who had gone into discount pricing.

Still markup pricing remains popular for a number of reasons. First, sellers have more certainty about costs than about demand. By tying the price to cost, sellers simplify their own pricing task; they do not have to make frequent adjustments as demand changes. Second, where all firms in the industry use this pricing method, their prices tend to be similar. Price competition is therefore minimized, which it would not be if firms paid attention to demand variations when they priced. Third, many people feel that cost-plus pricing is fairer to both buyers and sellers. Sellers do not take advantage of buyers when the latter's demand becomes acute; yet the sellers earn a fair return on their investment.

Break-even analysis and target-profit pricing. Another cost-oriented pricing approach is that of *target-profit pricing*. The firm tries to determine the price that would produce the profit it is seeking. Target pricing is used by General Motors, which prices its automobiles to achieve a 15 to 20 percent profit on its investment. This pricing method is also used by public utilities that are constrained to make a fair return on their investment.

Target pricing uses the concept of a *break-even chart*. A break-even chart shows the total cost and total revenue expected at different sales-volume levels. Figure 16–6 shows a hypothetical break-even chart. Fixed costs are $6 million regardless of sales volume. Variable costs are superimposed on the fixed costs and rise linearly with volume. The total revenue curve starts at zero and rises linearly with each unit sold. The slope of the total revenue curve reflects the price. Here the price is $15 (for example, the company's revenue is $12 million on 800,000 units, or $15 a unit).

At $15, the company must sell at least 600,000 units to break even, that is, for total revenue to cover total cost. If the company seeks a target profit of $2 million, it must sell at least 800,000 units at a price of $15 each. If the company is willing to charge a higher price, say $20, then it would not need to sell as many units to achieve its target profit. However, the market may not buy even this lower volume at the higher price: Much depends on the price elasticity of demand. This is not shown in the break-even chart. The company must consider different prices and estimate their impacts on sales volume and profits.

Perceived-value pricing. An increasing number of companies are basing their price on the product's *perceived value*. They see the buyers' perception of value, not the

[10] See Lee E. Preston, *Profits, Competition, and Rules of Thumb in Retail Food Pricing* (Berkeley: University of California Institute of Business and Economic Research, 1963), p. 31.

[11] Ibid., pp. 29–40.

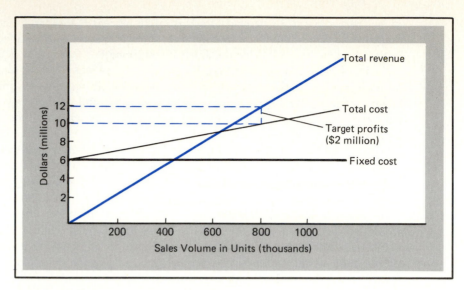

FIGURE 16–6
Break-Even Chart for Determining Target Price

seller's cost, as the key to pricing. They use the nonprice variables in the marketing mix to build up perceived value in the buyers' minds. Price is set to capture the perceived value.[12]

Perceived-value pricing fits in well with modern product-positioning thinking. A company develops a product concept for a particular target market with a planned quality and price. Then management estimates the volume it hopes to sell at this price. This indicates the needed plant capacity, investment, and unit costs. Management then figures out whether the product will yield a satisfactory profit at the planned price and cost. If the answer is yes, the company goes ahead with product development. Otherwise, the company drops the idea.

Two major practitioners of perceived-value pricing are Du Pont and Caterpillar. When Du Pont developed its new synthetic fiber for carpets, it demonstrated to carpet manufacturers that they could afford to pay Du Pont as much as $1.40 a pound for the new fiber and still make their current profit. Du Pont calls this the *value-in-use price*. Du Pont recognized, however, that pricing the new material at $1.40 a pound would leave the market indifferent. So they set the price lower than $1.40, the amount depending on the rate of market penetration they wanted. Du Pont did not use its unit-manufacturing cost to set the price but only to judge whether there was enough profit to go ahead in the first place.

Caterpillar uses perceived value to set prices on its construction equipment. It might price a tractor at $24,000 although a similar competitor's tractor might be priced at $20,000. And Caterpillar will get more sales than the competitor! When a

---

[12] See Daniel A. Nimer, "Pricing the Profitable Sale Has a Lot to Do with Perception," *"Sales Management,"* May 19, 1975, pp. 13–14.

prospective customer asks a Caterpillar dealer why he should pay $4,000 more for the Caterpillar tractor, the dealer answers:

$20,000 is the tractor's price if it is only equivalent to the competitor's tractor
$ 3,000 is the price premium for superior durability
$ 2,000 is the price premium for superior reliability
$ 2,000 is the price premium for superior service
$ 1,000 is the price premium for the longer warranty on parts
$28,000 is the price to cover the value package
−$ 4,000 discount
$24,000 final price

This stunned customer learns that although he is being asked to pay a $4,000 premium for the Caterpillar tractor, he is in fact getting a $4,000 discount! He ends up choosing the Caterpillar tractor because he is convinced that the lifetime operating costs of the Caterpillar tractor will be smaller.

The key to perceived-value pricing is to accurately determine the market's perception of the offer's value. Sellers with an inflated view of the value of their offer will overprice their product. Or they might underestimate the perceived value and charge less than they could. Market research is needed to establish the market's perception of value as a guide to effective pricing. Methods for estimating perceived value are described in Exhibit 16–3.

Going-rate pricing. In *going-rate pricing*, the firm bases its price largely on competitors' prices, with less attention paid to its own costs or demand. The firm might charge the same, more, or less than its major competitor(s). In oligopolistic industries that sell a commodity such as steel, paper, or fertilizer, firms normally charge the same price. The smaller firms "follow the leader." They change their prices when the market leader's prices change rather than when their own demand or cost changes. Some firms may charge a slight premium or slight discount, but they preserve the amount of difference. Thus minor gasoline retailers usually charge a few cents less than the major oil companies, without letting the difference increase or decrease.

Going-rate pricing is quite popular. Where costs are difficult to measure, or competitive response is uncertain, firms feel that the going price represents a good solution. The going price is thought to reflect the collective wisdom of the industry as to the price that would yield a fair return and not disturb industrial harmony.

Sealed-bid pricing. Competitive-oriented pricing also dominates where firms bid for jobs. The firm bases its price on expectations of how competitors will price rather than on a rigid relation to the firm's costs or demand. The firm wants to win the contract, and this requires pricing lower than the other firms.

Yet the firm cannot set its price below a certain level. It cannot price below cost without worsening its position. On the other hand, the higher it sets its price above its costs, the lower the chance of getting the contract.

The net effect of the two opposite pulls can be described in terms of the *expected profit* of the particular bid. (See Table 16–1.) Suppose a bid of $9,500 would yield

Exhibit 16-3

METHODS FOR ESTABLISHING PERCEIVED VALUE
—AN ILLUSTRATION

Three companies, A, B, and C, produce rapid-relay switches. Industrial buyers are asked to examine and rate the respective companies' offers. Here are three alternative methods:

☐ **Direct price-rating method.** Here the buyers estimate a price for each switch that they think reflects the total value of buying the switch from each company. For example, they may assign $2.55, $2.00, and $1.52, respectively.

☐ **Direct perceived-value-rating method.** Here the buyers allocate 100 points to the three companies to reflect the total value of buying the switch from each company. Suppose they assign 42, 33, and 25, respectively. If the average market price of a relay switch is $2.00, the three firms could charge, respectively, $2.55, $2.00, and $1.52, to reflect the variation in perceived value.

☐ **Diagnostic method.** Here the buyers rate the three offers on a set of attributes. They allocate 100 points to the three companies with regard to each attribute. They also allocate 100 points to reflect the relative importance of the attributes. Suppose the results are

Importance Weight	Attribute	Products		
		A	B	C
25	Product durability	40	40	20
30	Product reliability	33	33	33
30	Delivery reliability	50	25	25
15	Service quality	45	35	20
100	(Perceived value)	(41.65)	(32.65)	(24.9)

By multiplying the importance weights against each company's ratings, we find that company A's offer is perceived to be above average (at 42), company B's offer is average (at 33), and company C's offer is below average (at 25).

Company A can set a high price for its switches because it is perceived to offer more. If it wants to price proportionally to its perceived value, it can charge around $2.55 (= $2.00 for an average quality switch $\times \frac{42}{33}$). If all three companies set their price proportional to their perceived value, they will all enjoy some market share since they all offer the same value-to-price.

If a company prices at less than its perceived value, it will gain a higher-than-average market share because buyers will be getting extra value for their money. This is illustrated in the figure below.

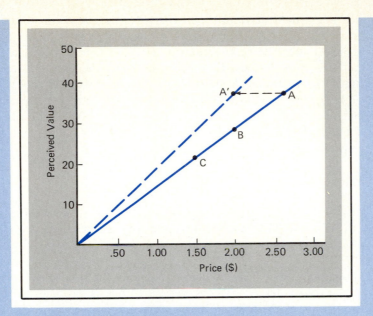

The three offers, A, B, and C, initially lie on the same value/price line. Respective market shares will depend upon the relative density of ideal points (not shown) surrounding the three locations. Now suppose company A lowers its price to A'. Its value/price will be on a higher line (the dashed line), and it will pull market share away from both B and C, particularly B because it offers more value at the same price as B. In self-defense, B will either lower its price or try to raise its perceived value by adding more service, quality, communication, and so on. If the cost of doing this is less than the loss in revenue that would result from a lower price, B should strengthen its perceived value.

a high chance of getting the contract, say .81, but only a low profit, say $100. The expected profit with this bid is therefore $81. If the firm bid $11,000, its profit would be $1,600, but its chance of getting the contract might be reduced, say to .01. The expected profit would be only $16. One logical bidding criterion would be to bid

TABLE 16-1

EFFECT OF DIFFERENT BIDS ON EXPECTED PROFIT

Company's Bid	Company's Profit	Probability of Getting Award with This Bid (Assumed)	Expected Profit
$ 9,500	$ 100	0.81	$ 81
10,000	600	0.36	216
10,500	1,100	0.09	99
11,000	1,600	0.01	16

the price that would maximize the expected profit. According to Table 16–1, the best bid would be $10,000, for which the expected profit is $216.

Using expected profit as a criterion for setting price makes sense for the large firm that makes many bids. In playing the odds, the firm will achieve maximum profits in the long run. The firm that bids only occasionally or that needs a particular contract badly will not find it advantageous to use the expected-profit criterion. The criterion, for example, does not distinguish between a $1,000 profit with a 0.10 probability and a $125 profit with an 0.80 probability. Yet the firm that wants to keep production going would prefer the second contract to the first.

Selecting the Final Price

The purpose of the previous pricing methods is to narrow the price range from which to select the final price. In selecting the final price, the company must bring in some additional considerations.

Psychological pricing. Sellers should consider the psychology of prices and not simply their economics. Many consumers use price as an indicator of quality. When Fleischmann raised the price of its gin from $4.50 to $5.50 a fifth, its liquor store sales went up, not down. Prestige pricing is especially effective with ego-sensitive products such as perfumes and expensive cars. A $100 bottle of perfume may contain $10 worth of scent, but people are willing to pay $100 because this price suggests something special.

Many sellers believe that prices should end in an odd number. Instead of pricing a stereo amplifier at $300, it should be priced at $299.99. The customer sees this as a price in the $200 range rather than $300 range. Or to be sure, the price might be set at $285. Newspaper ads are dominated by prices ending in odd numbers.[13] Some psychologists have argued that each digit has symbolic and visual qualities that should be considered in pricing. Thus 8 is symmetrical and creates a soothing effect, and 7 is angular and creates a jarring effect.

Company pricing policies. The contemplated price should be checked for consistency with company pricing policies. Many companies define the price image they want, their policy on price discounts, and their philosophy of meeting competitors' prices.

Impact of price on other parties. Management must also consider the reactions of other parties to the contemplated price. How will the *distributors and dealers* feel about it? Will the *company salesforce* be willing to sell at that price or complain that it is too high? How will *competitors* react to this price? Will *suppliers* raise their prices when they see the company's price? Will the *government* intervene and prevent this price from being charged? In the last case, marketers need to know the laws affecting price and make sure that their pricing policies are defensible.

---

[13] For further discussion, see Edward R. Hawkins, "Price Policies and Theory," *Journal of Marketing*, January 1954, pp. 233–40.

Companies do not set a single price but set a pricing structure that covers different products and items in the line and that reflects variations in geographical demand and costs, market-segment intensity of demand, purchase timing, and other factors. We will examine the following price modification strategies: geographical pricing, price discounts and allowances, promotional pricing, discriminatory pricing, new-product pricing, and product-mix pricing.

Geographical Pricing

Geographical pricing involves the company in deciding how to price its products to customers located in different parts of the country. Should the company charge higher prices to distant customers to cover the higher shipping costs and thereby risk losing their business? Or should the company charge the same to all customers regardless of location? We will examine five major geographical pricing strategies in connection with the following hypothetical situation:

> The Peerless Paper Company is located in Atlanta, Georgia, and sells paper products to customers all over the United States. The cost of freight is high and affects from whom customers buy their paper. Peerless wants to establish a geographical pricing policy. Management is trying to think through how to price a $100 order to three specific customers: customer A (Atlanta), customer B (Bloomington, Indiana), and customer C (Compton, California).

FOB origin pricing. Peerless can ask each customer to pay the shipping cost from the Atlanta factory to the specific destination. All three customers would pay the same factory price of $100, with customer A paying, say, $10 additional shipping, customer B paying $15 additional, and customer C paying $25 additional. Called FOB origin pricing, it means that the goods are placed free on board a carrier, at which point the title and responsibility passes to the customer, who pays the freight from the factory to the destination.

Advocates of FOB pricing feel that it is the most equitable way to allocate freight charges, because each customer picks up his own cost. The disadvantage, however, is that Peerless will be a high-cost firm to distant customers. If Peerless's main competitor is in California, this competitor will outsell Peerless in California. In fact, the competitor will outsell Peerless in most of the West, while Peerless will dominate the East. A vertical line could be drawn on a map connecting the cities where the two companies' price plus freight will just be equal. Peerless will have the price advantage east of this line, and its competitor will have the price advantage west of this line.

Uniform delivered pricing. Uniform delivered pricing is the exact opposite of FOB pricing. Here the company charges the same price plus freight to all customers regardless of their location. It is called "postage stamp pricing" after the fact that the U.S. government sets a uniform delivered price on first class mail anywhere in the country. The freight charge is set at the average freight cost. Suppose this is $15. Uniform delivered pricing therefore results in a high charge to the Atlanta customer (who pays $15 freight instead of $10) and a subsidized charge to the Compton customer (who pays $15 instead of $25). The Atlanta customer would prefer to buy paper from another local paper company that uses FOB origin pricing. On the other hand, Peerless has a better chance to win the California customer. Other advantages are that uniform delivered pricing is relatively easy to administer and allows the firm to maintain a nationally advertised price.

Zone pricing.   Zone pricing falls between FOB origin pricing and uniform delivered pricing. The company establishes two or more zones. All customers within a zone pay the same total price; and this price is higher in the more distant zones. Peerless might set up an East zone and charge $10 freight to all customers in this zone, a Midwest zone and charge $15, and a West zone and charge $25. In this way, the customers within a given price zone receive no price advantage from the company; thus a customer in Atlanta and Boston pay the same total price to Peerless. The complaint, however, is that the Atlanta customer is subsidizing the freight cost of the Boston customer. In addition, a customer just on the west side of the line dividing the East and Midwest pays substantially more than one just on the east side of the line, although they may be within a few miles of each other.

Basing-point pricing.   Basing-point pricing allows the seller to designate some city as a basing point and charge all customers the freight cost from that city to the customer location regardless of the city from which the goods are actually shipped. For example, Peerless might establish Chicago as the basing point and charge all customers $100 plus the appropriate freight from Chicago to their destination. This means that Atlanta customers pay the freight cost from Chicago to Atlanta even though the goods may be shipped from Atlanta. They are paying a "phantom charge." In its favor, using a basing-point location other than the factory raises the total price to customers near the factory and lowers the total price to customers far from the factory.

If all the sellers used the same basing-point city, delivered prices would be the same for all customers, and price competition would be eliminated. Such industries as sugar, cement, steel, and automobiles used basing-point pricing for years, but this method is less popular today because of adverse court ruling charging collusive pricing by competitors. Some companies establish multiple basing points to create more flexibility. They would quote freight charges from the basing-point city nearest to the customer.

Freight-absorption pricing.   The seller who is anxious to do business with a particular customer or geographical area might absorb all or part of the actual freight charges in order to get the business. Sellers might reason that if they can get more business, their average costs will fall and more than compensate for the extra freight costs. Freight-absorption pricing is used for market penetration and also to hold on to increasingly competitive markets.

Price Discounts and Allowances

Most companies will modify their basic price to reward customers for certain acts, such as early payment of bills, volume purchases, buying off season, and so on. These price adjustments—called discounts and allowances—are described below.

Cash discounts. A cash discount is a price reduction to buyers who pay their bills promptly. A typical example is "2/10, net 30," which means that payment is due within thirty days but the buyer can deduct 2 percent from the cost by paying the bill within ten days. The discount must be granted to all buyers meeting these terms. Such discounts are customary in many industries and serve the purpose of improving the sellers' liquidity and reducing credit collection costs and bad debts.

Quantity discounts. A quantity discount is a price reduction to buyers who buy large volumes. A typical example is "$10 per unit for less than 100 units; $9 per unit for 100 or more units." Quantity discounts must be offered to all customers and must not exceed the cost savings to the seller associated with selling large quantities. These savings include reduced expenses of selling, inventory, and transportation. They may be offered on a noncumulative basis (on each order placed) or a cumulative basis (on the number of units ordered over a given period). Discounts provide an incentive to the customer to buy more from a given seller rather than buying from multiple sources.

Functional discounts. Functional discounts (also called trade discounts) are offered by the manufacturer to trade-channel members if they will perform certain functions such as selling, storing, and record keeping. Manufacturers may offer different functional discounts to different trade channels because of the varying services they perform, but manufacturers must offer the same functional discounts within each trade channel.

Seasonal discounts. A seasonal discount is a price reduction to buyers who buy merchandise or services out of season. Seasonal discounts allow the seller to maintain steadier production during the year. Ski manufacturers will offer seasonal discounts to retailers in the spring and summer to encourage early ordering. Hotels, motels, and airlines will offer seasonal discounts in their slower selling periods.

Allowances. Allowances are other types of reductions from the list price. For example, *trade-in allowances* are price reductions granted for turning in an old item when buying a new one. Trade-in allowances are most common in the automobile industry and are also found in some other durable-goods categories. *Promotional allowances* are payments or price reductions to reward dealers for participating in advertising and sales-support programs.

Promotional Pricing

Under certain circumstances, companies will temporarily price their products below the list price and sometimes even below cost. Promotional pricing takes several forms.

☐ Supermarkets and department stores will price a few products as *loss leaders* to attract customers to the store in the hope that they will buy other things at normal markups.

☐ Sellers will also use *special-event pricing* in certain seasons to draw in more customers. Thus linens are promotionally priced every January to attract shopping-weary customers into the stores.

☐ Manufacturers will sometimes offer *cash rebates* to consumers who buy the product from dealers within a specified time period. The manufacturer sends the rebate directly to the customer. Rebates are a flexible tool for trimming inventories during difficult selling periods without cutting list prices. They have been popular recently with Chrysler and other auto makers and also with other big-ticket-item sellers, such as Fedders, Polaroid, and Minolta.

☐ *Psychological discounting* is another promotion-pricing technique, where the seller puts an artificially high price on a product and offers it at substantial savings; for example, "Was $359, Is $299." Illegitimate discount tactics are fought by the Federal Trade Commission and the Better Business Bureau. On the other hand, discounts from normal prices are a legitimate form of promotional pricing.

Discriminatory Pricing

Companies will often modify their basic price to accommodate differences in customers, products, locations, and so on. *Discriminatory pricing* describes the situation where the company sells a product or service at two or more prices that do not reflect a proportional difference in costs. Discriminatory pricing takes several forms:

☐ **Customer basis.** Here different customers pay different amounts for the same product or service. Museums will charge a lower admission fee to students and senior citizens.

☐ **Product-form basis.** Here different versions of the product are priced differently but not proportionately to their respective costs. SCM Corporation prices its most expensive Proctor-Silex steam/dry iron at $54.95, $5 above its next most expensive iron. The top model has a light that signals when the iron is ready. Yet the extra feature costs less than $1 to make.

☐ **Place basis.** Here different locations are priced differently even though the cost of offering each location is the same. A theatre varies its seat prices because of audience preferences for certain locations.

☐ **Time basis.** Here prices are varied seasonally, by the day, and even by the hour. Public utilities vary their prices to commercial users by time of day and weekend versus weekday.

For price discrimination to work, certain conditions must exist.[14] First, the market must be segmentable, and the segments must show different intensities of demand. Second, members of the segment paying the lower price should not be able to turn around and resell the product to the segment paying the higher price. Third, competitors should not be able to undersell the firm in the segment being charged

---

[14] See George Stigler, *The Theory of Price*, rev. ed. (New York: Macmillan Co., 1952), pp. 215ff.

the higher price. Fourth, the cost of segmenting and policing the market should not exceed the extra revenue derived from price discrimination. Fifth, the practice should not breed customer resentment and ill will. Sixth, the particular form of price discrimination should not be illegal.

With the current deregulation taking place in certain industries, such as airlines and trucks, companies in these industries have increased their use of discriminatory pricing. Consider the price discrimination introduced by airlines:

> The passengers on a plane bound from Cleveland to Miami may be paying as many as eleven different fares for the same flight. Those who checked carefully are benefiting from the heated-up competition between Eastern, United, and three other airlines flying this route. Many of the fares are aimed at segments of the market. The eleven possible fares are (1) $218 for first class, (2) $168 for standard economy class, (3) $136 for night coach, (4) $134 for weekend excursion, (5) $130 for Job Corps volunteers, (6) $128 for midweek excursion, (7) $118 for group-excursion tour, (8) $112 for military personnel, (9) $112 for youth fares, (10) $103 for weekend fares, and (11) $95 for charter.

New-Product Pricing

A company normally modifies its price as the product passes through the product life cycle. The introductory stage is especially challenging. We can distinguish between pricing a genuine product innovation that is patent protected and pricing a product that imitates existing products.

Pricing an innovative product. Companies launching a patent-protected innovative product can choose between market-skimming pricing and market-penetration pricing.

Market-skimming pricing. Many companies that invent new patent-protected products set high prices initially to "skim" the market. Du Pont is a prime practitioner of market skimming. On their discoveries—cellophane, nylon, and so on—they estimate the highest price they can charge given the comparative benefits of their new product versus the available substitutes. They set a price that makes it just worthwhile for some segments of the market to adopt the new material. After the initial sales slow down, they lower the price to draw in the next price-sensitive layer of customers. In this way, Du Pont skims a maximum amount of revenue from the various segments of the market. Polaroid also practices market skimming: It first introduces an expensive version of a new camera and gradually introduces simpler, lower-priced models to draw in new segments.

Market skimming makes sense under the following conditions: (1) A sufficient number of buyers have a high current demand; (2) the unit costs of producing a small volume are not so much higher that they cancel the advantage of charging what the traffic will bear; (3) the high initial price will not attract more competitors; (4) the high price supports the image of a superior product.

Market-penetration pricing. Other companies set a relatively low price on their innovative product, hoping to attract a large number of buyers and win a large market

Product Quality	Price: High	Price: Medium	Price: Low
High	1. Premium strategy	2. Penetration strategy	3. Superb-value strategy
Medium	4. Overcharging strategy	5. Average strategy	6. Good-value strategy
Low	7. Rip-off strategy	8. Borax strategy	9. Cheap-value strategy

FIGURE 16-7
Nine Marketing-Mix Strategies on Price/Quality

share. Texas Instruments (TI) is a prime practitioner of market-penetration pricing. TI will build a large plant, set its price as low as possible, win a large market share, experience falling costs, and cut its price further as costs fall.

The following conditions favor setting a low price:[15] (1) The market is highly price sensitive, and a low price stimulates more market growth; (2) production and distribution costs fall with accumulated production experience; and (3) a low price discourages actual and potential competition.

Pricing an imitative new product. A company that plans to develop an imitative new product faces a product-positioning problem. It must decide where to position the product on quality and price. Figure 16–7 shows nine possible price/quality strategies. If the existing market leader has preempted cell 1 by producing the premium product and charging the highest price, the newcomer might prefer to use one of the other strategies. The newcomer could design a high-quality product and charge a medium price (cell 2), design an average quality product and set an average price (cell 5), and so on. The newcomer must consider the size and growth rate of the market in each cell and the particular competitors.

Product-Mix Pricing

The logic of setting a price on a product has to be modified when the product is part of a product mix. In this case, the firm searches for a mutual set of prices that maximize the profits on the total product mix. Pricing is difficult because the various products have demand and cost interrelationships and are subject to different degrees of competition. We will distinguish four situations.

[15] See Joel Dean, *Managerial Economics* (Englewood Cliffs, N.J.: Prentice-Hall, 1951), pp. 420ff.

Product-line pricing. Companies normally develop product lines rather than single products. For example, Panasonic offers five different color video sound cameras, ranging from a simple one weighing 4.6 pounds to a complex one weighing 6.3 pounds that includes auto focusing, fade control, and two-speed zoom lens. Each successive camera in the line offers additional features. Management must decide on what price steps to establish between the various cameras. The price steps should take into account cost differences between the cameras, customer evaluations of the different features, and competitors' prices. If the price difference between two successive cameras is small, buyers will buy the more advanced camera, and this will increase company profits if the cost difference is smaller than the price difference. If the price difference is large, customers will buy the less advanced cameras.

In many lines of trade, sellers use well-established price points for the products in their line. Thus men's clothing stores might carry men's suits at three price levels: $150, $220, and $310. The customers will associate low-, average-, and high-quality suits with the three price "points." Even if the three prices are moderately raised, men will normally buy suits at their preferred price point. The seller's task is to establish perceived-quality differences that lend support to the price differences.

Optional-product pricing. Many companies offer optional products or features along with their main product. The automobile buyer can order electric window controls, defoggers, and light dimmers. However, pricing these options is a sticky problem. Automobile companies have to decide which items to build into the price and which ones to offer as options. General Motors' normal pricing strategy is to advertise a stripped-down model for $6,000, to pull people into the showrooms, and devote most of the showroom space to a display of loaded cars at $8,000 or $9,000. The economy model is stripped of so many comforts and conveniences that most buyers will reject it. When GM launched its new front-wheel drive J-cars in the spring of 1981, they took a clue from the Japanese auto makers and included in the sticker price a number of useful items previously sold only as options. Now the advertised price represented a well-equipped car. Unfortunately, however, the price was over $8,000 and many car shoppers balked.

Restaurants face a similar pricing problem. Restaurant customers can order liquor in addition to the meal. The seller needs to price the optional items. Management can price these options high to make them independently profitable or price them low to act as a traffic builder. Many restaurants price their liquor high and their food low. The food revenue covers the food and other costs of operating the restaurant, and the liquor produces the profit. This explains why waiters press hard to get customers to order drinks. Other restaurants will price their liquor low and food high to draw in a drinking crowd.

Captive-product pricing. Companies in certain industries produce products that must be used with the main product. Examples of captive products are razor blades and camera film. Manufacturers of the main products (razors and cameras) often price them low and set high markups on the supplies. Thus Kodak prices its cameras low because it makes its money on selling film. Those camera makers who do not sell film have to price their cameras higher in order to make the same overall profit.

By-product pricing. In producing processed meats, petroleum products, and other chemicals, there are often by-products. If the by-products have no value and in fact are costly to dispose of, this will affect the pricing of the main product. The manufacturer will seek a market for these by-products and should accept any price that covers more than the cost of storing and delivering the by-products. This will enable the seller to reduce the main product's price to make it more competitive.

INITIATING AND RESPONDING TO PRICE CHANGES

After developing their price structure and strategies, companies will face occasions when they will want to cut or raise prices.

Initiating Price Cuts

Several circumstances may lead a firm to consider cutting its price, even though this might provoke a price war. One circumstance is *excess capacity.* Here the firm needs additional business and cannot generate it through increased sales effort, product improvement, or other alternative measures. In the late 1970s various companies abandoned "follow-the-leader pricing" and turned to "flexible pricing" to boost their sales.[16]

Another circumstance is *falling market share* in the face of vigorous price competition. Several American industries—automobiles, consumer electronics, cameras, watches, and steel—have been losing market share to Japanese competitors whose high-quality goods carry lower prices than American products. Zenith, General Motors, and other American companies have resorted to more aggressive pricing action. General Motors, for example, cut its subcompact car prices by 10 percent on the West Coast, where Japanese competition is strongest.

Companies will also initiate price cuts in a *drive to dominate the market through lower costs.* Either the company starts with lower costs than its competitors or it initiates price cuts in the hope of gaining market share, which would lead to falling costs through larger volume.

Initiating Price Increases

Many companies have had to raise prices in recent years. They do this knowing that the price increases will be resented by customers, dealers, and the company's own sales force. Yet a successful price increase can increase profits considerably. For example, if the company's profit margin is 3 percent of sales, a 1 percent price increase will increase profits by 33 percent if sales volume is unaffected.

A major circumstance provoking price increases is the persistent worldwide *cost inflation.* Rising costs unmatched by productivity gains squeeze profit margins and lead companies to regular rounds of price increases. Companies often raise their prices by more than the cost increase in anticipation of further inflation or government

---

[16] See "Flexible Pricing," *Business Week*, December 12, 1977, pp. 78–88.

price controls. Companies hesitate to make long-run price commitments to customers, fearing that cost inflation will erode their profit margins. Pricing strategies that companies use to meet inflation are discussed in chapter 13, pp. 428–29.

Another factor leading to price increases is *overdemand*. When a company cannot supply all of its customers' needs, it can raise its prices, put customers on allocation, or both. Prices can be raised relatively invisibly by dropping discounts and adding higher-priced units to the line. Or prices may be pushed up boldly.

> U.S. Gypsum faced this problem when it fell into an oversold position on wallboard, fully recognizing that it would catch up with demand in six months and move to an undersold position. The issue was whether to put through a sharp price increase followed by a sharp price decrease six months later, or a small price increase followed by a small price decrease six months later. It chose the former because dealers were more concerned with availability than price and would make good money even at the higher price.

In passing price increases on to the customers, the company should avoid acquiring the image of price gouger. The price increases should be supported with a company communication program telling customers why prices are being increased. The company's sales force should help customers find ways to economize.

Buyers' Reactions to Price Changes

Whether the price is raised or lowered, the action will surely affect buyers, competitors, distributors, and suppliers and may interest government as well. Here we will consider buyers' reactions.

Customers do not always put a straightforward interpretation on price changes.[17] A price cut can be interpreted in the following ways:[18] The item is about to be replaced by a later model; the item has some fault and is not selling well; the firm is in financial trouble and may not stay in business to supply future parts; the price will come down even further and it pays to wait; or the quality has been reduced.

A price increase, which would normally deter sales, may carry some positive meanings to the buyers: The item is very "hot" and may be unobtainable unless it is bought soon; the item represents an unusually good value; or the seller is greedy and is charging what the traffic will bear.

Buyers' reactions to price changes also vary with their perception of the product's cost in relation to their total expenditures. Buyers are most price sensitive to products that cost a lot and/or are bought frequently, whereas they hardly notice higher prices on small items that they buy infrequently. In addition, buyers are normally less concerned with the product's *price* than the *total costs* of obtaining, operating, and servicing the product. A seller can charge more than competition and still get the business if the customer can be convinced that the total costs are lower.

---

[17] For an excellent review, see Kent B. Monroe, "Buyers' Subjective Perceptions of Price," *Journal of Marketing Research*, February 1973, pp. 70–80.

[18] See Alfred R. Oxenfeldt, *Pricing for Marketing Executives* (San Francisco: Wadsworth, 1961), p. 28.

Competitors' Reactions to Price Changes

A firm contemplating a price change has to worry about competitors' as well as customers' reactions. Competitors are very likely to react where the number of firms is small, the product is homogeneous, and the buyers are highly informed.

How can the firm anticipate the likely reactions of its competitors? Assume that the firm faces one large competitor. The competitor's reaction can be estimated from two vantage points. One is to assume that the competitor reacts in a set way to price changes. In this case, his reaction can be anticipated. The other is to assume that the competitor treats each price change as a fresh challenge and reacts according to self-interest at the time. In this case, the company will have to figure out what lies in the competitor's self-interest at the time. His current financial situation should be researched, along with recent sales and capacity, customer loyalty, and corporate objectives. If the competitor has a market-share objective, he is likely to match the price change. If he has a profit-maximization objective, he may react on some other strategy front, such as increasing the advertising budget or improving the product quality. The task is to read the mind of the competitor by using inside and outside sources of information.

The problem is complicated because the competitor can put different interpretations on, say, a company price cut: The competitor can surmise that the company is trying to steal the market, that the company is doing poorly and trying to boost its sales, or that the company wants the whole industry to reduce prices to stimulate total demand.

When there are several competitors, the company must estimate each competitor's likely reaction. If all competitors behave alike, this estimate amounts to an analysis of a typical competitor. If the competitors do not react uniformly because of critical differences in size, market shares, or policies, then separate analyses are necessary. If some competitors will match the price change, there is good reason to expect the rest will also match it. Exhibit 16–4 shows how a major chemical company analyzed the probable reactions of various parties to a contemplated price reduction.

Responding to Price Changes

Here we reverse the question and ask how a firm should respond to a price change initiated by a competitor. In some market situations the firm has no choice but to meet a competitor's price change. This is true for price reductions in a homogeneous product market. Unless the firm meets the price reduction, most buyers will buy from the lowest-price competitor.

When a firm raises its price in a homogeneous product market, the other firms may not match it. They will comply if the price increase will benefit the industry as a whole. But if one firm does not think that it or the industry would gain, its noncompliance can make the leader and the others rescind the price increases.

In nonhomogeneous product markets, a firm has more latitude in reacting to a competitor's price change. Buyers choose the vendor on a multiplicity of considerations: service, quality, reliability, and other factors. These factors desensitize buyers to minor price differences.

Exhibit 16-4

HOW A LARGE CHEMICAL COMPANY ASSESSED LIKELY COMPETITORS' REACTIONS TO A CONTEMPLATED PRICE CUT AND USED DECISION THEORY TO GUIDE ITS DECISION MAKING

A large chemical company had been selling a plastic substance to industrial users for several years and enjoyed a 40 percent market share. The management became worried about whether its current price of one dollar per pound could be maintained for much longer. The main source of concern was the rapid buildup of capacity by its three competitors and the possible attraction of further competitors by the current price. Management saw the key to the problem of possible oversupply to lie in further market expansion. The key area for market expansion lay in an important segment of the market that was closely held by a substitute plastic product produced by six firms. This substitute product was not as good, but it was priced lower. Management saw a possible solution in displacing the substitute product in the recalcitrant segment through a price reduction. If it could penetrate this segment, there was a good chance it could also penetrate three other segments, which had resisted the displacement.

The first task was to develop a decision model for the problem. This required defining the objectives, price alternatives, and key uncertainties. The chosen objective was to maximize the present value of future profits over the next five years. Management considered four price alternatives: maintaining the price at one dollar, or reducing the price to ninety-three, eighty-five, and eighty cents. The key uncertainties were:

- ☐ How much penetration in the key segment would take place without a price reduction?
- ☐ How would the six firms producing the substitute plastic react to each possible price reduction?
- ☐ How much key-segment penetration would take place for each possible price reaction by the suppliers of the substitute plastic?
- ☐ How much would key segment penetration speed up penetration of the other segments?
- ☐ If the key segment was not penetrated, what is the probability that the company's competitors would initiate price reduction soon?
- ☐ How would a price reduction affect the decision of existing competitors to expand their capacity and potential competitors to enter the industry?

The data-gathering phase consisted in asking sales personnel to place subjective probabilities on the possible states of the key uncertainties. For example, one question asked for the probability that the producers of the substitute product would retaliate if the company reduced its price to ninety-three cents per pound. On the average, the sales personnel felt that there was a 5 percent probability of a full match, a 60 percent probability of a half match and a 35 percent probability of no retaliation. They were also asked for probabilities if price were reduced to eighty-five and to eighty cents. The sales personnel indicated, as expected, that the probability of retaliation increased with the size of the price reduction.

The next step was to estimate the payoff associated with each price alternative. A decision-tree analysis revealed over four hundred possible outcomes. For this reason, the estimation of expected payoffs was programmed on a computer. The results indicated that all price reductions had a higher expected payoff than no price reduction, and a price reduction to eighty cents had the highest expected payoff. To check the sensitivity of these results, they were recomputed for alternative assumptions about the rate of market growth and the cost of capital. The ranking of the strategies was not affected by the change in assumptions. The analysis confirmed the desirability of a price reduction.

Source: See Paul E. Green, "*Bayesian Decision Theory in Pricing Strategy,*" Journal of Marketing, *January 1963,* pp. 5–14.

Before reacting, the firm needs to consider the following issues: (1) Why did the competitor change the price? Is it to steal the market, to utilize excess capacity, to meet changing cost conditions, or to lead an industrywide price change? (2) Does the competitor plan to make the price change temporary or permanent? (3) What will happen to the company's market share and profits if it doesn't respond? Are other companies going to respond? and (4) What are the competitor's and other firms' responses likely to be to each possible reaction?

Market leaders frequently face aggressive price cutting by smaller firms trying to build market share. Using price, Fuji attacks Kodak, Bic attacks Gillette, and Datril attacks Tylenol. When the attacking firm's product is comparable to the leaders, its lower price will cut into the leader's share. The leader at this point has several options.

☐ **Price maintenance.** The leader might maintain its price and profit margin, believing that (a) it would lose too much profit if it reduced its price; (b) it would not lose much market share; and (c) it could regain market share when necessary. The leader feels that it could hold on to good customers, giving up the poorer ones to the competitor. The argument against price maintenance is that the attacker gets more confident as its sales increase, the leader's sales force gets demoralized, and the leader loses more share than expected. The leader panics, lowers price to regain share, and finds it more difficult and costly than expected.

☐ **Price maintenance with nonprice counterattack.** The leader could maintain price but strengthen the value of its offer. It could improve its product, services, and communications so that customers see more value per dollar. The firm may find it cheaper to maintain price and spend money to improve its offer than to cut price and operate at a lower margin.

☐ **Price reduction.** The leader might lower its price to the competitor's price. It may do this because (a) its costs fall with volume; (b) it would lose a lot of share because the market is price sensitive; and (c) it would be hard to rebuild market share once it is lost. This action will cut its profits in the short run. Some firms will reduce their product quality, services, and marketing communications to maintain profits but this will ultimately hurt their long-run market share. The company should try to maintain the value of its offer as it cuts prices.

☐ **Price increase with product counterattack.** The leader might raise its price and introduce some new brands to bracket the attacking brand. Heublein, Inc., used this strategy when its Smirnoff's vodka, which had 23 percent of the American vodka market, was attacked by another brand, Wolfschmidt, priced at one dollar less a bottle. Instead of Heublein's lowering the price of Smirnoff by one dollar, it raised the price by one dollar and put the increased revenue into its advertising. Heublein set up another brand, Relska, to compete with Wolfschmidt and still another, Popov, to sell for less than Wolfschmidt.

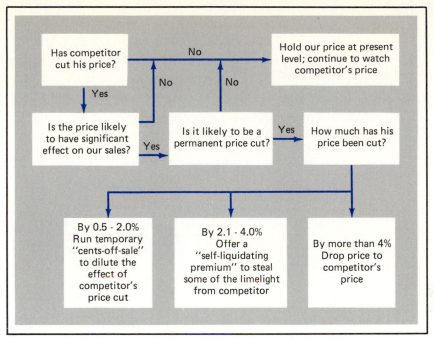

Source: Redrawn, with permission, from an unpublished paper by Raymond J. Trapp, Northwestern University, 1964.

FIGURE 16-8
Price-Reaction Program for Meeting a Competitor's Price Cut

This strategy effectively bracketed Wolfschmidt and gave Smirnoff an even more elite image.

The best response requires an analysis of the particular situation. The company under attack has to consider the product's stage in the life cycle, its importance in the company's product portfolio, the intentions and resources of the competitor, the price and value sensitivity of the market, the behavior of costs with volume, and the company's alternative opportunities.

An extended analysis of company alternatives is not always feasible at the time of a price change. The competitor may have spent considerable time in preparing this decision, but the company may have to react decisively within hours or days. About the only way to cut down price-reaction decision time is to anticipate possible competitors' price changes and to prepare contingent responses. Figure 16–8 shows a company price-reaction program to be used if a competitor cuts prices. Reaction programs for meeting price changes find their greatest application in industries where price changes occur with some frequency and where it is important to react quickly. Examples can be found in the meat-packing, lumber, and oil industries.[19]

---

[19] See, for example, William M. Morgenroth, "A Method for Understanding Price Determinants," *Journal of Marketing Research*, August 1964, pp. 17–26.

SUMMARY

In spite of the increased role of nonprice factors in the modern marketing process, price remains an important element and is especially challenging in markets characterized by monopolistic competition or oligopoly.

In setting the price of a product, the company follows a six-step procedure. First, the company carefully establishes its marketing objective(s), such as survival, current profit maximization, market-share leadership, or product-quality leadership. Second, the company determines the demand schedule, which shows the probable quantity purchased per period at alternative price levels. The more inelastic the demand, the higher the company can set its price. Third, the company estimates how its costs vary at different output levels and with different levels of accumulated production experience. Fourth, the company examines competitors' prices as a basis for positioning its own price. Fifth, the company selects one of the following pricing methods: cost-plus pricing, break-even analysis and target-profit pricing, perceived-value pricing, going-rate pricing, and sealed-bid pricing. Sixth, the company selects its final price, expressing it in the most effective psychological way, checking that it conforms to company pricing policies, and making sure it will prevail with distributors and dealers, company sales force, competitors, suppliers, and government.

Companies apply a variety of price modification strategies to the basic price. One is geographical pricing, where the company decides on how to price to distant customers, choosing from such alternatives as FOB pricing, uniform delivered pricing, zone pricing, basing-point pricing, and freight-absorption pricing. A second is price discounts and allowances, where the company establishes cash discounts, quantity discounts, functional discounts, seasonal discounts, and allowances. A third is promotional pricing, where the company decides on loss-leader pricing, special-event pricing, and psychological discounting. A fourth is discriminatory pricing, where the company establishes different prices for different customers, product forms, places, and times. A fifth is new-product pricing, where the company decides between introducing a patent-protected product innovation with skimming or market-penetration pricing; and it decides on one of nine price/quality strategies for introducing an imitative product. A sixth is product-mix pricing, where the company decides on the price zones for several products in a product line and on the pricing of optional products, captive products, and by-products.

When a firm considers initiating a price change, it must carefully consider customers' and competitors' reactions. Customers' reactions are influenced by the meaning customers see in the price change. Competitors' reactions flow either from a set reaction policy or from a fresh appraisal of each situation. The firm initiating the price change must also anticipate the probable reactions of suppliers, middlemen, and government.

The firm that faces a price change initiated by a competitor must try to understand the competitor's intent and the likely duration of the change. If swiftness of reaction is desirable, the firm should preplan its reactions to different possible price actions by competitors.

QUESTIONS

1. Under what circumstances would a manufacturer initiate price cuts?

2. In an effort to stimulate sales during a recessionary period, small-appliance manufacturers offered rebates, and auto makers offered low-interest-rate loans. What are the respective advantages and disadvantages of these two methods of price reduction?

3. Predatory pricing—pricing below costs to damage or destroy a competitor—is illegal. The Supreme Court ruled in the 1960s that total costs were the criteria for determining predatory pricing; in the 1970s a Harvard Law Review article proposed that average variable costs be the level below which pricing would be considered predatory. What are the consequences for large and small companies for adoption of either test?

4. Armco, a major steel company, has developed a new process for galvanizing steel sheets so that they can be painted (previously not possible) and used in car-body parts to prevent rust. What factors should Armco consider in setting a price for this product?

5. A firm might set a low price on a product to discourage competitors from coming in. Are there any situations when a firm might deliberately want to attract competitors into a new market and set a high price for this reason?

6. Xerox developed an office copying machine called 914. The machine was more expensive than competitive machines but offered the user superior copy and lower variable costs: 1¢ per copy as opposed to between 4¢ and 9¢ for competing processes. The machine cost $2,500 to produce, and management considered pricing it at either $3,500 or $4,500. How could management estimate unit sales at the two alternative price levels.

7. In principle, a reduction in price is tantamount to an increase in marketing effort. How can the price reduction be monetized into its equivalent in increased marketing effort?

8. How can a company increase its profits without raising price or lowering any of its costs?

9. Four companies, W, X, Y, and Z, produce electric can openers. Consumers were asked to allocate 100 points among the companies' products for each of four attributes. The results are shown below:

		Company Products			
Importance Weight	Attribute	W	X	Y	Z
0.35	Durability	30	15	40	15
0.15	Attractiveness	20	20	30	30
0.25	Noiselessness	30	15	35	20
0.25	Safety	25	25	25	25

An average electric can opener sells for $20. What should company W do about the pricing of its product if company Y charges $22?

Marketing-Channel Decisions

17

The middleman is not a hired link in a chain forged by a manufacturer, but rather an independent market, the focus of a large group of customers for whom he buys. . . . As he grows and builds a following, he may find his prestige in his market is greater than that of the supplier whose goods he sells.

PHILLIP MCVEY

In today's economy most producers do not sell their goods directly to the final users. Between them and the final users stand a host of marketing intermediaries performing a variety of functions and bearing a variety of names. Some intermediaries—such as wholesalers and retailers—buy, take title to, and resell the merchandise; they are called *merchant middlemen*. Others—such as brokers, manufacturers' representatives, and sales agents—search for customers and may negotiate on behalf of the producer but do not take title to the goods; they are called *agent middlemen*. Still others—such as transportation companies, independent warehouses, banks and advertising agencies—assist in the performance of distribution but neither take title to goods nor negotiate purchases or sales; they are called *facilitators*.

Marketing-channel decisions are among the most critical decisions facing management. *The company's chosen channels intimately affect all other marketing decisions.* The company's pricing depends upon whether it uses large, high-quality dealers or medium-size, medium-quality dealers. The firm's sales-force and advertising decisions depend upon how much training and motivation the dealers need. In addition, the company's channel decisions *involve relatively long-term commitments to other firms*. When an auto maker signs up independent dealers to sell its automobiles, it cannot buy them out the next day and replace them with company-owned outlets. When a drug manufacturer relies on independent retail druggists to sell its products, it must heed them when they object to its selling through mass-distribution outlets. Corey observed:

> A distribution system . . . is a key *external* resource. Normally it takes years to build, and it is not easily changed. It ranks in importance with key *internal* resources such as manufacturing, research, engineering, and field sales personnel and facilities. It represents a significant corporate commitment to large numbers of independent companies whose business is distribution—*and* to the particular markets they serve. It represents, as well, a commitment to a set of policies and practices that constitute the basic fabric on which is woven an extensive set of long-term relationships.[1]

Thus there is a powerful inertial tendency in channel arrangements. Therefore management must choose channels with an eye on tomorrow's likely selling environment as well as today's.

In this chapter we will examine: What is the nature of marketing channels and what trends are taking place? What issues do companies face in designing, managing, evaluating, and modifying their channels? In the next chapter we will examine marketing-channel issues from the perspective of retailers, wholesalers, and physical-distribution agencies.

THE NATURE OF MARKETING CHANNELS

Most producers work with marketing intermediaries to bring their products to market. The marketing intermediaries make up a *marketing channel* (also called trade channel or distribution channel). We shall use Bucklin's definition of a marketing channel:

> A *channel of distribution* shall be considered to comprise a set of institutions which performs all of the activities (functions) utilized to move a product and its title from production to consumption.[2]

Why Are Marketing Intermediaries Used?

Why is the producer willing to delegate some of the selling job to intermediaries? The delegation means relinquishing some control over how and to whom the products are sold. The producer appears to be placing the firm's destiny in the hands of intermediaries.

Since producers could sell directly to final customers, they must feel they gain certain advantages in using middlemen. These advantages are described below.

---

[1] E. Raymond Corey, *Industrial Marketing: Cases and Concepts* (Englewood Cliffs, N.J.: Prentice-Hall, 1976), p. 263.

[2] Louis P. Bucklin, *A Theory of Distribution Channel Structure* (Berkeley: Institute of Business and Economic Research, University of California, 1966), p. 5.

Many producers lack the financial resources to carry out direct marketing. For example, General Motors' sells its automobiles through over eighteen thousand independent dealers; even General Motors would be hard pressed to raise the cash to buy out its dealers.

Direct marketing would require many producers to become middlemen for the complementary products of other producers in order to achieve mass-distribution economies. For example, the Wm. Wrigley Jr. Company would not find it practical to establish small retail gum shops throughout the country or to sell gum door to door or by mail order. It would have to sell gum along with many other small products and would end up in the drugstore and grocery store business. Wrigley finds it easier to work through the extensive network of privately owned distribution institutions.

Producers who can afford to establish their own channels can often earn a greater return by increasing their investment in their main business. If a company earns a 20 percent rate of return on manufacturing and foresees only a 10 percent return on retailing, it will not want to undertake its own retailing.

The use of middlemen largely boils down to their superior efficiency in making goods widely available and accessible to target markets. Marketing intermediaries, through their contacts, experience, specialization, and scale of operation, offer the firm more than it can usually achieve on its own.

From the point of view of the economic system, the basic role of marketing intermediaries is to transform the heterogeneous supplies found in nature into meaningful goods assortments desired by people. According to Alderson:

> The materials which are useful to man occur in nature in heterogeneous mixtures which might be called conglomerations since these mixtures have only random relationship to human needs and activities. The collection of goods in the possession of a household or an individual also constitutes a heterogeneous supply, but it might be called an assortment since it is related to anticipated patterns of future behavior. The whole economic process may be described as a series of transformations from meaningless to meaningful heterogeneity.[3]

Alderson adds: "The goal of marketing is the matching of segments of supply and demand."[4]

Figure 17–1 shows one major source of the economies effected by the use of middlemen. Part (a) shows three producers, each using direct marketing to reach three customers. This system requires nine different contacts. Part (b) shows the three producers working through one distributor, who contacts the three customers. This system requires only six contacts. In this way, middlemen reduce the amount of work that must be done.

---

[3] Wroe Alderson, "The Analytical Framework for Marketing," *Proceedings—Conference of Marketing Teachers from Far Western States* (Berkeley: University of California Press, 1958).

[4] Wroe Alderson, *Marketing Behavior and Executive Action: A Functionalist Approach to Marketing Theory* (Homewood, Ill.: Richard D. Irwin, 1957), p. 199.

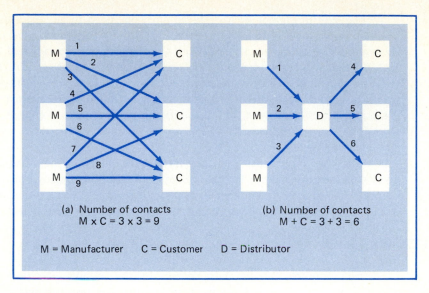

(a) Number of contacts
M x C = 3 x 3 = 9

(b) Number of contacts
M + C = 3 + 3 = 6

M = Manufacturer   C = Customer   D = Distributor

FIGURE 17–1
How a Distributor Effects an Economy of Effort

Marketing-Channel Functions

A marketing channel performs the work of moving goods from producers to consumers. It overcomes the major time, place, and possession gaps that separate goods and services from those who would use them. Members of the marketing channel perform a number of key functions:[5]

- ☐ **Research.** The gathering of information necessary for planning and facilitating exchange.
- ☐ **Promotion.** The development and dissemination of persuasive communications about the offer.
- ☐ **Contact.** The searching out and communicating with prospective buyers.
- ☐ **Matching.** The shaping and fitting of the offer to the buyer's requirements. This includes such activities as manufacturing, grading, assembling, and packaging.
- ☐ **Negotiation.** The attempt to reach final agreement on price and other terms of the offer so that transfer of ownership or possession can be effected.
- ☐ **Physical distribution.** The transporting and storing of the goods.
- ☐ **Financing.** The acquisition and dispersal of funds to cover the costs of the channel work.
- ☐ **Risk taking.** The assumption of risks in connection with carrying out the channel work.

The first five functions help consummate transactions; the last three help fulfill the completed transactions.

---

[5] For other lists, see Edmund D. McGarry, "Some Functions of Marketing Reconsidered," in *Theory in Marketing*, ed. Reavis Cox and Wroe Alderson (Homewood, Ill.: Richard D. Irwin, 1950), pp. 269–73; and Louis P. Bucklin, *A Theory of Distribution Channel Structure* (Berkeley: Institute of Business and Economic Research, University of California, 1966), pp. 10–11.

The question is not *whether* these functions need to be performed—they must be—but rather *who* is to perform them. All of the functions have three things in common: They use up scarce resources; they can often be performed better through specialization; and they are shiftable among channel members. To the extent that the manufacturer performs the functions, the manufacturer's costs go up, and its prices have to be higher. When some functions are shifted to middlemen, the producer's costs and prices are lower, but the middlemen must add a charge to cover their work. The issue of who should perform various channel tasks is one of relative efficiency and effectiveness.

Marketing functions, then, are more basic than the institutions that at any given time perform them. Changes in channel institutions largely reflect the discovery of more efficient ways to combine or separate economic functions that must be carried out to provide meaningful assortments of goods to target customers.

Number of Channel Levels

Marketing channels can be characterized by the number of channel levels. Each middleman that performs some work in bringing the product and its title closer to the final buyer constitutes a *channel level*. Since the producer and the final consumer both perform some work, they are part of every channel. We will use the number of *intermediary levels* to designate the *length* of a channel. Figure 17–2 illustrates several marketing channels of different lengths.

A *zero-level channel* (also called a *direct-marketing channel*) consists of a manufacturer selling directly to consumers. The three major ways of direct selling are door to door, mail order, and manufacturer-owned stores. Avon's sales representatives

FIGURE 17-2
Examples of Different-Level Channels

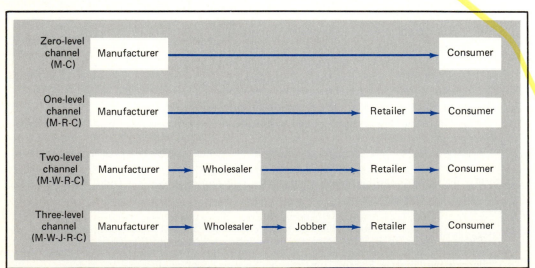

sell cosmetics to women on a door to door basis; Franklin Mint sells collectible objects through mail order; and Singer sells its sewing machines through its own stores.

A *one-level channel* contains one selling intermediary. In consumer markets this intermediary is typically a retailer; in industrial markets it is often a sales agent or a broker.

A *two-level channel* contains two intermediaries. In consumer markets they are typically a wholesaler and a retailer; in industrial markets they may be an industrial distributor and dealers.

A *three-level channel* contains three intermediaries. For example, in the meat-packing industry a jobber usually intervenes between the wholesalers and the retailers. The jobber buys from wholesalers and sells to the smaller retailers who generally are not serviced by the large wholesalers.

Higher-level marketing channels are also found but with less frequency. From the producer's point of view the problem of control increases with the number of channel levels, even though the manufacturer typically deals only with the adjacent level.

Types of Channel Flows

The institutions that make up a marketing channel are connected by several types of flows. The most important are the physical flow, title flow, payment flow, information flow, and promotion flow. These are illustrated in Figure 17–3 for the marketing of forklift trucks.

The *physical flow* describes the movement of physical products from raw materials to final customers. In the case of a forklift-truck manufacturer, such as Clark Equipment, raw materials, subassemblies, parts, and engines flow from suppliers via transportation companies (transporters) to the manufacturer's warehouses and plants. The finished trucks are warehoused and later shipped to dealers in response to their orders. The dealers sell and ship them to customers. Large orders may be shipped directly from the company warehouses or plant. One or more modes of shipment may be used, including railroads, trucks, and air freight.

The *title flow* describes the actual passage of ownership from one marketing institution to another. In the case of forklift trucks, title to the raw materials and components passes from the suppliers to the manufacturer. Title to the finished trucks passes from the manufacturer to the dealers and then to the customers. If the dealers only hold the trucks on *consignment*, they are not be included in the title flow.

The *payment flow* shows customers paying their bills through banks and other financial institutions to the dealers, the dealers remitting payment to the manufacturer (less the commission), and the manufacturer making payments to the various suppliers. Payments are also made to transporters and independent warehouses (not shown).

The *information flow* describes directed flows of influence (advertising, personal selling, sales promotion, and publicity) from one party to other parties in the system. Suppliers promote their name and products to the manufacturer and also to final customers in the hope of influencing the manufacturer to adopt their products. Manu-

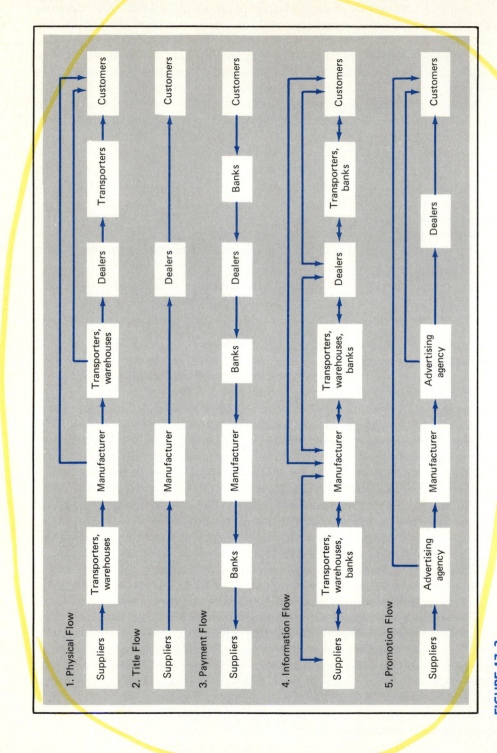

1. Physical Flow

2. Title Flow

3. Payment Flow

4. Information Flow

5. Promotion Flow

FIGURE 17-3
Five Different Marketing Flows in the Marketing Channel for Forklift Trucks

544

facturers direct a promotion flow to dealers (trade promotion) and final customers (end-user promotion).

If all of these flows were superimposed on one diagram, the tremendous complexity of even simple marketing channels would be apparent. This complexity goes even further, once we start distinguishing among different types of retailers, wholesalers, and others (see Chapter 18).

Channels in the Service Sector

The concept of marketing channels is not limited to the distribution of physical goods. Producers of services and ideas also face the problem of making their output *available* and *accessible* to target populations. They develop "educational dissemination systems" and "health delivery systems." They must figure out agencies and locations for reaching a spatially distributed population:

> Hospitals must be located in geographic space to serve the people with complete medical care, and we must build schools close to the children who have to learn. Fire stations must be located to give rapid access to potential conflagrations, and voting booths must be placed so that people can cast their ballots without expending unreasonable amounts of time, effort, or money to reach the polling stations. Many of our states face the problem of locating branch campuses to serve a burgeoning and increasingly well educated population. In the cities we must create and locate playgrounds for the children. Many overpopulated countries must assign birth control clinics to reach the people with contraceptive and family planning information.[6]

Marketing channels also are used in "person" marketing. Before 1940 professional comedians could reach audiences through seven channels: vaudeville houses, special events, nightclubs, radio, movies, carnivals, and theatres. In the 1950s television emerged as a strong channel, and vaudeville disappeared. Politicians also must find cost-effective channels—mass media, rallies, coffee hours—for distributing their messages to voters.

Channels normally describe a forward movement of products. One can also talk about *backward channels*. According to Zikmund and Stanton:

> The recycling of solid wastes is a major ecological goal. Although recycling is technologically feasible, reversing the flow of materials in the channel of distribution—marketing trash through a "backward" channel—presents a challenge. Existing backward channels are primitive, and financial incentives are inadequate. The consumer must be motivated to undergo a role change and become a producer—the initiating force in the reverse distribution process.[7]

The authors identify several middlemen that can play a role in "backward" channels, including (1) manufacturers' redemption centers, (2) "Clean-up Days" community groups, (3) traditional middlemen such as soft-drink middlemen, (4) trash-collection

---

[6] Ronald Abler, John S. Adams, and Peter Gould, *Spatial Organizations: The Geographer's View of the World* (Englewood Cliffs, N.J.: Prentice-Hall, 1971), pp. 531–32.

[7] William G. Zikmund and William J. Stanton, "Recycling Solid Wastes: A Channels-of-Distribution Problem," *Journal of Marketing*, July 1971, p. 34.

specialists, (5) recycling centers, (6) modernized "rag and junk men," (7) trash-recycling brokers, and (8) central-processing warehousing.

CHANNEL DYNAMICS

Distribution channels don't stand still. New wholesaling and retailing institutions keep emerging, and whole new channels systems evolve. Here we will look at the recent growth of vertical, horizontal, and multichannel marketing systems and how these systems cooperate, conflict, and compete.

Growth of Vertical Marketing Systems

One of the most significant recent channel developments are *vertical marketing systems* which have emerged to challenge conventional marketing channels. A conventional marketing channel consists of an independent producer, wholesaler(s), and retailer(s). Each is a separate business entity seeking to maximize its own profits, even if it is at the expense of maximizing the profits for the system as a whole. No channel member has complete or substantial control over the other members. McCammon characterizes conventional channels as "highly fragmented networks in which loosely aligned manufacturers, wholesalers, and retailers have bargained with each other at arm's length, negotiated aggressively over terms of sale, and otherwise behaved autonomously."[8]

A vertical marketing system (VMS), by contrast, consists of the producer, wholesaler(s), and retailer(s) acting as a unified system. Either one channel member owns the others or franchises them or has so much power that they all cooperate. The vertical marketing system can be dominated by the producer, the wholesaler, or the retailer. McCammon characterizes VMSs as "professionally managed and centrally programmed networks, preengineered to achieve operating economies and maximum market impact."[9] VMS came into being to control channel behavior and eliminate the conflict that results from independent channel members pursuing their own objectives. They achieve economies through their size, bargaining power, and elimination of duplicated services. VMSs have become the dominant mode of distribution in consumer marketing, serving as much as 64 percent of the total market.

We shall now examine three major types of VMSs, those shown in Figure 17–4.

Corporate VMS.   A *corporate VMS* combines successive stages of production and distribution under single ownership. As examples:

. . . Sherwin-Williams currently owns and operates over 2,000 retail outlets. . . . Sears reportedly obtains 50 percent of its throughput from manufacturing facilities in which

---

[8] Bert C. McCammon, Jr., "Perspectives for Distribution Programming," in *Vertical Marketing Systems*, ed. Louis P. Bucklin (Glenview, Ill.: Scott, Foresman, & Co., 1970), pp. 32–51.

[9] Ibid.

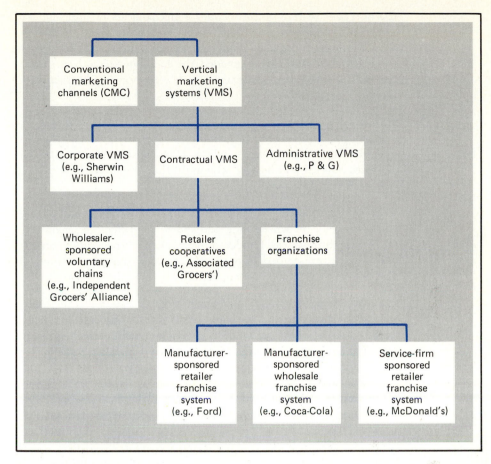

FIGURE 17–4
Conventional and Vertical Marketing Channels

it has an equity interest. . . . Holiday Inns is evolving into a self-supply network that includes a carpet mill, a furniture manufacturing plant, and numerous captive redistribution facilities. In short, these and other organizations are massive, vertically integrated systems. To describe them as "retailers," "manufacturers," or "motel operators" oversimplifies their operating complexities and ignores the realities of the marketplace.[10]

Administered VMS. An *administered VMS* coordinates successive stages of production and distribution not through common ownership but through the size and power of one of the parties. Manufacturers of a dominant brand are able to secure strong trade cooperation and support from resellers. Thus General Electric, Procter & Gamble, Kraftco, and Campbell Soup are able to command unusual cooperation from their resellers in connection with displays, shelf space, promotions, and price policies.

---

[10] Ibid., p. 45.

Contractual VMS. A *contractual VMS* consists of independent firms at different levels of production and distribution integrating their programs on a contractual basis to obtain more economies and/or sales impact than they could achieve alone. Contractual VMSs have expanded the most in recent years and constitute one of the most significant developments in the economy. Contractual VMSs are of three types.

Wholesaler-sponsored voluntary chains. Wholesalers organize voluntary chains of independent retailers to help them compete with large chain organizations. The wholesaler develops a program in which independent retailers standardize their selling practices and achieve buying economies that enable the group to compete effectively with chain organizations.

Retailer cooperatives. Retailers may take the initiative and organize a new business entity to carry on wholesaling and possibly production. Members concentrate their purchases through the retailer co-op and plan their advertising jointly. Profits are passed back to members in proportion to their purchases. Nonmember retailers may also buy through the co-op but do not share in the profits.

Franchise organizations. A channel member called a franchiser might link several successive stages in the production-distribution process. Franchising has been the fastest-growing and most interesting retailing development in recent years. Although the basic idea is an old one, some forms of franchising are quite new. Three forms of franchises can be distinguished.

The first is the *manufacturer-sponsored retailer* franchise system, exemplified by the automobile industry. Ford, for example, licenses dealers to sell its cars, the dealers being independent business people who agree to meet various conditions of sales and service.

The second is the *manufacturer-sponsored wholesaler* franchise system, which is found in the soft-drink industry. Coca-Cola, for example, licenses bottlers (wholesalers) in various markets who buy its syrup concentrate and then carbonate, bottle, and sell it to retailers in local markets.

The third is the *service-firm-sponsored retailer franchise system*. Here a service firm organizes a whole system for bringing its service efficiently to consumers. Examples are found in the auto rental business (Hertz, Avis), fast-food service business (McDonald's, Burger King), and motel business (Howard Johnson, Ramada Inn). This type of franchising system is discussed further in Chapter 18.

Many independent retailers, if they have not joined VMSs, have developed specialty stores that serve market segments that are not attractive to the mass merchandisers. The result is a polarization in retailing between large vertical marketing organizations, on the one hand, and specialty independent stores, on the other. This development creates a problem for manufacturers. They are strongly tied to independent middlemen whom they cannot easily give up. But they must eventually realign themselves with the high-growth vertical marketing systems and have to accept less attractive terms. Vertical marketing systems constantly threaten to bypass large manufacturers and set up their own manufacturing. *The new competition in retailing is no longer between independent business units but between whole systems of centrally programmed networks (corporate, administered, and contractual) competing against each other to achieve the best cost economies and customer response.*

Growth of Horizontal Marketing Systems

Another channel development is the readiness of two or more companies to join together to exploit an emerging marketing opportunity. Each company lacks the capital, know-how, production, or marketing resources to venture alone; or it is afraid of the risk; or it sees a substantial synergy in joining with another company. The companies may work with each other on a temporary or permanent basis or create a separate company. Adler calls this *symbiotic marketing*.[11] Here are two examples:

> Although Pillsbury had good acceptance in grocery outlets, it lacked the resources to market its new line of refrigerated dough for biscuits, cookies, and rolls because these products required special refrigerated display cases. But Kraft Foods Company was expert at selling its cheeses in this manner. The two firms set up an arrangement whereby Pillsbury makes and advertises its dough line while Kraft sells and distributes it.
>
> **Million Market Newspapers, Inc.**, is a sales company held in common by five newspapers—St. Louis Post-Dispatch, Washington Star, Boston Globe, Philadelphia Bulletin, and Milwaukee Journal-Sentinel. By selling these five markets in one convenient advertising package, the five newspapers all benefit.

Growth of Multichannel Marketing Systems

Companies are increasingly adopting multichannel systems to reach the same or different markets. For example, J. C. Penney operates department stores, mass-merchandising stores (called The Treasury), and specialty stores. Tillman has labeled multichannel retailing organizations *merchandising conglomerates* and defined them as "a multiline merchandising empire under central ownership, usually combining several styles of retailing with behind-the-scenes integration of some distribution and management function."[12]

Many companies operate multichannels that serve two different customer levels. Called *dual distribution*, this can breed conflicts for the sponsoring company.[13] For example, General Electric sells large home appliances through independent dealers (department stores, discount houses, catalog retailers) and also directly to large housing-tract builders, thus competing with retailers. The independent dealers would like General Electric to get out of the business of selling to tract builders. General Electric defends its position by pointing out that builders and retailers need very different marketing approaches.

---

[11] Lee Adler, "Symbiotic Marketing," *Harvard Business Review*, November-December 1966, pp. 59–71.

[12] Rollie Tillman, "Rise of the Conglomerchant," *Harvard Business Review*, November-December 1971, pp. 44–51.

[13] See Robert E. Weigand, "Fit Products and Channels to Your Markets," *Harvard Business Review*, January-February 1977, pp. 95–105.

Roles of Individual Firms in a Channel

Vertical, horizontal, and multichannel marketing systems underscore the dynamic and changing nature of channels. Each firm in an industry has to define its role in the channel system. McCammon has distinguished five roles:[14]

☐ **Insiders** are members of the dominant channel who enjoy access to preferred sources of supply and high respect in the industry. They want to perpetuate the existing channel arrangements and are the main enforcers of the industry code.

☐ **Strivers** are firms seeking to become insiders. They have less access to preferred sources of supply, which can handicap them in periods of short supply. They adhere to the industry code because of their desire to become insiders.

☐ **Complementors** are not part of the dominant channel. They perform functions not normally performed by others in the channel, or serve smaller segments of the market, or handle smaller quantities of merchandise. They usually benefit from the present system and respect the industry code.

☐ **Transients** are outside the dominant channel and do not seek membership. They go in and out of the market and move around as opportunities arise. They have short-run expectations and little incentive to adhere to the industry code.

☐ **Outside innovators** are the real challengers and disrupters of the dominant channels. They develop a new system for carrying out the marketing work of the channel; if successful, they force major channel realignments. They are companies like McDonald's, Avon, and Holiday Inn, which doggedly develop new systems to challenge the old.

Another important channel role is that of *channel captain*. The channel captain is the dominant member of a particular channel, the one who organized it and leads it. For example, General Motors is the channel captain of a system consisting of a huge number of suppliers, dealers, and facilitators. The channel captain is not always a manufacturer, as the examples of McDonald's and Sears indicate. Some channels do not have a channel captain in that each firm proceeds on its own.

Channel Cooperation, Conflict, and Competition

Different degrees of cooperation, conflict, and competition can be found within and between marketing channels.

Channel cooperation is usually the dominant theme among vertical members of the same channel. The channel represents a coalition of dissimilar firms that have banded together for mutual advantage. Manufacturers, wholesalers, and retailers complement each other's needs, and their cooperation normally produces greater profits than each participant could have obtained individually. By cooperating, they can more effectively sense, serve, and satisfy the target market.

Channel conflict, however, often arises within the channel. *Horizontal* channel *conflict* describes conflict occurring between member firms at the same level of the channel. Some Ford car dealers in Chicago complain about other Ford dealers in

---

[14] Bert C. McCammon, Jr., "Alternative Explanations of Institutional Change and Channel Evolution," in *Toward Scientific Marketing*, ed. Stephen A. Greyser (Chicago: American Marketing Association, 1963), pp. 477–90.

the city being too aggressive in their pricing and advertising and stealing sales from them. Some Pizza Inn franchisees complain about other Pizza Inn franchisees cheating on the ingredients, maintaining poor service, and hurting the overall Pizza Inn image. In these cases, the *channel captain* must establish clear and enforceable policies and take quick action to control this type of conflict.

Vertical channel conflict is even more common and refers to conflicts of interest between different levels of the same channel. For example, General Motors came into conflict with its dealers some years ago in trying to enforce policies on service, pricing, and advertising. And Coca-Cola came into conflict with its bottlers who agreed to bottle Dr. Pepper. Some amount of vertical channel conflict is inevitable, and the problem is not one of eliminating it but of managing it better. The channel captain should develop *superordinate goals* that everyone could support. Superordinate goals would include trying to minimize the total cost of moving the product through the system, improving information flows within the system, and cooperating to increase consumer acceptance of the product. Also *administrative mechanisms* should be developed to increase participation and trust and to help resolve conflicts; examples are dealer and distributor councils and conciliation, mediation, and arbitration mechanisms.[15]

Channel competition is another aspect of channel relations and describes the normal competition between firms and systems trying to serve the same target markets. *Horizontal channel competition* occurs between competitors at the same channel level seeking sales in the same market. Thus department stores, discount stores, and catalog houses all compete for the consumer's appliance dollar. This competition should result in consumers' enjoying a wider range of choice of products, prices, and services. *Channel system competition* describes the competition between different whole systems serving a given market. For example, food consumers are served by conventional marketing channels, corporate chains, wholesaler-sponsored voluntary chains, retailer cooperatives, and food franchise systems. Each system will have some loyal followers, but the share of the different systems in the total food business will shift over time toward those systems that are best able to meet changing consumer needs.

CHANNEL-DESIGN DECISIONS

We will now examine several channel-decision problems facing manufacturers. In designing marketing channels, manufacturers have to struggle between what is ideal and what is available. A new firm typically starts as a local or regional operation selling in a limited market. Since it has limited capital, it usually uses existing middlemen. The number of middlemen in any local market is apt to be limited: A few manufacturer's sales agents, a few wholesalers, several established retailers, a few trucking companies, and a few warehouses. Deciding on the best channels might not be a problem. The problem might be to convince one or a few available middlemen to handle the line.

---

[15] For an excellent summary of interorganizational conflict and power in marketing channels, see Louis W. Stern and Adel I. El-Ansary, *Marketing Channels*, 2nd. ed., (Englewood Cliffs, N.J.: Prentice-Hall, 1982), Chap. 7.

If the new firm is successful, it might branch out to new markets. Again, the manufacturer will tend to work through the existing intermediaries, although this might mean using different types of marketing channels in different areas. In the smaller markets the firm might sell directly to retailers; in the larger markets it might sell through distributors. In rural areas it might work with general-goods merchants; in urban areas, with limited-line merchants. In one part of the country it might grant exclusive franchises because the merchants normally work this way; in another, it might sell through all outlets willing to handle the merchandise. Thus the manufacturer's channel system evolves in response to local opportunities and conditions.

Designing a channel system calls for establishing the channel objectives and constraints, identifying the major channel alternatives, and evaluating them.

Establishing the Channel Objectives and Constraints

Effective channel planning begins with a determination of which markets are to be reached with what objectives. The objectives include the desired level of customer service, the desired functions that intermediaries should perform, and so on. Each producer develops its channel objectives in the context of constraints stemming from the customers, products, intermediaries, competitors, company policies, and the environment.

Customer characteristics. Channel design is greatly influenced by customer characteristics. When trying to reach a large and/or widely dispersed customer population, long channels are needed. If customers buy small amounts frequently, long channels are needed because of the high cost of filling small and frequent orders.

Product characteristics. *Perishable* products require more direct marketing because of the dangers associated with delays and repeated handling. *Bulky* products, such as building materials or soft drinks, require channel arrangements that minimize the shipping distance and the number of handlings in the movement from producer to consumers. *Nonstandardized* products, such as custom-built machinery and specialized business forms, are sold directly by company sales representatives because middlemen lack the requisite knowledge. Products requiring installation and/or maintenance services are usually sold and maintained by the company or exclusively franchised dealers. *High unit value* products are often sold through a company sales force rather than through middlemen.

Middlemen characteristics. Channel design reflects the strengths and weaknesses of different types of intermediaries in handling various tasks. For example, manufacturers' representatives are able to contact customers at a low cost per customer because the total cost is shared by several clients. But the selling effort per customer is less intense than if the company's sales representatives did the selling. In general, marketing intermediaries differ in their aptitude for handling promotion, negotiation, storage, contact, and credit.

Competitive characteristics. Channel design is influenced by the competitors' channels. The producers may want to compete in or near the same outlets carrying the competitors' products. Thus food processors want their brands to be displayed next to competitive brands; and Burger King wants to locate next to McDonald's. In other industries, producers may want to avoid the channels used by competitors. Avon decided not to compete with other cosmetics manufacturers for scarce positions in retail stores and established instead a profitable door-to-door selling operation.

Company characteristics. Company characteristics play an important role in channel selection. The company's *size* determines the size of its markets and its ability to secure desired dealers. Its *financial resources* determine which marketing functions it can handle and which to delegate to intermediaries. The company's *product mix* influences its channel pattern. The wider its product mix, the greater the company's ability to deal with customers directly. The greater the depth of the company's product mix, the more it might favor exclusive or selective dealers. The more consistent the company's product mix, the greater the homogeneity of its marketing channels. The company's *marketing strategy* will influence channel design. Thus a policy of speedy customer delivery affects the functions the producer wants intermediaries to perform, the number of final-stage outlets and stocking points, and the choice of transportation carriers.

Environmental characteristics. When *economic conditions* are depressed, producers want to move their goods to market in the most economical way. This means using shorter channels and dispensing with inessential services that add to the final price of the goods. *Legal regulations and restrictions* also affect channel design. The law has sought to prevent channel arrangements that "may tend to substantially lessen competition or tend to create a monopoly."

Identifying the Major Channel Alternatives

Suppose a manufacturing company has defined its target market and desired positioning. It should next identify its major channel alternatives. A channel alternative is described by three elements: the *types of business intermediaries*, the *number of intermediaries*, and the *terms and mutual responsibilities* of each channel participant.

Types of intermediaries. The firm should identify the types of intermediaries available to carry on its channel work. Consider the following example:

> A manufacturer of test equipment developed an audio device for detecting poor mechanical connections in any machine with moving parts. The company executives felt that this product would have a market in all industries where electric, combustion, or steam engines were used or manufactured. This meant such industries as aviation, automobiles, railroads, food canning, construction, and oil. The company's sales force was small, and the problem was how to reach these diverse industries effectively. The following channel alternatives came out of management discussion:

> **Company sales force.** Expand the company's direct sales force. Assign sales representatives to territories and give them responsibility for contacting all prospects in the area. Or develop separate company sales forces for the different industries.
>
> **Manufacturer's agency.** Hire manufacturer's agencies in different regions or end-use industries to sell the new test equipment.
>
> **Industrial distributors.**[16] Find distributors in the different regions and/or end-use industries who will buy and carry the new line. Give them exclusive distribution, adequate margins, product training, and promotional support.

Here is another example:

> A consumer electronics company decided to use its excess capacity to produce FM car radios. In considering channels of distribution, it came up with the following alternatives:
>
> **OEM market.** The company could seek a contract with one or more automobile manufacturers to buy its radios for factory installation on original equipment. OEM stands for **original equipment manufacture**.
>
> **Auto dealer market.** The company could sell its radios to various auto dealers for replacement sales when they service cars.
>
> **Retail automotive parts dealers.** The company could sell its radios to the public through retail automotive parts dealers. They could reach these dealers through a direct sales force or through distributors.
>
> **Mail-order market.** The company could arrange to have its radios advertised in mail-order catalogs.

Companies should also search for more innovative marketing channels. This happened when the Conn Organ Company decided to merchandise organs through department and discount stores, thus drawing more attention than organs ever enjoyed in small music stores. A daring new channel was exploited when the Book-of-the-Month Club decided to merchandise books through the mails. Other sellers followed soon after with record-of-the-month clubs, candy-of-the-month clubs, and dozens of others.

Sometimes a company has to develop a channel other than the one it prefers because of the difficulty or cost of breaking into the preferred channel. The decision sometimes turns out extremely well. For example, the U.S. Time Company originally tried to sell its inexpensive Timex watches through regular jewelery stores. But most jewelry stores refused to carry them. The company looked for other channels, and managed to get its watches into mass-merchandise outlets. This turned out to be a great decision because of the rapid growth of mass merchandising.

Number of intermediaries.   Companies have to decide on the number of middlemen to use at each channel level. Three strategies are available.

Intensive distribution.   Producers of convenience goods and common raw materials typically seek *intensive distribution*—that is, stocking their product in as many outlets

---

[16] For reading on industrial distributors, see James D. Hlavacek and Tommy J. McCuistion, "Industrial Distributors—When, Who, and How?" *Harvard Business Review*, March-April, 1983, pp. 96–101.

as possible. These goods must have place utility. Cigarettes, for example, sell in over one million outlets to create maximum brand exposure and convenience.

Exclusive distribution.   Some producers deliberately limit the number of intermediaries handling their products. The extreme form of this is *exclusive distribution*, where a limited number of dealers are granted the exclusive right to distribute the company's products in their respective territories. It often goes with *exclusive dealing*, where the manufacturer requires these dealers not to carry competing lines. Exclusive distribution is found to some extent in the distribution of new automobiles, some major appliances, and some women's apparel brands. Through granting exclusive distribution, the manufacturer hopes for more aggressive and knowledgeable selling and more control over intermediaries' policies on prices, promotion, credit, and various services. Exclusive distribution tends to enhance the product's image and allow higher markups.

Selective distribution.   Between intensive and exclusive distribution stands *selective distribution*—the use of more than one but less than all of the intermediaries who are willing to carry a particular product. It is used both by established companies and by new companies seeking to obtain distributors by promising them selective distribution. The company does not have to dissipate its efforts over many outlets, including many marginal ones. It can develop a good working relation with the selected middlemen and expect a better than average selling effort. Selective distribution enables the producer to gain adequate market coverage with more control and less cost than intensive distribution.

Terms and responsibilities of channel members.

The producer must determine the conditions and responsibilities of the participating channel members. The main elements in the "trade-relations mix" are the *price policies*, the *conditions of sale*, the *territorial rights*, and the *specific services to be performed by each party*.

Price policy calls for the producer to establish a list price and schedule of discounts. The producer must be sure that discounts strike the middleman as equitable and sufficient.

Conditions of sale refer to the payment terms and to producer guarantees. Most producers grant cash discounts to their distributors for early payment. Producers may also extend guarantees to distributors regarding defective merchandise or price declines. A guarantee against price declines is used to induce distributors to buy larger quantities.

Distributors' territorial rights are another element in the trade-relations mix. Distributors want to know where the producer will enfranchise other distributors. They would also like to receive full credit for all sales taking place in their territory, whether or not these sales occurred through their personal efforts.

Mutual services and responsibilities must be carefully spelled out, especially in franchised- and exclusive-agency channels. For example, the Howard Johnson Company provides restaurant leaseholders with a building, promotional support, a record-keeping system, training, and general administrative and technical assistance. In turn, leaseholders are expected to satisfy company standards regarding physical facilities, cooperate with new promotional programs, furnish requested information, and buy specified food products.

Evaluating the Major Channel Alternatives

Suppose a producer has identified several channel alternatives and wants to determine the one that would best satisfy the firm's long-run objectives. Each alternative needs to be evaluated against *economic*, *control*, and *adaptive* criteria. Consider the following situation:

A Memphis furniture manufacturer wants to sell its line to retailers on the West Coast. The manufacturer is trying to decide between two alternatives.

1. One alternative calls for hiring ten new **sales representatives** who would operate out of a sales office in San Francisco. They would receive a base salary plus commissions based on their sales.

2. The other alternative would use a San Francisco **manufacturer's sales agency** that has extensive contacts with retailers. The agency has thirty sales representatives, who would receive a commission based on their sales.

Economic criteria. Each channel alternative will produce a different level of sales and costs. The first issue is whether more sales will be produced through a company sales force or through a sales agency. Most marketing managers believe that a company sales force will sell more. Company sales representatives concentrate entirely on the company's products; they are better trained to sell the company's products; they are more aggressive because their future depends on the company; they are more successful because customers prefer to deal directly with the company.

On the other hand, the sales agency could conceivably sell more than a company sales force. First, the sales agent has thirty sales representatives, not just ten. Second, the agency's sales force may be just as aggressive as a direct sales force. That depends on how much commission the line offers in relation to the other lines carried. Third, some customers prefer dealing with agents who represent several manufacturers rather than with salespersons from one company. Fourth, the agency has extensive contacts, whereas a company sales force would have to build them up from scratch.

The next step is to estimate the costs of selling different volumes through each channel. The cost schedules are shown in Figure 17–5. The fixed costs of engaging a sales agency are lower than those of establishing a company sales office. But costs rise faster through a sales agency because sales agents get a larger commission than company sales people.

There is one sales level (S_B) at which selling costs are the same for the two channels. The sales agency would be the preferred channel at any sales volume below S_B, and the company sales branch would be preferred at any volume higher than S_B. In general, sales agents tend to be used by smaller firms, or by larger firms in their smaller territories wherever the sales volume is too low to warrant a company sales force.

Control criteria. The evaluation must be broadened to consider control issues with the two channels. Using a sales agency poses more of a control problem. A sales agency is an independent business firm interested in maximizing its profits. The agent

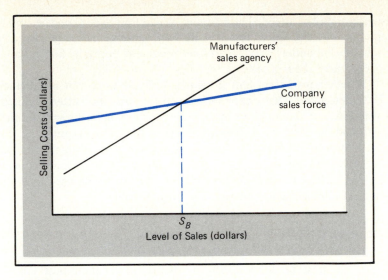

FIGURE 17-5
Break-Even Cost Chart for the Choice Between a Company Sales Force
and a Manufacturer's Sales Agency

may concentrate on the customers who are the most important in terms of the assortment they buy rather than for their level of interest in the particular manufacturer's goods. Furthermore, the agent's sales force may not master the technical details concerning the company's product or handle its promotion materials effectively.

Adaptive criteria. Each channel involves some duration of commitment and loss of flexibility. A manufacturer using a sales agency may have to offer a five-year contract. During this period, other means of selling, such as direct mail, may become more effective, but the manufacturer is not free to drop the sales agency. A channel involving a long commitment should be greatly superior on economic or control grounds to be considered.

CHANNEL-MANAGEMENT DECISIONS

After a company has chosen a channel alternative, individual middlemen must be *selected*, *motivated*, and *evaluated*.

Selecting Channel Members

Producers vary in their ability to attract qualified middlemen for the proposed channel. Some producers have no trouble recruiting middlemen. For example, Ford was able to attract 1,200 new dealers for its ill-fated Edsel. In some cases the promise of exclusive or selective distribution will draw a sufficient number of applicants.

At the other extreme are producers who have to work hard to line up the desired number of qualified middlemen. When Polaroid started, it could not get photographic-equipment stores to carry its new cameras and was forced to go to mass-merchandising outlets. And small food producers normally find it hard to get grocery stores to carry their products.

Whether producers find it easy or difficult to recruit middlemen, they should at least determine what characteristics distinguish the better middlemen. They will want to evaluate the middlemen's number of years in business, the other lines carried, growth and profit record, solvency, cooperativeness, and reputation. If the middlemen are sales agents, producers will want to evaluate the number and character of other lines carried and the size and quality of the sales force. If the middleman is a department store that wants exclusive distribution, the producer will want to evaluate the store's location, future growth potential, and type of clientele.

Motivating Channel Members

Middlemen must be continuously motivated to do their best job. The terms that lead them to join the channel provide some of the motivation, but these must be supplemented by continuous supervision and encouragement from the producer. The producer must sell not only through the middlemen but to them.

Stimulating channel members to top performance must start with the manufacturer's attempting to understand the needs and wants of the particular middleman. According to McVey, manufacturers often criticize middlemen "for failure to stress a given brand, or for the poor quality of his salesman's product knowledge, his disuse of supplier's advertising materials, his neglect of certain customers (who may be good prospects for individual items but not for the assortment), and even for his unrefined systems of record keeping, in which brand designations may be lost."[17] However, these shortcomings from the manufacturer's point of view may be understandable from the middleman's point of view. McVey listed the following propositions to help understand middlemen:

The middleman is not a hired link in a chain forged by a manufacturer, but rather an independent market. . . . After some experimentation, he settles upon a method of operation, performing those functions he deems inescapable in the light of his own objectives, forming policies for himself wherever he has freedom to do so. . . .

[The middleman often acts] as a purchasing agent for his customers and only secondarily as a selling agent for his suppliers. . . . He is interested in selling any product which these customers desire to buy from him. . . .

The middleman attempts to weld all of his offerings into a family of items which he can sell in combination, as a packaged assortment, to individual customers. His selling efforts are directed primarily at obtaining orders for the assortment, rather than for individual items. . . .

Unless given incentive to do so, middlemen will not maintain separate sales records by brands sold. . . . Information that could be used in product development, pricing,

---

[17] Phillip McVey, "Are Channels of Distribution What the Textbooks Say?" *Journal of Marketing*, January 1960, pp. 61–64.

packaging, or promotion-planning is buried in nonstandard records of middlemen, and sometimes purposely secreted from suppliers.[18]

Producers vary greatly in how they handle their distributor relations. We can distinguish three approaches: *cooperation, partnership*, and *distribution programming*.[19]

Most producers see the problem as finding ways to gain middleman *cooperation*. They will use the carrot-and-stick approach. They will use such positive motivators as higher margins, special deals, premiums, cooperative advertising allowances, display allowances, and sales contests. At times they will apply negative sanctions, such as threatening to reduce the margins, slow down delivery, or terminate the relationship. The weakness of this approach is that the producer has not really studied the needs, problems, strengths, and weaknesses of the distributors. Instead the producer applies miscellaneous motivators based on crude stimulus-response thinking. McCammon notes that many manufacturer programs "consist of hastily improvised trade deals, uninspired dealer contests, and unexamined discount structures."[20]

More sophisticated companies try to forge a long-term *partnership* with their distributors. The manufacturer develops a clear sense of what it wants from its distributors and what its distributors can expect in terms of market coverage, product availability, market development, account solicitation, technical advice and services, and market information. The manufacturer seeks an agreement from its distributors on these policies and may base compensation on their adhering to these policies. In one case, the company, instead of paying a straight 25 percent sales commission, pays the following:

> Five percent for carrying the proper level of inventory
> Another 5 percent for meeting the sales quotas
> Another 5 percent for servicing the customers effectively
> Another 5 percent for proper reporting of customer-purchase levels
> Another 5 percent for proper accounts-receivables management

Distribution programming is the most advanced arrangement. McCammon defines this as building a planned, professionally managed, vertical marketing system that incorporates the needs of both the manufacturer and the distributors.[21] The manufacturer establishes a department within the marketing department called distributor relations planning, and its job is to identify the distributors' needs and build up merchandising programs to help each distributor operate as optimally as possible. This department and the distributors jointly plan the merchandising goals, inventory

[18] Ibid.

[19] See Bert Rosenbloom, *Marketing Channels: A Management View* (Hinsdale, Ill.: Dryden Press, 1978), pp. 192–203.

[20] McCammon, "Perspectives for Distribution Programming," p. 32.

[21] Ibid., p. 43.

levels, space and visual merchandising plans, sales-training requirements, and advertising and promotion plans. The aim is to convert the distributors from thinking that they make their money primarily on the buying side (through an adversary relation with the supplier) to seeing that they make their money on the selling side by being part of a sophisticated vertical marketing system.

Evaluating Channel Members

The producer must periodically evaluate middlemen's performance against such standards as sales-quota attainment, average inventory levels, customer delivery time, treatment of damaged and lost goods, cooperation in company promotional and training programs, and middleman services owed to the customer.

The producer typically sets sales quotas for the middlemen. After each period, the producer should check the sales-to-quota performance of each middleman. Diagnostic and motivational effort should then be focused on the underachieving middlemen.

CHANNEL-MODIFICATION DECISIONS

A producer must do more than design a good channel system and set it into motion. The system will require periodic modification to meet new conditions in the marketplace.

This fact struck a large household-appliance manufacturer who had been marketing exclusively through franchised dealers and was losing market share. Several distribution developments had taken place since the original channel was designed:

☐ An increasing share of major-brand appliances were being merchandised through discount houses.
☐ An increasing share of major appliances were being sold on a private-brand basis through large department stores.
☐ A new market was developing in the form of volume purchases by tract home builders who preferred to deal directly with the manufacturers.
☐ Door-to-door and direct-mail solicitation of orders was being undertaken by some dealers and competitors.
☐ The only strong independent dealers were located in small towns, but rural families were increasingly making their purchases in large cities.

These developments led this manufacturer to undertake a major review of possible channel modifications.

Three levels of channel modification should be distinguished. The change could involve adding or dropping individual channel members, adding or dropping particular market channels, or developing a totally new way to sell goods in all markets.

Adding or dropping specific middlemen requires an incremental analysis. What would the firm's profits look like with and without this middleman? An automobile manufacturer's decision to drop a dealer would require subtracting the dealer's sales and estimating the possible loss or gain of sales to the manufacturer's other dealers.

Sometimes a producer contemplates dropping all middlemen whose sales are below a certain amount. For example, a truck manufacturer noted that 5 percent of its dealers were selling fewer than three or four trucks a year. It cost the company more to service these dealers than their sales were worth. However, the decision to drop these dealers could have large repercussions on the system as a whole. The unit costs of producing trucks would be higher since the overhead would be spread over fewer trucks; some employees and equipment would be idled; some business in these markets would go to competitors; and other dealers might become insecure. All of this would have to be taken into account.

The most difficult decision involves revising the overall channel strategy. For example, an automobile manufacturer may consider replacing independent dealers with company-owned dealers; a soft-drink manufacturer may consider replacing local franchised bottlers with centralized bottling and direct sales. These decisions would require revising most of the marketing mix and would have profound consequences.

A Conceptual Approach to the Problem of Channel Modification

In analyzing a proposed channel modification, the issue is whether the channel is in equilibrium. A channel is in equilibrium when there is no structural or functional change that would lead to increased profits. A structural change involves adding or eliminating some middleman level in the channel. A functional change involves reallocating one or more channel tasks among the channel members. A channel is ripe for change when it is in disequilibrium.

Assume there is a channel of the manufacturer-wholesaler-retailer type (M-W-R). (See Figure 17–6.) Each channel member makes decisions on price, advertising, and distribution (P,A,D), which affect the succeeding stage decisions. Thus the producer makes decisions $(P,A,D)_1$, which influence the quantity (Q_1) ordered by the wholesaler. The producer calculates net profits (Z_1) by subtracting its costs from its revenue from the wholesaler. Each channel member makes independent decisions that influence its revenue and cost and bring about a particular net profit.

Looking at the channel as a whole, a set of independent decisions is made

FIGURE 17–6
Conceptual Picture of the Profits in a Marketing Channel

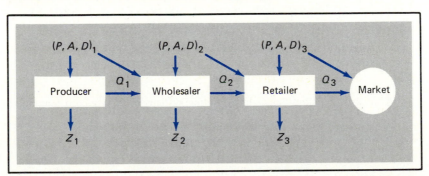

Source: Redrawn, with modifications, from Stanley Stasch, "A Method of Dynamically Analyzing the Stability of the Economic Structure of Channels of Distribution" (Ph.D. dissertation, School of Business, Northwestern University, 1964), p. 63.

$[(PAD)_1, (PAD)_2, (PAD)_3]$ that results in some total channel profit $(Z_1 + Z_2 + Z_3)$. The channel is in disequilibrium if there exists an alternative set of decisions $[(P,A,D)_1, (P,A,D)_2, (P,A,D)_3]^*$ that would result in higher channel profits $(Z_1 + Z_2 + Z_3)^*$. If this is the case, the channel presents an opportunity for increased profit. But the alternative decisions are not likely to be made as long as the channel members make their decisions independently. The greater the difference between $(Z_1 + Z_2 + Z_3)^*$ and $(Z_1 + Z_2 + Z_3)$, the greater the channel members' incentive to pursue joint planning or for some channel member to absorb one or more of the others to achieve the extra profits gained from coordinated decision making.[22]

SUMMARY

Marketing-channel decisions are among the most complex and challenging decisions facing the firm. Each channel system creates a different level of sales and costs. Once a particular marketing channel is chosen, the firm must usually adhere to it for a substantial period. The chosen channel will significantly affect and be affected by the other elements in the marketing mix.

Each firm needs to identify alternative ways to reach the market. They vary from direct selling to using one, two, three, or more intermediary-channel levels. The organizations making up the marketing channel are connected by physical, title, payment, information, and promotion flows. Marketing channels are characterized by continuous and sometimes dramatic change. Three of the most significant trends are the growth of vertical, horizontal, and multichannel marketing systems. These trends have important implications for channel cooperation, conflict, and competition.

Channel design calls for establishing the channel objectives and constraints, identifying the major channel alternatives (types and number of intermediaries), and the channel terms and responsibilities. Each channel alternative has to be evaluated according to economic, control, and adaptive criteria.

Channel management calls for selecting particular middlemen and motivating them with a cost-effective trade-relations mix. Individual channel members must be periodically evaluated against their own past sales and other channel members' sales.

Channel modification must be performed periodically because of the continuously changing marketing environment. The company has to evaluate adding or dropping individual middlemen or individual channels and possibly modifying the whole channel system.

QUESTIONS

1. Describe the multichannel marketing systems used by record manufacturers.

2. "In a battle between giants like Procter & Gamble and Safeway (supermarket chain) five years ago, P&G would have prevailed. Now Safeway can call the tune." What has caused the change in power?

---

[22] See Stanley Stasch, "A Method of Dynamically Analyzing the Stability of the Economic Structure of Channels of Distribution," (Ph.D. dissertation, Graduate School of Management, Northwestern University, 1964).

3. Sears acquired Dean Witter Reynolds, the fifth largest stock brokerage firm, in 1981, in order to capitalize on the growing demand for financial services. They have opened financial service centers in their stores, offering money market funds, casualty and life insurance, credit cards, auto and boat installment loans, etc. What forces are working for and against the success of such a venture?

4. In a market consisting of five producers and five customers, how many contacts would have to be made (a) without a middleman? (b) with a middleman? What are the general formulas?

5. Explain how the characteristics of (a) peaches and (b) cement affect the channels for them.

6. Suggest some alternative channels for (a) a small firm that has developed a radically new harvesting machine, (b) a small plastic manufacturer who has developed a picnic pack for keeping bottles and food cold, and (c) a manufacturer of expensive watches.

7. Can you think of a radically different way to organize the distribution of (a) automobiles? (b) beer?

8. "Middlemen are parasites." This charge has been made by many over the centuries. Is this likely to be the case in a competitive economic system? Why or why not?

9. There is often conflict between manufacturers and retailers. What does each party really want from the other, and why does this give rise to conflict?

Retailing, Wholesaling, and Physical-Distribution Decisions

18

*When is a refrigerator not a refrigerator? . . . . when
it is in Pittsburgh at the time it is desired in Houston.*

J. L. HESKETT, N. A. GLASKOWSKY, R. M. IVIE

In this chapter, we will look at the specific institutions that make up marketing channels, among them, retailers, wholesalers, transportation carriers, and warehouses. We will examine these institutions from two perspectives. First, we will look at them through the eyes of a producer who has to select and link these institutions to carry the final product to consumers. Producers need to know the nuances of each type of institution, especially given the rapid changes going on in distribution. Second, we will look at them from the point of view of marketing intermediaries, who also face challenging marketing problems. Intermediaries have to define their target clients, develop appropriate assortments, and formulate effective marketing strategies.

We will ask the following questions about each sector (retailers, wholesalers, and physical-distribution firms): What is the nature and importance of this sector? What are the major types of institutions within this sector? What marketing decisions do institutions in this sector make? and What is the future of this sector?

Nature and Importance of Retailing

Retailing includes all the activities involved in selling goods or services directly to final consumers for their personal, nonbusiness use. Any institution that does this selling—whether a manufacturer, wholesaler, or retailer—is doing retailing. It does not matter *how* the goods or services are sold (by person, mail, telephone, or vending machine) or *where* they are sold (in a store, on the street, or in the consumer's home). On the other hand, a *retailer* or *retail store* is any business enterprise whose sales volume primarily comes from retailing.

Retailing is one of the major industries in the United States. Retail stores constitute approximately 18 percent of all U.S. businesses, outnumbering manufacturing and wholesaling establishments by more than seven to one, and representing the third-largest source of employment in the nation, with over 15 million employees. The industry is composed of over 1.5 million single-unit establishments and over 332,000 multiunit establishments, and it generated a total of approximately $886 billion in sales in 1979. The largest retailers and their sales in billions in 1981 were Sears Roebuck ($27.4), Safeway Stores ($16.6), K-Mart ($16.5), J. C. Penney ($11.9), Kroger ($11.3), F. W. Woolworth ($7.2), Lucky Stores ($7.2), American Stores ($7.1), and Federated Department Stores ($6.1).

Types of Retailers

Retailing institutions exhibit great variety and new forms keep emerging. Several classifications have been proposed. Before getting to the one we will use, we will look at some others.

Retailing institutions can be classified into four groups according to their *level of service*. (See Table 18–1.)

☐ **Self-service retailing.** Used in many retailing operations, especially for obtaining convenience goods and, to some extent, shopping goods. Self-service is the cornerstone of all discount operations. Many customers are willing to carry out their own locate-compare-select process to save money.

☐ **Self-selection retailing.** Involves customers in finding their own goods, although they can ask for assistance. Customers complete their transactions by finding a salesperson to take the money for the item. Self-selection institutions have higher operating expenses than self-service operations because of the additional staff requirements.

☐ **Limited-service retailing.** Provides more sales assistance because these stores carry more shopping goods, and customers need more information. The stores also offer services, such as credit and merchandise return, not normally found in less service-oriented stores and hence have higher operating costs.

☐ **Full-service retailing.** Provides sales people who are ready to assist in every phase of the locate-compare-select process. Customers who like to be waited on prefer this type of store. The high staffing cost, along with the higher proportion of specialty goods and slower-moving items (fashions, jewelry, cameras), the more liberal merchandise-return policies, various credit plans, free delivery, home servicing of durables, and customer facilities such as lounges and restaurants, results in high-cost retailing.

TABLE 18-1

CLASSIFICATION OF RETAILERS BASED ON THE AMOUNT OF CUSTOMER SERVICE			

Decreasing Services ────────────────────► Increasing Services

	Self-service	Self-selection	Limited-service	Full-service
Attributes	Very few services Price appeal Staple goods Convenience goods	Restricted services Price appeal Staple goods Convenience goods	Small variety of services Shopping goods	Wide variety of services Fashion merchandise Specialty merchandise
Examples	Warehouse retailing Grocery stores Discount stores Mail-order retailing Automatic vending	Discount retailing Variety stores Mail-order retailing	Door-to-door sales Department stores Telephone sales Variety stores	Speciality stores Department stores

SOURCE: Adapted from Larry D. Redinbaugh, Retailing Management: A Planning Approach (New York: McGraw-Hill Book Co., 1976), p. 12.

FIGURE 18-1
Classification Schemes for Types of Retailers

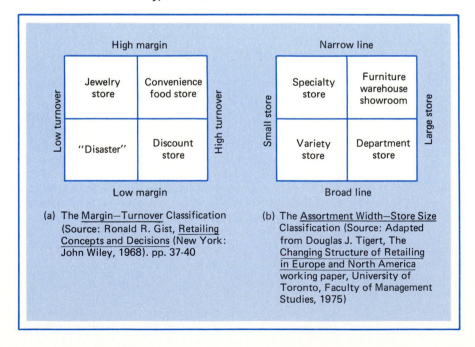

(a) The Margin–Turnover Classification (Source: Ronald R. Gist, Retailing Concepts and Decisions (New York: John Wiley, 1968). pp. 37-40

(b) The Assortment Width–Store Size Classification (Source: Adapted from Douglas J. Tigert, The Changing Structure of Retailing in Europe and North America working paper, University of Toronto, Faculty of Management Studies, 1975)

Two other schemes for classifying retailers are shown in Figure 18–1. Gist has developed a margin-turnover classification that distinguishes retail store types according to their margins and volumes. [See Figure 18–1(a).] A discount store, for example, works on low margins and high turnover. Other combinations of profitable retailing are possible, except a low-margin–low-turnover strategy.

Tigert proposed classifying retailers by assortment width and store size. [See Figure 18–1(b).] For instance, a furniture showroom warehouse is a large store featuring a narrow product line. Other types of stores can be located in this grid.

Thus we see that there are several ways to classify retailing institutions. We will use the following principles of classification: *product line sold*, *relative price emphasis*, *nature of business premises*, *control of outlets*, and *type of store cluster*. The corresponding retailer types are shown in Table 18–2 and described below.

Product line sold.   The first basis for classifying retailing institutions is according to the product line sold. Thus one finds grocery stores, liquor stores, furniture stores, and so on. More broadly, we can look at the length and depth of the product assortment and distinguish some major store types. Among the most important ones are the specialty store, department store, supermarket, convenience store, superstore, combination store, hypermarche, and service business.

Specialty store.   A specialty store carries a narrow product line with a deep assortment within that line. Examples of specialty retailers are apparel stores, sporting goods stores, furniture stores, florists, and bookstores. Specialty stores can be subclassified by the degree of narrowness in their product line. A clothing store would be a *single-line store*; a men's clothing store would be a *limited-line store*; and a men's custom-shirt store would be a *superspecialty store*. Some analysts contend that superspecialty

TABLE 18–2

DIFFERENT WAYS TO CLASSIFY RETAIL OUTLETS				
Product Line Sold	Relative Price Emphasis	Nature of Business Premises	Control of Outlets	Type of Store Cluster
Specialty store	Discount store	Mail-and-telephone-order retailing	Corporate chain	Central business district
Department store	Warehouse store		Voluntary chain and retailer cooperative	Regional shopping center
Supermarket	Catalog showroom	Automatic vending	Consumer cooperative	Community shopping center
Convenience store		Buying service	Franchise organization	Neighborhood shopping center
Combination store, superstore, and hypermarche		Door-to-door retailing	Merchandising conglomerate	
Service business				

stores will grow the fastest in the future, to take advantage of increasing opportunities for market segmentation, market targeting, and product specialization. Some of the successful current examples are Athlete's Foot (sport shoes only), Tall Men (tallmen's clothing), The Gap (primarily jeans), and Calculators, Inc. (primarily calculators).

The recent growth of specialty stores is tied to the boom of shopping centers, which typically have one or two anchor department stores and numerous specialty stores, the latter occupying 60 to 70 percent of the total shopping space. Although most specialty stores are independently owned, chain specialty stores are showing the strongest growth. The most successful chain specialty stores zero in on the needs of specific target markets.

> The Limited specializes in high-fashion clothes for the woman who is eighteen to thirty-five years old and is willing to pay a little more to get just the right look. The merchandise is presented in coordinated outfits, the employees are fashionably dressed and of the same age as the target market, and the store has a contemporary atmosphere. Having defined its target market carefully, The Limited can study the fashion interests of eighteen- to thirty-five-year-old women; it can pretest new fashion ideas; it can build a unique image; it can aim its advertising carefully; and it can locate in shopping centers.

Department store.   A department store carries several product lines, typically clothing, home furnishings, and household goods, where each line is operated as a separate department managed by specialist buyers or merchandisers. Examples of well-known department stores are Bloomingdale's (New York), Marshall Field (Chicago), and Filene's (Boston).

The Bon Marché, established in Paris in 1852, was the first department store.[1] It introduced several innovative principles, including low markups and rapid turnover, marking and displaying the prices of merchandise, encouraging customers to look around without any pressure or obligation to purchase, and a liberal complaints policy. The earliest department stores in America included Jordan Marsh, Macy's, Wanamaker's, and Stewart's. These stores were housed in huge, impressive buildings in fashionable central locations. They sold the concept of "shopping for enjoyment." With urban growth, the department store developed as the major retailing institution in the downtown areas. *Specialty department stores* also emerged, carrying only clothing, shoes, cosmetics, gift items, and luggage; examples are Saks Fifth Avenue and I. Magnin.

Starting in the post-World War II period, department stores declined in their share of total retailing and in their profitability. Many observers believe that these stores are in the declining stage of the *retail life cycle*. They point to the increased competition among department stores, which has escalated their operating and overhead costs to about 35 percent of sales; the increased competition coming from other types of retailers, particularly discount houses, specialty-store chains, and warehouse retailers; and the heavy traffic, poor parking, and deterioration of central cities, which have made downtown shopping less appealing.

---

[1] Ernest Samhaber, *Merchants Make History*, (New York, Harper & Row, 1964), pp. 345–48.

The result has been the closing of some department stores and the amalgamation of others. Department stores are waging a "comeback" war that is taking several forms. Many have opened branches in suburban shopping centers, where there is better parking, and the shoppers come from areas with more population growth and higher incomes. Others have added "bargain basements" to meet the discount threat. Still others are remodeling their stores, including "going boutique." Some are experimenting with mail-order and telephone shopping. Others, like Dayton-Hudson, have diversified into other store types, such as discount and specialty stores, thus becoming merchandising conglomerates. Some department stores are retrenching on the number of employees, product lines, and customer services, such as delivery and credit, but this strategy may hurt their major appeal, namely, better service. Department stores need to find more effective ways to increase their thinning profit margins.

Supermarket. A supermarket is a relatively large, low-cost, low-margin, high-volume, self-service operation "designed to serve the consumer's total needs for food, laundry, and household maintenance products."[2] A supermarket store can be independently owned, although most supermarket stores are operated by supermarket chains, of which the largest ones (in billions of 1975 dollars) are Safeway ($15.1), Kroger ($10.3), A&P ($6.8), Lucky ($6.4), American Stores ($6.4), Winn-Dixie ($5.9), and Jewel ($4.1). Today there are over 37,000 supermarkets in operation, accounting for 76 percent of total grocery sales. Supermarkets earn an operating profit of only about 1 percent on their sales and 10 percent on their net worth.

Supermarkets have moved in several directions to further build their sales volume. They have opened *larger stores*, with today's selling space occupying approximately 18,000 square feet as opposed to 11,700 square feet in the mid-1950s. Most of the chains now operate fewer but larger stores. Supermarkets carry a large *number and variety of items*. A typical supermarket handled 3,000 items in 1946 and now handles around 8,000. The most significant increase has been in the number of nonfood items carried—nonprescription drugs, beauty aids, housewares, magazines, books, toys—which now account for 8 percent of total supermarket sales. This "scrambled merchandising" is continuing, and many supermarkets are moving into prescriptions, appliances, records, sporting goods, hardware, garden supplies, and even cameras, hoping to find high-margin lines to improve profitability. Supermarkets are also *upgrading their facilities* through more expensive locations, larger parking lots, carefully planned architecture and decor, longer store hours and Sunday openings, and a wide variety of customer services, such as check cashing, restrooms, and background music. Supermarkets have also increased *promotional competition* in the form of heavy advertising, trading stamps, and games of chance. And supermarkets have moved heavily into *private brands* to reduce their dependence on national brands and increase their profit margins. Supermarket chains are also expanding their outlets in the Sunbelt states where economic growth is stronger.

Supermarkets have been hit hard by a number of innovative competitors (see

---

[2] The quoted part of the definition is from Walter J. Salmon, Robert D. Buzzell, Stanton G. Cort, and Michael R. Pearce, *The Super Store—Strategic Implications for the Seventies* (Cambridge, Mass.: Marketing Science Institute, 1972), p. 83.

Product Assortment \ Price	High	Medium	Low
Narrow	Convenience stores		"Box" stores
Large		Super markets	Discount stores
Broad		Combination stores	Superstores and hypermarches

Source: Developed from Fred C. Allvine, "The Supermarket Challenged: New Competitive Strategies Needed," *Business Horizons*, October 1968, p. 65. Copyright 1968 by the Foundation for the School of Business at Indiana University. Reprinted by permission.

FIGURE 18–2
Basic Store Types in Food Retailing

Figure 18–2) that meet better-defined customer needs with respect to product assortments and price levels. The food market is becoming more segmented, and no longer is it likely to be dominated by one major type of food retailer. Another challenge has been the rapid growth of out-of-home eating, with Americans now spending nearly 40 percent of their food budgets outside the food stores.

"Supermarketing" has recently spread to other types of business, particularly in the drug, home improvement, toy, and sporting goods fields. According to McCammon, the supermarket concept involves self-service and self-selection displays; centralization of customer services, usually at the checkout counter; large-scale physical facilities; a strong price emphasis; and a broad assortment and wide variety of merchandise to facilitate multiple-item purchases.[3] These principles, for example, are applied by Standard Brands in the home improvement retailing field and Walgreen's in the drug retailing field.

Convenience store. Convenience food stores are relatively small stores, located near residential areas, open long hours and seven days a week, that carry a limited line of high-turnover convenience products. Examples are Seven-Elevens and White Hen Pantries. Their long hours and their use by consumers mainly for "fill-in" purchases make them relatively high-price operations. Yet they fill an important consumer need, and people seem willing to pay for the convenience. Convenience stores have increased from approximately 2,000 in 1957 to 34,125 in 1977, with sales of $12.7 billion in 1979.

Convenience food retailing has spread recently to the food-gasoline store. Customers drive up to a service station that carries about one hundred convenience

[3] See Bert McCammon, "High Performance Marketing Strategies," unpublished paper.

items—bread, milk, cigarettes, coffee, and soft drinks—and can charge the purchase to their oil credit card.

Superstore, combination store, and hypermarche.   At the other end of the spectrum are three types of stores that are larger than the conventional supermarket. *Superstores* are larger than conventional supermarkets (30,000 instead of 18,000 square feet of selling space) and aim at meeting the consumers' total needs for routinely purchased food and nonfood items. They usually offer services such as laundry, dry cleaning, shoe repair, check cashing and bill paying, and bargain lunch counters.[4] *Combination stores* represent a diversification of the supermarket store into the growing drug and prescription field. Combination food and drug stores average 55,000 square feet of selling space. *Hypermarches* are even larger than combination stores, ranging between 80,000 and 220,000 square feet. The hypermarche combines supermarket, discount, and warehouse retailing principles. Its product assortment goes beyond routinely purchased goods and includes furniture, heavy and light appliances, clothing items, and many other things. The hypermarche uses a price-discount appeal in contrast to the normal pricing by superstores. It also operates on warehouse principles, with many products coming prepacked in wire "baskets" direct from manufacturers and then stacked on five-tier metal racks to a height of twelve to fifteen feet. The restocking is done by forklift trucks, which move through the wide aisles during selling hours. The basic approach is bulk display and minimum handling by store personnel, with discounts offered to customers who are willing to carry heavy appliances and furniture out of the store.

Service business.   Business enterprises whose main "product line" is *service* include hotels and motels, banks, airlines, colleges, hospitals, movie theatres, tennis clubs and bowling alleys, restaurants, repair services, and various personal-service businesses such as barber and beauty shops, dry cleaners, and funeral homes. Service retailers in the United States are growing at a faster rate than product retailers. Each service industry has its own drama. Banks are looking for new ways to distribute their services efficiently, including the use of automatic tellers and payment by telephone systems. Health-maintenance organizations (HMOs) are revolutionizing the way consumers get and pay for their health services. Groups such as Transcendental Meditation, est, and Silva Mind Control have applied franchise and chain-organization principles to mass distribute personal-growth services. And H&R Block has built a franchised network of accountants and tax specialists ready to help consumers pay as little as possible to Uncle Sam.

Relative price emphasis.   Retail stores can also be classified according to their price image. Most stores offer medium prices and normal levels of customer service. Some stores offer higher-quality goods and service, along with higher prices. Gucci's justifies its high prices by saying, "You will remember the goods long after the prices are forgotten." Discount stores, on the other hand, sell goods for less than their normal prices (called off-list pricing) because they run lower-cost, lower-service operations. Here we will examine discount stores, warehouse stores, and catalog showrooms.

---

[4] Salmon and others, *The Super Store*, p. 4.

Discount store. A discount store sells standard merchandise at lower prices than conventional merchants by accepting lower margins and working on higher volume. The mere use of discount pricing and specials from time to time or the selling of cheap and inferior goods at low prices does not make a discount store. A true discount store exhibits five elements: (1) The store regularly sells its merchandise at lower prices than those prevailing in high-margin, low-turnover outlets; (2) the store emphasizes national brands, so that low price does not suggest inferior quality; (3) the store operates on a self-service, minimum-facilities basis; (4) the location tends to be a low-rent area, and the store draws customers from relatively long distances; and (5) the fixtures are spartan and functional.[5] In 1981 there were an estimated 8,164 discount department stores, with almost $67 billion in sales.

The real explosion of discount retailing took place in the late 1940s, when it moved from soft goods (clothing, toiletries) to hard goods (refrigerators, appliances, washing machines, dishwashers, air conditioners, furnishings, sporting goods). The early discount stores operated from almost warehouse facilities in low-rent but heavily traveled districts, slashing services, advertising widely, and carrying a reasonable width and depth of branded products. They operated with expenses of 12 to 18 percent of sales compared with 30 to 40 percent for the department and specialty stores. By 1960, discount stores accounted for one-third of all sales of household appliances, and the average stockturn was fourteen per year compared with four for a conventional department store.

In recent years, intense competition among discount houses and between discount houses and department stores, has led many discount retailers to trade up. They have improved their decor, added new lines such as wearing apparel, added more services such as check cashing and easy returns, and opened new branches in suburban shopping centers, all leading to higher costs and forcing higher prices. Furthermore department stores often cut their prices to compete with the discounters, with the distinction between the two growing progressively blurry. Several major discount chains folded in the 1970s as a result of rising costs and the loss of their price edge.

On the other hand, a chain such as K-Mart has been spectacularly successful. It is the nation's second-largest retailer and operates 1,968 stores. K-Mart's success is based on sticking to discount traditions: Decor is minimal, the sales staff is sparse, and consumers wander about a huge one-story building to find what they want, put their selections into shopping carts, and wheel them to checkout counters. Shoppers can choose among fifteen thousand items and are treated to many national brands rather than the "seconds" and "irregulars" featured by other discount stores.[6]

Discount retailing has moved beyond general merchandise into special merchandise stores, such as discount sporting goods stores, discount stereo-equipment stores, and discount bookstores. A recent development in discount food retailing is the "box" food stores. Pioneered by Aldi Discount Food, Aldi stores carry about 450 high-turnover items; none are perishable, thus eliminating the need for costly refrigeration.

---

[5] Ronald R. Gist, *Retailing Concepts and Decisions* (New York: John Wiley & Sons, 1968), pp. 45–46. The list of elements is slightly modified from Gist.

[6] See "K-Mart's Plan to be Born Again, Again," *Fortune*, September 21, 1981, pp. 75–85.

Prices are posted on signs rather than on merchandise, thus saving marking costs. Customers pay cash and bring their own bags. These box stores represent another innovative way to segment the market and meet underserved consumer needs.

Warehouse store. A warehouse store is a no-frill, discount, reduced-service operation, which seeks to move high volume at low prices. In its broad form, it includes hyper-marches and box food stores. One of its most interesting forms is the *furniture show-room warehouse* (such as Levitz or Wickes). Shoppers enter a football field-size ware-house located in a suburban low-rent area and pass by a huge inventory of furniture piled in neat tiers. They enter a showroom containing approximately two hundred rooms of attractively displayed furniture. Customers make their selections and place orders with sales people. By the time the customer pays, leaves, and drives to the loading entrance, the merchandise is ready. Heavy goods can be delivered in a few days or loaded on the customer's vehicle at a saving of many dollars. The whole operation is targeted to buyers of medium-priced brand-name furniture who are seeking discount prices and immediate availability.[7]

Catalog showroom A catalog showroom applies catalog and discounting principles to a wide selection of high-markup, fast-moving, brand-name goods. These include jewelry, power tools, luggage, cameras, and photographic equipment. These stores emerged in the late 1960s and have become one of retailing's hottest new forms, even posing a threat to the traditional discounter, who has moved too much into improved decor, more service, and higher markups. Catalog showrooms such as Best Products Company and Service Merchandise issue four-color catalogs, often five hundred pages long, and supplement them with smaller seasonal editions. Each item's list price and discount price are shown. The customer can order an item over the phone and pay delivery charges or drive to the showroom, examine it firsthand, and buy it out of stock. The customer who buys at the catalog showroom has to put up with certain inconveniences, such as driving some distance, standing in line to see a particular item (many are locked in cases), waiting for the item to be supplied from the back room, and finding little service if there are problems. The rapid growth of catalog showrooms, however, indicates that customers want the savings and are willing to accept less service.

Nature of business premises. Although the overwhelming majority of goods and services are sold through stores, *nonstore retailing* has been growing much faster than store retailing. In 1977 nonstore retailing amounted to $75 billion, or 12 percent of all consumer purchases. Some observers foresee as much as a third of all general-merchandise retailing being done through nonstore channels by the end of the century.[8] Others predict *remote retailing*, where consumers will order their goods using home computers and receive them or pick them up, without stepping into stores.[9] Here

---

[7] See Jonathan N. Goodrich and Jo Ann Hoffman, "Warehouse Retailing: The Trend of the Future?" *Business Horizons*, April 1979, pp. 45–50.

[8] Leo Bogart, "The Future in Retailing," *Harvard Business Review*, November-December 1973, p. 26.

[9] Belden Menkus, "Remote Retailing a Reality by 1985?" *Chain Store Age Executive*, September 1975, p. 42.

we will examine: mail-and-telephone-order retailing, automatic vending, buying service, and door-to-door retailing.

Mail-and-telephone-order retailing. Mail-and-telephone-order retailing covers any selling that involves using the mail or telephone to get orders and/or to facilitate delivery of the goods. There are 11,000 mail-and-telephone-order houses, with total sales of over $8 billion. The mail-and-telephone-order business takes several forms.

☐ **Mail-order catalog.** Here the seller mails a catalog to a select list of customers and makes the catalog available on its premises. This approach is used by *general-merchandise* mail-order houses carrying a full line of merchandise. Sears is the industry giant, with over $3 billion in catalog operations, and it sends out 300 million catalogs annually.[10] Recently specialty department stores, such as Neiman-Marcus and Saks Fifth Avenue, have begun sending catalogs to cultivate an upper-middle-class market for high-priced, often exotic, merchandise such as "his and her" bathrobes, designer jewelry, and gourmet foods. Several major corporations have also acquired or developed mail-order divisions. Xerox offers children's books; Avon sells women's apparel; W. R. Grace sells cheese; American Airlines offers luggage; General Foods offers needlework kits; and General Mills sells sports shirts.[11]

☐ **Direct response.** Here the direct marketer runs an ad in a newspaper or magazine or on radio or television describing some product, and the customer can write or phone for it. The direct marketer selects the media vehicles that maximize the number of orders for a given advertising expenditure. This strategy works well with such products as phonograph records and tapes, books, and small appliances.

☐ **Direct mail.** Here the direct marketer sends single mail pieces—letters, fliers, and foldouts—to prospects whose names are on mailing lists of high-potential buyers of the product category. The mailing lists are purchased from mailing-list brokerage houses. Direct mail has proved very successful in promoting books, magazine subscriptions, and insurance and is increasingly being used to sell novelty items, clothing apparel, and even gourmet foods. The major charities use direct mail to raise $21.4 billion, or over 80 percent of their total contributions.[12]

☐ **Telephone selling.** Direct marketers are increasingly using the telephone to sell everything from home-repair services to newspaper subscriptions to zoo memberships. Some telephone marketers have developed computerized phoning systems where households are dialed automatically and computerized messages presented.

Today the mail-and-telephone-order business is booming. The movement of women into the work force has substantially cut down on their available shopping time. Other factors have made shopping less pleasant: the higher costs of driving; traffic congestion and parking headaches; shoppers retreating to the suburbs and aversion to visiting crime-plagued urban shopping areas; and the shortage of sales help and having to queue at checkout counters. In addition, many chain stores have dropped slower-moving specialty items, thus creating an opportunity for direct marketers to promote these items. Finally, the development of toll-free phone numbers and

---

[10] "Millions by Mail," *Forbes*, March 15, 1976, p. 82.

[11] See Rita Reif, "Mail Order: Old Road to New Sales," *New York Times*, August 24, 1975.

[12] For an excellent text on direct-mail techniques, see Bob Stone, *Successful Direct Marketing Methods*, 2nd ed., (Chicago: Crain Books, 1979).

the willingness of direct marketers to accept telephone orders at night or on Sundays has boosted this form of retailing.

Automatic vending. Automatic vending through coin-operated machines has been a major post-World War II growth area. By 1979 total sales had soared to $13 billion (1.5 percent of total retail trade). Automatic vending has been applied to a considerable variety of merchandise, including impulse goods with high convenience value (cigarettes, soft drinks, candy, newspapers, hot beverages) and other products (hosiery, cosmetics, food snacks, hot soups and food, paperbacks, record albums, film, T-shirts, insurance policies, shoeshines, and even fishing worms). Vending machines are found in factories, offices, large retail stores, gasoline stations, and even railway dining cars. According to the National Automatic Merchandising Association, over seven thousand machine operators in the United States operate more than 6 million machines.

Vending machines offer to customers the advantages of twenty-four-hour selling, self-service, and unhandled merchandise. At the same time, automatic vending is a relatively expensive channel, and prices of vended merchandise are often 15 to 20 percent higher. Vendor costs are high because of frequent restocking at widely scattered locations, frequent machine breakdowns, and the high pilferage rate in certain locations. For the customer the biggest irritations are machine breakdowns, out-of-stocks, and the fact that merchandise cannot be returned.

Vending machines are increasingly supplying entertainment services—pinball machines, slot machines, juke boxes, and the new electronic computer games. A highly specialized machine is the *automatic teller* that allows bank customers twenty-four-hour service on checking, savings, withdrawals, and transfer of funds from one account to another.

Buying service. A buying service is a storeless retailer serving specific clienteles—usually the employees of large organizations such as schools, hospitals, unions, and government agencies. The organization's members become members of the buying service and are entitled to buy from a selective list of retailers who have agreed to give discounts to members of the buying service. Thus a customer seeking a video recording machine would get a form from the buying service, take it to an approved retailer, and buy the appliance at a discount. The retailer would then pay a small fee to the buying service. United Buying Service, for example, offers its nine hundred thousand members the opportunity to buy merchandise at "cost plus 8 percent."

Door-to-door retailing. This form of selling—which started centuries ago with itinerant peddlers—has burgeoned into a $6 billion industry, with over six hundred companies selling either *door to door*, *office to office*, or at *home sales parties*. The pioneers include the Fuller Brush Company (brushes, brooms, and the like), Electrolux (vacuum cleaners), Southwestern Company of Nashville (bibles), and World Book (encyclopedias). Door-to-door selling improved considerably with Avon's entry into the industry, with the concept of the homemakers' friend and beauty consultant—the Avon lady. Its army of 995,000 representatives produced over $1.6 billion in sales in 1978, making it the world's largest cosmetics firm and the number one door-to-door marketer. Tupperware, on the other hand, helped popularize the home-sales-parties method of selling, in which several friends and neighbors are invited to a party in someone's home where Tupperware products are demonstrated and sold.[13]

Door-to-door selling is expensive (the salespersons get a 20 to 50 percent commission), and there are the costs of hiring, managing, and motivating the sales force. The future of door-to-door retailing is somewhat uncertain, with more women at work during the day. The door-to-door salesperson may well be replaced by home computer ordering in the future.

Control of outlets. Retailing institutions can be classified according to their form of ownership. About 80 percent of all retail stores are independents, and they account for two-thirds of all retail sales. Several other forms—the corporate chain, voluntary chain and retailer cooperative, consumer cooperative, franchise organization, and merchandising conglomerate—represent alternative ownership forms.

Corporate chain. The chain store is one of the most important retail developments of the twentieth century. Gist has defined *chain store* as *two or more outlets that are commonly owned and controlled, sell similar lines of merchandise, have central buying and merchandising, and may use a similar architectural motif.*[14] Corporate chains have appeared in all types of retail operations: supermarkets and discount, variety, specialty, and department stores. In terms of product line, the corporate chains (when defined as having eleven or more units) are strongest in department stores (94 percent of the total sales volume of 1979), variety stores (80 percent), food stores (54 percent), drug stores (50 percent), shoe stores (48 percent), women's apparel (37 percent), and tire, battery, and auto-accessory stores (20 percent).

The success of corporate chains is based on their ability to achieve a price advantage over independents by moving toward high volume and lower margins. Chains achieve their efficiency in several ways. First, their size allows them to buy large quantities to take maximum advantage of quantity discounts and lower transportation costs. Second, chains are able to hire good managers and develop scientific procedures in the areas of sales forecasting, inventory control, pricing, and promotion. Third, the chains can integrate wholesaling and retailing functions, while independent retailers have to deal with many wholesalers. Fourth, the chains achieve promotional economies by buying advertising that benefits all of their stores and spreading the cost over a large volume. And fifth, the chains permit their units some freedom to meet variations in consumer preferences and competition in local markets.

Voluntary chain and retailer cooperative. The chains triggered a competitive reaction from the independents, who began to form two types of associations. One is the *voluntary chain*, which consists of a wholesaler-sponsored group of independent retailers engaged in bulk buying and common merchandising. Examples include the Independent Grocers Alliance (IGA) in groceries, ACE in hardware, and Western Auto in auto supplies. The other is the *retailer cooperative*, which consists of a set of

[13] See "How the 'New Sell' is Raking in Billions," *U.S. News and World Report*, May 8, 1978, pp. 74–75.

[14] See Ronald R. Gist, *Marketing and Society*: *Text and Cases*, 2nd ed. (Hinsdale, Ill.: Dryden Press, 1974), p. 334.

independent retailers who set up a central buying organization and conduct joint promotion efforts. Examples include Associated Grocers in groceries and True Value in hardware. These organizations achieved the needed merchandising economies and became effective in meeting the price challenge of the corporate chains.

Consumer cooperative. A consumer cooperative (or co-op) is any retail firm owned by its customers. Consumer co-ops are started by community residents who feel that local retailers are not serving them well, either charging too high prices or providing poor-quality products. The residents contribute money to open their own store, and they vote on its policies and elect a group to manage it. The store may set its prices low or, alternatively, set normal prices with members receiving a patronage dividend based on their individual level of purchases.

Franchise organization. A franchise organization is a contractual association between a franchiser (a manufacturer, wholesaler, or service organization) and franchisees (independent business people who buy the right to own and operate one or more units in the franchise system). Franchise organizations are normally based on some unique product, service, or method of doing business, or on a trade name, or on patent, or on goodwill that the franchiser has developed.

The franchiser's compensation can consist of the following elements: an initial fee; a royalty on gross sales; rental and lease fees on equipment and fixtures supplied by the franchiser; a share of the profits; and sometimes a regular license fee. In a few cases franchisers have also charged management consulting fees, but usually the franchisee is entitled to this service as part of the total package. McDonald's charges franchisees an initial fee of $150,000 and receives a 3.0 percent royalty fee and a rental charge of 8.5 percent of the franchisee's volume. It also requires its new franchisees to attend "Hamburger University" for three weeks to learn how to manage the business. The franchisees must also adhere to certain procedures in buying raw materials and in preparing and selling the product.

In 1980 there were approximately 488,300 franchise outlets, with sales of $338 billion. McDonald's and other fast-food franchisers are currently facing difficult challenges in rising labor costs (due to higher minimum wages) and food costs, forcing them to raise their prices to the customers. New competitors continue to emerge, offering new foods, such as tacos and gyros. Some major franchisers are now opening units in smaller towns, where there is less competition. Others are moving into large factories, office buildings, colleges, and even hospitals. Others are experimenting with new products that they hope will appeal to the public and be profitable to the firm.

Merchandising conglomerate. Merchandising conglomerates are free-form corporations that combine several diversified retailing lines and forms under central ownership, along with some integration of their distribution and management functions.[15] Major examples include Federated Department Stores, Allied Stores, Dayton-Hudson, and J. C. Penney. In the 1980s diversified retailing is likely to be adopted by more corporate chains. The major question is whether diversified retailing produces management systems and economies that benefit all of the separate retail lines.

---

[15] See Rollie Tillman, "Rise of the Conglomerchant," *Harvard Business Review*, November-December 1971, pp. 44–51.

Type of store cluster. The last retail classification is the single store versus several clustered stores. Most stores today cluster in shopping districts, both because of zoning ordinances and to offer more convenience through one-stop shopping. Just as supermarkets and department stores save consumers time and energy in finding what they need, so do clustered stores. The four main types of retail clusters are the central business district, the regional shopping center, the community shopping center, and the neighborhood shopping center.

Central business district. Central business districts were the dominant form of retail cluster until the 1950s. Every large city and town had a central business district containing department stores, specialty stores, banks, and major movie houses. And smaller business districts were found in neighborhood and outlying areas. Then in the 1950s people began to migrate to the suburbs. Suburbanites reduced their shopping in the central business district, wishing to avoid the heavy traffic, expensive parking, and the deteriorating urban scene. These central business districts deteriorated further and forced centrally located merchants to open branches in the growing suburban shopping centers. They also made an effort to revitalize the downtown area by building shopping malls and underground parking and renovating their stores. Some central business districts have made a comeback, but others are in a state of slow and possibly irreversible decline.

Regional shopping center. A *shopping center* is "a group of commercial establishments planned, developed, owned, and managed as a unit related in location, size, and type of shop to the trade area that it services, and providing on-site parking in definite relationship to the types and sizes of stores it contains."[16] There are various size shopping centers. The one known as the regional shopping center is the most dramatic and most competitive with the central (downtown) business district on the one hand, and local neighborhood shopping areas on the other hand.

A regional shopping center is like a minidowntown and contains from forty to over one hundred stores. To be profitable, it must serve a population of from one hundred thousand to one million customers who live within thirty minutes' driving time. In its early form, the regional shopping center often contained two strong department stores at the two ends of a mall and a set of specialty stores in between. This arrangement encouraged comparison shopping because the specialty stores typically carried goods that competed with the lines carried by the department stores. Thus a customer wishing to buy jeans could comparison shop at Sears, Lord and Taylor, Just Jeans, The Gap, and The County Seat. Regional shopping centers have added new types of retailers over the years, such as dentists, health clubs, and even branch libraries. Larger regional malls now have several department stores and are laid out to encourage freely moving traffic so that all the stores can get exposure. Many of the newer malls in the North are enclosed.

Community shopping center. A community shopping center contains fifteen to fifty retail stores serving between twenty thousand and one hundred thousand residents, where 90 percent live within one and one-half miles of the center. One primary

---

[16] This definition by the Urban Land Institute can be found in Roger A. Dickinson, *Retail Management: A Channels Approach* (Belmont, Calif.: Wadsworth, 1974), p. 9.

store is normally found, usually a branch of a department store or a variety store. The shopping center is likely to include a supermarket, convenience-goods stores, and professional offices—and sometimes a bank. The primary store will usually be located at the corner of the L in the case of L-shaped shopping centers and in the center in the case of line-shaped shopping centers. The stores nearest to the primary store normally sell shopping goods, and the more distant stores normally sell convenience goods.

Neighborhood shopping center. The largest number of shopping centers are those serving neighborhoods. Neighborhood shopping centers contain five to fifteen stores and serve a population of less than twenty thousand residents. Customers walk to these centers or drive for no more than five minutes. These are convenience shopping centers, with the supermarket as the principal tenant and several service establishments, such as a dry cleaner, self-service laundry, shoe repair store, and a beauty shop. In contrast to the larger shopping centers, this is usually an unplanned strip of stores.

Shopping centers now account for approximately one-third of all retail sales, but they may be reaching their saturation point. Sales per square foot are dropping, and vacancy rates are climbing; some bankruptcies have occurred. Shopping center developers are planning to build smaller shopping centers in the 400,000-square-foot range, in medium-sized and smaller cities, and in the fastest-growing areas such as the Southwest.[17]

Retailer Marketing Decisions

We will now examine retailer marketing decisions in the areas of target market, product assortment and services, price, promotion, and place.

Target-market decision. A retailer's most important decision concerns the target market. Until the target market is defined and profiled, the retailer cannot make consistent decisions on product assortment, store decor, advertising messages and media, price levels, and so on. Some stores are able to define their target market quite well. A fashionable women's apparel store in Palm Springs knows that its primary market is upper-income women, primarily between thirty and fifty-five years of age, living within thirty minutes' driving time from the store. Many retailers, however, have not clarified their target market or are trying to satisfy too many markets, satisfying none of them well. Even Sears, which serves so many different people, must develop a better definition of which groups it will make its major target customers so that it can achieve more precision in its product assortment, prices, locations, and promotion with these groups.

A retailer should carry out periodic marketing research to check that it is satisfying its target customers. Consider a store that seeks to attract affluent consumers but whose image is the one shown by the solid line in Figure 18–3. The store's image does not appeal to its target market, and it has to serve either the mass market or redesign itself into a "classier store." Suppose it decides on the latter. Some time

---

[17] David Elsner, "Shopping Center Boom Appears to be Fading Due to Overbuilding," *Wall Street Journal*, September 7, 1976.

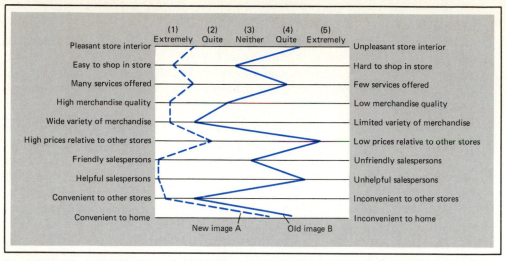

	(1) Extremely	(2) Quite	(3) Neither	(4) Quite	(5) Extremely	
Pleasant store interior						Unpleasant store interior
Easy to shop in store						Hard to shop in store
Many services offered						Few services offered
High merchandise quality						Low merchandise quality
Wide variety of merchandise						Limited variety of merchandise
High prices relative to other stores						Low prices relative to other stores
Friendly salespersons						Unfriendly salespersons
Helpful salespersons						Unhelpful salespersons
Convenient to other stores						Inconvenient to other stores
Convenient to home						Inconvenient to home

New image A   Old image B

Source: Adapted from David W. Cravens, Gerald E. Hills, and Robert B. Woodruff, *Marketing Decision Making: Concepts and Strategy* (Homewood, Ill.: Richard D. Irwin, 1976), p. 234. © 1976 by Richard D. Irwin, Inc.

FIGURE 18–3
A Comparison Between the Old and New Image of a Store Seeking to Appeal to a Class Market

later the store interviews customers again. The store image is now shown by the dashed line in Figure 18–3. The store has succeeded in bringing its image closer to its target market.

Product-assortment-and-services decision.   Retailers have to decide on three major "product" variables: product assortment, services mix, and store atmosphere.

The retailer's *product assortment* must match the shopping expectations of the target market. In fact, it becomes a key element in the competitive battle among similar retailers. The retailer has to decide on product assortment *width* (narrow or wide) and *depth* (shallow or deep). Thus in the restaurant business, a restaurant can offer a narrow and shallow assortment (small lunch counters), a narrow and deep assortment (delicatessen), a wide and shallow assortment (cafeteria), or a wide and deep assortment (large restaurants). Another product-assortment dimension is the quality of the goods. The customer is interested not only in the range of choice but also in the quality of the product.

Retailers must also decide on the *services mix* to offer customers. The old "mom and pop" grocery stores offered home delivery, credit, and conversation, services that today's supermarkets have completely eliminated. Table 18–3 lists some of the major services that full-service retailers can offer. The services mix is one of the key tools of nonprice competition for differentiating one store from another.

The *store's atmosphere* is a third element in its product arsenal. Every store has a physical layout that makes it hard or easy to move around. Every store has a "feel"; one store is dirty, another is charming, a third is palatial, a fourth is somber. The store must embody a planned atmosphere that suits the target market and leans them toward purchase. A funeral parlor should be quiet, somber, and peaceful, and

TABLE 18–3

TYPICAL RETAIL SERVICES		
Prepurchase Services	**Postpurchase Services**	**Ancillary Services**
1. Accepting telephone orders	1. Delivery	1. Check cashing
2. Accepting mail orders (or purchases)	2. Regular wrapping (or bagging)	2. General information
3. Advertising	3. Gift wrapping	3. Free parking
4. Window display	4. Adjustments	4. Restaurants
5. Interior display	5. Returns	5. Repairs
6. Fitting rooms	6. Alterations	6. Interior decorating
7. Shopping hours	7. Tailoring	7. Credit
8. Fashion shows	8. Installations	8. Restaurants
9. Trade-ins	9. Engraving	9. Baby-attendant service
	10. COD delivery	

SOURCE: Carl M. Larson, Robert E. Weigand, and John S. Wright, Basic Retailing (Englewood Cliffs, N.J.: Prentice-Hall, 1976), p. 364. Reprinted by permission of Prentice-Hall, Inc., Englewood Cliffs, N.J.

a discotheque should be bright, loud, and vibrating. The atmosphere is designed by creative people who know how to combine visual, aural, olfactory, and tactile stimuli to achieve the desired effect.[18]

Price decision.   The retailers' prices are a key competitive factor and reflect the quality of goods carried and services offered. The cost of merchandise is the basis for their pricing, and their ability to buy intelligently is a key ingredient in successful retailing. Retailers can often make as much money through smart buying as through smart selling. Beyond this, they must price carefully in a number of other ways. Low markups can be set on some items so they can work as *traffic builders* or *loss leaders*, in the hope that customers will buy additional items that bear a higher markup, once they are in the store. In addition, retail management has to be adept in its use of markdowns on slower-moving merchandise. Shoe retailers, for example, expect to sell 50 percent of their shoes at the normal markup, 25 percent at a 40 percent markup, and the remaining 25 percent at cost. Their initial pricing anticipates these expected markdowns.

Promotion decision.   Retailers use the normal promotional tools—advertising, personal selling, sales promotion, and publicity—to reach consumers. Retailers advertise in newspapers, magazines, radio, and television. The advertising is occasionally supplemented by hand-delivered circulars and direct-mail pieces. Personal selling requires careful training of the sales people in how to greet customers, meet their needs, and handle their doubts and complaints. Sales promotion may take the form of in-

---

[18] For more discussion, see Philip Kotler, "Atmospherics as a Marketing Tool," *Journal of Retailing*, winter 1973–74, pp. 48–64.

store demonstrations, trading stamps, grand prizes, and visiting celebrities. Publicity is always available to retailers who have something interesting to say.

Place decision. The retailer's choice of location is a key competitive factor in its ability to attract customers. For example, customers primarily choose a bank that is nearest to them. Department-store chains, oil companies, and fast-food franchisers are particularly careful in selecting locations. The problem breaks down into selecting regions of the country in which to open stores, then particular cities, and then particular sites. A supermarket chain, for example, may decide to operate in the Midwest and Southeast; within the Midwest, in the cities of Chicago, Milwaukee, and Indianapolis; and within Chicago, in fourteen locations, mostly suburban.

Large retailers must wrestle with the problem of whether to locate several small stores in many locations or larger stores in fewer locations. Generally speaking, the retailer should locate enough stores in each city to gain visibility and distribution economies. The larger the individual stores, the greater their trading area or reach. Firms use a variety of methods to assess locations, including traffic counts, surveys of consumer shopping habits, analysis of competitive locations, and so on. Nelson has published an elaborate checklist containing over thirty factors pertaining to a proposed site, including the site's trading-area potential, accessibility, growth potential, competitive interception, and site economics.[19] Several models for site location have been formulated.[20]

The Future of Retailing

Retailing is one of the most dynamic and challenging areas of the economy. Today's retailer, looking ahead to tomorrow, has to take into account the following major trends: the slowdown in population and economic growth; the increasing cost of capital, labor, and energy; the changing consumer lifestyles, shopping patterns, and attitudes toward shopping; the emergence of new technologies such as computerized checkout, electronic shopping, and more advanced automatic vending; the growing strength of major retailers; and the rise of consumerism and environmentalism and the increase in government regulations affecting retailing. Clearly these trends call for more *professional management* in retailing that goes beyond good merchandising skills. Top management will have to be skilled in designing and implementing profit-performance systems. The key need will be to find ways to increase *retail productivity*.

The search for more productivity in the 1980s will favor the development of retailing forms that keep costs down. Many retailing innovations have come about as solutions to high-cost, high-price retailing. They are partially explained by the

[19] Richard L. Nelson, *The Selection of Retail Locations* (New York: F. W. Dodge Corporation, 1958), pp. 349–50.

[20] See William J. Baumol and Edward A. Ide, "Variety in Retailing," *Management Science*, October 1956, pp. 93–101; and David L. Huff, "Defining and Estimating a Trading Area," *Journal of Marketing*, July 1964, pp. 34–38.

wheel of retailing hypothesis.[21] According to this hypothesis, many new types of retailing institutions begin as low-margin, low-price, low-status operations. They become effective competitors of more conventional outlets, which have grown "fat" over the years. Their success leads them to upgrade their facilities and offer additional services. This increases their costs and forces price increases until they resemble the conventional outlets that they displaced. They, in turn, become vulnerable to newer types of low-cost, low-margin operations. This hypothesis appears to explain the initial success and later troubles of department stores, supermarkets, and more recently, discount houses. On the other hand, it does not explain the growth of suburban shopping centers and automatic vending, both of which started out as high-margin and high-cost operations.

Nevertheless, one can be sure that new retailing forms will emerge to meet new needs:

> A soft-drink manufacturer opened a chain of soft-drink stores for the take-home market at substantial savings. American Bakeries started Hippopotamus Food Store outlets that feature large institutional-sized packages at a 10 to 30 percent savings. One of the large New York banks recently instituted "house-call loans" for which it will qualify a customer over the phone and then deliver the money in person. Adelphi University in Garden City, New York, developed a "commuter-train classroom" in which business people who commute daily between Long Island and Manhattan can get their M.B.A.'s by sitting in on fifty-minute classes held in specially reserved cars on the commuter train.

Marketers are continually seeking new ways to distribute their products and services. The longevity of the new retail forms, however, is likely to be less than that of the previous great forms, such as the department store and the supermarket. Table 18–4 lists the life-cycle characteristics of some major retailing institutions and indicates that the more recent ones are reaching their maturity much faster.[22]

WHOLESALING

Nature and Importance of Wholesaling

Wholesaling includes *all activities involved in selling goods or services to those who buy for resale or business use.* A retail bakery selling pastry to a local hotel is engaged in wholesaling at that point. We will use the term *wholesalers*, however, to describe

---

[21] Malcolm P. McNair, "Significant Trends and Developments in the Postwar Period," in *Competitive Distribution in a Free, High-Level Economy and Its Implication for the University*, ed. A. B. Smith (Pittsburgh: University of Pittsburgh Press, 1958), pp. 1–25. Also see the critical discussion by Stanley C. Hollander, "The Wheel of Retailing," *Journal of Marketing*, July 1960, pp. 37–42. For other theories of retail change, see Ronald R. Gist, *Retailing Concepts and Decisions* (New York: John Wiley & Sons, 1968), chap. 4.

[22] For additional articles on the future of retailing, see William R. Davidson, Albert D. Bates, and Stephen J. Bass, "The Retail Life Cycle," *Harvard Business Review*, November-December 1976, pp. 89–96; Albert D. Bates, "The Troubled Future of Retailing," *Business Horizons*, August 1976, pp. 22–28; and Malcolm P. McNair and Eleanor G. May, "The Next Revolution of the Retailing Wheel," *Harvard Business Review*, September-October 1978, pp. 81–91.

TABLE 18–4

LIFE CYCLES OF RETAIL INSTITUTIONS			
Retail Institutions	Early Growth	Maturity	Approximate Time Required to Reach Maturity
Department stores	Mid-1860s	Mid-1960s	100 years
Variety stores	Early 1900s	Early 1960s	60 years
Supermarkets	Mid-1930s	Mid-1960s	30 years
Discount department stores	Mid-1950s	Mid-1970s	20 years
Fast-food service outlets	Early 1960s	Mid-1970s	15 years
Home improvement centers	Mid-1960s	Late 1970s	15 years
Furniture warehouse showrooms	Late 1960s	Late 1970s	10 years
Catalog showrooms	Late 1960s	Late 1970s	10 years

SOURCE: From Bert C. McCammon, Jr., "The Future of Catalog Showrooms: Growth and Its Challenges to Management," Marketing Science Institute working paper (1975), p. 3.

firms that are engaged primarily in wholesaling activity. It excludes manufacturers and farmers because they are engaged primarily in production, and it excludes retailers.

Wholesalers differ from retailers in a number of ways. First, wholesalers pay less attention to promotion, atmosphere, and location because they are dealing with business customers rather than final consumers. Second, wholesale transactions are usually larger than retail transactions, and wholesalers usually cover a larger trade area than retailers. Third, the government deals with wholesalers and retailers differently in regard to legal regulations and taxes.

Why are wholesalers used at all? Manufacturers could bypass them and sell directly to retailers or final consumers. The answer lies in several efficiencies that wholesalers bring about. First, small manufacturers with limited financial resources cannot afford to develop direct-selling organizations. Second, even manufacturers with sufficient capital may prefer to use their funds to expand production rather than carry out wholesaling activities. Third, wholesalers are likely to be more efficient at wholesaling because of their scale of operation, their wider number of retail contacts, and their specialized skills. Fourth, retailers who carry many lines often prefer to buy assortments from a wholesaler rather than to buy directly from each manufacturer.

Thus retailers and manufacturers have reasons to use wholesalers. Wholesalers are used when they are more efficient in performing one or more of the following functions:

□ **Selling and promoting.** Wholesalers provide a sales force enabling manufacturers to reach many small customers at a relatively low cost. The wholesaler has more contacts and is often more trusted by the buyer than is the distant manufacturer.

□ **Buying and assortment building.** Wholesalers are able to select items and build assortments needed by their customers, thus saving the customers considerable work.

□ **Bulk-breaking.** Wholesalers achieve savings for their customers through buying in carload lots and breaking the bulk into smaller units.

- ☐ **Warehousing.** Wholesalers hold inventories, thereby reducing the inventory costs and risks to suppliers and customers.
- ☐ **Transportation.** Wholesalers provide quicker delivery to buyers because they are closer than the manufacturer.
- ☐ **Financing.** Wholesalers finance their customers by granting credit, and they finance their suppliers by ordering early and paying their bills on time.
- ☐ **Risk bearing.** Wholesalers absorb some risk by taking title and bearing the cost of theft, damage, spoilage, and obsolescence.
- ☐ **Market information.** Wholesalers supply information to their suppliers and customers regarding competitors' activities, new products, price development, and so on.
- ☐ **Management services and counseling.** Wholesalers often help retailers improve their operations by training their sales clerks, helping with stores' layouts and displays, and setting up accounting and inventory-control systems.

A number of factors have contributed to wholesaling's growth over the years: the growth of mass production in large factories located away from the principal users of the output; the growth of production in advance of orders rather than in response to specific orders; an increase in the number of levels of intermediate producers and users; and the increasing need for adapting products to the needs of intermediate and final users in terms of quantities, packages, and forms.

Types of Wholesalers

In 1977 there were 383,000 wholesaling establishments in the United States doing a total annual volume of $1,258 billion. The wholesalers fall into the four groups shown in Table 18–5.

Merchant wholesalers.   Merchant wholesalers are independently owned businesses that take title to the merchandise they handle. In different trades they are called

TABLE 18–5

CLASSIFICATION OF WHOLESALERS			
Merchant Wholesalers	**Brokers and Agents**	**Manufacturers' and Retailers' Branches and Offices**	**Miscellaneous Wholesalers**
Full-service wholesalers	Brokers	Sales branches and offices	Agricultural assemblers
Wholesale merchants	Agents	Purchasing offices	Petroleum bulk plants and terminals
Industrial distributors			Auction companies
Limited-service wholesalers			
Cash-and-carry wholesalers			
Truck wholesalers			
Drop shippers			
Rack jobbers			
Producers' cooperatives			
Mail-order wholesalers			

jobbers, distributors, or mill supply houses. They are the largest single group of wholesalers, accounting for roughly 50 percent of all wholesaling (in sales volume and in number of establishments). Merchant wholesalers can be subclassified into full-service wholesalers and limited-service wholesalers.

Full-service wholesalers. Full-service wholesalers provide such services as carrying stock, a sales force, offering credit, making deliveries, and providing management assistance. They include two types: wholesale merchants and industrial distributors.

WHOLESALE MERCHANTS. Wholesale merchants sell primarily to retailers and provide a full range of services. They vary mainly in the width of their product line. *General-merchandise wholesalers* carry several merchandise lines to meet the needs of both general-merchandise retailers and single-line retailers. *General-line wholesalers* carry one or two lines of merchandise in a greater depth of assortment. Major examples are hardware wholesalers, drug wholesalers, and clothing wholesalers. *Specialty wholesalers* specialize in carrying only part of a line in great depth. Examples are health-food wholesalers, seafood wholesalers, and automotive-item wholesalers. They offer customers the advantage of deeper choice and greater product knowledge.

INDUSTRIAL DISTRIBUTORS. Industrial distributors are merchant wholesalers who sell to manufacturers rather than to retailers. They provide several services, such as carrying stock, offering credit, and providing delivery. They may carry a broad range of merchandise (often called a mill supply house), a general line, or a specialty line. Industrial distributors may concentrate on such lines as MRO items (maintenance, repair, and operating supplies), OEM items (original-equipment supplies such as ball bearings, motors), or equipment (such as hand and power tools, fork trucks). There are about twelve thousand industrial distributors in the United States, and their sales were approximately $23.5 billion in 1974.

Limited-service wholesalers. Limited-service wholesalers offer fewer services to their suppliers and customers. There are several types of limited-service wholesalers.

CASH-AND-CARRY WHOLESALERS. Cash-and-carry wholesalers have a limited line of fast-moving goods and sell to small retailers for cash and normally do not deliver. A small fish-store retailer, for example, normally drives at dawn to a cash-and-carry fish wholesaler and buys several crates of fish, pays on the spot, and drives the merchandise back to the store and unloads it.

TRUCK WHOLESALERS. Truck wholesalers (also called truck jobbers) perform a selling and delivery function primarily. They carry a limited line of semiperishable merchandise (such as milk, bread, snack foods), which they sell for cash as they make their rounds of supermarkets, small groceries, hospitals, restaurants, factory cafeterias, and hotels.

DROP SHIPPERS. Drop shippers operate in bulk industries, such as coal, lumber, and heavy equipment. They do not carry inventory or handle the product. Once an order is received, they find a manufacturer, who ships the merchandise directly to the customer on the agreed terms and time of delivery. The drop shipper assumes title and risk from the time the order is accepted to its delivery to the customer. Because drop shippers do not carry inventory, their costs are lower, and they can pass on some savings to customers.

RACK JOBBERS. Rack jobbers serve grocery and drug retailers, mostly in the area of nonfood items. These retailers do not want to order and maintain displays of hundreds of nonfood items. The rack jobbers send delivery trucks to stores, and the delivery person sets up toys, paperbacks, hardware items, health and beauty aids, and so on. They price the goods, keep them fresh, set up point-of-purchase displays, and keep inventory records. Rack jobbers sell on consignment, which means that they retain title to the goods and bill the retailers only for the goods sold to consumers. Thus they provide such services as delivery, shelving, inventory carrying, and financing. They do little promotion because they carry many branded items that are highly advertised.

PRODUCERS' COOPERATIVES. Producers' cooperatives are owned by farmer members and assemble farm produce to sell in local markets. Their profits are distributed to members at the end of the year. They often attempt to improve product quality and promote a co-op brand name, such as Sun Maid raisins, Sunkist oranges, or Diamond walnuts.

MAIL-ORDER WHOLESALERS. Mail-order wholesalers send catalogs to retail, industrial, and institutional customers featuring jewelry, cosmetics, specialty foods, and other small items. Their main customers are businesses in small outlying areas. No sales force is maintained to call on customers. The orders are filled and sent by mail, truck, or other efficient means of transportation.

Brokers and agents. Brokers and agents differ from merchant wholesalers in two ways: They do not take title to goods, and they perform only a few functions. Their main function is to facilitate buying and selling, and for this they will earn a commission of anywhere from 2 to 6 percent of the selling price. Like merchant wholesalers, they generally specialize by product line or customer types. They account for 10 percent of the total wholesale volume.

Brokers. The chief function of a broker is to bring buyers and sellers together and assist in negotiation. They are paid by the party who hired them. They do not carry inventory, get involved in financing, or assume risk. The most familiar examples are food brokers, real estate brokers, insurance brokers, and security brokers.

Agents. Agents represent either buyers or sellers on a more permanent basis. There are several types.

Manufacturers' agents (also called manufacturers' representatives) are more numerous than other types of agent wholesalers. They represent two or more manufacturers of complementary lines. They enter into a formal written agreement with each manufacturer covering pricing policy, territories, order-handling procedure, delivery service and warranties, and commission rates. They know each manufacturer's product line and use their wide contacts to sell the manufacturer's products. Manufacturers' agents are used in such lines as apparel, furniture, and electrical goods. Most manufacturers' agents are small businesses, with only a few employees, who are skilled sales people. They are hired by small manufacturers who cannot afford to maintain their own field sales forces and by large manufacturers who want to use agents to open new territories or to represent them in territories that cannot support full-time salespeople.

Selling agents are given contractual authority to sell the entire output of a manufacturer. The manufacturer either is not interested in the selling function or feels unqualified. The selling agent serves as a sales department and has significant influence over prices, terms, and conditions of sale. The selling agent normally has no territorial limits. Selling agents are found in such product areas as textiles, industrial machinery and equipment, coal and coke, chemicals, and metals.

Purchasing agents generally have a long-term relationship with buyers and make purchases for them, often receiving, inspecting, warehousing, and shipping the merchandise to the buyers. One type consists of *resident buyers* in major apparel markets, who look for suitable lines of apparel that can be carried by small retailers located in small cities. They are knowledgeable and provide helpful market information to clients as well as obtaining the best goods and prices available.

Commission merchants (or houses) are agents who take physical possession of products and negotiate sales. Normally they are not employed on a long-term basis. They are used most often in agricultural marketing by farmers who do not want to sell their own output and do not belong to producers' cooperatives. A commission merchant would take a truckload of commodities to a central market, sell it for the best price, deduct a commission and expenses, and remit the balance to the producer.

Manufacturers' and retailers' branches and offices.

The third major type of wholesaling consists of wholesaling operations conducted by sellers or buyers themselves rather than through independent wholesalers. There are two types.

Sales branches and offices. Manufacturers often set up their own sales branches and offices to improve inventory control, selling, and promotion. *Sales branches* carry inventory and are found in such industries as lumber and automotive equipment and parts. Sales offices do not carry inventory and are most prominent in dry goods and notion industries. Sales branches and offices account for about 11 percent of all wholesale establishments and 36 percent of all wholesale volume.

Purchasing offices. Many retailers set up purchasing offices in major market centers such as New York and Chicago. These purchasing offices perform a role similar to that of brokers or agents but are part of the buyer's organization.

Miscellaneous wholesalers.

A few specialized types of wholesalers are found in certain sectors of the economy.

Agricultural assemblers. Agricultural assemblers gather farm products from farmers and build them into larger lots for shipment to food processors, bakers, and government. By taking advantage of carload or truckload rates and differences in area market prices, the assembler makes a profit.

Petroleum bulk plants and terminals. Petroleum bulk plants and terminals sell and deliver petroleum products to filling stations, other retailers, and business firms. Many are owned by major petroleum producers and others by independent companies.

Auction companies. Auction houses are important in industries where buyers want to see and inspect goods prior to purchase, such as in the tobacco and livestock markets. The buyers come together and bid until one bidder is left. This bidder gets the products if the bid exceeds the reserve price.

Wholesaler Marketing Decisions

Wholesalers must make decisions on their target market, product assortment and services, pricing, promotion, and place.

Target-market decision. Wholesalers, like retailers, need to define their target markets and should not try to serve everyone. They can choose a target group of customers according to size criteria (e.g., only large retailers), type of customer (e.g., convenience food stores only), need for service (e.g., customers who need credit), or other criteria. Within the target group they can identify the more profitable customers and design stronger offers and build better relationships with them. They can propose automatic reordering systems, set up management training and advisory systems, and even sponsor a voluntary chain. They can discourage less-profitable customers by requiring larger orders or adding surcharges to smaller ones.

Product-assortment-and-services decision. The wholesalers' "product" is their assortment. Wholesalers are under great pressure to carry a full line and maintain sufficient stock for immediate delivery. But this can kill profits. Wholesalers today are reexamining how many lines to carry and are choosing to carry only the more profitable ones. They are grouping their items on an ABC basis, with A standing for the most profitable items and C for the least profitable. Inventory-carrying levels are varied for the three groups.

Wholesalers are also examining which services count most in building strong customer relationships and which ones should be dropped or charged for. The key is to find a distinct mix of services valued by their customers.

Pricing decision. Wholesalers usually mark up the cost of goods by a conventional percentage, say 20 percent to cover their expenses. Expenses may run 17 percent of the gross margin, leaving a profit margin of approximately 3 percent. In grocery wholesaling the average profit margin is often less than 2 percent. Wholesalers are beginning to experiment with new approaches to pricing. They may cut their margin on some lines in order to win important new customers. They will ask suppliers for a special price break when they can turn it into an opportunity to increase the supplier's sales.

Promotion decision. Most wholesalers are not promotion minded. Their use of trade advertising, sales promotion, publicity, and personal selling is largely haphazard. Personal selling is particularly behind the times in that wholesalers still see selling as a single salesperson talking to a single customer instead of a team effort to sell, build, and service major accounts. As for nonpersonal promotion, wholesalers would benefit from adopting some of the image-making techniques used by retailers. They need to develop an overall promotion strategy. They also need to make greater use of supplier promotion materials and programs.

Place decision. Wholesalers typically locate in low-rent, low-tax areas and put little money into their physical setting and offices. Often the materials-handling systems and order-processing systems lag behind the available technologies. To meet rising costs, progressive wholesalers have been making time and motion studies of materials-handling procedures. The ultimate development is the automated warehouse, where the orders are key punched on tabulating cards, which are then fed into a computer. The items are picked up by mechanical devices and conveyed on a belt to the shipping platform, where they are assembled. This type of mechanization is progressing rapidly, and so is the mechanization of many office activities. Many wholesalers are turning to computers and word-processing machines to carry out accounting, billing, inventory control, and forecasting.

The Future of Wholesaling

Changes in wholesaling have been less dramatic than in retailing, but no less important. In the nineteenth century wholesalers held the dominant position in marketing channels. Most manufacturers were small, and dependent on major wholesalers to distribute their products to the many small retailers who dotted the land. Wholesalers' power began to diminish in the twentieth century as manufacturers grew larger and giant chains and franchise systems emerged in retailing. Large manufacturers sought ways to sell direct to the major retailers, and the major retailers sought ways to buy direct from the manufacturers. The opportunity to go direct, even though not used most of the time, increased the power of the manufacturers and retailers and forced wholesalers to become more efficient. Wholesalers declined in relative importance in the 1930s and 1940s and did not regain their position until the mid-1950s. Wholesale sales volume has continued to grow, but in relative terms, wholesalers have just held their own.

Manufacturers always have the option of bypassing wholesalers or of replacing an inefficient wholesaler with a more dynamic one. Manufacturers' major complaints against wholesalers are as follows: They do not aggressively promote the manufacturer's product line, acting more like order takers; they do not carry enough inventory and therefore fail to fill customers' orders fast enough; they do not supply the manufacturer with up-to-date market and competitive information; they do not attract high-caliber managers and bring down their own costs; and they charge too much for their services.

These complaints are justified in many cases. Wholesalers must adapt to a rapidly changing environment. According to Lopata:

> Technological advances, product line proliferation, changing retail structures, and social adjustments are only a few of the real problems that complicate the wholesaler's life. Each improved product passing through the wholesale level generates a new demand for investments in warehouse space, market analysis, and sales training and for myriad adjustments in the wholesaler's information systems. Each major retailing shift designed to satisfy customer needs obliges him to adjust his selling patterns, to review his customer service levels, to study product assortments, and to revise his strategies.[23]

---

[23] Richard S. Lopata, "Faster Pace in Wholesaling," *Harvard Business Review*, July-August 1969, p. 131.

Progressive wholesalers are those who are willing to change their ways to meet the challenges of chain organizations, discount houses, and rising labor costs. They are adapting their services to the needs of target customers and finding cost-reducing methods of transacting business.

PHYSICAL DISTRIBUTION

We are now ready to examine the institutions involved in physical distribution. Producers use these institutions to help them stock and move goods so that they will be available to customers at the right time and place. Customer attraction and satisfaction is highly influenced by the seller's physical-distribution capabilities and decisions. We will consider the nature, objectives, systems, and organizational aspects of physical distribution.

Nature of Physical Distribution

Physical distribution involves planning, implementing, and controlling the physical flows of materials and final goods from points of origin to points of use to meet customer needs at a profit.

A large number of tasks are involved in physical distribution, and they are shown in Figure 18–4. The first task is sales forecasting, on the basis of which the company schedules production and inventory levels. The production plans indicate the materials that the purchasing department must order. These materials arrive through inbound transportation, enter the receiving area, and are stored in raw material inventory. Raw materials are converted into finished goods. Finished-goods inventory is the link between the customers' orders and the company's manufacturing activity. Customers' orders draw down the finished-goods inventory level, and manufacturing activity builds it up. Finished goods flow off the assembly line and pass through packing, in-plant warehousing, shipping-room processing, outbound transportation, field warehousing, and customer delivery and servicing.

The main elements of total physical-distribution costs are transportation (46 percent), warehousing (26 percent), inventory carrying (10 percent), receiving and shipping (6 percent), packaging (5 percent), administration (4 percent), and order processing (3 percent). Management has become concerned about the total cost of physical distribution, which amounts to 13.6 percent of sales for manufacturing companies and 25.6 percent for reseller companies.[24] Experts believe that substantial savings can be effected in the physical-distribution area, which has been described as "the last frontier for cost economies"[25] and "the economy's dark continent."[26] Physical-distribution decisions, when uncoordinated, result in high costs. Not enough use is being made of modern decision tools for coordinating inventory levels, transportation modes, and plant, warehouse, and store locations.

---

[24] B. J. LaLonde and P. H. Zinszer, *Customer Service*: *Meaning and Measurement* (Chicago: National Council of Physical Distribution Management, 1976).

[25] Donald D. Parker, "Improved Efficiency and Reduced Cost in Marketing," *Journal of Marketing*, April 1962, pp. 15–21.

[26] Peter Drucker, "The Economy's Dark Continent," *Fortune*, April 1962, pp. 103ff.

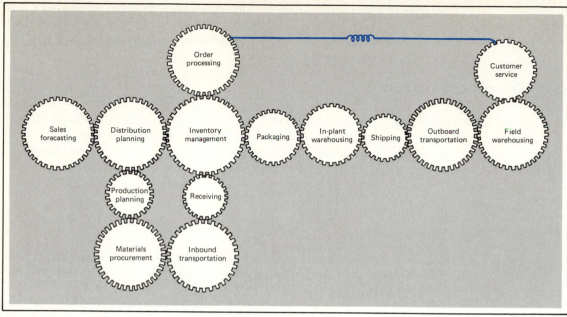

Source: Redrawn, with modifications, from Wendell M. Stewart, "Physical Distribution: Key to Improved Volume and Profits," *Journal of Marketing*, January 1965, p. 66.

FIGURE 18–4
Major Activities Involved in Physical Distribution

Physical distribution is not only a cost, it is a potent tool in demand creation. Companies can attract additional customers by offering better service or lower prices through physical-distribution improvements. Companies lose customers when they fail to supply goods on time. In the summer of 1976 Kodak launched its national advertising campaign for its new instant camera before it had delivered enough cameras to the stores. Customers found that it was not available and bought a Polaroid instead.

Traditional physical-distribution thinking starts with goods at the plant and tries to find low-cost solutions to get them to customers. Marketers prefer *market logistics* thinking that starts with the marketplace and works backward to the factory. Here is an example of market logistics thinking:

> German consumers typically purchase separate bottles of soft drinks. A soft-drink manufacturer decided to design and test a six-pack. Consumers responded positively to the convenience aspect of carrying a six-pack home. Retailers responded positively because the bottles could be loaded faster on the shelves, and more bottles would be purchased per occasion. The manufacturer designed the six-packs to fit comfortably on the store shelves. Then cases and pallets were designed for bringing these six-packs efficiently to the store's receiving rooms. Factory operations were redesigned to produce the new six-packs. The purchasing department let out bids for the new needed materials. Once implemented, this new packaging of soft drinks was an instant hit with consumers, and the manufacturer's market share rose substantially.

The Physical-Distribution Objective

Many companies state their physical-distribution objective as *getting the right goods to the right places at the right time for the least cost*. Unfortunately, this provides little actual guidance. No physical-distribution system can simultaneously maximize customer service and minimize distribution cost. Maximum customer service implies large inventories, premium transportation, and multiple warehouses, all of which raise distribution cost. Minimum distribution cost implies cheap transportation, low stocks, and few warehouses.

A company cannot achieve physical-distribution efficiency by letting each physical-distribution manager keep down his or her own costs. Physical-distribution costs interact, often in an inverse way:

☐ The traffic manager favors rail shipment over air shipment whenever possible. It reduces the company's freight bill. However, because the railroads are slower, rail shipment ties up working capital longer, delays customer payment, and may cause customers to buy from competitors offering faster service.

☐ The shipping department uses cheap containers to minimize shipping costs. This leads to a high rate of damaged goods in transit and customer ill will.

☐ The inventory manager favors low inventories to reduce inventory cost. However, this policy increases stockouts, back orders, paperwork, special production runs, and high-cost fast-freight shipments.

Given that physical-distribution activities involve strong tradeoffs, decisions must be made on a total system basis.

The starting point for designing the physical-distribution system is to study what the customers want and what competitors are offering. Customers are interested in several things: on-time delivery; supplier willingness to meet customer emergency needs; careful handling of merchandise; supplier willingness to take back defective goods and resupply them quickly; and supplier willingness to carry inventory for the customer.

The company has to research the relative importance of these services to customers. For example, service-repair time is very important to buyers of copying equipment. Xerox therefore developed a service-delivery standard that "can put a disabled machine anywhere in the continental United States back into operation within three hours after receiving the service request." Xerox runs a service division consisting of twelve thousand service and parts personnel.

The company must look at competitors' service standards in setting its own. It will normally want to offer at least the same level of service as competitors. But the objective is to maximize profits, not sales. The company has to look at the costs of providing higher levels of service. Some companies offer less service but charge a lower price. Other companies offer more service than competitors and charge a premium price to cover their higher costs.

The company ultimately has to establish physical-distribution objectives to guide its planning. For example, Coca-Cola wants to "put Coke within an arm's length of desire." Companies go further and define standards for each service factor. One appliance manufacturer has established the following service standards: to deliver at least 95 percent of the dealer's orders within seven days of order receipt; to fill the dealer's orders with 99 percent accuracy; to answer dealer inquiries on order status within three hours; and to ensure that damage to merchandise in transit does not exceed 1 percent.

Given a set of physical-distribution objectives, the company is ready to design a physical-distribution system that will minimize the cost of achieving these objectives. Each possible physical-distribution system implies a total distribution cost given by the expression:

$$D = T + FW + VW + S \qquad (18\text{--}1)$$

where:

    D = total distribution cost of proposed system
    T = total freight cost of proposed system
    FW = total fixed warehouse cost of proposed system
    VW = total variable warehouse costs (including inventory) of proposed system
    S = total cost of lost sales due to average delivery delay under proposed system

Choosing a physical-distribution system calls for examining the total distribution cost associated with different proposed systems and selecting the system that minimizes total distribution cost. Alternatively, if it is hard to measure S in (18–1), the company should aim to minimize the distribution cost $T + FW + VW$ of reaching a *target level of customer service*.

We will now examine the following major decision issues: (1) How should orders be handled? (*order processing*) (2) Where should stocks be located? (*warehousing*) (3) How much stock should be kept on hand? (*inventory*), and (4) How should goods be shipped? (*transportation*).

Order Processing

Physical distribution begins with a customer order. The order department prepares multicopy invoices and dispatches them to various departments. Items out of stock are back ordered. Shipped items are accompanied by shipping and billing documents with copies going to various departments.

The company and customers benefit when these steps are carried out quickly and accurately. Ideally sales representatives send in their orders every evening, in some cases phoning them in. The order department processes these quickly. The warehouse sends the goods out as soon as possible. Bills go out as soon as possible. The computer is used to expedite the order-shipping-billing cycle.

Industrial engineering studies of how sales orders are processed can help shorten this cycle. Some of the key questions are: What happens after receiving a customer purchase order? How long does the customer credit check take? What procedures are used to check inventory and how long does this take? How soon does manufacturing hear of new stock requirements? How long does it take for sales managers to get a complete picture of current sales?

Ringer and Howell reported a study that cut down the time between the receipt and issuance of an order from sixty-two hours to thirty hours without any change in costs.[27] General Electric operates a computer-oriented system that, upon receipt of a customer's order, checks the customer's credit standing and whether and where the items are in stock. The computer issues an order to ship, bills the customer, updates the inventory records, sends a production order for new stock, and relays the message back to the sales representative that the customer's order is on its way, all in less than fifteen seconds.

Warehousing

Every company has to store its goods while they wait to be sold. A storage function is necessary because production and consumption cycles rarely match. Many agricultural commodities are produced seasonally, while demand is continuous. The storage function overcomes discrepancies in desired quantities and timing.

The company must decide on a desirable number of stocking locations. More stocking locations means that goods can be delivered to customers more quickly. Warehousing costs go up, however. The number of stocking locations must strike a balance between the level of customer service and distribution costs.

Some company stock is kept at or near the plant, and the rest is located in warehouses around the country. The company might own *private warehouses* and rent space in *public warehouses*. Companies have more control in owned warehouses, but they tie up their capital and face some inflexibility if desired locations change. Public warehouses, on the other hand, charge for the rented space and provide additional services (at a cost) for inspecting goods, packaging them, shipping them, and invoicing them. In using public warehouses, companies have a wide choice of locations and warehouse types, including those specializing in cold storage, commodities only, and so on.

Companies use storage warehouses and distribution warehouses. *Storage warehouses* store goods for moderate to long periods of time. *Distribution warehouses* receive goods from various plants and suppliers and move them out as soon as possible. For example, Wal-Mart Stores, Inc., a regional discount-store chain, operates four distribution centers. One center covers 400,000 square feet on a 93-acre site. The shipping department loads fifty to sixty trucks daily, delivering merchandise on a twice-weekly basis to its retail outlets. This is less expensive than supplying each retail outlet from each plant directly.

The older multistoried warehouses with slow elevators and inefficient materials-handling procedures are receiving competition from newer single-storied *automated warehouses* with advanced materials-handling systems under the control of a central computer. The computer reads store orders and directs lift trucks and electric hoists to gather goods, move them to loading docks, and issue invoices. These warehouses have reduced worker injuries, labor costs, pilferage, and breakage and have improved inventory control.

[27] Jurgen F. Ringer and Charles D. Howell, "The Industrial Engineer and Marketing," in *Industrial Engineering Handbook*, 2nd ed., ed. Harold Bright Maynard (New York: McGraw-Hill Book Company, 1963), pp. 10, 102–3.

Inventory

Inventory levels represent another physical-distribution decision affecting customer satisfaction. Marketers would like their companies to carry enough stock to fill all customer orders immediately. However, it is not cost-effective for a company to carry this much inventory. *Inventory cost increases at an increasing rate as the customer-service level approaches 100 percent.* Management would need to know whether sales and profits would increase enough to justify higher inventories.

Inventory decision making involves knowing when to order and how much to order. As inventory draws down, management must know at what stock level to place a new order. This stock level is called the *order (or reorder) point.* An order point of twenty means reordering when the stock of the item falls to twenty units. The order point should be higher the higher the order lead time, the usage rate, and the service standard. If the order lead time and customer usage rate are variable, the order point should be set higher to provide a *safety stock.* The final order point should balance the risks of stockout against the costs of overstock.

The other decision is how much to order. The larger the quantity ordered, the less frequently an order has to be placed. The company needs to balance order-processing costs and inventory-carrying costs. Order-processing costs for a manufacturer consist of *setup costs* and *running costs* for the item. If setup costs are low, the manufacturer can produce the item often, and the cost per item is pretty constant and equal to the running costs. If setup costs are high, however, the manufacturer can reduce the average cost per unit by producing a long run and carrying more inventory.

Order-processing costs must be compared with inventory-carrying costs. The larger the average stock carried, the higher the inventory-carrying costs. These carrying costs include storage charges, cost of capital, taxes and insurance, and depreciation and obsolescence. Inventory-carrying costs may run as high as 30 percent of inventory value. This means that marketing managers who want their companies to carry larger inventories need to show that the larger inventories would produce incremental gross profit that would exceed incremental inventory-carrying costs.

The optimal order quantity can be determined by observing how order-processing costs and inventory-carrying costs sum up at different possible order levels. Figure 18–5 shows that the order-processing cost per unit decreases with the number of units ordered, because the order costs are spread over more units. Inventory-carrying charges per unit increase with the number of units ordered, because each unit remains longer in inventory. The two cost curves are summed vertically into a total-cost curve. The lowest point on the total-cost curve is projected down on the horizontal axis to find the optimal order quantity Q*.[28]

---

[28] The optimal order quantity is given by the formula $Q* = 2DS/IC$ where D = annual demand, S = cost to place one order, and IC = annual carrying cost per unit. Known as the economic-order quantity formula, it assumes a constant ordering cost, a constant cost of carrying an additional unit in inventory, a known demand, and no quantity discounts. For further reading on this subject, see Stephen F. Love, *Inventory Control: Mathematical Models* (New York: McGraw-Hill Book Co., 1979).

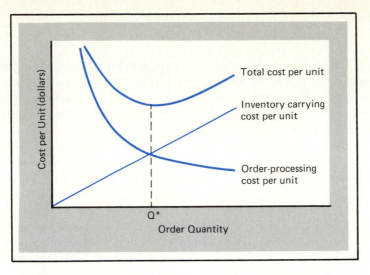

FIGURE 18-5
Determining Optimal Order Quantity

Transportation

Marketers need to take an interest in their company's transportation decisions. The choice of transportation carriers will affect the pricing of the products, on-time delivery performance, and the condition of the goods when they arrive, all of which will affect customer satisfaction.

In shipping goods to its warehouses, dealers, and customers, the company can choose among five transportation modes: *rail*, *water*, *truck*, *pipeline*, and *air*.

Rail. In spite of a shrinking share of total transportation, railroads remain the nation's largest transportation carrier, accounting for 30 percent of the nation's total cargo ton-miles. Railroads are one of the most cost-effective modes for shipping carload quantities of bulk products—coal, sand, minerals, farm and forest products—over long land distances. The rate costs for shipping merchandise are quite complex. The lowest rate comes from shipping carload rather than less-than-carload quantities. Manufacturers will attempt to combine shipments to common destinations to take advantage of lower carload rates. Railroads have recently begun to increase customer-oriented services. They have designed new equipment to handle special categories of merchandise more efficiently, provided flatcars for carrying truck trailers by rail (piggyback), and provided in-transit services such as diversion of shipped goods to other destinations en route and processing of goods en route.

Water. A substantial amount of goods move by ships and barges on coastal and inland waterways. Water transportation is very low in cost for shipping bulky, low-value, nonperishable products such as sand, coal, grain, oil, and metallic ores. On the other hand, water transportation is the slowest transportation mode and is dependent on climatic conditions.

Truck. Motor trucks have steadily increased their share of transportation and now account for 21 percent of total cargo ton-miles. They account for the largest portion of intracity as opposed to intercity transportation. Trucks are highly flexible in their routing and time schedules. They can move merchandise door to door, saving shippers the need to transfer goods from truck to rail and back again at a loss of time and risk of theft or damage. Trucks are an efficient mode of transportation for short hauls of high-value merchandise. Their rates are competitive with railway rates in many cases, and trucks can usually offer faster service.

Pipeline. Pipelines are a specialized means of shipping petroleum, coal, and chemicals from sources to markets. Pipeline shipment of petroleum products is less expensive than rail shipment, although more expensive than waterway shipment. Most pipelines are used by their owners to ship their own products, although they are technically available for use by any shipper.

Air. Air carriers transport less than 1 percent of the nation's goods but are becoming more important as a transportation mode. Although air freight rates are considerably higher than rail or truck freight rates, air freight is ideal where speed is essential and/or distant markets have to be reached. Among the most frequently air-freighted products are perishables (e.g., fresh fish, cut flowers) and high-value, low-bulk items (e.g., technical instruments, jewelery). Companies find that air freight reduces their required inventory levels, number of warehouses, and costs of packaging.

In choosing a transportation mode for a particular product, shippers consider such criteria as speed, frequency, dependability, capability, availability, and cost. If a shipper seeks speed, air and truck are the prime contenders. If the goal is low cost, then water and pipeline are the prime contenders. Trucks stand high on most of the criteria, and this accounts for their growing share.

Shippers are increasingly combining two or more transportation modes, thanks to containerization. *Containerization* consists of putting the goods in boxes or trailers that are easy to transfer between two transportation modes. *Piggyback* describes the use of rail and trucks; *fishyback*, water and trucks; *trainship*, water and rail; and *airtruck*, air and trucks. Each coordinated mode of transportation offers specific advantages to the shipper. For example, piggyback is cheaper than trucking alone and yet provides flexibility and convenience.

In choosing transportation modes, shippers can decide between private, contract, and common carriers. If the shipper owns its own truck or air fleet, the shipper becomes a *private carrier*. A *contract carrier* is an independent organization selling transportation services to others on a contract basis. A *common carrier* provides services between predetermined points on a schedule basis and is available to all shippers at standard rates.

Transportation decisions must consider the complex tradeoffs between various transportation modes and their implications for other distribution elements such as warehousing and inventory. As the relative costs of different transportation modes change over time, companies need to reanalyze their options in the search for optimal physical-distribution arrangements.

Organizational Responsibility for Physical Distribution

We see that decisions on warehousing, inventory, and transportation require the highest degree of coordination. A growing number of companies have set up a permanent committee composed of managers responsible for different physical-distribution activities. This committee meets periodically to develop policies for improving overall distribution efficiency. Some companies have appointed a vice-president of physical distribution, who reports to the marketing vice-president or manufacturing vice-president in most cases, or to the president. Here are two examples:

> The Burroughs Corporation organized the Distribution Services Department to centralize control over its physical-distribution activities. This department reported to the marketing vice-president because of the great importance Burroughs attached to good customer service. Within 2½ years following the reorganization, the company achieved savings of over $2 million annually (on $200 million of sales), plus a higher level of service to field branches and customers.
>
> Heinz created a new department of coordinate stature with marketing and production, which was headed by a vice-president of distribution. Heinz felt that this arrangement would guarantee respect for the department, develop a greater degree of professionalism and objectivity, and avoid partisan domination by marketing or production.

The location of the physical-distribution department within the company is a secondary concern. The important thing is that the company coordinates its physical-distribution and marketing activities in order to create high market satisfaction at a reasonable cost.

SUMMARY

Retailing and wholesaling consists of many organizations designed to bring goods and services from the point of production to the point of use.

Retailing includes all the activities involved in selling goods or services directly to final consumers for their personal, nonbusiness use. Retailing is one of the major industries in the United States. Retailers can be classified in several ways: by product line sold (specialty stores), department stores, supermarkets, convenience stores, combination stores, superstores, hypermarches, and service businesses); relative price emphasis (discount stores, warehouse stores, and catalog showrooms); nature of the business premises (mail-and-telephone-order retailing, automatic vending, buying services, and door-to-door retailing); control of outlets (corporate chains, voluntary chains and retailer cooperatives, consumer cooperatives, franchise organizations, and merchandising conglomerates); and type of store cluster (central business districts, regional shopping centers, community shopping centers, and neighborhood centers). Retailers make decisions on their target market, product assortment and services, pricing, promotion, and place. Retailers need to find ways to improve their professional management and increase their productivity.

Wholesaling includes all the activities involved in selling goods or services to those who are buying for the purpose of resale or for business use. Wholesalers help manufacturers deliver their products efficiently to the many retailers and industrial users across the nation. Wholesalers perform many functions, including selling and promoting, buying and assortment building, bulk-breaking, warehousing, transporting, financing, risk bearing, supplying market information, and providing management services and counseling. Wholesalers fall into four groups. Merchant wholesalers take possession of the goods. They can be subclassified as full-service wholesalers (wholesale merchants, industrial distributors) and limited-service wholesalers (cash-and-carry wholesalers, truck wholesalers, drop shippers, rack jobbers, producers' cooperatives, and mail-order wholesalers). Agents and brokers do not take possession of the goods but are paid a commission for facilitating buying and selling. Manufacturers' and retailers' branches and offices are wholesaling operations conducted by nonwholesalers to bypass the wholesalers. Miscellaneous wholesalers include agricultural assemblers, petroleum bulk plants and terminals, and auction companies. Wholesaling is holding its own in the economy. Progressive wholesalers are adapting their services to the needs of target customers and are seeking cost-reducing methods of transacting business.

The marketing concept calls for paying increased attention to the physical-distribution concept. Physical distribution is an area of potentially high cost savings and improved customer satisfaction. When order processors, warehouse planners, inventory managers, and transportation managers make decisions, they affect each other's costs and demand-creation capacity. The physical-distribution concept calls for treating all these decisions within a unified framework. The task becomes that of designing physical-distribution arrangements that minimize the total cost of providing a desired level of customer service.

QUESTIONS

1. A burgeoning market for discount direct-mail personal computers has evolved in the 1980s despite the fact that manufacturers like IBM, Osborne, Apple, and Hewlett-Packard refuse to sell to such dealers. Given the additional fact that the product's complexity suggests the need for extensive technical and instructional support by the local retailer for the consumer, how do you account for such dramatic growth of the direct-mail discount business for personal computers?

2. In two of its San Diego outlets, Montgomery Ward opened "Law Store" booths that provide a one-shot consultation for a $10 fee. Customers are ushered to a telephone-boothlike enclosure, where operators connect them to a central office of lawyers who respond to queries over the telephone. Discuss the retailer marketing decisions for the "Law Store."

3. Wholesalers typically do not invest much in the promotional part of their marketing mix. Why has this been a weak area for wholesalers?

4. Does it follow that the company offering high customer service bears high physical-distribution costs in relation to sales?

5. What are the two inventory-production policy alternatives facing a seasonal producer?

6. A company's inventory-carrying cost is 30 percent. A marketing manager wants the company to increase its inventory investment from $400,000 to $500,000, believing this would lead to increased sales of $120,000 because of greater customer loyalty and service. The gross profit on sales is 20 percent. Does it pay the company to increase its inventory investment?

7. You are the marketing manager of a medium-sized manufacturing company. The president has just made the following statement: "The distribution activity is not a concern of the marketing department. The function of the marketing department is to sell the product . . . let the rest of the company handle production and distribution." How would you reply to this statement?

Communication- and Promotion-Mix Decisions 19

People no longer buy shoes to keep their feet warm and dry. They buy them because of the way the shoes make them feel—masculine, feminine, rugged, different, sophisticated, young, glamorous, "in." Buying shoes has become an emotional experience. Our business now is selling excitement rather than shoes.

FRANCIS C. ROONEY

Modern marketing calls for more than developing a good product, pricing it attractively, and making it accessible to target customers. Companies must also communicate with their customers. Every company is inevitably cast into the role of communicator and promotor.

What is communicated, however, should not be left to chance. To communicate effectively, companies hire advertising agencies to develop effective ads; sales promotion specialists to design sales incentive programs; and public relations firms to develop the corporate image. They train their sales people to be friendly and knowledgeable. For most companies the question is not whether to communicate but how much to spend and in what ways.

A modern company manages a complex marketing communications system. The company communicates with its middlemen, consumers, and various publics. Its middlemen communicate with their consumers and various publics. Consumers engage in word-of-mouth communication with each other and with other publics. Meanwhile each group provides communication feedback to every other group.

TABLE 19–1

SOME COMMON PROMOTION TOOLS

Advertising	Sales Promotion	Publicity	Personal Selling
Print and broadcast ads	Contests, games, sweepstakes, lotteries	Press kits	Sales presentations
Packaging—outer	Premiums	Speeches	Sales meetings
Packaging inserts	Sampling	Seminars	Telemarketing
Mailings	Fairs and trade shows	Annual reports	Incentive programs
Catalogs	Exhibits	Charitable donations	Salesmen samples
Motion pictures	Demonstrators	Public relations	
House magazines	Couponing		
Brochures and booklets	Rebates		
Posters and leaflets	Low-interest financing		
Directories	Entertainment		
Reprints of ads	Trade-in allowances		
Billboards	Trading stamps		
Display signs			
Point-of-purchase displays			
Audiovisual material			
Symbols and logos			

The marketing communications mix (also called the promotion mix) consists of four major tools:

☐ **Advertising.** Any paid form of nonpersonal presentation and promotion of ideas, goods, or services by an identified sponsor.

☐ **Sales promotion.** Short-term incentives to encourage purchase or sale of a product or service.

☐ **Publicity.** Nonpersonal stimulation of demand for a product, service, or business unit by planting commercially significant news about it in a published medium or obtaining favorable presentation of it upon radio, television, or stage that is not paid for by the sponsor.

☐ **Personal selling.** Oral presentation in a conversation with one or more prospective purchasers for the purpose of making sales.[1]

Within these categories are numerous specific tools, such as those listed in Table 19–1. At the same time, communication goes beyond these specific communication tools. The product's styling, its price, the package's shape and color, the salesper-

---

[1] These definitions, except for sales promotion, are from *Marketing Definitions: A Glossary of Marketing Terms* (Chicago: American Marketing Association, 1960). The AMA definition of *sales promotion* covered, in addition to incentives, such marketing media as displays, shows and exhibitions, and demonstrations that can better be classified as forms of advertising, personal selling, or publicity. Some marketing scholars have also suggested adding *packaging* as a fifth element of the promotion mix, although others classify it as a product element.

son's manner and dress—all communicate something to the buyers. The whole marketing mix, not just the promotional mix, must be orchestrated for maximum communication impact.

This chapter examines three major questions: How does communication work? What are the major steps in developing effective marketing communication? Who should be responsible for marketing communication planning? Chapter 20 deals with advertising; Chapter 21, with sales promotion and publicity; and Chapter 22, with the sales force.

THE COMMUNICATION PROCESS

Marketers need to understand how communication works. Some years ago, Lasswell said that a communication model will answer (1) who (2) says what (3) in what channel (4) to whom (5) with what effect.[2] Over the years, a communication model with nine elements has evolved, that shown in Figure 19–1. Two elements represent the major parties in a communication—*sender* and *receiver*. Another two represent the major communication tools—*message* and *media*. Four represent major communication functions—*encoding*, *decoding*, *response*, and *feedback*. The last element represents noise in the system. These elements are defined as follows:

☐ **Sender.** The party sending the message to another party (also called the *source or communicator*).

☐ **Encoding.** The process of putting thought into symbolic form.

☐ **Message.** The set of symbols that the sender transmits.

☐ **Media.** The communication channels through which the message moves from sender to receiver.

☐ **Decoding.** The process by which the receiver assigns meaning to the symbols transmitted by the sender.

☐ **Receiver.** The party receiving the message sent by another party (also called the *audience* or *destination*).

☐ **Response.** The set of reactions that the receiver has after being exposed to the message.

☐ **Feedback.** The part of the receiver's response that the receiver communicates back to the sender.

☐ **Noise.** Unplanned static or distortion during the communication process, resulting in the receiver's receiving a different message than the sender sent.

The model underscores the key factors in effective communication. Senders must know what audiences they want to reach and what responses they want. They must be skillful in encoding messages that take into account how the target audience tends to decode messages. They must transmit the message through efficient media that reach the target audience. They must develop feedback channels so that they can know the audience's response to the message.

For a message to be effective, the encoding process of the sender must mesh with the decoding process of the receiver. Schramm sees messages as essentially signs

---

[2] Harold D. Lasswell, *Power and Personality* (New York: W. W. Norton & Co., 1948), pp. 37–51.

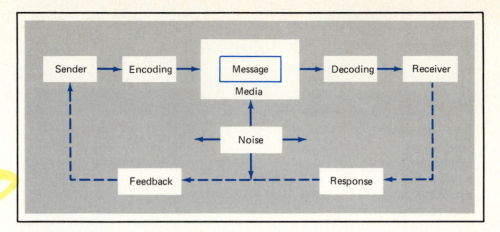

FIGURE 19–1
Elements in the Communication Process

that must be familiar to the receiver. The more the sender's field of experience overlaps with that of the receiver, the more effective the message is likely to be. (See Figure 19–2.) "The source can encode, and the destination can decode, only in terms of the experience each has had."[3] This puts a burden on communicators from one social stratum—like advertising people—who want to communicate effectively with another stratum—such as factory workers.

The sender's task is to get his or her message through to the receiver. There is considerable noise in the environment—people are exposed to over fifteen hundred commercial messages a day, aside from everything else they must attend to. Members of the audience may not get the intended message for any of three reasons. The first is *selective attention*, in that they will not notice everything around them. The second is *selective distortion*, in that they will twist the message to hear what they want to hear. The third is *selective recall*, in that they will retain only a small fraction of the messages that reach them.

The challenge to the communicator is to design a message that wins attention in spite of the surrounding distractions. Schramm suggested that the likelihood that a potential receiver will attend to a message is given by:[4]

$$\frac{\text{Likelihood}}{\text{of attention}} = \frac{\text{Perceived reward strength—Perceived punishment strength}}{\text{Perceived expenditure of effort}}$$

This explains why ads with bold headlines promising something, such as "How to Make a Million," along with an arresting illustration and little copy have a high

---

[3] Wilbur Schramm, "How Communication Works," in Wilbur Schramm and Donald F. Roberts, eds., *The Process and Effects of Mass Communication* (Urbana: University of Illinois Press, 1971), p. 4.

[4] Schramm, "How Communication Works," p. 32.

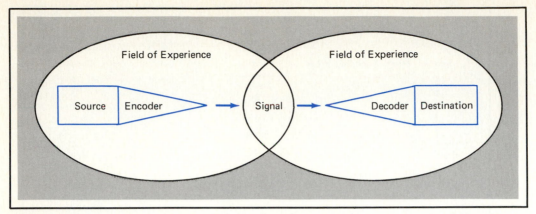

Source: Wilbur Schramm, "How Communication Works," in Wilbur Schramm and Donald F. Roberts, eds., *The Process and Effects of Mass Communication*, (Urbana, Ill.: University of Illinois Press, 1971), p. 4.

FIGURE 19-2
Elements Affecting Shared Meaning

likelihood of grabbing attention. For very little effort, the reader has an opportunity to gain a great reward.

As for selective distortion, receivers have set attitudes, which lead to expectations about what they will hear or see. They will hear what fits into their belief system. As a result, receivers often add things to the message that are not there (*amplification*) and do not notice other things that are there (*leveling*). The communicator's task is to strive for message simplicity, clarity, interest, and repetition, to get the main points across.

As for selective recall, the communicator aims to get the message into the receiver's long-term memory. Long-term memory is the repository for all information one has ever processed. In entering the receiver's long-term memory, the message has a chance of modifying the receiver's beliefs and attitudes. But first the message has to enter the receiver's short-term memory, which is a limited-capacity store that processes incoming information. Whether the message passes from the receiver's short-term memory to his or her long-term memory depends upon the amount and type of *message rehearsal* by the receiver. Rehearsal does not mean simple message repetition but rather the receiver's elaborating on the meaning of the information in a way that brings into short-term memory related thoughts in the receiver's long-term memory. If the receiver's initial attitude toward the object is positive and he or she rehearses support arguments, the message is likely to be accepted and have high recall. If the receiver's initial attitude is negative and the person rehearses counterarguments, the message is likely to be rejected but to stay in long-term memory. If there is no rehearsal of arguments but simply, "I've heard this before" or "I don't believe it," there is not likely to be high recall or any attitude change. Generally speaking, much of what is called persuasion is self-persuasion.[5]

---

[5] A. Greenwald, "Cognitive Learning, Cognitive Response to Persuasion, and Attitude Change," in *Psychological Foundations of Attitudes*, ed., A. Greenwald, T. Brock, and T. Ostrom (New York: Academic Press, 1968).

Communicators have been looking for audience traits that correlate with their degree of persuasibility. People of high education and/or intelligence are thought to be less persuasible, but the evidence is inconclusive. Women have been found to be more persuasible than men, but men who feel socially inadequate also show this trait.[6] Persons who accept external standards to guide their behavior and who have a weak self-concept appear to be more persuasible. Persons who are low in self-confidence are also thought to be more persuasible. However, research by Cox and Bauer and later by Bell showed a curvilinear relation between self-confidence and persuasibility, with those moderate in self-confidence being the most persuasible.[7] The communicator should look for audience traits that correlate with persuasibility and use them to guide message and media development.

Cartwright has outlined what must happen for a message to influence the behavior of another person:[8]

1. The "message" (that is, information, facts, and so on) must reach the sense organs of the persons who are to be influenced.
2. Having reached the sense organs, the "message" must be accepted as a part of the person's cognitive structure.
3. To induce a given action by mass persuasion, this action must be seen by the person as a path to some goal that he has.
4. To induce a given action, an appropriate cognitive and motivational system must gain control of the person's behavior at a particular point in time.

STEPS IN DEVELOPING EFFECTIVE COMMUNICATIONS

We will now examine the major steps in developing a total communication and promotion program. The marketing communicator must (1) identify the target audience; (2) determine the communication objectives; (3) design the message; (4) select the communication channels; (5) develop the total promotion budget; (6) decide on the promotion mix; (7) measure the promotion's results; and (8) manage and coordinate the total marketing communication process.

Identifying the Target Audience

A marketing communicator must start with a clear target audience in mind. The audience may be potential buyers of the company's products, current users, deciders, or influencers. The audience may be individuals, groups, particular publics, or the

---

[6] I. L. Janis and P. B. Field, "Sex Differences and Personality Factors Related to Personality," in *Personality and Persuasibility*, ed. C. Hovland and I. Janis (New Haven: Yale University Press, 1958), pp. 55–68.

[7] Donald F. Cox and Raymond A. Bauer, "Self-confidence and Persuasibility in Women," *Public Opinion Quarterly*, fall 1964, pp. 453–66; and Gerald D. Bell, "Self-Confidence and Persuasion in Car Buying," *Journal of Marketing Research*, February 1967, pp. 46–52. However, see the attempted refutation by Abe Shuchman and Michael Perry, "Self-confidence and Persuasibility in Marketing: A Reappraisal," *Journal of Marketing Research*, May 1969, pp. 146–54.

[8] Dorwin Cartwright, "Some Principles of Mass Persuasion," *Human Relations* 2 (1949): 253–67, here 255.

general public. The target audience will critically influence the communicator's decisions on *what* is to be said, *how* it is to be said, *when* it is to be said, *where* it is to be said, and *who* is to say it.

The communicator should research the audience's needs, attitudes, preferences, and other characteristics as a prelude to setting communication objectives. One of the most important things to establish is the audience's current *image* of the object.

Image analysis.   A major part of audience analysis is to assess the audience's current image of the company, its products, and its competitors. People's attitudes and actions toward an object are highly conditioned *by their beliefs about* the object. *Image* is the *set of beliefs, ideas, and impressions that a person holds of an object*.

It is important to measure the audience's image of the marketable object before any communication planning takes place. The first step is to measure the target audience's familiarity with the object, using the following scale:

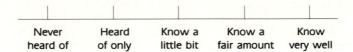

| Never | Heard | Know a | Know a | Know |
| heard of | of only | little bit | fair amount | very well |

If most of the respondents circle the first two categories, then the company's task will be to build awareness.

Respondents who are familiar with the product should be asked how favorable they feel toward it by checking one of the following:

| Very | Somewhat | Indifferent | Somewhat | Very |
| unfavorable | unfavorable | | favorable | favorable |

If most of the respondents check the first two or three categories, then the organization must overcome a negative image problem.

The two scales can be combined to develop insight into the nature of the communication problem. To illustrate, suppose area residents are asked about their familiarity and attitude toward four local hospitals, A, B, C, and D. Their responses are averaged and shown in Figure 19–3. Hospital A has the most positive image: Most people know it and like it. Hospital B is less familiar to most people, but those who know it like it. Hospital C is viewed negatively by those who know it, but fortunately not too many people know it. Hospital D is seen as a poor hospital, and everyone knows it.

Clearly each hospital faces a different task. Hospital A must work at maintaining its good reputation and high community awareness. Hospital B must gain the attention of more people since those who know it find it to be a good hospital. Hospital C needs to find out why people dislike it and take steps to improve its performance

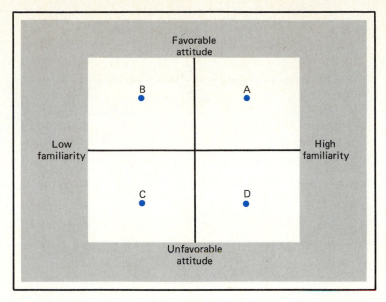

FIGURE 19–3
Familiarity-Favorability Analysis

while keeping a low profile. Hospital D should lower its profile (avoid news), improve its quality, and then seek public attention again.

Each hospital needs to go further and research the specific content of its image. The most popular tool for this is the *semantic differential*.[9] It involves the following steps:

1. **Developing a set of relevant dimensions.** The researcher asks people to identify the dimensions they would use in thinking about the object. People could be asked: "What things do you think of when you consider a hospital?" If someone suggests "quality of medical care," this would be turned into a bipolar adjective scale—say, "inferior medical care" at one end and "superior medical care" at the other. This could be rendered as a five- or seven-point scale. A set of additional dimensions for a hospital are shown in Figure 19–4.

2. **Reducing the set of relevant dimensions.** The number of dimensions should be kept small to avoid respondent fatigue in having to rate *n* objects on *m* scales. Osgood and his co-workers feel that there are essentially three types of scales:
   · evaluation scales (good-bad qualities)
   · potency scales (strong-weak qualities)
   · activity scales (active-passive qualities)
   Using these scales as a guide, the researcher can remove redundant scales that fail to add much information.

3. **Administering the instrument to a sample of respondents.** The respondents are asked to rate one object at a time. The bipolar adjectives should be randomly arranged so as not to list all of the poor adjectives on one side.

---

[9] The semantic differential was developed by C. E. Osgood, C. J. Suci, and P. H. Tannenbaum, *The Measurement of Meaning*, (Urbana: University of Illinois Press, 1957).

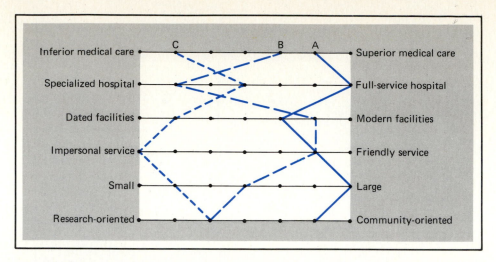

FIGURE 19–4
Images of Three Hospitals (Semantic Differential)

4. **Averaging the results.** Figure 19–4 shows the results of averaging the respondents' pictures of hospitals A, B, and C (hospital D is left out). Each hospital's image is represented by a vertical "line of means" that summarizes how the average respondent sees that institution. Thus hospital A is seen as a large, modern, friendly, and superior hospital. Hospital C, on the other hand, is seen as a small, dated, impersonal, and inferior hospital.

5. **Checking on the image variance.** Since each image profile is a line of means, it does not reveal how variable the image actually is. If there were 100 respondents, did they all see hospital B, for example, exactly as shown, or was there considerable variation? In the first case we would say that the image is highly *specific* and in the second case, highly *diffused*. An institution may not want a very specific image. Some organizations prefer a diffused image so that different groups can project their needs into this organization. The organization will want to analyze whether a diffused image is possibly the result of different subgroups rating the organization, with each subgroup having a highly specific image.

The marketers should now develop a picture of the *desired image* in contrast to the *current image*. Suppose hospital C would like the public to have a more favorable view of the quality of its medical care, facilities, friendliness, and so on. It is not aiming for perfection because the hospital recognizes its limitations. The desired image must be feasible in terms of the hospital's present reality and resources.

Management must decide which image gaps it wants to close first. Is it more desirable to improve the hospital's image of friendliness (through staff training programs and the like) or the look of its facilities (through renovation)? Each image dimension should be reviewed in terms of the following questions:

☐ What contribution to the organization's overall favorable image would be made by closing that particular image gap to the extent shown?
☐ What strategy (combination of real changes and communication changes) would help close the particular image gap?
☐ What would be the cost of closing that image gap?
☐ How long would it take to close that image gap?

An organization seeking to change its image must have great patience. Images are "sticky" and persist long after the organization has changed. Thus a hospital's medical care might have deteriorated, and yet it continues to be highly regarded in the public mind. Image persistence is explained by the fact that once people have a certain image of an object, they tend to be selective perceivers of further data. Their perceptions are oriented toward seeing what they expect to see. It will take highly disconfirming stimuli to raise doubts and open them to new information. Thus an image enjoys a life of its own, especially when people do not have new first-hand experiences with the changed object.

Determining the Communication Objectives

Once the target audience and its characteristics are identified, the marketing communicator must determine what response is sought. The ultimate response, of course, is purchase. But purchase behavior is the end result of a long process of consumer decision making. The marketing communicator needs to know how to move the target audience from where it now stands to a higher state of readiness-to-buy.

The marketer may be seeking a *cognitive, affective,* or *behavorial* response from the target audience. In other words, the marketer may want to put something into the consumer's mind, change the consumer's attitude, or get the consumer to undertake a specific action. Even here, there are different models of consumer-response stages. Figure 19–5 shows the four best known *response hierarchy models*.

The AIDA model shows the buyer as passing through awareness, interest, desire, and action. The "hierarchy-of-effects" model shows the buyer as passing through awareness, knowledge, liking, preference, conviction, and purchase. The "innovation-adoption" model shows the buyer as passing through awareness, interest, evaluation, trial, and adoption. The "communications" model shows the buyer as passing through exposure, reception, cognitive response, attitude, intention, and behavior. Most of these differences are semantic. All of these models assume that the buyer passes through a cognitive, affective, and behavioral stage, in that order. We will work with the "hierarchy-of-effects" model and describe the six *buyer-readiness states— awareness, knowledge, liking, preference, conviction,* and *purchase.* (Other sequences of states are possible, depending upon the degree of consumer involvement and the degree of brand differences. See the discussion in Chapter 4, p. 145, on how communication would be modified for low-involvement products.)

Awareness.   If most of the target audience is unaware of the object, the communicator's task is to build awareness, perhaps just name recognition. This can be accomplished with simple messages repeating the name. Even then, building awareness takes time.

> Suppose a small Iowa college called Pottsville seeks applicants from Nebraska but has no name recognition in Nebraska. And suppose there were thirty thousand high school seniors in Nebraska who might potentially be interested in Pottsville College. The college might set the objective of making 70 percent of these students aware of Pottsville's name within one year.

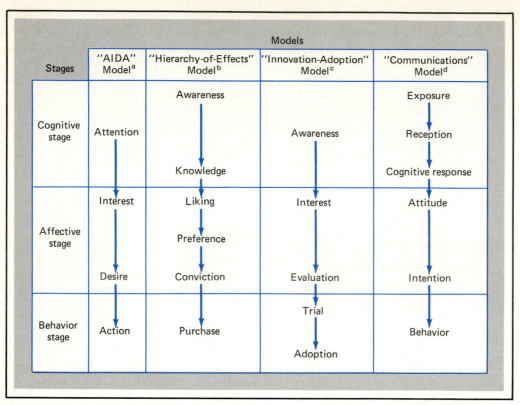

Models

Stages	"AIDA" Model[a]	"Hierarchy-of-Effects" Model[b]	"Innovation-Adoption" Model[c]	"Communications" Model[d]
Cognitive stage	Attention	Awareness ↓ Knowledge	Awareness	Exposure ↓ Reception ↓ Cognitive response
Affective stage	Interest ↓ Desire	Liking ↓ Preference ↓ Conviction	Interest ↓ Evaluation	Attitude ↓ Intention
Behavior stage	Action	Purchase	Trial ↓ Adoption	Behavior

Sources: (a) E. K. Strong, *The Psychology of Selling* (New York: McGraw-Hill Book Co., 1925), p. 9; (b) Robert J. Lavidge and Gary A. Steiner, "A Model for Predictive Measurements of Advertising Effectiveness," *Journal of Marketing*, October 1961, p. 61; (c) Everett M. Rogers, *Diffusion of Innovations* (New York: Free Press, 1962), pp. 79–86; (d) Various sources.

FIGURE 19–5
Response Hierarchy Models

Knowledge. The target audience might have company or product awareness but not know much more. Pottsville may want its target audience to know that it is a private four-year college in eastern Iowa with excellent programs in ornithology and thanatology. Pottsville College needs to learn how many people in the target audience have little, some, and much knowledge about Pottsville. The college may decide to build up product knowledge as its immediate communication objective.

Liking. If the target audience knows the object, how do they feel about it? If much of the audience looks unfavorably on Pottsville College, the communicator has to find out why and then develop a communications campaign to build up favorable feeling. If the unfavorable view is rooted in real inadequacies of the college, then a communication campaign will not do the job. The task requires improving the college and then communicating its quality. Good public relations call for "good deeds followed by good words."

Preference. The target audience might like the product but not prefer it to others. In this case the communicator seeks to build consumer preference. The communicator will tout the product's quality, value, performance, and other attributes. The communicator can check on the campaign's success by remeasuring the audience's preferences after the campaign.

Conviction. A target audience might prefer a particular product but not develop a conviction about buying it. Thus some high school seniors might prefer Pottsville but not be sure they want to go to college. The communicator's job is to build conviction that going to college is the right thing to do.

Purchase. Some members of the target audience might have conviction but not quite get around to making the purchase. They may be waiting for additional information, plan to act later, and so on. The communicator must lead these consumers to take the final step. Among purchase-producing devices are offering the product at a low price, offering a premium, offering an opportunity to try it on a limited basis, or indicating that it will soon be unavailable.

Determining the response sought is critical in developing a communication program. Exhibit 19–1 shows how the communicator can determine simultaneously both the target audience and the response sought.

Designing the Message

Having defined the desired audience response, the communicator moves to developing an effective message. Ideally the message should get *attention*, hold *interest*, arouse *desire*, and obtain *action* (**AIDA model**). In practice, few messages take the consumer all the way from awareness through purchase, but the AIDA framework suggests the desirable qualities.

Formulating the message will require solving four problems: what to say (*message content*), how to say it logically (*message structure*), how to say it symbolically (*message format*), and who should say it (*message source*).

Message content. The communicator has to figure out what to say to the target audience to produce the desired response. This has been variously called the *appeal*, *theme*, *idea*, or *unique selling proposition*, (USP). It amounts to formulating some kind of benefit, motivation, identification, or reason why the audience should think or do something. Three types of appeals can be distinguished. *Rational appeals* appeal to the audience's self-interest. They show that the product will produce the claimed functional benefits. Examples would be messages demonstrating a product's quality, economy, value, or performance. It is widely believed that industrial buyers are most responsive to rational appeals. They are knowledgeable about the product class, trained to recognize value, and accountable to others for their choice. Consumers, when they buy big-ticket items, are also thought to gather information and carefully compare the alternatives. They will respond to quality, economy, value, and performance appeals.

Exhibit 19–1

DETERMINING THE TARGET AUDIENCE AND RESPONSE SOUGHT

Communication objectives depend heavily on how many people already know about a product and may have tried it. Ottesen has developed a device called a *market map* to be used as a guide to choosing the target audience and eliciting the response sought. The market map is shown below:

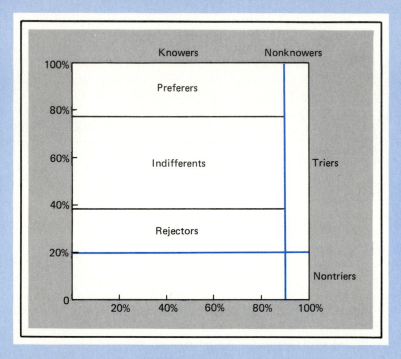

The horizontal dimension shows the current percentage of the market that knows the brand, here 90 percent. The vertical dimension shows the percentage of the market that have tried the brand, here 80 percent. From these two measures, we know that the brand is mature. The knowers-triers further divide into those who prefer (25 percent), are indifferent (50 percent), and have rejected (25 percent) the brand. The knower-nontriers can also be assumed to divide into those who have a positive, indifferent, and negative attitude toward the brand.

The task is to set communication objectives for this brand. Since 90 percent of the target market already know the brand, it would not make sense to build awareness in the remaining 10 percent. The 10 percent who do not know this brand consist of persons who are unaware of many things and probably don't have much income. It is expensive to reach these people and usually is not worth it.

What about getting more knower-nontriers to try the product? That is a worthwhile objective and can be best accomplished through sales promotion (free samples, cents-off coupons, and so on) rather than through additional advertising or personal selling. Since 25 percent of the current triers prefer the brand, we cannot expect that more than 25 percent of the new triers will stay with the brand. The marketer should calculate whether achieving this number of new-trier preferrers would be worth the cost of the sales promotion campaign.

Another plausible communication objective is to increase the proportion of triers who prefer this brand to other brands. This is difficult because consumer attitude is a function of how the consumer experiences the performance and price of the brand. If the company wants to increase preference, what is required is product improvement and lower prices rather than more advertising.

The following conclusions can be drawn about the three trier groups. Communication to those who already prefer the brand is usually not very productive unless there is high consumer forgetfulness or a high level of competitors' expenditure aimed at preferers. Communication directed to the rejectors is probably wasted because the rejectors are not likely to pay attention to the advertising and probably would not re-try the brand. Communication directed to the indifferents will probably be effective in attracting some proportion of their purchases, especially if the advertising makes some strong point to this audience.

Thus the communication objectives depend very much on the state of the market. When a brand is new, there are few knowers and triers, and communication can be very effective in increasing their number. When the brand is mature, it makes sense to try to convert nontriers into triers through sales promotion and to fight for a normal share of the indifferent triers; it makes less sense to try to increase the percentage of knowers to reinforce preferers, or to try to get rejectors to re-try the brand.

Source: See Otto Ottesen, "The Response Function," in Current Theories in Scandinavian Mass Communications Research, ed. Mie Berg (Grenaa, Demark: G.M.T., 1977).

Emotional appeals attempt to stir up some negative or positive emotion that will motivate purchase. Communicators have worked with fear, guilt, and shame appeals in getting people to do things they should (e.g., brushing teeth, taking an annual health checkup) or stop doing things they shouldn't (e.g., smoking, overimbibing, drug abuse, overeating). Fear appeals are effective up to a point, but if the audience anticipates too much fear in the message, they will avoid it. (See Exhibit 19–2.) Communicators also use positive emotional appeals such as humor, love, pride, and joy. Evidence has not established that a humorous message, for example, is necessarily more effective than a straight version of the same message. Humorous messages probably attract more attention and create more liking and belief in the sponsor, but humor may also detract from comprehension.[10]

Moral appeals are directed to the audience's sense of what is right and proper. They are often used to exhort people to support social causes, such as a cleaner environment, better race relations, equal rights for women, and aid to the disadvantaged. An example is the March of Dimes appeal: "God made you whole. Give to help those He didn't." Moral appeals are less often used in connection with everyday products.

Message structure. A message's effectiveness depends on its structure as well as its content. Hovland's research at Yale has shed much light on conclusion drawing, one- versus two-sided arguments, and order of presentation.

---

[10] See Brian Sternthal and C. Samuel Craig, "Humor in Advertising," *Journal of Marketing*, October 1973, pp. 12–18.

Exhibit 19-2

DO FEAR APPEALS WORK?

Fear appeals have been studied more than any other emotional appeal, not only in marketing communications but also in politics and child rearing. For many years marketing communicators believed that a message's effectiveness increased with the level of fear produced. Then the famous study of Janis and Feshbach, in which they tested the effectiveness of different fear levels in a dental-hygiene message directed to high school students, indicated that the strong fear appeal was less effective than a moderate one in producing adherence to a recommended dental-hygiene program. This finding, that neither extremely strong nor extremely weak fear appeals were as effective as moderate ones, became widely accepted. Ray and Wilkie supported this finding by hypothesizing two types of effects as fear increases:

First, there are the facilitating effects that are most often overlooked in marketing. If fear can heighten drive, there is the possibility of greater attention and interest in the product and message than if no drive were aroused. . . . But fear also brings the important characteristic of inhibition into the picture. . . . If fear levels are too high, there is the possibility of defensive avoidance of the ad, denial of the threat, selective exposure or distortion of the ad's meaning, or a view of the recommendations as being inadequate to deal with so important a fear.

But other researchers found cases where high fear appeals were very effective. This may mean that the buyers have different levels of tolerance for fear appeals, and the level of the fear message should be set separately for different segments. Further, if the fear message is to be effective, the communication should promise to relieve, in a believable and efficient way, the fear it arouses; otherwise buyers will ignore or minimize the threat.

Sources: Irving L. Janis and Seymour Feshbach, "Effects of Fear-Arousing Communications," Journal of Abnormal and Social Psychology, January 1953, pp. 78–92; Michael L. Ray and William L. Wilkie, "Fear: The Potential of an Appeal Neglected by Marketing," Journal of Marketing, January 1970, pp. 55–56; Carl I. Hovland, Irving L. Janis, and Harold H. Kelley, Communication and Persuasion (New Haven: Yale University Press, 1953), pp. 87–88; and Brian Sternthal and C. Samuel Craig, "Fear Appeals: Revisited and Revised," Journal of Consumer Research, December 1974, pp. 22–34.

Conclusion drawing is the question of whether the communicator should draw a definite conclusion for the audience or leave it to them. In a laboratory experiment, Hovland and Mandell found that more than twice as many persons changed in the direction advocated when the conclusion was stated than when they were left to draw their own conclusions.[11] Later studies, however, produced conflicting results. Conclusion drawing is less effective in the following situations:

☐ If the communicator is seen as untrustworthy, the audience may resent the attempt to influence them.

---

[11] Carl I. Hovland and Wallace Mandell, "An Experimental Comparison of Conclusion-Drawing by the Communication and by the Audience," *Journal of Abnormal and Social Psychology*, July 1952, pp. 581–88.

- ☐ If the issue is simple or the audience is intelligent, they may be annoyed at the attempt to explain the obvious.
- ☐ If the issue is highly personal, the audience may resent the communicator's attempt to draw a conclusion.

Drawing too explicit a conclusion can limit a product's acceptance. If Ford had hammered away that the Mustang was for young people, this strong definition might have blocked other age groups who were attracted to it. *Stimulus ambiguity* can lead to a broader market definition and more spontaneous uses of certain products. Conclusion drawing seems better suited for complex or specialized products where a single and clear use is intended.

One- or two-sided arguments raises the question of whether the communicator should only praise the product or also mention some shortcomings. One would think that the best effect is gained in one-sided presentations, which predominate in sales presentations, political contests, and child rearing. Yet the answer is not clear-cut. Here are some findings:[12]

- ☐ One-sided messages work best with audiences that are initially predisposed to the communicator's position, and two-sided arguments work best with audiences who are opposed.
- ☐ Two-sided messages tend to be more effective with better-educated audiences.
- ☐ Two-sided messages tend to be more effective with audiences who are likely to be exposed to counterpropaganda.

Order of presentation raises the question of whether a communicator should present the strongest arguments first or last. In the case of a one-sided message, presenting the strongest argument first has the advantage of establishing attention and interest. This is important in newspapers and other media where the audience does not attend to the whole message. However, it means an anticlimactic presentation. With a captive audience, a climactic presentation may be more effective. In the case of a two-sided message, the issue is whether to present the positive argument first (primacy effect) or last (recency effect). If the audience is initially opposed, the communicator would be smart to start with the other side's argument. This will disarm the audience and allow concluding with his strongest argument. Neither primacy nor recency effect dominates in all situations, and more research is needed.

Message format. The communicator must develop a strong format for the message. In a print ad, the communicator has to decide on the headline, copy, illustration, and color. To attract attention, advertisers use such devices as *novelty and contrast*, *arresting pictures and headlines*, *distinctive formats*, *message size and position*, and *color*, *shape*, and *movement*.[13] If the message is to be carried over the radio, the communicator has to carefully choose words, voice qualities (speech rate, rhythm,

---

[12] See C. I. Hovland, A. A. Lumsdaine, and F. D. Sheffield, *Experiments on Mass Communication* (Princeton, N.J.,: Princeton University Press, 1948), vol. III, chap. 8.

---

[13] For a discussion of these devices, see James F. Engel, Roger D. Blackwell, and David T. Kollat, *Consumer Behavior*, 3rd ed. (Hinsdale, Ill.: Dryden Press, 1978), pp. 346–48.

pitch, articulation), and vocalizations (pauses, sighs, yawns). The "sound" of an announcer promoting a used automobile has to be different from one promoting a quality mattress. If the message is to be carried on television or in person, then all of these elements plus body language (nonverbal clues) have to be planned. Presenters have to pay attention to their facial expressions, gestures, dress, posture, and hair style. If the message is carried by the product or its packaging, the communicator has to pay attention to color, texture, scent, size, and shape.

> Color plays an important communication role in food preferences. When housewives sampled four cups of coffee that had been placed next to brown, blue, red, and yellow containers (all the coffee was identical, unknown to the housewives), 75 percent felt that the coffee next to the brown container tasted too strong: nearly 85 percent judged the coffee next to the red container to be the richest: nearly everyone felt that the coffee next to the blue container was mild and the coffee next to the yellow container was weak.

Message source.   The message's impact on the audience is also influenced by how the audience perceives the sender. Messages delivered by highly credible sources are more persuasive. Pharmaceutical companies want doctors to testify about their products' benefits because doctors have high credibility. Antidrug crusaders will use ex-drug addicts to warn high school students against drugs because ex-addicts have higher credibility than teachers. Marketers will hire well-known personalities such as newscasters or athletes to deliver their messages.

But what factors underlie source credibility? The three factors most often identified are expertise, trustworthiness, and likability.[14] *Expertise* is the specialized knowledge the communicator appears to possess, which backs the claim. Doctors, scientists, and professors rank high on expertise in their respective fields. *Trustworthiness* is related to how objective and honest the source is perceived to be. Friends are trusted more than strangers or salespeople. *Likability* describes the source's attractiveness to the audience. Such qualities as candor, humor, and naturalness make a source more likable. The most highly credible source, then, would be a person who scored high on all three dimensions.

If a person has a positive attitude toward a source and a message, or a negative attitude toward both, a state of congruity is said to exist. What happens if the person holds one attitude toward the source and the opposite toward the message? Suppose a homemaker hears a likable celebrity praise a brand that she dislikes. Osgood and Tannenbaum posit that *attitude change will take place in the direction of increasing the amount of congruity between the two evaluations.*[15] The homemaker will end up respecting the celebrity somewhat less and respecting the brand somewhat more. If she encounters the same celebrity praising other disliked brands, she will eventually develop a negative view of the celebrity and maintain her negative attitudes toward the brands. The *principle of congruity* says that communicators can use their good

[14] Herbert C. Kelman and Carl I. Hovland, "Reinstatement of the Communication in Delayed Measurement of Opinion Change," *Journal of Abnormal and Social Psychology*, 48 (1953): pp. 327–35.

[15] C. E. Osgood and P. H. Tannenbaum, "The Principle of Congruity in the Prediction of Attitude Change," *Psychological Review* 62 (1955): 42–55.

image to reduce some negative feelings toward a brand but in the process may lose some audience regard.

Selecting the Communication Channels

The communicator must select efficient channels of communication to carry the message. Communication channels are of two broad types, *personal* and *nonpersonal*.

Personal communication channels.
Personal communication channels involve two or more persons communicating directly with each other. They might communicate face to face, person to audience, over the telephone, through the medium of television, or even through the mails on a personal correspondence basis. Personal communication channels derive their effectiveness through the opportunities the individuals have for personal addressing and feedback.

A further distinction can be drawn between advocate, expert, and social channels of communication. *Advocate* channels consist of company sales people contacting buyers in the target market. *Expert* channels consist of independent persons with expertise making statements to target buyers. *Social* channels consist of neighbors, friends, family members, and associates talking to target buyers. This last channel, known as *word-of-mouth influence*, is the most persuasive in many product areas.

Personal influence carries great weight especially in the following two situations:

☐ **Where the product is expensive, risky, or purchased infrequently.** Here buyers are likely to be high information seekers. They are likely to go beyond mass-media information and seek the opinions of knowledgeable and trusted sources.

☐ **Where the product has a significant social character.** Such products as automobiles, clothing, and even beer and cigarettes have significant brand differentiation that implies something about user status or taste. Consumers are likely to choose brands acceptable to their groups.

Companies can take several steps to stimulate personal influence channels to work on their behalf. They can (1) identify influential individuals and companies and devote extra effort to them; (2) create opinion leaders by supplying certain people with the product on attractive terms; (3) work through community influentials, such as disc jockeys, class presidents, and presidents of women's organizations; (4) use influential people in testimonial advertising; and (5) develop advertising that has high "conversation value."[16]

Nonpersonal communication channels.
Nonpersonal communication channels are media that carry messages without personal contact or feedback. They include mass and selective media, atmospheres, and events. *Mass and selective media* consist of print media (newspapers, magazines, direct mail), electronic media (radio, television),

---

[16] These and other points are discussed in Thomas S. Robertson, *Innovative Behavior and Communication* (New York: Holt, Rinehart & Winston, 1971), Chap. 9.

and display media (billboards, signs, posters). Mass media are aimed at large, often undifferentiated, audiences; selective media are aimed at specialized audiences. *Atmospheres* are designed environments that create or reinforce the buyer's leanings toward purchase or consumption of the product. Thus law offices and banks are designed to communicate confidence and other things that might be valued by the clients.[17] *Events* are occurrences designed to communicate particular messages to target audiences. Public relations departments arrange news conferences or grand openings to achieve specific communication effects on an audience.

Although personal communication is often more effective than mass communication, mass media may be the major way to stimulate personal communication. Mass communications affect personal attitudes and behavior through a *two-step flow-of-communication process*. "Ideas often flow from radio and print to opinion leaders and from these to the less active sections of the population."[18]

This two-step communication flow has several implications. First, the influence of mass media on public opinion is not as direct, powerful, and automatic as supposed. It is mediated by *opinion leaders*, persons who belong to primary groups and whose opinions are sought in one or more product areas. Opinion leaders are more exposed to mass media than those they influence. They carry messages to people who are less exposed to media, thus extending the influence of the mass media; or they may carry altered messages or none at all, thus acting as *gatekeepers*.

Second, the hypothesis challenges the notion that people's consumption styles are primarily influenced by a "trickle-down" effect from higher-status classes. To the contrary, people primarily interact within their own social class and acquire their fashion and other ideas from people like themselves who are opinion leaders.

A third implication is that mass communicators would be more efficient by directing their messages specifically to opinion leaders, letting the latter carry the message to others. Thus pharmaceutical firms try to promote their new drugs to the most influential physicians first.

Communications researchers are moving toward a social-structure view of interpersonal communication.[19] They see society as consisting of *cliques*, small social groups whose members interact with each other more frequently than with others. Clique members are similar, and their closeness facilitates effective communication but also prevents new ideas from entering the clique. The challenge is to create more system openness whereby cliques exchange more information with each other and in the larger environment. This openness is helped by persons who function as liaisons and bridges. A *liaison* is a person who connects two or more cliques without belonging to either. A *bridge* is a person who belongs to one clique and who is linked to a person in another clique. Word-of-mouth communications flow most readily within cliques, and the problem is to facilitate communication between cliques.

---

[17] See Philip Kotler, "Atmospherics as a Marketing Tool," *Journal of Retailing*, winter 1973–74, pp. 48–64.

[18] P. F. Lazarsfeld, B. Berelson, and H. Gaudet, *The People's Choice*, 2nd ed. (New York: Columbia University Press, 1948), p. 151.

[19] See Everett M. Rogers, "New Product Adoption and Diffusion," *The Journal of Consumer Research*, March 1976, pp. 290–301.

Establishing the Total Promotion Budget

One of the most difficult marketing decisions facing companies is how much to spend on promotion. John Wanamaker, the department-store magnate, said: "I know that half of my advertising is wasted, but I don't know which half. I spent $2 million for advertising, and I don't know if that is half enough or twice too much."

Thus it is not surprising that industries and companies vary considerably in how much they spend on promotion. Promotion spending may amount to 30 to 50 percent of sales in the cosmetics industry and only 10 to 20 percent in the industrial machinery industry. Within a given industry, low- and high-spending companies are found. Philip Morris is a high spender. When it acquired the Miller Brewing Company, and later the Seven-Up Company, it substantially increased total promotion spending. The additional spending at Miller's raised its market share from 4 to 19 percent within a few years.

How do companies decide on their promotion budget? We will describe four common methods used to set the total budget or any component, such as advertising.

Affordable method. Many companies set the promotion budget at what they think the company can afford. One executive explained this method as follows: "Why it's simple. First, I go upstairs to the controller and ask how much they can afford to give us this year. He says a million and a half. Later, the boss comes to me and asks how much we should spend and I say 'Oh, about a million and a half.' "[20]

This method of setting budgets completely ignores the impact of promotion on sales volume. It leads to an uncertain annual promotion budget, which makes long-range market planning difficult.

Percentage-of-sales method. Many companies set their promotion expenditures at a specified percentage of sales (either current or anticipated) or of the sales price. A railroad company executive said: "We set our appropriation for each year on December 1 of the preceding year. On that date we add our passenger revenue for the next month, and then take 2 percent of the total for our advertising appropriation for the new year."[21] Automobile companies typically budget a fixed percentage for promotion based on the planned car price. Oil companies set the appropriation at some fraction of a cent for each gallon of gasoline sold under their own label.

A number of advantages are claimed for this method. First, the percentage-of-sales method means that promotion expenditures are likely to vary with what the company can "afford." This satisfies the financial managers, who feel that expenses should bear a close relation to the movement of corporate sales over the business cycle. Second, this method encourages management to think in terms of the relationship between promotion cost, selling price, and profit per unit. Third, this method encourages competitive stability to the extent that competing firms spend approximately the same percentage of their sales on promotion.

---

[20] Quoted in Daniel Seligman, "How Much for Advertising?" *Fortune*, December 1956, p. 123.

[21] Albert Wesley Frey, *How Many Dollars for Advertising?* (New York: Ronald Press, 1955), p. 65.

In spite of these advantages, the percentage-of-sales method has little to justify it. It uses circular reasoning in viewing sales as the cause of promotion rather than as the result. It leads to an appropriation set by the availability of funds rather than by the opportunities. It discourages experimenting with countercyclical promotion or aggressive spending. The dependence of the promotion budget on year-to-year sales fluctuations interferes with long-range planning. The method does not provide a logical basis for choosing the specific percentage, except what has been done in the past or what competitors are doing. Finally, it does not encourage building up the promotion budget by determining what each product and territory deserves.

Competitive-parity method.   Some companies set their promotion budget to match competitors' outlays. This thinking is illustrated by the executive who asked a trade source: "Do you have any figures which other companies in the builders' specialties field have used which would indicate what proportion of gross sales should be given over to advertising?"[22]

Two arguments are advanced for this method. One is that competitors' expenditures represent the collective wisdom of the industry. The other is that maintaining a competitive parity helps prevent promotion wars.

Neither argument is valid. There are no grounds for believing that competition knows better what a company should be spending on promotion. Company reputations, resources, opportunities, and objectives differ so much that their promotion budgets are hardly a guide. Furthermore there is no evidence that budgets based on competitive parity discourage promotional wars from breaking out.

Objective-and-task method.   The objective-and-task method calls upon marketers to develop their promotion budgets by defining their specific objectives, determining the tasks that must be performed to achieve these objectives, and estimating the costs of performing these tasks. The sum of these costs is the proposed promotion budget.

Ule showed how the objective-and-task method could be used to establish an advertising budget for a new filter-tip cigarette, Sputnik (*name fictitious*).[23] The steps are as follows:

1. **Establish the market-share goal.** The advertiser wants 8 percent of the market. Since there are 50 million cigarette smokers, the company wants to switch 4 million smokers to Sputnik.
2. **Determine the percent of the market that should be reached by Sputnik advertising.** The advertiser hopes to reach 80 percent (40 million smokers) with the advertising.
3. **Determine the percent of aware smokers that should be persuaded to try the brand.** The advertiser would be pleased if 25 percent of aware smokers, or 10 million smokers, tried Sputnik. This is because he estimates that 40 percent of all triers, or 4 million persons, would become loyal users. That is the market goal.

---

[22] Ibid., p. 49.

[23] G. Maxwell Ule, "A Media Plan for 'Sputnik' Cigarettes," *How to Plan Media Strategy* (American Association of Advertising Agencies, 1957 Regional Convention), pp. 41–52.

4. **Determine the number of advertising impressions per 1 percent trial rate.** The advertiser estimates that 40 advertising impressions (exposures) for every 1 percent of the population would bring about a 25 percent trial rate.

5. **Determine the number of gross rating points that would have to be purchased.** A gross rating point is one exposure to 1 percent of the target population. Since the company wants to achieve 40 exposures to 80 percent of the population, it will want to buy 3,200 gross rating points.

6. **Determine the necessary advertising budget on the basis of the average cost of buying a gross rating point.** To expose 1 percent of the target population to one impression costs an average of $3,277. Therefore, 3,200 gross rating points would cost $10,486,400 (= $3,277 × 3,200) in the introductory year.

This method has the advantage of requiring management to spell out its assumptions about the relationship between dollars spent, exposure levels, trial rates, and regular usage.

The overall answer to how much weight promotion should receive in the total marketing mix (as opposed to product improvement, lower prices, more services, and so on) depends on where the company's products are in their life cycles, whether they are commodities or highly differentiable products, whether they are routinely needed or have to be "sold," and other considerations. In theory, the total promotional budget should be established where the marginal profit from the last promotional dollar just equals the marginal profit from the last dollar in the best nonpromotional use. Implementing this principle, however, is not easy.

Deciding on the Promotion Mix

Companies face the task of distributing the total promotion budget over the four promotion tools of advertising, sales promotion, publicity, and sales force. Companies within the same industry can differ considerably in how they divide their promotional budget. Avon concentrates its promotional funds on personal selling (its advertising is only 1.5 percent of sales), while Revlon spends heavily on advertising (about 7.0 percent of sales). In selling vacuum cleaners, Electrolux spends heavily on a door-to-door sales force while Hoover relies more on advertising. Thus it is possible to achieve a given sales level with various mixes of advertising, personal selling, sales promotion, and publicity.

Companies are always searching for ways to gain efficiency by substituting one promotional tool for another as its economics become more favorable. Many companies have replaced some field sales activity with ads, direct mail, and telephone calls. Other companies have increased their sales promotion expenditures in relation to advertising, to gain quicker sales. The substitutability among promotional tools explains why marketing functions need to be coordinated in a single marketing department.

Designing the promotion mix is even more complicated when one tool can be used to promote another. Thus when McDonald's decides to run Million Dollar Sweepstakes in its fast-food outlets (a form of sales promotion), it has to take out newspaper ads to inform the public. When General Mills develops a consumer advertising/sales promotion campaign to launch a new cake mix, it has to also develop a campaign directed to the trade, to win their support.

Many factors influence the marketer's choice of promotional tools. We will examine these factors in the following paragraphs.

Nature of each promotional tool. Each promotional tool—advertising, personal selling, sales promotion, and publicity—has its own unique characteristics and costs. Marketers have to understand these characteristics in selecting them.

Advertising. Because of the many forms and uses of advertising, it is difficult to make all-embracing generalizations about its distinctive qualities as a component of the promotional mix. Yet the following qualities can be noted:[24]

☐ **Public presentation.** Advertising is a highly public mode of communication. Its public nature confers a kind of legitimacy to the product and also suggests a standardized offering. Because many persons receive the same message, buyers know that their motives for purchasing the product will be publicly understood.

☐ **Pervasiveness.** Advertising is a pervasive medium that permits the seller to repeat a message many times. It also allows the buyer to receive and compare the messages of various competitors. Large-scale advertising by a seller says something positive about the seller's size, popularity, and success.

☐ **Amplified expressiveness.** Advertising provides opportunities for dramatizing the company and its products through the artful use of print, sound, and color. Sometimes the tool's very success at expressiveness may, however, dilute or distract from the message.

☐ **Impersonality.** Advertising cannot be as compelling as a company sales representative. The audience does not feel obligated to pay attention or respond. Advertising is able to carry on only a monologue, not a dialogue, with the audience.

Advertising can be used on the one hand to build up a long-term image for a product (such as Coca-Cola ads), and on the other, to trigger quick sales (as in Sears' advertising a weekend sale). Advertising is an efficient way to reach numerous geographically dispersed buyers at a low cost per exposure. Certain forms of advertising, such as TV advertising, can require a large budget, while other forms, such as newspaper advertising, can be done on a small budget.

Personal selling. Personal selling is the most effective tool at certain stages of the buying process, particularly in building up buyers' preference, conviction, and action. The reason is that personal selling, when compared with advertising, has three distinctive qualities:[25]

☐ **Personal confrontation.** Personal selling involves an alive, immediate, and interactive relationship between two or more persons. Each party is able to observe each other's needs and characteristics at close hand and make immediate adjustments.

☐ **Cultivation.** Personal selling permits all kinds of relationships to spring up, ranging from a matter-of-fact selling relationship to a deep personal friendship. Effective sales

---

[24] See Sidney J. Levy, *Promotional Behavior* (Glenview, Ill.: Scott, Foresman, & Co., 1971), Chap. 4.
[25] Ibid.

representatives will normally keep their customers' interests at heart if they want long-run relationships.

☐ **Response.** Personal selling makes the buyer feel under some obligation for having listened to the sales talk. The buyer has a greater need to attend and respond, even if the response is a polite "thank you."

These distinctive qualities come at a cost. Personal selling is the company's most expensive contact tool, costing companies an average of $153 a sales call in 1982.[26] In 1981, American firms spent over $150 billion on personal selling compared with $61 billion on advertising. This money supported over 6.4 million Americans who are engaged in sales work.

Sales promotion. Although sales promotion tools—coupons, contests, premiums, and the like—are a collection, they have three distinctive characteristics:

☐ **Communication.** They gain attention and usually provide information that may lead the consumer to the product.

☐ **Incentive.** They incorporate some concession, inducement, or contribution that gives value to the consumer.

☐ **Invitation.** They include a distinct invitation to engage in the transaction now.

Companies use sales promotion tools to create a stronger and quicker response. Sales promotion can be used to dramatize product offers and to boost sagging sales. Sales promotion effects are usually short run, however, and not effective in building long-run brand preference.

Publicity. The appeal of publicity is based on its three distinctive qualities:

☐ **High credibility.** News stories and features seem more authentic and credible to readers than ads do.

☐ **Off guard.** Publicity can reach many prospects who might avoid sales people and advertisements. The message gets to the buyers as news rather than as a sales-directed communication.

☐ **Dramatization.** Publicity has, like advertising, a potential for dramatizing a company or product.

Marketers tend to underuse product publicity or use it as an afterthought. Yet a well-thought-out publicity campaign coordinated with the other promotion-mix elements can be extremely effective.

Factors in setting the promotion mix. Companies consider several factors in developing their promotion mix. These factors are examined below.

Type of product market. The effectiveness of promotional tools vary between consumer and industrial markets. The differences are shown in Figure 19–6. Consumer-goods companies normally devote most of their funds to advertising, followed by sales promotion, personal selling, and finally publicity. Industrial-goods companies

---

[26] *Sales and Marketing Management*, February 21, 1983, p. 36.

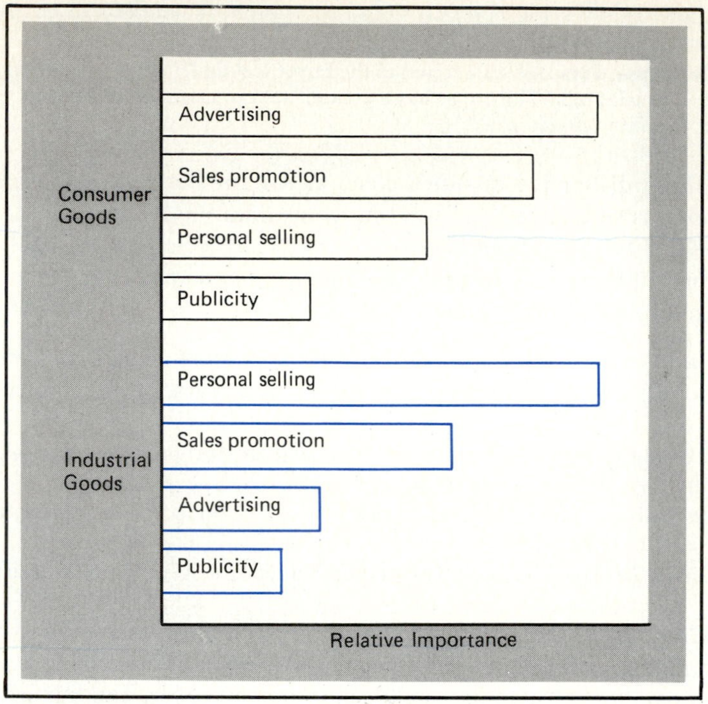

FIGURE 19-6
Relative Importance of Promotion Tools in Consumer versus Industrial Markets

devote most of their funds to personal selling, followed by sales promotion, advertising, and publicity. In general, personal selling is more heavily used with expensive and risky goods and in markets with fewer and larger sellers (hence, industrial markets).

While advertising is less important than sales calls in industrial markets, it still plays a significant role. Advertising can perform the following functions:

- ☐ **Awareness building.** Prospects who are not aware of the company or product may refuse to see the sales representative. Furthermore the sales representative may have to use up a lot of time describing the company and its products.
- ☐ **Comprehension building.** If the product embodies new features, some of the burden of explaining them can be effectively carried on by advertising.
- ☐ **Efficient reminding.** If prospects know about the product but are not ready to buy, advertisements reminding them of the product would be much more economical than sales calls.
- ☐ **Lead generation.** Advertisements carrying return coupons are an effective way to generate leads for sales representatives.
- ☐ **Legitimation.** Sales representatives can use tear sheets of the company's ads in leading magazines to legitimatize their company and products.
- ☐ **Reassurance.** Advertising can remind customers how to use the product and reassure them about their purchase.

Advertising's important role in industrial marketing is underscored in a number of studies. Morrill showed in his study of industrial commodity marketing that adver-

Exhibit 19-3

ROLE OF CORPORATE ADVERTISING IN INDUSTRIAL MARKETING

Theodore Levitt sought to determine the relative contribution of the company's reputation (built mainly by advertising) and the company's sales presentation (personal selling) in producing industrial sales. Purchasing agents were shown filmed sales presentations of a new, but fictitious, technical product for use as an ingredient in making paint. The variables were the quality of the sales presentation and whether the salesperson came from a well-known company, a less-known but creditable company, or an unknown company. Purchasing-agent reactions were collected after seeing the films and again five weeks later. The findings were as follows:

1. A company's reputation improves the chances of getting a favorable first hearing and an early adoption of the product. Therefore, corporate advertising that can build up the company's reputation (other factors also shape its reputation) will help the company's sales representatives.

2. Sales representatives from well-known companies have an edge in getting the sale, if their sales presentations are adequate. If a sales representative from a lesser-known company makes a highly effective sales presentation, that can overcome the disadvantage. Smaller companies should use their limited funds to select and train good sales representatives rather than spend the money on advertising.

3. Company reputations have the most effect where the product is complex, the risk is high, and the purchasing agent is less professionally trained.

Source: *Theodore Levitt*, Industrial Purchasing Behavior: A Study in Communication Effects, (*Boston*: *Division of Research*, *Harvard Business School, 1965*).

tising combined with personal selling increased sales 23 percent over what they were with no advertising. The total promotional cost as a percent of sales was reduced by 20 percent.[27] Freeman developed a formal model for dividing promotional funds between advertising and personal selling on the basis of the selling tasks that each performs more economically.[28] Levitt's research also showed the important role that advertising can play in industrial marketing. (See Exhibit 19–3.) More recently Lilien carried out a series of investigations in a project called ADVISOR in which he sought to determine and critique the practices used by industrial marketers to set their marketing communication budgets. (See Exhibit 19–4.)

Conversely personal selling can make a strong contribution in consumer-goods marketing. Some consumer marketers play down the role of the sales force, using them mainly to collect weekly orders from dealers and to see that sufficient stock is on the shelf. The common feeling is that "salesmen put products on shelves and

---

[27] *How Advertising Works in Today's Marketplace*: *The Morrill Study* (New York: McGraw-Hill Book Co., 1971), p. 4.

[28] Cyril Freeman, "How to Evaluate Advertising's Contribution," *Harvard Business Review*, July-August 1962, pp. 137–48.

Exhibit 19-4

THE ADVISOR PROJECT PROBES INTO HOW INDUSTRIAL MARKETERS SET THEIR MARKETING EXPENDITURES—AND HOW THEY SHOULD SET THEM

Professor Gary L. Lilien of M.I.T. directed a five-year study in the 1970s called the ADVISOR project, which examined how industrial marketers set their advertising budgets. ADVISOR ultimately consisted of two projects—ADVISOR 1 and ADVISOR 2.

ADVISOR 1

ADVISOR 1 was jointly sponsored by M.I.T. and the Association of National Advertisers. Data on various marketing factors were collected on sixty-six diversified industrial products from twelve cooperating companies. The study sought to develop marketing expenditure norms for industrial marketers. Industrial marketers tended to make a two-step decision in setting their advertising budgets. They decided, first, how much to spend on total marketing as a percentage of sales (the M/S ratio) and, second, how much to spend on advertising as a percentage of the marketing budget (the A/M ratio). When these ratios are multiplied, they give the A/S ratio, namely the advertising-to-sales-ratio.

The data yielded the following norms:

	Advertising	A/S	M/S	A/M
Median:	$92,000	0.6%	6.9%	9.9%
Range for 50% of products:	$16,000–$272,000	0.1%–1.8%	3%–14%	5%–19%

Thus the average industrial company in the sample spent $92,000 on advertising each product, and in 50 percent of the cases this figure ranged from $16,000 to $272,000. The average industrial company spent only 0.6 percent of its sales on advertising; it budgeted about 7 percent of its sales for total marketing; and it budgeted about 10 percent of its total marketing budget for advertising. The table also shows the 50 percent ranges for each ratio.

A company could use this table to check whether its M/S and A/M ratios are within a 50 percent range of most companies. If one or both ratios are outside of the range, either too low or too high, then management should ask why. If good reasons cannot be found, the advertising and marketing budgets should be revised.

There could be good reasons for spending outside of the typical range. Lilien investigated a large number of factors suggested by marketing managers that would lead them to spend more or less than the normal amount on advertising and/or marketing. He found that six factors had a major influence on marketing budgets: stage in life cycle; frequency of purchase; product quality, uniqueness, and identification with the company; market share; concentration of sales; and growth rate of customers. Here are some findings:

☐ The M/S ratio fell as the product life cycle progressed.
☐ The higher the purchase frequency, the greater the A/M.

☐ The higher the product quality or uniqueness, the higher the A/M.

☐ The higher the market share, the lower the M/S.

☐ The higher the sales concentration (few customers accounting a high share of the purchases), the lower the M/S ratio.

☐ The higher the customer growth rate, the higher the M/S and A/M ratios.

Next ADVISOR investigated how industrial companies allocated their advertising budgets to the following four media:

☐ **Space:** trade, technical press, and house journals (41 percent)

☐ **Direct mail:** leaflets, brochures, catalogs, and other direct-mail pieces (24 percent)

☐ **Shows:** trade shows and industrial films (11 percent)

☐ **Promotion:** sales promotion (24 percent)

The numbers show the median percentage that industrial companies spent on each of the media. Lilien tested four variables that influence the allocation percentages that companies make to each media, namely, sales volume, life cycle, sales concentration, and number of customers. Here are some conclusions:

☐ The higher the sales volume, the more the use of shows and sales promotion and the less the use of space and direct mail.

☐ Products in later stages of the life cycle spend more on direct mail and less on sales promotion.

☐ The higher the sales concentration, the more the sales promotion and the less the use of trade shows.

☐ The greater the number of customers, the less the use of direct mail.

ADVISOR 2

ADVISOR 2 was launched subsequently with a two-fold objective: to extend and verify the results of ADVISOR 1 and to determine the best level of spending and the best split of the spending between advertising and personal selling. Data was collected from 22 companies instead of 12 and covered 131 products instead of 66. When analyzed, the data confirmed the earlier ratios of A/S, A/M, and M/S. Several of the independent variables were confirmed and a few new variables were added to the analysis. ADVISOR 2 led to the building of some optimization models for setting marketing and advertising budgets.

Sources: Gary L. Lilien and John D. C. Little, "*The ADVISOR Project: A Study of Industrial Marketing Budgets,*" Sloan Management Review, *spring 1976, pp. 17–32*; and Gary L. Lilien, "*ADVISOR 2: Modeling the Marketing Mix Decision for Industrial Products,*" Management Science, *February 1979, pp. 191–204.*

advertising takes them off." Yet even here an effectively trained sales force can make three important contributions:

☐ **Increased stock position.** Persuasive sales representatives can influence dealers to take more stock and devote more shelf space to the company's brand.

☐ **Enthusiasm building.** Persuasive sales representatives can build dealer enthusiasm for a new product by dramatizing the planned advertising and sales promotion back-up.

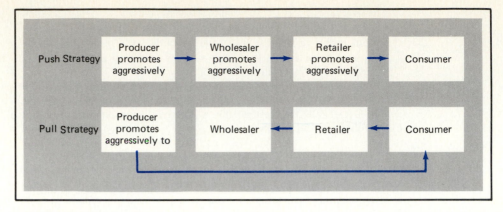

FIGURE 19-7
Push-versus-Pull Strategy

    ☐ **Missionary selling.** Sales representatives play a crucial role in signing up more dealers to carry the company's brands.

    Push-versus-pull strategy. The promotional mix is heavily influenced by whether the company chooses a push or pull strategy to create sales. The two strategies are contrasted in Figure 19–7. A *push strategy* calls for using the sales force and trade promotion to push the product through the channels. The producer aggressively promotes the product to wholesalers; the wholesalers aggressively promote the product to retailers; and the retailers aggressively promote the product to consumers. A *pull strategy* calls for spending a lot of money on advertising and consumer promotion to build up consumer demand. If the strategy is effective, consumers will ask their retailers for the product, the retailers will ask their wholesalers for the product, and the wholesalers will ask the producers for the product. Companies differ in their predilection for push or pull. For example, Lever Brothers relies more heavily on push, and Procter and Gamble on pull.

Buyer-readiness stage.   Promotional tools vary in their cost-effectiveness at different stages of buyer readiness. Figure 19–8 shows the relative effectiveness of four promotional tools.[29] Advertising, along with publicity, plays the most important roles in the awareness stage, more than is played by "cold calls" from sales representatives. Customer comprehension is primarily affected by education, with advertising and personal selling playing secondary roles. Customer conviction is influenced most by personal selling followed closely by advertising. Finally, closing the sale is predominantly a function of the sales call. Clearly personal selling, given its expensiveness, should be focused on the later stages of the customer buying process.

---

    [29] "What IBM Found about Ways to Influence Selling," *Business Week*, December 5, 1959, pp. 69–70. Also see Harold C. Cash and William J. Crissy, "Comparison of Advertising and Selling," in *The Psychology of Selling* (Flushing, N.Y.: Personnel Development Associates, 1965), Vol. 12.

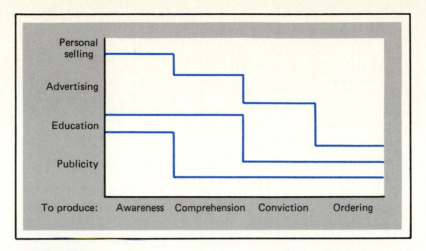

FIGURE 19-8
Relative Effectiveness of Four Promotional Tools at Different Stages of the Customer
Buying Process

Product life-cycle stage.   The promotional tools vary in their effectiveness at different stages of the product life cycle. In the introduction stage, advertising and publicity are cost effective in producing high awareness, and sales promotion is useful in promoting early trial. Personal selling is relatively expensive, although it must be used to get the trade to carry the product.

In the growth stage, advertising and publicity continue to be potent, while sales promotion can be reduced because fewer incentives are needed.

In the mature stage, sales promotion resumes in importance relative to advertising. Buyers know the brands and need only a reminder level of advertising.

In the decline stage, advertising is kept at a reminder level, publicity is eliminated, and sales people give the product only minimal attention. Sales promotion, however, might continue strong.

Measuring Promotion's Results

After implementing the promotional plan, the communicator must measure its impact on the target audience. This involves asking the target audience whether they recognize or recall the message, how many times they saw it, what points they recall, how they felt about the message, and their previous and current attitudes toward the product and company. The communicator would also want to collect behavioral measures of audience response, such as how many people bought the product, liked it, and talked to others about it.

Figure 19-9 provides an example of good feedback measurement. Looking at brand A, we find 80 percent of the total market are aware of brand A, 60 percent have tried it, and only 20 percent of those who have tried it are satisfied. This indicates that the communication program is effective in creating awareness, but the product fails to meet consumer expectations. On the other hand, only 40 percent of the total market are aware of brand B, only 30 percent have tried it, but 80 percent of those

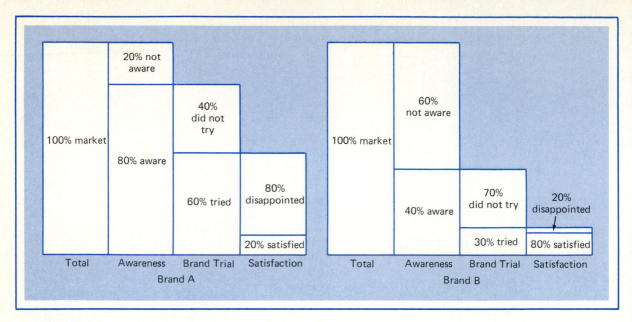

FIGURE 19-9
Current Consumer States for Two Brands

who have tried it are satisfied. In this case the communication program needs to be strengthened to take advantage of the brand's satisfaction-generating power.

Managing and Coordinating the Marketing Communication Process

The wide range of communication tools and messages available for reaching the target audience makes it imperative that they be coordinated. Otherwise the messages might be ill timed in terms of the availability of goods; they may lack consistency; or they might not be cost effective. Left alone, each manager of a communication resource will fight for more budget irrespective of the relative merits of each tool. The sales manager will want to hire two extra sales representatives for $80,000, while the advertising manager will want to spend the same money on a prime-time television commercial. Meanwhile the public relations manager feels that he or she can do wonders with more money for publicity.

Today companies are moving toward the concept of *coordinated marketing communications*. This concept calls for:

☐ Appointing a marketing communications director who has overall responsibility for the company's persuasive communications efforts
☐ Working out a philosophy of the role and the extent to which the different promotional tools are to be used
☐ Keeping track of all promotional expenditures by product, promotional tool, stage of product life cycle, and observed effect, as a basis for improving further use of these tools

☐ Coordinating the promotional activities and their timing when major campaigns take place

Coordinated marketing communications will produce more consistency in the company's *meaning* to its buyers and publics. It places a responsibility in someone's hand—where none existed before—to unify the company's image as it comes through the thousand activities the company carries on. It leads to a total marketing communication strategy aimed at showing how the company can help customers solve their problems.

SUMMARY

Marketing communications is one of the four major elements of the company's marketing mix. Marketers must know how to use advertising, sales promotion, publicity, and personal selling to communicate the product's existence and value to the target customers.

The communication process itself consists of nine elements: sender, receiver, encoding, decoding, message, media, response, feedback, and noise. Marketers must know how to get through to the target audience in the face of the audience's tendencies toward selective attention, distortion, and recall.

Developing the promotion program involves eight steps. The communicator must first identify the target audience and its characteristics, including the image it carries of the product. Next the communicator has to define the communication objective, whether it is to create awareness, knowledge, liking, preference, conviction, or purchase. Then a message must be designed containing an effective content, structure, format, and source. Then communication channels—both personal and nonpersonal—must be selected. Next the total promotion budget must be established. The promotion budget must be divided among the main promotional tools. The communicator must then monitor to see how much of the market becomes aware and tries the product and is satisfied in the process. Finally all of the communications must be managed and coordinated for consistency, good timing, and cost effectiveness.

QUESTIONS

1. Based on your understanding of the communication process, suggest some guidelines for the effective use of visual and verbal content in the creation of both print and broadcast advertising.

2. In 1982 Lite Beer commercials by Miller were the most often noticed, remembered, and liked ads on TV. Oscar Meyer commercials ranked twelfth on the list of most remembered commercials. Can we claim that Miller ads were considerably more successful than Oscar Meyer ads? Why or why not?

3. Apply the four major tools in the marketing communication mix to professional sports teams.

4. An advertising agency is preparing a cake-mix commercial. It is trying to choose between two copy versions. Version A allows the audience to share the entire product experience from

5. The major mass media—newspapers, magazines, radio, television, and outdoor media—show striking differences in their capacity for dramatization, credibility, attention getting, and other valued aspects of communication. Describe the special characteristics of each media type.

6. Develop a set of thematic guidelines that laundry detergent companies might follow in preparing detergent ads aimed at upper-lower- and lower-middle-class homemakers in the 24 to 45 age bracket.

7. What types of consumer responses should be aimed at in communication strategies for the following products: legal services, frozen pizza, veterinarian services, sewing machines, pianos, telephone answering services, hammers?
the moment of purchase through the act of baking the cake and the family's enthusiastically receiving it. Version B stops short of completing the process, hoping to involve the audience in imagining the rest. Which version do you think will be more effective and why?

Advertising Decisions

If you think advertising doesn't pay—we understand there are twenty-five mountains in Colorado higher than Pike's Peak. Can you name one?

THE AMERICAN SALESMAN

Advertising is one of the four major tools companies use to direct persuasive communications to target buyers and publics. It consists of *nonpersonal forms of communication conducted through paid media under clear sponsorship*. In 1981 advertising ran up a bill of over $61 billion. The spenders included not only commercial firms but museums, fund raisers, and various social-action organizations seeking to advertise their causes to various target publics. In fact, the twenty-sixth-largest advertising spender is a nonprofit organization—the U.S. government.

Within the commercial sector, the top 100 national advertisers account for nearly one-fourth of all national advertising. Procter & Gamble is the leading spender, accounting in 1981 for $672 million, or 5.6 percent of its total sales of $12 billion. The other major spenders, in order, are Sears ($544), General Foods ($457), Philip Morris ($433), General Motors ($401), and K-Mart ($350) (all figures in millions). Advertising as a percent of sales is lowest in the automobile industry and highest in the food and drug industries. The highest-percentage spenders overall are in drugs, toiletries, and cosmetics, followed by gum, candy, and soaps. Jeffery Martin, Inc., spent a record 54.7 percent of its sales on advertising in 1981.

The advertising dollars go into various media: magazine and newspaper space; radio and television; outdoor displays (posters, signs, skywriting); direct mail; novelties (matchboxes, blotters, calendars); cards (car, bus); catalogs; directories; and circulars. And advertising has many uses: long-term buildup of the organization's image (*institutional advertising*), long-term buildup of a particular brand (*brand advertising*), information dissemination about a sale, service, or event (*classified advertising*), announcement of a special sale (*sale advertising*), and advocacy of a particular cause (*advocacy advertising*).

Although advertising is primarily a private-enterprise marketing tool, it is used in all the countries of the world, including socialist countries. Advertising is a cost-effective way to disseminate messages, whether it is to build brand preference for Coca-Cola all over the world or to motivate a developing nation's consumers to drink milk or practice birth control.

Organizations obtain their advertising in different ways. In small companies, advertising is handled by someone in the sales department, who works with an advertising agency. Large companies set up their own advertising departments, whose managers report to the vice-presidents of marketing. The advertising department's job is to develop the total budget, approve advertising agency ads and campaigns, and handle direct-mail advertising, dealer displays, and other forms of advertising not ordinarily performed by the agency. Most companies use an outside advertising agency because they offer several advantages.

Marketing managers must make five decisions in developing an advertising program

☐ What are the advertising objectives? (mission)
☐ How much can be spent? (money)
☐ What message should be sent? (message)
☐ What media should be used? (media)
☐ How should the results be evaluated? (measurement)

We will examine these decisions in the following sections.

SETTING THE ADVERTISING OBJECTIVES

The first step in developing an advertising program is to set the advertising objectives. These objectives must flow from prior decisions on the target market, market positioning, and marketing mix. The marketing-positioning and mix strategy defines the job that advertising must do in the total marketing program.

Many specific communication and sales objectives can be assigned to advertising. Colley lists fifty-two possible advertising objectives in his well-known *Defining Advertising Goals for Measured Advertising Results*.[1] He outlines a method called DAGMAR

---

[1] See Russell H. Colley, *Defining Advertising Goals for Measured Advertising Results* (New York: Association of National Advertisers, 1961).

TABLE 20-1

POSSIBLE ADVERTISING OBJECTIVES

To inform:

Telling the market about a new product	Describing available services
Suggesting new uses for a product	Correcting false impressions
Informing the market of a price change	Reducing consumers' fears
Explaining how the product works	Building a company image

To persuade:

Building brand preference	Persuading customer to purchase now
Encouraging switching to your brand	Persuading customer to receive a sales call
Changing customer's perception of product attributes	

To remind:

Reminding consumers that the product may be needed in the near future	Keeping it in their minds during off seasons
Reminding them where to buy it	Maintaining its top-of-mind awareness

(after the book's title) for turning advertising objectives into specific measurable goals. An *advertising goal* is a specific communication task to be accomplished with a specific audience in a specific period of time. DAGMAR outlines an approach to measuring whether advertising goals have been achieved.

Advertising objectives can be classified as to whether their aim is to inform, persuade, or remind. Table 20–1 lists examples of these objectives.

Informative advertising figures heavily in the pioneering stage of a product category, where the objective is to build *primary demand*. Thus the yogurt industry initially had to inform consumers of yogurt's nutritional benefits and many uses.

Persuasive advertising becomes important in the competitive stage, where a company's objective is to build *selective demand* for a particular brand. Most advertising falls into this category. Some persuasive advertising has moved into the category of *comparison advertising*, which seeks to establish the superiority of one brand through specific comparison with one or more other brands in the product class.[2] Comparison advertising has been used in such product categories as deodorants, toothpastes, tires, and automobiles.

Reminder advertising is highly important in the mature stage of the product to keep the consumer thinking about the product. Expensive four-color Coca-Cola ads in magazines have the purpose not of informing or persuading but of reminding people about Coca-Cola. A related form of advertising is *reinforcement advertising*, which seeks to assure current purchasers that they have made the right choice. Automobile ads will often depict satisfied customers enjoying some special feature of the car they bought.

---

[2] See William L. Wilkie and Paul W. Farris, "Comparison Advertising: Problem and Potential," *Journal of Marketing*, October 1975, pp. 7–15.

DECIDING ON THE ADVERTISING BUDGET

After determining advertising objectives, the company can proceed to establish its advertising budget for each product. The role of advertising is to shift upward the product's demand curve. The company wants to spend the amount required to achieve the sales goal. Four commonly used methods for setting the advertising budget were described earlier. (See Chapter 19, pp. 621–23.) Here we will describe some advanced models.

Sales-Response and Decay Model

One of the best models of the response of sales to advertising was developed by Vidale and Wolfe.[3] In their model, the change in the *rate of sales* at time t is a function of four factors: the *advertising budget*, the *sales-response constant*, the *saturation level of sales*, and the *sales-decay constant*. Their basic equation is:

$$\frac{dS}{dt} = rA\frac{M-S}{M} - \lambda S \qquad (20\text{--}1)$$

where:

$$
\left.
\begin{aligned}
S &= \text{rate of sales at time } t \\
\frac{dS}{dt} &= \text{change in the rate of sales at time } t \\
A &= \text{rate of advertising expenditure at time } t
\end{aligned}
\right\} \quad \textit{variables}
$$

$$
\left.
\begin{aligned}
r &= \text{sales-response constant (defined as the sales generated per} \\
&\quad \text{advertising dollar when } S = 0) \\
M &= \text{saturation level of sales} \\
\lambda &= \text{sales-decay constant (defined as the fraction of sales per time} \\
&\quad \text{unit when } A = 0)
\end{aligned}
\right\} \quad \textit{parameters}
$$

The equation says that the rate of sales increase will be higher, the higher the sales-response constant, the higher the advertising expenditure, the higher the untapped sales potential, and the lower the decay constant. Suppose the sales response to advertising dollars is estimated at 4, current sales are $40,000, saturation-level sales are $100,000, and the company loses .1 of its sales per period if no advertising expenditure is made. In this case, by spending $10,000 in advertising, the company can hope to achieve an additional $20,000 of sales.

$$\frac{dS}{dt} = 4(10,000)\frac{100,000 - 40,000}{100,000} - .1(40,000) = \$20,000$$

If the profit margin on $20,000 is better than 50 percent, it pays to spend the $10,000 on advertising.

[3] M. L. Vidale and H. B. Wolfe, "An Operations-Research Study of Sales Response to Advertising," *Operations Research*, June 1957, pp. 370–81.

The Vidale-Wolfe model can be used to estimate the profit consequences of alternative advertising-budgeting strategies. It brings together and interrelates three useful concepts for determining the advertising budget.[4]

Adaptive-Control Model

An adaptive advertising-budgeting model assumes that the advertising sales-response function is not stable but changes through time. If it was stable, the company should make one large effort to measure it, and the benefits would extend far into the future. But there is good reason to believe that the parameters are not stable because of changing competitive activity, advertising copy, product design, and economic climate. It would not pay to invest heavily in researching the parameters of the current sales-response function. If the parameters change through time, it would pay to collect new information each period and combine it with the old information to produce new estimated parameters for the sales-response function on which to base the new advertising budget.

Little proposed the following adaptive-control method for setting advertising expenditures.[5] Suppose the company has set its advertising expenditure rate for the coming period based on its most current information on the sales-response function. It spends this rate in all markets except in a subset of $2n$ markets randomly drawn. In n of the test markets the company spends at a lower rate, and in the other n it spends at a higher rate. This will yield information on the average sales created by low, medium, and high rates of advertising that can be used to update the parameters of the sales-response function. The updated function is used to determine the best advertising expenditure rate for the next period. If this side experiment is carried out each period, advertising expenditures will closely track optimal advertising expenditures.

Competitive-Share Model

The preceding models do not explicitly take competitors' expenditures into account. This omission is valid where there are many competitors, none of whom is large; or where it is difficult to know what competitors are spending for advertising. In many situations, however, firms know their competitors' expenditures and try to maintain competitive parity. In these situations a firm must consider competitive reactions in determining its advertising appropriation.

The problem can be viewed in terms of game theory. Friedman has developed some models to show how duopolists should allocate advertising budgets to different territories to take maximum advantage of the other's mistakes.[6] He distinguishes

---

[4] For another interesting model, see Alfred A. Kuehn, "A Model for Budgeting Advertising," in *Mathematical Models and Methods in Marketing*, ed. Frank M. Bass *et al*. (Homewood, Ill.: Richard D. Irwin, 1961), pp. 302–53.

[5] John D. C. Little, "A Model of Adaptive Control of Promotional Spending," *Operations Research*, November 1966, pp. 1075–97.

[6] Lawrence Friedman, "Game Theory Models in the Allocation of Advertising Expenditures," *Operations Research*, September-October 1958, pp. 699–709.

two situations: where company sales are proportional to the company's share of total advertising expenditures and where the company with 50-plus percent of the total advertising takes the whole market (as when a single customer is at stake).

DECIDING ON THE MESSAGE

Many studies of the sales effect of advertising expenditures neglect the message creativity factor. Some analysts argue that large advertising agencies are equally creative, and therefore differences in individual campaigns "wash out." But it is precisely the differences in individual campaigns that advertisers seek. By leaving out the creative factor, a substantial part of the market-share movement is unexplained. One study that included the creativity factor found that a campaign's quality is more important than the number of dollars spent.[7] There is little doubt that differences in creative strategy are very important in advertising success.

Advertisers go through the following steps to develop a creative strategy: message generation, message evaluation and selection, and message execution.

Message Generation

Many things can be said about any product. No ad should say more than a few things, and a case could even be made that an ad, to gain distinctiveness, should emphasize one thing. The challenge is to generate some alternative messages and pretest them to find the best one.

Creative people use different methods to generate advertising ideas to carry out the advertising objectives. Many creative people proceed *inductively* by talking to consumers, dealers, experts, and competitors. Consumers are the most important source of good ideas. Their feelings about the strengths and shortcomings of existing brands provide important clues to creative strategy. A leading hair-spray company carries out consumer research annually to determine consumer satisfaction with existing brands. If consumers want stronger holding power, the company reformulates its product and uses this appeal.

Some creative people use a *deductive* framework for generating advertising messages. Maloney proposed one framework. (See Table 20–2.)[8] He saw buyers as expecting one of four types of reward from a product: *rational*, *sensory*, *social*, or *ego-satisfaction*. And buyers may visualize these rewards from *results-of-use experience*, *product-in-use experience*, or *incidental-to-use experience*. Crossing the four types of rewards with the three types of experience generates twelve types of advertising messages.

The advertiser can generate a theme for each of the twelve cells as possible messages for his product. For example, the appeal "gets clothes cleaner" is a rational-

---

[7] See "New Study Tells TV Advertisers How Advertising Builds Sales and Share of Market," *Printer's Ink*, May 8, 1964, pp. 27–38.

[8] John C. Maloney, "Marketing Decisions and Attitude Research," in *Effective Marketing Coordination*, ed. George L. Baker, Jr. (Chicago: American Marketing Association, 1961), pp. 595–618.

TABLE 20-2

EXAMPLES OF TWELVE TYPES OF APPEALS				
Types of Potentially Rewarding Experience with a Product	**Potential Type of Reward**			
	Rational	**Sensory**	**Social**	**Ego Satisfaction**
Results-of-Use Experience	1. Get clothes cleaner	2. Settles stomach upset completely	3. When you care enough to serve the best	4. For the skin you deserve to have
Product-in-Use Experience	5. The flour that needs no sifting	6. Real gusto in a great light beer	7. A deodorant to guarantee social acceptance	8. The shoe for the young executive
Incidental-to-Use Experience	9. The plastic pack keeps the cigarette fresh	10. The portable television that's lighter in weight, easier to lift	11. The furniture that identifies the home of modern people	12. Stereo for the man with discriminating taste

SOURCE: Adapted from John C. Maloney, "Marketing Decisions and Attitude Research," in *Effective Marketing Coordination*, ed. George L. Baker, Jr. (Chicago: American Marketing Association, 1961) pp. 595–618.

reward promise following results-of-use experience; and the phrase "real gusto in a great light beer" is a sensory-reward promise connected with product-in-use experience.

How many possible ad themes should the agency create before making a choice? The more ads created, the higher the probability that the agency will find a first-rate one. Yet the more time it spends creating ads, the higher the costs. There must be some optimal number of alternative ads that an agency should create and test for the client. Under the present commission system, the agency does not like to go to the expense of creating and pretesting many ads. In an ingenious study, Gross concluded that agencies generally create too few advertisement alternatives for their clients.[9] Gross estimates that advertising agencies spend from 3 to 5 percent of their media income on creating and testing advertising, whereas he estimates they should spend closer to 15 percent. He thinks agencies should devote a larger part of their budgets to finding the best ad and somewhat less to buying media. He even proposed that a company should hire several creative agencies to create advertisements, from which the best one is selected.

Message Evaluation and Selection

The advertiser needs to evaluate the possible messages. Twedt suggested that messages be rated on *desirability*, *exclusiveness*, and *believability*.[10] The message must first

---

[9] Irwin Gross, "An Analytical Approach to the Creative Aspect of Advertising Operations," (Ph.D. dissertation, Case Institute of Technology, November 1967).

[10] Dik Warren Twedt, "How to Plan New Products, Improve Old Ones, and Create Better Advertising," *Journal of Marketing*, January 1969, pp. 53–57.

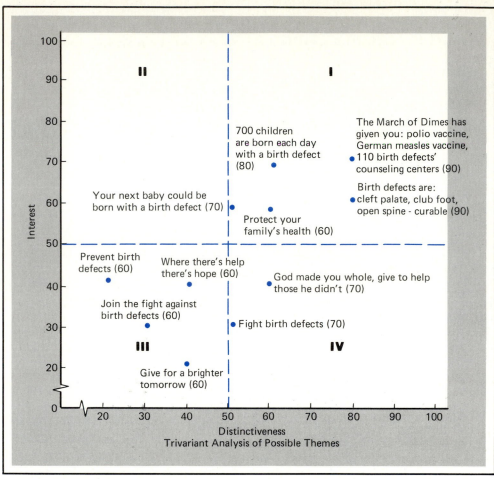

Source: William A. Mindak and H. Malcolm Bybee, "Marketing's Application to Fund Raising, *Journal of Marketing*, July 1971, pp. 13–18.

FIGURE 20–1
Advertising Message Evaluation

say something desirable or interesting about the product. The message must also say something exclusive or distinctive that does not apply to every brand in the product category. Finally, the message must be believable or provable.

For example, the March of Dimes searched for an advertising theme to raise money for its fight against birth defects.[11] Several messages came out of a brainstorming session. A group of young parents were asked to rate each message for interest, distinctiveness, and believability, assigning up to 100 points for each. (See Figure

---

[11] See William A. Mindak and H. Malcolm Bybee, "Marketing Application to Fund Raising," *Journal of Marketing*, July 1971, pp. 13–18.

20–1.) For example, "Five hundred thousand unborn babies die each year from birth defects" scored 70, 60, and 80 on interest, distinctiveness, and believability, while "Your next baby could be born with a birth defect" scored 58, 50, and 70. The first message outperformed the second and was preferred for advertising purposes.

Consumer ratings of ad appeals are not that reliable, however; they reflect opinion and not necessarily behavior. The advertiser should employ some pretest to determine which appeal is the strongest. For example, the Washington State Apple Commission was trying to decide which advertising theme appealed more to housewives:[12] One stressed the various *uses* of apples; the other, the *healthful* qualities of apples. An experiment was carried out in seventy-two self-service food stores in six midwestern cities for sixteen weeks. The results showed that the apple-use theme significantly outperformed the other theme in promoting sales.

Message Execution

The message's impact depends not only upon what is said but also on how it is said. Message execution can be decisive for those products that are highly similar, such as detergents, cigarettes, coffee, and beer. The advertiser has to put the message across in a way that wins the target audience's attention and interest. Execution is also gaining in importance for some industrial products that are becoming increasingly undifferentiated, such as pharmaceuticals in certain mature categories (antibiotics, and so on). Companies like Pfizer have launched aggressive campaigns designed to promote product *image* as well as quality.

The advertiser usually prepares a *copy strategy statement* describing the objective, content, support, and tone of the desired ad. Here is the strategy statement for a Pillsbury product called 1869 Brand Biscuits:

> The *objective* of the advertising is to convince biscuit users that now they can buy a canned biscuit that's as good as homemade—Pillsbury's 1869 Brand Biscuits. The *content* consists of emphasizing the following product characteristics: they look like homemade biscuits; they have the same texture as homemade biscuits; and they taste like homemade biscuits. *Support* for the "good as homemade" promise will be twofold: (1) 1869 Brand Biscuits are made from a special kind of flour (soft wheat flour) used to make homemade biscuits but never before used in making canned biscuits, and (2) the use of traditional American biscuit recipes. The *tone* of the advertising will be a news announcement, tempered by a warm, reflective mood emanating from a look back at traditional American baking quality.

Creative people must now find a *style*, *tone*, *words*, and *format* for executing the message.

Any message can be presented in different *execution styles*, such as

- ☐ **Slice-of-life.** This shows one or more persons using the product in a normal setting. A family seated at the dinner table might express satisfaction with a new biscuit brand.
- ☐ **Lifestyle.** This emphasizes how a product fits in with a lifestyle. A Scotch ad shows a

---

[12] See Peter L. Henderson, James F. Hind, and Sidney E. Brown, "Sales Effect of Two Campaign Themes," *Journal of Advertising Research*, December 1961, pp. 2–11.

handsome middle-aged man holding a glass of Scotch in one hand and steering his yacht with the other.

- ☐ **Fantasy.** This creates a fantasy around the product or its use. Revlon's ad for Jontue features a barefoot woman wearing a chiffon dress coming out of an old French barn, crossing a meadow, and confronting a handsome young man on a white steed, who carries her away.
- ☐ **Mood or image.** This builds an evocative mood or image around the product, such as beauty, love, or serenity. No claim is made about the product except through suggestion. Many cigarette ads, such as those for Salem and Newport cigarettes, create moods.
- ☐ **Musical.** This shows one or more persons or cartoon characters singing a song involving the product. Many cola ads have used this format.
- ☐ **Personality symbol.** This creates a character that personifies the product. The character might be *animated* (Green Giant, Cap'n Crunch, Mr. Clean) or *real* (Marlboro man, Morris the Cat).
- ☐ **Technical expertise.** This shows the company's expertise and experience in making the product. Thus Hills Brothers shows one of its buyers carefully selecting the coffee beans, and Italian Swiss Colony emphasizes its many years of experience in winemaking.
- ☐ **Scientific evidence.** This presents survey or scientific evidence that the brand is preferred to or outperforms one or more other brands. For years Crest toothpaste has featured scientific evidence to convince toothpaste buyers of Crest's superior anticavity-fighting properties.
- ☐ **Testimonial evidence.** This features a highly credible or likable source endorsing the product. It could be a celebrity like O. J. Simpson (Hertz Rent-a-Car) or ordinary people saying how much they like the product.

The communicator must also choose an appropriate *tone* for the ad. Procter & Gamble is consistently positive in its tone; its ads say something superlatively positive about the product. Humor is avoided so as not to take attention away from the message. On the other hand, Volkswagen's ads for its famous "Beetle" typically took on a humorous and self-depreciating tone ("the Ugly Bug").

Memorable and attention-getting *words* must be found. The themes listed below on the left would have had much less impact without the creative phrasing on the right:[13]

Theme	Creative Copy
7-Up is not a cola.	*"The Un-Cola"*
Let us drive you in our bus instead of driving your car.	*"Take the bus, and leave the driving to us."*
Shop by turning the pages of the telephone directory.	*"Let your fingers do the walking."*
If you drink a beer, Schaefer is a good beer to drink.	*"The beer to have when you're having more than one."*
We don't rent as many cars, so we have to do more for our customers.	*"We try harder."*

Creativity is especially required for headlines. There are six basic types of headlines: *news* ("New Boom and More Inflation Ahead . . . and What You Can Do About

---

[13] L. Greenland, "Is This the Era of Positioning?" *Advertising Age*, May 29, 1972.

It"); *question* ("Have You Had It Lately?"); *narrative* ("They Laughed When I Sat Down at the Piano, but When I Started to Play!"); *command* ("Don't Buy Until You Try All Three"); 1–2–3 *ways* ("12 Ways to Save on Your Income Tax"); and *how-what-why* ("Why They Can't Stop Buying"). Look at the care exercised by airlines to find the right way to describe their planes as safe without mentioning safety: "The Friendly Skies of United" (United); "The Wings of Man" (Eastern); and "The World's Most Experienced Airline" (Pan American).

Format elements such as ad size, color, and illustration will make a difference in an ad's impact as well as its cost. A minor rearrangement of mechanical elements within the ad can improve its attention-gaining power by several points. Larger-size ads gain more attention though not necessarily by as much as their difference in cost. Four-color illustrations instead of black and white increase ad effectiveness and ad cost.

In 1982 an industry study about television and print advertising's ability to change brand preference listed the following characteristics for ads that scored above average in recall and recognition: innovation (new product or new uses), "story appeal" (as an attention-getting device), before-and-after illustration, demonstrations, problem solution, and the inclusion of relevant characters that become emblematic of the brand (these may be cartoon figures such as the Jolly Green Giant or actual people, who may or may not be celebrities).[14]

DECIDING ON THE MEDIA

The advertiser's next task is to chose advertising media to carry the advertising message. The steps are deciding on desired reach, frequency, and impact; choosing among major media types; selecting specific media vehicles; and deciding on media timing.

Deciding on Reach, Frequency, and Impact

Media selection is the *problem of finding the most cost-effective way to deliver the desired number of exposures to the target audience*. But what do we mean by the desired number of exposures? Presumably the advertiser is seeking a certain response from the target audience, for example, a certain level of *product trial*. Now the rate of product trial will depend, among other things, on the level of audience brand awareness. Suppose the rate of product trial increases at a diminishing rate with the level of audience awareness, as shown in Figure 20–2(a). If the advertiser seeks a product trial rate of (say) T^*, it will be necessary to achieve a brand awareness level of A^*.

The next task is to find out how many exposures, E^*, will produce a level of audience awareness of A^*. The effect of exposures on audience awareness depends on the exposures' reach, frequency, and impact:

[14] David Ogilvy and Joel Raphaelson, "Research on advertising techniques that work—and don't work," *Harvard Business Review*, July-August 1982, pp. 14–18.

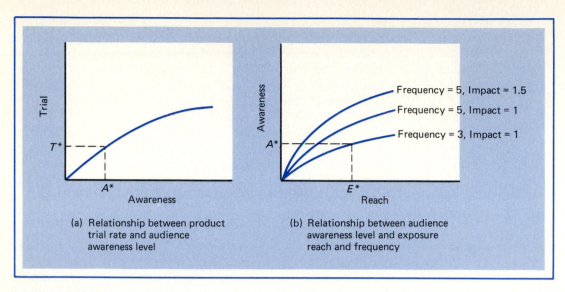

FIGURE 20-2
Relationship Between Trial, Awareness, and the Exposure Function

- □ **Reach (R).** The number of different persons or households exposed to a particular media schedule at least once during a specified time period.
- □ **Frequency (F).** The number of times within the specified time period that an average person or household is exposed to the message.
- □ **Impact (I).** The qualitative value of an exposure through a given medium (thus a food ad in *Good Housekeeping* would have a higher impact than in the *Police Gazette*).

Figure 20–2(b) shows the relationship between audience awareness and reach. Audience awareness will be greater, the higher the exposures' reach, frequency, and impact. The media planner recognizes important trade-offs between reach, frequency, and impact. Suppose the media planner has an advertising budget of $1,000,000 and the cost per thousand exposures of average quality is $5. This means that the advertiser can buy 200,000,000 exposures (= $1,000,000 ÷ $5/1000). If the advertiser seeks an average exposure frequency of 10, then the advertiser can reach 20,000,000 people (= 200,000,000 ÷ 10) with the given budget. Now if the advertiser wants higher-quality media costing $10 per thousand exposures, the advertiser will be able to reach only 10,000,000 people unless he or she is willing to lower the desired exposure frequency.

The relationship between reach, frequency, and impact is captured in the following concepts:

- □ **Total number of exposures (E).** This is the reach times the average frequency, that is, $E = R \times F$. It is also called the *gross rating points* (GRP). If a given media schedule reaches 80 percent of the homes with an average exposure frequency of 3, the media schedule is said to have a GRP of 240 (= 80 × 3). If another media schedule has a GRP of 300, it is said to have more weight, but we cannot tell how this weight breaks up into reach and frequency.

□ **Weighted number of exposures (WE).** This is the reach times average frequency times average impact, that is $WE = R \times F \times I$.

The media planning challenge is as follows. With a given budget, what is the most cost-effective combination of reach, frequency, and impact to buy? Suppose the media planner is willing to use average-impact media. This leaves the task of deciding how many people to reach with what frequency. It would make sense to settle the issue of frequency first. How many exposures does an average member of the target audience need for the advertising to work? Once this target frequency is decided, then reach will fall into place.

Many advertisers believe that the target audience needs a large number of exposures for the advertising to work. Too few repetitions may be a waste, according to Lucas and Britt: "It can be reasoned that introductory advertisements make too weak an impression to initiate much interest in buying. Succeeding advertisements may sometimes be more effective by building up already established weak impressions to the action level."[15] Other advertising researchers doubt the value of many exposures. They feel that after people see the same ad a few times, they either act on it, get irritated by it, or stop noticing it. Krugman has made the case that three exposures may be enough:

> The first exposure is by definition unique. As with the initial exposure to anything, a "What is it?" type of cognitive response dominates the reaction. The second exposure to a stimulus . . . produces several effects. One may be the cognitive reaction that characterized the first exposure, if the audience missed much of the message the first time around. . . . More often, an evaluative "What of it?" response replaces the "What is it?" response. . . . The third exposure constitutes a reminder, if a decision to buy based on the evaluations has not been acted on. The third exposure is also the beginning of disengagement and withdrawal of attention from a completed episode.[16]

Krugman's thesis favoring three exposures has to be qualified. He is using exposures to mean actual attention episodes on the part of the target audience. The advertiser would have to buy more exposures than three to insure that the audience actually sees three ads. Also there is a forgetting factor that operates. The job of advertising repetition is partly to put the message back into memory. The higher the forgetting rate associated with that brand, product category, or message, the higher the warranted level of repetition.

Choosing Among Major Media Types

The media planner has to know the capacity of the major media types to deliver reach, frequency, and impact. The major advertising media are profiled in Table 20–3. The major media types, in order of their advertising volume, are *newspapers*, *television*, *direct mail*, *radio*, *magazines*, and *outdoor*. Each medium has certain advan-

[15] Darrell B. Lucas and Steuart Henderson Britt, *Measuring Advertising Effectiveness* (New York: McGraw-Hill Book Co., 1963), p. 218.

[16] See Herbert E. Krugman, "What Makes Advertising Effective?" *Harvard Business Review*, March-April 1975, pp. 96–103, here p. 98.

TABLE 20-3

	PROFILES OF MAJOR MEDIA TYPES				
Medium	**Volume in Billions (1980)**	**Percentage (1980)**	**Example of Cost (1981)**	**Advantages**	**Limitations**
Newspapers	$15.6	28.5%	$11,128 one page, weekday Chicago Tribune	Flexibility; timeliness; good local market coverage; broad acceptance; high believability	Short life; poor reproduction quality; small "pass-along" audience
Television	11.3	20.7	$2,000 for thirty seconds of prime time in Chicago	Combines sight, sound, and motion; appealing to the senses; high attention; high reach	High absolute cost; high clutter; fleeting exposure; less audience selectivity
Direct mail	7.7	14.0	$1,190 for the names and addresses of 34,000 veterinarians	Audience selectivity; flexibility; no ad competition within the same medium: personalization	Relatively high cost; "junk mail" image
Radio	3.7	6.7	$400 for one minute of prime time in Chicago	Mass use; high geographic and demographic selectivity; low cost	Audio presentation only; lower attention than television; nonstandardized rate structures; fleeting exposure
Magazines	3.2	5.9	$57,780 one page, four-color in Newsweek	High geographic and demographic selectivity; credibility and prestige; high-quality reproduction; long life; good pass-along readership	Long ad purchase lead time; some waste circulation; no guarantee of position
Outdoor	0.6	1.1	$8,000 prime billboard coast per month in Chicago	Flexibility; high repeat exposure; low cost; low competition	No audience selectivity; creative limitations
Miscellaneous	12.6	23.1			
Total	$54.7	100.0%			

Miscellaneous media include media expenditures of the first six types that were not classified.
SOURCE: Columns 2 and 3 are from Advertising Age. February 16, 1981. Reprinted with permission.
Copyright © 1981, Crain Communications, Inc.

tages and limitations. Media planners make their choice among these media categories by considering several variables, the most important ones being

- [ ] **Target-audience media habits.** For example, radio and television are the most effective media for reaching teenagers.
- [ ] **Product.** Women's dresses are best shown in color magazines, and Polaroid cameras are best demonstrated on television. Media types have different potentials for demonstration, visualization, explanation, believability, and color.
- [ ] **Message.** A message announcing a major sale tomorrow will require radio or newspapers. A message containing a great deal of technical data might require specialized magazines or mailings.
- [ ] **Cost.** Television is very expensive, while newspaper advertising is inexpensive. What counts, of course, is the cost-per-thousand exposures rather than the total cost.

Ideas about media impact and cost must be reexamined regularly. For a long time, television enjoyed the dominant position in the media mix, and other media were neglected. Then media researchers began to notice television's reduced effectiveness due to increased commercial clutter. Advertisers beamed shorter and more numerous commercials at the television audience, resulting in poorer attention and impact. Furthermore television advertising costs rose faster than other media costs. Several companies found that a combination of print ads and television commercials often did a better job than television commercials alone. This illustrates that advertisers must periodically review the different media to determine their best buys.

Given the media characteristics, the media planner must decide on how to allocate the budget to the major media types. For example, Pillsbury might decide in launching its new biscuit to allocate $3 million to daytime network television, $2 million to women's magazines, and $1 million to daily newspapers in twenty major markets.

Selecting Specific Media Vehicles

Now the media planner chooses the specific media vehicles that would be most cost effective. The media planner turns to several volumes published by Standard Rate and Data that provide circulation and costs for different ad sizes, color options, ad positions, and quantities of insertions in different magazines. The six leading women's magazines are *Better Homes & Gardens*, *Family Circle*, *Women's Day*, *McCall's*, *Ladies' Home Journal*, and *Good Housekeeping*. The media planner evaluates the magazines on qualitative characteristics such as credibility, prestige, geographical editioning, occupational editioning, reproduction quality, editorial climate, lead time, and psychological impact. The media planner decides which specific vehicles deliver the best reach, frequency, and impact for the money.

The cost-per-thousand criterion. Media planners calculate the *cost per thousand persons reached* by a particular vehicle. If a full-page, four-color advertisement in *Newsweek* costs $58,000 and *Newsweek's* estimated readership is 6 million people, the cost of reaching each one thousand persons is approximately $10. The same advertisement in *Business Week* may cost $26,000 but reach only 2 million persons, at a cost per thousand of $13. The media planner would rank the various magazines according to cost per thousand and favor those magazines with the lowest cost per thousand.

Several adjustments have to be applied to this initial measure. First, the measure should be adjusted for *audience quality*. For a baby lotion advertisement, a magazine read by one million young mothers would have an exposure value of one million, but if read by one million old men would have a zero exposure value. Second, the exposure value should be adjusted for the *audience attention probability*. Readers of *Vogue*, for example, pay more attention to ads than readers of *Newsweek*. Third, the exposure value should be adjusted for the *editorial quality* (prestige and believability) that one magazine might have over another. Fourth, the exposure value should be adjusted for the magazine's ad placement policies and extra services.

Media planners are increasingly using more sophisticated measures of media effectiveness and employing them in mathematical models for arriving at the best media mix. Many advertising agencies use a computer program to select the initial media and then make further improvements based on subjective factors omitted in the model.[17] (See Exhibit 20–1.)

Deciding on Media Timing

The advertiser faces a macroscheduling problem and a microscheduling problem.

Macroscheduling problem. The advertiser has to decide how to schedule the advertising over the year in relation to seasonality and expected economic developments. Suppose a product's sales peak in December and wane in March. The seller has three options. The firm can vary its advertising expenditures to follow the seasonal pattern, to oppose the seasonal pattern, or to be constant throughout the year. Most firms pursue a policy of seasonal advertising. Even here the firm has to decide whether its advertising expenditures should lead or coincide with seasonal sales. It also has to decide whether its advertising expenditures should be more intense, proportional, or less intense than the seasonal amplitude of sales.

Forrester has proposed using his "industrial dynamics" methodology to test seasonal advertising policies.[18] He sees advertising as having a lagged impact on consumer awareness; awareness has a lagged impact on factory sales; and factory sales have a lagged impact on advertising expenditures. These time relationships can be studied and formulated mathematically into a computer-simulation model. Alternative timing strategies would be simulated to assess their varying impact on company sales, costs, and profits.

Kuehn developed a model to explore how advertising should be timed for frequently purchased, highly seasonal, low-cost grocery products.[19] Kuehn showed that the appropriate timing pattern depends upon the *degree of advertising carryover* and

---

[17] See Dennis H. Gensch, *Advertising Planning* (New York: Elsevier Publishing Co.), 1973.

[18] See Jay W. Forrester, "Advertising: A Problem in Industrial Dynamics," *Harvard Business Review*, March-April 1959, pp. 100–110.

[19] See Alfred A. Kuehn, "How Advertising Performance Depends on Other Marketing Factors," *Journal of Advertising Research*, March 1962, pp. 2–10.

Exhibit 20-1

COMPUTER MODELS FOR MEDIA SELECTION

Advertising researchers have built mathematical models for media selection, some of which are in active use by advertising agencies. Here are four types of models.

Linear programming. Linear programming can be used to select the media mix that will maximize the number of effective exposures subject to a set of constraints. A linear-programming statement of the media-selection problem is shown below.

$$
\begin{aligned}
\text{Maximize:} \quad & E = 3{,}100X_1 + 2{,}000X_2 + 2{,}400X_3 \\
\text{Subject to:} \quad & 15{,}000X_1 + 4{,}000X_2 + 5{,}000X_3 \leq 500{,}000 \\
& 15{,}000X_1 \geq 250{,}000 \\
& X_1 \geq 0 \\
& X_1 \geq 52 \\
& X_2 \geq 1 \\
& X_2 \leq 8 \\
& X_3 \geq 6 \\
& X_3 \leq 12
\end{aligned}
$$

There are three media vehicles, X_1, X_2, X_3. Vehicle 1 gives 3,100 (in thousands) effective exposures per issue, vehicle 2 gives 2,000, and vehicle 3 gives 2,400. The media planner will seek to buy the number of issues of each vehicle that will maximize the total number of effective exposures, E. The media planner has an advertising budget of $500,000, which cannot be exceeded. Vehicle 1 costs $15,000 per issue, vehicle 2, $4,000, and vehicle 3, $5,000. Furthermore, the media planner wants to spend at least $250,000 on vehicle 1. Vehicle 1 puts out fifty-two issues a year, vehicle 2, eight issues, and vehicle 3, twelve issues. The media planner wants to buy at least one issue of vehicle 2 and six issues of vehicle 3.

A mathematical-solution technique is used to find the media mix.* The limitations of this model are (1) linear programming assumes that repeat exposures have a constant marginal effect; (2) it assumes constant media costs (no discounts); (3) it cannot handle the problem of audience duplication; and (4) it does not schedule the ads.

Heuristic programming. This model selects media sequentially rather than simultaneously. The model selects the single best buy the first week. The remaining media choices are reevaluated to take into account audience duplication and potential media discounts. A second selection is made for the same week if the exposure rate for the week is below the *optimal* rate. The latter is a function of several marketing and media variables. This process continues until the optimal exposure rate for the week is reached, at which point new media choices are considered for the following week. This cycling process continues until the year's schedule is completed.†

The sequential procedure has the following advantages: (1) It develops a schedule simultaneously with the selection of media; (2) it handles the audience-duplication problem; (3) it handles the media-discount problem; and (4) it incorporates important variables such as brand-switching rates and multiple-exposure coefficients.

* See James F. Engel and Martin R. Warshaw, "Allocating Advertising Dollars by Linear Programming," *Journal of Advertising Research*, September 1964, pp. 41–48.
† For an example, see William T. Moran, "Practical Media Decisions and the Computer," *Journal of Marketing*, July 1963, pp. 26–30.

Simulation model. A simulation model estimates the exposure value of any given media plan. For example, the Simulmatics media model consists of 2,944 make-believe media users representing a cross section of the American population by sex, age, type of community, employment status, and education. Each person's media choices are determined probabilistically as a function of the person's socioeconomic characteristics and location. A particular media schedule is exposed to all the persons in this hypothetical population. The computer tabulates the number and types of people exposed. Summary graphs and tables are prepared at the end of the hypothetical year's run, and they supply a picture of the schedule's probable impact. The advertiser decides whether the audience profile and the reach and frequency characteristics of the proposed media schedule are satisfactory.

Simulation complements rather than competes with the preceding models. Its major limitations are (1) simulation normally does not include an overall effectiveness function; (2) it lacks a procedure for finding better schedules; and (3) the representativeness of the hypothetical population can be questioned.

MEDIAC. Little and Lodish created a model called MEDIAC.‡ MEDIAC handles in an analytical fashion a large number of marketing and advertising variables in the real media problem, such as market segments, sales potentials, exposure probabilities, diminishing marginal response rates, forgetting, seasonality, and cost discounts. MEDIAC asks questions, and the user supplies data and receives in a matter of seconds an optimal media schedule. The user can change the data inputs and note the effect on the media schedule.

Computerized media selection is an aid, not a substitute, for executive judgment. The plan is only a starting point, because the model cannot capture all the variables. The final media plan should be the joint product of the machine's ultralogical mind and people's imagination and judgment.

‡ John D. C. Little and Leonard M. Lodish, "A Media Planning Calculus," *Operations Research*, January–February 1969, pp. 1–35.

the *amount of habitual behavior in customer brand choice*. Carryover refers to the rate at which the effect of an advertising expenditure decays with the passage of time. A carryover of 0.75 per month means that the current effect of a past advertising expenditure is 75 percent of its level·last month, while a carryover of 0.10 per month means that 10 percent of last month's effect is carried over. Habitual behavior indicates how much brand holdover occurs independently of the level of advertising. High habitual purchasing, say 0.90, means that 90 percent of the buyers repeat their purchase of the brand regardless of the marketing stimuli.

Kuehn found that when there is no advertising carryover or habitual purchasing, the decision maker is justified in using a percentage-of-sales rule to budget advertising. The optimal timing pattern for advertising expenditures coincides with the expected seasonal pattern of industry sales. But if there is advertising carryover and/or habitual purchasing, the percentage-of-sales budgeting method is not optimal. It would be better to time advertising to lead the sales curve. The peak in advertising expenditures should come before the expected peak in sales, and the trough in advertising expenditures should come before the trough in sales. Lead time should be greater, the higher the carryover. Furthermore the advertising expenditures should be steadier, the greater the extent of habitual purchasing.

Microscheduling problem. The microscheduling problem calls for allocating a set of advertising exposures over a short period of time to obtain the maximum impact. Suppose the firm decides to buy thirty radio spots in the month of September.

One way to classify the multitude of possible patterns is shown in Figure 20–3. The left side shows that advertising messages for the month can be concentrated in a small part of the month ("burst" advertising), dispersed continuously throughout the month, or dispersed intermittently throughout the month. The top side shows that the advertising messages can be beamed with a level frequency, a rising frequency, a falling frequency, or an alternating frequency. The advertiser's problem is to decide which distribution pattern would be the most effective.

The most effective pattern depends upon the advertising communication objectives in relation to the nature of the product, target customers, distribution channels, and other marketing factors. Consider the following cases:

> A **retailer** wants to announce a preseason sale of skiing equipment. She recognizes that only certain people will be interested in the message. She thinks that the target buyers need to hear the message only once or twice. Her objective is to maximize the **reach** of the message, not the **repetition**. She decides to concentrate the messages on the days of the sale at a level rate but to vary the time of day to avoid the same audiences. She uses pattern (1).
>
> A **muffler manufacturer-distributor** wants to keep his name before the public. Yet he does not want his advertising to be too continuous because only 3 to 5 percent of the cars on the road need a new muffler at any given time. He chooses to use intermittent advertising. Furthermore he recognizes that Fridays are paydays, so he sponsors a few messages on a midweek day and more messages on Friday. He uses pattern (12).

The timing pattern should consider three factors. *Buyer turnover* expresses the rate at which new buyers appear in the market; the higher this rate, the more continuous the advertising should be. *Purchase frequency* is the number of times during the period that the average buyer buys the product; the higher the purchase frequency, the more continuous the advertising should be. The *forgetting rate* is the rate at which the buyer forgets the brand; the higher the forgetting rate, the more continuous the advertising should be.

In launching a new product, the advertiser has to choose between ad continuity and ad pulsing. *Continuity* is achieved by scheduling exposures evenly within a given period. *Pulsing* refers to scheduling exposures unevenly over the same time period. Thus fifty-two exposures could be scheduled continuously at one a week throughout the year, or flighted in several concentrated bursts. Those who favor pulsing feel that the audience will learn the message more thoroughly and money could be saved. Anheuser-Busch's research indicated that Budweiser could suspend advertising in a particular market and experience no adverse sales effect for at least a year and a half.[20] Then the company could introduce a six-month burst of advertising and restore the previous growth rate. This analysis led Budweiser to adopt a pulsing advertising strategy.

---

[20] Philip H. Dougherty, "Bud 'Pulses' the Market," *New York Times*, February 18, 1975.

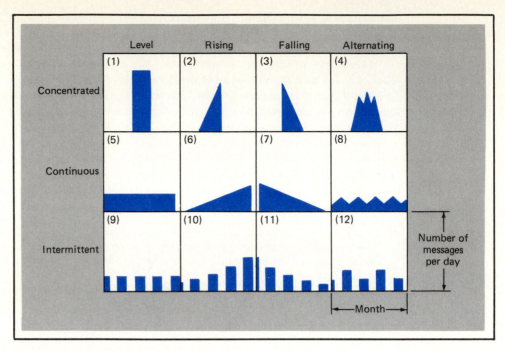

FIGURE 20-3
Classification of Advertising Timing Patterns

EVALUATING ADVERTISING EFFECTIVENESS

Good planning and control of advertising depend critically on measures of advertising effectiveness. Yet the amount of fundamental research on advertising effectiveness is appallingly small. According to Forrester:

> I doubt that there is any other function in industry where management bases so much expenditure on such scanty knowledge. The advertising industry spends 2 or 3 percent of its gross dollar volume on what it calls "research," and even if this were really true research, the small amount would be surprising. However, I estimate that less than a tenth of this amount would be considered research plus development as these terms are defined in the engineering and product research departments of companies . . . probably no more than ⅕ of 1 percent of total advertising expenditure is used to achieve an enduring understanding of how to spend the other 99.8 percent.[21]

Most of the measurement of advertising effectiveness is of an applied nature, dealing with specific ads and campaigns. Most of the money is spent by agencies on *pretesting* the given ad, much less is spent on postevaluation of its effects.

Most advertisers try to measure the *communication effect* of an ad, that is, its

---

[21] Forrester, "Advertising," p. 102.

effect on awareness, knowledge, or preference. They would like to measure the *sales effect* but often feel it is too difficult to measure. Yet both can be researched.

Communication-Effect Research

Communication-effect research seeks to determine whether an ad is communicating effectively. Called *copy testing*, it can be done before an ad is put into actual media and after it is printed or broadcast. There are three major methods of *ad pretesting*:

- ☐ **Direct ratings.** Here a panel of consumers or advertising experts are exposed to alternative ads and asked to rate them. The question might be: "Which ad do you think would influence you to buy the product?" Or a form with rating scales may be used, such as the one shown in Figure 20–4. Here the person evaluates the ad's attention strength, read-through strength, cognitive strength, affective strength, and behavioral strength, assigning a number of points up to a maximum in each case. An ad must score high on all of these if it is to stimulate buying action. Too often ads are evaluated only on their attention- or comprehension-creating abilities. At the same time, direct ratings are less reliable than hard evidence of an ad's actual impact, but they help to screen out poor ads.

- ☐ **Portfolio tests.** Here consumers are asked to look over a portfolio of ads, taking as much time as they want. The respondents are then asked to recall all the ads and as much of their content as they remember—unaided or aided by the interviewer. The results indicate an ad's ability to stand out and its message to be understood and remembered.

- ☐ **Laboratory tests.** Some researchers use equipment to measure consumers' physiological reactions—heartbeat, blood pressure, pupil dilation, perspiration—to an ad. These tests measure attention-getting power rather than beliefs, attitudes, or intentions.

Two popular methods of *ad posttesting* are:

- ☐ **Recall tests.** The researcher asks people who have been exposed to the media vehicle to recall advertisers and products contained in the last issue or installment. They are asked to play back everything they can remember. Recall scores indicate the ad's power to be noticed and remembered.

- ☐ **Recognition tests.** Here readers of a given issue of, say, a magazine, are asked to point out what they recognize as having seen before. For each ad, three different Starch readership scores (named after Daniel Starch, who provides the leading service) are prepared: (a) *noted*, the percentage of readers who say they previously saw the ad in the magazine; (b) *seen/associated*, the percentage who correctly identify the product and advertiser with the ad; and (c) *read most*, the percentage who say they read more than half of the written material in the ad. Starch also furnishes *adnorms* showing the average scores for each product class for the year, and separately for men and women for each magazine, to enable advertisers to compare their ad's impact to competitors' ads. A 1981 study examined the accuracy of Starch score predictors in testing ad and brand recognition. The relative importance of "noted" (ad recognition), "associated" (brand recognition via the ad), and "read most" in determining communication effectiveness was related to the consumer decision process. For low-involvement decisions, brand recognition ("associated") may be sufficient, whereas actual readership is probably necessary in high-involvement cases.[22]

---

[22] John Rossiter, "Predicting Starch Scores," *Journal of Advertising Research*, October 1981, pp. 63–68.

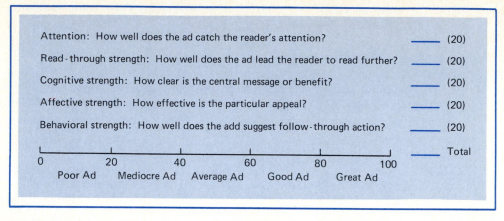

Attention: How well does the ad catch the reader's attention? ____ (20)

Read-through strength: How well does the ad lead the reader to read further? ____ (20)

Cognitive strength: How clear is the central message or benefit? ____ (20)

Affective strength: How effective is the particular appeal? ____ (20)

Behavioral strength: How well does the add suggest follow-through action? ____ (20)

						____ Total
0	20	40	60	80	100	
Poor Ad	Mediocre Ad	Average Ad	Good Ad	Great Ad		

FIGURE 20-4
Rating Sheet for Ads

Sales-Effect Research

Communication-effect advertising research helps advertisers assess the communication effects of an ad but reveals little about its sales impact. What sales are generated by an ad that increases brand awareness by 20 percent and brand preference by 10 percent?

The sales effect of advertising is generally harder to measure than the communication effect. Sales are influenced by many factors besides advertising, such as the product's features, price, and availability and competitors' actions. The fewer or more controllable these other factors, the easier it is to measure advertising's impact on sales. The sales impact is easiest to measure in mail-order situations and hardest to measure in brand or corporate-image-building advertising. Researchers try to measure the sales impact either through historical or experimental analysis.

The *historical approach* involves correlating past sales to past advertising expenditures on a current or lagged basis using advanced statistical techniques. For example, Palda studied the effect of advertising expenditures on the sales of Lydia Pinkham's Vegetable Compound between 1908 and 1960.[23] He calculated the short-term and long-term marginal sales effects of advertising. The marginal advertising dollars increased sales by only fifty cents in the short term, seeming to suggest that Pinkham spent too much on advertising. But the long-term marginal sales effect was three times as large. Palda calculated the posttax marginal rate of return on company advertising to be 37 percent over the whole period.

Montgomery and Silk estimated the sales effectiveness of three communication tools used in the pharmaceutical industry.[24] A drug company spent 38 percent of

[23] Kristian S. Palda, *The Measurement of Cumulative Advertising Effect* (Englewood Cliffs, N.J.: Prentice-Hall, 1964), p. 87.

[24] David B. Montgomery and Alvin J. Silk, "Estimating Dynamic Effects of Market Communications Expenditures," *Management Science*, June 1972, pp. 485–501.

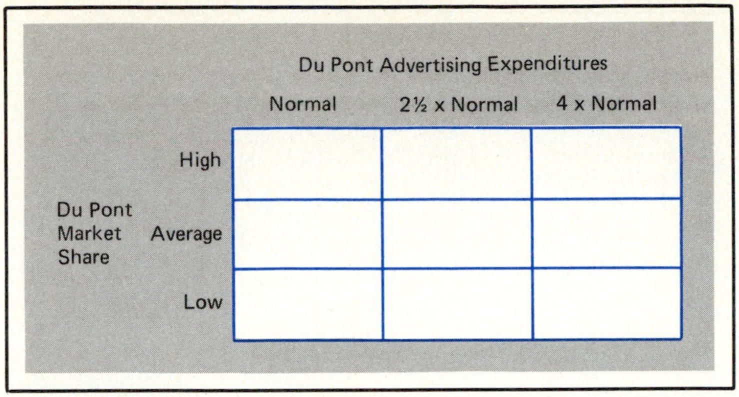

Du Pont Advertising Expenditures

		Normal	2½ x Normal	4 x Normal
	High			
Du Pont Market Share	Average			
	Low			

Source: From p. 166, *Mathematical Models and Marketing Management*, by Robert Buzzell. Boston: Division of Research, Graduate School of Business Administration, Harvard University, 1968. Reprinted by permission.

FIGURE 20–5
Experimental Design for Testing the Effect of Three Levels of Advertising Expenditure on Market Share

its communication budget on direct mail, 32 percent on samples and literature, and 29 percent on journal advertising. Yet the sales-effects research indicated that journal advertising, the least used communication tool, had the highest long-run advertising elasticity, here .365; samples and literature had an elasticity of .108; and direct mail had an elasticity of only .018. They concluded that the company spent too much on direct mail and too little on journal advertising.[25]

Other researchers use *experimental design* to measure the sales impact of advertising. Du Pont was one of the first companies to design advertising experiments. Du Pont's paint division divided fifty-six sales territories into high, average, and low market-share territories.[26] Du Pont spent the normal amount for advertising in one-third of the group; in another third, two and one-half times the normal amount; and in the remaining third, four times the normal amount. (See Figure 20–5.) At the end of the experiment, Du Pont estimated how much extra sales was created by higher levels of advertising expenditure. Du Pont found that higher advertising expenditure increased sales at a diminishing rate, and that the sales increase was weaker in Du Pont's high market-share territories.

In general, a growing number of companies are striving to measure the sales effect of advertising expenditures instead of settling for lower-order approaches such as testing ad recall or noting scores.

Figure 20–6 summarizes the major decisions and variables reviewed in this chapter in connection with the effective use of advertising.

[25] At the same time, the results from historical analysis must be carefully interpreted because of problems of high intercorrelation among the explanatory elements, insufficient number of years of sales data, and other problems.

[26] See Robert D. Buzzell, "E. I. Du Pont de Nemours & Co.: Measurement of Effects of Advertising," in his *Mathematical Models and Marketing Management* (Boston: Division of Research, Graduate School of Business Administration, Harvard University, 1964), pp. 157–79.

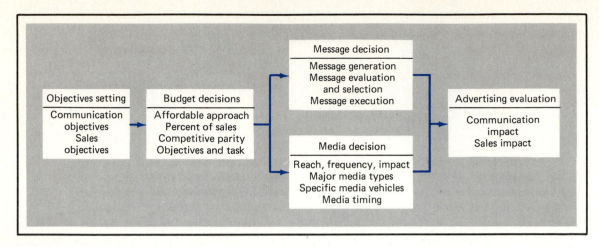

FIGURE 20-6
Major Decisions in Advertising Management

SUMMARY

Advertising—the use of paid media by a seller to communicate persuasive information about its products, services, or organization—is a potent promotional tool. American marketers spend over $61 billion annually on advertising, and it takes many forms (national, regional, local; consumer, industrial, retail; product, brand, institutional; and so on) designed to achieve a variety of objectives (immediate sales, brand recognition, preference, and so on).

Advertising decision making is a five-step process consisting of objectives setting, budget decision, message decision, media decision, and campaign evaluation. Advertisers should establish clear goals as to whether the advertising is supposed to inform, persuade, or remind buyers. The advertising budget can be established on the basis of what is affordable, as a percentage budget of sales, on the basis of competitors' expenditures, or on the basis of objectives and tasks; and more advanced decision models are available. The message decision calls for generating messages, evaluating and selecting among them, and executing them effectively. The media decision calls for defining the reach, frequency, and impact goals; choosing among major media types; selecting specific media vehicles; scheduling the media. Finally, campaign evaluation calls for evaluating the communication and sales effects of advertising, before, during, and after the advertising.

QUESTIONS

1. Consumer protection is one of the major rationales used for regulating advertising around the world. What other global forces should be monitored for their potential impact on advertising regulation?

2. Advertisers often do research to test for the effectiveness of an ad before it is placed in the media. Suggest some principles that should be followed when testing ad copy.

3. Comparative advertising—in which an advertiser directly compares his product to that of a competitor who is identified by name—has been allowed by the FTC since 1972. What are some of the advantages and dangers in using this form of advertising?

4. Consider the following two statements: "The purpose of advertising is to create sales." "The purpose of advertising is to improve the buyers' disposition toward the company's products." Which comes closer to the truth?

5. The advertising manager of a large firm asks the executive committee to approve a $100,000 increase in the advertising budget. She submits that this extra money will probably increase company sales by $500,000 over what they would otherwise be. What other information would you want in order to judge the budget request?

6. A company's advertising expenditures average $5,000 a month. Current sales are $29,000, and the saturation sales level is estimated at $42,000. The sales-response constant is $2, and the sales-decay constant is 6 percent per month. Use the Vidale-Wolfe formula to estimate the probable sales increase next month.

7. A canned-dog-food manufacturer is trying to choose between media A and B. Medium A has 10,000,000 readers and charges $20,000 for a full-page ad ($2 per 1,000). Medium B has 15,000,000 readers and charges $25,000 for a full-page ad ($1.67 per 1,000). Is there any other calculation that might be made before assuming that B is the better medium?

8. A large oil company allocates its advertising budget to its territories according to current territorial sales. The advertising manager justifies using a constant advertising-to-sales ratio by saying that the company loses a certain percentage of its customers in each market each year and that advertising's most important job is to get new customers to replace them. What assumptions underlie this reasoning?

9. Hershey Foods for many years did not advertise. In spite of this, its candy bar sales continued to grow. Does that suggest that companies with excellent products need little or no advertising?

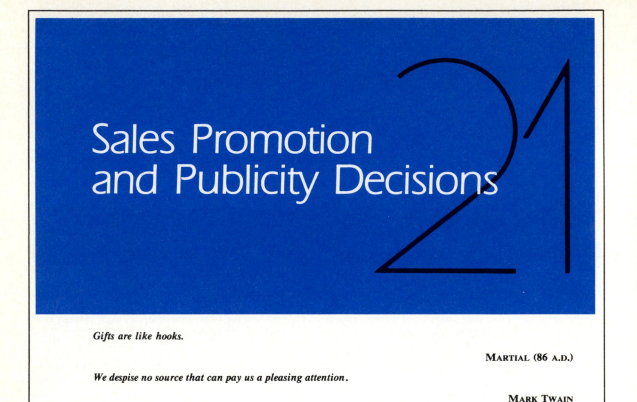

Sales Promotion and Publicity Decisions

21

Gifts are like hooks.

MARTIAL (86 A.D.)

We despise no source that can pay us a pleasing attention.

MARK TWAIN

In this chapter, we turn to sales promotion and publicity. They are often viewed as playing a secondary role to the major tools of advertising and personal selling. Yet these tools can contribute strongly to marketing performance. They are not well understood by marketing practitioners. Although some companies have created sales promotion departments, most companies lack a sales promotion manager and leave it to product and brand managers to choose sales promotions. And many companies lack a product publicity director and must get help from the company's public relations department. The recent difficult economic times, however, have led companies to use these promotional tools more aggressively.

SALES PROMOTION

Sales promotion consists of a wide variety of promotional tools designed to stimulate earlier and/or stronger market response. They include tools for *consumer promotion* (e.g., samples, coupons, money-refund offers, prices-off, premiums, contests, trading stamps, demonstrations), *trade promotion* (e.g., buying allowances, free goods, merchandise allowances, cooperative advertising, push money, dealer sales contests), and *sales-force promotion*, (e.g., bonuses, contests, sales rallies).

Sales promotion tools are used by most organizations, including manufacturers, distributors, retailers, trade associations, and nonprofit institutions. As examples of the last, churches sponsor bingo games, theatre parties, testimonial dinners, and raffles.

Rapid Growth of Sales Promotion

Sales promotion has grown rapidly in recent years. Between 1969 and 1976 sales promotion expenditures increased 9.4 percent per year compared with advertising's increase of 5.4 percent. Sales promotion exceeded $30 billion in 1976.[1] Furthermore, sales promotion expenditures are expected to continue to grow faster than advertising. Consider the following:

> A technique of particularly high growth has been consumer couponing. The A. C. Nielsen Company reports that the number of consumer coupons distributed jumped from 23.4 billion in 1972 to 45.8 billion in 1976. The proportion of households using coupons rose from 58 percent to 77 percent between 1971 and 1977. However, redemption rates for coupons were relatively low, in the 2.8 percent to 5.4 percent range for newspapers and magazines, 10.2 percent for direct mail, and up to 22.2 percent for "in" or "on" rack couponing.[2]

Several factors contributed to the rapid growth of sales promotion, particularly in consumer markets.[3] Internal factors include the following: Promotion is now more accepted by top management as an effective sales tool; more product managers are qualified to use sales promotion tools; and product managers are under greater pressure to increase their sales. External factors include the following: The number of brands has increased; competitors have become more promotion minded; inflation and recession have made consumers more deal oriented; the trade has demanded more deals from manufacturers; advertising efficiency has declined because of rising costs, media clutter, and legal restraints.

Purpose of Sales Promotion

No single purpose can be advanced for sales promotion tools, since they are so varied in form. A free sample stimulates consumer trial, while a free management-advisory service cements a long-term relationship with a retailer.

Sellers use incentive-type promotions to attract new triers and to reward loyal customers. New triers are of two types—users of another brand and those who are frequent brand switchers. Sales promotions primarily attract the brand switchers because users of other brands do not always notice or act on the promotion. Brand

---

[1] Roger A. Strang, "Sales Promotion—Fast Growth, Faulty Management," *Harvard Business Review*. July-August 1976, pp. 115–24, here pp. 116–17.

[2] "A Look at Sales Promotion," *The Nielsen Researcher*, no. 4, 1977, p. 8.

[3] Strang, "Sales Promotion," pp. 116–19.

switchers are primarily looking for low price or premiums. Sales promotions are unlikely to turn them into loyal brand users. Sales promotions used in markets of high brand similarity produce a high sales response in the short run but little permanent gain. In markets of high brand dissimilarity, sales promotions may alter market shares more permanently.

Sellers often think of sales promotion as designed to break down brand loyalty and advertising as designed to build up brand loyalty. Therefore an important issue for marketing managers is how to divide the budget between sales promotion and advertising. Companies use ratios of anywhere from 20:80 to 80:20. This sales promotion/advertising ratio has risen in recent years in response to consumers' heightened price sensitivity. Management should not let this ratio get too high. When a brand is price promoted too much of the time, the consumer begins to think of it as a cheap brand. No one knows when this happens, but probably there is risk in putting a well-known brand on promotion more than 30 percent of the time. Dominant brands use dealing infrequently, since most of it would only subsidize current users.

Most observers feel that dealing activities do not build long-term consumer franchise, as does advertising. Brown's study of 2,500 instant coffee buyers concluded that:

- [ ] Sales promotions yield faster responses in sales than advertising does.
- [ ] Sales promotions do not tend to yield new, long-term buyers in mature markets because they attract mainly deal-prone consumers who switch among brands as deals become available.
- [ ] Loyal brand buyers tend not to change their buying patterns as a result of competitive promotion.
- [ ] Advertising appears to be capable of increasing the "prime franchise" of a brand.[4]

Prentice, however, divides sales promotion tools into two groups, those that are "consumer-franchise building" and those that are not.[5] The former imparts a selling message along with the deal, as in the case of free samples, coupons when they include a selling message, and premiums when they are related to the product. Sales promotion tools that are not consumer-franchise building include price-off packs, consumer premiums not related to a product, contests and sweepstakes, consumer refund offers, and trade allowances. Seller should use consumer-franchise-building promotions because they reinforce the consumer's brand understanding.

Sales promotion seems most effective when used together with advertising. "In one study, point-of-purchase displays related to current TV commercials were found to produce 15 percent more sales than similar displays not related to such advertising. In another, a heavy sampling approach along with TV advertising proved more successful than either TV alone or TV with coupons in introducing a product."[6]

---

[4] Robert George Brown, "Sales Response to Promotions and Advertising," *Journal of Advertising Research*, August 1974, pp. 33–39, here pp. 36–37.

[5] See Roger A. Strang, Robert M. Prentice, and Alden G. Clayton, *The Relationship between Advertising and Promotion in Brand Strategy*, (Cambridge, Mass.: Marketing Science Institute, 1975), Chap. 5.

[6] Strang, "Sales Promotion," p. 124.

Major Decisions in Sales Promotion

In using sales promotion, a company must establish the objectives, select the tools, develop the program, pretest the program, implement and control it, and evaluate the results. We will examine these steps in the following paragraphs.

Establishing the Sales Promotion Objectives

Sales promotion objectives are derived from basic *marketing communication objectives*, which are derived from more basic *marketing objectives* developed for the product. The specific objectives set for sales promotion will vary with the type of target market. For *consumers*, objectives include encouraging more usage and purchase of larger-size units, building trial among nonusers, and attracting competitors' brand users. For *retailers*, objectives include inducing retailers to carry new items and higher levels of inventory, encouraging off-season buying, encouraging stocking of related items, offsetting competitive promotions, building brand loyalty of retailers, and gaining entry into new retail outlets. For the *sales force*, objectives include encouraging support of a new product or model, encouraging more prospecting, and stimulating off-season sales.

Selecting the Sales Promotion Tools

Many sales promotion tools are available to accomplish these objectives. The promotion planner should take into account the type of market, sales promotion objectives, competitive conditions, and cost effectiveness of each tool. The main tools are described below.

Samples, coupons, price packs, premiums, and trading stamps. These tools make up the bulk of consumer promotions. *Samples* are offers of a free amount or trial of a product to consumers.[7] The sample might be delivered door to door, sent in the mail, picked up in a store, found attached to another product, or featured in an advertising offer. Sampling is the most effective and most expensive way to introduce a new product. For example, Lever Brothers had so much confidence in its new mouthwash called Signal that in 1978 it distributed free samples to two out of three American households, at a cost of $15 million.

Coupons are certificates entitling the bearer to a stated saving on the purchase of a specific product. Over 81 billion coupons were distributed in 1979, about 1,200 per household. Only 4 percent were redeemed. Coupons can be mailed, enclosed in other products, or inserted in ads. They can be effective in stimulating sales of a mature brand and inducing early trial of a new brand. Experts believe they should provide a 15 to 20 percent saving to be effective. P&G's plan for breaking into the Pittsburgh market in 1977 with its Folger brand included a thirty-five-cent *discount*

---

[7] Most of the definitions in this section have been adapted from John F. Luick and William Lee Siegler, *Sales Promotion and Modern Merchandising* (New York: McGraw-Hill Book Co., 1968).

coupon on a one-pound can mailed to area homes and a *coupon in can* for ten cents off.

Price packs (also called cents-off deals) are offers to consumers of savings off the regular price of a product, flagged on the label or package. They may take the form of a *reduced-price pack*, which is single packages sold at a reduced price (such as two for the price of one), or a *banded pack*, which is two related products banded together (such as a toothbrush and toothpaste). Price packs are very effective in stimulating short-term sales, even more than coupons.

Premiums are merchandise offered at a relatively low cost or free as an incentive to purchase a particular product. A *with-pack premium* accompanies the product inside (in-pack) or (on-pack) the package. The package itself, if a *reusable container*, may serve as a premium. A *free-in-the-mail premium* is an item mailed to consumers who send in a proof of purchase, such as a box top. A *self-liquidating premium* is an item sold below its normal retail price to consumers who request it. Manufacturers now offer consumers all kinds of premiums bearing the company's name: The Budweiser fan can order T-shirts, hot-air balloons, and hundreds of other items with Bud's name on them.[8]

Trading stamps are a special type of premium received by customers making purchases, which they can redeem for merchandise through stamp redemption centers. The first merchants who adopt trading stamps usually attract new business. The other merchants adopt them defensively, and eventually they become a burden to everyone, with some merchants deciding to drop them and offer lower prices instead.[9]

Point-of-purchase displays and demonstrations. POP displays and demonstrations take place at the point of purchase or sale. A five-foot-high cardboard display of Cap'n Crunch next to Cap'n Crunch cereal boxes is an example. Unfortunately many retailers do not like to handle the hundreds of displays, signs, and posters they receive from manufacturers. Manufacturers are responding by creating better POP materials, tying them in with television or print messages and offering to set them up. The L'eggs pantyhose display is one of the most creative in the history of POP materials and a major factor in the success of this brand.[10]

Trade promotion. Manufacturers use a number of techniques to secure the cooperation of wholesalers and retailers. Manufacturers may offer a *buying allowance*, which is an offer of cents-off on each case purchased during a stated period of time. The offer encourages dealers to buy a quantity or carry a new item that they might not ordinarily buy. The dealers can use the buying allowance for immediate profit, advertising, or price redemptions.

Manufacturers may offer a *merchandise allowance* to compensate dealers for featuring the manufacturer's products. An *advertising allowance* compensates dealers

---

[8] For further reading, see Carl-Magnus Seipel, "Premiums—Forgotten by Theory," *Journal of Marketing*, April 1971, pp. 26–34.

[9] See Fred C. Allvine, "The Future for Trading Stamps and Games," *Journal of Marketing*, January 1969, pp. 45–52.

[10] "Our L'eggs Fit Your Legs," *Business Week*, March 27, 1972.

for advertising the manufacturer's product. A *display allowance* compensates them for carrying special displays of the product.

Manufacturers may offer *free goods*, which are extra cases of merchandise, to middlemen who buy a certain quantity. They may offer *push money*, which is cash or gifts to dealers or their sales force to push the manufacturer's goods. Manufacturers may offer free *specialty advertising* items that carry the company's name, such as pens, pencils, calendars, paperweights, matchbooks, memo pads, ashtrays, and yardsticks.[11]

Food retailers strongly prefer trade deals to consumer deals. They are unhappy about the amount of consumer deals they have to handle. According to Chevalier and Curhan:

> Retailers view promotional efforts initiated by manufacturers as encouraging profitless brand switching rather than increasing sales or profits. Manufacturers, on the other hand, complain that retailer-initiated promotions sometimes damage brand franchises which have been carefully and expensively nurtured over many years. Worse yet, manufacturers complain that retailers frequently take advantage of them by "absorbing" deals without passing their benefits along to consumers.[12]

Business conventions and trade shows. Industry associations organize annual conventions and typically sponsor a trade show at the same time. Firms selling to the particular industry display and demonstrate their products at the trade show. Over fifty-six hundred trade shows take place every year, drawing approximately 80 million people. The participating vendors expect several benefits, including generating new sales leads, maintaining customer contacts, introducing new products, meeting new customers, and selling more to present customers.[13]

Contests, sweepstakes, and games. These devices present to consumers, dealers, or sales forces the chance to win something—such as cash, trips, or goods—as a result of luck or extra effort. A *contest* calls for consumers to submit an entry—a jingle, estimate, suggestion—to be examined by a panel of judges who will select the best entries. A *sweepstake* calls for consumers to submit their names in a drawing. A *game* presents consumers with something every time they buy—bingo numbers, missing letters—which may or may not help them win a prize. A *sales contest* is a contest involving dealers or the sales force to induce them to redouble their sales efforts over a stated period, with prizes going to the top performers.

Developing the Sales Promotion Program

The marketer must make some additional decisions to define the full promotion program.

---

[11] See Walter A. Gaw, *Specialty Advertising* (Chicago: Specialty Advertising Association, 1970).

[12] See Michel Chevalier and Ronald C. Curhan, *Temporary Promotions as a Function of Trade Deals: A Descriptive Analysis* (Cambridge, Mass.: Marketing Science Institute, 1975), p. 2.

[13] See Suzette Cavanaugh, "Setting Objectives and Evaluating the Effectiveness of Trade Show Exhibits," *Journal of Marketing*, October 1976, pp. 100–105.

Size of incentive.   The marketer has to determine how much to offer. A certain minimum incentive is necessary if the promotion is to succeed. A higher incentive level will produce more sales response but at a diminishing rate. Some of the large consumer-packaged-goods firms have a sales promotion manager who studies the effectiveness of past promotions and recommends appropriate incentives to brand managers.

Conditions for participation.   Incentives might be offered to everyone or to select groups. A premium might be offered only to those who turn in box tops. Sweepstakes might not be offered in certain states or to families of company personnel or to persons under a certain age.

Distribution vehicle for promotion.   The marketer must decide how to promote and distribute the promotion program. A fifteen-cents-off coupon could be distributed in the package, store, mail, or advertising media. Each distribution method involves a different level of reach and cost.

Duration of promotion.   If the sales promotion period is too short, many prospects will not be able to take advantage, since they may not be repurchasing at the time. If the promotion runs too long, the deal will lose some of its "act now" force. According to one researcher, the optimal frequency is about three weeks per quarter, and optimal duration is the length of the average purchase cycle.[14]

Timing of promotion.   Brand managers need to develop calendar dates for the promotions. The dates will be used by production, sales, and distribution. Some unplanned promotions will also be needed and will require cooperation on a short notice.

Total sales promotion budget.   The sales promotion budget can be developed in two ways. It can be built from the ground up, where the marketer chooses the individual promotions and estimates their total cost. The cost of a particular promotion consists of the *administrative cost* (printing, mailing, and promoting the deal) and the *incentive cost* (cost of premium or cents-off, including rate of redemption), multiplied by the *expected number of units* that will be sold on the deal.

> Suppose a brand of after-shave lotion will be marked down 9¢ for a limited period. The item regularly sells for $1.09, of which 40¢ represents a contribution to the manufacturer's profit before marketing expense. The brand manager expects a million bottles to be sold under this deal. Thus the incentive cost of the deal will be $90,000 (= 0.09 × 1,000,000). Suppose the administrative cost is estimated at $10,000. Then the total cost is $100,000. In order to break even on this deal, the company will have to sell 250,000 (= $100,000 ÷ 0.40) more units than would have occurred over the same period without the deal.

In the case of a coupon deal, the cost would take into account the fact that only a fraction of the consumers will redeem the coupons. In the case of an in-pack premium,

---

[14] Arthur Stern, "Measuring the Effectiveness of Package Goods Promotion Strategies" (paper presented to the Association of National Advertisers, Glen Cove, N.Y., February 1978).

the deal cost must include the costs of procurement and packaging of the premium, offset by any price increase on the package.

The more common way to develop the sales promotion budget is to use a conventional percentage of the total promotion budget. For example, toothpaste may get a sales promotion budget of 30 percent of the total promotion budget, whereas shampoo may get 50 percent. These percentages vary for different brands in different markets and are influenced by the stages of the product life cycle and competitive expenditures on promotion.

Multiple-brand companies should coordinate their sales promotion activities, such as making single mailings of multiple coupons to consumers. Strang, in his study of company sales promotion practices, found three major budgeting inadequacies:[15]

☐ Lack of consideration of cost effectiveness.
☐ Use of simplistic decision rules, such as extensions of last year's spending, percentage of expected sales, maintenance of a fixed ratio to advertising, and the "left-over approach" where promotion gets what is left after advertising is set.
☐ Advertising and promotional budgets being prepared independently.

Pretesting the Sales Promotion Program

Although sales promotion programs are designed on the basis of experience, pretests should be conducted to determine if the tools are appropriate, the incentive size optimal, and the presentation method efficient. A survey by the Premium Advertisers Association indicated that fewer than 42 percent of premium offerers ever tested their effectiveness.[16] Strang maintains that promotions can usually be tested quickly and inexpensively and that some large companies test alternative strategies in selected market areas with each of their national promotions.[17]

Sales promotions directed at consumer markets can be readily pretested. Consumers can be asked to rate or rank different possible deals. Or trial tests can be run in limited geographical areas.

Implementing and Controlling the Sales Promotion Program

Implementation and control plans for individual promotion should be established. Implementation planning must cover lead time and sell-off time. Lead time is the time necessary to prepare the program prior to launching it.

It covers initial planning, design, and approval of package modifications or material to be mailed or distributed to the home, preparation of conjunctive advertising and point-of-sale materials, notification of field sales personnel, establishment of allocations for individual distributors, purchasing and printing of special premiums or packaging materi-

---

[15] Strang, "Sales Promotion," p. 119.

[16] Russell D. Bowman, "Merchandising and Promotion Grow Big in Marketing World," *Advertising Age*, December 1974, p. 21.

[17] Strang, "Sales Promotion," p. 120.

als, production of advance inventories and staging at distribution centers in preparation for release at a specific date, and finally, the distribution to the retailer.[18]

Sell-off time begins with the launch and ends when approximately 95 percent of the deal merchandise is in the hands of consumers, which may take one to several months, depending on the deal duration.

Evaluating the Sales Promotion Results

Evaluation is a crucial requirement, and yet, according to Strang, "evaluation of promotion programs receives . . . little attention. Even where an attempt is made to evaluate a promotion, it is likely to be superficial. . . . Evaluation in terms of profitability is even less common."[19]

Manufacturers can use four methods to measure sales promotion effectiveness. The most common method is to compare sales before, during, and after a promotion. Suppose a company has a 6 percent market share in the prepromotion period, which jumps to 10 percent during the promotion, falls to 5 percent immediately after the promotion, and rises to 7 percent after some time. (See Figure 21–1.) The promotion evidently attracted new triers and also stimulated more purchasing by existing customers. After the promotion sales fell, as consumers worked down their inventories. The long-run rise to 7 percent indicates that the company gained some new users. If the brand's share returned to the prepromotion level, then the promotion only altered the time pattern of demand rather than the total demand.

Consumer panel data would reveal the kinds of people who responded to the promotion and what they did after the promotion.[20] If more information is needed, *consumer surveys* can be conducted to learn how many recall the promotion, what they thought of it, how many took advantage of it, and how it affected their subsequent brand-choice behavior. Sales promotions can also be evaluated through *experiments* that vary such attributes as incentive value, duration, and distribution media.

Clearly sales promotion plays an important role in the total promotion mix. Its systematic use requires defining the sales promotion objectives, selecting the appropriate tools, constructing the sales promotion program, pretesting it, implementing it, and evaluating the results.

PUBLICITY

Another major promotion tool is publicity. *Publicity* involves "securing editorial space, as divorced from paid space, in all media read, viewed, or heard by a company's

---

[18] Kurt H. Schaffir and H. George Trenten, *Marketing Information Systems*, (New York: Amacom, 1973), p. 81.

[19] Strang, "Sales Promotion," p. 120.

[20] See Joe A. Dodson, Alice M. Tybout, and Brian Sternthal, "Impact of Deals and Deal Retraction on Brand Switching," *Journal of Marketing Research*, February 1978, pp. 72–81. They found that deals generally increase brand switching, the rate depending on the type of deal. Media-distributed coupons induce substantial switching, cents-off deals induce somewhat less switching, and package coupons hardly affect brand switching. Furthermore consumers generally return to their preferred brands after the deal.

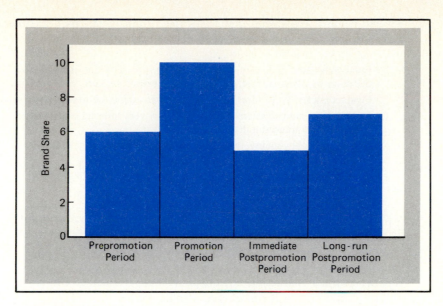

FIGURE 21-1
Effect of Consumer Deal on Brand Share

customers or prospects, for the specific purpose of assisting in the meeting of sales goals."[21] Publicity's results can sometimes be spectacular. Consider the following:

Promoting Paramount Pictures' **Saturday Night Fever** began months before its scheduled release. Robert Stigwood, the producer, issued the motion picture's sound track six weeks before the film's release. The records and tapes generated high-volume sales and received saturation radio play. When the film opened, moviegoers queued at the box office. Stigwood capitalized on America's fascination with celebrities by engineering a prime-time television "special" on the night of the Hollywood premiere of **Saturday Night Fever** to honor the film's star, John Travolta. The film's success was phenomenal. Stigwood's achievement was his ability to recognize a musical trend ("disco") and a talented performer (John Travolta) and to use publicity effectively to "hype" mass-market interest in the film.

Publicity is used to promote brands, products, persons, places, ideas, activities, organizations, and even nations. Trade associations have used publicity to rebuild interest in declining commodities such as eggs, milk, and potatoes. Organizations have used publicity to attract attention or to counter a poor image. Nations have employed publicity to attract more tourists, foreign investment, and international support.

Publicity is part of a larger concept, that of *public relations*. Company public relations has several objectives, including obtaining favorable publicity for the company, building up a good "corporate citizen" image for the company, and handling

---

[21] George Black, *Planned Industrial Publicity* (Chicago: Putnam Publishing, 1952), p. 3.

adverse rumors and stories that break out. Public relations departments use several tools to carry out these objectives:[22]

☐ **Press relations.** The aim of press relations is to place newsworthy information into the news media to attract attention to a person, product, or service.
☐ **Product publicity.** Product publicity involves various efforts to publicize specific products.
☐ **Corporate communications.** This activity covers internal and external communications and promotes understanding of the institution.
☐ **Lobbying.** Lobbying involves dealing with legislators and government officials to promote or defeat legislation and regulation.
☐ **Counseling.** Counseling involves advising management about public issues and company positions and image.

Those skilled in publicity are usually found not in the company's marketing department but in its public relations department. The public relations department is typically located at corporate headquarters; and its staff is so busy dealing with various publics—stockholders, employees, legislators, city officials—that publicity to support product marketing objectives may be neglected. One solution is to add a publicity specialist to the marketing department.

Publicity is often described as a marketing stepchild because of its limited and sporadic use. Yet publicity can create a memorable impact on public awareness at a fraction of the cost of advertising. The company does not pay for the space or time in the media. It pays for a staff to develop and circulate the stories. If the company develops an interesting story, it could be picked up by all the media and be worth millions of dollars in equivalent advertising. Furthermore it would have more credibility than advertising.

Major Decisions in Publicity

In considering when and how to use product publicity, management should establish the publicity objectives, choose the publicity messages and vehicles that will implement the publicity plan, and evaluate the publicity results.

Establishing the Publicity Objectives

Publicity can contribute in a number of ways to the overall promotion program. Publicity's potential contribution can be especially strong in the following circumstances:

☐ **Newsworthiness.** Products with interesting stories are the best candidates for publicity.
☐ **Stimulus for sales force and dealers.** Publicity can help boost sales-force and dealer enthusiasm. Stories about a new product before it is launched will help the sales force sell it to retailers.
☐ **Need for credibility.** Publicity adds credibility by communicating the message in an editorial context.

---

[22] Adapted from Scott M. Cutlip and Allen H. Center, *Effective Public Relations*, 3rd. ed. (Englewood Cliffs, N.J.: Prentice-Hall, 1964), pp. 10–14.

☐ **Small budget.** Publicity costs less than direct mail and media advertising. The smaller the company's promotion budget, the stronger the case for using publicity to gain share of mind.

Specific objectives should be set for every publicity campaign. The Wine Growers of California hired the public relations firm of Daniel J. Edelman, Inc., to develop a publicity campaign to convince Americans that wine drinking is a pleasurable part of good living and to improve the image and market share of California wines. The following publicity objectives were established: (1) develop magazine stories about wine and get them placed in top magazines (*Time, House Beautiful*) and in newspapers (food columns, feature sections); (2) develop stories about wine's many health values and direct them to the medical profession; and (3) develop specific publicity for the young adult market, college market, governmental bodies, and various ethnic communities. These objectives were refined into specific goals so that final results could be evaluated.

Choosing the Publicity Messages and Vehicles

The publicist next identifies interesting stories to tell about the product. Suppose a relatively unknown college wants more public recognition. The publicist will search for possible stories. Do any faculty members have unusual backgrounds, or are any working on unusual projects? Are any new and unusual courses being taught? Are any interesting events taking place on campus? Usually this search will uncover hundreds of stories that can be fed to the press. The stories chosen should reflect the image this college wants.

If the number of stories is insufficient, the publicist should propose newsworthy events that the college could sponsor. Here the publicist gets into *creating news* rather than *finding news*. The ideas include hosting major academic conventions, inviting celebrity speakers, and developing news conferences. Each event is an opportunity to develop a multitude of stories directed at different audiences.

Event creation is a particularly important skill in publicizing fund-raising drives for nonprofit organizations. Fund raisers have developed a large repertoire of special events, including *anniversary celebrations*, *art exhibits*, *auctions*, *benefit evenings*, *bingo games*, *book sales*, *cake sales*, *contests*, *dances*, *dinners*, *fairs*, *fashion shows*, *parties in unusual places*, *phonathons*, *rummage sales*, *tours*, and *walkathons*. No sooner is one type of event created, such as a walkathon, than competitors spawn new versions, such as readathons, bikathons, and jogathons.

A publicist is able to find or create stories on behalf of even mundane products. Here are two examples:

Some years ago the Potato Board decided to finance a publicity campaign to encourage more potato consumption. A national attitude and usage study indicated that many consumers perceived potatoes as too fattening, not nutritious enough, and not a good source of vitamins and minerals. These attitudes were disseminated by various opinion leaders, such as food editors, diet advocates, and doctors. Actually potatoes have far fewer calories than most people imagine, and they contain several important vitamins and minerals. The Potato Board decided to develop separate publicity programs for consumers, doctors and dieticians, nutritionists, home economists, and food editors. The consumer program consisted of disseminating many stories about the potato for network television and women's magazines, developing and distributing **The Potato Lover's Diet Cookbook**, and placing articles and recipes in food editors' columns. The food editors' program consisted of food-editor seminars, conducted by nutrition experts.

Publicity can be highly effective in brand promotion. One of the top brands of cat food is Star-Kist Foods' 9-Lives. Its brand image revolves around Morris the Cat. The advertising agency of Leo Burnett, which created Morris for its ads, wanted to make him more of a living, breathing, real-life feline to whom cat owners and cat lovers could relate. It hired a public relations firm, which then proposed and carried out the following ideas: (1) Launch a Morris "look-alike" contest in nine major markets, with Morris booked for personal appearances and extensive stories appearing about the search for a look-alike: (2) write a book called **Morris, an Intimate Biography,** describing the adventures of this famous feline: (3) establish a coveted award called "The Morris," a bronze statuette given to the owners of award-winning cats at local cat shows: (4) sponsor an "Adopt-a-Cat Month," with Morris as the official "spokescat" urging people to adopt stray cats as Morris was once adopted: and (5) distribute a booklet called "The Morris Method" on cat care. These publicity steps strengthened the brand's market share in the cat food market.

Implementing the Publicity Plan

Implementing publicity requires care. Take the matter of placing stories in the media. A great story is easy to place. But most stories are less than great and may not get past busy editors. One of the chief assets of publicists is their personal relationship with media editors. Publicists are often ex-journalists who know many media editors and know what they want. Publicists look at media editors as a market to satisfy so that these editors will continue to use their stories.

Publicity requires extra care when it involves staging special events such as testimonial dinners, news conferences, and national contests. Publicists need a good head for detail and for coming up with quick solutions when things go wrong.

Evaluating the Publicity Results

Publicity's contribution is difficult to measure because it is used along with other promotion tools. If it is used before the other tools come into action, its contribution is easier to evaluate.

Exposures.   The easiest measure of publicity effectiveness is the number of *exposures* created in the media. Publicists supply the client with a clipping book showing all the media that carried news about the product and a summary statement such as the following:

Media coverage included 3,500 column inches of news and photographs in 350 publications with a combined circulation of 79.4 million; 2,500 minutes of air time of 290 radio stations and an estimated audience of 65 million; and 660 minutes of air time on

160 television stations with an estimated audience of 91 million. If this time and space had been purchased at advertising rates, it would have amounted to $1,047,000.[23]

This exposure measure is not very satisfying. There is no indication of how many people actually read or heard the message and what they thought afterward. There is no information on the net audience reached, since publications overlap in readership.

Awareness/comprehension/attitude change.   A better measure is the change in product *awareness/comprehension/attitude* resulting from the publicity campaign (after allowing for the impact of other promotional tools). This requires surveying the before-and-after levels of these variables. The Potato Board learned, for example, that the number of people who agreed with the statement "Potatoes are rich in vitamins and minerals" went from 36 before the campaign to 67 percent after the campaign, a significant improvement in product comprehension.

Sales and profit contribution.   Sales and profit impact is the most satisfactory measure, if obtainable. For example, 9-Lives sales increased 43 percent at the end of the "Morris the Cat" publicity campaign. However, advertising and sales promotion had also been stepped up, and their contribution has to be allowed for. Suppose total sales have increased $1,500,000, and management estimates that publicity contributed 15 percent of the total sales increase. Then the return on publicity investment is calculated as follows:

Total sales increase	$1,500,000
Estimated sales increase due to publicity (15%)	225,000
Contribution margin on product sales (10%)	22,500
Total direct cost of publicity program	−10,000
Contribution margin added by publicity investment	$ 12,500
Return on publicity investment ($12,500/$10,000) =	125%

SUMMARY

Sales promotion covers a wide variety of short-term incentive tools—coupons, premiums, contests, buying allowances—designed to stimulate consumer markets, the trade, and the organization's own sales force. Sales promotion expenditures have been growing at a faster rate than advertising in recent years. Sales promotion calls for establishing the sales promotion objectives, selecting the tools, developing, pretesting, and implementing the sales promotion program, and evaluating the results.

Publicity—which is the securing of free editorial space or time—is the least utilized of the major promotion tools, although it has great potential for building awareness and preference in the marketplace. Publicity involves establishing the publicity objectives, choosing the publicity messages and vehicles, and evaluating the publicity results.

---

[23] Arthur M. Merims, "Marketing's Stepchild: Product Publicity," *Harvard Business Review*, November-December 1972, pp. 111–12.

QUESTIONS

1. In 1982 approximately 120 billion coupons were distributed by American manufacturers, only 5.4 billion of which were redeemed. What factors influence the rate of coupon redemption?

2. Companies annually spend over $6 billion a year on trade shows. What questions should marketing managers ask themselves when determining how much of the marketing budget to allocate to trade shows?

3. Many firms have had to contend with negative rumors about their products in recent years (e.g., "McDonald's has worms in its hamburger meat."). How can a company best deal with these rumors through public relations and advertising?

4. A major basketball team experienced a decline in home-game attendance. The team's owner decided to hire a marketer to stimulate attendance. What are some of the steps that can be taken?

5. Joe Pringle, a product manager at the XYZ Snacks Company, is concerned about falling sales in recent months. His inventory is high. He is contemplating a sales promotion to reverse the sales trend and reduce inventories. He is thinking of offering a case allowance to the trade. He expects sales to be 40,000 cases in the absence of promotion. The case price is $10 and the gross profit contribution is 40 percent. He is currently thinking of offering a $1 case allowance. He expects increased sales of 20,000 cases during the promotion period. The estimated cost of developing this promotion is $12,000. (a) Will he make a profit on this promotion? (b) What is the break-even sales increase that will justify this case allowance? (c) If he offers only a 50¢ case allowance, he expects additional net sales of 12,000. Should he offer a $1 or 50¢ case allowance?

6. Much of the public relations work done by business firms consists of miscellaneous and unrelated activities. Can you suggest an underlying public relations orientation a company could adopt that would provide a focus for many publicity activities?

7. Select a product or service and recommend which sales promotion tools should be used to build its consumer franchise.

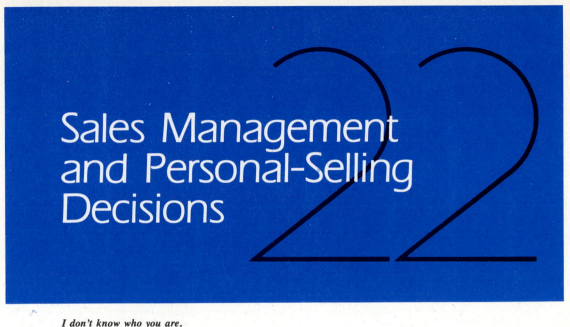

Sales Management and Personal-Selling Decisions

22

I don't know who you are.
I don't know your company.
I don't know your company's product.
I don't know what your company stands for.
I don't know your company's customers.
I don't know your company's record.
I don't know your company's reputation.
Now—what was it you wanted to sell me?

McGraw-Hill Publications

Robert Louis Stevenson observed that "everyone lives by selling something." In 1981 American firms spent approximately $150 billion on personal selling compared with $61 billion on advertising. Over 6.4 million Americans are employed in sales and related occupations. Sales forces are found in nonprofit as well as profit organizations. College recruiters are the college's sales-force arm for attracting students. Churches use membership committees to attract new members. The U.S. Agricultural Extension Service sends agricultural specialists to sell farmers on using new farming methods. Hospitals and museums use fund raisers to contact and raise money from donors. Selling is one the world's oldest professions.

People who sell are called by various names: saleswomen and salesmen, sales representatives, salespersons, account executives, sales consultants, sales engineers, field representatives, agents, service representatives, and marketing representatives. The public tends to carry many stereotypes about sales representatives. *Salesman* may conjure up an image of Arthur Miller's pitiable Willy Loman in *Death of a Salesman* or Meredith Wilson's cigar-smoking, back-slapping, joke-telling Harold

Hill in *The Music Man*. Sales representatives are typically pictured as loving sociability—although many sales representatives actually dislike it. They are criticized for foisting goods on people—although buyers often search out sales representatives.

Actually the term *sales representative* covers a broad range of positions in our economy, where the differences are often greater than the similarities. McMurry devised the following classification of sales positions:

1. Positions where the salesperson's job is predominantly to deliver the product, e.g., milk, bread, fuel, oil.
2. Positions where the salesperson is predominantly an inside order-taker, e.g., the haberdashery salesperson standing behind the counter.
3. Positions where the salesperson is also predominantly an order-taker but works in the field, as the packing-house, soap, or spice salesperson does.
4. Positions where the salesperson is not expected or permitted to take an order but is called on only to build goodwill or to educate the actual or potential user . . . the distiller's "missionary person" or the medical "detailer" representing an ethical pharmaceutical house.
5. Positions where the major emphasis is placed on technical knowledge, e.g., the engineering salesperson who is primarily a consultant to the "client" companies.
6. Positions which demand the creative sale of tangible products like vacuum cleaners, refrigerators, siding, and encyclopedias.
7. Positions requiring the creative sale of intangibles, such as insurance, advertising services, or education.[1]

The positions range from the least to the most creative types of selling. The first jobs call for maintaining accounts and taking orders, while the latter require hunting down prospects and influencing them to buy. Our discussion will focus on the more creative types of selling.

This chapter is divided into three parts. The first and second parts deal with several issues in designing and managing an effective sales force. (See Figure 22–1.) The third part deals with three issues in the effective conduct of personal selling, namely, salesmanship, negotiation, and relationship building.

DESIGNING THE SALES FORCE

Sales personnel serve as the company's unique link to the customers. The sales representative *is* the company to many of its customers and in turn brings back to the company much needed intelligence about the customer. Therefore the company needs to give its deepest thought to issues in sales-force design, namely, developing sales-force objectives, strategy, structure, size, and compensation.

Sales-Force Objectives

Sales-force objectives must be based on the character of the company's target markets and the company's sought position in these markets. The company must consider

---

[1] Robert N. McMurry, "The Mystique of Super-Salesmanship," *Harvard Business Review*, March-April 1961, p. 114.

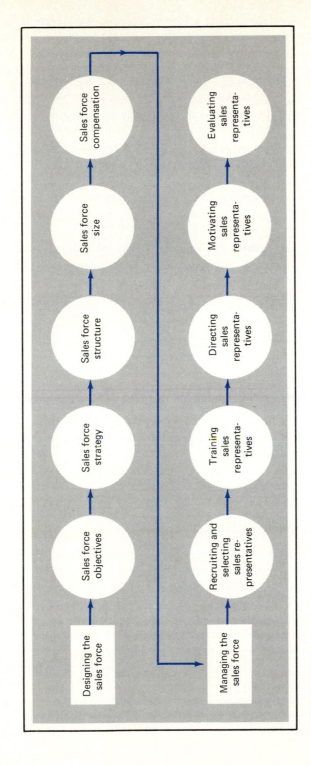

FIGURE 22–1
Steps in Designing and Managing the Sales Force

the unique role that personal selling can play in the marketing mix to serve customer needs in a competitively effective way. Personal selling happens to be the most expensive contact and communications tool of the company, costing companies an average of $127 a sales call in 1980.[2] Therefore it must be used sparingly. Personal selling is also the most effective tool at certain stages of the buying process, such as the buyer-education, negotiation, and sales-closing stages. It is important that the company think out carefully when and how to use sales representatives to facilitate the marketing task.

Companies set different objectives for their sales force. IBM's sales representatives are responsible for *selling, installing,* and *upgrading* customer computer equipment; AT&T sales representatives are responsible for *developing, selling,* and *protecting* accounts. Sales representatives perform one or more of the following tasks for their companies:

- ☐ **Prospecting.** Sales representatives find and cultivate new customers.
- ☐ **Communicating.** Sales representatives skillfully communicate information about the company's products and services.
- ☐ **Selling.** Sales representatives know the art of "salesmanship"—approaching, presenting, answering objections, and closing sales.
- ☐ **Servicing.** Sales representatives provide various services to the customers—consulting on their problems, rendering technical assistance, arranging financing, and expediting delivery.
- ☐ **Information gathering.** Sales representatives carry out market research and intelligence work and fill in call reports.
- ☐ **Allocating.** Sales representatives are able to evaluate customer quality and allocate scarce products during product shortages.

Companies get more specific about their sales-force objectives and activities. One company advises its sales representatives to spend 80 percent of their time with current customers and 20 percent with prospects, and 85 percent of their time on established products and 15 percent on new products.[3] If norms are not established, sales representatives tend to spend most of their time selling established products to current accounts and neglect new products and new prospects.

The sales representative's mix of tasks varies with the state of the economy. When widespread product shortages occurred in 1973, sales representatives in many industries found themselves with nothing to sell. Some observers jumped to the conclusion that sales representatives were redundant and could be retrenched. But this thinking overlooked the other roles of the salesperson—allocating the product, counseling unhappy customers, communicating company plans on remedying the shortage, and selling the company's other products that were not short in supply.

As companies increase their market orientation, their sales forces need to become more market oriented. The traditional view is that sales people should worry about

---

[2] *Sales and Marketing Management*, February 23, 1981, p. 34.

[3] See William R. Dixon, "Redetermining the Size of the Sales Force: A Case Study," in *Changing Perspectives in Marketing Management*, ed. Martin R. Warshaw (Ann Arbor: University of Michigan, Michigan Business Reports, 1962) no. 37, p. 58.

volume and sell, sell, sell and that the marketing department should worry about marketing strategy and profitability. The newer view is that sales people should know how to produce customer satisfaction and company profit. They should know how to analyze sales data, measure market potential, gather market intelligence, and develop marketing strategies and plans. Sales representatives need analytical marketing skills, and this becomes especially critical at the higher levels of sales management. Marketers believe that a market-oriented rather than a sales-oriented sales force will be more effective in the long run.

Sales-Force Strategy

Companies compete with each other to get orders from customers. They must deploy their sales forces strategically so that they are calling on the right customers at the right time and in the right way. Sales representatives can approach customers in several ways:

☐ **Sales representative to buyer.** A sales representative talks to a prospect or customer in person or over the phone.

☐ **Sales representative to buyer group.** A sales representative makes a sales presentation to a buying group.

☐ **Sales team to buyer group.** A sales team (such as a company officer, a sales representative, and a sales engineer) makes a sales presentation to a buying group.

☐ **Conference selling.** The sales representative brings resource people from the company to meet with one or more buyers to discuss problems and mutual opportunities.

☐ **Seminar selling.** A company team conducts an educational seminar for a technical group in a customer company about state-of-the-art developments.

Thus the sales representative often acts as the "account manager" who arranges contacts between various people in the buying and selling organizations. Selling increasingly calls for teamwork, requiring the support of other personnel, such as *top management*, which is increasingly involved in the sales process, especially when *national accounts*[4] or *major sales*[5] are at stake; *technical people*, who supply technical information to the customer before, during, or after the purchase of the product; *customer-service representatives*, who provide installation, maintenance, and other services to the customer; and an *office staff*, consisting of sales analysts, order expediters, and secretaries.

Once the company decides on a desirable selling approach, it can use either a direct or a contractual sales force. A *direct* (or *company*) *sales force* consists of full- or part-time paid employees who work exclusively for the company. This sales force includes *inside sales personnel*, who conduct business from their office using the telephone and receiving visits from prospective buyers, and *field sales personnel*,

[4] Roger M. Pegram, *Selling and Servicing the National Account* (New York: Conference Board, 1972).

[5] William H. Kaven, *Managing the Major Sale* (New York: American Management Association, 1971); and Benson P. Shapiro and Ronald S. Posner, "Making the Major Sale," *Harvard Business Review*, March-April 1976, pp. 68–78.

who travel and visit customers. A *contractual sales force* consists of manufacturers, reps, sales agents, or brokers, who are paid a commission based on their sales.

Sales-Force Structure

The sales-force strategy will have implications for structuring the sales force to have maximum impact in the market. Sales-force structure is simple if the company sells one product line to one end-using industry with customers in many locations; the company would use a territorial-structured sales force. If the company sells many products to many types of customers, it might need a product-structured or customer-structured sales force. These alternative sales-force structures are discussed below.

Territorial-structured sales force. In the simplest sales organization each sales representative is assigned an exclusive territory in which to represent the company's full line. This sales structure has a number of advantages. First, it results in a clear definition of the salesperson's responsibilities. As the only salesperson working the territory, he or she bears the credit or blame for area sales to the extent that personal selling effort makes a difference. Second, territorial responsibility increases the sales representative's incentive to cultivate local business and personal ties. These ties contribute to the sales representative's selling effectiveness and personal life. Third, travel expenses are relatively small, since each sales representative travels within a small geographical area.

Territorial sales organization is supported by a hierarchy of sales management positions. Several territories will be supervised by a *district sales manager*; several districts will be supervised by a *regional sales manager*; and several regions will be supervised by a *national sales manager* or *sales vice-president*. Each higher-level sales manager takes on increasing marketing and administrative work in relation to the time available for selling. In fact, sales managers are paid for their management skills rather than their selling skills. The new sales trainee, in looking ahead at the career path, can expect to become a sales representative and then a district manager and, depending on his or her ability and motivation, may move to higher levels of sales or general management.

In designing a set of territories, the company seeks certain territorial characteristics: The territories are easy to administer; their sales potential is easy to estimate; they keep down total travel time; and they provide a sufficient and equitable workload and sales potential for each sales representative. These characteristics are achieved through decisions about the size and shape of territorial units.

Territory size. Territories can be designed to provide either *equal sales potential* or *equal workload*. Each principle offers advantages at the cost of some dilemmas.

Territories of *equal potential* provide each sales representative with the same income opportunities and provide the company with a means to evaluate performance. Persistent differences in sales yield by territory are assumed to reflect differences in ability or effort of individual sales representatives. Salespersons are encouraged to work at their top capacity.

But because customer density varies by territory, territories with equal potential can vary widely in area. The potential for selling a large drill press in Chicago is larger than in several western states. A sales representative assigned to Chicago can cover the same sales potential with far less effort than the sales representative who sells in the Far West.

Either the sales representative assigned to the larger and sparser territory is going to end up with fewer sales and less income for equal effort or with equal sales through extraordinary effort. One solution is to pay the western sales representatives more compensation for the extra effort. But this reduces the profits on sales in the western territories. Another solution is to acknowledge that territories differ in attractiveness and assign the better or more senior sales representatives to the better territories.

Alternatively, territories could be designed to *equalize the sales workload*. Each sales representative can then cover his or her territory adequately. This principle, however, results in some variation in territory sales potentials. That does not concern a sales force on straight salary. But where sales representatives are compensated partly on their sales, territories will vary in their attractiveness even though their workloads are equal. A lower compensation rate can be paid to sales representatives in the territories with the higher sales potential, or the territories with the better potential can go to the higher performers.

Territory shape. Territories are formed by combining smaller units, such as counties or states, until they add up to a territory of a given sales potential or workload. They take into account the location of natural barriers, the compatibility of adjacent areas, the adequacy of transportation, and so forth. Many companies prefer a certain territory shape because this can influence the cost and ease of coverage and the sales representatives' job satisfaction. Most common are circular, cloverleaf, and wedge-shaped territories.

Computer models are being used to design sales territories that balance workload, sales potential, compactness, and routing efficiency.[6] The efficient routing of sales calls through a territory to reduce travel time or cost is being assisted by computer programs based on the "traveling salesman problem."[7]

Product-structured sales force. The importance of sales representatives' knowing their products, together with the development of product divisions and product management, has led many companies to structure their sales force along product lines. Product specialization is particularly warranted where the products are technically complex, highly unrelated, or very numerous.

The mere existence of different company products, however, is not a sufficient argument for specializing the sales force by product. Such specialization may not

---

[6] A computer-based method that creates territories that are compact and equal in workload is described in Sidney W. Hess and Stuart A. Samuels, "Experiences with a Sales Districting Model: Criteria and Implementation," *Management Science*, December 1971, pp. 41–54. Also see Leonard M. Lodish, "Sales Territory Alignment to Maximize Profit," *Journal of Marketing Research*, February 1975, pp. 30–36; and Andris A. Zoltners, "Integer Programming Models for Sales Territory Alignment to Maximize Profit," *Journal of Marketing Research*, November 1976, pp. 426–30.

[7] See John D. C. Little et al., "An Algorithm for the Traveling Salesman Problem," *Operations Research*, November-December 1963, pp. 972–89.

be the best course if the company's separate product lines are bought by the same customers. For example, the American Hospital Supply Corporation has several product divisions, each with its own sales force. It is possible that several sales representatives from the American Hospital Supply Corporation could call on the same hospital on the same day. This means that company sales personnel travel over the same routes, and each waits to see the customer's purchasing agents. These extra costs must be weighed against the benefits of more knowledgeable product representation.

Customer-structured sales force. Companies often specialize their sales forces along customer lines. Separate sales forces may be set up for different industries, for major versus regular accounts, and for current versus new-business development. The most obvious advantage of customer specialization is that each sales force can become knowledgeable about specific customer needs. At one time General Electric's sales representatives specialized in products (fan motors, switches, and so forth), but it later changed to specialization in markets, such as the air-conditioning market and auto market, because that is how customers saw the purchase of fan motors, switches, and so forth. A customer-specialized sales force can sometimes reduce total sales-force costs. A pump manufacturer at one time used highly trained sales engineers to sell to original-equipment manufacturers (who needed to deal with technical representatives) and jobbers (who did not need to deal with technical representatives). Later the company split its sales force and staffed the jobber sales force with lower paid, less technical sales personnel.

The major disadvantage of customer-structured sales forces arises when the various types of customers are scattered throughout the country. This means extensive travel by each of the company's sales forces.

Complex sales-force structures. When a company sells a wide variety of products to many types of customers over a broad geographical area, it often combines several principles of sales-force structure. Sales representatives may be specialized by territory-product, territory-customer, product-customer, or ultimately by territory-product-customer. A sales representative may then report to one or more line managers and staff managers. One of the most interesting developments is the growth of national account management divisions. (See Exhibit 22–1.)

Sales-Force Size

Once the company clarifies its sales-force strategy and structure, it is ready to consider sales-force size. Sales representatives are one of the company's most productive and expensive assets. Increasing their number will increase both sales and costs.

Most companies use the *workload approach* to establish sales-force size. This method consists of the following steps:

1. Customers are grouped into size classes according to their annual sales volume.
2. The desirable call frequencies (number of sales calls on an account per year) are established for each class. They reflect how much call intensity the company seeks in relation to competitors.

Exhibit 22-1

NATIONAL ACCOUNT MANAGEMENT—WHAT IT IS AND HOW IT WORKS

When a company sells to many small accounts, it uses a traditional sales force, with each sales representative handling several accounts. If the company has one large account, this account is often assigned to a high-level manager to watch or sell to. This large account is variously called a key account, a major account, or a house account. If this account is a large complex company with many divisions operating in many parts of the country and subject to many buying influences (such as Sears or General Motors), it is likely to be handled as a *national account* with a specific individual or sales team assigned to it. If the seller has several such accounts, it is likely to organize a *national account management (NAM) division*. The company will then sell its larger customers through this division and its smaller customers through its regular sales force. A company such as Xerox handles about 250 national accounts through its NAM division.

National account management is growing for a number of reasons. As buyer concentration increases through mergers and acquisitions, fewer buyers account for a larger share of a company's sales. Thus the largest 10 percent of accounts may account for more than 50 percent of a company's revenue. Another factor is that many buyers are centralizing their purchases of certain items instead of leaving those purchases to the local units. This gives them more bargaining power with the sellers. The sellers in turn need to devote more attention to these major buyers. Still another factor is that, as products grow more complex, more groups in the buyer's organization get involved in the purchase choice and the typical salesperson may not have the needed authority or coverage to be effective in selling to the buyer.

In organizing a national account program, a company has to face a number of issues, including: how to select national accounts; how to manage them; how to develop, manage, and evaluate national account managers; how to organize a structure for national account management, and where to locate national account management in the organization.

Essentially a company wants its national account managers to be good at a number of things. They must be able to reach all of the buying influences in the buyer's organization. They must be able to reach all the groups in their own organization—sales people, R&D staff, manufacturing people, and so on—to coordinate them in meeting the buyer's requirements. Thus national account managers link all the complex parts of their company with all the complex parts of the buying company. In many organizations they are, in fact, called "relationship managers."

Sources: For further discussion, see the working papers on National Account Management prepared by Benson P. Shapiro and Rowland T. Moriarty under the sponsorship of the Marketing Science Institute, Cambridge, Mass., published in 1980–83.

3. The number of accounts in each size class is multiplied by the corresponding call frequency to arrive at the total workload for the country, in sales calls per year.
4. The average number of calls a sales representative can make per year is determined.
5. The number of sales representatives needed is determined by dividing the total annual calls required by the average annual calls made by a sales representative.

Suppose the company estimates that there are one thousand A accounts and two thousand B accounts in the nation; and A accounts require thirty-six calls a year and B accounts twelve calls a year. This means the company needs a sales force that can make sixty thousand sales calls a year. Suppose the average sales representative can make one thousand calls a year. The company would need sixty full-time sales representatives.

Sales-Force Compensation

To attract the desired number of sales representatives, the company has to develop an attractive compensation plan. Sales representatives would like income regularity, reward for above-average performance, and fair payment for experience and longevity. On the other hand, management would emphasize control, economy, and simplicity. Management objectives, such as economy, will conflict with sales representatives' objectives, such as financial security. It is understandable why compensation plans exhibit a tremendous variety, not only among industries but among companies within the same industry.

Management must determine the level and components of an effective compensation plan. The *level of compensation* must bear some relation to the "going market price" for the type of sales job and abilities required. For example, the average earnings of the experienced salesperson in 1981 amounted to $30,444.[8] If the market price for sales people is well defined, the individual firm has little choice but to pay the going rate. To pay less would bring forth less than the desired quantity or quality of applicants, and to pay more would be unnecessary. The market price for sales people, however, is often not well defined. For one thing, company plans vary in the importance of fixed and variable salary elements, fringe benefits, and expense allowances. And data on the average take-home pay of sales representatives working for competitive firms can be misleading because of significant variations in the average seniority and ability levels of the competitors' sales forces. Published data on industry sales-force compensation levels are infrequent and generally lack sufficient detail.

The company must determine the *components of compensation*—a fixed amount, a variable amount, expenses, and fringe benefits. The *fixed amount*, which might be salary or a drawing account, is intended to satisfy the sales representatives' need for some stability of income. The *variable amount*, which might be commissions, bonus, or profit sharing, is intended to stimulate and reward greater effort. *Expense allowances* enable the sales representatives to undertake selling efforts that are considered necessary or desirable. And *fringe benefits*, such as paid vacations, sickness or accident benefits, pensions, and life insurance, are intended to provide security and job satisfaction.

Top sales management must decide on the relative importance of these components in the compensation plan. A popular rule favors making about 70 percent of the salesperson's total income fixed and allocating the remaining 30 percent among the other elements. But the variations around this average are so pronounced that it can hardly serve as a guide. Fixed compensation should have more emphasis in jobs with a high ratio of nonselling to selling duties and in jobs where the selling

---

[8] *Marketing News*, February 5, 1982, p. 1.

task is technically complex. Variable compensation should have more emphasis in jobs where sales are cyclical or depend on sales-force initiative.

Fixed and variable compensation give rise to three basic types of sales-force compensation plans—straight salary, straight commission, and combination salary and commission. In one study, 28 percent of the companies paid straight salary, 21 percent paid straight commission, and 51 percent paid salary plus commission.[9] The advantages and disadvantages of each plan are described below.

Straight salary. With this plan, sales representatives receive a fixed salary and an amount to cover expenses in performing various duties. Occasionally there will be additional compensation through discretionary bonuses or sales-contest prizes.

Management gains a number of advantages under a straight salary plan. The primary one is that management can alter sales duties without strong objection. Straight salary plans are also easier to explain and less costly to administer. They simplify the task of projecting the sales payroll for the coming year. Finally, by providing the sales force with a stable income, the straight salary plan may lead to higher sales-force morale and spirit.

The chief weakness of the straight salary plan is that it does not present the sales force with an incentive to do a better-than-average selling job. This puts a greater supervision burden on management to control, evaluate, and reward the performances of individual sales representatives. Other problems posed by straight salary plans are an inflexible selling-expense burden during business downswings; the danger that during upswings sales representatives on fixed salaries will not have sufficient incentive to exploit the increased business potential; thorny questions in salary adjustment for ability, rising living costs, and length of service; and the probability that the company will not attract or hold on to the more aggressive sales representatives.

Straight commission. This plan pays sales representatives some fixed or sliding rate related to their sales or profit volume. They may or may not receive reimbursement for expenses incurred in performing the selling function. Straight commission plans are prominent in the selling of insurance and investment securities, furniture, office equipment, small office machines, and clothing and in the textile and shoe industries and in drug and hardware wholesaling.

The straight commission plan offers three advantages. First, it provides an incentive for sales representatives to work at maximum capacity. Second, it ties selling expenses more closely to current revenue. Third, management can set different commissions on different products and sales tasks, thereby influencing how the salespersons spend their time.

These advantages come at a substantial cost, however. Management encounters great resistance when it tries to get the sales force to do things that do not generate immediate income, such as following up leads, filling out reports, or providing customer service. The salesperson's financial stake in getting the sale may lead to high-pressure tactics or price discounting, which may damage customer goodwill. Straight commis-

---

[9] Ibid.

sion plans are more costly to administer. Also they provide little security and cause morale to drop when sales fall through no fault of the sales force.

Management has several options regarding the commission base, commission rates, and the commission starting point. The *commission base* may be gross sales volume, net sales after returns, gross margins, or net profits. The *commission rates* may be identical for all sales or differentiated by customers and/or products; they may be constant with sales volume or vary in a progressive or regressive fashion. The *commission starting point* may be the first sale or sales over a minimum quota. Most companies base sales commissions on sales volume, for administrative simplicity. But sales commissions based on sales volume fail to relate selling effort to company profitability. The payment of commissions on *gross margin* should do a superior job of motivating sales representatives to improve their product and customer mix and, therefore, company profits.[10]

Combination salary and commission.
The great majority of firms pay a combination of salary and commission, in the hope of achieving the advantages of each while avoiding the disadvantages. The combination plan is appropriate where sales volume depends upon the sales representative's motivation and yet management wants some control over nonselling duties performed by the sales representative. The plan means that during downswings the company is not stuck with inflexible selling costs, and sales representatives do not lose their whole income.

Bonus.
Many companies pay *bonuses* as a supplement or a substitute for commission-type incentives. Bonuses are noncontractual payments for extra effort, merit, or results. They reward sales representatives for performing tasks that are desirable but not rewardable through commissions, for example, preparing prompt reports, supplying useful selling ideas, and developing unusual product or market knowledge. The main problem with bonuses is that managerial judgment enters into their determination, and sales representatives can raise questions of fairness.

Other costs.
Besides salary, commission, and bonus, the company's selling costs include the following additional elements: *selling expenses* (travel, lodging, telephone, entertainment, samples promotion, and office and/or clerical expenses); *fringe benefits* (hospitalization insurance, life insurance, pension plan, association memberships, and moving expenses); *special incentives* (contests, service awards); and *staff back-up costs* (cost of technical and customer-service people, sales analysts, computer time, and sales-training programs). Thus the cost of running a sales force adds up to much more than the direct compensation elements alone.

---

[10] See Ralph L. Day and Peter D. Bennett, "Should Salesmen's Compensation Be Geared to Profits?" *Journal of Marketing Research*, May 1964, pp. 39–43; and John U. Farley and Charles B. Weinberg, "Inferential Optimization: An Algorithm for Determining Optimal Sales Commissions in Multiproduct Sales Forces," *Operational Research Quarterly*, June 1975, pp. 413–18.

Having established the objectives, strategy, structure, size, and compensation of the sales force, the company has to move to recruiting and selecting, training, directing, motivating, and evaluating sales representatives. Various policies and procedures guide these decisions.

Recruiting and Selecting Sales Representatives

Importance of careful selection.   At the heart of a successful sales-force operation is the selection of effective sales representatives. The performance levels of an average and a top sales representative are quite different. A survey of over five hundred companies revealed that 27 percent of the sales force brought in over 52 percent of the sales.[11] Beyond the differences in sales productivity are the great wastes in hiring the wrong persons. Of the sixteen thousand sales representatives who had been hired by the surveyed companies, only 68 percent still worked for the company at the end of the year, and only 50 percent were expected to remain throughout the following year.

The financial loss due to turnover is only part of the total cost. The new sales representative who remains with the company receives a direct income averaging around half of the direct selling cost. If he or she receives $20,000 a year, another $20,000 may go into fringe benefits, expenses, supervision, office space, supplies, and secretarial assistance. Consequently the new sales representative needs to produce sales on which the gross margin at least covers the selling expenses of $40,000. If the gross margin is 10 percent, he or she would have to sell at least $400,000 for the company to break even.

What makes a good sales representative?   Selecting sales representatives would not be a problem if one knew what traits to look for. If effective sales representatives were always outgoing, aggressive, and energetic, these characteristics could be checked in applicants. But many successful sales representatives are introverted, mild mannered, and far from energetic. Successful sales representatives include men and women who are tall and short, articulate and inarticulate, well groomed and slovenly.

Nevertheless the search continues for the magic combination of traits that spells sure-fire sales ability. Numerous lists have been drawn up. McMurry wrote: "It is my conviction that the possessor of an *effective* sales personality is a *habitual 'wooer,' an individual who has a compulsive need to win and hold the affection of others*."[12] McMurry listed five additional traits of the super salesperson: "a high level of energy, abounding self-confidence, a chronic hunger for money, a well-established habit of industry, and a state of mind that regards each objection, resistance, or obstacle as a challenge."[13]

---

[11] The survey was conducted by the Sales Executives Club of New York and was reported in *Business Week*, February 1, 1964, p. 52.

[12] McMurry, "Mystique of Super-Salesmanship," p. 117.

[13] Ibid., p. 118.

Mayer and Greenberg offered one of the shortest lists of traits.[14] They concluded that the effective salesperson has at least two basic qualities: (1) *empathy*, the ability to feel as the customer does; and (2) *ego drive*, a strong personal need to make the sale. Using these two traits as criteria led to fairly good predictions of the subsequent performance of applicants for sales positions in three different industries.

How can a company determine the characteristics necessary for sales representatives in its industry? The job duties suggest some of the characteristics to look for. Is there a lot of paper work? Does the job call for much travel? Will the salesperson confront a high proportion of rejections? The company should also examine the traits of its most successful sales representatives for possible clues.

Recruitment procedures.

After management develops its selection criteria, it must recruit. The personnel department seeks applicants by various means, including soliciting names from current sales representatives, using employment agencies, placing job ads, and contacting college students. As for college students, companies have found it hard to sell them on selling. A survey of one thousand male college students indicated that only one in seventeen showed an interest in selling.[15] The reluctant ones gave such reasons as, "Selling is a job and not a profession," "It calls for deceit if the person wants to succeed," and "There is insecurity and too much travel." To counter these objections, company recruiters emphasize starting salaries, income opportunities, and the fact that one-fourth of the presidents of large U.S. corporations started out in marketing and sales.

Applicant-rating procedures.

Recruitment procedures, if successful, will attract many applicants, and the company will need to select the best ones. The selection procedures can vary from a single informal interview to prolonged testing and interviewing, not only of the applicant but of the applicant's family.

Many companies give formal tests to sales applicants. Although test scores are only one information element in a set that includes personal characteristics, references, past employment history, and interviewer reactions, they are weighted quite heavily by such companies as IBM, Prudential, Procter & Gamble, and Gillette. Gillette claims that tests have reduced turnover by 42 percent and have correlated well with the subsequent progress of new sales representatives in the sales organization.

Training Sales Representatives

Many companies send their new sales representatives into the field almost immediately after hiring them. They are supplied with samples, order books, and a description of their territory. And much of their selling is ineffective. A vice-president of a major food company spent one week watching fifty sales presentations to a busy buyer for a major supermarket chain. Here is what he observed:

---

[14] David Mayer and Herbert M. Greenberg, "What Makes a Good Salesman?" *Harvard Business Review*, July-August 1964, pp. 119–25.

[15] "Youth Continues to Snub Selling," *Sales Management*, January 15, 1965, p. 69. Also see Donald L. Thompson, "Stereotype of the Salesman," *Harvard Business Review*, January-February 1972, p. 21.

I watched a soap company representative come in to the buyer. He had three separate new promotional deals to talk about with six different dates. He had nothing in writing. . . . After the salesman left, the buyer looked at me and said, "It will take me fifteen minutes to get this straightened out."

I watched another salesman walk in to the buyer and say, "Well, I was in the area, and I want you to know that we have a great new promotion coming up next week." The buyer said, "That's fine. What is it?" He said, "I don't know. . . . I'm coming in next week to tell you about it." The buyer asked him what he was doing there today. He said, "Well, I was in the area."

Another salesman came and said, "Well, it's time for us to write that order now . . . getting ready for the summer business." The buyer said, "Well, fine, George, how much did I buy last year in total?" The salesman looked a little dumbfounded and said, "Well, I'll be damned if I know. . . ."

The majority of salesmen were ill prepared, unable to answer basic questions, uncertain as to what they wanted to accomplish during the call. They did not think of the call as a studied, professional presentation. They didn't have a real idea of the busy retailer's needs and wants.[16]

It is true that training programs are costly. They involve large outlays for instructors, materials, and space; paying a person who was not yet selling; and losing opportunities because he or she was not in the field. Yet they are essential. Today's new sales representatives may spend a few weeks to several months in training. The median training period is twenty-eight weeks in industrial-products companies, twelve in service companies, and four in consumer-products companies.[17] In IBM, new sales representatives are not on their own for two years! And IBM expects its sales representatives to spend 15 percent of their time each year in additional training.

The annual sales-training bill for major U.S. corporations runs into millions of dollars. Yet sales management sees training as adding more value than cost. Today's sales representatives are selling to more cost- and value-conscious buyers. Furthermore they are selling technically complex products. The company wants and needs mature and knowledgeable sales representation.

The training programs have several goals:

- ☐ **Sales representatives need to know and identify with the company.** Most companies devote the first part of the training program to describing the company's history and objectives, the organization and lines of authority, the chief officers, the company's financial structure and facilities, and the chief products and sales volume.
- ☐ **Sales representatives need to know the company's products.** Sales trainees are shown how the products are produced and how they function in various uses.
- ☐ **Sales representatives need to know customers' and competitors' characteristics.** Sales representatives learn about the different types of customers and their needs, buying motives, and buying habits. They learn about the company's and competitors' strategies and policies.
- ☐ **Sales representatives need to know how to make effective sales presentations.** Sales representatives receive training in the principles of salesmanship. In addition, the company

---

[16] From an address given by Donald R. Keough at the twenty-seventh annual conference of the Super-Market Institute in Chicago, April 26–29, 1964.

[17] "Double-Digit Hikes in 1974 Sales Training Costs," *Sales and Marketing Management*, January 6, 1975, p. 54.

outlines the major sales arguments for each product, and some provide a sales script.

☐ **Sales representatives need to understand field procedures and responsibilities.** Sales representatives learn how to divide time between active and potential accounts; how to use the expense account, prepare reports, and route effectively.

New methods of training are continually being explored. Among the instructional approaches are role playing, sensitivity training, cassette tapes, videotapes, programmed learning, and films on salesmanship and company products. There is no one way to evaluate the training results, but training departments need to collect as much evidence of improved sales performance as possible. There should be a measurable impact on such variables as sales-force turnover, sales volume, absenteeism, average sale size, calls-to-close ratio, customer complaints and compliments, new accounts per time unit, and volume of returned merchandise.

The substantial costs of company training programs raise the question of whether a company could do better by hiring experienced sales representatives away from other companies. The gain is often illusory, however, because the experienced salesperson is brought in at a higher salary. Some of the representatives' specific training and company experience is wasted when they transfer to other companies. Within some industries, companies tacitly agree not to hire sales personnel away from each other.

Directing Sales Representatives

New sales representatives are given more than a territory, a compensation package, and training—they are given supervision. Supervision is the fate of everyone who works for someone else. It is the expression of the employers' natural and continuous interest in the activities of their agents. Through supervision, employers hope to direct and motivate the sales force to do a better job. Exhibit 22–2 indicates that much work still needs to be done.

Companies vary in how closely they direct their sales representatives. Sales representatives who are paid mostly on commission and who are expected to hunt down their own prospects are generally left on their own. Those who are salaried and must cover definite accounts are likely to receive substantial supervision.

Developing customer targets and call norms. Most companies classify customers into A, B, and C accounts, reflecting the sales volume, profit potential, and growth potential of the account. They establish the desired number of calls per period on each account class. A accounts may receive nine calls a year; B, six calls; and C, three calls. The call norms depend upon competitive call norms and expected account profitability.

The real issue is how much sales volume could be expected from a particular account as a function of the annual number of calls. Magee described an experiment where similar accounts were randomly split into three sets.[18] Sales representatives

---

[18] See John F. Magee, "Determining the Optimum Allocation of Expenditures for Promotional Effort with Operations Research Methods," in *The Frontiers of Marketing Thought and Science*, ed. Frank M. Bass (Chicago: American Marketing Association, 1958), pp. 140–56.

Exhibit 22-2

HOW EFFICIENTLY DO COMPANIES MANAGE THEIR SALES FORCE?

There is much evidence of inefficiency in the way companies manage their sales force. A survey of 257 "Fortune 500" companies revealed the following:

☐ 54 percent have not conducted an organized study of sales representatives' use of time, even though most respondents felt that time utilization represents an area for improvement.

☐ 25 percent do not have a system for classifying accounts according to potential.

☐ 30 percent do not use call schedules for their sales force.

☐ 51 percent do not determine the number of calls it is economical to make on an account.

☐ 83 percent do not determine an approximate duration for each call.

☐ 51 percent do not use a planned sales presentation.

☐ 24 percent do not set sales objectives for accounts.

☐ 72 percent do not set profit objectives for accounts.

☐ 19 percent do not use a call report system.

☐ 63 percent do not use a prescribed routing pattern in covering territories.

☐ 77 percent do not use the computer to assist in time and territorial management.

Source: Robert Vizza, "Managing Time and Territories for Maximum Sales Success," Sales Management, July 15, 1971, pp. 31–36.

were asked to spend less than five hours a month with accounts in the first set, five to nine hours a month with those in the second set, and more than nine hours a month with those in the third set. The results demonstrated that additional calls produced more sales, leaving only the question of whether the magnitude of sales increase justified the additional cost.

Developing prospect targets and call norms.   Companies often specify how much time their sales force should spend prospecting for new accounts. Spector Freight wants its sales representatives to spend 25 percent of their time prospecting and to stop calling on a prospect after three unsuccessful calls.

Companies set up prospecting standards for a number of reasons. If left alone, many sales representatives will spend most of their time with current customers. Current customers are better-known quantities. Sales representatives can depend upon them for some business, whereas a prospect may never deliver any business. Unless sales representatives are rewarded for opening new accounts, they may avoid new-account development. Some companies rely on a missionary sales force to open new accounts. (Exhibit 22–3 describes a model for estimating the value of a sales prospect.)

Exhibit 22-3

ESTIMATING THE VALUE OF A SALES PROSPECT

Salespersons need a method to estimate the value of calling on different prospects in order to target the right accounts and use their time effectively. The method draws on investment theory, since call time will be invested in each prospect. First, the sales representative estimates the value of the prospect's business if the prospect were converted to a customer. The value of the prospect's business is seen as a discounted income stream lasting so many years. Specifically,

$$Z = \sum_{t=1}^{\bar{t}} \frac{mQ_t - X}{(1 + r)^t}$$

(22-1)

where:

Z = present value of the future income from a new customer
m = gross margin on sales
Q_t = expected sales from new customer in year t
X = cost of maintaining customer contact per year
r = company discount rate
t = a subscript for a year
$\bar{t}$ = number of years that this new customer is expected to remain a customer

Thus the sales representative estimates that if this prospect were converted to a customer, he would annually purchase from the company Q_t units with a profit per unit of m less a customer-contact cost (X) and that this last for t periods. Future income is discounted at an interest rate, r.

The next step is to consider the investment necessary to convert this prospect to a customer. The investment can be described as:

$$I = nc$$

(22-2)

where:

I = investment in trying to convert the prospect to a customer
n = the number of calls to convert the prospect into a customer
c = cost per call

The number of calls to the prospect will influence the probability of conversion—that is,

$$p = p(n)$$

(22-3)

The value of the prospect's business should be scaled down by this probability. Putting the previous elements together, the following investment formula emerges for the value (V) of a prospect:

$$V = p(n) \sum_{t=1}^{i} \frac{mQ_t - X}{(1 + r)^t} - nc \qquad (22\text{--}4)$$

Thus the value of a prospect depends on the expected present value of the income stream less the investment cost in prospect conversion. Both the expected present value and the investment cost depend on the planned number of calls, n, upon the prospect. The planned or optimal number of calls can be found mathematically if the probability-of-conversion function is known.

The formula could be incorporated into a computer program. The sales representative would sit down at a terminal, type in estimates for each prospect regarding the expected volume of the prospect's business, the maximum probability of conversion, and so on, and receive back a ranking of all the prospects in order of their investment value along with the suggested number of calls to make on each.

Using sales time efficiently. Sales representatives need to know how to use their time efficiently. One tool is the *annual call schedule* showing which customers and prospects to call on in which months and which activities to carry out.

Sales representatives of Bell Telephone companies plan their calls and activities around three concepts. The first is *market development*—various efforts to educate customers, cultivate new business, and gain greater visibility in the buying community. The second is *sales-generating activities*—direct efforts to sell particular products to customers on particular calls. The third is *market-protection activities*—various efforts to learn what competition is doing and to protect relations with existing customers. The sales force aims for some balance among these activities, so that the company does not achieve high current sales at the expense of long-run market development.

The other tool is *time-and-duty* analysis. The sales representative spends time in the following ways:

☐ **Travel.** In some jobs travel time amounts to over 50 percent of total time. Travel time can be cut down by using faster means of transportation—recognizing, however, that this will increase costs. More companies are encouraging air travel for their sales force, to increase their ratio of selling to total time.

☐ **Food and breaks.** Some portion of the sales force's workday is spent in eating and taking breaks.

☐ **Waiting.** Waiting consists of time spent in the outer office of the buyer. This is dead time unless the sales representative uses it to plan or to fill out reports.

☐ **Selling.** Selling is the time spent with the buyer in person or on the phone. It breaks down into "social talk" (the time spent discussing other things) and "selling talk" (the time spent discussing the company's products).

☐ **Administration.** This is a miscellaneous category consisting of the time spent in report writing and billing, attending sales meetings, and talking to others in the company about production, delivery, billing, sales performance, and other matters.

No wonder actual selling time may amount to as little as 15 percent of total working time! If it could be raised from 15 percent to 20 percent, this would be a 33 percent improvement. Companies are constantly seeking ways to use sales-force time effectively. Their methods take the form of training sales representatives in the use of "phone power," simplifying the record-keeping forms, using the computer to develop call and routing plans, and supplying marketing research reports on customers.

Motivating Sales Representatives

Some sales representatives will do their best without any special coaching from management. To them selling is the most fascinating job in the world. They are ambitious and self-starters. But the majority of sales representatives require encouragement and special incentives to work at their best level. This is especially true of field selling, for the following reasons:

- ☐ **The nature of the job.** The selling job is one of frequent frustration. Sales representatives usually work alone; their hours are irregular; and they are often away from home. They confront aggressive, competing sales representatives; they have an inferior status relative to the buyer; they often do not have the authority to do what is necessary to win an account; they lose large orders that they have worked hard to obtain.
- ☐ **Human nature.** Most people operate below capacity in the absence of special incentives, such as financial gain or social recognition.
- ☐ **Personal problems.** Sales representatives are occasionally preoccupied with personal problems, such as sickness in the family, marital discord, or debt.

Management can influence the sales force's morale and performance through its organizational climate, sales quotas, and positive incentives.

Organizational climate.   Organizational climate describes the feeling that the sales representatives get regarding their opportunities, their value, and their rewards for a good performance. Some companies treat sales representatives as if they were of minor importance. Other companies treat their sales representatives as the prime movers and allow unlimited opportunity for income and promotion. The company's attitude toward its sales representatives acts as a self-fulfilling prophecy. If the representatives are held in low esteem, there is much turnover and poor performance; if they are held in high esteem, there is little turnover and high performance.

The personal treatment by the sales representative's immediate superior is an important aspect of organizational climate. An effective sales manager keeps in touch with the sales force through correspondence and phone calls, personal visits in the field, and evaluation sessions in the home office. At different times the sales manager acts as the sales person's boss, companion, coach, and confessor.

Sales quotas.   Many companies set sales quotas for their sales representatives specifying what they should sell during the year and by product. Compensation is often related to the degree of quota fulfillment.

Sales quotas are developed in the process of developing the annual marketing plan. The company first decides on a sales forecast that is reasonably achievable. This becomes the basis for planning production, work-force size, and financial requirements. Then management establishes sales quotas for its regions and territories, which typically add up to more than the sales forecast. Sales quotas are set higher than the sales forecast in order to stretch the sales managers and sales people to their best effort. If they fail to make their quotas, the company nevertheless may make its sales forecast.

Each area sales manager divides the area's quota among the area's sales representatives. There are three schools of thought on quota setting. The *high-quota school* sets quotas higher than what most sales representatives will achieve but that are nevertheless attainable. Its adherents believe that high quotas spur extra effort. The *modest-quota school* sets quotas that a majority of the sales force can achieve. Its adherents feel that the sales force will accept the quotas as fair, attain them, and gain confidence. The *variable-quota school* thinks that individual differences among sales representatives warrant high quotas for some, modest quotas for others. According to Heckert:

> Actual experience with sales quotas, as with all standards, will reveal that sales representatives react to them somewhat differently, particularly at first. Some are stimulated to their highest efficiency, others are discouraged. Some sales executives place considerable emphasis upon this human element in setting their quotas. In general, however, good men will in the long run respond favorably to intelligently devised quotas, particularly when compensation is fairly adjusted to performance.[19]

Factors that influence the setting of sales quotas for individual sales persons are described in Exhibit 22-4.

Positive incentives.   Companies use several motivators to stimulate sales-force effort. Periodic *sales meetings* provide a social occasion, a break from routine, a chance to meet and talk with "company brass," and a chance to air feelings and to identify with a larger group. Companies also sponsor *sales contests* to spur the sales force to a special selling effort above what would be normally expected. Other motivators include honors, awards and profit-sharing plans.

Evaluating Sales Representatives

We have been describing the *feed-forward* aspects of sales supervision—how management communicates what the sales representatives should be doing and motivates them to do it. But good feed-forward requires good feedback. And good feedback means getting regular information from sales representatives to evaluate their performance.

Sources of information.   Management obtains information about its sales representatives in several ways. The most important source is sales reports. Additional information comes through personal observation, customers' letters and complaints, customer surveys, and conversations with other sales representatives.

Sales reports are divided between *plans for future activities* and *writeups of completed activities*. The best example of the former is the *salesperson's work plan*, which sales representatives submit a week or month in advance. The plan describes

---

[19] J. B. Heckert, *Business Budgeting and Control* (New York: Ronald Press, 1946), p. 138.

Exhibit 22-4

FACTORS TO USE IN SETTING A VARIABLE SALES QUOTA

The variable-quota school will base sales quotas on a number of considerations, including the person's sales performance in the previous period, her territory's estimated potential, and a judgment of her aspiration level and reaction to pressure and incentive. Some propositions in this area are:

1. The sales quota for salesperson j at time t, Q_{jt}, should be set above her sales in the year just ending, $S_{j,t-1}$; that is,

$$Q_{jt} > S_{j,t-1}$$

2. The sales quota for salesperson j at time t should be higher, the greater the positive gap between the estimated sales potential of the salesperson's territory, S_{Pjt}, and her sales in the year just ending; that is,

$$Q_{jt} \sim (S_{Pjt} - S_{j,t-1})$$

3. The sales quota for salesperson j at time t should be higher, the more positively she responds to pressure, E_j; that is,

$$Q_{jt} \sim E_j$$

These three propositions can be combined in an equation for setting a salesperson's quota:

$$Q_{jt} = S_{j,t-1} + E_j (S_{Pjt} - S_{j,t-1})$$

Thus salesperson j's quota at time t should be at least equal to her actual sales in the previous period, plus some fraction, E_j, of the difference between estimated territorial sales potential and her sales last year; the more positively she reacts to pressure, the higher the fraction.

---

intended calls and routing. This report leads the sales force to plan and schedule their activities, informs management of their whereabouts, and provides a basis for comparing their plans and accomplishments. Sales representatives can be evaluated on their ability to "plan their work and work their plan." Occasionally management contacts individual sales representatives after receiving their plans to suggest improvements.

Companies are beginning to require their sales representatives to develop an annual *territory marketing plan* in which they outline their program for developing new accounts and increasing business from existing accounts. The formats vary considerably, some asking for general ideas on territory development and others asking for detailed volume and profit estimates. This type of report casts sales representatives into the role of market managers and profit centers. Their sales managers study these plans, make suggestions, and use them to develop sales quotas. Both sales representatives and sales managers are making increasing use of microcomputers to help plan their sales activities.[20]

Sales representatives write up their completed activities on *call reports*. Call reports keep sales management informed of the salesperson's activities, indicate the status of the customers' accounts, and provide information that might be useful in subsequent calls. Sales representatives also submit expense reports, for which they are partly or wholly reimbursed. Additional types of reports that some companies require are reports on new business, reports on lost business, and reports on local business and economic conditions.

These reports supply the raw data from which sales managers can extract key indicators of sales performance. The key indicators are (1) average number of sales calls per salesperson per day, (2) average sales call time per contact, (3) average revenue per sales call, (4) average cost per sales call, (5) entertainment cost per sales call, (6) percentage of orders per hundred sales calls, (7) number of new customers per period, (8) number of lost customers per period, and (9) sales-force cost as a percentage of total sales. These indicators answer several useful question: Are sales representatives making too few calls per day? Are they spending too much time per call? Are they spending too much on entertainment? Are they closing enough orders per hundred calls? Are they producing enough new customers and holding on to the old customers?

Formal evaluation of performance.

The sales force's reports along with other reports and observations supply the raw materials for evaluating members of the sales force. Formal evaluation leads to at least three benefits. First, management has to develop and communicate clear standards for judging sales performance. Second, management is motivated to gather well-rounded information about each salesperson. And third, sales representatives know they will have to sit down one morning with the sales manager and explain their performance or failure to achieve certain goals.

Salesperson-to-salesperson-comparisons.   One type of evaluation is to compare and rank the sales performance of the various sales representatives. Such comparisons, however, can be misleading. Relative sales performances are meaningful only if there are no variations in territory market potential, workload, degree of competition, company promotional effort, and so forth. Furthermore sales are not the indicator of achievement. Management should be more interested in how much each sales representative contributes to net profits. And this requires examining each sales representative's sales mix and sales expenses.

Current-to-past-sales comparisons.   A second type of evaluation is to compare a sales representative's current performance with his or her past performance. This should provide a direct indication of progress. An example is shown in Table 22–1.

---

[20] For a description of several applications of microcomputers to sales management, see G. David Hughes, "Computerized Sales Management," *Harvard Business Review*, March-April 1983, pp. 102–12.

TABLE 22-1

FORM FOR EVALUATING SALES REPRESENTATIVE'S PERFORMANCE

Territory: Midland
Sales Representative: John Smith

	1979	1980	1981	1982
1. Net sales product A	$251,300	$253,200	$270,000	$263,100
2. Net sales product B	$423,200	$439,200	$553,900	$561,900
3. Net sales total	$674,500	$692,400	$823,900	$825,000
4. Percent of quota product A	95.6	92.0	88.0	84.7
5. Percent of quota product B	120.4	122.3	134.9	130.8
6. Gross profits product A	$ 50,260	$ 50,640	$ 54,000	$ 52,620
7. Gross profits product B	$ 42,320	$ 43,920	$ 55,390	$ 56,190
8. Gross profits total	$ 92,580	$ 94,560	$109,390	$108,810
9. Sales expense	$ 10,200	$ 11,100	$ 11,600	$ 13,200
10. Sales expense to total sales (%)	1.5	1.6	1.4	1.6
11. Number of calls	1,675	1,700	1,680	1,660
12. Cost per call	$ 6.09	$ 6.53	$ 6.90	$ 7.95
13. Average number of customers	320	324	328	334
14. Number of new customers	13	14	15	20
15. Number of lost customers	8	10	11	14
16. Average sales per customer	$ 2,108	$ 2,137	$ 2,512	$ 2,470
17. Average gross profit per customer	$ 289	$ 292	$ 334	$ 326

The sales manager can learn many things about John Smith in this table. Smith's total sales increased every year (line 3). This does not necessarily mean that Smith is doing a better job. The product breakdown shows that he has been able to push the sales of product B further than the sales of product A (lines 1 and 2). According to his quotas for the two products (lines 4 and 5), his success in increasing product B sales may be at the expense of product A sales. According to gross profits (lines 6 and 7), the company earns about twice as much on A as B. Smith may be pushing the higher-volume, lower-margin product at the expense of the more profitable product. Although he increased total sales by $1,100 between 1981 and 1982 (line 3), the gross profits on his total sales actually decreased by $580 (line 8).

Sales expense (line 9) shows a steady increase, although total expense as a percentage of total sales seems to be under control (line 10). The upward trend in

Smith's total dollar expense does not seem to be explained by any increase in the number of calls (line 11), although it may be related to his success in acquiring new customers (line 14). There is a possibility, however, that in prospecting for new customers, he is neglecting present customers, as indicated by an upward trend in the annual number of lost customers (line 15).

The last two lines show the level and trend in Smith's sales and gross profits per customer. These figures become more meaningful when they are compared with overall company averages. If John Smith's average gross profit per customer is lower than the company's average, he may be concentrating on the wrong customers or may not be spending enough time with each customer. A look back at his annual number of calls (line 11) shows that Smith may be making fewer annual calls than the average salesperson. If distances in his territory are not much different from those of the average salesperson, this may mean he is not putting in a full workday, he is poor at planning his routing or minimizing his waiting, or he spends too much time with certain accounts.

Qualitative evaluation of sales representatives. The evaluation usually includes the salesperson's knowledge of the company, products, customers, competitors, territory, and responsibilities. Personality characteristics can be rated, such as general manner, appearance, speech, and temperament. The sales manager can also review any problems in motivation or compliance. The sales manager should check that the sales representative knows the law. Each company must decide what would be most useful to know. It should communicate these criteria to the sales representatives so that they know how their performance is judged and can make an effort to improve it.

PRINCIPLES OF PERSONAL SELLING

We turn now from designing and managing a sales force to the purpose of a sales force, namely, to make a sale. Personal selling is an ancient art, which has spawned a large literature and many principles. Effective salespersons have more than instinct; they are trained in a method of analysis and customer interaction. Selling today is a profession that involves mastering and using a whole set of principles. There are many different styles of personal selling, some very consistent with the marketing concept and some antithetical to the spirit of the marketing concept. We will examine three major aspects of personal selling in the remainder of this chapter: salesmanship, negotiation, and relationship management.

Salesmanship

Today's companies spend hundreds of millions of dollars each year to train their sales people in the art of salesmanship. Almost a million copies of books on selling are purchased annually, with such tantalizing titles as *How to Outsell the Born Salesman*, *How to Sell Anything to Anybody*, *How Power Selling Brought Me Success in 6 Hours*, *Where Do You Go from No. 1?* and *1000 Ways a Salesman Can Increase His Sales*. One of the most enduring books is Dale Carnegie's *How to Win Friends and Influence People*.

All of the sales-training approaches try to convert a salesperson from being a passive *order taker* to an active *order getter*. *Order takers* operate on the following assumptions: Customers know their needs; they would resent any attempt at influence; and they prefer salespersons who are courteous and self-effacing. An example of an order-taking mentality would be a Fuller brush salesman who knocks on dozens of doors each day, simply asking if the consumer needs any brushes.

In training salespersons to be *order getters*, there are two basic approaches, a *sales-oriented approach* and a *customer-oriented approach*. The first one trains the salesperson in *high-pressure selling techniques*, such as those used in selling encyclopedias or automobiles. The techniques include overstating the product's merits, criticizing competitive products, using a slick canned presentation, selling yourself, and offering some concession to get the order on the spot. This form of selling assumes that the customers are not likely to buy except under pressure, that they are influenced by a slick presentation and ingratiating manners, and that they will not be sorry after signing the order, or if they are, it doesn't matter.

The other approach trains sales personnel in *customer problem solving*. The salesperson learns how to identify customer needs and propose effective solutions. This approach assumes that customers have latent needs that constitute company opportunities, that they appreciate good suggestions, and that they will be loyal to sales representatives who have their long-term interests at heart. The problem solver is a more compatible image for the salesperson under the marketing concept than the hard seller or order taker.

No sales approach works best in all circumstances. (See Exhibit 22–5.) Yet most sales-training programs agree on the major steps involved in any effective sales process. These steps are shown in Figure 22–2 and discussed below.[21]

Prospecting and qualifying.   The first step in the selling process is to identify prospects. Although the company supplies leads, sales representatives need skill in developing their own leads. Leads can be developed in the following ways:

☐ Asking current customers for the names of prospects.
☐ Cultivating other referral sources, such as suppliers, dealers, noncompeting sales representatives, bankers, and trade association executives.
☐ Joining organizations to which prospects belong.
☐ Engaging in speaking and writing activities that will draw attention.
☐ Examining data sources (newspapers, directories) in search of names.
☐ Using the telephone and mail to track down leads.
☐ Dropping in unannounced on various offices (cold canvassing).

Sales representatives need to know how to screen out poor leads. Prospects can be qualified by examining their financial ability, volume of business, special requirements, location, and likelihood of continuous business. The salesperson should phone or write to prospects to see if they are worth pursuing.

---

[21] Some of the following discussion is based on W. J. E. Crissy, William H. Cunningham, and Isabella C. M. Cunningham, *Selling: The Personal Force in Marketing* (New York: John Wiley & Sons, 1977), pp. 119–29.

Exhibit 22-5

THE VARIETY OF SELLING STYLES AND BUYING STYLES

Blake and Mouton distinguish various selling styles by examining two dimensions, the salesperson's *concern for the sale* and *concern for the customer*. These two dimensions give rise to the *sales grid* shown below, which describes five types of salespersons. Type 1, 1 is very much the order taker and 9, 1 is the hard seller. Type 5, 5 is a soft seller, while the 1, 9 is "sell myself." Type 9, 9 is the problem-solving mentality, which is most consistent with the marketing concept.

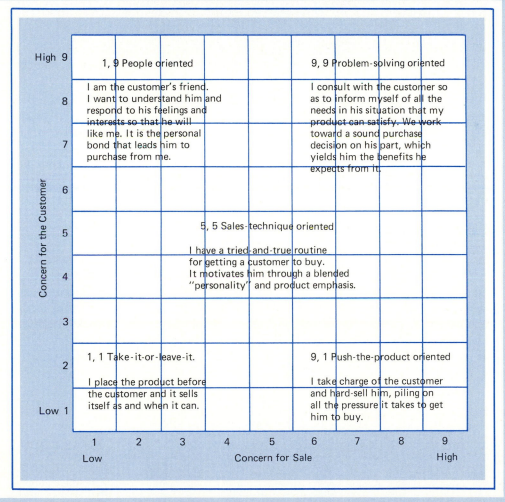

1, 9 People oriented

I am the customer's friend. I want to understand him and respond to his feelings and interests so that he will like me. It is the personal bond that leads him to purchase from me.

9, 9 Problem-solving oriented

I consult with the customer so as to inform myself of all the needs in his situation that my product can satisfy. We work toward a sound purchase decision on his part, which yields him the benefits he expects from it.

5, 5 Sales-technique oriented

I have a tried-and-true routine for getting a customer to buy. It motivates him through a blended "personality" and product emphasis.

1, 1 Take-it-or-leave-it.

I place the product before the customer and it sells itself as and when it can.

9, 1 Push-the-product oriented

I take charge of the customer and hard-sell him, piling on all the pressure it takes to get him to buy.

Concern for the Customer (vertical axis: High 9, 8, 7, 6, 5, 4, 3, 2, Low 1)

Concern for Sale (horizontal axis: 1 Low, 2, 3, 4, 5, 6, 7, 8, 9 High)

Source: *Robert R. Blake and Jane S. Mouton,* The Grid for Sales Excellence: Benchmarks for Effective Salesmanship (*New York: McGraw-Hill Book Co., 1970*), p. 4.

Blake and Mouton argue that no one type of sales style will be effective with all buyers. Buying styles are just as varied as selling styles. Buyers vary in their concern for the purchase and concern for the sales person. Some buyers couldn't care less; some are defensive; some will only listen to salespersons from well-known companies.

The view that effective selling depends on matching the seller's style to the buyer's style means that salespersons should not be trained in only one style of selling. Evans sees selling as a *dyadic process*, where the outcome depends on the match of *buyer and seller characteristics* as well as on *buying and selling styles*. He found that people bought insurance from people very much like themselves in such factors as age, height, income, political opinions, religious beliefs, and smoking. What mattered was the perceived similarity more than the actual similarity. Evans proposed that insurance companies should hire all types of salespersons if they want to achieve broad market penetration. The only requirement is that they exhibit the intelligence and kinds of abilities effective in selling insurance. (See Franklin B. Evans, "Selling as a Dyadic Relationship—a New Approach," *The American Behavioral Scientist*, May 1963, pp. 76–79, at pp. 76 and 78. Also see Harry L. Davis and Alvin J. Silk, "Interaction and Influence Processes in Personal Selling," *Sloan Management Review*, winter 1972, pp. 59–76.)

Preapproach. The salesperson should learn as much as possible about the prospect company (what it needs, who is involved in the purchase decision) and its buyers (their personal characteristics and buying styles). The salesperson can consult standard sources (*Moody's, Standard and Poor, Dun and Bradstreet*), acquaintances, and others, to learn about the company. The salesperson should set *call objectives*, which might be to qualify the prospect or gather information or make an immediate sale. Another task is to decide on the best *approach*, which might be a personal visit, a phone call, or a letter. The best *timing* should be thought out because many prospects are busy at certain times. Finally, the salesperson should give thought to an *overall sales strategy* for the account.

Approach. The salesperson should know how to meet and greet the buyer to get the relationship off to a good start. This involves the salesperson's appearance, the opening lines, and the follow-up remarks. The salesperson should wear clothes similar to what buyers wear (for instance, in Texas the men wear open shirts and no ties); show courtesy and attention to the buyer; and avoid distracting mannerisms, such as pacing the floor or staring at the customer. The opening line should be positive,

FIGURE 22-2
Major Steps in Effective Selling

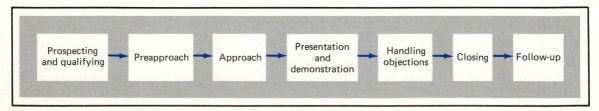

such as "Mr. Smith, I am Bill Jones from the ABC Company. My company and I appreciate your willingness to see me. I will do my best to make this visit profitable and worthwhile for you and your company." This might be followed by some key questions or the showing of a display or sample to attract the buyer's attention and curiosity.

Presentation and demonstration.   The salesperson now tells the product "story" to the buyer, following the AIDA formula of getting *attention*, holding *interest*, arousing *desire*, and obtaining *action*. The salesperson emphasizes throughout *customer benefits*, bringing in *product features* as evidence of these benefits. A benefit is any advantage, such as lower cost or less work. A feature is a characteristic of a product, such as its weight and size. A common mistake in selling is to dwell on product features (a product orientation) instead of customer benefits (a marketing orientation).

Companies use three styles of sales presentation. The oldest is the *canned approach*, which is a memorized sales talk covering the main points. It is based on stimulus-response thinking; that is, the buyer is passive and can be moved to purchase by the use of the right stimulus words, pictures, terms, and actions. Thus an encyclopedia salesperson might describe the encyclopedia as "a once-in-a-lifetime buying opportunity" and focus on some beautiful four-color pages of sports pictures, hoping to trigger desire for the encyclopedia. Canned presentations are used primarily in door-to-door and telephone selling.

The *formulated approach* is also based on stimulus-response thinking but identifies early the buyer's needs and buying style and then uses a formulated approach to this type of buyer. The salesperson initially draws the buyer into the discussion in a way that indicates the buyer's needs and attitudes. Then the salesperson moves into a formulated presentation that shows how the product will satisfy the buyer's needs. It is not canned but follows a general plan.

The *need-satisfaction approach* starts with a search for the customer's real needs by encouraging the customer to do most of the talking. This approach calls for good listening and problem-solving skills. It is well described by an IBM sales representative: "I get inside the business of my key accounts. I uncover their key problems. I prescribe solutions for them, using my company's systems and even, at times, components from other suppliers. I prove beforehand that my system will save money or make money for my accounts. Then I work with the account to install the system and make it prove out."[22]

Sales presentations can be improved with demonstration aids such as booklets, flip charts, slides, movies, and actual product samples. To the extent that the buyer can see or handle the product, he or she will better remember its features and benefits. During the demonstration, the salesperson can draw on five influence strategies:[23]

---

[22] Mark Hanan, "Join the Systems Sell and You Can't Be Beat," *Sales and Marketing Management*, August 21, 1972, p. 44. Also see Mark Hanan, James Cribbin, and Herman Heiser, *Consultative Selling* (New York: American Management Association, 1970).

[23] See Rosann L. Spiro and William D. Perreault, Jr., "Influence Use by Industrial Salesmen: Influence Strategy Mixes and Situational Determinants," unpublished paper, Graduate School of Business Administration, University of North Carolina, 1976.

☐ **Legitimacy.** The salesperson emphasizes the reputation and experience of his or her company.

☐ **Expertise.** The salesperson shows deep knowledge of the buyer's situation and company's products, doing this without being overly "smart."

☐ **Referent power.** The salesperson builds on any shared characteristics, interests, and acquaintances.

☐ **Ingratiation.** The salesperson provides personal favors (a free lunch, promotional gratuities) to strengthen affiliation and reciprocity feelings.

☐ **Impression management.** The salesperson manages to convey favorable impressions of himself or herself.

Handling objections. Customers almost always pose objections during the presentation or when asked to place an order. Their resistance can be psychological or logical. Psychological resistance includes resistance to interference, preference for established habits, apathy, reluctance to giving up something, unpleasant associations about the other person, tendency to resist domination, predetermined ideas, dislike of making decisions, and neurotic attitude toward money.[24] Logical resistance might consist of objections to the price, delivery schedule, or certain product or company characteristics. To handle these objections, the salesperson maintains a positive approach, asks the buyer to clarify the objection, questions the buyer in a way that the buyer has to answer his or her own objection, denies the validity of the objection, or turns the objection into a reason for buying. The salesperson needs training in the broader skills of negotiation, of which handling objections is a part.[25]

Closing. Now the salesperson attempts to close the sale. Some sales people don't get to this stage, or don't do it well. They lack confidence or feel guilty about asking for the order or do not recognize the right psychological moment to close the sale. Salespersons need to know how to recognize closing signals from the buyer, including physical actions, statements or comments, and questions. Salespersons can use one of several closing techniques. They can ask for the order, recapitulate the points of agreement, offer to help the secretary write up the order, ask whether the buyer wants A or B, get the buyer to make minor choices such as the color or size, or indicate what the buyer will lose if the order is not placed now. The salesperson may offer the buyer specific inducements to close, such as a special price, an extra quantity at no charge, or a gift.

Follow-up. This last step is necessary if the salesperson wants to ensure customer satisfaction and repeat business. Immediately after closing, the salesperson should complete any necessary details on delivery time, purchase terms, and other matters. The salesperson should schedule a follow-up call when the initial order is received, to make sure there is proper installation, instruction, and servicing. This visit would detect any problems, assure the buyer of the salesperson's interest, and reduce any cognitive dissonance that might have arisen.

---

[24] Crissy, Cunningham, and Cunningham, *Selling*, pp. 289–94.

[25] See Gerald I. Nierenberg, *The Art of Negotiation* (New York: Hawthorn Books, 1968); and Chester L. Karrass, *The Negotiating Game* (Cleveland: World Publishing Co., 1970).

Negotiation

Salespersons who have stimulated customer interest in their product must now apply their negotiation skills. The two parties need to reach agreement on the price and the other terms of sale. Salespersons need to win the order without making concessions that will hurt profitability.

This section will focus on negotiation skills. These skills apply to dealing not only with customers but also with suppliers, middlemen, and agencies, store buying committees, other departments in the company, and various publics. We will define negotiation, describe some negotiation models, and examine the major decisions facing negotiators.

Negotiation defined.   Marketing is concerned with exchange activities and the manner in which the terms of exchange are established. We can distinguish two general types of exchange: *routinized exchange*, where the terms are established by administered programs of pricing and distribution, and *negotiated exchange*, where price or other terms of exchange are set via bargaining behavior. Arndt has observed that a growing number of markets are coming under negotiated exchange, in which two or more parties negotiate long-term binding agreements (e.g., joint ventures, franchises, subcontracts, vertical integration). These markets are moving from being highly competitive to being highly "domesticated," that is, being less available to competitors.[26]

Although price is most frequently considered to be the object of negotiation activities, it is by no means the only one. Other objects of negotiation include time of contract completion; quality of goods or service offered; volume of goods sold; responsibility for financing, risk taking, promotion, and title; and safety of product with government agencies. The number of negotiation-related topics and parties is virtually unlimited.

We will use the terms *bargaining* and *negotiation* interchangeably.[27] Bargaining has the following features:

- [ ] At least two parties are involved.
- [ ] The parties have a conflict of interest with respect to one or more issues.
- [ ] The parties are at least temporarily joined together in a special kind of voluntary relationship.
- [ ] Activity in the relationship concerns the division or exchange of one or more specific resources and/or the resolution of one or more intangible issues among the parties or among those whom they represent.
- [ ] The activity usually involves the presentation of demands or proposals by one party and evaluation of these by the other, followed by concessions and counterproposals. The activity is thus sequential rather than simultaneous.[28]

---

[26] Johan Arndt, "Toward a Concept of Domesticated Markets," *Journal of Marketing,* fall 1979, pp. 69–75.

[27] For some references, see Ian Morley and Geoffrey Stephenson, *The Social Psychology of Bargaining* (London: George Allen and Unwin Ltd., 1977); and John G. Cross, *The Economics of Bargaining* (New York: Basic Books, 1969).

[28] Jeffrey Z. Rubin and Bert R. Brown, *The Social Psychology of Bargaining and Negotiation* (New York: Academic Press, 1975), p. 18.

In these situations, the marketing managers must have negotiation skills if successful implementation of marketing strategies is to occur.

Bargaining/negotiation models and paradigms. Bargaining has received attention in a variety of disciplines, including economics, applied mathematics, international relations, industrial relations, and social psychology. We will briefly describe the contribution of game theory, economics, social psychology, and experimental perspective.

Beginning with the work of von Neumann and Morgenstern,[29] game theorists have examined the results of rational actors' strategies in situations involving interdependent decision making.[30] Game theory assumes that each actor has an objective (typically, loss minimization), and the payoffs depend on the decisions of his or her opponent. The major purpose of game theory is to describe the set of decision rules by which rational actors choose the best strategy. (For an example, see Chapter 6, pp. 217–18.)[31]

Economists study the bargaining process through the concept of "bilateral monopoly." They see the process as a sequence of offers and counteroffers by the participants. They pay less attention to manipulative tactics, power, and bargaining skills of the participants.[32]

Social psychologists have studied the effect of several independent variables on bargaining effectiveness.[33] Rubin and Brown, in their exhaustive review of social-psychological studies on bargaining behavior, summarized the impact of four major variables—the structural context of bargaining, the behavioral predispositions of bargainers, the interdependence of bargainers, and the use of social-influence strategies—on bargaining effectiveness.[34] Bargaining effectiveness is usually measured by the number of cooperative or competitive choices made throughout the total number of trials and/or the magnitude of the outcomes obtained by the bargainers. The behavioral approach focuses on the concepts of power, tactical action, and bargaining settlements.[35]

Several models of the bargaining process have been published by experienced negotiators, who also offer courses to train executives in their approach to negotiation.[36]

---

[29] John von Neumann and Oscar Morgenstern, *Theory of Games and Economic Behavior* (Princeton, N.J.: Princeton University Press, 1944).

[30] For a well-written general survey of game theory, see R. Duncan Lace and Howard Raiffa, *Games and Decisions* (New York: John Wiley & Sons, 1957).

[31] The following books have applied game-theoretic models to analyzing actual bargaining situations: John Dennis McDonald, *The Game of Business* (New York: Doubleday & Co., 1975); and Thomas C. Schelling, *The Strategy of Conflict* (Cambridge, Mass.: Harvard University Press, 1960).

[32] See Howard Raiffa, *The Art and Science of Negotiation* (Cambridge: Harvard University Press, 1982).

[33] See for example R. E. Walton and R. B. McKenzie, *A Behavioral Theory of Labor Negotiations* (New York: McGraw Hill Book Co., 1965).

[34] See Rubin and Brown, *Social Psychology of Bargaining*, esp. Chapter 3.

[35] Samuel B. Bacharach and Edward J. Lawler, *Bargaining: Power, Tactics, and Outcome* (San Francisco: Jossey-Bass, 1981).

[36] See Herb Cohen, *You Can Negotiate Anything* (New York: Bantam Books, 1980); Nierenberg, *Art of Negotiation*, and Karass, *Negotiating Game*.

The experiential approach to the discussion of bargaining has the advantage of being based on first-hand experience in negotiation settings but lacks rigorous analysis.[37]

Bargaining decisions. Marketers who find themselves in bargaining situations must make a number of decisions about when to negotiate and how to negotiate.

When to negotiate. The question of when bargaining is an appropriate procedure for concluding a sale has been addressed in several ways. Lee and Dobler have listed the following instances when negotiation is appropriate for purchasing agents:

1. When many variable factors bear not only on price, but also on quality and service.
2. When business risks involved cannot be accurately predetermined.
3. When a long period of time is required to produce the items purchased.
4. When production is interrupted frequently because of numerous change orders.[38]

Young has developed a "bargainers' calculus," which mathematically demonstrates the point at which bargaining is an appropriate method of accomplishing objectives.[39]

For our purposes we will propose that bargaining is appropriate whenever the five definitional conditions are met (see p. 705), and a *zone of agreement* exists.[40] A zone of agreement can be considered as the range of acceptable outcomes that exists simultaneously for all bargaining parties. This concept is illustrated in Figure 22–3. If two parties, say a manufacturer and one of its dealers, are negotiating a price, each privately establishes the threshold value that he or she needs. That is, the seller has a reservation price, s, which is the *minimum* he or she will accept. Any final-contract value, x, that is below s represents a price that is worse than not reaching an agreement at all. For any $x > s$, the seller receives a surplus. Obviously the seller (manufacturer) desires as large a surplus as possible while maintaining good relations with the buyer (dealer). Likewise the buyer has a reservation price, b, that is the *maximum* he or she will pay; any x that is above b represents a price that is worse than no agreement. For any $x < b$, the buyer receives a surplus. If the seller's reservation price is below the buyer's, that is, $s < b$, then a zone of agreement exists, and bargaining will determine where x will fall within the zone.

There is an obvious advantage in knowing or probabilistically assessing the other party's reservation price and in making one's own reservation price seem higher (for a seller) or lower (for a buyer) than it really is. However, the openness with which buyers and sellers reveal and use their reservation prices or otherwise practice

---

[37] This literature lists the traits that effective negotiators should possess. The most important traits are preparation and planning skill, knowledge of subject matter being negotiated, ability to think clearly and rapidly under pressure and uncertainty, ability to express thoughts verbally, listening skill, judgment and general intelligence, integrity, ability to persuade others, and patience. See Karrass, *Negotiating Game*, pp. 242–44.

[38] Lamar Lee and Donald W. Dobler, *Purchasing and Materials Management* (New York: McGraw Hill Book Co., 1977), pp. 146–47.

[39] Oran R. Young, ed., *Bargaining: Formal Theories of Negotiation* (Urbana, Ill., University of Illinois Press, 1975), pp. 364–90.

[40] This discussion of zone of agreement is fully developed in Raiffa, *Art and Science of Negotiation*.

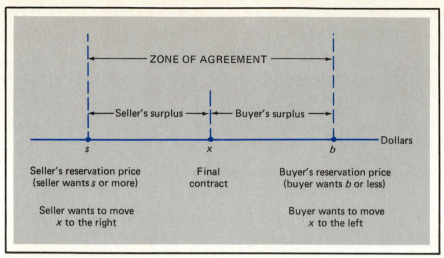

ZONE OF AGREEMENT

Seller's surplus ——— Buyer's surplus

Dollars

s   *x*   *b*

Seller's reservation price
(seller wants *s* or more)

Final
contract

Buyer's reservation price
(buyer wants *b* or less)

Seller wants to move
x to the right

Buyer wants to move
x to the left

SOURCE: Reprinted by permission of the publishers from *The Art and Science of Negotiation*, by Howard Raiffa, Cambridge, Mass.: the Belknap Press of Harvard University Press, copyright © 1982 by the President and Fellows of Harvard College.

FIGURE 22–3
The Zone of Agreement

strategic misrepresentation is often dictated by the personalities of the bargainers, the circumstances of the negotiation, and the expectation of future relations.

Formulating a bargaining strategy.   Bargaining involves strategic decisions before bargaining begins and tactical decisions during the bargaining sessions.

A bargaining strategy can be defined as a commitment to an overall approach that has a good chance of achieving the negotiator's objectives.

For example, some negotiators advise pursuing a "hard" strategy with opponents, while others maintain that a "soft" strategy yields more favorable results. Fisher and Ury propose still another strategy, that of "principled negotiation."[41] They claim that this strategy will result in outcomes favorable to its adopter regardless of the strategy selected by the other party. The strategy of principled negotiation is:

. . . to decide issues on their merits rather than through a haggling process focused on what each side says it will and won't do. It suggests that you look for mutual gains wherever possible, and that where your interests conflict, you should insist that the results be based on some fair standards independent of the will of either side. The method of principled negotiations is hard on the merits, soft on the people.[42]

[41] Roger Fisher and William Ury, *Getting to Yes: Negotiation Agreement Without Giving In* (Boston: Houghton Mifflin Co., 1981).

[42] Ibid., p. xii.

Exhibit 22-6

THE PRINCIPLED NEGOTIATION APPROACH TO BARGAINING

In research known as the Harvard Negotiation Project, Roger Fisher and William Ury arrived at four points for conducting "principled negotiations" that have a high chance of concluding successfully for both parties. They are described below.

1. **Separate the people from the problem.** Because people, not machines, are conducting the face-to-face bargaining, it is easy for emotions to become entangled with the objective merits of the issue being negotiated. Framing negotiation issues in terms of the personalities involved rather than the interests of the parties can lead to ineffective bargaining. Negotiation deteriorates when it becomes a test of wills instead of a joint problem-solving activity. Separating the people from the problem first involves making accurate perceptions. Each party must understand empathetically the power of the opponent's viewpoint and try to feel the level of emotion with which they hold it. Second, emotions brought into or evolving out of negotiations should be made explicit and acknowledged as legitimate. Openly discussing emotions of both parties while not reacting to an emotional outburst helps keep negotiations from degenerating into unproductive name-calling sessions. Third, clear communications must exist between parties. Listening actively and acknowledging what is being said, communicating about problems rather than the opponent's shortcomings, and directly addressing interests rather than speaking first just to be heard are methods of improving the chances of jointly beneficial solutions by better communication techniques. In general, separating the people from the problem means looking at the issues side by side rather than face to face.

2. **Focus on interests, not positions.** The difference between positions and interests is that one's position is something one decided upon, while one's interests are what caused one to adopt the position. Thus a bargaining *position* may be that a contract must include a stiff penalty for late shipment; but the party's *interest* is to maintain an unbroken flow of raw materials. Reconciling interests works better because for every interest there usually exist several possible positions that could satisfy that interest. Also, opposing positions may hide shared and compatible interests (e.g., we want the predictability of a steady flow of orders, you want the security of an unbroken flow of raw materials). Making certain that interests are understood by all parties and then being flexible as to the means of achieving these interests, while negotiating firmly for the interests themselves, is an effective strategy. As Fisher and Ury state it:

   > Fighting hard on the substantive issues increases the pressure for an effective solution; giving support to the human beings on the other side tends to improve your relationship and to increase the likelihood of reaching agreement. It is the combination of support and attack which works; either alone is likely to be insufficient.*

3. **Invent options for mutual gain.** Inventing options for mutual gain involves searching for a larger pie rather than arguing over the size of each slice.† Developing options requires innovative thinking such as brainstorming sessions where judgment of options is undertaken only after many options have been invented. Looking for options which offer mutual gain facilitates the desirable condition of side-by-side bargaining and helps identify shared interests.

4. **Insist on objective criteria.** When an opposing negotiator is intransigent and argues his position rather than his interests, a good strategy is to insist that the agreement

must reflect some fair objective criteria independent of the position of either side. This will help reach solutions on principle, not pressure. By discussing objective criteria instead of stubbornly held positions, neither party is yielding to the other; both are yielding to a fair solution. Such objective criteria may be market value, depreciated book value, competitive prices, replacement costs, wholesale price index, etc. This approach works best when each issue is seen as requiring a joint search for objective criteria, and each party is open to reason as to the standards best reflecting objectivity. Deviation from a fair, objective standard should be made only when a better one is offered, not because the opposing party is applying pressure, threats, or other means of imposing his will.

* Adaptation, Fisher and Ury, *Getting to Yes*, p. 57.
† For a discussion of the differences between integrative (larger pie) and distributive bargaining (size of slice), see Walton and McKenzie, *A Behavioral Theory of Labor Negotiation*.

Similarly stated strategies have been referred to as "win/win" strategies, integrative bargaining, or using a strategy of flexible rigidity (flexible with respect to bargaining means, rigid with respect to goals). Exhibit 22–6 describes the four basic points of the principled negotiation strategy.

Bargaining tactics during negotiations

Bargaining tactics **can be defined as maneuvers to be made at specific points in the bargaining process.**

Threats, bluffs, last-chance offers, hard initial offers, and other tactics are discussed in both scholarly and "how-to" books. Many sources offer checklists of tactical dos and don'ts, such as "Don't tip your hand too early" and "Do negotiate on home ground whenever possible." These lists of possible tactics are usually a shotgun blast of widely varied actions and are rarely consistent with a specific overriding bargaining strategy. (For a list of some classic tactics, see Exhibit 22–7.)

On the other hand, Fisher and Ury have offered some tactical advice that is consistent with their strategy of principled negotiation. Their first piece of tactical advice concerns what should be done if the other party is more powerful. The best tactic is to know one's BATNA—Best Alternative To a Negotiated Agreement. By identifying one's alternatives if a settlement is not reached, it sets a standard against which any offer can be measured. It protects one from being pressured into accepting unfavorable terms by a more powerful opponent.

Another tactic comes into play when the opposing party insists on arguing his or her position instead of his or her interests and attacks one's proposals or person. While the tendency is to push back hard when pushed against, the better tactic is to deflect the attack from the person and direct it against the problem. Look at the interests that motivated the opposing party's position and invent options that can satisfy both parties' interests. Invite the opposing party's criticism and advice ("If you were in my position, what would you do?").

Another series of bargaining tactics concerns responses to opposition tactics

Exhibit 22-7

SOME CLASSIC BARGAINING TACTICS

Here are several standard bargaining tactics:

- ☐ **Acting Crazy.** Put on a good show by visibly demonstrating your emotional commitment to your position. This increases your credibility and may give the opponent a justification to settle on your terms.

- ☐ **Big Pot.** Leave yourself a lot of room to negotiate. Make high demand at the beginning. After making concessions, you'll still end up with a larger payoff than if you started too low.

- ☐ **Get a Prestigious Ally.** The ally can be a person or a project that is prestigious. You try to get the opponent to accept less because the person/object he or she will be involved with is considered "prestigious."

- ☐ **The Well Is Dry.** Take a stand and tell the opponent you have no more concessions to make.

- ☐ **Limited Authority.** You negotiate in good faith with the opponent, and when you're ready to sign the deal, you say, "I have to check with my boss."

- ☐ **Whipsaw/Auction.** You let several competitors know you're negotiating with them at the same time. Schedule competitors' appointments with you for the same time and keep them all waiting to see you.

- ☐ **Divide and Conquer.** If you're negotiating with the opponent's team, sell one member of the team on your proposals. That person will help you sell the other members of the team.

- ☐ **Get Lost/Stall for Time.** Leave the negotiation completely for a while. Come back when things are getting better and try to renegotiate then. Time period can be long (say you're going out of town) or short (go to the bathroom to think).

- ☐ **Wet Noodle.** Give no emotional or verbal response to the opponent. Don't respond to his or her force or pressure. Sit there like a wet noodle and keep a "poker face."

- ☐ **Be Patient.** If you can afford to outwait the opponent, you'll probably win big.

- ☐ **Let's Split the Difference.** The person who first suggests this has the least to lose.

- ☐ **Play the Devil's Advocate.** Argue against the opponent's proposal by stating, "Before I say yes or no, let's look at all the bad things that could possibly happen if we did what you want." This lets you show the opponent your better way of achieving his or her objectives without directly opposing the opponent's viewpoint.

- ☐ **Trial Balloon.** You release your decision through a so-called reliable source before the decision is actually made. This enables you to test reaction to your decision.

- ☐ **Surprises.** Keep the opponent off balance by a drastic, dramatic, sudden shift in your tactics in general. Never be predictable—keep the opponent from anticipating your moves.

Source: From a list of over 200 tactics prepared by Professor Donald W. Hendon of the University of Hawaii in his seminar, 'How to Negotiate and Win.'

that are intended to deceive, distort, or otherwise influence the bargaining to their own advantage. What tactic should be used when the other side uses a threat or a take-it-or-leave-it tactic or puts the other party on the side of the table with the sun in her eyes? To respond, a negotiator should recognize the tactic, raise the issue explicitly, and question the tactic's legitimacy and desirability—in other words, negotiate over it. Negotiating the use of the tactic follows the same principled negotiation procedure: Question the tactic, ask for the reasons why the tactic was used, suggest alternative courses of action to mutually pursue, suggest the principle behind the tactic as a negotiation rule. Finally, resort to one's BATNA if all else fails and terminate the negotiation until the other side ceases to employ these tricky tactics. Meeting these tactics by defending principles is more productive than counterattacking with tricky tactics.

Relationship Management

The principles of personal selling and negotiation are transaction oriented, that is, their aim is to help marketers effect an immediate sale to a customer. There is a larger concept, however, that should guide the seller's dealings with its customers, namely, that of *relationship management*. The seller who knows how to build and manage strong relationships with key customers will have plenty of future sales from these customers. Relationship management is a key skill needed by marketers.

Relationship management is most appropriate with those customers and publics who can most affect the organization's future. For many companies, the top five or ten customers account for a disproportionate share of the company's sales. Sales people working with key customers must do more than call when they think customers might be ready to place orders. They should call or visit at other times, taking customers to dinner, making useful suggestions about their business, and so on. They should follow the fortunes of these key accounts, know their problems and opportunities, and be ready to serve them in a number of ways. This type of salesperson is often called a *relationship manager* (also called national account manager or customer manager).

The relationship manager represents the latest step in the evolution of the salesperson. Originally salespersons were *order takers*. Then they evolved into *order getters*, aggressively seeking business from purchasing agents. Later they evolved to *account representatives*, who dealt with a number of people in the buying organization who could influence purchases. Now they are evolving into *relationship managers*, who plan and service the entire relationship with the customers. Here are two examples:

> The marketing vice-president of an Atlanta construction firm has as a major account a large fast-food franchiser headquartered in New York. When he travels to New York, he always contacts the marketing vice-president of the fast-food franchising firm and takes him out to dinner or a show. He also invites this manager on skiing trips and golf outings. He rarely asks the fast-food franchiser for any business. Some people have called this LGD marketing: "lunch, golf, and dinner marketing."
>
> A major consulting firm observed that it had repeat business from certain clients and no repeat business from others. It discovered that some of its consultants were good at managing

relationships and getting repeat business, and others were good at managing projects but not relationships. The consulting firm identified its key clients and made sure that consultants skilled in relationship building were assigned to them.

Relationship management will undoubtedly play a larger role in the future, because of increased buyer concentration, among other things. As the buyers in an industry become fewer and larger, each one counts more. It is highly desirable that a relationship manager be assigned to each important customer. The relationship manager would plan and coordinate the company's services to serve the customer well.

Here are the main steps in establishing a relationship management program in a company:

- **Identify the key customers meriting relationship management.** The company can choose the five or ten largest customers and designate them for relationship management. Additional customers can be added who show exceptional growth or who pioneer new developments in the industry, and so on.
- **Assign a skilled relationship manager to each key customer.** The salesperson who is currently servicing the customer should receive training in relationship management or be replaced by someone who is more skilled in relationship management. The relationship manager should have characteristics that match or appeal to the customer.
- **Develop a clear job description for relationship managers.** It should describe their reporting relationships, objectives, responsibilities, and evaluation criteria. The relationship manager is responsible for the client, is the focal point for all information about the client, and is the mobilizer of company services for the client. Each relationship manager will have only one or a few relationships to manage.
- **Appoint an overall manager to supervise the relationship managers.** This person will develop job descriptions, evaluation criteria, and resource support to increase the effectiveness of this function.
- **Each relationship manager must develop long-range and annual customer-relationship plans.** The annual relationship plan will state objectives, strategies, specific actions, and required resources.

The main point about relationship management is that the company's managers need skill in managing their relationship with the managers of other organizations. Under the marketing concept, an organization must focus as much on managing its customers as its products.

SUMMARY

Most companies use sales representatives, and many companies assign them the pivotal role in the marketing mix. Sales people are very effective in achieving certain marketing objectives. At the same time they are very costly. Management must give careful thought to designing and managing its personal-selling resources.

Sales-force design calls for decisions on objectives, strategy, structure, size and compensation. Sales-force objectives include prospecting, communicating, selling and servicing, information gathering, and allocating. Sales-force strategy is a question of what types and mix and selling approaches are most effective (solo selling, team selling, and so on). Sales-force structure is a choice between organizing by territory, product, customer, or some hybrid combination and developing the right territory size and shape. Sales-force size involves estimating the total workload and how many sales hours—and hence salespersons—would be needed. Sales-force compensation involves determining the pay level and pay components such as salary, commission, bonus, expenses, and fringe benefits.

Managing the sales force involves recruiting and selecting sales representatives and training, directing, motivating, and evaluating them. Sales representatives must be recruited and selected carefully to hold down the high costs of hiring the wrong persons. Sales-training programs familiarize new sales people with the company's history, its products and policies, the characteristics of the market and competitors, and the art of selling. Sales people need supervision and continuous encouragement because they must make many decisions and are subject to many frustrations. Periodically the company must evaluate their performance to help them do a better job.

The purpose of the sales force is to produce sales, and this involves the art of personal selling. One aspect is salesmanship, which involves a seven-step process: prospecting and qualifying, preapproach, approach, presentation and demonstration, handling objections, closing, and follow-up. Another aspect is negotiation, the art of arriving at transaction terms that satisfy both parties. The third aspect is relationship management, the art of creating a closer working relation and interdependence between two organizations.

QUESTIONS

1. What are some ways in which a microcomputer can be of help to a sales manager?

2. Select a bargaining situation between a marketing agent and another party (internal or external to the firm) and discuss how the principled-negotiation approach could be used to successfully reach agreement for both parties.

3. You are a member of a marketing team negotiating with a potential customer over a robotics system for her production line. The other party is attempting to use the "divide and conquer" tactic described in Exhibit 22–7. What is your response to this tactic?

4. A district sales manager voiced the following complaint at a sales meeting: "The average salesperson costs our company $40,000 in compensation and expenses. Why can't we buy a few less $40,000 full-page advertisements in *Time* magazine and use the money to hire more people? Surely one individual working a full year can sell more products than a one-page ad in one issue of *Time*." Evaluate this argument.

5. The text described some of the characteristics that might be looked for in sales representatives. What characteristics should be looked for in selecting district sales managers? What about the national sales manager?

6. A sales manager wants to determine how many sales calls per month the sales force should make to average-size accounts. Describe how an experiment might be set up to answer the question.

7. A sales manager is trying to figure out the most that should be spent to win a particular account. This account would produce sales of $10,000 a year, and the company is likely to retain it for at least four years. The company's profit margin on sales is 15 percent. The company wants its various investments to earn 8 percent. What is the most that the company should spend to win this account?

8. Suppose a salesperson can make 1,600 calls a year. If he or she has been writing $420,000 worth of business a year, how many calls can the sales person make to a $10,000-a-year account without diluting the total business written during the year?

9. Describe several types of selling situations where a straight salary plan seems appropriate.

10. Should sales representatives participate in the establishment of sales quotas for their territories? What would be the advantages and disadvantages of their participation?

Marketing Organization and Implementation

Success is a product of unremitting attention to purpose.

BENJAMIN DISRAELI

Do your work with your whole heart and you will succeed—there is so little competition!

ELBERT HUBBARD

We now turn to the administrative side of marketing management to examine how firms organize, implement, and control their marketing activities. In this chapter we will deal with marketing organization and implementation, and in the next chapter, with marketing control.

MARKETING ORGANIZATION

We will first look at marketing organization and examine how marketing departments evolve in companies, how they are organized, and how they interact with the company's other departments.

The Evolution of the Marketing Department

The modern marketing department is the product of a long evolution. At least five stages can be distinguished, and companies can be found today in each stage.

Simple sales department. All companies start out with four simple functions. Someone must raise and manage capital (finance), produce the product or service (operations), sell it (sales), and keep the books (accounting). The selling function is headed by a sales vice-president, who manages a sales force and also does some selling. When the company needs some marketing research or advertising, the sales vice-president also handles those functions. This stage is illustrated in Figure 23–1(a).

Sales department with ancillary functions. As the company expands, it needs marketing research, advertising, and customer service on a more continuous and expert basis. The sales vice-president hires specialists to perform these functions. The sales vice-president may also hire a marketing director to plan and control the nonselling functions. [See Figure 23–1(b).]

Figure 23-1
Stages in the Evolution of the Marketing Department

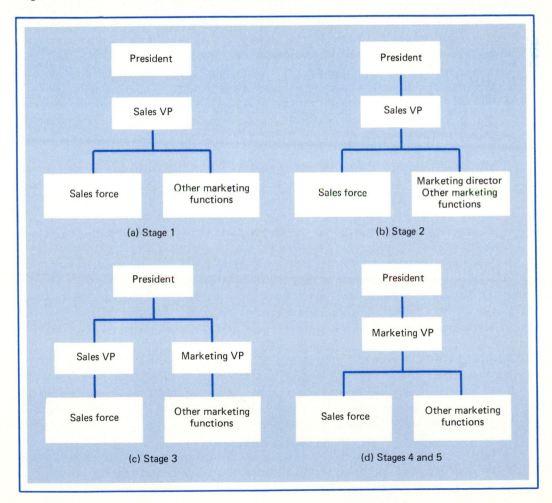

Separate marketing department.   The continued growth of the company increases the importance of other marketing functions—marketing research, new-product development, advertising and sales promotion, customer service—relative to sales-force activity. Nevertheless the sales vice-president continues to give disproportionate time and attention to the sales force. The marketing director will argue that more budget should go into the other marketing functions. The company president will eventually see the advantage of establishing a marketing department that is relatively independent of the sales vice-president. [See Figure 23–1(c).] The marketing department will be headed by a marketing vice-president, who reports, along with the sales vice-president, to the president or executive vice-president. At this stage, sales and marketing are separate and equal functions in the organization that are supposed to work closely together.

Modern marketing department.   Although the sales and marketing vice-presidents are supposed to work harmoniously, their relationship is often characterized by rivalry and distrust. The sales vice-president resists letting the sales force become less important in the marketing mix; and the marketing vice-president seeks more power for the nonsales-force functions. The sales vice-president tends to be short-run oriented and preoccupied with achieving current sales. The marketing vice-president tends to be long-run oriented and preoccupied with planning the right products and marketing strategy to meet the customers' long-run needs.

If there is too much conflict between sales and marketing, the company president may place marketing activities back under the sales vice-president, or instruct the executive vice-president to handle conflicts that arise, or place the marketing vice-president in charge of everything, including the sales force. The last solution is eventually chosen in many companies and forms the basis of the modern marketing department, a department headed by a marketing vice-president with subordinates reporting from every marketing function, including sales management. [See Figure 23–1(d).]

Modern marketing company.   A company can have a modern marketing department and yet not operate as a modern marketing company. The latter depends upon how the other company officers view the marketing function. If they view marketing as primarily a selling function, they are missing the point. Only when they see that all of the departments are "working for the customer" and that marketing is the name not of a department but of a company philosophy will they become a modern marketing company.

Ways of Organizing the Marketing Department

Modern marketing departments show numerous arrangements. All marketing organizations must accommodate to four basic dimensions of marketing activity: *functions, geographical areas, products,* and *customer markets.*

Functional organization.   The most common form of marketing organization consists of functional-marketing specialists reporting to a marketing vice-president, who coordinates their activities. Figure 23–2 shows five specialists: marketing administra-

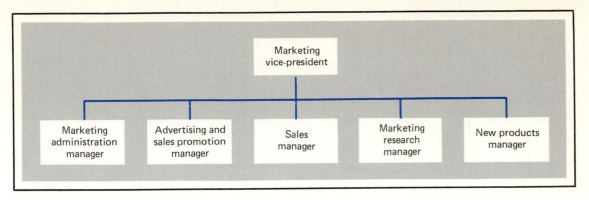

FIGURE 23–2
Functional Organization

tion manager, advertising and sales promotion manager, sales manager, marketing research manager, and new-products manager, respectively. Additional functional specialists might include a customer-service manager, a marketing-planning manager, and a physical-distribution manager.

If the number of functions reporting to the marketing vice-president becomes too large, they may be subgrouped into *resource functions* and *program functions*. Marketing resource managers handle the sales force, customer services, advertising, sales promotion, and marketing research. Marketing program managers handle specific products, industries, and ventures. Thus the marketing vice-president has two areas to oversee, resources and programs.

The main advantage of a functional marketing organization is its administrative simplicity. On the other hand, this form loses effectiveness as the company's products and markets grow. First, there is inadequate planning for specific products and markets, since no one has full responsibility for any product or market. Products that are not favorites of various functional specialists get neglected. Second, each functional group competes to gain more budget and status vis-à-vis the other functions. The marketing vice-president has to constantly sift the claims of competing functional specialists and faces a difficult problem in coordination.

Geographical organization. A company selling in a national market often organizes its sales force (and sometimes other functions) along geographical lines. Figure 23–3 shows 1 national sales manager, 4 regional sales managers, 24 zone sales managers, 192 district sales managers, and 1,920 salespersons. The span of control increases as we move from the national sales manager down toward the district sales managers. Shorter spans allow managers to give more time to subordinates and are warranted when the sales task is complex, the salespersons are highly paid, and the salesperson's impact on profits is substantial.

Some companies are now adding *local marketing specialists* to support the sales efforts in high-volume markets. The local marketing specialist for Cleveland, for example, would know everything there is to know about Cleveland's marketing environment.

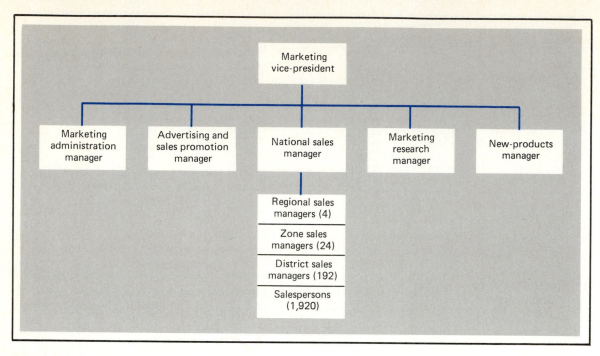

FIGURE 23–3
Geographical Organization

The specialist would prepare and implement a long-range and short-range marketing plan for developing the Cleveland market for the company's products.

Product management organization.   Companies producing a variety of products and/or brands often establish a product or brand management organization. The product management organization does not replace the functional management organization but serves as another layer of management. The product management organization is headed by a products manager, who supervises several product group managers, who supervise product managers in charge of specific products. (See Figure 23–4.)

A product management organization makes sense if the products are quite different and/or if the sheer number of products is beyond the capacity of a functional marketing organization to handle.

Product management first appeared in the Procter and Gamble Company in 1927. A new company soap, Camay, was not doing well, and one of the young executives, Neil H. McElroy (later president of P&G), was assigned to give his exclusive attention to developing and promoting this product. He did it successfully, and the company soon added other product managers.

Since then many firms, especially in the food, soap, toiletries, and chemical industries, have established product management organizations. General Foods, for example, uses a product-management organization in its Post Division. There are separate product group managers in charge of cereals, pet food, and beverages. Within

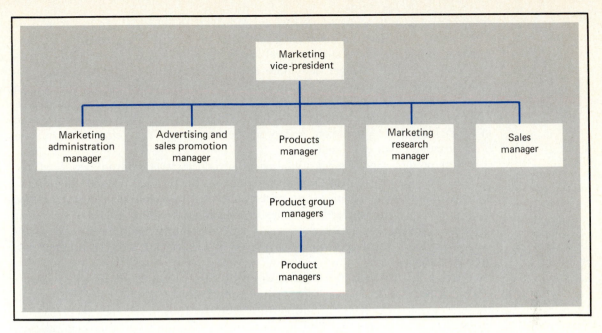

FIGURE 23-4
Product Management Organization

the cereal product group, there are separate product managers for nutritional cereals, children's presweetened cereals, family cereals, and miscellaneous cereals. In turn, the nutritional-cereal product manager supervises brand managers.[1]

The product manager's role is to develop product plans, see that they are implemented, monitor the results, and take corrective action. This responsibility breaks down into six tasks:

☐ Developing a long-range and competitive strategy for the product
☐ Preparing an annual marketing plan and sales forecast
☐ Working with advertising and merchandising agencies to develop copy, programs, and campaigns
☐ Stimulating interest in and support of the product among the sales force and distributors
☐ Gathering continuous intelligence on the product's performance, customer and dealer attitudes, and new problems and opportunities
☐ Initiating product improvements to meet changing market needs

These basic functions are common to both consumer- and industrial-product managers. Yet there are some differences in their jobs and emphases.[2] Consumer-

---

[1] For details, see "General Food Corporation: Post Division," in *Organization Strategy: A Marketing Approach*, ed. E. Raymond Corey and Steven H. Star (Boston: Division of Research, Graduate School of Business Administration, Harvard University, 1971), pp. 201–30.

[2] See Elmer E. Waters, "Industrial Product Manager . . . Consumer Brand Manager: A Study in Contrast," *Industrial Marketing*, January 1969, pp. 45–49.

product managers typically manage fewer products than industrial-product managers. They spend more time on advertising and sales promotion. They spend more time working with others in the company and various agencies and little time with customers. They are often younger and more educated. Industrial-product managers, by contrast, think more about the technical aspects of their product and possible design improvements. They spend more time with laboratory and engineering personnel. They work more closely with the sales force and key buyers. They pay less attention to advertising, sales promotion, and promotional pricing. They emphasize rational product factors over emotional ones.

The product management organization introduces several advantages. First, the product manager harmonizes the marketing mix for the product. Second, the product manager can react more quickly to problems in the marketplace than a committee of specialists. Third, smaller brands are less neglected because they have a product advocate. Fourth, product management is an excellent training ground for young executives, for it involves them in almost every area of company operations. (See Figure 23–5.)

But a price is paid for these advantages. First, product management creates some conflict and frustration.[3] Typically product managers are not given enough authority to carry out their responsibilities effectively. They have to rely on persuasion to get the cooperation of advertising, sales, manufacturing, and other departments. They are told they are "minipresidents" but are often treated as low-level coordinators. They are burdened with a great amount of "housekeeping" paperwork. They often have to go over the heads of others to get something done.

Second, product managers become experts in their product but rarely become experts in any functions. They vacillate between posing as experts and being cowed by real experts. This is unfortunate when the product depends on a specific type of expertise, such as advertising.

Third, the product-management system often turns out to be costlier than anticipated. Originally one person is appointed to manage each major product. Soon product managers are appointed to manage even minor products. Each product manager, usually overworked, pleads for and gets an *assistant brand manager*. Later, both overworked, they persuade management to give them a *brand assistant*. With all these personnel, payroll costs climb. In the meantime the company continues to increase its functional specialists in copy, packaging, media, promotion, market surveys, statistical analysis, and so on. The company becomes saddled with a costly structure of product management people and functional specialists.

Fourth, product managers tend to stay a short time on their jobs. Either product managers move up in a few years to another brand or product, or they transfer to another company, or they leave product management altogether. Their short-term involvement with the product leads to short-term marketing planning and plays havoc with building up the product's long-term strengths.

---

[3] See David J. Luck, "Interfaces of a Product Manager," *Journal of Marketing,* October 1969, pp. 32–36.

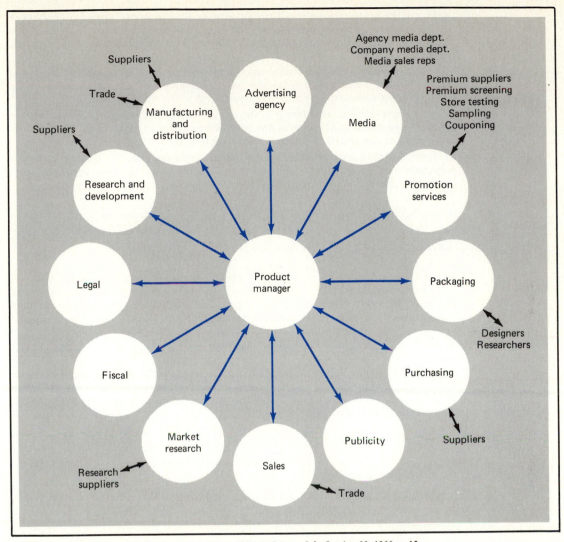

Adapted from "Product Managers: Just What do They Think?" *Printers Ink*, October 28; 1966, p. 15.

FIGURE 23–5
The Product Manager's Interactions

Pearson and Wilson have suggested five steps to make the product management system work better:[4]

☐ **Clearly delineate the limits of the product manager's role and responsibility for the management of a product.** (They are essentially proposers, not deciders.)

---

[4] Andrall E. Pearson and Thomas W. Wilson, Jr., *Making Your Organization Work* (New York: Association of National Advertisers, 1967), pp. 8–13.

☐ **Build a strategy development and review process to provide an agreed-to-framework for the product manager's operations.** (Too many companies allow product managers to get away with shallow marketing plans featuring a lot of statistics but little strategic rationale.)

☐ **Take into account areas of potential conflict between product managers and functional specialists when defining their respective roles.** (Clarify which decisions are to be made by the product manager, which by the expert, and which will be shared.)

☐ **Set up a formal process that forces to the top all conflict-of-interest situations between product management and functional line management.** (Both parties should put the issues in writing and forward them to general management for settlement.)

☐ **Establish a system for measuring results that is consistent with the product manager's responsibilities.** (If product managers are accountable for profit, they should be given more control over the factors that affect their profitability.)

A second alternative is to switch from a product-manager to a product-team approach. In fact there are three types of product-team structures in product management. (See Figure 23–6.)

☐ **Vertical product team.** This consists of a product manager, assistant product manager, and product assistant. [See Figure 23–6(a).] The product manager is the leader and primarily deals with other executives, to gain their cooperation. The assistant product manager assists in these tasks and also does some paper work. The product assistant does most of the paperwork and runs errands.

☐ **Triangular product team.** This consists of a product manager and two specialized product assistants, one who takes care of (say) marketing research and the other, marketing communications. [See Figure 23–6(b).] This design is used at the Illinois Central Railroad, where various three-person teams manage different commodities. Also the Hallmark Company uses a "marketing team" consisting of a market manager (the leader), a marketing manager, and a distribution manager.

FIGURE 23–6
Three Types of Product Teams

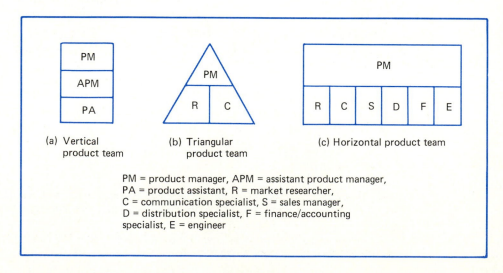

(a) Vertical product team

(b) Triangular product team

(c) Horizontal product team

PM = product manager, APM = assistant product manager, PA = product assistant, R = market researcher, C = communication specialist, S = sales manager, D = distribution specialist, F = finance/accounting specialist, E = engineer

□ **Horizontal product team.** This consists of a product manager and several specialists from within and outside marketing. [See Figure 23–6(c).] Thus the 3M Company divided its commercial tape division into nine business-planning teams, each team consisting of a team leader and representatives from sales, marketing, laboratory, engineering, accounting, and marketing research. Instead of a product manager's bearing the entire responsibility of product planning, he or she shares it with representatives from key parts of the company. Their input is critical in the marketing-planning process, and furthermore each team member could bring influence to bear in his or her own department. The ultimate step after a horizontal product team is organized is to form a product division around the product.

A third alternative is to eliminate product-manager positions for minor products and load two or more products on each remaining product manager. This is feasible especially where the products appeal to a similar set of needs. Thus a cosmetics company does not need separate product managers because cosmetics serve one major need—beauty—whereas a toiletries company needs different managers for headache remedies, toothpaste, soap, and shampoo because these products differ in their use and appeal.

A fourth alternative is to turn major company products into product divisions and set up functional resources within divisions. Pearson and Wilson feel that a functional marketing organization "is the oldest, simplest and, in many respects, the soundest form of organization for marketing."[5]

The product-manager position is undergoing important changes.[6] Three trends have been accelerated by recent company experiences with shortages, rapid inflation, recession, and consumerism. The first is that product managers have assumed more responsibility for profit. Rising costs have led companies to be less satisfied with volume attainment and more concerned with profit attainment. The product manager is seen as operating a profit center and must put a profit test to the various items in the budget. Some companies are holding their product managers responsible for excessive costs of inventory and receivables. The second trend is that product managers are working more closely with other managers to secure scarce supplies, develop substitute ingredients, engineer product economies, smooth production, and keep total costs down. The third trend is toward giving higher management more authority over brand managers. These trends reflect the need for more coordinated planning of whole product lines rather than simply of brands and the need for greater responsiveness to consumerists' concerns with advertising truthfulness and product safety.[7]

Market management organization. Many companies will sell a product line to a highly diverse set of markets. For example, Smith Corona sells its electric typewriters to consumer, business, and government markets. U.S. Steel sells its steel to the railroad, construction, and public utility industries. When the customers fall into different

---

[5] Ibid., p. 5.

[6] See Richard M. Clewett and Stanley F. Stasch, "Shifting Role of the Product Manager," *Harvard Business Review*, January-February 1975, pp. 65–73; Victor P. Buell, "The Changing Role of the Product Manager in Consumer Goods Companies," *Journal of Marketing*, July 1973, pp. 3–11; "The Brand Manager: No Longer King," *Business Week*, June 9, 1973.

[7] See Joseph A. Morein, "Shift from Brand to Product Line Marketing," *Harvard Business Review*, September-October 1975, pp. 56–64.

user groups with distinct buying practices or product preferences, a market management organization is desirable.

A market management organization is similar to the product-management organization shown earlier in Figure 23–4. A *markets manager* supervises several *market managers* (also called *market development managers*, *market specialists*, or *industry specialists*). The market managers draw upon functional services from the rest of the organization as needed. Market managers of important markets may even have some functional specialists reporting to them.

Market managers are essentially staff, not line, people, with similar duties to product managers. Market managers develop long-range and annual plans for their markets. They must analyze where their market is going and what new products their company should offer to this market. Their performance is often judged by their contribution to market-share growth rather than to current profitability in their market. This system carries many of the same advantages and disadvantages of product management systems. Its strongest advantage is that the marketing activity is organized to meet the needs of distinct customer groups rather than focusing on marketing functions, regions, or products per se.

Many companies are reorganizing along market lines. Hanan calls these *market-centered organizations* and argues that "the only way to ensure being market-oriented is to put a company's organizational structure together so that its major markets become the centers around which its divisions are built."[8] Xerox has converted from geographical selling to selling by industry. The Mead Company has clustered its marketing activities around home building and furnishings, education, and leisure markets.

One of the most dramatic changes to market centeredness has occurred at the Heinz Company. Before 1964 Heinz was organized around a brand-management system, with separate brand managers for soups, condiments, puddings, and so on. Each brand manager was responsible for both grocery sales and institutional sales. Then in 1964 Heinz created a separate marketing organization for institutional sales. Thus selling ketchup to institutions would be handled by institutional product managers rather than the brand managers. More recently Heinz created three broad market groups: groceries, commercial restaurants, and institutions. Each group contains further market specialists. For example, the institutional division contains market specialists for schools, colleges, hospitals, and prisons.

Product management/market management organization. Companies that produce many products flowing into many markets face a dilemma. They could use a product management system, which requires product managers to be familiar with highly divergent markets. Or they could use a market management system, which means that market managers would have to be familiar with highly divergent products bought by their markets. Or they could install both product and market managers, that is, a *matrix organization*.

---

[8] Mark Hanan, "Reorganize Your Company around Its Markets," *Harvard Business Review*, November–December 1974, pp. 63–74.

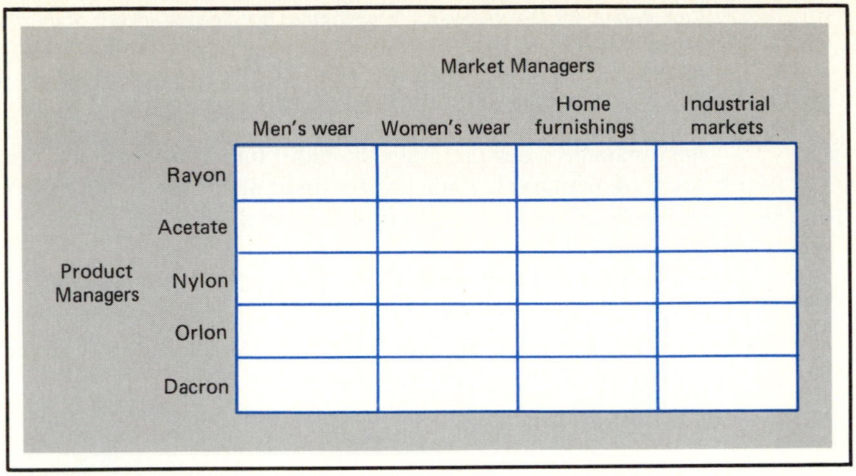

FIGURE 23–7
Product/Market Management System

Du Pont is a company that has done the latter.[9] (See Figure 23–7.) Its textile fibers department consists of separate product managers for rayon, acetate, nylon, orlon, and dacron; and also separate market managers for men's wear, women's wear, home furnishings, and industrial markets. The product managers have responsibility for planning the sales and profits of their respective fibers. These managers concentrate on improving current profit performance and finding more uses of their fiber. Their job is to contact each market manager and ask for an estimate of how much material can be sold in each market. The market managers, on the other hand, have the responsibility for developing profitable markets for existing and potential Du Pont fibers. They take a long view of market needs and care more about evolving the right products for their market than about pushing specific fibers. In preparing their market plan, they contact each product manager to learn about planned prices and availabilities of different materials. The final sales forecasts of the market managers and the product managers should add to the same grand total.

A product management/market management organization would seem desirable in a multiple-product, multiple-market company. The rub is that this system is both costly and conflictual. There is the cost of supporting a three-dimensional *matrix organization* (i.e., two layers of program management in addition to one layer of resource management). There are also questions about where authority and responsibility should reside. Here are two of the many dilemmas:

☐ **How should the sales force be organized?** Should there be separate sales forces for rayon, nylon, and each of the other fibers? Or should the sales forces be organized according to men's wear, women's wear, and other markets? Or should the sales force not be specialized?

---

[9] For details, see Corey and Star, *Organization Strategy*, pp. 187–96.

□ **Who should set the prices for a particular product/market?** Should the nylon product manager have final authority for setting nylon prices in all markets? What happens if the men's wear market manager feels that nylon will lose out in this market unless special price concessions are made on nylon?

Most managers feel that only the more important products and markets would justify separate managers. Some are not upset about the conflicts and cost and believe that the benefits of product and market specialization outweigh the costs.[10]

Corporate/divisional organization. As multiproduct companies grow in size, they often turn their larger product groups into separate divisions. The divisions set up their own departments and services. This raises the question of what marketing services and activities should be retained at corporate headquarters.

Divisionalized companies have reached different answers to this question. Corporate marketing staffs follow one of four models:[11]

□ **No corporate marketing.** Some companies lack a corporate marketing staff. They don't see any useful function for marketing to perform at the corporate level. Each division has its own marketing department.

□ **Minimal corporate marketing.** Some companies have a small corporate marketing staff that performs a few functions, primarily (a) assisting top management with overall opportunity evaluation, (b) providing divisions with consulting assistance on request, (c) helping divisions that have little or no marketing, and (d) promoting the marketing concept to other departments of the company.

□ **Moderate corporate marketing.** Some companies have a corporate marketing staff that, in addition to the preceding activities, also provides various marketing services to the divisions. The corporate marketing staff might provide specialized *advertising services* (e.g., coordination of media buying, institutional advertising, review of division advertising from a taste and image standpoint, auditing of advertising expenditures), *sales promotion services* (e.g., companywide promotions, central buying of promotional materials), *marketing research services* (e.g., advanced mathematical analysis, research on marketing development cutting across divisional lines), *sales-administration services* (e.g., counsel on sales organization and sales policies, development of common sales-reporting systems, management of sales forces selling to common customers), and some miscellaneous services (e.g., counseling of marketing planning, hiring and training of marketing personnel).

□ **Strong corporate marketing.** Some companies have a corporate marketing staff that, in addition to the preceding activities, participates strongly in the planning and control of divisional marketing activities.

The question arises as to whether companies are converging toward one of these models of the corporate marketing department. The answer is no. Some companies have recently installed a corporate marketing staff for the first time; others have expanded their department; others have reduced its size and scope; and still others have eliminated it altogether. The potential contribution of a corporate marketing staff varies in different stages of the company's evolution. Most companies begin

---

[10] See B. Charles Ames, "Dilemma of Product/Market Management," *Harvard Business Review*, March-April 1971, pp. 66–74.

[11] See Watson Snyder, Jr., and Frank B. Gray, *The Corporate Marketing Staff: Its Role and Effectiveness in Multi-Division Companies* (Cambridge, Mass.: Marketing Science Institute, April 1971).

with weak marketing in their divisions and often establish a corporate marketing staff to bring marketing into the various divisions through education and supplying various services. Some members of the corporate marketing staff later join the divisions to head marketing departments. As the divisions grow strong in their marketing, corporate marketing has less to offer them. Some companies decide that corporate marketing has done its job and eliminate the department.

A corporate marketing staff generally has three justifications. The first is to serve as a corporate focus for review and leadership of overall company marketing activities and opportunities. The second is to offer certain marketing services that could be provided more economically on a centralized basis than by being duplicated in the different divisions. The third is to take responsibility for educating divisional managers, sales managers, and others in the company on the meaning and implementation of the marketing concept.

Exhibit 23–1 summarizes some of the preceding discussion by showing how company marketing evolves in fast-growth, high-tech companies.

Marketing's Relations with Other Departments

In principle, business functions should mesh harmoniously to achieve the overall objectives of the firm. In practice, departmental relations are often characterized by deep rivalries and misunderstandings. Some interdepartmental conflict stems from differences of opinion as to what is in the best interests of the firm, some from real trade-offs between departmental well-being and company well-being, and some from unfortunate departmental stereotypes and prejudices.

In the typical organization each department has an effect on customer satisfaction through its activities and decisions. Under the marketing concept, it is desirable to coordinate those activities and decisions because customer satisfaction depends on the *totality* of customer-impinging stimuli, not simply the stimuli managed by the marketing department.

The marketing department is willing to accept this responsibility and use its influence. A marketing vice-president has two tasks: to coordinate the marketing activities of the company, and to deal with the vice-presidents of finance, operations, and so on, on a regular basis so that they develop a deeper appreciation of the benefits of a customer orientation. But there is little agreement on how much influence and authority marketing should have over other departments to bring about coordinated marketing.

Other departments may resist bending their efforts to the will of the marketing department. Just as marketing stresses the customer's point of view, other departments stress the importance of their tasks. Inevitably departments define company problems and goals from their point of view. As a result, conflicts of interest are unavoidable. Table 23–1 summarizes the main point-of-view differences between marketing and other departments. We will examine briefly the typical concerns of each department.

R&D. The company's desire for successful new products is often thwarted by poor working relations between R&D and marketing. In many ways these groups represent two different cultures in the organization. The R&D department is staffed with scien-

Exhibit 23-1

THE EVOLUTION OF THE MARKETING FUNCTION IN FAST-GROWTH HIGH-TECH COMPANIES

A company will reorganize its marketing function several times through the course of the company's growth. Each time the marketing function will be adapted to the company's needs at that stage. The evolution of the marketing department was described by Tyebjee, Bruno, and McIntyre based on their interviewing several high-tech companies. They identified four stages in the evolution of company marketing.

Entrepreneurial Marketing

The high-tech company starts as a new venture headed by an entrepreneur possessing technical expertise but little marketing knowledge. That entrepreneur designs some initial products for some specialized customers and personally markets them. The company's low production volume does not justify the overhead of a formal marketing organization. The product line and customer base is narrow, and selling is based on the entrepreneur's personal marketing to a few major accounts.

Opportunistic Marketing

The company now wants to expand its customer base by developing a more standardized product line. The company is willing to start competing against larger companies. It establishes an infant marketing department staffed mainly with sales people, who deal with tactical issues. This department does not handle product planning and pricing; these functions stay in top management's hands.

Responsive Marketing

The company now has several products that need more individual attention. This leads to the appointment of product managers, who act as advocates for their products and manage budgets for marketing research, promotion, and customer service. Marketing is now driven by customer needs, which are researched more adequately.

Diversified Marketing

The company cannot expand much more in its core product areas because of market saturation or antitrust considerations. The company starts new businesses and divisions, each staffed with product managers and marketing staffs. Now marketing emerges at the corporate level to perform a number of neglected functions, such as monitoring divisional marketing, providing specialized services to divisional marketing departments, and proposing and investigating new ventures.

Source: Based on Tyzoon T. Tyebjee, Albert V. Bruno, and Shelby H. McIntyre, "Growing Ventures Can Anticipate Marketing Stages," Harvard Business Review, *January-February 1983, pp. 2–4.*

TABLE 23-1

SUMMARY OF ORGANIZATIONAL CONFLICTS
BETWEEN MARKETING AND OTHER DEPARTMENTS

Department	Their Emphasis	Marketing's Emphasis
R&D	Basic research	Applied research
	Intrinsic quality	Perceived quality
	Functional features	Sales features
Engineering	Long design lead time	Short design lead time
	Few models	Many models
	Standard components	Custom components
Purchasing	Narrow product line	Broad product line
	Standard parts	Nonstandard parts
	Price of material	Quality of material
	Economical lot sizes	Large lot sizes to avoid stockouts
	Purchasing at infrequent intervals	Immediate purchasing for customer needs
Manufacturing	Long production lead time	Short production lead time
	Long runs with few models	Short runs with many models
	No model changes	Frequent model changes
	Standard orders	Custom orders
	Ease of fabrication	Aesthetic appearance
	Average quality control	Tight quality control
Finance	Strict rationales for spending	Intuitive arguments for spending
	Hard and fast budgets	Flexible budgets to meet changing needs
	Pricing to cover costs	Pricing to further market development
Accounting	Standard transactions	Special terms and discounts
	Few reports	Many reports
Credit	Full financial disclosures by customers	Minimum credit examination of customers
	Low credit risks	Medium credit risks
	Tough credit terms	Easy credit terms
	Tough collection procedures	Easy collection procedures

tists and technicians who pride themselves on scientific curiosity and detachment, like to work on challenging technical problems without much concern for immediate sales payoffs, and like to work without much supervision or accountability for research costs. The marketing/sales department is staffed with business-oriented persons, who pride themselves on a practical understanding of the world, like to see many new products with sales features that can be promoted to customers, and feel compelled to pay attention to costs. Each group often carries negative stereotypes of the other group. Marketers see the R&D people as impractical, long-haired, mad-scientist types who don't understand business, while R&D people see marketers as gimmick-oriented hucksters who are more interested in sales than in the technical features of the product. These stereotypes get in the way of productive teamwork.

Companies turn out to be either R&D dominated, marketing dominated, or balanced. In *R&D-dominated companies* the R&D staff researches fundamental problems, looks for major breakthroughs, and strives for technical perfection in product development. R&D expenditures are high, and the new-product success rate tends to be low, although R&D occasionally comes up with major new products.

In *marketing-dominated companies*, the R&D staff designs products for specific market needs, much of it involving product modification and the application of existing technologies. A higher ratio of new products succeed, but they represent mainly product modifications with relatively short product lives.

A *balanced R&D/marketing company* is one in which effective organizational relations have been worked out between R&D and marketing to share responsibility for successful market-oriented innovation. The R&D staff takes responsibility not for invention alone but for successful innovation. The marketing staff takes responsibility not for new sales features alone but also for helping identify new ways to satisfy needs. R&D/marketing cooperation is facilitated in several ways: (1) Joint seminars are sponsored to build understanding and respect for each other's goals, working styles, and problems; (2) each new project is assigned to an R&D person and a marketing person, who work together through the life of the project; (3) R&D and marketing personnel are interchanged so that they have a chance to experience each other's work situations (some R&D people may travel with the sales force, while some marketing people might hang around the lab for a short time); and (4) conflicts are worked out by higher management, following a clear procedure.[12]

Engineering.   Engineering is responsible for finding practical ways to design new products and new production processes. Engineers are interested in achieving technical quality, cost economy, and manufacturing simplicity. They come into conflict with marketing personnel when the latter want several models to be produced, often with product features requiring custom rather than standard components. Engineers see marketers as wanting "bells-and-whistles" on the products, rather than intrinsic quality. These problems are less pronounced in companies where marketing executives have engineering backgrounds and can communicate effectively with engineers.

Purchasing.   Purchasing executives are responsible for obtaining materials and components at the lowest possible cost and in the right quantities and quality. They see marketing executives pushing for several models in a product line, which requires purchasing small quantities of many inventory items rather than large quantities of a few items. They think that marketing insists on too high a quality of ordered materials and components. They dislike marketing's forecasting inaccuracy; it causes them to place rush orders at unfavorable prices and at other times to carry excessive inventories.

---

[12] For further discussion, see William E. Souder, "Effectiveness of Nominal and Interacting Group Decision Processes for Integrating R&D and Marketing," *Management Science*, February 1977, pp. 595–605.

Manufacturing. There are several potential conflicts between manufacturing and marketing. Manufacturing people are responsible for the smooth running of the factory to produce the right products in the right quantities at the right time for the right cost. They have spent their lives in the factory, with its attendant problems of machine breakdowns, inventory stockouts, and labor disputes and slowdowns. They see marketers as having little understanding of factory economics or politics. Marketers will complain about insufficient plant capacity, delays in production, poor quality control, and poor customer service. Yet marketers often turn in inaccurate sales forecasts, recommend products that are difficult to manufacture and come in too many versions, and promise more factory service than is reasonable.

Marketers do not see the factory's problems but rather they see the problems of their customers, who need the goods quickly, who receive defective merchandise, and who can't get factory service. Marketers often don't show enough concern for the extra factory costs involved in helping a customer. The problem is not only poor communication but an actual conflict of interest.

Companies settle these conflicts in different ways. In *manufacturing-dominant* companies, everything is done to ensure smooth production and low costs. The company prefers simple products, narrow product lines, and high-volume production. Sales campaigns calling for a hasty production buildup are kept to a minimum. Customers on back order have to wait.

Other companies are *marketing dominant*, in that the company goes out of its way to satisfy customers. In one large toiletries company the marketing personnel call the shots, and the manufacturing people have to fall in line, regardless of overtime costs, short runs, and so on. The result is high and fluctuating manufacturing costs, as well as variable product quality.

Companies need to develop a *balanced manufacturing/marketing orientation* in which both sides feel important and in which they codetermine what is in the best interests of the company. Solutions include joint seminars to understand each other's viewpoint, joint committees and liaison personnel, personnel exchange programs, and analytical methods to determine the most profitable course of action.[13]

Finance. Financial executives pride themselves on being able to evaluate the profit implications of different business actions. When it comes to marketing expenditures, they feel frustrated. Marketing executives ask for substantial budgets for advertising, sales promotions, and sales force, without being able to prove how much sales will be produced by these expenditures. Financial executives suspect that the marketers' forecasts are self-serving. They think that marketing people don't spend enough time relating expenditures to sales and shifting their budgets to more profitable areas. They think that marketers are too quick to slash prices to win orders, instead of pricing to make a profit.

Marketing executives, on the other hand, often see financial people as controlling the purse strings too tightly and refusing to invest funds in long-term market development. Financial people seem overly conservative and risk averse, causing many oppor-

---

[13] See Benson P. Shapiro, "Can Marketing and Manufacturing Coexist?" *Harvard Business Review*, September-October 1977, pp. 104–14.

tunities to be lost. The solution lies in giving marketing people more financial training and giving financial people more understanding of how markets respond to different types of marketing effort.

Accounting. Accountants see marketing people as lax in providing their sales reports on time. They dislike the special deals sales people make with customers, because these require special accounting procedures. Marketers, on the other hand, dislike the way accountants allocate fixed-cost burdens to different products in the line. Brand managers may feel that their brand is more profitable than it looks, the problem being high overhead assigned to it. They would also like accounting to prepare special reports on sales and profitability by different channels, territories, order sizes, and so on.

Credit. Credit officers check out the credit standing of potential customers and deny or limit credit to the more doubtful ones. They think that marketers will sell to anyone, even to those from whom payment is doubtful. Marketers, on the other hand, often feel that credit standards are too high. They think that "zero bad debts" really means that the company lost a lot of sales and profits. They feel they work too hard to find customers to hear that they are not good enough to sell to.

Strategies for Building a Companywide Marketing Orientation

Only a handful of American companies—such as P&G, IBM, McDonald's—are truly marketing oriented. A much larger number of companies are sales oriented. These companies sooner or later experience some market shock. They may lose a major market, experience slow growth or low profitability, or find themselves facing more sophisticated competitors.

> For years, General Motors prided itself on a marketing orientation and pointed to its huge sales volume and market share as evidence. However, as management witnessed the growing share of small foreign cars, they realized that they had not fully monitored the market and responded to consumer desires. They still have to learn how to design small cars with the quality and fuel economy that Americans have found in Japanese cars.[14]
>
> In the early 1970s, American Telephone and Telegraph (AT&T) suddenly found itself facing keen competition in selling switchboards and ancillary telephone equipment. AT&T was totally unprepared to meet the new competition. They lacked marketing personnel and marketing muscle. They realized that they had been pushing sales when they should have been paying attention to changing market forces. They are now involved in a crash effort to acquire marketing know-how.[15]
>
> American Hospital Supply Company enjoys market leadership in the hospital-supplies business, based largely on their extensive distribution and sales coverage. They are now facing new sophisticated competitors, such as P&G, who are attacking their established markets. AHS is now committed to transforming itself from a sales company to a marketing company.

---

[14] See J. Patrick Wright, *On a Clear Day You Can See General Motors* (New York: Avon Books, 1979), especially chapter 8.

[15] Bro Uttal, "Selling Is No Longer Mickey Mouse at A.T.&T.," *Fortune*, July 17, 1978, pp. 98–104.

The Chase Manhattan Bank of New York has watched Citibank, its main competitor, make one smart move after another, each time leaving Chase behind. Citibank has been systematically developing a marketing culture at the bank, while Chase has operated along traditional financial lines. Recently Chase started a whole program to educate its officers in modern marketing thinking.

These companies realized that they were weak in marketing and at a great disadvantage when competing against topflight marketing companies. Responding with traditional sales tactics was not enough. Sales managers want to spend more money and/or reduce prices. They think the answer lies in sales controls to get the sales force to work harder. But top management is becoming less confident in pure sales power. They want those responsible for sales to get smarter, not work harder. They want better analyses of the changing forces in the marketplace; they want better marketing strategies and plans; they want products that meet new and emerging customer needs.

Top management's challenge is to convert the company from a sales company into a modern marketing company. Management has to take several steps to create a genuine marketing culture in their company.

Presidential leadership. The president's leadership is a key prerequisite to establishing a modern marketing company. The vice-president of marketing cannot unilaterally direct other company officers to bend their efforts to serve customers. The company president must appreciate how marketing differs from sales, believe that marketing is a key to company growth and prosperity, and build marketing into speeches and decisions.

Marketing task force. The president should appoint a marketing task force to develop a plan for bringing modern marketing practices into the company. The task force should include the president, executive vice-president, the vice-presidents of sales, marketing, manufacturing, and finance, and a few other key individuals. They should examine the need for marketing, set objectives, anticipate problems in introducing it, and develop an overall strategy. For the next few years, this committee should meet periodically to measure progress and take new initiatives.

Outside marketing consultant. The marketing task force would probably benefit from outside consulting assistance in building a marketing culture at the company. Consulting firms have considerable experience in the problems of, and approaches to, bringing marketing thinking into a company.

A corporate marketing department. A key step is to establish a corporate marketing department. This department should review each division's marketing resources and needs. Often the division's general manager does not understand marketing and confuses it with sales. The division's sales group is usually headed by a sales vice-president who is not marketing oriented. To appoint a marketing vice-president over this person would be asking for trouble. Alternatives might be to add the outside marketer to the division as the executive vice-president, or to add this person as a marketing vice-president on a parallel level to the sales vice-president, or to put this person in charge of the division's planning. Ultimately each division will need a strong marketing vice-president if it wants to make marketing headway.

In-house marketing seminars.   The new corporate marketing department should sponsor in-house marketing seminars for top corporate management, divisional general managers, marketing and sales personnel, manufacturing personnel, R&D personnel, and so on. The seminars should first be presented to the higher levels of management and move to lower levels. The marketing seminars should aim to change the marketing beliefs, attitudes, and behavior of various executive groups.

Hiring marketing talent.   The company should consider hiring marketing talent away from leading marketing companies and also new M.B.A.s receiving their degrees in marketing. When Citibank got serious about marketing some years ago, they hired away several brand managers from General Foods.

Promoting market-oriented executives.   The company should try to promote market-oriented individuals to positions as division managers. A large public-accounting firm is currently sending out signals that it will give preference to market-oriented partners for branch manager positions.

Installing a modern marketing-planning system.   An excellent way to train people to think marketing is to install a modern market-oriented planning system. The planning format will require managers to first think about the marketing environment, marketing opportunities, competitive trends, and other marketing issues. Then marketing strategies and the sales forecast can be developed on a hard-data marketing base.

The job of creating a marketing orientation throughout the company is an uphill and never-ending battle. The purpose is not to resolve every issue in favor of the customer, no matter what the cost, but rather to help the other managers see that customers are the foundation of the company's business.[16]

Introducing Marketing in Nonbusiness Organizations

Most of the marketing examples in this book have been drawn from the business sector. Starting in the 1970s, there has been a "broadening of marketing" to cover all organizations because all organizations have marketing problems that can be aided by the application of marketing principles. The nonprofit and public sectors account for more than a quarter of the American economy and badly need improved management and marketing practices.

Lovelock and Weinberg have identified four characteristics of the nonbusiness sector:[17]

---

[16] For further discussion, see Edward S. McKay, *The Marketing Mystique* (New York: American Management Association, 1972), pp. 22–30.

[17] Christopher H. Lovelock and Charles B. Weinberg, "Public and Nonprofit Marketing Comes of Age," in *Review of Marketing 1978*, ed. Gerald Zaltman and Thomas V. Bonoma (Chicago: American Marketing Association, 1978), pp. 413–52.

☐ **Multiple publics.** Nonbusiness organizations have two major publics to market to: clients and funders. The former pose the problem of resource allocation and the latter, the problem of resource attraction. In addition, other publics surround the nonbusiness organization that require marketing planning. Thus a college directs marketing programs to prospective students, current students, parents of students, alumni, faculty, staff, local business firms, and local government agencies.

☐ **Multiple objectives.** Nonbusiness organizations tend to pursue several objectives rather than one, such as profits. This makes the task of strategy formulation more difficult.

☐ **Services rather than physical goods.** Most nonbusiness organizations produce services rather than goods. They therefore need to apply the principles of services marketing.

☐ **Public scrutiny and nonmarket pressures.** Nonbusiness organizations are subject to close public scrutiny because they are subsidized, tax exempt, and sometimes mandated into existence. They experience pressures from various publics and are expected to operate in the public interest. This means that their marketing activities will come under public scrutiny.

Many nonbusiness organizations—colleges, hospitals, social service organizations, charities, museums, performing arts groups, churches, government agencies—are experiencing difficult times. They are losing clients, on the one hand, and finding it more difficult to raise funds, on the other hand. This has increased their interest in the subject of marketing. Where marketing at one time was alien to these organizations, many are now embracing it almost uncritically as a possible panacea to their problems. Many nonbusiness organizations initially think of marketing as synonymous with promotion. They think their problems will be solved by creating more advertising, sales promotion, trained sales personnel, and publicity. Consider what several colleges did when they discovered "marketing":

☐ The admissions office at North Kentucky State University planned to release 103 balloons filled with scholarship offers; another college passed out promotional frisbees to high school students vacationing in Fort Lauderdale, Florida, during the Easter break.

☐ St. Joseph's College in Rensselaer, Indiana, achieved a 40 percent increase in freshmen admissions through advertising in *Seventeen* and on several Chicago and Indianapolis rock radio stations. The admissions office also planned to introduce tuition rebates for students who recruited new students ($100 finders' fee), but this was canceled.

☐ Bard College developed a same-day admission system for students who came to the campus and qualified.

☐ Worcester Polytechnic Institute offered to negotiate credit for previous study or work experience to shorten the degree period.

☐ The University of Richmond spent $13,000 to create a twelve-minute film to show to high school students.

☐ Drake University advertised on a billboard near Chicago's O'Hare Airport that "Drake is only 40 minutes from Chicago" (if one flies).

There are several dangers in equating marketing with intensified promotion. Aggressive promotion can create negative reactions among the school's constituencies, especially the faculty, who regard hard selling as offensive. Also hard promotion may turn off as many prospective students as it turns on. Aggressive promotion can attract the wrong students to the college—students who drop out when they discover they don't have the qualifications to do the work or that the college is not what it was advertised to be. Finally, this kind of marketing creates the illusion that the college has taken sufficient steps to reverse declining enrollment—an illusion that slows down the needed work on market definition and product improvement—the basis of all good marketing.

When a nonbusiness organization recognizes the need to adopt a thoroughgoing marketing orientation that includes all four Ps, it should appoint a marketing committee. The marketing committee's objectives are to identify the marketing problems and opportunities facing the organization, the major needs of various administrative units for marketing services, and the institution's possible need for a full-time director of marketing. As a part of this process, the marketing committee might be helped by a marketing consultant, who will point out some of the ways the organization can use marketing to improve its performance.

Eventually the organization should consider adding a marketing director or a marketing vice-president. A marketing director occupies a middle-management position and primarily provides marketing services to others in the institution, such as marketing research, advertising, publicity, and product testing. The institution might ultimately appoint a marketing vice-president, who will have more authority and influence. A marketing vice-president not only coordinates and supplies marketing services but also is in a position to influence the vice-presidents of personnel, operations, and finance as to the importance of focusing their effort on satisfying the organization's customers. Thus in a college setting, the marketing vice-president would try to get the deans, faculty, maintainance people, food-service managers, dormitory managers et al. to see their task as promoting the well-being and satisfaction of the student body.

MARKETING IMPLEMENTATION

Having looked at how business and nonbusiness organizations handle the marketing function, we now turn to the question of how marketing personnel can effectively implement marketing plans. A brilliant strategic marketing plan will count for little if it is not implemented properly.

> *Marketing implementation* **is the process that turns marketing plans into action assignments and ensures that such assignments are executed in a manner that accomplishes the plan's stated objectives.**

Whereas strategy addresses the *what* and *why* of marketing activities, implementation addresses the *who*, *where*, *when*, and *how*. Strategy and implementation are closely related in that one "layer" of strategy implies certain tactical implementation assignments at a lower level. For example, top management's strategic decision to "harvest" a product in the decline stage of its life cycle must be translated into specific budgeting changes allocating fewer funds for marketing programs, directions to sales people to change their selling emphasis, a reprinting of price lists with perhaps higher prices for the product, reassignment of personnel by ad agencies to different products in the line, and so on. Also implementation is tied to strategy in that anticipated difficulties in implementing a strategy may influence the choice of strategy.

Bonoma, in a study of the implementation problems of sixteen organizations, identified four areas that can influence the effective implementation of marketing programs:[18]

☐ Skills in recognizing and diagnosing a problem
☐ Skills in assessing the company level where the problem exists
☐ Skills in implementing plans
☐ Skills in evaluating implementation results

We will examine these areas in the following paragraphs.

Diagnostic Skills

The close interrelationship between strategy and implementation can pose difficult diagnostic problems when marketing program results do not fulfill their expectations. Was the low sales rate the result of poor strategy or poor implementation? Moreover, is the issue to determine what the problem *is* (diagnosis) or what should be *done* about it (action)? For each problem there are different sets of management "tools" and solutions.

Company Levels

Problems in marketing implementation can occur at any of three corporate levels.[19] One level is that of the *marketing functions* that must be performed in executing the marketing task—selling, licensing, advertising, new-product planning, channels of distribution, and so on. For example, how should the new-product-development function of a late entrant be organized in a high-loyalty market?

Another level is that of *marketing programs*—the synergistic blending of the marketing functions into a set of integrated activities. Pricing, promoting, and distributing a product line of oil filters to auto-parts retailers would exemplify a marketing program concern.

A third level of implementation is that of *marketing policies.* Here management is concerned with the directives that lead the marketing actors to understand what the organization stands for and does in marketing. Marketing leadership as well as the more concrete variables of compensation, recruiting, training, and selling policies communicates the marketing culture of the organization. The adoption of the societal marketing concept by company personnel in their dealings with customers, dealers, suppliers, and others requires clear marketing policies toward that end. Procter & Gamble is a good example of a company whose policies on handling customer complaints, developing new products, and so on, permeate all levels of operation. Bonoma

---

[18] Thomas V. Bonoma, "Marketing Implementation: Getting the Marketing Job Done," unpublished manuscript, 1982. Much of this section is based on Bonoma's work.

[19] Ibid., p. 6.

found that marketing policies had the greatest impact on effective implementation, followed by the competence with which the marketing functions were executed. Therefore the successful implementation of marketing programs depends upon establishing and implementing sound policies.

Marketing Implementation Skills

A set of skills must be practiced at each corporate "level"—functions, programs, policies—to achieve effective implementation. The four primary skills are allocating, monitoring, organizing, and interacting.[20]

Allocating skills are manifested in the competence with which marketing managers budget time, money, and personnel to functions, policies, or programs. For example, allocating field sales personnel to geographical regions is a common problem facing industrial products companies. Determining how much money to spend on trade shows (functions level) or what warranty work to perform on "marginal" products (policies level) are other problems demanding allocation skills.

Monitoring skills consists of developing and managing a system of controls to give feedback on the results of marketing actions. Controls may be of three types: annual-plan control, profitability control, and strategic control. (See Chapter 24.) From an implementation standpoint, we are primarily concerned with the first two types of controls.

Organizing skills are concerned with specifying the structure of relationships among marketing personnel to accomplish corporate objectives. Managing the degree of centralization and formalization built into the system and also understanding the informal marketing organization are important prerequisites to the development of effective implementation procedures. The interaction of the informal and formal systems will influence the effectiveness of many implementation activities.

Interacting skills involve the manager's ability to get things done by influencing others. Marketers must not only be capable of motivating the organization's own people toward effectively implementing the desired strategy, they must also motivate outsiders—marketing research firms, ad agencies, dealers, wholesalers, agents—whose objectives may not exactly parallel those of the organization. Managing conflict within a channel of distribution, for example, demands a high level of interaction skill.

By examining the four skills for each of the three levels, it is possible to identify many of the problem areas inherent in marketing implementation. The frequency with which each problem area arises in an organization may be related to the firm's size, its market position, or the industry growth rate in which the firm competes. However, excellence in marketing implementation requires management skill in each of the four areas (allocating, monitoring, organizing, interacting) at each of the three levels (functions, programs, policies).

Implementation-Evaluation Skills

Good performance in the marketplace does not necessarily prove that there was good marketing implementation. It is difficult to use performance to differentiate

---

[20] Ibid., p. 9.

between good strategy/poor implementation and poor strategy/good implementation. We can, however, do the spadework to evaluate a company's implementation effectiveness. Evidence of effective marketing implementation practice would include positive responses to the following questions:[21]

☐ Is there a clear marketing theme, strong marketing leadership, and a culture that promotes and provokes excellence?
☐ Is there subfunctional soundness in the company's marketing activities? Are the selling function's distribution, pricing, and advertising well managed?
☐ Do the company's marketing programs integrate and deliver marketing activities in a focused fashion to various customer groups?
☐ How good is marketing management at interacting with (a) other marketing-related staff, like sales, (b) other functions in the company, and (c) the customers and trade?
☐ What monitoring efforts are used by management to inform itself about not only its own moves but also customer and prospect groups?
☐ How good is management at allocating time, money, and people to marketing tasks?
☐ How is management organized, both to do marketing tasks and to deal with customer interactions? Are there easily accessed "organizational doors" open to the customers and the trade?

Separating the effects of strategy and implementation on market results will always be a difficult task. But stressing the need for corporate excellence in both marketing implementation activities and strategic marketing planning will lead to improved overall performance.

SUMMARY

This chapter examined how the marketing function is organized and marketing plans implemented in the modern organization.

The modern marketing department evolved through several stages. It started as a sales department, and later this department took on ancillary functions, such as advertising and marketing research. As the ancillary functions grew in importance, many companies created a separate marketing department to manage these other marketing activities. But the heads of sales and marketing often disagreed, and eventually the two departments were merged into a modern marketing department headed by a marketing vice-president. A modern marketing department, however, does not automatically create a modern marketing company unless the other officers accept and practice a customer orientation.

Modern marketing departments are organized in a number of ways. The most common form is the functional marketing organization in which marketing functions are headed by separate managers reporting to the marketing vice-president. Another form is the product management organization in which products are assigned to product managers, who work with functional specialists to develop and achieve their plans. Another form is the market management organization in which major markets are assigned to market managers, who work with functional specialists to develop and achieve their plans. Some large compa-

---

[21] For these and the following questions, see ibid., pp. 15–17.

nies use a product management and market management organization. Finally, multidivision companies usually operate a corporate marketing department and divisional marketing departments, with some variations as to the division of tasks.

Marketing must work smoothly with the other functions in a company. In its pursuit of customers' interests, marketing may come into conflict with R&D, engineering, purchasing, manufacturing, inventory, finance, accounting, credit, and other functions. These conflicts can be reduced when the company president commits the company to a customer orientation and when the marketing vice-president learns to work effectively with the other officers. Acquiring a modern marketing orientation requires presidential support, a marketing task force, outside marketing consulting help, a corporate marketing department, in-house marketing seminars, marketing talent hired from the outside and promoted inside, and a market-oriented marketing-planning system.

Those responsible for the marketing function must not only develop effective marketing plans but also implement them successfully. Marketing implementation is the process of turning plans into action assignments describing who does what, when, and how. Effective implementation requires skills in allocating monitoring, organizing, and interacting at the level of marketing functions, programs, and policies.

QUESTIONS

1. Choose a product or service and list some strategy-stage issues and some implementation-stage issues.

2. For the product or service discussed in question 1, indicate some specific problems of diagnosis and problems of action that could occur at the strategy and implementation stages.

3. For the product or service discussed in question 1, give an example of the problems that could arise at the function, program, and policy levels when implementing a marketing strategy.

4. In order to carry out a proposed national sales promotion, describe some of the departments whose efforts must be coordinated with those of the marketing department. Through what kind of planning device might these efforts be integrated?

5. Does it make organizational sense to combine the company's marketing department and public relations department under one vice-president?

6. A major airline's marketing department is presently organized on a functional basis: advertising, field sales, customer services, and so on. The airline is considering setting up a route-manager organization, with a manager assigned to each major route who would be to a route what a brand manager is to a brand. Do you think this is a good idea?

7. The General Electric Company does not have a corporate vice-president of marketing. Its vice-presidents of marketing are found in various sectors, groups, and divisions. General Electric does have a corporate vice-president of strategic planning. Do you think a corporate vice-president of marketing should be added?

8. In large railroads, the operations department usually holds dominant power. The needs of freight customers are accorded less weight than achieving operational efficiency. Suggest a strategy for establishing a companywide marketing orientation.

9. Describe some industrial situations where local marketing specialists would be of particular assistance to a company.

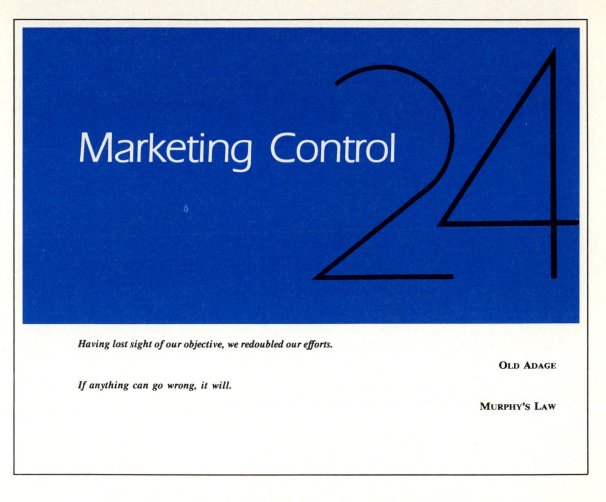

Marketing Control

24

Having lost sight of our objective, we redoubled our efforts.

OLD ADAGE

If anything can go wrong, it will.

MURPHY'S LAW

The marketing department's job is to plan and control marketing activity. Because many surprises will occur during the implementation of marketing plans, the marketing department has to engage in continuous monitoring and control of marketing activities. Marketing control systems are essential to make sure the company operates efficiently and effectively.

In spite of the need for effective marketing control, many companies have inadequate control procedures. This conclusion was reached in a private study of seventy-five companies of varying sizes in different industries. The main findings were:

☐ Smaller companies have poorer controls than larger companies. They do a poorer job of setting clear objectives and establishing systems to measure performance.

☐ Fewer than half of the companies know the profitability of their individual products. About one-third of the companies have no regular review procedure for spotting and deleting weak products.

☐ Almost half of the companies fail to compare their prices to competition, to analyze their warehousing and distribution costs, to analyze the causes of returned merchandise,

743

to conduct formal evaluations of advertising effectiveness, and to review their sales-force call reports.

☐ Many companies take four to eight weeks to develop control reports, and they are often inaccurate.

Marketing control, however, is far from being a single process. Four types of marketing control can be distinguished (Table 24–1).

In *annual-plan control* marketing personnel check ongoing performance against the annual plan and take corrective actions when necessary. *Profitability control* consists of efforts to determine the actual profitability of different products, territories, end-use markets, and trade channels. *Efficiency control* involves searching for ways to improve the impact of different marketing tools and expenditures. *Strategic control* consists of periodically examining whether the company's basic strategies are well matched to its opportunities. We now turn to these four types of marketing control.

TABLE 24–1

TYPES OF MARKETING CONTROL			
Type of Control	**Prime Responsibility**	**Purpose of Control**	**Approaches**
I. Annual-plan control	Top management Middle management	To examine whether the planned results are being achieved	Sales analysis Market-share analysis Sales-to-expense ratios Financial analysis Attitude tracking
II. Profitability control	Marketing controller	To examine where the company is making and losing money	Profitability by: product territory customer group trade channel order size
III. Efficiency control	Line and staff management Marketing controller	To evaluate and improve the spending efficiency and impact of marketing expenditures	Efficiency of sales force advertising sales promotion distribution
IV. Strategic control	Top management Marketing auditor	To examine whether the company is pursuing its best opportunities with respect to markets, products, and channels	Marketing-effectiveness rating instrument Marketing audit

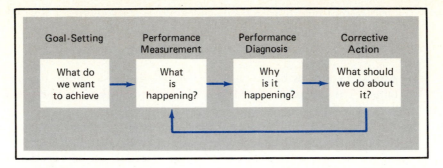

FIGURE 24-1
The Control Process

ANNUAL-PLAN CONTROL

The purpose of annual-plan control is to ensure that the company achieves the sales, profits, and other goals established in its annual plan. The heart of annual-plan control is *management by objectives*. Four steps are involved. (See Figure 24-1.) First, management must set monthly or quarterly goals in the annual plan as benchmarks. Second, management must monitor its performance in the marketplace. Third, management must determine the causes of any serious performance deviations. Fourth, management must take corrective action to close the gaps between its goals and performance. This may require changing the action programs or even changing the goals.

This model of control applies to all levels of the organization. Top management sets certain sales and profit goals for the year. These goals are elaborated into specific goals for each lower level of management. Thus each product manager is committed to attaining specified levels of sales and costs. Each regional and district sales manager and each sales representative is also committed to specific goals. Each period, top management sees the results and can ascertain where any short falls occurred and seek to find out why they occurred.

Managers use five tools to check on plan performance. They are sales analysis, market-share analysis, marketing expense-to-sales analysis, financial analysis, and customer-attitude tracking.

Sales Analysis

Sales analysis consists of measuring and evaluating actual sales in relation to sales goals. There are two specific tools in this connection.

Sales-variance analysis measures the relative contribution of different factors to a gap in sales performance. Suppose the annual plan called for selling 4,000 widgets in the first quarter at $1 a widget, or $4,000. At quarter's end, only 3,000 widgets were sold at .80¢ a widget, or $2,400. The sales performance variance is $1,600, or 40 percent of expected sales. The question arises: How much of this underperformance is due to the price decline and how much to the volume decline? The following calculation answers this question:

$$\text{Variance due to price decline} = (\$1.00 - .80\cent)(3,000) \qquad = \$\ \ 600 \qquad 37.5\%$$
$$\text{Variance due to volume decline} = (\$1.00)(4,000 - 3,000) = \$1,000 \qquad \underline{\ \ 62.5\%}$$
$$\hphantom{\text{Variance due to volume decline} = (\$1.00)(4,000 - 3,000) =} \underline{\$1,600} \qquad 100.0\%$$

Almost two-thirds of the sales variance is due to a failure to achieve the volume target. The company should look closely into why its expected sales volume was not achieved.[1]

Micro-sales analysis may provide the answer. *Micro-sales analysis* looks at specific products, territories, and so forth, that failed to produce their expected share of sales. Suppose the company sells in three territories, and expected sales were 1,500 units, 500 units, and 2,000 units, respectively, adding up to 4,000 widgets. The actual sales volume was 1,400 units, 525 units, and 1,075 units, respectively. Thus territory 1 showed a 7 percent shortfall in terms of expected sales; territory 2, a 5 percent surplus; and territory 3, a 46 percent shortfall! Territory 3 is causing most of the trouble. The sales vice-president can check into territory 3 to see which hypothesis explains the poor performance: Territory 3's sales representative is loafing or has a personal problem; a major competitor has entered this territory; or GNP is depressed in this territory.

Market-Share Analysis

Company sales do not reveal how well the company is doing relative to competitors. Suppose a company's sales increase. This could be due to improved economic conditions wherein all companies gained. Or it could be due to improved company performance in relation to its competitors. Management needs to track its market share. If the company's market share goes up, the company is gaining on competitors; if it goes down, the company is losing relative to competitors.

These conclusions from market-share analysis, however, are subject to certain qualifications:[2]

☐ **The assumption that outside forces affect all companies in the same way is often not true.** The U.S. surgeon general's report on the harmful consequences of cigarette smoking caused total cigarette sales to falter but not equally for all companies. Companies with a reputation for better filters were hurt less.

☐ **The assumption that a company's performance should be judged against the average performance of all companies is not always valid.** A company with greater than average opportunities should register a growing market share. If its market share remains constant, this may imply poor rather than average management.

☐ **If a new firm enters the industry, then every existing firm's market share may fall.** Here a decline in a company's market share does not mean that the company is performing any worse than other companies.

☐ **Sometimes a market-share decline is deliberately engineered by a company to improve**

---

[1] For further discussion, see James M. Hulbert and Norman E. Toy, "A Strategic Framework for Marketing Control," *Journal of Marketing*, April 1977, pp. 12–20.

[2] See Alfred R. Oxenfeldt, "How to Use Market-Share Measurement," *Harvard Business Review*, January-February 1969, pp. 59–68.

profits. For example, management may drop unprofitable customers or products to improve its profits.

☐ **Market share can fluctuate for many adventitious reasons.** For example, the market share can be affected by whether a large sale is made on the last day of the period or at the beginning of the next period. Not all shifts in market share have marketing significance.

The first step in using market-share analysis is to define which measure(s) of market share will be used. Four different measures are available:

☐ **Overall market share.** The company's overall market share is its sales expressed as a percentage of total industry sales. Two decisions are necessary to use this measure. The first is whether to use unit sales or dollar sales to express market share. Any changes in unit market share reflect volume changes among competitors, whereas changes in dollar market share reflect a combination of volume and price changes.

The other decision has to do with defining the total industry. For example, suppose Harley-Davidson wants to measure its share of the American motorcycle market. If motor scooters and motorized bikes are included, then Harley-Davidson's market share will be lower, since it does not produce these. The issue hinges on whether consumers perceive lighter cycles to be highly substitutable for standard motorcycles.

☐ **Served-market share.** The company's served-market share is its sales expressed as a percentage of the total sales to its served market. Its served market is the market that would be interested in the company's offering and is reached by the company's marketing effort. If Harley-Davidson only produces and sells expensive motorcycles on the East Coast, its served-market share would be its sales as a percentage of the total sales of expensive motorcycles sold on the East Coast. A company's served-market share is always larger than its overall market share. A company could have close to 100 percent of its served market and yet a relatively small percentage of the overall market. A company's first task is to try to get the lion's share of its served market. As it approaches this goal, it should add new product lines and territories to enlarge its served market.

☐ **Relative market share (to top three competitors).** This involves expressing the company's sales as a percentage of the combined sales of the three largest competitors. For example, if this company has 30 percent of the market, and its three largest competitors have 20, 10, and 10 percent, then this company's relative market share is 75 percent (=30/40). If each of the four companies had 25 percent of the market, then any company's relative market share would be 33 percent. Relative market shares above 33 percent are considered to be strong.

☐ **Relative market share (to leading competitor).** Some companies track their sales as a percentage of the leading competitor's sales. A relative market share greater than 100 percent indicates a market leader. A relative market share of exactly 100 percent means that the firm is tied for the lead. A rise in the company's relative market share means that it is gaining on its leading competitor.

After choosing which market share measure(s) to use, the company must find the necessary data. Overall market share is normally the most available measure, since it requires only total industry sales, and these are often available in government or trade association publications. Estimating served-market share is harder in that the company will have to keep track of its served market, which will be affected by changes in the company's product line and geographical market coverage, among other things. Estimating relative market shares is still harder, because the company will have to estimate the sales of specific competitors, who guard these figures. The company has to use indirect means, such as learning about competitors' purchase rate of raw materials or the number of shifts they are operating. In the consumer-goods area, individual brand shares are available through syndicated store and consumer panels.

The final requirement is to be able to interpret market share movements correctly. Market-share analysis, like sales analysis, increases in value when the data is disaggregated along various dimensions. The company might watch the progress of its market share by product line, customer type, region, or other breakdowns.

A useful way to analyze market-share movements is in terms of the following four components:

$$\begin{matrix}\text{Overall} \\ \text{market} \\ \text{share}\end{matrix} = \begin{matrix}\text{Customer} \\ \text{penetration}\end{matrix} \times \begin{matrix}\text{Customer} \\ \text{loyalty}\end{matrix} \times \begin{matrix}\text{Customer} \\ \text{selectivity}\end{matrix} \times \begin{matrix}\text{Price} \\ \text{selectivity}\end{matrix} \qquad (24\text{--}1)$$

where:

Customer penetration is the percentage of all customers who buy from this company.
Customer loyalty is the purchases from this company by its customers expressed as a percentage of their total purchases from all suppliers of the same products.
Customer selectivity is the size of the average customer purchase from the company expressed as a percentage of the size of the average customer purchase from an average company.
Price selectivity is the average price charged by this company expressed as a percentage of the average price charged by all companies.

Now suppose the company's dollar market share falls during the period. Equation (24–1) provides four possible explanations:

☐ The company lost some of its customers (lower customer penetration).
☐ Existing customers are buying a smaller share of their supplies from this company (lower customer loyalty).
☐ The company's remaining customers are smaller in size (lower customer selectivity).
☐ The company's price has slipped relative to competition (lower price selectivity).

By tracking these factors through time, the company can diagnose the underlying causes of market-share changes. Suppose at the beginning of the period, customer penetration was 60 percent, customer loyalty 50 percent, customer selectivity 80 percent, and price selectivity 125 percent. According to (24–1), the company's market share was 30 percent. Suppose that at the end of the period, the company's market share fell to 27 percent. In checking, the company finds customer penetration at 55 percent, customer loyalty at 50 percent, customer selectivity at 75 percent, and price selectivity at 130 percent. Clearly the market-share decline was due mainly to a loss of some customers (fall in customer penetration) who normally made larger-than-average purchases (fall in customer selectivity). The manager can now investigate why these customers were lost.

Marketing Expense-to-Sales Analysis

Annual-plan control requires making sure that the company is not overspending to achieve its sales goals. The key ratio to watch is *marketing expense-to-sales.* In one company this ratio was 30 percent and consisted of five component expense-to-sales ratios: *sales force-to-sales* (15 percent); *advertising-to-sales* (5 percent); *sales promotion-to-sales* (6 percent); *marketing research-to-sales* (1 percent); and *sales administration-to-sales* (3 percent).

Management needs to monitor these marketing-expense ratios. They will exhibit small fluctuations that can well be ignored. But fluctuations in excess of the normal range are a cause for concern. The period-to-period fluctuations in each ratio can be tracked on a *control chart* (Figure 24–2). This chart shows that the advertising expense-to-sales ratio normally fluctuates between 8 and 12 percent, say ninety-nine out of one hundred times. In the fifteenth period, however, the ratio exceeded the upper control limit. One of two hypotheses can explain this occurrence:

☐ **Hypothesis A:** The company still has good expense control, and this situation represents one of those rare chance events.

☐ **Hypothesis B:** The company has lost control over this expense and should find the cause.

FIGURE 24–2
The Control-Chart Model

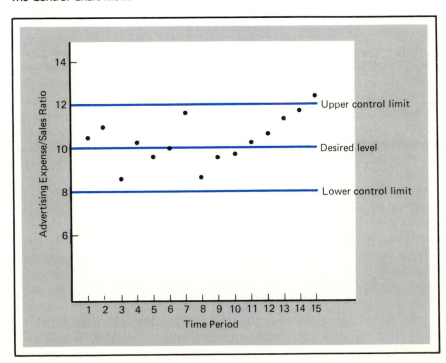

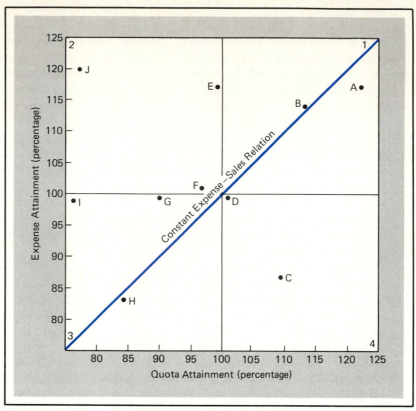

Source: Adapted from D. M. Phelps and J. H. Westing, *Marketing Management*, 3rd ed. (Homewood, Ill.: Richard D. Irwin, Inc., 1968), p. 754. © 1968 by Richard D. Irwin, Inc.

FIGURE 24–3
Comparison of Expense and Revenue Deviations by District

If hypothesis A is accepted, no investigation is made to determine whether the environment has changed. The risk in not investigating is that some real change may have occurred, and the company will fall behind. If hypothesis B is accepted, the environment is investigated at the risk that the investigation will uncover nothing and be a waste of time and effort.

The behavior of successive observations even within the control limits should be watched. Note that the level of the expense-to-sales ratio rose steadily from the ninth period onward. The probability of encountering six successive increases in what should be independent events is only one out of sixty-four.[3] This unusual pattern should have led to an investigation sometime before the fifteenth observation.

When an expense-to-sales ratio gets out of control, disaggregative data is needed to track down the problem. An *expense-to-sales deviation chart* can be used. Figure 24–3 shows the performances of different sales districts in terms of their sales-quota

---

[3] There is a ½ chance that a successive observation will be higher or lower. Therefore the probability of finding six successively higher values is given by $(\frac{1}{2})^6 = \frac{1}{64}$.

attainment and expense attainment in percentages. For example, district D achieved its sales quota close to the expected expense level. District B exceeded its quota, and its expenses are proportionately higher. The most troubling districts are in the second quadrant. For example, district J achieved less than 80 percent of its quota, and its expenses are disproportionately high. The next step is to prepare a chart for each deviant district showing sales representatives' standings. Within district J, for example, the poor performance might be associated with a few sales representatives.

Financial Analysis

The expenses-to-sales ratios should be analyzed in an overall financial framework to determine how and where the company is making its money. Marketers are increasingly using financial analysis to find profitable strategies and not just sales-building strategies.

Financial analysis is used by management to identify the factors that affect the company's *rate of return on net worth*. The main factors are shown in Figure 24–4 along with some illustrative numbers, for a large chain-store retailer. The retailer is earning a return on net worth of 12.5 percent. Many retailers would argue that this is too low and that retail organizations need at least a 15 percent return to fully satisfy their profit requirements. Some successful retailers routinely earn over 20 percent.

Next we notice that the return on net worth is the product of two ratios, the company's *return on assets* and its *financial leverage*. To improve its return on net worth, the company must either increase the ratio of its net profits to its assets or increase the ratio of its assets to its net worth. The company should analyze the

FIGURE 24–4
Financial Model of Return on Net Worth

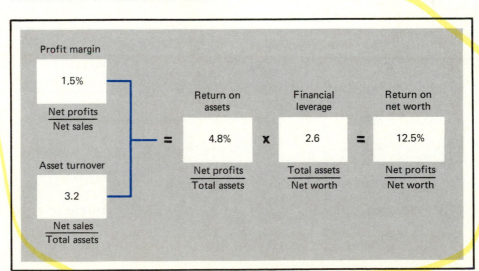

composition of its assets (i.e., cash, accounts receivable, inventory, and plant and equipment) and see if it can improve its assets management.

The return on assets is the product of two ratios, namely, the *profit margin* and the *asset turnover*. The profit margin seems low, while the asset turnover is more normal for retailing. Given the low profit margin, the marketing executive's task is to find ways to increase sales and/or lower costs.

Customer-Attitude Tracking

The preceding annual-plan control measures are largely financial and quantitative in character. They are important but not sufficient. Needed are qualitative measures that provide early warnings to management of impending market-share changes. Alert companies set up systems to track the attitudes of customers, dealers, and other marketing-system participants. By monitoring changing customer attitudes before they

FIGURE 24–5
A Consumer-Survey Feedback System

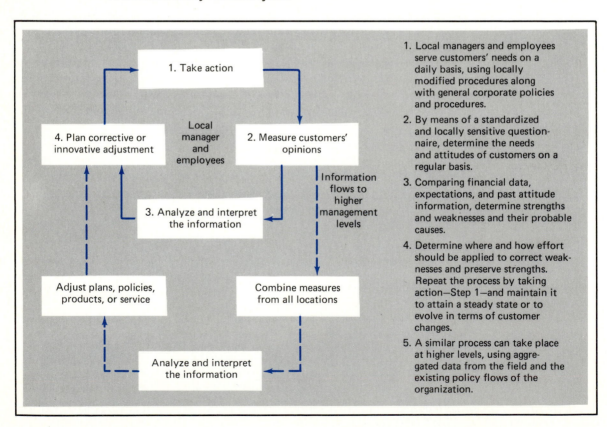

Source: Arthur J. Daltas, "Protecting Service Markets with Consumer Feedback," *The Cornell Hotel and Restaurant Administration Quarterly*, May 1977, p. 73–77.

affect sales, management can take earlier action. The main customer-attitude tracking systems are:

☐ **Complaint and suggestion systems.** Market-oriented companies record, analyze, and respond to written and oral complaints that come from customers. The complaints are tabulated, and management attempts to correct whatever is causing the most frequent types of complaints. Many retailers, such as hotels, restaurants, and banks, provide suggestion cards to encourage customer feedback. Market-oriented companies try to maximize the opportunities for consumer complaining so that management can get a more complete picture of customer reactions to their products and services.[4]

☐ **Customer panels.** Some companies run panels consisting of customers who have agreed to communicate their attitudes periodically through phone calls or mail questionnaires. These panels are more representative of the range of customer attitudes than customer complaint and suggestion systems.

☐ **Customer surveys.** Some companies periodically send out questionnaires to a random sample of customers to evaluate the friendliness of the staff, the quality of the service, and so on. The customers answer these questions on a five-point scale (very dissatisfied, dissatisfied, neutral, satisfied, very satisfied). The responses are summarized and go both to local managers and to higher-management levels, as illustrated in Figure 24–5. Local managers see how the various components of their service were rated in the current period compared to the last period, to the average of all the local units, and to the standard. This system improves the staff's motivation to provide good customer service in the knowledge that their ratings will go to higher management.[5]

Corrective Action

When performance starts deviating too much from the plan's goals, management needs to undertake corrective actions. Consider the following case:

> A large fertilizer company's sales were lagging behind its goals. The industry was marked by excess capacity and rampant price cutting.

In dealing with the situation, the company went through a cycle of increasingly drastic actions:

1. **Production cutting.** The company ordered cutbacks in production.
2. **Price cutting.** The company began to cut its prices selectively.
3. **Increased pressure on sales force.** The company put more pressure on its sales force to meet their quotas. The sales representatives started "beating down" doors, pressuring customers to buy more or to buy before the end of the year.
4. **Fringe expenditure cutting.** The company cut the budgets for personnel hiring and training, advertising, public relations, charities, and research and development.
5. **Personnel cuts.** The company began to lay off, retire, or fire personnel.
6. **Bookkeeping adjustment.** The company undertook some fancy bookkeeping to produce a better picture, including changing the depreciation base, recording purchases as capital

---

[4] See Claes Fornell, "Complaint Management and Marketing Performance," unpublished paper, Graduate School of Management, Northwestern University, Evanston, Ill., October 1978.

[5] For an application to a hotel chain, see Arthur J. Daltas, "Protecting Service Markets with Consumer Feedback," *The Cornell Hotel and Restaurant Administration Quarterly*, May 1977, pp. 73–77.

items rather than as expenses, selling some company assets for leaseback, and recording sales to phantom buyers.

7. **Investment cutting.** The company began to cut its investment in plant and equipment.

8. **Selling property.** The company decided to sell some of its product lines to other companies.

9. **Selling the company.** The company started to consider selling out or merging with another company.

PROFITABILITY CONTROL

Besides annual-plan control, companies need to measure the profitability of their various products, territories, customer groups, trade channels, and order sizes. This information will help management determine whether any products or marketing activities should be expanded, reduced, or eliminated.

Methodology of Marketing-Profitability Analysis

We shall illustrate the steps in marketing-profitability analysis with the following example:

> The marketing vice-president of a lawnmower company wants to determine the profitability of selling its lawnmower through three types of retail channels: hardware stores, garden supply shops, and department stores. Its profit-and-loss statement is shown in Table 24–2.

Step 1: Identifying the functional expenses. Assume that the expenses listed in Table 24–2 are incurred to sell the product, advertise it, pack and deliver it, and bill and collect for it. The first task is to measure how much of each expense was incurred in each activity.

Suppose that most salary expense went to sales representatives and the rest went to an advertising manager, packing and delivery help, and an office accountant.

TABLE 24–2

A SIMPLIFIED PROFIT-AND-LOSS STATEMENT

Sales		$60,000
Cost of goods sold		39,000
Gross margin		$21,000
Expenses		
Salaries	$9,300	
Rent	3,000	
Supplies	3,500	
		15,800
Net profit		$ 5,200

TABLE 24–3

MAPPING NATURAL EXPENSES INTO FUNCTIONAL EXPENSES					
Natural Accounts	Total	Selling	Advertising	Packing and Delivery	Billing and Collecting
Salaries	$ 9,300	$5,100	$1,200	$1,400	$1,600
Rent	3,000	—	400	2,000	600
Supplies	3,500	400	1,500	1,400	200
	$15,800	$5,500	$3,100	$4,800	$2,400

Let the breakdown of the $9,300 be $5,100, $1,200, $1,400, and $1,600, respectively. Table 24–3 shows the allocation of the salary expense to these four activities.

Table 24–3 also shows the rent account of $3,000 as allocated to the four activities. Since the sales representatives work away from the office, none of the building's rent expense is assigned to selling. Most of the expenses for floor space and rented equipment are in connection with packing and delivery. A small portion of the floor space is used by the advertising manager and office accountant.

Finally, the supplies account covers promotional materials, packing materials, fuel purchases for delivery, and home-office stationery. The $3,500 in this account is reassigned to the functional uses made of the supplies. Table 24–3 summarizes how the natural expenses of $15,800 were translated into functional expenses.

Step 2: Assigning the functional expenses to the marketing entities.   The next task is to measure how much functional expense was associated with selling through each type of channel. Consider the selling effort. The selling effort is indicated by the number of sales made in each channel. This is found in the selling column of Table 24–4. Altogether 275 sales calls were made during the period. Since the total selling expense amounted to $5,500 (see Table 24–4), the selling expense per call averaged $20.

Advertising expense can be allocated according to the number of ads addressed to the different channels. Since there were 100 ads altogether, the average ad cost $31.

The packing and delivery expense is allocated according to the number of orders placed by each type of channel; this same basis was used for allocating billing and collection expense.

Step 3: Preparing a profit-and-loss statement for each marketing entity.   A profit-and-loss statement can now be prepared for each type of channel. The results are shown in Table 24–5. Since hardware stores accounted for one-half of total sales ($30,000 out of $60,000), this channel is charged with half of the cost of goods sold ($19,500 out of $39,000). This leaves a gross margin from hardware stores of $10,500. From this must be deducted the proportions of the functional expenses

Marketing Control   **755**

TABLE 24-4

BASES FOR ALLOCATING FUNCTIONAL EXPENSES TO CHANNELS

Channel Type	Selling	Advertising	Packing and Delivery	Billing and Collecting
	No. of Sales Calls in Period	No. of Advertise- ments	No. of Orders Placed in Period	No. of Orders Placed in Period
Hardware	200	50	50	50
Garden supply	65	20	21	21
Department stores	10	30	9	9
	275	100	80	80
Functional expense	$5,500	$3,100	$4,800	$2,400
No. of units	275	100	80	80
Equals	$20	$31	$60	$30

that hardware stores consumed. According to Table 24–5, hardware stores received 200 out of 275 total sales calls. At an imputed value of $20 a call, hardware stores have to be charged with a $4,000 selling expense. Table 24–5 also shows that hardware stores were the target of 50 ads. At $31 an ad, the hardware stores are charged with $1,550 of advertising. The same reasoning applies in computing the share of the other functional expenses to charge to hardware stores. The result is that hardware

TABLE 24-5

PROFIT-AND-LOSS STATEMENTS FOR CHANNELS

	Hardware	Garden Supply	Dept. Stores	Whole Company
Sales	$30,000	$10,000	$20,000	$60,000
Cost of goods sold	19,500	6,500	13,000	39,000
Gross margin	$10,500	$ 3,500	$ 7,000	$21,000
Expenses				
Selling ($20 per call)	$ 4,000	$ 1,300	$ 200	$ 5,500
Advertising ($31 per advertisement)	1,550	620	930	3,100
Packing and delivery ($60 per order)	3,000	1,260	540	4,800
Billing ($30 per order)	1,500	630	270	2,400
Total expenses	$10,050	$ 3,810	$ 1,940	$15,800
Net profit (or loss)	$ 450	$ (310)	$ 5,060	$ 5,200

stores gave rise to $10,050 of the total expenses. Subtracting this from the gross margin, the profit of selling through hardware stores is only $450.

This analysis is repeated for the other channels. The company is losing money in selling through garden supply shops and makes virtually all of its profits in selling through department stores. Notice that the gross sales through each channel are not a reliable indicator of the net profits being made in each channel.

Determining the Best Corrective Action

It would be naive to conclude that garden supply shops and possibly hardware stores should be dropped in order to concentrate on department stores. The following questions would need to be answered first:

☐ To what extent do buyers buy on the basis of the type of retail outlet versus the brand? Would they seek out the brand in those channels that are not eliminated?
☐ What are the trends with respect to the importance of these three channels?
☐ Have company marketing strategies directed at the three channels been optimal?

On the basis of the answers, marketing management can evaluate a number of alternative actions:

☐ **Establish a special charge for handling smaller orders to encourage larger orders.** This move assumes that small orders are a cause of the relative unprofitability of dealing with garden supply shops and hardware stores.
☐ **Give more promotional aid to garden supply shops and hardware stores.** This assumes that the managers of these stores could increase their sales with more training or promotional materials.
☐ **Reduce the number of sales calls and the amount of advertising going to garden supply shops and hardware stores.** This assumes that some costs can be saved without seriously reducing sales to these channels.
☐ **Do nothing.** This assumes that current marketing efforts are optimal and either that marketing trends point to an imminent profit improvement in the weaker channels or that dropping any channel would reduce profits because of repercussions on production costs or on demand.
☐ **Don't abandon any channel as a whole but only the weakest retail units in each channel.** This assumes that a detailed cost study would reveal many profitable garden shops and hardware stores whose profits are concealed by the poor performance of other stores in these categories.

In general, marketing-profitability analysis indicates the relative profitability of different channels, products, territories, or other marketing entities.[6] It does not prove that the best course of action is to drop the unprofitable marketing entities, nor does it capture the likely profit improvement if these marginal marketing entities are dropped.

---

[6] For another example, see Leland L. Beik and Stephen L. Buzby, "Profitability Analyses by Market Segments," *Journal of Marketing*, June 1973, pp. 48–53.

Direct versus Full Costing

Like all information tools, marketing-profitability analysis can lead or mislead marketing executives, depending upon the degree of their understanding of its methods and limitations. The example showed some arbitrariness in the choice of bases for allocating the functional expenses to the marketing entities being evaluated. Thus the "number of sales calls" was used to allocate selling expenses, when in principle "number of sales man-hours" is a more accurate indicator of cost. The former base was used because it involves less record keeping and computation. These approximations may not involve too much inaccuracy, but marketing executives should perceive this judgmental element in determining distribution costs.[7]

Far more serious is another judgmental element affecting the computation of marketing costs, namely, whether to allocate *full costs* or only *direct and traceable costs.* The example sidestepped this problem by assuming only simple costs that fit in with marketing activities. But the question cannot be avoided in the actual analysis of marketing costs. Three types of costs have to be distinguished:

☐ **Direct costs.** These are costs that can be assigned directly to the marketing entities that give rise to them. For example, sales commissions are a direct cost in a profitability analysis of sales territories, sales representatives, or customers. Advertising expenditures are a direct cost in a profitability analysis of products to the extent that each advertisement promotes only one company product. Other direct costs for specific purposes are sales-force salaries, supplies, and traveling expenses.

☐ **Traceable common costs.** These are costs that can be assigned only indirectly, but on a plausible basis, to the marketing entities. In the example rent was analyzed in this way. The company's floor space was needed for three different marketing activities, and an estimate was made of how much floor space supported each activity.

☐ **Nontraceable common costs.** These are costs whose allocation to the marketing entities is highly arbitrary. Consider "corporate image" expenditures. To allocate them equally to all products would be arbitrary because all products do not benefit equally from corporate image making. To allocate them proportionately to the sales of the various products would be arbitrary because relative product sales reflect many factors besides corporate image making. Other typical examples of difficult-to-assign common costs are management salaries, taxes, interest, and other types of overhead.

There is no controversy concerning the inclusion of direct costs in marketing cost analysis. There is a small amount of controversy concerning the inclusion of traceable common costs. Traceable common costs lump together costs that would change with the scale of marketing activity and costs that probably would not change in the near future. If the lawnmower company drops garden supply shops, it is likely to continue to pay the same rent for contractual reasons. In this event its profits would not rise immediately by the amount of the present loss in selling to garden supply shops ($310). The profit figures are more meaningful when traceable costs can be eliminated.

The major controversy concerns whether the nontraceable common costs should be allocated to the marketing entities. Such allocation is called the *full-cost approach,*

---

[7] For common bases of allocation, see Charles H. Sevin, *Marketing Productivity Analysis* (New York: McGraw-Hill Book Co., 1965).

and its advocates defend it on the grounds that all costs ultimately must be imputed in order to determine true profitability. But this argument confuses the use of accounting for financial reporting with the use of accounting to provide a quantitative basis for decision making and profit planning. Full costing has three major weaknesses:

☐ The relative profitability of different marketing entities can shift quite radically when an arbitrary way to allocate nontraceable common costs is replaced by another. This weakens confidence in the tool.
☐ The arbitrariness demoralizes managers, who feel that their performance is judged adversely.
☐ The inclusion of nontraceable common costs may weaken efforts at real cost control. Operating management is most effective in controlling direct costs and traceable common costs. Arbitrary assignments of nontraceable common costs may lead them to spend their time fighting the arbitrary cost allocations rather than managing their controllable costs well.

EFFICIENCY CONTROL

Suppose a profitability analysis reveals that the company is earning poor profits in connection with certain products, territories, or markets. The question is whether there are more efficient ways to manage the sales force, advertising, sales promotion, and distribution in connection with these poorer-performing marketing entities.

Sales-Force Efficiency

Sales managers at each level—regional, district, and area—should keep track of several key indicators of sales-force efficiency in their territory. They are:

☐ Average number of sales calls per salesperson per day
☐ Average sales-call time per contact
☐ Average revenue per sales call
☐ Average cost per sales call
☐ Entertainment cost per sales call
☐ Percentage of orders per 100 sales calls
☐ Number of new customers per period
☐ Number of lost customers per period
☐ Sales-force cost as a percentage of total sales

An analysis of these statistics will raise useful questions such as: Are sales representatives making too few calls per day? Are they spending too much time per call? Are they spending too much on entertainment? Are they closing enough orders per hundred calls? Are they producing enough new customers and holding onto the old customers?

When a company starts investigating sales-force efficiency, it can often find a number of areas for improvement. General Electric was able to reduce the size of one of its divisional sales forces without any sales loss after discovering that sales representatives were making too many calls on customers. A large airline found that its sales representatives were both selling and servicing and transferred the servicing function to lower-paid clerks. Another company conducted time-and-duty studies and found ways to reduce the ratio of idle-to-productive time.

Advertising Efficiency

Many managers feel that it is almost impossible to measure what they are getting for their advertising dollars. But an effort should be made to keep track of at least the following statistics:

☐ Advertising cost per thousand buyers reached overall, for each media category, and each media vehicle
☐ Percentage of audience who noted, saw/associated, and read most for each media vehicle
☐ Consumer opinions on the ad content and effectiveness
☐ Before-after measures of attitude toward the product
☐ Number of inquiries stimulated by the ad
☐ Cost per inquiry

Management can undertake a number of steps to improve advertising efficiency, including doing a better job of positioning the product, defining advertising objectives, pretesting messages, using the computer to guide the selection of advertising media, looking for better media buys, and doing advertising posttesting.

Sales Promotion Efficiency

Sales promotion includes dozens of devices for stimulating buyer interest and product trial. In order to improve the sales promotion efficiency, management should keep records on each sales promotion, its costs, and its impact on sales. Management should watch the following statistics:

☐ Percentage of sales sold on deal
☐ Display costs per sales dollar
☐ Percentage of coupons redeemed
☐ Number of inquiries resulting from a demonstration

If a sales promotion manager is appointed, that manager can observe the results of different sales promotions and advise product managers on the most cost-effective promotions to use.

Distribution Efficiency

Management needs to search for distribution economies. Several models are available for improving inventory control, warehouse locations, and transportation modes. Improvement of local delivery costs is also possible, as the following example shows:

> **Wholesale bakers** face increased competition from chain bakers. They are especially at a disadvantage in the physical distribution of bread. The wholesale bakers must make more stops and deliver less bread per stop. Furthermore the driver typically loads each store's shelf, while the chain bakery leaves the bread at the chain's unloading platform to be placed on the shelf by store personnel. This led the American Bakers' Association to investigate whether more efficient bread handling procedures were achievable. A systems engineering study was conducted. The bread delivery operation was studied in minute detail from the time of truck loading to the time of shelving. As a result of riding with the drivers and observing procedures, the engineers recommended several changes. Economies could be secured from more scientific routing; from a relocation of the truck's door from the back of the trailer to the driver's side; and from the development of preshelved racks. These economies were always available but not recognized until competitive pressure increased the need for improved efficiency.

STRATEGIC CONTROL

From time to time, companies must undertake a critical review of their overall marketing effectiveness. Marketing is an area where rapid obsolescence of objectives, policies, strategies, and programs is a constant possibility. Each company should periodically reassess its overall approach to the marketplace. Two tools are available, namely a *marketing-effectiveness rating review* and a *marketing audit*.

Marketing-Effectiveness Rating Review

Here is an actual situation.

> The president of a major industrial-equipment company reviewed the annual business plans of various divisions and found several divisional plans lacking in marketing substance. He called in the corporate vice-president of marketing and said:
>
> > I am not happy with the quality of marketing in our divisions. It is very uneven. I want you to find out which of our divisions are strong, average, and weak in marketing. I want to know if they understand and are practicing customer-oriented marketing. I want a marketing score for each division. For each marketing-deficient division, I want a plan for improving its marketing effectiveness over the next few years. I want evidence next year that each marketing-deficient division is making progress toward a marketing orientation.
>
> The corporate marketing vice-president agreed, recognizing that it was a formidable task. His first inclination was to base the evaluation of marketing effectiveness on each division's performance in sales growth, market share, and profitability. His thinking was that high-performing divisions had good marketing leadership and poor-performing divisions had poor marketing leadership.

Actually marketing effectiveness is not necessarily revealed by current marketing performance. Good results may be due to a division's being in the right place at the right time, rather than having effective marketing management. Improvements in that division's marketing might boost results from good to excellent. Another division might have poor results in spite of excellent marketing planning. Replacing the present marketing managers might only make things worse.

The marketing effectiveness of a company or division is reflected in the degree to which it exhibits five major attributes of a marketing orientation: *customer philosophy, integrated marketing organization, adequate marketing information, strategic orientation*, and *operational efficiency*. Each attribute can be measured. Table 24–6

TABLE 24–6

MARKETING-EFFECTIVENESS RATING INSTRUMENT (CHECK ONE ANSWER TO EACH QUESTION)

CUSTOMER PHILOSOPHY

    A. Does management recognize the importance of designing the company to serve the needs and wants of chosen markets?

Score

0 ☐ Management primarily thinks in terms of selling current and new products to whoever will buy them.

1 ☐ Management thinks in terms of serving a wide range of markets and needs with equal effectiveness.

2 ☐ Management thinks in terms of serving the needs and wants of well-defined markets chosen for their long-run growth and profit potential for the company.

    B. Does management develop different offerings and marketing plans for different segments of the market?

0 ☐ No.

1 ☐ Somewhat.

2 ☐ To a good extent.

    C. Does management take a whole marketing system view (suppliers, channels, competitors, customers, environment) in planning its business?

0 ☐ No. Management concentrates on selling and servicing its immediate customers.

1 ☐ Somewhat. Management takes a long view of its channels although the bulk of its effort goes to selling and servicing the immediate customers.

2 ☐ Yes. Management takes a whole marketing systems view recognizing the threats and opportunities created for the company by changes in any part of the system.

INTEGRATED MARKETING ORGANIZATION

    D. Is there high-level marketing integration and control of the major marketing functions?

0 ☐ No. Sales and other marketing functions are not integrated at the top and there is some unproductive conflict.

1 ☐ Somewhat. There is formal integration and control of the major marketing functions but less than satisfactory coordination and cooperation.

2 ☐ Yes. The major marketing functions are effectively integrated.

    E. Does marketing management work well with management in research, manufacturing, purchasing, physical distribution, and finance?

0 ☐ No. There are complaints that marketing is unreasonable in the demands and costs it places on other departments.

1 ☐ Somewhat. The relations are amicable although each department pretty much acts to serve its own power interests.

2 ☐ Yes. The departments cooperate effectively and resolve issues in the best interest of the company as a whole.

TABLE 24–6 Cont.

F. How well-organized is the new product process?

0 ☐ The system is ill-defined and poorly handled.

1 ☐ The system formally exists but lacks sophistication.

2 ☐ The system is well-structured and professionally staffed.

ADEQUATE MARKETING INFORMATION

G. When were the latest marketing research studies of customers, buying influences, channels, and competitors conducted?

0 ☐ Several years ago.

1 ☐ A few years ago.

2 ☐ Recently.

H. How well does management know the sales potential and profitability of different market segments, customers, territories, products, channels, and order sizes?

0 ☐ Not at all.

1 ☐ Somewhat.

2 ☐ Very well.

I. What effort is expended to measure the cost effectiveness of different marketing expenditures?

0 ☐ Little or no effort.

1 ☐ Some effort.

2 ☐ Substantial effort.

STRATEGIC ORIENTATION

J. What is the extent of formal marketing planning?

0 ☐ Management does little or no formal marketing planning.

1 ☐ Management develops an annual marketing plan.

2 ☐ Management develops a detailed annual marketing plan and a careful long-range plan that is updated annually.

K. What is the quality of the current marketing strategy?

0 ☐ The current strategy is not clear.

1 ☐ The current strategy is clear and represents a continuation of traditional strategy.

2 ☐ The current strategy is clear, innovative, data-based, and well-reasoned.

L. What is the extent of contingency thinking and planning?

0 ☐ Management does little or no contingency thinking.

1 ☐ Management does some contingency thinking although little formal contingency planning.

2 ☐ Management formally identifies the most important contingencies and develops contingency plans.

OPERATIONAL EFFICIENCY

M. How well is the marketing thinking at the top communicated and implemented down the line?

0 ☐ Poorly.

1 ☐ Fairly.

2 ☐ Successfully.

TABLE 24–6 Cont.

N. Is management doing an effective job with the marketing resources?

0 ☐ No. The marketing resources are inadequate for the job to be done.

1 ☐ Somewhat. The marketing resources are adequate but they are not employed optimally.

2 ☐ Yes. The marketing resources are adequate and are deployed efficiently.

O. Does management show a good capacity to react quickly and effectively to on-the-spot developments?

0 ☐ No. Sales and market information is not very current and management reaction time is slow.

1 ☐ Somewhat. Management receives fairly up-to-date sales and market information; management reaction time varies.

2 ☐ Yes. Management has installed systems yielding highly current information and fast reaction time.

TOTAL SCORE

The instrument is used in the following way. The appropriate answer is checked for each question. The scores are added—the total will be somewhere between 0 and 30. The following scale shows the level of marketing effectiveness:

0–5 = None	16–20 = Good
6–10 = Poor	21–25 = Very good
11–15 = Fair	26–30 = Superior

SOURCE: Philip Kotler, "From Sales Obsession to Marketing Effectiveness," **Harvard Business Review,** November-December 1977, pp. 67–75. Copyright © 1977 by the President and Fellows of Harvard College: all rights reserved.

presents a *marketing-effectiveness rating instrument* based on these five attributes. This instrument is filled out by marketing and other managers in the division. The scores are then summarized.

The instrument has been tested in a number of companies, and very few achieve scores within the superior range of 26 to 30 points. The few include well-known master marketers such as Procter & Gamble, Avon, McDonald's, IBM, General Electric, and Caterpillar. Most companies and divisions receive scores in the fair-to-good range, indicating that their own managers see room for marketing improvement. The scores of each attribute indicate which elements of effective marketing action need the most attention. Divisional management can then establish a plan for correcting its major marketing weaknesses.[8]

The Marketing Audit

Those companies and divisions that discover marketing weakness through applying the marketing-effectiveness rating review should undertake a more thorough study known as a *marketing audit.*[9]

---

[8] For further discussion of this instrument, see Philip Kotler, "From Sales Obsession to Marketing Effectiveness," *Harvard Business Review*, November-December 1977, pp. 67–75.

[9] See Philip Kotler, William Gregor, and William Rodgers, "The Marketing Audit Comes of Age," *Sloan Management Review*, winter 1977, pp. 25–43.

We define *marketing audit* as follows:

A *marketing audit* is a *comprehensive*, *systematic*, *independent*, and *periodic* examination of a company's—or business unit's—marketing environment, objectives, strategies, and activities with a view to determining problem areas and opportunities and recommending a plan of action to improve the company's marketing performance.

Let us examine the marketing audit's four characteristics:

☐ **Comprehensive.** The marketing audit covers all the major marketing activities of a business, not just a few trouble spots. It would be called a functional audit if it covered only the sales force, or pricing, or some other marketing activity. Although functional audits are useful, they sometimes mislead management as to the real source of its problem. Excessive sales-force turnover, for example, may be a symptom not of poor sales-force training or compensation but of weak company products and promotion. A comprehensive marketing audit usually is more effective in locating the real source of the company's marketing problems.

☐ **Systematic.** The marketing audit involves an orderly sequence of diagnostic steps covering the organization's marketing environment, internal marketing system, and specific marketing activities. The diagnosis is followed by a corrective-action plan involving both short-run and long-run proposals to improve the organization's overall marketing effectiveness.

☐ **Independent.** A marketing audit can be conducted in six ways:[10] (1) self-audit, (2) audit from across, (3) audit from above, (4) company auditing office, (5) company task-force audit, and (6) outsider audit. Self-audits, where managers use a checklist to rate their own operations, may be useful, but most experts agree that the self-audit lacks objectivity and independence.[11] The 3M Company has made good use of a corporate auditing office, which provides marketing audit services to divisions on request.[12] Generally speaking, however, the best audits are likely to come from experienced outside consultants, who have the necessary objectivity and independence, broad experience in a number of industries, some familiarity with this industry, and the undivided time and attention to give to the audit.

☐ **Periodic.** Typically marketing audits are initiated only after sales have turned down, sales-force morale has fallen, and other company problems have occurred. Ironically companies are thrown into a crisis partly because they failed to review their marketing operations during good times. A periodic marketing audit can benefit companies in good health as well as those in trouble. "No marketing operation is ever so good that it cannot be improved. Even the best can be made better. In fact, even the best *must* be better, for few if any marketing operations can remain successful over the years by maintaining the status quo."[13]

Marketing audit procedure.   A marketing audit starts with a meeting between the company officer(s) and the marketing auditor(s) to work out an agreement on the objectives, coverage, depth, data sources, report format, and the time period

---

[10] Some of these approaches are briefly discussed by Alfred Oxenfeldt and Richard D. Crisp in their respective articles in *Analyzing and Improving Marketing Performance*, report no. 32 (New York: American Management Association, 1959).

[11] However, a very useful set of checklists for a marketing self-audit can be found in Mike Wilson, *The Management of Marketing* (Westmead, England: Gover Publishing Co., 1980).

[12] Kotler, Gregor, and Rodgers, "Marketing Audit Comes of Age," p. 31.

[13] Abe Shuchman, "The Marketing Audit: Its Nature, Purposes, and Problems," in Oxenfeldt and Crisp, *Marketing Performance*, pp. 16–17.

for the audit. A detailed plan as to who is to be interviewed, the questions to be asked, the time and place of contact, and so on, is carefully prepared so that auditing time and cost are kept to a minimum. The cardinal rule in marketing auditing is, don't rely solely on the company's executives for data and opinion. Customers, dealers, and other outside groups must be interviewed. Many companies do not really know how their customers and dealers see them, nor do they fully understand customer needs.

When the data-gathering phase is over, the marketing auditor presents the main findings and recommendations. A valuable aspect of the marketing audit is the process that the managers go through to assimilate, debate, and develop new concepts of needed marketing action.

Components of the marketing audit.   The marketing audit consists of examining six major components of the company's marketing situation. The six components are described below, and the major auditing questions are listed in Table 24–7.

☐ **Marketing-environment audit.** This audit calls for analyzing major macroenvironment forces and trends in the key components of the company's task environment: markets, customers, competitors, distributors, and dealers, suppliers, and facilitators.

☐ **Marketing-strategy audit.** This audit calls for reviewing the company's marketing objectives and marketing strategy to appraise how well these are adapted to the current and forecasted marketing environment.

☐ **Marketing-organization audit.** This audit calls for evaluating the capability of the marketing organization implementing the necessary strategy for the forecasted environment.

☐ **Marketing-systems audit.** This audit involves examining the quality of the company's systems for analysis, planning, and control.

☐ **Marketing-productivity audit.** This audit calls for examining the profitability of different marketing entities and the cost effectiveness of different marketing expenditures.

☐ **Marketing-function audits.** These audits consist of in-depth evaluations of major marketing-mix components, namely products, price, distribution, sales force, advertising, promotion, and publicity.

Example of a marketing audit.[14]   O'Brien Candy Company is a medium-sized candy company located in the Midwest. In the last two years, its sales and profits have barely held their own. Top management feels that the trouble lies with the sales force; they don't "work hard or smart enough." To correct the problem, management plans to introduce a new incentive-compensation system and hire a sales-force trainer to train the sales force in modern merchandising and selling techniques. Before doing this, however, they decide to hire a marketing consultant to do a marketing audit. The auditor conducts a number of interviews with management, customers, sales representatives, and dealers and examines various data. Here is what the auditor finds:

☐ The company's product line consists primarily of eighteen products, mostly candy bars. Its two leading brands are in the mature stage of their life cycles and account for 76

---

[14] This case is adapted with permission from the excellent article by Dr. Ernst A. Tirmann, "Should Your Marketing be Audited?" *European Business,* Autumn 1971, pp. 49–56.

TABLE 24-7

COMPONENTS OF A MARKETING AUDIT

Part I. Marketing Environment Audit

MACROENVIRONMENT

A. Demographic

1. What major demographic developments and trends pose opportunities or threats to this company?
2. What actions has the company taken in response to these developments and trends?

B. Economic

1. What major developments in income, prices, savings, and credit will affect the company?
2. What actions has the company been taking in response to these developments and trends?

C. Ecological

1. What is the outlook for the cost and availability of natural resources and energy needed by the company?
2. What concerns have been expressed about the company's role in pollution and conservation, and what steps has the company taken?

D. Technological

1. What major changes are occurring in product technology? In process technology? What is the company's position in these technologies?
2. What major generic substitutes might replace this product?

E. Political

1. What laws are being proposed that could affect marketing strategy and tactics?
2. What federal, state, and local actions should be watched? What is happening in the areas of pollution control, equal employment opportunity, product safety, advertising, price control, and so forth, that affects marketing strategy?

F. Cultural

1. What is the public's attitude toward business and toward the products produced by the company?
2. What changes in consumer and business lifestyles and values have a bearing on the company?

TASK ENVIRONMENT

A. Markets

1. What is happening to market size, growth, geographical distribution, and profits?
2. What are the major market segments?

B. Customers

1. How do customers and prospects rate the company and its competitors on reputation, product quality, service, sales force, and price?
2. How do different customer segments make their buying decisions?

C. Competitors

1. Who are the major competitors? What are their objectives and strategies, their strengths and weaknesses, their sizes and market shares?
2. What trends will affect future competition and substitutes for this product?

D. Distribution and Dealers

1. What are the main trade channels for bringing products to customers?

TABLE 24–7 Cont.

2. What are the efficiency levels and growth potentials of the different trade channels?

E. Suppliers

1. What is the outlook for the availability of key resources used in production?

2. What trends are occuring among suppliers in their pattern of selling?

F. Facilitators and Marketing Firms

1. What is the cost and availability outlook for transportation services?

2. What is the cost and availability outlook for warehousing facilities?

3. What is the cost and availability outlook for financial resources?

4. How effective are the company's advertising agencies and marketing research firms?

G. Publics

1. What publics represent particular opportunities or problems for the company?

2. What steps has the company taken to deal effectively with each public?

Part II. Marketing Strategy Audit

A. Business Mission

1. Is the business mission clearly stated in market-oriented terms? Is it feasible?

B. Marketing Objectives and Goals

1. Are the corporate and marketing objectives stated in the form of clear goals to guide marketing planning and performance measurement?

2. Are the marketing objectives appropriate, given the company's competitive position, resources, and opportunities?

C. Strategy

1. Is management able to articulate a clear marketing strategy for achieving its marketing objectives? Is the strategy convincing? Is the strategy appropriate to the stage of the product life cycle, competitors' strategies, and the state of the economy?

2. Is the company using the best basis for market segmentation? Does it have sound criteria for rating the segments and choosing the best ones? Has it developed accurate profiles of each target segment?

3. Has the company developed a sound positioning and marketing mix for each target segment? Are marketing resources allocated optimally to the major elements of the marketing mix—i.e., product quality, service, sales force, advertising, promotion, and distribution?

4. Are enough resources or too many resources budgeted to accomplish the marketing objectives?

Part III. Marketing Organization Audit

A. Formal Structure

1. Does the marketing officer have adequate authority over and responsibility for company activities that affect the customer's satisfaction?

2. Are the marketing activities optimally structured along functional, product, end-user, and territorial lines?

TABLE 24-7 Cont.

B. Functional Efficiency

1. Are there good communication and working relations between marketing and sales?

2. Is the product management system working effectively? Are product managers able to plan profits or only sales volume?

3. Are there any groups in marketing that need more training, motivation, supervision, or evaluation?

C. Interface Efficiency

1. Are there any problems between marketing and manufacturing, R&D, purchasing, finance, accounting, and legal that need attention?

Part IV. Marketing Systems Audit

A. Marketing Information System

1. Is the marketing intelligence system producing accurate, sufficient, and timely information about marketplace developments with respect to customers, prospects, distributions and dealers, competitors, suppliers, and various publics?

2. Are company decision makers asking for enough marketing research, and are they using the results?

3. Is the company employing the best methods for market and sales forecasting?

B. Marketing Planning Systems

1. Is the marketing planning system well conceived and effective?

2. Is sales forecasting and market potential measurement soundly carried out?

3. Are sales quotas set on a proper basis?

C. Marketing Control System

1. Are the control procedures adequate to ensure that the annual-plan objectives are being achieved?

2. Does management periodically analyze the profitability of products, markets, territories, and channels of distribution?

3. Are marketing costs periodically examined?

D. New-Product-Development System

1. Is the company well organized to gather, generate, and screen new-product ideas?

2. Does the company do adequate concept research and business analysis before investing in new ideas?

3. Does the company carry out adequate product and market testing before launching new products?

Part V. Marketing Productivity Audit

A. Profitability Analysis

1. What is the profitability of the company's different products, markets, territories, and channels of distribution?

2. Should the company enter, expand, contract, or withdraw from any business segments and what would be the short- and long-run profit consequences?

B. Cost-Effectiveness Analysis

1. Do any marketing activities seem to have excessive costs? Can cost-reducing steps be taken?

Part VI. Marketing Function Audits

A. Products

1. What are the product-line objectives? Are these objectives sound? Is the current product line meeting the objectives?

TABLE 24–7 Cont.

2. Should the product line be stretched or contracted upward, downward, or both ways?

3. Which products should be phased out? Which products should be added?

4. What is the buyers' knowledge and attitudes toward the company's and competitors' product quality, features, styling, brand names, etc? What areas of product strategy need improvement?

B. Price

1. What are the pricing objectives, policies, strategies, and procedures? To what extent are prices set on cost, demand, and competitive criteria?

2. Do the customers see the company's prices as being in line with the value of its offer?

3. What does management know about the price elasticity of demand, experience curve effects, and competitors' prices and pricing policies?

4. To what extent are price policies compatible with the needs of distributors and dealers, suppliers, and government regulation?

C. Distribution

1. What are the distribution objectives and strategies?

2. Is there adequate market coverage and service?

3. How effective are the following channel members: distributors, dealers, manufacturers' representatives, brokers, agents, etc.?

4. Should the company consider changing its distribution channels?

D. Advertising, Sales Promotion, and Publicity

1. What are the organization's advertising objectives? Are they sound?

2. Is the right amount being spent on advertising? How is the budget determined?

3. Are the ad themes and copy effective? What do customers and the public think about the advertising?

4. Are the advertising media well chosen?

5. Is the internal advertising staff adequate?

6. Is the sales promotion budget adequate? Is there effective and sufficient use of sales promotion tools such as samples, coupons, displays, sales contests?

7. Is the publicity budget adequate? Is the public relations staff competent and creative?

E. Sales Force

1. What are the organization's sales-force objectives?

2. Is the sales force large enough to accomplish the company's objectives?

3. Is the sales force organized along the proper principles of specialization (territory, market, product)? Are there enough (or too many) sales managers to guide the field sales representatives?

4. Does the sales-compensation level and structure provide adequate incentive and reward?

5. Does the sales force show high morale, ability, and effort?

6. Are the procedures adequate for setting quotas and evaluating performances?

7. How does the company's sales-force compare to competitors' sales forces?

percent of total sales. The company has looked at the fast-developing markets of chocolate snacks and candies but has not made any moves yet.

☐ The company recently researched its customer profile. Its products appeal especially to lower-income and older people. Respondents who were asked to assess O'Brien's chocolate products in relation to competitors' products described them as "average quality and a bit old-fashioned."

☐ O'Brien sells its products to candy jobbers and large chains. Its sales force call on many of the small retailers reached by the candy jobbers, to fortify displays and provide ideas; its sales force also call on many small retailers not covered by jobbers. O'Brien enjoys good penetration of small retailing, although not in all segments, such as the fast-growing restaurant area. Its major approach to middlemen is a "sell-in" strategy: discounts, exclusively contracts, and stock financing. At the same time O'Brien does not do too well in penetrating the various chains. Its competitors rely more heavily on mass consumer advertising and store merchandising and are more successful with the large chains.

☐ O'Brien's marketing budget is set at 15 percent of its total sales, compared with competitors' budgets of close to 20 percent. Most of the marketing budget supports the sales force, and the remainder supports advertising; consumer promotions are very limited. The advertising budget is spent primarily in remainder advertising for the company's two leading products. New products are not developed often, and when they are, they are introduced to retailers by using a "push" strategy.

☐ The marketing organization is headed by a sales vice-president. Reporting to the sales vice-president is the sales manager, the marketing research manager, and the advertising manager. Having come up from the ranks, the sales vice-president is partial to sales-force activities and pays less attention to the other marketing functions. The sales force is assigned to territories headed by area managers.

The marketing auditor concluded that O'Brien's problems would not be solved by actions taken to improve its sales force. The sales-force problem was symptomatic of a deeper company malaise. The auditor prepared and presented a report to management consisting of the findings and recommendations shown in Table 24–8.

THE MARKETING CONTROLLER CONCEPT

We have examined how an outside marketing auditor can contribute to strategic control. Some companies have established inside positions known as *marketing controllers* to monitor marketing expenses and activities. Marketing controllers are persons working in the controller office who have specialized in the marketing side of the business. In the past controller offices concentrated on watching manufacturing, inventory, and financial expenses and did not include staff that understood marketing very well. The new marketing controllers are trained in finance and marketing and can perform a sophisticated financial analysis of past and planned marketing expenditures. A survey by Goodman showed that:

Large sophisticated companies, such as General Foods, Du Pont, Johnson & Johnson, Trans World Airlines, and American Cyanamid, have all instituted financial control positions which directly oversee advertising and, in some selected cases, merchandising policies. The major functions of these individuals are to verify advertising bills, ensure

TABLE 24-8

SUMMARY OF MARKETING AUDITOR'S FINDINGS AND RECOMMENDATIONS FOR O'BRIEN CANDY COMPANY

Findings

The company's product lines are dangerously unbalanced. The two leading products accounted for 76 percent of total sales and have no growth potential. Five of the eighteen products are unprofitable and have no growth potential.

The company's marketing objectives are neither clear nor realistic.

The company's strategy is not taking changing distribution patterns into account or catering to rapidly changing markets.

The company is run by a sales organization rather than a marketing organization.

The company's marketing mix is unbalanced, with too much spending on sales force and not enough on advertising.

The company lacks procedures for successfully developing and launching new products.

The company's selling effort is not geared to profitable accounts.

Short-Term Recommendations

Examine the current product line and weed out marginal performers with limited growth potential.

Shift some marketing expenditures from supporting mature products to supporting the more recent ones.

Shift the marketing-mix emphasis from direct selling to national advertising, especially for new products.

Conduct a market-profile study of the fastest growing segments of the candy market and develop a plan to break into these areas.

Instruct the sales force to drop some of the smaller outlets and not to take orders for under twenty items. Also, cut out the duplication of effort of sales representatives and jobbers calling on the same accounts.

Initiate sales-training programs and an improved compensation plan.

Medium-to-Long-Term Recommendations

Hire an experienced marketing vice-president from the outside.

Set formal and operational marketing objectives.

Introduce the product manager concept in the marketing organization.

Initiate effective new-product-development programs.

Develop strong brand names.

Find ways to market its brands to the chain-stores more effectively.

Increase the level of marketing expenditures to 20 percent of sales.

Reorganize the selling function by specializing sales representatives by distribution channels.

Set sales objectives and base sales compensation on gross profit performance.

the optimization of agency rates, negotiate agency contracts, and perform an audit function regarding the client's agency and certain of the suppliers.[15]

Goodman feels that this step is in the right direction and advocates an even fuller role for the marketing controller. The marketing controller would:

- ☐ Maintain record of adherence to profit plans
- ☐ Maintain close control of media expense
- ☐ Prepare brand manager's budgets
- ☐ Advise on optimum timing for strategies
- ☐ Measure the efficiency of promotions
- ☐ Analyze media production costs
- ☐ Evaluate customer and geographic profitability
- ☐ Present sales-oriented financial reports
- ☐ Assist direct accounts in optimizing purchasing and inventory policies
- ☐ Educate the marketing area to financial implications of decisions

The Nestlé Company took a step in this direction when a specific segment of the controller operation was made available for marketing planning and control. Marketing-service analysts were assigned to each of Nestlé's six marketing divisions to work for the marketing head. They carried out diverse assignments designed to improve marketing efficiency and performance. Their reports proved helpful, and the position served as a training ground for future general managers because of their exposure to marketing, production, and finance.

The marketing controller position is desirable, particularly in organizations where marketing is still oriented toward sales rather than profits. The marketing controller can help analyze how and where the company is making its money. As future marketing managers acquire greater financial training, they can do more of this work themselves, with marketing controllers providing primarily a monitoring function of marketing expenditures.

SUMMARY

Marketing control is the natural sequel to marketing planning, organization, and implementation. Companies need to carry out four types of marketing control.

Annual-plan control consists of monitoring the current marketing effort and results to make sure that the annual sales and profit goals will be achieved. The main tools are sales analysis, market-share analysis, marketing expense-to-sales analysis, financial analysis, and customer-attitude tracking. If underperformance is detected, the company can implement several corrective measures, including cutting production, changing prices, increasing sales-force pressure, and cutting fringe expenditures.

Profitability control calls for determining the actual profitability of the firm's products, territories, market segments, and trade channels. Marketing-profitability analysis reveals

---

[15] Sam R. Goodman, *Increasing Corporate Profitability* (New York: Ronald Press, 1982), chapter 1.

the weaker marketing entities, although it does not indicate whether the weaker units should be bolstered or phased out.

Efficiency control is the task of increasing the efficiency of such marketing activities as personal selling, advertising, sales promotion, and distribution. Managers must watch certain key ratios that indicate how efficiently these functions are being performed and must also introduce resources to improve performance.

Strategic control is the task of making sure that the company's marketing objectives, strategies, and systems are optimally adapted to the current and forecasted marketing environment. One tool, known as the marketing-effectiveness rating instrument, profiles a company's or a division's overall marketing effectiveness in terms of customer philosophy, marketing organization, marketing information, strategic planning, and operational efficiency. Another tool, known as the marketing audit, is a comprehensive, systematic, independent, and periodic examination of the organization's marketing environment, objectives, strategies, and activities. The purpose of the marketing audit is to determine marketing problem areas and recommend a corrective short-run and long-run action plan to improve the organization's overall marketing effectiveness.

A growing number of companies have established marketing controller positions to monitor marketing expenditures and develop improved financial analyses of the impact of these expenditures.

QUESTIONS

1. In many instances marketing control requires comparison of a performance measure to an established standard of measurement. Suggest some steps that could be taken by marketing managers to establish a performance standard.

2. What are the relative advantages and disadvantages of consumer-attitudes tracking when compared with other annual-plan control approaches?

3. Do you foresee a professional marketing auditing association, which licenses practitioners, on the model of professional certified public accountants? Why or why not? Do you think it is a good idea?

4. A sales manager examined his company's sales by region and noted that the East Coast sales were about 2 percent below the quota. To probe further, the sales manager examined district sales figures. He discovered that the Boston sales district within the East Coast region was responsible for most of the underachievement. He then examined the individual sales of the four sales people in the Boston sales district. This examination revealed that the top salesman, Roberts, had filed only 69 percent of his quota for the period. Is it safe to conclude that Roberts is loafing or having personal problems?

5. Suppose a company's market share falls for a couple of periods. The marketing vice-president, however, refuses to take any action, calling it a random walk. What does he mean? Is he justified?

6. Company XYZ produces five products, and its sales people represent the full product line on each sales call. In order to determine the profit contribution of each product, sales representatives' costs (salary, commission, and expenses) have to be allocated among the five products. How should this be done?

7. A large manufacturer of industrial equipment has a salesperson assigned to each major city. Regional sales managers supervise the sales representatives in several cities. The chief marketing officer wants to evaluate the profit contribution of the different cities. How might each of the following costs be allocated to the cities: (a) billing; (b) district sales manager's expenses; (c) national magazine advertising; (d) marketing research?

8. A company conducts a marketing cost study to determine the minimum size order for breaking even. After finding that size, should the company refuse to accept orders below it? What issues and alternatives should be considered?

9. The idea of treating the marketing department as a profit center raises some difficult problems. Name them and suggest possible solutions.

10. What is the difference between the job of a marketing auditor and of a marketing controller?

Company Index

A

A & P, 73, 178, 485, 487
ACE, 576
Alabe Products, 255
Alberto-Culver, Inc., 312
Aldi Discount Food, 572–73
Allied Stores Corporation, 577
American Airlines, Inc., 197, 201
American Baker's Association, 761
American Bell, Advanced Information Systems (AIS) Division, 22
American Cyanamid Company, 771
American Hospital Supply Corporation, 167, 279, 682, 734
American Oil Company, 98
American Research Bureau (ARB), 194
American Telephone and Telegraph Company (AT&T), 24, 43–44, 101, 678, 734
Anheuser-Busch, Inc., 408, 435, 484, 653
Apple Computer, Inc., 478
Arm & Hammer, 388
Armour Company, 487
Armstrong Cork Company, 393
Armstrong Rubber Company, 35
Atari, Inc., 20
Avis Rent A Car, 273, 389, 397, 407
Avon, 23, 408, 469, 553, 623, 764

B

Bang & Olufsen Company, 481
Bank of America, 27
Bayer Aspirin, 386, 389
Beatrice Foods Company, 309
Beecham, Inc., 31, 270
Bell Laboratories, 317
Best Foods, 311
Bic, 389, 400
Bissell Company, 336
Bobbie Brooks, Inc., 271
Boeing Corporation, 101, 387
Book-of-the-Month Club, 554
Booz, Allen & Hamilton, 309–10, 313–16
Borden, Inc., 103
Boston Consulting Group, 51–52, 74
Bowmar Company, 476–77
Bristol-Meyers Company, 122, 311, 372
Browning-Ferris Company, 435
Bulova Watch Company, 450
Burger King, 22, 389
Burnett, Leo, Company, Inc., 672
Burroughs Corporation, 410, 599

C

Campbell's Soups, 311, 393, 439, 455, 485, 486, 547

(continued)

Case, J. I., Company, 184
Caterpillar Tractor Company, 10–11, 23, 39, 169, 386, 397, 398–400, 443, 475, 508, 518–19, 764
Celanese Company, 278
Chase Econometrics, 244
Chase Manhattan Bank, 735
Chrysler Corporation, 38, 73, 101, 169, 391, 439
Ciba-Geigy Corporation, 456
Citicorp, 443, 735, 736
Coca-Cola, Inc., 250–51, 268, 364, 368, 386, 389–90, 408–9, 443, 448, 453, 455, 593, 636, 637
Colgate-Palmolive Company, 122, 262–63, 311, 340, 397, 405, 443, 486
Conn Organ Company, 554
Continental Bank of Chicago, 28
Crown Cork & Seal Company, 410
Crown Zellerbach Corporation, 421
Cummins Engine Company, Inc., 439
Curtis, Helene, 402, 457
Curtis Candy Company, 260
Curtis Publishing Company, 21

D

Daimler-Benz, Inc., 9
Data Resources, Inc., 244

Name Index

Subject Index

Shortages, 70, 97, 99, 416–24
Simple ranking, 337
Simulated store technique, 339–40
Simulation model, 652
Single market concentration, 65
Small-car market, 40–41
Social audits, 108
Social class, 126, 127, 258
Social factors, consumer behavior and, 126, 128–31
Social needs, 138
Societal marketing concept, 28–30
Socio/cultural environment, 106–10
Soft drink industry, 29
Space allocation, 180
Specialization, 411
Specialty goods, 467
Specialty stores, 567–68
S-shaped product life cycle, 354–55
Stages in buying decision process, 147–59
Stagflation economy, 416
Standard Industrial Classification System (S.I.C.), 235–36
Star, 53
Statistical bank, 211–13
Statistical decision theory (Bayesian decision theory), 214, 217
Statistical demand analysis, 246–47
Status, 130–31
Steel industry, 470
Stimuli, 140, 141
Stimulus ambiguity, 617
Stimulus-response model, 123–24
Stock control, 180
Straight extension, 455
Straight rebuy, 164
Strategic business units (SBUs), 51–57
Strategic control, 744, 761–71
Strategic planning, 34–75, 279–80
Strategic planning gap, 57
Strategic remarketing, 419
Strategic window, 40
Strengths/weaknesses analysis, 285
Strong inflation, 424
Style, 357
Style improvement, 369
Subcultures, 107, 125
Subsegmentation, 65
Success requirements, 42–43
Supermarkets, 178–79, 569–70
Supersegments, 271, 272
Superstores, 571
Supervision of sales force, 690–94
Suppliers, 79–80, 172–74

Supply planning, 169
Survey research, 201
Survival, 508
Sweepstakes, 665
Symbiotic marketing, 549
Synectics, 319–20
Systems buying, 165–66

T

Tachistoscope, 205
Tangible product, 463
Target audience, 607–11, 614–15
Target marketing, 64–67, 251–52, 302–5, 579–80, 589
  (see also Market segmentation; Market targeting; Product positioning)
Target-profit pricing, 517
Tariff, 446
Technology, 2–3, 99–102
Telephone-order retailing, 574–75
Television, 647–49, 662
Territorial-structured sales force, 680–81
Territory marketing plan, 696–97
Test marketing, 340–42
Time-and-duty analysis, 693
Time-series analysis, 244–46
Time utility, 80
Timing, 343–44
Top-down planning, 278
Total costs, 512
Total market potential, 234–35
Trademark, 482
Trade marketing mix, 115
Trade-off analysis, 326, 329–30
Trade promotion, 661, 664–65
Trade shows, 343, 665
Trading stamps, 664
Training sales representatives, 688–90
Transaction, 8–11
Transfer, 10
Transportation, 81, 597–99
Trend correlation, 241
Trend extrapolation, 240
Truck manufacturing industry, 384–85, 470
Truck transportation, 598
Truth-in-Lending Act (1968), 105
Turnkey operation, 165
20–80 rule, 419

U

Undifferentiated marketing, 267–69
Unemployment, 415, 416
Uniform delivered pricing, 523–24
Unsought goods, 467
Usage rate, 261–62
User, 143, 166
User status, 261

V

Value, 6–8
Value analysis, 172–74
Values, cultural, 106–10
Variable costs, 512
Variety-seeking buying behavior, 144, 145–46
Verbal models, 214, 218
Vertical marketing systems, 546–49
Volume segmentation, 261
Voluntary chains, 576
Voter markets, 12

W

Warehouse stores, 573
Warehousing, 81, 595
Water transportation, 597–98
Wheeler-Lea Act (1938), 104
Wholesalers, 70
Wholesaler-sponsored voluntary chains, 548
Wholesaling, 583–91
Work ethic, 108
Working wives, 90

Z

Zero-based budgeting, 305
Zip-code centers, 238–39
Zone pricing, 524